THE FUTURE
A Guide to Information Sources
SECOND EDITION

WORLD FUTURE SOCIETY

4916 St. Elmo Avenue
Washington, D.C. 20014 • U.S.A.

Published by

WORLD FUTURE SOCIETY
4916 St. Elmo Avenue
Washington, D.C. 20014 • U.S.A.

Copyright © 1979 by
World Future Society

Library of Congress Cataloging in Publication Data

World Future Society.
  The future: A guide to information sources

  Includes indexes.
   1. Forecasting—Societies, etc.—Directories.
2. Forecasting—Bibliography. I. Title.
CB 158.W67   1979   309'.06'2   79-19398
ISBN 0-930242-07-6

Library of Congress Catalog Number 79-19398
International Standard Book Number 0-930242-07-6

Price: $25.00
$19.50 to members of the World Future Society

CONTENTS

INTRODUCTION

This directory covers the wide range of information resources—organizations, individuals, books, films, courses, etc.— now available in the field of futuristics, or "the study of the future." Preparation of the first edition of this directory was supported in part by a grant from the National Science Foundation and the Library of Congress, Congressional Research Service. This second edition of *The Future: A Guide to Information Sources* represents an extensive revision and includes considerably more information than the first edition published in 1977. This volume contains some 560 individuals, 270 organizations, 120 research projects, 587 books and reports, 105 periodicals, 93 films, 109 audiotapes and tape series, 45 games and simulations, 17 mixed media presentations, and more than 280 courses and programs offered by educational institutions. The total number of sources is close to 2200.

The volume also features a glossary of terms frequently found in writings about the future, and separate indexes identifying individuals and organizations according to their special interests and geographic location. By consulting these indexes, readers can quickly identify promising sources of information on a particular topic, or determine which of several different sources of information is most accessible.

The directory is not, of course, an exhaustive inventory of every resource in the field. Many individuals, organizations, and other sources are omitted only because the required information on them had not been received by press time.

Every section of the directory is prefaced by brief guidelines for its use. The length of an entry is not a judgment on the relative importance of the subject. In most cases, the descriptions of the aims and interests of the individuals and organizations listed in the directory are given as they appeared on the returned questionnaire.

We hope that readers will find this second edition of the directory useful, and we invite suggestions for improvements in future editions. We would also like to thank the scores of scholars around the world who freely contributed their knowledge and advice.

Readers seeking a general introduction to the rapidly growing field of futuristics may consult *The Study of the Future* by Edward S. Cornish (World Future Society, 1977, $8.50 to Society members, $9.50 to non-members). The task of writing this descriptive volume was carried on simultaneously with the production of the first edition of this directory, and was also funded in part by the National Science Foundation and the Library of Congress.

ACKNOWLEDGEMENTS

More than 1,000 people contributed to the preparation of this directory, many of them by taking time from their busy schedules to supply information about themselves or their organizations. Without these essential contributions, this directory could never have been prepared.

Primary responsibility for coordinating the collection of data fell to Janet Carson and Nancy B. McLane, who worked tirelessly to verify facts and obtain information from experts in many countries around the world.

Special acknowledgement is also due to two U.S. Government agencies: The National Science Foundation's Office of Government and Public Programs and the Congressional Research Service of the Library of Congress. These two agencies provided support for a preliminary study entitled *Resources Directory for America's Third Century* that was completed early in 1977 and from which the present publication evolved.

PROJECT STAFF

EDITOR
Edward S. Cornish

PROJECT MANAGER
Peter Zuckerman

RESEARCH COORDINATOR
Janet Carson

RESEARCH CONSULTANT
Nancy B. McLane

STAFF WRITERS AND RESEARCHERS
Julie Ramsey Bigelow
Vicki Boyer
Sally Cornish
Ellen Dudley
Tom Fischmann
Jean Hollister
Lane Jennings
Virginia Kerney
Hugh Myers
Frances Segraves

GRAPHIC DESIGN
Peggy Bates
Diane Smirnow
Carol Wade

PROOFREADERS
Virginia Fry
Jean Ruffin

CONSULTANTS
Roy C. Amara
David J. Berry
Bruce Bigelow
Mihai C. Botez
Joseph F. Coates
Vary T. Coates
Duane Dale
Penny Damlo
Hugues de Jouvenel
Denison Simulation Center

Howard F. Didsbury, Jr.
Gregg Edwards
John Eggers
William R. Ewald, Jr.
Margaret P. Fowler
Jib Fowles
Betty Barclay Franks
Jerome C. Glenn
Hazel Henderson
Lance Holthusen
Frank Snowden Hopkins
Robert Horn
Tibor Hottovy
Earl C. Joseph
Anthony J.N. Judge
Robert Jungk
Robert W. Lamson
Harold A. Linstone
Thomas Madeira
Michael Marien
Marie Martin
Eleonora Masini
Robert Maston
Yoneji Masuda
John McHale
Jay S. Mendell
Graham T.T. Molitor
Burt Nanus
Charles Plummer
David Potter
David Snyder
Hugh A. Stevenson
Richard Stock
Andre van Dam
Richard Wakefield
Jerry Ward
James Webber
James Wellesley-Wesley

DEDICATION

To those individuals listed in the first edition who have since died and are therefore not listed in this second edition. These distinguished futurists include Ward Allen, Raymond Bauer, Dennis Gabor, Peter Goldmark, Carl Madden, John McHale, Margaret Mead, and E.F. Schumacher.

ORGANIZATIONS

ORGANIZATIONS

While there are hundreds of corporations and businesses who carry on certain future-oriented activities, this listing is limited to groups whose *major* focus is on the future. The list includes certain future-oriented units within larger organizations. Emphasis is given to organizations that take a broad-gauge look at the future rather than those which are highly specialized or cause-oriented (e.g., environmental groups, political action groups, etc.).

Where available, the following information has been provided for each organization listed:
Name
Mailing address
Telephone number
Year founded
Principal officers, directors, and staff specialists
Type of organization (government, business, etc.)
Staff size
Principal sources of funding
Approximate annual budget
Primary objectives and special interests
Major programs and projects
Special facilities (libraries, data banks, etc.)
Other activities
Principal publications (periodicals, books, reports)

THE ABEND GROUP

120 East Genesee Street
Syracuse, New York 13202, U.S.A.

Telephone: (315) 425-9555

Founded: 1976

Officers: C. Joshua Abend, Executive Director; N.E. Gelston, Business Advisor.

Private organization. Staff: Two. **Sources of support:** Private. **Annual Budget:** No answer.

Objectives and interests: Innovation management as a tool for opportunity finding in new markets and products; application of "product futures"—a method of developing attributes and product specifications for advanced development programs and next generation directions; risk reduction by means of using forecasting to determine product decisions and choices.

Major programs and projects: "Anticipating Tomorrow's Markets and Identifying Tomorrow's Products"—a study and analysis done for Corning Glass Consumer Products Group to pinpoint new product opportunities. "Directions and Opportunities in Plastic Products"—development of more quantifiable basis for business decisions based on forecasting and monitoring techniques.

Special facilities: —

Activities: In-house seminars.

Publications: —

THE ACADEMY FOR CONTEMPORARY PROBLEMS

1501 Neil Avenue
Columbus, Ohio 43201, U.S.A.

Telephone: (614) 421-7700

Founded: 1971

Officers: Ralph R. Widner, President; Kenneth Rainey, Vice-President for Operations (Columbus); Herrington Bryce, Vice-President for Operations (Washington, D.C.); Joseph White, Senior Fellow in Social Policy; Frederick D. Stocker, Fellow in Public Finance; James Coke, Fellow in Public Management.

Independent, not-for-profit public foundation. Staff: About 65. **Sources of support:** Foundation, contracts, private contributions. **Annual Budget:** $2.5 million.

Objectives and interests: As the policy research and conference center of its seven member organizations (Council of State Governments, International City Management Association, National Association of Counties, National Conference of State Legislatures, National Governors' Association, National League of Cities, and U.S. Conference of Mayors), the Academy seeks to assist citizens, technical experts, and decision-makers in working together toward solving urgent public problems; issues selected for Academy attention must have impact on the state, county, and local governments of the United States.

Major programs and projects: "Great Lakes Development Project"—six reports describing potential economic development strategies for the six Great Lakes states. "Tri-National Project"—compares urban problems and alternative policies in the U.S., Great Britain, and West Germany. "Comprehensive Community Energy Management Program"—to determine the effectiveness of energy conservation management methodology. "Project 'MIJJIT'"—describes and analyzes major issues in juvenile justice training and information. "Neighborhood Response"—encourages and assists life and health insurance companies to become involved in urban neighborhood revitalization projects.

Special facilities: The Academy provides its facilities and equipment as a conference center for nonprofit, nonsectarian, community groups.

Activities: National Urban Policy Roundtable—A forum meeting several times annually in which leaders from the public and private sectors, academia, and civic groups meet to develop more effective programs and policies for U.S. cities.

Publications: *Clearinghouse Reporter*, Harry M. Griggs, editor, free, quarterly; *Clearinghouse Memoranda*, Harry M. Griggs, editor, free, Academy research summarized as reports are issued; *Revitalizing the Northeastern Economy*, 1977; *Stimulating the Economy of the Great Lakes States*, 1978; *America Growing*, a multimedia color presentation narrated by Henry Fonda, produced for the 1978 White House Conference on Balanced National Growth and Economic Development; *State-Local Fiscal Incentives and Economic Development*, F. D. Stocker, 1978; *The Impact of Inflation on State and Local Government;* Robert Crider,1978.

4

ACADEMY FOR EDUCATIONAL DEVELOPMENT

680 Fifth Avenue
New York, New York 10019, U.S.A.

Telephone: (212) 397-0040

Founded: 1961

Officers: Gerald R. Ford, Chairman of the Board; James A. Perkins, Vice Chairman; Alvin C. Eurich, President and Chief Executive Officer; Merrell M. Clark, Executive Vice President (New York); Stephen F. Moseley, Executive Vice President (Washington, D.C.).

Independent, non-profit, research and service organization. **Staff:** 125. **Sources of support:** Approximately 50% U.S. Government; 20% foundations; 16% educational organizations and other non-profit organizations and associations; remainder from state, city and local government, foreign organizations, agencies, individuals and corporations. **Annual Budget:** Approximately $5 million.

Objectives and interests: To assist institutions, organizations, and states in planning their future; to help institutions solve some of their most pressing problems in education, communications and international affairs; to improve educational management; to improve the process of negotiating disputes between nations.

Major Programs and projects: "Iran"—planning institutions for technical education; "Saudi Arabia"—planning a new University of Mecca; "Developing countries"—planning the use of instructional technology to improve health; "Ivory Coast"—evaluating in-school television for future use; "Several states (Alabama, Mississippi, South Carolina, and others)" —the future of higher education.

Special facilities: Instructional Technology Library, 1414 Twenty-Second Street, N.W., Washington, D.C. 20037, U.S.A.

Activities: Conducts conferences on a variety of problems in education, communication, and international affairs. Conducts a wide variety of studies for educational institutions, government agencies, organizations and associations. Assists institutions in finding key executive officers; counsels communication media on current problems.

Publications: *Academy Quarterly Newsletter; You Are Never Too Old to Learn* (1978); *Never Too Old to Teach* (1978); *How to Plan a College Program for Older People* (1978); *The Middle Years: A Multidisciplinary View* (1978); *Major Transitions in the Human Life Cycle* (1977); *A Reason to Read* (1975).

ACADEMY OF SCIENCES OF THE UKRAINIAN SSR, SCIENCE POLICY STUDIES DEPARTMENT OF THE INSTITUTE OF CYBERNETICS

Telephone: 63-11-60

109 Nauka Avenue
252028 Kiev, U.S.S.R.

Founded: 1966

Officers: G. M. Dobrov, Head; V. N. Klimenyuk, Department Chief; L. P. Smirnov, Senior Research Worker; B. Ya. Brusilovski, Senior Research Worker; Yu. V. Yershov, Senior Research Worker; A. A. Korennoy, Senior Research Worker.

Research Institute Department. **Staff:** 100. **Sources of support:** Budget of the Academy of Sciences of the Ukrainian SSR. **Annual Budget:** 0.5-0.8 million roubles.

Objectives and interests: Science policy studies; technological forecasting; technology assessment of research and development; management information systems for research and development organizations.

Major programs and projects: Management by Objectives in R & D Organizations; improving the system of organization of science in the Ukrainian SSR; development of methodology of forecasting the future of computers.

Special facilities: Maintains a library of books and periodicals on mathematics, cybernetics, information science, etc.

Activities: Research, conferences, seminars, postgraduate courses.

Publications: *Naukovedeniye i Informatika [Science and Information Systems]* (quarterly journal); *Nauka o Nauke [Science of Science]*, G. M. Dobrov (1970); *Prognozirovaniye Nauki i Tekhniki [Forecasting Science and Technology]*, G. M. Dobrov (1969); *Matematycheskíyie Modeli v Planirovanii i Organizatsii Nauki [Mathematical Models in Planning and Organization of Science]*, B. Ya. Brusilovski (1975); *Upravleniye razvitiyem i ispolzovaniyem nauchnogo potentsiala [Management, Development and Utilization of Scientific Potential]*, V. N. Klimenyuk (1974).

(From the first edition. Corrections not received by press time.)

ACADEMY OF WORLD STUDIES
2820 Van Ness Avenue
San Francisco, California 94109, U.S.A.

Telephone: (415) 441-1404

Founded: 1968

Officers: Bennet Skewes-Cox, President; Felicia Bock, Chairman, Board of Directors; Barry L. Smail, Treasurer; Sandra D. Shattuck, Registrar; Robert Kluender, Director of English Language Studies; Daniel T. Linger, Director of Foreign Language Studies.

Non-profit educational institution promoting world education. **Staff:** 21, including part-time foreign language faculty. **Sources of support:** Tuition, private contributions and grants. **Annual Budget:** No answer.

Objectives and interests: Introduction and promotion of the synoptic (over-all) approach to world problems; future studies on global affairs; development of international communication through language studies.

Major programs and projects: "World Ombudsman Training Program"—Internship for high school, college, and graduate students preparing for world service. "Towards Century 21"—Ongoing college futures course now offered at Merritt College, Oakland, California. "World Studies Curricula"—A worldwide interrogatory by the Academy of World Studies, prepared for and distributed by the Association for World Education, New York. "Worldview Perspective"—Future-oriented college course, primarily for social studies teachers, on major world problems.

Special facilities: Maintains a private (open to members only) library of books, periodicals, and file cards on world affairs. The file card research, adaptable to microfiche, is one of the world's most extensive collections on the synoptic approach to world problems. Has a considerable collection of material on the specific topic of world federal government for global peace-keeping.

Activities: Courses in all languages; synoptic research on major world problems; headquarters of the California Council for the United Nations University; seminars and colloquia on the U.N. University, on world studies curricula, etc. Translator and interpreter services.

Publications: *Worldview/San Francisco* (newsletter, four or five times per year); *The Worldview*, B. Skewes-Cox (1962, mimeo); *Report on the United Nations University Colloquim* (1974); *Exploring the Potential of the U.N. University*, James Cox and Alfred Gilbert, editors (1975).

AD HOC INTERAGENCY COMMITTEE ON FUTURES RESEARCH
c/o Richard P. Wakefield
Room 15-99, National Institute of Mental Health
5600 Fishers Lane
Rockville, Maryland 20857, U.S.A.

Telephone: (301) 443-3373

Founded: 1969

Officers: Richard P. Wakefield, Dean and Chairman, Program Committee.

An unofficial, informal, and fluid group, composed chiefly of Executive Branch civil servants in policy-related positions, who meet regularly to discuss matters relating to the future and their governmental responsibilities, especially long-range planning. **Staff:** None. **Sources of support:** None. **Annual Budget:** None.

Objectives and interests: To generate awareness and understanding of futures research and long-range governmental planning among executive branch civil servants.

Major programs and projects: "A Federal Budget for the Year 2000" (incomplete)—Eight sub-task forces developing general forecasts. "Bureaucrats' Views of the Future of Governance" (in process)—A Delphi survey of federal employees by federal employees.

Special facilities: None.

Activities: Monthly meetings to hear and discuss talks on futures research, technology assessment, social impact assessment, forecasting, and related topics (e.g., human values).

Publications: *Bureaucrats' Views of the Future of Governance: A Report on a Pilot Study* (1975).

6

UNIVERSITY OF AKRON
INSTITUTE FOR FUTURE STUDIES AND RESEARCH
Akron, Ohio, 44325 U.S.A.

Telephone: (216) 375-7887

Founded: 1978

Officers: A. Al-Rubaiy, Acting Director; D.J. Guzzetta, University President and Chairman, Advisory Committee; F.S. Buchtel, Assistant to the President.

Non-profit, teaching and research institute. Staff: Three. **Sources of support:** Internal budgeting.
Annual Budget: No answer.

Objectives and interests: Teaching and research activities in the area of future studies. Special emphases are being defined.

Major programs and projects: Programs and projects are in the process of development.

Special facilities: The Institute is developing a specialized library of books, periodicals, and reports with emphasis on teaching and research.

Activities: A semi-annual lecture series of prominent futurists, for the University and the community. (The first lecture series was in the fall of 1978 with Buckminster Fuller as the speaker.)

Publications: Publications are in the process of development.

AMERICAN COUNCIL OF LIFE INSURANCE,
TREND ANALYSIS PROGRAM
1850 K Street, N.W.
Washington, D.C. 20006, U.S.A.

Telephone: (202) 862-4134

Founded: 1970

Officers: Ronna Klingenberg, Project Director, Trend Analysis Program.

Non-profit. Staff: No answer. **Sources of support:** Life insurance business. **Annual Budget:** No answer.

Objectives and interests: Monitors the broad environment, including: science and technology, social sciences, politics and government, business and economics.

Major programs and projects: "Death, Dying and Life Extension"; "Citizen Participation in Public Policy Decision Making"; "Special Report on Health."

Special facilities: Collection of abstracts of thousands of articles from publications monitored by program participants (over 100 executives in the life insurance business). Not for public access.

Activities: One conference annually for participants in program.

Publications: Trend Reports are issued approximately three times a year and contain themes presented in thesis, scenario and statistical forms. Some subjects which have appeared to date are: *Aging and the Aged, Social Security: Future Prospects,* and *The Future of Inflation.*

AMERICAN ENTERPRISE INSTITUTE FOR
PUBLIC POLICY RESEARCH
1150 17th Street, N.W.
Washington, D.C. 20036, U.S.A.

Telephone: (202) 862-5800

Founded: 1943

Officers: William J. Baroody, Jr., President; Herman J. Schmidt, Chairman of the Board of Trustees; Charles T. Fisher, III, Treasurer.

Non-partisan, non-profit, tax exempt, educational research organization. Staff: 120. **Sources of support:** Foundation grants and contributions from corporations and individuals. **Annual Budget:** Approximately $7 million.

Objectives and interests: To assist policy makers, scholars, businessmen, thé press, and the public by providing objective analysis of national and international issues.

Major programs and projects: "Minimum Wage Studies Project"—to analyze the effects on the economy and in society of enforcement of legal minimum wage standards. "Center for Health Policy Research"—to examine the adequacy of the present health care system of the United States. "Legal Policy Studies Program"—to examine the growing controversy over the role of the courts and the law itself in American society. "Tax Policy Studies Project"—devoted to providing the best possible analytic foundation for the continuing debate over tax reform. "Project on the Future Conduct of American Foreign Policy"—focuses on the changing nature of American relations with the rest of the nations of the world. "Public Policy Project on National Defense"—focuses on problems related to promoting peace and, if necessary, assuring the safety of the United States. "Project on Major Economic Problems"—to analyze many of the difficulties the nation is likely to encounter as it attempts to achieve a sustainable rate of economic growth, coupled with an acceptable behavior on price level. "Center for the Study of Government Regulation"—to provide better public understanding of the costs and benefits of government regulation. "Social Security Studies"—long-range research by recognized authorities exploring problems related to the administration and financing of the social security system.

Special facilities: Social sciences library.

Activities: Public Policy Forums—a continuing series of televised public affairs programs featuring face-to-face discussions of major public issues by authorities of varying views. Conferences—Designed to focus on issues of unusual complexity, these sessions provide a forum for leading scholars to discuss critical subjects before invited audiences. "Discussions With . . ." —Provides an opportunity for scholars and other experts on major public policy problems and issues to meet informally and examine ideas with persons from government, business, labor, and the news media.

Publications: *AEI Memorandum* (bimonthly); *Public Opinion* magazine; *Regulation* magazine; *The AEI Economist* newsletter; *AEI Defense Review;* approximately 100 annual monographs and studies.

APPLIED FUTURES, INC.

22 Greenwich Plaza
Greenwich, Connecticut 06830, U.S.A.

Telephone: (203) 661-9711

Founded: 1972

Officers: William W. Simmons, President; John R. Moore, Director of Marketing.

Private consulting/marketing firm. Staff: Four. **Sources of support:** Private investment. **Annual Budget:** No answer.

Objectives and interests: The primary objective is marketing the CONSENSOR, which facilitates better communication and exchange in a variety of meetings and formats. The second major objective is increasing business awareness and understanding of the future.

Major programs and projects: "The CONSENSOR is a planning tool which enables any task group to apply the principles of the Delphi decision technique to its planning process by means of instantly displayed electronic consensus and anonymous weighted voting."

Special facilities: —

Activities: Major activities on a one-to-one basis with clients depending on their particular needs and uses of the CONSENSOR. Applied Futures also sponsors meetings with corporate planners from Fortune 500 companies to discuss the "future" of planning, ranging from basic problems and techniques to the use and impact of futurist techniques and forecasting.

Publications: *Exploratory Planning Briefs,* published by the Planning Executives Institute—an index of activities by corporations, government (international, federal, and state) and private institutions and individuals; "A Strategic Planning Program for the Next Decade" (*American Management Journal,* January 1975); "Main Forms of Futures Research" (*European Business,* Summer 1972); "Practical Planning" (*Long Range Planning,* Vol. 5, No. 2, June 1972); "So You Want To Have A Long-Range Plan" (Planning Executives Institute).

ARAB LEAGUE EDUCATIONAL, CULTURAL AND SCIENTIFIC ORGANISATION (ALECSO)

109 Tahrir Street, Dokki, Giza
Cairo, Egypt

Telephone: 846072

Founded: 1970

Officers: Mohi El-Din Saber, Director General; Ussama Amin El-Kholy, Assistant Director General for Science and Technology; Safieddin Abul-Ezz, Director, Institute for Arab Research and Studies; Saber Selim, Director,

Department of Science; Saad Labib Mekkawi, Director, Department of Communication and Mass Media.

Intergovernmental.   **Staff:** 180 at Cairo office; about 50 in branch organisations in Iraq, Kuwait, Bahrain, Sudan, Libya, Morocco and Somalia.   **Sources of support:** Member state contributions.   **Annual Budget:** Approximately $7,000,000.

Objectives and interests: Promotion of regional efforts in the fields of education, culture and science.

Major programs and projects: "Science and Technology in the Arab Region in the Year 2000"—environmental considerations in development planning. "Technologies for the Satisfaction of Basic Human Needs in the Arab Region." "Scientific-Technological Plan of Action for the Arab Region." "An Arab Educational Strategy"—program of environmental research and studies of the Red Sea and Gulf of Aden (PERSGA). "An Arab Strategy in Communication and Flow of Information"—an Arab strategy for conservation of natural resources.

Special facilities: Libraries.

Activities: Research, studies, courses, seminars, conferences, publications (books and periodicals), field work.

Publications: *Arab Culture* (annual); *Arab Documentation and Information* (annual); *The Teaching of Science and Mathematics* (every 6 months); *Education of the Masses* (quarterly); *Aquatic Resources of the Arab Countries: Science Monograph Series No. 1* (1972); *Groundwater Resources in the Arab Countries: Science Monograph Series No. 2* (1973); *Man, Environment, Development: Proceedings Khartoum Symposium, February 1972; Environmental Education: A Source-Book for General Level,* edited by M. A. Mostafa (1976); *Man and Environment: A Source-Book for Higher Institutes and Universities,* edited by M. A. Mostafa (1978).

ASSOCIATION INTERNATIONALE FUTURIBLES
[FUTURIBLES INTERNATIONAL]

55 rue de Varenne
75007 Paris, France

Telephone: (01) 222 63 10 +

Founded: 1960 as International Committee
of Futuribles;
1967 as International Association
Futuribles

Officers: Philippe de Seynes, Chairman of the Board; Hugues de Jouvenel, Executive Director (Delegue General); Guy Poquet, Research Associate, in charge of Documentation Department; Christine de Guebriant, Assistant to the Director; Francoise Robinet, Assistant to the Editor, in charge of the Publications Department.

Independent, private, non-profit, international.   **Staff:** 12 full-time; 20 part-time.   **Sources of support:** Membership fees and subscriptions (25%); public agencies (40%); private corporations (35%).   **Annual Budget:** 1,600,000 French francs.

Objectives and interests: The aim of the Association is to act as a center for information, documentation and coordination in futures studies (who is doing what, where, how), as well as to analyze, stimulate and undertake research on the facts, ideas, and options on which the future of our society depends.

Major programs and projects: "Active Citizenship and Participation"—Public choices and human values/process of decision making. "Social Experiments and Innovation"—Identify them and analyze how relevant they might be as social indicators. "Futures in Government"—How can a government take into account the long range? "Research on Research"—Comparative analysis of futures studies and elaboration of synopsis. Research in the area of human values, lifestyles and household consumption patterns.

Special facilities: Specialized library—about 5,000 volumes in the futures field. Reference Service—more than 60,000 entries relating to published or unpublished documents, conference reports, etc. Index of Who's Who in the futures field—about 10,000 entries. International network of experts and correspondents—1500 experts from about 65 countries.

Activities: The Association is currently organizing international conferences (next one will be on the future of international relations), training seminars (three per year), and round-tables (every month). Its general activities include: clearinghouse, research training, and publications.

Publications: *Futuribles,* a bimonthly journal on economic, social and political issues which are important for the future; *Futur-Informations,* monthly. More than 600 studies and 18 books have been published since 1960. Among the most recent studies: growth and inequalities; the participation of the public in collective choices; the management of raw materials and the current crisis; European futurism; social change in Europe 1950-1990; the economy of raw materials.

ASSOCIATION FOR THE STUDY OF MAN ENVIRONMENT RELATIONS

P.O. Box 57
Orangeburg, New York 10962, U.S.A.

Telephone: (212) 948-2410
Founded: 1969

Officers: Aristide H. Esser, President; Alton J. DeLong, Secretary; Dennis Falk, Treasurer; D. Michael Murtha.

Non-profit, educational, membership organization. **Staff:** Three. **Sources of support:** Membership subscriptions, government contracts. **Annual Budget:** $15,000.

Objectives and interests: Synergy between behavior scientists and (design) professionals; development of a theory of man-environment relations; information dissemination.

Major programs and projects: Publication of bimonthly journal and of the *International Directory of Behavior and Design Research.*

Special facilities: —

Activities: Regular workshops at conferences of national professional organizations; publications.

Publications: *Man-Environment Systems* (bimonthly journal); M-ES Focus Series: *Environmental Design Perspectives, International Directory of Behavior and Design Research, Psyche and Design; The Stable Society,* Edward Goldsmith; *Health Promotion through Designed Environment,* Health and Welfare Canada; *Spatial Structures in Everyday Face-to-Face Behavior,* R. Deutsch.

ASSOCIAZIONE TEILHARD DE CHARDIN: CENTRO DI RICERCA SUL FUTURO DELL'UOMO
[TEILHARD DE CHARDIN ASSOCIATION: CENTER FOR RESEARCH ON THE FUTURE OF MAN]

Viale Don Minzoni, 25/A
Florence 50129, Italy

Telephone: (055) 576.551

Founded: 1964

Officers: Italo Mancini, President; Alessandro Dall'Olio, Secretary-General and Director of the Stensen Institute.

Private, non-profit research association, founded by the Stensen Institute. **Staff:** None—the Association is composed of a small number of research professors. **Sources of support:** Stensen Institute. **Annual Budget:** $1,000.

Objectives and interests: The Association conducts social-religious and philosophical-scientific research to further the work and thinking on the future which Teilhard de Chardin outlined in his works.

Major programs and projects: Publication of *Il Futuro dell'Uomo [The Future of Man]*.

Special facilities: The Association has access to the facilities of the Stensen Institute, a cultural institute, which has a library with a specialized section on Teilhard de Chardin, reading rooms, meeting rooms and conference hall.

Activities: Conferences, congresses, seminars.

Publications: *Il Futuro dell'Uomo [The Future of Man]* (quarterly).

BALAI SENI TOYABUNGKAH

Jalan Dr. Saharjo 290, Tebet
Jakarta, Indonesia

Telephone: 584845

Founded: 1973

Officers: Sutan Takdir Alisjahbana, Chairman; Zulkarnain, Sugita, Ibu Reneng.

Private, non-profit. **Staff:** 35, including dancers and musicians. **Sources of support:** Private of the Director, plus income from restaurant and rooms. **Annual Budget:** $20,000.

Objectives and interests: Creating an art for the future which should express human responsibility, human solidarity and the joy of a continuously expanding creative life.

10

Major programs and projects: "International Association for Art and the Future"—a permanent contact among the various art centers, art academies, colleges, artists and scholars the world over, who are interested in or concerned with the problems of art and the future.

Special facilities: Library on art and culture, containing about 600 volumes from Bali and other countries.

Activities: Experimenting in art creativities, conferences, seminars, courses.

Publications: *Art and the Future*, a newsletter; *Balai Seni Toyabungkah; A Futuristic Experimental Art Center at Lake Batur, Kintamani, Bali*, by S. Takdir Alisjahbana (1977).

BATTELLE GENEVA RESEARCH CENTERS

7, route de Drize
CH-1227 Carouge-Geneva, Switzerland

Telephone: (022) 43 98 31

Founded: 1952

Officers: V. Stingelin, Director General; R. Adoutte, Associate Director and Head of Business Administration and Services Centre; K. D. Beccu, Director of Marketing; F. Trojer, Head, Industrial Technology Centre; R. Haroz, Head, Toxicology and Biosciences Centre; J. C. Masson, Head, Applied Economics Centre.

Non-profit research institute. **Staff:** 420. **Sources of support:** Contract research. **Annual Budget:** No answer.

Objectives and interests: The Battelle-Geneva Centre performs technical and scientific research for industries and governments. In the area of futures research, it performs studies of technological forecasting and social and economic simulation modeling.

Major programs and projects: "Input-Output Chemistry 1980-85"—model of the European industry analyzing the characteristic interdependence of this sector. "Social Audit"—study aimed at developing a system permitting private companies to assume their social responsibility at a management, negotiations and public relations level. "Explor-Multitrade 1985"—an economic forecasting model of Europe, the U.S.A., and Japan. "Prospect"—short-term models, forecasts, and policy analysis of European economics. "Forsys"—a dynamic input-output model for the main OECD countries providing forecasts on an annual basis.

Special facilities: Documentation centers on the main techno-economics sector, data banks on chemical plants, gas turbines, drinks, etc.; central economic information center; library.

Activities: Small number of conferences. Studies are conducted for individual sponsors which use or diffuse their results.

Publications: Periodicals—*Battelle Research Outlook*, published twice a year in Columbus, Ohio, and *Research Futures*, published quarterly in Columbus, Ohio; *Battelle Multiclient Studies*, inputs to corporate planning.

BATTELLE-INSTITUT e.V.

Am Romerhof 35
6000 Frankfurt am Main, Federal Republic of Germany

Telephone: (0611) 79081

Founded: 1952

Officers: H. Haeske.

Independent, non-profit, research institute; one of the research centers of the Battelle Memorial Institute. **Staff:** 863, including 330 scientists and engineers. **Sources of support:** Contract research sponsored by industry, business associations, and government authorities. **Annual Budget:** 62 Mio. DM.

Objectives and interests: Research and development and scientific studies in the physical, life, and engineering sciences, as well as in the economic and social sciences.

Major programs and projects: Electronic Funds Transfer Systems (6 projects): includes such topics as "Worldwide Investigation of Attitudes Towards Payment Methods and Forecast of the Demand for New Payment Systems." Raw Materials Studies include: "Future World Markets for Non Coking Coal"; "The Production of Formed Coke and Its Future"; "Impact on Conventional Coke-Making and Blast Furnace Operations in the World"; "Future World Markets for Coking Coal."

Special facilities: —

Activities: Most activities are related to contract research. Some courses are also sponsored—for example, a recent course on acoustic emission.

Publications: *Battelle Information* (bulletin, three times a year); results of research are published for the sponsor of the project.

BATTELLE MEMORIAL INSTITUTE
505 King Avenue
Columbus, Ohio 43201, U.S.A.

Telephone: (614) 424-6424

Founded: 1925

Officers: Clair E. Fultz, Chairman of the Board; S. L. Fawcett, President; Ronald S. Paul, Senior Vice President; T. W. Ambrose, Director, Pacific Northwest Division; John M. Batch, General Manager, Battelle Project Management Division; Horst Haeske, Managing Director, Battelle-Institut e.V. (Frankfurt).

Public purpose, not-for-profit organization engaged in research and educational activities. **Staff:** 6,300. **Sources of support:** Industry and government. **Annual Budget:** $224.4 million.

Objectives and interests: To benefit mankind by the advancement and utilization of science through technological innovation and educational activities; research is centered in the physical, life, engineering, and social/behavioral sciences.

Major programs and projects: Conducts over 2,700 studies and research programs annually, in the following areas: "Community Life"—encompassing studies aimed at improved housing, safer and more convenient mass transportation, better highways, more effective ways of dealing with complex community problems, and enhanced business and economic activities. "Environment"—including studies in air pollution, water quality, noise pollution, and solid waste treatment. "Energy"—concerned with present-day and potential sources of energy—coal, gas, nuclear, laser fusion, solar, geothermal—and involved with the generation, storage and use of energy, and related environmental and economic considerations. "Food-Agriculture"—studies in land use, new sources of food, use of agricultural by-products, and methods of enhancing food products. "Health"—development of new drugs, better diagnostic tools, and materials and devices to replace diseased or damaged parts of the body. "Manufacturing Technology"—including planning studies to assist industry in anticipating future demands and constraints.

Special facilities: Maintains a 150,000 volume library and various information analysis services, including Materials and Ceramics Information Center, Magnesium Research Information Center, Iron Information Center, and Battelle's Automated Search Information System, an on-line interactive information data storage, retrieval, and analysis software system.

Activities: Organizes and presents a wide variety of workshops, seminars, and special courses that are supported by sponsoring organizations or by attendees through payment of fees. These are conducted mainly through the Center for Improved Education at Battelle-Columbus and the Human Affairs Research Centers in Seattle, Washington.

Publications: *Battelle Today* (quarterly). Each year the Battelle staff authors hundreds of reports, published articles, papers, and books—890 articles and papers and 18 books in 1977. A list of published papers and articles is issued annually and is available upon request.

THE BROOKINGS INSTITUTION
1775 Massachusetts Avenue, N.W.
Washington, D.C. 20036, U.S.A.

Telephone: (202) 797-6000

Founded: 1927

Officers: Bruce K. MacLaury, President; Joseph A. Pechman, Director of Economic Studies; Martha Derthick, Director of Governmental Studies; John D. Steinbruner, Director of Foreign Policy Studies; Walter G. Held, Director of Advanced Study Program.

Non-profit organization for research and education in public policy. **Staff:** 50 senior fellows and research associates; about 175 supporting staff. **Sources of support:** Foundations, corporations, endowment, U.S. government. **Annual Budget:** $9,300,000 estimated for FY 79.

Objectives and interests: Policy-oriented research, education, and publication in economics, government, foreign policy, and the social sciences generally.

Major programs and projects: "The Future of Social Security"—Analysis of major issues in financing the social security system. "Long-Term Growth of Output and Productivity"—Analysis of proposals for maximizing U.S. economic growth. "The Future of the Navy"—Examines the optimum size and composition of the U.S. Navy in the year 2000. "Future Problems in U.S.-Japanese Relations"—Examines economic and security problems in U.S.-Japanese relations over the next ten years.

Special facilities: Library of 45,000 volumes supports research in the Institution's main fields of interest (not open to the public); Social Science Computation Center provides computing services to research staff and to other non-profit organizations in Washington, D.C. engaged in quantitative social science research. Publications program publishes over 250,000 volumes a year in sales.

Activities: Through its conferences, seminars, roundtables, and other educational activities, the Advanced Study Program aids leaders in government, business, and the professions in increasing their understanding of public policy issues. Conferences include: "Public Policy Issues," "Business in Contemporary Society," "Issues in Science and Technology," "Federal Government Operations," "Government, the Economy, and American Society," "Critical Public Policy Issues." Educational programs may be conducted upon request for groups of scholars participating in special fellowship programs. The Institution also sponsors Economic Policy Fellowships, Research Fellowships, Guest Scholar Program, Federal Executive Fellowships, and Visiting Professor and Younger Scholar Programs.

Publications: *Brookings Bulletin* (quarterly); *Brookings Papers on Economic Activity* (journal, three times a year). Brookings publishes 25 to 30 books and papers annually. Some of the more recent of these include: *Modernizing the Strategic Bomber Force: Why and How*, Alton H. Quanbeck and Archie L. Wood (1976); *Transportation for the Cities*, Wilfred Owen (1976); *Setting National Priorities: The Coming Decade*, Henry Owen and Charles Schultze, editors (1976); *Regimes for the Oceans, Outer Space, and Weather: The Impact of Technological Change*, Seyom Brown, Nina W. Cornell, Larry L. Fabian, Edith Weiss (1976).

BUREAU D'INFORMATIONS ET DE PREVISIONS ECONOMIQUES
[BUREAU OF ECONOMIC DATA AND FORECASTS]   **Telephone:** 747 1166
122 Avenue Charles de Gaulle
Neuilly 92522, France   **Founded:** 1958

Officers: Claude Gruson, President; Rene Mercier, Administrator; Jean Hauchecorne, Managing Director; Henri Aujac, Scientific Consultant; Jean Malsot, Director.

Non-profit research organization. Staff: 50 professionals. **Sources of support:** Membership dues; research contracts with private companies and government agencies. **Annual Budget:** Ten million francs.

Objectives and interests: To analyze the principal factors that affect economic growth; to improve forecasting methods.

Major programs and projects: Technological forecasting; medium-term sectoral forecasts; new growth and long-term construction technology; futuristic research on the economic and social situation of major countries, both developed and developing, and the structure of international relations; long-term substitution of steel and other materials; long-term world demand with regard to different industries.

Special facilities: Information service; data bank.

Activities: Lectures; special task forces; seminars.

Publications: *Prevision a un an de l'activite de l'economie francaise [One Year Forecast of the French Economy]* (annual); *Projections detaillees glissantes a cinq ans [Rolling Five-Year Projections for 200 Products]* (annual); *Evaluation de la capacite strategique des industries prioritaires au regard de leur aptitude a exercer des effets de domination dans les filieres industrielles [Evalatuion of the Strategic Capacity of Leading Industries with Regard to Their Ability to Dominate Industrial Procedures]* (1977); *Prospective et voies de recherche en matiere de prevision technologique sur la base d'une evaluation critique des prevision realisees par le BIPE au cours de annees 60 [Prospects and Avenues of Research for Technological Forecasting on the Basis of a Critical Evaluation of Forecasts Made by the BIPE during the 1960s]* (1977); *La specialisation internationale a l'horizon 1985 - Recherches methodologiques et scenarios chiffres a l'echelle mondiale [International Specialization to the Year 1985: Methodological Research and Scenarios Quantified on a World Scale]* (1978); *Les automatismes -Analyse approfondie des conditions de developpement de l'industrie francaise [Automation: A Deeper Analysis of the Conditions for Growth in French Industry]* (1978).

BUSINESS INTERNATIONAL CORPORATION   **Telephone:** (212) 750-6300
1 Dag Hammarskjold Plaza
New York, New York 10017, U.S.A.   **Founded:** 1954

Officers: Orville L. Freeman, President and Chief Executive Officer; Elliot Haynes, Chairman of the Board; Sol M. Linowitz, Director; William Persen, Senior Vice-President; Erika Izakson, Vice-President, Research.

Privately-held corporation. **Staff:** 230 fulltime worldwide; about 100 part-time located in 75 countries. **Sources of support:** Sales of research, publishing, educational, conference and other services to clients, private and public. **Annual Budget:** No answer.

Objectives and interests: Business International is an independent research, publishing and advisory organization serving corporations doing business across borders and those who support and govern them, including bankers, attorneys, consultants, colleagues, etc.

Major programs and projects: "The World Automotive Industry to 1995"-multi-client supported private study completed in December 1975, slated for updating in 1979, over 3,000 pages. "Latin American Forecasting Study/ European Forecasting Study/Asia-Pacific Forecasting Study"-each year, Business International presents a series of regional forecasting studies covering a total of 35 countries, proving five-year forecasts of political and economic developments in each country. "Business International Forecasts for 35 World Markets"-regularly updated, short-term forecasts of political, social and economic conditions. Individual, proprietary research projects for clients, both political/economic, industry/market, and issues.

Special facilities: Business International Data Service (BI/Data), a statistical database containing more than 120,000 entries dating back to 1960 for 70 countries. BI/Metrics, a currency forecasting service, model-based, which takes a "general equilibrium" approach to currency forecasting rather than standard partial equilibrium.

Activities: For special clients, Business International organizes informal roundtable meetings with heads of state of individual countries and their cabinets, as well as functional meetings among clients themselves to exchange ideas and opinions on various areas of operations; Business International Institute is a separate unit providing courses in international business and international finance, east-west trade, etc.

Publications: *Business Eastern Europe* (weekly); *Business International* (weekly); *Business Asia* (weekly); *Business Latin America* (weekly); *Business Europe* (weekly); *Business International Money Report* (weekly); *Operating in a Changing Canada: A Rich Market, An Uncertain Future; Cuba at the Turning Point; International Licensing: Opportunities and Challenges in Worldwide Technology Management; Italy: How International Companies View It.*

UNIVERSITY OF CALIFORNIA-LOS ANGELES, DEPARTMENT OF PSYCHIATRY, PROGRAM ON PSYCHOSOCIAL ADAPTATION AND THE FUTURE (PSAF)

Telephone: (213) 825-0463

760 Westwood Plaza, NPI C8-831B
Los Angeles, California 90024, U.S.A.

Founded: 1971

Officers: Roderic Gorney, Director, PSAF; David Loye, Research Director, PSAF.

University program. **Staff:** Six professionals, many volunteers and student assistants. **Sources of support:** — **Annual Budget:** No answer.

Objectives and interests: To discover psychosocial means of enhancing the achievement and psychological strength of both children and adults, and of decreasing the incidence of violence and mental illness; to find means of helping large numbers of people to make soon enough those changes in themselves and their environment which accumulating information shows are necessary for the survival of our species; to reinforce the ability and determination of people to endure the rigorous efforts required of learning to live with uncertainty in the turbulent future, resisting the temptation of all spurious promises to relieve us of this obligation; as a first step in enabling everyone to participate in creating the future, to disseminate the results of rational inquiry to as broad an audience as possible, and to develop techniques for encouraging, collecting, and utilizing feedback from this audience.

Major programs and projects: Researching effects of dramatized television on children and adults; researching cultural patterns leading to high and low levels of achievement, mental illness, and aggression.

Special facilities: —

Activities: Research and courses on The Human Agenda.

Publications: *The Human Agenda*, Roderic Gorney (1973).

(From the first edition. Corrections not received by press time.)

CALIFORNIA STATE DEPARTMENT OF EDUCATION
OFFICE OF SUPPORT SERVICES
721 Capitol Mall
Sacramento, California 95814, U.S.A.

Telephone: (916) 445-7456

Founded: 1975

Officers: Ramiro Reyes, Assistant Superintendent, Office of Support Services; Gerald Hamrin, Administrator, Planning Section; Don Glines, Consultant, Planning Section.

State education agency. **Staff:** Three, all part-time. **Sources of support:** Federal. **Annual Budget:** General allocation.

Objectives and interests: Examining alternative futures and studying the potential implications for education.

Major programs and projects: Development of resource bibliographies related to societal and educational futures; technical assistance to the field upon request.

Special facilities: —

Activities: In-service seminars and workshops for local school districts and county educational agencies.

Publications: Special papers and bibliographies prepared as requested for various components of State Department of Education.

CALIFORNIA TOMORROW
681 Market Street, Room 1059
San Francisco, California 94105, U.S.A.

Telephone: (415) 391-7544

Founded: 1961

Officers: Weyman L. Lundquist, President; Joseph C. Houghteling, Vice President (Northern California); Ronald L. Olson, Vice President (Southern California); Clarence E. Heller, Secretary/Treasurer; Richard A. Grant, Executive Secretary, Editor, *Cry California* reports; Walt Anderson, Editor, *Cry California* annual review.

Private, non-profit educational organization. **Staff:** Eight. **Sources of support:** Private foundations, individual contributions, membership dues. **Annual Budget:** No answer.

Objectives and interests: To explore and throw light upon the major problems Californians must face in order to protect California's natural environment, improve its man-made environment, and at the same time guarantee opportunities for economic strength and personal fulfillment to all its people; to demonstrate ways of solving these problems, emphasizing that a system of state and regional planning and administration, highly responsive to the public's interest in the quality of life, is practical and essential to society; to inform and educate the public about these goals.

Major programs and projects: Currently engaged in a 4-year program (1978/81) to evaluate government processes at state and regional levels and to recommend programs that will answer the often conflicting needs of environmental conservation, economic growth and social well being. The initial phase will look at planning and budgeting procedures of state government and formulate a political mechanism able to oversee a comprehensive planning process. The second phase will consist of a series of regional meetings around the state to consider the implications of the program's study and research to date. A final product is expected to be a further refinement of *The California Tomorrow Plan.*

Special facilities: —

Activities: An environmental intern program screens and places qualified applicants in subsidized internships with government agencies, businesses and non-profit groups throughout California. Interns are able to apply their academic and community experience to environmentally related tasks and to gain valuable on-the-job knowledge that can direct and enhance their future careers. Sponsoring organizations receive professionally oriented, enthusiastic workers who are willing to tackle special projects for relatively low pay.

Publications: *Cry California* (quarterly journal); *California Going, Going,* Samuel E. Wood and Alfred E. Heller (1962); *Phantom Cities of California,* Samuel E. Wood and Alfred E. Heller, (1963); *The Federal Threats to the California Landscape,* Samuel E. Wood and Daryl Lembke (1967); *The California Tomorrow Plan,* edited by Alfred Heller (1972); *Democracy in the Space Age: Regional Government under a California State Plan,* edited by John W. Abbott (1973).

CAMBRIDGE RESEARCH INSTITUTE, INC.
15 Mt. Auburn Street
Cambridge, Massachusetts 02138, U.S.A.

Telephone: (617) 492-3800

Founded: 1959

Officers: Gerald A. Simon, Managing Director; John D. Glover; Carl W. Thieme; David B. Kiser; Bertrand Fox; J. Keith Butters; Dan T. Smith.

Private research institute. **Staff:** 50. **Sources of support:** Client engagements. **Annual Budget:** No answer.

Objectives and interests: CRI provides services to help executives understand the future, plan for it, and manage change. CRI provides these services through research, consultation, and educational programs, within an overall framework of Environmental Analysis and Planning. The major interest of CRI is in *applying* key information regarding the environment—past, present, and future—to practical problems of business strategy and policy, including the impact of changes in public policy on private and public institutions.

Major programs and projects: "Trends Affecting the U.S. Health Care System." "Trends Affecting the U.S. Banking System."

Special facilities: —

Activities: CRI conducts seminars and conferences for clients, and participates in in-house management development programs. Subject areas include environmental analysis, strategy formulation and organizational change.

Publications: *Chief Executive's Handbook,* John D. Gover and Gerald A. Simon, editors (1976); *Omnibus Copyright Revision: Comparative Analysis of the Issues* (1973); *What You Should Know About the Value-Added Tax,* Dan Throop Smith, James B. Webber, Carol M. Cerf (1973).

CANADIAN ASSOCIATION FOR FUTURES STUDIES
No. 302 - 100 Gloucester, Street
Ottawa, Ontario K2P OA4, Canada

Telephone: (613) 236-9712

Founded: 1976

Officers: Ruben F.W. Nelson, President; Lou D'Amore, Vice-President; Roy Woodbridge, Secretary; Frank Feather, Treasurer; Barbara Moore, Membership Secretary; Richard M. Henshel, Editor, *Futures Canada.*
National, non-profit, voluntary association with affiliated regional associations in Canada. **Staff:** One, plus eight executives, three editorial board members, and twelve regional coordinators. **Sources of support:** Membership fees. **Annual Budget:** No answer.

Objectives and interests: To encourage members to recognize and accept responsibility for shaping Canada's future; to provide an interdisciplinary, critical forum for Canadians interested in futures studies; to provide information on futures studies in Canada and elsewhere in the world; to publish such information and research results; to encourage serious study of the future and cooperation with other national and international organizations.

Major programs and projects: Fourth Annual National Conference, Kingston, Ontario, June 7-9, 1979; further development of regional affiliated associations and provision of assistance to them; an international Futures Conference, "Through the 80s," July 20-25, 1980, Toronto, Ontario, in conjunction with the World Future Society.

Special facilities: —

Activities: Annual conferences; regular meetings and other programs sponsored by regional affiliated associations; publication program for members; courses and speakers bureau under consideration.

Publications: *Futures Canada* (quarterly bulletin, French and English); *CAFS News.*

CENTER FOR FUTURE MANAGEMENT
c/o Tom O'Brien
4605 W. Frankfort Drive
Rockville, Maryland 20853, U.S.A.

Telephone: (301) 871-7180 (evenings)
(202) 523-6341 (daytime)

Founded: 1976

Officers: Tom O'Brien, Chairperson; Emilie Heller, Co-Chairperson; Kent Myers, Secretary/Treasurer; Robert Maston; Annette Hartenstein; Pauline Frederick.

Non-profit. **Staff:** No full time staff — all volunteers. **Sources of support:** Current funding from occasional workshops and seminars. **Annual Budget:** No answer.

Objectives and interests: To develop, within systems and institutions, a safe and healthy environment in which all participants have appropriate opportunities for growth, receive appropriate rewards, realize their full potentialities, and harmoniously perform at their best.

Major programs and projects: "Dialogues with Futurists" — a series of intermittent dialogues with pioneers in the evolution of the concepts of future management. Workshops and seminars — occasional sessions held in conjunction with other organizations to promote the concepts of future management (may vary in length from one day to one week). Public programs — occasional one evening sessions in which Associates of the Center provide information to the general public as well as invited guests.

Special facilities: —

Activities: Conferences, seminars, lectures, dialogues with futurists, journal articles and technical assistance directed to individuals and managers. All Center activities lead to the development, evolution and promotion of an all-inclusive concept of management as the role and responsibility of participants in a system, employees in an enterprise, members of a group, etc.

Publications: Currently seeking funding for a projected newsletter, *Tomorrow's Management.*

CENTER FOR INTEGRATIVE STUDIES

Telephone: (713) 749-1121

Library Building, Room 571
University of Houston
Houston, Texas 77004, U.S.A.

Founded: 1968

Officers: John McHale, Founding Director; Magda Cordell McHale, Acting Director and Senior Research Associate, Guy F. Streatfeild, Assistant Director.

Research institute. **Staff:** Six. **Sources of support:** University; federal; foundations. **Annual Budget:** No answer.

Objectives and interests: Primary objectives — global development of future studies and long-range planning. Special interests — human needs and priorities assessment, world trends, resource projections, and social and cultural futures.

Major programs and projects: "Basic Human Needs: A Framework for Action"; "Human Requirements, Supply Levels and Outer Bounds" — assessment of global human needs over time and capacity to meet them within biospheric constraints. "International Survey of Future Studies" — world survey of individuals and organizations in the field. "The Timetable Project" — a continuing assessment of projected relationships between population, resources and technologies. "The Changing Information Environment" — impact of information /communications technologies on society in the next 25 years. "Women in World Terms: Facts and Trends" — comparative study of historical, present, and projected data on women. "The Anatomy of Change" — comprehensive review and projection of major changes in the 20th Century. "The Structure of Conceptual Revolutions" — interrelationships of scientific, social and cultural change. "Children in World Terms" — comprehensive review of present and future data on children worldwide.

Special facilities: Data on world trends; social; cultural; resources. Project files in specialized areas such as sociology of future study and major programs above. Personal library holdings in futures studies, resources and trend data.

Activities: Educational — undergraduate/graduate coursework and independent study; conferences organized in cosponsorship with other institutions.

Publications: *The Future of the Future,* John McHale (George Braziller, Inc., 1969); *The Ecological Context,* John McHale (George Braziller, Inc., 1970); *World Facts and Trends,* John McHale (Collier Books, Inc., 1972); *The Changing Information Environment,* John McHale (Westview Press, 1976); *The Futures Directory,* John McHale and Magda Cordell McHale (Westview Press, 1977); *Basic Human Needs: A Framework for Action,* John McHale and Magda Cordell McHale (Transaction Books, 1977); *The World of Children, 1979 World's Children Data Sheet,* and *Children in the World,* John McHale and Magda Cordell McHale (Population Reference Bureau, 1979). In addition, since 1968, the Center has produced numerous reports, papers, articles and studies. Some of these are available from the Center.

CENTER FOR POLICY PROCESS

Telephone: (202) 387-5700

1755 Massachusetts Avenue N.W.
Washington, D.C. 20036, U.S.A.

Founded: 1974

Officers: John Naisbitt, Chairman of Board of Directors, Acting Director; Nicholas Zumas, Carlton Spitzer, Directors; Jane Chrisbaum, Administrative Director.

Non-profit, tax-exempt, educational. **Staff:** 11. **Sources of support:** Membership fees, Conference grants (foundation). **Annual Budget:** No answer.

Objectives and interests: Forecast social trends by means of content analysis of daily local press and assist members in understanding, anticipating and managing change.

Major programs and projects: —

Special facilities: Microfiche data bank of local press stories used in publication of the *Trend Report*. For members' use only.

Activities: National conferences, open to the public. Seminars for members, three times a year.

Publications: *Trend Report* (three times a year for members).

CENTER FOR POLICY RESEARCH, INC.

Telephone: (212) 870-2135

475 Riverside Drive
New York, New York 10027, U.S.A.

Founded: 1968

Officers: Amitai Etzioni, Director; Edward W. Lehman, Associate Director; Emanuel S. Savas, Associate Director; Clara Shapiro, Executive Officer; Sophie Sa, Administrator.

Independent, non-profit research institution. **Staff:** Approximately 50. **Sources of support:** Government grants and contracts; foundations. **Annual Budget:** No answer.

Objectives and interests: To provide the intellectual environment and the facilities for social research dealing with issues of public policy, particularly health education, crime, incarceration, manpower, environment, aging.

Major programs and projects: "Evaluating Deinstitutionalization: Willowbrook's Case." "New Methods of Health and Medical Responsibility: A Critical Analysis." "The Ethical Preparation of the Next Generation of Americans." "Parole Alternatives."

Special facilities: Conference rooms for groups up to 300.

Activities: Conference on Dependency and Institutions (Spring 1976).

Publications: *The Active Society,* Amitai Etzioni (1968); *Genetic Fix,* Amitai Etzioni (1973); *Technological Short Cuts to Social Change,* Amitai Etzioni and Richard Remp (1973); *Computers and Bureaucratic Reform,* Kenneth C. Laudon (1975).

THE CENTER FOR STRATEGIC AND INTERNATIONAL STUDIES
GEORGETOWN UNIVERSITY

Telephone: (202) 833-8595

1800 K Street, N.W., Suite 520
Washington, D.C. 20006, U.S.A.

Founded: 1962

Officers: David M. Abshire, Chairman of the Center; Ray S. Cline, Amos A. Jordan, John Richardson, Jr., Michael A. Samuels, Executive Directors; M. Jon Vondracek, Director of Communications.

Private non-profit research institute. **Staff:** 60. **Sources of support:** Foundations. **Annual Budget:** $2.5 million.

Objectives and interests: To examine and call public attention to emerging public policy issues with international implications.

Major programs and projects: "National Coal Policy Project"—environmentalists and industrialists seeking environmentally acceptable uses of U.S. coal resources. "Future of Business Project"—a civilizational look at business over the next three decades.

Special facilities: None.

Activities: Conferences, seminars, roundtables, publications.

Publications: *The Washington Review of Strategic and International Studies*, edited by Michael Ledeen, (quarterly); *The Washington Papers*, edited by Walter Laqueur, (10 issues annually); *World Power Assessment*, by Ray S. Cline (1975); *Energy: A National Issue*, by Francis X. Murray (1977); *Energy: A National Issue*, film featuring Flintstones characters, narration by Charleton Heston, 1977 CINE Award winner; *Futurology: Promise, Performance, Prospects*, by Victor C. Ferkiss, one of The Washington Papers series.

CENTER FOR THE STUDY OF DEMOCRATIC INSTITUTIONS: THE FUND FOR THE REPUBLIC, INC.

Telephone: (805) 969-3281

P.O. Box 4068, 2056 Eucalyptus Hill Road
Santa Barbara, California 93103, U.S.A.

Founded: 1953

Officers: Morris L. Levinson, Chairman of the Board; Maurice Mitchell, President; Peter Tagger, Secretary and Treasurer; Donald McDonald, Editor of *The Center Magazine* and *World Issues*.

Non-profit, educational institution. **Staff:** 26. **Sources of support:** Contributions from members. **Annual Budget:** $1,200,000.

Objectives and interests: To clarify basic issues and widen the circles of discussion about them, principal fields of research being the social, economic and political aspects of democratic society and impact of government, corporations, trade unions and religious institutions on individual members of society, including studies on the American character, war and peace, relations between American problems and world problems, church-state relationships, constitutional privileges, scientific and technological development, law, labor, and other basic issues facing a free society.

Major programs and projects: Conferences, dialogues, and publications.

Special facilities: Maintains a library.

Activities: Conferences, dialogues, publications.

Publications: *World Issues* (bimonthly newsletter); *The Center Magazine* (bimonthly); *Ecocide . . . and Thoughts Toward Survival*, Clifton Fadiman and Jean White, editors (1971); *The Presidency Reappraised*, Rexford C. Tugwell and Thomas Cronin, editors (1974); *Pacem in Maribus*. Elisabeth Mann Borgese, editor (1972); *Rural Development: World Frontiers*. Laurence Hewes (1974); *The Emerging Constitution*, Rexford G. Tugwell (1974).

CENTER FOR THE STUDY OF THE FUTURE

Telephone: (317) 264-3984

925 W. Michigan
Indianapolis, Indiana 46202, U.S.A.

Founded: 1975

Officers: Richard K. Curtis, President.

Non-profit institution engaged in research, publication, and public conferences, affilated with the Central Indiana Chapter of the World Future Society. Staff: All volunteers. **Sources of support:** Gifts. **Annual Budget:** No answer.

Objectives and interests: To foster combinations of public and private cooperation; to work closely with state and metropolitan area planning bodies, as well as with colleges and universities.

Major programs and projects: —

Special facilities: —

Activities: Mainly research to link together representatives of various organizations in the Indianapolis area.

Publications: Occasional newsletter.

CENTER FOR THE STUDY OF THE FUTURE

Telephone: (503) 282-5835

4110 N.E. Alameda
Portland, Oregon 97212, U.S.A.

Founded: 1973

Officers: Carl Townsend, President and Director; Floyd Pennington, Vice-President; Sandy Townsend, Secretary-Treasurer.

Non-profit research institute. Staff: — **Sources of support:** Publications; grants. **Annual Budget:** No answer.

Objectives and interests: To serve as a resource and educational center for Christians studying the future and how the body of Christ should relate to it.

Major programs and projects: "The ENABLER System"—Microcomputer-based information retrieval system. "Christian Survival Kits"—Cassette tapes/workbook study programs for churches and individuals.

Special facilities: Specialized library on the future, change, and the church.

Activities: Seminars and consulting available on request.

Publications: *Patterns* (bimonthly newsletter); *Future Shock and the Christian* (1976); *300 Ways to Fight Inflation; The Church in the Near Future* (cassette tape and report).

CENTRAL PLANNING BUREAU

Van Stolkweg 14
The Hague, The Netherlands

Telephone: (070) 514151

Founded: 1945

Officers: C. A. van den Beld, Director; H. den Hartog, Deputy Director; J. Weitenberg, Deputy Director; J. Sandee, Advisor.

Governmental, non-profit, research institute. Staff: 140. **Sources of support:** Netherlands Government. **Annual Budget:** No answer.

Objectives and interests: Public policy research on the economic aspects of domestic and international issues; short-, medium-, and long-term forecasting on economic matters; national economic cost-benefit analysis.

Major programs and projects: "Macro-economische Verkenning" [Macro-economic Outlook]—Annual publication, together with the Budget. "Centraal Economisch Plan" [Central Economic Plan]— Annual publication. "De Nederlandse Economie in 19-" [The Netherlands Economy in 19-]—Medium-term (five year) forecast of The Netherlands economy.

Special facilities: —

Activities: Research.

Publications: (See "Major Programs and Projects.) Reports and studies are published in several series: "CPB-Monographs," "Occasional Papers," and "CPB-Reprints." Official publications are on sale at the Staatsuitgeverij, Christ. Plantijnstraat, The Hague.

CENTRE DE RECHERCHE SUR LE BIEN-ETRE (CEREBE)
[CENTER OF RESEARCH ON WELL-BEING]
140, Rue du Chevaleret
75013 Paris, France

Telephone: (1) 584-14-20

Founded: 1967

Officers: Philippe d'Iribarne, Director.

Non-profit, research institute. Staff: 10. **Sources of support:** Centre National de la Recherche Scientifique. **Annual Budget:** No answer.

Objectives and interests: Research aimed at analysing the mechanisms, especially those of a psychological and sociological kind, by which people's physical and social environment influence their personal well-being.

Major programs and projects: "The Influence of Consumption Upon Personal Well-being." "The Socio-cultural Factors of 'Economic' Behavior."

Special facilities: —

Activities: —

Publications: *La Politique du Bonheur [The Politics of Happiness]*, Ph. d'Iribarne (Le Seuil, 1973); *L'invasion pharmaceutique [The Pharmaceutical Invasion]*, J-P. Dupuy and S. Karsenty (Le Seuil, 1974); *Le gaspillage et le desir*

20

[*Waste and Desire*], Ph. d'Iribarne (Fayard, 1975); *Valeur sociale et encombrement du temps* [*Social Value and the Pressure on People's Time*], J-P. Dupuy (Centre National de la Recherche Scientifique, 1975); "La consommation et le bien-etre, problemes de theorie et de methodes" ["Consumption and Well-being: Problems of Theory and Methods"], Ph. d'Iribarne (*Rapport CEREBE*, 1977).

CENTRE D'ETUDE DES CONSEQUENCES GENERALES DES GRANDES TECHNIQUES NOUVELLES
[CENTER FOR THE STUDY OF THE GENERAL CONSEQUENCES OF NEW TECHNOLOGY]

Telephone: 260 30 48

5, rue d'Alger
75001 Paris, France

Founded: 1956

Officers: Georges Gueron, Director of Publications; Jean Jacques Ballan, Executive Committee; Jeannine Gueron, Executive Committee; Armand Braun; Jean Claude Roumanteau.

Private, non-profit association. Staff: — **Sources of support:** Membership dues and private grants. **Annual Budget:** No answer.

Objectives and interests: To study the consequences for the individual of scientific and technological progress.

Major programs and projects: Established, in conjunction with Mankind 2000, the International Foundation for Social Innovation (Paris).

Special facilities: —

Activities: Study groups, lectures, workshops.

Publications: *L'Homme et les techniques nouvelles* [*Man and New Technology*] (bimonthly).

CENTRE INTERNATIONAL DE RECHERCHE SUR L'ENVIRONNEMENT ET LE DEVELOPPEMENT
[INTERNATIONAL CENTER FOR RESEARCH ON DEVELOPMENT AND THE ENVIRONMENT]

Telephone: 544.38.49, poste 219

54, boulevard Raspail
75270 Paris Cedex 06, France

Founded: 1973

Officers: Ignacy Sachs, Director; Krystyna Vinaver, Research Coordinator.

Academic research institute. Staff: 15. **Sources of support:** Ecole des hautes etudes en sciences sociales, Secretariat d'Etat aux Universites [School of Higher Studies in the Social Sciences, State Secretariat of Universities]; also research contracts. **Annual Budget:** No answer.

Objectives and interests: Interdisciplinary research, particularly related to long-term socio-economic planning and strategies for economic and social growth, with rational administration of natural resources and the environment; the definition of strategies of ecological development for developing countries. Areas of interest include lifestyle and patterns of consumption, technology, and the management of space.

Major programs and projects: "Ecodevelopment"—an alternative approach to various subjects (health care, habitats, etc.). "Alternative Energy Strategies for Developing Countries." "Life Styles and Time Management." "Global Management of Natural Resources." "Substitutions Within Natural Resources."

Special facilities: A unit of documentation and liaison on ecodevelopment.

Activities: Seminars: "Life Styles and Planning," "Third World Industrial Futures," "Appropriate Technology and Development Strategies," and "Ecodevelopment and Habitat".

Publications: *Ecodevelopment Newsletter*, edited by D. Thery (quarterly); *Energie et Division Internationale du Travail* [*Energy and International Division of Work*], J. C. Hourcade (1978); *Elements pour une Nouvelle strategie de Sante au Tiers Monde* [*Elements in a New Health Strategy for the Third World*], S. Sigal (1978); *Pour une Economie Politique du Developpement* [*For a New Political Economy of Development*], I. Sachs (1977); *Nourrir en harmonie avec l'environnement* [*To Feed in Harmony with the Environment*], A. Berger, O. Godard, H. L. Morales, S. Passaris, C. Romanini (1975).

CENTRE FOR POLICY RESEARCH

Telephone: 672774/672295

C-6 Commercial Area
Paschimi Marg, Vasant Vihar
New Delhi 110057, India

Founded: 1973

Officers: V.A. Pai Panandiker, Director; Satish K. Arora, P. D. Malgavkar.

Non-profit research institution. **Staff:** 22. **Sources of support:** Annual membership of State Governments, public sector undertakings, grants-in-aid from Government of India. **Annual Budget:** 10 million Indian rupees.

Objectives and interests: Study policy issues in crucial areas of national importance and help develop a body of knowledge about policy making.

Major programs and projects: "Towards an Industrial Policy—2000 A.D." "Meeting the Foodgrains Prospects—2000 A.D." "Investment Policy for Agricultural Development." "Employment Policy." "Population Policy—2000 A.D."—a study of the relationship between population and economic development.

Special facilities: Maintains a library of books and periodicals on policy sciences, bureaucracy, futurology, etc.

Activities: Research projects, seminars and conferences three to four times a year on topics of policy issues of national importance, and occasional training courses.

Publications: *C.P.R.* (quarterly) free newsletter edited by V.A. Pai Panandiker; *Towards an Industrial Policy—2000 A.D.*, P. D. Malgavkar and V. A. Pai Panandiker (1977); *Cybernetic Analysis of Indian Social System*, P. N. Rastogi (1978); *Bureaucracy and Development Administration*, V. A. Pai Panandiker and S. S. Kshirsagar (1978); *Towards a Theory of Development Administration*, V. A. Pai Panandiker (1977); *Policy Implications of Incentives and Disincentives in Family Planning*, V. A. Pai Panandiker, R. N. Bishnoi, O. P. Sharma (1977).

CENTRUM FOR TVARVETENSKAPLIGA STUDIER AV MANNISKANS VILLKOR [CENTER FOR INTERDISCIPLINARY STUDIES OF THE HUMAN CONDITION]

Telephone: (031) 168691

Molndalsvagen 85
Gothenburg, Sweden

Founded: —

Officers: Emin Tengstrom; Britta Jungen; Olof Janson; Dick Larsson.

Non-profit research institute, part of the University of Gothenburg. **Staff:** — **Sources of support:** — **Annual Budget:** —

Objectives and interests: Matters of energy and resources, future studies and interdisciplinary studies of the human condition in a wide perspective.

Major programs and projects: "The Swedish Future Energy Provision in a Historical and Global Perspective." "The Valsviken Project" — an attempt to create a self-reliant area of work and housing in an ordinary town. "Alternative Production Groups" — in cooperation with the trade unions trying to solve some of the problems in the Swedish shipbuilding industry.

Special facilities: Institution library. Admission to the facilities of the university in the field.

Activities: Seminars on problems of development, conferences on different subjects, and a few courses.

Publications: *Informationsbladet. [Information Paper]* Eva Ekehorn, editor (seven times a year); *Alternativbladet [Alternative Paper]* Ulla Wall, editor (somewhat irregular, about four times a year); *Rapport om Surte [Report about Surte]*, members of the Center (1976); *Sveriges Framtida energiforsorjning i ett historiskt och globalt perspektiv [The Swedish Future Energy Provision in a Historical and Global Perspective]*, K.E. Eriksson (1977); *Valsviken*, Emin Tengstrom and Kare Olsson (1976).

CENTRUM VOOR VRAAGSTUKKEN VAN WETENSCHAP EN SAMENLEVING, "DE BOERDERIJ" [CENTER FOR PROBLEMS OF SCIENCE AND SOCIETY, "DE BOERDERIJ"]

Telephone: (053) 892985

Twente University of Technology
Postbus 217
Enschede, The Netherlands

Founded: 1975

Officers: P. Boskma; W. A. Smit; G. H. de Vries.

Research and educational institution. Staff: Three. **Sources of support:** Twente University of Technology. **Annual Budget:** 500,000 Dutch guilders.

Objectives and interests: Research on subjects of science and society, including environmental and energy problems, nuclear proliferation, technical arms race and disarmament, philosophy of science.

Major programs and projects: Problems on acceptability of risks and risk evaluation; nuclear proliferation problems; future ethical problems connected with the development of science; internal and external factors in the development of science.

Special facilities: —

Activities: Courses for students; information provided for political parties, parliament, and pressure groups on subjects which have been studied at the Institute.

Publications: Reports published by the Institute are known as "Boerderijcahiers." Included in this series are *Uraniumverrijking [Uranium Enrichment]*, P. Boskma, W. A. Smit and G. H. de Vries (No. 7501); *Kernenergie in discussie [Nuclear Energy in Discussion]*, P. Boskma et. al. (No. 7502); *Kleine kansen— grote gevolgen—of gevolgen van een groot ongeluk met een kerncentrale [Consequences of a Nuclear Reactor Accident]*, G. van Dijk, W. A. Smith (No 7601); *Beheersing van technologische ontwikkeling: Noodzaak en Mogelijkheden [Control of Technological Development]* (No. 7602); *Een regeringsadviseur en een rebel: J. Robert Oppenheimer—Bertrand Russell en de maatschappelijke verantwoordelijkheid van de natuurwetenschapper [The Social Responsibility of the Scientist: J. Robert Oppenheimer and Bertrand Russell]*. D. Stemerding (No. 7603); *Technological Innovation: A Socio-Political Problem*, C. Freeman, B.V.A. Roling, A. M. Weinberg, H. F. York (No. 7701), *De Neutronenbom [The Neutron Bomb]*, J. D. Bosch, P. Boskma, J. Mellema (No. 7702); *Laserfusie: Verwevenheid van civiel en militair onderzoek [Laserfusion: The Connection Between Civil and Military Research]*, W.A. Smit (No. 7801.)

CHAMPOEG II—OREGON 2000 PROJECT
Room 306, State Library Building
Salem, Oregon 97310, U.S.A.

Telephone: (503) 378-3732

Founded: 1978

Officers: Leonard Rice, Chairman; James Breithaupt, Staff Director.

Public, State Government. Staff: Four. **Sources of support:** Pacific Northwest Regional Commission. **Annual Budget:** No answer.

Objectives and interests: To recommend to the Governor and Legislature growth policies for the State of Oregon.

Major programs and projects: Group was established by the Governor as a means to identify growth policy issues and recommend new legislation and changes in existing programs.

Special facilities: —

Activities: Oregon 2000 Commission meetings; public involvement meetings; research on growth and development.

Publications: *Preliminary Report of the Oregon 2000 Commission* (1979).

CLUB DE AMIGOS DE LA FUTUROLOGIA
[CLUB OF FRIENDS OF FUTUROLOGY]
Gran Via, 608, 80 D
Barcelona 7, Spain

Telephone: 302 46 35

Founded: 1972

Officers: Josep Perena, President; Albert Oliva, Secretary-General; Rosa Palet, Treasurer; Josefa Majoral, First Vice-Secretary; Conchita Bargallo, Second Vice-Secretary; Maria Luisa Cots, Third Vice-Secretary.

Private, non-profit, volunteer, membership organization for those desiring a better future. Staff: Volunteer. **Sources of support:** Member dues and donations. **Annual Budget:** 250,000 pesetas.

Objectives and interests: To identify and assimilate new trends in the world in general and in Europe in particular; to disseminate information on futurology; to conduct investigations of and formulate new answers to world problems.

Major programs and projects: "Energy Alternatives"—study of the problem of energy and energy use. "Power Structures and the World Problematique"—study of the present situation and possible alternatives.

Special facilities: Library containing books and journals related to futurology.

Activities: Conduct weekly study sessions on relevant themes for club members; conduct public sessions on special topics.

Publications: Newsletter of the club's activities.

THE CLUB OF ROME
163, Via Giorgione
00147 Rome, Italy

Telephone: (06) 54671

Founded: 1968

Officers: Executive Committee: Maurice Guernier; Alexander King; Saburo Okita; Aurelio Peccei, President; Eduard Pestel; Hugo Thiemann; Victor Urquidi.

Non-profit civil association (Canton of Geneva). **Staff:** None. **Sources of support:** Voluntary work, plus some royalties on publications. **Annual Budget:** No budget.

Objectives and interests: World problematique.

Major programs and projects: "Food for Doubling World Population" (Hans Linnemann)—how to feed eight billion people by the beginning of the 21st century. "Goals for Global Society" (Ervin Laszlo)—where a multi-billion society can, should and wants to go. Human Learning. Capital Requirements and Capital Formation.

Special facilities: —

Activities: Research and reflection projects; international conferences; contacts with social groups and decision-makers.

Publications: *The Limits to Growth* by Dennis L. Meadows et al., 1972; *Mankind at the Turning Point* by Mihajlo Mesarovic and Eduard Pestel, 1974; *RIO—Reshaping the International Order* by Jan Tinbergen (coordinator), 1976; *Beyond the Age of Waste* by Dennis Gabor, Umberto Colombo, et al, 1978; *Goals for Mankind* by Ervin Laszlo et al,1977; *Energy: The Countdown; The New Threshold* by the Executive Committee (1973), out of stock; *The Limits to Growth in Perspective* by Aurelio Peccei and Manfred Siebker (1973).

THE COLLEGE BOARD, FUTURE DIRECTIONS FOR A LEARNING SOCIETY
Telephone: (212) 582-6210

888 Seventh Avenue
New York, New York 10019, U.S.A.

Founded: 1977

Officers: Rexford G. Moon, Jr., Managing Director; Carol B. Aslanian, Associate Director; Ronald H. Miller, Assistant Director; Donna M. Pokorny, Assistant to the Director.

Non-profit organization. **Staff:** 10 **Sources of support:** Exxon Education Foundation; Sears Roebuck Foundation. **Annual Budget:** Approximately $600,000.

Objectives and interests: To develop consensus and support for strategies, services, and policies that can best meet current and projected needs of participants and providers in a learning society.

Major programs and projects: "National Forum on Learning and the American Future"—surveying 2,000 decision makers on their impressions of future societal trends and goals.

Special facilities: Lifelong Learning Library.

Activities: National Invitational Conference on Educational Information Services I and II (1977, 1978); National Institute on the Management of Lifelong Learning in Postsecondary Education (beginning in 1979)—10-day workshop each summer; one-day workshops at selected national conferences/meetings; one- to three-day workshops at selected sites; Policy Seminar on Lifelong Learning Adulthood (Aspen Institute, 1979).

Publications: *Learning Times*, Ronald Gross, editor (four times/year); *40 Million Americans in Career Transition*, Arbeiter, Aslanian, Schmerbeck, and Brickell (July 1978); *Telephone Counseling for Home-based Adults*, Arbeiter, Aslanian, Schmerbeck, and Brickell (July 1978); *Lifelong Learning During Adulthood: An Agenda for Research* (Panel on Research Needs in Lifelong Learning During Adulthood, August 1978); *The Missing Link: Connecting Adult Lear-*

24

ners to Learning Resources, K. Patricia Cross (September 1978); *Planning for a Statewide Educational Information Center Network*, William D. Van Dusen, Ronald H. Miller, and Donna M. Pokorny (December 1978).

COMMISSARIAT GENERAL DU PLAN
[GENERAL COMMISSION FOR THE PLAN]   **Telephone:** 551 75 70
18, rue de Martignac
75007 Paris, France   **Founded:** 1946

Officers: Jean Ripert, Commissaire au Plan; Michel Albert, Commissaire Adjoint.

Government agency. Staff: About 70. **Sources of support:** 100% State budget. **Annual Budget:** No answer.

Objectives and interests: Five-year Plans and future-oriented studies relevant for the preparation thereof.

Major programs and projects: "Development of an Economic and Social Plan 1976-80 for France."

Special facilities: Documentation unit on problems of planning.

Activities: Individual staff member participation in conferences and seminars.

Publications: *Plan et Prospectives [Plan and Prospects]:* A collection of nine reports on economic and social future issues (Armand Colin Publishing Co., Paris, 1971-73); *Vivre Demain [To Live Tomorrow]:* A follow-up of the aforementioned collection; *Prospective du travail [The Future of Work]* (to be published by Documentation Francaise).

(From the first edition. Corrections not received by press time.)

COMMISSION FOR THE FUTURE   **Telephone:** 725033
P.O. Box 5053
Wellington, New Zealand   **Founded:** 1978

Officers: R. F. Ryan, Director; M. Hunn, Executive Officer; N. Zepke, Social Science Investigating Officer; D. Hunt, Science Investigating Officer.

Non-profit, independent but government-sponsored. Staff: Six. **Sources of support:** New Zealand Treasury. **Annual Budget:** No answer.

Objectives and interests: Study social and economic options for the nation and initiate public debate on them.

Major programs and projects: "New Zealand in the Future World"—an initial study.

Special facilities: In-house library.

Activities: Research projects, contributors' seminars, etc., in conjunction with areas of study.

Publications: Newsletter (biannual), brochures and pamphlets as required; first year study expected to be published in March 1979.

COMMISSION ON THE YEAR 2000 (STATE OF HAWAII)   **Telephone:** (808) 523-2500
P.O. Box 656
Honolulu, Hawaii 96809, U.S.A.   **Founded:** 1970

Officers: Gerald A. Sumida, Chairman; Doreen Leland, Program Director.

Public agency of the State of Hawaii. Staff: One. (Administrative support provided by University of Hawaii.) **Sources of support:** State of Hawaii legislative appropriations. **Annual Budget:** $45,000.

Objectives and interests: Public policy research and recommendations on issues confronting Hawaii in statewide, Pacific and global contexts.

Major programs and projects: "Alternative Economic Futures for Hawaii," a five-year conference to explore alternative economic futures for Hawaii, with recommendations for public and private policies; the development of futures-oriented educational programs for use in secondary school curricular programs; "International Uses of the Pacific," a three-year future-oriented exploration of public policy options for the Pacific Ocean and region; exploration of the future of a multicultural society and social value system (including both prospects for conflict and possibilities for cooperation).

Special facilities: In cooperation with the Hawaii Research Center for Futures Research, the Commission maintains a library of books, periodicals, films, and related materials on futures-oriented issues and problems.

Activities: Sponsors and promotes public policy-oriented conferences, seminars, lecture series and programs for specialized and general audiences, with a distinctive futures-planning orientation. The Commission is the first publicly established and funded agency of its type. It has been followed by numerous other and similar efforts in several other states, Puerto Rico, Malaysia, and other countries.

Publications: *Annual Report,* submitted to the Office of the Governor, the Hawaii State Legislature, public libraries and others; *Hawaii 2000: Continuing Experiment in Anticipatory Democracy* edited by George Chaplin and Glenn D. Paige (University Press of Hawaii, 1973).

COMMITTEE FOR ECONOMIC DEVELOPMENT   **Telephone:** (202)296-5860 D.C.
Headquarters
477 Madison Avenue
New York, New York 10022, U.S.A.
and
1700 K Street, N.W.
Washington, D.C. 20006, U.S.A.   **Founded:** 1942

Officers: Fletcher L. Byrom, Chairman; Franklin A. Lindsay, Chairman, Research and Policy Committee; Robert C. Holland, President; Sol Hurwitz, Vice President, Administration/Information; Frank W. Schiff, Vice President and Chief Economist; S. Charles Bleich, Vice President, Finance.

Private, non-profit research and education organization composed of 200 national business leaders. **Staff:** 44. **Sources of support:** Contributions from business; foundation grants. **Annual Budget:** $2,006,547.

Objectives and interests: To propose policies that will help bring about steady economic growth at high employment and reasonably stable prices, increase productivity and living standards, provide greater and more equal opportunity for every citizen, and improve the quality of life for all.

Major programs and projects: "Jobs for the Hard-to-Employ"—calls for a renewed public/private commitment to reduce structural unemployment, making national policy recommendations to achieve that goal. "Revitalizing America's Cities"—a "superproject" which will include a series of studies aimed at highlighting the major forces that are altering the viability of major American cities and developing recommendations as to how public policies should be altered to meet various needs. "Regulation and the Role of Government Intervention in the Economy"—developing criteria for judging the appropriateness of government intervention in and the costs of regulation to the economy. "Technology Policy"—this study in progress will describe the trend of technological progress in the U.S. and discuss the implications for future economic growth.

Special facilities: —

Activities: Currently holding six policy forums on Jobs for the Hard-to-Employ in cities across the country to focus attention and stimulate an exchange between business, government and citizen's groups on the local level in order to foster a stronger public-private partnership to alleviate the plight of the severely disadvantaged job-seeker.

Publications: *CED Newsletter* (annual); *Improving Management of the Public Work Force* (1978); *Jobs for the Hard-to-Employ: New Directions for a Public-Private Partnership* (1978); *An Approach to Federal Urban Policy* (1977); *Key Elements of a National Energy Strategy* (1977). Publications list available; updated annually. Film for rental or purchase: "Inflation." Filmstrip for purchase: "Jobs for the Hard-to-Employ."

THE COMMITTEE FOR THE FUTURE
2325 Porter Street
Washington, D.C. 20008, U.S.A.

Telephone: (202) 966-8776

Founded: 1970

Officers: Barbara Marx Hubbard, Chairman; John J. Whiteside, Vice-Chairman.

Non-profit public foundation. **Staff:—** **Sources of support:** U.S. governmental agencies, individual donations, corporations, and foundations. **Annual Budget:** No answer.

Objectives and interests: To bring the positive options for the future into the public arena for decision and action. Public policy research on domestic and international issues, with special emphasis on the need for an open system perspective in a policy setting.

Major programs and projects: Theater for the Future—an hour and fifteen minute multi-media show presenting positive options for the future through an evolutionary perspective. ACT III—a two day seminar follow-on to the Theater for the Future. Evolutionary network.

Special facilities: Video Tape Library containing video tapes in various formats of futuristic thinkers in all fields, live documentaries of all previously held Syncons, panel discussions with nation's leading thinkers, and special productions.

Activities: Developed conference technique known as Syncon. The Committee also holds seminars with futuristic thinkers and decision-makers. Both Syncons and seminars are open to the public.

Publications: *The Evolutionary Journal; The Hunger of Eve,* by Barbara Marx Hubbard.

COMMITTEE FOR FUTURE ORIENTED RESEARCH
Fack, 10310 Stockholm, Sweden

Telephone: (08) 141000

Founded: 1974

Officers: Torsten Hagerstrand, Chairman; Anders Karlqvist, Secretary; Sture Oberg, Deputy Secretary.

Research Council. **Staff:** Five. **Sources of support:** Ministry of Education. **Annual Budget:** $450,000.

Objectives and interests: Initiate and sponsor research of basic, interdisciplinary, future-oriented research.

Major programs and projects: "Technology and Social Change." "Dependent Population Groups in Society (Especially Aged People)." "The Individual in the Information and Communication Society." "Changing Health Conditions and Individual Health." "Cultural Change and Landscape Evolution."

Special facilities: —

Activities: Projects, conferences, seminars, publications.

Publications: *Communication, Social Organization, Human Resources* (1977); *Work Exchange,* by Sven Lindqvist (1978); newsletters in Swedish, free of charge, approximately 4-5 issues a year; population and health reports in preparation.

THE CONFERENCE BOARD
845 Third Avenue
New York, New York 10022, U.S.A.

Telephone: (212) 759-0900

Founded: 1916

Officers: Kenneth A. Randall, President; George Brown, Corporate Secretary; Vera Reap, Treasurer; Albert Sommers, Senior Vice President and Chief Economist; David G. Moore, Executive Vice President; Leonard A. Lecht, Director, Special Projects Research.

Independent, non-profit, business research and educational organization—a membership corporation. **Staff:** 250. (The Conference Board in Canada has an additional staff of 50.) **Sources of support:** Organization subscriptions, conferences, sales of publications. **Annual Budget:** Approximately $11 million.

Objectives and interests: To foster broader understanding of business and the economy for the enlightenment and practical benefit of those who manage business enterprises and of the society which shapes the business system. Major areas of research include business economics, general administration, finance, personnel administration, marketing, international operations management, and public affairs.

Major programs and projects: The Senior Executives Council consists of 37 chief executive officers from business, foundations, universities, and quasi-public organizations, who meet to examine emerging trends and forces in society. The Public Affairs Research Council of The Conference Board consists of 50 public affairs officers, who hold an annual Public Affairs Outlook Conference. (In 1976 the Council examined the role of business in improving public management.) "Games Managers Should Play": Research report on scenario writing and organizational responsiveness to emerging issues. "Changes in Occupational Characteristics in the Next Decade: Their Implication for Planning." "Impact of Slow and Rapid Recovery on an Occupational Employment, 1975-83."

Special facilities: Comprehensive business library.

Activities: Conducts 20 conferences per year on various topics, e.g., antitrust, credibility, economic outlook; regional seminars and meetings are held on topics such as company contributions and non-discrimination in employment. In addition, Subscribing Associates are encouraged to make full use of the Conference Board's information services, making telephone or written inquiries which are answered by the staff.

Publications: *Across the Board* (monthly magazine); Conference Board Associates receive 40 to 50 major research reports a year, a monthly digest of studies and conferences, and monthly, bimonthly, and quarterly statistical series on a range of indicators. Some selected titles of reports include: *Future Trends in Employee Benefits; Perspectives for the 70s and 80s; Tomorrow's Marketing; The Free Society and Planning: A Conversation on the Future of the Mixed Economy; Planning and Forecasting in the Smaller Company; Human Resources: Toward Rational Policy Planning;* and *Nationalism or Interdependence: The Alternatives.*

CONGRESSIONAL CLEARINGHOUSE ON THE FUTURE

Telephone: (202) 225-3153

3564 House Annex No. 2
Washington, D.C. 20515, U.S.A.

Founded: 1976

Officers: 27 Members of Congress, including Charlie Rose, Mike Gravel and Millicent Fenwick; Anne W. Cheatham, Director; Marilyn Gadzuk, Coordinator, Talent bank, Underside Project, *What's Next*; Lena Lupica, Administrator TEAM program.

Unofficial Congressional study group. **Staff:** Six. **Sources of support:** Approximately 150 Members of Congress. **Annual Budget:** Annual Budget: $125,000.

Objectives and interests: To provide information about the future to Members of Congress and their staffs by way of a monthly newsletter, an early identification of trends, and by in-depth seminars on issues undergoing change.

Major programs and projects: "Dialogues on America's Future"—monthly seminars on issues likely to be important in the future. "Congressional Talent Bank"—network of futurists around the country who discuss legislation with Hill personnel. "TEAM (Trend Evaluation and Monitoring)"—a trend analysis program which reviews 70+ publications in 5 subject areas. "Underside Project"—designed to involve children in the Congressional process.

Special facilities: See Congressional Talent Bank.

Activities: Monthly seminars for Members of Congress and their staffs which focus on particular issues.

Publications: *What's Next?* (monthly newsletter), Marilyn Gadzuk, editor; *Trends* (six times a year), Lena Lupica, editor, not available outside Congress.

CONGRESSIONAL RESEARCH SERVICE

Telephone: (202) 287-6498

OF THE LIBRARY OF CONGRESS,
THE FORESIGHT TEAM
Washington, D.C. 20540, U.S.A.

Founded: 1975

Officers: Walter A. Hahn, Senior Specialist in Futures Research (Coordinator); Dennis L. Little, Executive Secretary; and representatives from each division.

Government agency. **Staff:** 13. **Sources of support:** U.S. Government. **Annual Budget:** No answer.

Objectives and interests: To answer specific congressional requests for general futures information, sources and consultation; to alert, counsel, and teach CRS and congressional professional staff about the concepts, techniques, processes, information sources, and display techniques of futures research and forecasting; to design, develop, and implement a futures information system "add-on" to the CRS's existing research, documentation, and reference systems.

Major programs and projects: Having matured and accomplished many of their original objectives, the Futures Research Group has been disbanded and replaced by the Foresight Team with one or more representatives from each division. Foresight team seminars in 1979 included Herman Kahn, Hudson Institute, "World Economic Development 1978-2000"; Kathleen Newland, Worldwatch Institute, "The Changing Role of Women"; Jerome Rosow, The Work in America Institute, "Work in the Coming Decade"; and William Ascher, Johns Hopkins University, "An Appraisal for the Policy Maker of Forecasting." Reports have been prepared on various science and technology questions, demographic shifts, labor issues, and emerging issues in the area of renewable natural resources.

Special facilities: The Futures Information Retrieval System (FIRST), when completed, is expected to include futures bibliographic information, trends, forecasts, directory-type data, and interactive programs/models. The first level of design work has been completed and the initial stages of implementation have begun.

Activities: Research, seminars, and conferences related to forecasting.

Publications: *Renewable Natural Resources, Some Emerging Issues* (1979); *The United States and the World Economy: World Population Growth and United States Labor Market Issues* (1979); *Special Study on Economic Change, A Review of the Panel Meetings May 31 to June 22, 1978 (1979); Science, Technology, and American Diplomacy: An Extended Study of the Interactions of Science and Technology with United States Foreign Policy* (1977).

CONTRACULTURA CENTER
C C Central 1332
1000 Buenos Aires, Argentina

Telephone: —

Founded: 1970

Officers: Miguel Grinberg, Director; Aldo Sorenson, Coordinator; David Grinberg, Secretary General.

Independent, non-profit research center. Staff: Irregular, on a voluntary basis. **Sources of support:** Donations and subscriptions; no official support. **Annual Budget:** No answer.

Objectives and interests: Documentation on environmental, educational, and futures matters. Short- and medium-term forecasting on cultural and social developments in Argentina related to the post-industrial societies.

Major programs and projects: "Utopos 1"—A study of alternative, non-authoritarian ways of development. "Futuromania"—A study of the uses of U.S. futures research related to Argentina.

Special facilities: Library of books and periodicals on futures research, ecology, and alternative education, for use by members only.

Activities: Seminars and courses, on a formative level, for undergraduates; no degrees.

Publications: *Contracultura Journal* (bimonthly); *Precursores de Futuros [Futures Forerunners]*, Miguel Grinberg (1974).

CORNELL UNIVERSITY PROGRAM ON
SCIENCE, TECHNOLOGY, AND SOCIETY
628 Clark Hall
Cornell University
Ithaca, New York 14853, U.S.A.

Telephone: (607) 256-3810

Founded: 1969

Officers: Lawrence Scheinman, Director, Professor of Government; Stuart M. Brown, Jr., Associate Director, Professor of Philosophy; Lloyd Carter, Administrative Manager; Raymond Bowers, Professor of Physics; Franklin A. Long, Henry R. Luce, Professor of Science and Society; Dorothy Nelkin, Professor of City and Regional Planning.

University-wide, non-profit program. Staff: 11 faculty, 4 post-doctoral fellows, 2 support staff. **Sources of support:** Cornell University, private foundations and corporations, federal agencies. **Annual Budget:** Approximately $500,000.

Objectives and interests: Research, teaching, and promotion of public understanding of the interactions of science and technology with social and political institutions, as well as the effect of these interactions on individual lives; special interests include biology and society, electronic message transfer, and international science policy.

Major programs and projects: "An Exploratory Analysis of Electronic Message Transfer"—exploring the use of electronic communication as a substitute for present mail freight transportation needs, and the potential which electronic mail handling schemes have for conserving energy and other resources (funded by the National Science Foundation). "The Biology and Society Program"—examining the interactions between biological and sociocultural forces.

Special facilities: Small specialized library (primarily faculty research facility).

Activities: The Program sponsors 19 courses (1978-79 academic year), as well as weekly seminars covering a wide variety of STS-related topics. The Program is also actively involved in research in the above-mentioned areas as well as in environmental law, nuclear non-proliferation and nuclear export policy, and science policy.

Publications: *Communications for a Mobile Society*, R. Bowers, A. Lee and C. Hershey (1978); *Controversies: The Politics of Science and Technology*, Dorothy Nelkin (1978); *Science Textbook Controversies and the Politics of Equal Time*, Dorothy Nelkin (1978), *Technological Innovation for the U.S. Civilian Economy*, Franklin A. Long (1978); *The Environmental Impact Statement Process*, Neil A. Orloff (1978).

JAMES L. CREIGHTON
15415 Pepper Lane
Saratoga, California, 95070, U.S.A.

Telephone: (408) 354-6070

Founded: 1969

Officers: James L. Creighton, Founder.

Private consulting firm. Staff: Two. **Sources of support:** 90% government (federal and state); 10% private industry. **Annual Budget:** $150,000.

Objectives and interests: Application of the social sciences to the solution of organizational and social problems. Special interests in citizen participation, alternative futures planning, values, and belief systems.

Major programs and projects: "Procedures for Alternative Futures Planning: A Demonstration Study"—Development of techniques for planning to protect options identified through scenario writing, public participation, and cross impacting, conducted for the U.S. Bureau of Reclamation. "Alternative Futures"—Training courses in alternative futures planning for such clients as the U.S. Forest Service, U.S. Bureau of Reclamation, U.S. Bureau of Land Management, and Wickes Corporation.

Special facilities: —

Activities: Alternative futures training courses; developing manuals and designing training programs in citizen participation, used by federal and state agencies.

Publications: Annual newsletter; *Procedures for Alternative Futures Planning*, James L. Creighton (1976); *Advanced Training Course in Public Involvement—Participants Workbook*, James L. Creighton.

L.J. D'AMORE AND ASSOCIATES, LTD.
3680 Mountain Street
Montreal, Quebec, Canada H3G 2A8

Telephone: (514) 281-1822

Founded: 1969

Officers: Lou D'Amore, President; Carl Johnston, Vice-President; Richard Hamilton, Secretary-Treasurer; Sheila Rittenberg, Senior Consultant; John Farina and Francis Bregha, Associates.

Private research and planning firm. Staff: Eight. **Sources of support:** Contracts. **Annual Budget:** No answer.

Objectives and interests: Tourism, social research and planning; social impact assessment; recreation planning; public participation.

Major programs and projects: "The Saint John Human Development Projects"—a city-wide public participation project establishing goals to 1986 and an action plan to achieve them. "Tourism in Canada—1986"—a Delphi study of the future. "Social Trends and Their Implications for North Pickering"—social dimensions of the plan for a new city of 200,000. "Towards a Conserver Society"—total community efforts in three Canadian cities to set goals and strategies for energy conservation. "Tourism Trends to 1990" — societal trends and their implications for tourism.

Special facilities: Specialized collections on tourism trends and on social dimensions of environmental planning.

Activities: Seminars on community development, social dimensions of environmental planning and social impact assessment.

Publications: *Social Dimensions of Environmental Planning; An Executive Guide to Social Impact Assessment* (1978 and 1979); *The Significance of Tourism to Canada* (1977); *Saint John 1986: Anticipatory Democracy in Action* (1977).

THE DANISH COMMITTEE ON FUTURES STUDIES

Telephone: (01) 11 43 00

c/o Secretariate of Danish Research Councils
Holmens Kanal 7
1060 Copenhagen K, Denmark

Founded: 1974

Officers: Herborg Nielsen, Chairman; Allan George Ottsen, Secretary.

Committee within the Danish Research Policy Structure. **Staff:** Two plus project group. **Sources of support:** The Danish Research Councils. **Annual Budget:** 200,000 Danish Kroner.

Objectives and interests: To coordinate and initiate futures studies and provide information and documentation in the field.

Major programs and projects: "Shortcomings in Research Strategy and Methodology in Futures Research" — proceedings from a conference. "The Hudson Report — Denmark in Europe 1990" — a futures study in cooperation with the Hudson Institute (six full-time researchers). A state-of-the-art report to the field of futures research.

Special facilities: —

Activities: —

Publications: *Orientering*, edited by the Institute for Futures Studies (six issues per year).

UNIVERSITY OF DAYTON RESEARCH INSTITUTE

Telephone: (513) 229-3036

Technological Forecasting Group
300 College Park Drive
Dayton, Ohio 45469, U.S.A.

Founded: 1951

Officers: George Noland, Dean, Graduate Studies and Research; John R. Westerheide, Director, Research Institute; Joseph Militello, Associate Director, Interdisciplinary Research; Ralph C. Lenz, Head, Technological Forecasting Group; Joseph P. Martino, Research Scientist; Kuei-Lin Chen, Associate Systems Engineer.

University connected, non-profit, research institute. **Staff:** 300 (Research Institute.) **Sources of support:** U.S. Government 93%, industry 7%. **Annual Budget:** $10 million, futures-related $500,000.

Objectives and interests: Multi-disciplinary research; medium and long-range forecasting on technological and social change (particularly energy, defense and space matters); technology assessment.

Major programs and projects: "Assessment and Forecasting of Future Influences on the Development of Flight Vehicle Technology (USAF Flight Dynamics Laboratory.)" "Computer Conference for Technological Forecasting Methodology (NSF)." "Technology Assessment of Satellite Communications (NASA-Lewis Lab)" — cross-impact model and trend analysis of satellite communications. "NSF Sponsored Workshop in Technology Assessment Methodology." "Comprehensive Community Energy Management Program" — survey and plan for meeting future regional energy needs.

Special facilities: University of Dayton Library, 380,000 volumes. Member of Dayton-Miami Valley Consortium, combining library resources of 20 institutions of higher learning and research. On-line information retrieval systems section.

Activities: Technological forecasting courses (graduate level,) seminars on strategic planning for technological change, workshops on technology assessment, consultation to industry and government. All cover futures related work only.

Publications: *Technological Forecasting for Decision-Making*, Martino (1972); *Predicting the Diffusion Rate of Industrial Innovations*, Martino, Chen, Lenz (1978).

DCM ASSOCIATES
908 Fox Plaza
San Francisco, California 94102, U.S.A.

Telephone: (415) 626-3125

Founded: 1966

Officers: David C. Miller, Partner; Virginia F. Miller, Partner.

Private, for-profit, futures education materials publisher; futures educational and futures studies consulting. **Staff:** Two; project and support staff retained as required. **Sources of support:** — **Annual Budget:** No answer.

Objectives and interests: Conception, design, development, testing, and publication of learning materials for futures education; application of qualitative conjectural futures methods in top-management planning programs (public and private sectors).

Major programs and projects: "The Advent Program"—Curriculum Guide, Learning Resources Guide, Hopes and Fears Switchboard.

Special facilities: Extensive knowledge of futures films, as documented in special reports published by the University of California Extension Media Center, Berkeley.

Activities: Instruction in graduate-level futures courses in Cybernetic Systems Program and School of Education, San Jose State University; consultation to Corporate Planners Association (Project FORETHOUGHT); futures consultant to management consultant firms, e.g., New Management Center, Palo Alto; sub-contract research, futures studies projects to major contract research organizations.

Publications: Co-author of *Handbook of Forecasting Techniques* (1975), submitted to the U.S. Army Engineers Institute for Water Resources.

DECISIONS AND DESIGNS, INCORPORATED (DDI)
Suite 600, 8400 Westpark Drive
P.O. Box 907
McLean, Virginia 22101, U.S.A.

Telephone: (703) 821-2828

Founded: 1971

Officers: Robert A. Eidson, President; Clinton W. Kelly, Director, Decision Systems and Applications; Cameron R. Peterson, Director, Decision Analysis and Systems Evaluation; Joseph M. Fox, Director, Computer Systems.

Private corporation. **Staff:** 70. **Sources of support:** Government and commercial. **Annual Budget:** 1977 annual sales—$4 million.

Objectives and interests: Specializing in the application of decision-analytic techniques and methodologies and in basic and advanced research in the field of decision theory.

Major programs and projects: "Conditional Forecasting"—prediction of economic and political outcomes of national policy options in energy, foreign policy and defense. "Contingent Action Planning"—development of pre-programmed action responses to possible future contingencies (e.g., political and military crises.) "A Hazard Index for Radioactive Waste"—nuclear waste management involving the assessment of public attitudes towards radiological risks affecting future generations.

Special facilities: DDI maintains a technical library designed to support the research staff.

Activities: Executive training seminars.

Publications: *Issues in the Value of Decision Analysis*, by Rex V. Brown and Stephen R. Watson (1975); *On Using Scenarios in the Evaluation of Complex Alternatives*, by Michael F. O'Connor and Ward Edwards (1976); *Crisis Forecasting and Crisis: A Critical Examination of the Literature*, by Richard W. Parker (1976); *The Value of Improved Forecasts of Climate for Agriculture Decision Making*, by Lawrence D. Phillips (1978).

DELEGATION A L'AMENAGEMENT DU TERRITOIRE ET A L'ACTION REGIONALE (D.A.T.A.R.)
[AGENCY FOR NATIONAL AND REGIONAL LAND USE PLANNING]

Telephone: 783 61 20

1, Avenue Charles Floquet
75007 Paris, France

Founded: D.A.T.A.R., 1963; S.E.S.A.M.E., 1968

Officers: Andre Chadeau, Delegue a l'Amenagement du Territoire; Jacques Durand, Directeur de Systeme d'Etudes du Scheme d'Amenagement de la France.

Government agency. Staff: No answer. **Sources of support:** Government. **Annual Budget:** Four million francs.

Objectives and interests: Land use planning; the international socio-economic situation; the development of French society.

Major programs and projects: The redistribution of industry in France; the problems of regional research and planning; forecasting methods; population forecast studies; future changes in employment and activities; manpower mobility and people's new aspirations; the role of tertiary activities in the economy.

Special facilities: Special collection of books and reports on forecasting: "Travaux et Recherches de Prospective" ["Books and Reports on Forecasting"].

Activities: Course at the National Foundation for Political Sciences; national seminars; various conferences; future-oriented seminars on industrial, political, social, and international problems.

Publications: *Une image de la France en l'an 2000 [An Image of France in the Year 2000]; Paris, ville internationale [Paris, The International City]; La methode des scenarios [The Scenario Method]; Regard prospectif sur le Bassin Mediterraneen [A Future-Oriented Look at the Mediterranean Basin]; Sur l'emploi: activities et regions [Employment: Types and Regions]; Une image de la France en l'an 2000: sept ans apres [An Image of France in the Year 2000: Seven Years Later]; Villes internationales, villes mondiales [International Cities; World Cities].*

DELFT UNIVERSITY OF TECHNOLOGY, INSTITUTE FOR TOWN PLANNING RESEARCH

Telephone: (015) 761088

Berlageweg 1
Delft—2208, The Netherlands

Founded: 1959

Officers: P. Drewe, Chairman of the Board; J. den Draak, Director.

Research institute. Staff: 14. **Sources of support:** University budget (government). **Annual Budget:** 60,000 Dutch guilders (excluding salaries).

Objectives and interests: Fundamental research into various fields of physical planning, especially housing, transportation planning, shopping models, traffic noise, and information theory.

Major programs and projects: "The Residential Function of the Inner City"—developments and perspectives, on the basis of statistical data and on analysis of plans. "Implications of Socio-Cultural Developments for Physical Planning"—literature study.

Special facilities: Maintains a library of books, periodicals, and reports on physical planning (open to the public).

Activities: Organizes transportation planning research colloquia, in cooperation with other research institutes.

Publications: *Mededelingen* (announcements of new publications of the Institute, published once or twice a year); *Living in New Residential Areas—Summary of the Results*, K. Brouwer and M. Tacken; *A Travel Time Model for Urban Road Networks*, P. Bovy and G. Jansen; *Interregional Migration and Population Redistribution Policy*, P. Drewe; *The Prediction of Traffic Noise Levels with the Aid of a Scale Model*, L. Nijs; *Some Trends in the Housing Situation in the Netherlands*, Wivan der Windt.

DELPHI COMMUNICATIONS GROUP

Telephone: (207) 236-4742

P.O. Box 243
Rockport, Maine 04856, U.S.A.

Founded: 1978

Officers: James Ruddy, Travis Charbeneau, Directors; Matt Matthews, Associate; Jennifer Bonning, Research Associate.

Private. Staff: — **Sources of support:** Private business. **Annual Budget:** No answer.

Objectives and interests: Delphi is a small group of communications people which has evolved from a commercial media background; primary objective is to provide responsible communication on futures-related topics for mainly business and industry clients.

Major programs and projects: "The Future: The Perennial Frontier"—a six-hour film series for Public Broadcasting Service. "Health: A New Kind of High"—an educational film about holistic health. "I've Seen That Face"— a multi-media module which introduces the future. "Full Circle"—a film dealing with man's synergism with nature through technology. "Apres nous le deluge?"—an insurance-related futures seminar package.

Special facilities: —

Activities: —

Publications: —

DEPARTMENT OF SCIENCE AND TECHNOLOGY

Telephone: 0-662626 and R-384016

Technology Bhavan
New Mehrauli Road
New Delhi-110029, India

Founded: 1973

Officers: A. Ramachandran, Secretary; B. D. Tilak, Chairman; S. C. Seth, Member-Secretary; K. K. Ayra, Resource Personnel and Secretary to the Member-Secretary.

Policy-making ministry of the Government of India. Staff: — **Sources of support:** Government funding. **Annual Budget:** No answer.

Objectives and interests: Undertake exercise in technology assistance; promote quantitative research-based futuristic studies; promote teaching and research programs in Indian Institutes of Technology, universities and other institutes of advanced learning.

Major programs and projects: "Ahmedabad 2000 A.D."—a project in the field of urban development conducted by National Institute of Design, Ahmedabad, and sponsored by Department of Science and Technology to examine various aspects of future of the city. "India Model 2000 A.D."—a three-year, inter-institutional research study program. Eleven technology sub-groups of the Futurology Panel are working in the fields of energy, food, housing, urbanology, transportation, communication, rural development, management, health, water, and education. Indian Institute of Technology, Powai, Bombay, held an International Workshop on Technology Assessment to develop the venue of the World Futures Conference in 1980.

Special facilities: Various libraries in India, the Census Report and other government documentations.

Activities: Futurology Panel has set up six Centers of Futures Studies; it has commissioned more than 30 thematic and awareness workshops. In consultation with the Indian Council of Management and Future, it has organized workshops and discussion groups.

Publications: *ScienceTech Bulletin; Indian Review of Management and Future* (quarterly); *Base Document on Futurology*, by S. C. Seth; *Developing a Strategy for Mass Communication in India: A Futuristic View*, by Shri Ashok Chatterjee; *Integration Document: A Discussion Paper*, by S. C. Seth.

THE DIEBOLD GROUP, INC.

Telephone: (212) 755-0400

430 Park Avenue
New York, New York 10022

Founded: 1954

Officers: John Diebold, Chairman; Theodore J. Freiser, Vice-President; Robert C. Murray, Vice-President; Liesa Bing, Vice-President and General Counsel; Joseph Ferreira, Vice-President.

Private, international management consulting firm. Staff: — **Sources of support:** — **Annual Budget:** No answer.

Objectives and interests: Specialize in assisting business and governmental organizations to benefit from the opportunity of changing technology and environment.

34

Major programs and projects: "The Diebold Research Program"; "The Diebold Automated Office Program", "The Diebold Corporate Issues Program."

Special facilities: —

Activities: Consulting assignments and multi-sponsored research.

Publications: *Tomorrow's Enterprise and Its Management*, 3 volumes, *Beyond Automation, Business Decisions and Technological Change,* and *Man and the Computer*, John Diebold; *The World of the Computer*, John Diebold, editor (Random House); *Automated Data Processing Handbook*, The Diebold Group, editors (McGraw-Hill).

UNIVERSITY OF EDINBURGH
CENTRE FOR HUMAN ECOLOGY
Edinburgh EH8 9LN Scotland, U.K.

Telephone: 031-667-1011
Ext. 6696
Founded: 1972

Officers: J. Loraine, Executive Director; L.J. Hale; J. Higgs, Honorary Research Fellow; T. Birley; H. Dickinson; U.E. Loening; C. Pritchard.

A non-profit, cross-disciplinary research and teaching unit within the University of Edinburgh. **Staff:** eight part-time. **Sources of support:** University of Edinburgh. **Annual Budget:** 1500 pounds sterling to date.

Objectives and interests: The study of man's impact on and place in the environment in developed and developing countries; the study of the ethical and moral issues of technology.

Major programs and projects; Lecture course and seminars on Population and Society and on Energy and Society; others from time to time on subjects of interest in human ecology.

Special facilities: None.

Activities: Occasional lectures and seminars on subjects of current interest in human ecology.

Publications: *Global Signposts to the 21st Century*, J. Loraine (due 1979); *2050: Perspectives on the Future*, J. Loraine and T. Birley (in preparation); *Ecology and the Future of Man*, edited by J. Loraine (in press); *Life and Death Before Birth*, L.J. Hale et al. (in press); *The Human Ecology of Settlements*, edited by L.J. Hale (1978).

EDUCATIONAL FUTURES PROJECTS
P.O. Box 2977
Sacramento, California 95812, U.S.A.

Telephone: (916) 442-2772
Founded: 1976

Officers: Don Glines, Director; Michael Barkhurst, Associate Director.

Private consulting group. **Staff:** Four part-time, four on-call part-time, adjunct consultants available by contract as needed. **Sources of support:** Contract and consulting fees. **Annual Budget:** Variable.

Objectives and interests: Assist educators, school boards, students, and communities make the personal and professional transitions that appear to be essential in this period of global transformation; provide leadership toward the creation of preferable societal and educational futures.

Major programs and projects: Continuously update a 50-page non-annotated bibliography on societal and educational futures, listing books, resources, materials, journals with implications for education. Maintain an educational change bibliography. Develop occasional papers and articles regarding phases of the futures of education.

Special facilities: None.

Activities: Organizing workshops, seminars, and inservice education courses; presenting keynote and sectional addresses by invitation of school districts, schools, and educational conferences; providing information "free" by answering mail and telephone inquiries.

Publications: *Educational Futures I: Imagining and Inventing; Educational Futures II: Options and Alternatives; Educational Futures III: Change and Reality* (1978).

THE ELECTRICAL RESEARCH ASSOCIATION LTD.
Cleeve Road
Leatherhead, Surrey KT22 7SA U.K.

Telephone: 03723-74151

Founded: 1920

Officers: B.C. Lindley, Managing Director; R.C. Peattie, Engineering Director; K. Sedgwick, Commercial Director.

Private limited liability contract R&D company. **Staff:** 285. **Sources of support:** Contracts. **Annual Budget:** 3.5 M pounds sterling.

Objectives and interests: Contract research and development in electrical, electronic and related topics.

Major programs and projects: "660 Volts in Industry (Project No. 0034)"—evaluation of advantages of higher industrial distribution voltages. "The Selection and Efficient Use of Electric Motor Drives (0126)". "Electric Power Plant International (2700)"—reference report on rotary and static generating plant. "Creep of Plastics Used in Generators (0100)"—3-year program to evaluate properties of plastic insulation.

Special facilities: Information center; library; technical reports.

Activities: Seminars in various areas of electrotechnology, e.g., batteries, motors, switchgear.

Publications: *ERA News* (10 issues yearly, free); reports list available.

EPISCOPAL DIOCESE OF CALIFORNIA, FUTURES PLANNING COUNCIL

Telephone: (415) 776-6611

1055 Taylor Street
San Francisco, California 94108, U.S.A.

Founded: 1967

Officers: The Right Reverend C. Kilmer Myers; Cecil Hudson, Chairman; The Venerable John J. Weaver, Archdeacon for Futures Planning.

Non-profit. **Staff:** Two. **Sources of support:** The Protestant Episcopal Church. **Annual Budget:** No answer.

Objectives and interests: The stance of the church as we move into the 21st century.

Major programs and projects: The Futures Planning Council is made up of separate task forces studying a wide range of problems affecting the human condition today and likely to influence it in the future: work and leisure, a guaranteed income, amniocentesis, the energy crisis, alternative forms of education, new forms of religious awareness, drug abuse, etc.

Special facilities: A library of booklets on subjects under study by the task forces.

Activities: Once a year the entire Council meets at the Vallombrosa Retreat Center in Menlo Park, California, for a three-day session on a specific subject. In the past these matters have included "Economics," "Community," "Is Technology Programming Us or Are We Programming Technology?" and others.

Publications: 67 booklets have been produced. A list of past reports is available from the Futures Planning Council. Titles include: *Visions of the Future of Man, Alternative Futures and Educational Policy, Institutional Change, Toward Human Futuristics,* etc.

FEDERAL AVIATION ADMINISTRATION, OFFICE OF AVIATION POLICY, SYSTEM CONCEPTS BRANCH (AVP-110)

Telephone: (202) 426-3220

800 Independence Avenue, S.W.
Washington, D.C. 20591, U.S.A.

Founded: 1974

Officers: Lynn E. Jackson, Chief, System Concepts Branch; Wesley Carson, Chief, Policy Development Division; Duane W. Freer, Director, Office of Aviation Policy; Kenneth W. Harris, Senior Policy Analyst; Yong Keun Cha, Economist; Pamela Kruzic, Senior Policy Analyst.

Government. **Staff:** Nine. **Sources of support:** Federal Aviation Administration appropriations. **Annual Budget:** No answer.

Objectives and interests: Demographic, economic, social, and technical trends affecting aviation, and other factors leading to long-range aviation policy development.

Major programs and projects: Socioeconomic Impact Assessment: Communications Industry (TF&A for Aviation Impacts).

Special facilities: —

Activities: —

Publications: *Aviation Futures to the Year 2000* (1976); *The Impact of Microcomputers on Aviation: A Technology Forecasting and Assessment Study* (1977); forecasts and assessments of technology trends and aviation applications in alternative socioeconomic scenarios to 2000.

THE FINDHORN FOUNDATION UNIVERSITY OF LIGHT

The Park, Forres
IV 36 OTZ Scotland

Telephone: Findhorn 311

Founded: 1962

Officers: Peter Caddy, Founder-Director; R. Ross Stewart, Chairman, Board of Trustees; Sir George Trevelyan, Bart. Trustee; Bruce Davidson, Core Group Focaliser; James Micheal Shaw, Management Group Focaliser; Michael Lindfield, Education Branch Focaliser.

Registered charitable trust, non-profit. **Staff:** Approximately 200 community members. **Sources of support:** Members' contributions, guests' payments, publications sales. **Annual Budget:** No answer.

Objectives and interests: The Findhorn Foundation is a community of some 200 people formed in the realization that the earth and all humanity are entering a new age, a new cycle of evolution. Findhorn is a place where people can come to have the inner seeds of potential nourished and a new consciousness developed and thereby help foster the emergence of a new consciousness and culture throughout the earth.

Major programs and projects: "Onearth Gathering" (annually in October) — a conference of people from around the world focusing on New Age themes, the challenge of growth and transformation and the synthesis of divergent views. "Erraid Island" — an experiment by 8 community members in self-sufficient living "in tune with the Earth" on a small island off the west coast of Scotland.

Special facilities: Extensive list of tapes and books on the themes of the New Age, Wholeness, Integration, Spiritual Living; a 7,500 volume library specializing in spiritual and metaphysical works.

Activities: Findhorn is a place where people can obtain education and experience in New Age concepts and consciousness. Activities for this purpose include non-traditional work programs and college courses relating to New Age themes. Among the workshops and classes offered are "Creating a New Age Community," "Education in the New Age," "Cooperation with the Nature Kingdoms," Teilhard de Chardin's "Phenomenon of Man," "The Birth of a New Age," etc.

Publications: *Onearth* (semi-annual magazine); *Open Letter* (newsletter, 6 times yearly); *The Findhorn Garden*, Findhorn Community (1976); *Revelation—The Birth of a New Age*, David Spangler (1976); *Reflections on the Christ*, David Spangler (1978); *God Spoke to Me*, Eileen Caddy (1976); *Foundations of Findhorn*, Eileen Caddy (1978).

FONDATION CLAUDE NICOLAS LEDOUX POUR LES REFLEXIONS SUR LE FUTUR
[CLAUDE NICOLAS LEDOUX FOUNDATION FOR REFLECTION ON THE FUTURE]

Saline de Chaux
Arc et Senans 25610, France

Telephone: (16) 81 80 2543

Founded: 1972

Officers: Denis Gradjean, "Directeur"; Louis-Bertrand Raffour, "Adjoint".

Private, non-profit association. **Staff:** Three. **Sources of support:** Private. **Annual Budget:** 2,000,000 francs.

Objectives and interests: To support awareness in Europe and throughout the world of long-term problems and innovations.

Major programs and projects: —

Special facilities: Library.

Activities: Seminars and meetings in the area of prospective research; publications.

Publications: *Futur Informations* (eight times a year, published in collaboration with Futuribles).

FONDATION EUROPEENNE DE LA CULTURE
[EUROPEAN CULTURAL FOUNDATION]
Jan van Goyenkade, 5
1075 HN Amsterdam, The Netherlands

Telephone: (20) 760222

Founded: 1954

Officers: Raymond Georis; Jacques E. Chabert; L. Cerych; K. von Moltke; M. Martinez Cuadrado.

Non-profit research institute. Staff: 38. **Sources of support:** Private and public sources. **Annual Budget:** 5,800,000 Dutch guilders.

Objectives and interests: To promote cultural, scientific, and educational activities of a multinational nature and of a European character.

Major programs and projects: "Youth, Education, and Employment"; "Regional Development and Post-Secondary Education"; "Contribution of New Forms of Higher Education to the Equalization of Educational Opportunity"; "How Are Parliamentary Assemblies Informed on Environmental Policy?"; Cultural values and new international economic order; Study of the political problems specific to pluralistic societies.

Special facilities: —

Activities: Research in the field of education, environment; international cooperation; policies; grants to scientific and cultural activities.

Publications: *European Journal of Education* (newsletter, 3 times a year).

FONDATION INTERNATIONALE DE L'INNOVATION SOCIALE
[INTERNATIONAL FOUNDATION FOR SOCIAL INNOVATION]
5, rue d'Alger
75001 Paris, France

Telephone: 260 30 48

Founded: 1975

Officers: Georges Gueron, President; Robert Jungk, Vice-President; Anthony Judge, Secretary-General; Armand Braun; Jean-Jacques Ballan; Jeannine Gueron.

Non-profit association. Staff: Ten. **Sources of support:** Private grants. **Annual Budget:** No answer.

Objectives and interests: —

Major programs and projects: "The Role of the Postal Administration in Small Communities"; "Social Innovation in Business."

Special facilities: —

Activities: Studies, lectures, workshops, reports.

Publications: *Bulletin de la Fondation [Bulletin of the Foundation],* (newsletter, published irregularly).

FORECASTING INTERNATIONAL, LTD.
1001 North Highland Street—Penthouse
Arlington, Virginia 22201, U.S.A.

Telephone: (703) 527-1311

Founded: 1971

Officers: Marvin J. Cetron, President and Chairman of the Board; Norman Nisenoff, Vice President; Audrey Clayton, Senior Scientist and Corporate Secretary; Anne Nelsen, Senior Research Analyst; Charles McFadden, Senior Research Analyst, Sharon Sugarek, Senior Research Analyst.

Private research organization. Staff: 15. **Sources of support:** U.S. Government and commercial. **Annual Budget:** No answer.

Objectives and interests: Futures studies, technological forecasts, technology assessments, resource allocation models, corporate planning (especially concerning energy, technology transfer, and scientific and technical communication).

Major programs and projects: "A Study of Future U.S. Coast Guard Surveillance Requirements"—determination of requirements and capabilities, and development of R&D program, for next 25 years. "The Potential Influence of Social, Economic, Regulatory and Technical Factors on Scientific and Technical Communication"—a study of the interaction of technological and non-technological factors influencing future changes in processing and access needs and capabilities.

Special facilities: Data compilations on over 15,000 key events: technological, economic, energy and other resource related, environmental, social, legal, and political; computer with word processing and terminal capability.

Activities: Seminars and workshops designed for specific clients; consultancy; and specific tasks for customers electing not to do their own forecasts.

Publications: *Technological Forecast of the Future Environment and Its Effects on the Tobacco Industry*, M.J. Cetron, S. Sugarek (1978); *Forecasting the Effects of Events on Consumer Affairs*, N. Nisenoff, A. Clayton, E. Bishop (1978); *Prediction of Naval Aviation Logistics Requirements*, A. Clayton, N. Nisenoff (1978); *Three Alternative Future Scenarios for New York City*, Anne Nelsen (1978).

FORMEDLINGSCENTRALEN FOR FRAMTIDSSTUDIER AB
[THE SWEDISH ASSOCIATION OF FUTURES STUDIES]   Telephone: (8) 22 07 60
Box 5073
S-102 42 Stockholm, Sweden   Founded: 1971

Officers: Gunnar Hambraeus, Chairman of the Board; Daniel Sundstrom, Managing Director; Goran Lundgren.

Non-profit subsidiary to the Royal Swedish Academy of Engineering Sciences.   Staff: Four professionals.
Sources of support: Contract research and information subscription system.   **Annual Budget:** No answer.

Objectives and interests: To support long-term study teams in Swedish government offices and industrial firms with information from the futures studies field.

Major programs and projects: "Sweden 2000"—Broad survey of projections and prospects for Swedish long-term development. "Technology Assessment"—Monitoring methodology and practical applications of technology assessment. "Scenario Techniques for Industrial Planning"—Input of basic information for long-term planning processes. "Prospects for Energy, Raw Materials, and Food"—Studies of basic long-term trends. "Technological Forecasting of Major Innovation Areas"—Exploratory studies.

Special facilities: Small specialized library on futures studies.

Activities: Seminars and roundtable discussions; joint studies financed by the 70 industrial and governmental members of the association.

Publications: *Futures Studies News* (10 issues per year, issued primarily to members of the association). Other in-depth studies and reports are also disseminated to members.

FORSVARETS FORSKNINGSANSTALT (FOA)
[SWEDISH NATIONAL DEFENSE RESEARCH INSTITUTE]   Telephone: 08-63-1800
Linnegatan 89
104 50 Stockholm 80, Sweden   Founded: 1945

Officers: N.H. Lundquist, Director General; G. Franzen, Head of Department for Planning and Operations Research; Nils Andren, Head of Division for International and Social Studies; Gunnar Jervas; E. Block; L. Hogberg, Head of Division for Documentation.

Public, non-profit government agency.   Staff: FOA, approximately 1,400; Department for Planning and Operations Research, approximately 140; Division for International and Social Studies, approximately 15. **Sources of support:**   Government.   **Annual Budget:**   Department for Planning and Operations Research: 20 million Swedish crowns; FOA total: 219 million Swedish crowns.

Objectives and interests: FOA's research is concerned with the short- and long-range problems of the total national defense of Sweden (military, economic, civil, etc.).

Major programs and projects: A quarterly index of defense research reports, with brief abstracts in Swedish, is published under the title "Forsvarsforskningsreferat," of which a major part is unclassified. FOA also participates with the Ministry of Defense in publishing studies on future national defense problems in a series entitled "Forsvars—och sakerhetspolitik" *[*Defense and Security Policy*]*.

Special facilities: —

Activities: Apart from *internal* activities (supporting the authorities of the national defense and, to some extent, other governmental bodies), there are *external* activities, especially in the form of unclassified reports on various research activities.

Publications: *Trends in Planning*, C.G. Jennergren, S. Schwarz, and O. Alvfeldt, editors (1977); *Knowledge and Concepts in Futures Studies*, S. Schwarz, editor (1976).

FORUM FOR THE ADVANCEMENT OF STUDENTS IN SCIENCE AND TECHNOLOGY, INC.

Telephone: (202) 466-3860

2030 M Street, N.W., Suite 402
Washington, D.C. 20036, U.S.A.

Founded: 1972

Officers: Alan Ladwig, President.

Non-profit, educational organization. **Staff:** Three. **Sources of support:** Contracts, contributions, grants, subscriptions. **Annual Budget:** $70,000.

Objectives and interests: To create an environment for active student participation in the discussion of science and technology issues.

Major programs and projects: "An Assessment of Methods to Initiate Student Participation in the Discussion of Satellite Power Systems"—study for DOE to analyze student participation methods. "Student Participation in National Conference on Science, Technology, and the Human Perspective"—contract to select student participants in conference to celebrate 100th anniversary of the electric light. "Student Payload Program"—study to determine how best to give students opportunities to have their experiments flown aboard the space shuttle.

Special facilities: Library containing 3000 volumes, periodicals, brochures, speeches, and reports relevant to broad range of science and technology topics, particularly in aerospace/aviation, energy/environment, and biomedical technologies—open to the public.

Activities: The Forum's activities are focused on publications, conferences, internships, a clearinghouse for student science education activities, and testimony before congressional committees and federal agencies.

Publications: *FASST News* (quarterly tabloid); *FASST News Service* (periodic press release service for campus and educational media editors).

FOUNDATION RESHAPING THE INTERNATIONAL ORDER (RIO)

Telephone: (10) 116181, Ext. 28150

3000 AG, P.O. Box 299
3014 DA, Weena 700
Rotterdam, The Netherlands

Founded: 1976

Officers: Jan van Ettinger, Director; Antony J. Dolman, Senior Fellow; Dick A. Leurdijk, Fellow.

Private, non-profit, action-oriented research institute. **Staff:** Four. **Sources of support:** Contributions from the Governments of Canada, Norway, The Netherlands, Sweden and Venezuela. **Annual Budget:** Approximately $250,000.

Objectives and interests: Goal is to promote a widening and deepening dialogue on the creation of a more equitable international order; objective is to make a substantive contribution to the formulation and implementation of the International Development Strategy for the 1980's and Beyond.

Major programs and projects: "RIO—A 'Second Round'"—an evaluation of the various kinds of reaction to the many proposals contained in the RIO Report, with a view to generating a "second round" of debate. "World Order Studies"—a project designed to compare and coherently link major "world order" studies. "The 'Like-Minded' Countries"—a project seeking to identify the main elements of possible strategies for joint action by the "like-minded" in the 1980's and beyond.

Special facilities: Small library, microfiche documentation service on the New International Order.

Activities: Action-oriented research, publications.

Publications: *Reshaping the International Order*, Jan Tinbergen, coordinator (1976); *Partners in Tomorrow, Strategies for a New International Order*, edited by Antony J. Dolman and Jan van Ettinger (1978).

FUNDACION AMERICA LATINA 2001
[LATIN AMERICAN FOUNDATION 2001]
Apartado Aereo 854
Calle 10 No. 3-61
Bogota, Colombia

Telephone: 242.16.06

Founded: 1976

Officers: Horacio H. Godoy, President; Claire Liekens, Secretary.

Private, non-profit. Staff: — **Sources of support:** Grants. **Annual Budget:** Approximately $50,000.

Objectives and interests: Development of science and technology and future research.

Major programs and projects: "Theoretical Foundations and Methodological Significance"—a prospective analysis. "Holdings of Public Enterprises"—an instrument for future development in Latin America. "Science, Technology and the Future: Towards an Iberoamerican Scientific Community."

Special facilities: —

Activities: Publishing, participation in seminars and courses.

Publications: *America Latina 2001, Editora Guadalupe*, (4 issues per year).

FUNDACION ARGENTINA ANO 2000
[ARGENTINA FOUNDATION FOR THE YEAR 2000]
Leandro Alem 36—Piso 11
Buenos Aires, Argentina 1003

Telephone: 33-8051 ext. 28
Founded: 1973

Officers: Jorge Luis Guerra, President of the Administrative Council; Horacio J. Gomez Beret, Secretary-General; Armando Turano, Voter; Michel J. P. Ramlot; Ramon G. Diaz Bessone; Nicanor Saleno.

Independent, non-profit, private research institute. Staff: 12 members. **Sources of support:** Contributions from private enterprise. **Annual Budget:** No answer.

Objectives and interests: Studies and research on futurology, and prospective on domestic and international issues, in particular South America and the South Cone; short-, medium- and long-term forecasting on economics, politics, technology; studies for private enterprise.

Major programs and projects: "Rol de America del Sur en la produccion de alimentos para el ano 2000" ["The Role of South America in the Production of Food in the Year 2000"]. "Proyecto Nacional. Futurible No. 2"—scenario for the future of the Argentine Republic. "El krill. Proteinas para el mundo" ["The Krill Proteins for the World"]. "La integracion de America del Sur" ["South America's Integration"].

Special facilities: Private library of books, periodicals and reports on domestic and international issues.

Activities: Two courses per year on planning; seminars on topics in futurology and prospective.

Publications: *Proyecto Nacional. Futurible No. 1.*, Ramon G. Diaz Bessone and others (1973); *Estudios sobre el desarrollo de la cuenca inferior del Rio Uruguay [Studies for the Development of the Lower Basin of the Uruguay River]*, Michael J. P. Ramlot (1974).

FUNDACION BARILOCHE
Casilla de Correo 138
San Carlos de Bariloche, Provincia de Rio Negro
8400 Argentina

Telephone: 48017, 48322, 48321

Founded: 1963

Officers: Carlos Alberto Mallmann, Executive President; Ramon A. Aguirre, General Secretary; Oscar Nudler, Senior Fellow; Carolos E. Suarez; Gilberto Gallopin.

Private, non-profit, research organization. **Staff:** 30 associated. **Sources of support:** International organizations. **Annual Budget:** No answer.

Objectives and interests: Synergic developments research; quality of life and development alternatives, energy economics, ecological systems analysis.

Major programs and projects: "Latin American World Model"—Long-term global normative model developed during the last four years. "Model of Latin America"—Four-year project to be started in the near future; "Further Development of the Latin American World Model"—Uses and applications of the same.

Special facilities: Libraries.

Activities: Research.

Publications: *Catastrophe or New Society?—Latin American World Model.* Extensive publication list available from the institution.

FUNDACION JAVIER BARROS SIERRA, A.C.

Tacuba 5, Centro
Mexico 1, D.F., Mexico

Telephone: 520-49-18

Founded: 1975

Officers: Daniel Ruiz, Chairman of the Board; Jose Manuel Covarrubias Solis, Director; Felipe Lara Rosano, Scientific Coordinator; Eduardo Rivera Porto, Chief of Methodological Organization Tools and Mathematical Models; Raul Delgado Wise, Chief of Rural Development Studies; Napoleon Serna Solis, Chief of Educational Area.

Non-profit organization. **Staff:** Seven. **Sources of support:** Mexican government, corporations and foundations. **Annual Budget:** : $750,000.

Objectives and interests: Prospective studies for the future development of the country and long-term planning in the following areas: urban transition, rural development, education, human and natural resources.

Major programs and projects: "Physical Planning" — regional planning for two areas: U.S. border and tropical Gulf of Mexico. "Livestock Prospective" — building of livestock scenarios and recommended actions. "Science and Technology Prospective" — definition of science and technology and recommended actions. "Basic Education Prospective" — long-term planning to cover educational priorities. "Economic Development" — development simulation model.

Special facilities: Library; data terminal.

Activities: Conferences; four annual seminars.

Publications: *Diseno de un futuro para el futuro [Sketch of a Future for the Future]*, Wladimir Sachs; publish approximately 12 papers per year covering special issues.

THE FUTURE ASSOCIATES AND THE KANSAS CITY REGIONAL DEVELOPMENT ASSOCIATION

P.O. Box 912
Shawnee Mission, Kansas 66201, U.S.A.

Telephone: (913) 432-8743

Founded: 1974

Officers: Jim Brown, President; Fannie Webster, Vice-President; Dennis Murphy, Secretary; Joe Falk, General Manager; Bob Vancrum, Legal Counsel.

The Future Associates is a not-for-profit cooperative publishing association; K.C.R.D.A. is a not-for-profit cooperative management association. Staff: All services by volunteers. **Sources of support:** Private. **Annual Budget:** No answer.

Objectives and interests: To develop and disseminate multimedia educational material related to cooperative activities at the neighborhood level and help organize and finance self-sufficient self-help activities at the neighborhood level.

Major programs and projects: Creating audiovisual materials, syndicated newspaper stories, radio talk show formats, and how-to-do-it manuals on cooperative success stories that will stimulate discussion and decision-making at the neighborhood level. Developing a working model of cooperative community development in the metropolitan market area of Kansas City, Missouri/Kansas. "Cooperative Community Development"—A 300-page guidebook outlining why and how to organize not-for-profit neighborhood development associations. "Dialogues on What Could Be in a Cooperative Future"—Six dialogues which explain the "evocative" dialogue method of conducting meetings and learning to cooperate.

Special facilities: —

Activities: Introductory talks and seminars on cooperative community development to interested groups of people.

Publications: *Cooperative Community Development,* Joe Falk, editor (1975); *Dialogues on What Could Be in a Cooperative Future,* Joe Falk (1974).

FUTURE OPTIONS ROOM
1223 Connecticut Avenue, N.W.
Washington, D.C. 20036, U.S.A.

Telephone: (202) 393-1970

Founded: 1975

Officers: Jerry Glenn, Executive Director; Roy Mason, Director of Planning; Scott Dankman, Director of Information Systems.

Private firm. Staff: Three full-time professionals. **Sources of support:** One-third U.S. government; one-third Canadian government; one-third corporations. **Annual Budget:** No answer.

Objectives and interests: To condense the complex future into simple options and designs by synthesizing high quality information from a variety of fields and conceiving new ideas and designs.

Major programs and projects: "Philosophy and Methodology of Futures Research"—Why, what, and how to integrate futures into Canadian Ministry of Urban Affairs. "Policy Analysis and Future Briefing/Strategy Room Design"—Identifying technology and design for Canadian Ministry of Urban Affairs policy rooms. "Aerospace Impact on U.S. GNP, Inflation, Employment, and Balance of Payments"—For Rockwell and Seaman/Clark Associates. "Briefing on Aquaculture and HR 370"—Analysis of impact of current and future U.S. fishing and aquaculture on economy, for Congressional Research Service. Futuristic curriculum for 7th-12th grades—National program integrating ecology, technology, and economy in the future, for Seaman/Clark Associates.

Special facilities: Wholistic taxonomy of the future, with option cards, briefing and option sheets. Physical environment designed as options room, including special briefing room, extensive futures library, and diverse bank of future-oriented authorities.

Activities: Briefings in major policy areas such as growth, energy, information systems, agriculture, environment, finance, education, and technology. Public speaking and futures courses for government agencies and corporations.

Publications: *Architecture Beyond 2000* (film, in development); *Energy Beyond 2000* (film, in development); *Why Space?* (slide show, in development); *Briefing Sheets on the Future,* Jerry Glenn, Roy Mason, and Scott Dankman (1976).

FUTURE SYSTEMS
P.O. Box 14067
Minneapolis, Minnesota 55414, U.S.A.

Telephone: —

Founded: 1977

Officers: Earl C. Joseph, Chairman of the Board; Scott W. Erickson, President; Michael DeWane, Vice-President.

Non-profit, research institute. Staff: Nine. **Sources of support:** Corporations, foundations, government. **Annual Budget:** No answer.

Objectives and interests: Futures research and policy analysis on economic, political, social and technological matters; special emphasis on future studies in education.

Major programs and projects: —

Special facilities: —

Activities: —

Publications: —

FUTUREMICS, INC.
1629 K Street, N.W.
Washington, D.C. 20006

Telephone: (202) 667-5620

Founded: 1970

Officers: Robert E. Maston, President; Marilyn Gadzuk, Director of Publications; Kent Myers, Co-editor, *Future Abstracts;* Laura Bukkila, Co-editor, *Future Abstracts.*

Private, for-profit, research, publication, and educational consulting firm. Staff: Five; six part-time. **Sources of support:** Subscriptions, contracts with public and private sectors. **Annual Budget:** No answer.

Objectives and interests: To assist individuals, groups, and organizations in programming their activities toward the definition and achievement of preferable and desirable futures. The structure of Futuremics is itself experimental, in that the company attempts to embody concepts which the staff believes to be relevant to the future, such as democratic decision-making, worker self-management, and maximization of personal growth.

Major programs and projects: Futures Curriculum Center—Develops materials and programs and establishes networks in support of futures education. Workshop Training Programs—Emphasize participation and goal-directedness; subjects include management by objectives, management of time, management of change, management by creativity, and self-management. Futures Education Survey—A continuing survey of future-related courses in higher education, including publication of the results. College of the Potomac—A university-without-walls program featuring learner-determined objectives and self-assessment.

Special facilities: Futures library of approximately 2,000 volumes, plus selected periodicals and reports, on topics pertinent to the future; the Dartmouth College (Eldredge) Files—Futuremics is the repository of survey materials collected by H. Wentworth Eldredge on futures courses in higher education throughout the United States.

Activities: The staff members design and run programs, conferences, and workshops, do individual counseling and write and publish materials on subjects related to the future; Futuremics contracts to provide services of management and technical specialists, psychologists, speakers, writers, planners, and evaluators.

Publications: *Footnotes to the Future* (monthly newsletter); *Future-Abstracts* (monthly abstracting service).

THE FUTURES GROUP, INC.
76 Eastern Blvd.
Glastonbury, Connecticut 06033, U.S.A.

Telephone: (203) 633-3501

Founded: 1971

Officers: Theodore J. Gordon, President; Harold S. Becker, Executive Vice-President and Treasurer; Lillian Deitch, Vice-President; Robert H. Smith, Vice-President; John G. Stover, Herbert Gerjuoy.

Independent, profit-making, research and management consulting company. Staff: — **Sources of support:** — **Annual Budget:** No answer.

Objectives and interests: Policy analysis and forecasting; assisting management in anticipating the consequences of change; bringing futures research to the solution of practical problems of short-term and long-range planning.

Major programs and projects: "Hybrid Probabilistic System Dynamics Model of U.S. Agriculture"; "The Future Psychotropes Effects Desired and Means to Achieve Them"; "Important Urethane Foam Developments in the United States: A Forecast Through 1990"; "Key Characteristics of the Energy Environment"; "Airport Demand-Capacity Relationships: Policy Implications of Alternative Future Scenarios for the National Aviation System."

Special facilities: Maintains a library of books, periodicals and reports in a variety of fields with special emphasis on futurology, futures research, and futurics. The SCOUT Information File is a unique data bank of forecasted events which are extracted from published material (both serial and monographs).

Activities: Proprietary studies, policy and forecasting seminars, workshops, data services (Pharmaceutical Prospects, Hospital Prospects, Consumer Prospects, Scout) daily consulting on methods and substantive items, lectures to industry, government, and academia.

Publications: *Pharmaceutical Prospects* (six times a year); *American Consumer: Purchasing Patterns in the Late 1970s; The Impact of Legalized Gambling: Lotteries and Off-Track Betting,* D. Weinstein, L. Deitch, with H. Becker (Praeger 1974); *Prepaid Legal Services; Socioeconomic Consequences,* L. Deitch, D. Weinstein, with H.

Becker and W. Renfro (D.C. Heath and Co.); *A Technology Assessment of Life-Extending Technologies*, H. Gerjuoy, T. Gordon, et. al. (available from NTIS).

THE FUTURES-INVENTION ASSOCIATES

1250 South Williams Street
Denver, Colorado 80210, U.S.A.

Telephone: (303) 733-1854

Founded: 1977

Officers: Warren L. Ziegler, President and Director of Research; Grace M. Healy, Vice-President and Director of Training.

Private, independent, futures-action research and education. **Staff:** — **Sources of support:** Contracts, grants and sale of publications. **Annual Budget:** No answer.

Objectives and interests: Prepare citizens and leaders in communities, cities, states and organizations to invent future alternatives and take present actions to bring them about.

Major programs and projects: "The Futures of the Sisters of Mercy"—various projects with Mercy Sisters around the country. "The Memphis Conference"—a collaboration with Southwestern-citizen participation. "The Learning Stance"—a fundamental research project in collaboration with Syracuse Research Corporation and National Institute of Education. "The Club of Athens"—participatory research and action on the future of the world in collaboration with other agencies and persons.

Special facilities: —

Activities: Workshops, seminars and longer-term futures-invention and social action strategy invention projects with communities, colleges, schools, religious, civic, voluntary and non-profit organizations. Fields covered include civic literacy, education, law and justice, environment, race relations, urban development, economy, goverance, etc.

Publications: *A Mindbook for Futures-Inventors*, by W. L. Ziegler (1978); *The Art of Futures-Invention*, W. L. Ziegler (1977); *Adult Learning and the Future of Post-Secondary Education*, W. L. Ziegler and Grace M. Healy (1977); *The Future of Adult Education and Learning*, W. L. Ziegler (1976).

FUTURES NETWORK

Deneswood, Wilmerhatch Lane
Epsom, Surrey KT18-7EQ, England

Telephone: Epsom 25502

Founded: 1977

Officers: J. Michael Williamson, Chairman of Council (20 Members).

Informal, non-profit network. **Staff:** None. Michael and Marion Williamson administer the network on a part-time basis with help from other members. **Sources of support:** Subscriptions. **Annual Budget:** None.

Objectives and interests: Futures Network is an informal association of people interested in futures studies and the use of futures thinking and concerned with examining longer-term developments (e.g. social change, technological change) and their implications regarding some or all aspects of society.

Major programs and projects: —

Special facilities: —

Activities: Ad hoc meetings. There are few full network activities, the purpose of the network being to help members help themselves.

Publications: Quarterly newsletter.

FUTURES STUDIES CENTRE

15 Kelso Road
Leeds, England LS2 9PR

Telephone: 0532 459865

Founded: 1974

Officers: Roland Chaplain, Secretary.

Independent, non-profit. **Staff:** The Centre acts as an information and contact point within a self-developing international network. It is democratically run by volunteers who find a role for themselves within its structure. In this respect, it attempts to reflect in its mode of working some of the insights of those with whom it is linked through information gathering and exchange. **Sources of support:** Subscriptions, private donations, bartering of skills and knowledge. **Annual Budget:** No answer.

Objectives and interests: Popularizing futures studies; education for participation; acting as a "look-out" center for significant new "indicators" and threats.

Major programs and projects: Two studies to be undertaken on an international scale in cooperation with the World Future Studies Federation: (1) Gathering and exchange of information about the growing dialogue between environmentalists, consumer groups, futurists, trade unionists, and factory workers; (2) Gathering and exchange of information about "Alternative Technology" and "Alternative Lifestyle" experiments, communes, cooperatives, workers' control, and other social experiments which might provide significant indicators for alternative futures.

Special facilities: Library (no loans), cross-indexed contact list of several thousand people, organizations, interests, skills, and locations.

Activities: Conferences and seminars conducted as an integral part of projects.

Publications: Bimonthly newsletter; other occasional publications, conference and working group reports, exchange of articles.

FUTURONTO, INC.
1207 Linbrook Road
Oakville, Ontario, Canada L6J 2L5

Telephone: (416) 844-4959

Founded: 1969

Officers: Frank Feather, President and Director of Research; Joyce Feather, Secretary-Treasurer and Director of Publications; Joyce A. Coltart, Senior Research Fellow and Project Leader.

Private, non-profit, research, publication and educational consulting organization. **Staff:** Four. **Sources of support:** Subscriptions, contracts with public and private sector. **Annual Budget:** No Answer.

Objectives and interests: Anticipatory planning and environmental scanning research and consulting, using general systems techniques and split-grain research findings in designing appropriate futures which are flexible, open and evolutionary.

Major programs and projects: "Futuronto: Antidote to Future Shock in Business and Management"—seminar program series emphasizing environmental systems approach. "Futuronto Management Centre"—developing programs and support material and establishing networks in support of business management education. "Futuronto Business Survey"—continuing survey of future-oriented activities in business organizations around the world. "Futuronto General System"—development of universal general system for application in fields of business and management.

Special facilities: Futures library of essential and relevant futures material. Also management, planning and business library of selected periodicals and future-pertinent reports/material.

Activities: Conduct seminars and programs on management and planning, and contract to provide services of management specialists, speakers, writers and planners.

Publications: *Futuronto Quarterly*, a quarterly journal of futures research, business planning and management, and general systems research, etc. Also numerous reports based on contract work available to supporting organizations. List available on request.

GAMMA GROUP
University of Montreal and McGill University
3535 Queen Mary, Suite 210
Montreal, Quebec, Canada

Telephone: (514) 343-7020

Founded: 1975

Officers: Kimon Valaskakis, Director; J. G. Smith, Assistant Director; P.S. Sindell, Senior Associate; Iris Martin, P. Arnopoulos, R. Jouandet, Research Associates.

Inter-university forecasting and planning institute. **Staff:** Five permanent, 20 part-time (variable). **Sources of support:** Canadian Government, Quebec Government. **Annual Budget:** About $250,000.

Objectives and interests: Public policy planning; conservation; forecasting methodology.

Major programs and projects: "The Information Society in Canada"—(research in progress). "Re-thinking Development"—project co-sponsored by U.N. University and affiliated to Galtung's Geneva project, "GPID."

Special facilities: —

Activities: "Technological Challenge of Conservation" (April 1978) and "The Future of Quebec" (March 1978).

Publications: *Conserver Society*, by K. Valaskakis, P.S. Sindell, J. G. Smith, E. Martin (1978); *The Implications of a Conserver Society*, 15 researchers involved, 4 volumes (1976); *The Future of Quebec*, 40 researchers involved, 26 volumes.

THE GEORGE WASHINGTON UNIVERSITY, PROGRAM OF POLICY STUDIES IN SCIENCE AND TECHNOLOGY

Telephone: (202) 676-7380
(202) 676-7292

The George Washington University
2130 H Street, N.W., Suite 714
Washington, D.C. 20052, U.S.A. **Founded:** 1966

Officers: Louis H. Mayo, Director; Vary T. Coates, Associate Director; John Logsdon, Director, Graduate Program in Science, Technology, and Public Policy; Joseph B. Margolin, Director, Behavioral Sciences and Educational Policy Group.

University-related research institute. **Staff:** 10-15 professionals. **Sources of support:** Federal grants and contracts. **Annual Budget:** Approximately $750,000 to $1 million.

Objectives and interests: Science policy analysis, technology assessment, and futures research.

Major programs and projects: "Evaluating the Institutional Aspects of the Introduction of Non-Proliferation Alternative Nuclear Systems." "Videoconferencing for Congress: An Experimental Application of the Communications Technology Satellite." "Manpower Policies for the Use of Science and Technology in Development." "Preliminary Technology Assessment of Computer-Assisted Makeup and Imaging Systems (CAMIS)." "Basic Research Foundations for Public Education in Energy Conservation: The Case of the Appliance Labeling Program."

Special facilities: Innovation Information Center: a collection of over 6,500 books, periodicals, government publications, etc., dealing with innovation in the private and public sector and the impacts of public policy. Includes structured abstracts of approximately 5,000 articles. Accession lists available. Open to scholars by appointment (telephone: 676-6392 or 676-7380). Bibliographic searches can be arranged for a fee.

Activities: Government/academic seminars and conferences; associated M.A. degree program in Science, Technology, and Public Policy.

Publications: Publications list available on request.

GESELLSCHAFT FUR ZUKUNFTSFRAGEN e.V.

Telephone: 030-8838874

[ASSOCIATION FOR FUTURE STUDIES]
Giesebrechtstrasse 15
1000 Berlin 12, Federal Republic of Germany **Founded:** 1967

Officers: Peter Menke-Glueckert, Chairman; Hans Buchholz, Manager.

Private membership association of approximately 600 members. **Staff:** — **Sources of support:** Membership dues. **Annual Budget:** 100,000 German marks.

Objectives and interests: To support and coordinate efforts in futures research and to make the results of such research available to the public.

Major programs and projects: World Future Studies Conference (WFSC), 8-10 May 1979 at Berlin.

Special facilities: —

Activities: Working teams and project groups; joint meetings with other organizations; conferences, seminars, and symposia.

Publications: *Analysen und Prognosen [Analyses and Forecasts]* (bimonthly); *Sachbuch: Zukunftenergie [Factbook on Energy Futures]* (1975).

GOALS FOR DALLAS
2004 Davis Building
1309 Main Street
Dallas, Texas 75202, U.S.A.

Telephone: (214) 741-1738

Founded: 1966

Officers: Floyd A. Norman, Chairman, Board of Trustees; Louis J. Weber, Jr., Vice-Chairman, Board of Trustees; Marjorie Allan, Staff Director; Norma Mecaskey, Office Administrator.

Independent, non-profit, nonpartisan, non-political citizen involvement program. **Staff:** Four, supplemented by additional staff when necessary. **Sources of support:** Donations from foundations, businesses, individuals. **Annual Budget:** $135,000 to $215,000, depending on activities.

Objectives and interests: Provide a mechanism through which all interested citizens can work with community leaders from both the public and private sectors to identify issues, set goals and develop plans and priorities for achieving the goals; progress in achieving goals is evaluated annually.

Major programs and projects: "Tanglewood Conference," 1976 (170 goals proposed). "Goals Revision Conferences," 1976 to 1977. "Publication of New Goals for Dallas, 1977." "Development of Plans and Priorities for Achievement of New Goals." "Formation of Goals Achievement Committees to Monitor Progress on Goals."

Special facilities: Maintains a library of reports, studies and papers prepared by Goals for Dallas Task Forces in identifying major issues facing the community and plans and priorities for achieving the goals. Available to public upon request.

Activities: Goals-setting conferences; task forces to identify issues, develop plans and set priorities; neighborhood meetings for citizen review and revision of goals; goals achievement committees for monitoring goals achievement.

Publications: *Newsletter* (semiannual), circulated free of charge to Goals volunteers and Task Force members; *Goals for Dallas, Submitted for Consideration by Dallas Citizens* (1966); *Goals for Dallas, Proposals for Achieving the Goals* (1969); *Goals for Dallas, Achieving the Goals* (1970); *Economic Potentials Handbook,* Third Edition (1973); *New Goals for Dallas* (1977).

GOALS FOR THE GREATER AKRON AREA
One Cascade Plaza - 8th Floor
Akron, Ohio 44308, U.S.A.

Telephone: (216) 375-2176

Founded: 1973

Officers: M. G. O'Neil, Chairman; Barbara Hiney, Vice-Chairman and Executive Director.

Non-profit. **Staff:** Three, plus consultants retained, and hundreds of volunteers. **Sources of support:** Public contributions; in-kind matching services provided by industry and the City of Akron. **Annual Budget:** No answer.

48

Objectives and interests: Improving the quality of life and sense of community in the Akron area by bringing together representatives of public and private power structures and the general citizenry in order to achieve effective communication, improve levels of knowledge and understanding, and provide mechanisms for mutual problem-solving.

Major programs and projects: Implementation of the recommendations of the Task Forces; providing an effective forum for public discussion of major issues, and continuing to serve the community with innovative efforts to improve communication among the public and private power structures and the citizenry.

Special facilities: None.

Activities: Formation of Board of Trustees and Executive Committee, reflecting the character of the Akron area in terms of race, sex, geography, economic level and occupation; organization of 20 neighborhood meetings to discuss community problems and goals; commissioning of 16 essays on community problems by professionals in various fields; sponsorship of three-day goals-setting conference involving 74 area citizens—corporate officers, union leaders, white and blue collar workers, teachers, students, etc.

Publications: Task Force reports, issued in 1978, on Housing, Public Safety, Education, Local Government, Health, Social Services, The Economy, Transportation, Recreation, and Culture and Entertainment.

HARRIS INTERNATIONAL
Box 2321
La Jolla, California 92038, U.S.A.

Telephone: (714) 453-7321

Founded: 1971

Officers: Philip R. Harris, President; Dorothy L. Harris, Vice-President.

Private research and training organization. **Staff:** 45 consultants. **Sources of support:** Government and corporate contracts. **Annual Budget:** Confidential.

Objectives and interests: Action research, training, and consulting on management and organization development; special focus on the management of change, preventing organization shock, and human resource/potential development, and future studies.

Major programs and projects: "Professional Development Institutes on Human Behavior"—under contract to the Office of Naval Research, this three year study was for human resource specialists and criminal justice personnel. "Management Development and Team Building for Los Angeles County Fire and Park Department"—focus on management of change in a county fire department. "Cultural Awareness Workshops for Westinghouse Electric Corporation and the U.S. Customs Service"—cross-cultural training research for multinational managers and customs officials. "Management of Change for Union Leaders, Western Federation of Butchers"—research on new meat processing plants and development of union leadership. "Management of Change in Naval Systems"—a series of programs on change and behavioral sciences for Naval Units.

Special facilities: Five-year study on human emergence—summary article available upon request.

Activities: Conducts client-sponsored workshops, institutes, seminars, and conferences, using custom designs and pilot testing, evaluation and follow-up studies; action research on manpower and organizational problems, such as communication, conflict, motivation, and other behavioral science management topics; associated with The Innovative Group of La Jolla in studies of top performers and high achievers at work; organization development consulting.

Publications: *Effective Management of Change,* Philip R. Harris (three audio cassettes and a manual, 1977); *Improving Management Communication Skills,* Philip and Dorothy Harris, (three audio cassettes and a manual, 1978); *Organization Dynamics: An Instructor's Manual for Human Resource Specialists* (1973); *Leadership Effectiveness with People,* Philip and Dorothy Harris (an album of audio cassettes, 1978); *Managing Cultural Differences* (1979).

HAZAN INTERNATIONAL
38 rue de Moscou
Paris 75008, France

Telephone: 293 4809

Founded: 1963

Officers: Joseph Hazan, President; Monique Castelin; Christiane Roulin.

Private, for-profit organization. **Staff:** Four. **Sources of support:** Contracts with clients. **Annual Budget:** —

Objectives and interests: To provide consulting services for diversification, product search, agreements between firms, interfacing R and D industry, future market definition, and joint ventures.

Major programs and projects: On-going indentification of fast growth, high profit opportunities in Europe. World-wide product search, both existing and at prototype stage. International Club of Consultants and Researchers in all industrial countries and all branches of industry.

Special facilities: —

Activities: —

Publications: *International Business Proposals* (quarterly, presents business offers and requests for licensing, distribution, mergers, acquisitions, joint ventures, services offered by research centers, and services of consultants.).

HOUSTON CHAMBER OF COMMERCE
FUTURE STUDIES COMMITTEE AND DIVISION
1100 Milam Building
Houston, Texas 77002, U.S.A.

Telephone: (713) 651-1313 ext. 188 or 189

Founded: 1965-66

Officers: John H. Crooker, Jr., Chamber of Commerce (CofC) Board Chairman; Louie Welch, CofC President and Chief Executive Officer; Leonard S. Patillo, CofC Executive Vice-President and General Manager; Harry A. Golemon, Future Studies Chairman; Floyd Martin, Director, Future Studies Division; Robin Rose, Secretary, Future Studies Division.

Non-profit organization. Staff: Two. **Sources of support:** CofC General Fund, which is supported by voluntary-member subscriptions and has no government support. **Annual Budget:** No answer.

Objectives and interests: Identify significant trends and indicate possible impacts—favorable or unfavorable—on the Houston region in the future.

Major programs and projects: "Staff Executives Workshop"—two-day hideaway think-tank relating CofC role in this region to anticipated changes, both positive and negative, during the next decade.

Special facilities: In-house files and resource materials; working files of three-dozen CofC committees and task forces.

Activities: Leadership opinion surveys to help set future-studies guidelines and priorities; conduct staff executive workshop to relate CofC role to identified trends; forecast-consolidation seminars to achieve consensus among 10-year forecasts made annually by three-dozen specialized committees and a task force of CofC; CofC Board-level executive assemblies—top-leadership review of forecasts, impacts, and plans for managing the process of change; annual program-of-work development for entire CofC; cooperate with other planning agencies in the region, providing inputs and reviewing draft/plans for comment.

Publications: *Houston Magazine*, Richard Stanley, editor (monthly, business-news magazine); *At Work*, Mary Midkiff, editor (CofC monthly newsletter).

HUDSON INSTITUTE, INC.
Quaker Ridge Road
Croton-on-Hudson, New York 10520, U.S.A.

Telephone: (914) 762-0700

Founded: 1961

Officers: Herman Kahn, Director and Chairman of the Board; Rudy L. Ruggles, Jr., President; Leon C. Martel, Executive Vice-President; Donald G. Brennan, Frank Armbruster, Colin S. Gray.

Non-profit research institute. Staff: 25 research, plus 40 support staff. **Sources of support:** Government contracts, corporate support, grants. **Annual Budget:** No answer.

Objectives and interests: Policy studies in the public interest.

Major programs and projects: "Future of Australia"—several scenarios of the social, political and economic future of Australia. "Future of Westchester"—demographic and economic analysis of Westchester. "Future of Arizona"—Indian problems, water and energy issues, business and social trends, illegal immigration. "The Japanese

Challenge"—economic, political, social and international analysis of Japan. "Long Term Prospects for Developments in Space (A Scenario Approach)"—for the National Aeronautics and Space Administration.

Special facilities: Library.

Activities: Lecture-seminars annually; round table discussion meetings; Corporate Environment Program intelligence briefings; three-area Corporate Environment Program meetings (U.S., Japan, Europe) annually; annual meeting of Members.

Publications: *The Next 200 Years*, by Kahn, Brown and Martel (1976); *Our Children's Crippled Future*, by Armbruster, Bracken (1977); *World Food Prospects and Agricultural Potential*, by Chou, Harmon and Kahn (1977); *EDA Report—The Future of the U.S. and its Regions*, by Leveson and Newitt (1978); *Suggestions for a Phase II National Energy Policy*, by Brown (1978).

HUNGARIAN ACADEMY OF SCIENCES, INSTITUTE FOR SCIENCE ORGANIZATION
Telephone: 123-022

Munnich Ferenc Street 18
1051 Budapest V, Hungary   **Founded:** 1967

Officers: Lajos Szanto, Director; Vince Grolmusz, Candidate of Economic Sciences; Judith Mosoni, Research Associate; Ildiko Fogarasi, Research Associate.

Research institute. Staff: 30 members.   **Sources of support:** State budget.   **Annual Budget:** N answer.

Objectives and interests: Studies on science policy and science organization; preparation of decision making for the Hungarian Academy of Sciences and governmental bodies; forecasting research.

Major programs and projects: Forecasting of the main research branches in science and technology; forecasting of the Hungarian R and D potential to 1990; methodology of forecasting.

Special facilities: —

Activities: Postgraduate seminars.

Publications: *Prognosztika [Prognosis]* (scientific periodical on forecasting; in Hungarian); "Tudomanypolitika es tomanyszervezes Magyarorszagon" ["Science Policy and Science Organization in Hungary"], Csondes, Szanto, and Vas-Zoltan (*Tudomanyszervezesi fuzetek [Journal of Science Organization]*, 1971); *Jovokutatasi modszertani utmutato [Guide to Futures Research Methodology]* (1973); *Politique des sciences sociales en Hongrie [Social Science Policy in Hungary]*, Szanto (1975).

HUNGARIAN ACADEMY OF SCIENCES, PRESIDENTIAL COMMITTEE ON THE SOCIAL IMPACT OF SCIENCE AND TECHNOLOGY.
Telephone: 123-022, 318-385

Munnich Ferenc-u 18
1051 Budapest, Hungary   **Founded:** 1973

Officers: Alexander Szalai, President; Istvan Lang, Vice-President; Gyorgy Pethes, Secretary.

Academy group.   Staff: Several members of the Academy staff.   **Sources of support:** Academy budget.
Annual Budget: No answer.

Objectives and interests: Study of the social impact of science and technology; prognostics of the development, especially the national development of scientific research and of the social consequences of the introduction of new technologies.

Major programs and projects: Prognostication of major new tasks and topics of Hungarian research up to 1990; contributions to the assessment of the potential national and ecological resources of Hungary; studies on the applicability of global and regional "world models."

Special facilities: Academy library.

Activities: Plenary meetings of the Presidential Committee, sub-committees and staff; preparation of special studies in the field of futures research; preparation of memoranda and expertises for the presidium of the Academy and for other authorities.

Publications: *Prognosztika* (a periodical in Hungarian).

IDAHO'S TOMORROW
Division of Budget Policy and Planning
State House
Boise, Idaho 83720, U.S.A.

Telephone: (208) 384-3900

Founded: 1975

Officers: Paul S. Card, Project Director.

Public goal-setting effort. Staff: — **Sources of support:** Pacific Northwest Regional Commission. **Annual Budget:** $60,000.

Objectives and interests: To develop a consensus on Idaho's future with input from citizens, under the direction of a planning consortium appointed by the governor; to provide educational and policy guidance for state action to implement recommendations.

Major programs and projects: Statewide surveys of citizens' ideas regarding the future of Idaho; statewide, regional, and local conferences to discuss major topics of concern; review conference to consolidate findings; trend analysis project to determine what state will be like in 1995.

Special facilities: —

Activities: Meetings and conferences to report results of original survey to the citizens and to solicit their recommendations for implementing goals; additional workshops that are issue specific to update and clarify information received in 1975.

Publications: Reports and monographs related to the major goals identified in Idaho's Tomorrow.

ILLINOIS 2000 FOUNDATION
20 North Wacker Drive
Suite 1960
Chicago, Illinois 60606, U.S.A.

Telephone: (312) 372-7373

Founded: 1977

Officers: David E. Connor, Chairman; Lester W. Brann, Vice-Chairman; David E. Baker, Executive Director; Linda Bruce, Administrative Assistant.

Private, non-profit, tax exempt, operating foundation. Staff: Two. **Sources of support:** Economic Development Program, Illinois Chamber of Commerce. **Annual Budget:** $100,000.

Objectives and interests: Set long-range economic goals for State of Illinois, set trends and economic alternatives; use public participation processes to generate widespread understanding of future economic issues and gain consensus on directions for the state.

Major programs and projects: "Program to Analyse Long-range Trends and Alternatives for the Illinois Economy." "Goals Conference on Illinois' Economic Future."

Special facilities: Library on economic issues. In process of assembling data bank on Illinois economy in association with University of Illinois-Urbana Champaign.

Activities: Board meetings; issue area team research process (includes meetings, research and review of major economic issues, goals-setting conferences, polls, surveys, balloting on goals, and local goals projects in communities related to state program).

Publications: *Annual Report,* issued each October at no charge; *Illinois 2000 Update,* (periodic) edited by Linda Bruce, no charge; *Illinois Economy: Trends and Statistics,* staff of Illinois 2000 (1977).

INDIAN INSTITUTE OF TECHNOLOGY
Powai, Maharashtra
Bombay 400 0076, India

Telephone: 581772

Founded: 1958

Officers: A. K. De, Director; J. T. Panikar, Civil Engineering Department; B.D. Mishra, Humanities and Social Sciences Department.

National, non-profit institute for teaching and research. Staff: 317 faculty, 1,830 other. **Sources of support:** Grant-in-aid from Government of India. **Annual Budget:** No answer.

Objectives and interests: Undergraduate and postgraduate training, and postdoctoral research.

Major programs and projects: "Vital Resources for the Future"—research and assessment of modern technology in the context of a depletion rate of non-renewable resources. "Crises and Disasters, Early Warning System"—need to sense the signals of excessive stress on the environmental system due to human interventions to monitoring the natural recycling time for a recovery to prevent permanent damage. "Technology and Development"—development as a process of emergence from subservience to the hazards and uncertainties of the natural state and cycle of events to an organized and planned effort to greater flexibility, freedom and security. "Social and Technological Alternatives for the Future"—systematic studies of major sectors like food, energy, population, non-renewable resources and the integration of these with scenarios related to the future quality of life and implications related to science policy.

Special facilities: Central library and departmental libraries.

Activities: International Workshop on Technology Assessment, January and April 1978; Workshop of Futurology, November 1976.

Publications: *Annual Report; Research Bulletin* (annual); *Newsletter* (quarterly); *Courses of Study Bulletins* (annual).

INDUSTRIAL MANAGEMENT CENTER, INC.

Telephone: (207) 633-4082

River Road
North Edgecomb, Maine 04566, U.S.A.

Founded: 1967

Officers: James R. Bright, President; John Vanston, Associate Director; Ralph Swalm, Associate Director; James Apple, Associate Director; Mary E. Bright, Financial Secretary; Patricia Olson, Administrative Director.

Private educational and consulting firm. Staff: Three full-time, 20 part-time consultants. **Sources of support:** Private. **Annual Budget:** No answer.

Objectives and interests: Post-university education and consulting in topics related to the management of technology.

Major programs and projects: The Center offers several courses, conducted in the U.S. and abroad, which train delegates from industry, government, and academia in the systematic analysis of future technology and its impacts. Among its regularly scheduled courses are the following: "Technology Forecasting Workshop"—One-week course in technology forecasting techniques. "Socio-Political Change and Technology"—One-week course in socio-political changes and institutional response. "Impact Analysis and Technology Assessment"—One-week course in technology assessment and analysis. "Managing Technological Innovation"—One-week course in improving the management of technological innovation.

Special facilities: Numerous exercises in technology forecasting and technology assessment methods.

Activities: Short courses open to the public; in-house courses for private firms and government agencies; consulting assignments with top management.

Publications: *Brief Introduction to Technology Forecasting: Concepts and Exercises,* James R. Bright (1973, revised, 1976); *Guide to Practical Technological Forecasting,* James R. Bright and Milton E. Schoeman (1973); *Technological Forecasting for Industry and Government,* James R. Bright (1968); *Political Technology Forecasting: With Notes on Socio-Political Change and Technology,* James R. Bright (1978).

INFOMEDIA CORPORATION

Telephone: (415) 321-2682

530 Lytton Avenue
Palo Alto, California 94301, U.S.A.

Founded: 1976

Officers: Jacques Vallee, Raymond Williams, Jr., Principal Officers and Directors; Salvatore Suniga, Vice-President; Richard Miller, Director of Research; Aleda Womack, Executive Assistant.

Private. Staff: Six. **Sources of support:** Public and private sector clients. **Annual Budget:** No answer.

Objectives and interests: Electronic message systems; tele-conferencing; networking.

Major programs and projects: "Office Communications in 1985"—a study of future environments and product opportunities.

Special facilities: Series of information brochures, describing computer-based message systems.

Activities: Computer conferences are created by client organizations, using the "planet" and "notepad" systems, in support of management control activites and international networking.

Publications: *Planet News,* newsletter (monthly), free to clients, sample copies on request.

INFORMATION FUTURES
2217 College Station
Pullman, Washington 99163, U.S.A.

Telephone: (509) 332-5726

Founded: 1974

Officers: Gerald R. Brong, President.

Private business. Staff: Two plus 30 associates. **Sources of support:** Sale of publications; conference registration fees. **Annual Budget:** No answer.

Objectives and interests: To explore the alternative futures in education and library/information-service fields in an attempt to facilitate a selection of the future that meets the needs of an information-rich society.

Major programs and projects: "Media in Higher Education: The Critical Issues" — a critical issues conference culminating in publication of issue-papers collection. "Educational Technology: The Alternative Futures" — publication of issue-papers collection.

Special facilities: —

Activities: Critical-issues conferences, seminars and research study sessions; publication.

Publications: *Instructional Improvement: An Assessment of Programs at Sixteen Universities,* John A. Davis (1978); *Copyright and the Teaching/Learning Process,* Jerome K. Miller, editor (1977); *The Selection, Acquisition, and Utilization of Audiovisual Materials* (2nd Edition), William J. Quinly (1978); *Media Programs and Their Management Related to the Information Cycle,* Gerald R. Brong (1977).

INFORMATION FOR POLICY DESIGN
Webster Road
LaFayette, New York 13084, U.S.A.

Telephone: (315) 677-9278

Founded: 1974

Officers: Michael Marien, Director.

Private. Staff: One, and part-time help. **Sources of support:** Majority of work contracted to World Future Society. **Annual Budget:** Not applicable.

Objectives and interests: Seeks to contribute to a comprehensive forum addressing domestic and global problems by identifying and commenting upon the relevant literature. Also seeks to improve policy-making and curriculum relevant to public policy and future studies.

Major programs and projects: —

Special facilities: Special compilations prepared upon request.

Activities: Publications; consultation.

Publications: *Future Survey* (January 1979—), monthly bibliographic review published by the World Future Society; *Public Policy Book Forecast,* Michael Marien, editor (7 issues, October 1977-October 1978), bibliographic newsletter on forthcoming and recently published books and reports, succeeded by WFS *Future Survey,* full set of back issues available; *Societal Directions and Alternatives: A Critical Guide to the Literature,* Michael Marien (1976), critical annotations and ratings of 1,015 items, overview essays to 16 chapters, and nine indexes to names, organizations, and ideas.

INSEAD
[EUROPEAN INSTITUTE OF BUSINESS ADMINISTRATION]
Boulevard de Constance
77305 Fontainebleau
France

Telephone: Paris 422 4827

Founded: 1958

Officers: Pierre Cailliau, Director General; Uwe Kitzinger, Dean; Jean Claude Thoenig, Associate Dean, Research and Course Development; Claude Rameau, Associate Dean, MBA and Continuing Education Programmes.

Private. Staff: 65 including full-time and part-time members. **Sources of support:** 50 percent programme revenue; 50 percent external fund raising companies, foundations, etc. **Annual Budget:** 1.8 million FF.

Objectives and interests: Education of managers (MBA and Continuing Education); research; pedagogical innovation.

Major programs and projects: "Management of Human Resources in a Changing World"—several projects. "Transfer of Technology from EEC to Asian Enterprises." "The Current Evolution and Future of Europe." "Markets as Social Systems." "Forecasting and Quantitative Data"—several projects.

Special facilities: —

Activities: —

Publications: —

INSTITUT DE PROSPECTIVE ET POLITIQUE DE LA SCIENCE
[INSTITUTE OF SCIENCE POLICY AND FORECASTING]   **Telephone:** —
Universite des Sciences Sociales
Grenoble Cedex 38040, France   **Founded:** 1971

Officers: Yves Barel, Scientific Director.

Research team of the National Center for Scientific Research. Staff: — **Sources of support:** — **Annual Budget:** —

Objectives and interests: Theory of social change.

Major programs and projects: "The Evolution of Technology and Work: Toward an Ecology of Work."

Special facilities: —

Activities: Research, graduate courses in science policy, conferences, training programs directed toward public and governmental agencies.

Publications: *La reproduction sociale [Social Reproduction]*, Yves Barel (1973); *Le rapport humain a la matiere [Man's Relationship to Matter]*, Yves Barel (French edition, 1978, English edition, 1979).

INSTITUT FUR WELTWIRTSCHAFT
[THE KIEL INSTITUTE OF WORLD ECONOMICS]   **Telephone:** (0431) 8841
Duesternbrooker Weg 120/22
D-2300, Kiel, Federal Republic of Germany   **Founded:** 1914

Officers: Herbert Giersch, President; Gerhard Fels, Vice President; Juergen B. Donges, Martin Hoffmeyer, Klaus Schatz, and Norbert Walter, Heads of the Research Departments.

Non-profit research institute. Staff: 230 (75 professionals). **Sources of support:** Public funds, grants from foundations and international organizations. **Annual Budget:** 13 million German marks.

Objectives and interests: Empirical research on economic relations among industrial countries, industrial and developing countries, and industrial and socialist countries. In addition, analyses of current business cycles (including forecasts), and country studies in various economic issues, such as trade, industrial structure, employment, foreign investment, raw materials.

Major programs and projects: Production and employment adjustment in industrial countries due to changes in the world economic structure, technological innovations, and long-term industrial cycles; an appraisal of the implications of the "new international economic order" and possible alternatives; strategies for employment oriented development in developing countries; prospects of private direct investment in developing countries; potential for future economic growth in industrial countries.

Special facilities: Economic Library, one of the largest in the world, with a detailed cataloging system classifying works by subject, author, corporations, and regions. Economic Archive, which has collected German and foreign newspaper clippings and other sources of daily information since 1920. These facilities are open to the public.

Activities: International conferences on issues of major concern; lectures by eminent persons; international roundtable discussions on the business cycle (twice a year); seminars, frequently with participation from invited academic experts.

Publications: *Weltwirtschaftliches Archiv [Review of World Economics]* (quarterly, in German, English, and French); *Die Weltwirtschaft [The World Economy]* (biannual, in German); *Kiel Discussion Papers* (ad hoc, in German or English); *Reshaping the World Economic Order*, (1977); *Capital Shortage and Unemployment in the World Economy* (1978), *The Case for a European Parallel Currency*, Roland Vaubel (1978).

INSTITUT TECHNIQUE DE PREVISION ECONOMIQUE ET SOCIALE
[TECHNICAL INSTITUTE FOR ECONOMIC AND SOCIAL FORECASTING]
292, rue Saint-Martin **Telephone:** 271.24.14
poste 523
Paris 75141
Cedex 03, France **Founded:** 1962

Officers: Etienne Hirsch; Jean Fourastie; Raymond Saint-Paul; P. Brossard, Secretary-General.

Non-profit institute. Staff: — **Sources of support:** Government subsidy and student registrations. **Annual Budget:** No answer.

Objectives and interests: To provide theoretical education and practical training for specialists in economic and social forecasting; to organize advanced seminars; to undertake research on the methods of economic and social forecasting in order to implement and update these teaching methods.

Major programs and projects: —

Special facilities: Specialized library.

Activities: Evening courses and seminars on demand.

Publications: *Outil et procedure de planification dans une entreprise de fabrication automobile [Method and Procedure of Planning in an Automobile Manufacturing Firm]*, M. Pietrois; *Le machines-outils a metaux - Previsions a l'horizon 1980 de la consommation interieure Francaise [Metal-Working Machine Tools - Forecasts to 1980 of French Domestic Consumption]* M. Wanegue; *Prevision et controle de gestion: un instrument efficace au service de la direction des entreprises: application a un service d'entretien de materiel automobile militaire [Forecasting and Management Control: A Useful Tool in Business Management: Application to a Maintenance Service for Military Automobile Materiel]*, M. Defali; *Le bois et le developpement economique en republique populaire du Congo 1960-1982 - Bilan et Perspectives [Wood and Economic Development in the People's Republic of the Congo 1960-1982 - Facts and Commentary]*, M. Soumbou; *Prevision synchronique et asynchronique. Une approche de la prevision de la demande du telephone [Synchronous and Asynchronous Forecasting. An Approach to Forecasting the Demand for Telephones]*, M. Burtschy.

INSTITUTE FOR ALTERNATIVE FUTURES **Telephone:** (202) 265-0346
Antioch College/Antioch School of Law
1624 Crescent Place, N.W.
Washington, D.C. 20009, U.S.A. **Founded:** 1977

Officers: Clement Bezold, Director; Jim Dator, Associate; Robert Olson, Energy Consultant.

Educational unit of Antioch University. Staff: Two-four. **Sources of support:** Antioch University, government, business and foundation funds. **Annual Budget:** No answer.

Objectives and interests: The purpose of IAF is to encourage more systematic consideration of the future within government policy making and more effective citizen participation in that process.

Major programs and projects: "Legislative Foresight" — working within Congress and state legislatures to develop futures research capacities. "Anticipatory Democracy" — monitor and aid state and local efforts to involve citizens in exploring alternative futures and setting goals. "Energy." "Future of Law." "Health."

Special facilities: —

Activities: Consultants on Congressional Foresight Hearings; testimony requested for Senate Judiciary Committee; developed national network for preparing and evaluating impact statements; presentations for Congress at Congressional Foresight Fair.

56

Publications: *Anticipatory Democracy: The People in the Politics of the Future,* Clement Bezold, editor, Introduction by Alvin Toffler (1978); "Citizen Participation in Congressional Foresight," Clement Bezold (THE FUTURIST, April 1978).

INSTITUTE FOR APPLIED SYSTEMS ANALYSIS AND PROGNOSIS (ISP)
Medizinische Hochschule Haus W3G
D 3000 Hannover 61
Federal Republic of Germany

Telephone: (0511) 5325406

Founded: 1975

Officers: Eduard Pestel, President; Lothar Hubl, Vice-President; Hartmut Bossel, Research Director; Rolf Bauerschmidt, Wolfgang Oest, Peter Moller.

Independent, non-profit, research institute. **Staff:** Eight. **Sources of support:** 60% from German Federal Government, 30% from foundations, and 10% state and industry. **Annual Budget:** No answer.

Objectives and interests: Public policy research on domestic and international issues; global and national models (population, education and labor, economy, energy, plus materials); cognitive systems analysis; value change and social change.

Major programs and projects: "Simulation Model of the Federal Republic of Germany"—a simulation model of the demographic, economic, technological development for the next decades. "Nonnumerical Modeling of the Cognitions Determining Political Behavior"—computer-processing of formalized energy and growth related concepts to determine behavioral trends of selected interest groups. "Assessment of the Environmental Impact of Energy Regulations"—development of systems analytical instrument for use by government agencies. "Software for Computer-Assisted Policy Analysis"—various software for the efficient use of numerical and nonnumerical models by non-experts. "University Planning in the State of Lower Saxony"—a simulation model of student development.

Special facilities: Computer software.

Activities: No regular activities.

Publications: *Mankind at the Turning Point,* by M. Mesarovic and E. Pestel (1974); *Concepts and Tools of Computer-Assisted Policy Analysis,* H. Bossel (1977); *Das Deutschland-Modell* (Simulation model of the F.R. Germany), E. Pestel et al (1978); *Burgerinitiativen Entwerfen Die Zukunft [Citizen Initiatives Sketch the Future: The Economistic vs. the Ecological Alternative],* H. Bossel (1978).

INSTITUTE FOR CANADIAN FUTURES
2323 Confederation Parkway, Suite 206
Mississauga, Ontario, Canada L5B 1R6

Telephone: (416) 276-2660

Founded: 1977

Officers: Don Wilson, President; Wayne Beach, Secretary; Bruce McNeely, Assistant Secretary.

Non-profit, research organization. **Staff:** Two, plus contract consultants. **Sources of support:** Government, business, and membership. **Annual Budget:** No answer.

Objectives and interests: Public policy, domestic issues, technological forecasting, energy systems, urban systems.

Major programs and projects: —

Special facilities: —

Activities: Spring and fall seminars.

Publications: *Canadian Futures,* Don Wilson, editor (bimonthly).

INSTITUTE FOR THE FUTURE
2740 Sand Hill Road
Menlo Park, California 94025, U.S.A.

Telephone: (415) 854-6322

Founded: 1968

Officers: Henry David, Chairman of the Board; Bruce Palmer, Vice-Chairman; Roy Amara, President; Andrew Lipinski, Senior Research Fellow; Gregory Schmid, Senior Research Fellow; Robert Johansen, Senior Research Fellow.

Independent, non-profit research institute. **Staff:** 20-25. **Sources of support:** Half private corporations and foundations; half U.S. Government. **Annual Budget:** No answer.

Objectives and interests: Futures planning on domestic and international issues for both the public and private sector. Primary focus on social environment, economic trends, consumer attitudes, regulatory matters, and technological (primarily energy, computer communications) developments.

Major programs and projects: "The Corporate Environment"—linking futures information to current operating decisions. "Public Policy"—examining the effects of public participation in social choices. "Communications"—applications of teleconferencing and assessment of social and political effects of interactive media in a variety of environments. "Education"—analyzing factors shaping the future of post-secondary education, such as uses of new technology and the role of the corporation. "International Studies"—examining international and cross-cultural developments, with emphasis on the impact of the corporation in an interdependent world.

Special facilities: Maintains a library of books, periodicals, and journals monitoring demographic, social, economic, regulatory, technological, and international developments (not for public use).

Activities: Annual meeting of Corporate Associates including presentations and workshops on the corporate environment ahead. Special seminars between Institute staff, client groups, and Institute consultants (drawn from active file of 300 individuals). Teleconferences on wide range of topics including transportation, agriculture, and minerals.

Publications: *Cap Report* (six issues a year), available to Corporate Associates only; *Newsletter* (four issues a year), available to the public without charge; *Technological Alternatives and Social Choices*, Robert Johansen, Jacques Vallee, and Kathleen Spangler (1978); *Forecasting Attractive Acquisition Areas*, Michael Palmer and Gregory Schmid (1978); *Climate Change to the Year 2000: A Survey of Expert Opinion*, Roy Amara and Hubert Lipinski (1978); *Group Communication through Computers*, Volume 5, Robert Johansen, Robert De Grasse, Jr., and Thaddeus Wilson (1978); *The Insurance World of 1990: Environmental Scenarios*, Gregory Schmid and Roy Amara (1977).

THE INSTITUTE ON MAN AND SCIENCE
Rensselaerville, New York 12147, U.S.A.

Telephone: (518) 797-3783
Founded: 1962

Officers: Oscar S. Strauss, II, Chairman, Board of Trustees; Everett R. Clinchy, Chairman, Executive Committee; Harold S. Williams, President and Director of Community Renewal; Gordon A. Enk, Director, Environmental and Economic Studies.

Independent, non-profit, education and research center. **Staff:** 20. **Sources of support:** Private, corporate, and foundation contributions; project grants and contracts. **Annual Budget:** Approximately $1 million.

Objectives and interests: Critical examination and research on selected social problems in which science and technology affect the quality of human life; seeks to develop closer relationships between those who generate knowledge and the policy makers and practitioners who influence its use.

Major programs and projects: "Community Process"—Applied research and special demonstration projects on the renewal of small towns and urban neighborhoods. "Economic and Environmental Studies"—Research and training for professionals in the field of environmental decision-making. "Educational Services"—Research, conferences, and courses directly related to current and future issues facing American education. "International Affairs"—At least one annual seminar for senior officials and diplomats throughout the world focusing on varied international issues. "The Sciences and Humanities"—A continuing Institute theme concerned with the uses of science to advance human values and ends.

Special facilities: Maintains a library of selected materials in its fields of interest and endeavor (not for public use).

Activities: Conferences, research and evaluative studies, demonstration projects, courses, invitational and public seminars, a continuing education program.

Publications: *News* (IMS Newsletter, irregular); *Annual Report and Program Review, The Institute on Man and Science* (annual); *Beyond NEPA: Criteria for Environmental Impact Review*, G. A. Enk (1973); *Assessing the Social Impacts of Oil Spills*, G. A. Enk (1973); *The Revitalization of Stump Creek*, H. S. Williams (1973, 1975); *Reports of International Seminars*, R. N. Gardner.

THE INSTITUTE OF MANAGEMENT SCIENCES (TIMS)   **Telephone:** (401) 274-2525
146 Westminster Street
Providence, Rhode Island 02903, U.S.A.   **Founded:** 1953

Officers: Frank M. Bass, President; Paul Gray, Secretary; H. Martin Weingartner, Vice President-Finance; M. R. DeMelim, Executive Director; Mary Lou Grant, Administrative Assistant to Executive Director.

International non-profit professional organization.   **Staff:** Five.   **Sources of support:** Dues and subscriptions.   **Annual Budget:** $450,000.

Objectives and interests: To identify, extend, and unify scientific knowledge pertaining to management.

Major programs and projects: National and international meetings, generally two each year, are held to communicate ideas and stimulate thinking on significant topics. The colleges of TIMS are special interest groups which provide forum and platform for discussion and analysis of problems in specifically identified areas of management science. College meetings are generally held in conjunction with national and international meetings.

Special facilities: —

Activities: TIMS College on the Practice of Management Science Summer Conference, Bowdoin College, July 22-27, 1979. TIMS XXIV International Meeting will be held in Honolulu, Hawaii, June 18-22 1979.

Publications: *Management Science* (monthly); *Interfaces* (quarterly); *Mathematics of Operations Research* (quarterly); *The OR/MS Index*, compiled by Kneale T. Marshall and F. Russell Richards (1978); The North Holland/ TIMS Studies in the Management Sciences include the following: Volume 1—*Logistics*, Murray A. Geisler, editor (1975); Volume 2—*World Modeling: A Dialogue*, C. West Churchman and Richard O. Mason, editors; Volume 3—*Economic Modeling for Water Policy Evaluation*, Robert M. Thrall, Russ Thompson, Ted Schad, and Earl Heady, editors.

INSTITUTE FOR POLICY STUDIES   **Telephone:** (202) 234-9382
1901 Q Street, N.W.
Washington, D.C., 20009, U.S.A.   **Founded:** 1963

Officers: Robert L. Borosage, Director; Peter Weiss, Chairman of the Board of Trustees; Richard J. Barnet, Senior Fellow; Marcus G. Raskin, Senior Fellow; Howard M. Wachtel, Director, International Economic Order Project.

Non-profit, transnational center for research and education. Staff: 50. **Sources of support:** Foundation grants and individual donors; no government funds accepted.   **Annual Budget:** No answer.

Objectives and interests: Research and analysis on issues related to the international economic order and the policies of multinational banks and lending agencies; national security, arms control policy, and U.S. arms sales policy; issues related to Southern Africa and Latin America; futures studies *per se* not an area of study.

Major programs and projects: —

Special facilities: Periodical collection; collection of volumes including Helen Lamb Memorial Collection of books, documents, and periodicals on Southeast Asia and U.S. policy in Vietnam; Militarism and Disarmament Project maintaining a data base on U.S. arms sales to Third World countries and handling inquiries from researchers, congressional offices, and other interested parties.

Activities: Regular seminars; frequent conferences (recently on nuclear war, U.S. arms sales policy, U.S. policy towards Korea; upcoming on NATO, debt and dependency, Soviet "threat"); establishing IPS Academy to offer courses in Spring 1979 on such topics as political journalism, politics and film-making, the U.S. Senate, the corporation and the State.

Publications: Pamphlet and issue paper series appears irregularly (usually several each month); *Supplying Repression: U.S. Support for Authoritarian Regimes Abroad*, Michael T. Klare (1978); *Derailing Development: The IMF in Jamaica*, Michael Moffitt (January 1979); *Food and the International Economic Order*, Susan George (January 1979); *The New Gnomes; Multinational Banks in the Third World*, Howard Wachtel (1978); *Toward World Security: A Program for Disarmament*, Earl C. Ravenal (1978).

INSTITUTE ON RELIGION IN AN AGE OF SCIENCE   **Telephone:** (312) 643-5131
1524 E. 59th Street
Chicago, Illinois 60637, U.S.A.   **Founded:** 1954

Officers: Solomon H. Katz, President; Ralph W. Burhoe, Treasurer.

Independent, non-profit, voluntary association of members seeking to provide a channel of communication between the religious and scientific communities. Staff: No paid staff. **Sources of support:** Membership dues, conference fees, occasional small foundation grants. **Annual Budget:** $15,000.

Objectives and interests: To promote creative efforts leading to the formulation, in the light of contemporary knowledge, of effective doctrines and practices for human welfare; to formulate dynamic and positive relationships between the concepts developed by science and the goals and hopes of man expressed through religion; to apply the sciences to the interpretation and revitalization of religion.

Major programs and projects: At least once a year there is a conference or symposium examining human values in the light of the sciences and seeking ways of applying this to the advancement of the institutions that transmit and enculturate human values. Such symposia in the past have included: "The Human Prospect," "Science, Religion, and Social Change," "The Humanizing and Dehumanizing of Man," "Science and Human Purpose." IRAS has a sister organization, the Center for Advanced Study in Religion and Science (at the same address), which conducts courses of study in the field.

Special facilities: —

Activities: Annual meeting and summer conference each summer for one week; special conferences or regional meetings.

Publications: *Zygon, Journal of Religion and Science* (quarterly); *Newsletter* (irregular); *Science Ponders Religion,* Harlow Shapley, editor (1960); *Religion Ponders Science,* Edwin Prince Booth, editor (1964).

INSTITUTE FOR RESEARCH ON PUBLIC POLICY

Telephone: (514) 342-9121

3535 Queen Mary Road, Suite 514
Montreal, Quebec, Canada H3V 1H8

Founded: 1974

Officers: Michael J.L. Kirby, President; Raymond Breton, Director, Ethnic and Cultural Diversity Program; David Hoffman, Director, Futures Studies Program; William T. Stanbury, Director, Regulation and Government Intervention Program.

Non-profit, research institute. **Staff:** 31. **Sources of support:** Endowment fund contributions from federal and provincial governments and private sector. **Annual Budget:** 1,938,474 Canadian dollars (1978).

Objectives and interests: To find practical solutions to important public policy problems; to act as a catalyst within the national community by helping to facilitate informed public debate on issues of major public interest; to stimulate participation by all segments of the national community in the process that leads to decision-making.

Major programs and projects: "Social Impacts of Canada's Alternative Energy Futures: 1975-2025" — identifies the political, economic and lifestyle impacts that are implied by each option. "Canadian Social Trends Report" — focus on trends in lifestyles, political and social attitudes, health status, income and education; with projections of future directions. "Impacts of Technological and Economic Changes on Canadian Society" — a series of probes to examine the effects of prospective technological and economic changes on Canadian society. "Computers, Microelectronics and the Future of Employment Opportunities in Canada." "Canada-Japan Issues" — near-term future. "Canada-U.S. Transborder Data Flows" — issues and prospects.

Special facilities: Documentation center; on-line access to the data bases of QL Systems (Canadian Data bases), *Globe and Mail* (Toronto daily), SDC-ORBIT, Lockheed-DIALOG, *New York Times,* CANSIM (selected time series from Statistics Canada), Informatech France-Quebec; 1976 population and death data for Montreal by census tract (tape and disc storage).

Activities: In 1978-79 will hold four national conferences on government processes; 5 to 8 seminars per year on government operations, aimed at improving ability of private sector leaders to perceive trends and anticipate training and impact of government decisions.

Publications: *Profile,* Robert Miller, editor (newsletter; 6 times per year); "Nodule Shock? Seabed Mining and the Future of the Canadian Nickel Industry," W.E. Cundiff, in *Proceedings of the Conference on Issues in Canada-U.S. Transborder Data Flows,* W.E. Cundiff and Mado Reid, editors (1978); *The Electronic Briefcase;Text Processing in the Office of the Future,* R. Russel (1978); *Canada in the New Monetary Order,* M. Hudson (1978); *Computers in the Home,* C. Gotlieb (1978); *Canadian Population Trends and Public Policy Through the 1980's,* Leroy O. Stone and Claude Marceau (1977); *The Canadian Condition: A Guide to Research in Public Policy,* Raymond Breton (1977); *Une orientation de la recherche politique dans le contexte canadian [An Orientation to Public Policy Research in the Canadian Context],* Raymond Breton (1978).

INSTITUTE FOR SOCIAL ENGINEERING, INC.

Akasaka Palace Building,
1-4-21 Moto-Akasaka, Minato-ku
Tokyo 107, Japan

Telephone: (03) 403-9051

Founded: 1969

Officers: Jiro Ushio, President; Kisho Kurokawa, Principal; Takeyoshi Nakamura, Vice-President; Takahiko Furuta, Chief of Research Department; Hideaki Tatebayashi, Chief of Administration; Susumu Iwasaki, Senior Researcher.

Independent, private, for-profit research institute. **Staff:** 30. **Sources of support:** Investments by 26 large Japanese corporations. **Annual Budget:** Approximately 250,000,000 yen.

Objectives and interests: Public policy research on urban and regional development; short-, medium-, and long-term forecasting on economic, social, technological, and political matters; surveys of opinions.

Major programs and projects: Long-term time series analysis of population distribution in Japan, with forecasts from present to 2000 A.D. (1974-75, National Land Agency). Factor structural analysis of J-turn and U-turn phenomena of population movement; analysis of psychological, social, and economic causes of U-turn phenomenon (1975-76, National Institute for Research Advancement). Research on public use of land in the Tokyo area, including process of preparing land-use proposals for publicly-owned land (1974, Ministry of Finance). Research and development of science and technology related to social welfare—pilot study on the application of the human intellect to welfare-oriented science and technology (1973-74, Science and Technology Agency). Research on the role of V/STOL planes in inter-city transportation—technology assessment, forecasting demand, and developing "area navigation systems" (1971-73, Ministry of International Trade and Industry).

Special facilities: Library of books, periodicals, and reports.

Activities: Mirai Club (Future Club)—250 members; ten seminars and one conference a year. Kisho Kai (Kisho Kurokawa Club)—170 members, four seminars a year.

Publications: Mirai Club Information Cassette Tape (members only, twice a month); Kisho Kai Information Cassette Tape (members only, once a month); *Metabolism in Architecture,* K. Kurokawa (1976); *The Future of Informative Archipelago-Japan,* K. Kurokawa (1972); *Dialogue for Futurology,* K. Kurokawa (1972); *Challenge to the Interdisciplinary Zone* (1971).

INSTITUTE FOR SOCIETY, ETHICS AND THE LIFE SCIENCES—THE HASTINGS CENTER

360 Broadway
Hastings-on-Hudson, New York 10706, U.S.A.

Telephone: (914) 478-0500

Founded: 1969

Officers: Willard Gaylin, President; Daniel Callahan, Director; Robert Veatch, Senior Associate; Margaret Steinfels, Editor; Ruth Macklin, Associate for Behavioral Studies.

Research institute. **Staff:** 22 full-time, six part-time. **Sources of support:** Private foundations, U.S. Government, associate members. **Annual Budget:** $1 million.

Objectives and interests: Examine the ethical and moral implications of advances in bio-medicine and the behavioral sciences.

Major programs and projects: "Health Policy"—to examine the ethical issues raised by the efforts to establish an equitable health care system. "Behavior Control"—to study the dynamics of controversy surrounding the efforts to research the bio-psychological roots of violence. "Death and Dying"—to study the ethical, moral and policy implications of the efforts to define death. "Teaching of Ethics"—to study the significance of the resurgence of interest in ethical inquiry in undergraduate, graduate and professional schools. "Genetics"—to study the dilemmas attendant upon the advances in technology for prenatal diagnosis.

Special facilities: A small, specialized library on ethical issues in bio-medicine and behavioral science is available to the public only upon special request.

Activities: Publication of the *Hastings Center Report,* a Bibliography on Bio-Ethics, summer workshops on selected issues, annual general meeting. In addition to these activities which are open to the public, the Institute conducts research meetings and conferences for its fellows and invited experts.

Publications: *The Foundation of Ethics and Its Relationship to Science* - 3 volumes; *Case Studies in Medical Ethics,* Robert Veatch; *Operating on the Mind,* Willard Gaylin; *Abortion,* Daniel Callahan; *The American Population Debate.*

INSTITUTE FOR THE STUDY OF THE HUMAN FUTURE, INC.

Telephone: (415) 527-6679

2000 Center Street, Suite 1362
Berkeley, California 94704

Founded: 1978

Officers: Arlen Teresa Wilson, President and Director; Robert Anton Wilson, Vice-President; John Holmdahl, Jr., Coordinator.

Private non-profit educational organization. **Staff:** Three. **Sources of support:** Activity fees, private contributions. **Annual Budget:** $10,000.

Objectives and interests: To expedite the flow in information between the scientific community and non-specialists concerning present scientific research and experiment which may contribute positively to the world of tomorrow; to encourage individual, group and media awareness of the future as a realm of increasing rather than decreasing options.

Major programs and projects: Provide a forum for the sharing of scenarios for the human future growing largely out of present work in various sciences and technology; presentations by specialists; audiences invited to raise questions and evaluate the projections from standpoints that may concern them such as, ethical, environmental, religious, humanistic, so that in the interchange new perspectives and the bases for an informed consensus may emerge.

Special facilities: Access to members of the scientific community at work on such future-oriented projects as space settlement and industrialization, genetics and the extension of the average human lifespan.

Activities: Seminars, colloquia, lectures, classes, study groups.

Publications: *ISHF Newsletter;* cassette tapes.

INSTITUTE FOR THEOLOGICAL ENCOUNTER WITH SCIENCE AND TECHNOLOGY (ITEST)

Telephone: (314) 535-3300

221 North Grand Boulevard
St. Louis, Missouri 63103, U.S.A.

Founded: 1968

Officers: Robert A. Brungs, S.J., Director; Robert Bertram, Vice-Director; Richard Stith, Jr., Treasurer; Bernice Morris, Administrative Assistant.

Non-profit, interfaith, interdisciplinary organization. **Staff:** Two full-time; several part-time volunteers. **Sources of support:** Dues and gifts. **Annual Budget:** No answer.

Objectives and interests: To assess the impact of science and technology (particularly bioscience and biotechnology) on the Christian faith and to alert institutions to this impact.

Major programs and projects: "Fabricated Man"—Series of conferences to investigate aspects of the biotechnological revolution and its impact on society.

Special facilities: —

Activities: Semi-annual conferences; some workshops; network of 320 members in 22 countries.

Publications: *Newsletter of the International Secretariat for Science/Theology Dialogue* (quarterly); Proceedings of Semi-annual Conferences.

INSTITUTE FOR 21ST CENTURY BUSINESS

Telephone: (216) 672-2170

Kent State University
Kent, Ohio 44242, U.S.A.

Founded: 1970

Officers: Donald F. Mulvihill, Coordinator.

Research institute. **Staff:** Part-time coordinator and graduate assistants. **Sources of support:** Released time and foundations. **Annual Budget:** Depending on number of projects being carried out.

Objectives and interests: To examine trends in all areas of activity and attempt to determine alternative effects on business in the world of the future.

Major programs and projects: "Incidence of Futures Research in Fortune 500 Companies"—to determine if futures research is being done, who is responsible for it, particular projects being carried out. "Courses in Futures Activity Being Offered by Colleges of Business Administration"—to determine the number of schools of business offering courses of this nature, what they are, and what is planned in the near future for additional courses or the dropping of existing ones. "Impact of the Laser on Business, Particularly the Machine Tool Industry"—to determine how the laser is being substituted for other devices in the production of goods, particularly of machine tools, and the recognition of what changes may be taking place in the long run within a given industry.

Special facilities: Maintenance of references in periodicals dealing with future trends and how they are being met by business.

Activities: "21st Century Business," a course offered to all seniors in the university; participation in conferences and seminars related to the objective.

Publications: *An Annotated Bibliography of Business Articles in the Future, 1965-76; Institute for 21st Century Business Monograph Series,* 12 publications dealing with the fisheries industry, plans for restructuring the states of the United States, and similar subjects.

INSTITUTE FOR WORLD ORDER, INC.
777 United Nations Plaza
New York, New York 10017, U.S.A.

Telephone: (212) 490-0010

Founded: 1948

Officers: James Rouse, Chairman of the Board; Robert C. Johansen, President; Harry Hollins, Chairman, Executive Committee; Saul H. Mendlovitz, Director, World Order Models Project; Virginia Heiserman, Director of Public Education Program.

Private, non-profit, education and research organization. **Staff:** 20. **Sources of support:** Private donors, foundations. **Annual Budget:** $934,400.

Objectives and interests: Through a broad program of education and policy research, the Institute seeks to develop an awareness among academic and non-academic audiences of the need for new systems of social/political/economic institutions built on humane values. The scholars and educators who compose the Institute look at world problems from an analytical perspective, looking to advance the first part of a process that may be used to initiate an effective, continuing public discussion of these matters in the U.S. and the world. The Institute is undertaking the mobilization of political constituencies toward world order goals.

Major programs and projects: "Public Education Program"—to help to initiate and to support a citizens' movement to abolish war as an accepted human institution. "The World Order Models Project, Phase One" —an enterprise that has brought together scholars from different parts of the world to create models of their "preferred worlds." "The World Order Models Project, Phase Two" — a transition model of the world, a common product by a group of global scholars.

Special facilities: —

Activities: University Program: works with world order centers in various universities to conduct symposia, seminars, and transnational conferences in connection with research on global values (e.g., food and hunger, war/peace, social and economic justice, ecological concerns); coordinates workshops for teachers and teacher-trainers.

Publications: Over 95 different books, pamphlets, reprints, multimedia kits available. *Alternatives* (quarterly journal); *Transition* (newsletter); *Peace Education News; On the Creation of a Just World Order,* Saul Mendlovitz, editor (1975); *A Study of Future Worlds,* Richard A. Falk (1975); *Footsteps into the Future,* Rajni Kothari (1975); *First State of the Globe Report* (1974); *A World Federation of Cultures,* Ali Mazrui (1976); *The Revelation of Being,* Gustavo Lagos and Horacio H. Godoy (1977); *The True Worlds,* Johan Galtung (forthcoming, 1979).

INSTITUT FUR ZUKUNFTSFORSCHUNG
[INSTITUTE FOR FUTURE RESEARCH]
Giesebrechtstrasse 15
1000 Berlin 12, Federal Republic of Germany

Telephone: 030-883 88 74

Founded: 1968

Officers: Ossip K. Flechtheim; Hans Buchholz; Dieter Kolb; Rolf Kreibich.

Private, non-profit, research institute. **Staff:** 25. **Sources of support:** Research contracts. **Annual Budget:** 2 million German marks.

Objectives and interests: Content analysis; studies on methodology, future-diagnosis and therapy; education of future-oriented generalists.

Major programs and projects: Results of research are made available through publications (see below).

Special facilities: —

Activities: Sponsors lectures, seminars, and symposia on future research.

Publications: *Analysen und Prognosen [Analyses and Forecasts]* (bimonthly); *Energiesektorales Informationssystem [An Information System for the Energy Sector]*, J. Burstenbinder, H. Illing, F. Opalla, and P. Rosolski (1975); *Alternativen fur die Verstadterung Europas [Alternatives for the Urbanization of Europe]* V. R. v. Bieberstein, K. Lederer, R. Mackensen, R. Schroter, M. Wend (1975); *Zukunftenergie [Future of Energy]* (1975); *Verfahren zur Erfolgskontrolle von Massnahmen des Umweltschutzes [Proceedings for the Control of Results of Environmental Protection Measures]*, W. Bormann, R. Schroter, H. Buchholz (1976); *Verfahren zur Bestimmung der Prioritaten bei den Investitionen im Fernstrassenbau unter Berucksichtigung der Ziele der Raumordnung [Proceedings for Establishing Investment Priorities for Highway Construction in Accordance with the Objectives of Regional Planning]*, H. Dichlmayer (1976).

INSTITUTTET FOR FREMTIDSFORSKNING
[INSTITUTE FOR FUTURES STUDIES]
Vester Farimagsgade 3
DK-1606 Copenhagen V, Denmark

Telephone: 01 11 71 76

Founded: 1969

Officers: Thorkil Kristensen, Chairman of the Board; Erik Juul Jorgensen, Deputy Director; Torben Bo Jansen, Editor of *Orientering;* Soren Rasmussen, cand. polit.; Bent Ryd Svensson, cand. polit.; Allan Ottsen, cand. oecon.

Private, independent, non-profit research institute.   **Staff:** 15.   **Sources of support:** One-half membership fees, one-half contractual research.   **Annual Budget:** 1.8 million Danish kroner.

Objectives and interests: Short-, medium-, and long-term forecasting on economic and political, national and international development.

Major programs and projects: "Perspectives for the Economic and Political Development"—forecasts for the short, medium and long-term economic and political developments. "Delphi Study of Danish Agricultural Research"—to pinpoint the most important research breakthroughs to 2000. "International Economic Interdependence and Influence." "Future Conditions for the Iron and Metalworking Industry in 10-15 Years and Connected Development Trends."

Special facilities: Library of books, magazines, press clippings, and other material on economics and related fields (for members); data bank.

Activities: Biannual seminars on the perspectives for economic and political development.

Publications: *Orientering om Fremtidsforskning [Survey of Future Studies]*, (newsletter, issued 9-11 times a year); *Evaluations for Occupation and Education 1975 to 2000*, Gert Strande-Sorensen (1975); *Population and Labour Force in the EEC to 1990*, Erik Juul Jorgensen, et al. (1975); *Design for Innovation: A Cybernetic Approach*, Bjarne Rugy (1974); *Perspectives for Danish Foreign Trade*, Bent Jorgensen (1972); *Problems of Inflation in the EEC*, Niels Mengel (1977).

INTERDISCIPLINARY CENTER FOR TECHNOLOGICAL ANALYSIS AND FORECASTING
Telephone: (03) 410984

Tel Aviv University, Ramat Aviv
Tel Aviv, Israel

Founded: 1971

Officers: B. Raz, Director; Z. Hirsch; J. Baal-Schem, R. Horesh, Senior Researchers.

Non-profit research institute.   **Staff:** 30.   **Sources of support:** Grants and contracts from government and other agencies.   **Annual Budget:** 10 million Israeli lirot.

Objectives and interests: Promotion of methodolgy and practice of technological forecasting as a planning tool and analysis of the interaction of technology with the social, behavioral and environmental aspect in an integrative plan.

Major programs and projects: "Exporting R & D Intensive Goods." "Technological Aspects of Secure Borders." "Innovation in the Public Housing Sector." "Solar Energy in Housing."

Special facilities: Library specializing in publications on technology and forecasting. A variety of relevant data banks on topics like government support of technological innovation.

Activities: Research activities and seminars and symposia on subjects ranging from new forecasting methods to management problems, research and development planning, establishing new plants in Israel, import-export policy, etc.

Publications: *Materials Research and Development Policy—Case of Copper; Materials Research and Development Policy—Case of Aluminum; Export of R & D Intensive Industrial Products—Preliminary Forecast & Evaluation; Innovation and Improvement in a Housing Project: The Pharmaceutical Industry in Israel in the Year 2000.*

INTERDISCIPLINARY SYSTEMS GROUP

Telephone: (916) 752-1558

Department of Zoology
University of California
Davis, California 95616, U.S.A.

Founded: 1968

Officers: Kenneth E. F. Watt.

Research. Staff: One professor, plus up to 40 support staff (varies with funding). **Sources of support:** Ford Foundation, National Science Foundation, U.S. Congress, corporations. **Annual Budget:** Varies widely from $12,000 to $400,000.

Objectives and interests: Building national and global economic model using greater variety of variables than in existing models; exploring the consequences of public policy, particularly with respect to prices of labor and other resources.

Major programs and projects: "Development of Global Economic Model"—model deals with seven categories of variables, from physical environment to culture, and three hierarchical levels, from metropolitan area to international trading system. Principal focus is exploring full panoply of impacts of various national energy pricing or taxing or rationing policies.

Special facilities: In process of buying own computer center with multiple disc drives.

Activities: 180 lectures a year to university, corporation and government audiences. Offers five courses, including global and regional modelling. External advisor to White House Global 2000 project and past consultant to U.S. House of Representatives Subcommittee on Energy and Power.

Publications: *The Titanic Effect; The Unsteady State; The Structure of Post-Industrial Economies,* 1978. Many articles have been published in *Simulation* and elsewhere.

INTERFUTURE

Telephone: (212) 682-8955
596-9576

420 Lexington Avenue
New York, New York 10017, U.S.A.

Founded: 1969

Officers: Paul W. Conner, President; W.B. Ofuatey-Kodjoe, Vice-President for Academic Affairs; Graham Irwin, Chairman; Harry M. Matthews, Jr., Vice-President for Overseas Relations; Carol-June V. Cassidy, Vice Chairman.

Private, non-profit, educational organization facilitating undergraduate intercultural futures studies. Staff: Ten. **Sources of support:** Student participation fees. **Annual Budget:** $45,000—$60,000.

Objectives and interests: To offer select undergraduates the opportunity to design and carry out independent study projects—in North America, Europe, and the Third World—on issues important to the human future and the world community.

Major programs and projects: Participants may focus their projects in several areas, including the following: "Internationalism"—how can a more humane world order be achieved? "Individual and Society"—how can individuality be reconciled with the growing need for human cooperation? "Habitat"—how can humankind live in harmony with the planet?

Special facilities: Copies of research projects completed by InterFuture participants are available to InterFuture Associates for the cost of duplication and mailing.

Activities: Services provided for the students include three preparatory conferences, continuous counseling during the seven-month preparatory phase, an individual tutorial advisor in each overseas locale, student or host-family housing overseas, and general administrative support (transportation, contacts, etc.). A network of campus coordinators aids in identifying potential participants.

Publications: *News from InterFuture* (occasional newsletter); *InterFuture Reports*, 750-1,000 word summaries of completed projects, written by student participants and distributed annually.

INTERNATIONAL COUNCIL OF SCIENTIFIC UNIONS (ICSU)   Telephone: (1) 5277702
51 Boulevard de Montmorency
Paris 75016 France   **Founded:** 1931 (from International Research Council, 1919)

Officers: C. de Jager (Netherlands), President; D.A. Bekoe (Ghana), Vice-President; Sir John Kendrew (U.K.), Secretary-General; F.W. Baker, Executive Secretary.

Non-profit, non-governmental, research organization. **Staff:** Eight in Paris, 25 worldwide. **Sources of support:** National contributions, UNESCO subvention. **Annual Budget:** About $3 M.

Objectives and interests: To encourage international scientific activity for the benefit of mankind.

Major programs and projects: Environmental Subjects, organized by Scientific Committee on Problems of the Environment. Global Atmospheric Research Programme (with World Meteorological Organization)—Concerned with weather forecasting and climate dynamics. International Magnetospheric Study.

Special facilities: Maintains small library (not for public use).

Activities: The ICSU family organizes more than 200 international conferences, meetings, seminars, and workshops per year. ICSU has a sub-committee on Scientific Priorities which examines proposals for future studies in ICSU family.

Publications: *ICSU Bulletin* (quarterly); *ICSU Yearbook* (annual).

INTERNATIONAL CREATIVE CENTER (ICC)   Telephone: (022) 98.35.87
Colladon 20
Geneva, CH-1209 Switzerland   **Founded:** 1943

Officers: Dali Schindler, President; Richard Walsh, General Secretary; Nicolas Kaloy, Cultural Director; Jean Naef, Treasurer; Graziella Celante, Executive Officer; Cornelia Moesching, Assistant Executive Officer.

Independent, non-profit, research institute. **Staff:** — **Sources of support:** Membership fees, donations. **Annual Budget:** 500,000 Swiss francs.

Objectives and interests: Study and promotion of problems concerning the future in the sciences, economics, and the arts; research aiming at synthesis of most advanced techniques as well as new truths to bridge the gap between technology and spiritual values.

Major programs and projects: "Summit of Futurologists"—Creation of regular conventions in cooperation with American futurologists; exhibitions of American and European technology. "TV-Debates"—Organization of TV debates in Switzerland with international experts in science, economics, education, and the arts. "Corporate Environment Programs"—Coordination and unification of various Swiss programs. "Life-long Education Center"—Construction of a village on ecological patterns offering facilities for interdisciplinary refresher courses. "Creation of Vacation Courses"—Courses in French, English, German, Italian, Spanish, and cultural courses for young people of all countries.

Special facilities: Library of books, periodicals, and reports on futurology, economics, education, medicine, ecology, ecumenical studies, philosophy, architecture, and the arts.

Activities: Seminars and "Biennales of Futurology," with participants from around the world; "Chair of Futurology"—Creation of a chair on Futurology and Philosophy of Science in cooperation with local universities.

Publications: *Futurology* (quarterly review).

(From the first edition. Corrections not received by press time.)

INTERNATIONAL FEDERATION OF INSTITUTES FOR ADVANCED STUDY (IFIAS)

Telephone: (08) 85 01 15

Ulriksdals Slott
Solna, Sweden S-171 71

Founded: 1972

Officers: Alexander King, Chairman; Walter Orr Roberts, Program Coordinator; Sam Nilsson, Director and in charge of the Executive Secretariat.

Non-profit, non-governmental. **Staff:** Six. **Sources of support:** Membership dues, private foundations, industry. **Annual Budget:** Core budget of $250,000; current projects on separate fundings.

Objectives and interests: To further transnational, transdisciplinary research programs with the aid of a network of cooperating institutes, distinguished in their respective fields; to present the results to the general public and policy makers.

Major programs and projects: "Save Our Soils (SOS)"—soil management based on case studies. "Self-Reliant Development"—to determine the optional energy budget a self-reliant community can attain via an integrated system of biological and physical solar-energy conversion. "Science and Technology for Development"—three sub-projects; one related to the UNCSTD, one concerning the Muslim World, and a third related to this role of transnational corporations. "Basic Research Trends with a Bearing on Basic Human Needs." "The Impact of Climate Change on The Character and Quality of Human Life."

Special facilities: —

Activities: Study projects on selected major global problems in a long-range perspective, considering natural sciences, technology, social sciences and humanity.

Publications: *The State of the Planet*, a book by Alexander King on the evolution of global problems and measures taken to face them; fifteen reports on current projects and programs also are available.

INTERNATIONAL GRADUATE SCHOOL OF EDUCATION, CENTER FOR FUTURISTIC STUDIES

Telephone: (303) 841-3826

University Park Place
Parker, Colorado 80134, U.S.A.

Founded: 1974

Officers: Ed Pino, President, International Graduate School of Education.

The International Graduate School of Education is a non-profit, tax-exempt open university chartered by the State of Colorado. The Center for Futuristic Studies is that part of ISGE which focuses its concern on the future of the world. **Staff:** Varies, depending on projects. **Sources of support:** International Graduate School of Education. **Annual Budget:** Varied.

Objectives and interests: To assist educators in developing and implementing futuristic educational programs on the elementary and secondary level. This is achieved through research and development, curriculum and instructional strategies development and implementation, analysis and interpretation of futurist writing, and publication and dissemination of materials and information.

Major programs and projects: "Alternative Futures in Education"—Graduate course for K-12 teachers and administrators. Futuristic oriented K-12 curricular program—Process oriented, competency based futuristic curriculum. Resources Index—Annotated non-human and human resources index in futuristics. Futuristic-educational research and development—Finding solutions to education's unmet needs. Dissemination of futuristic-educational resources—Providing a resource center for educators interested in futurizing their schools.

Special facilities: Annual comprehensive futuristic-educational resources index; listing of K-12 schools in U.S. involved in futuristic programs, and names of futurist-educators.

Activities: Regional and national workshops and symposiums; K-12 program development and implementation; development of model school programs; assessment of futuristic movement in education; publication of futuristic resources index.

Publications: *Futuristic Resources Index,* Third Edition, John Eggers and Don Glines (1976); *Futuristic K-12 Curricular Competencies,* Ed Pino and John Eggers (1976); *Futurism in Education,* John Eggers and Ed Pino (1975); *Futuristic Instructional Activities,* John Eggers and Ed Pino (1976).

INTERNATIONAL INSTITUTE FOR APPLIED SYSTEMS ANALYSIS (IIASA)

Schloss Platz 1   **Telephone:** 02236-75210
Laxenburg, A-2361 Austria   **Founded:** 1972

Officers: Jermen Gvishiani (USSR), Chairman of the Council; Roger Levien (U.S.), Director; Oleg Vasiliev (USSR), Deputy Director; Andrei Bykov (USSR), Secretary.

Non-profit, independent, non-governmental, research institute. Staff: 300. **Sources of support:** Scientific institutions in National Member Organization Countries (USSR, Canada, Czechoslovakia, France, German Democratic Republic, Japan, Federal Republic of Germany, Bulgaria, U.S.A., Italy, Poland, UK., Austria, Hungary, Sweden, Finland, Netherlands). **Annual Budget:** No answer.

Objectives and interests: To bring together scientists of different disciplines, cultures and ideologies to work together on problems of concern to mankind; to create a network of research institutions with coordinated objectives; to function as a catalyst for the dissemination, exchange, initiation and critique of concepts in systems analysis; to raise the level of analytical techniques and of decision processes; and to bridge the gap between scientists and decision-makers.

Major programs and projects: "Energy Systems Program"—a comparison of the available options to satisfy future energy demands, 50 and more years from now. "Food and Agriculture Program"—addresses the problem of meeting the nutritional needs of the growing global population through improved national and international programs. "Resources and Environment Area"—deals with the earth's natural endowment. "Human Settlements and Services Area"—concerned with the earth's human endowment. "Management and Technology Area"—concerned with man-made social, economic, and technological mechanisms. "Systems and Decision Sciences Area"—concerned with mathematical and computational methods of analyzing system and decision problems.

Special facilities: Reference library, program library.

Activities: IIASA conducts and supports collaborative and individual research in relation to problems of modern societies arising from scientific and technological development, and undertakes its own studies into both methodological and applied research in the fields of systems analysis, cybernetics, operations research, and management techniques.

Publications: *Options*, edited by P. Schlifke (quarterly newsletter, free). Recent publications include: *On 10^{12}: A Check on Earth Carrying Capacity for Man*, C. Marchetti; *Regional Multiplier Analysis: A Demometric Approach*, J. Ledent; *The Bratsk-Ilimsk Territorial Production Complex: A Field Study Report*, H. Knop; *Nonsmooth Optimization and Descent Methods*, C. Lemarechal; *A Review of Energy Models No. 4*, J.M. Beaujean and J.P. Charpentier.

INTERNATIONAL INSTITUTE FOR STRATEGIC STUDIES

                                                                   Telephone: (01) 930 3757 & 1102
18 Adam Street
London WC2N 6AL England   **Founded:** 1958

Officers: Christoph Bertram, Director; J. Alford, Deputy Director; A.M. Majendie, Administrative Director; P. Evans, Assistant Administrative Director; S. Chubin, Assistant to the Director; D.J. Cutfield, Information Officer.
Non-profit research institute. Staff: 28. **Sources of support:** Two-thirds foundations; one-third membership, sales. **Annual Budget:** Approximately 135,000 pounds sterling.

Objectives and interests: Independent study into all aspects of the role of force in international relations; national and international strategy, arms control, military technology, defense economics, peacekeeping alliances, civil-military relations, and domestic violence.

Major programs and projects: "Strategic Survey"—Annual review of strategic events during the past calendar year. "The Military Balance"—Annual listing of armed forces strengths, equipment, and budgets of some 126 countries; comparison of East/West strengths.

Special facilities: Press clippings library, including English and major German and French newspapers; periodicals and book library of strategic and strategy-associated material (open to public, small charge).

Activities: Regular series of lectures and private discussion meetings in London; one annual general meeting; briefings, seminars, and specialist discussions, including lectures as required.

Publications: *Survival* (bimonthly magazine); *Adelphi Papers Series* (ten per year, 25,000-word monographs).

THE ISRAELI INSTITUTE FOR THE STUDY OF INTERNATIONAL AFFAIRS (IISIA)

Telephone: —

P.O. Box 17027
Tel Aviv 61170, Israel

Founded: 1963

Officers: Charles Bloch, Council Chairman; Marion Mushkat, Chairman of the Board and Academic Director; Leon Boim, Vice-Chairman of the Board; Zvi Tamir, Research Assistant, Mibi Moser, Research Assistant, Paulette Kurzer, Research Assistant and Librarian.

Non-profit research and information institute. **Staff:** Five. **Sources of support:** Research grants and member-fees. **Annual Budget:** $15,000.

Objectives and interests: International affairs, peace research, futures research, and problems of developing countries.

Major programs and projects: "The Metamorphosis of the Political and Economic World Order." "The Impact of the Oil Issue." "The Future of the Regime of the Seas and Oceans." "The Environmental Issue and International Organizations." "State-centric versus Global Approach in the Shape of the World Order of the Future."

Special facilities: Library.

Activities: Conferences, seminars, roundtables, publications, research studies.

Publications: *International Problems* (quarterly review); *International Cooperation and International Organizations: The Future Trend,* M. Mushkat; *Israel-Africa Cooperation: The Past, the Present, and the Future,* Y.Z. Hershlag, editor (1976).

M. S. IYENGAR AND ASSOCIATES (PRIVATE) LIMITED

Telephone: 584018

Post Box No. 2817
13/15 Multistoreyed Building
Seventh Floor, NPL Colony
New Delhi 110 060, India

Founded: 1974

Officers: M. S. Iyengar, Managing Director; Vinod A. Iyengar, Director; Azra Seema Iyengar, Director.

Private consulting firm. **Staff:** Ten. **Sources of support:** Consultant fees. **Annual Budget:** No answer.

Objectives and interests: Industrial consultancy, long-term projections, and technology forecasting.

Major programs and projects: "Long-term Energy Studies for India"—The study would cover fossil, non-fossil, and non-traditional energy sources and indicate at the anticipatory, operational, and tactical levels the policies that could be pursued. "Alternative Models for Development"—To determine the most plausible models for development in India, after full comprehension of the various possible and desirable alternatives.

Special facilities: Library of books on technological forecasting, technology assessment, problems of industrialization.

Activities: Industrial consultancy work, long-term studies of policy-making on energy, food, alternative models of growth. Member of the Executive Council and the Scientific Council of the World Future Studies Federation and member of the Futurology Panel of the Government of India.

Publications: *Can Countries of the Third World Transform into a Post-Industrial Society?,* M. S. Iyengar (1973); *Technology Assessment and Its Relevance to the Developing Countries,* M. S. Iyengar (1973); *The Challenge of Growth in the Developing Countries,* M. S. Iyengar; "Technology and Economic Development in India" in *Chemical Processing and Engineering,* M. S. Iyengar; "Can We Transform into a Post-Industrial Society?" in THE FUTURIST, M. S. Iyengar; currently engaged in writing a book on "India in the Year 2000."

JAPAN ASSOCIATION FOR FUTURE RESEARCH

Telephone: (983) 4345

Faculty of Law
Gakushuin University
1-5-1 Mejiro, Toshima-ku
Tokyo, Japan 171

Founded: 1968

Officers: Ichiro Nakayama, President; Yujiro Hayashi, Chairman; Hidetoshi Kato, Secretary-General.

Professional association. **Staff:** — **Sources of support:** Membership fees. **Annual Budget:** No answer.

Objectives and interests: Future research on interdisciplinary basis.

Major programs and projects: —

Special facilities: —

Activities: Conferences are held twice a year on various subjects related to future research.

Publications: *Proceedings of International Future Research Conference* (Kyoto, 1970) 3 volumes (in English); newsletters (in Japanese) are circulated among members several times a year.

THE JAPAN ECONOMIC RESEARCH CENTER
Nikkei Bldg., No. 9-5, Ohtemachi 1-Chome
Chiyoda-ku, Tokyo 100, Japan

Telephone: (270) 5541

Founded: 1964

Officers: Hiromi Arisawa, Advisor; Saburo Okita, Chairman; Hiaso Kanamori, President; Nobuyoshi Namiki, Chief Economist; Sueo Sekiguchi, Senior Economist; Kiyoo Ishimoto, Executive Secretary.

Private, non-profit research institute. **Staff:** 130, including branch office in Osaka. **Sources of support:** Corporations and others. **Annual Budget:** $1,980,000.

Objectives and interests: Economic research, with particular emphasis on economic forecasting.

Major programs and projects: "Human being and society" of the 21st century; studies on the socioeconomic framework to analyze the energy supply-demand situation in the year 2000.

Special facilities: Library of books, magazines, newspapers, and other materials on economics and related fields (not for public use).

Activities: Organizes joint economic research; sponsors economic study courses, seminars, lectures, and symposia, with participation and assistance from leading scholars and economists in academic, business, and government circles; trains junior businessmen in advanced economics and research; undertakes research projects on contractual basis.

Publications: *Bulletin* (semimonthly in Japanese); *Quarterly Forecast of Japan's Economy* (thrice yearly); *A Five-Year Forecast of the Japanese Economy*, 1977-82, Y. Moriya, editor; *The Future of World Economy and Japan*, H. Kanamori, editor (1975); *The Experience of Economic Planning in Japan*, Saburo Okita (1974); *The Future of the Japanese Economy and Its Primary Commodity Requirements*, H. Kanamori, et al. (1975); *Technology Transfer in Pacific Economic Development* (1974); *A Collection of Essays*, Saburo Okita (1975); *Recent Developments of Japanese Economy and Its Differences from Western Advanced Economics* (1976); *The 1974-75 Recession and Economic Stabilization Policy Commodity Requirements*, Hisao Kanamori and Sueo Sekiguchi (1977); *Japanese Economic Growth and Economic Welfare*, Hisao Kanamori (1977); *Japanese Direct Foreign Investment*, Sueo Sekiguchi (1977); *The Japanese Economy in 1985* (1976); *The Future of Labor Problems in Japan* (1977); *The Japanese Labor Market in 1990* (1978); *Income Distribution Employment and Economic Development in Southeast and East Asia* (1975); *Cooperation and Development in the Asia/ Pacific Region* (1976); *Basic Problems for Postwar Reconstruction of Japanese Economy*, Saburo Okita (1977).

JAPAN TECHNO-ECONOMICS SOCIETY
4-5, Iidabashi, 2-Chome, Chiyoda-ku
Tokyo, Japan

Telephone: (03) 263-5501

Founded: 1966

Officers: Shoichi Moriyama, Executive Director, Bunya Tadano, Managing Director; Osamu Yoshida, Secretary-General; Mitsuo Iinuma, Vice Secretary-General; Guiichi Matsuo, Chief of International Department; Hisayuki Nimiya, Chief of Research Department.

Non-profit. **Staff:** About 20. **Sources of support:** Contributions from member companies. **Annual Budget:** 172 million yen.

Objectives and interests: To research the holistic structure of techno-economic activities in Japan and the world.

Major programs and projects: "Industrial Technical Level Indicator Research Project"—to establish an indicator measuring the industrial technical level. "Research Project on Major R&D Theme in Japan"—to select the major field of R&D which has the highest priority in Japan. "Project for the Appropriate Information Society"—to predict the emergence of new industrial fields related to the trade of information.

Special facilities: Library.

Activities: Conferences, seminars, symposiums, research projects, dissemination of relevant materials to membership.

Publications: *Technology and Economy,* Shoichi Moriyama, editor (monthly); *Environmental Management and Public Participation,* T. Hoshi, et al., (1977); *R&D Motivation Know-how Book,* K. Mizuno, et al., (1977); *Technology in Japan: Past Decade and Future Decade,* N. Makino, et al., (1977); *Soft Technology,* B. Tadano, et al., (1972).

KENILWORTH INSTITUTE
316 Richmond Road
Kenilworth, Illinois 60043, U.S.A.

Telephone: (312) 251-3910

Founded: 1975

Officers: Raymond P. Ewing, President; Roy R. Anderson and James Hathaway, Directors; Jane A. Ewing, Researcher.

Non-profit. Staff: Two to ten, according to project. **Sources of support:** Varied. **Annual Budget:** No answer.

Objectives and interests: To foster, encourage, and promote business, professional, civic, and individual participation in the formulation and development of public policies and relevant alternatives, as they affect the quality of human life.

Major programs and projects: "Futurists and the Public Policy Process"—a study of the participation and impact of futurists in public policy debate. "Social Inventions Centers"—a feasibility study of social invention R and D centers to keep pace with science and technology. "Implications of the Holistic Movements"—public policy implications of the holistic movements (health, education, etc.). "Corporations and the Public Policy Process"—a study of how modern corporations participate in the public policy process. "Futurist Education for the Gifted and the Talented"—futurist curricula for the gifted and talented at primary and secondary education levels.

Special facilities: —

Activities: Work-in-progress seminars, at which unpublished papers and research are presented and discussed.

Publications: *Futurescope* (quarterly newsletter); *Why We Need Two GNPs: Gross National Product and Gross National Poverty,* Raymond P. Ewing (1976); *The Future of Futurists,* Raymond P. Ewing (1979); *The Future: A Challenge to Our Systems of Compensation,* Roy A. Anderson (1978); *A Clear and Present Danger: Federal Bureaucracy,* James Hathaway (1978); *Social Inventions and Solar Energy,* Raymond P. Ewing (1978); *The Public Policy Process,* Raymond P. Ewing (1979).

KOMMUNIKATIONSZENTRUM FUR ZUKUNFTS- UND FRIEDENSFORSCHUNG IN HANNOVER GmbH [ZFF] [COMMUNICATION CENTER FOR FUTURE AND PEACE RESEARCH IN HANNOVER]
Glockseestr. 33 i.Hs. Gaswerk
3000 Hannover 1, German Federal Republic

Founded: 1964

Officers: Lothar Schulze, Director; Hildegard Anschutz, Secretary; Muthgard Hinkelmann; Kate Ledig-Schon.

Non-profit private limited company. The ZFF is a successor organization of the earlier Gesellschaft zur Forderung von Zukunftsund Friedensforschung e.V. [Society for the Advancement of Future and Peace Research], and carries on the activity of the latter society. The ZFF is now a suborganization of the Gesellschaft fur Zukunftsfragen e.V. Berlin. Staff: Four. **Sources of support:** Membership contributions, gifts. **Annual Budget:** 30,000 DM.

Objectives and interests: Documentation and information; communication by workshops.

Major programs and projects: Research projects are in preparation.

Computer searching service regarding the literature included in the Peace Research Abstracts; data bank for futurology (projected).

Special facilities: Computer searching service regarding the literature included in the Peace Research Abstracts; data bank for futurology (projected).

Activities: The center offers the possibility for technical organization of meetings in Hannover.

Publications: *Information - Zunkunfts - und Friedensforschung [Futures and Peace Research Information]*, edited by Gesellschaft fur Zukunftsfragen e. V. Berlin (quarterly, 2.70 DM per copy); *Die Zukunft geht uns alle an—eine Dokumentation von Auberungen zum Thema Zukunfts—und Friedenssicherung 1965-1975 [The Future Is Everybody's Concern—A Documentation of Remarks on Securing Peace and the Future]*, Lothar Schulze (1976).

KOREA INSTITUTE OF SCIENCE AND TECHNOLOGY

Telephone: (967) 8801, 8901, 8931

39-1, Hawolgok-dong Sungbuk-ku
Seoul 132, Korea

Founded: 1966

Officers: Byong Doo Chun, President; Tai-Wan Kwon, Vice-President for Research; Won Hee Park, Vice-President for Technical Services; Chun Juh Rhee, Vice-President for Administration; Yeo Gyeong Yun, Vice-Chairman for Planning and Control Committee.

Independent, non-profit, integrated, contract research institute. **Staff:** 1,000. **Sources of support:** Research Contracts (Government 50 percent, industry 50 percent). **Annual Budget:** Approximately $20 million (Research Volume).

Objectives and interests: To contribute to national development by meeting the technical needs of industry through research and development and technical services.

Major programs and projects: "Localization of Basic Materials and Development of Processes." "Development of Technologies for Indigenous Industries of Technology and Knowledge Intensive Nature." "Development of Comprehensive Technologies for Solving Energy and Resources Problems." "Development of Technologies for Environmental Protection and Social Hygiene." "Comprehensive Study on Overall Regional Development."

Special facilities: A library of books, periodicals, and reports on research results; Technical Information Department; Technical Transfer Center; EDPS Room.

Activities: Conduct international conferences, seminars and other meetings; e.g., "Joint Symposium on Science and Technology"; "ASCA Meeting"; "New Capital Workshop."

Publications: Newsletters (quarterly); collected reprints (annually); reports, papers and documents on its research results (frequently).

THE KOREAN SOCIETY FOR FUTURE STUDIES

Telephone: (87) 0101 Ext. 2847

Room 211, Graduate School of Environmental Studies
Seoul National University
Seoul, Korea 151

Founded: 1967

Officers: Young-Hwan Hahn, Dean, The Graduate School of Social Development, Chungang University, Seoul, Korea; An-Jae Kim, Professor, The Graduate School of Environmental Studies, Seoul National University, Seoul, Korea; Jin-Hyen Kim, Deputy Editor, The Dong-A Daily Newspaper, Seoul, Korea; Sang-Chuel Choe, Professor, The Graduate School of Environmental Studies, Seoul National University, Seoul, Korea.

Non-profit, research institute. Staff: Two full-time research assistants. **Sources of support:** Individual and corporate membership fees. **Annual Budget:** $16,000.

Objectives and interests: Exchange of information primarily between members; counseling for public and private institutions on either individual or association base. Current interests are in quality of life in the rapidly changing society of Korea.

Major programs and projects: "Exploration into a Method of Predicting the Future"—intensive workshop focused on method to be applied to the proposed extensive research on predicting Korea's future to the year 2010.

Special facilities: —

Activities: Hold seminars, primarily for members, several times a year; held three symposia on "Challenge to the Year 1990 and the Creative Future of Korea" under co-sponsorship of The Federation of Korean Industries.

Publications: *Inquiry into the Future*, Vol's. 1-6, Sang-Chuel Choe, editor (annual, not for sale); *Challenge to the Year 1990 and the Creative Future of Korea* (Korean Society for Future Studies and Federation of Korean Industries; in Korean; 1978).

72

LABORATOIRE DE PROSPECTIVE APPLIQUEE
[LABORATORY OF APPLIED FUTURISTICS]
6 rue Dante
Paris 75005, France

Telephone: 3548265, 3256061

Founded: 1971

Officers: Andre-Clement Decoufle, Gerard Klein, Jean-Claude Collard.

Non-profit research institute. Staff: One full-time; 10-12 part-time. **Sources of support:** Contracts. **Annual Budget:** $100,000.

Objectives and interests: Medium- and long-term social and geo-political forecasting; theoretical research in forecasting methodology; application of forecasting to the problems of corporations.

Major programs and projects: "L'environnement social de l'entreprise en 1985" ["The Social Environment of Business in 1985"]—General review of current social change, particularly as it applies to business; the future of business in global society. "Elements d'un vocabulaire de la prevision" ["Elements of a Forecasting Vocabulary]—An effort to define the concepts of "future," "crisis," "discontinuity," "evolution," "future-bearing fact," etc.

Special facilities: Library.

Activities: Seminars conducted for clients (e.g., on geo-political aspects of the energy crisis, futuristics and the problem of crises, objectives and missions of a forecasting group within a corporation). Also conducts university courses and research studies.

Publications: *Cahiers du Laboratoire de Prospective Appliquee [Notebooks of the Laboratory of Applied Futuristics]* (bimonthly, mimeographed); *L'An 2000: une anti-histoire de la fin du monde [The Year 2000: An Anti-History of the End of the World]* (1975); *Sociologie de le prevision [Sociology of Forecasting]* (1976); *Les moeurs en l'an 2000: essai de speculation prospective [Morals in the Year 2000: An Attempt at Future Speculation]* (1976); *La Prospective [The Future]* (1972); *Prospective de l'Espace habite [Forecasting About Land Use]* (1976); *Traite Elementaire de Prevision et de Prospective [A Treatise on Forecasting and Futures Research]* (1978).

MANAGEMENT HORIZONS, INC.
450 West Wilson Bridge Road
Worthington, Ohio 43085, U.S.A.

Telephone: (614) 846-9555

Founded: 1966

Officers: William R. Davidson, Chairman of the Board; Byron L. Carter, President; Cyrus C. Wilson, Vice-President.

Private consulting firm. Staff: 50. **Sources of support:** Private. **Annual Budget:** Not available.

Objectives and interests: Management Horizons is a distribution-focused professional consulting firm serving North American and European retailers, wholesalers, manufacturers and service organizations, specializing in marketing and distribution strategy, retail merchandising, consumer behavior and marketing research, personal selling, data processing and information systems, financial management and applied management technology.

Major programs and projects: "Shopping Trends Conference"—an annual event devoted to evaluation information gleaned from 6,000 consumer buying preference interviews. "Retail Outlook Conference"—provides forecasts of consumer goods sales and profitability. "Executive Development Series—Three Days"—first day—"Profit Modeling," second day— "Strategic Distribution Planning," third day— "Environmental Review." "Annual Management Conference"—an annual briefing on critical topics, such as "Life Cycle Management" "Long Term Outlook," or "View From the Top."

Special facilities: Slide library covering distribution/consumer goods marketing fields with 200,000 35mm slides cataloged; a Distribution/Consumer Goods Marketing Library containing more than 3,000 books, 5,000 government reports, 450 business publications, subscriptions to 1,000 company annual reports, and 500 10K reports.

Activities: Conferences.

Publications: *Retail Yearbook* (yearly); *Retail Performance Update* (quarterly); *Retail Focus* (quarterly); *Pulse* (bimonthly); *DataScan* (bi-monthly); *Critique* (bi-monthly); *How's Retailing?* (quarterly); *Retail Forecast* (annually); *Regional Retail Forecast* (annually); *Critical Issues in Retailing* (3 reports per year); *Retailing Management,* William Davidson, Alton F. Doody, Daniel J. Sweeney; *Marketing,* William R. Davidson, W. Wayne Talarzyk, Theodore H. Beckman; *The Retail Life Cycle,* William R. Davidson, Albert D. Bates, Stephen J. Bass; *The Product Life Cycle: A Key to Strategic Marketing Planning,* John E. Smallwood.

MANKIND 2000

Telephone: Brussels 511 83 96

1 rue aux Laines
1000 Brussels, Belgium **Founded:** Originally 1966 in Holland; subsequently transferred to Brussels in 1973.

Officers: A.J.N. Judge, Executive Secretary.

Non-profit, independent, transnational cultural, scientific, and educational association. **Staff:** None on a permanent basis. **Sources of support:** Membership and other private donations. **Annual Budget:** No answer.

Objectives and interests: To support and promote all aspects of human development in the individual, within and between groups, and in the emerging world community, with special reference to the mental, moral, and essential well-being of each person and of the human community as a whole. Also to encourage such conditions and techniques that will ensure that the future development of mankind becomes centered on the person as a human being.

Major programs and projects: Established the International Foundation for Social Innovation in Paris (1975); International Study Meeting on Social Innovation (September 1975, Paris); development of the World Forum for Social Innovation, in collaboration with the Centre d'etude des Consequences generales des grandes Techniques Nouvelles in Paris; International Futures Research Inaugural Conference, Oslo, 1967; played a role in the international futures conferences in Kyoto, 1970, and Rome/Frascati, 1973; continuing dialogue on human development, re-creation processes, and facilitative environments.

Special facilities: Data gathered in connection with the compilation of the *Yearbook of World Problems and Human Potential,* on world problems, human development concepts, intellectual disciplines and sciences, integrative unitary and interdisciplinary concepts, human values, multinational corporations and enterprises, multilateral treaties and agreements, human diseases, occupations, jobs, and professions, etc.

Activities: Being essentially experimental, organic, decentralized, and non-directive itself, Mankind 2000 seeks to function as a catalyst/facilitator through meetings, publications, correspondence and relevant visualization means.

Publications: *Limits to Human Potential* (1976); *Yearbook of World Problems and Human Potential,* in collaboration with the Union of International Associations, Brussels (May 1976).

K. MARX UNIVERSITY OF ECONOMIC SCIENCES, DEPARTMENT OF NATIONAL ECONOMIC PLANNING, GROUP FOR FUTURE RESEARCH
Telephone: 186-855/246

Dimitrov ter 8
1093 Budapest, Hungary

Founded: 1968

Officers: Geza Kovacs; Erzsebet Novaky; Attila Korompai; Eva Hideg; Gabor Nemethi.

State university. **Staff:** Six. **Sources of support:** University and academy budget. **Annual Budget:** No answer.

Objectives and interests: Very long-range futures research; the problems of the consistency of complex forecasts and prognoses; the connection between futures research and social planning.

Major programs and projects: "Hungary in the Year 2000"—investigations of the connection between the forecasted frame of the future in Hungary around the year 2000 and long-range planning, development and structure, mutual effects of natural/technical economic and social systems, and their regional aspects in the future. "Theoretical and Methodological Problems of Future Research"—summarizing research experiences and writing up research results.

Special facilities: Specialized library on future research.

Activities: Research on long-term economic planning and forecasting for various organizations; courses and special seminars for students and post-graduates.

Publications: *Practice of Future Research and Forecasting—A Handbook of Methodology,* Lajos Besenyei, Erzsebet Gidai, and Erzsebet Novaky (Kozgazdasagi es Jogi Konyvkiado, 1977).

MASSACHUSETTS INSTITUTE OF TECHNOLOGY, RESEARCH PROGRAM ON COMMUNICATIONS POLICY

Telephone: (617) 253-3124

53-401 Massachusetts Institute of Technology
Cambridge, Massachusetts 02139, U.S.A.

Founded: 1973

Officers: Ithiel de Sola Pool, Director; Wilbur Davenport, Professor of Electrical Engineering; Marvin Sirbu, Center for Policy Alternatives.

Research center. **Staff:** 12 **Sources of support:** AT&T, IBM, Hughes, Markle Foundation, contracts. **Annual Budget:** No answer.

Objectives and interests: Study of policies affected by new communications technologies.

Major programs and projects: "Electronic Mail"—an evaluation of the prospects. "Transborder Data Flows"— policy issues. "Telecommunications Capital Mobilization"—comparison of systems. "New Communications Technologies and the First Amendment"—an examination of the implications. "Broadband Satellite Switched Networks"—an evaluation of prospects.

Special facilities: —

Activities: Seminars, research.

Publications: Annual report and publications list.

MASSACHUSETTS INSTITUTE OF TECHNOLOGY, SYSTEM DYNAMICS GROUP

Telephone: (617) 253-1550

Massachusetts Institute of Technology, E40-253
Cambridge, Massachusetts 02139, U.S.A.

Founded: 1956

Officers: Jay W. Forrester, Germeshausen Professor of Management; Nathaniel J. Mass, Director, Systems Dynamics National Modeling Project; Gilbert W. Low, Assistant Professor of Management; Peter Senge, Assistant Professor of Management; Alan K. Graham, Assistant Professor of Management.

Private educational and research institute. **Staff:** 40. **Sources of support:** Public and private sector funding. **Annual Budget:** No answer.

Objectives and interests: Development and teaching of system dynamics methodology; building computer simulation models of social systems.

Major programs and projects: "Systems Dynamics National Modeling Project"—Computer simulation model of socio-economic change in the United States.

Special facilities: —

Activities: Research; conferring of degrees; seminars, conferences, and workshops.

Publications: *System Dynamics Newsletter* (annually); *The Limits to Growth,* Donella H. Meadows, *et al.* (1972); *World Dynamics,* Jay W. Forrester (1971, Revised 1973); *Urban Dynamics,* Jay W. Forrester (1969); *Industrial Dynamics,* Jay W. Forrester (1961); *Principles of Systems,* Jay W. Forrester (1968).

JAY S. MENDELL AND ASSOCIATES

Telephone: (305) 753-1138

11295 N.W. 38th Street
Coral Springs, Florida 33065, U.S.A.

Founded: 1973

Officers: Jay S. Mendell, Principal; Donald Cooper, Paul Guglielmino, William John Upjohn, Associates.

Consulting and training in long range thinking and business strategy. **Staff:** Variable; will remain very small. **Sources of support:** Consulting fees; fees for workshops and speeches. **Annual Budget:** No answer.

Objectives and interests: Consulting, training, and organization development devoted to solving the psychological and philosophical barriers to setting up futures groups in large and small companies.

Major programs and projects: Consulting, corporate planning, and early warning systems.

Special facilities: Negotiating for participation in large data-base of social, political, economic, technological, and ecological information.

Activities: Consulting on planning and scanning systems, corporate identity, emerging issues and corporate response; workshops and speeches; lecture bureau.

Publications: —

MIDWEST RESEARCH INSTITUTE
425 Volker Boulevard
Kansas City, Missouri 64110, U.S.A.

Telephone: (816) 753-7600

Founded: 1944

Officers: John McKelvey, President; John A. Dinwiddie, Vice-President and Treasurer; Harold Hubbard, Vice-President for Technical Operations; Paul Rappapert, Vice-President and Director, Solar Energy Research Institute; Eugene Vandegrift, Director of Economics and Management Science Division; James D. Maloney, Jr., Manager, Planning and Policy Analysis; Edward Lawless, Manager, Technology Assessment Section.

Private, not-for-profit research institute. **Staff:** 960, including the Solar Energy Research Institute, Golden, Colorado. **Sources of support:** Contract research and development with industry and government agencies. **Annual Budget:** $40 million.

Objectives and interests: Research on public policy issues of national and regional importance, including policy analysis, delivery of public services, regional development, and technology and social assessments; and futures analyses.

Major programs and projects: "Econometric Supply/Demand Modeling of Helium Resources of 2000"—an examination of projected supply and demand for helium. "A Survey of Technology Assessment in the Private Sector"—an interview-questionnaire survey and analyses of TA in industry. "A Preliminary TA of Jojoba Bean Development"—an analysis of the impact of the development of the Jojoba bean. "A Technology Assessment of the Integration of the Pork Industry"—an examination of the social impacts of changes in pork production. "Forecasting Emerging Environmental Problems: Development of a Plan"—an analysis of some anticipated needs on environmental problems.

Special facilities: American Industrial Development Council Library; Resource and Environmental Profile Analysis (REPA) Data Bank; Quality of Life Data Bank; Leisure/Recreation Data Bank; Environmental Profiles of LDC's Data Bank; Technology Assessment and Planning in the Private Sector Data Bank; The Solar Energy Research Institute (SERI) has become a division of MRI and all solar energy research will be funded through this laboratory.

Activities: "Midcontinent Perspectives: Year 2001" — a lecture series on issues of importance to the midcontinent region with monthly sessions, attendance by invitation.

Publications: *MRI Quarterly; Midcontinent Perspectives* (monographs, published irregularly); *Quality of Life in the United States; Quality of Life in the U.S. Metropolitan Areas; Technology and Social Shock*, Edward Lawless (1977).

MISSISSIPPI 1990
P.O. Box 1990
University, Mississippi 38677, U.S.A.

Telephone: (601)232-7195

Founded: 1977

Officers: Walter Mathews, Director; Patricia Christian, Coordinator; Naree Hiranyachatri.

Non-profit organization. **Staff:** — **Sources of support:** Grants. **Annual Budget:** No answer.

Objectives and interests: To promote an interest in the future among Mississippians.

Major programs and projects: —

Special facilities: —

Activities: Twelve community workshops/seminars on the future of Mississippi.

Publications: —

MOVEMENT FOR A NEW SOCIETY (MNS)
4722 Baltimore Avenue
Philadelphia, Pennsylvania 19143, U.S.A.

Telephone: (215) 724-1464

Founded: —

Officers: No officers or directors; roles and jobs rotated frequently.

Network of collectives. **Staff:** No paid staff. **Sources of support:** Mainly from publication sales. **Annual Budget:** No answer.

Objectives and interests: Our vision for a new society includes maximum decentralization and democracy in both political and economic sectors; social ownership of productive capital; no rich and no poor; guaranteed social services; and production based on human needs.

Major programs and projects: "Fatted Sprout"—an alternative, catering food-collective; catering and raising consciousness on food and hunger issues. "Keystone Alliance"—group of local groups working on the issue of nuclear power. "Marvelous Toys"—worker owned and controlled business; anti-profit collective that makes toys. "MACRO Analysis Seminars"—study group that gives a macro view of world problems.

Special facilities: —

Activities: Training in non-violence for a number of different groups; conferences on issues including nuclear power, world hunger, and simple living.

Publications: *Wine* (internal newsletter); *Dandelion* (outreach newsletter); *Strategy for a Living Revolution*, George Lakey (1973); *Moving Toward a New Society*, Gowan, Lakey, Moyer, and Taylor (1976); *Resource Manual*, Esser, Cooper, Moore, and Deacon (1977); *MNS Packet*.

MPI INTERNATIONAL, INC. (MOTIVATION PROGRAMMERS, INC.)

Telephone: (212) 421-7040

770 Lexington Avenue
New York, New York 10021, U.S.A.

Founded: 1961

Officers: Emanuel H. Demby, Chairman; Marvin Schoenwald, President; Edward Cohen, Executive Vice-President; Sharyn Chick, Senior Vice-President; Leonard Resnicoff, Senior Vice-President; Betty Demby, Director, Future Projects; Michael A. Carraher, Director, Qualitative Studies.

Private, profit-making organization. Staff: 85 (affiliated offices in London, Paris, Rome, Milan, Duesseldorf, Sao Paolo, and Tokyo). **Sources of support:** Private and government contracts. **Annual Budget:** No answer.

Objectives and interests: Development of decision-making processes; the study of the effect of changes in decision-making on business and social developments.

Major programs and projects: "Today and Tomorrow"—Analysis of current problems and potential methods of solution. "Five Years from Now"—Continuing study of decision-making changes expected in five years and the effect of these changes on business and society. "New Product Idea Generation"—Generating new product ideas on the basis of today's unsatisfied needs.

Special facilities: Data gathering in the U.S., Latin America, Europe, and Asia on a continuing basis.

Activities: Research and private seminars conducted for clients in Europe, Latin America, Asia, Africa, and the U.S.

Publications: *Psychographics,* Emanuel H. Demby; *Sensory Testing,* Howard Moscowitz.

NATIONAL COUNCIL FOR THE SOCIAL STUDIES (NCSS)
SPECIAL INTEREST GROUP IN FUTURE STUDIES

Telephone: (216) 491-4366

c/o History Department
John Carroll University
University Heights, Ohio 44118, U.S.A.

Founded: 1977

Officers: Betty Barclay Franks, Chairperson; Mary Kay Howard, Program Chairperson; Michael Rockler, Secretary-Treasurer.

Non-profit; membership limited to members of NCSS. **Staff:** — **Sources of Support:** Membership dues. **Annual Budget:** No answer.

Objectives and interests: Create a network of educators interested in adding the futures perspective to the social studies curriculum; exchange ideas and information concerning futures-oriented materials, activities, and resources; support members who need assistance in adding futures studies to the curriculum; promote public awareness of futures issues.

Major programs and projects: Compiling bibliography of media and materials useful to social studies teachers.

Special facilities: —

Activities: Yearly business meeting and program held at national meeting of NCSS; speakers' bureau being developed to present programs and plan workshops.

Publications: *The Futures Perspective* (newsletter for members; twice yearly).

NATIONAL INSTITUTE FOR RESEARCH ADVANCEMENT

Telephone: 03-344-3371

37 F. Shinjuku Mitsui Bldg. 2-1-1
Nishi-Shinjuku-ku
Tokyo 160, Japan

Founded: 1974

Officers: Tadashi Sasaki, Chairman; Masao Sakisaka, President; Akira Yamamoto, Vice-President; Tetsuo Matsumuro; Tetsutaro Suzuki; Yukio Suzuki; Atsushi Ueda.

Research institute. **Staff:** 47 **Sources of support:** Central government, local governments and private contributions. **Annual Budget:** 1,412 million yen.

Objectives and interests: The central purpose of NIRA is to promote and conduct interdisciplinary research that focuses on the problems facing modern society and their alleviation.

Major programs and projects: NIRA makes its research facilities available to researchers, disseminates information and provides opportunities for research training and education.

Special facilities: NIRA intends to establish a data bank by continuing to accumulate reports and documents; NIRA is developing a network of researchers in Japan and abroad, consisting of the staff of research institutes, university researchers and specialists from government bodies and private corporations.

Activities: "Toward the 21st Century" — focused on defining the problems Japan will face toward the 21st century and providing all the relevant information to the Japanese people so that they can reflect on the future development of their country. "Energy Project" — since completion in 1977, has contributed to the formulation of Japanese medium and long-term energy policy. NIRA also conducts research projects in five major areas: Long-term Energy Problems; Problems Toward the 21st Century; International Economic and Industrial Problems; Regional, Urban and Environmental Problems; and Social Problems.

Publications: *21 Seiki Eno Senryaku [Strategy of Japan Toward 21st Century]* (1978); *Jiten: Nippon No Kadai [Japan's Tomorrow]* (1978); *2000 Nen No Enerugi [Energy Crisis and Japan's Option]* (1977); *Chiho Jichitai Kenyu Yoran [Summary of Researches and Surveys Conducted by Local Autonomy]* (1978); *Choki Enerugi Senryaku No Sentaku [Choice of a Long-Term Energy Strategy]* (1977); *A Proposal on International Monetary Problems* (1977); *Japan Toward the 21st Century* (1978); and reports of research projects conducted by NIRA.

NATIONAL PLANNING ASSOCIATION

Telephone: (202) 265-7685

1606 New Hampshire Avenue, N.W.
Washington, D.C. 20009, U.S.A.

Founded: 1934

Officers: M. Frederik Smith, Chairman; John F. Miller, President and Assistant Chairman of the Board; Everard Munsey, Executive Vice-President; Theodore Geiger, Director of International Studies; Robert W. Rafuse, Jr., Acting Director, Research Center; Michael Koleda, Director, Center for Health Policy Studies.

Private, non-profit planning and research organization. **Staff:** 90. **Sources of support:** Private contributions, foundation grants, government contracts. **Annual Budget:** $3 million.

Objectives and interests: Planning, research, and policy analysis on domestic and international issues; fostering planning and development of planning techniques and data. Specializes in economic and demographic trend analysis and projections, public policy research, technical research in human and social resources development, and studies on domestic and international economic topics.

Major programs and projects: "National and Regional Economic Projections"—Economic and demographic projections for 10 years ahead for the U.S. multi-state regions, states, and Standard Metropolitan Statistical Areas. "National Manpower Survey"—Projection and analysis of manpower needs and related training and education requirements in law enforcement and criminal justice through 1985. "Goals Accounting System"—Development of a system relating change in future social conditions, measured by selected indicators, to combinations of public and private activities and available resources. "National Goals Research"—Estimation of dollar and manpower requirements for achievement of specified national goals. "Energy-related Manpower"—Projection of manpower requirements by occupation associated with alternative scenarios of domestic energy production.

Special facilities: Regional economic and demographic data bank.

Activities: Sponsors some 20 meetings every year of policy committees composed of leaders in business, labor, agriculture, and the professions.

Publications: *Looking Ahead/Projection Highlights* (newsletter, monthly); *New International Realities* (newsletter, three times a year); *National Economic Projection Series* (semi-annually); *Regional Economic Projection Series* (semi-annually); *Improvements in the Quality of Life: Estimates of Possibilities in the United States, 1974-1983,* Nestor E. Terleckyj (1975); *Clash of Culture: Management in an Age of Changing Values,* Carl H. Madden (1975); *Federal Health Spending, 1969-74,* Louise B. Russell *et al.* (1974); *Dollars for National Goals: Looking Ahead to 1980,* Leonard A. Lecht (1974); *Technical Change and American Enterprise,* J. Herbert Hollomon (1974). (From the first edition. Corrections not received by press time.)

NATIONAL RESEARCH COUNCIL OF CANADA
Montreal Road
Ottawa, Ontario K1A OR6, Canada

Telephone: (613) 993-9101

Founded: 1916

Officers: W.G. Schneider, President; W.A. Cumming, Senior Vice-President; K. Glegg, Vice-President, Industry; B.A. Gingras, Vice-President, External Relations; P.J. Choquette, Vice-President, Personnel and Administrative Services.

Federal government agency. **Staff:** 3,000. **Sources of support:** Federal government of Canada. **Annual Budget:** $272 million.

Objectives and interests: The National Research Council (NRC) is a national research agency established by Parliament to undertake, assist or promote scientific and engineering research to further Canada's economic and social development. A governing Council of 21 members appointed by the federal cabinet provides the overall supervision and direction to NRC's research programs and policies. It reports to Parliament through a designated Minister.

Major programs and projects: Projects are undertaken at the request of, or in cooperation with, industries, utilities, federal government departments, or provincial or municipal governments. Projects within the Engineering and Natural Sciences Research Program include: "Basic and Exploration Research"—to acquire new knowledge and expertise and to discover new applications of science of potential economic and social benefit; "Research on Long-term Problems of National Concern"—directed towards the solution of problems such as energy, food, transportation, building and construction; "Research in Direct Support of Industrial Innovation and Development"; "Research to Provide Technological Support of Social Objectives"—in areas such as health, law, public safety, environmental quality and quality of Canadian life; "National Facilities"—developed and managed as unique research facilities as a service to industry, governments and universities; "Research and Services Related to Standards." Projects within the Scientific and Technical Information Program include: "Provision of Information Services"—with the aid of the expertise and resources of the Canada Institute for Scientific and Technical Information (CISTI); and "Network Implementation."

Special facilities: —

Activities: The Council operates ten laboratory divisions and the Canada Institute for Scientific and Technical Information.

Publications: Canadian Journals of Research in biochemistry, botany, chemistry, earth sciences, forest research, geotechnology, microbiology, physics, physiology and pharmacology, zoology and civil engineering; *Science Dimension* (six times a year); *Research News* (monthly); *Canadian Building Abstracts; Building Research News; Report of the President* (annual); reports on research and development published by each division.

NATIONAL SCIENCE FOUNDATION, APPLIED SCIENCE AND RESEARCH APPLICATIONS DIRECTORATE
1800 G Street, N.W.
Washington, D.C. 20550, U.S.A.

Telephone: (202) 632-7424

Founded: 1971

Officers: Jack T. Sanderson, Assistant Director; Richard J. Green, Director of Operations.

Government agency. **Staff:** 124. **Sources of support:** U.S. Government. **Annual Budget:** No answer.

Objectives and interests: The ASRA program is designed to increase the contribution of science and technology to the nation by identifying and supporting research and related activities having the highest potential for contribution to the understanding and resolution of significant problems.

Major programs and projects: ASRA supports research in the following areas: problem analysis; integrated basic research; applied research in the applied social and behavior sciences involving public policy and regulation, public service delivery and urban problems, industrial organizations and markets, individual and group processes and applied physical, mathematical and biological sciences and engineering involving physical, mathematical and engineering, biological and ecological, and geophysical and environmental applications; problem-focused research applications involving earthquake hazards mitigation, chemical threats to man and environment, alternative biological sources of materials, and science and technology to aid the physically handicapped; inter-governmental science and research and development incentives.

Special facilities: Applied Science and Research Applications Document Center and through the National Technical Information Service.

Activities: Periodic workshops, conferences and symposia.

Publications: ASRA publications are available through the ASRA Information Resources Activity and through the National Technical Information Service.

NATIONAL SPACE INSTITUTE

Telephone: (703) 525-3103

1911 N. Ft. Myer Drive, Suite 408
Arlington, Virginia 22209, U.S.A.

Founded: 1974

Officers: Huge Downs, President; James C. Fletcher, Vice-President; Charles C. Hewitt, Executive Director; Thomas A. Gorski, Director of Communications; Cathy Lesser, Membership Director; Roger Lewis, Director of Development.

Non-profit; educational. **Staff:** Eight. **Sources of support:** Publication donations and grants. **Annual Budget:** $300,000.

Objectives and interests: As an independent forum, to communicate news of developments in space, future planning, and other areas of potential significance for this planet; to educate the public concerning the current and potential uses of space as a resource in solving earthly problems.

Major programs and projects: Developing lists of direct and indirect space benefits and their current/future impacts; developing space oriented curriculum package for use at all school levels.

Special facilities: File system based on direct/indirect space benefits—including relevant audio-visual materials; reference file on selected space topics and organizations.

Activities: SPACEWATCH Programs—educational/mass communications programs designed to bring an awareness of space and how it effects a particular area (CHICAGO SPACEWATCH held October 1978); preparation of Issue Guides by high school/college debate teams.

Publications: *Insight,* Courtney A. Stadd, editor (monthly mini-magazine); preparation of magazine articles, i.e., "The Space Program: Luxury or Necessity," Alan Shepard (*Braniff International,* Vol. 7, No. 6); press releases on space activities/benefits.

NEW YORK CENTER FOR WORLD GAME STUDIES, INC.

Telephone: (212) 288-9119

345 East 69th Street
New York, New York 10021

Founded: 1970

Officers: Mico Delianova, President; Charles Ross, Vice-President in Charge of Solar Center Project; Maris Ambats, Vice-President in Charge of Research.

Non-profit, tax exempt, educational and scientific organization. **Staff:** Seven. **Sources of support:** Contributions from the general public and individuals. **Annual Budget:** No answer.

Objectives and interests: Concerned with developing strategies and comprehensive anticipatory design systems aimed at making the world work for 100% of humanity. Sponsors and executes transdisciplinary seminars, workshops, research, and experiments, and engages in developing access to non-redundant information and tools with which to make such information available.

Major programs and projects: "The New City: A Syncon on Urban Horizons"—Used the SYNCON process to develop a consensus on the New City, then took this consensus to the decision-makers to act on. "Values and the Future"—A symposium conducted in cooperation with the World Future Society (New York City Chapter) to explore the contemporary dilemma and to focus on developing possible new value systems for the future.

Special facilities: General library, with books, periodicals, and reports on future studies and research; special solar energy library; special communications library (not for public use).

80

Activities: Conducting research and experiments in solar energy.

Publications: None.

(From the first edition. Corrections not received by press time.)

NORTH AMERICAN SOCIETY FOR CORPORATE PLANNING

Telephone: (513) 223-0419

1406 Third National Building
Dayton, Ohio 45387, U.S.A.

Founded: 1966

Officers: Robert H. Donaldson, President; O. Frederick Heider, Vice-President for Programs; G. A. Graham Hardman, Secretary; Francine W. Rickenbach, Administrative Coordinator; Gerald M. Bell.

Professional association. **Staff:** Five. **Sources of support:** Membership fees. **Annual Budget:** No answer.

Objectives and interests: —

Major programs and projects: —

Special facilities: —

Activities: Annual conference held by national society. Local chapters (16) hold a variety of meetings on monthly basis, as well as sponsoring study groups and special interest seminars.

Publications: *Planning Review,* (bimonthly) edited by Robert Allio; a series of articles from *Planning Review* is to be published in book form in cooperation with American Management Association.

NORTHWEST REGIONAL FOUNDATION

Telephone: (509) 455-9255

P.O. Box 5296
Spokane, Washington 99205, U.S.A.

Founded: 1974

Officers: Edward B. Lindaman, President; Robert Stilger, Executive Director; Roseanne Nolan, Materials Editor; Susan Virnig, Program Manager.

Non-profit, educational corporation. **Staff:** Seven. **Sources of support:** Grants, contracts, sales, contributions. **Annual Budget:** $125,000.

Objectives and interests: To encourage and assist people in taking a more active and responsible role in preparing for their future.

Major programs and projects: Consultant services—Community development block grants, emphasizing the development and implementation of citizen participation. Habitat—Varied educational programs relative to the United Nations Habitat Conference. Community Dialogues—Use of media and discussion groups to promote communication. Seminars for Community Understanding—Business/community dialogues.

Special facilities: Extensive files of articles, books, and videotapes relating to quality of life, futures, environment; vertical file library, including 150 items (articles, manuscripts, other materials).

Activities: Publication of various materials; consultant services for citizen participation programs; development and management of conferences, symposia, and workshops.

Publications: *Future Set,* a collection of packages of information on futures topics; *Alternative Futures for America III,* Robert Theobald (1975); other papers and books by Robert Theobald.

NUCLEO ROLANROC

Telephone: —

Casilla 60 - Surcursal 14
Buenos Aires, 1414 Argentina

Founded: 1974

Officers: Miguel Grinberg, Director; Carlos Ponce, Secretary

Non-profit, private, club-type informative nucleus. **Staff:** Variable. **Sources of support:** Donations, subscriptions, memberships. **Annual Budget:** No answer.

Objectives and interests: The dissemenation of information in Spanish; topics include: futures research, environmental affairs, and spiritual growth.

Major programs and projects: Pro-World 99 — combined activities (courses and publications) for responsible individual actions and educational patterns for young futurists.

Special facilities: Library.

Activities: Courses entitled "Consciousness of the Future" and "A Media for Coming Events" are included as a part of the Pro-World 99 Program.

Publications: *Pro-World 99* (newsletter devoted to information on futures research); *Rolanroc* (bulletin devoted to environmental affairs); *Nueva Sincronia* (bulletin devoted to spiritual growth). (All publications are in Spanish).

OFFICE OF SCIENCE AND TECHNOLOGY POLICY

Telephone: (202) 395-4692

Executive Office of the President
Washington, D.C. 20500, U.S.A.

Founded: 1976

Officers: Frank Press, Director; Benjamin Huberman, Assistant Director for National Security, International, and Space Affairs; Gilbert Omenn, Assistant Director for Human Resources, Social and Economic Services; Phillip Smith, Assistant Director for Natural Resources and Commercial Services.

U.S. Government Agency. **Staff:** 24. **Sources of support:** U.S. Government appropriation. **Annual Budget:** No answer.

Objectives and interests: Provides advice to the President concerning policies in science and technology and on the utilization of science and technology in addressing important national problems.

Major programs and projects: —

Special facilities: —

Activities: —

Publications: —

THE OPEN UNIVERSITY, DESIGN GROUP

Telephone: (0908) 63970

Walton Hall
Milton Keynes, England

Founded: 1972

Officers: Nigel Cross and Robin Roy, Course Team Chairmen; David Elliott; Godfrey Boyle.

Educational program **Staff:** 10. **Sources of support:** Government. **Annual Budget:** No answer.

Objectives and interests: Preparation of multimedia undergraduate courses in futures/design; research in alternative technology.

Major programs and projects: "Man-made Futures"—Undergraduate open university course.

Special facilities: —

Activities: The Open University provides a nationwide undergraduate degree program for part-time adult students, using correspondence texts and BBC TV and radio broadcasts. The Design Group is part of this effort.

Publications: *The Politics of Technology*, G. Boyle, D. Elliott, R. Roy, editors (1977); *Man-made Futures*, course texts (1975); *Control of Technology*, course texts (1978); *Man-made Futures*, N. Cross. D. Elliott, R. Roy, editors (1974); *Designing the Future*, N. Cross, D. Elliott, and R. Roy (1975); *Technology and Society*, R. Roy and N. Cross (1975); *Policy and Participation*, D. Elliott (1975); *Design and Technology*, N. Cross (1975).

THE OPEN UNIVERSITY OXFORD RESEARCH UNIT

Telephone: (0865) 730731

Community Participation by Children in Futures Project
Boars Hill
Oxford, United Kingdom

Founded: —

Officers: Simon Nicholson, Chairperson, Art and Environment Faculties of Technology, Arts and Social Science; Raymond Lorenzo, Faculty of Technology.

University research unit. **Staff:** Two. **Sources of support:** U.K. government. **Annual Budget:** $10,000.

Objectives and interests: Participatory ideas and actions in futures, including full awareness of futures colonization.

Major programs and projects: "Community Participation by Children in Futures Project"—participation in futures by children in Oxford, Napoli and Toronto.

Special facilities: Multimedia databank of futures generated by children in Oxford, Napoli, Toronto, and Ottawa.

Activities: Coordinator, "Today's Child, Tomorrow's World," Child Participation Project, United Nations International Year of the Child, 1979. Futures Exhibitions: "Le Jeu dans les Establissements Humains," ["Play in Human Establishments,"] Seventh World Conference, Ottawa, August 1978; "The Child in the World of Tomorrow," Athens International Symposium, Institute of Child Health, Athens, July 1978.

Publications: *Forty Futures*, Simon Nicholson (1979); "No Vanished Futures" in *The Future of Communication: Cultural Identity in an Interdependent World*, World Future Studies Federation (1979); "Art and the Future: The 80's and 90's" in *National Society for Art Education Journal*, United Kingdom (1978); "Children as Planners" in *The Children's Rights Movement*, Beatrice and Ronald Gross, editors (1977); "Art is not Yesterday" in *New Destinations: The Arts and Education*, Greater London Arts Association (1976).

ORGANIZATION FOR ECONOMIC COOPERATION AND DEVELOPMENT (OECD), DEVELOPMENT CENTRE

Telephone: 524 82 00

94 rue Chardon-Lagache
75016 Paris, France

Founded: 1962

Officers: Louis Sabourin, President; Yves Berthelot, Head of Research; Christian Heimpel, Head of Publication, Documentation and Dissemination; Giulio Fossi; Nicolas Jequier; Julien Conde.

International governmental organization. **Staff:** 81. **Sources of support:** Member governments of the OECD. **Annual Budget:** Approximately 15 million francs.

Objectives and interests: To serve as an informal link between OECD member countries and developing countries in terms of their economic and social development, taking into account the economic interdependency of all countries.

Major programs and projects: Multinational Corporations: Transfer of Technology and Absorptive Capacity of Developing Countries. Changing Attitudes to Population Assistance. Planning for Growing Populations. Wind and Water-mills, Solar Energy Equipment, Biogas Generators, and Ethanol Plants: Problems in the Diffusion of Appropriate, Non-Conventional Energy Technology. Scope and Conditions for Improved Use of Food Aid for Development.

Special facilities: Library of books, periodicals, and documents in the general field of economic and social development of developing countries.

Activities: Economic and social research; conferences and seminars for experts from both developed and developing countries on research results on specific topics in the field of development.

Publications: *Liaison Bulletin* (quarterly); *Latest Information on National Accounts of Less Developed Countries* (two or three times yearly); *Trilateral Cooperation: Vol. I, Arab Development Funds and Banks: Approaches to Trilateral Cooperation; Vol. II, Special Approaches to Trilateral Cooperation*, Traute Schart (Paris, 1978); *A Management Approach to Project Appraisal and Evaluation* (with special reference to nondirectly productive projects). Nicholas Imboden (Paris, 1978); *The Social Costs of Urban Surplus Labour*, R.H. Sabot (Paris, 1977); *Elements de bibliographie sur la secheresse au Sahel [Elements for a Bibliography of the Sahel Drought]*, Update No. 1, Francoise Beudot (November 1977); *Borrowing by Developing Countries on the Euro-currency Market*, P.A. Wellens (Paris, 1977); *Industry and Trade in Some Developed Countries*, Little, Scott, and Scitovsky (1970); *Employment, Unemployment in Developing Countries; National Objectives and Project Appraisal in Developing Countries*, H. Schneider (1975).

ORI, INC.
1400 Spring Street
Silver Spring, Maryland 20910, U.S.A.

Telephone: (301) 588-6180

Founded: 1953

Officers: Harvey D. Kushner, President; Howard Eisner, Executive Vice-President; Art. R. Milkes, Senior Vice-President, Finance; Howard Lefkowitz, Senior Vice-President; Bernard J. Buc, Vice-President; Patrick J. Steen, Vice-President.

Private organization (employee stock ownership trust). **Staff:** 250 plus 100 consultants. **Sources of support:** Revenue from contract work. **Annual Budget:** $10-$11 million.

Objectives and interests: Solving problems for government and industry in defense, management systems, space and transportation, safety in energy fields, and environmental pollution.

Major programs and projects: Projection of demand for air-traffic to be handled by the National Aviation System; investigations of the long-range needs for civil aviation; technology projections to the 1980's and 1990's for NASA and the Department of Defense; space-tracking and data-acquisition requirements based upon user mission needs to the 1980's; air-quality and environmental and health-impact projections.

Special facilities: Private library of published reports on strategic defense systems and weapons, communications and space technology, transportation systems design and safety, computer science technology, environmental and energy plans, safety programs, and educational research; collection of over 130 tested, generalized, computer programs and subprograms; in-house PRIME 400 computer and Harris Corporation 1620 remote, batch terminal with eight 10-30 cps terminals for connection to CDC 6500, 6600 and 6700 computers outside.

Activities: Conducted first International Teleconference on Space Shuttle Utilization; provide logistics and technical support for three-day NASA workshops concerning spacecraft in the 1980's; customer courses as requested in special areas such as education and computer science applications.

Publications: *Research in Education* (monthly abstract journal); newsletter (company business quarterly); prepare bulletin on upper atmospheric programs for bimonthly distribution by NASA/Federal Aviation Administration.

OSRODEK BADAN PROGNOSTYCZNYCH [FORECASTING RESEARCH CENTER]
Wybrzeze Wyspianskiego 27
53-370 Wroclaw, Poland

Telephone: 484-238

Founded: 1971

Officers: Karol I. Pelc, Director; Ludwik J. Baworowski, Assistant Director; Jozef A. Kosinski; Tomasz Kocowski; Stanislaw Rowecki; Ryszard Wasniowski.

Research institute at Technical University of Wroclaw (state-owned). Staff: 40. **Sources of support:** Government and industry. **Annual Budget:** Approximately 30,000 man-hours a year.

Objectives and interests: Methodology of exploratory and normative forecasting; technological forecasts; long-term research and development planning; management of research and development projects; management of technological innovation.

Major programs and projects: "Science and Technology in Poland in the Year 2020." "Theory of Active Systems and Its Application to Forecasting and Management of R&D." "Simulation Techniques in Scientific Manpower Forecasting." "Methodology of International Forecasting in CMEA Countries." "Forecasting in the Domain of Electronics."

Special facilities: Library of approximately 3,500 volumes on social, economic, and technological forecasting.

Activities: Winter school of forecasting; International Conference on Management of Research and Education; postgraduate course on technological forecasting.

Publications: *Prace Naukoznawcze i Prognostyczne [Papers on Science of Science and Forecasting]* (quarterly; abstracts in English); *Prace Naukowe Osrodka Badan Prognostycznych [Scientific Publications of Forecasting Research Center]*.

OSTERREICHISCHE AKADEMIE DER WISSENSCHAFTEN, INSTITUT FUR SOZIO-OKONOMISCHE ENTWICKLUNGSFORSCHUNG[AUSTRIAN ACADEMY OF SCIENCES, INSTITUTE FOR RESEARCH IN SOCIO-ECONOMIC DEVELOPMENT]

Telephone: 52 94 89

Fleischmarkt 20
Vienna A-1010, Austria **Founded:** 1973

Officers: Robert Reichardt, Director; Hans Hornich, Chairman of the Board; Peter Fleissner, Deputy Director; Frank Landler, Education; Peter Sint, Energy; Rene Dell'Mour, Education.

Non-profit, research institute. **Staff:** Six. **Sources of support:** Ministry of Science and Research. **Annual Budget:** 2 million schillings.

Objectives and interests: Analysis of domestic developments in the economy, education, health care, energy, and information systems.

Major programs and projects: A simulation model of the Austrian health care system. A model of the educational system of Austria. Alternatives in energy production. Cost-effectiveness study of psychiatry in Austria.

Special facilities: —

Activities: Research.

Publications: *Ein Simulationsmodell des Osterreichischen Gesundheitswesen [A Simulation Model of the Austrian Health System]*, P. Fleissner (1974); *Das Osterreichischen Bildungswesen [The Austrian Educational System]*, P. Landler.

OSTERREICHISCHE GESELLSCHAFT FUR LANGFRISTIGE ENT-WICKLUNGSFORSCHUNG [AUSTRIAN SOCIETY FOR FUTURE RESEARCH] Telephone: —

c/o Institute fur Sozio-okonomische Entwicklungsforschung
[Institute for Research in Socio-economic Development]
Fleischmarkt 20
Vienna A-1010, Austria **Founded:** 1973

Officers: Gerhart Bruckmann, President; P. Blau, Vice-President; Peter Fleissner, Acting Director.

Non-profit association with about 80 members. Staff: None. **Sources of support:** Membership fees. **Annual Budget:** About 10,000 schillings.

Objectives and interests: Clearinghouse for persons interested in futures research.

Major programs and projects: —

Special facilities: —

Activities: Seminars and conferences on future research at the University of Vienna.

Publications: Newsletter published about five times a year containing internal information.

OSTERREICHISCHEN INSTITUT FUR WIRTSCHAFTSFORSCHUNG
[AUSTRIAN INSTITUTE FOR ECONOMIC RESEARCH] **Telephone:** 65 66 61

A-1103 Wien, Postfach 91, Arsenal
Vienna, Austria **Founded:** 1927

Officers: Hans Seidel; Helmut Kramer; Felix Butschek; Karl Musil.

Non-profit, research institute. **Staff:** 90. **Sources of support:** Government, associations, corporations. **Annual Budget:** 30 million schillings.

Objectives and interests: Economic research and short- and medium-term forecasting.

Major programs and projects: "Austrian Agriculture in 1985"; "The Austrian Labor Market in 1980-85"; "Demand for Energy in 1990."

Special facilities: Library; data bank containing data on the Austrian economy.

Activities: —

Publications: *Monatsberichte des Osterreichischen Instituts fur Wirtschaftsforschung [Monthly Report of the Austrian Institute for Economic Research]; Empirica* (biannual); "Der Osterreichische Arbeits-markt bis 1991" ["The Austrian Labor Market up to 1991"], G. Biffl (*Monatsbericht des Osterreichischen Instituts fur Wirtschaftsforschung,* No. 2/78); *Internationaler Reiseverkehr und Wirtschaftswachstum [International Tourist Traffic and Economic Growth]* — forecast up to 1985, Stefan Schulmeister (1975).

OVERSEAS DEVELOPMENT COUNCIL

1717 Massachusetts Avenue, N.W.
Washington, D.C. 20036, U.S.A.

Telephone: (202) 234-8701

Founded: 1969

Officers: Theodore M. Hesburgh, Chairman of the Board; James P. Grant, President; John W. Sewell, Executive Vice-President; Michael V. O'Hare, Controller; James W. Howe, Senior Fellow; Robert Ayers, Senior Fellow; Martin M. McLaughlin, Senior Fellow; Valeriana Kallab, Executive Editor; Jayne Millar Wood, Director, Public Education.

Private, non-profit education and research organization. **Staff:** 35. **Sources of support:** Foundations, corporations, and private individuals. **Annual Budget:** No answer.

Objectives and interests: To increase American understanding of the economic and social problems confronting the developing countries and of the importance of these countries to the United States; to promote consideration of development issues by the American public, policy makers, specialists, educators, and the media through its research, conferences, publications, and liaison with U.S. mass membership organizations interested in U.S. relations with the developing world.

Major programs and projects: "A Global Approach to Energy" — develop a framework for analysis of energy problems from global point of view and examine alternative energy sources in the Third World. "International Economic Systems and the U.S. Interest" — studies and analyses that trace the interrelations and mutual benefits of a new international economic order for the U.S. and developing countries. "Alternative Development Stratagies and Basic Human Needs" — analyses of development strategies that stress the achievement of basic human needs on an increasingly self-reliant basis. "Development Education and the U.S. Public" — designing and coordinating educational programs with different sectors of the American public to enhance their understanding of development issues. "Population, Health and Development" — studies designed to stimulate innovative approaches to developing goals with greater progress toward reducing mortality and fertility rates.

Special facilities: Maintains small library.

Activities: Fellowship program sponsors studies by Development Fellows from U.S. and Third World universities and agencies. Conducts a program of research, analysis, communication, and public education. Conducts conferences and seminars with groups including private and voluntary organizations, women's groups, and similar organizations.

Publications: ODC regularly publishes monographs, occasional papers, development papers and communiques, selected titles of which are as follows: *Accelerating Population Stabilization Through Social and Economic Progress,* Robert S. McNamara; *Negotiations on Two Fronts: Manufactures and Commodities,* Guy F. Erb; *Debt and Developing Countries: New Problems and New Actors,* Paul M. Watson; *The PQLI: Measuring Progress in Meeting Human Needs,* Morris D. Morris and Florizelle B. Liser; *International Commodity Agreements: An Evaluation of the UNCTAD Integrated Commodity Programme,* Jere R. Behrman; *Looking At Guinea-Bissau: A New Nation's Development Strategy,* Denis Goulet; *Development As If It Mattered* (Bibliography), May Rihani; *U.S. and World Development: Agenda 1977,* John W. Sewell and the staff of ODC: *U.S. and World Development: Agenda 1978,* Martin McLaughlin and the staff of ODC: *The Uncertain Promise: Value Conflicts in Technology Transfer,* Denis Goulet; *Beyond Charity: U.S. Voluntary Aid for A Changing Third World,* John G. Sommer; *Beyond Dependency: The Developing World Speaks Out,* Guy F. Erb and Valeriana Kallab, editors.

DAVID OWEN CENTRE FOR POPULATION GROWTH STUDIES

51 Park Place
University College
Cardiff, Wales, United Kingdom CF1-1XL

Telephone: Cardiff (0222) 44211

Founded: 1973

Officers: Caspar Brook, Director; Jack Parsons, Senior Lecturer and Deputy Director; Betty Murch, Programme Officer.

University teaching and research institute. **Staff:** Seven. **Sources of support:** University Grants Committee, Ministry of Overseas Development, United Nations Fund for Population Activities.   **Annual Budget:** 100,000 pounds sterling (national, partly hidden).

Objectives and interests: Further world social-economic development by balancing population and resources; improve population awareness and public policy in the United Kingdom.

Major programs and projects: "POPTRAN"—a new, computer-based population education tool being developed by Charles Mercer, lecturer in psychology at the Centre's sister institution, the University of Wales Institute of Science and Technology; development of population program management training aids; development of population awareness, policy and integrated family planning in the Sudan; personal research by Jack Parsons in competitive breeding and population optimisation.

Special facilities: Technical Information Centre (for academic and public use) and a modified PLATO population simulation program.

Activities: Running 10-month post graduate diploma course in population studies; furthering population research, awareness, interest and education; publishing list of relevant material.

Publications: *Population Fallacies,* by Jack Parsons (1977); *Towards Integrated Family Planning in the Sudan,* by Caspar Brook (1977); *Choice Not Chance,* by B. Bewley, J. Cook, P. Kane (1977); *Newsletter,* published each term for alumni; reprints of annual Sir David Owen Memorial Lecture.

PLANNING DYNAMICS, INCORPORATED

Telephone: (412) 321-6000

850 Ridge Avenue
Babb Building
Pittsburgh, Pennsylvania 15212, U.S.A.

Founded: 1965

Officers: Colin H. Hershey, President; Robert F. Glass, Vice-President; Charles A. Tulloh, Vice-President.

Private.   Staff: 10.   **Sources of support:** Corporate contracts.   **Annual Budget:** $150,000.

Objectives and interests: To help corporations, educational institutions, health care service organizations, and government agencies plan for the future in a more practical and purposeful manner; to enable organizations to manage the future by optimizing when there is a significant deviation in anticipated developments or results; to assist in strategic planning, communications, and management effectiveness.

Major programs and projects: "Westwood Program"—the development of a prototype planning program for the American College of Hospital Administrators. "Planning Seminar for Colleges and Universities"—developed a prototype for future planning under the auspices of the Ford and Exxon Educational Foundations. "Management Training Program"—corporate planning program designed for managers to assist in the understanding of planning.

Special facilities: Library of information on future planning concepts and processes in corporations, public utilities, government agencies, educational institutions, and health-care service organizations.

Activities: Consultation, conferences, seminars, workshops, task-force support.

Publications: *Corporate Planning Workbook* (1970); *Management Planning for Hospitals* (1971).

PLANNING EXECUTIVES INSTITUTE

Telephone: (513) 523-4185

5500 College Corner Pike
Oxford, Ohio 45056, U.S.A.

Founded: 1951

Officers: Charles Courey, President; Warren Sladky, Senior Vice-President; James Thomson, Executive Director; Henry C. Doofe, Administrative Assistant; Shirley Taylor, Office Manager.

Non-profit membership society.   Staff: Nine   **Sources of support:** Dues, publications, conferences and seminars.   **Annual Budget:** $210,000.

Objectives and interests: Financial and corporate planning.

Major programs and projects: -—

Special facilities: Library of planning books for loan to members.

Activities: Annual conference, two corporate planning conferences, 30 chapter seminars, and monthly chapter meetings.

Publications: *Managerial Planning* (bimonthly), edited by Henry C. Doofe; *Research Series*, monographs published frequently; *Educational Series*, monographs and books published occasionally. (10 titles of both series in print)

PLANNING AND FORECASTING CONSULTANTS

908 Town and Country Boulevard
Suite 120
Houston, Texas 77024, U.S.A.

Telephone: (713) 467-4732

Founded: 1973

Officers: Dale W. Steffes, President and Founder; Paul Strain, Senior Consultant; senior staff consists of highly qualified professions in all fields on a part-time basis.

Private forecasting firm, assist with planning (strategic). Staff: Four consultants on a part-time basis. **Sources of support:** Private corporations (clients operate 12% of U.S. electric generation, including major and independent oil companies and several OPEC countries). **Annual Budget:** $100,000 to $150,000.

Objectives and interests: To provide managements with unbiased information for their planning process; to critique corporate plans. Work generally relates to the energy field, both national and international, with emphasis on the transportation of coal.

Major programs and projects: "A Coal Slurry Pipeline from the Western Coal Reserves of the United States"—macro view of what coal slurry industry could look like in the 1980's. "World Petroleum Supply and Demand, 1973-1985"—illustrates the discontinuity in the supply and demand curves. "Rail Transportation of Western Coal and Other Commodities, 1975-1995" — evaluation of Western Railroads' ability to haul the massive projected coal movements. "Optimum Speed of a Coal Unit Train (1976)"; "The New United States Energy Playbook (1976)." "United States Refinery Requirements to 1990"—multi-client study to be completed in December 1978. "World Energy Supply and Demand to 1990"—multi-client study to be completed in December 1978. "Market Study for Railcars 1978 and to 1985."

Special facilities: Maintain a library of books, publications, internal reports, and data divided into the six influences—social, political, technological, ecological, economic, and natural resources; Data Bank on Markets for Western Coal; building a world data bank on population, and economics.

Activities: Seminars pertaining to current topics, with participation by invitation.

Publications: *Trend Discontinuities* (published at irregular intervals); *Western (U.S.) Coal Market Study* (1978); *United States Refinery Requirements to 1990* (1978); *World Energy Supply and Demand to 1990* (1978).

POLICY STUDIES INSTITUTE

½ Castle Lane
London SW1, United Kingdom

Telephone: 235-5271 or 242-7295

Founded: 1978

Officers: John Pinder, Director; Michael Fogarty, Deputy Director; Richard Davies, Director of Administration; Roger Morgan, Head; and David Coombes, Staff Member; European Centre for Studies in Democratic Politics.

Non-profit, research institute. **Staff:** Approximately 50. **Sources of support:** Joseph Rowntree Memorial Trust; subscriptions; donations; convenants; revenue from publications; government departments; trust. **Annual Budget:** Approximately 500,000 pounds sterling.

Objectives and interests: Implications for economic and social policy of changes in population size; family structure; employment activity; geographical distribution; and economic, social and environmental policies.

Major programs and projects: Establishment of European Centre for Studies in Democratic Policies with a grant from European Cultural Foundation; Educational Policy Unit in collaboration with the University of Lancaster.

Special facilities: Library.

Activities: Lunchtime seminars; conferences.

Publications: Annual report; bulletin (twice yearly).

POLICY STUDIES ORGANIZATION

Telephone: (217) 359-8541

361 Lincoln Hall
University of Illinois
Urbana, Illinois 61801, U.S.A.

Founded: 1972

Officers: Stuart Nagel, Secretary-Treasurer and Journal Coordinator; Kenneth Dolbeare, Vice-President and President-Elect; Joyce Nagel, Business Manager; Marian Neef, Research Associate; Kathleen Burkholder, Directory Editor.

Non-profit, tax-exempt, educational organization. Staff: 10. **Sources of support:** Dues, government grants, foundation grants, royalties, single-issue sales. **Annual Budget:** $40,000.

Objectives and interests: To promote the application of political and social science to important policy problems.

Major programs and projects: "Science and Technology Policy"—symposium by Joseph Haberer. "Using Social Research in Public Policy Making"—symposium by Carol Weiss. "Policy Studies in America and Elsewhere"—symposium by Stuart Nagel. "Methodologies for Analyzing Public Policies"—symposium by Frank Scioli and Tom Cook. "Population Policy Analysis"—symposium by Michael Kraft and Mark Schneider.

Special facilities: —

Activities: Sponsor convention panels, information clearing house, legislation, academic-practitioner interaction, and other policy-relevant activities.

Publications: *Policy Studies Journal*, Stuart Nagel, editor (4 or 5 times/year). Series of directories describing policy studies people and institutions: *Policy Studies Directory* (survey of teaching programs); *Political Science Utilization Directory* (government agencies); *Policy Grants Directories* (funding sources); *Policy Research Centers Directory*; *Policy Studies Personnel Directory*; *Directory of Policy Journals, Associations, and Publishers*. Book series: Lexington Books series includes such books as *Policy Analysis and Deductive Reasoning*, Gordon Tullock and Richard Wagner, editors; Sage series includes such books as *Public Policies in America*, Ted Lowi and Allan Stone, editors; Praeger series includes *Environmental Politics*, Stuart Nagel, editor; Transaction Books series included *Policy Studies and the Social Sciences*, Stuart Nagel, editor; SIU Press series includes *Economic Regulatory Policies*, James Anderson, editor.

POLISH ACADEMY OF SCIENCES, INSTITUTE OF PHILOSOPHY AND SOCIOLOGY, DIVISION FOR LIFESTYLES STUDIES

Telephone: 26-76-42

Nowy Swiat 72
Warsaw 00-330, Poland

Founded: 1969

Officers: Andrzej Sicinski, Head of the Division; Anna Pawelczynska, Head of a Section; Marcin Czerwinski, Docent; Aleksander Wallis, Docent.

Research institute. Staff: 17. **Sources of support:** Government. **Annual Budget:** No answer.

Objectives and interests: Problems of cultural change; changes in lifestyle.

Major programs and projects: Changes in lifestyle in Poland and in Scandinavian countries.

Special facilities: —

Activities: Seminar on problems of the style of life; seminar on spatial problems of culture.

Publications: *Studies in Social Prognostics*, A. Razniewski and A. Sicinski, editors (1972, in Polish); *Prognostication in Culture*, A. Wallis (1973, in Polish); *Methodological Problems of Prognostication of Human Behavior*, A. Sicinski and A. Razniewski, editors (in Polish); *Style of Life: Conceptions and Proposals*, A. Sicinski, editor (1976, in Polish); *Style of Life: Changes in Contemporary Poland*, A. Sicinski, editor (1978, in Polish).

POLISH ACADEMY OF SCIENCES, RESEARCH AND PROGNOSTICS COMMITTEE "POLAND 2000"

Telephone: Warsaw 200-211 ext. 4074, 2677

Palac Kultury i Nauki
Warsaw, Poland

Founded: 1969

Officers: Wladyslaw Markiewicz, Chairman; Julius Gorynski, Deputy Chairman; Kazimierz Secomski, Deputy Chairman and Vice-Premier; Jozef Pajestka, Council of Ministries Planning Commission; Jan Danecki, Scientific Secretary; Danuta Markowska, Chief, Research and Coordination Unit.

Research organization. Staff: 12. **Sources of support:** Polish Academy of Sciences. **Annual Budget:**No answer.

Objectives and interests: Social and cultural forecasting; research and expert advising.

Major programs and projects: "Criteria of Progress"—Delphi research, Jan Danecki, director. "Model of Educated Pole"—B. Suchodolski, director. "Verification of Demographic Prognoses for Poland"—K. Secomski, director. "Prognoses on Future Demand for Qualified Cadres"—J. Tynowski and J. Kordaszewski, directors. "Evolution of Needs of Various Categories of Families in Poland in the Light of Socio-political Development"—A. Rajkiewicz, director. The Committee Poland 2000 also participates in the following international research projects: UNU, Establishment of a New International Economic Order, and UNITAR.

Special facilities: Books, periodicals, reports, data collected in areas of interest.

Activities: Methodological seminar for researchers from various centers; symposiums on special topics organized by Commissions of the Committee "Poland 2000."

Publications: *Polska 2000*, A. Rajkiewicz, editor (journal, published irregularly, 3-4 times per year); *Kultura polska a socjalistyczny system wartosci [Polish Culture and Socialist System of Values]* B. Suchodolski, editor (1977); *Kultura a wiez przestrzenna [Culture and Spatial Ties]* A. Wallis (1978); *Toward Poland 2000: Problems of Social Development Until the Year 2000*, J. Danecki, editor (collective volume to be published in English in 1979).

PORTLAND STATE UNIVERSITY, FUTURES RESEARCH INSTITUTE

Telephone: (503) 229-4960

P.O. Box 751
Portland, Oregon 97207, U.S.A.

Founded: 1973

Officers: Harold A. Linstone, Director; James Wilson; Dan Schwartz; Rias Van Wyk.

Research institute. Staff: 4-6. **Sources of support:** Portland State University. **Annual Budget:** No answer.

Objectives and interests: Futures research; publications; conferences and seminars.

Major programs and projects: "The Use of Structural Modeling for Technology Assessment."

Special facilities: Forecast data file; library for futures research.

Activities: Conference, "Oregon Tomorrow/Trends and Options" (1974); various research studies; visiting scholars and lecturers.

Publications: *Technological Forecasting and Social Change* (8 issues a year); *The Delphi Method*, H. Linstone and M. Turoff (1975); *Technological Substitution*, H. Linstone and D. Sahal (1976); *Futures Research: New Directions*, H. Linstone and W.H.C. Simmonds (1977); *Oregon Tomorrow*—background summary (1974); *QSIM 2*, W. Wakeland (1975); *Planning—Toy or Tool?*, H. Linstone (1974); *On Discounting the Future*, H. Linstone (1973); *Technology Forecasting: The Gap Between Theory and Practice*, H. Linstone (1975).

PREDICASTS, INC.

Telephone: (216) 795-3000

200 University Circle Research Center
11001 Cedar Avenue
Cleveland, Ohio 44106, U.S.A.

Founded: 1960

Officers: Samuel A. Wolpert, President; William M. Weiss, Executive Vice-President/Research; Robert M. Baumgartner, Vice-President/Information; Fern S. Pomerantz, Vice-President/Market Promotion; Paul E. Owen, Vice-President/Sales; Ramune Kubiliunas, Vice-President/Information Center.

Privately-held, fully integrated business information and research firm. Staff: 110. **Sources of support:** Subscriptions, service fees. **Annual Budget:** No answer.

Objectives and interests: A major contributor to the development of information technology, Predicasts is devoted to helping clients access business and economic information. Services are directed toward providing librarians with comprehensive indexes to business information and bibliographies of pertinent material; satisfying the analysts' need for reliable reports on the status of technology, the marketing climate, and the economy; giving the planner rapid access to rational forecasts—both general and specific; and bringing to executives the sophisticated studies needed to evaluate alternate strategies and determine policy.

Major programs and projects: *Predicasts*—a quarterly publication which presents statistical abstracts to forecasts to the year 2020 published in over 1,000 sources; forecasts cover the full range of U.S. business and economic activity and are arranged by subject; composite forecasts to 1990 are derived and presented for 500 key economic series. *Predicasts' Basebook* — companion publication which presents historical time series data from 1960-77. *Worldcasts*—published quarterly in two editions, this is the international edition of *Predicasts;* forecasts are arranged by geographic region/ country and by subject, with composites to 1990 included. "Industry and Statistical Studies"—about 30 published annually, analyzing the full economy and selected industries, with emphasis on plastics, electronics, and paper; list includes studies covering U.S. and worldwide industries. "Market Reports"—titles fall under resource, growth, U.S., world or regional classification; hundreds of key digests derived from Predicasts' computerized database; cover past and future industry structure, facilities, technology, regulation markets and end-uses; summary of findings including consensus forecasts.

Special facilities: Predicasts' Information Center contains over 5,000 worldwide titles, including newspapers, government and industry reports, bank letters, corporate reports. All documents are abstracted and indexed for periodicals and databases. "Predicasts Terminal System" (PTS) is an on-line database compiled in a joint venture with Lockheed Information Systems (DIALOG) and System Development Corporation (ORBIT). PTS files contain over one million statistical, index, abstract, and bibliographic records. It is worldwide in scope and includes computational capabilities, accessible to clients in North America and Europe on a subscription basis.

Activities: Three types of seminars held throughout U.S. and Europe: "Introductory"—to acquaint participants with on-line systems and capabilities, participation open, no charge; "Literature Retrieval Training"—teaches how to search PTS files, participation open, fee charged; "Advanced Training"—a review of search skills and training on computational mode of PTS, participation open, fee charged. Custom PTS training sessions, fee charged plus expenses.

Publications: *Promt* (monthly); *Predi-Briefs* (monthly); *Marketing Ideas* (biweekly); *Financial Ideas* (biweekly); *Technical Survey* (weekly); *Federal Index* (monthly); *Source Directory* (quarterly); *F&S Index International* (monthly, quarterly); *F&S Index of Corporations and Industries* (weekly, monthly, quarterly); *F&S Index Europe* (monthly, quarterly); *F&S Index of Corporate Change* (quarterly); *Reinforced Plastics*, J. Wimberly (1978); *World Automotive Aftermarket*, J. Pirnat (1978); *Industrial Packaging*, J. Brock (1978); *U.S. Energy Outlook to 1990*, J. Pirnat (1978); *World Rubber and Tire Markets*, J. Vetter (1978).

PRINCETON CENTER FOR ALTERNATIVE FUTURES, INC.   Telephone: (609) 921-2280
60 Hodge Road
Princeton, New Jersey 08540, U.S.A.   Founded: 1967

Officers: Carter Henderson, Co-Director; Hazel Henderson, Co-Director.

Privately-owned, tax-paying corporation. Staff: Two. **Sources of support:** Writing, lecturing, and research fees from voluntary and professional associations, colleges and universities, church groups, corporations, and government. **Annual Budget:** No answer.

Objectives and interests: Exploring alternative futures for citizens of industrialized countries in a planetary context of human interdependence.

Major programs and projects: "Resources and the Future of Wealth and Scarcity"—On-going study of production and consumption analyzed in terms of the planet's worsening population/resource ratio. "Human Values in an Era of Radical Change"—Continuing examination of values as the dominant, driving variables in all human systems—both technological and social—in today's era of radical change.

Special facilities: None.

Activities: Writing, lecturing, small private conferences, and futures research.

Publications: *Creating Alternative Futures*, Hazel Henderson, with a foreword by E.F. Schumacher (G.P. Putnam's, 1978); *The Inevitability of Petroleum Rationing in the U.S.*, Carter Henderson (Princeton Center for Alternative Futures, Inc., 1978); publications list of more than 50 articles and papers in major journals, speeches, and congressional testimony updated bimonthly and individually available at cost.

PROGNOS AG, EUROPEAN CENTER FOR APPLIED ECONOMIC RESEARCH
Telephone: (061) 22.40.70

Viaduktstrasse 65
Basle CH-4011, Switzerland
Founded: 1959

Officers: Heik Afheldt, General Manager; Alois Schwietert; Dieter Schroder; R. Chr. Meier, R. Boos; Jurgen Hogeforster; Gerd Bernsau.

Private research institute. Staff: 120. **Sources of support:** Commercial clients, on project basis. **Annual Budget:** 10 million Swiss francs.

Objectives and interests: Industrial market research and marketing; management consulting for industry (particularly industrial structure and growth), trade, services, and public administration; urban and regional planning; economic and public policy consulting; general economic research.

Major programs and projects: Approximately 100 projects annually, the results of which are generally of a confidential nature.

Special facilities: Large socioeconomic and technological library and documentation system.

Activities: Staff members engage in management education and training, as well as in general lectures on economics and business, both at universities and training institutions and at PROGNOS' own seminars throughout Europe.

Publications: *Euro-report: Future Trends in Western Europe* (annually); *PROGNOS Reports* (economic and demographic data, issued yearly); *PROGNOS Studies* (concentrating on macroeconomic topics).

PROJECT FORETHOUGHT NETWORK
Telephone: (713) 493-7885

c/o Shell Development Company
Westhollow Research Center, P.O. Box 1380
Houston, Texas 77001, U.S.A.
Founded: 1975

Officers: George T. Coker, Jr., and David C. Miller, Co-Directors.

Informal group of corporate planners. Staff: — **Sources of support:** — **Annual Budget:** —

Objectives and interests: To maintain a network of future-oriented corporate planners.

Major programs and projects: "Survey '79: Consumer Goods Probe—21st Century Overview"—poll of Forethought, plus Planning Executives Institute, North American Society of Corporate Planners, Academy of Management, and selected congressional staffers.

Special facilities: List of 300-400 future-oriented corporate planners.

Activities: Survey '77 completed and reported in "Alternate Futures for the Corporation," presented at The Society of General Systems Research, February 1978.

Publications: *Thresholds & Turningpoints* (monthly).

PROSPECTIVE, INTERNATIONAL CENTER OF RESEARCH AND COMMUNICATION
Telephone: (02) 648-2766

Rue E. Cattoir, 16
Brussels 1050 Belgium
and
Prospective, U.S. Center
106 W. 56 Street
New York, New York 10019, U.S.A.
(212)586-5016 (N.Y.)

Founded: 1969

Officers: Alexandre Lagasse De Locht, International President; Charles M. Grace, President, U.S. Board of Directors; Charles Lagasse, International Director; Bernadette Kenny, Executive director, U.S. Center.

Private, non-profit, research and communication center. Staff: Brussels-15; U.S. Center-3. **Sources of support:** Foundation grants and special gifts. **Annual Budget:** $120,000.

Objectives and interests: Development of a network of horizonal communication among church leaders throughout the world by providing data from diverse cultures and disciplines from which they can develop pastoral solutions to major human problems in order to assist in shaping a better future for humankind.

Major programs and projects: "Development in the Service of Humankind"—file of research from many countries on the cultural, ministerial, political, and economic dimensions of development especially regarding Third World growth. "Childhood and Society"—file presenting the psychological, sociological, pastoral, and cultural dimensions of the role assigned to children in diverse areas of the world. "The Future of Religious Life"—update of file previously published presenting results of five conferences held in 1977-78 on four continents. "Conference on European Legislation on Life Issues"—conference for candidates to the European Legislation on Life Issues —conference for candidates to the European Parliament on moral and ethical implications of current legislation on such issues as abortion, euthanasia, and manipulation of life. "The Church and Development"—a study of the Church as the hope of the poor. "The Church and the Socialization of the Child."

Special facilities: Approximately 80 centers of research in the world have agreed to exchange of documentation. Also maintains a library of books, periodicals, and reports on seminars. Complete sets of files are available for review at the office in Brussels and in New York.

Activities: Abstracts of research data printed on index cards in three languages mailed to subscribers world-wide, four to five times each year; seminars on various topics co-sponsored with other organizations in various countries.

Publications: The Center publishes dossiers in four subject areas: Growth and Progress; Family and Population; Liberation and Society; and Church and Religious Phenomena. A dossier contains 100 four-page files, each of which is the synthesis of a book, an article, or a seminar in the subject area.

PUBLIC POLICY RESEARCH ORGANIZATION

Telephone: (714) 833-5449

University of California, Irvine
Irvine, California 92717, U.S.A.

Founded: 1966

Officers: Kenneth L. Kraemer, Director; Ralph A. Catalano, Associate Director; David G. Schetter, Research Administrator; John L. King and Debora Dunkle, Research Specialists.

University-organized research unit. **Staff:** 30. **Sources of support:** National Science Foundation, National Institute of Mental Health, U.S. Department of Health, Education and Welfare. **Annual Budget:** No answer.

Objectives and interests: Information technology and public policy, environmental policy, administration of public policy, methodological problems of scientific policy studies.

Major programs and projects: "Evaluation of Information Systems in Local Government." "Economy as Stressor of Metropolitan Populations." "Concepts and Issues in Instrumental Computer Use." "Cross-National Comparative Study of Computer Policies and Impacts in Cities." "Diffusion and Adoption of Computer Application Software in Local Government."

Special facilities: Automated data base on management of information technology in local government.

Activities: Presentations at various conferences and seminars; sponsors colloquiums for benefit of University faculty and student researchers.

Publications: *Technology and Public Policy: The Case of EFT*, K. Colton and K.L. Kraemer (forthcoming); *Diffusion and Adoption of Technical Innovation: Computing in American Local Government*, J.L. Perry and K.L. Kraemer (forthcoming); *Computers, Bureaucrats, and Politicians: High Technology in American Local Governments*, URBIS Group (in process); *The Management of Information Systems: Implementation Policy for Computing in American Local Governments*, URBIS Group (in process).

PUGWASH CONFERENCE ON SCIENCE AND WORLD AFFAIRS

Telephone: (01) 405-6661

9 Great Russell Mansions
60 Great Russell Street
London WC1B 3BE, England

Founded: 1957

Officers: Dorothy C. Hodgkin, President; Martin M. Kaplan, Director-General; Edith Salt, Secretary; Madeleine Satin, Secretary.

Private, non-profit. **Staff:** Three. **Sources of support:** Contributions. **Annual Budget:** No answer.

Objectives and interests: To promote international discussions and studies on arms control, disarmament, international security issues, and problems of development.

Major programs and projects: "29th Pugwash Conference on Science and World Affairs"—Mexico City, 18-23 July, 1979: development and security. "33rd Pugwash Symposium"—Helsinki, Finland, 19-21 April, 1979: impact of current political developments and arms control efforts on European security. "Pugwash Workshop on Disarmament and Development"—Vienna, Austria, 21-23 March, 1979. "7th CW Workshop"—joint meeting Pugwash/SIPRI.

Special facilities: Collection of proceedings of 28 conferences since 1957; records of 32 symposia.

Activities: Annual conferences, symposia, workshops (all on an international level).

Publications: *Impacts of New Technologies on the Arms Race*, B. T. Feld, editor (1972); *Future of the Sea-Based Deterrent*, B.T. Feld, editor (1973); *Scientists in the Quest for Peace: History of Pugwash Conferences*, J. Rotblat (1972; supplement, 1977); *A New Design for Nuclear Disarmament*, W. Epstein and T. Toyoda, editors (1977); *Pugwash on Self-Reliance*, W. K. Chagula, B. T. Feld, A. Parthasarathi, editors (1977).

QUANTUM SCIENCE CORPORATION

Telephone: (212) 997-0070

1114 Avenue of the Americas
New York, New York 10036, U.S.A.

Founded: 1961

Officers: John S. Brennan, Vice-President, Operations; Donald Haback, Vice-President, International Marketing; William W. Cain, Executive Vice-President; Mirek J. Stevenson, Chairman of the Board; Donald J. Maguire, Director, European Operations; Thomas Mandel, Director, Computer Studies; Daniel Lavery, Director, Office Studies.

Private research organization. **Staff:** 75, including branch in London. **Sources of support:** All programs are funded by corporations and financial institutions. **Annual Budget:** $4 million.

Objectives and interests: Analyses and forecasts of technology-based industries, such as computer equipment, communications, computer services, and office systems.

Major programs and projects: "Integrated Workstations"—multi-client study defining various occupationally-defined devices incorporating voice, data, text and graphic interfaces (1978-1985). "Consumer Entertainment and Information Systems"—multi-client study analyzing the penetration of digital technology into home markets (1978-1985). "Worldwide Technology Impact"—multi-client study analyzing all new technologies which will impact the information industry (1977-1985).

Special facilities: Maintains extensive data bank on U.S. and European markets, formatted using input-output methodologies.

Activities: Management Action Program in Technology (MAPTEK) U.S.A. and MAPTEK Europe strategy programs, including conferences, reports, inquiry services; multi-cleint studies in areas of technology or product analysis; custom studies carried out by Quantum Consultants, Inc., subsidiary.

Publications: MAPTEK Service is published on a monthly basis with an annual series of major reports on all technological areas. Subscriptions are available on a variety of technologies and geographical areas.

RAAD VIR GEESTESWETENSKAPLIKE NAVORSING
[HUMAN SCIENCES RESEARCH COUNCIL]

Telephone: (012) 483944

Private Bag X41
Pretoria 0001, Transvaal, Republic of South Africa

Founded: 1969

Officers: A. L. Kotzee, President; J. D. Venter, Vice-President; A. J. van Rooy, Vice-President.

Non-profit, research body. **Staff:** Approximately 450. **Sources of support:** South African Treasury. **Annual Budget:** Variable.

Objectives and interests: The Council undertakes, promotes and coordinates research in the human sciences, advises the government and other bodies on the utilization of research findings, and disseminates information on the human sciences.

Major programs and projects: Publication of journal, *RSA 2000*.

Special facilities: Reference library; data banks on information in specialized fields.

Activities: Occasional seminars.

Publications: *Humanitas* (3 to 4 issues/year); *Research Bulletin* (10 issues/year); *RSA 2000* (2 issues/year); *Contree* (2 issues/year); Newsletter (10 issues/year).

THE RAND CORPORATION

1700 Main Street
Santa Monica, California 90406, U.S.A.

Telephone: (213) 393-0411

Founded: 1948

Officers: Donald B. Rice; President; Gustave H. Shubert, Senior Vice-President and Head, Domestic Research Division; William E. Hoehn, Jr., Vice-President, Project Air Force Division; Dale M. Landi, Vice-President, National Security Research Division; George K. Tanham, Vice-President, Washington, D. C. Operations.

Private, non-profit research institution. **Staff:** 1,037: 564 research professionals; 450 professional consultants. **Sources of support:** Federal, state, and local governments; private foundations and other philanthropic sources; funds drawn from fees earned. **Annual Budget:** $36.7 million (fiscal year 1978).

Objectives and interests: To perform research and analysis of matters affecting national security and the public welfare.

Major programs and projects: Emphasis in Rand programs is more on application than on basic research and centers on problems of policy, planning, and development. Domestic programs: criminal justice; education and human resources; energy policy; health sciences; housing; labor and population; regulatory policies and institutions; urban policy. National security programs: applied science and technology; strategic assessment; international security policy; ground warfare; manpower, mobilization, and readiness; information processing systems. Project Air Force programs: technology applications; strategic systems; operations and readiness improvements; theater conflict; manpower, personnel, and training; systems acquisition management.

Special facilities: Library of 63,000 books, 220,000 reports, and 1,700 periodical titles.

Activities: Conferences, seminars, and courses for employees in computer science; Rand Graduate Institute (accredited) offers an innovative graduate program leading to a doctoral degree in policy analysis which couples formal training with on-the-job training in applied analysis through work on Rand research projects.

Publications: *Selected Rand Abstracts* (quarterly journal); Rand publications, including some 300 new titles each year, are placed in subscription libraries worldwide, and individual titles may be purchased directly from Rand. Some titles include: *Giant Oil Fields and World Oil Resources*, Richard Nehring (June 1978); *Doctors, Damages, and Deterrence: An Economic View of Medical Malpractice*, William B. Schwartz and Neil K. Komesar (June 1978); *Nuclear Reactor Spent Fuel Valuation: Procedure, Applications, and Analysis*, Kenneth A. Solomon (November 1978); *Race Differences in Earnings: A Survey and New Evidence*, James P. Smith and Finis Welch (March 1978); *The California Health Facilities Commission: A Case Study of Government Regulation*, Albert J. Lipson (November 1977).

REGIONAL RESEARCH LABORATORY SYSTEMS PLANNING AND RESEARCH MANAGEMENT GROUP

Industrial Estate
Trivandrum 19
Kerala State 695019, India

Telephone: —

Founded: 1977

Officers: P.K. Rohatgi.

Research institute. **Staff:** Four (laboratory strength 80). **Sources of support:** Government funds. **Annual Budget:** Rs. 150 lakhs for the whole laboratory.

Objectives and interests: To carry out strategic planning exercises through forecasting and assessment exercises for identification of research imperatives.

Major programs and projects: "Kerala 2000 A.D."—to forecast the economic and social future of Kerala. "An Assessment of the Solar Water-heater Technology"—to evaluate the cost-benefit of the technology. "Normative Forecasting and Assessment Exercises"—preparing capability and gap profiles with respect to national goals.

Special facilities: Library of books, periodicals and reports.

Activities: Staff members have participated in national and international seminars and training courses.

Publications: "Technology Assessment for India," P.K. Rohatgi, S. Mohan, and R.V.G. Menon (paper, *U.N. Conference of Technology Assessment for Development,* Bangalore, 1978).

RESEARCH FOR BETTER SCHOOLS, INC.

1700 Market Street, Suite 1700
Philadelphia, Pennsylvania 19103, U.S.A.

Telephone: (215) 561-4100

Founded: 1966

Officers: Robert G. Scanlon, Executive Director; John E. Hopkins, Director of Planning and Evaluation; Louis Maguire, Director, Research and Development Division; Richard McCann, Director, Dissemination Division; JoAnn Weinberger, Assistant to the Executive Director.

Private, non-profit, educational research laboratory. Staff: 125. **Sources of support:** National Institute of Education; federal agencies; corporations. **Annual Budget:** No answer.

Objectives and interests: To help elementary and secondary schools improve their educational programs through the design, development and dissemination of school improvement models.

Major programs and projects: "Planning Schools for the Future"—A project designed to conduct systematic research into what student needs will be in 1985 and the setting of clear and defined directions for education so that schools will be able to meet the identified needs.

Special facilities: Maintains a library of books, periodicals, and reports on the future and education.

Activities: National institutional symposia on Anticipating Tomorrow's Schools; technical assistance to education agencies.

Publications: *Planning Schools for the Future* (newsletter, quarterly); *Planning Schools for the Future,* JoAnn Weinberger (1976); *Anticipating Tomorrow's Schools,* Robert G. Scanlon and JoAnn Weinberger (1975); *A Curriculum for Personalized Education,* Robert G. Scanlon (1974); *The Future of Education: Perspectives on Tomorrow's Schools,* Louis J. Rubin (1975); *Educators' Guide for the Future,* Glen Heathers, Jane Roberts, and JoAnn Weinberger (1977); *Educational Reform for a Changing Society,* Louis J. Rubin (1978).

RESEARCH PROGRAM ON TECHNOLOGY AND PUBLIC POLICY

H. B. 8000
Dartmouth College
Hanover, New Hampshire 03755, U.S.A.

Telephone: (603) 646-3551

Founded: 1972

Officers: Dennis Meadows, Director; Thomas Adler, Director, Transportation Systems; Daniel Lynch, Director, Water Resource Systems; Charles Hewett, Director, Forest Resource Systems.

Research and teaching institute. Staff: 30. **Sources of support:** State and Federal organizations, private foundations. **Annual Budget:** No answer.

Objectives and interests: Forecast the long-term dynamics of population-resource interactions; especially interested in the design of steady state systems for resource use.

Major programs and projects: "Power: Potential of Wood Energy Resources"—identify environmental, economic, technical and institutional constraints on increased use of wood for energy. "Case Study in Low-Head Hydropower"—determining the factors that constrain use of low head dams. "Dynamics of Long-Term Fossil Energy Availability"— develop FOSSIL1, a model for long-range forecasting of energy supply.

Special facilities: Operation of a time-sharing computer system that makes models available throughout the United States via Telenet. A collection of more than 100 books and reports are available, with a report list and order form upon request.

Activities: Annual conferences on resource simulation modeling, and a graduate program on the use of computer simulation models for policy assessment.

Publications: *System Dynamics Newsletter* (annual); *The Limits to Growth,* by D.H. Meadows et al (1972); *Dynamics of Growth in a Finite World,* D. L. Meadows et al (1974); *Alternatives to Growth,* D. L. Meadows (1977); *Managing the Energy Transition,* R. N. Naill (1976); *The Electronic Oracles,* D. H. Meadows (in press, 1978).

RESOURCES FOR THE FUTURE
1755 Massachusetts Avenue, N.W.
Washington, D.C. 20036, U.S.A.

Telephone: (202) 462-4400

Founded: 1952

Officers: Charles J. Hitch, President; Emery N. Castle, Vice-President; Gilbert F. White, Chairman of the Board of Directors; Walter Spofford, Director of Quality of the Environment Division; Hans Landsberg, Director, Center for Energy Policy Research; Kenneth Frederick, Director, Renewable Resources Division.

Private, non-profit, research organization. **Staff.** Approximately 90. **Sources of support:** Ford Foundation; other foundations; government and private grants and contracts. **Annual Budget:** No answer.

Objectives and interests: To advance the development, conservation, and use of natural resources and the improvement of the quality of the environment through research and education, with energy as a special concern.

Major programs and projects: Study of alternative national energy policies; environmental policy assessment; examination of differences in international energy consumption and gross national product; assessment of hazardous materials policy issues; studies of forest economics and policies.

Special facilities: Maintains an energy library, including documents of Ford Foundation Energy Policy Project, with limited access to scholars.

Activities: Conferences and seminars, both regularly scheduled and occasional, are held throughout the year, with participants from academe, government, and the private sector. Subjects of these in the past have included U.S. oil import policy; materials modeling; Regional Environmental Quality Management Modeling; Metropolitan Growth and Collective Choice; The International Research Conference on Public Policy and the Quality of Life in Cities; Conference on Population Policy from a Socioeconomic Perspective.

Publications: *Resources* (bulletin, 3 times per year); also publish about 12 books per year.

RISK STUDIES FOUNDATION
205 East 42nd Street
New York, New York 10017, U.S.A.

Telephone: (212) 557-3210

Founded: 1975

Officers: E. W. Altstaetter, Director and President; Rita Epstein, Director and Secretary.

Non-profit, research institute. **Staff:** One. **Sources of support:** The Risk and Insurance Management Society. **Annual Budget:** No answer.

Objectives and interests: To research the multifaceted fields of risk and insurance management in order to contribute to a more universal understanding of the nature of risks facing the community now and in the future.

Major programs and projects: "Decision Making Under Uncertainty with Particular Reference to Risk Management"—study by Gordon Dickson, Glasgow College of Technology, Glasgow, Scotland.

Special facilities: Currently developing library.

Activities: —

Publications: *The Future of Risk* (December 1978); "A Comparative Analysis of Alternative Maximum Probable Loss Estimators," J. David Cummins and Leonard R. Freifelder (*The Journal of Risk and Insurance*, March 1978); *Risk Management in International Corporations*, Norman A. Baglini (April 1976).

RUSSELL SAGE FOUNDATION
230 Park Avenue
New York, New York 10017, U.S.A.

Telephone: (212) 949-8990

Founded: 1907

Officers: Oscar M. Ruebhausen, Chairman of the Board of Trustees; David B. Truman, President, Arnold Shore, Vice-President.

Private, non-profit research foundation. **Staff:** 35, including professional staff, research assistants and full- and part-time administrative staff. **Sources of support:** Endowment. **Annual Budget:** $2.5 million.

Objectives and interests: Established in 1907 by Mrs. Margaret Olivia Sage for the "improvement of social and living conditions in the United States," the Foundation conducts and supports social science research relevant to public policy issues.

Major programs and projects: "Culture"—a program that explores the ways in which shared values and preferences arise. "Citizenship"—a program that examines how particular notions of commitment, obligation, and service to community or nation arise from shared values and preferences. "Institutions"—a program that assesses the structural mechanisms which translate the values and preferences of citizens into public policies. "Policy Analysis"—a program that attempts to impove the practice and theory of public policy formulation: sub-areas include New York City, Human Resources, and Tehnical Policy Analysis (energy studies).

Special facilities: —

Activities: The four research program areas currently supported by the Foundation are: culture, citizenship, institutions, and policy analysis. Each of these programs is under the direction of a resident scholar. In addition to conducting research in their own areas of interest, program directors solicit and evaluate proposals for projects consistent with the objectives of each program area and sponsor special seminars in these areas.

Publications: *Regulatory Justice: Implementing a Wage-Price Freeze*, Robert A. Kagan (1978); *Models in the Policy Process: Public Decision Making in the Computer Era*, Martin Greenberger, Matthew A. Crenson, and Brian L. Crissey (1976); *Union Representation Elections: Law and Reality*, Julius G. Getman, Stephen B. Goldberg, and Jeanne B. Herman (1976); *The Quality of American Life: Perceptions, Evaluations, and Satisfactions*, Angus Campbell, Philip E. Converse, and Willard L. Rodgers (1976); *The New Presidential Elite: Men and Women in National Politics*, Jeane Kirkpatrick (1976).

SCHOOL OF LIVING

Deep Run, RD 7, Box 388A
York, Pennsylvania 17402, U.S.A.

Telephone: (717) 755-1561

Founded: 1936

Officers: Jean Petty Austin, Chairman of the Board; Jubal Stucki, President; Evan Lefver, Secretary; Mildred J. Loomis, Director of Education; Arnold Greenberg, School of Homesteading; Rri Ho Wats, Editor, *The Green Revolution.*

Independent, non-profit educational association. **Staff:** Four and four assistants. **Sources of support:** Membership fees and subscriptions to the monthly journal. **Annual Budget:** No answer.

Objectives and interests: Adult education in objectively defining and dealing with universal, major problems of living.

Major programs and projects: Apprenticeships in rural-community living; nine-month School of Homesteading in learning self-reliant lifestyle and modern homesteading.

Special facilities: Maintains a library of books catalogued under Major Universal Problems of Living.

Activities: Monthly public workshops in universal major problems.

Publications: *The Green Revolution* (monthly journal); *School of Living Monthly News* (free to members); *The Decentralist Manifesto*, Ralph Borsodi (reprinted, 1979); *Flight from the City*, Ralph Borsodi (1933); *This Ugly Civilization*, Ralph Borsodi (1928); *Seventeen Major Problems of Living*, Ralph Borsodi (1977); *What to Do About Inflation* (December, 1978); *School of Living* (free brochure).

SCHWEIZERISCHE VEREINIGUNG FUR ZUKUNFTSFORSCHUNG
[SWISS ASSOCIATION FOR FUTURES RESEARCH]

Weinbergstrasse 17
CH-8623 Wetzikon, Switzerland

Telephone: (01) 930 40 27

Founded: 1971

Officers: B. Fritsch, President; G. Kocher, Vice-President; Paul Dubach, Secretary.

Membership organization. **Staff:** One. **Sources of support:** Membership dues. **Annual Budget:** 40,000 Swiss francs.

Objectives and interests: Coordination of future research in Switzerland; understanding of future problems; development of new methods of research; bulletin on future research subjects; cooperation with other international organizations.

Major programs and projects: "Delphi Survey on Traffic Development in Switzerland"—36 questions, 90 partici-

98

pants. "Future of the Health System in Switzerland"—publication of the 1973 seminar. "Study on Cost-effectiveness Methods in Process." "Innovation Processes."

Special facilities: Library of Swiss titles on futures research.

Activities: Seminars, working teams, methodology courses, delphi surveys.

Publications: *Bulletin* (bimonthly); *Zukunft Schweiz [The Future of Switzerland]*, B. Fritsch and P. Dubach (1971); *Die Zukunft des Verkehrs in der Schweiz [The Future of Transportation in Switzerland]*, H. Schloch, editor (1975); *Grenzen der Forschung und Innovation [Limits of Research and Innovation]* (1976); *Praktische Zukunftsforschung [Practical Futures Research]* (1978).

SCIENCE COUNCIL OF CANADA
100 Metcalfe Street, 17th Floor
Ottawa, Ontario K1P 5MI, Canada

Telephone: (613) 996-1729

Founded: 1966

Officers: Claude Fortier, Chairman; J.J. Shepherd, Vice-Chairman and Executive Director; R.D. Voyer, Research and Administration Director; R.W. Jackson, Science Advisor; J. Miedzinski, Secretary.

Crown corporation, advisory council. Staff: 15-20 professionals. **Sources of support:** Government of Canada. **Annual Budget:** $2 million.

Objectives and interests: To assess Canada's scientific and technological resources and to make recommendations thereon to the Minister; to improve political and public awareness of issues involving science and technology.

Major programs and projects: "Industrial Prospects"—an analysis of Canada's manufacturing industries. "Canada's Transportation Future"—studies on an integrated freight and passenger transportation system for Canada. "Canada's Energy Opportunities"—studies on Canada's options for energy supply. "Canada's Role in a World Short of Food"—development of a food policy for Canada.

Special facilities: Library.

Activities: Studies, reports, committees, seminars.

Publications: *Agenda* (quarterly); *Annual Report;* continuing series of Reports, with policy recommendations (e.g., *Policies and Poisons; Canada as a Conserver Society: Resource Uncertainties and the Need for New Technologies*, No. 27); continuing series of Background Studies (e.g., *The Weakest Link: A Technological Perspective on Canadian Industrial Underdevelopment*, No. 43; *Human Goals and Science Policy*, No. 38; *Knowledge, Power and Public Policy*, No. 31); *Uncertain Prospects: Canadian Manufacturuing Industry 1971-1977.*

SCIENCE POLICY FOUNDATION
Benjamin Franklin House
36 Craven Street
London WC2N 5NG England

Telephone: (01) 839-4985

Founded: 1966

Officers: Herman Bondi, President; Harry Melville, Chairman; Maurice Goldsmith, Director.

Non-profit educational trust. Staff: Five. **Sources of support:** Membership, endowments, special contracts, publications. **Annual Budget:** No answer.

Objectives and interests: To promote the study of science and technology: internally, to seek to determine science and technology laws of growth; externally, to study the impact on social institutions and behavior, both industrial and political.

Major programs and projects: "British Economic Predicament"—economic, industrial and social policy for the next 25 years. "Creation of Federation of European Science Policy Organizations."

Special facilities: Specialized collections in libraries at the University of Sussex, Brunel University, Manchester University, and the CSIR (India).

Activities: Annual lecture; biennial conference; eight to ten seminars per year.

Publications: *Science and Public Policy*, Maurice Goldsmith, editor (bimonthly); *Outlook on Science Policy*, Maurice

Goldsmith, editor (monthly newsletter); *Strategies for Europe: Proposals for Science and Technology Policies*, European Economic Community (1977); *A Strategy for Resources*, Maurice Goldsmith, et al., editors (1976); *Decisionmaking in Science Policy*, De Reuck, M. Goldsmith and J. Knight, editors (1968); *Science and Social Responsibility*, M. Goldsmith, editor (1975); *Forward Planning in the Service Sectors*, M. Goldsmith, editor (1975).

SECRETARIAT FOR FUTURE STUDIES

Box 7502
103 92 Stockholm
Sweden

Telephone: (08) 763 10 00

Founded: 1973

Officers: Lars Ingelstam; Goran Backstrand; Ola Johansson; Ann-Kristin Wentzel.

Government. Staff: Secretariat—Seven; Project members—about 20. **Sources of support:** Swedish government. **Annual Budget:** 3.62 million Swedish kronor.

Objectives and interests: Background material for decision-making in a long-term perspective; promotion of public debate on future-oriented questions.

Major programs and projects: "Care in Society." "Sweden in a New Economic World Order." "The Vulnerable Society." "Forecasting and Political Futures Planning."

Special facilities: —

Activities: Conferences with participation from government administration and from researchers; seminars for government employees; symposia with university participation.

Publications: Publications within each futures study project.

SECRETARIAT FOR FUTURES STUDIES, GOVERNMENT OF CANADA MINISTRY OF STATE FOR SCIENCE AND TECHNOLOGY

270 Albert Street
Ottawa, Ontario, Canada K1A 1A1

Telephone: (613) 996-0601

Founded: 1976

Officers: H. Alan Raymond, Head of the Secretariat.

Governmental organization. Staff: Five full-time, two part-time. **Sources of support:** Federal Government. **Annual Budget:** No answer.

Objectives and interests: Futures studies; alternative futures; policy research; futures methodology; resource utilization; social priorities; population.

Major programs and projects: Futures workshops on specific topics such as energy and methodology; annual review of Canadian and related futures research, describing all current futures research related to Canada; a summary and analysis of futures research in the Canadian federal government—Lamontagne I.

Special facilities: Futures Reference Centre, tapes of meetings and workshops.

Activities: Secretariat holds a number of meetings of the Interdepartmental Committee on Futures Research and a number of futures workshops for the Canadian federal government in general.

Publications: A summary and analysis of futures research in the Canadian federal government published by the Canadian Senate Committee on Science Policy.

SELSKAPET FOR FREMTIDSSTUDIER (SEFREM)
[NORWEGIAN SOCIETY FOR FUTURE STUDIES]

Teatergaten 1
Oslo 1, Norway

Telephone: (02) 11 27 96

Founded: 1972

Officers: Jan Henrik Nyheim, Director; Oivind Due Trier; Steinar Tangeraas; Guri Berg, Accountant, Head of Secretariat; Daniel Liseth, Editor, Information Activities.

Private, non-profit membership organization. Staff: Two. **Sources of support:** Membership fees. **Annual Budget:** $50,000.

100

Objectives and interests: To serve as main forum for futures studies in Norway; to provide an information service and library on the future.

Major programs and projects: "Word Processing and the Future Office"—seminar. "Long-range Planning Methods"—seminar. "The Inter-dependence of Telecommunications and Society, and Planning of New Telecommunications Networks"—committee, seminar. "The Relationship (If Any) Between Economic Depressions and Planning/Forecasting Activities"—meeting/seminar. "Review of Long-range Planning Activities Within Institutional Members"—initiated 1978, probably complete 1979.

Special facilities: Library.

Activities: Seminars, study groups, funding of future research.

Publications: *SEFREM-Kontakt* (newsletter, six times a year); *Communication and the Future* (1975, in Norwegian); *Oil and the Norwegian Economy* (1975, in Norwegian).

THE SIMULATION AND GAMING ASSOCIATION (SAGA)
4833 Greentree Road
Lebanon, Ohio 45036, U.S.A.

Telephone: (513) 423-0036

Founded: 1972

Officers: Michael J. Raymond, Executive Director; Gerry Malueg, President; Mary Jane Rodabaugh, Vice-President; Betty Barclay Franks, Game Designer; Harvard W. McLean, Researcher-Designer; Anna Mayans, Researcher.

Non-profit, teacher-controlled, educational association. Staff: One full-time; one part-time. **Sources of support:** Donations, subscriptions, and purchases of products. **Annual Budget:** Variable.

Objectives and interests: To improve classroom instruction through the use of simulation and gaming techniques, through game design, research, and the publication of teacher-made materials.

Major programs and projects: "Future Decisions: The I.Q. Game" (second edition). "Design Your Own Game" (second edition)—A booklet to guide the step-by-step design of a simulation or game. "Kibbutz!"—A simulation dealing with the various decisions necessary for the creation of a kibbutz in Israel.

Special facilities: All facilities are restricted to members.

Activities: Co-sponsor Simulation and Gaming Workshops throughout Ohio; participate in various national conventions; serve as consultants to various local school districts.

Publications: *The Saga Journal* (quarterly); *Kama* (a simulation dealing with a post-colonial African Country) Michael J. Raymond (1973); *A Directory of Environmental Simulations and Games,* Harvard W. McLean and Steven Hawley (1973); *Reapportionment* (deals with Congressional reapportionment in a hypothetical state of the union) Tom Ryan (1973); *Mortgage* (simulation of house purchasing) Jack W. Reynolds (1976); *Southern Mountaineer* (a simulation of family life in the Southern mountains in the early 20th century) Michael J. Raymond and Anna Mayans; *Programa de Integracao Nacional: The Conference for Amazonian Development* Edwin R. Smith (1977).

SIMULATION IN THE SERVICE OF SOCIETY
8484 La Jolla Shores Drive
La Jolla, California 92037, U.S.A.

Telephone: (714) 454-0966

Founded: 1970

Officers: Suzette McLeod, Managing Editor; John McLeod, Technical Editor.

Private organization. Staff: Two. **Sources of support:** Sale of publication. **Annual Budget:** No answer.

Objectives and interests: Promote the use of simulation for the study of societal systems.

Major programs and projects: —

Special facilities: Specialized collection of books, proceedings, and papers related to the use of models and simulation.

Activities: Compiling, editing and writing the newsletter *Simulation in the Service of Society.*

Publications: *Simulation in the Service of Society,* John McLeod, editor (published monthly as a special feature of *Simulation,* the technical journal of the Society for Computer Simulation).

SOCIAAL EN CULTUREEL PLANBUREAU
[SOCIAL AND CULTURAL PLANNING OFFICE]
J. C. van Markenlaan 3
Rijswijk, The Netherlands

Telephone: (070) 949330

Founded: 1974

Officers: A.J.v.d.Staay, Director; A.P.N. Nauta, Deputy Director

Government planning office. **Staff:** 28. **Sources of support:** Government budget. **Annual Budget:** 3 million Dutch florin.

Objectives and interests: National planning in the field of social and cultural policy.

Major programs and projects: "Social and Cultural Report" (English translation available) — periodical analysis of the social and cultural situation. "Survey of Living Conditions in the Netherlands" — produced by the Central Bureau of Statistics. "Norms and Values in the Netherlands" — measurement of cultural change in the Netherlands.

Special facilities: Specialized library, data-tapes of research projects for further analysis.

Activities: Primarily research.

Publications: A series of cahiers on specialized subjects. "Manpower Planning for the Public Sector." "The Budget Incidence."

SOCIAL IMPACT ASSESSMENT NETWORK
c/o C.P. Wolf
Environmental Psychology Program
CUNY Graduate Center
33 West 42nd Street
New York, New York 10036, U.S.A.

Telephone: (212) 790-4553

Founded: 1974

Officers: C.P. Wolf, Coordinator.

Voluntary interest group. **Staff:** None. **Sources of support:** None. **Annual Budget:** None.

Objectives and interests: To stimulate interest in social impact assessment among government and corporate officials and the general public; to develop the methodology of social impact assessment and encourage its application in technology assessment, cultural resources, environmental design and related fields; and to improve communication among practitioners and interested others.

Major programs and projects: None.

Special facilities: None.

Activities: Annual and special conferences; informal consultations.

Publications: *Social Impact Assessment* (monthly newsletter), C.P. Wolf, editor.

SOCIAL SCIENCE RESEARCH COUNCIL (UK)
1 Temple Avenue
London EC4Y OBD United Kingdom

Telephone: (01) 353 5252

Founded: 1965

Officers: Michael V. Posner, Chairman of Council; Cyril S. Smith, Secretary.

Incorporated by Royal Charter. **Staff:** 218, including Research Units in Oxford, Cambridge, Warwick, and Bristol. **Sources of support:** Her Majesty's Government, by grant-in-aid through the Department of Education and Science. **Annual Budget:** 15.5 million pounds (research grants, about 4 million pounds).

Objectives and interests: The encouragement and support of research in the social sciences; the provision and operation of services in carrying out research; the provision of grants for post-graduate instruction in the social sciences; the dissemination of knowledge concerning the social sciences.

Major programs and projects: The support of research, through the subject committees in Area Studies, Computing, Economic and Social History, Economics, Education, Human Geography, Management and Industrial Relations, Linguistics, Planning, Political Science and International Relations, Psychology, Social Anthropology, Social Sciences and the Law, Sociology and Social Administration, and Statistics. The Research Initiatives Board explores issues of topical and interdisciplinary concern.

Special facilities: Library, information services; final reports of SSRC programs and projects are filed in the British Library Lending Division.

Activities: Conferences and seminars in the areas indicated under "Major Programs and Projects."

Publications: *Forecasting and the Social Sciences,* Michael Young, editor (1968); *Progress and Problems in Social Forecasting,* Freeman, Jahoda, and Miles, editors (1976); *Forecasting in Urban and Regional Planning,* Donald Cross (1976); *Research Supported by the SSRC 1975.*

SOCIAL SCIENCE RESEARCH COUNCIL, CENTER FOR COORDINATION OF RESEARCH ON SOCIAL INDICATORS

Telephone: (202) 667-8884

1755 Massachusetts Avenue, N.W.
Washington, D.C. 20036, U.S.A.

Founded: 1972

Officers: Eleanor Bernert Sheldon, President, Social Science Research Council; Robert Parke, Director, Center for Coordination of Research on Social Indicators; Nancy Carmichael, Librarian and Newsletter Editor.

Private, non-profit research organization. Staff: Eight. **Sources of support:** U.S. National Science Foundation, Division of Social Sciences, Office of Special Projects and Social Indicators. **Annual Budget:** No answer.

Objectives and interests: The Social Science Research Council seeks to advance research in the social sciences, primarily through the planning, appraisal, and stimulation of research that offers promise of increasing knowledge in social science or of increasing its usefulness to society. The Center for Coordination of Research on Social Indicators seeks to enhance the contribution of social science research to the development of a broad range of indicators of social change.

Major programs and projects: —

Special facilities: Research library on social indicators, open to those engaged in research on social indicators and social change.

Activities: The Center provides communications about research in the social indicators field through its library, the *Social Indicators Newsletter,* journal articles and papers, and other means, and seeks to identify and advance the interests of the field through research planning in the field generally and in the specific areas of criminal justice indicators, science indicators, and the measurement of neighborhood quality.

Publications: *Survey Data for Trend Analysis: An Index to Repeated Questions in U.S. National Surveys Held by the Roper Public Opinion Research Center,* Philip K. Hastings and Jessie Southwick, editors (1974); *Basic Background Items for U.S. Household Surveys,* Roxann A. Van Dusen and Nicholas Zill, editors (1975); *Towards a Metric of Science,* Yehuda Elkana, Joshua Lederberg, Robert K. Merton, and Harriet Zuckerman, editors (1978); *A Research Agenda for the National Longitudinal Surveys of Labor Market Experience: A Report on the Social Science Research Council's Conference on the National Longitudinal Surveys,* October 1977 (May 1978).

SOCIETE D'ETUDES ET D'EXPANSION [SOCIETY OF STUDIES AND EXPANSION]

Telephone: (41) 32 0600

Avenue Rogier, 12
4000 Liege, Belgium

Founded: 1902

Officers: P. Latteur, Chairman of the Board; M. Aldenhoff, Director; J. C. Lahaut, Manager; M. Desamory, General Secretary.

Non-profit, international, scientific association consulative to the Council of Europe and ECOSOC of the U.N. Staff: Five. **Sources of support:** Members (including corporations and governments). **Annual Budget:** No answer.

Objectives and interests: Main socio-economic problems in relation to the future.

Major programs and projects: "Persons and Society." "Citizens and Community." "Personnel and Companies." "International Economic Order."

Special facilities: 25,000-volume library on human sciences, economy, management, and international law and policy.

Activities: Conferences; seminars; library (main languages French and English).

Publications: *Etudes et Expansion* (review; 4 times/year).

SOCIETY FOR COMPUTER SIMULATION (SCS)

Telephone: (714) 459-3888

P.O. Box 2228
La Jolla, California 92038, U.S.A.

Founded: 1952

Officers: President and national officers elected annually; R. R. Favreau, Director of Publications; C. G. Stocton, Manager of Operations; Natalie Fowler, Managing Editor; Stanley Rogers, Publisher.

Non-profit organizations. Staff: 10. Sources of support: Membership; sales of publications; advertising.
Annual Budget: No answer.

Objectives and interests: Advancing the state-of-the-art and science of computer modeling and simulation.

Major programs and projects: —

Special facilities: Specialized collection of books, proceedings, and papers related to simulation.

Activities: Publishing; conferences; seminars; courses.

Publications: *Simulation*, N. Fowler, editor (monthly); *SCS Proceedings*, S. Rogers, editor; proceedings of conferences sponsored or co-sponsored by SCS.

SOCIETY FOR THE INVESTIGATION OF RECURRING EVENTS

Telephone: —

Box 477
Linden, New Jersey 07036, U.S.A.

Founded: 1960

Officers: Donald D. MacAlpine, President; Susan Hardt, Vice President; Cecelia K. Walzer, Vice President; Arthur A. Merrill, Secretary; Basil Shanahan, Treasurer; Michael G. Zahorchak, President Emeritus.

Non-profit membership organization. Staff: Volunteers. **Sources of support:** Membership dues.
Annual Budget: No answer.

Objectives and interests: To study cyclical (recurring) phenomena; to provide a forum where proponents of various rhythms can present their views and be questioned on them. All members of SIRE, whether scientists, investment counselors, journalists, educators, or medical doctors, share "the same basic interest in what causes the rhythmic, or at least quasi-rhythmic, fluctuations in moods, markets, tides, typhoons, hurricanes, and horse races."

Major programs and projects: Monthly dinner meetings in New York City with speaker on some aspect of recurring events, e.g., "Commodity Cycle Forecasting," "Rhythms in Human Moods," "Is Earthquake Occurrence Cyclic?"

Special facilities: —

Activities: —

Publications: Monthly digest of speaker's remarks.

SOCIETY FOR LONG RANGE PLANNING

Telephone: (01) 730 0466

8th Floor, Terminal House, Grosvenor Gardens
London SW1W OAR, England

Founded: 1965

Officers: S. Temple, Administrative Secretary.

Non-profit, professional, educational organization. Staff: Two. **Sources of support:** Subscriptions. **Annual Budget:** No answer.

Objectives and interests: To exchange and extend information pertinent to long range planning available to corporate planners, industry, government, and the academic world; to enhance the skills of long range planners.

Major programs and projects: Futures Study Group.

Special facilities: —

Activities: Conferences, seminars, regional groups, study groups, and general meetings, held regularly on various aspects of planning.

Publications: *Long Range Planning* (bimonthly); Newsletter (bimonthly); *Case Studies in Corporate Planning,* Peter Baynes (1973); *Corporate Planner's Yearbook,* David Hussey (1974).

(From the first edition. Corrections not received by press time.)

SOCIOCYBERNEERING, INC.

2919 S. W. 36th Avenue
Miami, Florida 33133, U.S.A.

Telephone: (305) 443-2895

Founded: 1971

Officers: Jacque Fresco, President; Josephy Fasula, Vice-President; Birgit Lahaye, Secretary/Treasurer; Don Gillette, Karl Geissler, Roxanne Meadows.

Non-profit. Staff: 13. **Sources of support:** Donations. **Annual Budget:** No answer.

Objectives and interests: Finding alternative solutions to present day social problems.

Major programs and projects: Conservation of energy; international cooperation in all areas of social endeavor; overall social design in accordance with the highest standard of science and technology and humanities.

Special facilities: Collection and assimilation of a systems approach in design for major cities.

Activities: Lectures, seminars, films.

Publications: *Introduction to Sociocyberneering* (1977); *Determinance of Behavior* (1978); *Cities in Transition* (1978); *Introduction to Sociocyberneering* (1978).

UNIVERSITY OF SOUTHERN CALIFORNIA, CENTER FOR FUTURES RESEARCH

Graduate School of Business Administration
Los Angeles, California 90007, U.S.A.

Telephone: (213) 741-5229

Founded: 1971

Officers: Burt Nanus, Director; Selwyn Enzer, Associate Director; Wayne I. Boucher, Senior Research Associate and Director of Publications; James O'Toole, Senior Research Associate; Paul Gray, Senior Research Associate; Olaf Helmer, Harold Quinton Professor of Futures Research (Emeritus).

University research institute. Staff: Approximately 20 full- and part-time professionals. **Sources of support:** 80 percent corporations and foundations; 20 percent government. **Annual Budget:** Approximately $300,000.

Objectives and interests: To develop methodologies to study social change; conduct multi-disciplinary policy analyses and forecasts in major economic, technological, social, and business areas.

Major programs and projects: "The Future Environments of International Trade"—sponsored by 15 corporations. "Emerging Social and Worker Entitlements"—sponsored by 18 corporations. "Technology Assessment of the Personal Computer"—National Science Foundation. "The Future of Network Information Services"—sponsored by 10 corporations. "Interax: Interactive Cross-impact Simulation"—sponsored by 10 corporations.

Special facilities: —

Activities: Holds workshop on "futures research techniques for corporate planners" three or four times a year; occasional seminars for businessmen, academics and government officials; regular graduate courses in long-range planning and futures research.

Publications: Annual report and bimonthly newsletter available free; approximately 70 other working papers available at cost; *Energy and Social Change,* James O'Toole (MIT Press, 1976); *Neither Feast Nor Famine,* Selwyn Enzer et al. (Lexington Books, 1978); *The Telecommunications-Transportation Tradeoff,* Nilles et al. (Wiley, 1976); *The Social Implications of the Use of Computers Across National Boundaries,* Burt Nanus et al. (AFIPS Press, 1973).

SQUARE ONE MANAGEMENT, LTD.

No. 302 - 100 Gloucester Street
Ottawa, Ontario, Canada K2P OA4

Telephone: (613) 236-9712

Founded: 1970

Officers: Ruben F.W. Nelson, President; Betty Weinstein, Senior Consultant.

Private consulting firm. **Staff:** Four. **Sources of support:** Government and corporate clients. **Annual Budget:** No answer.

Objectives and interests: To seek out, generate and develop ideas, understandings, institutional forms and practices which contribute to, rather than threaten, a future fit to live in.

Major programs and projects: "Cultural Paradigms Project" — the largest Canadian survey and evaluation of futures literature. "Selection, Transaction and Promotion of Non-Theatrical Film" — development of a system to provide information and distribution of non-theatrical film in Canada. "Cope with Change: Get a Grip on the '80s" — an intensive, limited enrollment, two or three day seminar on fundamental change. "Alternative Social Futures" — a university-level course, designed to get at alternative foundations for an alternative future. "Understanding and Using Futures Thinking" — a one-day seminar presenting a substantial and critical introduction to futures studies.

Special facilities: In-house library focussing on social foundations and alternative futures.

Activities: Consulting, social research, conference designing, public participation advisement, public and in-house seminars.

Publications: *The Illusions of Urban Man*, Ruben F.W. Nelson (1976).

ST. GALLER ZENTRUM FUR ZUKUNFTSFORSCHUNG
[ST. GALLER CENTER FOR FUTURES RESEARCH]

Guisanstrasse 92
CH-9010 St. Gallen, Switzerland

Telephone: (071) 25 58 88

Founded: 1968

Officers: F. Kneschaurek; H.G. Graf.

Non-profit organization. **Staff:** 10. **Sources of support:** National government; industry. **Annual Budget:** 350,000 Swiss francs.

Objectives and interests: Long-term economic development of Switzerland.

Major programs and projects: Population and the working force; alternative trends of long-term economic development in Switzerland; the qualification of the working force in Switzerland; the structure of the Swiss economy; political action and economic trends.

Special facilities: Library, computerized data collection on international, national, structural, and regional economically relevant materials.

Activities: Seminars; publications.

Publications: *Mitteilungen* (newsletter, published quarterly); *Demographic Trends in Switzerland Until 2000* (1978); *Swiss Long-Term Growth-Potential* (1978); *Economic Development by Branches of Activity in Switzerland, 1960-1990,* (1978); *Perspectives and Problems of Swiss Economic Development* (forthcoming).

STANFORD RESEARCH INSTITUTE, BUSINESS INTELLIGENCE PROGRAM

Telephone: (415) 326-6200

333 Ravenswood Avenue
Menlo Park, California 94025, U.S.A.

Founded: 1958

Officers: Paul E. Shay, Director; Nevin K. Hiester, Associate Director; John M. Stearns, Director, Marketing; Frank Rosten, Director, BIP Europe; Jean W. Nelson, Manager, Reserach Reports Group; Rosemarie Short, Manager, Inquiry Services.

Division of a non-profit research institute. **Staff:** 70. **Sources of support:** Program membership fees. **Annual Budget:** $3 million.

Objectives and interests: An ongoing, international, multiclient, research program, studying the business world and reporting on any change—economic, social, technological, or political—that will have major implications for corporate management.

Major programs and projects: "Secure ADP Auditing"—provides guidelines for a systematic and intensive audit of automated data-processing systems and activities. "New Approaches to Long-term Medical Care"—a comparison of eight alternative settings, now in operation, which are better suited to health needs than are nursing homes and similar hospital-like settings. "Strategic Planners Scan the Future"—discusses today's trends—economic, political, social and technological—and how they can produce changes that will powerfully affect a company's future.

Special facilities: Information centers in Menlo Park, California, London, and Tokyo. Backup files and reference collections. Intensive literature surveillance in Menlo Park and London, both qualitative and quantitative.

Activities: Seminars and meetings; consulting; special information searches for clients.

Publications: *Datalog* (monthly)—informs members of work in progress, and research of interest to the business community; *Research Reports*—in-depth analyses and forecasts on vital subjects for the next 10-year period; *Guidelines*—brief reports on the next two- to five-year period; *World Diesel Engine Markets*, N. Stoller (April 1978); *Personal Computers: Future Uses in Home and Office* (October 1978); *Vulnerability Analysis in Business Planning*, D. Hurd (November 1977); *U. S. Economic Growth to 1990*, D. Baron (February 1978).

STANFORD RESEARCH INSTITUTE, CENTER FOR THE STUDY OF SOCIAL POLICY

333 Ravenswood Avenue
Menlo Park, California 94025, U.S.A.

Telephone: (415) 326-6200

Founded: 1967

Officers: Thomas C. Thomas, Director; Willis W. Harman, Associate Director.

Independent, non-profit research institute. **Staff:** 30. **Sources of support:** Government, foundations, corporations. **Annual Budget:** No answer.

Objectives and interests: Assisting government and business leaders in their assessment and formulation of policies that will simultaneously address current needs and help direct the nation's institutions toward a workable, high quality future.

Major programs and projects: "Transportation Energy Demand in Alternative Futures" (Department of Energy)—four alternative scenarios, 1978-2025, transportation energy demand projections by mode and methodology. "Potential Changes in the Use and Characteristics of the Automobile" (Office of Technology Assessment)—impact assessment of potential future federal automobile policies in the context of alternative futures scenarios. "Transportation in America's Future: Potentials for the Next Half Century" (Department of Transportation)—long range projections of U. S. transportation technology, infrastructure, and modal demand in the context of alternative scenarios, 1975-2025. "Future Technology in the California Desert" (Bureau of Land Management)—technology forecasts to the year 2000 in eight topic areas, including recreations, transportation, energy, and agriculture. Studies of the future of the U.S. automobile industry for various corporate clients, emphasizing social and institutional as well as traditional factors.

Special facilities: Maintain special collection of books, periodicals, reports, and clippings on futures, social policy, images of man, societal problems, energy policy, education research, and social trends. (Not for public use.) Access to extensive professional staff and facilities of Stanford Research Institute.

Activities: Mainly research studies.

Publications: *A Methodology for Developing Alternative Futures Scenarios*, T. F. Mandel (1978); *Solar Energy in America's Future: A Preliminary Assessment*, John S. Reuvl et al. (1977); *Handbook of Forecasting Techniques*, Mitchell, Arnold et al. (1975); *Minimum Standards for Quality of Life*, O. W. Markley and M. D. Bagley (1975); *Plausibility of a Restricted Energy Use Scenario*, J. Armstrong and Willis Harman (1975); *City Size and the Quality of Life*, Duane Elgin (1974); *Changing Images of Man*, O. W. Markley et al. (1974).

UNIVERSITY OF STELLENBOSCH, UNIT FOR FUTURES RESEARCH

Stellenbosch, Cape Province
7600 South Africa

Telephone: (02231) 72862

Founded: 1974

Officers: J. L. Sadie, Director, Bureau of Economic Research; R. J. van Wyk, Deputy-Director, Bureau for Economic Research; E. Dostal, Research Officer.

Research institute. **Staff:** Five. **Sources of support:** 33 Associates, mainly corporations, plus public utilities and foundations. **Annual Budget:** No answer.

Objectives and interests: To analyze future trends in order to identify possible opportunities for threats to, or constraints on, the business community; to prepare useful management information on the basis of these analyses.

Major programs and projects: Provision of management information to 33 associated organizations; special project on housing requirements and supply; special project on manpower demand and supply; special project on resources, waste accumulation, and recycling.

Special facilities: Reading room for the Unit for Futures Research and its Associates.

Activities: Special interest meetings for Associates; Annual General Meeting.

Publications: Issues periodic bulletins and newsletters to Associates; *Some Long-Term Trends in South Africa*, R.J. van Wyk; *A Management Guide to Futures Studies; The Future—A Maker's Handbook*, A. T. Williams (forthcoming).

STICHTING TOEKOMSTBEELD DER TECHNIEK   **Telephone:** (070) 646800
[THE FUTURE SHAPE OF TECHNOLOGY FOUNDATION]
Prinsessegracht 23
The Hague, The Netherlands   **Founded:** 1868

Officers: A.E. Pannenborg, Chairman; J.H.F. van Apeldoorn, Project Engineer; H.K. Boswijk, Project Engineer; R.G.F. De Groot, Project Engineer.

Independent, private, non-profit, research institute.   **Staff:** Seven.   **Sources of support:** The Netherlands Government, Netherlands industry and business, and the Royal Institute of Engineers in The Netherlands.   **Annual Budget:** Approximately 700,000 guilders.

Objectives and interests: The aims of the Foundation are twofold: to study, from the viewpoint of the engineering sciences, possible future technological developments and explore their interaction with other social trends; and to give wide publicity to the findings of the studies, thereby contributing to the construction of a more integrated picture of the future pattern of life in the Netherlands.

Major programs and projects: "Data Handling and the Medical Profession"; "Distribution of Consumer Goods": "The Impact of the Electronic Revolution"; "Industry"; "Forestry."

Special facilities: —

Activities: Holds conferences about study results for business, government, academia, and all those who have an interest in the specific subject. Publishes study results in book format.

Publications: *Feeding the World: Place and Role of the European Economic Community*, several authors (1976); *New Approaches of Urban Transportation Problems*, many authors, edited by J. Overeem (1976); *Materials for Our Society*, many authors, edited by J.A. Over (1976); *Industry in The Netherlands: A Survey of Problems and Options*, H.K. Boswijk, editor (1978); *Future of Industry in The Netherlands*, H.K. Boswijk, editor (1978).

UNIVERSITY OF SUSSEX, SCIENCE POLICY RESEARCH UNIT
                                        Telephone: (0273) 686758
Mantell Building, Falmer
Brighton, Sussex BN1 9RF, U.K.   **Founded:** 1966

Officers: Christopher Freeman, Director; C. H. G. Oldham, Deputy Director; J. K. Fuller, Secretary.

University research unit.   **Staff:** 35-40   **Sources of support:** Foundations, research councils, international organizations, government agencies, industry.   **Annual Budget:** 360,000 pounds sterling.

Objectives and interests: To contribute to the advancement of knowledge of the complex social process of research, invention, development, innovation, and diffusion of innovations, and thereby to a deeper understanding of policy for science and technology. To study the research-innovation complex of events in industry and in government, as well as in universities, and in the context of the environment in developing countries, as well as in industrialized societies. The range of interests inherently has an important forecasting component, since any innovative activity requires imaginative guesswork about the future.

Major programs and projects: "Forecasting Techniques"—A range of sub-projects enabling the Unit to make some original contributions to the development and improvement of various forecasting methods and to test out their feasibility for a variety of applications. "Future Patterns of Social Organization"—

108

Projects on the quality of life, on Britain and the post-industrial society, and on future forms of participation. "Socio-technical Sectors"—Long-term global forecasting in relation to three key sectors of the world economy: energy, food, and materials. "Technology Assessment"—Specific technologies being assessed are transport (electric car) and chemical weapons; includes some methodological studies.

Special facilities: Specialized research library.

Activities: Primarily research; also some undergraduate and postgraduate teaching, mainly in the "History and Social Studies of Science" subject group.

Publications: *Research Policy* (quarterly journal, together with colleagues from the Federal Republic of Germany and France); *Models of Doom: A Critique of The Limits to Growth* (1973); *The Art of Anticipation* (1975); *Global Simulation Models* (1975); *The Poverty of Prediction* (1975); *World Futures: The Great Debate* (1978); *The Uses and Abuses of Forecasting* (1979).

SYSTEME D'ETUDES DU SCHEMA GENERAL D'AMENAGEMENT DE LA FRANCE (SESAME)
[STUDY SYSTEM OF THE FRENCH REGIONAL PLANNING SCHEME]

48, Boulevard de Latour-Maubourg
75007 Paris, France

Telephone: 705 93 50
Founded: 1968

Officers: Jacques Durand, Charge de mission a la Delegation a l'Amenagement du Territoire et a l'Action Regionale (DATAR); Philippe Barret, Charge de mission a la DATAR; Jean-Francois Langumier; Michelle Laperrousaz; Antoine Valeyre; Jean-Louis Muron; Jehanne Piona; Florence Bas.

Public research organization. Staff: Seven. **Sources of support:** Government. **Annual Budget:** No answer.

Objectives and interests: Long-term studies related to territorial planning.

Major programs and projects: "Prospective of Tertiary Activities"—research on the content of these activities in the future and their economic and social function in society. "Scenario on Employment"—2,000 projections on the structure of employment in France. "Corporate City"—the new roles of municipalities in economic life. "Scenarios on Transportation"—the future French industrial-productive apparatus.

Special facilities: —

Activities: Several seminars and conferences per year.

Publications: Our studies are generally published in *Travaux et Recherches de Prospective*, Documentation Francaise, 29, Quai Voltaire, 75340 Paris Cedex 07, France, and sometimes in *Futuribles*, 55, rue de Varenne, 75007 Paris, France.

SYSTEMPLAN E.V. INSTITUT FUR UMWELTFORSCHUNG UND ENTWICKLUNGSPLANUNG
[INSTITUTE FOR ENVIRONMENTAL RESEARCH AND DEVELOPMENT PLANNING]

Telephone: 06221/49021

Tiergartenstrasse 15
6900 Heidelberg 1, Federal Republic of Germany

Founded: 1971

Officers: Peter Dietze, Chairman of the Board; Otto Graf Praschma, Member of the Board; Gerhard J. Stoeber, Member of the Board.

Private, non-profit, research institute. Staff: 30 (including field offices in Nepal and Brazil). **Sources of support:** Governments, foundations, international organizations. **Annual Budget:** 3 million marks.

Objectives and interests: Public policy research and development planning, mainly in matters of urban and regional development, technology assessment and technology transfer, institution building, European integration, organization of planning in developing countries.

Major programs and projects: "Integrated Regional Planning in Developing Countries"—field studies and evaluation projects. "Integrated Town Development Planning in Developing Countries"—projects; evaluation of programs and projects. "Evaluation of Politics, Programs and Projects"—e.g., social infrastructure. "Technology Transfer in Developing Countries"—field studies. "Studies in Environmental Planning."

Special facilities: Collection of evaluation projects and methods.

Activities: Research and planning projects; ad hoc consulting; seminars, symposia, and workshops on selected issues in various countries, partly in collaboration with similar institutions.

Publications: *Evaluation of Political Planning,* (Huebner et al. 1976); *Regional Planning in Developing Countries* (Systemplan, 1974); *Social Infrastructure: Analysis of Planning Processes* (Systemplan, 1978); *Regional Planning in the Countries of EC* (Systemplan, 1977); *System Analysis of New York City Building Concepts* (Systemplan, 1976).

TALOUDELLINEN SUUNNITTELUKESKUS
[ECONOMIC PLANNING CENTRE]
Erottaja 15-17
00130 Helsinki 13, Finland

Telephone: 647 901

Founded: 1970

Officers: Eero Tuomainen, Director; Erkki Hellsten, Head of Section; Seppo Leppanen, Head of Section; Seppo Suokko, Head of Section.

Government research institute subordinated to the Ministry of Finance, working also as the Secretariat of the Economic Council. Staff: 25. **Sources of support:** State budget. **Annual Budget:** $514,000.

Objectives and interests: Long-term macro-economic forecasting and planning; structural problems of the economy.

Major programs and projects: "Challenge of the New International Division of Labour to the Finnish Economy." "Long-term Macroeconomic and Regional Planning Models." "The Finnish Manufacturing Industry in 1960-1990." "Macroeconomic Impacts of Energy Policy." "Housing Policy Alternatives up to 2000."

Special facilities: Library of books, periodicals, and reports on economic planning and forecasting and related matters.

Activities: Research work, publications, lectures.

Publications: *Finland 1990: Economic Prospects* (1977, in Finnish and English); *Factors Affecting the Development of Raw Material Markets* (1977, in Finnish); *Economic and Technological Trends of Ferrous Metals* (1977, in Finnish); *Regional Model for Population and Labour Force* (1978, in Swedish); *Inflation: Causes, Consequences, Policy* (1975, in Finnish).

THOMSON—CSF, GROUPE D'ETUDES PROSPECTIVES
[THOMSON CORPORATION, FUTURE STUDIES GROUP]
49 bis, avenue Hoche
Paris 75008, France

Telephone: 561 96 00

Founded: 1968

Officers: Lucien A. Gerardin, Research Director.

Private corporation. Staff: Three. **Sources of support:** Internal. **Annual Budget:** No answer.

Objectives and interests: Exploratory planning for the benefit of the Thomson Corporation.

Major programs and projects: Most research conducted is of a proprietary nature.

Special facilities: —

Activities: Research.

Publications: —

UNION OF INTERNATIONAL ASSOCIATIONS
1 rue aux Laines
1000 Brussels, Belgium

Telephone: (02) 511.83.96

Founded: 1910

Officers: Robert Fenaux, Secretary-General; Anthony J. N. Judge, Assistant Secretary-General; Genevieve Deville, Assistant Secretary-General.

International non-profit, non-governmental research organization. Staff: 15. **Sources of support:** Sale of publications produced by the organization. **Annual Budget:** No answer.

Objectives and interests: To serve as a clearinghouse for information on international associations (particularly nongovernmental), world problems, and related topics. Particularly interested in new forms of organization and organizational networks and their relation to problems and societal resources.

Major programs and projects: Publication of *Yearbook of International Organizations*, a 1000-page computer-based publication in English and French editions. Publication of *Yearbook of World Problems and Human Potential*, a 1000-page computer-based publication, published jointly with Mankind 2000. "World Forum on Transnational Associations"—1980 meeting, with preparatory studies in 1979, on the future role of "international associations."

Special facilities: Data for two yearbooks listed above is held on computer files; other information on international meetings also available.

Activities: Conferences, symposia, publication of reference books and periodicals.

Publications: *Transnational Associations* (10 times per year); *Yearbook of International Organization; Yearbook of World Problems and Human Potential.*

UNITED NATIONS ASIAN AND PACIFIC DEVELOPMENT INSTITUTE   Telephone: 2815400

P. O. Box 2-136, Sri Ayudhya Road
Bangkok, Thailand   **Founded:** 1964

Officers: Vinyu Vichit-Vadakan, Director; Ram C. Malhotra, Deputy Director; D. V. Ramana, Development Economist; J. H. Rhee, Agricultural Economist; A. Kintanar, Expert on Financial Policies and Institutions.

Non-profit, research and training institute. **Staff:** 15 professionals, 40 general service. **Sources of support:** United Nations Development Program and member governments. **Annual Budget:** Approximately $1.5 million.

Objectives and interests: To work in close collaboration with national institutions and with individuals engaged in development work in the countries of the Asian and Pacific region, with a view to identifying development needs and priorities, and to building and strengthening national capabilities for planning and implementation of development programs through research, training, and advisory services.

Major programs and projects: The Institute is now in Phase III (1976-1980), during which time it will concentrate its efforts on the problems of poverty, unemployment, and social inequality.

Special facilities: Maintains a library and documentation center. Library collections pertain to the social sciences, particularly development planning. Services include reference and loan facilities, bibliographical search services, and dissemination of information service in the field of development information.

Activities: Conducts about ten regional training courses and five to ten country courses a year for member government personnel within the ESCAP region; undertakes research, the results of which are mainly for use in training; renders advisory services on request to governments and agencies.

Publications: Newsletter (quarterly); *An Approach to Micro-level Development, Designing and Evaluation of Rural Development Projects*, W. Haque, N. Mehta, A. Rahman and P. Wignaraja (1977); *Asian Rethinking on Development* (UNESCO/APDI, 1977); *Social Structure in Asia*, N. K. Sarkar (1975); *Social Development in Asia*, R. Pieris (1974); *Towards a Theory of Rural Development*, W. Haque, N. Mehta, A. Rahman, and P. Wignaraja (1975); *Towards a Unified Approach to Development Planning*, D.V. Ramana and R.C. Malhotra; *Industrial Structure of Greater Bangkok*; N.K. Sarkar (1974).

UNITED NATIONS DEPARTMENT OF INTERNATIONAL ECONOMIC AND SOCIAL AFFAIRS, POPULATION DIVISION   Telephone: (212) 754-1234

New York, New York, 10017, U.S.A.   **Founded:** 1946

Officers: Leon Tabah, Director; M. A. El-Badry, Assistant Director, Research; P. S. Menon, Senior Population Affairs Officer.

International. **Staff:** 35 professional staff. **Sources of support:** United Nations regular budget, supplemented by U. N. Fund for Population Activities. **Annual Budget:** No answer.

Objectives and interests: Studies and research in trends and structure of population, population and development, population policy, estimates and projections, fertility and family planning; programs and projects which coordinate and support substantive aspects of technical cooperation in the population field, including training of demographers.

Major programs and projects: Projections, including studies on which the assumptions of these projections are based; monitoring of world population trends and policies (every two years); review and appraisal of World Population Plan of Action; review and appraisal of progress made towards achieving goals and recommendations of World Population Plan of Action.

Special facilities: Population Reference Center; data bank on population policies.

Activities: Conduct seminars, expert groups, etc., on different aspects of work program; reports to Population Commission (which meets every two years), a functional commission of the Economic and Social Council, and to the Economic and Social Council, and the General Asssembly; 20th session of the Population Commission, 29 January to 9 February 1979; Expert Group on Measuring the Impact of Family Planning Programmes on Fertility, 19-26 March 1979; WHO/ UN Meeting on Socio-Economic Determinants of Mortality, 19-25 June 1979.

Publications: *Population Newsletter* (biannual); *Population Bulletin* (biannual); *Working Papers of the Population Division; Concise Report of the World Population Situation in 1977 — New Beginnings and Uncertain Ends; World Population Trends and Policies —* 1977 Monitoring Report; *Methods of Measuring the Impact of Family Planning Programmes on Fertility — Problems and Issues; Trends and Characteristics of International Migration Since 1950.*

UNITED NATIONS EDUCATIONAL, SCIENTIFIC AND CULTURAL ORGANIZATION(UNESCO)
Telephone: 577-16-10

7, place de Fontenoy
75007 Paris, France **Founded:** 1946

Officers: Amadau-Mahtar M'Bow, Director-General; Federico Mayor, Deputy Director-General; Abdul Razzak Kaddoura, Assistant Director-General for Science; Y. Novozhilov, M. Batisse, H. Harada, Deputy Assistant Directors-General for Science; Y. de Hemptinne, Director, Division of Science and Technology Policies.

Intergovernmental organizations belonging to the United Nations System. **Staff:** Approximately 2,400. **Sources of support:** Governments of the 145 member states. **Annual Budget:** Approximately $150 million.

Objectives and interests: Encouraging international intellectual cooperation through the communication of knowledge, the comparison of experiences, and the exchange of ideas; operational assistance to member states; and the promotion of peace, human rights, and mutual understanding among peoples. Interests focus on education, science and technology, culture, communications, etc.

Major programs and projects: Research on organization and performance of research units, aimed at better understanding of factors affecting productivity and effectiveness of research groups; research on indicators of scientific and technological development, aimed at determining best indicators of S&T development level of given countries; studies on methods of budgeting and programming of S & T activities at the national level; preparatory studies for forthcoming ministerial Conference on the Application of Science and Technology to Development of Asia (CASTASIA II); applications of specific planning in terms of scientific research resources and infrastructure in relation to human resources in technology; work in the field of socio-economic analysis, in particular in relation to measuring quality-of-life indicators.

Special facilities: UNESCO Library; UNESCO data banks, numerous collections of scientific and technological periodicals, including those in the field of "futures," forecasting, etc.

Activities: International conferences, assistance to member states, research, elaboration of international instruments such as conventions, recommendations, organization of training courses, awarding of fellowships, clearinghouse activities, publication of books, periodicals.

Publications: *The UNESCO Courier* (monthly magazine); *UNESCO Chronicle* (monthly bulletin); *Prospects* (quarterly review of education); *Impact of Science on Society* (quarterly journal); *Nature and Resources* (quarterly newsletter); *Internationl Social Science Journal* (quarterly); UNESCO's own Medium-Term Plan (1977-1982), major exercise in application of futures research to the organization's own programmes (published in paperback form as *Thinking Ahead: UNESCO and the Challenges of Today and Tomorrow*); forthcoming publication of booklet *Science for Man* in connection with UN Conference on Science and Technology for Development; numerous other books and publications.

UNITED NATIONS INSTITUTE FOR TRAINING AND RESEARCH (UNITAR)
Telephone: (212) 754-8637 (New York)
98 58 50 (Geneva)

801 United Nations Plaza
New York, New York 10017, U.S.A.
and
Palais des Nations
CH-1211 Geneva 10 Switzerland **Founded:** 1963

Officers: Davidson Nicol, Executive Director; Philippe de Seynes, Director, Project on the Future; Robert S. Jordan, Director of Research; Abdul-Ghani Al-Rafei, Director of Training; Zamir Ahmad, Chief, Finance and Administration; Joseph Barnea, Special Fellow; Laurel Isaacs, Publications Officer; Hans-Jorg Geiser, Officer-in-Charge of Geneva Office.

International training and research organization (autonomous United Nations Institute). **Staff:** About 50

112

(New York) and 5 (Geneva).   **Sources of support:** Voluntary contributions from governments and foundations.
Annual Budget: No answer.

Objectives and interests: To enhance the effectiveness of the United Nations in achieving its major objectives, in particular the maintenance of peace and security and the promotion of economic and social development, through research, training and studies on future problems of the world.

Major programs and projects: "Technology Choices, Domestic Distribution and North-South Relations"—an intensive research project into development alternatives within the framework of an econometric model. "Regional Approaches to the Problematique of the Future—Africa and the Future." "Conference on Development Scenarios for South East Asia." "Progress in the Establishment of a New International Economic Order." "Conference on Long-term Energy Planning." "Development of Off-shore Oil and Gas."

Special facilities: Maintains a selective and specialized collection of books, periodicals, fugitive and source material on subjects dealing generally with problems of the future which have particular relevance to U.N. organizations.

Activities: Short-term intensive courses for U.N. delegates on such subjects as peaceful settlement of disputes, U.N. development programmes, and regional structure; regional training programs on development assistance, international procurement, and international law (with fellowships for practical training in the latter); seminars for international officials on management and development.

Publications: A catalogue of UNITAR publications is available from the Publications Officer on request. Titles include: *The United Nations and Decision-Making: The Role of Women,* edited by Davidson Nicol and Margaret Croke (UNITAR, 1978); *The Objectives of the New International Economic Order,* edited by Ervin Laszlo (1978); *The Brain Drain: Emigration and Return,* by William A. Glaser with G. Christopher Habers (1978); *Multinational Co-operation for Development in West Africa,* by John P. Renninger (coming out early 1979); *Arab Development Funds in the Middle East,* by Soliman Demir (coming out early 1979); *Disaster Preparedness and the United Nations: Advanced Planning for Disaster Relief,* by Barbara Brown, (coming out early 1979); *Important for the Future,* edited by Joseph Barnea (journal issued six times a year); *UNITAR News,* (last issued September 1978, distributed free).

UNITED STATES CONGRESS, OFFICE OF TECHNOLOGY ASSESSMENT
Telephone: (202) 224-8996
Washington, D.C. 20510, U.S.A.   **Founded:** 1973 (authorizing legislation enacted October 1972)

Officers: Morris K. Udall, Chairman, Technology Assessment Board (96th Congress); John H. Gibbons Director;   Daniel V. DeSimone, Deputy Director; Lionel S. Johns, Assistant Director for Energy, Materials, and Global Security; Joyce Lashof, Assistant Director for Health and Life Sciences; Gerald O. Barney, Assistant Director for Science, Information, and Transportation.

Public agency; research arm of the Congress.   Staff: 140.   **Sources of support:** Congressional appropriations.   **Annual Budget:** Approximately 11.3 million for FY 1979.

Objectives and interests: Public policy research to provide early indications of the probable beneficial and adverse impacts of the applications of technology, and to develop other coordinate information which may assist the Congress.

Major programs and projects: "Alternative Energy Futures." "Global Food Futures." "Effects of Nuclear War." "Future Use and Characteristics of the Automobile." "Future Availability of Imported Materials."

Special facilities: Assessment activities are supported by an Information Services staff, which maintains an in-house library containing basic background materials and current data resources and provides on-line access to several computerized data-retrieval networks. Liaison with the Library of Congress, including use of its facilities and services.

Activities: OTA assessment activity is under way in 11 principal areas: energy, food, health, materials, oceans, R&D, policies and priorities, transportation, national security affairs, genetics and world population, information systems, and technology and foreign affairs (formerly technology and world trade).

Publications: *Application of Solar Technology to Today's Energy Needs,* Volumes I & II (October 1978); *Assessing the Efficacy and Safety of Medical Technologies* (September 1978); *Renewable Energy from the Oceans—Ocean Thermal Energy Conversion* (June 1978); *Government Involvement in the Innovation Process* (August 1978); *Emerging Food Marketing Technologies* (October 1978).

U.S. ARMY WAR COLLEGE, STRATEGIC STUDIES INSTITUTE
Telephone: (717) 245-3230
Carlisle Barracks, Pennsylvania 17013, U.S.A.   **Founded:** 1962

Officers: Andrew C. Remson, Jr., Director; John R. Cameron, Assistant to Director; Anthony L. Wermuth; Lloyd D. Bryant; Robert H. Donaldson.

Government research institute. Staff: Approximately 40 professional military and civilian analysts. **Sources of support:** U.S. government. **Annual Budget:** No answer.

Objectives and interests: Primarily policy research on major issues of current and probable future interest to the Army, the Defense Department, and the larger national security community concerned with functional and/or regional security. Primary emphasis on national military strategy and options, but complementary interest in political, economic, and technological factors with likely impact on national security policy.

Major programs and projects: Analysis of mid-term politico-military conflict environment. Analysis of dynamics of national security policy formulation.

Special facilities: —

Activities: Basic emphasis is on studies for Defense Department use, covering a range of topics both functionally and geographically diverse. About 20% of study workload is internally generated. Conducts occasional joint projects with educational institutions (e.g., one on Civilian Based Defense, with Harvard University, 1975).

Publications: *Strategies, Alliances and Military Power: Changing Roles* (1977); *National Strategy and Detente* (1976); *New Dynamics in National Strategy: The Paradox of Power* (1975); *Being Number One Nation: Primacy and Detente*, Anthony Wermuth (1975).

U.S. DEPARTMENT OF AGRICULTURE, ECONOMIC RESEARCH SERVICE, NATIONAL ECONOMIC ANALYSIS DIVISION, ECONOMIC PROJECTIONS AND ANALYTICAL SYSTEMS

Telephone: (202) 447-7681

Room 248, 500 12th Street, S.W.
Washington, D.C. 20250, U.S.A.

Founded: 1973

Officers: Leroy Quance, Program Leader and ERS Coordinator for Projections; Allen Smith, Y.C. Lu, Austin Fox, and Karen Lin, Project Leaders.

Federal government office. Staff: Nine. **Sources of support:** Economic Service's Research Budget (USDA). **Annual Budget:** $400,000.

Objectives and interests: To simulate and analyze alternative futures for U.S. agriculture under scenarios differing with respect to major uncertainties impacting on the supply and demand for U.S. farm output.

Major programs and projects: National-Interregional Agricultural Projections; Projecting Linkages between the General Economy and the Food and Agricultural System; Projecting Technological Change in Food and Agriculture; Agricultural Projections Research and Management Information System; Projecting Agricultural Inputs.

Special facilities: National-Interregional Agricultural Projections (NIRAP) System, with significant on-line conversational gaming capability.

Activities: Conducts research and disseminates information useful to public and private decision-makers in food and agriculture.

Publications: *Monthly Report; Agriculture in the Third Century: Introduction to the Economic Projections Program; Commodity Production and Utilization Projections to 1985; Historical Perspective of Supply and Demand Projections in the U.S. Department of Agriculture.*

USSR ACADEMY OF SCIENCES, INSTITUTE FOR SOCIOLOGICAL RESEARCH, SECTION ON SOCIAL FORECASTING

Telephone: 128-91-22

Novo-Cheremushki, 46
Moscow 117418, USSR

Founded: 1968

Officers: Igor V. Bestuzhev-Lada.

Research institute. Staff: Ten. **Sources of support:** USSR government. **Annual Budget:** No answer.

Objectives and interests: Social forecasting methodology; forecasting of social needs and societal way of life.

Major programs and projects: "Forecasting in Sociology: Methodological Problems"—theoretical research. "Forecasting of Changes in the System of Social Needs"—empirical research. "Forecasting of Changes in Societal Way of Life"—empirical research. "Conceptions and Trends in Modern Futurology"—theoretical research. "History of Future Thought"—theoretical research.

Special facilities: Bibliography on social forecasting.

Activities: Seminars for heads of futures research sections in several institutes; seminars for postgraduate students in futures studies.

Publications: Yearbooks on Social Forecasting (in Russian): *Problems of General and Social Forecasting* (1968), *Futures Research and Operations Research* (1969), *Social Forecasting* (1975), *Forecasting the Social Needs* (1976), *Problems of Building a Societal Way of Life Indicators System* (1977), *Problems of the Measurement and Modelling of Societal Way of Life* (1978); *The Window into the Future*, I.V. Bestuzhev-Lada (1970, in Russian); *Forecasting in Sociology: Some Paradigms*, I.V. Bestuzhev-Lada, editor (Publishing House Mysl, Moscow, 1978, in Russian); *Modelling in Sociological Research*, I.V. Bestuzhev-Lada (Publishing House Nauka, Moscow, 1978, in Russian); *Forecasting the Social Needs of Youth*, I.V. Bestuzhev-Lada, editor (Publishing House Nauka, Moscow, 1978, in Russian); "The Development of Alternative Futures," I.V. Bestuzhev-Lada, in *The Future Society* (Publishing House Progress, Moscow, 1973, in English); *Forecasting the Way of Life of Society*, I.V. Bestuzhev-Lada (1974, in English); *Social Needs: Analysis and Prognosis*, I.V. Bestuzhev-Lada (1974, in English); *Construction of a System of Indictors of the Level, Quality, Pattern, Style, and Way of Life of Society: Methodological Problems*, I.V. Bestuzhev-Lada (1978, in English).

UTAH FUTURE STUDY

Telephone: (801) 581-5903

T.E.K.
DCE Annex 1152
University of Utah
Salt Lake City, Utah 84112, U.S.A.

Founded: —

Officers: Thom Kearin, Director.

Private. Staff: Each "team" developed from local professors for each project. **Sources of support:** Private contracts. **Annual Budget:** No answer.

Objectives and interests: Perform consulting services to inter-mountain area institutions and corporations.

Major programs and projects: "Utah Future Study" — planning a 20-year horizon for state agencies. "Welfare Assessment" — planning and research for major institution. "Future Site Purchase Methodologies" — planning and research for a major institution. "Operation and Maintenance Survey" — reevaluation of traditional operation and maintenance for a major institution using previous growth patterns.

Special facilities: —

Activities: —

Publications: —

UTAH STATE PLANNING COORDINATOR'S OFFICE

Telephone: (801) 533-5245

124 State Capitol Building
Salt Lake City, Utah 84114, U.S.A.

Founded: 1963

Officers: Kent Briggs, State Planning Coordinator; Don H. Nielson, Utah State Science Adviser; Chauncey G. Powis, Associate State Planning Coordinator (Natural Resources); Paul Parker, Associate State Planning Coordinator (Planning); Lorayne Tempest, Associate State Planning Coordinator (Intergovernmental Relations); Marilyn McKay Nath, Associate State Planning Coordinator (Human Resources).

State government office. Staff: 27. **Sources of support:** State legislative appropriation; federal grants. **Annual Budget:** No answer.

Major programs and projects: "Recalibration of the Utah Process Economic and Demographic (UPED) Impact Model"—updating of economic/demographic alternative futures projections.

Objectives and interests: To coordinate planning efforts in the state; to provide technical assistance in economic and demographic modeling.

Activities: —

Special facilities: Utah State Planning Library—provides reference, literature research, and acquisition services for the department and to any other official state or local planning entity requesting such services; services to private and out-of-state requesters provided only as time and resources available. Federal Resources Information Center—branch of the Division of Intergovernmental Relations; provides technical and research assistance statewide to those seeking federal, state, or private funding assistance.

Publications: *The Utah Process: Alternative Futures 1975-1990*, Weaver, Rodger et al. (1975; revision forthcoming, 1979). An index to a project carried on from 1975 to 1977, *The Utah Natural Resources and Land Use Information System*, is available free to libraries and serious researchers in microform only (COM-fiche) — over 8,000 publications are indexed by subject, author, title, and geographic area.

VARIFLEX CORPORATION
2905 Davenport Street, N. W.
Washington, D. C. 20008, U.S.A.

Telephone: (202) 244-1519

Founded: 1977

Officers: Leslie W. Ayres, President; Robert U. Ayres, Vice-President and Chairman of the Board.

Private. Staff: Two. **Sources of support:** Contracts. **Annual Budget:** Approximately $100,000.

Objectives and interests: Medium and long-term forecasts with special emphasis on resource and technology issues.

Major programs and projects: "World Steel Industry to 2000"—forecast and model development. "World Auto Industry to 2000"—forecast and model development.

Special facilities: —

Activities: —

Publications: *Uncertain Futures—Challenge to Decision-Makers* (1979); *Resources, Environment and Economics* (1978).

WAKEFIELD WASHINGTON ASSOCIATES, INC.
1129 20th Street, N.W.
Washington, D.C. 20036

Telephone: (202) 833-9880

Founded: —

Officers: Rowan A. Wakefield, President; Charles Cohen, Vice-President; Carol Pudliner Sweeny, Research Associate; Susan Brown, Co-editor, *American Family;* Gail Washchuck, Research Associate.

Private management consulting firm. Staff: Six. **Sources of support:** Client fees, subscription to newsletter, project contracts. **Annual Budget:** $200,000.

Objectives and interests: Providing Washington representation for universities and private companies; determining future macro trends and policy alternatives for ourselves and for clients; publishing newsletter, reports, books; developing improved corporate/Washington relations programs.

Major programs and projects: *American Family* — bimonthly newsletter carries column on "Future Trends." "Future Direction and Nature of Corporate Washington Relations" — in the past five to six years there has been a major transition in the nature of the relationship of business to the federal government. The nature of this change and possible future directions are examined in this report to be completed in March 1979.

Special facilities: Maintains a Federal Program Documents reference library; specialized reference collection on Family and Public Policy; electronically stored and retrievable appropriate technology publications; and core reference library.

Activities: Planning several conferences on international issues, graphics for management, federal relations, and appropriate technology; operating Career Development Internship program for entry-level and mid-career liberal arts graduates; developing classification system for Appropriate Technology library; conducting Washington marketing surveys for several clients; representing Adelphi University Center for Energy Studies, Rochester Institute of Technology, Alaska Pacific University, Inupiat University, U Form Systems and Technology and public affairs of the National Distillers and Chemical Corporation in Washington; studying specific future trends with changing society, relative to energy and appropriate technology, the family, the corporation, education and work, and native American and traditional Third World cultures.

Publications: *American Family*, Susan Brown and Rowan Wakefield, co-editors (bimonthly); *Family Research: An Analysis and Guide to Federal Funding*, Catherine Allen, Rowan Wakefield, and Gail Washchuck (forthcoming in 1979, Greenwood Press); "Survey of Family Conference Being Planned by 50 States in Preparation for White House Conference on Families" Rowan Wakefield and Debra Slack (September, 1978).

WEINER, EDRICH, BROWN, INC.
303 Lexington Avenue
New York, New York 10016, U.S.A.

Telephone: (212) 889-7007

Founded: 1977

Officers: Arnold Brown, President; Edith Weiner, Harold Edrich, Executive Vice-Presidents; Kathy O'Connell, Office Manager.

Private, management consultant. **Staff:** Four. **Sources of support:** Clients, primarily corporate. **Annual Budget:** No answer.

Objectives and interests: To help organizations develop their own capacities to anticipate and understand changes in the social, political, economic and technological environment and to develop appropriate strategic responses.

Major programs and projects: "Team" (Trend Evaluation and Monitoring)—participatory environmental scanning system using the organization's own personnel in all phases. "Implement"—evaluating an organization's purchased research reports to help maximize their effectiveness. "Environmental Analysis"—a comprehensive study of the organization's social, political, economic and technological environment with specific implications and recommendations for action.

Special facilities: —

Activities: Develop and install environmental scanning systems; prepare environmental analyses for organizations or their specific departments; develop conferences and seminars with futures orientation.

Publications:

WERNER-REIMERS-STIFTUNG
[WERNER-REIMERS FOUNDATION]
Am Wingertsberg 4
638 Bad Homburg, Federal Republic of Germany

Telephone: (06172) 2 40 58/9

Founded: 1963

Officers: Konrad Muller, State Secretary (retired).

Private, non-profit foundation. **Staff:** Seven. **Sources of support:** — **Annual Budget:** No answer.

Objectives and interests: Arts and humanities, including language and philosophy; education, including educational research; religion and social sciences, including anthropology; economics; history; human ethology; political science; psychology; sociology and urban studies.

Major programs and projects: Human Ecology—Particularly concerned with urban and suburban problems. Urban Planning and Urban Sociology—Development of theories and methods for measuring, explaining, and influencing urban design and social structures. Social Indicators—Development of instruments for describing social infrastructure and social problems. Sex Roles—Main questions are the generation of sex roles and possibilities for change. Human Ethology—Survey of state of research is intended.

Special facilities: Resource materials on social indicators, social planning, and the reconstruction of cities. Publications and materials on human ecology, sex roles, and human ethology.

Activities: Sponsors interdisciplinary study groups in which 10-25 scientists work together on relevant subjects, particularly with reference to present problems of mankind; each study group holds two to four meetings every year to which other individuals can be invited. The results of their work are published. The Foundation also sponsors international symposia.

Publications: *Arbeitskonferenz "Sociale Indikatoren" [Working Conference on "Social Indicators"]*, Wolfgang Zapf (1972); *Soziale Indikatoren: Konzeption und Forschungsansatze, Berichte und Diskussionen [Social Indicators: Conception and Research Arrangements, Reports, and Discussions]*, Wolfgang Zapf, editor (1972-73, two volumes); *Symposion 1975: Okologische Perspektiven in der Psychologie [Symposium 1975: Ecological Perspectives in Psychology]*, Carl F. Graumann, publisher (Huber, Bern, 1978); *Symposium 1976: Income Distribution and Economic Inequality*, Zvi Griliches and Wilhelm Krelle et al., editors (Campus-Verlag, Frankfurt, 1978); *Symposium 1977: Humanethology: Claims and Limits of a New Discipline* (Cambridge University Press, 1979).

WICKERT INSTITUTE TUBINGEN FUR MARKT-, MEINUNGS- UND WIRTSCHAFTLICHE ZUKUNFTSFORSCHUNG
[THE WICKERT INSTITUTE OF TUBINGEN FOR MARKET, OPINION, AND ECONOMICS FUTURES RESEARCH]

Telephone: (07071) 22318
(08337) 8044

Wilhelmstrasse 102
7400 Tubingen, Federal Republic of Germany
and

Kirchplatz 5
7919 Illereichen, Federal Republic of Germany **Founded:** 1964

Officers: Horst Wagenfuhr, Gunter Wickert.

Private research institute. Staff: 37. **Sources of support:** Private firms, universities, governments. **Annual Budget:** 4.2 million marks.

Objectives and interests: Futures research in economics, in connection with market and opinion research.

Major programs and projects: Projects, most of which are highly confidential, have included the following: "Gesellschaft und wirtschaft im zukunftigen deutschland" *["Society and the Economy in the Future Germany"]*; "Gegenwartige Situation und Zukunftsfragen" *["The Future of the Drug Industry in Germany"]* (including medical and social factors); "Report Technik 1999: Dynamik von morgen" *["The Future of Technology in 1999: The Dynamics of Tomorrow"]*.

Special facilities: —

Activities: Conducts futures research in topics related to economics and sociology; operates educational center in Illereichen for 200 people.

Publications: *Zeitschrift fur Markt-, Meinungs- und Zukunftsforschung [Periodical for Market, Opinion, and Futures Research]* (in German, English, and French); *Wirtschaftliche Zukunftsforschung [Economic Futures Research]*, by Horst Wagenfuhr; *Who Is Who in Futurology? An International Reference and Bibliography of Futures Research; Zukunft in Wort und Zahl: Deutschlands Wirtschaft 1970-2000 [The Future in Words and Numbers: Germany's Economy 1970-2000]*, by Horst Wagenfuhr.

CHARLES W. WILLIAMS, INC.
Telephone: (703) 548-2501

801 N. Pitt Street, Suite 117
Alexandria, Virginia 22314, U.S.A. **Founded:** 1973

Officers: Charles W. Williams, Jr., President; Kendall W. Simmons and Robert Crane, Research Directors; Peter M. De Arcangelis, Joseph L. Lipman, and Ronald Shalita, Senior Research Analysts.

Private research and consulting firm. Staff: 14-16. **Sources of support:** Private industry 60%; public sector 40%. **Annual Budget:** No answer.

Objectives and interests: Strategic policy research and assistance to complement planning units in their effort to develop, formulate, and implement programs and plans; work closely with a core of clients for anticipatory planning and policy management, recommending procedures and action programs to enhance the efficiency and effectiveness of their operations.

Major programs and projects: "Technology Forecasting"—conceptualization and innovative development of a system to consider and forecast relevant technical and scientific developments on key segments of industrial community. "Design of Forecasting System for Planning and Resource Management Units"—design of processes and procedures whereby planning and budgeting units can use alternative futures and various forecasting-related information in day-to-day operations. "Competitive/Competitor Assessments"—key assessment studies to determine future competitive posture of corporations and technologies. "Development of Key Growth Strategies"—development and recommendation of alternative growth strategies for business. "Alternative Futures in the Marine Environment"—analysis and assessment of possible future marine environment uses, resources, restrictions and viability.

Special facilities: Internal library with specialized collections on forecasting methodologies and approaches; future of the environment; planning and management theory; and the marine environment.

Activities: Conceptualization and initial development of system to forecast technical and scientific developments and assess impacts upon key segments of industrial community; determination of processes and procedures as a point of linkage between mid-and long-range futures and resource planning and management; conceptualization and preliminary design of ideal process to consider and include long-range alternative futures in the planning system.

Publications: Most publications are under client propriety and must be obtained directly through the client.

WISSENSCHAFTSZENTRUM BERLIN
[INSTITUTE FOR SCIENTIFIC STUDY, BERLIN] **Telephone:** (030) 313 40 81
Steinplatz 2
1000 Berlin 12, Federal Republic of Germany **Founded:** 1969

118

Officers: Helmut G. Meier; Frieder Naschold; Karl W. Deutsch; Walter Goldberg; Fritz W. Scharpf.

Non-profit, research institute. Staff: 130. **Sources of support:** Federal Republic of Germany and West Berlin. **Annual Budget:** 11 million German marks.

Objectives and interests: Policy-oriented, social-science research focused on problems common to highly industrialized nations.

Major programs and projects: "International Institute of Management." "International Institute for Comparative Studies." "International Institute for Environment and Society."

Special facilities: Book series; institute papers.

Activities: Conferences; workshops; international cooperation.

Publications: Newsletter (in German; bimonthly); *Union Organization and Militancy: Conclusions from a Study of the United Mine Workers of America*, Makoto Takamiya (Autumn 1978); *Alternative Raumpolitik [Alternative Outer-Space Politics]*, Frieder Naschold (June 1978); *Strategien zur Regulierung von Automobilemissionen [Strategy for the Regulation of Automobile Emissions]*, Herwig Gabriel and Klaus Zimmermann (June 1978); *Dynamik der Arbeitslosigkeit [Dynamics of Unemployment]*, Dieter Freiburghaus (Winter 1978).

WORLD FUTURE SOCIETY
4916 St. Elmo Avenue
Washington, D.C. 20014, U.S.A.

Telephone: (301) 656-8274

Founded: 1966

Officers: Edward S. Cornish, President; Frank Snowden Hopkins, Vice-President; Peter Zuckerman, Secretary-Treasurer.

Non-profit, scientific and educational association. **Staff:** 21. **Sources of support:** Members' dues, sales of books and publications, occasional gifts and grants. **Annual Budget:** $972,000.

Objectives and interests: To contribute to a reasoned awareness of the future and of the importance of its study, without advocating particular ideologies or engaging in political activities; to advance responsible and serious investigation of the future; to promote the development and improvement of methodologies for the study of the future; to increase public understanding of future-oriented activities and studies.

Major programs and projects: "Resources Directory for America's Third Century" — a survey of individuals, organizations, educational programs, research projects, etc., conducted by the World Future Society under grants from the National Science Foundation and Library of Congress, Congressional Research Service (1975-76). "Futurizing the U.S. Government" — a series of future-creating workshops with Robert Jungk, April 1976, and Joseph Coates, June 1976. "The Next Twenty-Five Years: Crisis and Opportunity" — The Second General Assembly of the World Future Society, Washington, D.C., June 1975. "Energy: Today's Choices, Tomorrow's Opportunities" — a forum on energy held in Washington, D.C., April 1974. "Teacher's Workshop" — a conference on teaching futures held in Bethesda, Maryland, October 1974. "The Future: A Comprehensive Look at What Tomorrow Holds by the World Future Society" — prepared as a special section on the future for the 1979 edition of the *Hammond Almanac*. A similar feature is now being prepared for the 1980 edition.

Special facilities: Book store.

Activities: Chapters, committees, or coordinators in approximately 100 cities of the world, with local groups sponsoring lectures and other activities. Occasional regional meetings. Courses on such topics as introduction to future studies, technology forecasting, etc. The Society's Book Service identifies and sells future-oriented books and other materials. The Society has also organized special-studies sections in Business, Education, and Technology, and sponsored section meetings on Business Tomorrow in New York, October 1976, Communications Tomorrow in New York, November 1977, and Education Tomorrow in Houston, October 1978 (a second education meeting is planned for October 1979 in Minnesota). Planning is currently underway for the Society's Third General Assembly, to be held July 20-25, 1980 in Toronto, Canada.

Publications: THE FUTURIST: *A Journal of Forecasts, Trends and Ideas About the Future* (bimonthly); *The World Future Society* BULLETIN (bimonthly); FUTURE SURVEY: *A Monthly Abstract of Books, Articles and Reports of Special Interest to the Futurist Community* (monthly); *Education Tomorrow, Business Tomorrow, Technology Tomorrow* (bimonthly newsletters); *The Study of the Future*, Edward S. Cornish (1977); *The Future: A Guide to Information Sources*, Edward S. Cornish, editor (1977, revised edition forthcoming in 1979); *1999: The World of Tomorrow*, Edward S. Cornish, editor (1978); *Instructor's Manual for The Study of the Future*, Howard Didsbury (forthcoming in 1979); *Student Handbook for the Study of the Future*, Howard Didsbury (forthcoming in 1979); *Toward the Future*, film, Marc Chinoy and Roy Mason (1978); *The Next 25 Years: Crisis and Opportunity*, Andrew Spekke, editor (1975); *Energy: Today's Choices, Tomorrow's Opportunities*, Anton B. Schmalz, editor (1974); *Films on the Future*,

Marie Martin (1977, revised edition forthcoming); *World Future Society Catalog* (published approximately twice yearly).

WORLD FUTURE STUDIES FEDERATION (WFSF)

Casella Postale 6203
Roma Prati
Rome 00195, Italy

Telephone: (06) 872529

Founded: 1973

Officers: Mahdi Elmandjra, President; Eleonora Masini, Secretary General; Serge Antoine, Hernan Santa Cruz, Bogdan Suchodolski, Romesh Thapar, Vice-Presidents; Annarosa Arista, Staff Member.

Non-profit, international federation. **Staff:** One part time. **Sources of support:** Membership fees. **Annual Budget:** No answer.

Objectives and interests: To promote and encourage future studies so that they are open to all scientific initiatives in different disciplines and areas; to serve as an umbrella organization or network of organizations and individuals engaged in future studies; to provide a forum for generating ideas concerning the future; to organize advisory teams and models of integrated future analysis by setting up a data bank of future research capacities; to analyze crucial global problems.

Major programs and projects: "The Future of Communication, Cultural Identity in an Interdependent World"—world conference. "Visions of Desirable Societies"—a subproject of the United Nations University project, "Goals Processes and Indicators for Development." "Forecasting Methodology in the Field of Education"—for UNESCO.

Special facilities: —

Activities: Sixth World Conference on Future Studies in Cairo "The Future of Communication, Cultural Identity in an Interdependent World"; Berlin meeting on "Science and Technology and the Future," May 8-10 1979; Regional reference in developing countries.

Publications: *WFSF Newsletter* (bimonthly); proceedings of Fifth and Sixth World Future Studies Conferences.

WORLD INSTITUTE COUNCIL

171 West Street
Brooklyn, New York 11222, U.S.A.

Telephone: (212) 383-5000

Founded: 1946

Officers: Julius Stulman, President; Landrum Bolling, Vice-President; Robert Triffin; Stephen Stulman.

Non-profit research institute. **Staff:** Varies from 2 to 50, according to projects. **Sources of support:** Self-supporting. **Annual Budget:** No answer.

Objectives and interests: "Creative problem solving"; basic research on specific problems of mankind; and counseling government bodies, public and private educational institutions. Deals with specific problems with supporting grants.

Major programs and projects: "The World Institute"—The establishment of a methodology for creative problem-solving—the world's most gifted people, having access to the most modern information-handling technology, working together as a kind of world brain. "III Industrial Revolution"—The creation of a supplement to the monetary system, enabling developing countries to more easily enter the money markets. "Distribution Systems"—Creating new distribution systems based on new concepts such as containerization; the development of Cargo City concepts. "Creative Systems and Housing"—New methods of creating values in integrative system approaches to urban and suburban areas. "Executive Brain Center"—Practical method of integrating on an interdisciplinary basis all factors applying to given problems, creating abilities that small corporations and nations are incapable of.

Special facilities: —

Activities: Research; publications; counseling and working with government bodies and educational institutions.

Publications: *Fields Within Fields* (quarterly journal); *Evolving Mankind's Future,* Julius Stulman (1967); *World Brain: New Formula for World Peace and Prosperity,* Julius Stulman (1969); *The Third Industrial Revolution,* Julius Stulman (1973); *The Methodology of Pattern,* Julius Stulman (1972); *The World Institute: Key to Mankind's Emergence,* Julius Stulman (1974).

WORLD MAN

P.O. Box 30341
Bethesda, Maryland 20014, U.S.A.

Telephone: (202) 387-4735

Founded: 1970

120

Officers: Lorenz K. Y. Ng, President; Michael R. Klein, Secretary-Treasurer; Harold D. Lasswell; Virginia Dwan; Emily Mudd.

Non-profit foundation. Staff: Three. **Sources of support:** Private donations. **Annual Budget:** $10,000.

Objectives and interests: To foster a transnational world view with Man as its central focus; to develop paradigms for a systematic study of Man and behavior; to explore approaches which can transcend the barriers of traditional thought and attempt to devise methods by which conceptual and bureaucratic rigidity can be prevented or surmounted.

Major programs and projects: "Health and Human Behavior: A Perspective for U.S. Policy." "Man in Transition"—To explore the various alternative images of man in the process of evolving. "Violence and Aggression"—With particular emphasis on the biological basis of destructive behavior.

Special facilities: —

Activities: Sponsors seminars and workshops (e.g., "Man in Transition," 1974); sponsors projects dealing with health and human behavior.

Publications: *Incentives for Health: Report of a Working Conference,* L.K.Y.Ng and D.L. Davis (1977); *The Promotion of Health: New Trends and Perspectives,* L.K.Y. Ng and D.L. Davis, editors (in press).

WORLD PROBLEMS PROJECT

1 rue aux Laines
1000 Brussels, Belgium

Telephone: (02) 511.83.96

Founded: 1972

Officers: Anthony J. N. Judge, Project Director.

International, non-profit, non-governmental permanent working group. Staff: Cyclic, according to preparation of publications. **Sources of support:** Union of International Associations and Mankind 2000. **Annual Budget:** No answer.

Objectives and interests: To collect information on world problems and to produce adequate descriptions of them and their interrelationships, the organizations and disciplines concerned with them, and the values which make them visible as problems.

Major programs and projects: "Representation of Complex Issues"—use of data bases to provide more comprehensible representatives of complex issues. Publication of *Yearbook of World Problems and Human Potential,* which interrelates, for the first time, the following distinct series: world problems, international organizations, intellectual disciplines, interdisciplinary concepts, concepts of human development and potential, human values, international periodicals, human diseases, occupations, traded commodities, economic sectors, multinational corporations, and multilateral treaties.

Special facilities: —

Activities: —

Publications: *Yearbook of World Problems and Human Potential* (1976).

WORLDWATCH INSTITUTE

1776 Massachusetts Avenue, N.W.
Washington, D.C. 20036, U.S.A.

Telephone: (202) 452-1999

Founded: 1974

Officers: Orville L. Freeman, Chairman of the Board of Directors; Lester R. Brown, President and Senior Researcher; Erik Eckholm, Senior Researcher; Denis Hayes, Senior Researcher; Bruce Stokes, Director of Outreach.

Private, non-profit, research organization. Staff: 12. **Sources of support:** Foundations; United Nations Environment Program and United Nations Fund for Population Activities (for specific projects). **Annual Budget:** No answer.

Objectives and interests: To identify emerging global issues and encourage a reflective approach to global problem-solving; to bring these issues to the attention of decision-makers and the general public through the media and through Worldwatch publications.

Major programs and projects: "The Sisterhood of Man"—women's changing roles in a changing world. "The God That Limped"—impact of technology on society. "The Participatory Society"—community initiatives and ability to solve problems. "The Sustainable Society"—policies that will lead to a sustainable society from an energy and environmental standpoint. Ecological undermining of food production as a result of over-grazing, deforestation, desert encroachment, soil erosion and abandonment, flooding, and silting of irrigation systems; economic, demographic, and political discontinuities facing the world in the last quarter of this century; global strategies for energy equilibrium, with particular attention to possibilities for conservation and alternatives to fossil fuels and nuclear power.

Special facilities: Library of books, periodicals, and reports on the issues of food production and distribution, population growth, environmental issues, the status of women, energy options, and health. (Not for public use.).

Activities: Worldwatch publications program.

Publications: Worldwatch research results are communicated through Worldwatch Papers, which are available from the Institute, and through articles and books, including the following: *Worldwatch Paper Series* (on population, food, women, and energy); *Losing Ground: Environmental Stress and World Food Prospects*, Erik Eckholm (1976); *Rays of Hope: The Transition to a Post-Petroleum World*, Denis Hayes (1977); *The Picture of Health: Environmental Sources of Disease*, Erik Eckholm (1977); *The Twenty Ninth Day: Accommodating Human Needs and Numbers to the Earth's Resources*, Lester R. Brown (1978); *The Sisterhood of Man*, Kathleen Newland (1979); *The God That Limped*, Colin Norman (in preparation); *The Participatory Society*, Bruce Stokes (in preparation); *The Sustainable Society*, Denis Hayes (in preparation).

YANKELOVICH, SKELLY AND WHITE, INC.

Telephone: (212) 752-7500 (NY)
(203) 327-6990 (CT)

575 Madison Avenue
New York, New York 10022, U.S.A.
and
1234 Summer Street
Stamford, Connecticut 06905, U.S.A.   **Founded:** 1959

Officers: Daniel Yankelovich, President; Arthur H. White, Executive Vice-President; Florence R. Skelly, Executive Vice-President.

Private study group specializing in survey research. **Staff:** 110. **Sources of support:** Corporations and foundations. **Annual Budget:** No answer.

Objectives and interests: Commercial market research; public opinion research for media and non-profit organizations; research on social problems.

Major programs and projects: "Social Trends Monitor"—An annual census of changing social values and how new social values can affect consumer marketers, available on a subscription basis to sponsors. "Corporate Priorities"—An annual study of what the American people and their leaders want and are expected to want from business and from particular industries, available on a subscription basis to sponsors.

Special facilities: —

Activities: Slide-show presentations on the Monitor and Corporate Priorities programs are made available to sponsors.

Publications: —

YOUTH MOVEMENT FOR A NEW INTERNATIONAL ORDER (NIO YOUTH)

Telephone: (020)227502

Leliegracht 21
Amsterdam 1016 GR, The Netherlands   **Founded:** 1947

Officers: Jesper Grolin, Chairperson; Gabriella Battaini, Vice-Chairperson; Wim Frankenmolen, Treasurer; Jos Lemmers, Member, Coordinating Team; Karen Seabrooke, Member, Coordinating Team; Howard Huxter, Part-time Publications Officer.

Non-governmental, non-profit, non-aligned, political, youth/student organization.   **Staff:** Four.

Sources of support: Membership fees; grants; project subsidies; ad hoc support.   **Annual Budget:** No answer.

Objectives and interests: Working for principles of federalism; autonomy, cooperation, adequate allocation of decision-making power to "problem level," and participation; working for a New International Order (NIO) based on above principles.

Major programs and projects: "Towards a Strategy for a New International Order"—research project to evaluate work being done and methods employed on NIO. "Young Workers and the NIO"—research project to evaluate out-of-school education programs to inform young workers on development, NIO-related problems. "Follow-up Project on the Special Session on Disarmament (SSD)"—project to evaluate SSD and discover ways to assure implementation of (positive) results; New York City, (October 1978). "Dimensions of European Democratization"—research project based on results of four meetings held by NIO Youth since 1974 on aspects of democratization in Europe. "Mass Media and the New International Information Order"—conference to study how the right to communicate (ethically and legally) can be achieved; Bonn, 1978.

Special facilities: Collection of historical, world-federalist materials dating back to 1947; documentation file on NIO issues.

Activities: Organizes two to three conferences a year for youth and students on NIO-related issues, such as human rights, food and basic needs, democratization, mass media and the new international information order, and qualitative growth and citizen participation in industrialized countries; also concentrates on energy, law of the seas, U.N. reform.

Publications: *Transnational Perspectives*, Rene Wadlow, editor (quarterly journal); *Progress Report*, Karen Seabrooke, editor (monthly, internal report); *Federalism and Non-alignment*, Finn Laursen, editor (1972); *Federalism and World Order, Compendiums I and II*, F. Laursen, editor (1972); *Europe and the NIO* (documentation file edited by NIO Youth, 1977); *Human Rights*, H. Lannung, editor (booklet, 1978).

INDIVIDUALS

INDIVIDUALS

The individuals listed here are the authors of books dealing with the future, serve as officers of important future-oriented groups, or are otherwise prominent in the field. Certain prominent futurists are not included because the necessary autobiographical information had not been received by press time.

Where available, the listing for each individual includes the following information:

Name
Mailing address
Telephone number
Date and place of birth
Profession
Interests and field of specialization
Education
Professional employment
Professional activities
Publications

ABBOTT, WILLIAM LATHAM

Born: 1925, Milwaukee, Wisconsin, U.S.A.

Director
Labor Center
American Association of Community and Junior Colleges
One DuPont Circle
Washington, D.C. 20036, U.S.A.   **Telephone:** (202) 293-7050

Profession: Adult educator

Field of specialization: World of work; employment and training; adult and worker education; self-management and the quality of work life; labor relations; occupational education; life-cycle planning; non-traditional education.

Education: B.A., 1948, M.A., 1951, History, University of Wisconsin.

Professional employment: American Association of Community and Junior Colleges, Labor Center: Director (1976-). Federal City College, Labor Studies Center: Assistant Director (1975-76). Hawaii Federation of College Teachers: Executive Secretary (1971-74). Hawaii American Federation of Laborers and Congress of Industrial Organizations (AFL-CIO): Executive Secretary-Treasurer (1969-71). University of Hawaii, Labor-Management Education Program: Associate Specialist (1967-69). United Rubber Workers: Education Director (1960-67).

Professional activities: Editor, *Careers Tomorrow*, World Future Society; research project with United Auto Workers on educational attitudes of local union leaders (1978); consultant, U.S. Department of Labor's book, *The American Worker* (1975-76); member, Honolulu Manpower Area Planning Council (1973-74); consultant to Hawaii community organization training program "dynamics of social change."

Publications: *The American Labor Heritage* (Industrial Relations Center, University of Hawaii, 1967); *Union Administration* (Industrial Relations Center, University of Hawaii, 1968); "Reporting the Labor Story" (*New Republic*, April 1960); "Politics Towmorrow: The New Coalitions" (*The Nation*, September 23, 1968); "Work in the Year 2001" (THE FUTURIST, Vol. II, No. 1, February 1977).

ABRAMS, MARK ALEXANDER

Born: 1906, London, England

Age Concern
60 Pitcairn Road
Mitcham, Surrey CR4 3LL, England   **Telephone:** (01) 640-5431

Profession: Sociologist

Field of specialization: Social policy planning with special reference to rapid increase in future elderly population.

Education: B.Sc., Economics, London School of Economics, 1927; Ph.D., Economic History, London School of Economics, 1929; Research Fellow, Economics, Brookings Institution (U.S.A.).

Professional employment: Age Concern: Research Director (1977-). Social Science Research Council: Director, Survey Research (1970-77); Chairman, Research Services (1946-69).

Professional activities: Sample surveys of elderly in various English cities (1977-78); longitudinal survey of "young elderly" to identify predictors of non-survival, poor survival and good survival (1977-).

Publications: *Beyond Three Score and Ten* (Age Concern, 1978); "Future of the Old" (*Proceedings of the Annual Conference of the British Association for the Advancement of Science*, 1979); *Profiles of the Elderly* (Age Concern, 1978); *Overview of Problems, Methods, and Use of Subjective Social Indicators* (European Economic Community, 1975); "Changing Social Values in Britain" (*Encounter*), 1975).

ABT, CLARK C.

Born: 1929, Cologne, Germany

President and Treasurer
Abt Associates, Inc.
55 Wheeler Street
Cambridge, Massachusetts 02138, U.S.A.   **Telephone:** (617) 492-7100

Profession: Social scientist; company executive

Field of specialization: Social science research; social policy analysis and evaluation; systems engineering; operations research.

Education: B.S., Engineering, Massachusetts Institute of Technology, 1951; M.A., Literature and Philosophy, Johns Hopkins University, 1952; Ph.D., Political Science, Massachusetts Institute of Technology, 1965.

Professional employment: Abt Associates, Inc.: President and Treasurer (1965-). Raytheon Company: Manager, Advanced Systems Department (1957-64). U.S. Air Force: Navigator; Intelligence Officer (1952-57). Johns Hopkins University: Instructor (1951-52).

Professional activities: President, Council for Applied Social Research (1978-79); Visiting Professor, State University of New York, Binghamton (1975-76); directed development of the Social Audit, a method of measuring the social assets and liabilities of a corporation (1971-74); consultant to U.S. Department .of Health, Education and Welfare, U.S. Department of Housing and Urban Development, and other agencies; designed model for the technology transfer process; has directed research programs on long-range technology forecasting, labor productivity, welfare reform.

Publications: Editor, *The Evaluation of Social Programs* (Sage, 1976); editor with Kenneth Arrow and S. Fitzsimmons, *German-American Social Policy Research* (Abt Books, in press); editor, *Benefits and Costs of Applied Social Research* (Abt Books, in press); *Social Audits* (American Management Association, 1976); contributing author, "The Issue of Social Costs in Benefit/Cost Analysis of Surgery" (Chapter three in *Costs, Risks and Benefits of Surgery*, Oxford University Press, 1977); "The Social Costs of Cancer" (*Social Indicators Research*, 1975); *Serious Games* (The Viking Press, 1970).

ACKOFF, RUSSELL L.

Born: 1919, Philadelphia, Pennsylvania, U.S.A.

Chairman
Social Systems Sciences Unit and Graduate Faculty
University of Pennsylvania
Busch Center, Vance Hall
3733 Spruce Street
Philadelphia, Pennsylvania 19173, U.S.A.

Telephone: (215) 243-6541

Profession: Professor

Field of specialization: Social Systems Sciences

Education: B. Architecture, University of Pennsylvania, 1941; Ph.D., Philosophy of Science, University of Pennsylvania, 1947.

Professional employment: University of Pennsylvania: Chairman, Social Systems Sciences Unit and Graduate Faculty (Current); Chairman, Department of Statistics and Operations Research (1964-69); Director, Management Science Center (1964-71). Case Western Reserve: Associate Professor and Professor of Operations Research (1955-64).

Professional activities: Editorial Board, *Human Relations* (1972-); Editorial Board, *General Systems* (1973-). Memberships: Operations Research Society, The Institute of Management Science, American Statistical Association, Society for General Systems Research, Peace Science Society. Has conducted research and provided consulting services for more than 200 corporations and government agencies. Organizes management education for a variety of institutions.

Publications: *The Art of Problem Solving, Accompanied by Ackoff's Fables* (John Wiley, New York, 1978); *Redesigning the Future* (John Wiley, New York ,1974); *Systems and Management Annual* (Mason and Charter, New York, 1974); co-author, *On Purposeful Systems* (Aldine-Atherton, Chicago, 1972); "Does Quality of Life Have to Be Quantified?" (*General Systems*, Volume II, 1975).

ACQUAVIVA, SABINO

Born: 1927, Padova, Italy

Professor
University of Padova
26, Via del Santo
Padova 35 100, Italy

Telephone: 33 663

Profession: Sociologist

Field of specialization: Value systems; social planning and social and economic development.

Education: Laurea, 1951, Ph.D., Sociology, 1959, University of Padova.

Professional employment: University of Padova: Full Professor (1968-); Assistant Professor (1959); Director of Laboratory of Sociology (1972). All Souls College, Oxford: Visiting Fellow (1975-76).

Professional activities: Currently working on studies on ethnical minorities and crisis of values in Italian society; field research in underdevelopment in Italy for the Institute of Sociology, University of Bonn (1970-76), and for the Italian National Research Council (1973-76).

Publications: *In Principio Era Il Corpo [At the Beginning was the Body]* (Borla, Rome, 1978); *The Eclipse of the Holy in Industrial Society* (Blackwell, Oxford, 1976); co-author, *The Structure of Italian Society: Crisis of a System* (Robertson, London, 1976); *Una scommessa sul futuro: sociologia e programmazione [A Wager on the Future: Sociology and Planning]* (Isedi, Milan, 1972); co-author, *Telescuola [Teleschool]* (Enke Verlag, Stuttgart, 1974); *La montagna del sole [Mountain of the Sun]* (Comunita, Milano, 1971).

ADELSON, MARVIN

Born: 1926, Brooklyn, New York, U.S.A.

Professor
School of Architecture and Urban Planning
University of California-Los Angeles
405 Hilgard Avenue
Los Angeles, California 90024, U.S.A.

Telephone: (213) 825-7932

Profession: Professor of Architecture/Urban Design

Field of specialization: Organizational change strategies and practices; imaging the future; decision-making; creative problem solving; management; educational futures.

Education: B.S., Electrical Engineering, Virginia Polytechnic Institute and State University, 1947; M.A., 1950, Ph.D., 1952, Psychology, University of Illinois.

Professional employment: University of California-Los Angeles: Professor, School of Architecture and Urban Planning (1970-). Information Transfer Corporation: Co-founder and Vice President (1969-70). Institute for the Future: Co-founder (1968-69). System Development Corporation: Principal Scientist and Consultant to President (1961-69). Committee on Utilization of Scientific and Engineering Manpower, National Research Council: Executive Director (1963-64). National Science Foundation: Consultant to Director for Research (1960-). Hughes Aircraft Company: Manager, Command Control and Information Systems Department (1955-61).

Professional activities: Director, Creative Problem-Solving Program for UCLA undergraduates (1971-76); teaches courses on "Imaging the Future" and "Decision Making in Planning and Design"; participant and consultant in workshops and colloquia regarding Management and the Future; has conducted research on social change, future images and forecasting, and in human factors design of complex equipment and human information handling characteristics; principal investigator of a USOE-sponsored research project to develop an evaluation plan for the Creative Problem-Solving Curriculum.

Publications: "Perceptions of the Year 2000" in *Long Range Planning for Special Education, Part I: A Statewide Planning Process* (University of Michigan, 1975); co-author, "Differential Images of the Future" in *The Delphi Method: Techniques and Applications* (Addison Wesley Publishing Company, 1975); "On Changing Higher Education from Within" (*American Behavioral Scientist*, November-December 1974); co-author, "Group Images of the Future," paper presented at the Third World Futures Research Conference, Bucharest, Romania (1972); "Education at the Crossroads of Decision" in *Information Technology—Some Critical Implications for Decision-Makers* (The Conference Board, New York, 1972).
(From the first edition. Corrections not received by press time.)

ADLER-KARLSSON, GUNNAR

Born: 1933, Karlshamn, Sweden

Professor
Roskilde University Center
Box 260' Roskilde, Denmark 4000

Telephone: (03) 363611

Profession: Researcher

Field of specialization: International economic and political relations; comparative social systems.

Education: Dr. of Law, 1962, Ph.D., Economics, 1968, University of Stockholm.

Professional employment: Roskilde University Center: Professor (1974-). UNIDO Consultant (1978). International Institute for Comparative Economic Studies, Vienna: Research Fellow (1971-74). Institute for International Economic Studies, Stockholm University: Research Assistant (1962-68).

Professional activities: Writing a book on how population, material standard, natural resources, technical development, institutional changes, values and violence interact in the shaping of the global future.

Publications: *Der Kampf gegen die absolute Armut [The Struggle Against Absolute Poverty]* (Frankfurt A.M.: S. Fischer Verlag, 1978); *Tankar om den Fulla Sysselsattningen [Thoughts on Full Employment]* (Prisma, Stockholm, 1977, 1978); co-author, with W.H. Wriggins, *Reducing Global Inequities* (McGraw-Hill with Council on Foreign Relations, 1978); *Larobok for 80-Tale [Textbook for the 1980's]* (Prisma, 1975); *Harrying and Carrying Capacity* (Ministry of Foreign Affairs, Stockholm 1974); *Kuba Report — Sieg Older Niederlag? [Kuba Report — Victory or Defeat]* (Europaverlag, 1972); *Western Economic Warfare 1947-1967* (Almquist, 1968); *Functional Socialism* (Prisma, 1967).

AFHELDT, HEIK

General Manager
PROGNOS AG, European Center for Applied Economic Research
Steinengraben 42
CH-4011 Basel, Switzerland

Born: 1937, Insterburg, Germany

Telephone: (061) 22 23 00

Profession: Economist; urbanist

Field of specialization: Urban and regional planning; long-range planning.

Education: Diploma in Business Administration, 1961, Doctor of Public Affairs, 1964, University.

Professional employment: PROGNOS AG: General Manager (1977-); Member of the Board (1970-); Project Manager (1964-). University of Hamburg: Assistant (1962). EWG Brussels: Practitioner (1961).

Professional activities: General Manager of staff of 80 to 100 scientists and consultants; member, steering committee, Robert-Bosch Program for Urban Research; consultant to companies and government; member, advisory committee to West German Ministry on Research Programs; consultant to Organization for Economic Cooperation and Development on industrial development project in Greece.

Publications: *Infrastrukturbedarf bis 1980, Eine Bedarfs—und Kostenschatzung notwendiger Verkehrs—, Bildungs—und Versorgungseinrichtungen fur die BRD [Infrastructure Requirements to 1980: An Estimate of Demand and Costs for Essential Transportation, Education, and Public Service Facilities in the Federal Republic of Germany]* (Kohlhammer Verlag, Stuttgart, Germany, 1967); "Grunde fur die Verkehrsmittelwahl im Nahverkehr und ihre Veranderungstendenzen: in Grundsatzprobleme bei Langfristprognoseng im Personenverkehr" |"Grounds for a Choice of Transportation Options for Short-Distance Traffic, and Changing Trends"| (Schriftenreihe der DVWG e.V., Reihe B25 Koln/Berlin, 1975); "Erfahrungen mit der Beteiligung von Burgern an der Planung" | "Examples of Citizen Involvement in the Planning Process"| (*Garten und Landschaft*, Publication No. 4, 1973).

ALDRIDGE, ALEXANDRA

Lecturer
Alternative Futures
102 Rackham Bldg.
University of Michigan
Ann Arbor, Michigan 48109, U.S.A.

Born: Chicago, Illinois, U.S.A.

Telephone: (313) 764-2199

Profession: Editor, educator

Field of specialization: Utopian/dystopian literature; futures studies.

Education: B.A., Sociology, Millikin University, 1961; M.A., English, Northwestern University, 1963; Ph.D., Comparative Literature, University of Michigan. 1978.

Professional employment: University of Michigan: Lecturer (1975). Wayne State University: Instructor (1968-72).

Professional activities: Principal consultant, University of Wisconsin-Milwaukee to develop project "Technology and the Social Imagination" (1978); Science Fiction Research Association (1977-); Science, Technology and Future Societies, University of Michigan Faculty Association (1975-); lecturer, panelist, Ohio University, University of Missouri-St. Louis, Utopias Conferences (1977-78); lecturer, panelist, consultant, teamed with John W. Aldridge, on a tour of American colleges and universities (1970-71), European Universities and Institutes (1972-73); writer and consultant, Westdeutsche Rundfunk (1972-73); taught various courses in utopias, science fiction and alternative futures, University of Michigan (1975-); organized academic activities relating to utopias and future studies (1974-).

Publications: Co-editor, *Alternative Futures: The Journal of Utopian Studies* (Rensselaer Polytechnic Institute/University of Michigan, Spring 1978); co-author, "Pie in the Sky: Do We Really Want Colonies in Space?" (*The Ecologist*, December 1977); co-editor, special utopias issue of *Extrapolation* (December 1977); "Myths of Origin and Destiny in Utopians Literature: Zamiatin's We" (*Extrapolation*, December 1977); "Scientising Society: The Dystopian Novel and the Scientific World View" (University of Michigan, 1978).

ALTENPOHL, DIETER G.

Born: 1923, Wuppertal, Germany

Vice President, Technology
Swiss Aluminium Ltd.
Feldeggstrasse 4
CH-8034 Zurich, Switzerland

Telephone: (01) 34 9090

Profession: Head of Group Staff "Perspectives and Innovations"

Field of specialization: Technology assessment; technology planning; technology transfer; energy; environmental questions.

Education: Dr. of Science, Physics and Metallurgy, University of Gottingen, 1948.

Professional employment: Swiss Aluminium Limited: Vice President, Head of Group Staff "Perspectives and Innovations" (1975-); Department Director (1968-74); Head of the Process Development Division (1960-67).

Professional activities: Visiting Professor of Materials Science at the University of Virginia, Charlottesville (1978-); Visiting Fellow of the Department of Materials Science and Engineering at MIT, Cambridge (1978-); lecturer at the College of Economy and Social Science in St. Gallen on "The Interaction of Industry and Its Environment"; appointed Professor to the Institut fur Werkstoffkunde at the Technological University of Berlin (1965); lecturer at the Max-Planck-Institut fur Metallforschung at the University of Stuttgart (1968-74).

Publications: *Materials in World Perspective—Technological Assessment of the Materials Industry* (Springer Verlag, Berlin, 1979); *TP—Die Zukunftsformel [TP—The Future Formula]* (Umschau-Verlag, Frankfurt, 1975); *Aluminium von innen betrachtet [Aluminum Viewed from Within]* (Aluminium-Verlag GmbH, Dusseldorf, 4th edition, 1979—also available in French edition); "Tomorrow Begins Today" (Papers presented at the Joint Meeting of the Chemical Marketing Research Association and the Commercial Development Association in St. Louis, 1973); *Technology Transfer* (NATO Advanced Study Institute Series E, No. 6, 1974).

AMARA, ROY

Born: 1925, Boston, Massachusetts, U.S.A.

President/Sr. Research Fellow
Institute for the Future
2740 Sand Hill Road
Menlo Park, California 94025, U.S.A.

Telephone: (415) 854-6322

Profession: Systems scientist; research executive

Field of specialization: Social impact of information systems; future corporate environment; emerging societal issues; methods of long-range planning and futures research.

Education: B.S., Management, M.I.T., 1948; M.A., Arts and Sciences, Harvard University, 1949; Ph.D., Systems Engineering, Stanford University, 1958

Professional employment: Institute for the Future: President/Sr. Research Fellow, (1970-). Stanford Research Institute: Vice President (1968-69); Asst. to the President (1964 and 1968); Executive Director, Systems Sciences (1964-68); Manager, Systems Engineering (1959-64); Senior Research Engineer (1952-59)

Professional activities: Appointed member of Long-Range Planning Committee of United Way of America to study role of United Way in context of future of volunteerism in U.S. to the year 2000 (1976); Assessment of Political and Social Risks of Investment in South Africa (1975); Group Communication through Computers (1972-76); *The Future as Present* (book in preparation); extensive work in computer and communication systems planning and design; first full-scale computer for banking (1955); first passenger space reservation system (1956-58); theory of distributed communication networks (1959-64); member of Steering Committee of Systems, Man, and Cybernetics Group (1972-75).

Publications: Co-author, *Climate Change to the Year 2000: A Survey of Expert Opinion* (Government document, 1978); "Strategic Planning in a Changing Corporate Environment" (*Long Range Planning,* 1978); "Five Emergent Features of U.S. Society and Their Impact on Management in the Next Decade" (*Planning Review,* March 1978); *Planning, Futures and the Skeptics* (Institute for the Future, P-59, 1978); "Probing the Future" (*Handbook of Futures Research,* 1978); co-author, *Linking the Corporation to the Future,* with A.J. Lipinski, Institute for the Future P-58,1977); "Looking Ahead at the Third Century" (*World,* Spring 1976).

ANTOINE, SERGE

Fondation Claude Nicolas Ledoux
  pour les Reflexions sur le Futur
Arc et Senans 25610, France

Born: 1927, Strasbourg, France

Telephone: (16 81) 802563

Profession: Lawyer; environmentalist

Field of specialization: —

Education: Institut d'etudes Politiques *[* Institute for Political Studies*]*, Paris; Faculte de Droit *[* Law Faculty*]*, Paris.

Professional employment: —

Professional activities: Secretary-General of the High Committee for the Environment.

Publications: Publisher of the journal *2000* and co-publisher of the bulletin *Futur Informations*.

APOSTOL, PAVEL A.

71224 Bucharest I
Post Office 63
Casuta postala 58
Romania

Born: 1919, Arad, Romania

Telephone: 795958

Profession: Philosopher; educational forecaster

Field of specialization: Educational forecasting; changing mentalities in developing countries and their impact upon international relationships (social forecasting); new integrative intellectual approaches.

Education: M.A., Philosophy of Culture, 1945, Ph.D., Philosophy, 1948, University of Cluj.

Professional employment: Central Institute for Post-Graduate Teacher's In-Service Training, Bucharest: Methodology of Philosophy and Social Sciences (1970-). Polytechnical Institute, Bucharest: Philosophy, Logic and Methodology of Science (1963-70). University of Cluj: Professor, Philosophy and Methodology of Social Sciences (1948-52).

Professional activities: Project Director, Academy of Social and Political Sciences of the S.R. of Romania, studying social dynamics in Romania; Director for obtaining the Doctor of Philosophy degree at the University of Bucharest; member of the Board of the State Commission for Prognostics in Education and Manpower Development (1970-74); Association Internationale Futuribles: correspondent of the Conseil d'Administration (1975-), Vice-President (1972-75); World Futures Studies Federation: member of the Executive Board (1976-), Vice President (1973-76); Senior Fellow of the Academy of Social and Political Sciences, S.R. of Romania (1970); lectures and courses at numerous universities and other organizations;

research project in France, Centre National de Recherche Scientifique, laboratoire de prospective appliquee (1977-78).

Publications: *Omul anului 2000 [The Man of the Year 2000]* (The Romanian Encyclopaedical Publishing House and Junimea Publishing House, 1969 first edition, 1972 second edition); *Calitatea Vietii si Explorarea Viitorului [The Quality of Life and the Exploring of the Future]* (Political Publishing House, 1975); *Viitorul [The Future]* (Romanian Scientific and Encyclopaedical Publishing House, 1977); *Trei Meditatii Asupra Culturii [Three Meditations about the Culture of Tomorrow]* (Dacia Publishing House, 1970); *Cibernetica, Cunoastere, Actiune [Cybernetics, Knowledge, Action]*, 1969; *Educatie si Pedagogie in Perspectiv Operational [Education and Pedagogy in an Operational Approach]* (Pedagogical and Didactical Publishing House, 1969).

ARMER, PAUL

Born: 1924, Montebello, California, U.S.A.

President
Armer Associates
105 Hillside Avenue
Menlo Park, California 94025, U.S.A.

Telephone: (415) 854-3063

Profession: Computer scientist

Field of specialization: Social implications of technology and science, particularly of computers and information processing technology; obsolescence of knowledge and its impact on individuals and institutions; impact of electronic funds transfer systems.

Education: A.B., Meteorology, University of California-Los Angeles, 1946; U.C.L.A. Executive Program, Graduate School of Business, 1960.

Professional employment: Armer Associates: President (1976-). Harvard University: Research Associate and Lecturer in the Business School (1970-72). Stanford University: Director, Computation Center (1968-70); Lecturer, Computer Science Department (1973-); Fellow and Program Coordinator, Center for the Advanced Study in the Behavioral Sciences (1972-76).

Professional activities: Chairman, Association for Computing Machinery (ACM) Committee on Computers and Public Policy (1978-); member of ACM Committee on Self-Assessment (1974-); President, American Federation of Information Processing Societies (AFIPS) (1968-69); consultant to three presidential commissions (1964, 1965, and 1976).

Publications: Co-author, "A Self-Assessment Procedure" *(Communications of the ACM, May 1976)*; co-author, "A Problem-List of Issues Concerning Computers and Public Policy" *(Communications of the ACM, September 1974)*; "Electronic Funds Transfer Systems and the Consumer" *(Computers and People , June 1976)*; "Obsolescence and Self-Assessment" *(Proceedings of the ACM Special Interest Group on Computer Personnel Research, June 1972)*; "The Individual: His Privacy, Self-Image, and Obsolescence" in *Management of Knowledge* (U.S. Government Printing Office, 1970).

ARNSTEIN, SHERRY PHYLLIS

Born: 1930, New York, New York, U.S.A.

2500 Virginia Avenue No. 417
Washington, D.C. 20036, U.S.A.

Telephone: (301) 443-5134

Profession: Policy analyst

Field of specialization: Technology assessment, particularly in the field of health care.

Education: B.A., Group Work, University of California-Los Angeles, 1951; M.A., Communications, American University, 1963.

Professional employment: National Center for Health Services Research, Department of Health, Education, and Welfare: Senior Service Fellow (1975-). Self-Employed: Consultant on Public Policy (1968-75). Department of Housing and Urban Development: Chief Advisor on Citizen Participation (1967-68). Department of Health, Education, and Welfare: Special Assistant to the Assistant Secretary (1965-66). President's Committee on Juvenile Delinquency: Staff Consultant (1963-65). *Current Magazine:* Washington Editor (1961-63).

Professional activities: Currently designing a program on Technology Assessment for the National Center for Health Services Research (HEW); Member, International Society for Technology Assessment (1976); preparing a paper on "State of the Art of Technology Assessment"; participated in a technology assessment on solar energy (1974-75); designed a national workshop on technology assessment (1975); lectured on citizen participation in public programs (1969-).

Publications: Co-author with A. Christakis, *Perspectives on Technology Assessment* (Science and Technology Publishers, 1975); "Technology Assessment: A Working Model for Public Participation" (*Public Administration Review,* January 1975); "A Ladder of Citizen Participation" (*Journal of the American Institute of Planners,* July 1969).

ARVAY, STEPHEN
Sheridan College
Trafalgar Road
Oakville, Ontario
L6H 2L1 Canada

Born: 1937, Hamilton, Ontario, Canada

Telephone: (415) 362-5861

Profession: Sociologist

Field of specialization: Value systems; technology assessment; modernization—industrialization; developing nations; political models and ideologies.

Education: B.A., 1963, M.A., 1973, McMaster University; M.Ed., University of Toronto, 1968; Ph.D., Waterloo University, 1976; York University, Ph.D Candidate, 1979.

Professional employment: Sheridan College: Master of Sociology (1968-75). Western Technical High School: Academic—Tech. Teacher (1964-67).

Professional activities: Presently designing college courses in the technology, Third World, values and ideologies area.

Publications: *The Future as a Social Problem: A Video-Based System* (Sheridan 1978); editor, *Sociology: Learning by Objectives — A Programmed Course* (Sheridan, 1971); *Anthropology: Learning by Objectives — A Programmed Course* (Sheridan, 1972).

ASIMOV, ISAAC
10 West 66th Street, 33-A
New York, New York 10023, U.S.A.

Born: 1920, Petrovichi, USSR

Telephone: (212) 362-1564

Profession: Author; educator

Field of specialization: Science fiction; science writing

Education: B.S., Chemistry, Columbia University, 1939; M.A., Chemistry, Columbia University, 1941; Ph.D., Chemistry, Columbia University, 1948.

Professional employment: Self-employed

Professional activities: To date has published 195 books in all fields, including futurics; Associate professor of biochemistry at Boston University School of Medicine.

Publications: *Biochemistry and Human Metabolism* (Williams and Wilkins, 1952); *Foundation* (1951); *Foundation and Empire* (1952); *Second Foundation* (1953); *Today and Tomorrow and ...* (1973).

AUERBACH, LEWIS E.
Executive Director
Research and Media Services
166 Clemow Avenue
Ottawa K1S 2B4 Ontario, Canada

Born: 1941, New York, New York, U.S.A.

Telephone: (613) 233-4355 or 232-8850

Profession: Consultant and Writer

Field of specialization: Implications of demographic change; aging, northern development, presentation of science and futures in the media.

Education: A.B., *magna cum laude*, History and Science, Harvard University, 1963; A.M., History of Science, Harvard University, 1965.

Professional employment: Research and Media: Executive Director (1978-); Science Council of Canada: Science Advisor (1974-1978). Television Ontario: Producer and Education Supervisor (1971-74). Canadian Broadcasting Corporation: Producer (1967-71). American Institute of Physics: Research Associate (1967). Harvard University Teaching Fellow (1964-67).

Professional activities: Conducting seminar in Science and Technology Policies at the Graduate School of Public Administration, Carleton University, Ottawa, (1979); studying geotechnical problems of the gas pipeline in the Arctic; consultant and seminar organization activities; numerous articles in press or in process of completion about Canada in the 1980's; has produced a large number of radio and television shows, mainly of the "intellectual" and documentary variety; lectured at several universities and professional societies on current activities and research interests.

Publications: "Implications of the Changing Age Structure of the Canadian Population" (*Information Canada*, May 1976); co-author, "Discussion Paper on Northern Development" (*Issues in Canadian Science Policy*, May 1976); "To Choose a Future — Future Studies in Sweden (A Review)" (*Science Forum*, March 1975); "Report of Senate Committee on Science Policy" (*Canadian Forum*, April 1971); "Scientists in the New Deal..." (*Minerva*, Vol. 3, 1967); "Berger Report Sets a New Precedent in Assessing Technology's Effects" (*Science Forum*, August 1977).

AUERBACH, PHILIP HONE

By-Products, Inc. Route 66 and Joliet Avenue
McCook, Illinois 60525 U.S.A.

Born: 1940, New York, New York, U.S.A.

Telephone: (312) 242-3641

Profession: Planner

Field of specialization: Government planning and policy-making; political socialization; values, ideologies, and belief-systems; theory and methodology of futures research.

Education: B.A., Anthropology, Harvard College, 1961; M.A., Political Science, University of Chicago, 1967.

Professional employment: By-Products, Inc.: Director of Planning (1976-). World Future Society: Research Director (1975-76). Cornell University: Assistant Professor of Government (1970-74).

Professional activities: Research, editing, and writing for the World Future Society report describing the theory and practice of futures research; consultant for the structure and format of the World Future Society's Resources Directory (1975-76); taught graduate and undergraduate seminars on the politics of the future of Europe, political speculations about the future, and the politics of imaginary societies (1971-74); research on the development of political reasoning among French school children (1964-).

Publications: A review of *Things to Come: Thinking about the Seventies and Eighties* (*The American Political Science Review*, Volume LXX, March 1976); co-author, *Prehistoric Maya Settlements in the Beliza Valley* (Harvard University, 1965); co-author, "On Studying Anthropology in Paris" (*Anthropology Tomorrow*, 1964).

AUJAC, HENRI

Scientific Advisor to the President
Bureau d'Informations et de Previsions Economiques
/Bureau of Economic Information and Forecasts/ (BIPE)
122, avenue Ch. de Gaulle
92522 Neuilly sur Seine, France

Born: 1919, Fez, Morocco

Ecole des Hautes Etudes en Sciences Sociales
/Institute for Advanced Research in the Social Sciences/
54, boulevard Raspail
75006 Paris, France

Telephone: 747 11 66 (BIPE)

Profession: Economist

Field of specialization: National planning and technical, economic and social evolution and long-term projection.

Education: Ecole des Mines, Nancy; Faculte de Droit, University of Grenoble; Ecole des Sciences Politiques, Paris.

Professional employment: Ecole des Hautes Etudes en Sciences Sociales: Study Director. Bureau d'Informations et de Previsions Economiques: Scientific Advisor to the President. Ministry of Finance: Economist. C.E.C.A.: Researcher in the Economics Section. I.S.E.A.: Researcher.

Professional activities: Currently conducting research on the development of France's economy and society; research on energy problems; supervising doctoral theses dealing with technical progress and economic and social development; has conducted research on inflation considered as a consequence of the behavior of social groups; research on the use of input-output tables in the preparation of France's national development plans.

Publications: "L'influence et le comportement des groupes sociaux sur le developpement d'une inflation" ["The Influence and Behavior of Social Groups in the Development of Inflation"]; "Towards a New Social Input-Output Table: The Dynamics of Social Groups and Institutions" (Sixth International Conference on Input-Output Techniques, Vienna, April 1974); "A New Approach to Technological Forecasting in French National Planning" in *Science and Technology in Economic Growth*, B.R. Williams, ed., (Proceedings of a conference held by the International Economic Association, St. Anton, Austria, 1973); "Comparaisons des potentiels respectifs de developpement de la RFA et de la France" ["Companion of Development Potentials of West Germany and France"] (Documentation Francaise); *Les Chances d'une Communaute Mediterraneenne* [Chances of a Mediterranean Community] (to be published in 1979).

AYRES, ROBERT UNDERWOOD

Professor of Engineering and Public Policy
Carnegie-Mellon University
Department of Engineering and Public Policy
Schenley Park
Pittsburgh, Pennsylvania 15213, U.S.A.

Born: 1932, Plainfield, New Jersey, U.S.A.

Telephone: (412) 578-2672

Profession: Economist; systems analyst

Field of specialization: Resource/environmental economics; technology; long-range forecasting; public policy analysis; model development.

Education: B.S., Mathematics, University of Chicago, 1954; M.S., Physics, University of Maryland, 1956; Ph.D., Mathematical Physics, University of London, 1958.

Professional employment: Carnegie-Mellon University: Professor of Engineering and Public Policy (1979-). Variflex Corporation: Vice-President and Chairman (1978-). Delta Research Corporation: Vice-President (1976-1978). International Research and Technology Corporation: Vice President and Director of Research (1968-). Resources for the Future, Inc.: Visiting Scholar (1967-68); Non-resident staff member (1966-67). Hudson Institute: Research staff member (1962-67). Yeshiva University Graduate School of Science: Research Associate (1961-62). G.C. Dewey Corporation, New York City: Research Associate (1960-61). University of Maryland: Research Associate, Department of Physics (1958-60).

Professional activities: Forecast of worldwide transportation energy demand, Department of Energy (1977-); forecast of world auto industry to 1995, Business International (1974-75); forecast of world steel industry to 2000 for UN (1977-1978); development of world process encyclopedia for UN (1978-79); development of programming models for technology choice for World Bank (1973-).

Publications: *Uncertain Futures: Challenge to Decision-makers* (Wiley-Interscience, New York, 1979); *Resources, Environment and Economics* (Wiley-Interscience, New York, 1978); *Technology Forecasting and Long Range Planning* (McGraw-Hill Book Company, New York, 1969); co-author, *Aspects of Environmental Economics: A Materials Balance-General Equilibrium Approach* (Johns Hopkins University Press, 1970); co-author with R.P. McKenna, *Alternatives to the Internal Combustion Engine* (Johns Hopkins University Press, 1972); co-author, "World Auto Study to 1996" (multi-client study, 1975); co-author, "Use of Explicit Technological Forecasts in Long Range Input-Output Models" (*Technology Forecasting and Social Change*, 1976).

BACKSTRAND, GORAN KARL

Head of Section
Secretariat for Futures Studies
Regeringsgatan 65
Stockholm, Sweden

Born: 1937, Lund, Sweden

Telephone: (08) 763-3818

Profession: Civil servant

Field of specialization: International relations

Education: B.L., University of Lund, Sweden, 1961; Diploma, European Institute for Business Administration, Fontainebleau, France, 1962.

Professional employment: Secretariat for Future Studies: Head of Section (1973-). Ministry for Foreign Affairs: Head of Section (1967-73). Swedish Embassy, Algiers, Algeria: First Secretary (1965-67). Swedish Embassy, Bonn, Federal Republic of Germany: First Secretary (1963-65).

Professional activities: Participated in four major future studies sponsored by the Secretariat for Future Studies in 1974-75 (resources and raw material, working life in a future perspective, energy and society, and Sweden and the world society); responsible for undertaking an information service to the government and to the public in the field of future studies; diplomatic service (1962-73); secretary to the research committee responsible for Swedish preparations for the 1972 UN Conference on the Human Environment.

Publications: Co-author, "How much is enough? How much is lagom?" (essay in *Development Dialogue's* special issue "What now," Dag Hammarskjold Foundation, Uppsala, 1976); co-author, *Utveckling och miljo i u-landerna [Development and Environment in Developing Countries]* (Bokforlaget Prisma, Stockholm, 1972); *Debatten om tillvaxtens granser [The Debate about Limits to Growth]* (Secretariat for Future Studies, 1974).

BAIER, KURT E.

Department of Philosophy
University of Pittsburgh
Forbes and Bigelow
Pittsburgh, Pennsylvania 15260, U.S.A.

Born: 1917, Vienna, Austria

Telephone: (412) 624-5776

Profession: Professor of Philosophy

Field of specialization: Ethical theory; ethics of life and death; political theory; medical ethics; business ethics; quality of life.

Education: Law, University of Vienna, 1935-38; B.A., Philosophy, University of Melbourne, 1945; M.A., University of Melbourne, 1947; D. Phil., Oxford University, 1952.

Professional employment: University of Pittsburgh: Professor of Philosophy (1967-); Chairman, Department of Philosophy (1962-67). Canberra U. College, Australian National University: Foundation Professor (1957-62). University of Melbourne: Senior Lecturer (1955-56); Lecturer (1947-49, 1953-55); Assistant Lecturer (1945-47).

Professional activities: President, American Philosophical Association, Eastern Division (1977); Consulting Editor to *The American Philosophical Quarterly, Metaphilosophy, Philosophical Research Archives*, and *Philosophical Monographs*. Consultant for the National Commission for the Protection of Human Subjects of Biomedical and Behavioral Research; Member of the Assembly of Behavioral and Social Sciences of the National Research Council.

Publications: *Moral Point of View* (Cornell University Press, 1958); *Values and the Future* (The Free Press, 1969); "The Meaning of Life" (Inaugural Lecture, Canberra University College, 1957); "Moral Obligation" (*American Philosophical Quarterly*, 1966); "Towards a Definition of Quality of Life" (*Environmental Spectrum*, D. Van Nostrand Company, 1973).

BAKER, DAVID EDWIN

Executive Director
Illinois 2000
Suite 1960, 20 North Wacker Drive
Chicago, Illinois 60606, U.S.A.

Born: 1942, Oakland, California, U.S.A.

Telephone: (312) 372-7373

Profession: Administrator of futures planning programs

Field of specialization: Citizen involvement in futures planning; alternative futures; population; food and environmental futures; state and national growth policy; business long range planning.

Education: A.B., History and Economics, Stanford University, 1964, M.A., International Affairs, School of Advanced International Studies, 1968.

Professional employment: Executive Director: Illinois 2000 (1977-); The Population Institute: Director, Intern Program (1973-77); Governmental Affairs Institute: Special Assistant, Management Services (1969-73); Program Officer, International Visitor Service (1968-69).

Professional activities: Seminar leader, "The Future: A Macro View" for Illinois Bell Telephone (1978-79); member, Economic Development and Jobs Committee, Illinois Employment and Training Council; member, Steering Committee, Illinois Environmental Education Task Force; member, Board of Directors, and Treasurer, The Population Institute, Washington, D.C., guest lecturer, "Man and Environment Series" Waterloo University, Waterloo, Ontario (February 1978).

Publications: "Anticipatory Democracy Experiments at the State and Local Level" in Clement Bezold, ed., *Anticipatory Democracy* (Random House, 1978); "The States Experiment with Anticipatory Democracy" (THE FUTURIST, October, 1976); "State Goals Groups: Performance and Potential" (The World Future Society BULLETIN, March-April, 1976); "State Futures Commissions: Planning for the Quality of Life" (*State Planning Issues*, June 1975); "Unclouding the Crystal Ball, Fourteen States Are Leading the Way in Futures Planning" (*AAUW Journal*, April, 1976).

BARACH, ARNOLD B.

Editor, Special Projects
Kiplinger Washington Editors, Inc.
1729 H Street, N.W.
Washington, D.C. 20006, U.S.A.

Born: 1913, Wallingford, Connecticut, U.S.A.

Telephone: (202) 298-6400

Profession: Writer; economist

Field of specialization: Economic and technological trends and their impact on individuals and families; population growth and implications; futures methodology.

Education: B.A., Economics, Wesleyan University, 1935; M.S., Journalism, Columbia University, 1936.

Professional employment: Kiplinger Washington Editors, Inc.: Editor, Special Projects (1978-). *Changing Times* Magazine: Executive Editor (1948-). Department of Defense: Information Head, Munitions Board (1947-48). Robert R. Nathan Associates: Writer (1946-47). Office of War Information: Information Specialist, Psychological Warfare (1943-46). U.S. Department of Agriculture: Information Specialist (1938-43).

Professional activities: Member of Boards of World Future Society and National Mental Health Association; occasional lecturer on future economic trends; consultant for Spartansburg, S.C., in Transition Project (1973-75); lecturer and panel participant on future trends at several college campuses and community symposia (1960-70).

Publications: *1975 and The Changes to Come* (Harper and Row, 1962); *The New Europe and Its Economic Future* (Macmillan, 1964); *U.S.A. and Its Economic Future* (Macmillan, 1964), "The Fabulous Fifteen Years Ahead" (*Changing Times*, January 1961); *Famous American Trademarks* (Public Affairs Press, 1970).

BARKER, JOEL A.

President
Infinity Limited, Inc.
1301 Cherokee Avenue
West St. Paul, Minnesota 55118, U.S.A.

Born: 1944, Rochester, Minnesota, U.S.A.

Telephone: (612) 457-5543

Profession: Futurist, educator.

Field of specialization: Futures methodology, paradigm conflict resolution, new designs for educational curricula.

Education: B.S., English Education, University of Minnesota, 1966.

Professional employment: Infinity Limited: President (1978-). Science Museum of Minnesota: Director, Future Studies Department (1976-); Education Specialist (1975-76). St. Paul Academy: Teacher (1968-75).

Professional activities: Co-director, Horizons Seminar, IBM Corporation; Minnesota Project for Quality Education (1973-76); Director of Futures Workshops for teachers (1974-77); Consultant for corporations, religious and educational institutions; Chairman, Steering Committee, Minnesota State Department of Educational Futures Studies (1975-76).

Publications: —

BARRETT, FRANCIS DERMOT

Born: 1924, Ottawa, Ontario, Canada

President
Management Concepts Limited
31 Pineridge Drive
Scarborough, Ontario
M1M 2X6 Canada

Telephone: (416) 264-4361

Profession: Management consultant

Field of specialization: Organization and management; creativity and innovation; planning; time management; industrial relations; communications; international management.

Education: B.Sc., Psychology, McGill University, 1948; Ph.D., Industrial Economics, Massachusetts Institute of Technology, 1953.

Professional employment: Management Concepts Limited: President (1969-). York University: Professor and Director, Executive Development Division (1966-69). Queen's University: Professor and Chairman, Executive Development Program (1960-66). Banff School of Advanced Management: Associate Director (1959-60).

Professional activities: Conducting research, consulting and teaching future-focused management methods in Canada, United States and the United Kingdom for corporations, governments and public institutions; writing, editing and publishing a bimonthly newsletter entitled *Insights and Innovations for the Manager of Change;* founding chairman of the Toronto chapter of the World Future Society (1971); Advisory Committee to the president of the Institute for the Future (1972-76).

Publications: "Creativity Techniques: Past, Present and Future" (*Advanced Management Journal,* Winter 1978); "Metamorphoses by MBO" (*C.A. Magazine,* August 1975); "Perspectives on Time Management" (*Management by Objectives Journal,* 1977); "The Management of Time" (*The Business Quarterly,* University of Western Ontario, Spring 1969); "Communication: What Does It Mean in Business?" (*Canadian Textile Journal,* 1972).

BARUCHELLO TERENZI, BARBARA

Born: 1949, Rome, Italy

Coadiuture
Office for Regional Coordination
Italian Foreign Ministry
20, Via Luigi Siciliani
Rome 00137, Italy

Telephone: 82 75 169

Profession: Future studies educator

Field of specialization: Future studies education; relationships; social and human forecasting.

Education: Political science, Universita Degli Studi di Roma.

Professional employment: Italian Foreign Ministry, Office for Regional Coordination; Coadiutore (1977-). IRADES, Education and Relationships Section, Center for Future Studies (1974-77).

Professional activities: Presently a consultant for futures studies education and relationships to IRADES (in re-organization).

Publications: Collaborator, *Goals for Humanity: A Report to the Club of Rome* (Mondadori EST, 1978); collaborator, *Goals for Mankind: A Report to the Club of Rome* (E.P. Dutton, 1977); co-author, *Social and Human Forecasting* (Edizioni Previsionali, Rome, 1975); editor, *Social and Human Forecasting Newsletter* (Edizioni Previsionali, Rome, 1974-75).

BAWOROWSKI, LUDWIK JERZY
Project Director
Forecasting Research Center
Technical University of Wroclaw
Wybrzeze Wyspianskiego 27
50-370 Wroclaw, Poland

Born: 1927, Krakow, Poland

Telephone: 48-42-38

Profession: Economist; technology policy analyst

Field of specialization: Futures methodology; methodological problems and experiments in forecasting of science and technology, especially in a planned economy.

Education: M.A., Industrial Economics, Highschool of Economics, 1960; Ph.D., Industrial Economics, The Oscar Lange Academy, 1968.

Professional employment: Technical University of Wroclaw, Forecasting Research Center: Project Director (1972-). Institute for Environmental Protection—Wroclaw Division: Assistant Director (1968-71). Polish Economics Society: Director of Wroclaw Division (1962-67).

Professional activities: Project Director, systems and procedures of international science and technology forecasting, Technical University of Wroclaw (1978-); Head of Postgraduate Studies in Science and Technology Forecasting; lecturer, Technical University of Wroclaw (1975-); Project Director, R and D Forecasting 2020 (1975-78); lecturer in the TNOIK on forecasting process, technology and methodology (1973-75); conception of a national forecasting system, Technical University of Wroclaw, Forecasting Research Center (1972-75).

Publications: "Goals and Values in Poland" in *Goals in a Global Community* (Pergamon Press, New York, 1977); *Technological Forecasting in the Seventies* (Humboldt Universitat, Berlin, 1978); "Forecast of a Demand for Scientific Staff for R and D Process in the System of Social, Scientific and Economic Forecasting" (Praha, 1974); "Some Future Problems of Technology Equilibrium in a Planned Economy" (V SAINT Conference, Salzburg, 1975); "The Impact of Technological Forecasting on Programming of Education and Research at a Technical University"—Papers of the International Conference "Management of Research and Education" (Technical University Wroclaw, 1976).

BEAN, LOUIS H.
3714 N. Randolph Street
Arlington, Virginia 22207, U.S.A.

Born: 1896, Lithuania

Telephone: (703) 243-3360

Profession: Economist; statistician

Field of specialization: Economic analysis; political analysis; weather and crop forecasting (a year or more ahead).

Education: B.A., Mathematics, Chemistry, University of Rochester, 1919; M.B.A., Factory management, Harvard School of Business, 1922.

Professional employment: Consultant in economic and statistical analyses (1953-). U.S. Budget Bureau: Fiscal Analyst (1943-46). Board of Economic Warfare: Assistant to Administrator (1940-43). Economic Advisor to three Secretaries of Agriculture (1933-40, 1946-53). U.S. Department of Agriculture: Economic analyst (1923-33).

Professional activities: Consultant in economic and statistical analyses (1953-).

Publications: "A Simplified Method of Graphic Carvilinear Correlation" (*Journal of American Statistical Association*, December 1929 and December 1930); "Crop Yields and Weather" (U.S. Dept. of Agriculture, 1942); *How to Predict Elections* (Knopf, 1948); *Carvilinear Correlation* (A. M. Kelly, 1969); "International Industrialization and Per Capita Income" (National Bureau of Economic Research, Vol. 8, *Income and Wealth*, 1946).

BECKER, HAROLD S.
Executive Vice President and Treasurer
The Futures Group
124 Hebron Avenue
Glastonbury, Connecticut 06033, U.S.A.

Born: 1929, Chicago, Illinois, U.S.A.

Telephone: (203) 633-3501

Profession: Policy analysis; forecaster

Field of specialization: Technology assessment; futures research; futures methodology; policy analysis.

Education: Aeronautical Engineering, Georgia Institute of Technology; Master of Engineering, University of California-Los Angeles; graduate courses in management and advanced mathematics.

Professional employment: The Futures Group: Executive Vice-President and Treasurer (1971-). Institute for the Future: Treasurer and Senior Fellow (1969-71). National Aeronautics and Space Administration: Director Advanced Projects Office and Deputy Director Advanced Systems (1966-69). North American Aviations: Director, Launch Vehicles, Advanced Systems (1963-66).

Professional activities: Currently directing studies with The Futures Group on consumer lifestyles and spending patterns as they relate to banking and financial services; work for industrial and governmental clients has included studies of corporate strategies of U.S. automative manufacturers, vegetable substitutes for animal protein, energy supply and demand, consumer purchasing patterns and household appliances, trends in determinants of electrical energy and natural gas consumption in the state of California, alternative socioeconomic scenarios of conditions in the United States related to demand for air travel and approaches to policy analysis for the national aviation system; has taught and lectured for industry and academia on policy analysis, technology assessment, forecasting, futures research, industrial planning and decision-making, community goals and development planning, management and organization concepts and personnel motivation techniques.

Publications: Co-author, *Alternative Socioeconomic Conditions in the United States and Their Associated Energy Targets* (The Futures Group, April 1978); co-author, *Incorporating Uncertainty in Energy Supply Models,* two volumes (Electric Power Research Institute, February 1978); "Government Spending and Tomorrow's Marketplace" *(Executive,* Vol. 4, No. 3, June 1978); *An Assessment of Socioeconomic and Demographic Determinants of Electrical Energy and Gas Consumption in California* (Five volumes, December 1976); "The Thrust of National Civil Aviation R and D Policy in the United States: The Role of Federal Funding of R and D" (invited testimony submitted to the U.S. House of Representatives Committee on Science and Technology, Subcommittee on Aviation and Transportation R and D, May 1976).

BECKWITH, BURNHAM PUTNAM

656 Lytton Avenue (C430)
Palo Alto, California 94301, U.S.A.

Born: 1904, Carthage, Missouri, U.S.A.

Telephone: (415) 324-0342

Profession: Economist; independent author

Field of specialization: Welfare economics; price theory; future social, political, and economic trends.

Education: B.A., Philosophy, Stanford University, 1926; Business Administration, Harvard University, 1926-28; M.A., Economics, University of Southern California, 1930; Ph.D., Economics, University of Southern California, 1932.

Professional employment: Private study, travel, writing (1949 to date). OMGUS, Berlin: Economist and Statistician (1946-49). Biarritz American University, France: Instructor (1945-46). University of Georgia: Associate Professor of Economics (1938-40).

Professional activities: Manuscripts in progress: book of essays on social reform; book on ideal income determination; a utopian novel; a critical review of literature on futurism.

Publications: *Free Goods—The Theory of Free Distribution* (self-published, 1977); *Liberal Socialism Applied* (self-published, 1978); *The Next 500 Years* (Exposition Press, 1967); *Government by Experts: The Next Step in Political Evolution* (Exposition Press, 1972); *Liberal Socialism* (Exposition Press, 1974); *The Case for Liberal Socialism* (Exposition Press, 1976); *Religion, Philosophy, and Science* (Philosophical Library, 1957).

BELL, DANIEL

370 William James Hall
Harvard University
33 Kirkland Street
Cambridge, Massachusetts 02138

Born: 1919, New York, New York, U.S.A.

Telephone: (617) 495-3843

Profession: Sociologist

Field of specialization: Macro-historical change

Education: B.S., Economics, City College of New York, 1939; Ph.D., Sociology, Columbia University, 1960.

Professional employment: Harvard University: Professor of Sociology (1969-). Columbia University: Professor of Sociology (1959-69). *Fortune*: Editorial Board (1948-58). University of Chicago: Instructor, Social Science (1945-48). *Common Sense*: Managing editor (1945). *The New Leader*: Staff writer; managing editor (1940-45).

Professional activities:

Publications: *The Cultural Contradictions of Capitalism* (Basic Books, 1976); *The Coming of Post-Industrial Society* (Basic Books, 1973); editor, *Towards the Year 2000* (Daedalus/Beacon Press 1967); *The End of Ideology* (Free Press, 1960); *Marxian Socialism in the U.S.* (Princeton University, 1952).

BELL, WENDELL   **Born:** 1924, Chicago, Illinois, U.S.A.
Professor
Department of Sociology
Yale University
New Haven, Connecticut 06520, U.S.A.   **Telephone:** (203) 436-8251

Profession: Sociologist

Field of specialization: Social futuristics; theories of social change; beliefs, attitudes and values; decisions of nationhood in the new states of the Caribbean.

Education: B.A., Social Science, Fresno State University, 1948; M.A., Sociology, University of California, Los Angeles, 1951; Ph.D., Sociology, UCLA, 1952.

Professional employment: Yale University: Professor of Sociology (1963-); Director of Undergraduate Studies (1976-); Director of Comparative Sociology Training Programs (1969-77). University of California, Los Angeles: Associate Professor to Professor (1957-63). Northwestern University: Associate Professor (1954-57). Stanford University: Assistant Professor of Sociology and Director, Survey Research Facility (1952-54). U.S. Navy: Naval Aviator (1943-46).

Professional activities: President, Caribbean Studies Association (1979); member-at-large, Section on Social and Economic Sciences of the American Association for the Advancement of Science (1978-82); consultant, The Future of Corrections, for the National Institute of Law Enforcement and Criminal Justice (1978); research grant for a study of democracy in Jamaica, Social Science Research Council (1978-79); National Science Foundation grant for a comparative study of nationhood, social stratification, and the ideology of equality.

Publications: "Equality, Social Justice, and the Future," in *Focus on the Future* (University of Houston, College of Education, 1978); co-author "Equality, Success, and Social Justice in England and the United States" (*American Sociological Review*, April 1978); co-author and editor, *The Sociology of the Future* (Russell Sage Foundation, Basic Books, 1971); co-author and editor, *The Democratic Revolution in the West Indies* (Schenkman, 1967); *Jamaican Leaders: Political Attitudes in a New Nation* (University of California Press, 1964); co-author, *Social Area Analysis* (Stanford University Press, 1955).

BELLMAN, RICHARD ERNEST   **Born:** 1920, New York, New York, U.S.A.
Professor
University of Southern California
University Park
Department of Electrical Engineering
Los Angeles, California 90007, U.S.A.   **Telephone:** (213) 741-2015

Profession: Professor

Field of specialization: Dynamic Programming and invariant imbedding; mathematics; applied mathematics.

Education: B.A., Brooklyn College, 1941; M.A., University of Wisconsin, 1943; Ph.D., Princeton University, 1946.

Professional employment: University of Southern California: Professor of Mathematics, Electrical Engineering and Medicine (1965-). RAND Corporation, Santa Monica, California: (1953-65). Stanford University: Professor and Associate Professor of Mathematics (1948-52). Princeton University: Associate Professor of Mathematics (1946-48).

Professional activities: National Academy of Engineering (1977); American Academy of Arts and Sciences (1975).

Publications: *Methods of Nonlinear Analysis*, Vol. 11 (Academic Press, Inc., 1973); co-author with C.P. Smith, *Simulation in Human Systems: Decision-Making in Psychotherapy* (John Wiley and Sons, 1973); co-author with G.M. Wing, *An Introduction to Invariant Imbedding* (John Wiley and Sons, 1975); *Can Computers Think?* (Boyd and Fraser Publishing Co., 1978); *Introduction to Analytic Number Theory* (in process).

BENDER, ALLAN DOUGLAS
Vice President, R and D Operations
Smith Kline Corporation
1500 Spring Garden Street
Philadelphia, Pennsylvania 19101, U.S.A.

Born: 1936, Iowa City, Iowa, U.S.A.

Telephone: (215) 854-5640

Profession: Biologist

Field of specialization: R & D planning and management; technological forecasting.

Education: B.A., Biology, Williams College, 1957; M.S., Physiology, University of Iowa, 1959; Ph.D., Physiology, Thomas Jefferson University, 1962.

Professional employment: Smith Kline and French Laboratories: Vice President, R and D Operations (1978-); Vice President, Planning and Operations (1971-78); Director, Science Information (1967); Coordinator, Long Range Planning (1966); Group Leader (1964-66); Senior Scientist (1962-64).

Professional activities: Member, American Physiological Society, World Future Society, Institute of Management Science; Fellow, American College of Cardiology; Fellow, Gerontological Society.

Publications: Co-author, "Delphic Study Examines Developments in Medicine" (*Futures*, 1969); co-author, *Delphi Study of the Future of Medicine* (Smith Kline and French, 1969); "Simulation of R & D Investment Strategies" (*Omega*, 1976); "Investment Model for R & D Project Evaluation and Selection" (*IEEE Transactions* 1971).

BENNIS, WARREN
240 Lake Avenue
Aspen, Colorado 81611, U.S.A.

Born: 1925, New York, New York, U.S.A.

Telephone: (303) 925-8137

Profession: Educator

Field of specialization: Future of institutional environments.

Education: A.B., Antioch College, 1951; Honors Certificate, London School of Economics, 1952; Ph.D., Social Sciences and Economics, 1955, Hicks Fellow, 1952, Massachusetts Institute of Technology.

Professional employment: Centre d'etudes Industrielles, Geneva, Switzerland: U.S. Professor of Corporations and Society (1978-). Pepperdine University: Executive-in-Residence (1978-). University of Cincinnati: President and University Professor (1971-78). State University of New York at Buffalo: Provost, Faculty of Social Sciences and Administration; Vice President for Academic Development; Acting Executive Vice President, Provost of Natural Sciences (1967-70). Massachusetts Institute of Technology: Associate Professor of Industrial Management; Professor of Organizational and Management Psychology; Chairman, Organization Studies Group, Alfred P. Sloan School of Management (1959-67).

Professional activities: Currently writing a monthly column for *Technology Review;* Advisory Board, National Council, American Society for Public Administration; Visiting Committee in Philosophy, Massachusetts Institute of Technology, National Training and Development Services; member, American Academy for the Advancement of Science (Fellow), American Board of Professional Psychologists (Diplomate), American Psychological Association (Fellow), and the American Sociological Association (Fellow).

Publications: "Toward a Learning Society: A Basic Challenge to Higher Education" *(New Directions for Education and Work,* Summer 1978); *Backing Into the Future* (University of Houston Press, 1978); "Encounters of a 4th Kind" *(Journal of Applied Behavioral Sciences); The Unconscious Conspiracy: Why Leaders Can't Lead* (American Management Association, 1976); *Beyond Bureaucracy: Essays on the Development and Evolution of Human Organization* (formerly titled *Changing Organizations,* McGraw—Hill, 1973); co-author with John Thomas, *Management of Change and Conflict* (Penguin Publishers, 1973); co-author with P.E. Slater, *The Temporary Society* (Harper and Row, 1968); editor, with K.D. Benne and R. Chin, *The Planning of Change: Readings in the Behavioral Sciences* (Holt, Rinehart and Winston, Third edition, 1976).

BERMAN, LOUISE M.   **Born:** 1928, Hartford, Connecticut, U.S.A.
Professor of Education
Department of Administration, Supervision and Curriculum
College of Education
University of Maryland
College Park, Maryland 20742, U.S.A.   **Telephone:** (301)454-5864
Profession: Educator

Field of specialization: Curriculum planning; decision-making.

Education: A.B., English, Wheaton College, 1950; M.A., 1953, Ed. D., 1960, Curriculum and Teaching, Teachers College, Columbia University.

Professional employment: University of Maryland: Professor of Education (1967-); Acting Associate Dean (1978-). Association for Supervision and Curriculum Development: Associate Secretary (1965-67). University of Wisconsin-Milwaukee: Assistant and Associate Professor (1960-65). Central Connecticut State College: Instructor (1954-58).

Professional activities: Investigator on research project on children's involvement and decision making; co-editor, *Feeling Valuing, and the Art of Growing,* ASCD 1977 Yearbook; assisted in planning World Conference on Education, Instanbul, Turkey (1977); President, Board of Directors, Association for Supervision and Curriculum Development (1979-82); Community Development Project, Brazil (1963); Director, Center for Young Children (1967-75).

Publications: *New Priorities in the Curriculum* (Charles E. Merrill, 1968); *Supervision, Staff Development and Leadership* (Charles E. Merrill, 1971); *From Thinking to Behaving* (Teachers College Press, 1966); co-author, *Personalized Supervision* (Association for Supervision and Curriculum Development, 1966); co-author, *Curriculum: Teaching the How, What, and Why of Living* (Charles E. Merrill, 1977).

BERRY, ADRIAN M.   **Born:** 1937, London, England
Daily Telegraph
135 Fleet Street
London EC4, England   **Telephone:** 353-4242
Profession: Author and journalist

Field of specialization: The extreme long-term future of mankind; astronautics; astronomy; cosmology; astrophysics; space travel; planetology.

Education: Honours, History, Oxford University, 1959.

Professional employment: *Daily Telegraph* (British newspaper): Science Correspondent (1977-). *Sunday Telegraph* (British newspaper): Assistant Editor (1972-77); Science Correspondent (1969-72).

Professional activities: Fellow of the Royal Astronomical Society (1973-); Senior Member of the British Interplanetary Society (1973-); reported for *London Daily Telegraph*, covering many important stories, including Apollo 11 in 1969, the first moon-landing mission, and other manned space missions.

Publications: *The Iron Sun: Crossing the Universe through Black Holes* (E.P. Dutton, New York, 1977); Warner paperbacks, 1979); *The Next Ten Thousand Years: A Vision of Man's Future in the Universe* (Saturday Review Press. E.P. Dutton, New York, 1974; New American Library, 1975); articles in U.S. and British magazines.

BERRY, DAVID JOHN   **Born:** 1939, Kampala, Uganda
Lecturer
Mass Media and Communications Department
Stockwell College of Education
Rochester Avenue
Bromley, Kent, United Kingdom   **Telephone:** (01) 460 2355

Profession: University lecturer (film, T.V., communications)

Field of specialization: Communications and global society; education and the future; role of audio-visual communications in teaching and publicizing alternative futures studies; science fiction literature and (film/t.v.) images of the future; utopian thought and contemporary communities; values and the future.

Education: B.A. Moral Sciences Modern European and American History, 1962, M.A., 1966, Christ's College, Cambridge; Postgraduate Cert. Ed., History, Institute of Education, London University, 1963; M.A., Birmingham University Centre for Contemporary Culture Studies, 1974.

Professional employment: Stockwell College of Education, London University: Lecturer, Mass Media and Communications (1966-). Ravensbourne College of Art and Design: Lecturer, Moving Picture Communications (1965-67). Swedish-British Centre, Sweden: Lector, English as a foreign language (1963-64). British Council and Karachi Grammar School: Teacher (1958-59).

Professional activities: Coordinator, London Group of the World Future Society (1971-76); organized a series of six seminars titled "Futures Forum" at the Institute of Contemporary Arts, London (April 1975); lecturing in film and TV studies, developing courses, encouraging research in film and TV, Stockwell College of Education (1972-); research on the role of science fiction literature and film TV image of the future, and development of a "contemporary cultural studies approach" to science fiction literature (1969-74); conducted courses on utopian thought and futures studies at the Teilhard Centre for the Future of Man (1972), and man and the future at Marylebone Institute of Education (1975); supervised a student exhibition "Designing for the Future" (1975).

Publications: *The Science Fiction Novel, 1930-70* (Masters thesis, 1974); *Herbert Marcuse, Exposition and Analysis of His Theories* (Mimeo, 1970); "Man-made Futures: Readings in Society, Technology and Design" — review of an Open University course (*Futures*, February 1975).

BEST, FRED JOSEPH   **Born:** 1944, Oakland, California, U.S.A.
Associate
National Commission for Manpower Policy
1522 K Street, N.W. Suite 300
Washington, D.C. 20005, U.S.A.   **Telephone:** (202) 724-1571

Profession: Sociologist, policy analyst

Field of specialization: Social forecasts; flexible life scheduling; future of work; family structure and sex roles; industrial sociology; sociology of education.

Education: B.A., History and Economics, University of California, Berkeley, 1967; M.B.A., Complex Organization and Industrial Relations, University of California, Berkeley, 1972; Ph.D., Sociology, University of Massachusetts, 1978.

Professional employment: National Commission for Manpower Policy: Associate (1977-). United States Department of Commerce, Economic Development Administration: Special Assistant to Deputy Assistant Secretary for Economic Development (1977). Quality of Life Research Associates: Director (1973-77). United States Department of Health, Education and Welfare: Resident Consultant, Office of the Assistant Secretary for Education (1975).

Professional activities: Member of the Board of Directors, National Council for Alternative Work Patterns (1977-); Member of the Steering Committee, Committee for Dialogue on Work Sharing (1977-).

Publications: Editor, *The Future of Work* (Prentice-Hall, 1973); co-author, "Education, Work and Leisure—Must They Come in That Order?" (*Monthly Labor Review*, July 1977); "Recycling People: Work Sharing Through Flexible Life Scheduling" (THE FUTURIST, February 1978); "The Effect of Work Scheduling on Time-Income Trade-offs" (*Social Forces*, September 1978); *Recycling People: The Case for Flexible Life Scheduling* (forthcoming).

BESTUZHEV-LADA, IGOR VASSILIEVICH   **Born:** 1927, Lada (Pensa), USSR
Head, Department of Forecasting
Institute for Sociological Research
Section on Social Forecasting
USSR Academy of Sciences
Novo-Cheremushki, 46
Moscow 117418, USSR   **Telephone:** 128 91 22

Profession: Historian and sociologist

Field of specialization: History of futurology — social forecasting; theory of futurology — futures research; futures research in sociology.

Education: Dipl. Historian, Institute of International Relations, Moscow Institute of History, 1950; Candidate of Sciences, 1954, Dr. of Historical Sciences, 1963, Academy of Sciences, Moscow.

Professional employment: Institute for Sociological Research, USSR Academy of Sciences: Head, Department of Forecasting (1969-). Institute for Labor Movement: Head, Department of Forecasting (1967-69). Institute of History: Research Fellow (1954-66).

Professional activities: Research project "The Society Way of Life: A System of Social Indicators for the Year 1990" (1976-80); course on social forecasting at the Moscow University; President, Section of Social Forecasting, Soviet Sociological Association (1967-); Co-President, Research Committee on Futures Research, International Sociological Association (1970-); consulting in several state offices (1967-).

Publications: Editor and co-author, *Forecasting in Sociology: Some Paradigms* (in Russian, Publishing House Mysl, 1978); editor and co-author, *Forecasting the Social Needs of Youth* (in Russian, Publishing House Nauka, 1978); *Family: Yesterday, Today, Tomorrow* (in Russian and English, Publishing Houses Znanie and Novosti, 1978); *Forecasting the Way of Life* (Publishing House Znanie, Kiev, 1975); *The Window into the Future* (Publishing House Mysl, Moscow, 1970); "Utopias of Bourgeois Futurology" (THE FUTURIST, December 1970); "Evolution of American Futurology" (in Russian, *USA: Economics, Politics, Ideology*, No. 3, 1977).

BEZOLD, CLEMENT   **Born:** 1948, Coral Gables, Florida, U.S.A.
Director
Institute for Alternative Futures
1624 Crescent Place, N.W.
Washington, D.C. 20009 U.S.A.   **Telephone:** (202) 265-0346

Profession: Futurist, political scientist, public interest activist

Field of specialization: Anticipatory democracy; legislative foresight; alternative futures planning; citizen participation.

Education: B.S.F.S., International Affairs, Georgetown University, 1970; M.A., 1973, Ph.D., Political Science, 1976, University of Florida.

Professional employment: Institute for Alternative Futures: Director (1977-). University of Florida Law School, Center for Governmental Responsibility: Assistant Director (1975-77); Social Science Coordinator (1974-75); Graduate Assistant, Research (1973-74); Graduate Assistant, Department of Political Science (1971-72).

Professional activities: Research on state and local citizen futures projects; research, seminars and workshops on legislative foresight for Congress and state legislatures; research on citizen education and the future; work with public interest groups, other voluntary organizations and corporations to develop their futures planning capacity; co-editor of *Government Tomorrow*, a newsletter of The World Future Society.

Publications: Editor, *Anticipatory Democracy: People in the Politics of the Future* (Random House, 1978); "Citizen Education: Participation in Shaping the Future" in Willis Harman, *Citizen Education and the Future* (U.S. Office of Education/Task Force on Citizen Education, 1978); "Congress and the Future" (THE FUTURIST, Vol. 9, No. 3, July 1975).

BIDERMAN, ALBERT D.
Research Associate
Bureau of Social Science Research, Inc.
1990 M Street, N.W.
Washington, D.C. 22207, U.S.A.

Born: 1923, Paterson, New Jersey, U.S.A.

Telephone: (202) 223-4300

Profession: Sociologist

Field of specialization: Social indicators; institutions for social knowledge; military institutions; crime.

Education: B.A., Economics, New York University, 1946; M.A., Sociology, University of Chicago, 1952; Ph.D. Sociology, University of Chicago, 1964.

Professional employment: Bureau of Social Science Research: Research Associate (1958-); Assistant Director (1970-). Society for the Investigation of Human Ecology: Research Fellow (1957-58). United States Air Force: Research Social Psychologist (1952-57). Illinois Institute of Technology: Instructor, Sociology (1948-52).

Professional activities: Chairman, Ad Hoc Committee on Statistical Graphics, American Statistical Association; Vice-Chairman, Council on Social Graphics; Member of Executive Committee, Inter-University Seminar on Armed Forces and Society; Member, International Editorial Board, *Victimology: An International Journal;* Committee on Government Statistics, American Sociological Association (1973-); Panel for the Evaluation of Crime Surveys, Committee on National Statistics, National Research Council (1974-76); Advisory Board, National Criminal Justice Manpower Survey, National Planning Association (1974-75); Howard Ikenberry Jensen Lecturer in Sociology, Duke University (1975).

Publications: Co-editor, *Measuring Work Quality for Social Reporting* (Halsted Press, 1976); co-editor, *Social Scientists and International Affairs* (John Wiley and Sons, 1969); co-author, *An Inventory of Surveys of the Public on Crime, Justice and Related Topics* (United States Government Printing Office, 1973); co-author, "Evaluation Research Procurement and Method" (*Social Science Information*, June-August 1972); "Victimology and Victimization Surveys" chapter in *Victimology: A New Focus*, Drapkin and Viano, eds. (Lexington Books, 1975).

BIGELOW, BRUCE EDWARD
Associate Professor of History
Denison University
Granville, Ohio 43023, U.S.A.

Born: 1944, Bluffton, Ohio, U.S.A.

Telephone: (614) 587-0810 ext. 239

Profession: Historian; educational analyst

Field of specialization: East European history and politics (special emphasis on Yugoslavia); values systems and cultural norms; space and space technology; simulation; audio-visual development; educational development.

Education: B.A., Mathematics and History, College of Wooster, 1966; M.A., 1967, Ph.D., 1972, History, University of Chicago.

Professional employment: Denison University: Associate Professor (1971-). Colgate University: Director, Yugoslav Study Group (1975, 1978). Denison Simulation Center: Director (1977-78). Great Lakes Colleges Association: Yugoslav Representative (1970, 1972, 1973, 1978).

Professional activities: Consulting on educational futures, simulation use and development (1977-); teaching courses on East Europe, Middle East, futures and ethics (1971-); lecturing on Yugoslavia, simulation, educational futures (1971-); writing on history and futuristics, Yugoslavia as model of world development (1978-); developed and directed work on simulation use and evaluation (1971-78); wrote and produced two 16mm 30-minute films (1973-77); directed four summer seminars in Yugoslavia for faculty and students (1970-78); member, World Future Society.

Publications: "History Simulation" in *The Guide to Simulations and Games* (4th edition, 1978-79); "Simulation in History" (*Simulations and Games*, 1978); co-author, "Values, History and Simulation" (*Proceedings of Denison Simulation Center*, 1978); "Centralization Versus Decentralization in Interwar Yugoslavia" (*Southeast Europe*, 1974); *Essays on Yugoslav History and Culture* (Colgate University, 1975).

BIZE, RENE
60 avenue de la Bourdonnais
75007 Paris, France

Born: 1901, Paris, France

Telephone: 551-63-38

Profession: Physician

Field of specialization: Scientific study of needs, i.e., "chreiology."

Education: M.S.; Neuropsychiatry.

Professional employment: Conservatoire National des Arts et Metiers: Professor of Work Psychology (1948-70). School of Anthropology: Professor (1948-). Now honorary.

Professional activities: Current research on "chreiology," cybernetics and systems; member, International Society for Science and Society, Yugoslavia; member, French Society of Neurology, Psychology and Cybernetics; Neuropsychologist (1950-75); work psychology (1948-75).

Publications: *Le Penser Efficace [Effective Thinking]* (Paris, 1966); *L'equilibre de corps et de la pensee [Body and Thought Equilibrium]* (C.E.P.L., Paris, 1969); *Journees Francaises de chreiologie [French Days of Chreilogy]* (U.F.O.D., Paris, 1968); *L 'Homme dans l'Entreprise [Man in Business]* (Paris, 1958); *Le Troisieme Age [The Third Age]* (C.E.P.L., Paris, 1970).

BLOCK, A. ESKIL
Director of Research
National Defence Research Institute
Linnegatan 89
Stockholm 10450, Sweden

Born: 1932, Goteborg, Sweden

Telephone: (08) 63 1500

Profession: Political scientist; scientific reporter

Field of specialization: Futures methology, especially scenarios; conflicts; values; resources; organized crime.

Education: Diploma Engineer, Electronics, 1954, Dr. of Engineering, Physics, 1959, Chalmers Goteborg; M. of Science, Physics, 1958, M. of Politics (almost completed 1964), Lund University.

Professional employment: National Defence Research Institute: Director of Research (1969-71 and 1973-); Coordinator of Belgian Project (1971-73). SW Educational Television: Producing Director (1967-69). SW Radio Television: Producer and Reporter (1964-67). Technical University of Lund: Lecturer (1961-64).

Professional activities: Projects on Herman Kahn and methodology (1974-79), earth resources (1976-82), organized crime (1976-82), and low-level conflicts (1972-); currently producing a report on methodology documentation for scenarios; lecturing; journalism in several papers and radio.

Publications: Co-author, *Framtiden—Hot Eller Lofte? [The Future — Threat or Promise?]* (Bonniers, 1971); *Framtidsmiljt fur Utbildning [Future Environment for Training]* (Liber, 1971); *Forskare ser Framat [Scientists Look Forward]* (Forum fur Samtallsdebatt, 1976); *Om Jordens Resurser [On World Resources]* (Ultrikespolitiske Institutet, 1978; *Tempus Futurum [Future Time]* (1970); co-author, *Manniskan och Tekniken i Framtidssamtallet [Man and Technology in Future Society]* (Liber, 1976); several articles on organized crime.

BONNER, JAMES
Professor of Biology
California Institute of Technology
1201 E. California Boulevard
Pasadena, California 91125, U.S.A.

Born: 1910, Ansley, Nebraska, U.S.A.

Telephone: (213) 795-6811

Profession: Biologist

Field of specialization: Molecular biology of the chromosomes; control of gene expression in higher organisms.

Education: A.B., Chemistry and Mathematics, University of Utah, 1931; Ph.D., Biology, California Institute of Technology, 1934.

Professional employment: California Institute of Technology: Professor of Biology (1946-); Associate Professor (1943-46); Assistant Professor (1938-43); Instructor (1935-38). National Research Council: Postdoctoral Fellow in Europe (1934-35).

Professional activities: Research in molecular biology and control of gene expression (1960-); consultant to various American corporations; Consultant and Member, Advisory Committee, Malaysian Rubber Research Institute, Kuala Lumpur (1965-); Advisor, Commonwealth Bank of Australia (1949-62).

Publications: Co-author, *The Next 90 Years* (1967); co-author, *The Next 80 Years* (1977); editor, *Plant Biochemistry* (Academic Press, 1950, second edition, 1965, third edition, 1976); co-author, *Principles of Plant Physiology* (Freeman Publishing Company, 1952); co-author, *The Next 100 Years* (Viking Press, 1957); editor, *The Nucleohistones* (Holden-Day, 1964); *The Molecular Biology of Development* (Oxford Press, 1965).

BOOKCHIN, MURRAY

Born: 1921, New York, New York, U.S.A.

Professor
Ramapo College of New Jersey
Ramapo Valley Road
Mahwah, New Jersey 07430, U.S.A.

Telephone: (201) 825-8200

Profession: Social ecologist

Field of specialization: Alternate technology; urban sociology; social ecology.

Education: Educated at City College of New York and New School for Social Research.

Professional employment: Ramapo College: Full Professor (1974-). Goddard College, Institute for Social Ecology: Director (1972-). City University of New York, Richmond College: Visiting Professor (1970-72). Alternate University of New York: Lecturer (1969-71).

Professional activities: Research in aquaculture and alternate energy patterns (1974-); pioneered in application of social theory to environmental problems; founder of Institute for Social Ecology at Goddard College, Plainfield, Vermont.

Publications: *Post-scarcity Anarchism* (Ramparts Press, 1971); *The Limits of the City* (Harper and Row, 1977); *The Spanish Anarchist* (Harper and Row, 1978); "Toward an Ecological Society" (*Philosophica,* 1976).

BORGESE, ELISABETH MANN

Born: 1918, Munich, Germany

Associate
Center for the Study of Democratic Institutions
Box 4068
Santa Barbara, California 93103, U.S.A.

Telephone: (805) 969-3281

Profession: Author

Field of specialization: Marine resources; ocean management; law of the sea.

Education: Abitur, Classical Studies, Freies Gymnasium, Zurich; Mathematics, University of Chicago; Diploma, Piano, Conservatory of Music, Zurich.

Professional employment: Center for the Study of Democratic Institutions: Associate (1964-). Encyclopedia Britannica: Executive Secretary, Board of Editors (1964-67). International Publications, Inc.: Editor (1952-.62). University of Chicago: Research Associate (1945-51).

Professional activities: Chairman, Planning Council, International Ocean Institute (1971-); Projects on the law of the sea, Mediterranean, Caribbean, and the new international economic order; Member, Club of Rome; Member, Board of Trustees, RIO Foundation; Editor, Ocean Yearbook.

Publications: *The Drama of the Oceans* (Harry Abrams, 1976); *The Ocean Regime* (Center for the Study of Democratic Institutions, 1968); co-author with Arvid Pardo, *The Law of the Sea and the New International Economic Order* (University of Malta Press, 1976); editor, *Pacem in Maribus* (Dodd, Mead, 1972); editor with David Krieger, *Tides of Change* (Charter and Mason, 1974); also published many books and articles in other fields.

BOSSEL, HARTMUT H.   **Born:** 1935, Braunschweig, Germany
Director of Research
ISP-Institute for Applied Systems Analysis and Prognosis
Medizinsche Hochschule Haus W3G
D3 Hannover 61, Federal Republic of Germany   **Telephone:** (0511) 5325410

Profession: Engineer; systems analyst

Field of specialization: Computer-assisted policy analysis; numerical and nonnumerical models; cognitive systems analysis.

Education: Dipl. Ing., Mechanical Engineering, Technical University, Darmstadt, 1961; Ph.D., Aeronautical Science, University of California, Berkeley, 1967.

Professional employment: ISP-Institute for Applied Systems Analysis and Prognosis, Hannover: Director of Research (1978-). ISI, Karlsruhe: Senior Scientist (1972-78). University of California, Santa Barbara: Associate Professor (1970-72); Assistant Professor (1967-70). Northrop Corporation: Engineer (1962-63).

Professional activities: Development of formalized methods for cognitive analysis, including nonnumerical computer processing; development of orientation theory for forecasting behavior tendencies; development of instruments for environmental impact assessment of legal codes; energy modeling (1973-75); modeling of value-oriented behavior (1974-77).

Publications: Author and editor, *Concepts and Tools of Computer-assisted Policy Analysis* (Birkhauser, Basel 1977); *Burgerinitiativen entwerfen die Zukunft [Citizens Initiative Sketch the Future: The Economistic vs. the Ecological Alternative]* (S. Fischer, Frankfurt 1978); author and editor, *Systems Theory in the Social Sciences* (Birkhauser, Basel, 1976); author and editor, *Energie richtig gentzt [Energy Alternatives]* (C.F. Miller, Karlsruhe, 1976); co-author, "Experiments with an 'Intelligent' World Model" (*Futures*, June 1978).

BOTEZ, MIHAI C.   **Born:** 1940, Bucharest, Romania
Senior Research Fellow
Systems Studies Division
University of Bucharest
14, Academiei Street
Bucharest 70109, Romania   **Telephone:** (90) 15-15-16

Profession: Mathematician; policy analyst

Field of specialization: Forecasting and planning methodology; systems and prospective logic; operation research and systems analysis and design; applications in development strategies.

Education: M.A., Operations Research, University of Bucharest, 1963; Ph.D., Statistics and Operations Research, Institute for Mathematics, Romanian Academy of Science, 1966.

Professional employment: University of Bucharest, Systems Studies Division: Senior Research Fellow (1977-). International Center for Methodology of Futures and Development Studies: Director (1974-77). Romanian National Committee for Futures Studies: Executive Secretary (1973-). University of Bucharest, Systems Studies Division: Head of Department (1974-).

Professional activities: "Evolution through societal learning," a technical contribution to the "learning report" to The Club of Rome (1977-); "alternative logics and ethics in international behavior" (1976-77); member of the Advisory Board, *Technological Forecasting and Social Change* (1977-); Head, Bucharest Chapter, Society for General Systems Research, Washington, D.C.; member, Executive Committee, World Future Studies Federation (1976-).

Publications: *Mathematical Tools in Forecasting Techniques* (University of Bucharest Press, 1975); *An Introduction to Prospective Research* (CIDSP Publishing House, 1971); co-author and editor, *A Course in Prognosis* (CIDSP Publishing House, 1972); "Social Framework for Technological Change" (*Philosophical Review*, 1975); co-author, *Prognosis and Military Conflicts* (Romanian Army Publishing House, 1973).

BOTKIN, JAMES W.
Project Director and Co-author
The Club of Rome Learning Project
26 Grozier Road
Cambridge, Massachusetts 02138, U.S.A.

Born: 1943, New Jersey, U.S.A.

Telephone: —

Profession: Educator

Field of specialization: Learning; education; global issues.

Education: B.A., International Relations, Harvard College, 1965; M.B.A., 1968, D.B.A., 1973 University Administration and Computer Based Systems, Harvard Business School.

Professional employment: Club of Rome: Project Director and Co-author (1977-). Salzburg Seminar: Academic Director (1972-77). Harvard Business School: Research Associate (1970-72).

Professional activities: Associate in Education, Harvard Graduate School of Education (1977-79); member, U.S. Commissioner's Task Force on Global Education (1978); Fellowship Award, The German Marshall Fund of the U.S. (1977-78); member, World Future Studies Federation and World Association for Social Perspectives.

Publications: Co-author, *Learning to Bridge the Human Gap* (Pergamon Press, forthcoming).

BOUCHER, WAYNE I.
Senior Research Associate
Center for Futures Research
Graduate School of Business Administration
University of Southern California
Los Angeles, California 90007, U.S.A.

Born: 1934, Bay City, Michigan, U.S.A.

Telephone: (213) 742-5229

Profession: Analyst and Research Administrator

Field of specialization: Conceptual issues in futures research; role of the humanities in futures research; implementation of futures research results in the private sector and in government; continued development of such methods as the Interview Delphi and the Focused Planning Effort (FPE).

Education: B.A., 1956, M.A., 1960, English Language and Literature, University of Michigan; Graduate work in philosophy, University of Missouri.

Professional employment: Center for Futures Research, Graduate School of Business Administration, University of Southern California; Senior Research Associate (1978-). National Commission on Electronic Fund Transfers: Deputy Director and Director of Research (1976-78). The Futures Group: Vice-President and Secretary (1971-76). Institute for the Future: Research Associate (1969-71). The Rand Corporation: Deputy Assistant to the President (1963-69). University of Missouri: Instructor in English (1958-63).

Professional activities: Studies of the Future of the Consumer Finance Industry to the Year 2000 (1978-) and Technology Assessment of the Personal Computer (1978-); member, Editorial Board, *Business Tomorrow* (WFS); member, Advisory Board, *Technological Forecasting and Social Change*.

Publications: More than 65 reports, papers, and book chapters; author and editor *The Study of the Future: An Agenda for Research* (U.S. Government Printing Office, 1977); co-author and editor, with E.S. Quade, *Systems Analysis and Policy Planning* (American Elsevier, New York, 1968).

BOULADON, GABRIEL ANTOINE
Director
PRESI S.A.
2 ave Hector Berlioz
Poisat, Grenoble, Isere, France F 38.320

Born: 1927, St. Etienne, Loire, France

Telephone: (76) 25.32.72

Profession: Director

150

Field of specialization: Technological forecasting; technology assessment; new systems of transportation and energy

Education: Ecole Centrale, Lyon, 1951; Sec. Education (Baccalaureate in France).

Professional employment: PRESI S.A.: Director (1978-). Battelle Institute, Geneva: Director of Programs (1972-77); Head of Engineering Department (1965-72); Head of Mechanical Group (1957-65); Engineer (1955-57). Swiss Industry (turbines): Engineer (1952-55).

Professional activities: Consultant for Organization for Economic Cooperation and Development in Paris and Battelle Geneva in the field of transportation; inventor of various new systems of transportation (including pneumatic tube train, an accelerated moving pavement); has given a course in Technology Forecasting in Milan, Italy; is a member of the Editorial Boards of *Futures* and *Transportation Planning and Technology;* has lectured in Paris, Tokyo, London, and the U.S.

Publications: "European Transport Over the Next 25 Years" *(Futures,* August 1977); "Potential for Energy Savings in European Transport" (Asahi Shimbum, Second International Symposium on Man and Transport, May 1978); "The Transport Gaps" *(Science Journal,* Vol. 3, No. 4, April 1967); "Transport: Forecasting the Future" *(Science Journal,* Vol. 3, No. 10, October 1967); "Technological Forecasting as Applied to Transport" *(Futures,* March 1970).

BOULDING, ELISE
Professor
Institute of Behavioral Science, No. 1
University of Colorado
Boulder, Colorado 80302, U.S.A.

Born: 1920, Oslo, Norway

Telephone: (303) 492-6836

Profession: Sociologist

Field of specialization: Localist, community-centered world order modeling; development of androgynous society; replacement of public school systems by community-wide education.

Education: B.A., English, Douglass College, 1940; M.S., Sociology, Iowa State College, 1949; Ph.D., Sociology, University of Michigan, 1969.

Professional employment: Dartmouth College, Department of Sociology: Visiting Professor (1978-79). University of Colorado, Department of Sociology: Professor (1973-); Associate Professor (1969-73); Assistant Professor (1968-69); Lecturer (1967-68). Eastern Michigan University: Instructor (1966-67).

Professional activities: Council, American Sociological Association (1977-); U.S. Commission for UNESCO (1978-); Advisory Council, United Nations University Program in Human and Social Development (1977-); research network convenor, Consortium on Peace Research, Education and Development (1975-); Board, Institute of World Order (1973-).

Publications: *Childrens Rights and the Wheel of Life* (Transaction Press, 1978); co-author, *The Social System of the Planet Earth* (Addison-Wesley, 1979); translator, *Image of the Future,* Fred Polak, Utrecht, 1955 (English translation, Oceana Press, 1961); "Futuristics and the Imaging Capacity of the West" (in *Human Futuristics,* M. Maruyama and J. Dator, eds., University of Hawaii, Social Science Research Institute, 1971); "Societal Complexity and Religious Potential"; *Underside of History* (Westview Press, 1976); *Women in the Twentieth Century World Community* (Sage Publications, 1976); *International Data Handbook on Women* (Sage Publications, 1976).

BOULDING, KENNETH EWART
Professor of Economics
Institute of Behavioral Science No. 3
University of Colorado
Boulder, Colorado 80302, U.S.A.

Born: 1910, Liverpool, England

Telephone: (303) 492-7526

Profession: Economist

Field of specialization: Peace research; international systems; grants economics.

Education: B.A., First Class Honours, School of Philosophy, Politics, and Economics, 1931, M.A., 1939, Oxford University.

Professional employment: University of Colorado: Professor of Economics (1968-); Director of the Program of Research on General Social and Economic Dynamics, Institute of Behavioral Science (1967-). University of Michigan: Co-Director, Center for Research on Conflict Resolution (1961-64); Research Director (1964-65); Director (1965-66); Professor of Economics (1949-67). McGill University: Angus Professor of Political Economy and Chairman of Department (1946-47).

Professional activities: President, American Association for the Advancement of Science (1979); teaching and research at the University of Colorado; extensive writing and lecturing; President, American Economic Association (1968); President, International Studies Association (1974-75); President, Association for the Study of the Grants Economy (1970-); President, Society for General Systems Research (1957-59).

Publications: *Ecodynamics, A New Theory of Societal Evolution* (Sage, Inc., Beverly Hills, 1977); *Stable Peace* (University of Texas Press, 1978); *Economy of Love and Fear: A Preface to Grants Economics* (Wadsworth, 1973); *A Primer on Social Dynamics* (Free Press, 1970); *The Meaning of the Twentieth Century* (Harper and Row, 1964); *Economics as a Science* (McGraw—Hill, 1970); *Economic Analysis* (Harper, 1941).

BOWERS, RAYMOND

Born: 1927, London, England

Director
Program on Science, Technology and Society
Cornell University
614 Clark Hall
Ithaca, New York 14853, U.S.A.

Telephone: (607) 256-3810

Profession: Physicist; Director, Science, Technology and Society Program

Field of specialization: Technology assessment, particularly in the area of electronic communications.

Education: B.Sc., Physics, London University, 1948; Ph.D., Physics, Oxford University, 1951; Postdoctoral Fellow, Physics, University of Chicago, 1951-53.

Professional employment: Cornell University: Director, Program on Science, Technology and Society (present); Professor of Physics (1960-). Westinghouse Electric Corporation: Research Physicist (1954-60).

Professional activities: Fellow of the American Physical Society, the Institute of Physics (U.K.), and the American Academy of Arts and Sciences; Member of the Association for the Advancement of Science; formerly chairman of the Solid State Division of the American Physical Society.

Publications: Co-author with Edward Dickson, *The Video Telephone* (Praeger Publishers); principal author, *Communications for a Mobile Society* (Sage Publications).

BRADLEY, HELEN GENEVIEVE

Born: 1932, Cleveland, Ohio, U.S.A.

Research Associate
Center for Futures Research
University of Southern California
University Park
Los Angeles, California 90007, U.S.A.

Telephone: (213) 741-5229

Profession: Planner

Field of specialization: Urban studies, telecommunications, public broadcasting.

Education: B.A., Architecture, Radcliffe College, 1953; Urban Studies, Loyola University; Public Administration, Roosevelt University; Master of Management, Management Information Systems, Northwestern University, 1976.

Professional employment: Center for Futures Research: Research Associate (1976-). Metropolitan Structures: Systems Manager (1970-76). Cook County Department of Public Aid: Social Worker (1969-70). Urban Training Center: Training Staff (1968-69). Louis C. Holloway, Jr., Architect: Draftswoman (1962-68).

Professional activities: Study on The Future of Network Information Services (1976-78); Guide to Telecommunications Technologies for the Corporation for Public Broadcasting (1978); study of alternative delivery systems for instructional television in Spokane for the Corporation for Public Broadcasting (1977-78); study of the impact of forthcoming satellite capability on a public television station (1977); brochure on new communications technologies for Pacific Telephone (1977).

Publications: Co-author, *Maximizing Diversity in Public Broadcasting through Satellite Technology* (The Corporation for Public Broadcasting, 1978); editor, "Satellite New Communities" (*The Center Magazine*, 1972); co-author, *The Future of Network Information Services* (forthcoming).

BRAND, STEWART   **Born:** 1938, Rockford, Illinois, U.S.A.
The CoEvolution Quarterly
Box 428
Sausalito, California 94965 U.S.A.   **Telephone:** (415) 332-1716

Profession: Editor; event organizer

Field of specialization: Cybernetics; soft technology; epistemology; cultural evolution

Education: B.A., Stanford, 1960; San Francisco Art Institute, San Francisco State College, University of California Extension, art.

Professional employment: Portola Institute/POINT: Editor, Director (1968-76). Merry Pranksters: artist (1964-66). USCO: artist (1964-66). Gordon Ashby and Associates: researcher (1964). U.S. Infantry: Lieutenant (1960-62).

Professional activities: Editor of *CoEvolution Quarterly*; Special Consultant to Edmund G. Brown, Jr., Governor of California; lecturer, panelist, etc.; organized "New Games Tournament" (1973);

Publications: Co-editor, *Soft Tech* (Viking Penguin, 1978); editor, *Space Colonies* (Viking Penguin, 1977); editor, *The (Updated) Last Whole Earth Catalog* (Portola Institute/Random House/Viking Penguin, 1971-76); editor, *Whole Earth Epilog* (Viking Penguin, 1973); *Two Cybernetic Frontiers* (Random House, 1974).

BRENNAN, DONALD GEORGE   **Born:** 1926, Waterbury, Connecticut, U.S.A.
Director of National Security Studies
Hudson Institute
Croton-on-Hudson, New York 10520, U.S.A.   **Telephone:** (914) 762-0700

Profession: Strategist, mathematician

Field of specialization: Arms control; military policy; strategic and tactical nuclear policy issues; alliance relationships.

Education: B.S., 1955, Ph.D., 1959, Mathematics, Massachusetts Institute of Technology.

Professional employment: Hudson Institute: Director of National Security Studies (1964-); President (1962-64). Massachusetts Institute of Technology, Lincoln Laboratory: Research Mathematician and Communications Theorist (1953-62).

Professional activities: Conducts research on various strategic and theater nuclear-weapon policy issues, civil defense policy issues, and arms control matters; served as a consultant to various government agencies, the Los Alamos Scientific Laboratory, and the Laurence Livermore Laboratory; presently active in Council on Foreign Relations; conducted mathematics research (1955-62) engaged in communications theory and engineering (1953-58), and radio engineering (1945-53).

Publications: Co-author and editor, *Arms Control, Disarmament, and National Security* (Braziller, 1961); "A Comprehensive Test Ban: Everybody or Nobody" (*International Security*, 1976); "When the SALT Hit the Fan" (*National Review*, June 1972); "Linear Diversity Combining Techniques" (*Proceedings of the Institute of Radio Engineers* (now International Institute of Electrical and Electronic Engineers,) (June 1959); "On the Pathological Character of Independent Random Variables" (Ph.D. dissertation, Massachusetts Institute of Technology, 1959).

BRIGHT, JAMES R.
President
Industrial Management Center, Inc.
River Road
N. Edgecomb, Maine 04556, U.S.A.

Born: 1917, Pittsburgh, Pennsylvania, U.S.A.

Telephone: (207) 633-4088

Profession: Consultant on technology forecasting and innovation

Field of specialization: Technology forecasting; management of technological innovation.

Education: B.S., Industrial Engineering, Lehigh University, 1939; M.S., Industrial Engineering, Columbia University, 1950; A.M. (Hon.), Harvard University, 1960.

Professional employment: Industrial Management Center Inc.: President (1954-). Graduate School of Business Administration, University of Texas: Professor of Technology Management and Associate Dean (1969-76). Harvard Business School: Professor (1954-69). *Modern Materials Handling*: Chief Editor (1950-54). *Product Engineering*: Managing Editor (1946-50). U.S. Army: Second Lt., Bg. Gen. Ret. 1970 (1940-46). General Electric: Test Engineer (1939-40).

Professional activities: Director, semi-annual Technology Forecasting Workshops (1967-); consultant to many firms and government agencies in the U.S. and abroad on technology forecasting; current research and writing in field of technological innovation and management; member, American Society of Mechanical Engineers; Society for History of Technology; pioneered the teaching of management of technology in graduate schools of business (1960-); launched first civilian seminar on technology forecasting (1967); author of some 100 papers in the technology and management area.

Publications: *Practical Technology Forecasting: Concepts and Exercises* (Industrial Management Center, 1978); "Technological Forecasting Literature: Emergence and Impact on Technological Innovation," in Patrick Kelly and Melvin Kranzberg, *Technological Innovation: A Critical Review of Current Knowledge* (San Francisco Press, 1978); *Automation and Management* (Harvard Business School, 1958); *Research, Development and Technological Innovation* (Richard Irwin, 1964); editor, *Technological Forecasting for Industry and Government* (Prentice Hall, 1968); *Brief Introduction to Technology Forecasting, Concepts and Exercises* (Industrial Management Center, 1972).

BRONWELL, ARTHUR B.
University of Connecticut
32 Hillyndale Road
Storrs, Connecticut 06268, U.S.A.

Born: Drexel, Illinois, U.S.A.

Telephone: (203) 429-5330

Profession: Formerly Dean of Engineering, University of Connecticut (retired).

Field of specialization: Industrial consultant on management; specialist in global political evolution theories.

Education: B.S. and M.S., Electrical Engineering, Illinois Institute of Technology, 1933; Master of Business Administration, Northwestern University, 1942.

Professional employment: University of Connecticut: Dean of Engineering (1962-70); currently on faculty. Worcester Polytechnic Institute: President (1955-62). Northwestern University: Faculty of

Electrical Engineering Department (1938-55).

Professional activities: College administrator; educator; management consultant; author; holds honorary doctoral degrees (LL.D., Northeastern University, 1955; D.Sc., Wayne State University, 1958); has presented papers before six international conferences on global technological development, political evolution in the future, and requirements for civilization's survival; consultant, Bell Telephone Laboratories, Allen B. Dumont Company, Motorola Company, and others; formerly Executive Secretary, American Society for Engineering Education and editor of *Journal of Engineering Education* (1947-55).

Publications: *Freedom—The Democracy of the Future* (to be published 1979); author and editor, *Science and Technology in the World of the Future* (John Wiley and Sons, 1970); *Advanced Mathematics in Physics and Engineering* (McGraw Hill, 1955).

BROWN, ARNOLD
President
Weiner, Edrich, Brown, Inc.
303 Lexington Avenue
New York, New York 10016, U.S.A.

Born: 1927, Boston, Massachusetts, U.S.A.

Telephone: (212) 889-7007

Profession: Management consultant

Field of specialization: Environmental scanning; systemic analysis; values; socio-political forecasting.

Education: B.A., English, University of California, Los Angeles, 1950.

Professional employment: Weiner, Edrich, Brown, Inc.: President (1977-). Institute of Life Insurance: Vice President (1961-77). Mutual Benefit Life Insurance Company: Assistant Director of Sales Promotion. Book Guild of America: Secretary-Treasurer. Radio Television Training Association: Assistant Vice-President.

Professional activities: Planning Committee, 1979 Conference on Re-writing Communications Act; member, North American Society for Corporate Planning; member, Analysis Committee, Trend Analysis Program, Institute of Life Insurance; Vice-president, New York Chapter, World Future Society; Co-Chair, General Electric/Institute of Life Insurance Symposium; spoke at First and Second General Assemblies, World Future Society; lectured and spoke on futures research at Universityity of Massachusetts, Wharton School, New School for Social Research, and to various business and government groups; developer of Trend Analysis, Institute of Life Insurance.

Publications: "A Discouraging Word?" in *Focus on the Future: Implications for Education* (University of Houston, 1978); "How to Get the Jump on Your Future" *(Management Review,* June 1977); "Will Banks Control Insurance Sales?" *(The National Underwriter,* July 1978); "The Challenge to Democracy" (article in *The Next 25 Years: Crisis and Opportunity,* World Future Society, 1975).

BROWN, HARRISON SCOTT
Professor of Geochemistry
Division of Humanities and Social Sciences
California Institute of Technology
Pasadena, California 91125, U.S.A.

Born: 1917, Sheridan, Wyoming, U.S.A.

Telephone: (213) 795-6811, Ext. 1073

Profession: Geochemist

Field of specialization: Resources; population; economic development; the human future in general.

Education: B.S., Chemistry, University of California-Berkeley, 1938; Ph.D., Chemistry, Johns Hopkins University, 1941.

Professional employment: California Institute of Technology: Professor of Geochemistry (1951-); Professor of Science and Government (1967-); Director, Caltech Population Program (1970-75). University of Chicago: Assistant Professor of Chemistry in the Institute for Nuclear Studies (1946-48); Associate Professor in the Institute for Nuclear Studies (1948-51). Oak Ridge Laboratory, Oak Ridge, Tennessee: Assistant Director of Chemistry, Plutonium Project (1943-46). University of Chicago: Research Associate, Plutonium Project (1942-43). Johns Hopkins University: Instructor of Chemistry (1941-42).

Professional activities: Has conducted research on transuranium elements, meteorites, geochronology, physics and chemistry of the solar system, science and public policy, population problems, environmental problems, and natural resources. Member, Commission on Critical Choices for Americans. Member, Commission on U.S. Latin American Relations. Chairman, Finance Committee, International Institute for Applied Systems Analysis. President, International Council of Scientific Unions (1974-). Trustee, Resources for the Future, Inc. Trustee, Charles F. Kettering Foundation.

Publications: *The Challenge of Man's Future* (Viking Press, 1954); *Must Destruction Be Our Destiny?* (1946); *The Cassiopeia Affair* (Doubleday, 1968); "The Fissioning of Human Society" (*Quarterly Journal of Economics*, May 1975); "Energy in Our Future" (*Annual Review of Energy*, 1976). (From the first edition. Corrections not received by press time.)

BROWN, LESTER R.
President
Worldwatch Institute
1776 Massachusetts Avenue, N.W.
Washington, D.C. 20036, U.S.A.
Profession: Agriculturalist

Born: 1934, Bridgeton, New Jersey, U.S.A.

Telephone: (202) 452-1999

Field of specialization: World food/population situation; global problem solving; early warning systems.

Education: B.S., Agricultural Science, Rutgers University, 1955; M.A. Economics, University of Maryland, 1959; M.P.A., Public Administration, Harvard University, 1962.

Professional employment: Worldwatch Institute: President and Senior Researcher (1974-). Overseas Development Council: Senior Fellow (1969-74). Department of Agriculture: Administrator of the International Agricultural Development Service (1966-69); Secretary's Staff, Advisor on Foreign Agricultural Policy (1964-66); International Agricultural Economist with the Economic Research Service (1959-64).

Professional activities: Author of numerous articles and frequent guest lecturer on world food/population interdependence; faculty member, Salzburg Seminar in American Studies (1971); guest scholar, Aspen Institute (1972); recipient Arthur S. Flemming award (1965); named one of 10 outstanding young men in America by the U.S. Jr. Chamber of Commerce (1966) for his anticipation of the 1965 crop failure in India early enough to initiate a massive and successful food rescue effort; member of the Council on Foreign Relations, the U.S. Committee for UNICEF, the Board of Directors of the Overseas Development Council, the Federation of American Scientists, the World Future Society, the Society for International Development, and Zero Population Growth.

Publications: *The Twenty Ninth Day: Accommodating Human Needs and Numbers to the Earth's Resources* (W.W. Norton and Co., 1978); *Man, Land and Food* (USDA, 1963); *Seeds of Change* (Praeger, 1970); *World Without Borders* (Random House, 1972); *In The Human Interest* (Norton, 1974); *By Bread Alone* (Praeger, 1974). His books have been published in a dozen languages.

BROWN, SEYOM
Professor of Politics
Brandeis University
Waltham, Massachusetts 02154, U.S.A.

Born: 1933, Hightstown, New Jersey, U.S.A.

Telephone: (617) 647-2905

Profession: Foreign policy analyst

Field of specialization: World society and politics; international relations; U.S. foreign policy.

Education: B.A., 1955, M.A., 1957, Political Science, University of Southern California; Ph.D., Political Science, University of Chicago, 1963.

Professional employment: Brandeis University: Professor of Politics (current position). Carnegie Endowment for International Peace: Director, U.S.-Soviet Relations Program (1976-78). Brookings Institution: Senior Fellow (1969-). Rand Corporation: Social Scientist (1962-69),

Professional activities: Current research projects on U.S.-Soviet Relations, U.S. foreign policy options, world order issues, and arms control; research and writing on military strategy (1962-69).

Publications: *Regimes for the Ocean, Outer Space and Weather* (Brookings Institution, 1977); *New Forces in World Politics* (Brookings Institution, 1976); *The Faces of Power* (Columbia University Press, 1968).

BROWN, WILLIAM M.
Director of Technological Studies
Hudson Institute, Inc.
Quaker Ridge Road
Croton-on-Hudson, New York 10520, U.S.A.

Born: 1919, Philadelphia, Pennsylvania, U.S.A.

Telephone: (914) 762-0700

Profession: Policy analyst; physicist

Field of specialization: National security issues; world resource supplies; long-term technological trends; energy issues.

Education: B.S., M.A., Ph.D., Theoretical Physics, University of California, Los Angeles.

Professional employment: Hudson Institute, Inc.: Director, Technological Studies (1975-). Independent Consultant (1970-75). RAND Corporation: Senior Scientist (1958-61) (1967-70). Hudson Institute, Inc.: Director, Civil Defense (1961-67).

Professional activities: Currently working on a study of geopressurized zones for the Department of Energy; prepared a study entitled "A Perspective on Unconventional Sources of Natural Gas" for Consolidated Edison of New York (November 1977); prepared a study entitled "Long-Term Prospects for Developments in Space (A Scenario Approach)" for NASA (October 1977).

Publications: Co-author, *The Next 200 Years: A Scenario for America and the World* (William Morrow and Company, Inc. 1976); co-author, *Suggestions for a Phase II National Energy Policy* (Hudson Institute for Energy Research and Development Administration, 1977); "A Huge New Reserve of Natural Gas Comes Within Reach" (*Fortune*, October 1976).

BRUCKMANN, GERHART D.
Professor of Statistics
Institute for Statistics
University of Vienna
Rathausstrasse 19
Vienna, Austria A-1010

Born: 1932, Vienna, Austria

Telephone: (222) 434159

Profession: Professor of Statistics

Field of specialization: Methodology; economic and social systems of tomorrow; global modeling.

Education: Technical University Graz; Antioch College; B.A., Engineering, Technical University, Vienna, 1953; B.A., Actuarial Mathematics, Technical University, Vienna, 1953; M.A., Mathematics, University of Vienna, 1955; Dr. in Statistics and Actuarial Sciences, University of Rome, 1956.

Professional employment: University of Vienna: Full Professor of Statistics (1968-). Institute for Advanced Studies: Director (1968-73). University of Linz: Full Professor of Statistics (1967-68). Federal Chamber of Commerce: Head, Statistical Office (1957-67).

Professional activities: Part-time consultant to the International Institute for Applied Systems Analysis (1973-); Director, Institute for Socio-Economic Forecasting (1967-69); member, Executive Council, World Future Studies Federation (1975-); Chairman, the Austrian Futures Research Society (1973-); Fellow, the Austrian Academy of Sciences (1972-); projects in long-range forecasting include: supervision of several projects of the Institute for Advanced Studies; head of a working group on housing forecasts; member of the (former) working group on labor force forecasting; Director, Institute for Socio-Economic Forecasting, Austrian Academy of Sciences; part-time consultant for the International Institute for Applied Systems Analysis, entrusted with the preparation of a series of conferences on global modeling.

Publications: *Sonnenkraft statt Atomenergie [Solar Power Instead of Nuclear Energy]* (Molden-Verlag, 1978); co-author, *Langfristige Prognosen [Long-term Forecasting]* (Physica-Verlag, 1978); *Auswege in die Zukunft [Loopholes in the Future]* (Molden-Verlag, 1974); editor, *Prognose des Wohnungsbedarfes in Osterreich [Forecasts of Housing Demand in Austria]* (Trauner-Verlag, 1976).

BUCHEN, IRVING H.

Born: 1930, New York, New York, U.S.A.

Director
Division of the Future
Fairleigh Dickinson University
285 Madison Avenue
Madison, New Jersey 07940, U.S.A.

Telephone: (201) 377-4700, Ext. 243

Profession: Professor of English and futures studies

Field of specialization: Educational futures; curriculum design

Education: B.A., New York University, 1952; M.A., New York University, 1955; Ph.D., The Johns Hopkins University, 1960.

Professional employment: Fairleigh Dickinson University: Director, Division of the Future (1977-); Chairman, Department of English (1974-77); Instructor to Professor (1960-). Maryland Institute: Director of English (1958-60). The Johns Hopkins University: Junior Instructor (1956-60). Pennsylvania State University: Instructor (1955-56).

Professional activities: Has served as a consultant in futurism to Campus-Free College, Boston, Massachusetts; Educational Policy Research Center, Syracuse, New York; Academic Council, Committee for the Future, Washington (Syncon conference technique, extra-terrestrial colonization); Planning Group, Teilhard de Chardin Association; Center for Technology Assessment, Newark College of Engineering; editor of Futures Department, *Intellect*; has served as Northeast Modern Language Association President (1972-73), Vice President (1971-72), and Chairman, Romantic Section (1970).

Publications: "Towards a 21st Century Curriculum" *(Cutting Edge,* Winter 1978); "The Limits to Individuality: Past and Future Mass Models" *(Intellect,* October 1974); "Towards a History of Futurism: The Greeks" *(Futures,* October 1974); "Humanism and Futurism: Enemies or Allies?" (in Alvin Toffler's *Learning for Tomorrow,* New York, 1974); "The Future of Technology and Human Destiny" (Science and Society Convention, Yugoslavia, 1973); "Education for the Future: A Universal Curriculum" (World Future Research Conference, Bucharest, Romania, September 1972).

BUCHHOLZ, HANS

Born: 1939, Berlin, Germany

Institute of Futures Research
Giesebrechtstr. 15
D-1000 Berlin 12, Federal Republic of Germany

Telephone: (030) 883 8874

Profession: Economist, planner

Field of specialization: Futures methodology; futures planning.

Education: M.B.A., Free University of Berlin.

Professional employment: Institute of Futures Research: Director (1974-). Congena, Inc.: Planning consultant and Partner (1970-74). Quickborner Team, Inc.: Planning consultant and Partner (1969-70). German Institute of Economic Research, Berlin: Research scientist (1967-69).

Professional activities: General Secretary for the Association for Future Questions (1974-); editor, *Analysen und Prognosen* (1975-).

Publications: "Zukunftsforschung—eine komplemtare Prognosekapaz" ["Futures Research—a complimentary Prognosis Capability"] *(Analysen und Prognosen,* 6, 37, S.5., 1974); "Berlin im Jahr 2000—eine qualitative Prognose" ["Berlin in the Year 2000—A Qualitative Prognosis"] *(Analysen und Prognosen,* 10,55, 1978); Der influss der Informationstechnik auf die Zukunft der Gesellschaft" ["The Influence of Information Technology on the Future of Society"] (Lecture at the Rabunus-Maurus Academy, Konigstein, 1978); "Zukunftsforschung—Die nachsten zehn Jahre" ["Futures Research—The Next Ten Years"] *(Analysen und Prognosen,* 10, 58, 1978); co-author with Rolf Kreibich, "Berlin als uberregionales Zentrum fur Zukunftsforschung" ["Berlin as a Supra-regional Center for Futures Research"] *(Der Arbeitgeber,* September 1978).

BUNDY, ROBERT FRANKLIN

Born: 1932, Watertown, New York, U.S.A.

147 Hathaway Road
Syracuse, New York 13214, U.S.A.

Telephone: (315) 446-9164

Profession: Educational futurist; teacher, poet

Field of specialization: New systems of formal education for a post-industrial society; the influence of images of the future on educational practice and theory; new approaches to defining literacy for the educated person of the future.

Education: B.S., Physics, LeMoyne College, 1958; Ph.D., Education, Syracuse University, 1968; Theology and Philosophy, Catholic University and Wadhams Hall Seminary, 1951-56.

Professional employment: Self employed Educational Planning Consultant (1969-). Educational Policy Research Center at Syracuse University: Manager, Educational Services (1968). Xerox Corporation: Marketing Administration; New Product Planner in Office of the President; Sales Training Supervisor; R and D Analyst (1958-65).

Professional employment: Currently consulting and offering futures workshops for school districts, private colleges, state education departments, professional educational organizations, community educational planning groups, and non-educational groups in the U.S. and Canada; has conducted many hundreds of workshops and taught 14 graduate/undergraduate courses on the future; authored a number of publications on reform of education and new models of schooling for the future; reviewed books for several major journals; currently involved in developing a post-industrial lifestyle.

Publications: "Social Visions and Educational Futures" *(Phi Delta Kappan,* September 1976); editor and contributor, *Images of the Future: The 21st Century and Beyond* (Prometheus Press, 1976); "Images of the Future: Health Occupations in Transition to a New Age" *(American Vocational Journal,* February 1978); "Accountability: A New Disneyland Fantasy" *(Phi Delta Kappan,* November 1974); "The Possible Dream" *(The Humanities Journal,* February 1974).

CALDER, NIGEL

Born: 1931, London, United Kingdom

8 The Chase, Furnace Green
Crawley, West Sussex
United Kingdom

Telephone: 0293-26693

Profession: Science writer

Field of specialization: Current advances in fundamental scientific knowledge and their potential implications.

Education: M.A., Natural Sciences, University of Cambridge, 1957.

Professional employment: Freelance TV scriptwriter and author (1966-). *New Scientist:* Editor-in-chief (1962-66); Science Editor (1960-62); Staff Writer (1956-60). Mullard Research Laboratories: Research physicist (1954-56).

Professional activities: Writing and sometimes presenting major science documentaries (1966-); productions for the BBC-TV and overseas co-producers (e.g. PBS); writing books associated with these productions; chairman, Association of British Science Writers (1960-62); chairman, Continiung Committee of the International Futures Research Congress (1967-68); awarded UNESCO Kalinga Prize for the popularization of science (1972).

Publications: Editor, *The World in 1984* (Penguin, 1965); *The Environment Game* (United States title was *Eden was no Garden)* (Secker and Warburg/Holt, Reinhart, 1967); editor, *Unless Peace Comes* (Allen Lane/Viking, 1968); *Technopolis: Social Control of the Uses of Science* (McGibbon and Kee/Simon and Schuster, 1969); *Spaceships of the Mind* (BBC/Viking, 1978) and numerous other books less directly oriented to future studies.

CALHOUN, JOHN BUMPASS

Born: 1917, Elkton, Tennessee, U.S.A.

Research Psychologist
National Institute of Mental Health
Building 110, NIHAC
9000 Rockville Pike
Bethesda, Maryland 20014, U.S.A.

Telephone: (301) 496-9556

Profession: Ecology; psychology.

Field of specialization: Population; evolution; social behavior; environmental design; communication.

Education: B.S., Biology, University of Virginia, 1939; Ph.D., Zoology, Northwestern University, 1943.

Professional employment: National Institute of Mental Health: Research Psychologist (1954-). Walter Reed Army Medical Center: Research Psychologist (1951-54). Jackson Memorial Laboratory: NIMH Fellow (1949-51). Johns Hopkins University: Research Associate (1946-51). Ohio State University: Instructor (1944-46). Emory University: Instructor (1943-44).

Professional activities: Currently preparing a revised version of his past-to-future evolutionary model of the human course; editing a volume with prospective title *Adaptation, Population, Environment: Design of Evolution* on researchable problems relating to the megacrisis that marks the transition into a new era of evolution; over the past 30 years studied mammalian populations in natural and experimental settings — results have been translated into insights about past and future human evolution.

Publications: "A Scientific Quest for a Path to the Future" (*Populi*, Vol. 3, 19-28, U.N. Fund for Population Activities, 1976); "Population Density and Social Pathology" (*Scientific American*, February 1962); "The Social Use of Space" in W.V. Mayer and R. Van Gelder, editors, *Physiological Mammalogy*, Volume 1 (Academic Press, 1963); "Space and the Strategy of Life" in A.H. Esser, editor, *Behavior and Environment* (Plenum Press, 1971); "Revolution, Tribalism and the Cheshire Cat" (*Technological Forecasting and Social Change*, Volume 4, 1973).

CALVERT, GEOFFREY NEIL

Born: 1912, New Zealand

525 Towner Park Road, RR1
Sidney, British Columbia
Canada V8L 3R9

Telephone: (604) 656-2543

Profession: Consulting actuary; economist; futurist.

Field of specialization: General field of futures studies; actuarial, economic and demographic forecasts.

Education: M.A., Economics and Political Science, University of New Zealand; Fellow of the Institute of Actuaries, Institute of Actuaries, London.

Professional employment: Self employed: Consulting Actuary, economist, futurist (1973-). Tomenson-Alexander, Ltd.: Senior Consulting Actuary (1971-73). Alexander and Alexander, New York: Director-Founder, Actuarial Division (1949-70). World Bank: Economist (1947-49). New Zealand Government, Prime Minister's Department: Statistician to War Cabinet and Chief Research Officer, Organization for National Development (1940-46).

Professional activities: Researching the funding of the Canada Pension Plan and the outlook for electricity (consumption versus capacity); research and writing in futures studies field (1973-); consulting actuary to British Columbia Forest Industries (1972-); research studies for Canadian Institute of Actuaries (1975) and Canadian Pension Conference (1975-76); research into U.S. social security system (1973-76); currently writing a series of leaflets, "Thinking About the Future," published by Alexander and Alexander Inc., New York.

Publications: *Pensions and Survival* (Financial Post Books, Toronto, 1977); *Twelve Faces of Inflation* (Thinking about the Future Series, Alexander and Alexander, Inc., New York, 1978); *Energy, Power and Survival* (Thinking about the Future Series, Alexander and Alexander Inc., New York, 1977); *Population, Food, Inflation and Power* (Thinking about the Future Series, Alexander and Alexander Inc., New York, 1976); *The Future Population of New Zealand* (New Zealand Government, 1946); *Land and Real Estate as Field of Investment for Pension Funds* (Alexander and Alexander, Inc., New York, 1966).

CARLETON, THOMAS JAMES

Born: 1944, Ann Arbor, Michigan, U.S.A.

Co-Director
Earthrise, Inc.
P.O. Box 120, Annex Station
Providence, Rhode Island 02901, U.S.A.

Telephone: (401) 274-0011

Profession: Designer; educator

Field of specialization: Value systems and paradigms; alternative education and design.

Education: B.A., Futures Studies and Design, Union for Experimenting College and Universities, 1972; School of Architecture, University of Detroit.

Professional employment: Earthrise, Inc.: Co-Director (1972-); New Life Enterprises: Vice-President (1978-); Educational and Administrative Director of Futures Lab undergraduate program (1973-76); Lecturer for Earthrise's traveling Futures Workshops (1972-); co-designer of *Global Futures Game,* a simulation of present and future world conditions to year 2020; regular contributions to Earthrise Newsletter; editor of "Capitol Life," a neighborhood magazine; lectured at dozens of colleges around the country on historical and contemporary views of alternative social and environmental futures; presented series of lectures called "Project Earthrise" for Hawaii State Commission on Year 2000; compiled several surveys on women and Third World Futurists.

Professional activities: Educational and Administrative Director of Futures Lab undergraduate program (1973-); Lecturer and Workshop Coordinator for Earthrise's traveling Futures Workshops (1972-); Co-designer of *Global Futures Game*, a simulation of present and future world conditions to year 2020; designing a multi-media presentation on "Images of Alternative Futures"; regular contributor to *Earthrise Newsletter*; lectured at dozens of colleges around the country on historical and contemporary views of alternative social and environmental futures; compiled several surveys on women and Third World futurists.

Publications: *Futures Lab Prospectus* (Earthrise Document ER-8, 1974); co-author, *Global Futures Game* (Earthrise Document ER-7, 1975); co-author, *Rhode Island 2000* (Earthrise Document ER-3, 1973); "Global Futures: A Planetary Paradigm" (*Journal of World Education,* Summer 1975); "Are Future Studies for Whites Only?" (Earthrise Newsletter, November 1974); "Images of the Future" (*Earthrise Newsletter,* April 1976); "In Search of an Appropriate Paradigm" (*Earthrise Newsletter,* December 1978).

CASE, FRED E.
Professor
Graduate School of Management
University of California
Los Angeles, California 90024, U.S.A.

Born: 1918, Logansport, Indiana, U.S.A.

Telephone: (213) 825-3977

Profession: Professor

Field of specialization: Futures methodology (Delphi, scenarios); urban planning; land use forecasting.

Education: B.S., 1942, M.B.A., 1948, D.B.A., 1951, Business management and Urban Land Economics, Indiana University.

Professional employment: University of California, Los Angeles: Professor (1951-). University of Florida: Assistant Professor (1950-51). Indiana University: Assistant Dean and Instructor (1946-50).

Professional activities: Various research projects on land uses and land values (since 1951), California 2000 (1975), housing and land values, California 1975-1980 (1977), impact of government controls on home prices (1977), the California real estate brokerage industry—present and future (1976); consulting for State of California Legislative Analyst Office, San Franscisco Home Loan Bank, city of Palm Springs, city of Los Angeles, Los Angeles City Council; member of Los Angeles City Planning Commission (1974).

Publications: *Investment Guide to Home and Land Purchases* (Prentice-Hall, 1977); *The Real Estate Investment Game* (Prentice-Hall, 1978); co-author, *Real Estate Appraisal and Investment* (Wiley, 1977); "Home Ownership-Nightmare or Dream (a view to 1980)" (*California Management Review,* 1978); co-author, *Real Estate Finance* (Wiley, 1978).

CASSIRER, HENRY REINHARD
Les Moulins
Menthon Street Bernard nr. Annecy
74290, France

Born: 1911, Berlin, Germany

Telephone: (50) 44 88 53

Profession: International consultant for communication and education.

Field of specialization: Policies and planning for communciation and education; particular concern with social (adult) education in both developed and developing countries; application of communication media to development in the Third World; the future of communication industries which serve man rather than dominate him.

Education: B.A., Honors, 1936, Ph.D., History, 1940, London University—London School of Economics.

Professional employment: Free lance: International consultant for communication and education (1971-). U.N. Educational, Scientific and Cultural Organization (UNESCO): Director, Mass Media in Education (1952-71). Free lance: Producer/Writer in TV and film (1949-52). Columbia Broadcasting System, New York: Assistant Director, Shortwave Listening Station (1941-44); Television News Editor (1944-49). British Broadcasting Corporation, London: Announcer/Translator (1938-40).

Professional activities: Consultant on rural communication for World Bank in Morocco and Ghana (1975); consultant on rural broadcasting for German government in French West Africa (1976); Visiting Professor, Ontario Institute for Studies in Education (1974); advisory missions, organization of training courses, conferences, and seminars in 16 countries (1957-71); participated in World Futures Conference, Bucharest (1973); Visiting Professor, University of Southern California (1962); teacher of TV Public Affairs, New School for Social Research, and New York University (1947-51); working to assure that one-way authoritarian and elitist communication, and the separation among ideas, disciplines and social practices be replaced in the future by democratic communication, and the integration of man's knowledge and experience.

Publications: *Kommunikation und die Zukunft der Bildung [Communication and the Future of Education]* (Deutsche Vérlagsanstalt, 1974); *Television Teaching Today* (UNESCO, 1960); *Television, a World Survey* (UNESCO, 1953); *Communications, Key to Man's Self Awareness* (New York Academy of Sciences, 1970).

CAZES, BERNARD
Head, Division of Long-Term Studies
Commissariat General du Plan
18 Rue de Martignac
75007 Paris, France

Born: 1927, Hanoi, Vietnam

Telephone: 705 10 77

Profession: Senior Civil Servant

Field of specialization: Futures research for government planning purposes.

Education: M.A., History, Bordeaux University, 1948; Ecole Nationale d'Administration, 1954.

Professional employment: Commissariat General du Plan: Head, Division of Long-Term Studies (1960-). Ministry of Finance: Junior Civil Servant (1955-59).

Professional activities: Long-term studies for Commissariat General du Plan; course on social forecasting at the College of Europe, Bruges (1972-75); seminars on applied futures research, European University Institute, Florence (1977-).

Publications: *La vie economique [Economic Life]* (Armand Colin, 1966); *La face cachee de l'histoire [The Hidden Face of History]* (Robert Laffont, forthcoming); "Social Indicators: A Survey" in Shonfield and Shaw, eds., *Heinemann Educational* (1972); "Applied Futures Research in France" (*Futures*, June 1973); "Condorcet's True Paradox" (*Daedalus*, 1975).

CEPEDE, MICHEL
Professor
Department of Sociologie
Institut National Agronomique
16 Rue Claude Bernard
75231 Paris, France, Cedex 05

Born: 1908, Wimereux, France

Telephone: (1) 551 61 38

Profession: Socio-economist

Field of specialization: Rural sociology; agricultural development; food economics.

Education: Ingenieur Agronome, Economics, Institut National Agronomique, 1928; Certif. Etudes Superieur, Geology, 1930, M.L., Economics and Political Science, 1932, Ph.D., 1944, Universite de Paris; Hon. Dr. es. Sc., Faculte Agronomique Gembleux, 1967.

Professional employment: Institut National Agronomique: Professor, Head of Service (1959-); Professor (1947-59); Assistant (1931-39). Ministere de l'Agriculture: Administrator (1944-59).

162

Professional activities: President, Comite Francais of the Food and Agriculture Organization (1957-); Directeur, Laboratoire Econ. Soc. et Development, INRA (1959-); Chairman, I.L.O. Commission on Rural Development (1974-); President, Comite Francais Contre la Faim (1970-); Independent Chairman of the Council of F.A.O. (1969-73); Chairman, Committee on Agriculture, Organization for Economic Cooperation and Development; President, Societe Francaise d'Economie Rurale (1960-65).

Publications: *Du prix de revient au produit net en agriculture [Raw Material Cost and Net Product in Agriculture]* (C.N.I.E., Presses Universitaires de France, Paris, 1946); co-author, with Maurice Lengelle, *Economie alimentaire du globe [The Food Economy of the World]* (M. Th. Genin, Paris, 1953); editor, *Agriculture et alimentation en France pendant la II Guerre Mondiale [Agriculture and Food in France During the Second World War]* (M. Th. Genin, Paris, 1961); *Le science contre la faim [Science Against Hunger]* (Presses Universitaires de France, 1970); *La solidarite [Solidarity]* (Martinsart, 1973).

CETRON, MARVIN JEROME
President
Forecasting International, Ltd.
1001 North Highland Street
Arlington, Virginia 22201, U.S.A.

Born: 1930, Brooklyn, New York, U.S.A.

Telephone: (703) 527-1311

Profession: Technological Forecaster and Technology Assessor

Field of specialization: Technological forecasting and assessment

Education: B.S., Industrial Engineering, Pennsylvania State University, 1952; M.S., Economics and Production Management, Columbia University, 1957; Ph.D., R&D Management, American University, 1969.

Professional employment: Forecasting International, Ltd.: President (June, 1971-). U.S. Navy: Assistant to Technical Director; completed a career in R and D planning and forecasting, both in laboratories as Assistant to the Technical Director at the Applied Science Laboratory and Head of Planning at the Marine Engineering Laboratory, and as Head of Planning for Exploratory Development at Headquarters, Naval Materiel Command in Washington, D.C.; in charge of the design, development, and implementation of a comprehensive technological forecast in the United States (1952-71).

Professional activities: Adjunct Professor at American University and teaches at MIT, Georgia Tech, and George Washington University; has lectured extensively on technological forecasting, technology assessment, and R&D planning; has consulted with Institute of Electrical and Electronic Engineers, Clorox, Johnson and Johnson, Brown and Williamson, Holiday Inns, General Motors, GT&E, Union Carbide, Xerox, IBM, Mead-Johnson, International Research and Technology Corporation, the U.S. National Academy of Engineering, the Royal Swedish Academy of Engineering Science, National Science Foundation, UNESCO, OECD, the Common Market, and to foreign governments; Editor-in-Chief of the *Technology Assessment Journal* and on Editorial Advisory Board of *Technological Forecasting and Social Change.*

Publications: Co-author, "Investigating Potential Value Changes," in Linstone and Simmonds, eds., *Futures Research: New Directions* (Addison-Wesley, 1977); co-editor, *Industrial Technology Transfer* (Noordhof, Leyden, The Netherlands, 1977); *Technological Forecasting: A Practical Approach* (Gordon and Breach, 1969); co-author, *Technical Resource Management: Quantitative Methods* (MIT Press, 1970); editor, *The Science of Managing Organized Technology*, 4 volumes (Gordon and Breach, 1971).

CHACKO, GEORGE K.
Professor of Systems Management
University of Southern California
Washington Center
6809 Barr Road
Washington, D.C. 20016, U.S.A.

Born: 1930, Trivandrum, India

Telephone: (301) 229-6266

Profession: Operations researcher; systems scientist.

Field of specialization: Systems approach to large, unstructured problems; systems methodology; technological forecasting and control.

Education: B. Commerce, Commerce and Accounting, Calcutta University, 1952; M.A., Economics and

Political Science, Madras University, 1950; Post-Master's Training in Statistics, Indian Statistical Institute, Calcutta, 1950-51; Ph.D., Econometrics, The New School for Social Research Graduate Faculty, 1959.

Professional employment: University of Southern California, Washington Center: Professor of Systems Management (1970-). TRW Systems Group: Senior Staff Scientist (1967-70). Mitre Corporation: Staff Member (1965-67). Research Analysis Corporation: Staff Member (1963-65). Union Carbide Corporation: Operations Research Consultant (1962-63).

Professional activities: Editor, special issue of *Journal of Research Communication Studies on Forward Computer Networks for Editorial Processing* (1979); Vice-Chairman of the Committee on Representation of Operations Research Society of America to the American Association for the Advancement of Science (1972-); representative of the Institute of Management Sciences to the International Institute for Applied Systems Analysis (1976-); Vice-President, Publications, American Astronautical Society (1969-71).

Publications: *Technological Forecontrol—Prospects, Problems and Policy* (North-Holland Publishing Co., Amsterdam, 1975); *Management Information Systems* (Petrocelli Books, Princeton, 1979); *Computer-Aided Decision-Making* (American Elsevier, New York, 1971); *Health Handbook: An International Reference on Care and Cure* (North-Holland Publishing Co., Amsterdam, in preparation); *Systems Acquisitions Management: A Handbook* (Petrocelli Books, 1979, in preparation).

CHAPLAIN, ROLAND   **Born:** 1941, Bournemouth, England
Secretary
Future Studies Centre
15 Kelso Road
Leeds LS2 9PR, England   **Telephone:** 0532 459865

Profession: Futurist; meteorologist

Field of specialization: Applied weather forecasting; social, political, environmental, ecological, and other implications of intentional/inadvertent weather/climate modification; alternatives to unemployment.

Education: B.A., Theology, Birmingham University, 1963; Fellowship of Royal Meteorological Society, 1964; Certificate of Education, Huddersfield College of Education (Technical), 1970-71.

Professional employment: Futures Studies Centre, Leeds: Secretary (1974-). Bradford College: Liberal Studies Part Time Lecturer (1973). Nottinghamshire County Education Authority: Teacher (1971-72). Edgbaston Meteorological Observatory: Research Assistant, Deputy Director, Acting Director (1963-69).

Professional activities: "Industry, the Community and Appropriate Technology" Conference, Leeds, 1977; involved in two studies in cooperation with the World Future Studies Federation: (1) the interaction between environmentalists, futurists, consumer groups and trade unionists and factory workers—particular initiatives towards the production of more socially desirable goods and joint action such as the "green ban" movement to oppose and find alternatives to socially or environmentally undesirable developments; and, (2) "alternative technology" and "alternative lifestyle" experiments which might provide significant indicators for alternative futures; organized Leeds "Food Event" (1974) and "Industry, The Community and Alternative Technology Conference," Bradford, 1975. The Leeds Center acts as an information and contact point about alternatives for the future.

Publications: *Future Studies Centre Newsletter* (occasional from 1974; bi-monthly from September 1977).

CHAPLIN, GEORGE   **Born:** 1914, Columbia, South Carolina, U.S.A.
Editor-in-Chief
The Honolulu Advertiser
P.O. Box 3110
Honolulu, Hawaii 96802, U.S.A.   **Telephone:** (808) 525-8080

Profession: Newspaper editor

Field of specialization: Alternative economic futures for states (such as Hawaii).

Education: B.S., Chemistry, Clemson University, 1935; Nieman Fellow, Race relations and nationality problems, Harvard University, 1940.

Professional employment: *The Honolulu Advertiser*: Editor-in-Chief (1958-). *The New Orleans Item*: Editor (1949-58). *San Diego Journal*: Managing Editor (1947-48). *Courier-Post*, Camden, New Jersey: Managing Editor (1946-47). *The Stars and Stripes*, Pacific: Editor, Office-in-Charge (World War II). *Piedmont*, Greenville, South Carolina: Reporter, City Editor (1935-42).

Professional activities: Co-chairman, Alternative Economic Futures for Hawaii (1973-); Chairman, Hawaii Governor's Conference on the Year 2000 (1970); Chairman, Hawaii State Commission on the Year 2000 (1971-74); speaker, Conference on Malaysia 2001, Kuala Lumpur (1975); President, American Society of Newspaper Editors (1976-77); member, World Future Society, American Committee of the International Press Institute, Society of Nieman Fellows, National Conference of Editorial Writers.

Publications: Co-editor, *Hawaii 2000: Continuing Experiment in Anticipatory Democracy* (University Press of Hawaii, 1973).

CHASE, STUART

Box 422
Georgetown, Connecticut 06829, U.S.A.

Born: 1888, Somersworth, New Hampshire, U.S.A.

Telephone: —

Profession: Free lance writer on social subjects

Field of specialization: Economics; semantics; planning; technology assessment; one world.

Education: S.B. *cum laude*, Economics, Harvard University, 1910

Professional employment: Labor Bureau, Inc., New York: Research (1921-30). U.S. Food Administration (World War I). Federal Trade Commission (1917-1920).

Professional activities: Member, National Institute of Arts and Letters; Secretary, Town Planning Commission, Redding, Connecticut (1956-); member of Trade Union Delegation to Russia (1927); worked with State Department Cultural Exchange with USSR ("Dartmouth" Conferences) in U.S. and USSR (1961-); reported on "Operation Bootstrap," Puerto Rico, for National Planning Association (1950); acted as consultant to Tennessee Valley Authority, Department of Agriculture, Security and Exchange Commission, National Resources Board.

Publications: 32 books published to date. *The Tyranny of Words* (Harcourt-Brace, 1937); *The Most Probable World* (Harper and Row, 1968); *The Proper Study of Mankind* (Harper and Row, 1956); *The Tragedy of Waste* (Macmillan, 1925); *Some Things Worth Knowing* (Harper, 1958).

CHEATHAM, ANNE WILSON

Director
Congressional Clearinghouse on the Future
3692 House Annex No. 2
Washington, D.C. 20515, U.S.A.

Born: 1944, Smithfield, North Carolina, U.S.A.

Telephone: (202) 225-3153

Profession: Public service

Field of specialization: Implementation of foresight in U.S. Congress by building information networks between Congress and futures community.

Education: B.A., Religion, University of North Carolina, Chapel Hill, 1966; M.A.T., English and Education, University of North Carolina, Chapel Hill, 1968.

Professional employment: Congressional Clearinghouse on the Future: Director (1976-). Taipei American School, Taiwan: Counselor and teacher (1971-1974).

Professional activities: Advisory Board, Futures Studies Program, University of Massachusetts, Amherst, Massachusetts.

Publications: "Helping Congress to Cope with Tomorrow" (THE FUTURIST, April 1978).

CHEN, KAN

Born: 1928, Hong Kong

Professor of Electrical and Computer Engineering
4520 East Engineering
525 East University
The University of Michigan
Ann Arbor, Michigan 48109, U.S.A.

Telephone: (313) 764-4332

Profession: Professor; engineer; policy analyst

Field of specialization: Technology assessment; value systems; futures methodology; urban planning; social systems engineering; decision analysis; public policy studies.

Education: BEE, Cornell University, 1950; SM, Massachusetts Institute of Technology, 1951; Sc.D., Massachusetts Institute of Technology, 1954.

Professional employment: The University of Michigan: Professor of Electrical and Computer Engineering and of Industrial and Operations Engineering (1973-); Paul G. Goebel Professor of Advanced Technology (1971-73). University of Pittsburgh: Professor of Environmental Systems Engineering (1970-71). Stanford Research Institute: Director, Institute-wide Program on Urban Development (1966-70). Westinghouse Electric Corporation: Manager, Systems Technology Research and Development (1954-65).

Professional activities: Teaching macro societal systems engineering, social decision making, values, epistemology, and policy, technology assessment; policy research on population and environment, on telecommunications research, on systems approach to social decision-making, comprehensive energy R and D evaluation; Fellow, IEEE; consultant to National Science Foundation, Acumenics Research and Technology, Inc., Whirlpool Corporation, The Futures Group, Decisions and Designs, Inc.,; Past President, IEEE Systems; Man and Cybernetic Society; co-editor, IEEE Proceedings special issue on Social Systems Engineering (March 1975).

Publications: Co-author, *Growth Policy: Population, Environment, and Beyond* (University of Michigan Press, 1974); co-author, "Technology Assessment Methodologies in Perspective" (*Perspectives on Technology Assessment*, 1975); co-author and editor, *Urban Dynamics: Extensions and Reflections* (San Francisco Press, 1972); editor, *Technology and Social Institutions* (IEEE Press, 1974); editor, *National Priorities* (San Francisco Press, 1970).

CHOUCRI, NAZLI

Born: 1943, Cairo, Egypt

Professor
Department of Political Science
Massachusetts Institute of Technology
30 Wadsworth Street
Cambridge, Massachusetts 02139, U.S.A.

Telephone: (617) 253-6198

Profession: Political scientist

Field of specialization: Futures methodology

Education: B.A., Social Science, American University, Cairo, 1962; M.A., 1964, Ph.D., 1967, Political Science, Stanford University.

Professional employment: Massachusetts Institute of Technology: Professor, Political Science (1978-); Associate Professor (1972-78); Assistant Professor (1969-72). Queen's University, Canada: Assistant Professor (1967-69).

Professional activities: Current research projects include "Interstate Migration in the Middle East" (1978-81), and "Technology Adaptation Program: Labor Management Project" (1977-78); other research projects included "Technology Adaption Program: Study of Political Determinants of Technical Choice in Developing Countries" (1975-76); committee, National Research Council, Panel for the 1979 U.S. Conference on Science and Technology for Development (1977-78); worked with grants from the Rockfeller Foundation "Project on Access, Availability, and Security of Mineral Supplies" (1976-77) and from the National Science Foundation "Project on International Consequences of Resource Constraints" (1972-76).

Publications: Co-author, *Nations in Conflict: National Growth and International Violence* (W.H. Freeman, 1975); *Population Dynamics and International Violence: Propositions, Insights, Evidence* (D.C. Heath, 1974); co-author, *The International Politics of Energy Interdependence* (D.C Heath, 1976); editor, *Forecasting in International Relations: Theory, Methods, Problems, Prospects* (W.H. Freeman, 1978).

CHRISTAKIS, ALEXANDER N.
Battelle Columbus Laboratories
2030 M Street, N.W.
Washington, D.C. 20036, U.S.A.

Born: 1937, Athens, Greece

Telephone: (202) 785-8400

Profession: Futures and Policy Research

Field of specialization: Technology assessment; human settlement planning; systems methodology.

Education: A.B., Physics, Princeton University, 1959; M.A., Physics, Yale University, 1961; Ph.D., Physics, Yale University, 1965.

Professional employment: Battelle Columbus Laboratories: Research Leader and Head of the Futures Group (1975-). Academy for Contemporary Problems: Fellow (1972-75). U.S. Department of Commerce: Staff Consultant (1970-72). Club of Rome: Consultant (1970). Doxiadis System Development Corporation: Director of Research (1967-70).

Professional activities: Chairman, 1976 International Society for Technology Assessment Congress (1975-76); holds seminars on "Anticipating the Future," U.S. Department of Agriculture Graduate Program (1975-76); taught Social Psychology of Planning, Georgetown University; worked on "Appropriate Technology" workshops for the Agency for International Development; Visiting Professor on Systems Planning, University of Virginia.

Publications: Co-author, *Perspectives on Technology Assessment* (Science and Technology Publishers, 1975); co-author, *Technology Assessment: Creative Futures* (Elsevier Publishing Co., 1979); "An Appreciation of Contemporary Settlement Morphology" *(Futures,* Vol. 8, No. 2, 1976); "A New Policy Science Paradigm" *(Futures,* Vol. 5, No. 6, 1973).

CHURCHMAN, C. WEST
Professor
University of California
Berkeley, California 94720, U.S.A.

Born: 1913, Philadelphia, Pennsylvania, U.S.A.

Telephone: (415) 642-3860

Profession: Philosopher; planner

Field of specialization: Systems approach (holism); ethics and epistemology of planning in public sector.

Education: Ph.D., Philosophy, University of Pennsylvania, 1938.

Professional employment: University of California; Professor of Business Administration (1958-). Case Institute of Technology: Professor of English Administration (1950-58). Wayne University: Associate Professor of Philosophy (1948-50). University of Pennsylvania: Assistant Professor of Philosophy.

Professional activities: Consulting for the U.S.A. Wildlife Service (1974-) and the California Dept. of Consumer Affairs (1978-); editor-in-chief, *Philosophy of Science* (1948-58); editor-in-chief, *Management Science* (1954-62); president, The Institute of Management Science (1963).

Publications: *Design of Inquiring Systems* (Basic Books, 1970); *The Systems Approach* (Delacorte Press, 1968); *Challenge to Reason* (McGraw Hill, 1968); *Prediction and Optimal Decision* (Prentice-Hall, 1964); co-author, *Introduction to Operations Research* (Wiley, 1957).

CLARK, JOHN ALBERT
Fellow
Science Policy Research Unit
University of Sussex
Falmer, Brighton
Sussex, England

Born: 1946, Carshalton, Surrey, England

Telephone: (0273) 686758

Profession: Systems Analyst

Field of specialization: Systems analysis applied to the process of technical change and its effects on the economy.

Education: B.Sc., Physics, 1968, D. Phil., Theoretical Physics, 1972, University of Sussex.

Professional employment: Science Policy Research Unit, University of Sussex: Fellow (1973-).

Professional activities: Study of the influence of technical change on employment (1978-); study of technology in North-South development (1977-); reviewing global computer models (1973-); study of use of materials in the United Kingdom (1975-); involved in Science Policy Research Unit work on food and agriculture (1975-); review of simulation modelling for United Kingdom Research Councils (1973); work on long-term trends in the European Economic Community (1973-74); participant in feasibility study for European Forecasting Institute, "Europe Plus Thirty" (1974-75).

Publications: Co-author, *Global Simulation Models* (John Wiley, 1975); co-author, "Models of World Food Supply, Demand and Nutrition" (*Food Policy*, February 1976); co-author, "Long-Term Forecasting in Western Europe" (*Futures*, December 1975); co-author, "Experimental Socio-Economic Models of Europe" (*Futures*, December 1974).

CLARKE, ARTHUR CHARLES
25 Barnes Place
Colombo 7, Sri Lanka

Born: 1917, Minehead, United Kingdom

Telephone: Columbo 94255

Profession: Science writer

Field of specialization: Astronautics; oceanology; science fiction.

Education: B.Sc., Physics, Mathematics, Kings College, London, 1948.

Professional employment: Self-employed since 1950. Institution of Electrical Engineers, London: Editor (1949-50). Royal Air Force: Flight Lieutenant (1941-46).

Professional activities: Technical advisor, Underwater Safaris, Colombo, Sri Lanka; Editor, *Physics Abstracts* (1949-50); Chairman, British Interplanetary Society (1949-50, 1953); originated proposal for use of satellites for communications (*Wireless World*, October, 1945); since 1954, engaged in underwater exploration on Great Barrier Reef of Australia and coast of Sri Lanka; has made numerous radio and TV appearances and lectured widely all over the world.

Publications: *The Fountains of Paradise* (Harcourt Brace Jovanovich, 1979); *The View from Serendip* (Random House, 1977); "Extra-terrestrial Relays" (*Wireless World*, October 1945); co-author, *2001: A Space Odyssey* (NAL, 1968); *Profiles of the Future* (Harper and Row, 1973); *Imperial Earth* (Harcourt Brace Jovanovich, 1976); *The Exploration of Space* (Harper, 1952).

CLARKE, IAN FREDERICK
Chairman of English Department
Department of English Studies
University of Strathclyde
George Street
Glasgow, Scotland

Born: 1918, Wallasey, Cheshire, United Kingdom

Telephone: (041) 552 4400

Profession: Professor of English Studies

Field of specialization: Futuristic fiction; origin and development of imaginary war stories; history of utopian fiction and of predictive literature.

Education: B.A. with Honours, 1950, M.A., 1953, English Literature, University of Liverpool.

Professional employment: University of Strathclyde: Chairman of English Department (1968-). Royal College of Science and Technology: Senior Lecturer (1958-68). Various schools: Head of English Department (1952-58). University of Liverpool: University Fellow (1950-52).

Professional activities: Editing series on "Prophecy and Prediction" for *Futures* (1969-); completing study of utopian fiction (1969-); currently teaching and supervising postgraduate students; has lectured and written widely on development of "the idea of the future," with special reference to movement of ideas since 1750.

Publications: *The Tale of the Future* (Library Association, 1961, second edition, 1972, third edition, 1978); *The Pattern of Expectation* (1979); *Voices Prophesying War* (Oxford University Press, 1966).

CLAWSON, MARION   **Born:** 1905, Elko, Nevada, U.S.A.
Resources for the Future
1755 Massachusetts Avenue, N.W.
Washington, D.C. 20036, U.S.A.   **Telephone:** (202) 462-4400

Profession: Economist

Field of specialization: Natural resources; land; forestry; urban planning.

Education: B.S., 1926, M.S., 1929, Agriculture, University of Nevada; Ph.D., Economics, Harvard University, 1943.

Professional employment: Resources for the Future: Consultant (1976); Vice-President (July-December 1975); Acting President (March 1974-June 1975); Director of Land and Water Program (1955-75). University of Washington: Walker-Ames Professor (April 1976). University of California-Berkeley: Regent's Professor (January-March 1976). Many years with the U.S. government.

Professional activities: Currently in consultant capacity to Resources for the Future; member of several committees, National Academy of Sciences; Secretary, Society for International Development (1959-63); Fellow, American Agricultural Economics Association; consultant to various organizations for missions to Pakistan, Israel, Venezuela, Chile, and India.

Publications: Co-author, *Planning for Urban Growth: An Anglo-American Comparison* (Johns Hopkins Press, 1972); *Suburban Land Conversion: An Economic and Political Process* (Johns Hopkins Press, 1970); co-author, *The Economics of Outdoor Recreation* (Johns Hopkins Press, 1965); *Forests for Whom and for What?* (Johns Hopkins Press, 1975); editor, *Forest Policy for the Future: Conflict, Compromise, Consensus* (Johns Hopkins Press, 1974).

CLEVELAND, HARLAN   **Born:** 1918, New York, New York, U.S.A.
Aspen Institute for Humanistic Studies
P.O. Box 2820, Rosedale Road
Princeton, New Jersey 08540, U.S.A.   **Telephone:** (609) 921-1141

Profession: Political scientist and political executive

Field of specialization: —

Education: A.B., Politics, Princeton, University, 1938; Rhodes Scholar, Oxford University, 1938-39.

Professional employment: Aspen Institute Program in International Affairs: Director (1974-). University of Hawaii: President (1969-74). Department of State: U.S. Ambassador to NATO (1965-69); Assistant Secretary of State for International Organization Affairs (1961-65). Syracuse University: Dean, Maxwell Graduate School of Citizenship and Public Affairs (1956-61).

Professional activities: Chairman, U.S. Weather Modification Advisory Board (1977-78); board member of Atlantic Council, Center for War/Peace Studies, Global Perspectives in Education, International Council for Educational Development, International Economic Studies Institute, and the Oceanic Society.

Publications: *The Third Try at World Order: U.S. Policy for an Interdependent World* (Aspen Institute, 1977); *China Diary* (Georgetown University, 1976); *Humangrowth: An Essay on Growth, Values and the Quality of Life* (Aspen Institute, 1978); *The Future Executive* (Harper and Row, New York, 1972); *NATO: The Transatlantic Bargain* (Harper and Row, 1970); *The Obligations of Power* (Harper and Row, 1966); co-author, *The Overseas Americans* (McGraw-Hill Book Co., 1960).

COATES, JOSEPH F.   **Born:** 1929, Brooklyn, New York, U.S.A.
Assistant to the Director
Office of Technology Assessment
U.S. Congress
Washington, D.C. 20510, U.S.A.   **Telephone:** (202) 224-6019

Profession: Policy Analyst; Adjunct Professor; Chemist

Field of specialization: Technology assessment; methodology; research and development; crime; revolution.

Education: B.S., Chemistry, Polytechnic Institute of Brooklyn, 1951; M.S., Organic Chemistry, Pennsylvania State University, 1953; Graduate study in Philosophy, University of Pennsylvania, 1954-57.

Professional employment: U.S. Congress, Office of Technology Assessment: Assistant to the Director (1975-). National Science Foundation: Professor Manager (1970-74). Institute for Defense Analyses: Senior Staff Member (1962-70). Onyx Chemical Company, New Jersey: Chief Research Chemist (1960-62). Atlantic Refining Company, Pennsylvania: Research Chemist (1953-60).

Professional activities: Secretary, General Section (X), The American Association for the Advancement of Science (1974-77); Member, Scientific Advisory Committee of the Sierra Club (1972-); Member, Program Committee of the Ad Hoc Interagency Futures Group (1971-); Member, the Expert Committee on Technology Assessment, OECD; "Coates' Corner," a quarterly column in *Technology Assessment*; liaison to the Advisory Committee on Alternative Automotive Power Systems (from National Science Foundation); has conducted under the auspices of the World Future Society a weekly half-hour program on the future over WAMU-FM, American University; frequently gives courses and lectures on technology assessment and the future.

Publications: "The Role of Formal Models in Technology Assessment" *(Technological Forecasting and Social Change,* 1976); *Demographic Trends Influencing the Elementary and Secondary School System* (U.S. Congress, Office of Technology Assessment, May 1977); "Technological Change and Future Growth" *(Technological Forecasting and Social Change,* Vol. 2, No. 1, 1977); "The Identification and Selection of Candidates and Priorities for Technology Assessment" *(Technology Assessment,* Vol. 2, No. 2, 1974); co-author, "Wanted: Weapons That Do Not Kill" *(New York Times Magazine,* September 1967, and *Readers Digest,* February 1968).

COATES, VARY T.

Born: 1930, Anderson, South Carolina, U.S.A.

Associate Director
U.S. Department of Energy — Division of Technology Assessment
20 Massachusetts Avenue, N.W.
Washington, D.C. 20001, U.S.A.

Telephone: (202) 376-4695

Profession: Policy analyst

Field of specialization: Technology assessment; environmental assessment; energy.

Education: A.B., Political Science, Furman University, 1951; M.A., Public Affairs, The George Washington University, 1967; Ph.D., Political Science, The George Washington University, 1972.

Professional employment: Department of Energy: Associate Director, Division of Technology Assessment, Office of Environment (1978-). The George Washington University: Associate Director, Program of Policy Studies in Science and Technology (1973-78); Head, Technology Assessment Group (1973-); Senior Staff Scientist (1970-73); Research Scientist (1969-70). AVCO Economic Systems Corporation: Housing Consultant (1968-69).

Professional activities: Worked on studies for the National Science Foundation on "A Retrospective Technology Assessment of Submarine Telegraphy" and "A Survey of Technology Assessment in the Federal Government"; President, International Society for Technology Assessment (1976); member, Washington, D.C. Chapter Council, World Future Society (1974-76); taught graduate courses on technology assessment at George Washington University; has lectured and written extensively on the future of science and technology and the role of women in the future.

Publications: *Technology and Public Policy: The Process of Technology Assessment in the Federal Government* (George Washington University, 1972); "Revitalization of Small Communities: Transportation Options," (Department of Transportation, First Report, May 1974, Second Report, December 1975); "Technology in the Balance," THE FUTURIST, April 1973; (with Joseph F. Coates), "Technology Assessment and Education," *Futurism in Education—Methodologies* (McCutchan Publishing Corporation 1974).

COLE, HUGH SAMUEL DAVID

Born: 1943, United Kingdom

Science Policy Research Unit
University of Sussex
Brighton, United Kingdom

Telephone: 686758

Profession: Mathematical physicist

Field of specialization: Alternative futures; forecasting methods; technological and social change; development studies; urban planning.

Education: B.Sc., Physics, Imperial College, London, 1965; ARCS., D. Philosophy, University of Sussex, 1968.

Professional employment: Science Policy Research Unit, University of Sussex: Research Fellow (1971-). Department of Environment: Senior Scientific Officer, Urban Planning Division (1969-71). Cavendish Laboratory, Cambridge: Research Assistant (1968-69).

Professional activities: Social and technological alternatives for the future program; consultancy and projects for the United Nations, European Community, and Europe + 30 team; research project on "The Latin American World Model as a Tool of Analysis and Integrated Planning at a National and Regional Level in Developing Countries," for UNESCO (1977); member of executive committee of the World Futures Studies Federation; member of editorial advisory board for the *Journal of Policy Modelling;* co-director of UNITAR project on "The Role of Technology in National Development and North-South Relations—An Inquiry into Policy and Social Choices"; consultant on technological and long run forecasting to FINEP, Brazil, sponsored by the British Council.

Publications: Contributor to *The Futures of Europe* (Cambridge University Press, 1977); *Global Models and the International Economic Order* (Pergamon Press, 1977); co-editor and author, *World Futures: The Great Debate* (Martin Robertson, 1978); author in *Business Decision, Forecasting and Uncertainty* (Fildes and Wook, Saxon House, 1978); co-editor and author, *Global Models, Planning and Basic Needs* (proceedings of a UNESCO-sponsored conference, to be published by Pergamon, 1978); co-author and editor, *Models of Doom* (Universe Books, New York, 1973); co-author and editor, *Global Simulation Models* (Wiley, 1975).

CONGER, D. STUART   **Born:** 1926, Ottawa, Ontario, Canada
Director
Occupational and Career Analysis and Development Branch
Department of Manpower and Immigration
Ottawa, Ontario, Canada   **Telephone:** 996-1428

Profession: —

Field of specialization: Social invention for human and social resource development.

Education: B.A., Psychology, University of British Columbia, 1949.

Professional employment: Department of Manpower and Immigration: Director, Occupational and Career Analysis and Development Branch (1975-); Director, Training Research and Development Station (1972-74). Saskatchewan Newstart: Chairman and Executive Director (1968-). Department of Trade and Commerce: Chief, Small Business Division (1962-68). R. L. Crain Limited: Director, Training (1957-62).

Professional activities: Current projects include: career guidance for future world work; job and organization redesign; quality of working life; lectures and writes extensively on social inventions; member of the Board of Directors of the International Foundation for Social Innovation, Paris, France; directed experimental projects to develop new methods and programs for training and counseling adults, including "Life Skills" (1969), "Individualized Instruction" (1970), "Literacy Training" (1971), "Career Guidance" (1972), "Business Management" (1973), "Community Economic Management (1974), and "Language Training" (1975).

Publications: *Social Inventions* (Information Canada, 1974); "Social Inventions" (THE FUTURIST, August 1973); editor *Canadian Open Adult Learning Systems* (Information Canada, 1973); editor, *Reading in Life Skills* (Information Canada, 1973); "Auch eine Gesellschaft kann kreativ sein" ["A Society, Too, Can Be Creative,"] in *Experiments for Society,* Rudolf Brun, ed., (Zurich: Gottlieb Duweiler Inst., 1976).

COOK, EARL   **Born:** 1920, Bellingham, Washington, U.S.A.
Dean, Geosciences
Texas A and M University
College Station, Texas 77843, U.S.A.   **Telephone:** (713) 845-3651

Profession: Resource geographer

Field of specialization: Future of nonrenewable resources, including energy; resource and environmental decision-making; social and political impacts of energy use.

Education: B.S., Mining Engineering, 1943, M.S., Geology, 1947, Ph.D., 1953, University of Washington.

Professional employment: Texas A and M University: Dean, Geosciences (1971-); Professor of Geology and Geography (1965-). National Academy of Sciences, National Research Council: Executive Secretary, Division of Earth Sciences (1963-66). College of Mines, University of Idaho: (1957-64); Professor of Geology (1951-64). Idaho Bureau of Mines and Geology: Director (1957-64); Acting Director (1956-57); Geologist (1953 and 54).

Professional activities: Teaching course on "Man and Nature" covering the evolution of man's attitudes toward his physical and biological environment, the role these attitudes have played in his decisions on the use of his environment, and a study of present and potential mechanisms for improved environmental decision-making; other current activities in the area of energy and the environment and volcanic geology.

Publications: *Man, Energy, Society* (W. H. Freeman and Company, 1976); "Limits to the Exploitation of Nonrenewable Resources" (*Science Magazine*, February 1976); "Ionizing Radiation"—chapter in *Environment, Resources, Pollution and Society* (Sinauer Associates, 1975); "Health Aspects of a High-Energy Society" (*Texas Reports on Biology and Medicine*, 1975); "The Flow of Energy in an Industrial Society" (*Scientific American*, September 1971).

(From the first edition. Corrections not received by press time.)

COOMER, JAMES CHESTER
Born: 1939, Evansville, Indiana, U.S.A.

Chairman, Studies of the Future, University of Houston/Clear Lake Campus
Executive Secretary, Third Biennial Woodlands Conference on Growth Policy
2700 Bay Area Boulevard
Houston, Texas 77058, U.S.A.
Telephone: (713) 488-9410

Profession: Political scientist

Field of specialization: Anticipatory policy making; impact assessment.

Education: B.A., Political Science, Carson-Newman College, 1965; M.A., Political Science, Georgia State University, 1968; Ph.D., Political Science, The University of Tennessee, 1974.

Professional employment: University of Houston/Clear Lake: Associate Professor (1974-). University of Tennessee: Instructor and Research Associate (1969-70; 1973-74). U.S. Senate: Special Assistant to Senator Vance Hartke (1972-74). Nashville-Davidson County, Tennessee: Administrative Assistant to the Mayor (1971-72). Office of Economic Opportunity, The Job Corps: Head, Assignment Section (1965-67).

Professional activities: Executive Secretary-Assistant to Chief Administrator, The Third Biennial Woodlands Conference on Growth Policy (1976-); Chairman, Studies of the Future Program, University of Houston/Clear Lake (1978-); Director, Energy Education Workshop—funded by a grant from the Shell Foundation (1978-); presently conducting graduate courses on public policy and the study of the future; member, World Future Society, Southern Political Science Association, American Political Association.

Publications: Co-author, *Nashville Metropolitan Government: The First Decade* (Bureau of Public Administration, University of Tennessee, November 1974); co-author, *Houston and Energy: Where Are We Going?* (The Energy Institute, University of Houston, November 1977); co-author, "Politicians' Attitudes Towards Planning" (*Long Range Planning*, December 1977); "Solving the Energy Dilemma" (THE FUTURIST, Vol. 11, No. 4, August 1977); co-author, "The Policy-Maps of Urban Decision Makers: Attitudes Toward Long Range Planning" (*The Journal of Political Science*, forthcoming).

COOPER, DONALD R.
Born: 1945, New York, New York, U.S.A.

Assistant Professor
Administration and Systems
College of Business and Public Administration
Florida Atlantic University
Boca Raton, Florida 33431, U.S.A.
Telephone: (305) 395-5100 ext. 2946

Profession: Professor of Organizational Behavior; research methodologist.

Field of specialization: Individual, small group and organizational behavior; decision making and priority-setting methodologies; futures methodology; social psychological/organizational psychological measurement and testing.

Education: B.A., 1967, M.A., 1968, University of Akron; Ph.D., Kent State University, 1977.

Professional employment: Florida Atlantic University: Assistant Professor, Administration (1976-). Kent State University: Graduate Teaching Fellow (1973-76). North American Air Defense Command (NORAD): Education and Training Officer (1968-72).

Professional activities: Currently working with a program planning/priority setting grant for county government; developing a program for the 1970 SCA Conference on "Communication in the Twenty-first Century"; Research Editor, *Business Tomorrow* (A WFS publication) (current); a survey of "The Organizational Development Specialist as a Futurist" (current); teaching graduate courses in Research Methodology and Organizational Behavior; conducted a survey of Fortune 500 CEO's on "The Future of the Free Enterprise System" (1977); presently doing consulting; working on a textbook with Jay Mendell, J.W. Upjohn, and P. Guglielmino, titled *A Skills Hierarchy for Management Development.*

Publications: *Application of Communication Resources to Problems of Social Significance* (ERIC/RCS, August 1978); *A Preliminary Report on Procedures for Ranking Decision Packages in Zero Base Budgeting* (Palm Beach County, Florida, Technical Report, April 1978).

CORDELL, ARTHUR JASON

Born: 1936, Montreal, Quebec, Canada

Economic Adviser
Science Council of Canada
100 Metcalfe Street
Ottawa, Ontario, Canada

Telephone: (613) 992-1151

Profession: Economist

Field of specialization: Conserver society; computer-communications and interactive information systems.

Education: B.A., Economics/Psychology, McGill University, 1960; M.A., 1963, Ph.D., 1965, Economics, Cornell University.

Professional employment: Science Council of Canada: Economic Adviser (1968-). General Foods Corporation, White Plains, New York: Assistant Manager of Economic Analysis (1967-68). Joel Dean Associates, New York City: Senior Associate (1966-67). U.S. National Commission on Food Marketing: Staff Economist (1965-66). Cornell University: Teaching Assistant (1961-65).

Professional activities: Projects at Science Council of Canada: science policy; the costs and benefits of the multinational firm; strategies of development for the Canadian computer industry; ownership, development of natural resources and benefits accruing to Canada; transfer of technology; structure and function of government laboratories; and the implications of changing from a consumer to a "conserver" society. Participant in a number of seminars and conferences concerned with: implications of the multinational corporation; environmental impact of economic growth; and level and rate of resource use, energy demands and patterns of consumption.

Publications: "Innovation, the Multinational Corporation: Some Implications for National Science Policy" (*Long Range Planning*, September 1973); "Technological Progress: Are We the Captives of a Monumental Myth?" (*Science Forum*, Vol. 5, No. 4, August 1972); "The Changing Nature of Industrial Economic Analysis" (*Indian Journal of Economics*, January 1969); co-author, *The Role and Function of Government Laboratories and the Transfer of Technology to the Manufacturing Sector* (Background study for the Science Council, in press); *The Multinational Firm, Foreign Direct Investment, and Canadian Science Policy* (Background study for the Science Council, December 1971).

CORNISH, EDWARD SEYMOUR

Born: 1927, New York, New York, U.S.A.

President
World Future Society
4916 St. Elmo Avenue (Bethesda)
Washington, D.C. 20014, U.S.A.

Telephone: (301) 656-8274

Profession: Journalist; association executive

Field of specialization: Social innovation; axiology; human destiny.

Education: Diplome d'Etudes, French Civilization, University of Paris (Sorbonne), 1948; B.A., Social Psychology, Harvard College, 1950.

Professional employment: World Future Society: President and Editor (1966-). National Geographic Society: Staff Writer (1957-69). United Press Associations (now UPI): Staff Correspondent in U.S., England, France, and Italy (1951-56).

Professional activities: Editor, *Resource Directory for America's Third Century* (1975-76); editor, THE FUTURIST (1966-); editor, World Future Society BULLETIN (1968-76); member, Organizing Committee, First (1970-71) and Second (1974-75) General Assembly of the World Future Society; Member of the Board of Directors, Worldwatch Institute (1975-); consultant to various business and governmental groups.

Publications: *The Study of the Future: An Introduction to the Art and Science of Understanding and Shaping Tomorrow's World* (World Future Society, 1977); editor, *1999: The World of the Future* (World Future Society, 1978); editor, *The Future: A Guide to Information Sources* (World Future Society, 1977).

CORNISH, SALLY WOODHULL   **Born:** 1927, Bethlehem, Pennsylvania, U.S.A.
World Future Society
4916 St. Elmo Avenue
Washington, D.C. 20014, U.S.A.   **Telephone:** (301) 656-8274

Profession: Journalist

Field of specialization: Value systems; future of the family; teaching futures.

Education: A.B., Journalism, University of North Carolina, 1949.

Professional employment: World Future Society: Program Director (1978-). World Future Society: Staff Writer (1967-). *Small World* (New York): Managing Editor (1956-57). *Realities* (Paris, France): Editorial Assistant (1953-54). United Press International: Staff Correspondent (1951-53). Raleigh (N.C.) *Times*: Reporter (1949-51).

Professional activities: Active in organizing the General Assemblies and other conferences of the World Future Society; member of the Washington, D.C., Chapter Council, World Future Society; has lectured frequently for university classes and other groups; has assisted in organizing seminars on teaching the future.

Publications: —

COX, HARVEY GALLAGHER, JR.   **Born:** 1929, Malvern, Pennsylvania, U.S.A.
Victor S. Thomas Professor of Divinity
Divinity School
Harvard University
Cambridge, Massachusetts 02138, U.S.A.   **Telephone:** (617) 495-5761

Profession: Theologian

Field of specialization: Church and society

Education: A.B., History, University of Pennsylvania, 1951; B.D., Divinity School at Yale University, 1955; Ordained in the Baptist Church, 1956; Ph.D., History and Philosophy of Religion, Harvard University, 1963.

Professional employment: Harvard University Divinity School: Victor S. Thomas Professor of Divinity (1970-); Associate Professor of Church and Society (1965-68); Professor of Divinity (1960-70). Andover-Newton Theological School: Assistant Professor of Theology and Culture (1963-65). American Baptist Home Mission Society: Program Associate (1958-63). Oberlin College: Director of Religious Activities (1958-63).

Professional activities: Serves on the editorial board of *Christianity and Crises;* lectured at the Pontifical Catholic University of Lima, Peru (1970); taught at the Seminario Bautista de Mexico (1974); maintained two-way communication between West and East in East Berlin as a Fraternal Worker for the Gossnor Mission (1962-63); taught at Naropa Institute during the summers of 1975 and 1976.

Publications: *Turning East* (1977); *God's Revolution and Man's Responsibility* (1965); *The Secular City* (1965); *On Not Leaving It to the Snake* (1965); editor, *The Church Amid Revolution* (1967); editor, *The Situation Ethics Debate* (1968); *The Feast of Fools* (Harvard, 1969, Harper Paperback, 1971).

CRAVER, J. KENNETH

Born: 1915, Jonesboro, Illinois, U.S.A.

Manager, Futures Research
Monsanto Company
761 W. Kirkham
Glendale, Missouri 63122, U.S.A.

Telephone: (314) 962-6704

Profession: Futurist; planner; analyst

Field of specialization: Corporate planning; long-range forecasting; technology assessment; cross-impact analysis.

Education: B.Ed., Chemistry, Education, So. Illinois University, 1937; M.S., Chemistry, Syracuse University, 1938.

Professional employment: Monsanto Company: Manager, Futures Research (1971-); Manager, Long-Range Forecasting (1967-71); Senior Research Associate, Technological Forecasts (1961-67); Senior Research Associate, Applied Ingenuity Research (1955-61); Commercial Development Manager (1945-55); Application Research Chemist (1938-45).

Professional activities: Chairman, Divisional Officers Group, American Chemical Society (1976); President, Commercial Development Association (1965); U.S. Program Chairman, International Society for Technology Assessment, Monaco Meeting (1975); Founding Chairman, Gordon Research Conference on Chemistry and Physics of Paper, American Association for the Advancement of Science (1966); extensive publications on ultra sonic impedometry, sonic modulus, physics of fiber webs, hydrogen-bonding phenomena, plasticizers and polymer-solvent interactions.

Publications: Editor, *Applied Polymer Science* (American Chemical Society, 1975); co-author, "Technology Assessment in Product Development" (*Chemical Technology*, Vol. 5, September 1975); co-author, "A Case Study of Technology Assessment in Industry" (*Proceedings of the International Conference on Technology Assessment,* , 1976); "Technological Innovation in the Corporate Environment" (*Technology Transfer*, 1974); editor, "Technological Forecasting for Corporate Growth" in *Planning for Profitable Growth* (Commercial Development Association, 1970).

CREALOCK, CAROL MARIE

Born: 1941, Hamilton, Ontario, Canada

Assistant Professor
Department of Educational Psychology
University of Western Ontario
London, Ontario, Canada N6G 1G7

Telephone: (519) 679-3489

Profession: Psychologist

Field of specialization: Creative problem solving; children with learning disabilities; the future for women.

Education: B.A., 1963, M.A., 1965, Psychology, University of Western Ontario; Ph.D., Educational Psychology, University of Toronto, 1973.

Professional employment: University of Western Ontario: Assistant Professor (1972-). Metropolitan Separate School Board: School Psychologist (1967-70). Child Guidance Clinic, Dublin, Eire: Psychologist (1965-66).

Professional activities: Doing research on problem solving skills with children who have learning disabilities; teaching undergraduate courses in Special Education; graduate courses in Curriculum Theory; consulting psychologist for Policy Analysis with Alexander Blake Associates; doing research on Teacher Practicum Programmes; member, Canadian Association for Studies in Education and Ontario Psychological Association (1970-).

Publications: "Juvenile Delinquency: The Canadian Perspective" (*Behavior Disorders*, 1979); "Sex, Vocational Stereotypes and Fear of Success" (*The Ontario Psychologist*, 1978); "Interaction Between Intelligence and Interstimulus Trace Interval" (*American Journal of Mental Deficiency*, 1966); "Risk Taking and Reading Test Performance" (*Proceedings of the Learned Societies*, CCSE, 1975).

CROSS, NIGEL   **Born:** 1942, Bristol, England
Senior Lecturer in Design
The Open University
Walton Hall
Milton Keynes, United Kingdom MK7 6AA   **Telephone:** (0908) 74066

Profession: Designer

Field of specialization: The role of design in creating alternative futures.

Education: B.Sc., Architecture, University of Bath, 1966; M.Sc., Design Technology, University of Manchester, 1967; Ph.D., Computer-aided Design, University of Manchester, 1974.

Professional employment: The Open University: Senior Lecturer in Design (1975-); Lecturer in Design (1970-75). University of Manchester: Lecturer in Design Technology (1968-70). University of London: Research Assistant (1967-68).

Professional activities: Chairman, "Man-made Futures" course team, Open University; educational work includes writing teaching texts and presenting television and radio broadcasts on design, technology, and society; Honorary General Secretary of Design Research Society (1971-74), Vice Chairman (1977-); director of Design Participation Conference (1971); consultant on Impact of Computers in Architecture, Department of the Environment (1968).

Publications: *The Automated Architect* (Pion Ltd., London, 1977); *Methods Guide* (Open University Press, 1978); co-author, with D. Elliott and R. Roy, *Man-made Futures* (Hutchinson Press, London, 1974); editor, *Design Participation* (Academy Editions, London, 1972); *Design and Technology* (Open University Press, 1975); co-author, with P. Murray, *The Future of Shelter* (Open University Press, 1975).

CROZIER, MICHEL JEAN   **Born:** 1922, Sainte Menehould, Marne, France
Director
Centre de Sociologie des Organizations
(Center for Organizational Sociology)
20, rue Geoffroy Saint Hilaire
75005 Paris, France   **Telephone:** 587 12 77/78

Profession: Sociologist; research director

Field of specialization: Organizational sociology.

Education: Doctor of Law, Faculty of Law, University of Paris; Doctor of Letters, Faculty of Letters, University of Paris.

Professional employment: Centre de Sociologie des Organisations: Founder and Director (1961-). Centre National de la Recherche Scientifique: Research (1970, 1964, 1954, 1952). Stanford University, Center for Advanced Study in the Behavioral Sciences: Fellow (1959-60, 1973-74). Faculty of Letters, Paris Nanterre: Professor of Sociology (1967-68). Harvard University: Professor of Sociology (1966-67 and 1968-70).

Professional activities: Chairman, Research Committee on Sociology of Organizations, International Sociological Association (1971-); Founding Member, Association pour le Developpement des Sciences Sociales appliquees (1972-); President, French Sociological Association (1970-72); Member, Executive Committee, Jean Moulin Club (1960-70).

Publications: Co-author, with Samuel Huntington and Joji Watanuki, *The Crisis of Democracy—Report on the Governability of Democracies to the Trilateral Commission*, New York (New York University Press, 1975); *Ou va l'Administration Francaise? [Where Is the French Civil Service Going?]* (Collection Sociologie des Organisations, Les Editions d'Organisation, 1974); *La Societe-Bloquee*

[Blocked Society] (Les Editions du Seuil, Paris, 1970, translated into English); *Le monde des employes de bureau [The World of Office Workers]* (Les Editions du Seuil, Paris, 1965, translated into English and Italian).
(From the first edition. Corrections not received by press time.)

CULVER, JOHN C.
Born: 1932, Rochester, Minnesota, U.S.A.

Member
United States Senate
2327 Dirksen Senate Office Building
Washington, D.C. 20510, U.S.A.

Telephone: (202) 224-3744

Profession: United States Senator

Field of specialization: Improving capacity of political institutions to anticipate problems; developing methods of involving private citizens in process of public goal-setting and future planning.

Education: B.A., with Honors, American Government, Harvard University; LL.B., Harvard Law School, 1962; Graduate Studies, Cambridge University, England.

Professional employment: U.S. Senate: Senator (1974-). U.S. House of Representatives: Congressman (1964-75). Practicing attorney in Iowa (1963-64). Senator Edward Kennedy: Legislative Assistant (1962-63).

Professional activities: Currently conducting a year-long series of hearings as Chairman of the Panel on Environmental Science and Technology (fact finding panel of the Senate Public Works Committee) on "Choosing our Environment: Can We Anticipate the Future?"; sponsored Congressional Conferences on "Outsmarting Crises: Futures Thinking in Congress" and "Long-Range Planning in a Free Society"; authored resolution adopted by Senate establishing Temporary Commission on the Operation of the Senate, citizens' panel charged with recommending improvements in the day-to-day functioning of the Senate; as member of Select Committee on Reorganization of Committees of the House of Representatives, authored "foresight provision" in the House Rules; originated "Iowa 2000," statewide program of private citizen participation in selection of future priorities and values.

Publications: "Information for Legislation: A Congressman Speaks" (*Bulletin for the American Society for Information Science*, April 1975).
(From the first edition. Corrections not received by press time.)

CURTIS, RICHARD KENNETH
Born: 1924, Worcester, Massachusets, U.S.A.

Professor of Speech and Communication
Indiana University and Purdue University at Indianapolis
925 West Michigan Street
Indianapolis, Indiana 46202, U.S.A.

Telephone: (317) 264-4796

Profession: Professor of speech and communication

Field of specialization: Systems theory; value systems; energy/information processing.

Education: Th.B., Religion and Speech, Northern Baptist Seminary, Chicago, 1950; M.S., Ph.D., Speech, Purdue University.

Professional employment: Indiana University and Purdue University at Indianapolis: Professor of Speech and Communication (1969-). Muskingum College, Ohio: Chairman, Department of Speech (1967-69). University of Missouri at Kansas City: Visiting Lecturer (1963-67). Immanuel Baptist Church, Kansas City: Senior Minister (1962-67). Bethel College and Seminary, Saint Paul: Chairman, Department of Speech (1956-62); Professor of Homiletics (1956-57). Barrington College, Rhode Island: Chairman, Department of Communication (1952-56).

Professional activities: Consultant to Office of Technology Assessment, Library of Congress (1977-); Founding Director, Center for the Study of the Future, Indianapolis, Indiana (1975-); coordinator, Indiana members of the World Future Society (1974-); President, Central Indiana Chapter of the World Future Society (1974-); currently writing a primer for the future; moderator, energy alternatives, appropriate technology regional meeting for the National Science Foundation (1978).

Publications: *They Called Him Mister Moody* (Doubleday, 1962, Wm. B. Ferdmans Company, 1967).

DADDARIO, EMILIO QUINCY
Hedrick and Lane
1211 Connecticut Avenue, NW
Washington, D.C. 20036, U.S.A.

Born: 1918, Newton Centre, Massachusetts, U.S.A.

Telephone: (202) 628-5923

Profession: Lawyer

Field of specialization: Technology assessment

Education: B.A., Wesleyan University, 1939; LL.B., University of Connecticut, 1942.

Professional employment: Hedrick and Lane: (1977-). Office of Technology Assessment, U.S. Congress: Director (1973-77). Gulf and Western Precision Engineering Group: Senior Vice President (1971-73). Daddario, Flitt, Jacobs and Sullivan—Attorneys: Senior Partner (1952-73). U.S. Congress, Member, House of Representatives (1959-71).

Professional activities: Chairman of the Board, American Association for the Advancement of Science (1978); member, Board of Directors, Institute for the Future; member, Council on Trends and Perspectives, National Chamber of Commerce; chaired the Subcommittee on Science, Research and Development while a member of the House; major interest in the House of Representatives was the establishment by Congress of a national policy for science and technology.

Publications: "Science Policy: Relationships Are the Key" (*Daedalus*, Journal of the American Academy of Arts and Sciences); "Congress and Science Policy"—chapter in *Science and Technology in the World of the Future*, A. Bronwell, Ed. (John Wiley and Sons, 1970).

DALKEY, NORMAN C.
Adjunct Professor
University of California-Los Angeles
405 Hilgard
Los Angeles, California 90272, U.S.A.

Born: 1915, Crowley, Colorado, U.S.A.

Telephone: (213) 825-4315

Profession: Decision theorist

Field of specialization: Delphi—group decision theory; value systems; futures methodology.

Education: A.B., Philosophy and Psychology, San Jose State College, 1937; Philosophy, University of Chicago, 1937-39; Ph.D., Philosophy, University of California-Los Angeles, 1942.

Professional employment: University of California-Los Angeles: Adjunct Professor (1972-). Rand Corporation: Senior Mathematician (1948-72). Sherman H. Dryer Products: Assistant Director (1946-48). Radiation Laboratory, Berkeley: Physicist (1943-46). University of California-Los Angeles: Instructor of Meteorology (1942-43).

Professional activities: Research on group decision analysis (1974-); Project Consultant, California Air Resources Board, Delphi study of human health damages from mobile source air pollution (1974-); consultant to various government and industrial organizations on Delphi and group judgment; experimental study of group judgment for Rand Corporation and UCLA (1966-74); large-scale computer simulation of military systems for Rand (1956-66); research on theory of games and decision theory (1948-56)

Publications: "Group Decision Analysis" in *Multidimensional Criteria Decision Making*, Milan Zeleny, Ed. (Springer Verlag, 1976); "Toward a Theory of Group Estimation" in *The Delphi Method*, Linstone and Turoff, Eds. (Addison Wesley, 1975); *Studies in the Quality of Life* (D. C. Heath, 1972); "An Experimental Study of Group Opinion" (*Futures*, Vol. 1, September and December 1969); "Delphi" in *An Introduction to Technological Forecasting*, Joseph Martino, Ed. (Gordon and Breach, 1972).
(From the first edition. Corrections not received by press time.)

DALY, HERMAN E.
Professor of Economics
Economics Department
Louisiana State University
Baton Rouge, Louisiana 70803, U.S.A.

Born: 1938, Houston, Texas, U.S.A.

Telephone: (504) 388-5211

Profession: Economist

Field of specialization: Limits to growth; economic development.

Education: B.A., Economics, Rice University, 1960; Ph.D., Economics, Vanderbilt University, 1967.

Professional employment: Louisiana State University: Professor of Economics (1974-). Yale University: Research Associate (1969-70).

Professional activities: Research in steady-state economy and costs of economic growth.

Publications: Editor, *Toward a Steady-State Economy* (Freeman Company, 1973); "Steady-State Economics" (*American Economic Review*, May 1974); "Energy Demand Forecasting" (*American Institute of Planners Journal*, January 1976); "On Economics as a Life Science" (*Journal of Political Economy*, June 1968); "A Marxian-Malthusian View of Poverty" (*Population Studies*, March 1971.). (From the first edition. Corrections not received by press time.)

DAMLO, PENNY ANN **Born:** 1948, Fargo, North Dakota, U.S.A.
Research Associate
Future Systems, Inc.
P.O. Box 14067
Minneapolis, Minnesota 55337, U.S.A. **Telephone:** (612) 222-2247 (612) 894-3873

Profession: Research Associate

Field of specialization: Futures education; futures methodology.

Education: B.A., Political Science and Education, Hamline University, 1970.

Professional employment: Future Systems, Inc.: Research Associate (1978-). Burnsville Senior High School: Futuristics Instructor (1973-78). Social Studies Instructor (1971-73).

Professional activities: Senior Vice President, Minnesota Futurists, a chapter of the World Future Society (1978); assistant editor, FUTURICS (1978).

Publications: Co-author, *Futuristics: Forecasting Techniques* (Burnsville Senior High School, 1976).

DANECKI, JAN **Born:** 1928, Kalisz, Poland
Scientific Secretary
Research and Prognostics Committee
"Poland 2000"
Polish Academy of Sciences
Palac Kultury i Nauki
Warsaw, Poland **Telephone:** 200-211 Ext. 2677

Profession: Sociologist

Field of specialization: Theory of social forecasting; social forecasting

Education: M.A., Sociology, Poznan University, 1951; Ph.D., Sociology, Higher School of Social Sciences, 1966; Professor Degree, Social Policy, Warsaw University, 1972.

Professional employment: Committee "Poland 2000," Polish Academy of Sciences: Scientific Secretary (1971-). Institute of Philosophy and Sociology, Polish Academy of Sciences: Head of Research Group (1975-76). Warsaw University: Associate Professor (1966-75). Journalistic work: Editor, writer (1952-65). Pozan University: Assistant (1950-51).

Professional activities: Social forecasting, research on theoretical and methodological premises of defining long-term social goals, studies on theory of social progress and social policy at the Committee "Poland 2000"; lectures and seminars in the Institute of Social Policy, Warsaw University; research on the theory of industrial civilization and on social structure (begun 1966); research on social progress; studies on premises of prospective social policy (1974-77).

Publications: *Unity of Divided Time: The Time of Work and the Time of Leisure in Industrialized Societies* (in Polish, 1972, 1974); *Problems of Social Progress in Socialist Industrialized Societies* (in Polish, Warsaw University Press, 1974); editor, *Social Development of Poland in Prognostic Works* (in Polish, "Poland 2000", 1974) (abridged edition in English); editor, *Social Aspects of Economic Growth* (in Polish, Polish Scientific Publishers, 1975); "Assumption of Perspective Policy in Income Distribution in Poland" in *Social Structure*, (in English, Ossolineum Publishers, 1977).

DARLING, CHARLES M., III

Vice President and Partner
C. Stewart Baeder Associates
10 East 53rd Street
New York, New York 10022, U.S.A.

Born: 1924, Burlington, Vermont, U.S.A.

Telephone: (212) 355-4310

Profession: Management policy consultant

Field of specialization: International systems design and management assessment and development.

Education: B.A., New York University, 1949; Career in-training programs at Harvard Business School, Foreign Service Institute (U.S. Department of State), and Bureau of Social Science Research; Equivalent of doctorate in policy sciences.

Professional employment: C. Stewart Baeder Associates: Vice President and Partner (1977-). The Intersect Group: Executive Director (1975-). The Conference Board: Director of Projects for Senior Executives Council (1966-72). International Marketing Institute: Associate Director (1964-65). Western Electric Company: Public Affairs Associate (1961-62). U.S. Department of State and Defense: Country Analyst Indochina (1950-52); Foreign Service Staff Officer, Thailand, Pakistan, Japan (1954-60).

Professional activities: Creating, financing The Intersect Group as an international network (1975-); initiated projects on "Major Decision Settings and Options Confronting the Information-Communications Industry Within the Emerging Global Context," "Resource Requirements Essential to Viability of Industrialized and Non-industrialized Regions and the Critical Trade-offs Between Wants and Needs Therein"; Member, World Future Society; helped establish The Institute for the Future in California (1967-68); Member, White House task force and coordinator of follow-up team to design Institute for Public Choices (1970-71); Consultant to Mayor of Dallas on "Goals for Dallas," and to National Science Foundation in "information sciences" and "Research Applied to National Needs (RANN)" programs; frequent guest lecturer and conference organizer on communications, management, and international relations.

Publications: Co-author, *Information Technology: Some Critical Implications for Decision Makers: Decisions That Cannot Wait* (The Conference Board, New York, 1971-72); Director of Study, *Challenge to Leadership: Managing in a Changing World* (Free Press, New York, and Macmillan, London, 1973); editor, *Perspectives for the '70s and '80s: Tomorrow's Problems Confronting Today's Management* (The Conference Board, New York, 1969).

DARROW, R. MORTON

Vice-President
The Prudential Insurance Company of America
15 Prudential Plaza
Newark, New Jersey 07101, U.S.A.

Born: 1926, New York, New York, U.S.A.

Telephone: (201) 877-7310

Profession: Political scientist; historian.

Field of specialization: Generalist with some concentration in future of corporations, new cities, and institutional change.

Education: B.S.S., History, City College of New York, 1946; M.A., History, Columbia University, 1948; Ph.D., Government/History, Columbia University, 1953.

Professional employment: Prudential Insurance Company: Vice-President (1956-). State of New Jersey: Secretary of Conservation and Development (1954-56). Princeton University: Instructor (1950-54). City College of New York: Lecturer (1947-50).

Professional activities: Member of Overseeing Committee of the Trend Analysis Program (TAP) of the Institute of Life Insurance (1970-); member of the World Future Society from inception of group; participated in study of world food problems at University of Southern California; problems of compulsory retirement at age 65 (AIR); technology assessment overseeing group, Washington, D.C.; member of the Council on Trends and Perspectives of the U.S. Chamber of Commerce (1970-75); Delosian and participant in the World Ekistics Society; lectures extensively on future of society to business organizations.

Publications: Co-author, *Religious Perspectives in American Culture* (Princeton University Press, 1961); co-author, *Social Indicators and Marketing* (American Marketing Association, 1974).

DATOR, JAMES ALLEN

Born: 1933, Newark, New York, U.S.A.

Professor and Head of Alternative Futures Program
Department of Political Science
University of Hawaii
2424 Maile Way
Honolulu, Hawaii 96822, U.S.A.

Telephone: (808)948-7979

Profession: Political scientist

Field of specialization: Public participation in futures design; teaching political futuristics; media communication of images of the future; future of law.

Education: A.B., History/Philosophy, Stetson University, Florida, 1954; M.A., Political Science, University of Pennsylvania, 1955; Ph.D., Political Science, The American University, 1959; (Cert.) Ethics, Virginia Theological Seminary, 1958.

Professional employment: University of Hawaii, Professor and Head, Alternative Futures Program (1969-). TV Ontario (Toronto): Head of Futures Project (1974-76). Virginia Polytechnic Institute: Associate Professor (1966-69). Rikkyo University (Tokyo): Assistant Professor (1960-66).

Professional activities: Production of TV shows about the future for TV Ontario and Hawaii (1974-); teaching introductory, advanced and graduate courses in futuristics, University of Hawaii (1969-); member, Scientific Committee of World Future Studies Federation (1973-); consultant to Hawaii Judiciary.

Publications: "The Transformation Society," in Johan Galtung, ed., *Alternative Visions of Desirable Societies* (Forthcoming). Paper given at a Conference on Alternative Visions of Desirable Societies, Mexico City, 1978; "Alternative Futures and the Future of Law," and "Alternative Futures for the Adversary System in American Law," in C. Bezold and J. Dator (eds.), *Alternative Futures for American Law* (Forthcoming); "The Future of Culture/Cultures of the Future," in Tony Marsella, ed., *Perspectives in Cross-Cultural Psychology* (Academic Press, 1979); *"The Future of Anticipatory Democracy,'* in C. Bezold, ed., *Anticipatory Democracy* (Random House, 1978); "The Pedagogy of the Oppressed: North American Style," (*McGill Journal of Education*, Spring 1977); "De-Colonizing the Future," in A. Spekke, ed., (*The Next 25 Years*, World Future Society, 1975); "Adult Education and the Invention of Alternative Futures," in J. Dator, ed., (*Convergence: International Journal for Adult Education*, Vol. VIII, No. 3, 1975).

DAUMAN, JAN VICTOR

Born: —

Matrix Corporate Affairs Consultants Ltd.
4 Cromwell Place
London S.W. 7, England

Telephone: (01) 581-2223

Profession: Engineer; public policy analyst

Field of specialization: International issue management; futures methodology; corporate responsibility; business-government relations; social impact analysis.

Education: B.Sc., Chemical Engineering, Imperial College, London, 1963; M.I.A., Industrial Administration, Yale University, 1965; Ph.D. candidate, Corporate Responsibility, Brunel University, England.

Professional employment: Inter-Corporate Services: President (1978-). Matrix Corporate Affairs Consultants Ltd.: Managing Director (1973-). Corporate Responsibility Centre: Executive Director (1976-). IBM United

Kingdom Ltd.: Manager, External Affairs (1969-73). Kellogg International Corporation: East Europe Sales Engineer (1965-68).

Professional activities: Research into business-society relations (1969-); Committee of London-Europe Society, Society of Chemical Industry (1968-); member, Royal Institute of International Affairs, Institute of Strategic Studies, Society of Long Range Planning; consultant to international business and government (1973-); European Architectural Heritage Year Industry Panel (1974-75).

Publications: Co-author, *Business Survival and Social Change* (Associated Business Programmes, 1975); editor, *Education and Industry* (IMB Occasional Paper, 1969); co-author, "Disclosure—Beware the Data Trap" (*Profile*, 1978); co-author, "Business and the Community" (*Journal of General Management*, 1974); several articles in various journals on the impact of technology on society (1969-73).

DAVIDOWITZ, MOSHE
115 Waverly Place
New York, New York 10011, U.S.A.

Born: 1934, New York, New York, U.S.A.

Telephone: (212) 673-5403

Profession: - -

Field of specialization: Values in the future; religion of the future; art in the future.

Education: B.S., History, City College of New York, 1955; Rabbi, Jewish Theological Seminary, 1959; Ph.D., Media Ecology, New York University, 1977.

Professional employment: Hofstra University, New York University: Adjunct Faculty (1970-). Iona College: Assistant Professor, Communications Department (1976-77). New York University: Assistant Director, Division of Continuing Education (1971-74). Spertus Museum of Judaica, Chicago: Director (1968-71). Temple Shalom, Greenwich, Conn.: Rabbi (1959-66).

Professional activities: President, New York Chapter of the World Future Society (1977-); teaching courses and lecturing in futuristics.

Publications: —

DAVIS, RICHARD C.
President
Richard C. Davis Associates, Inc.
P.O. Box 12346
Research Triangle Park, North Carolina 27709, U.S.A.

Born: 1920, Lexington, North Carolina, U.S.A.

Telephone: (919) 782-1552

Profession: Technology forecaster; technical planner

Field of specialization: Technology forecasting for industrial clientele; technology assessments of industrial products; technical planning for industrial research departments.

Education: B.S., Textile Chemistry, North Carolina State University, 1948; M.A., Political Science, Andrews University, 1968.

Professional employment: Richard C. Davis Associates, Inc.: President (1976-). Whirlpool Corporation: Manager, Technology Forecasting and Technology Assessment (1968-75); Manager, Technical Intelligence (1963-68); Senior Research Chemist (1957-63). Armour and Company: Technical Service Representative (1954-57).

Professional activities: Member, Forward Planning Committee, American Society of Agricultural Engineers (1974-76); Member, Executive Committee, American Association of Textile Chemists and Colorists (1970-73); Assistant Professor, North Carolina State University (1949-54); frequent speaker to technical and professional societies.

Publications: Co-author, with W. G. Cutler, *Detergency: Theory and Test Methods*, (Book I, 1972, Book II, 1975, Book III, 1976); Chapter XVI, *Practical Technology Forecasting*, Bright (Prentice-Hall,

1972); *A Monograph for Home Laundry* (American Association of Textile Technologists, 1974); approximately 40 articles in scientific and technological journals.

DAY, LAWRENCE HARVEY

Born: 1942, Halifax, Nova Scotia, Canada

Assistant Director
Business Planning Group
Bell Canada
Room 1105, 620 Belmont
Montreal, Quebec, Canada H3C 3G4

Telephone: (514) 870-3223

Profession: Manager, Policy Research Group

Field of specialization: Technology forecasting and assessment; computer and communications futures.

Education: B. Comm., Economics, Dalhousie University, 1964; M.B.A., Marketing, McMaster University, 1967.

Professional employment: Bell Canada: Assistant Director, Business Planning (1969-); Supervisor, Business Development (1967-69).

Professional activities: Currently manager of a corporate futures research group; conducting a wide variety of technology forecasting and assessment studies in the computer and telecommunications fields; Member of International Society for Technology Assessment, World Future Society, Association for Computing Machinery; frequent lecturer and author in a wide variety of national and international journals and conferences.

Publications: "The Corporate Role in Technology Assessment: A Case Example" (*Technology Assessment*, Vol. 2, No. 1, 1973); "An Assessment of Travel/Communications Substitutability" (*Futures*, December 1973); "Long Term Planning in Bell Canada" (*Long Range Planning*, September 1973); "Delphi Research in the Corporate Environment" in Linstone and Turoff, *The Delphi Method: Techniques and Applications* (Addison-Wesley, 1975).
(From the first edition. Corrections not received by press time.)

DE, NITISH R.

Born: 1927, Lakshmibassa (Bangla Desh)

Director
Public Enterprises Centre for Continuing Education
C-6/5 Safdarjang Development Area
New Delhi 110 016, India

Telephone: 653320

Profession: Social system designer

Field of specialization: Design of social systems with a view to moving towards ideal-seeking systems.

Education: B.A., 1st Class Hons. in Political Science, University of Dacca, Bangla Desh, 1947; M.A., 1st Class Hons in Economics, University of Calcutta, India, 1949.

Professional employment: Public Enterprises Centre for Continuing Education, New Delhi: Director (1977-). National Labour Institute, New Delhi: Dean (1974-77). Indian Institute of Management, Calcutta: Senior Professor (1965-74).

Professional activities: Action research in the field of rural organizations, industrial organizations and government administration systems (1973-); organization development in industrial organizations (1965-); development of network in the third world countries on study of futurology.

Publications: Editor, *Readings in Group Development for Managers and Trainers in India* (Asia Publishing House, Bombay, 1967); co-editor, *Readings in Personnel Management* (Orient Longmans, C Calcutta, 1970); *New Forms of Work Organization India* (I.L.O., Geneva, 1977).

DECOUFLE, ANDRE C.

Born: 1936, Paris, France

Chairman
Laboratoire de Prospective Appliquee
[Laboratory of Applied Futuristics]
Dante no. 6
75005 Paris, France

Telephone: (1) 0338265/3256061

Profession: Political scientist

Field of specialization: Social forecasting; the year 2000 to come; futures epistemology and methodology; geo-politics; land use planning.

Education: M.A., Institut d'Etudes Politiques, 1958; Ph.D., Political Science, 1960, Ph.D., Law, 1964, Faculty of Law, Paris.

Professional employment: Laboratoire de Prospective Appliquee: Chairman (1971-). United Nations: Regional Planning Officer (1967). Institut d'Etudes du Developpement, University of Paris: Director of Research (1958).

Professional activities: Writing and research projects with the Laboratoire de Prospective Appliquee.

Publications: *Sociologie des revolutions [Sociology of Revolutions]* (Presses Universitaires de France, 1968); *La Prospective [Foresight]* (Presses Universitaire de France, 1972); *L'an 2000 [The Year 2000]* (Gallinard, 1975); co-author, *Prospective de l'espace habite [Future of Living Space]* (La Documentation Francaise, 1976); editor and co-author, *Traite elementaire de prevision et de prospective [An Elementary Tract on Forecasting and Futuristics]* (Presses Universitaire de France, 1978); *Tableaux de la France en l'an 2000 [A Picture of France in the Year 2000]* (to appear in 1979, Robert Laffont).

DEDE, CHRISTOPHER JAMES

Born: 1947, Milwaukee, Wisconsin, U.S.A.

Associate Professor
University of Houston at Clear Lake City
2700 Bay Area Blvd.
Houston, Texas 77058, U.S.A.

Telephone: (713) 488-9400

Profession: Educator; scientist

Field of specialization: Education about issues of science and society in the future.

Education: B.S., Chemistry and English, California Institute of Technology, 1969; Ed.D., Science Education, Studies of the Future, University of Massachusetts, 1972.

Professional employment: University of Houston at Clear Lake City: Associate Professor (1976-); Assistant Professor (1974-76). University of Massachusetts: Assistant Professor (1972-74).

Professional activities: President, Education Section, World Future Society (1976-); co-chairman, Futures Research Committee, University of Houston at Clear Lake (1975-); teaching courses in sciences, education, human sciences and futures (1974-); chairman, University-wide committee to develop Institute for Educational Applications of Aerospace Research (1975-); extensive writing and lecturing on science, society, education and the future; co-founder and director of Program for the Study of the Future in Education, University of Massachusetts (first doctoral level futures program in country).

Publications: Co-author, *The Far Side of the Future* (World Future Society, Education Section, 1978); editor, *Proceedings of the First World Future Society Education Section Conference* (World Future Society, Education Section, 1978); "The Future of Technology" in *Handbook for Futures Research* (Greenwood, 1978); "Futures Research and the Secondary Science Curriculum" (*The Science Teacher*, 1974); "Coming Emergence of Education as Force for Conscious Social Change" (*Journal of Thought*, 1975).

DEDIJER, STEVAN

Born: 1911, Sarajevo, Yugoslavia

Research Policy Program
Forskningspolitska Programmet
Magistratsvagen 55 N
S-222 44 Lund, Sweden

Telephone: —

Profession: Social scientist

Field of specialization: Science and technology policy; social intelligence—processes and policies; comparative study of natural and social sciences.

184

Education: B.S., Mathematical Physics, Princeton University, 1934.

Professional employment: Research Policy Program, University of Lund: Founder and Former Director (1966-). Nuclear Institute "B. Kidrich": Director (1952-54); Researcher (1949-52). Nuclear Institute "R. Boskovic": Researcher (1954-56).

Professional activities: Research and teaching on "Social Intelligence" (1974-76) and science and technology policy (1956-74); has written articles on the future of R and D policy and the future of science in Alaska.

Publications: Co-author, "The East is READ" (*Nature*, August 1974); "The Knowledge Industry— Protocol of a Consumer's Day" (*Teknisk Dokumentation*, Sweden, January 1975); "Intelligence Policy" (*Public Science*, June 1974); "Past Brain Gain Policies" (*Journal of World History*, Number 4, 1967); "Underdeveloped Science in Underdeveloped Countries" (*Minerva*, Autumn, 1963).

DE JOUVENEL, BERTRAND
Chateau d'Anserville
60540 Bornel
Oise, France

Born: 1903, Paris, France

Telephone: (4) 452-51-52

Profession: Political scientist; economist; philosopher.

Field of specialization: —

Education: Educated in law, biology, and economics.

Professional employment: Author and professor

Professional activities: Launched Futuribles, an international group of scholars involved in futurist research, in 1960; edited the Bulletin of the Societe d'Etudes et de Documentation Economiques, Industrielles et Sociales from 1961-65; helped to create the International Futuribles Association in 1967; currently teaching at CEDEP; participated as an expert at the Conseil Economique de France, Commission des Comptes et de la Nation, and at the European Community; presided over a commission to advise on long-term policies for forests.

Publications: Twenty-nine books (excluding contributions to collective works) of which the following are available in English: *Du pouvoir [On Power]* (1947, many editions of which the latest is Beacon Press); *Problems of Socialist England* (Batchoworth Press, 1948); *Sovereignty* (Cambridge University and Chicago University Press, 1957); *De la politique pure [The Pure Theory of Politics]* (Cambridge and Yale, 1963); *L' art de la conjecture[The Art of Conjecture]* (Editions de Rocher, 1964, Basic Books, 1967); *La Civilisation de Puissance [The Power Civilization]* (Fayard, 1976); *Un voyageur dans le Siecle [A Traveler in Time]* (Laffont, 1979).

DE JOUVENEL, HUGUES ALAIN
General Delegate and Secretary-General
Association International Futuribles
55 rue de Varenne
Paris 75007, France

Born: 1946, Lausanne, Switzerland

Telephone: (01) 222 63 10+

Profession: Social scientist

Field of specialization: Value systems and public choices; development planning; futures methodology.

Education: Bachelor of Laws, Paris-Sorbonne University of Law, Economic and Political Science, 1969; Master of Laws, Paris-Sorbonne University of Law, Economic and Political Science, 1971; Training for practice as barrister, 1971-72; Thesis for Ph.D. in sociology and philosophy in progress.

Professional employment: International Association Futuribles (International Center of Research and Training on the Future): General Delegate and Secretary-General (1974-); Active Member (1969-71). SEDEIS (Center for Economic, Industrial and Social Studies and Documentation): Secretary-General and Acting Director (January-November 1974); Member and Secretary-General (1968-72). Association for the Development of Applied Social Sciences: (February-June 1974). United Nations Institute for Training and Research, New York: Visiting Scholar and Research Associate

(January-December 1973). French Ministry of Defense: News Editor and Press Attache (January-December 1972).

Professional activities: Free-lance journalist; translator of economic and social scholarly works including C.A. Doxiadis, *Between Dystopia and Utopia* and James S. Coleman, *Changes in Educational Structures;* special consultant to the United Nations Institute for Training and Research for Future Studies (January 1974-); contributor to various periodicals, including *Analyse and Prevision, Horizon du Futur, Futurology, Technological Forecasting and Social Change.*

Publications: "The Case of the Environment" *(Chroniques d'Actualite, 1973)*; "Planning and Forecasting in the U.N. System: Specific Opportunities and Constraints" *(Technological Forecasting and Social Change,* Volume 5, Number 3, 1973); "The Bluff of the Future: Hopes" *(Futurology,* Number 4, March 1975); "On French Prospective"; "Three Basic Assumptions of Forecasting"; Futures Studies, Decision and Action" *(Revue 2000);* "Social Dynamics" *(Futuribles,* Jan. 1978); "Education for Tomorrow" (a UNESCO mimeo); "The Evolution of Lifestyles in Europe and Social Change 1950-1990" (mimeo).

DELORS, JACQUES LUCIEN JEAN

Born: 1925, Paris, France

Professor
Universite Paris-Dauphine
Centre de Recherche "Travail et Societe"
Place Marechal de Lattre de Tassigny
75016 Paris, France

Telephone: 505 14 10

Profession: Economist

Field of specialization: Macro-economic and macro-social policies; work policy and industrial relations; relations between education, work and society; measurement of social progress (social indicators).

Education: Licence of Economy, University of Paris, 1945-47; Diplome, Centre d'Etudes Superieures de Banque, Institut d'Etudes Politiques, 1948-50.

Professional employment: University of Paris-Dauphine: Professor (1973-). Research Center "Work and Society": Director (1975-).

Professional activities: Director of seminars for doctoral students on "Comparison Between Social and Economic Policies in European Countries," and "Work Policy and Industrial Relations"; Consultant for the European Economic Community; Professor, Ecole Nationale d'Administration (1973-75); Chief of Social Affairs Department, French Planning Board (1962-68); currently President of a citizen's association, "Echange et Projects."

Publications: *The Social Indicators* (Futuribles, Hachette, 1971); *Changer* (Les Grands Leaders, Stock, 1975).

DERNOI, LOUIS ANTOINE

Born: 1925, Budapest, Hungary

Consulting Urbanologist
Parallel Development, Inc.
403-60 McLeod Street
Ottawa, Ontario
Canada K2P 2G1

Telephone: (613)238-5366

Profession: Urbanologist

Field of specialization: Urban planning; work and leisure; time planning and management.

Education: B. Architecture, University of Technology and Economics, Budapest, 1943; Housing History, Hungarian Academy of Arts and Sciences; M. Architecture, Urban Planning, McGill University; Doctorate, Leisure Studies, Universite d'Aix-Marseille, France, 1979.

Professional employment: Parallel Development, Inc.: Consulting Urbanologist (1978-). Department of Public Works: Senior Urban Planner (1976-77). Self-employed: Planning Consultant (1962-76). CMHC: Architect-planner (1958-62). Town of Beaconsfield, Quebec: Assistant Planner (1957-58). State Planning

Agency, BPT: Assistant Chief, Architect-planner (1951-56).

Professional activities: Professor of Leisure Science, Faculty of Social Sciences, University of Ottawa (1978-); study and analysis of parallel alternative ways of life and urban development (1977-); Research in the planning and management of time and its effects on the urban environment (1976-).

Publications: *Dimensions, Space and Time* (American Institute of Planners, 1978); "New Communities, New Ways of Life," (*Contact,* University of Waterloo, Ontario, 1977); "Applied Future Studies" (*WSFS Newsletter,* 1976); "Siege of the Fourth Dimension" (*Contact,* University of Waterloo, 1975); "Work and Leisure, Vision 2000" (*Analysen und Prognosen,* 1973); "The Leisure Element of Weekends" (International Union of Local Authorities, 1973).

DICKSON, PAUL ANDREW
Box 80
Garrett Park, Maryland 20766, U.S.A.

Born: 1939, Yonkers, New York, U.S.A.

Telephone: (301) 942-5798

Profession: Writer

Field of specialization: Reporting on future-related policy issues for the general reader.

Education: B.S., Psychology, Wesleyan University, 1961.

Professional employment: Self-employed writer (1969-). McGraw-Hill, Inc., *Electronics* magazine: Writer and Editor (1966-69). U.S. Navy: officer (1962-65).

Professional activities: Board member, Washington Independent Writers (1975-77); University Fellowship, American Political Science Association (1969).

Publications: *Think Tanks* (Atheneum, 1970); *Future File* (Rawson Associates, 1977); *The Electronic Battlefield* (Indiana University Press, 1976); *The Future of the Workplace* (Weybright and Talley, 1975); *Out of This World* (Delta Books, 1977).

DIDSBURY, HOWARD FRANCIS, JR.
Executive Director
Program for the Study of the Future
Kean College of New Jersey
Morris Avenue
Union, New Jersey 07083, U.S.A.

Born: 1924, Detroit Michigan, U.S.A.

Telephone: (201) 527-2190

Profession: Professor of History, Comparative Civilization

Field of specialization: Value systems; cultural change; planning.

Education: B.A., Philosophy and Government, Yale University, 1947; Diploma, Chinese Civilization, Yale Institute of Far Eastern Languages and Cultures, 1948; Chinese Government Scholarship, Asian Studies and Philosophy, University of Southern California, 1948-49; M.A., History and Social Relationships, Harvard University, 1949-51; Ph.D., History, The American University, 1960.

Professional employment: Kean College of New Jersey: Professor of History (1960-); Executive Director, Program for the Study of the Future (1971-). Educational Policies Commission, Washington, D.C.: Consultant (1964-66).

Professional activities: Teaches undergraduate courses: "Alternative Futures: Planning Tomorrow Today"; "Seminar on Futurism"; "Utopia and History: Dreams and Nightmares." Graduate course: "Impact of Science and Technology on Culture." Member, New Jersey Commission to Study Adolescent Education (1976-); research on Value-Shifts and Philosophical Aspects of Futurism; Director, Special Studies Division of the World Future Society (1975-); Educational Officer, Embassy of Pakistan, Washington, D.C. (1953-56); Professor of the History of Far Eastern Civilization and Philosophy of History (1962-).

Publications: Editor, *Student Handbook for the Study of the Future* (World Future Society, 1979); "Coalescence of Cultures" (the foundation research paper for the Educational Policies Commission Report, *Education and the Spirit of Science,* Washington, D.C., 1966); "Whitehead's Interpretation of History" (Lahore,

Pakistan: Pakistan Philosophical Congress); *Are European Schools Better Than Ours?* (National Educational Association, 1965); associate editor, *The Next 25 Years: Crisis and Opportunity* (World Future Society, 1975).

DIEBOLD, JOHN   **Born:** 1926, Weehawken, New Jersey, U.S.A.
Chairman
The Diebold Group, Inc.
430 Park Avenue
New York, New York 10022, U.S.A.   **Telephone:**   (212) 755-0400

Profession: Business executive

Field of specialization: Management and technology; automation

Education: B.S., Engineering, U.S. Merchant Marine Academy, 1946; B.A., Economics, Swarthmore College, 1949; M.B.A., Harvard, 1951; LL.D., Rollins College, 1965; Sc.D., Clarkson College, 1965; D. Engineering, Newark College of Engineering, 1970; D. Comml. Science, Manhattan College, 1973.

Professional employment: The Diebold Group, Inc.: Chairman and Founder (1954-). John Diebold Incorporated (Management and Investment Company): Chairman (1967-). Diebold Europe SA and Management Science Technology Institute: Founder (1958). With Griffenhagen and Associates (Management Consultants): (1951-57); owner (1957-60); merged with Louis J. Kroegar and Associates to become Griffenhagen-Kroegar, Inc. (1960).

Professional activities: Trustee, National Planning Association (1973-); Member, National Science Foundation Advisory Committee on Ethical and Human Value Implications of Science and Technology (1973-); Member, Advisory Council, Society for the Technological Advancement of Modern Man, Switzerland (1963-); Member, U.S. Chamber of Commerce, Council on Trends and Perspectives (1969-); Member, International Institute for Strategic Studies, London (1971-); Director, Academy for Educational Development (1972-); Member, Visiting Committee, Center for Research in Computing Technology and Office for Information Technology, Harvard University (1971-74).

Publications: *Automation: The Advent of the Automatic Factory* (1952); *Beyond Automation* (1964); *Man and the Computer: Technology as an Agent of Social Change* (1969); *Business Decisions and Technological Change* (1970); editor, *World of the Computer* (1973).

DIXON, JOHN   **Born:** 1928, France
Consultant
1421 Massachusetts Avenue, N.W.
Washington, D.C. 20005, U.S.A.   **Telephone:**   (202) 483-0637

Profession: Policy planning consultant

Field of specialization: Theological and historical perspectives necessary for planning policy; application of policy sciences value analysis to public interest issues; interaction between communication systems and society; political role of voluntary associations and cause and issue-oriented groups (e.g., consumer, environmental, peace) in identifying, shaping and guiding major public policy issues.

Education: Attended Harvard, 1949.

Professional employment: Consultant to (1974-): State Department; Congressional Research Service; Congressional Office of Technology Assessment; Joint Economic Committee; National Science Foundation; National Council on Philanthropy; Woodrow Wilson International Center for Scholars; Ruder and Finn Public Relations; American Telephone and Telegraph Company. Applied Futures, Inc.: Washington Representative (1974-). Center for a Voluntary Society: Director (1971-74); Consultant (1968-71). Xerox Corporation: Director, Washington Office, Public Affairs (1965-68). National Institute of Mental Health: Policy Planning Staff (1963-65). U.S. Information Agency: Foreign Service Officer (1960-63). R. Buckminster Fuller: Associate (1953-60).

Professional activities: Board Member, Kingsbury Center for Remedial Education. Advisory Committees of: Center for Theology and Public Policy; Center for Science in the Public Interest; National Committee for Responsive Philanthropy.

Publications: *Orthodox Catholic Spirituality* (Institute of Spirituality, St. John's University, Collegeville, Minnesota, 1979); co-author, *Communication and Interaction Between Citizens' Associations and the Department of State* (Department of State Publication No. 8837, November 1975); co-author, "The Voluntary Society" in *Challenge to Leadership: Managing in a Changing World* (Free Press, Macmillan, 1971); foreward to *Voluntary Sector Policy — Research Needs* (Center for a Voluntary Society, Washington, D.C. 1973).

DOBROV, GENNADY MIKHAYLOVICH

Born: 1929, Artemovsk, Ukrainian SSR, USSR

Deputy Director
Head, Science Policy Studies Department
Institute of Cybernetics
Academy of Sciences of the Ukrainian SSR
109, Nauka Avenue, Kiev, 252028, USSR

Telephone: 63-11-60

Profession: Science policy studies specialist; mechanical engineer

Field of specialization: Science policy studies; technological forecasting; technology assessment.

Education: Diploma, Mechanical Engineering, Mining, Kiev Polytechnical Institute, 1950; Candidate of Technical Sciences, Coal-Mining Machinery, Institute of Power Engineering, 1954; Doctor of Economics, Science Policy Studies, 1968; Professor, Science Policy Studies, 1971.

Professional employment: Academy of Sciences of the Ukrainian SSR: Deputy Director, Institute of Cybernetics and Head, Science Policy Studies Department (1971-). Council for Studies of Productive Forces of the Ukrainian SSR: Deputy Director and Head of Science Policy Studies Department (1968-71); Head and Deputy Director of the Science Policy Studies Department, Institute of Mathematics (1967-68); Head, Department for Machine Methods of Processing of Historio-Scientific Information, Institute of History (1961-67).

Professional activities: Currently working on science policy studies, technological forecasting methodology, technology assessment in R and D management; corresponding member of the International Academy of History of Sciences, Paris; conducts graduate courses on science policy studies; has lectured and written on technology forecasting, science policy studies, and R and D management.

Publications: *Nauka o Nauke [Science of Science]* (Naukova Dumka, Second Edition, 1970); *Prognozirovaniye nauki i tekhniki [Science and Technology Forecasting]* (Nauka, Moscow, 1969); *Wissenschafts-Organization und Effektivitat [Science Organization and Effectiveness]* (Akademie-Verlag, Berlin, 1971); *Wissenschaft Ihre Analyse und Prognose [Science: Its Analysis and Forecast]* (Deutsche Verlags-Anstalt GmbH, Stuttgart, 1974); "Forecasting as a Mean for Scientific and Technological Policy Control" (*Technological Forecasting and Social Change*, Volume 4, 1972).
(From the first edition. Corrections not received by press time.)

DOYLE, FRANK JOHN

Born: North Bay, Ontario, Canada

Chief, Technology Transfer Division
Department of Industry, Trade and Commerce
235 Queen Street
Ottawa, Ontario, Canada K1A 0H5

Telephone: (613) 593-7881

Profession: Policy analyst

Field of specialization: Futures methodology; global forecasting and planning; long-term technological policy development.

Education: B.A., Psychology, University of Toronto, 1963; M.B.A., McMaster University, 1969.

Professional employment: Government of Canada, Department of Industry, Trade and Commerce: Chief, Technology Transfer Division (1977-); Chief, Technological Strategy Division (1975-76); Acting Chief, Technological Forecasting Division (1974-75); Planning Advisor (1972-74). Bell Canada: Staff Supervisor, Market Planning (1971-72); Staff Supervisor, Long-term Planning (1969-71).

Professional activities: Policy development in the field of technology transfer; development of a long-term technological strategy for Canada; founding member, director, and past president, North American Society for Corporate Planning, Ottawa Chapter; long-term global forecasting (1973-75); long-term forecasts of key sectors, using Delphi methodology (1969-72).

Publications: "Long-Term Planning—Global Scale" (*Planning Review*, October/November 1974); "A Global Forecast of Changing Needs and Growth Patterns 1985-2000" (Internal Publication, Government of Canada, April 1973); "How to Design, Structure and Perform a Delphi Study" (Internal Publication, Government of Canada, July 1974); co-author, "An Exploration of the Future in Medical Technology" (Bell Canada Publication, April 1970); co-author, "An Exploration of the Future in Educational Technology" (Bell Canada Publication, January 1970).

DROBNICK, RICHARD LEE   Born: 1945, Waukegan, Illinois, U.S.A.
Staff Economist
Center for Futures Research
University of Southern California
Graduate School of Business Administration
Los Angeles, California 90007, U.S.A.   **Telephone:**   (213) 741-5229

Profession: Economist; policy analyst

Field of specialization: Economic development planning; world agricultural conditions; international macroeconomic policy analysis.

Education: B.S., Ecnomics, Bradley University, 1967; M.A., Economics, University of California, 1973.

Professional employment: Center for Futures Research: Staff Economist, (1976-). Peace Corps/Malaysia: Director, Agricultural Training Program (1971). Volunteer attached to the Malaysian Dept. of Agriculture (1967-69).

Professional activities: Co-principal investigator of Center for Future Research's Fourth Twenty Year Forecast Project entitled "Future Environments of International Trade" (1977-78); lecturer at Center for Future Research's workshops on "Future Research Techniques for Corporate Planners"; designer of international food systems models for Center for Future Research's Second Twenty Year Forecast Project on future world food conditions (1976-77); director of the Peace Corps Agricultural Training Programs in Malaysia (1971); management advisor to the State Supervisor of Farmers Associations in Perak, Malaysia (1967-69).

Publications: Co-author "Neither Feast nor Famine: World Food 20 Years On" (*Food Policy*, February 1978); co-author *Neither Feast nor Famine: Food Conditions to the Year 2000* (Lexington Books, in press); "Perak Farmers Associations: An Analysis and Evaluation" (Report to Malaysian Department of Agriculture, 1969); "Supervised Production Credit" (Report to the Malaysian Department of Agriculture, 1968).

DROR, YEHEZKEL   Born: 1928, Vienna, Austria
Professor of Political Science
The Hebrew University
Jerusalem, Israel   **Telephone:**   (02)31679

Profession: Policy scientist

Field of specialization: Policy-making; strategic planning; policy analysis.

Education: B.A., Political Science and Sociology, 1952, Mag. Jur., Public Law, 1953, Hebrew University of Jerusalem; LL.M., Public Law, 1954, S.J.D., Public Law, Legislation, 1955, Harvard University.

Professional employment: Hebrew University of Jerusalem: Professor of Political Science and Wolfson Professor of Public Administration (1954-). Israeli Ministry of Defense: Senior Advisor on Policy Analysis and Planning (1975-77). Israeli Labor Party: Chief Scientist (1977-78). Rand Corporation: Senior Staff Member (1968-70).

Professional activities: Advisor and consultant to various governments and international agencies on planning, policy-making and policy analysis; main teaching subjects have been policy making, public administration, Israeli government, and strategic studies; serves on the editorial boards of a number of scientific journals, including *Policy Sciences, Policy and Politics, Futures, Technological Forecasting and Social*

Change, Journal of the American Institute of Planners, Social Indicators Research, Policy Studies Journal and *International Journal of General Systems;* Fellow, Center for Advanced Study in the Behavioral Sciences, Palo Alto (1962-63).

Publications: *Public Policymaking Reexamined* (Chandler, New York, 1968, and Leonard Hill, U.K., 1973); *Design for Policy Sciences* (American Elsevier, 1971); *Ventures in Policy Sciences* (American Elsevier, 1971); *Crazy States: A Counter-conventional Strategic Problem* (Heath Lexington, 1971); *The Complete Policy Analyst* (Macmillan, London, 1979); *Handbook for Rulers* (Macmillan, London, 1979).

DROUIN, MARIE-JOSEE
Executive Director
Hudson Institute of Canada
666 Sherbrooke Street West, Room 701
Montreal, Quebec, Canada

Born: 1949, Ottawa, Ontario, Canada

Telephone: (514) 282-9676

Profession: Economist; policy analyst

Field of specialization: Economic development; international economics; futures methodology.

Education: B.A., Economics, Universite du Quebec a Montreal, 1970; M.A., Economics, University of Ottawa, 1973; Doctoral Candidate, McGill University.

Professional employment: Hudson Institute of Canada: Executive Director (1973-). Special Assistant to the Solicitor General of Canada (1971-73). Power Corporation of Canada Ltd.: Financial Analyst (1970-71).

Professional activities: Currently working on a study of the future of the province of Quebec and alternative scenarios (political and economic) for that province; conducting a study on the impacts of current international economic trends on key sectors of the Canadian economy; participating in a study of Australia's economic and social prospects to the year 1990; directing a research project on Canadian values; advisor to the board of the Canadian Association of Future Studies; member of the Communications Research Advisory Board of the federal government.

Publications: Co-author, *Canada Has a Future* (McLelland and Stewart, 1978); co-author, *The Future of Quebec* (Stanke International, 1978); "Australia's Economic Prospects" (Hudson Institute Research Memo, 1978); "Global Political Assessment: Canada" (Columbia University, Bi-annual).

DUBACH, PAUL
Secretary
Schweiz Vereinigung fur Zukunftsforschung
(Swiss Association for Futures Research)
Weinbergstr. 17
Ch-8623 Wetzikon, Switzerland

Born: 1925, Bern, Switzerland

Telephone: (01) 930 40 27

Profession: Engineer

Field of specialization: Technology assessment; value systems; futures methodology.

Education: Dipl. Ing., Mechanical Engineering, ETH (Tahn, Hochschule), 1951.

Professional employment: Consultant (1968-).

Professional activities: Consultant on developing countries and futures methodology; Secretary, Swiss Association for Futures Research.

Publications: *Zukunft Schweiz [Future of Switzerland]* (Benzinger Einsiedeln, 1971); co-author, "Zukunftsmethodik" ["Futures Methodology"] in Bruckmann (Physica Verlag, 1977).

DUBOS, RENE
Professor Emeritus
The Rockefeller University
66th Street and York Avenue
New York, New York 10021, U.S.A.

Born: 1901, Saint Brice, France

Telephone: (212) 360-1000

Profession: Microbiologist and experimental pathologist

Field of specialization: The effects that environmental forces—physicochemical, biological and social—exert on human life.

Education: College Chaptal, Paris, 1915-19; Institut National Agronomique, Paris, 1919-21; Ph.D., Rutgers University, 1927.

Professional employment: The Rockefeller University: Professor Emeritus (1971-); Faculty Member (1927-71). Harvard University Medical School: George Fabyan Professor of Comparative Pathology and Professor of Tropical Medicine (1942-44). International Institute of Agriculture (Rome): Assistant Editor (1924-27).

Professional activities: Author, lecturer and scientific investigator on the biological and mental effects of the total environment; editor, *Journal of Experimental Medicine* (1946-72); member, National Academy of Sciences, the Century Association of New York, and the American Philosophical Society; appointed by President Nixon to the Citizens' Advisory Committee on Environmental Quality (1970).

Publications: Co-author with Barbara Ward, *Only One Earth* (1972); *A God Within* (1972); *Beast or Angel: Choices That Make Us Human* (1974); *Man Adapting* (1965); *Man, Medicine and Environment* (1968).
(From the first edition. Corrections not received by press time.)

DUHL, LEONARD J.
Professor
Health and Medical Sciences Program
University of California
Building T-7, Room 106
Berkeley, California 94720, U.S.A.

Born: 1926, New York, New York, U.S.A.

Telephone: (415) 642-1715

Profession: Professor; psychiatrist

Field of specialization: Public health and urban social policy; holistic health; the new institution; health planning.

Education: A.B., Columbia University, 1945; M.D., Albany Medical College, 1948; Menninger School of Psychiatry, 1954; Washington Psychoanalytic Institute, 1964.

Professional employment: University of California-Berkeley: Director, Dual Degree Option, Health and Medical Sciences Program (1973-77); Professor, Public Health and Urban Social Policy (1968-). Department of Housing and Urban Development: Special Assistant to the Secretary (1966-68). National Institute of Mental Health: Chief Office of Planning (1964-66); Psychiatrist, Professional Services Branch (1954-64).

Professional activities: Organizer of courses on "Mental Health Activities" and "Deliberate Social Change" (1968-); Review Board, *Journal of Community Psychology* (1975-); Member, Group for the Advancement of Psychiatry (1963-); evaluation of Experimental Schools Program, Berkeley, California (1971-73); Member, Science and Technology Advisory Council, California Assembly (1969-74).

Publications: *The Urban Condition: People and Policy in the Metropolis* (Basic Books, New York, 1963); "The University and the Urban Crisis" in *The University and the Urban Crisis* (Behavioral Publications, Inc., New York, 1974); "The Process of Re-Creation: The Health of the I and the US" (in press, *Ethics in Science and Medicine*, 1976); "Participatory Democracy: Networks as a Strategy for Change" (*Urban and Social Change Review*, Vol. 3, No. 2, Spring 1970); *The Promotion and Maintenance of Health: Myth and Reality* (to be published by the Department of National Health and Welfare, Ottawa, 1976).

DUNCAN, JAMES FRANCIS
Professor, Department Head
New Zealand Commission for the Future
Box 5053
Wellington, New Zealand

Born: 1921, Liverpool, United Kingdom

Telephone: 725 033

Profession: Academic chemist

Field of specialization: A University professor of inorganic and theoretical chemistry with an active research commitment in applied science. As chairman of the New Zealand Commission for the Future, has an overview interest in all areas of future studies.

Education: B.Sc., 1943, M.A., 1945, Chemistry, Jesus College, Oxford; M.Sc., Chemistry, University of Melbourne, 1957.

Professional employment: Victoria University of Wellington, New Zealand: Professor, Head of Department (1962-). Melbourne University, Australia: Reader in Radio Chemistry (1952-62). Atomic Energy Research Establishment, Harwell United Kingdom: Scientist (1947-52).

Professional activities: Order of the British Empire, Fellow of the Royal Society of New Zealand.

Publications: —

DUNSTAN, MARYJANE
Instructor, Communications
College of Marin
Kentfield, California 94904, U.S.A.

Born: 1925, Bethlehem, Pennsylvania, U.S.A.

Telephone: (415) 454-3962

Profession: Educator

Field of specialization: Futures studies; curriculum development; community involvement in alternative futures.

Education: B.A., 1951, M.A., 1953, Language Arts, San Francisco State University.

Professional employment: College of Marin: Instructor, Communications (1963-). Artist's Proof Bookstore and Graphics Art Workshop: Partner (1974-). Fulbright Lecturer, Rangoon and Mandalay, Burma (1958-62).

Professional activities: Coordinator, Interdepartmental Futures Group, College of Marin (1974-); Instructor, Futures Perspectives, College of Marin (1968-); Special Project, "Scenario 1980", College of Marin (1975-).

Publications: Co-author, *Worlds in the Making* (Prentice-Hall, Inc., 1970); co-author, *Star Sight* (Prentice-Hall, October 1976); co-author, *Orange Robed Boy* (Viking Press, 1967); co-author, *The Boy Who Played Tiger* (Viking Press, 1968).

DURIE, ROBERT WESLEY
Director
Advanced Concepts Centre
Environment Canada
Ottawa, Ontario
K1A OH3 Canada

Born: 1931, Moose Jaw, Saskatchewan, Canada

Telephone: (819) 997-2347

Profession: Planner; engineer; manager

Field of specialization: —

Education: Engineering, University of Saskatchewan, 1953; M.Sc., Engineering, Ph.D., Petroleum Engineering, University of Texas, 1962; Diploma, International Industrial Management, University of Geneva, 1973.

Professional employment: Advanced Concepts Centre, Environment Canada: Director (1973-76) (1978-). Commission for the Environment, New Zealand: Visiting Senior Fellow, Advisor on Environmental Implications of Electric Power Development Planning (August 1976 to March 1978) (on leave exchange from Environment Canada).

Professional activities: —

Publications: —

ECKHOLM, ERIK P.
Senior Researcher
Worldwatch Institute
1776 Massachusetts Avenue, N.W.
Washington, D.C. 20036, U.S.A.

Born: 1949, Tuscon, Arizona, U.S.A.

Telephone: (202) 452-1999

Profession: Policy analyst

Field of specialization: Environment and development; environmental health.

Education: B.A., Political Science, Occidental College, 1971; M.A., Development Studies, Johns Hopkins School of Advanced International Studies, 1974.

Professional employment: Worldwatch Institute: Senior Researcher (1974-). Overseas Development Council: Associate Fellow (1973-74).

Professional activities: Current projects: endangered species and world forest trends.

Publications: *The Picture of Health: Environmental Sources of Disease* (W.W. Norton, 1977); *Losing Ground: Environmental Stress and World Food Prospects* (W.W. Norton, 1976).

EDRICH, HAROLD
Principal
Weiner, Edrich, Brown, Inc.
303 Lexington Avenue
New York, New York 10016, U.S.A.

Born: 1938, New York, New York, U.S.A.

Telephone: (201) 889-7007

Profession: Psychologist

Field of specialization: Value and attitude change; organizational behavior; environmental scanning.

Education: B.B.A., Psychology, City College of New York, 1960; Ph.D., Industrial and Social Psychology, New York University, 1966.

Professional employment: Weiner, Edrich, Brown, Inc.: Principal (1977-). American Council of Life Insurance: Director of Research (1965-77). Queens College: Adjunct Professor (1966-76). Research Center for Human Relations, New York University: Research Assistant (1963-65). City College of New York: Teaching Fellow (1960-63). Ted Bates Advertising: Intern.

Professional activities: Board of Advisors, East-West Center for Holistic Health (current); member, American Psychological Association and the American Association for Public Opinion Research; Director, Job Placement Office, Eastern Psychology Association (1970); interviewed on various radio programs; primary responsibility for development of Social Research Program at American Council of Life Insurance (1966-77).

Publications: "Americans are on the Move—And That's Part of the Problem" *(Viewpoint,* Issues for the Eighties, 1977); editor, Trend Analysis Report (TAP) (American Council of Life Insurance, 1974-77); "The Potential in All of Us" (Southwestern Life Insurance Co., 1971); co-author, "The Effects of Context and Raters Attitudes on Judgments of Favorableness of Statements About a Social Group" *(Journal of Social Psychology, 1966).*

EDWARDS, GREGG

Program Manager
Knowledge for National Productivity (SE)
National Science Foundation
Washington, D.C. 20550, U.S.A.

Born: —

Telephone: (202) 282-7910

Profession: Theoretical physics; education futures; cross-cultural communications; systems and computer engineering

Field of specialization: Knowledge systems; evaluation, methodology, ethnology of futures; communications technology and implications; evolutionary organizations.

Education: B.A., Liberal Arts (Mathematics, Psychology, and Philosophy), M.A., Ph.D., Physics, Rice University; D.Sc. (honoris causa), Davis and Elkins College; Fulbright-Hayes Fellowship (Italy).

Professional employment: National Science Foundation: Program Manager, Knowledge for National Productivity (current position). National Academy of Sciences: Consultant, Computer Systems (1969-70). Commission on College Physics: Associate Staff Physicist. University of Maryland: Senior Scholar and Visiting Assistant Professor of Physics (1967-69). Visitor with Stipend, Niels Bohr Institute, Copenhagen (1967); Laboratoire de Physique Nucleare, University of Grenoble, France (1965-67). Collins Radio Corporation: Senior Systems Engineer (1961-65).

Professional activities: Director, professional activities, World Future Society (1975-); organizing committee, Society for Art and Science (1977-); Past-President, Washington, D.C. Chapter of the World Future Society (1973-76); lectures extensively at universities on futury, values, knowledge organizations, and technology assessment; Co-Chairman and Program Committee, World Future Society General Assemblies (1971-75).

Publications: Papers on systems engineering, physics, education, urban studies,. organization theory, cosmology, family structures and science in the arts.

EIICHI, ISOMURA

President
Toyo University
3-16-2 Yagumo Meguroku
Tokyo 152, Japan

Born: 1903, Tokyo, Japan

Telephone: (03) 717-2869

Profession: Professor of Sociology

Field of specialization: Urban problems and policy; science of human settlements (ekistics).

Education: Graduate, Tokyo National University; Ph.D., Sociology, Tokyo National University, 1956.

Professional employment: Toyo University: President. Tokyo Metropolitan University: Professor of Sociology (1945-59). Assistant to Governors of Tokyo (1944-47). Tokyo Metropolitan Government: Director of Public Welfare Department (1940-44).

Professional activities: President, Japan Society of Ekistics; member and past president, World Society for Ekistics; adviser, Japan Sociological Society; director, Japan Society for Urban Affairs; visiting professor at Boston University; chairman, National Committee for Discrimination Problems; member, National Committee for Land Utilities Planning.

Publications: *Science of Urban Affairs* (Ryosho-Fukyukai, 1971); *Encyclopedia for Urban Science* (Kazima-Shuppan, 1965); *City Charter* (Kazima-Shuppan, 1978).

ELBOIM-DROR, RACHEL

Head
Division of Educational Planning and Administration
Hebrew University
Mount Scopus
Jerusalem, Israel

Born: 1931, Poland

Telephone: —

Profession: Professor of Educational Administration

Field of specialization: Educational administration and planning; educational futures.

Education: B.A., Sociology, Hebrew University, 1953; Ed.M., 1955, Ed.D., 1958, Educational Administration, Harvard University.

Professional employment: Hebrew University: Senior Lecturer in Educational Administration (1971-); Lecturer (1965-71); External Teacher (1963-65); Lecturer and Tutor, Inservice Training Department (1959-61). Teachers College: Teacher (1956-58). Harvard Graduate School of Education: Field Studies (1954-65). Teacher at various schools (1949-54).

Professional activities: Currently working on studies in education policy-making and on alternative futures for education in Israel; coordinator of group on Educational Futures at IRADES Conference in Rome (1973); coordinator of group on Educational Planning at World Future Research Conference in Bucharest, Rumania (1972); Director of Research on Decision-making Process in Education, supported by a grant from the Hebrew University Research and Development Authority (1970-73).

Publications: "Some Characteristics of the Education Policy Formation System" (*Policy Sciences*, Vol. 1, No. 2, 1970); "Organizational Characteristics of the Education System" (*Journal of Educational Administration*, Vol. 2, No. 1, 1973); "Two Cultures in Education" in *Studies in Education* (Hebrew University, 1977); *Status and Conditions of Work of Secondary School Teachers* (Hebrew University, 1962); "The Management System in Education and Staff Relations" (*Journal of Educational Administration and History*, Vol. 4, No. 1 and 2, 1972).

ELDREDGE, H. WENTWORTH
Department of Sociology
Dartmouth College
Hanover, New Hampshire 03755, U.S.A.

Born: 1909, New York, New York, U.S.A.

Telephone: (603) 646-2541

Profession: Sociologist emeritus

Field of specialization: Urban futures; university level education in future studies.

Education: A.B., Sociology, Dartmouth College, 1931; Ph.D., Sociology, Yale University, 1935.

Professional employment: Science Applications, Inc., Washington, D.C.: (1975-). Dartmouth College: Professor of Sociology (1935-75); Emeritus (1975-). Military Services: (1942-46).

Professional activities: Research for Science Applications, Inc., and Mathtech, Inc; university futures teaching; lectures and writes widely on political sociology, including the sociology of revolution and social change, city, metropolitan, regional, national and international holistic planning; delivered paper on "The Future as a University Discipline" at CIBA Foundation Symposium, London, 1975; two lectures at the Future Course, International University Centre for Graduate Studies, Dubrovnik, 1975; has published numerous studies of futures teaching.

Publications: Editor, *Taming Megalopolis: An Introduction to Urban Planning and Urbanism* (Anchor/Doubleday, 1967); editor, *World Capitals: Toward Guided Urbanism* (Anchor/Doubleday, 1975); "Education for Futurism in the U.S.A." (THE FUTURIST, December 1970; *Technological Forecasting and Social Change*, December 1970; updated versions published in THE FUTURIST, *Fields Within Fields, Futures,* etc., 1974-75).

ELGIN, DUANE S.
President
Center for Transformational Studies
534 Pope Street
Menlo Park, California 94025, U.S.A.

Born: 1943, Nampa, Idaho, U.S.A.

Telephone: (415) 329-9090

Profession: Self-employed consultant

Field of specialization: Evolving human consciousness and values (exploring present status and future social expression); problems of large, complex systems.

Education: B.A., Liberal Arts, College of Idaho, 1966; M.B.A., Business, 1968, M.A., Economic History, 1969, University of Pennsylvania.

Professional employment: Center for Transformational Studies: President (1977-). Stanford Research Institute: Senior Social Policy Analyst (1972-76). President's Commission on Population and the American Future: Professional Staff (1971-72). Department of Housing and Urban Development: Planning Intern (1967).

Professional activities: Research, consulting and seminars on problems of large complex systems (1976-78); co-leader of seminars for business on changing American values (1977-78); research and seminars on voluntary simplicity as a forerunner of incipient values change (1976-78); presently writing a book on voluntary simplicity for publication in 1979.

Publications: Co-author, "Voluntary Simplicity" (*Co-Evolution Quarterly* and THE FUTURIST, 1977); "The Limits to Complexity: Are Bureaucracies Becoming Unmanageable?" (Stanford Research Institute and THE FUTURIST, 1977); co-author, *Changing Images of Man* (Stanford Research Institute, 1974); co-author, *Alternative Futures for Environmental Planning: 1975-2000* (Stanford Research Institute and the U.S. Government Printing Office, 1975); *City Size and the Quality of Life* (Stanford Research Institute and the U.S. Government Printing Office, 1975).

EL-KHOLY, USSAMA AMIN
ALECSO
109, Tahrir Street, Dokki, Giza
Cairo, Egypt

Born: 1923, Cairo, Egypt

Telephone: 846072

Profession: Professor of engineering

Field of specialization: Technology assessment; science policies; informatics; futures methodology.

Education: B. Eng. (Hons.), Mechanical Engineering, Faculty of Engineering, Cairo University, 1944; D.I.C., Aero. Engineering, Imperial College, London University, 1946; Ph.D., Aero. Engineering, London University, 1951.

Professional employment: ALECSO: A.D.G., Science and Technology (1977-); Cairo University: Professor (1965-); Assistant Professor (1958-65). Alexandria University: Lecturer (1951-58).

Professional activities: Coordination of future industrialization plans in the Arabian Peninsula (1978-); Civil aviation in Egypt (long-term plan) (1978); Future of science and technology in the Arab region (1978); Analysis of Arab Industrialization Plans (1950-75); Establishment of Arab Industrial Information Network (1976); Establishment of Computer Centre in Cairo University (1967).

Publications: Co-author, *Science and Development in the Arab Region* (ALECSO, 1976); editor, *Assessment of Industrialization Effort in the Arab Region (1950-1975)* (IDCAS, 1977); *Application and Development of Research Results* (ALECSO, 1974); *The Scientific Technological Revolution and the Arab World* (Federation of Arab Engineers, 1968); "A Bridge Between the Physical and Social Sciences" (*Contemporary Thought*, 1970).

ELLIS, WILLIAM N.
Coordinator
TRANET
Box 567
Rangeley, Maine 04970, U.S.A.

Born: 1920, Rangeley, Maine, U.S.A.

Telephone: (207) 864-2252

Profession: Consultant

Field of specialization: Appropriate/alternative technology; economic development; intergovernmental relations; technology transfer; science policy.

Education: B.S., Engineering, University of Maine; M.S., Physics, University of Vermont.

Professional employment: TRANET: Coordinator (1976-). World Bank: Consultant (1977-). VITA: Consultant (1977-). U.N. HABITAT: Director, A.T. Program (1976). Governor's Office, State of Maine:

Professional activities: —

Publications: "A.T. The Quiet Revolution" (*Bulletin of the Atomic Scientists*); "The New Technology" (*Habitat*, January 1977); "The New Ruralism" (THE FUTURIST, August 1975); "The Crisis in Science" (*Bulletin of the Atomic Scientist*, February 1971); "Federalism and Science" (National Science Foundation, 1966).

ELMANDJRA, MAHDI   **Born:** 1933, Rabat, Morocco
President
World Future Studies Federation
B.P. 53
Rabat, Morocco   **Telephone:**   (7) 521-12

Profession: Economist

Field of specialization: Future studies, value systems, social change, international organization.

Education: B.A., Government, Cornell University, 1954; Ph.D., Economics and International Relations, London School of Economics and Political Sciences, 1957.

Professional employment: University Mohamed V, Rahat: Professor (1976-). UNESCO: Special Advisor to the Director General (1974-76); Assistant Director General for Pre-Programming and Prospective Studies (1971-74). London School of Economics: Visiting Fellow, Center of International Studies (1970). UNESCO: Assistant Director General for Social Sciences, Humanities and Culture (1966-70).

Professional activities: President, World Future Studies Federation (1977-); Pugwash Conference, Convener of group on "Disarmament and Development" (1978); Special Adviser to the International Federation of Institutes for Advanced Studies (1977); member, Steering Committee, North/South Roundtable (SID) (1977); co-author, the next report of the Club of Rome on "Learning" (1977); consultant for the preparation of the U.N. Conference on the Application of Science and Technology for Development (1979); fellow, World Academy of Art and Science; vice-president, Moroccan Japanese Association; president, Association for the Study of Moroccan-American Relations (ASMAR).

Publications: *The United Nations Systems: An Analysis* (Faber and Faber, London and Archon Books, Hamden Conn., 1973); "Alternatives for the Establishment of a New International Economic Order" *(Economas,* Rabat, 1976); *Political Facets of the North-South Dialogue* (SID, Rome 1978); *The Future Socio-Cultural Values in the Mediterranean* (National Institute of Prospective, Madrid, Spain, 1977); *Interaction between Western and Japanese Culture* (Japanese National Commission for UNESCO, Tokyo, 1968).

ELTON, MARTIN C.J.   **Born:** 1942, London, United Kingdom
Visiting Associate Professor
New York University, School of the Arts
144 Bleecker Street
New York, New York 10012, U.S.A.   **Telephone:**   (212) 598-3338

Profession: Systems scientist

Field of specialization: Telecommunications, applications research and planning; planning methodology.

Education: B.A., Mathematics, University of Cambridge, England, 1963; Ph.D., Operational Research, University of Lancaster, England, 1968.

Professional employment: New York University, School of the Arts: Visiting Associate Professor (1976-). Communications Studies and Planning, Ltd.: Director (1976-). University College, London: Senior Research Fellow (1972-76). Tavistock Institute of Human Relations (1969-72). Gallaher, Ltd., London: Consultant (1968). B.P., Ltd., London: Operational Research Analyst (1963-64).

Professional activities: Chairman, The Interactive Telecommunications Program, New York University (1978-); Research Director, Alternate Media Center, New York University (1977-); Principal Investigator of two projects sponsored by the National Science Foundation and one project sponsored by Health, Education and Welfare in the field of interactive telecommunications (1977-); varied consulting in telecommunications field (1972-); Director, symposium on interpersonal telecommunications systems sponsored by the North Atlantic Treaty Organization (1977); Visiting Associate Professor, Wharton Business School (1973-74; 1975-76).

Publications: Editor, *Evaluating New Telecommunications Services* (Plenum Publishing, 1978); editor and co-author, "Government Telecommunications Research and Policy Development" in *Refocusing Government Communications Policy* (Aspen Institute, 1977); *Tvavagskabel-TV och Telesamtraden [Two-Way Cable TV and Telecommunications]* (Bank of Sweden Tercentenary Foundation, 1978); editor and co-author, *The Effectiveness of Person-to-Person Telecommunications Systems* (Long Range Studies Divisions, British Post Office, 1975); co-author, "Microsimulation Models of Markets" *(Operational Research Quarterly,* 1971).

EMERY, FREDERICK EDMUND

Born: 1925, Narrogin, West Australia

Senior Research Fellow
Centre for Continuing Education
Australian National University
Box 4 P.O.
Canberra, Australia 2600

Telephone: 49 2892

Profession: Social Psychologist

Field of specialization: Futures methodology; design of social systems for participative democracy.

Education: B.Sc. (Honours), Psychology, University of West Australia, 1946; Ph.D., Psychology, University of Melbourne, 1953.

Professional employment: Centre for Continuing Education, Australian National University: Senior Research Fellow (1974-). Research School for Social Sciences, Australian National University: Senior Research Fellow (1969-74). Human Resources Centre, Tavistock Institute of Human Relations: Senior Social Scientist, Chairman (1958-69). Department of Psychology, University of Melbourne: Lecturer, Senior Lecturer (1948-58).

Professional activities: Study of the future of the telephone for Telecomm Australia; current work is carried out with a futures-oriented group in the Centre for Continuing Education; diagnosis of "futures we're in" — current emphasis is on future forms of governance (1967-);international consulting on democratized forms of work organization; Member of International Council for Quality of Work Life; design of matrix organization for the manufacturing sector; theory and practice of "search conferences"; has carried out futures research for a wide range of international, governmental and private corporations (the main practical strand has been with evolving adaptive socio-technical systems for the future).

Publications: *Limits to Choice* (Centre for Continuing Education, Australian National University, 1978); *The Emergence of a New Paradigm of Work* (Centre for Continuing Education, Australian National University, 1978); *Futures We're In* (Martinus Nijhoff, The Hague, 1976); co-author, *Democracy at Work* (Martinus Nijhoff, The Hague, 1976); co-author, *On Purposeful Systems* (Aldine Atherton and Tavistock Publications, 1972); editor, *Systems Thinking* (Penguin, 1969).

EMPAIN, LOUIS

Born: 1908, Bruxelles, Belgique

Editor
Art, vie, esprit
8 Bodenbroek
1000 Bruxelles, Belgique

Telephone: 02 513 36 23

Profession: Editor

Field of specialization: Education; modern art; forecasting a new way of living.

Education: Baccalaureat Sciences Langue; Baccalaureat Mathematiques; studied mathematics at Sorbonne University, Paris.

Professional employment: *Art, vie, esprit*: Editor (1970-71, 1974-). College de la Halle: Director (1945-59). Pro Juventute, Belgium: Chairman and Director (1938-72). Empain Group: Managing Director (1930-42).

Professional activities: "Animateur" of the Art, vie, esprit group (1968-); studied new modes of education (1938-); directed an art gallery (1964-73); Director, "Collection An 2000" (Editions du jour, Paris, 1972-74).

Publications: *Les saints vous parlent [The Saints Speak to You]* (Editions du Soleil Levant, Namur, 1955); *Demain le XXIe siecle [Tomorrow the Twenty-first Century]* (Editions Art vie esprit, Bruxelles, 1971); *Un module parcourt l'espace [A Module Travels Through Space]* (Paris, 1972); *Vers une nouvelle ethique [Towards a New Ethic]* (Editions du jour, Paris, 1975).

(From the first edition. Corrections not received by press time.)

ENCEL, SOLOMON
Professor of Sociology
Department of Sociology
University of New South Wales
P.O. Box 1
Kensington 2033
New South Wales, Australia

Born: 1925, Warsaw, Poland

Telephone: 662 2237

Profession: Sociologist

Field of specialization: Science, technology and society; theory and methodology of social forecasting; sex roles; class and status.

Education: B.A., 1949, M.A., 1952, Ph.D., 1960, Political Science, University of Melbourne.

Professional employment: University of New South Wales: Professor of Sociology (1966-). Australian National University: Reader in Political Science (1956-66). University of Melbourne: Lecturer in Political Science (1952-55).

Professional activities: Consultant to the Australian Telecommunications Commission (1974-76); Visiting Fellow, Science Policy Research Unit, University of Sussex (1973-); member of the Australian Science and Technology Council (1975-76). President, Sociological Association of Australia and New Zealand (1969-70).

Publications: Co-author, *Inside the Whale* (Pergamon Press, 1978); co-author, *Science, Technology and Public Policy* (Pergamon Press, 1979); contributor, *The Uses and Abuses of Forecasting* (Macmillan, 1979); co-author, *The Art of Anticipation* (Martin Robertson, 1975).

ENZER, SELWYN
Associate Director
Center for Futures Research
Graduate School of Business Administration
University of Southern California
Los Angeles, California 90007, U.S.A.

Born: 1928, Bronx, New York, U.S.A.

Telephone: (213) 741-5229

Profession: Futures researcher

Field of specialization: Futures methodology; strategic planning and technology assessment; philosophy of change.

Education: B.C.E., City College of New York, 1951; Ph.D., Business Administration, University of Southern California, 1979.

Professional employment: University of Southern California: Associate Director, Center for Futures Research (1975-). Institute for the Future: Senior Research Fellow (1969-75). McDonnell Douglas: Branch Manager (1967-69). Rockwell International: Project Manager (1962-67). Republic Aviation: Principal Structures Engineer (1955-62).

Professional activities: Project Director, INTERAX, Twenty-Year Forecast Projects concerning world trade and world food; member of the National Materials Advisory Board; engaged in development of interactive stochastic models for forecasting alternative futures; has conducted numerous research projects involving forecasting and impact assessments and methods development; has been engaged in development of many of the basic tools of futures research and has conducted seminars using these techniques in the United States and internationally.

Publications: "World Food Prospects" (THE FUTURIST, October 1978); "Cross-impact Analysis and Classical Probability" (*Futures*, June 1978); "Neither Feast Nor Famine" (Lexington Books, Lexington, Massachusetts, 1978); "Beyond Bounded Solutions" (*Education Research Quarterly*, Winter 1977); "Cross-impact Techniques in Technology Assessment" (*Futures*, March 1972); "Delphi and Cross-impact Techniques — An Effective Combination for Futures Analysis" (*Futures*, March 1971); "Some Views on Bankruptcy Reform" (*The American Bankruptcy Law Journal*, Fall 1973); co-author, "Shaping the Future" (*Chemtech*, May 1972); "Futures Research as an Aid to Government Planning in Canada" (Institute for the Future, Report R-22, August 1971).

ERICKSON, SCOTT WILLIAM

President
Future Systems
P.O. Box 14067
Minneapolis, Minnesota 55414, U.S.A.

Born: 1948, Brodhead, Wisconsin, U.S.A.

Telephone: —

Profession: Consultant, futurist

Field of specialization: Education; technology and sociocultural change.

Education: B.A., 1970, M.A., 1973, History, Ph.D., 1978, Education, University of Minnesota.

Professional employment: Future Systems: President (1977-). University of Minnesota: Instructor of Education (1973-77).

Professional activities: President (1978-80), Vice-President, Academics (1976-78), Minnesota Futurists, chapter of the World Future Society.

Publications: "Education and the Creation of the Future"(World Future Society BULLETIN, January-February 1978); "Space and the Exploring Spirits" *(Futurics, Spring 1977)*; "The High Frontier: Space Colonization and Human Values" *(Futurics, Fall 1976)*.

ESFANDIARY, F.M.

Box 61
Village Station
New York, New York 10014, U.S.A.

Born: —

Telephone: (212) 989-2827

Profession: Long-range planner; writer; designer; university lecturer

Field of specialization: Post-industrial social, economic, political, technological planning; value systems; telesphere designs; 21st century community designs; life-extension programs; cosmic scenarios; normative philosophy.

Education: Mr. Esfandiary describes himself as "teleducated."

Professional employment: New School for Social Research: Conducts seminars on long-range planning (ongoing). University of California at Los Angeles: Seminars in long-range planning (ongoing). United Nations: Seminars in long-range planning (1953-55).

Professional activities: Seminars in long-range planning in the U.S. and abroad; consulting with corporations and foreign governments; Up-Winger activities; teaching at the New School (Fall 1979) and University of California at Los Angeles (January 1979).

Publications: *Optimism One* (W.W. Norton, 1970; completely updated and revised, Fawcett/Popular Library, 1978); *Up-Wingers* (John Day Co., 1973; Fawcett/Popular Library, 1977); *Telespheres* (Fawcett/Popular Library 1977).

ESSIG, FRANCOIS BERNARD

DATAR
Avenue Charles Floquet
Paris, France 75007

Born: 1934, Paris, France

Telephone: 783 6120

Profession: —

Field of specialization: —

Education: Diploma, Institute of Political Science; Law Degree, Ecole Nationale d'Administration.

Professional employment: DATAR: Director (1975-78); Assistant Director (1969-75); Project Manager (1964-69). Conseil d'Etat: (1962-64).

Professional activities: —

Publications: —

ETZIONI, AMITAI W.   **Born:** 1929, Cologne, W. Germany
Director
Center for Policy Research
475 Riverside Drive
New York, New York 10027, U.S.A.   **Telephone:** (212) 870-2011

Profession: Sociologist

Field of specialization: Macro-sociology

Education: B.A., Sociology, Hebrew University (Jerusalem), 1954; M.A., Sociology, Hebrew University, 1956; Ph.D., Sociology, University of California (Berkeley), 1958.

Professional employment: Center for Policy Research: Director (1968-). Columbia University: Chairman, Department of Sociology (1969-71); Senior Staff Member, Bureau of Applied Social Research (1961-70); Research Associate, Institute of War and Peace Studies (part-time 1969-71); Faculty member (1958-). Social Science Research Council: Faculty Fellowship (1967-68 and 1960-61). Stanford University: Fellow, Center for Advanced Study in the Behavioral Sciences (1965-66).

Professional activities: American Association for the Advancement of Science: Fellow (1978-), Committee on Public Understanding of Science (1972-74); Guest Scholar, The Brookings Institution (1978); Consultant to President's Commission on the Causes and Prevention of Violence and the Advisory Committee on Campus Unrest and Change (Study of the American Council on Education); member, editorial board: *Journal of Peace Research* (1965-74), *Science* (1970-72), *Social Policy* (1970-); Fellow, American Sociological Association (1964-), Hudson Institute (1964-69); Founding Member, Research Advisory Group of the World Order Models Project (World Law Fund — 1969-71).

Publications: *Social Problems* (Prentice-Hall, Englewood Cliffs, New Jersey, 1976); *Genetic Fix: The Next Technological Revolution* (Macmillan, New York, 1973); *The Active Society: A Theory of Societal and Political Processes* (Free Press, New York, 1968); *Studies in Social Change* (Holt, Rinehart and Winston, New York, 1966); *Political Unification: A Comparative Study of Leaders and Forces* (Holt, Rinehart and Winston, New York, 1970); *Modern Organizations* (Prentice-Hall, Englewood Cliffs, New Jersey, 1964); *A Comparative Analysis of Complex Organizations* (Free Press, Glencoe, Illinois, 1961).

EURICH, ALVIN C.   **Born:** 1902, Bay City, Michigan, U.S.A.
President
Academy for Educational Development, Inc.
680 Fifth Avenue
New York, New York 10019, U.S.A.   **Telephone:** (212) 265-3350

Profession: Psychologist

Field of specialization: Technology assessment in education; educational planning; tests and evaluation.

Education: A.B., History, Psychology, North Central College, 1924; M.A., Education, Psychology, University of Maine, 1926; Ph.D., Psychology, University of Minnesota, 1929.

Professional employment: Academy for Educational Development, Inc.: President (1962-). Aspen Institute for Humanistic Studies: President (1964-67). Ford Foundation: Executive Director, Education Division (1958-64); Vice-President and Director, Fund for the Advancement of Education (1952-67). State University of New York: First President (1949-51). Stanford University: Professor (1938-48); Vice-President and Acting President (1944-48). Northwestern University: Professor (1937-38). University of Minnesota: all ranks from Assistant to Professor and Assistant to the President (1926-37).

Professional activities: Directing studies on future planning of individual colleges and universities in the United States and foreign countries, more effective management of educational institutions and state systems, and evaluation of the use of instructional technology in educational institutions; Trustee, Penn Mutual Life Insurance (1946-77); director, Lovelace Foundation and Clinic (1946-); lectured extensively in the United States and abroad; published seven books and over 300 articles in professional journals and general magazines; Vice-President and President, American Educational Research Association; Vice-Chairman of the Board, Educational Facilities Laboratories; member of various commissions, including the Hoover Commission, President Truman's Commission on Higher Education, President Kennedy's Task Force on Education, Surgeon General's Commission on Nursing.

Publications: *Reforming American Education* (Harper and Row, 1969); editor, *Campus 1980* (Delacort Press, 1968); editor, *High School 1980* (Pitman Publishing Company, 1970); co-author with H. A. Carroll, *Educational Psychology* (Educational Psychology, 1935); *Reading Abilities of College Students* (University of Minnesota Press, 1931); "Higher Education in the 21st Century" (*Atlantic Monthly*, June 1963).

EWALD, WILLIAM RUDOLPH
Development Consultant
1730 K Street, N,W.
Washington, D.C. 20006, U.S.A.

Born: 1923, Detroit, Michigan, U.S.A.

Telephone: (202) 659-8570

ACCESS Project
114 E. de la Guerra Street
Santa Barbara, California 93101, U.S.A.

(805) 963-0428

Profession: Policy analyst and communicator

Field of specialization: Environmental education; interactive regional telecommunication for regional policy making; policy research; perception; graphic communication.

Education: Sc. B., Civil Engineering, Brown University, 1944; post-graduate work, University of Michigan, 1947-48; Computer familiarization and programming, Cornell University and University of Michigan, 1968, 1966.

Professional employment: University of California, Santa Barbara: Professional Researcher Series VI, Community Organization and Research Institute (1974-1978); Development Consultant (1963-). Doxiadis Associates, Inc.: Senior Vice-President and Treasurer for North America (1961-63). Urban Renewal Administration: Assistant Commissioner for Technical Standards (1959-61). Arkansas Industrial Development Commission: Chief of Development (1955-59). Baltimore Association of Commerce: Assistant Manager, New Industry Location (1951-55). Detroit City Planning Commission: Planner (1949-51).

Professional activities: Principal investigator, ACCESS Project, Council on Social Graphics; Principal investigator, ACCESS project, Santa Barbara, for the National Science Foundation (1974); Public Member, Policy Board, Change in Liberal Education Project—Carnegie sponsored (1974-77); film, exhibitions, graphic designer, lecturer, author on environmental policy and long-term future; Visiting Fellow, Center for the Study of Democratic Institutions (1970); Danforth Foundation lecturer (1970-72); conception, organization and direction of American Institute of Planners' investigation into long-range policy questions facing nation over next 50 years (1966-70); member, American Institute of Planners, American Institute of Graphic Arts, Council on Social Graphics, and World Future Society.

Publications: Co-author, *Street Graphics* (book and film). (Landscape Architects Foundation, 1971); *ACCESS: Alternative Comprehensive Community Environmental Study System* (Ekistics, 1976); *Information, Perception, Regional Policy* (Government Printing Office, 1976); co-author, *Creating the Human Environment* (University of Illinois Press, 1970); *Change/Challenge/Response: A 60 Year Development of Policy for New York State* (State of New York, 1964); editor, *Environment for Man; Environment and Policy; Environment and Change—The Next Fifty Years* (University of Indiana Press, 1967-68); *The Next Fifty Years*—28 program video cassette series (Visual Information Systems/Ewald, 1970).

FABUN, DON
5932 Ocean View Drive
Oakland, California 94618, U.S.A.

Born: 1920, Moline, Illinois, U.S.A.

Telephone: (415) 652-4355

Profession: Author; editor; lecturer

Field of specialization: Translating advanced concepts in the sciences and the humanities into relatively simple, conversational English, with an emphasis on the probable future, alternative impacts of these concepts on a global society.

Education: A.B., Journalism, University of California-Berkeley, 1942.

Professional employment: Self-employed: Author, Consulting Editor, Lecturer on Future-Oriented Subjects (since July 1974). Kaiser Aluminum and Chemical Corporation, Oakland, California: Director of Publications (1952-74). McCann-Erickson, Inc.: Copy Writer (1946-52).

Professional activities: Author, consulting editor, lecturer on future-oriented subjects in science, socio-economics, communications, creativity, design of alternative future life-styles (micro- and macro-environments), practical applications of general semantics and general systems research theory in government and business. Wrote, edited, and had published, over a period of 15 years, a series of illustrated 32 to 48 page "monographs" on the impact of change on socio-economic systems and explorations of alternative futures that may result from social applications of scientific and humanistic "advances." Conducted seminars and workshops based on the "monograms."

Publications: *The Dynamics of Change* (Prentice-Hall, Inc., 1967); *Three Roads to Awareness— Motivation, Creativity, Communication* (Glencoe Press, Div. Macmillan Company, 1970); *Dimensions of Change* (Glencoe Press, Div. Macmillan Company, 1971); *Australia 2000!—A Look at Alternative Futures* (Cassell Australia Ltd., 1974).

FALK, RICHARD ANDERSON

Born: 1930, New York, New York, U.S.A.

Professor of International Law and Practice
Princeton University
Corwin Hall (110)
Princeton, New Jersey 08540, U.S.A.

Telephone: (609) 452-4864

Profession: Professor

Field of specialization: World order; the international legal order; U.S. foreign policy.

Education: B.S., Economics, University of Pennsylvania, Wharton School, 1952; Ll.B., Yale Law School, 1955; J.S.D., Harvard Law School, 1962.

Professional employment: Princeton University: Albert G. Millbank Professor of International Law and Practice (1965-); Associate Professor (1961-65). Lindisfarne Association: Fellow (1975-). College of Law, Ohio State University: Assistant, then Associate Professor (1955-61). Institute for World Order: Senior Fellow (1974-).

Professional activities: Co-Director, Project on Development and Authoritarianism, International Foundation for Alternative Development, Geneva, Switzerland; research director, North American Team, World Order Models Project, Institute for World Order (1968-); co-director, Project on the Future of the International Legal Order, Princeton University (1966-); Editorial Board, *The Nation* (1978-); Foreign Policy Editor, *Working Papers* (1977-); Editorial Board, *Foreign Policy Magazine* (1970-), *American Journal of International Law* (1961-), and *Alternatives* (1974-); Vice President, American Society of International Law (1969-71, 1974-75); chairman, Consultative Council, Lawyers' Committee on American Policy Toward Vietnam (1967-).

Publications: *A Study of Future Worlds* (Free Press, 1975); *A Global Conception of National Policy* (Harvard University Press, 1975); editor, *The Vietnam War in International Law,* Volumes I-IV (Princeton University Press, 1968-76); *This Endangered Planet* (Random House, 1971); "Contending Approaches to World Order" (*Journal of International Affairs,* January 1978); "Nuclear Policy and World Order" (World Order Models Working Paper No. 2, 1978).

FEATHER, FRANK

Born: 1943, Oxenhope, England

Controller - Domestic Regions
Canadian Imperial Bank of Commerce
Commerce Court West
Toronto, Ontario, Canada

Telephone: (416) 862-2680

Profession: Organizational planning

Field of specialization: Business environmental assessment and planning; general systems theory and left-brain/right-brain research as applied to organization structure, management techniques and creative futuristics.

Education: A.I.B., Banking and Economics, Institute of Bankers, U.K., 1968; B.A., Administrative Studies, York University, Toronto, 1976; P.Mgr., Management, Canadian Institute of Management, 1976.

Professional employment: Canadian Imperial Bank of Commerce: Superintendent—Domestic Relations (1979-); Controller—Domestic Relations (1977-79); Controller - Central Ontario (1976-77); Regional Controller (1974-76). Toronto-Dominion Bank: Assistant Manager, International Division (1970-73); Administrative Supervisor (1968-70). Barclays Bank Ltd.: Analyst (1965-68); Accountant (1959-65).

Professional activities: Conference Chairman, "Through the 80's, First Global Conference on the Future, co-sponsored by the World Future Society and the Canadian Futures Society at Toronto, Canada, July 1980; Editor, Business Tomorrow, World Future Society (1978-); President, Business Section, Special Studies Division, World Future Society (1979-); Senior Partner and Director of Research, FUTURONTO INC. (1973-); Chairman of the Toronto, Canada, Chapter of the World Future Society (1975-); charter member of the Canadian Association for Future Studies (founded 1976); member, Canadian Institute of Bankers; widely published and has lectured extensively to conferences, seminars, universities, schools, and other groups.

Publications: Editor, *Business Tomorrow* (World Future Society, Washington, D.C.); editor and publisher, *Futuronto Quarterly* (Futuronto, Inc., Oakville, Ontario); *Futuronto Handbook: Guide to the Future* (Futuronto, Inc., Oakville, Ontario, 1978).

FEINBERG, GERALD   **Born:** 1933, New York, New York, U.S.A.
Professor of Physics
Columbia University
538 W. 120th Street
New York, New York 10027, U.S.A.   **Telephone:** (212) 280-3337

Profession: Physicist

Field of specialization: Long-range goals; future materials resources; space program; energy.

Education: B.A., Physics, Columbia College, 1953; M.A., Physics, Columbia University, 1954; Ph.D., Physics, Columbia University, 1957.

Professional employment: Columbia University: Professor of Physics (1959-). Brookhaven Laboratory: Research Associate (1957-59).

Professional activities: Has written article on Future Sources of Materials for book on International Research Flow (1975); President, Prometheus Project Coordinating Agency (1972).

Publications: *The Prometheus Project* (Doubleday, 1969); "Long-Range Goals and Environmental Problems" (THE FUTURIST, 1971); "Post Modern Science" (*Journal of Philosophy*, 1969); *Consequences of Growth* (Seabury Press, 1977).

FELD, BERNARD T.   **Born:** 1919, New York, New York, U.S.A.
Professor of Physics
Massachusetts Institute of Technology (6-308)
Cambridge, Massachusetts 02139, U.S.A.   **Telephone:** (617) 253-5090

Profession: Physicist

Field of specialization: Elementary particle physics; armaments and arms control; technology transfer to developing nations; future energy technologies.

Education: B.S., Physics, City College of New York, 1939; Ph.D., Physics, Columbia University, 1945.

Professional employment: Massachusetts Institute of Technology: Professor of Physics (1954-); Instructor to Associate Professor (1946-54). Los Alamos Laboratories: Assistant Group Leader (1944-45). Metallurgical Laboratory, Chicago: Group Leader (1942-44). Columbia University: Research Associate (1941-42).

Professional activities: Research in theory of elementary particles; Head, Division of Nuclear and Elementary Particle Physics, MIT Physics Department (1975-); Secretary-General, Pugwash Conferences on Science and World Affairs (1973-76); Editor-in-Chief, *Bulletin of Atomic Scientists* (1976-); Vice President, Division of Mathematics and Physical Sciences, American Academy of Arts and Sciences (1973-75); Vice-President, Federation of American Scientists (1961-62); Director M.I.T. Laboratory for Nuclear

Sciences (1968-71); President, Council for a Livable World (1962-75); Associate Editor, *Annals of Physics* (1955-).

Publications: *Models of Elementary Particles* (Blaisdell-Ginn-Xerox, 1969); editor, *Impact of New Technologies on the Arms Race* (M.I.T. Press, 1970); editor, *Future of the Sea-Based Deterrent* (M.I.T. Press, 1973); *Experimental Nuclear Physics, Volume II—The Neutron* (Wiley and Sons, 1953); editor, *Collected Works of Leo Szilard—Scientific Works* (M.I.T. Press, 1972).

FERKISS, VICTOR CHRISTOPHER

Born: 1925, New York, New York, U.S.A.

Professor of Government
Georgetown University
Washington, D.C. 20057, U.S.A.

Telephone: (202) 625-4941

Profession: Political scientist

Field of specialization: Future politics; values and society; technology and society.

Education: A.B., Political Science, University of California-Berkeley, 1948; A.M., Political Science, University of California-Berkeley, 1949; M.A., Political Science, Yale University, 1950; Ph.D., Political Science, The University of Chicago, 1954.

Professional employment: Georgetown University: Professor of Government (1962-). St. Mary's College of California: Associate Professor of Political Science (1960-62); Assistant Professor of Political Science (1955-59). Boston University: Field Program Director, Personnel Training for Africa (1959-60). University of Montana: Assistant Professor of Political Science (1954-55).

Professional activities: Teaches courses in Political and Social Futures, Science, Technology, and International relations (1969-); Consultant to Forecasting International (1975-); research project on American images of future and their political implications (1976-); Program Chairman, Second General Assembly, World Future Society (1975); Eli Lilly Visiting Professor of Science, Theology and Human Values, Purdue University (Spring 1976); Fulbright Professor of Political Science, University of the West Indies-Trinidad (1968-69). Frequent lecturer on futures and technology and society to university groups, symposia, and mass media.

Publications: *Futurology: Promise, Performance, Prospects* (Sage Publications, 1977); *The Future of Technological Civilization* (George Braziller, 1974); *Technological Man* (George Braziller, 1969); *Africa's Search for Identity* (George Braziller, 1966); co-author "Creating Chosen Futures" (*Freedom: Then, Now, Tommorrow*, Pennsylvania State, 1977); "The Future of American Politics" (*Liberal Education*, May 1976).

FISHER, JOSEPH LYMAN

Born: 1914, Pawtucket, Rhode Island, U.S.A.

Member of Congress
U.S. House of Representatives
318 Cannon House Office Building
Washington, D.C. 20515, U.S.A.

Telephone: (202) 225-5136

Profession: Economist; member of Congress

Field of specialization: Economic problems of resource development and environmental quality.

Education: B.S., Bowdoin College; M.A., Education, George Washington University; Ph.D., Economics, Harvard University, 1947.

Professional employment: U.S. House of Representatives: Member of Congress (1975-). Resources for the Future, Inc.: President (1953-74). Council of Economic Advisors: Executive officer; senior economist (1947-53). U.S. Department of State: Economist (1942-43). National Resources Planning Board: Planner (1939-42).

Professional activities: Member, Board of Directors, American Forestry Association; member, Advisory Council, Electric Power Research Institute; member, American Economic Association; member, American Society for Public Administration; member, American Association for the Advancement of Science; has written, lectured, and consulted widely on economic problems of resource development and environmental quality.

Publications: Co-author, *Resources In America's Future* (Johns Hopkins, 1965); co-author, *World Prospects for Natural Resources* (Johns Hopkins, 1966); has written numerous professional articles.

FLECHTHEIM, OSSIP K.
Director
Institut fur Zukunftsforschung
*[*Institute for Futures Research*]*
Giesebrechtstrasse 15
D-1000 Berlin 12, Federal Republic of Germany

Born: 1909, Nikolaiev, Russia

Telephone: (030) 883 88 71

Profession: Political Scientist

Field of specialization: Futurology, especially the philosophy of the future, societal models of the future, and utopias.

Education: Doctor of Law, University of Cologne, 1934; Diploma, Graduate Institute of International Studies, 1940; Dr. of Philosophy, University of Heidelberg, 1947. Studied law and political science at the Universities of Freiburg, Paris, Heidelberg, Berlin and Cologne.

Professional employment: Institut fur Zukunftsforschung: Director (1976-). Free University of Berlin: Professor of Political Science (1959-74); Guest Professor (1951-52). Deutsche Hochschule fur Politik, Berlin: Professor (1952-54, 1955-9). Kansas City University: Guest Professor (1954-55). Colby College: Assistant Professor and Associate Professor (1947-51). Bates College: Instructor, Assistant Professor (1943-46). Atlanta University: Instructor (1940-43). U.S. Office of Chief of Counsel for War Crimes: Section and Research Chief (1946-47). Columbia University, Institute of Social Research: Research Associate (1939-40).

Professional activities: Advises the Institut fur Zukunftsforschung (1971-); co-editor, *Analysen und Prognosen* (1972-); editor, *Futurum* (1968-71); member, Scientific Council of the World Future Studies Federation (1976-). Coined the term "futurology" in 1943 in the U.S.

Publications: *Futurologie: Der Kampf um die Zukunft [Futurology: The Struggle Over the Future]* (Verlag Wissenschaft und Politik, Cologne, Germany, 1970, Second Edition, 1971); *History and Futurology* (Verlag Anton Hain, Meisenheim am Glan, Germany, 1966); co-author and editor, *Fundamentals of Political Science* (New York, 1952); *Zeitgeschichte und Zukunftspolitik [Contemporary History and Future Politics]* (Hoffman and Campe, Hamburg, Germany, 1974); *Ausblick in die Gegenwart [Prospects in the Present]* (1974). *Von Marse bis Kolakovski—Sozialismus oder Untergang in der Barbarei [From Marx to Kolakovski—Socialism or Descent into Barbarism]* (European Publishing Institute, Cologne (1958).

FONDERSMITH, JOHN
Chief, Special Projects Section
District of Columbia Municipal Planning Office
1329 E Street, N.W.
Washington, D.C. 20004, U.S.A.

Born: 1937, Washington, D.C., U.S.A.

Telephone: (202) 629-4861

Profession: Urban planner

Field of specialization: Urban planning; civic education.

Education: B.A., Government and Politics, University of Maryland, 1961; M.S., City Planning, University of Illinois, 1963.

Professional employment: District of Columbia Municipal Planning Office: Chief, Special Projects Section (1975-). D.C. Office of Planning and Management: Director, Transit Development Team (1970-74). Marcou, O'Leary and Associates: Associate (1965-70). Peace Corps: Volunteer, Peru (1963-65).

Professional activities: Currently helping to develop a Year 2000 Plan for Central Washington, including downtown; planning for Washington Civic Center; developing catalog of guidebooks to the built environment; publishing a newsletter on guidebooks; President, Washington, D.C., Chapter, World Future Society (1972).

Publications: "Architectural Guidebooks: Proliferating and Maturing" (AIA Journal, December 1976).

FONTELA, EMILIO

Born: 1938, Cauderan, Spain

Director
Department of Econometrics
University of Geneva
1211 Geneva 4, Switzerland

Telephone: —

Profession: Economist

Field of specialization: Futures methodology; structural modeling; econometrics.

Education: B.A., Economics, University of Geneva, 1959; Ph.D., Economics, University of Geneva, 1962.

Professional employment: University of Geneva: Director, Department of Econometrics (1978-); Professor (1974-). Battelle-Geneva: Director of the Applied Economics Department (1967-74); Economist (1961-67).

Professional activities: President of the European Association of Applied Economics (1978-); member of the Board of the Societe Suisse d'Economie Politique et de Statistique (1971-77); editorial board of the *European Economic Review;* Schweizerische Vereinigung fur Zukunsftsforschung (1976-); private consultant; editorial board of *Futures* and *Futuribles;* Visiting Professor, Case Institute of Technology, Cleveland (1966); Visiting Professor, Institute of Business Administration and Management, Tokyo (1970).

Publications: Co-author, "The Causal Structure of Economic Models" *(Futures,* December 1977); "L'enquete DEMATEL" [The DEMATEL Inquiry] *(Futuribles,* April 1978); co-author, "Forecasting Socio-Economic Change" *(Science Journal,* London, September 1965); co-author, "Forecasting Technical Coefficients and Changes in Relative Prices" *(Applications of Input-Output,* North Holland Publication, Amsterdam, 1969); co-author, "Future Prices in Long-Term Forecasting" *(Futures,* London, September 1968); co-author, "Current Perceptions of the World Problematique" *(World Modeling,* North-Holland, Amsterdam, 1976).

FORRESTER, JAY WRIGHT

Born: 1918, Climax, Custer, Nebraska, U.S.A.

Professor of Management
Sloan School of Management (Room E52-454)
Massachusetts Institute of Technology
50 Memorial Drive
Cambridge, Massachusetts 02139, U.S.A.

Telephone: (617) 253-1571

Profession: Professor of Management

Field of specialization: Systems dynamics as a methodology for understanding the behavior of social systems.

Education: B.S., Electrical Engineering, The University of Nebraska, 1939; S.M., Electrical Engineering, Massachusetts Institute of Technology, 1945.

Professional employment: Massachusetts Institute of Technology: Professor of Management (1956-); Research Staff (1939-56).

Professional activities: Development of a system dynamics model of social and economic change in the United States; developing field of system dynamics (1956-); directing development of SAGE Air Defense System (1951-56); Director of MIT Digital Computer Laboratory (1946-51); research in servomechanisms (1940-46).

Publications: *Industrial Dynamics* (M.I.T. Press, 1961); *World Dynamics,* Second Edition (M.I.T. Press, 1973); *Principles of Systems* (M.I.T. Press, 1968); *Urban Dynamics* (M.I.T. Press, 1969); *Collected Papers of Jay W. Forrester* (M.I.T. Press, 1975).

FOURASTIE, JEAN JOSEPH

Born: 1907, St. Benin d'Azy, France

Professor
Conservatoire Nationale des Arts et Metiers
rue Saint Martin No. 292
75161 Paris, Cedex 03, France

Telephone: TUR 37 38

Profession: Professor

Field of specialization: Economics

Education: Institut d'Etudes Politiques; Ingenieur, Ecole Centrale des Arts et Manufactures; Docteur, Faculte de Droit de Paris.

Professional employment: Conservatoire National des Arts et Metiers: Professor (1960-). Ecole Pratique des Hautes Etudes: Director of Studies (1950-). Ministere des Finances: Commissaire Controleur General (1935-50).

Professional activities: President, Manpower Commission of the Commissariat au Plan (1950-70).

Publications: *Le grand espoir du XX siecle [The Great Hope of the Twentieth Century]* (Gallimard, 1950); *La Productivite [Productivity]* (Presses Universitaires de France, 1955); *Les 40,000 heures [The 40,000 Hours]* (1960); *Idees majeures [Principal Ideas]* (Gonthier, 1965); *Lettre ouverte a quatre milliard d'hommes [Open Letter to Four Billion People]* (Albin Michel, 1970); *Le long chemin des hommes [The Long Road of Men]* (Robert Laffont, 1976); *La realite economique: Vers la revision des Idees dominantes en France [Economic Reality: Towards the Revision of Dominant Ideas in France]* (Robert Laffont, 1978).

FOWLES, JIB
Professor
Studies of the Future
University of Houston at Clear Lake City
2700 Bay Area Boulevard
Houston, Texas 77058, U.S.A.

Born: 1940, Hartford, Connecticut, U.S.A.

Telephone: (713) 488-9250

Profession: Professor, Studies of the Future

Field of specialization: Sociocultural change

Education: B.A., History and Literature, Wesleyan University, 1963; M.A., Linguistics, Columbia University, 1967; Ph.D., Mass Communications and Futures Research, New York University, 1974.

Professional employment: University of Houston at Clear Lake City: Professor, Studies of the Future (1978-); Chairman, Studies of the Future (1974-78). New York University: Instructor (1967-72).

Professional activities: Writes, consults, and lectures on the future of industrialization, multinational corporations, and the mass media.

Publications: Editor, *The Handbook of Futures Research* (Greenwood Press, 1978); *Mass Advertising as Social Forecast* (Greenwood Press, 1976); "Hands Off the Future" (World Future Society BULLETIN); co-author, "The Methodological Worth of the Delphi Forecasting Technique" (*Technological Forecasting and Social Change,* 1975); "On Chronocentrism" (*Futures,* 1974).

FRANCIS, JOHN MICHAEL
Principal, Scottish Office
Scottish Development Department
New St. Andrew's House
Edinburgh, Scotland EH2 4YN

Born: 1939, London, United Kingdom

Telephone: (031) 556-8400

Profession: Central government administration

Field of specialization: Transport policy; urban planning and rehabilitation of the inner city; housing; energy conservation.

Education: B.Sc., ARCS, Physical Chemistry, 1960, Ph.D., Nuclear Technology, 1963, Imperial College of Science and Technology, University of London.

Professional employment: Scottish Office, U.K. Department of State: Principal (1976-). Heriot Watt University: Senior Research Fellow in Energy Studies (1974-76). Church of Scotland Home Board: Director, Society, Religion and Technology Project (1970-74). Central Electricity Generating Board: Group Leader, Fuel Element Compatability Studies (1963-70).

Professional activities: Member, Oil Development Council for Scotland (1973-); Member, Scottish Advisory Committee of the Nature Conservancy Council (1974-); Adviser on Science and Technology, World Council of Churches, Geneva, Switzerland (1975-); Program Presenter, BBC and Scottish Television (1971-75); Investment Consultant, World Energy Market (1971-74); numerous papers in scientific journals and periodicals ranging from *Nature, The Proceedings of the Royal Society of London*, to *Futures* and *Environment and Change.*

Publications: Co-author, *The Future as an Academic Discipline* (Elsevier, 1975); co-author, *The Future of Scotland* (Croom Helm, 1977); co-author, *Hidden Factors in Technological Change* (Pergamon Press, 1976); editor, *Faith, Science and the Future* (World Council of Churches, 1977); co-author, *Scotland in Turmoil* (St. Andrew Press, 1973).

FRANCOEUR, ROBERT THOMAS

Chairperson of Biological and Allied Health Sciences
Fairleigh Dickinson University
285 Madison Avenue
Madison, New Jersey 07940, U.S.A.

Born: 1931 Detroit, Michigan, U.S.A.

Telephone: (201) 377-4700 Ext. 282

Profession: Embryologist; sexologist; ethicist

Field of specialization: Technology assessment, especially in the areas of human reproduction and genetic engineering; medical advances with a focus on (1) the impact of these technologies on sexual relations, images, life styles, and (2) the impact of these technologies on the general range of human values.

Education: B.A., Philosophy, Sacred Heart College, Detroit, 1953; M.A., Theology, St. Vicent College, Latrobe, Pennsylvania, 1957; M.S., Biology, University of Detroit, 1961; Ph.D., Embryology and Biology, University of Delaware, 1967.

Professional employment: Fairleigh Dickinson University: Chairperson of Biological and Allied Health Sciences (current position); Professor of Biological Sciences (1965-). Roman Catholic Diocese of Steubenville, Ohio: Assistant Pastor, Parish Administrator, and High School Instructor (1958-63).

Professional activities: Currently teaching courses in embryology, bioethics, medical genetics, human sexuality, and a variety of interdisciplinary courses in futuristics (1965-); member and consultant for "A comprehensive study of the ethical, social and legal implications of advances in biomedical and behavior research and technology," (The Center for Technology Assessment and Policy Research, Inc., 1975-76); founded the American Teilhard de Chardin Association in 1965; Delphi expert for a study of human relations and psychogenic drug usage in 1985 (The Futures Group and Monsanto); has contributed to over 30 books on such diverse subjects as Teilhard de Chardin, reproductive technologies, human evolution, futuristics, alternative life styles, women in the year 2000, and the future of human sexuality.

Publications: *An Operational Decision Workbook for Biomedical Ethics* (Harper and Row, 1979); co-author, *Hot and Cool Sex: Cultures in Conflict* (Harcourt Brace Jovanovich, 1974); editor, *The Future of Sexual Relations* (Prentice Hall, 1974); *Eve's New Rib: 20 Faces of Sex, Marriage and Family* (Harcourt Brace Jovanovich, 1972); *Utopian Motherhood: New Trends in Human Reproduction* (Doubleday, 1970); *Evolving World, Converging Man* (Holt Rinehart and Winston, 1970).

FRANCOIS, CHARLES OSCAR
Commercial Attache
Belgian Embassy in Argentina
Defensa 113, 8o p.
1065 Buenos Aires, Argentina

Born: 1922, Belgium

Telephone: 33.0066

Profession: Economist

Field of specialization: Cybernetics, general theory of systems, futures, methodology.

Education: Free University of Brussels (no degree because of war circumstances).

Professional employment: Belgian Embassy: Commercial attache (1966-). Personal business: Argentina (1963-66), Belgium (1961-62), Zaire (1945-60).

Professional activities: Scientific co-ordinator of the Grupo de Estudio de Sistemas Integrados (GESI). [Study Group for Integrated Systems]. The Group is a section of the of the Instituto de Cibernetica from the Sociedad Cientifica Argentina. It gives courses, organizes symposia, publishes reports and offers services to its members.

Publications: *Phenomenologie, Cybernetique et Prospective* (in French, International Association of Cybernetics, 1975); *Introduccion a la Prospectiva* (in Spanish, Pleamar, Buenos Aires, 1978); *Elements du Probleme Africain* (in French, *La Presse Africaine*, 1958); "Cybernetics and Systems" (8th International Congress of Cybernetics, 1976); "La dinamica de Sistemas de Forrester en el marco de la teoria genral de sistemas" (in Spanish, *Boletin de la Sociedad Argentina de Investigacion Operativa* nr. 34, 1977).

FRANKS, BETTY BARCLAY
Department Chairperson
Maple Heights High School
5500 Clement Drive
Maple Heights, Ohio 44137, U.S.A.

Born: 1941, Prescott, Arizona, U.S.A.

Telephone: (216) 587-3200

Profession: Social Studies teacher; consultant; futuristics education

Field of specialization: Futuristics curriculum development; simulation and gaming; workshops for futuristic educators.

Education: B.A., History, Arizona State University, 1963; University of Texas, John Carroll University, Institut Catholique, Paris, 1978-79.

Professional employment: Maple Heights High School: Social Studies Department Chairperson (1970-). Austin, Texas Public School System: Social Studies Teacher (1964-69). Glendale, Arizona Public School System: Social Studies Teacher (1963-64).

Professional activities: Chairperson of the Special Interest Group in Future Studies of the National Council for the Social Studies (1977-78); currently writing a text for secondary school students with co-author Dr. Mary Kay Howard of John Carroll University; presenting workshops on alternative educational futures which involves a new simulation entitled "Educational Horizons: Learning in the Future"; co-director, Three-Phase Futuristics Curriculum Development Project for the Greater Cleveland Area (1972-73); consultant, Science Museum of Minnesota Futures Workshops (1974-76, 1978), Frances Payne Bolton School of Nursing, Case Western Reserve University (1973); participant in several programs on futuristics education.

Publications: "Future Decisions: The IQ Game" (Simulation and Gaming Association, 1975); co-author, *The Biological Revolution: Examining Human Values Through the Futures Perspective* (National Education Association, 1976); co-author, *Looking Forward: A Mini-Course in Future Studies* (McGraw Hill Film Division, 1975); "Futuristics Education" in *The Creative Social Science Teacher*, Paul Tedesco, editor (Bantam Books, 1974); editor, "Futures Section" in *The Guide to Simulation/Games for Education and Training*, Robert Horn, editor, (Didactic Systems, Inc., 1977).

FREEMAN, CHRISTOPHER
Director
Science Policy Research Unit
University of Sussex
Falmer, Brighton, Sussex
BN1 9RF, United Kingdom

Born: 1921, Yorkshire, United Kingdom

Telephone: (0273) 686758

Profession: Economist

Field of specialization: Policy for research and development; industrial innovation studies.

Education: B.Sc. (Economics), Government, London School of Economics, 1948.

Professional employment: University of Sussex: Science Policy Research Unit, Director and R. M. Phillips Professor of Science Policy (1966-). National Institute of Economic and Social Research, London: Senior Research Officer (previously Research Officer, 1959-66); before 1959, mainly in teaching and research, including market research.

Professional activities: Consultant to various international agencies, including OECD and UNESCO (intermittent since 1966); co-editor of quarterly journal *Research Policy*, published by North-Holland (since 1971-).

Publications: *The Economics of Industrial Innovation* (Penguin, 1974); co-author, "The Goals of R and D in the 1970s" (*Science Studies*, Volume 1, Number 3, October, 1971); "Chemical Process Plant: Innovation and the World Market" (*National Institute Economic Review*, Number 45, August, 1968); co-author, *Thinking About the Future: A Critique of the Limits to Growth* (Chatto and Windus, Sussex University Press, 1973); co-author, *Success and Failure in Industrial Innovation* (Centre for the Study of Industrial Innovation, 1972).

FREEMAN, ORVILLE LOTHROP
President
Business International Corporation
1 Dag Hammarskjold Plaza
New York, New York 10017, U.S.A.

Born: 1918, Minneapolis, Minnesota, U.S.A.

Telephone: (212) 759-7700

Profession: Attorney; politican; businessman

Field of specialization: Global food and agricultural development and potential; global economic interdependence, i.e., multinational companies as the instruments for foreign investment, moving the world to a unified global economy.

Education: B.A., magna cum laude, Phi Beta Kappa, 1940, LLB, Law, 1946, University of Minnesota; honorary doctorates from Fairleigh Dickinson University, St. Josephs College, and University of Seoul.

Professional employment: Business International Corporation: President (1970-); Chief Executive Officer (1971-). EDP Technology International, Inc.: President (1969-70). U.S. Government: U.S. Secretary of Agriculture (1961-69). State of Minnesota: Governor (1955-61).

Professional activities: Member, Board of Directors, United Nations Association of the U.S.A.; Chairman, U.S.-India Businessmen's Advisory Council; member, Board of Directors, Committee for the Future, Natomas Corporation, Franklin Mint, FARMCO, Rural American Marketing, Multinational Agribusiness Systems, Inc., Worldwatch Institute, and the World Future Society; member, Executive Committee, International Executive Service Corp., Japan-U.S. Businessmen's Advisory Council.

Publications: *World Without Hunger* (Praeger, 1968); "America, A National Among Nations—Bicentennial Reflections" (Lutheran Brotherhood *Bond*, March 1976); "Interdependence: The Bottom Line—Global Crisis Spells Opportunity" (*Montana Business Quarterly*, Spring 1975); *Analyzing Corporate Impact: Some Innovative Approaches* (International Management and Development Institute, 1976); "Plough Without Prejudice" (*United Nations Development Forum*, August-September 1977).

FRIEDMAN, YONA

Born: 1923, Budapest, Hungary

42 Boulevard Pasteur
75015 Paris, France

Telephone: (1) 320-9923 (1) 566-0484

Profession: Architect; sociologist

Field of specialization: Communication; science popularization; user-design; self-planning.

Education: Technion, Haifa, Israel, 1949; Great Award, Academy of Berlin, 1972; Honorary Fellow, Royal Academy, The Hague, 1977.

Professional employment: Architect

Professional activities: Expert, U.N. Conference on Habitat, Vancouver (1976); leading seminars for United Nations Educational, Scientific, and Cultural Organization (UNESCO) on "no-cost housing," Cairo (1977), La Paz (1978); expert for U.N. University and Organization for Economic Cooperation and Development; organizing "self-planning in schools" for Ministry of Education, Paris (1978); member, Executive Committee, World Future Studies Federation; expert on housing problems, Algeria; scientific advisor, Massachusetts Institute of Technology (1973-).

Publications: *"No-cost" Housing* (UNESCO, Paris, 1977); *Habitat is Everyone's Concern, Particularly Yours* (UNESCO, Paris, 1977); *Utopies realisables [Realizable Utopias]*(Paris, 1975); *Towards a Scientific Architecture* (The MIT Press, 1975); French original, 1970); *Comment vivre entres les autres sans etre chef et sans etre esclave? [How to Live Among Others Without Being a Boss or a Slave?]* (J.J. Pauvert, Paris, 1974).

FRITSCH, BRUNO

Born: 1926, Prague, Czechoslovakia

Director
Center for Economic Research
Swiss Federal Institute of Technology
Weinbergstrasse 35
Zurich, Switzerland

Telephone: (01) 326211

Profession: Economist

Field of specialization: Global modelling; interaction between economic and ecological systems; technology assessment; futures methodology.

Education: Philosophy, University of Prague; Dr. Economics, University of Basel.

Professional employment: Center for Economic Research, Swiss Federal Institute of Technology: Director (current position); Full Professor (1965-). University of Heidelberg: Full Professor (1963-65). University of Karlsruhe: Full Professor (1960-63).

Professional activities: Head of an interdisciplinary post-graduate course on developing countries (1970-); President, Swiss Association for Future Research; Research Fellow at the Rasler Center for Economic and Financial Research (1953-58); Visiting Professor, Harvard Summer School (1963-); Visiting Professor, Australian National University (1971); has written numerous articles for professional journals.

Publications: *Die Seld Kredittheorie von Karl Marx [The Money and Credit Theory of Karl Marx]* (Poly. Verlag, Zurich, 1955); *Die Amerikanische Stabilisierungspolitik [American Stabilization Policy]* (Polygraphischer Verlag, Zurich, 1958); *Die Vierle Welt [The Fourth World]* (Deutsche Verlagsanstalt, Stuttgart, 1973); editor, *Entencklungslander [Developing Countries]* (Kiepenliener, Koln, 1968); *Growth Limitation and Political Power* (Ballinger, Cambridge, Massachusetts, 1976).

FUCHS, GEORG   **Born:** 1908, Vienna, Austria
President
International Institute for Peace
Mollwaldplatz 5
A-1040 Vienna, Austria   **Telephone:** (0222) 65 64 37

Profession: Radiologist and radiation physicist

Field of specialization: Social problems of radiobiology and nuclear energy.

Education: Dr. Med., 1933, Dr. Phil., 1947, University of Vienna; Dr. H.C., University of Rostock, 1973.

Professional employment: International Institute for Peace: President (1972-). Kaiser Franz Joseph Hospital, Vienna: Chief Radiology (1946-74).

Professional activities: Peace research, particularly sociological aspects of radiation.

Publications: *Die Strahlengefahrdung des Menschen in der Gegenwartigen Zivilisation [The Dangers of Radiation in Contemporary Civilization]* (Publishing House Akademie Verlag, Berlin, 1971); editor, *Kernenergie und Weltfrieden [Nuclear Energy and World Peace]* (Publishing House Gazetta, Vienna, 1976).

FULLER, R. BUCKMINSTER   **Born:** 1895, Milton, Massachusetts, U.S.A.
3500 Market
Philadelphia, Pennsylvania 19104, U.S.A.   **Telephone:** (215) 387-5400

Profession: Comprehensive anticipatory design science.

Field of specialization: Global planning; architecture; general systems; geometry/structure; cartography; value systems; shelter; urban planning.

Education: Harvard University, 1913-15; U.S. Naval Academy (Spec.) 1917; 40 Honorary Doctorates, 1954-78.

Professional employment: Southern Illinois University: University Professor Emeritus (1968-); Research Professor, Director of World Resources Inventory (1959-68). University of Pennsylvania: University Professor Emeritus (1975-). Haverford, Bryn Mawr, Swarthmore Colleges and University Science Center: World Fellow in Residence (1972-78).

Professional activities: Consultant, Architects Team 3, Penang, Malaysia, Penang Urban Center (1974-); Advisory Council on International Programs, Bryn Mawr (1975-); International President, World Society for Ekistics (1975); consultant, Earth Metabolic Design and Design Science Institute (1973); tutor in Design Science, International College, Los Angeles, California (1974); President, Synergetics, Inc. (1954-59); President, Geodesics, Inc. (1949-); Chairman, Board of Trustees, Fuller Research Foundation (1946-54); Chairman of the Board, Chief Engineer, Dymaxion Dwelling Machine Corporation (1944-46); Chief Mechanical Engineer, U.S. Board of Economic Warfare, W. W. II (1942-44); Technical Consultant, *Fortune Magazine* (1938-40); Assistant to Director, R and D, Phelps Dodge Corporation (1936-38); Director and Chief Engineer, Dymaxion Corporation (1932-36); Editor and Publisher, *Shelter Magazine* (1930-32); President, 4D Company, Chicago (1927-32); President, Stockade Building System, Chicago (1922-27).

Publications: *Synergetics: Explorations into the Geometry of Thinking* (MacMillan, 1975); *Operating Manual for Spaceship Earth* (Scribners, 1970); *Education Automation* (Doubleday, 1971); co-author, *Dymaxion World of Buckminster Fuller* (Doubleday, 1965); *Nine Chains to the Moon* (Doubleday, 1936).

GABEL, MEDARD A.   **Born:** 1946, Evanston, Illinois, U.S.A.
Director
Earth Metabolic Design
Box 2016, Yale Station
New Haven, Connecticut 06510, U.S.A.   **Telephone:** (203) 776-4921

Profession: Design scientist

Field of specialization: Global studies; global energy development; global food development; futures methodology; design science; regional planning; local planning.

Education: B.A., Design Science, Southern Illinois University, 1971; Ph.D., Design Science, International College, 1977.

Professional employment: Earth Metabolic Design, Inc.: Director (1972-). R. Buckminster Fuller: Research Associate, Archivist (1973-); Research Associate (1969-71). Southern Illinois University, Department of Design: Director, Design Science Laboratory (1971-72); Designer, Health Care Curriculum Development Project (1971-72).

Professional activities: Global energy development research project (1973-); global food development research project (1975-); World Game Workshop—course (1970-).

Publications: *Energy, Earth and Everyone* (Straight Arrow Books/Simon and Schuster, 1975); co-author, *Design Science Primer* (Earth Metabolic Design/Department of Health, Education and Welfare, Department of Environmental Education, 1976); co-author, *Introduction to the Design Science Information System* (Earth Metabolic Design, 1973); *Ho-Ping: Food for Everyone* (Earth Metabolic Design, 1976).

(From the first edition. Corrections not received by press time.)

GABUS, ANDRE M.W.   **Born:** 1931, Geneva, Switzerland
Senior Economist
Economic Analysis and Forecasting Research Group
Battelle, Geneva Research Center
7, route de Drize
Carouge - Geneva 1227, Switzerland   **Telephone:**   (022) 43 98 31

Profession: Economist; socio-economist

Field of specialization: Planning research and futures methodology (systematic use of human judgment on societal development).

Education: Licence (M.A.), Business Economics, University of Geneva, 1954.

Professional employment: Battelle, Geneva Research Center: Senior Economist, Economic Analysis and Forecasting (1977-); Head, Economic Planning Research Group (1974-77); Associate Chief, Division for Industrial and Economic Studies (1971-73); Head, Socio-Economics Research and Economic Group (1967-71). Batelle, Mission in Morocco: Head (1975-77); Program Director (1975-77).

Professional activities: Currently working on scenarios and regional studies; Principal Investigator, Associate Program Director, and Director of the **DEMATEL** (Decision-Making Trial and Evaluation Laboratory) Project, including a systematic approach to the so-called "world problematique" (1971-74); Associate Head, SIM-SPAIN Project, linking cross-impact evaluation and a dynamic econometric model (1970-73); Head ACT-EXLOR Program—a permanent research tool to the service of economic planning, including an input-output model for the major western countries (1966-70).

Publications: Co-author, "L'enquete DEMATEL" ["The DEMATEL Investigations"] (*Futuribles*, Paris, March-April 1978); co-author, "Events and Economic Forecasting Modelling" (*Futures*, August 1974); co-author, "Current Perception of the World Problematique" in *World Modelling: A Dialogue*, eds., C. West Churchman and R.O. Mason (North-Holland, 1976); "Problematique de la securite" ["The Security Puzzle"] (*Le Monde Diplomatique*, Paris, April 1974).

GAPPERT, GARY M.   **Born:** 1939 Chicago, Illinois U.S.A.
Director of Urban Development
Research for Better Schools, Inc.
1700 Market Street
Philadelphia, Pennsylvania 19103, U.S.A.   **Telephone:**   (215) 562-4100

Profession: Social economist; urbanist

Field of specialization: Urban systems; social-economic policy; education; management training.

Education: B.A., Chemistry, Colorado College, 1961; Grad. Diploma, Education, Makerere College, Uganda, 1962; Ph.D., Economics, Syracuse University, 1972.

Professional employment: New Jersey State Department of Education: Assistant Commissioner, Research, Planning, and Evaluation (1975-). University of Wisconsin: Assistant Professor, Urban Affairs (1970-75). Research Economist, Tanzania (1967-68).

Professional activities: Main research interests have been concerned with the development of planning and management systems, and human resource development in urban communities; professional affiliations include membership in the American Society of Planning Officials, American Institute of Planners, American Economic Association, and the International Society of Technology Assessment.

Publications: Editor, *The Social Economy of Cities, 99th Urban Affairs Annual* (Sage Publications, 1975); *The Future of Work in Post-Affluent America* (Manpower, Inc., 1974); "Post-Affluence: The Turbulent Transition" *(The Futurist,* Vol. 8 No. 5, 1974); "Assessment and Acceptability of Urban Futures" *(Futures,* Vol. 6, No.1, February 1974); *Post-Affluent America: The Social Economy of the Future* (Franklin Watts, 1979).

GARAUDY, ROGER
Director
Institut international pour le dialogue des civilisations
[International Institute for Conferences on Civilizations]
14 Rue Calvin
Geneva, Switzerland

Born: 1913, Marseille, France

Telephone: (022) 28 60 82

Profession: Writer

Field of specialization: Dialogue of civilizations; alternative futures; value systems; futures methodology.

Education: Masters in Philosophy, Doctor of Letters, University of Paris, Sorbonne; Doctor in Philosophical Sciences, Academy of Sciences, Moscow.

Professional employment: Institut international pour le dialogue des civilisations: Director (present position).

Professional activities: Current work on dialogue of civilizations for United Nations Educational, Scientific and Cultural Organization; French Deputy and Senator (1946-60); University Professor (until 1972); Director, Marxist Study and Research Center (1960-70).

Publications: *Perspectives de l'homme [Human Perspectives]* (Presses Universitaires de France, 1961); *Marxisme du XX Siecle [Twentieth Century Marxism]* (1968); *L'alternative [The Alternative]* (Robert Laffont, 1973); *Parole d'homme [Word of Honor]* (Robert Laffont, 1975); *Le Projet esperance [Project Hope]* (Robert Laffont, 1976).

(From the first edition. Corrections not received by press time.)

GERARDIN, LUCIEN A.
Research Director
Thomson—CSF
Corporate Management
49 bis, avenue Hoche
75008 Paris, France

Born: 1923, Nancy, France

Telephone: (1) 561 96 00

Profession: Research Director

Field of specialization: Exploratory planning

Education: Master, Mathematics, University of Toulouse; Engineer, Electronics, Superior School of Electricity, Paris.

Professional employment: Thomson—CSF: Research Director (current); from 1946 with the Corporation.

Professional activities: In charge of exploratory planning for Thomson Corporation; currently preparing a textbook for IIASA and John Wiley on structural modeling.

Publications: *Le Biofeedback au service de la maitrise et de la connaissance de soi [Biofeedback for Better Self-Control and Improved Self-Awareness]* (RETZ/CEPL, Paris, 1978); *Les Futurs Possible [Possible Futures]* (Hachette, Paris, 1971); *Bionics* (McGraw Hill, 1968); co-author, *Les Futures de l'Audio-Visuel: l'Audio-Viseul [Audio-Visual Futures]* (CEPL et Hachette, Paris, 1974); co-author, *Planifier l'Entreprise: Prevision et Prospective [Business Planning: Forecasting and Future Studies]* (Marabout - collection Monde Moderne, Bruxelles, 1974). Has written three books on Alchemy, Magic, Numbers, and numerous professional papers.

GERBA, JOHN
Office of the Administrator
U.S. Environmental Protection Agency (EPA)
401 M Street, S.W.
Washington, D.C. 20460, U.S.A.

Born: 1931 U.S.A.

Telephone: (202) 755-2933

Profession: Planning policy analyst; architect; viticulturalist

Field of specialization: National and regional growth and development issues; environmental policy assessment; planning issues identification.

Education: B. Architecture, Western Reserve University, 1955; M.C.P., Regional Planning, Yale University, 1961.

Professional employment: U.S. Environmental Protection Agency: Land Use Coordination, Office of the Administrator (1975-); Special Projects Coordinator, Office of R and D (1973-75); Chief, Exploratory Research, ORD (1972-73). U.S. Department of Commerce and Transportation: Regional Planning Analyst, North East Corridor Transportation Project (1965-72). City of West Haven, Connecticut: Director of Planning (1963-65). Yale University, Graduate Program in City/Regional Planning: Faculty (1961-63).

Professional activities: Conducting futures seminars for EPA; identifying auxillary public benefits of environmental programs through inter-agency program coordination; identifying interrelationships between environmental mandates to state and multi-state region growth objectives, including economic siting decisions; and personal interest in sensitizing program managers to long range considerations including the implications of their own objectives; member, American Planning Association (APA) and American Institute of Certified Planners (1963-); Chairman, APA's Environmental Planning Department (1976-77), and editor of the Department's *Environmental Quarterly;* member, State of Virginia Advisory Committee on the Future for Wine Grape Growing (1977-).

Publications: Co-author, *Futures Research Techniques Applicable to Environmental Analysis* (Environmental Protection Agency, pending); editor, *Alternative Futures and Environmental Quality* (Environmental Protection Agency, 1973); editor, *The Quality of Life Concept: A New Tool for Decision Makers* (Environmental Protection Agency, March 1973); contributor, *Report Set: Recommendations of the Northeast Corridor Transportation Project* (Department of Transportation, 1974-75).

GERKEN, WILLIAM, JR.
Tomorrow Studies
11616-2C Vantage Hill Road
Reston, Virginia 22090, U.S.A.

Born: 1936, New York, New York, U.S.A.

Telephone: (703) 437-3047

Profession: Engineer

Field of specialization: Impacts of present ('real') values and decisions on the evolving future; impacts of population growth on quality of life (including questions of energy and resource availability and usage; education for the future; role of space utilization in the future; development of slide, video and panel presentations (to heighten awareness of alternatives for the future) for school and general audiences.

Education: M.E., Mechanical Engineering, Stevens Institute of Technology, 1959; M.B.A., Management, Florida State University, 1971.

Professional employment: Naval Ship Engineering Center: Reliability Engineer, Ship Maintenance Program (1975-). Norfolk Naval Shipyard: Mechanical Engineer, nuclear ship overhaul supervision (1974-75). ILC Industries, Inc.: Senior Flight Systems Engineer, Kennedy Space Center (1969-73). Bell Aerosystems Company: Test Engineer and Field Engineering Representative (1961-69).

Professional activities: Developing computerized ship maintenance problem index as an engineering/management tool (1976-78); developing 'engineering memory' documentation for ship monitoring project (1976-78); developing and presenting slide shows concerning the future for school and general audiences in the Metropolitan Washington, D.C. area (1976-78); testing of rocket motors and engines for Mercury, Gemini and Apollo Programs (1961-66); spacesuit flight training and preparation for Apollo and Skylab Programs (1969-73); developed and taught continuing education course concerning Florida's future (1974); presented and discussed aspects of alternative futures with school, church and community groups in central Florida (1972-74); developed citizens values survey as a Florida county Bicentennial Committee project (1974).

Publications: "Terra Lune: A Frontier City-State" chapter in *Cultures Beyond Earth*, M. Maruyama and A. Harkins, editors (Random House, 1975).

GERSHUNY, JONATHAN ISRAEL
Fellow
Science Policy Research Unit
Sussex University, Brighton
Sussex, United Kingdom

Born: 1949, London England

Telephone: 02373 686758

Profession: Policy analyst; economist

Field of specialization: Employment futures in relation to changing patterns of consumption in the developed world; economic theories of social justice.

Education: B.Sc., Economics, Loughborough University; M.Sc., Politics, Strathllyde University; D.Phil., History and Social Studies of Science, Sussex University.

Professional employment: Sussex University, Science Policy Research Unit: Fellow (1976-).

Professional activities: Consultant to Research Unit for Ethnic Relations, Bristol University; consultant to Interfutures Project and research project "Social Assessment of Technology" at OECD, Paris; consultant to the U.K. Atomic Energy Authority on Technology Assessment.

Publications: *After Industrial Society? The Emerging Self-Service Economy* (Macmillans, Humanities Press in U.S., 1978); "Post-Industrial Society: The Myth of the Service Economy" (*Futures*, April 1977); "The Self-Service Economy" (*New Universities Quarterly*, Winter 1977); "Policymaking Rationality: A Reformation" (*Policy Sciences*, forthcoming); co-author, "Scenarios of World Development" (*Futures*, February 1978).

GHABBOUR, SAMIR IBRAHIM
Lecturer
Department of Natural Resources
Institute of African Research and Studies
Cairo University
Giza, Egypt

Born: 1933, Cairo, Egypt

Telephone: 980789

Profession: Animal ecologist

Field of specialization: Soil fauna; litter breakdown, arid and semi-arid lands; conservation and management of natural resources; environment and development; land use; urban ecology.

Education: B.Sc., 1954, M.Sc., 1964, Ph.D., 1971, Zoology, Cairo University, Faculty of Science; D.E.P., Education and Psychology, Ain Shams University, Institute of Education, 1955.

Professional employment: Cairo University: Lecturer, Department of Natural Resources (1971-); Part-time Demonstrator, Department of Zoology (1959). University of Kartoum: Part-time Demonstrator, Department of Zoology (1968-69). Higher Teachers' Training Institute, Sudan: Part-time Demonstrator, Department of Biology (1968-69). Ministry of Education, Egypt: Teacher of Biology (1955-71).

Professional activities: Organizer, ALECSO Symposium, "Environmental Considerations in Development Planning (for Arab States)," 1978; organizer, Egyptian Society for Environmental Sciences Second Symposium, "Ecological Studies on the River Nile," April 1978; Assistant Secretary-General, Egyptian Society for Environmental Sciences (since 1975); consultant, ALECSO/UNEP/ASPEN Institute Seminar, "Technologies for Sustainable Satisfaction of Basic Human Needs in the Arab Region," September-November 1978; participated in ALECSO/IDCAS project, "Environmental Considerations in Planning for Industrial Development in the Arab Region: An Environmental Industrial Development Strategy for Arab Countries."

Publications: Editor, *Environmental Considerations in Development Planning* (ALECSO, 1979); "Managing the Ecosystem of World Nations," in *Cultures of the Future*, M. Maruyama, ed. (Mouton Publishers, The Hague, 1978); "The Arab Regional Plan - Natural Resources and Environment," paper presented at the Regional Planning Project for Arab Countries, The Cairo Group (The National Planning Institute, Cairo, Egypt, May 1977); "World Environmental Problems," paper presented at the Long-term Planning in Egypt and in Arab Countries Training Course (UNIDO/Egypt National Planning Institute, April 1977).

GHOSH, SAMIR KUMAR
Professor of Sociology and Director
Indian Institute of Human Sciences
114 Sri Aurobindo Road
Konnagar, W. B., India 712235

Born: 1930, Calcutta, India

Telephone: 22-4546

Profession: Sociologist; policy analyst

Field of specialization: Long-term policies; impact of technology on family; biological model of future; neurolinguistic sociology.

Education: M.A., Social Anthropology, 1952, M.A., Linguistics, 1954, University of Calcutta; Ph.D., Sociology, Massachusetts Institute of Technology, 1964; D.Sc., Sociology, University of Munich, 1974.

Professional employment: Indian Institute of Human Sciences: Professor and Director (1973-). Panjab University: Visiting Professor of Sociology (1975-76). Max-Planck-Institute for Behavioral Sciences: Visiting Professor (1974-75). Institute z. Erfor. d. UdSSR, Munich: Professor of Sociology (1968-73). Indian Institute for Advanced Study, Simla: Senior Fellow (1967-68).

Professional activities: Research project on women and national development; survey to measure the potentialities of the children of the lower-middle-class and beggar children of the city of Calcutta; U.N. Educational, Scientific and Cultural Organization (UNESCO); Professor of Social Sciences, University of Berlin (1965-67); Visiting Professor, Foreign Service Institute, Washington, D.C. (1964-65); consultant to UNESCO, U.N. Human Rights Division; research and teaching in sociology, sociolinguistics, future methodologies, future of family, and sex roles in society (1955-73).

Publications: *The Grammar of Human Greeting Behavior: An Ethological Study* (R. Piper and Company, Verlag, Munich, 1979); *Sociolinguistics of Indian Nationalism* (Indian Publications, Calcutta, 1978); editor, *Man, Language and Society* (Mouton and Company, The Hague, 1970); *Biology, Language and Human Behavior* (University Park Press, Baltimore, Maryland 1976); "A Biological Model Future" (*Journal of Future Studies*, Vol. 3, No. 4, 1975).

GIDAI, ERZSEBET
Institute of Marxism
Semmelweis University
Nagyvarad ter 4
Budapest VIII, 1089
Hungary

Born: 1940, Budapest, Hungary

Telephone: 134-880 137-070

Profession: Economist; psychologist

Field of specialization: Future methodology; development of social-economy.

Education: University of Economics and Psychology at Faculty of Arts; Dr. oec, 1967; Dr. Sc., oec, 1975, Berlin.

Professional employment: Institute of Marxism, Semmelweis University: University Dozent (present).

Professional activities: Member of Prognostic Committee at the Academy of Sciences, Hungary (1969-73); currently lecturing on the methodology of prognostics; Secretary of Prognostic Committee at the Society of Organization and Planning; member of Future Committee at the Academy of Sciences, Hungary; member of Editorial Committee of *Prognostic.*

Publications: *The Principles of Economic Forecasting, Its Methods and Possibilities of Application* (OVK, Budapest, 1971); *Future Research* (MSZMP Oktatasi igazgatosag, Budapest, 1973); *What is Future Research?* (Kossuth, Kiad, 1974); co-author, with L. Besenyei, E. Novaky, *Methodology of Future Research* (KJK, 1977).

GILFILLAN, S. COLUM

615 Linda Vista
Pasadena, California 91105, U.S.A.

Born: 1889, St. Paul, Minnesota, U.S.A.

Telephone: (213) 684-2219

Profession: Social scientist

Field of specialization: Social science and psychological aspects of invention; human geography; long-range prediction, not only practising, but studying to improve the art.

Education: A.B., University of Pennsylvania, 1910; M.A., 1920, Ph.D., 1935, Sociology, Columbia University.

Professional employment: Employed or self-employed at research on invention and prediction (1938-). Purdue University: Assistant Professor of Sociology (1937-38). University of Chicago: Research Associate (1930-36). Museum of Science and Industry, Chicago: Curator of Transportation and Social Science (1928-29). Grinnell College: Assistant Professor of Social Sciences (1924-26). University of the South, Sewanee: Assistant Professor of Social Sciences (1921-24).

Professional activities: Currently completing a book to be entitled *Lead Poison Ruined Rome;*lectured at the University of California-Los Angeles on "Environmental and Population Problems Reconsidered"; chief life work has been on the social and psychological aspects of invention; started serious work on prediction (always long-range) in 1910, and published three predictive articles in 1912 and 1913. "My interest in prediction has always been in the long-range art, say over 40 years ahead, and often centuries. This is so different an art from the usual, short-run prediction that they should hardly be called by the same name. Perhaps prophecy for the long-range, and prediction for the short-range. I may be the only predictor in the world who can check on his predictions published 64 years ago. They were rather successful."

Publications: "Environmental and Population Problems Reconsidered" (*Technological Forecasting and Social Change,* Vol. 3, 1972); "Successful Social Prophecy in the Past" (Master's thesis, Columbia University, 1920); "Lead Poisoning and the Fall of Rome" (*Journal of Occupational Medicine,* Vol. 7, 1965); "A Sociologist Looks at Technical Prediction" (the opening paper at the first conference on prediction, published in *Technological Forecasting for Industry and Government,* James Bright, ed. (1968); *The Sociology of Invention* (1935, republished 1971 by MIT Press); *Supplement to the Sociology of Invention* (San Francisco Press, 1971); *Invention and the Patent System* (U.S. Government publication, 1964).

GLENN, JEROME CLAYTON

Executive Director
Future Options Room
9817 Inglemere Drive
Bethesda, Maryland 20034, U.S.A.

Born: 1945, Oak Park, Illinois, U.S.A.

Telephone: (301)365-2337

Profession: Futurist; policy analyst; educator

Field of specialization: Early warning indicators; interrelationship of consciousness and technology;

translation between futurist theory and current realities; tracking cutting-edge knowledge for cultural integration; design of policy analysis rooms.

Education: B.A., Philosophy, The American University, 1968; M.A.T., Social Science, Education, Antioch Graduate School, 1971; Doctoral Candidate (on leave), Future Studies, University of Massachusetts.

Professional employment: Future Options Room: Executive Director (1975-). Hudson Institute: Consultant (1974-). World Future Society: Research Writer (July-August, 1975). The Committee for the Future: Director, New Worlds Training Center (1973-75); SYNCON Coordinator (1973-75).

Professional activities: Teaching course on "How to Invent the Future," The American University (Fall 1978); nonmilitary futures for R and D associates (1978); consultant to Humanity Foundation World Symposium on Humanity (1978-79); policy analysis and alternatives for SALT II and III (1978).

Publications: Co-author, *Space Trek* (Stackpole Books, 1978); "Social Technologies of Freedom," chapter in *Anticipatory Democracy* (Random House, 1978); "Nonformal Futures Education" (*Education Tomorrow*, September, 1978).

GLINES, DON E.
Director
Educational Futures Projects
Box 2977
Sacramento, California 95812, U.S.A.

Born: 1930, Glendale, California, U.S.A.

Telephone: (916) 442-2772

Profession: Educational consultant

Field of specialization: Educational futures change and alternatives.

Education: B.A., Education, Springfield College, 1952; M.A., 1956, Ph.D., 1960, Education, University of Oregon.

Professional employment: California State Department of Education: Planning Consultant (1974-). Mankato State University: Director, Wilson Campus School and Professor of Education (1968-73). Lake Region, South Dakota, Planning Center: Consultant (1967-68). University City Schools, Missouri: Program Specialist (1965-67). Amphitheater Public Schools, Arizona: Principal (1963-65). American School, Haiti: Director (1963-64). American School, Taiwan: Assistant to the Superintendent (1962-63). American School, Spain (1962-63).

Professional activities: Education futures consultant; conducts workshops and seminars on futures; teaches college courses on futures; National Council on Year-Round Education, President (1975-76). Board of Directors (1972-77).

Publications: *Implementing Different and Better Schools* (D.M. Print Co., Mankato, Minnesota, 1969); *Creating Humane Schools* (D.M. Print Co., Mankato, Minnesota, 1970); *Education Futures I: Imagining and Inventing, Educational Futures II: Options and Alternatives, Educational Futures III: Change and Reality, Educational Futures IV: Updating and Overleaping* (Anvil Press, Millville, Minnesota, 1978-79).

GODOY, HORACIO HERMES
United Nations, Room 2236
P.O. Box 20
Grand Central Station
New York, New York 10017, U.S.A.

Born: 1925, Mendoza, Argentina

Telephone: (212) 754-8518

Profession: Lawyer; policy analyst; modern manager

Field of specialization: World politics; science and technology; international organization; Latin American integration.

Education: Lawyer, Doctorate in Law, School of Jurid. and Social Science, National University of La Plata, 1946; Master in Law, Yale Law School, 1959-60.

Professional employment: United Nations: Inter-Regional Adviser (1978-); Project Manager, Chief Adviser (1973-78); U.N. Expert in Advanced Methods in the Social Sciences (1973). United Nations Educational, Scientific, and Cultural Organization: Regional Expert in Flacso (1966-72); Scientific Director of Flacso (1967-72).

Professional activities: Founder and Director of *America Latina 2001*, A Journal on Science, Technology and Futurology (1976); Co-Director of the Latin American Section of the World Order Model Project in the Year 2000, sponsored by the Institute for World Order (1967-); Member of the New York Academy of Sciences (1970-72); Founder and Director of the Revista Latinoamericana de Ciencia Politica (1970-72); Organizer and Executive Secretary of the Action Committee for Latin American Integration (1969-72).

Publications: Editor, *America Latina 2001, Revista Latinoamericana de Ciencia, Tecnologia y Futurologia [Latin America 2001, Latin American Review of Science, Technology and Futurology]* (Editora Guadalupe, 1976); co-author and editor, *Politica Mundial, Siglo XXI [World Politics in the 2lst Century]* (Friederich Naumann Stiftung, 1973); co-author and editor, *Inversiones Extranjeras y Transferencia de Tecnologia en America Latina [Foreign Investments and Technology Transfer in Latin America]* (ILIS and Escuela Latinoamericana de Ciencia Pol. y Adm. Pub., 1972); "La Crisis del Estado Nacional Contemporanee" ["The Crisis of Today's Nation State"] (*America Latina 2001, Revista Latinoamericana de Ciencia, Tecnologia y Futurologia*, Editora Guadalupe, 1976); "Los Acuerdos de Moscu (1972) y de Washington (1973) entre los Estados Unidos y la Union Societica" ["The Moscow and Washington Agreements Between the U.S. and the USSR, 1972-73"] in *Politica Mundial Siglo XXI* (Friederich Naumann Stiftung, 1973).

GOLDSMITH, EDWARD RENE
Born: 1928, Paris, France

Editor
The Ecologist
73 Molesworth Street
Wadebridge, Cornwall, United Kingdom
Telephone: 2996

Profession: Editor; author; consultant

Field of specialization: Epistemology; general systems; anthropology; ecology.

Education: B.A. (Hons.), Politics, Philosophy, Economics, 1950, M.A. (Hons.), 1960, Magdalen College, Oxford.

Professional employment: *The Ecologist*: Editor (1969-). University of Michigan: Adjunct Assistant Professor (Fall 1975). Environment Canada: Consultant (Fall 1975).

Professional activities: Ecology Party Candidate, Cornwall County Council, Elections for Wadebridge (1977); Vice-Chairman, Ecoropa, Ecological Movement for Europe (1977); consultant to Atlanta 2000 (1973-); political campaigning with Ecology Party in Britain and Ecologie et Survie Party in Alsace; editing *The Ecologist;* co-published, with David Brower of Friends of the Earth, *Eco*, Stockholm Conference (1972).

Publications: *The Stable Society — Towards a Social Cybernetics* (Wadebridge Press, 1978); co-author, *A Blueprint for Survival* (Houghton Mifflin, U.S., 1972); part author and editor, *Can Britain Survive?* (Stacey, 1971); *The Epistemological and Behavioral Basis of Culturalism* (W.E.C., 1974); "The Limits of Growth in Natural Systems" (*General Systems Yearbook*, December 1971).

GORDON, THEODORE JAY
Born: 1930, New York, U.S.A.

President
The Futures Group, Inc.
124 Hebron Avenue
Glastonbury, Connecticut 06033, U.S.A.
Telephone: (203) 633-3501

Profession: Corporate executive in policy analysis, planning, and forecasting.

Field of specialization: Technology assessment; value systems; futures methodology; cross impact and probabilistic system dynamics.

Education: B.S., Aerodynamics, Louisiana State University, 1950; M.S., Aerodynamics, Georgia Institute of Technology, 1951.

Professional employment: The Futures Group: President (1971-). Institute for the Future: Vice President (1968-71). McDonnell-Douglass Astronautics Co.: Director, Advanced Space Systems and Launch Vehicles (1955-71).

Professional activities: Frequent lecturer in management seminars at Columbia University; Board of Advisors, Futures Options Room (1976); research projects at The Futures Group include a technology assessment of agricultural information systems performed for the Office of Technology Assessment and a technology assessment of geothermal energy resource development performed for the National Science Foundation; consulting work has included efforts concerned with the design and conduct of corporate and governmental forecasting activities, the development of forecasting capabilities within particular companies, and the social responsibility of business; one of the innovators of several methods of forecasting, including the cross-impact method, trend impact analysis, and probabilistic system dynamics.

Publications: Co-author, with Harry Harrison, *Ahead of Time* (St. Martin's Press, 1959); *The Future* (St. Martin's Press, 1965); *Ideas in Conflict* (1966); co-author, with Julian Scheer, *First Into Outer Space* (St. Martin's Press, 1959); "Current Methods of Futures Research" in Albert Somit (ed.) *Political Science and the Study of the Future* (Dryden Press, 1974); co-author, with Wayne Boucher, *Some Thoughts on the Future* (The Futures Group, 1975).

GORI, UMBERTO
Born: 1932, Pistoia, Italy

Co-Director
Centro Analisi Relazioni Internazionali [International Relations Research Center]
Via della Scala, 87
Florence 50123, Italy

Telephone: (055) 219923

Profession: Professor of International Relations; Director of Political Science Institute

Field of specialization: Forecasting methodology for foreign policy and international relations.

Education: Ph.D. (Libero Docente), International Organization, University of Florence, Faculty of Political Sciences.

Professional employment: Centro Analisi Relazioni Internazionali (C.A.R.I.): Co-Director (1975-). University of Florence: Full Professor of International Relations (1968-); Director of the Institute of Political Science (current). University of Macerata: Assistant Professor of International Law (1968-75). University of Rome: Assistant Professor of International Law (1958-68). Italian Society for International Organization: Deputy Director (until 1968).

Professional activities: Research project for the European Consortium for Political Research; workshop on "Forecasting in Foreign Policy" (Brussels, 1979); teacher at the Diplomatic Institute, Ministry of Foreign Affairs, Rome; consultant to the Ministry of Foreign Affairs, Rome; Director of the "Political Science and International Relations Series" of the F. Angeli Publishing House, Milan; working with C.A.R.I. on a Data Bank on International Events in Europe.

Publications: Co-author and editor, *Relazioni internazionali - metodi e tecniche di analisi [International Relations: Methods and Analytic Techniques]* (Etas Kompass, Milan, 1973, new edition, 1974); *L'organizzazione internazionale dalla Societa delle Nazionalle N.U. [The International Organization from the League of Nations to the United Nations]* (Cedam, Padova, 1969, new edition, 1971); *La 'diplomazia' culturale multilaterale dell'Italia [Multilateral Cultural 'Diplomacy' in Italy]* (Bizzarri, Rome, 1970); *L'Universita e la Comunita Europea [The University and the European Community]* (Cedam, Padova, 1964); co-author and editor, *La vicera sulla pace [Peace Research]* (F. Angeli, Milan, 1978); co-author and editor, *Tecniche di analisi per le decisioni politiche et economiche [Analytic Techniques for Political and Economic Decisions]* (F. Angeli, Milan, 1978); co-author and editor, *Analisi sistemica e previsione nelle relazioni internazionali [Systems Analysis and Forecasting in International Relations]* (F. Angeli, Milan, forthcoming).

GORNEY, RODERIC
Born: 1924, Grand Rapids, Michigan, U.S.A.

Program on Psychosocial Adaptation and the Future
Department of Psychiatry
University of California-Los Angeles
760 Westwood Plaza
Los Angeles, California 90024, U.S.A.

Telephone: (213) 825-0463

Profession: Professor of Psychiatry and Psychoanalysis

Field of specialization: Effects of dramatized television entertainment on children and adults; cultural patterns and achievement, mental illness, and aggression; future of values.

Education: B.A., Pre-med., M.D., 1949, Stanford University; Ph.D., Psychoanalysis, Southern California Psychoanalytic Institute, 1977,

Professional employment: Department of Psychiatry, University of California-Los Angeles, School of Medicine: Associate Professor of Psychiatry (1973-); Assistant Professor of Psychiatry (1962-73). Private Practice Psychiatry (1952-62). Stanford University, School of Medicine: Assistant Clinical Professor of Psychiatry (1953-62). University of California-San Francisco Medical Center: Assistant Clinical Professor of Psychiatry (1958-62).

Professional activities: Teaching courses on Mental Examination and Psychopathology, on "The Human Agenda," and on evolution and future of values; researching effects of dramatized television on children and adults; studying cultural patterns leading to high and low levels of achievement, mental illness, and aggression; frequent invited lecturer at conferences, symposia, meetings, and television seminars.

Publications: *The Human Agenda* (Simon and Schuster, 1972); "Interpersonal Intensity, Competition, and Synergy: Determinants of Achievement, Aggression, and Mental Illness"*(American Journal of Psychiatry, 128, 1971)*; "The New Biology and the Future of Man" *(UCLA Law Review, 15, 1968)*; co-author with Gary Steele, "Futurology, Psychiatric" *(Wolman's Encyclopedia of Psychiatry, Psychology, and Psychoanalysis, 1977)*; co-author with David Loye and Gary Steele, "Impact of Dramatized Television Entertainment on Adult Males" *(American Journal of Psychiatry, February 1977)*; co-author with David Loye and Gary Steele, "Effects of Television: An Experimental Field Study" *(Journal of Communication, Summer 1977)*.

GRAUL, EMIL HEINZ

Born: 1920, Zeitz, Germany

Director
Klinik und Poliklinik fur Nuklearmedizin
[Clinic and Polyclinic for Biophysics and Nuclear Medicine]
Philipps-University of Marbourg
355 Marburg (Lahn)
Lahnstrasse 4a, Federal Republic of Germany

Telephone: 06421 43 474

Profession: Director of the Institute for Biophysics and Nuclear Medicine

Field of specialization: Environtology; futurology; computer application in medicine.

Education: M.D., University of Marbourg, 1945; Ph.D., University of Munster.

Professional employment: Philipps-University of Marbourg: Director of Clinic and Polyclinic for Biophysics and Nuclear Medicine (1976). MEDICEF (International Center for Medical Environmental Sciences and Future Research): Director (1970-). Institute for Clinical Nuclear Medicine, Bad Wildungen: Director (1968-). University of Marbourg: Full Professor (1963); Associate Professor (1957).

Professional activities: Editor-in-Chief, *Atompraxis [Nuclear Medicine]*; Editor of *Deutsches Arzteblatt [German Physicians Journal]*, *Munchner Med. Wochenschrift [Munich Medical Weekly]*, *Nuccompact, Diagnostik [Diagnostics]*. President and Vice-President of numerous scientific medical societies in the field of aerospace medicine, computer medicine, environmental sciences, biophysics, and nuclear medicine.

Publications: *Strahlensyndrom—Radioaktive Verseuchung [Radiation Syndrome—Radioactive Contamination]* (Verlag Gasschutz u. Luftschutz, Koblenz, 1957); *Die unbewaltigte Zukunft—Blind in das dritte Jahrtausend [The Unconquered Future—Blind in the Third Millennium]*(Kindler-Verlag, Munchen, 1970); *Weltraummedizin—Der Mensch in der Zerreissprobe [Space Medicine—Man in the Breaking Test]* (Ullstein-Verlag, Berlin, 1970); *Der 29. Tag [The 29th Day]* (Jagerdruck Speyer, 1975); *Die menschlichen Lebensbedingungen [The Human Conditions for Life]* (Deutscher Arzteverlag, Koln, 1974); *Computersysteme in der Medizin [Computer Systems in Medicine]* (Deutscher Arzteverlag, Koln, 1973).

GRAY, COLIN S.   **Born:** 1943, Witney, Oxfordshire, England
Professional Staff Member
Hudson Institute
Quaker Ridge Road
Croton-on-Hudson, New York 10520, U.S.A.   **Telephone:** (914) 762-0700

Profession: Political scientist

Field of specialization: Strategic studies; foreign policy; international relations theory.

Education: B.A. Econ. (Hons.), Government, Manchester University, 1965; Ph.D., International Politics, Oxford University, 1970.

Professional employment: Hudson Institute: Professional Staff Member (1975-). International Institute for Strategic Studies, London: Assistant Director (1974-75). Department of War Studies, Kings College, London: Ford Fellow (1973-74). University of British Columbia, Vancouver: Associate Professor in Political Science (1972-73). Canadian Institute of International Affairs: Executive Secretary, Strategic and International Studies Commission (1970-72). York University, Toronto: Lecturer in Political Science (1970-72). Royal Military College of Canada: Associate Professor in Political Science (Spring 1971). University of Lancaster, England: Lecturer in Politics (1968-70).

Professional activities: Conducting research on Soviet and American defense issues (1978); contributes articles and papers on defense issues, the SALT negotiations, strategic doctrine and arms control theory to journals and symposia (1971-); completed a book, *Strategic Studies and Public Policy: The American Experience* (forthcoming); consultant to the RAND Corporation and Stanford Research Institute; lectured extensively at educational institutions, war colleges and various professional organizations (1975-); member of the International Institute for Strategic Studies, Royal United Services, Institute for Defense Studies and the Arms Control Association.

Publications: *The Soviet-American Arms Race* (Lexington Books, 1976); *Canadian Defence Priorities: A Question of Relevance* (Clark, Irwin, Toronto, 1972); *The Geopolitics of the Nuclear Era: Heartland, Rimlands, and the Technological Revolution* (monograph, Crane, Russak, New York, 1977); "The Future of Land-Based Missile Forces" (Adelphi Paper No. 140, IISS, London, 1977); "The Strategic Forces Triad: End of the Road?" (*Foreign Affairs*, Vol. 56, No. 4, July 1978).

GRAY, PAUL   **Born:** 1930, Vienna, Austria
Professor
Graduate School of Business Administration
Center for Futures Research
University of Southern California
Los Angeles, California 90007, U.S.A.   **Telephone:** (213) 741-2446

Profession: Professor

Field of specialization: Cross-impact analysis, scenarios, transportation, aviation, systems.

Education: B.A., Mathematics, New York University, 1950; M.A., Mathematics, University of Michigan, 1954, M.S., Electrical Engineering, Purdue University, 1962; Ph.D., Operations Research, Stanford University, 1968.

Professional employment: University of Southern California: Professor (1972-). Georgia Institute of Technology: Professor (1971-72). Stanford University: Consulting Associate Professor (1968-71). Stanford Research Institute: Director, Institute Transportation Program and Senior Research Engineer (1962-71). Purdue University: Instructor (1960-62).

Professional activities: Secretary, Institute of Management Sciences (1975-); Departmental Editor, *Management Science* (1977-); consultant to both government and industry organizations; Associate Editor, *Operations Research* (1972-77); Editor, *Bulletin of the Operations Research Society* (1969-71).

Publications: Co-author, *Telecommunications-Transportation Tradeoffs: Options for Tomorrow* (John Wiley and Sons, 1976); co-author, "The Uses of Futures Analysis for Transportation Policy Planning" (*Transportation Journal*, Winter 1976); co-author, "The Substitution of Communications for Transporation—A Case Study" (*Management Science*, July 1977); "The Use of Scenarios in Futures Modeling" (*Proceeding of the Western AIDS Meeting*, March 1978).

GREEN, THOMAS F.   **Born:** 1927, Lincoln, Nebraska, U.S.A.
Professor of Education
Division of Education and Social Policy
School of Education
Syracuse University
Syracuse, New York 13210, U.S.A.   **Telephone:** (315) 423-3343

Profession: Philosopher

Field of specialization: Value systems; theory of choice; the behavior of educational systems; problems of youth; educational policy.

Education: B.A., Philosophy/Government, 1948, M.A., Philosophy, 1949, University of Nebraska; Ph.D., Philosophy, Cornell University, 1953.

Professional employment: Syracuse University: Professor of Education (1964-). Michigan State University: Professor of Education (1955-64). South Dakota School of Mines: Instructor, English and Social Science (1952-55).

Professional activities: Research on the normative structure and behavior of national educational systems — the principles of policy choice; President, Philosophy of Education Society (1975-76); Trustee, Center for a Human Future, Inc., Syracuse (1973-); Director, Educational Policy Research Center, Syracuse University Research Corporation (1967-69), Co-Director (1970-73); consultant to the Organization for Economic Cooperation and Development, Paris (1970-71).

Publications: *The Activities of Teaching* (McGraw-Hill, 1971); *Educational Planning in Perspective*, a special issue of *Futures* (IPC Science and Technology Press, England, 1971); *Work, Leisure and the American Schools* (Random House, 1968); *Education and Pluralism: Ideal and Reality* (Syracuse University Press, 1966); "Stories and Images of the Future" in *Images of the Future: The Twenty-First Century and Beyond*, ed., Robert Bundy (Prometheus Books, Buffalo, 1975).

GRINBERG, MIGUEL   **Born:** 1937, Buenos Aires, Argentina
Director
Contracultura Center
C. C. Central 1332
1000 Buenos Aires, Argentina   **Telephone:** —

Profession: Educational scientist

Field of specialization: Futures research related to human resources (within a half-developed society); experimental educative seminars on the scarcity

Education: School of Medicine, University of Buenos Aires, 1955-58; M.A. Sciences Department, Instituto Central de Cordoba, 1963; Ph.D., Educational Sciences, Colegio Libre de Buenos Aires, 1971.

Professional employment: Contracultura Center: Director (1975-). Rolanroc Club: Researcher (1979-). "2001 Project": Coordinator (1971-73).

Professional activities: Research project, Proworld 99, a series of publications and courses (1979-); Editor, *Eco Contemporaneo* (1961-69; 1978-); columnist for *Vigencia* (monthly newspaper, Belgrano University, Buenos Aires, 1978-); Professor and researcher at the Colegio Libre de Buenos Aires (1971-78); researcher, "Futoromania Project" (1975-); columnist, *Diario "La Opinion"* (1975-); Director of Publicity, 20th Century-Fox Films, Buenos Aires (1973-); staff writer, Radio Ciudad de Buenos Aires (1972-74); Futures Editor, *Revista "2001"* (1970-73); Arts/Leisure Editor, *Revista "Panorama"* (1966-70).

Publications: *Ecologia del Alma [Ecology of the Soul]* (Utopos I, Rolanroc Press, 1979); *Precursores de Futuros [Futures Forerunners]* (Lumen Editores, 1974); *Utopos* (Eco Contemporaneo Press, 1975); editor, *La Sociedad Carnivora [Meat-eater Society]* (Editorial Galerna, 1969); *La Nueva Revolucion Norteamericana [New American Revolution]* (Editorial Galerna, 1968).

GROSS, BERTRAM

Born: 1912, Philadelphia, Pennsylvania, U.S.A.

Distinguished Professor of Public Policy and Planning
Hunter College
790 Madison Avenue
New York, New York 10021, U.S.A.

Telephone: (212) 570-5594

Profession: Political scientist; urbanist; systems synthesist

Field of specialization: Societal change in the U.S. within a global and historical perspective.

Education: B.A., English, 1933, M.A., 1935, University of Pennsylvania.

Professional employment: Hunter College: Professor of Public Policy and Planning (present position). Wayne State University: Director, Center for Urban Studies (1969-70). Syracuse University: Professor of Administration, Maxwell School of Citizenship and Public Affairs (1963-68, 1960-61). Hebrew University, Jerusalem: Visiting Professor of Administration (1956-60); External Lecturer (1955-56).

Professional activities: Has completed lengthy study of trends toward authoritarianism in the U.S.—to be published as *Friendly Fascism: The Logic of American Capitalism*; worked with the Congressional sponsors of the recent Humphrey-Hawkins Full Employment and Balanced Growth Act; teaches "futurology" as part of urban and national planning courses, with special attention to future of transnational corporations of capitalist and socialist systems, and of potentialities for large-scale participation in policy-making.

Publications: "Planning in an Era of Social Revolution" (*Public Administration Review,* June 1971); "Friendly Fascism: Model for America" (*Social Policy,* November-December, 1970); *State of the Nation: Social Systems Accounting* (Tavistock, 1966); *The Managing of Organizations* (Free Press/Macmillan, 1964); editor, *Social Intelligence for America's Future* (1960); *A Great Society?* (1968).

GUERON, GEORGES

Born: 1910, Tunis

Vice-President
Societe Internationale des Conseillers de Synthese
[International Society of Systems Consultants]
5, rue d'Alger
75001 Paris, France

Telephone: 26030 48

Profession: Systems consultant

Field of specialization: Thinking about the conditions for decision and action in our era.

Education: Diplome des Hautes Etudes Commerciales; Graduate in Business Studies

Professional employment: Societe Internationale des Conseillers de Synthese: Vice-President (1957-). M.T.O., Algerian textile industry: General Director (1928).

Professional activities: Centre de recherches et des grandes techniques nouvelles [Center for Research and New Technology] (1960-); President, Fondation internationale de l'Innovation Sociale [International Foundation for Social Innovation] (1973-).

Publications: —

GUERON, JEANNINE

Born: 1919, Nice, France

Centre d'Etudes des Consequences Generales des Grandes Techniques Nouvelles (C.T.N.)
5 rue d'Alger
75001 Paris, France

Telephone: 260 30 48

Profession: Documentalist

Field of specialization: Technology assessment; social innovation.

Education: Licence, Sciences Naturelles, Universite de Paris.

Professional employment: Centre d'Etude des Consequences Generales des Grandes Techniques Nouvelles: Documentalist (1957-).

Professional activities: —

Publications: Editor, *Bulletin CTN* (1962-74); editor, *L'Homme et les Techniques Nouvelles [Man and New Technology]* (1974-75).

GUY, CYNTHIA B.

Born: 1945, Boston, Massachusetts, U.S.A.

125 Marlborough Street
Boston, Massachusetts 02116, U.S.A.

Telephone: (617) 536-8918

Profession: Educator

Field of specialization: Pre-high school futures education

Education: B.A., Education, Goddard College, 1968; M.Ed., Environmental Education, Antioch College, 1971; Ed.D., Future Studies, University of Massachusetts, 1978.

Professional employment: Presently taking maternity leave. University of Massachusetts, Future Studies: Supervisor of Student Teachers (1972-78). Hanover, New Hampshire School System: Teacher (1968-74). Consultant.

Professional activities: —

Publications: Are We Educating Students for Their Future?" (*Teacher* Magazine, April 1977); co-author, "Helping Children to Think Futures" (THE FUTURIST, August 1974); "Survey of Pre-High School Futures Programs Completed" (*Education Tomorrow*, October 1978); numerous articles on pre-high school futures curriculum for the Futures Information Interchange, University of Massachusetts Futures Studies Program.

HAHN, WALTER A., JR.

Born: 1921, New York, New York, U.S.A.

Senior Specialist in Science, Technology and Futures Research
Congressional Research Service
Library of Congress
Washington, D.C. 20540, U.S.A.

Telephone: (202) 426-6082

Profession: Policy analyst

Field of specialization: Science policy; futures research; technology assessment; technology transfer.

Education: B.S., Physics, New York University; M.A., Public Administration, American University; Public Administration, Syracuse University.

Professional employment: Congressional Research Service, Library of Congress: Senior Specialist in Science, Technology and Futures Research (current position). U.S. Department of Commerce: Director of Policy Analysis (1971); Deputy Assistant Secretary for Science and Technology (1969). The White House: Senior Research Associate, National Goals Research Staff (1970). Other Government employment with ESSA, Weather Bureau, and National Aeronautics and Space Administration. Also with General Electric Company and the National Academy of Sciences.

Professional activities: Chairman, Board of Directors, International Society for Technology Assessment; member, National Conference for the Advancement of Research, American Society for Public Administration, World Future Society; elected member, National Academy of Public Administration; Board of Directors, U.S. Association for the Club of Rome.

Publications: Co-editor, with Kenneth F. Gordon, *Assessing the Future and Policy Planning* (Gordon and Breach, New York, 1973); contributing editor, *Technology Assessment for the Congress* (Government Printing Office, 1972); "The Future of Technology Assessment in Policy Formulation" in *Technological Assessment in a Dynamic Environment*, M. Cetron, *et al.*, eds. (Gordon and Breach, New York, 1973); Senior Research Associate, *Towards Balanced Growth: Quantity with Quality*, Report of the National Goals Research Staff (The White House, Washington, D.C. 1970); co-author, with S. L. Doscher, "Summary and Syntheses," in *Proceedings of the Second NATO Advanced Study Institute on Industrial Technology Transfer* (Nordhoff, Leiden, 1975).

HAKE, BARRY JOHN

Droogbloem 8
Castricum
The Netherlands

Born: 1943, Devonshire, Great Britain

Telephone: —

Profession: Sociologist, adult educationalist

Field of specialization: Value systems; macro-social systems; educational systems and educational policy analysis.

Education: B.A., Honours, Politics, Bristol, 1964; Post Graduate Certificate, Education, Exeter, 1965.

Professional employment: State University of Leiden: Lecturer in Adult Education (1976-). Tropical Museum Amsterdam: Head of Educational Services (1974-76). European Cultural Foundation: Research Worker with Plan Europe 2000 (1970-74).

Professional activities: Currently teaching and doing research in the area of adult education and community development — research directed to developing supportive infrastructures for systems of adult education provision.

Publications: Co-author, *Possible Futures of European Education* (M. Nijhoff, The Hague, 1973); co-author, *Does Education Have a Future?* (M. Nijhoff, The Hague, 1975); *Education for Social Emancipation* (M. Nijhoff, The Hague, 1975).

HALAL, WILLIAM EMITT

Chairman
Management Department
School of Business
American University
Washington, D.C. 20016, U.S.A.

Born: 1933, Beirut, Lebanon

Telephone: (202) 686-2152

Profession: Management scientist

Field of specialization: Long-range strategic planning and policy studies; complex organizations and institutional change; management of science and technology.

Education: B.S., Engineering, Purdue University, 1956; M.B.A., Management, 1970, Ph.D., Management, 1971, University of California-Berkeley.

Professional employment: American University: Associate Professor; Director of Doctoral Program; Chairman of Management Department (1971-). San Francisco State University: Assistant Professor (1970-71). State of California: Executive Staff Member (1968-70). Grumman Aerospace Corporation: Program Manager (1963-65). Curtiss-Wright Corporation: Systems Engineer (1960-63).

Professional activities: Management consultant in long-range strategic planning and organization design and development to major organizations such as General Motors, AT&T, and the National Institutes of Health; conducting workshops in strategic planning for organizations such as the Pharmaceutical Manufacturer's Association, Washington Council of Governments, and the U.S. Department of Labor; also active as a guest speaker on topics such as the changing role of major corporations, institutional change, and other future developments; winner of the 1977 Alternatives to Growth Competition, which is sponsored by the Club of Rome.

Publications: "Beyond the Profit Motive: The Post-Industrial Corporation" *(Technological Forecasting and Social Change,* June 1978); "Toward a General Theory of Leadership" *(Human Relations,* April 1974); "The Post-Industrial Organization" *(The Bureaucrat,* October 1974);"Organizational Development in the Future" *(California Management Review,* Spring 1974).

HALL, PETER GEOFFREY

Professor
Department of Geography
University of Reading
Whiteknights, Reading
Berkshire, England

Born: 1932, London, England

Telephone: (0734) 85123 Ext. 7845

Profession: Geographer; planner

Field of specialization: Urban planning

Education: B.A., 1953, M.A., 1958, Ph.D., 1959, Geography, University of Cambridge.

Professional employment: University of Reading: Professor, Department of Geography (1968-). London School of Economics: Reader (1966-67). Birkbeck College, University of London: Lecturer (1957-65).

Professional activities: Chairman, Integration Committee, Plan Europe 2000 (1974-76); editor, *Regional Studies Journal* (1967-); consultant and author, Resources for the Future, Washington, D.C. (1971); Visiting Professor, University of California, Berkeley (1974).

Publications: *London 2000* (Faber and Faber, 1963-69); *The World Cities* (World University Library, 1966); co-author, *The Containment of Urban England* (Allen and Unwin, 1973); *Urban and Regional Planning* (Penguin, 1975); editor, *Europe 2000* (Duckworth, 1977).

HAMIL, RALPH EDWARD

Born: 1939, New York, New York, U.S.A.

Specialist, Marketing Research
General Electric Company
570 Lexington Avenue
New York, New York 10022, U.S.A.

Telephone: (212) 750-2149

Profession: Specialist in marketing research

Field of specialization: Both national and international futures with no time-span limitations; special concentration on space, energy and other technologies, environmental issues, future of religion and Marxism.

Education: B.A., International Relations, Brown University, 1960; M.A., Government, University of Maryland, 1971.

Professional employment: World Future Society: Co-Representative to U.N. (1976-); Contributing Editor (1970-). General Electric Company: Specialist, Marketing Research (1973-); Specialist, Enviornmental Analysis (1971-73). U.S. State Department: Foreign Service Officer (1961-69).

Professional activities: Vice-President, New York City local chapter, World Future Society (1975-); completing book entitled Future Talk: A Glossary and Gazetteer of 21st Century English.

Publications: Author and editor of several articles, book reviews, listings and other items in THE FUTURIST and World Future Society BULLETIN (1970-78); "Terraforming the Earth" (*Analog*, July 1978); "The Vietnam War Centennial Celebration" (*Analog*, October 1972).

HANAPPE, PAUL

Born: 1931, Fayt-Lez Manage, Belgium

Research Director
Developpement et Amemagement [Development and Planning]
87, Avenue Denfert-Rochereau
Paris XIV
France

Telephone: (1) 329 5260

Profession: Economist

Field of specialization: Spatial economy (industry location, transportation); structural changes and long-term forecasting in international economics and industrial developments.

Education: Doctor in Law, Universite de Louvain, Belgium, 1953; Licence in Economic Science, Universite de Louvain, 1954; M.A., Economics, Princeton, 1960.

Professional employment: University of Paris-Dauphine IX: Director of Studies (1975-); University of Paris (Dauphine): Teaching Fellow (1971-); Associate Professor (1970-71). National School of Bridges and Roads: Instructor (1961-71).

Professional activities: Research Director at Developpement et Amenagement (1977-); founding member of the World Future Studies Federation; Director of Studies, Prospective et Amenagement (1973-); Editor-in-Chief, *La Vie Urbaine* (1971-72); Economic Engineer, later Chief Engineer, SETEC, Paris (1961-69); Attorney at Law, Mons, Belgium (1953-61).

Publications: Co-author, *Une image de la France en l'an 2000 [An Image of France in the Year 2000]* (Collection Travaux et Recherches de Prospective, No. 20 and 30, Documentation Francaise); *Ports industrielle et mutations economiques [Industrial Ports and Economic Changes]* (Ministry of Transport, Paris, 1977); *La genetique des branches dominante dans l'economie [The Origins of the Principal Sectors of the Economy]* (Cordes, Paris, 1978); *Transports industriels, l'internationalisation de l'economie et mouvements de Kondratieff [Industrial Transportation, Internationalization of the Economy and Kondratieff Movements]* (Research Section, Ministry of Transportation, Paris, 1978).

HARDIN, GARRETT

Born: 1915, Dallas, Texas, U.S.A.

Professor of Human Ecology
University of California
Santa Barbara, California 93106, U.S.A.

Telephone: (805) 967-1384

Profession: Ecologist

Field of specialization: Social and ethical consequences of technology

Education: Sc.B., Zoology, University of Chicago, 1936; Ph.D., Biology, Stanford University, 1941.

Professional employment: University of California, Santa Barbara: Professor of Human Ecology (1946-). Carnegie Institution of Washington: Staff Member (1942-46).

Professional activities: Teaching Human Ecology to undergraduates (1964-); active in the abortion law reform movement (1963-72).

Publications: *The Limits of Altruism* (Indiana University Press, 1977); "The Tragedy of the Commons" *(Science,* 1968); *Nature and Man's Fate* (Rinehart, 1959); *Exploring New Ethics for Survival* (Viking Press, 1972); *Mandatory Motherhood: The True Meaning of 'Right to Life'* (Beacon Press, 1974); *Managing the Commons* (W.H. Freeman and Company, 1976).

HARDING, MAY MAURY

Born: 1927, Memphis, Tennessee, U.S.A.

Director of Programs
Center for Continuing Education
Southwestern at Memphis
2000 North Parkway
Memphis, Tennessee 38112 U.S.A.

Telephone: (901) 274-6606

Profession: Educator

Field of specialization: Futures methodology; urban policy; long-range planning.

Education: B.A., Mathematics, Southwestern at Memphis, 1948; Certificates, Urban Policy Seminars, The Brookings Institution, 1968-75.

Professional employment: Southwestern at Memphis: Director of Programs, Continuing Education (1952-); Director of Programs, Urban Policy Institute (1962-); Director, Center for the Study of Alternative Futures (1973-); Associate Director, Continuing Education (1978-).

Professional activities: Consultant to Shelby County Goals Program (1978); consultant to Department of Housing and Community Development of City of Memphis (1978); served as academic humanist for "Mississippi 1990" project; co-chairman, Mid-South Chapter, World Future Society and program chairman of Chapter's first annual conference, "Education 1990"; founding member of the Association of Futures-Invention Facilitators (1978); leadership role in organizing "Futures Committee" of the Memphis Area Chamber of Commerce and working with them on a trend monitoring and analysis program (1976); Vice President (1976) and President-Elect (1977) of the Memphis Area Planners Club; conducts futures-invention workshops for organizations and cities in Mid-South Region.

Publications: —

HARKINS, ARTHUR MARTIN

Associate Professor
College of Education
University of Minnesota
203-B Burton Hall
Minneapolis, Minnesota 55455, U.S.A.

Born: 1936, Olean, New York, U.S.A.

Telephone: (612) 373-3178

Profession: Sociologist; anthropologist

Field of specialization: Anthropological and sociological aspects of culture transmission and creation; social design and alternative futures; applied social science.

Education: B.A., Sociology, University of Kansas, 1959; M.A., Sociology, University of Massachusetts, 1962; Ph.D., Sociology, University of Kansas, 1968.

Professional employment: University of Minnesota: Associate Professor of Education and Sociology (1972-); Assistant Professor (1968-72); Instructor (1967). Moorhead State College, Minnesota: Extension Instructor (1966-67). Peace Corps Project: Instructor in Community Development, University of Missouri at Kansas City (1965). University of Kansas: Assistant Instructor in Sociology (1964-65).

Professional activities: U.S. Office of Education project on future of K-12 education; Director, Program in Alternative Social and Educational Futures, University of Minnesota; Director, Office for Applied Social Science and the Future, University of Minnesota (1971-73); co-director of Delphic research project on leading 20th century general futurists conducted under contract with World Institute Council, New York City (1973-74); co-director of a Delphic research project on the future of water resources conducted with the Futures Group (1972); President, Minnesota Futurists, a chapter of the World Future Society; founding editor, *Kansas Journal of Sociology* (1964-66); associate editor, *Futurics* (1974-78).

Publications: "Controls, Paradigms, and Designs: Critical Elements in the Understanding of Cultural Dynamics" (Council on Anthropology and Education *Quarterly*, Vol. VI, No. 2, 1975); "The Birth of Cultural Futurology" (World Future Society BULLETIN,' November 1971); co-editor, with Magoroh Maruyama, *Cultures of the Future*, two volumes (Aldine, New York, 1978); co-editor, with Magoroh Maruyama, *Cultures Beyond the Earth* (Random House, New York, 1975); co-author and editor, *World Information Systems and Citizen Participation* (Office for Applied Social Science and the Future, University of Minnesota, 1972).

HARMAN, WILLIS W.

Associate Director
Center for the Study of Social Policy
Stanford Research Institute
333 Ravenswood Avenue
Menlo Park, California 94025, U.S.A.

Born: 1918, Seattle, Washington, U.S.A.

Telephone: (415) 326-6200

Profession: Policy analyst

Field of specialization: Futures methodology; social learning

Education: B.S., Electrical Engineering, University of Washington, 1939; M.S., Physics, Stanford University, 1948; Ph.D., Electrical Engineering, Stanford University, 1948.

Professional employment: Stanford Research Institute: Senior Scientist (1966-). Stanford University: Professor, Engineering-Economic Systems (1952-). University of Florida: Associate Professor, Electrical Engineering (1949-52).

Professional activities: Associate Director, Center for the Study of Social Policy, Stanford Research Institute (1966-); member, U.S. Department of Commerce Technical Advisory Board (1973-77).

Publications: *An Incomplete Guide to the Future* (Stanford Alumni Association, San Francisco Book Company, 1976); "On Normative Forecasting" (*Policy Sciences*, Vol. 6, 1975); "The Great Legitimacy Challenge" (*Vital Speeches*, Pages 147-149, December 1975); "Understanding Social Change" (*Futures*, Pages 143-147, April 1978).

HARMON, DAVID P., JR.

Born: 1937, New York, New York, U.S.A.

Professional Staff
Hudson Institute
Quaker Ridge Road
Croton-on-Hudson, New York, New York 10520, U.S.A.

Telephone: (914) 762-0700

Profession: Policy analyst; economist

Field of specialization: Food and agricultural policy issues, both domestic and foreign; specializing in developing-country, agricultural development.

Education: A.B., Slavic Languages and Literature, Harvard College, 1959; M.B.A., Accounting—C.P.A. Program, New York University, 1965.

Professional employment: Hudson Institute: Professional Staff (1971-). Adelphi University: Assistant Dean (1967-71). Mobil Oil Corporation: Marketer and Economic Analyst (1959-66).

Professional activities: Currently editing book *Critical Food Issues of the Eighties* for Hudson Institute food, agriculture and society research program; Co-Director, food, agriculture and society research program, Hudson Institute (1977-78); Co-Director, world food prospects and agricultural potential, Hudson Institute, funded by the National Science Foundation (1975-76); study of economic and political implications of U.S.-USSR technology transfer (1974).

Publications: Editor, *Critical Food Issues of the Eighties* (Pergamon Press, 1979); co-author, *World Food Prospects and Agricultural Potential* (Praeger, 1977); co-author, "Food Enough for All" (*World View*, September 1975); contributor, *The Price of a Future with Food for All* (The Lutheran Church, Missouri Synod, 1977); "An Optimistic View of Agriculture's Future" (*New York Times*, January 31, 1976).

HAYASHI, YUJIRO

Born: 1916, Tokyo, Japan

Vice Chairman
Institute for Future Technology
Science Museum, 2-1, Kitanomaru-Koen
Chiyoda-ku
Tokyo, Japan

Telephone: (03) 215-1911

Profession: Futurist

Field of specialization: Future methodology; technology assessment.

Education: B.S., Electrochemistry, Tokyo Institute of Technology, 1940.

Professional employment: Institute for Future Technology: Vice Chairman (1978-); President (1971-78). Toyota Foundation: Executive Director (1974-). Tokoyo Institute of Technology: Professor, Social Engineering (1967-75). Economic Planning Agency: President, Economic Research Institute (1964-67).

Professional activities: Member of Central Council for Environmental Pollution Control, Environmental Agency (1976-); overall direction of administration and research for Toyota Foundation and Institute for Future Technology.

Publications: *Toward a Mature Japanese Society* (Chuokeizaisha, 1975); *My Opinion* (Sangyo Noritsu Tandai Shuppanbu, 1975); translation of *The Cultural Contradictions of Capitalism* (Kodansha, 1977); *From Age of Knowledge to Age of Wisdom* (Sangyo Noritsu Tandai Shuppan-bu, 1978).

HEILBRONER, ROBERT L.

Born: 1919, New York, New York, U.S.A.

Professor
New School for Social Research
66 West 12th Street
New York, New York 10021, U.S.A.

Telephone: (212) 741-5717

Profession: Economist

Field of specialization: Evolution of capitalism

Education: B.A., Economics, Harvard, 1940; Ph.D., Economics, New School for Social Research, 1963.

Professional employment: New School for Social Research, Graduate Faculty: Norman Thomas Professor (1973-).

Professional activities: Executive Committee, American Economic Association, (1972-75); Chairman (1971-76), member of the Executive Committee (1971-), Council on Economic Priorities; Editorial Board, *Journal of Economic Issues* (1970-76); Editorial Board, *Journal of Post-Keynesian Economics.*

Publications: *The Future as History* (Harper and Row, 1959); *The Great Ascent* (Harper and Row, 1962); *The Limits of American Capitalism* (Harper and Row, 1962); *An Inquiry into the Human Prospect* (W.W. Norton, 1974); *Business Civilization in Decline* (W.W.Norton, 1976).

HELLMAN, HAL

Born: 1927, New York City, New York, U.S.A.

100 High Street
Leonia, New Jersey 07605, U.S.A.

Telephone: (201) 947-5534

Profession: Free lance writer

Field of specialization: Science and technology

Education: B.A., Economics, Hunter College, 1950; M.A., Industrial Management, City College of New York, 1955; M.S., Physics, Stevens Institute of Technology, 1961.

Professional employment: Free lance writer (1966-). General Precision, Inc.: Technical Information Officer (1956-66).

Professional activities: Conducts courses on "Technology, Society and the Future" and "Communications in the World of the Future" at Fordham University; delivers lectures on these subjects and other aspects of the future.

Publications: Co-author, *Understanding Physics* (Wadsworth Publishing Co., Inc., 1978); *Technophobia: Getting Out of the Technology Trap* (M. Evans and Co., 1976); *Energy in the World of the Future*, second edition (M. Evans and Co., 1975); *Communications in the World of the Future*, second edition (M. Evans and Co., 1974); *Feeding the World of the Future* (M. Evans and Co., 1972); numerous magazine and journal articles.

HELMER, OLAF

Born: 1910, Berlin, Germany

26180 Valley View
Carmel, California 93921, U.S.A.

Telephone: (408) 624-6337

Profession: Professor emeritus; consultant

Field of specialization: Futures methodology (especially Delphi and cross-impact analysis); applications of such methods to long-range planning.

Education: Dr. Philosophy, Mathematics, University of Berlin, 1934; Ph.D., Logic, University of London, 1936.

Professional employment: International Institute for Applied Systems Analysis: Research Scholar (1977-78); University of Southern California: Harold Quinton Professor of Futures Research (1973-76). Institute for the

Future: Director of Research (Part time: President) (1968-73). Rand Corporation: Senior Mathematician (1946-68). New York City College: Instructor (1941-44). University of Illinois: Instructor (1938-41).

Professional activities: Methodological research on cross-impact analysis; design of national and global simulation games; consulting on methods of long-range planning.

Publications: *Social Technology* (Basic Books, 1966); co-author, "On the Epistemology of the Inexact Sciences" *(Management Science 6, 1959)*; co-author, "An Experimental Application of the Delphi Method to the Use of Experts" *(Management Science 9, 1963)*; "Cross-Impact Gaming" *(Futures 4, 1972)*; On the Future State of the Union (Institute for the Future, R-27, 1972); *GEM: An Interactive Simulation Model of the Global Economy* (IIASA, forthcoming); "Problems in Futures Research: Delphi and Causal Cross-impact Analysis" *(Futures 9, February 1977)*.

HENDERSON, HAZEL   **Born:** 1933, Bristol, England
Co-Director
Princeton Center for Alternative Futures, Inc.
60 Hodge Road
Princeton, New Jersey 08540, U.S.A.   **Telephone:** (609) 921-2280

Profession: Author; social critic; civic activist

Field of specialization: Exploring cultural and social change in industrial societies in a planetary context of human interdependence. Asserting the primacy of value-assumptions underlying scientific disciplines; technological and economic systems. Developing conceptual rationale and organizing citizen participation in science and technology issues, technology assessments, etc. Critiquing traditional economics and proposing new models for managing steady-state economies.

Education: D.Sc., Hon. Causa, Worcester Polytechnic Institute, 1976; attended pre-college level private, English schools. (Note: Ms. Henderson describes herself as "auto-didact.")

Professional employment: Princeton Center for Alternative Futures, Inc: Co-proprietor and Co-director (1967-). Self-employed as a writer and community organizer and public sector entrepreneur.

Professional activities: Guest lecturer at U.S. universities, corporate executive seminars, and national organizations; Fellow, Scientists Institute for Public Information; member, Committee on Public Engineering Policy, National Research Council, National Academy of Sciences (1975-76); co-founder of Citizens for Clean Air, Inc., New York City, Public Interest Economics West, San Francisco, and Environmentalists for Full Employment, Washington, D.C.; co-organizer of Sun Day (1978); member, Advisory Council. U.S. Congress Office of Technology Assessment (1974-); member, Board of Directors, Worldwatch Institute, Washington, D.C. (1976-); member, Board of Directors, Council on Economic Priorities, New York City (1970-); member, U.S. Association of the Club of Rome (1977-); member, National Council of Churches Energy Task Force (1977-78); editorial advisory board, *Technological Forecasting and Social Change* (1977-).

Publications: *Creating Alternative Futures* (G.P. Putnam's Berkley Paperback, New York, 1978); "Risk, Uncertainty and Economic Futures" *(Best's Review, Casualty Insurance Edition, May 1978)*; "Science and Technology: The Revolution from Hardware to Software" *(Technological Forecasting and Social Change* Vol. 12, No. 4, November 1978)*; "The Legacy of E.F. Schumacher" *(Environment, Vol. 20, No. 4, May 1978)*; "Limits of Traditional Economics: New Models for Managing a Steady-State Economy" *(Financial Analysis Journal, May 1973)*; "Ecologists Versus Economists" *(Harvard Business Review, July-August 1973)*.

HENSHEL, RICHARD L.   **Born:** 1939, Dallas, Texas, U.S.A.
Associate Professor
Department of Sociology
The University of Western Ontario
London, Ontario, Canada   **Telephone:** (519) 679-3606

Profession: Sociologist

Field of specialization: Futures methodology; self-altering predictions; imaging the future; perception.
Education: B.A., Sociology, University of Texas, 1962; Ph.D., Sociology, Cornell University, 1969.
Professional employment: University of Western Ontario: Associate Professor (present).

Professional activities: Editor, *Futures Canada* (1976-); contributing editor, *Sociological Practice* (1976-78); Canada Council grant, "Prediction in the Social Sciences" (1972-73); occasional lecturer on social prediction.

Publications: *On the Future of Social Prediction* (Bobbs-Merrill Co., 1976); *Reacting to Social Problems* (Longmans Canada, 1976); "Self-Altering Predictions" in Fowles, ed., *Handbook of Futures Research* (Greenwood Press, 1978); "Effects of Disciplinary Prestige on Predictive Accuracy: Distortions from Feedback" (*Futures,* April 1975); "Sociology and Prediction" (*The American Sociologist,* August 1971).

HERRERA, AMILCAR OSCAR
Professor
Universidade de Campinas
Sao Paulo, Brazil

Born: 1920, Buenos Aires, Argentina

Telephone: —

Profession: Professor

Field of specialization: Science policy; natural resources.

Education: M.S., Economic Geography, Colorado School of Mines, 1951; Ph.D., Geology, Universidad de Buenos Aires, 1952.

Professional employment: Universidade de Campinas: Professor (1978-). Fundacion Bariloche: Professor (1969-76). University of Chile: Professor (1966-69). University of Buenos Aires: Professor (1956-66). Instituto Nacional de Geol. y Min.: Vice-President (1964-66). Banco Industrial de la Rep. Argentina: Chairman of Geology Department (1949-56).

Professional activities: Formerly Director of Latin American World Model (Fundacion Bariloche); research project on "Modern and Indigenous Technologies" (sponsored by IDRC, Canada); consultant of UNO, United Nations Conference on Trade and Development; has conducted research on economic geology and geochemistry.

Publications: *Ciencia y Politica en America Latina [Science and Politics in Latin America]* (Siglo XXI Editores, Mexico, 1971); *Los Recursos Minerales de America Latina [Mineral Resources of Latin America]* (Editorial Universitaria de Buenos Aires, 1965); *Los Recursos Minerales y los Limites del Desarrollo Economico [Mineral Resources and the Limits of Economic Development]* (Siglo XXI Argentina, Editores, 1974); co-author, *The Art of Anticipation*, Encel, Marstrand, Page, eds. (Martin Robertson, 1975); co-author, *Catastrophe or New Society? Latin American World Model* (Fundacion Bariloche, 1976).

HESS, KARL
P.O. Box 173
Kearneysville, West Virginia 25430, U.S.A.

Born: 1923, Washington, D.C., U.S.A.

Telephone: (304) 263-7526

Profession: Writer; welder

Field of specialization: Alternative technology; value systems; ethics; small-scale social organization.

Education: None.

Professional employment: None.

Professional activities: Writing, welding, working with tools, material, and techniques of alternative technologies, i.e., appropriate, low-impact technology; former speech writer and theorist for presidents, senators, congressmen, and corporate presidents; member, Appropriate Technology Task Force, Office of Technology Assessment.

Publications: *Dear America* (William Morrow, 1975); *Neighborhood Power* (Beacon, 1975); *Community Technology* (Harper & Row, 1979).

HETMAN, FRANCOIS
Principal Administrator
Directorate for Science, Technology and Industry

Born: 1917, Stranna

236

Organization for Economic Cooperation and Development
2, rue Andre Pascal
75016 Paris, France

Telephone: 524 93 63

Profession: Economist and policy analyst

Field of specialization: Science policy; technology assessment; research of future alternatives; methodology of futures research.

Education: Engineer, 1946, Ph.D., Economic Sciences, 1973, University of Grenoble.

Professional employment: Organization for Economic Cooperation and Development: Principal Administrator, Directorate for Science, Technology and Industry (1967-). Bureau d'Informations et de Previsions Economiques (1964-67). REXECO—Institute for Economic Research: 1958-64.

Professional activities: Responsible for programs on science policy perspectives, prospective analysis, social assessment of technology (1972-), and a review of national science policies (1967-71); research fellow and director of research responsible for macro-economic forecasting and planning (1958-67); published extensively in scientific reviews and various journals on economic growth and perspectives, future of science and technology, methodology of forecasting and futures research.

Publications: *Methods of Technological Forecasting* (AGARD Report No. 655, Paris, 1977); editor, *Methodological Guidelines for Social Assessment of Technology* (OECD, Paris, 1975); *L'Europe de l'abondance [Abundant Europe]* (Favard, Paris, 1967); *Les secrets des geants Americains [Secrets of American Giants]* (Seuil, Paris, 1969); *Le Langage de la prevision [The Language of Forecasting]* (SEDEIS, Paris, 1969); *La maitrise du futur [Mastering the Future]* (Seuil, Paris, 1971); *Society and the Assessment of Technology* (OECD, Paris, 1973); co-author, *Science Policy Formats* (Hearings, U.S. House of Representatives, Washington, D.C. 1974).

HITCH, CHARLES JOHNSTON

Born: 1910, Boonville, Missouri, U.S.A.

President
Resources for the Future
1755 Massachusetts Avenue, N.W.
Washington, D.C. 20036, U.S.A.

Telephone: (202) 462-4400

Profession: Economist; research administrator; former university president.

Field of specialization: Economic analysis; decision-making.

Education: B.A., with highest distinction, University of Arizona, 1931; Post-graduate, Harvard University, 1931-32; B.A. with first class honors (Rhodes Scholar), Oxford University, 1934; M.A., 1938; several honorary degrees.

Professional employment: Resources for the Future: President (1975-). University of California: President (1968-75); Vice President for Administration (1966-67); Vice President for Business and Finance (1965-66); Assistant Secretary of Defense (Comptroller) (1961-65). Rand Corporation: Head of Economics Division and later Chairman of Research Council (1948-61). Queens College, Oxford University: Fellow, Praelector, Tutor (1935-48); General Editor, Oxford Economic Papers (1941-48).

Professional activities: Trustee, Asia Foundation; Member of the Board of Directors, Aerospace Corporation; Member, Council on Foreign Relations; Fellow, American Association for the Advancement of Science, American Academy of Arts and Sciences, and the Econometric Society; President, Operations Research Society of America (1959-60); Vice-President of the American Economic Association (1965); organized panel "The Natural Resources Doomsayers: Was Malthus Right After All?" for the World Future Society's Second General Assembly, June 1975; author of articles on economics and education.

Publications: Editor, *Modeling Energy-Economy Interactions: Five Approaches* (Resources for the Future, 1977); editor, *Resources for an Uncertain Future* (Resources for the Future, 1978); editor, *Energy Conservation and Economic Growth* (Westview Press, 1978); *America's Economic Strength* (Claredon Press, 1941); co-author with Roland McKean, *The Economics of Defense in the Nuclear Age* (Harvard University Press, 1960).

HOFFMAN, BEN B.
Planning Officer
University Grants Commission
11-395 Berry Street
Winnipeg, Manitoba, Canada

Born: 1928, San Diego, California, U.S.A.

Telephone: (204) 889-7280

Profession: Educational Planner, Metro-Regional Economics

Field of specialization: Urban planning; housing options; decision making assisted by automated participant simulated learning; outcome planning applications; international affairs; innovative seed bed environments.

Education: Geography, University of California-Berkeley; B.A., Geography, State University of San Diego, 1953; Ph.D., Metropolitan Studies, Economics, Social Science, Syracuse University, 1968.

Professional employment: University Grants Commission: Planning Officer (1971-76); Department of Education, Research, Chairman and Co-Chairman (1972-76). Ontario Institute Studies Education: Research Associate (1970-71). Syracuse University: Associate Director, Institution Research (1964-67). U.S. Navy: Underwater Demolition, Operations Officer (1954-57).

Professional activities: Chair and Co-Chair, University Outcomes Committee (1976-78) and Manitoba Post-Secondary Research Reference Committee (1972-78); National Executive, Canadian Association for Future Studies (1977-78); Coordinator, Implementation Studies of University Outcomes (1978); Public Relations Chairman, United Nations Association (1977); Coordinator, Operational Research and R and D (1971-76).

Publications: *Forced Home Ownership: A National Study of the Circumstances of Elderly Home Owners with the Emphasis on Blighted Neighbourhoods, Property Tax Issues and Negative Voting Behavior* (Syracuse University, 1967); *A Question of Potential and Motivation: A Study of Submerged Talent and the Problems of Recognition and Development* (Syracuse University, 1967); *Search for a World Class Junior Tennis Program: Sections on Program Evaluation and Outcome Planning* (to be published); "Students' Decisions on Post-Secondary" *(Educational Planning,* October 1974); *Campus Environment* (Kansas City Regional Council, 1969); *Registration Roulette* (Syracuse University, 1967).

HOFFMAN, JOHN DAVID
Director
Institute for Research on Public Policy
3535 Queen Mary Road
Montreal, Quebec
H3V 1H8 Canada

Born: 1936, St. Catherines, Ontario, Canada

Telephone: (514) 342-9121

Profession: Political scientist; policy analyst

Field of specialization: Values; social trend analysis; public policy.

Education: B.A., Economics and Political Science, McMaster University, 1958; M.A., Political Science, University of Toronto, 1959; Ph.D., Political Science, London School of Economics, 1963.

Professional employment: Institute for Research on Public Policy: Director (1977-). Government of Canada: Director and Consultant (1974-77). York University: Professor and Department Chairman (1965-74). McMaster University: Assistant Professor (1963-65).

Professional activities: Directing Future Studies Program at IRPP (1977-); Executive, Canadian Political Science Association (1966-67; 1971-74); Review Editor (1967-71), Co-editor (1971-74), *Canadian Journal of Political Science;* member, Canada Council Negotiated Grants Committee (1975-77).

Publications: "Interacting with Government: The General Public and Interest Groups" in *Government and Politics* (Macmillan, 1975); "The Public's Opinion of the MPP" (Ontario Commission on the Legislature, 1974); "Liason Officers and Ombudsmen: Canadian MPs and the Federal Bureaucracy" in *The Apex of Power* (1971); co-author, *Bilingualism and Biculturalism in the Canadian House of Commons* (Queen's Printer, 1970); co-author, *Canadian Attitudes Towards Government Information Services* (Institute for Behavioral Research, 1969).

238

HOLTHUSEN, T. LANCE
President
TLH Associates, Inc.
Suite 900, Minnesota Building
St. Paul, Minnesota 55101, U.S.A.

Born: 1938, Two Rivers, Wisconsin, U.S.A.

Telephone: (612) 227-8866

Profession: Private consultant: research, education and planning for the future.

Field of specialization: Futures methodology; institutional planning; adult education; facilitating general systems approach to learning and planning models for the future.

Education: B.S., Political Science, Wisconsin State University-Stevens Point, 1963; M.Div., History and Theology, Luther Theological Seminary, 1968; M.A. candidate, Futures Education, St. Cloud State University.

Professional employment: TLH Associates, Inc., St. Paul, Minnesota: President (current position). Grace Lutheran Church, Eau Claire, Wisconsin: Pastor (1968-70).

Professional activities: Managing editor, *Futurics*, a quarterly journal of futurist research, published by the Minnesota Futurists, a chapter of the World Future Society; past president and a director of the Minnesota futurists; vice president, Education Section, World Future Society.

Publications: Editor, *The Role of Futures Studies in Public Education* (The Science Museum of Minnesota, January 1976); editor, *Museums and the Future* (The Science Museum of Minnesota, Fall 1973); "Museums and Futures Studies: An Alternative for the General Public's Participation in the Future" (Irades, 1974).

HOOS, IDA RUSSAKOFF
Space Sciences Laboratory
University of California
Berkeley, California 94720, U.S.A.

Born: 1912, Skowhegan, Maine, U.S.A.

Telephone: (415) 642-1347

Profession: Research Sociologist

Field of specialization: Technology and society; technology assessment; futures methodology.

Education: A.B., Sociology and Social Psychology, Radcliffe College, 1933; M.A., Sociology and Social Psychology, Harvard University, 1942; Ph.D., Sociology, University of California, 1959.

Professional employment: University of California Space Sciences Laboratory: Research Sociologist (1961-).

Professional activities: Co-investigator, Remote Sensing Technology as Applied to Earth Resources in California, sponsored by National Aeronautics and Space Administration (1970-); member, Special Task Force on Waste Management, Nuclear Regulatory Commission (1975-); consultant to National Science Foundation; member, C. Wright Mills Award Committee, Society for the Study of Social Problems (1976); consultant and participant, British Broadcasting System's Open University (1973-75); member, NASA Advisory Council, Space and Terrestrial Applications Advisory Committee; member, National Academy of Sciences, Committee on Advanced Energy Storage Systems; member, Solar Energy Panel, National Academy of Sciences; member, Hydrogen Energy Panel, National Academy of Sciences.

Publications: *Systems Analysis in Public Policy* (University of California Press, 1974); *Retraining the Work Force* (University of California Press, 1967); *Automation in the Office* (Public Affairs Press, 1961); "When the Computer Takes Over the Office" (*Harvard Business Review*, July-August, 1960); "Criteria for 'Good' Futures Research" (*Technological Forecasting and Social Change*, August, 1974).

HOPKINS, FRANK SNOWDEN
Vice-President
World Future Society
4916 St. Elmo Avenue (Bethesda)
Washington, D.C. 20014, U.S.A.

Born: 1908, Gloucester, Virginia, U.S.A.

Telephone: (301) 656-8274

Profession: Writer on world affairs; former long-range planner for U.S. Department of State.

Field of specialization: History and the future of the world community.

Education: A.B., English and Journalism, College of William and Mary, 1927; A.M., English and Comparative Literature, Columbia University, 1928; Courses in history, no degree, Johns Hopkins University, 1936-38; Nieman Fellow, Government, Economics, and Sociology, Harvard University, 1938-39.

Professional employment: U.S. Department of State: Special Assistant for Long-range Planning and Member, Policy Planning Council (1967-68); Director of U.S. Office, Bureau of Educational and Cultural Affairs (1964-67); Consul General, Melbourne, Australia (1960-63); Consul for French West Indies (1958-60); Deputy Director, UNESCO Relations Staff (1955-58); Public Affairs Officer, Stuttgart, Germany (1952-55); Member of Faculty, Army War College (1951-52); Assistant Director, Foreign Service Institute (1947-51). Prior to service with Department of State, Director of Training for Maryland Drydock Company, Baltimore (1941-45). Years from 1929 to 1941 spent as a newspaperman, magazine journalist, and publishing house editorial assistant.

Professional activities: Vice-President, World Future Society (1975); coordinator for chapters, World Future Society (1968-78); writing and lecturing on futurist subjects; completed a manuscript in 1975 on the world future, "Civilization on the Defensive: Planning for the World of 2000"; currently working on a fantasy novel about the future; numerous articles in THE FUTURIST.

Publications: "The Planning Mission Before Us," chapter in *Handbook of Futures Research*, Jib Fowles, ed. (Greenwood Press, 1978); "Two International Futures," in *The Next 25 Years: Crisis and Opportunity* (World Future Society, 1975); "Thoughts of a 130-Year-Old American" (THE FUTURIST, December 1975); review of *Mankind at the Turning Point*, Mesarovic and Pestel (THE FUTURIST, October 1975); "International Education in Tomorrow's World" (paper prepared for the U.S. Department of State, 1967).

HORHAGER, AXEL

18, ch. Sous Caran
CH 1222 Vesenaz, Geneva, Switzerland

Born: 1947, Kufstein, Tirol, Austria

Telephone: (022) 52 26 67

Profession: Consultant

Field of specialization: Economics; environmental economics; defense.

Education: B.A., Electrical Sciences, 1968, M.A., 1972, Churchill College, Cambridge University; D.E.S., Economics, Universite de Paris I, 1971; Doctorat d'Etat, Economics, Pantheon-Sorbonne, 1975.

Professional employment: Freelance consultant (1973-). University of Geneva: Charge d'enseignement in Economics (1972-73). Deutsche Shell A.G.: Employed in planning departments (1970, 1971).

Professional activities: Cost-benefit analysis of air quality management in Egypt for the United Nations Development Program and Institut Ecoplan, Geneva (1978); two market research studies for Gordon International Research Associates, Geneva (1977, 1978); research on European defense problems (1976); member of the Scientific Council of the World Future Studies Federation (1973-); member of a working group on the ethical foundations for futures studies (1976); member of a research group on spectral analysis, Paris (1971-74).

Publications: *Suez City Air Quality Study: Suez in the Year 2000* (Institut Ecoplan, for UNDP, 1979); *Etude du systeme de sante suisse - les hopitaux dans le canton de Zurich [Study of Hospital Planning in the Swiss Canton of Zurich]* (Institut Ecoplan, for Algerian Government, 1978); "Economie de l'environnement"["Environmental Economics"](Doctoral Thesis, Universite de Paris, 1975); "Une application de l'analyse spectrale en economie" ["An Application of Spectral Analysis to Economics"] (Dossier a l'Universite de Paris I, 1971); editor, "Qualite de la Vie" ["Quality of Life"] (*Revue 2000*, February 1973).

HOTTOVY, TIBOR C.

Senior Research Scientist
The National Swedish Institute for Building Research
Sodra Sjotullsgatan 3, Box 785
801 29 Gavle 1, Sweden

Born: 1923, Budapest, Hungary

Telephone: (026) 10 02 20

Profession: Architect and planner

Field of specialization: Urban and regional research; technology assessment (the potential impact of technological innovations on housing, building, and planning).

Education: Master of Architecture, University of Technology, School of Architecture, Budapest, 1945.

Professional employment: The National Swedish Institute for Building Research: Senior Research Scientist (1965-). Private Town Planning and Structural Engineering Office, Stockholm: Architect (1957-64). Ministry of Transport and Communication (1950-56). With authorities under the Ministry in Budapest (1947-49). Private Architect Office, Copenhagen (1946).

Professional activities: Working on a future study, "The Potential Impact of Telecommunication and Information Technology on Urban and Regional Structure"; Swedish Coordinator, World Future Society; Member, CIB International Council for Building Research, Commission on Forecasting Methods; one of the founders of the Swedish Association for Future Studies; research on "Future of Prefabrication in the Building Industry" (1953-54); lectured and wrote articles on "The Future of Plastics and Other New Materials in Building" (1966-67); articles and film on "The Future of Building Structures"; studies of building and planning research in the U.S. (1968), in Japan (1970), and in six European countries (1971).

Publications: *Future Studies and Forecasting in Swedish Housing Building and Planning* (The National Swedish Institute for Building Research, 1978); *The Potential Impact of Telecommunication and Information Technology on Future Housing and Settlement System* (The National Swedish Institute for Building Research, 1979); "Forecasting and Long-Term Planning in Sweden" World Future Society BULLETIN, Vol. IX, No. 4,5,6, 1975); *Forecasting and Long-Term Planning in Sweden — A Review* (The National Swedish Institute for Building Research, 1975); *Architectural Visions and the Expo 70* (20 minute color film, The National Swedish Institute for Building Research, 1970).

HUBBARD, BARBARA MARX
Director
The International Committee for the Future
2325 Porter Street, N.W.
Washington, D.C. 20008, U.S.A.

Born: 1929, New York, New York, U.S.A.

Telephone: (202) 966-8776

Profession: Futurist, educator

Field of specialization: Value systems; use of theatre, art, music, dance to help envision long-range futures; spiritual aspects of conscious evolution; using an understanding of evolutional process as predictive models.

Education: B.A. (*cum laude*), Political Science, Bryn Mawr, 1951.

Professional employment: The International Committee for the Future: Director (current position). The Committee for the Future, Inc: Co-founder and Chairperson of the Board (1970-76). The New Worlds Company: Chairperson of the Board (1971-76).

Professional activities: Conference design; the SYNCON process; organizing "Future Maps"—a new cartography for humanity as a conscious participant in designing the future; member of the Board, World Future Society (1970-); established a "Communications/Information Center"—The New Worlds Network—to gather information on all aspects of human activity and disseminate it in all media; member and organizer of the President's Commission on a National Curriculum for Antioch College (1976); narrator, The Theatre for the Future—Previews of Coming Attractions; co-organizer, with John Whiteside, Act III—an educational weekend on how to enact desirable futures.

Publications: *The Evolutionary Journal* (Futures Network, 1978); *The Hunger of Eve: A Woman's Odyssey Toward the Future* (Stackpole Books, 1976); editor, *The Search is On: A View of the Future from the Perspective of Space* (PACE, 1969); editor, *The Center Letter: A Network of Discovery* (self-published, 1967-69); "An Appetite for Evolution" (*The Futurist*, February 1973); "The Shift from Revolutionary to Evolutionary Activism" (*New Worlds*, March 1973).

HUBNER, KURT

Born: 1921, Prague, Czechoslovakia

Philosophisches Seminar
Olshausenstrasse
D-2300 Kiel
Federal Republic of Germany

Telephone: (0431) 8802231

Profession: Philosopher

Field of specialization: Critical investigations of the scientific and technological age.

Education: University of Prague, University of Rostock, University of Kiel.

Professional employment: University of Kiel: Full Professor (1971-). Technical University of Berlin: Full Professor (1960). Free University of Berlin: Honorary Professor (1961).

Professional activities: Arbeitskreis fur Wissenschaftsforschung [Working Group for Scientific Research] (1975-); Member of the Scientific Commission for the World Congress of Philosophy (1975-); President, Allgemeine Gesellschaft fur Philosophie in Deutschland e.V. [General Society for Philosophy in Germany] (1969-75); Member of the Kuratorium des Zentrums fur Kybernetik in Berlin [Member of the Board of Trustees of the Center for Cybernetics in Berlin] (1968-70).

Publications: *Philosophische Fragen der Zukunftsforschung [Philosophical Questions of Futures Research]* (Studium Generale 24, 1971); "Philosophische Probleme der Technick" [Philosophical Questions of Technology"] in H. Lenk, *Moser Techne-Technik-Technologies* (1973); "On the Question of Relativism and Progress in Science" (*Man and World*, Vol. 7, No. 4, 1974); "Outline of a Theory of Forecasting" in *Man in the Society of the 1980s* (1973); "On Modern Theories of Rational Decisions" in *Man in the Society of the 1980s* (1973).

HUMPHRIES, GEORGE E.

Born: 1923, Jacksonville, Florida, U.S.A.

President
Advanced Technology Management Associates
716 Fourth Street, S.E.
Washington, D.C. 20003, U.S.A.

Telephone: (202) 546-9659

Profession: Management consultant

Field of specialization: Management of R and D; organizational development; technology assessment, technology transfer; technology forecasting; policy analysis; public and congressional relations.

Education: Chemical Engineering, Clemson College, 1940-42; B.S., Public Communications, University of Maryland; M.S. equivalent, Political Science, Naval Intelligence Post-Graduate School; M.S.B.A., Business Administration, George Washington University, 1970.

Professional employment: Advanced Technology Management Associates: President (1970-). IITRI: Scientific Advisor (1976). Progress Management Services: Senior Associate (1967-76). George Washington University, Program of Policy Studies in Science and Technology: Senior Consultant (1974-76). Computer Command and Control Corporation: Scientific Consultant (1971-73). U.S. Navy: Commander, Aviator, Intelligence, Public Relations (1942-70).

Professional activities: Editor, *T. A.—Update*, Newsletter of the International Society for Technology Assessment; senior researcher on several technology assessment studies; Member, International Society for Technology Assessment, Technology Transfer Society, World Future Society, TIMS, Society for General Systems Research, and the Society for General Semantics; Co-chairman, T. A.—Update 1975, a five session conference on Technology Assessment sponsored by the World Future Society (February 1975); Co-chairman of two sessions on technology assessment at the World Future Society's Second General Assembly (June 1975); Co-chairman, T. A.—Update 1974, an eight session conference on Technology Assessment sponsored by ISTA (June 1974).

Publications: "Technology Assessment: A New Imperative in Corporate Planning" (*Planning Review*, March 1976); co-author with K. Finsterbusch *et al., A Methodology for the Analysis of Social Impacts* (Braddock, Dunn and McDonald, Vienna, Virginia, 1974).

(From the first edition. Corrections not received by press time.)

ILLICH, IVAN
APDO 479
Cuernavaca, Mexico

Born: 1926, Vienna, Austria

Telephone: —

Profession: Philosopher

Field of specialization: Alternatives to industrial society.

Education: Ph.D., History of Philosophy, Salzburg, Austria; Advanced degrees in Philosophy and Theology from Gregorian University, Rome.

Professional employment: None.

Professional activities: Member of Editorial Board and Founder of *Technologie und Politik*, Aktuell Magazine, Rohwolt Verlag, Hamburg—appears four times per year, deals with political analysis of technological dimensions; Co-founder and advisor to a series of books dealing with alternatives to industrial society, *Ideas in Progress*, Marion Boyars Publications, London; Co-editor of a series of books, *Technocritique*, published by Le Seuil, Paris; conducted at CIDOC (Center for Intercultural Documentation), Cuernavaca, a seminar on the multi-dimensional limits in growth to industrial institutions, particularly in the service sector; currently interested in a history of awareness among social critics of the mutual relationship between social structures supporting the informal production of use-values and those supporting the production of commodities.

Publications: *Towards a History of Needs* (Pantheon, 1978); *The Right to Useful Unemployment* (Marion Boyars, London, 1978); *De-Schooling Society*, a collection of essays (Harper and Row, 1971); *Tools for Conviviality* (Harper and Row, 1973); *Energy and Equity* (Marion Boyars, London, 1974); *Medical Nemesis — The Expropriation of Health* (Pantheon, 1976).

IMSLAND, DONALD ORLENE
Human Design, Inc.
5021 Belmont Avenue
Minneapolis, Minnesota 55419, U.S.A.

Born: 1931, McCallsburg, Iowa, U.S.A.

Telephone: (612) 825-8169

Profession: Business consultant

Field of specialization: Design of learning and planning programs concerned with the future; corporate planning process; environmental scanning; business and society relationships; corporate responsibility; social trends; religion and the future; intermediate technology.

Education: Agricultural Engineering, Iowa State University; B.A., Mathematics and Science, Luther College, 1958; B.D., Theology, Luther Theological Seminary, 1962.

Professional employment: CEO Project on Corporate Responsibility: Director (1978-). Northern States Power Campany: Consultant, Corporate Planning Staff (1976-78), Planning and Research (1975-76), Assistant to the President (1973-75), Environmental Affairs (1970-73).

Professional activities: Member, World Future Society, Minnesota Futurists, American Teilhard de Chardin Association; chairperson, Minnesota China Council; member, Board of Directors, Leisure Studies, Inc.; Advisory Editor, *Futurics*, Journal of the Minnesota Futurists; teaching a course on Business, Government, and Society in the Business School, University of Minnesota.

Publications: *Celebrate the Earth* (Augsburg, 1971); co-author, *Urban Problems and Techniques No. 2* (Chandler-Davis, 1970).

INGELSTAM, LARS E.
Director
Secretariat for Future Studies
P.O. Box 7502
S-10392, Stockholm, Sweden

Born: 1937, Uppsala, Sweden

Telephone: (08) 7631000

Profession: Research director; mathematician

Field of specialization: Future studies for political decision-making.

Education: M. Eng., Applied Physics, 1959, Ph.D., Mathematics, 1964, Royal Institute of Technology; M.Sc., Mathematics, University of Stockholm, 1960.

Professional employment: Secretariat for Future Studies: Director (1973-). Research Group for Planning Theory: Director (1969). Royal Institute of Technology: Associate Professor of Mathematics (1966).

Professional activities: Director of the Secretariat for Future Studies, a unit set up by the government (1973-); has conducted research in mathematics and planning theory.

Publications: Editor, *To Choose a Future* (Ministry of Foreign Affairs, Secretariat for Future Studies, 1972); "Systems Structure and Future Trends in a Long Term Environmental Study" (*Systems Engineering*, Vol. 3, No. 1, Summer 1972); "Zukunftsmoglichkeiten fur Organisation und Planung" *["Future Possibilities for Organization and Planning"]* in *Zeitschrift fur Zukunftsforschung* (Hanser, Verlag, Heft 2, 1971); co-author, "Air Pollution Across National Boundaries: The Impact on the Environment of Sulfur in Air and Precipitation," Sweden's case study for the United Nations conference on the human environment (Royal Ministry for Foreign Affairs/Royal Ministry of Agriculture, 1971); "Some Aspects of Long-Range Planning and Future Studies in Sweden" in *Forward Planning in the Service Sectors* (MacMillan, London, 1975).

IYENGAR, MADHUR SRINIVAS

Born: 1922, Hyderabad, Andhra Pradesh, India

Managing Director
M. S. Iyengar and Associates, Ltd.
13/15 Multistoreyed Building
N. P. L. Colony, Post Office Box 2817
New Delhi, 110060, India

Telephone: 584018

Profession: System and Engineering Consultant

Field of specialization: Science policy; technology assessment; futurology; industrial development.

Education: M.Sc., Organic Chemistry, Osmania University, India, 1944; Ph.D., Chemical Engineering, Leeds, 1948.

Professional employment: M. S. Iyengar and Associates, Ltd.: Managing Director (1974-). Regional Research Laboratory, Jorhat, Assam, India: Director (1964-73). Ministry of Defense: Director of Special Duty (1962-64). Central Fuel Research Institute, Jealgora, India: Assistant Director (1953-62). Regional Research Laboratory, Hyderabad, India: Scientist (1949-53).

Professional activities: Currently working on a project for India on "Alternative Model for Growth" for the Futurology Panel on Food Policies; has lectured and written extensively on social implications of science and technology, technology assessment and technology of future; Member, Scientific Council, World Future Studies Federation; likely to be associated with the "Society in Transformation" project of The Club of Rome; working on "Long-Term Food Policy Options"—a project sponsored by the Futurology Panel of the Department of Science and Technology.

Publications: "Can We Invent the Future?" (*Hindustan Times*, 1970); "Can We Transform Into a Post-Industrial Society?" (THE FUTURIST and Random House, New York, 1972); "Can Countries of the Third World Transform into a Post-Industrial Society?"(Paper presented at the Rome Special Conference on the Future, 1973); "Technology Assessment and Its Relevance to the Developing Countries" (Paper presented at the First International Conference on Technology Assessment, The Hague, 1973); "The Challenge of Our Time" (Paper presented at the Special Conference in Berlin by the World Future Studies Federation, 1975).

JACCACI, AUGUST T., JR.

Born: 1937, New York, New York, U.S.A.

President
Interrobang Ideas, Inc.
Common Street
Groton, Massachusetts 01450, U.S.A.

Telephone: (617) 448-5091

Profession: Social architect; educator

Field of specialization: General systems theory; cosmological modeling; learning environments; media; art; experimental future-oriented cultural-political events; consulting on General Systemic Growth Theory; T.V., film and conference producing and directing.

Education: A.B., English, Harvard College, 1960; M.A.T., English, Harvard Graduate School of Education, 1964; M.F.A., Painting, Rhode Island School of Design, 1965.

Professional employment: Interrobang Ideas, Inc.: President (1977-). Lawrence Academy: Director, Alternative School and Futures Project (1976-77). Boston College: Assistant to the President, Honors Instructor, Director of the Film Program (1969-76). Phillips Academy: Art Instructor, Coach (1965-69). Rhode Island School of Design: English Instructor, Admissions Assistant (1963-65). Harvard College: Admissions Officer, Coach, Proctor (1961-63).

Professional activities: Currently writing *Social Architecture and the Future* on the social use of the emerging beyong-light-speed paradigm of consciousness and cosmology; organized and hosted The First World Congress of the New Age in Florence, Italy, February 1978; organized the "Lawrence Project: Education for the Future" at Lawrence Academy (1976-77); President, World Future Society, Boston-Cambridge Chapter (1975); initiator and organizing coordinator of "Town Meeting on the Future" a Massachusetts Bicentennial event on WGBH—TV (April 20-21, 1975); initiator of the GENESA SYNCON on "The Future of Television" on WGBH—TV (1974); organizer and host of the 1970 "World Game Seminar" with R. Buckminster Fuller at Boston College; recently completed a film for television and general distribution *The Human Race.*

Publications: Editor, "Warrant Articles" from "Town Meeting of the Future" (*Massachusetts Bicentennial News* Supplement, 1975); "Lawrence Project Report" (privately published, 1977).

JACKSON, RAY W.   **Born:** 1921, Toronto, Ontario, Canada
Science Adviser
Science Council of Canada
100 Metcalfe Street
Ottawa, Ontario, Canada KIA ON2   **Telephone:**   (613) 992-9901

Profession: Physicist

Field of specialization: Science policy; futures scanning; goals and values; conserver society and development.

Education: B.A. Sc., Engineering Physics, University of Toronto, 1944; Ph.D., Nuclear Physics, McGill University, 1950; Phil. of Science, Yale University, 1952.

Professional employment: Science Council of Canada: Science Adviser (1969-). Privy Council Office, Government of Canada: Science Adviser (1966-69). McMaster University: Visiting Professor (1964-65). RCA Montreal: Laboratory Director (1956-66). Sprague Electric Company: Senior Engineer (1954-56).

Professional activities: Engaged in study "The Implications of a Conserver Society" (1974-78); staff function of future scanning and program planning, involving early identification in the interaction of science and technology with society.

Publications: Co-author, "A Nuclear Dialogue" (Science Council of Canada, 1978); *Human Goals and Science Policy* (Science Council of Canada, May 1976); co-author, *Projections of R and D Manpower and Expenditure* (Science Council of Canada, 1969); co-author, "The Rationalization of University Research" (*Issues in Science Policy,* 1974); "A New Model of The University" (*Science Forum,* 1973); "Technology Assessment: Seen from the Smaller Country," Chapter 8 in Cetron and Bartocha, eds., *Technology Assessment in a Dynamic Environment* (1973).

JAHODA, MARIE   **Born:** 1907, Vienna, Austria
Senior Research Consultant
Science Policy Research Unit
University of Sussex
Falmer, Brighton, England   **Telephone:**   Brighton 686758

Profession: Social psychologist

Field of specialization: Interdisciplinary approaches to forecasting.

Education: D. Phil., Psychology, University of Vienna, 1932.

Professional employment: University of Sussex, Science Policy Research Unit: Senior Research Consultant (1972-); Professor of Social Psychology (1965-73). Brunel University: Professor of Psychology (1958-65). New York University: Professor of Social Psychology (1949-58). Columbia University: Research Fellow (1947-49).

Professional activities: Coordinator of interdisciplinary team at Science Policy Research Unit (1971-); research and teaching (1932-73).

Publications: Editor, *Thinking About the Future* (Sussex University Press, 1973); *The Art of Anticipation* (Martin Robertson, 1975); co-editor and contributor, *World Futures: The Great Debate* (Martin Robertson, 1978, Universe Books, 1978); "Technicalities and Fantasy About Men and Women" (*Futures*, 1975); *Freud and the Dilemmas of Psychology* (Hogarth Press, 1977).

JANNE, HENRI GUSTAVE   **Born:** 1908, Brussels, Belgium
Chairman
Institut de Sociologia
Universite de Bruxelles
44 Avenue Jeanne
1050 Brussels, Belgium   **Telephone:** 6488158

Profession: Sociologist (Methodology and Sociology of Education)

Field of specialization: Research on education matters; value systems; models of global society.

Education: Ph.D., Rationalistic Origins, Faculty of Philosophy and Literature, University of Brussels, 1932.

Professional employment: Universite de Bruxelles: Honorary Professor (1978-); promoter for research projects (1949-); Professor (1949-78); Rector (1955-59); Chairman of the Scientific College, Institute of Sociology (1960-). Services of Prime Minister: Director General for Economic Coordination (1947-49); Minister of Education and Culture (1963-65); Member of Senate (1961-65).

Professional activities: Courses on sociology, social stratification; research on education matters; Director, Inspector General, and Director General in Social and Economic Administration of the State (1936-49); member, Belgian Royal Academy for Sciences, Literature and Fine Arts (President, 1974); Member of the Board, International Council for Educational Development, New York; corresponding member of the Institut de France, Paris.

Publications: *Le systeme social—Essai de theorie general [The Social System: An Essay in General Theory]* (Institute of Sociology, Brussels, 1968); *Le temps du changement [The Time of Change]* (Marabout Universite, 1971); co-editor, *L'education creatrice [Creative Education]* (Fondation Europeenne de la Culture, 1975); co-author, *Report on the Needs of the Youngsters of 16-19 Age Group* (for the Council of European Ministers of Education at Bern, 1973).

JANTSCH, ERICH   **Born:** Austria
Center for Research in Management Science
University of California
Berkeley, California 94720, U.S.A.   **Telephone:** —

Profession: Academic-at-large

Field of specialization: Self-organization paradigm; theory of evolution; dynamic system theory.

Education: Ph.D., Astrophysics, University of Vienna, 1951.

Professional employment: Visiting Professor: University of Bielefeld, Germany; University of Kassel, Germany; Technical University of Hannover, Germany; Technical University of Denmark; University of Lund, Sweden; University of Paris; Graduate School of Economic and Social Sciences, St. Gall, Switzerland; Institute of Advanced Studies, Vienna, Austria; Portland State University, Portland, Oregon.

Professional activities: Research in self-organization; seminars at various universities; seminars for government and business executives; course at the Wright Institute, Berkeley, California.

246

Publications: *The Self-Organizing Universe: Scientific and Human Implications of the Emerging Paradigm of Evolution* (Pergamon Press, Oxford and New York, forthcoming in 1979); co-editor with C.H. Waddington, *Evolution and Consciousness: Human Systems in Transition* (Addison-Wesley, Reading, Massachusetts, 1976); *Technological Planning and Social Futures* (ABP, London; Halsted Press, New York, 1974); editor, *Perspectives of Planning* (OECD, Paris, 1969); *Technological Forecasting in Perspective* (OECD, Paris, 1967); *Design for Evolution: Self-organization and Planning in the Life of Human Systems* (Braziller, New York, 1975).

JAUMIN-PONSAR, ANNE MARIE

Born: 1939, Brasschaat, Belgium

Associate Professor
Catholic University of Louvain
Unite Riap
1 Place Montesquieu
1348 Louvain-La-Neuve, Belgium

Telephone: (10) 418181, extension 4124

Profession: Policy analyst

Field of specialization: Governmental decision-making; social indicators; women's studies.

Education: Doctorate in Law and Doctorate in Political Science, University of Louvain; Master's Degree, Political Science, University of Wisconsin-Madison.

Professional employment: Catholic University of Louvain: Associate Professor (1973-); Assistant Professor (1968-70). Barrister (1964-68).

Professional activities: Presently teaching "Theories of Organizations in the Public Sector"; working on decision-making process of Belgian Government and studies on the status of women in Western Europe; Fellow, University of Wisconsin (1970-71).

Publications: *La policy science: une nouvelle ecole de la decision publique [Policy Science: A New School of Public Decision Making]* (1975); "Une nouvelle ecole en science administrative: la policy science" *["A New School of Administrative Science: Policy Science"] (Revue internationale des sciences administratives*, 1975); "Methodes et institutions administratives pour prevoir les effets de l'augment economique" *["Administrative Methods and Institutions to Forecast the Effects of Economic Growth"]*; "The Policy Science as an Alternative to the Heterogeneity of Social Sciences" in *Human Needs, New Societies, Supporting Technologies* (Rome, 1973).

JOHANSEN, ROBERT R.

Born: 1945, Geneva, Illinois, U.S.A.

Senior Research Fellow
The Institute for the Future
2740 Sand Hill Road
Menlo Park, California 94025, U.S.A,

Telephone: (415) 854-6322

Profession: Social scientist

Field of specialization: Social evaluation of teleconferencing systems; educational futures; futures methodology; religion and value systems.

Education: B.S., Commerce, University of Illinois, 1967; M.Div., Religion and Social Change, Crozer Theological Seminary, 1970; Ph.D., Sociology of Religion, Northwestern University, 1972.

Professional employment: The Institute for the Future: Senior Research Fellow (1973-). Upsala College: Assistant Professor of Sociology (1972-73). Garrett Theological Seminary: Director, Curriculum Evaluation Project (1970-72). Crozer/Martin Luther King School: Teaching Assistant (1969-70).

Professional activities: Research on social evaluation of computer conferencing (1973-), analysis of societal developments affecting education (1975-), future impacts of electronic media for group communication (1976-), evaluation of the use of computer conferencing for expert interaction for the National Science Foundation (1973-75), applications of futures research in education for Lilly Endowment, Inc. (1974-75), and developing a future-oriented evaluation process in a graduate school curriculum (1970-72); periodic teaching, lectures, workshops, primarily relating to future studies and communications.

Publications: Co-author, *Electronic Meetings: Technical Alternatives and Social Choices* (Addison-Wesley, Reading, Massachusetts, 1978); co-author, *Group Communication through Computers: Prag-*

matics and Dynamics (Institute for the Future, Final Report to National Science Foundation, October 1975); "Pitfalls in the Social Evaluation of Teleconferencing Media, "*The Telephone in Education* (University of Wisconsin Extension Press, 1976); co-author, "Mapping Views of the Future in a Small Group" (*Futures,* April 1976); co-author, "Group Communication through Electronic Media" (*Educational Technology,* August 1974; reprinted in *The Delphi Method,* Turoff and Linstone, editors).

JOHNSTON, DENIS F.   **Born:** 1924, Calgary, Canada
Senior Advisor on Social Indicators
Social Indicators Office
Bureau of the Census
Room 3442, FB 3
Washington, D.C. 20233, U.S.A.   **Telephone:** (301) 763-5145

Profession: Sociologist, statistician

Field of specialization: Social indicators, forecasting methods, social accounts.

Education: B.A., Social Institutions, University of California, 1947; M.A., Sociology, University of Oregon, 1950; M.A., Social Relations, Harvard University, 1952; Ph.D., Sociology, The American University, 1961.

Professional employment: Bureau of the Census: Senior Advisor on Social Indicators (1978-). Office of Management and Budget, Statistical Policy Division: Director, Social Indicators Project (1974-78). Department of Labor, Bureau of Labor Statistics: Senior Demographic Statistician (1969-74); Director, Office of Special Studies (1968-69). President's Commission on Income Maintenance Programs (1968-69). Georgetown University: Department of Sociology, Professional Lecturer (part-time, 1970-). Organization for Economic Cooperation and Development, Paris: U.S. Representative to Working Party on Social Indicators (1974-).

Professional activities: Preparing the third comprehensive United States social indicators report, due in 1980; course director, American Association for the Advancement of Science Chautauqua Short Course for College Teachers, on social indicators; teaching a spring semester 1979 course on social indicators at Georgetown University; consultant to the United Nations Economic and Social Commission for Asia and the Pacific (ESCAP) in September-October 1978, attended an Expert Group meeting in Manila, and presented a background paper, "Data Requirements for a System of Social Indicators in the areas of Income, Health, and Education."

Publications: "Social Indicators and Social Forecasting" in *Handbook of Futures Research,* Jib Fowles, ed. (Greenwood Press, 1978); editor, *Social Indicators 1976* (U.S. Government Printing Office, issued by Department of Commerce, 1977) *An Analysis of Sources of Information on the Population of the Navajo* (Smithsonian Institution, Bureau of American Ethnology, 1966); "Social Indicators and Social Forecasting" *(Cahiers du Centre de Recherches Science et Vie,* September 1971); "Forecasting Methods in the Social Sciences" in *Political Science and the Study of the Future,* Albert Somit, ed. (The Dryden Press, 1974); "The U.S. Labor Force: Projections to 1990" (U.S. Government Printing Office, *BLS Special Labor Force Report,* No. 156, 1973); "Basic Disaggregations of Main Social Indicators" (OECD Social Indicators Development Programme, Special Studies No. 4, 1977).

JONES, J. CHRISTOPHER   **Born:** 1927, Aberystwyth Wales, United Kingdom
Y Sylfaen Graig Ddychmygol-The Imaginary Rock Foundation
173 Walm Lane
London NW2 3AY, United Kingdom   **Telephone:** 01 450 4270

Profession: Non-specialist
Education: Various colleges and universities; studied engineering, art, and design.

Field of specialization: Non-specialist interested in industrial life and experimental arts.

Professional employment: Industrial design, ergonomics, teaching generalist design, futures research (1950-75). Since then free-lance lecturing and writing.

Professional activities: Free-lance lecturing and writing; publishing essays, plays, etc., as facsimile texts and microtexts (Jones Family Editions, London).

Publications: *Writings Remembered: A Review of Writings Past and Thoughts Present 1950-76* (Jones Family Editions, London 1976); *Design Methods: Seeds of Human Futures* (John Wiley and Sons, 1970); "Automation and

248

Design" (*Design*, 103, 104, 106, 108, 110, 1957-58); "Professions as Inhibitors of Socio-Technical Evolution" (*Futures*, March 1970); "Superman Has Had His Day," a play (Rome Special Conference on Future, Irades, 1973); several contributions of fiction to recent futures conferences.

JONES, MARTIN V.
President
Impact Assessment Institute
5400 Linden Court
Bethesda, Maryland 20014, U.S.A.

Born: 1918, La Salle, Illinois, U.S.A.

Telephone: (301) 530-0359

Profession: Economist

Field of specialization: Technology assessment; impact analysis; program evaluation.

Education: A.B., 1939, M.B.A., 1940, School of Business Administration, Ph.D., Economics, 1944, University of Chicago.

Professional employment: Impact Assessment Institute: President (1973-). Mitre Corporation: Member of Technical Staff (1960-69, 1970-73). Urban Institute: Senior Research Associate (1969-70). Several Federal Agencies: Economist (1944-60).

Professional activities: Currently working on several projects involving energy research, weather modification, and technology assessment methodology; Member of the American Economic Association, International Society for Technology Assessment, World Future Society, American Association for Advancement of Science, American Academy of Political and Social Science, and the Institute of Society, Ethics, and Life Sciences.

Publications: Co-author, *Twenty-Five National Science Foundation Technology Assessment Studies: An Analytical Bibliography* (Impact Assessment Institute, 1977); *A Technology Assessment Methodology: Some Basic Propositions* (Mitre Corporation, 1971); co-author, *Scientific Earthquake Prediction* (Impact Assessment Institute, 1975); *Generating Social Impact Scenarios, A Planning Tool for Meeting the Nation's Energy Needs* (Mitre Corporation, 1972); co-author, *Diagnostic Motor Vehicle Inspection: Potential, Indirect, Societal Impacts* (Impact Assessment Institute, 1975).

JONES, PETER MICHAEL SEATON
Head, Economics and Programmes Branch
United Kingdom Atomic Energy Authority
11 Charles II Street
London S W 1, United Kingdom

Born: 1932, Cardiff, South Wales

Telephone: (01) 930-5454 Ext. 576

Profession: Scientist, technical economist

Field of specialization: Energy demand and social and economic implications of alternative energy systems.

Education: B.Sc., Chemistry-Physics, 1953, Ph.D., Chemistry, 1956, Cardiff University.

Professional employment: United Kingdom Atomic Energy Authority: Head, Economics and Programmes Branch (1977-); Scientist (1956-67). Programmes Analysis Unit: Director (1972-77); Group Leader (1967-72).

Professional activities: Head of a team looking at current and future energy requirements and their implications.

Publications: Co-author, "One Organisation's Experience" in *Futures Research* (Addison-Wesley Publishing Co., 1977); "Basis for Selectivity in R and D" (*Chemistry and Industry*, 1975); co-author and editor, *Collected Essays by Programmes Analysis Unit Authors* (HMSD, London, 1974); co-author and editor, *An Economic and Technical Appraisal of Air Pollution in the U.K.* (HMSD, London, 1972); "Lessons from the Objective Appraisal of Programmes at the National Level" (*Research Policy*, 1971).

JONES, THOMAS EVAN

Adjunct Associate Professor
Polytechnic Institute of New York
Graduate School of Management
333 Jay Street
Brooklyn, New York 11201, U.S.A.

Born: 1937, Kenosha, Wisconsin, U.S.A.

Telephone: —

Profession: Professor; writer; lecturer; consultant

Field of specialization: The growth controversy; value-impact forecasting; future-oriented, comparative historical analysis of socio-cultural processes; comparative evaluation of forecasts in terms of their assumptions.

Education: B.A., Philosophy, Wheaton College, 1954, M.A., Philosophy, Harvard University, 1963; Ph.D., Philosophy, Johns Hopkins University, 1964; M.A., Theology, Wheaton Graduate School, 1965; D.S.Sc., Sociology, New School for Social Research, 1975.

Professional employment: Polytechnic Institute of New York, Graduate School of Management: Adjunct Associate Professor (1976-78). New School for Social Research, Futuristics Department: Member of the Faculty (1976-78). U.N. Institute for Training and Research: Research Fellow (1975-76).

Professional activities: Consultant, revision of the U.N. *World Plan of Action;* conducted and reported on a Delphi study for the Public Relations Society of America conference (1978); writing four future-oriented books: *Options for the Future* (a comparative analysis of forecasts), *Alternative Futures: Choice Among Possible Tomorrows* (co-authored by F. John Pessolano), *Global Goals for an Interdependent World,* and *Toward a Future of Selective Growth* (an analysis of the growth controversy, co-authored by James Martin and Anthony Wiener); finalist, Mitchell Prize international essay contest (1977); member, Core Group, Goals for Global Society Project, Club of Rome (1975-76); New York City Chapter of the World Future Society, Vice-President (1972-73), Board of Directors (1974-78).

Publications: "Current Prospects of Sustainable Economic Growth" in *Goals in a Global Community* (Vol. 1, Pergamon, 1977); co-author, with M. Washburn, "Anchoring Futures in Preferences" in Nazli Choucri and T. Robinson; editors, *Forecasting in International Relations* (W.H. Freeman and Company, August 1978); "Toward a Future of Selective Growth" in *The Next 25 Years: Crisis and Opportunity,* Spekke, ed., (World Future Society, 1975); "Outmoded Aspirations" (volume of the Fourth International Conference on the Unity of the Sciences, 1976); "Kahn and Wiener's 'Post-Industrial Culture'" (*Philosophy Forum,* special issue, 1977).

JOSEPH, EARL C.

Staff Scientist-Futurist
Sperry Univac-U2L28
P.O. Box 3525
St. Paul, Minnesota 55165, U.S.A.

Born: 1926, St. Paul, Minnesota, U.S.A.

Telephone: (612) 456-2395

Profession: Staff scientist, futurist

Field of specialization: Technology forecasting; future value systems; societal futures; futurics methodology; all-win futures; educational futures; basic futures research; computer futures; agricultural futures; medical futures.

Education: B.A., Math-Physics, University of Minnesota, 1951.

Professional employment: Sperry Univac: Staff Scientist-Futurist (1951-).

Professional activities: Director, Minnesota Futurists, a chapter of the World Future Society (1968-); visiting lecturer, University of Minnesota in Future Studies (1970-); basic futures research and long-range planning at Sperry Univac (1963-); futurist-in-residence at Science Museum of Minnesota (1973-); published over 100 papers and chapters in 20 books (1958-); distinguished lecturer for the Institute for Electrical and Electronic Engineers Computer Society (1975-); three computer patents; system architect of five major computer systems (1957-63); General Chairman for ACM (1975).

Publications: "An Introduction to Studying the Future" in *Futurism in Education* (McCutchan Publishing Corporation, 1974); co-author, "Some Projections" in *Future Alternatives for Industrial Arts* (McKnight, 1976); "Forecasts and Trends Pointing to Future Computer Systems" (*Technology Trends*, IEEE, 1975); "What Is Future Time?" (THE FUTURIST, August 1974).

JUDGE, ANTHONY JOHN
Assistant Secretary-General
Union of International Associations
1 rue aux Laines
1000 Brussels, Belgium

Born: 1940, Port Said, Egypt

Telephone: 511 83 96

Profession: "Appropriate label not yet discovered."

Field of specialization: Transnational (non-governmental) association, facilitative information systems, value systems, interdisciplinary approaches, human development concepts; networks of organizations, concepts, world problems; problems of registering networks, analyzing them as structures, and representing them in a comprehensible manner; implications of polyhedral and tensegrity structures as a basis for alternative forms of conceptual and human organization; interrelating incompatible viewpoints; tensed networks.

Education: Chemical Engineering, Imperial College of Science and Technology (1961, no degree); M.B.A. program, University of Cape Town, 1967.

Professional employment: Development of information system for *Yearbook of World Problems and Human Potential* and for *Yearbook of International Organizations.* Union of International Associations: Assistant Secretary-General (1970-); Editor (1962-). Mankind 2000: Projects Director (1973-).

Professional activities: Member, World Future Studies Federation; member, International Foundation for Social Innovation; consultant, Commonwealth Science Council; member, Society for General Systems Research, International Studies Association, Committee on Conceptual and Terminological Analysis (IPSA); writes extensively on networks and their representation and facilitation.

Publications: Editor, *Yearbook of World Problems and Human Potential* (Mankind 2000 and Union of International Associations, 1976); co-editor, *Yearbook of International Organizations* (Union of International Associations, 1978); "Transcending Duality Through Tensional Integrity" *(Transnational Associations,* 1978); "Representation, Comprehension and Communication of Sets: The Role of Number" *(International Classification,* 1978).

JUNGK, ROBERT
Technical University
Kurfuerstendamn 196
Berlin, Federal Republic of Germany

Born: 1913, Berlin Germany

Zentrum Berlin fur Zukunftsforschung
  Berlin Center for Futures Research
Giesebrechstrasse 15
D1 Berlin 15
Federal Republic of Germany

(home) Steingasse 31
A 5020 Salzburg, Austria

Telephone: (6222) 75127

Profession: Writer; Professor of Planning Sciences

Field of specialization: Citizen participation in futures design and planning; cultural forecasting.

Education: Ph.D., Modern History, University of Berlin, 1944 (also attended from 1932-33); University of Zurich, 1938-44.

Professional employment: Freelance writer and researcher.

Professional activities: Currently working on a book on social innovation; teaching course on "The Future of Democratic Institutions" (November-December, 1976); preparing book on "The New Tower of Babel," bridging the semantic gap between academia and the public. "Only a small part of my effort has resulted in publications, institutional appointments, and professional positions. The many personal contacts I have had all over the world, and my work for the organization of the first and following World Future Research Conferences (Oslo 1967, Kyoto 1970, Bucharest 1972, Rome 1973, Dubrovnik 1976) have been more central to my activities."

Publications: *Tomorrow is Already Here* (Simon and Schuster, New York, 1954, in German, 1952); *Brighter than a Thousand Suns* (Harcourt Brace, New York, 1958, in German, 1956); *Der Jahrau-*

sendmensch [Project Everyman]; The New Tyranny (Grosset and Dunlap, 1979); currently working on a book, *The Reformation of Science.*

JUPP, GEORGE ALEXANDER
Vice President, Public Affairs
The Molson Companies Limited
P.O. Box 6015
Toronto, A.M.F., Ontario
L5P 1B8 Canada

Born: 1927, Arcola, Saskatchewan, Canada

Telephone: (416) 675-5500

Profession: Corporate vice president and university teacher

Field of specialization: Futures education; alternative futures; futures methodology.

Education: B.A., Political Science and History, University of Saskatchewan, 1964; M.A., Sociology, University of Calgary, 1969.

Professional employment: Molson Companies: Vice President, Public Affairs (1964-). York University: Instructor (1972-). Sir George Williams University: Instructor (1970-71). University of Calgary (1964-69).

Professional activities: Taught a class in "Futurology" at York University (1973-78); lectures and papers to seminars on the future to various groups (1973-78); in process of establishing an environmental monitoring system within The Molson Companies, with particular regard to Canada 1981-1996.

Publications: —

KADE, GERHARD PAUL
Professor
Technical University Darmstadt
Schloss
Darmstadt, Federal Republic of Germany

Born: 1931, Berlin, Germany

Telephone: 06151/162095

Profession: Economist

Field of specialization: Futures methodology; environmental planning; long-term projections; energy research.

Education: Ph.D., Economics, Free University of Berlin, 1957.

Professional employment: Technical University Darmstadt: Professor (1966-). Free University of Berlin: Assistant Professor (1961-66).

Professional activities: Consultant to Organization for Economic Cooperation and Development, Paris (1960-76); consultant to several governments in developing countries and to private firms; Vice-President of the International Institute for Peace, Vienna.

Publications: "The Economics of Pollution and the Interdisciplinary Approach to Environmental Planning" (*International Social Science Journal*, 1970); "Kernenergie, Elektrizitat und Umwelt" *["Nuclear Power, Electricity and Environment"]* (*Blatter fur Deutsche und Internationale Politik [Journal of German and International Politics]*, 1971); co-author, "Estudio Socio-economico de Andalucia" *["Socio-Economic Studies in Andalusia"]* (Madrid, 1971); "On Some Fundamental Problems in the Analysis of Global Civilization" (*Peace and the Sciences*, 1974); "Krise des Kapitalismus" *["Crisis of Capitalism"]* (*Wirtschaftsdienst [Economic Service]*, 1976).

KAHN, HERMAN
Director
Hudson Institute
Quaker Ridge Road
Croton-on-Hudson, New York 10520, U.S.A.

Born: 1922, Bayonne, New Jersey, U.S.A.

Telephone: (914) 762-0700

Profession: Director of Research

Field of specialization: Physicist; specialist in public policy analyses; futurologist; long-term cultural, economic, political and technological change.

Education: B.A., Physics and Mathematics, University of California-Los Angeles, 1945; M.A., Physics, California Institute of Technology, 1948.

Professional employment: The Hudson Institute: Founder and Director (1961-). The Rand Corporation, Santa Monica, California: Research Analyst, Physics Division (1948-61).

Professional activities: Member, Center for Inter-American Affairs and Council on Foreign Relations; currently leading Hudson Institute studies on Corporate Environment Program and Prospects for Mankind; consultant, White House and Department of State.

Publications: *World Economic Development* (Westview Press, forthcoming 1979); co-author, with Thomas Pepper, *The Japanese Challenge* (Crowell, forthcoming 1979); *On Thermonuclear War* (Princeton University Press, 1960); *Thinking About the Unthinkable* (Horizon Press, 1962); *On Escalation: Metaphors and Scenarios* (Frederick A. Praeger, 1965); co-author, *The Year 2000* (The Macmillan Company, New York, 1967); co-author, *Can We Win in Vietnam?* (Praeger, 1968); *The Emerging Japanese Superstate* (Prentice-Hall, 1970); co-author, *Things to Come* (The Macmillan Company, 1972); editor, *The Future of the Corporation* (Mason and Lipscomb, 1974); co-author, *The Next 200 Years* (William Morrow and Company, May 1976).

KANAMORI, HISAO

Born: 1924, Tokyo, Japan

President
The Japan Economic Research Center
Nikkei Building, Number 9-5
Ohtemachi 1-chome
Chiyoda-ku, Tokyo, 100 Japan

Telephone: (03) 270-5543

Profession: Economist

Field of specialization: Economic forecasting

Education: Political Science, Faculty of Law, Tokyo University, 1948; Nuffield College, Oxford University, 1958-60.

Professional employment: The Japan Economic Research Center: President (1973-); Chief Economist (1967-70). The Economic Planning Agency: (1953-73); Chief, Domestic Economic Research Division (1964-67); Deputy Director, The Economic Research Institute (1970-73). The Ministry of International Trade and Industry (1948).

Professional activities: Member of BEISHIN (Rice Council, 1973-); member, Higher Education Council, Ministry of Education (1973-); wrote an economic survey of Japan for the Economic Planning Agency, Japan Government (1964-66).

Publications: Editor, *The Future of the World Economy and Japan* (Japan Economic Research Center, 1975); co-author, *The Future of the Japanese Economy and its Primary Commodity Requirements* (Japan Economic Research Center, 1975); *A Powerful Sun* (in Japanese, Diamond Inc., 1968); "A New Dimension of the Japanese Economy" (in Japanese, *Japan Economic Journal*, 1972); "The Future Prospects for the Japanese Economy" (in Japanese, *Japan Economic Journal*, 1973).

KANE, JULIUS

Born: 1935, Vorozenh, Russia

Professor of Mathematical Ecology
Institute of Resource Ecology
University of British Columbia, Hut B-8
Vancouver, British Columbia, Canada

Telephone: (604) 228-2080

Profession: Professor of Mathematical Ecology

Field of specialization: Environmental policy and manpower planning; future methodology.

Education: B.A., Physics, Brooklyn College, 1954; Ph.D., Mathematics, Courant Institute, New York University, 1960.

Professional employment: University of British Columbia: Professor of Mathematics/Zoology/Ecology (1968-). University of California-Los Angeles: Research Professor of Space Science (1965-68). California Institute of Technology: Associate Professor of Geophysics (1964-65). University of Rhode Island: Professor of Mathematics and Electrical Engineering (1960-65).

Professional activities: Developing interactive computer languages for structural analysis and policy decisions; consulting for U.S. and Canadian governments on environmental policy and manpower planning; design of alternative social systems; Senior Member, Institute for Electrical and Electronic Engineers (1960-); Sigma Xi (1960-).

Publications: "KSIM, Methodology for Resource Policy Simulation" (*Water Resources Research*, February 1973); "KSIM Primer in Delphi Method," ed. Linstone (Addison Wesley, 1975); "Dynamics of Peter Principle" (*Management Science*, 1970); "Health Care Delivery" (*Socio-Economic Planning Sciences*, 1972); "Hadamard Transform Image Coding" (*Proceedings IEEE*, 1969).

KAPUR, JAGDISH CHANDRA

Chairman
Danfoss (India) Limited
706-707 Surya Kiran
19 Kasturba Gandhi Marg
New Delhi 110001, India

Born: 1920, Lucknow, U.P., India

Telephone: 387422/387423

Profession: Technologist; futurist; industrial manager.

Field of specialization: Corporate planning; technology assessment; value systems; scenario-building.

Education: B.Sc., Mechanical Engineering, B.Sc., Electrical Engineering, Punjab University, India; M.S., Engineering, Cornell University; Post-Graduate Studies in Aeronautical Engineering, Indian Institute of Science, Bangalore.

Professional employment: Danfoss (India) Ltd.: Chairman (1977); Director (1966-). Kapcompany General, Ltd.: Chairman and Managing Director (1966-). Kapur Solar Farms: Founder and Proprietor (1963-).

Professional activities: Research and development work in solar energy technology and applications to meet the needs of rural development; has published numerous articles, reports, and studies on a wide diversity of subjects including climate and man, intermediate technology, management of research and technology, industrial management, energy and solar energy and also technology transfer, future of electronics and rural development; member, Panel on Futurology and Technology Assessment, National Committee on Science and Technology; member, Scientific Advisory Committee, Tata Energy Research Institute, Bombay; member, Publications Committee, International Solar Energy Society (1978); member, Threshold Award Advisory Council (1978).

Publications: "Human Future: Eastern and Western Perspectives" (*Whole Earth Paper*, U.S.A., 1978); "Future of Man: Eastern and Western View" (*Futurology*, 1977); "India 2000 A.D.: Strategy for Rural Transformation" (*Journal of the Institution of Engineers*, India, 1977); *Culture for Intermediate Technology* (Intermediate Technology Development Group, London, 1978); *India 2000* (India International Centre, New Delhi, 1975); "Socio-Economic Consideration in the Utilization of Solar Energy in Developing Societies" (Keynote address at U.N. Conference, Rome, 1961).

KASSAS, MOHAMED A.F.

Professor of Applied Botany
Faculty of Science
University of Cairo
Cario, Egypt

Born: 1921, Borg-el-Borollos, Egypt

Telephone: —

Profession: Plant ecologist

Field of specialization: Desert ecology; environment and development; application of science to development.

Education: B.Sc., Honours, Botany, 1944, M.Sc., Plant Ecology, 1947, University of Cairo; Ph.D., Plant Ecology, University of Cambridge, 1950.

Professional employment: University of Cairo: Professor of Applied Botany (1965-); Assistant Professor (1956-64); Lecturer (1950-53). University of Khartoum: Professor (1964-68). National Research Centre, Cairo: Head of Ecology Research Unit (1959-64). Science Council of Egypt: Assistant Secretary General (1956-59). ALECSO: Assistant Director General (1972-76).

Professional activities: Current research and studies in desert and marsh ecology; Member, Egyptian Academy of Science; Member, Club of Rome; President, International Union for the Conservation of Nature; Member, British Ecological Society and the American Ecological Society.

Publications: "Plant Life in Deserts" in *Arid Lands*, E. S. Hills, ed. (Methuen and UNESCO, 1966); "Impact of River Control Schemes on the Shoreline of the Nile Delta" in *Careless Technology*, J. Milton and M. T. Farvar, eds. (1972); "Ecological Consequences of Water Development Projects" in *Environmental Future*, N. Polunin, ed. (1972); "The Units of a Desert Ecosystem" (*Journal of Ecology*, 52, 1964).

KAUFFMAN, DRAPER LAURENCE, JR.
7707 Charing Square
St. Louis, Missouri 63119, U.S.A.

Born: 1946, Washington, D.C., U.S.A.

Telephone: (314) 968-0500 x405

Profession: Futurist; author; business and education consultant

Field of specialization: Future-oriented education; forecasting methods; systems theory; the "limits" issue; computers/communications impact; business futures; long-range consumer demand assessment; product innovation.

Education: B.A., Long-Range Social Forecasting, Prescott College, 1971; Ed.D., Education Policy, University of Massachusetts, 1975.

Professional employment: Webster College: Director of Research, Environmental Education (1977-78); Assistant Professor of Social Sciences and Director, Future Studies MAT (1975-77). University of Massachusetts: Director, Future Studies Teacher Preparation Program (1972-75); Coordinator, Doctoral Futuristics Program (1971-73). Stanford Research Institute, Education Policy Research Center: Education Policy Analyst (1970 and 1971).

Professional activities: Received U.S. Department Health, Education, and Welfare grant in environmental education (1977-78); taught "Future Values in a Global Society," Maryville College (Spring 1978); developed graduate future studies program for in-service teachers (1975-77); conducted futures workshop for West Virginia Superintendent of Education and senior staff (Spring 1977); contributor to "Making Changes" curriculum, RBS, Inc. (1976-77).

Publications: *The Human Environment: An Introduction to Environmental Systems* (Webster College, 1978); "Making the Future Count in Your Classroom" (*Teacher*, April 1977); *Teaching the Future* (ETC Publications, Palm Springs, California, 1976); *Futurism and Future Studies* (National Education Association, Washington, D.C., 1976) "The Role of Futuristics in Education" in Allen and Hecht, *Controversies in Education* (W.B. Saunders, Philadelphia, 1974).

KAUFMANN, FELIX
President
Science for Business
1160 Pauline Blvd.
Ann Arbor, Michigan 48103, U.S.A. (313)

Born: 1918, Berlin, Germany

Telephone: (313) 663-3129

Profession: International business consultant

Field of specialization: Acquisitions, ventures, foreign operations, forecasting (economic, social, political, technological), trend analysis, planning, decision-making and decision theory, management science innovations, technology assessment, health care and health economics, training client personnel.

Education: B.Sc. (Honors), Physiology, Biochemistry, 1940, D.I.C., Industrial Chemistry, 1943, University of London; Management, British Institute of Management, 1949-52; Alexander Hamilton Institute, New York (1957-60).

Professional employment: Science for Business: President (1963-). The Bendix Corporation: Director, International Strategic Planning (1974-). Hoffman-La Roche: Manager, Corporate Planning (1965-71). The Hudson Institute: Director, Futures Program (1962-65). Kerr Italia, Sp.A.: President (1959-62). Kerr Manufacturing Company: Executive Vice President, Kerr International (1957-62).

Professional activities: Consultant to governments, multinational corporations, the United Nations, and non-profit organizations; has taught future-oriented faculty seminars and university courses; delivered papers at future conferences in the U.S., Japan and Bucharest.

Publications: "Man and Medicine in the Year 2000" in *Peoples of the World Encyclopedia* (The Danbury Press, 1973); *Decisions* and *Organizational Decisions* (Future Life Press, Washington, D.C., 1972); "The Strategic Decisionmakers" *(Innovation,* New York, 1971); "Decisionmaking, Eastern and Western Style" *(Business Horizons,* 1969); "World Government and the U.S. National Interest" (Hudson Institute, 1965); editor and co-author, *Hypercyogenics* (Plenum Press, New York, 1963) and *The 1965-75 Strategic Debate* (Hudson Institute, 1963).

KAYA, YOICHI

Born: 1934, Sapporo, Japan

Professor
Department of Electrical Engineering
University of Tokyo
Hongo, 7-3-1, Bunkyo-ku
Tokyo, Japan 113

Telephone: (03) 812-2111, Ext. 7540

Profession: Systems scientist

Field of specialization: Global modeling; modeling methodology of social systems; energy system analysis; technological forecasting.

Education: B.S., 1957, M.S., 1959, Ph.D., 1962, Electrical Engineering, University of Tokyo.

Professional employment: The University of Tokyo: Professor (1978); Associate Professor (1963; 1964-78); Lecturer (1962). Massachusetts Institute of Technology: Instructor (1963-64).

Professional activities: Leader, Project FUGI (Future of Global Interdependence), a global modeling project; member, The Club of Rome; leader, study group on integrated social policy; leader, study group on long-range technological forecasting.

Publications: *Automatic Control Engineering* (Kyoritsu Publishing Company, 1970); "Global Constraints and a New Vision for Development" *(Technological Forecasting and Social Change,* Vol. 6, 1974); *Future of Global Interdependence* (5th Global Modeling Conference of the International Institute of Applied Systems Analysis, 1977); *Probability and Statistics* (Iwanami Publishing Company, 1978).

KELLER, SUZANNE

Born: 1932, Vienna, Austria

Professor
Department of Sociology and School of Architecture
Princeton University
Princeton, New Jersey 08540, U.S.A.

Telephone: (609) 452-4531

Profession: Sociologist

Field of specialization: Social architecture; family and sex roles; social stratification and elites.

Education: A.B., Literature and Physiology, Hunter College, 1950; Ph.D., Sociology, Columbia University, 1953.

Professional employment: Princeton University: Professor, Department of Sociology and School of Architecture (1968-). Athens Center of Ekistics, Greece: Research Associate (1964-68). Vassar College: Associate Professor (1961-62). Brandeis University: Assistant Professor (1957-60). New York Medical College: Research Associate (1960-61).

Professional activities: Research on a planned community (1973-76); teaching, public lectures, consulting, and extensive writing; Vice President, American Sociological Association (1976).

Publications: *Beyond the Ruling Class* (Random House, 1963); *The Urban Neighborhood* (Random House, 1968); co-author, *Sociology, A Text* (Random House, 1975); *Male and Female: A Sociological View* (A General Learning Corporation Module, 1975); "Does the Family Have a Future?"(*Journal of Comparative Family Studies*, Spring, 1971).

KELTY, MIRIAM FRIEDMAN
Psychologist
Commission for the Protection of Human Subjects
of Biomedical and Behavioral Research
5333 Westbard Avenue, Room 125
Bethesda, Maryland 20016, U.S.A.

Born: 1938, New York, New York, U.S.A.

Telephone: (301) 496-7526

Profession: Psychologist

Field of specialization: Health technology assessment; human services planning; values; future of health; health behavior; science policy.

Education: Psychology, Antioch College, University of Paris; B.A., 1960, M.A., 1962, Psychology, The City College of New York; Ph.D., Psychology and Psychobiology, Rutgers University, 1965.

Professional employment: National Commission for Protection of Research Subjects: Psychologist (1974-). American Psychological Association: Administrative Officer for Scientific Affairs (1970-74). National Institute of Mental Health: Psychologist (1968-70). Harvard School of Public Health: Research Fellow (1966-68). Boston Veterans Administration Hospital: Psychologist (1968). The City College of New York: Lecturer in Psychology (1962-65).

Professional activities: Currently working for a Congressionally mandated Commission in the area of science policy, particularly ethical issues in health research and health services; Project Officer for a Comprehensive Study of the Implications of Advances in Biomedical and Behavioral Research and Technology (1974-); President-Elect, Division of Environmental and Population Psychology, American Psychological Association (1978-79); Executive Committee Member, Division of Psychologists in Public Service, American Psychological Association (1976-); Associate Editor, *American Psycholgist* (1972-77); member, Washington D.C. Chapter, World Future Society and member, Planning Committee, First and Second General Assemblies of the World Future Society (1970-73); consultant, National Heart, Lung and Blood Institute and National Cancer Institute on behavioral aspects of health and illness (1972-); member, National Institutes of Health review committee on Behavioral Science and Population (1976-); member, ad hoc Interagency Committee.

Publications: Co-author, *The Special Study: Implications of Advances in Research and Technology* (Government Printing Office, forthcoming, 1978); co-author, *Research Involving the Institutionalized Mentally Infirm* (Government Printing Office, 1978); co-author, "Contributions of Psychology to Health Research" (*American Psycholgist*, 1976); *Ethical Requirements for Sex Research in Humans: Confidentiality Ethical Issues in Sex Research and Sex Therapy* (Little Brown and Co., 1977); co-author, "Report of the Task Force on Psychology, Family Planning and Population Policy" (*American Psychologist*, 1972).

KENNET (LORD), formerly WAYLAND YOUNG
House of Lords
London, S.W.1, England

Born: 1923, London, England

Telephone: —

Profession: Writer; journalist; politician

Field of specialization: Policy formation; application; evaluation.

Education: M.A., History, Cambridge University, 1946.

Professional employment: Quarterly Journal *Disarmament and Arms Control:* Founder-Editor (1962-65). *Guardian* Newspaper: Columnist (1960s). *Observer* Newspaper: Special and Diplomatic Correspondant (1953-55). Foreign Office: Third Secretary (1947-51).

Professional activities: Consultant to European Commission (1973-76); Director, Europe Plus Thirty Project (1974-75); President, International Parliamentary Conferences on the Environment (1971-); Member of European Assembly (1978-); T.V., broadcasting, journalism, pamphleteering (Fabian Society); Parliamentary Secretary, Ministry of Housing and Local Government, U.K. Government (1966-70); Opposition Spokesman, Foreign Affairs, Science/Technology, House of Lords (1970-74).

Publications: Editor, *The Future of Europe* (based on Europe Plus Thirty Report, Cambridge University Press, 1976); *Thirty Four Articles* (Weidenfeld and Nicolson, 1965); editor, *Existing Mechanisms of Arms Control* (Pergamon Press, 1965); *Strategy for Survival* (Penguin Books, 1959); three novels, history, administrative studies, etc.

KETTLE, JOHN

Born: 1928, London, England

President
John Kettle Incorporated
135 Maclean Avenue
Toronto, Ontario, Canada M4E 3A5

Telephone: (416) 699-1154

Profession: Writer, consultant, futurist

Field of specialization: Generalist

Education: —

Professional employment: John Kettle Incorporated: President (1975-). Self-employed: (1966-75).

Professional activities: Consulting futurist; forecasts, writes scenarios, conducts seminars, and helps many Canadian government departments and private corporations set up their own long-range planning and futures studies departments; consultant on information retrieval systems to Glenbow Museum, Calgary (1975-77); consultant, Institute for Research on Public Policy, Montreal; consultant, Hudson Institute, New York (1970-); consultant, "Footnotes on the Future," 10-part T.V. series, CBC-TV (1968-69); member, editorial board, *Business Tomorrow*, World Future Society (1978-); teaching course on futures studies, Queen's University, Kingston, Ontario (1977-78).

Publications: *Footnotes on the Future* (Methuen, Toronto, 1970); *Hindsight on the Future* (Macmillan of Canada for the Ministry of State for Urban Affairs, 1976); "Direction Canada" series (*Executive* magazine, (1976-79); Forewatch' series (*Executive* magazine, 1979-); "Footnotes on the Future" (monthly magazine series, *Monetary Times Magazine*, then *Executive* magazine, 1970-76); editor, *A Science Policy for Canada* (report of the Senate Special Committee on Science Policy, Queen's Printer, Ottawa, 1970-73); editor, *Beyond Habitat* by Moshe Safdie (Tundra, M.I.T., Cambridge, 1970).

KING, ALEXANDER

Born: 1909, Glasgow, Scotland

Chairman
The International Federation of Institutes of Advanced Study
168, Rue de Grenelle
75007 Paris, France

Telephone: (01) 705-2183

Profession: Scientist, global analyst

Field of specialization: Analysis of world trends and their interactions; formulation and inception of multidisciplinary research on longer-term world problems.

Education: B.Sc., 1930, Chemistry, M.Sc., 1932, Imperial College of Science and Technology, London; D.Sc., Chemistry, University of Munich, 1940.

Professional employment: The International Federation of Institutes of Advanced Study: Chairman (1974-). Organization of Economic Cooperation and Development, Paris: Director General for Scientific Affairs (1961-74). European Productivity Agency: Director (1957-60). Department of Industrial Research, London: Chief Scientist (1952-57). British Government Cabinet Scientific Secretariat: Head (1948-51). British Embassy, Washington, D.C.: Scientific counselor (1942-47). British Ministry of Production: Deputy Scientific Advisor (1940-41). Imperial College of London: Senior Lecturer in Physical Chemistry (1932-50).

Professional activities: Multidisciplinary research on long-term world problems for IFIAS; co-founded and still active with The Club of Rome; consultant to U.N. and UNESCO; advisor on science policy for government of Ontario; course of 25 lectures on "The State of the Planet," Brandeis University (1978); series of seminars on science policy, University of Montreal (1979); Vice Chairman, Steering Committee of the Non-Governmental Organizations on Science & Technology for Development (1978) which helped organize the International Symposium on this subject in Singapore (1979); Member of study group, Europe Plus Thirty, European Economic Community; Associate Fellow, Center for the Study of Democratic Institutions, Santa Barbara, California (1968-); as Director General of OECD, was responsible for organizing work on man-power and educational forecasting, technological forecasting and technology assessment; lectured in more than 40 countries on such matters.

Publications: *Science Policy—The International Stimulus* (Oxford University Press, 1974); co-author, *Beyond the Age of Waste* (Pergamon Press, 1978); *Report on the State of the Planet* (for IFIAS, Pergamon Press, 1979); co-author, *The RIO Report*, chapter on science and technology (Dutton, 1976).

KING-HELE, DESMOND GEORGE
Deputy Chief/Scientific Officer
Royal Aircraft Establishment
Farnborough, Hampshire, England

Born: 1927, Seaford, Sussex, England

Telephone: (0252) 24461

Profession: Mathematician; space scientist

Field of specialization: The future of the world in the widest sense; future of space exploration; evolution and its implications; weapons technology.

Education: B.A., First Class Honours, Mathematics, 1948, M.A., 1952, Trinity College, Cambridge University.

Professional employment: Royal Aircraft Establishment: Deputy Chief/Scientific Officer (1968-); at RAE since 1948.

Professional activities: Research on upper atmosphere and earth's gravitational field by analysis of satellite orbits.

Publications: *The End of the Twentieth Century?* (Macmillan, London; St. Martin's Press, New York 1970); "Has Man a Future?" (*Your Environment*, Volume II, 1971); "Evolution and Expectation" (*Futures*, Vol. 6, December 1974); *Shelley: His Thought and Work* (Macmillan, Second Edition, 1971); *Erasmus Darwin* (Macmillan, London; Scribners, New York, 1963).

KLAGES, HELMUT
Professor
Post-Graduate School of Administrative Sciences Speyer
Freiherr-vom-Stein-Strasse 2
6720 Speyer, Federal Republic of Germany

Born: 1930, Nurnberg, Germany

Telephone: 06232 106290

Profession: Sociologist

Field of specialization: Futures methodology; organizational development and planning; strategies and problems of societal modernization; value systems.

Education: Dipl. rer. pol., Universitat Erlangen, 1953; Dr. rer. pol., Universitat Hamburg, 1955.

Professional employment: Post-Graduate School of Administrative Sciences, Speyer: Professor (1974-). Technische Universitat Berlin: Professor (1964-74). Sozialforschungsstelle an der Universitat Munster: Head of Department (1962-64).

Professional activities: Co-Editor of *Research Policy* (1973-); Co-Editor of *Policy Sciences* (1974-); Member of the International Institute of Administrative Sciences (1975-); Associate Member of the Club of Rome (1975-); Member of the Club of Rome (1972-75); Co-Founder and Member (temporarily chairman) of the Board of Directors of the Berlin Center of Future Research (1968-75).

Publications: *Soziologie zwischen Wirklichkeit und Moglichkeit [Sociology Between Reality and Possibility]* (Koln und Opladen, Westdeutscher Verlag, 1968); "Assessment of an Attempt at a System of Social Indicators" (*Policy Sciences*, Vol. 4, No. 3, September 1973); *Planungspolitik [Planning Policies]* (Stuttgart-Berlin-Koln-Mainz, Verlag W. Kohlhammer, 1971); *Die unruhige Gesellschaft [The Unsilent Society]* (Beck'sche Verlagsbuchhandlung, Munchen, 1975); *Grenzen der Organisierbarkeit von Verwaltungsorganisationen [Limits to the Manageability of Administrative Organizations]* (Die Verwaltung, Heft 3, 1976); *Wettlauf mit dem Chaos [Race with Chaos]*, with H. Hermann and D. Seelmann (1972).

KNOPPERS, ANTONIE T.
St. Luke's Institute for Health Sciences
114 Amsterdam Avenue, Administration
New York, New York 10023, U.S.A.

Born: 1915, Kapelle, The Netherlands

Telephone: (212) 870-6661

Profession: Manager, science and technology

Field of specialization: Technology transfer; science management; environment and trade offs.

Education: M.D., University of Amsterdam, 1939; Dr. Pharmacology, University of Leyden, 1941; D.Sc. (Hon.), Worcester Polytechnic Institute.

Professional employment: St. Luke's Institute for Health Sciences, New York: President (1976-); Merck and Company, Inc.: Vice Chairman, Board of Directors (1974-75); President, Chief Operating Officer (1971-74); Senior Vice President (1967-71). Merck Sharp and Dohme International: President (1957-67); Vice President and General Manager (1955-57).

Professional Activities: Currently a director of John Wiley and Sons, Inc., Hewlett-Packard Co., Mathematica, Inc., Scott Paper Company, Humana, Inc.,; Trustee of Drew University and Salk Institute; Consultant to Drexel-Burnham and Co., Inc.; Member, International Chamber of Commerce; Director, Foreign Policy Association; President, Netherlands Chamber of Commerce; Trustee, Asia Society; served as a member of the Presidential Commission on International Trade and Investment Policy (1971); Chairman, The Salsbury Seminar for American Studies; Chairman, U.S. Council, International Chamber of Commerce (1971-72).

Publications: "Looking into the Grim Face of the Future" (*Fortune*, Books and Ideas Section, September 1975); "The Management and Sociology of Innovation" (*Science Journal*, London, 1972); "The Multinational Corporation in the Third World" (*Columbia Journal of World Business*, Vol. V, No. 4, July-August 1970); "The Transatlantic Technological Gap and U.S. Investment in Europe" (*Progress*, Unilever Quarterly, Vol. 53, No. 297, 1968); "The Role of Science and Technology" (*Commerce*, monthly review of American Chamber of Commerce, Belgium, November 1966).

KOCHER, GERHARD
Jonas-Furrer-Str. 21/62
8046 Zurich, Switzerland

Born: 1939, Bern, Switzerland

Telephone: (01) 57 93 93

Profession: Economist; political scientist

Field of specialization: Futurology; planning in politics; technology assessment; health planning; Delphi method; morphology; centralization-decentralization; organization and documentation of futures research.

Education: Dr. in Economics, University of Bern, 1966.

Professional employment: Independent consultant (1974-). Swiss Office for Development of Trade: Executive Secretary (1968-74). Tradax S.A.—Cargill Inc.: Trainee/Trader (1966-68).

Professional activities: Consultant and writer (1974-); Vice President, Swiss Association for Futures Research (1973-); Editor, Bulletin of the Swiss Association for Futures Research (1973-); Member of the Board, Societe d'Etudes de la Prevision et de la Planification, Lausanne (1974); Member, World Future Society (1971-); Member of Prospektivkonferenz of Neue Helvetische Gesellschaft (1971-75); organizer of conferences of futures research in Switzerland (1971-); Delphi survey of future of mass communication (1975-); Vice-President, Swiss Society for Health Policy (1976-); Editor, Bulletin of the Swiss Society for Health Policy (1977-).

Publications: *Zukunftsforschung in der Schweiz [Futures Research in Switzerland]* (Haupt, Bern, 1970);

editor, *Zukunftsaspekte unseres Gesudheitswesens [Future Aspects of Our Health System]* (SZF/Wetzikon, 1974); "Zur Kritik an der Zukunftsforschung" ["Against the Critique of Futures Research"] *(Analysen und Prognosen,* November 1974); "Glanz and Elend der Leitbilder" ["Brightness and Distress of the New Images"] *(Neue Zuercher Zeitung,* June 1974); has written numerous articles on futures research for a variety of journals and for Swiss radio broadcasts.

KOELLE, HEINZ HERMANN
Professor of Space Technology
Aerospace Institute
Technical University Berlin
Salzufer 17/19
D-1000 Berlin 45, Federal Republic of Germany

Born: 1925, Danzig, Germany

Telephone: (030) 3142307

Profession: Engineer

Field of specialization: Long range forecasting and planning; value systems; simulation.

Education: Diploma-Ing., Mechanical Engineering, University of Stuttgart, 1954; Dr.-Ing., Aeronautical Engineering, Technical University Berlin, 1963.

Professional employment: Technical University Berlin: Professor of Space Technology (1965-). NASA/MSFC: Director, Future Projects Office (1960-65). U.S. Army (ABMA): Chief, Preliminary Design Branch (1955-60).

Professional activities: Teaching courses on Systems Engineering, Space Propulsion/Transportation Systems, and Space Program Planning (annually); working on several research projects including Europe Plus Thirty; Apollo Program Planning (1959-61); Saturn Systems Design (1957-60).

Publications: Editor, *Handbook of Astronautical Engineering* (McGraw-Hill Book Company, 1961); plus more than 200 reports and articles.

KOJAROV, ASSEN TODOROV
Deputy Director
Institute for Contemporary Social Theories
"Pionerski Pat" 21
Sofia 35, Bulgaria

Born: 1911, Gotze, Delchev, Bulgaria

Telephone: 56-69-35

Profession: Philosopher; sociologist

Field of specialization: Futures methodology; value systems.

Education: Doctor of Philosophical Sciences, Sofia University, 1973, Professor, 1976.

Professional employment: Institute for Contemporary Social Theories, Academy of Sciences: Deputy Director (1968-). *Philosophska Missul* Magazine: Deputy Chief Editor (1952-72).

Professional activities: Member, Scientific Council of the World Futures Studies Federation. Currently working on 1) philosophical and sociological grounds of social forecasting; 2) futures methodology; 3) the perspectives of peaceful coexistance between socialist and capitalist world social systems.

Publications: *Monism and Pluralism in Ideology and in Politics* (Sofia Press, 1974); *The Social Forces Behind the Socialist Revolution* (Sofia Press, 1968); *Effectiveness of Thinking* (in Bulgarian, Partizdat, Sofia, 1961); "The Law as a Basic Logical Form" in *Wissenschaft, Philosophie, Ideologie* (Akademie Verlag, Berlin, 1973); "Forecasting and Transformation of the Contemporary World" *(Proceedings of the XVth World Congress of Philosophy,* September 1973); *Human Rights and the Ideology Struggle Today* (Sofia Press, 1978).

KOLLEN, JAMES H.

Policy Analyst
SRI International
333 Ravenswood Avenue
Menlo Park, California 94025, U.S.A.

Born: 1943, Minneapolis, Minnesota, U.S.A.

Telephone: (415) 326-6200

Profession: Corporate policy analyst

Field of specialization: Emerging corporate policy issue identification; corporate issue impact assessment.

Education: B.A., Political Science, University of Minnesota, 1966; M.P.A., Public Policy Studies, 1967, Ph.D., (C.D.), International Relations, 1970, University of Michigan.

Professional employment: SRI International: Policy Analyst (current). Bell of Canada: Manager, Business Planning Group; Supervisor, Environmental Studies Group; University of Michigan: Teaching Fellow of International Relations. Office of Management and Budget, Executive Office of the President: Program Evaluation Staff Member. Industrial Management Center, Inc.: Lecturer.

Professional activities: Research on management effectiveness of federal R and D programs, emphasizing guidelines for improvement; development of policy research programs assessing social, economic, and political issues confronting business; member, World Future Society, Honor Society Phi Kappa Phi, Corporate Planners Association.

Publications: —

KONETCHY, RONALD DEAN

Director
Schola Moderna, Inc.
P.O. Box 364
New Haven, Connecticut 06502, U.S.A.

Born: 1933, LaCrosse, Wisconsin, U.S.A.

Telephone: (203) 776-9942

Profession: Educator; producer; music director

Field of specialization: New liberal arts

Education: B.M., 1958, M.M., 1960, Music, Yale University.

Professional employment: Schola Moderna, Inc.: Director (1965-). Albertus Magnus College: Professor (1960-76).

Professional activities: Currently developing "Watershed—a new humanities for the emerging global civilization;" concurrently giving demonstrations at future-oriented conferences in the U.S.; writing *Tuning Fork*, a book featuring a symbol-based learning process for integrated study of the arts and humanities; member, Harford-New Haven Chapter Council, World Future Society (1977-).

Publications: Author and editor, *Tuning Fork: Towards a New Liberal Arts* (Choric Corporation, forthcoming in 1980); author and editor, *World Music: A Multimedia Inventory of Musical and Other Cultural Effects* (Albertus Magnus College, 1970); author and editor, *Luther Legacy* (two long-playing records, Schola Moderna, Inc., 1967); *Polish Heritage* (one long playing record, Schola Moderna, Inc., 1966).

KORNBLUH, MARVIN

Analyst in Futures Research
Congressional Research Service
U.S. Library of Congress
Washington, D.C. 20540, U.S.A.

Born: 1927, New York, New York, U.S.A.

Telephone: (202) 426-6036

Profession: Futurist; information systems analyst; planner

Field of specialization: Futures methodology; strategic planning; information systems development.

Education: B.S., 1950, Columbia University; M.A., 1956, New York University; additional graduate courses in business administration, operations research and computer sciences; Graduate, IBM Systems

Research Institute Graduate School.

Professional employment: Congressional Research Service, U.S. Library of Congress: Analyst in Futures Research (1975-). John Wiley and Sons, Inc., Wiley Systems, Inc.: President (1969-75). Contemporary Systems Corporation: President (1968-69).

Professional activities: As a member of Science Policy Research Division of the Congressional Research Service, answer specific requests and perform studies which have a futures orientation and an information systems orientation, develop and conduct seminars, workshops, briefings and individual consultations on futures and information topics and needs; conceive, develop and implement a comprehensive futures information retrieval system (FIRST).

Publications: *The Effective Executive and the Systems Challenge* (U.S. Savings and Loan League, Chicago, Illinois, 1978); co-author with Dennis Little, "The Nature of a Computer Simulation Model" (*Technological Forecasting and Social Change,* Vol. 9, No. 1/2, 1976); co-author with William Renfro, "Futures in Politics" in *Handbook of Futures Research,* J. Fowles, ed., (Greenwood Press, 1977).

KOSTELANETZ, RICHARD
P.O. Box 73, Canal Street
New York, New York, 10013, U.S.A.

Born: 1940, New York, New York, U.S.A.

Telephone: (212) 840-1234

Profession: Writer; artist

Field of specialization: Art; futuristic social thought.

Education: A.B., American Studies, Brown University, 1962; M.A., American History, Columbia University, 1966; Fulbright Scholar, King's College, University of London, 1964-65.

Professional employment: Assembling Press: Co-founder and President (1970-). The Future Press: Sole proprietor (1976-). *Precisely* (periodical); Co-editor and publisher (1977-). University of Texas, Austin: Visiting Professor (Spring, 1977). Indiana University Writers Conference: Senior staff (July, 1976). John Jay College, City University of New York: Program Associate, Thematic Studies (1972-73).

Professional activities: Editing anthologies about avant-garde art (1967-); creating art with words, numbers and lines, as books, drawings, prints, audiotapes, videotapes, holographs, photographs and films; editing anthologies of futuristic social thought (1967-73).

Publications: Editor, *Beyond Left and Right* (Morrow, 1968); editor, *Social Speculations* (Morrow, 1971); editor, *Human Alternatives* (Morrow, 1971); editor, *The Edge of Adaptation* (Prentice-Hall, 1973); editor, *Esthetics Contemporary* (Prometheus, 1978); *The End of Intelligent Writing: Literary Politics in America* (Sheed, 1974).

KOVACS, GEZA
Professor
University of Economics
Dimitrov Ter 8
Budapest
1093 Hungary

Born: 1928, Bohonye, Hungary

Telephone: 186-855/282

Profession: Economist

Field of specialization: Long range planning and futures research

Education: Undergraduate and Graduate, University.

Professional employment: University of Economics: Professor, Head of the Group of Futurology.

Professional activities: Teaching future research courses; forming of futures pictures; special seminars; lectures on long range planning; conducting research on relationship between prognoses, futures pictures and long range plans, and the leadership of "Complex Long Range Futures Research" projects.

Publications: *Economic Policy Targets and Mechanism* (Kozgazdasagi es Jogi Konyvkiado, Budapest, 1968); co-author and editor, *Planning and Regulation of National Economy* (Kozgazdasagi es Jogi Konyvkiado, Budapest, 1969); *Long Range Perspectives and Planning* (Kozgazdasagi es Jogi Konyvkiado, Budapest, 1970); *Critical Turning Points of Future Development* (Kozgazdasagi es Jogi Konyvkiado, Budapest, 1975); and approximately 100 studies in several Hungarian and foreign journals.

KOZMETSKY, GEORGE

Born: 1917, Seattle, Washington, U.S.A.

Dean and Professor
Graduate School of Business
The University of Texas at Austin
Austin, Texas 78712, U.S.A.

Telephone: (512) 471-5921

Profession: Educator

Field of specialization: Information technology; organization theory; systems analysis; systems management; asset management; futures, ethics and values systems; applications of digital computing.

Education: B.A., Political Science, University of Washington, 1938; M.B.A., 1947, D.C.S., Finance, 1957, Harvard University.

Professional employment: The University of Texas at Austin: Dean and Professor, Graduate School of Business (1966-). Teledyne, Inc.: Executive Vice President (1960-66). Litton Industries: Vice President and Assistant General Manager (1959-60); Director, Computers and Control Division (1954-59). Hughes Aircraft Company: Member, Technical Staff, Advisor, Electrical Laboratory (1952-54). Carnegie Institute of Technology: Assistant Professor (1950-52). Harvard University: Instructor (1947-50).

Professional activities: Currently conducting research and teaching on asset management, global management, ethics and value systems; Member, U.S. Commission on Supplies and Shortages (1975-76); Director, Student Loan Marketing Association (1973-); Past Chairman of the Board and President, The Institute of Management Sciences; Member, Presidential Advisory Committee on the National Data Center (1965-66); Consultant, National Science Foundation R and D Incentives Program (1972-75).

Publications: Co-author, *Electronic Computers and Management Control* (McGraw-Hill, 1956); co-author, *Centralization vs. Decentralization in Organizations* (American Book-Stratford Press, Ltd., 1954); *Financial Reports of Labor Unions* (The Andover Press, Ltd., 1950); co-author, *Information Technology: Initiatives for Today* (The Conference Board, 1972); co-author, "Information Requirements for Urban Systems: A View into the Possible Future" (*Management Science*, Vol. 9, No. 4, December 1972).

KRAEGEL, WILFRED A.

Born: 1924, Lansing, Illinois, U.S.A.

Associate Actuary
Northwestern Mutual Life Insurance Co.
720 East Wisconsin Avenue
Milwaukee, Wisconsin 53202, U.S.A.

Telephone: (414) 271-1444

Profession: Actuary

Field of specialization: Product development (life insurance), aging, business and society, education, health, population, work—and their futuristic aspects.

Education: A.B., Mathematics, University of Illinois, 1946; M.S., Actuarial Science, 1947; Fellow, Society of Actuaries, 1955.

Professional employment: Northwestern Mutual Life Insurance Co.: Associate Actuary (1970-); Director of Data Processing (1968-70); Manager of Data Processing (1956-68). University of Wisconsin, Milwaukee: Lecturer (1977-1978).

Professional activities: Committee on Futurism of Society of Actuaries, Chairman (1978-), member (1976-); Overseeing Committee of The Trend Analysis Program, American Council of Life Insurance, member (1978-), monitor (1970-78); co-president, Milwaukee Chapter of the World Future Society (1973-75, 1977-78).

Publications: "Futurizing a City" (World Future Society BULLETIN, June 1978; also publsihed in *Milwaukee's Economy*, 1978); co-author, "Policy Loans and Equity" (*Transactions*, Society of Actuaries, 1978).

KRISTENSEN, THORKIL

Born: 1899, Denmark

Director
Instituttet for Fremtidsforskning
*[*Institute for Futures Studies*]*
Vester Farmigsgade 3
DK-1606, Copenhagen V, Denmark

Telephone: (01) 11 71 76

264

Profession: Economist

Field of specialization: —

Education: Cand. Polit., University of Copenhagen, 1927.

Professional employment: Institute for Futures Studies: Director (1970-). Organization for Economic Cooperation and Development: Secretary General (1960-69). Danish Ministry of Finance: Minister (1950-53, 1945-47). Copenhagen School of Economics: Professor (1953-60, 1948-50). University of Aarhus: Professor (1938-45).

Professional activities: Currently active with The Institute for Futures Studies.

Publications: Co-author and editor, *The Economic World Balance* (Munksgaard, Copenhagen, 1960); *The Food Problem of Developing countries* (OECD, 1968); *Development in Rich and Poor Countries* (Praeger, New York, 1974).

KUMAR, JAGDISH KRISHAN
Senior Lecturer in Sociology
Keynes College
University of Kent
Canterbury, Kent, England

Born: 1942, Trinidad, West Indies

Telephone: 0227-66822

Profession: Sociologist

Field of specialization: Post-industrial theory; general futurology.

Education: B.A., History, St. John's College, Cambridge, 1964; M.Sc. (Econ.), Sociology, London School of Economics, 1965; Ph.D., Sociology, University of Kent, 1977.

Professional employment: University of Kent: Senior Lecturer in Sociology (1977-); Lecturer in Sociology (1967-77).

Professional activities: Research advisor, Acton Society Trust, London (1973-); writing and teaching.

Publications: *Prophecy and Progress: The Sociology of Industrial and Post-Industrial Society* (Penguin Books and Allen Lane, 1978); "Reflections on the Current Discontents in Britain: A Review and a Proposal" *(Theory and Society,* 1978); "Industrial and Post-Industrialism" *(Sociological Review,* England, 1976); "The Industrializing and the Post-Industrial Worlds: On Development and Futurology" in *Sociology and Development,* Kadt, ed. (Tavistock Publication, 1974).

LAGOS, GUSTAVO
Professor
Institute of International Studies
Condell 249
Santiago, Chile

Born: 1924, Santiago, Chile

Telephone: 42940

Profession: Political Scientist

Field of specialization: International relations.

Education: Licendiado in Juridicial and Social Sciences, Law School, University of Chile, 1948; Institut des Sciences Politiques, University of Paris.

Professional employment: Institute of International Studies: Professor (1972-). Institute for World Order: Co-Director for Latin America of World Order Models Project (1969-76). Institute for Latin American Integration (INTAL): Director (1965-69). Latin American Faculty of Social Sciences (FLACSO): Secretary General (1958-62).

Professional activities: Conducts graduate courses on International Relations (1974-); research project on "Latin America and the Future of the International System"(1973-77); Visiting Professor of International Relations, University of North Carolina (1961-62); Chief of Training, Interamerican Development Bank, Washington, D.C. (1962-65).

Publications: *International Stratification and Underdeveloped Countries.* (The University of North Carolina Press, 1963); editor, "L 'integration Latinoamericaine" ["Latin-American Integration"] (Tiers Monde, Presses Universitaire de France, Paris, 1966); *El Problema Historico del Trabajo [The Historical Problem of Work]* (Editorial Andres Bello, Santiago, Chili, 1950); "The Revolution of Being" in *On the Creation of a Just World Order*, Saul Mendlovitz, ed. (Free Press, 1975); "Latin America" in *International Organization World Politics*, Robert W. Cox, ed. (Macmillan, 1969); co-author, with Horacio H. Godoy, *Revolution of Being: A Latin American View of the Future* (Free Press, 1977).

LAMBERT-LAMOND, GEORGES M.

Born: 1910, Nice, France

Senior Adviser
Panafrican Institute for Development
3, rue de Varembe
1211 Geneva 20, Switzerland

Telephone: (022) 336016/17

Profession: Economic sociologist; political scientist

Field of specialization: Social development (urban, regional and rural); African and European affairs.

Education: Licence, Letters (Sociology), 1929, Licence, D.E.S., Law and Economics, 1931, Sorbonne; Diploma (honors), Diplomacy, Public Finance, Ecole des Sciences Politiques, 1931.

Professional employment: Panafrican Institute for Development: Senior Adviser (1972-). U.N. Research Institute for Social Development: Secretary General (1964-72). U.N. Economic and Social Department: Senior Officer (1945-64). UNTAB, International Labor Organization, etc.: Occasional consultant (1945-). Royal Marines, British Admiralty: Major (1940-45).

Professional activities: Senior adviser and Council Member on research, courses, consultation, and administration (present); Representative of Society for International Development in Geneva; Member or board member of several scientific societies.

Publications: Co-author of numerous U.N. or International Labor Organization reports, including *World Social Situation, World Employment Programme, Urbanization in Africa and Europe*, etc.

LAMBO, THOMAS ADEOYE

Born: 1923, Abeokura, Nigeria

Deputy Director-General
World Health Organization
Avenue Appia
1211 Geneva 27, Switzerland

Telephone: (022) 34 60 61

Profession: Doctor of Medicine

Field of specialization: Neuro-psychiatry; international administrator.

Education: M.B., Ch.B., 1948, M.D., 1954, Birmingham University, England; DPM, 1953, M.R.C.P.Ed., 1961, F.R.C.P.Ed., 1963, London University of Psychiatry; J.P., Western State, Nigeria, 1968.

Professional employment: World Health Organization (WHO): Deputy Director-General (1973-); Assistant Director-General (1971-73). University of Ibadan, Nigeria: Vice-Chancellor (1968-71); Dean, Medical School (1966-68); Professor of Psychiatry and Head of Department of Psychiatry, Neurology and Neurosurgery (1963-74). Western Region Ministry of Health, Nigeria: Senior Specialist, Neuropsychiatric Centre (1960-63).

Professional activities: Organizational research with special emphasis on disease, health and socio-economic development; currently a member of the Advisory Scientific Panel, Centre for Advanced Study in the Development Sciences, Scientific Council of the World Future Studies Federation, the World Society for Ekistics, The Club of Rome, and on the Advisory Board of EARTHSCAN; first African to be appointed to the Pontifical Academy of Sciences (1974); first African winner of the Haile Selassie African Research Award (1970); has taught and conducted research in the behavioral sciences and mental health.

Publications: "Psychiatry's New Challenges" (Address to the Annual Meeting of the American Psychiatric Association, May 1975); "Evaluation of Man's Progress of Humanization" in *Human Needs, New Societies, Supportive Technologies* (Collected documents at the Rome Special World Conference on Futures Research, 1973); "Changing Patterns of Mental Health Needs in Africa" (*Journal of Con-*

266

temporary Rev., London, February 1973); "New Strategies for Higher Education in Developing Countries" (Paper presented at the Director-General's Conference, WHO, March 1972).

LAMONTAGNE, MAURICE
Born: 1917, Mont-Joli, Quebec, Canada

Member
The Senate of Canada
Parliament Buildings
Ottawa, Ontario, Canada

Telephone: (613) 992-3046

Profession: Economist

Field of specialization: Science policy and futures methodology.

Education: B.A., Seminaire de Rimouski, 1937; Etudes Superieure en Philosophie, College Dominicain, 1939; M.A., Social Sciences, 1941; M.A., Economics, 1943, Harvard University.

Professional employment: Appointed to the Canadian Senate (1967). Secretary of State of Canada (1964-65). Chairman of the Privy Council of Canada (1963). Federal M.P. for Outremont-St. Jean (1963-67). Member of the Canada-U.S. Committee (1958-63). Special Counsellor to the Chief of the Opposition, Mr. Pearson (1959-63). Vice Dean of the Faculty of Social Science at Ottawa University (1960-61). Laval University: Part Time Professor of Economics (1957-59); Director, Department of Economics (1951-54); Professor of Social Sciences (1943-54).

Professional activities: Member, Club of Rome, Royal Society of Canada (1957-); Privy Council of Canada (1963-), Royal Society of the Arts of London (1964-); Special Counsellor of the Royal Commission on Economic Perspective in Canada (1957); Member, Canadian Delegation to European Economic Cooperation League, Brussels (1951).

Publications: *Role of the Legislator in Planning for Balanced Growth* (1975); *The Message of The Club of Rome* (1975); *The Loss of the Steady State* (1975); *Exponential Growth—Human Survival* (1973); *The New Social and Economic Priorities* (1973); *The Doom Debate* (1972); *Building Industrial Innovative Capacity* (1972); *The Impact of Science, Technology on Society* (1970).

LAMSON, ROBERT WARREN
Born: 1928, Shanghai, China

Program Manager
Division of Intergovernmental Science and Public Technology
Applied Science and Research Applications Directorate
National Science Foundation
1800 G Street, N.W.
Washington, D.C. 20550, U.S.A.

Telephone: (202) 634-4333

Profession: Policy analyst; research administrator.

Field of specialization: The improvement and use of various means (intellectual, technological and social) to solve social problems. Policy analysis in such areas as: the support and use of science and technology; national security and foreign affairs; and environment, resources, and population.

Education: A.B., 1951, M.A., 1952, Sociology, Boston University; Ph.D., Sociology, University of Chicago, 1960.

Professional employment: National Science Foundation: Program Manager, Applied Science and Research Applications Program (1977-); Program Manager, Research Applied to National Needs Program (1972-77); Program Manager, University Science Planning and Policy Program (1966-69). Department of Defense: Staff Assistant to Assistant Secretary for Civil Defense: (1962-66). United States Senate: Legislative Assistant (1960-62).

Professional activities: Organized symposium at 1975 Annual Meeting of the American Association for the Advancement of Science concerning "Citizen Involvement in Decision-Making"; Consultant to National Academy of Sciences Study Conference concerning Social Science Research Strategies on Environmental Problems and Policies (1969); advised special task force to the Secretary of the Department of Health, Education and Welfare concerning the report, *Strategy for a Livable Environment* (1967); Visiting Lecturer, American University (1963).

Publications: "Public Policy and Values Concerning Information and Ownership of Land" in *Secrecy and Disclosure of Wealth in Land* (U.S. Department of Agriculture, 1978); "National Goals and Science and Technology: Is a Better Synthesis Possible?" *(Congressional Record,* 120, December 18, 1974); "Corporate Accounting for Environmental Effects" in *Corporate Social Accounting,* M. Dierkes and R. Bauer, eds. (Praeger Publishers, 1973); "The Future of Man's Environment" *(The Science Teacher,* 36, January 1969); "Research on the Population Problem" (Statement in hearings before Senate Committee on Labor and Public Welfare, 1971); "Science Policy—Needed Research" *(Research Policy,* Vol. 1, No. 4, 1972).

LAND, GEORGE THOMAS LOCK
Chairman
The Hampton Institute
27 Henry Street
Southampton, New York 11968, U.S.A.

Born: 1933, Hot Springs National Park, U.S.A.

Telephone: (516) 283-6248
(800) 824-7888 ext. A3018

Profession: Consultant; author

Field of specialization: Organizational development through use of creative problem solving methods and systems: social trend and policy analysis; general education; development of general field theory and stage change models in analysis of discontinous trends.

Education: Political Science, Millsaps College, Jackson, Mississippi, 1952-53; Anthropology, University of Vera Cruz, Mexico, 1955-56; Ph.D., Anthropology and Psychology, Sussex Institute of Technology, 1973; Sc.D., Physics, Max Planck Institute, 1977.

Professional employment: The Hampton Institute: Chairman (1977-). American Telephone and Telegraph: Planning Consultant (1977-). Forest Hospital and Foundation: Consultant-in-residence and Trustee, Forest Institute of Professional Psychology (1978-). On-going assignments: Director, the Agape Clinic, Jamestown, New York; Consultant and Visiting Professor of Creative and Evolutionary Studies, Mankato State University, Minnesota; Consultant in Behavioral Sciences, George Washington University, Washington, D.C.; Consultant-in-Residence, Social Systems, Inc., Chapel Hill, North Carolina. Turtle Bay Institute and Innotek Corp.: Chairman of the Board (1964-74). Motivation Sciences, Inc.: President (1960-64). Television del Norte, Mexico: Vice President and General Manager (1958-60). Anthropological research in Latin America and Mexico (1954-58).

Professional activities: Research in evolution of social value system and policies (1977-); development of general systems education, elementary and secondary (1976-); research in developmental theory for diagnosis and treatment of mental illness (1977-); research in unified and general field theory (1978-); conducts seminars, lectures and workshops in creative thinking, policy analysis and interdisciplinary science; current work centers on the integration of physical laws with individual and social development theories, with special emphasis on the nature of phase change-discontinuity-phenomena.

Publications: "Creativity, Reality and General Systems" *(Journal of Creative Behavior,* Vol. 11, No. 1, 1977); "Toward a Unified Concept of Mind and Mental Illness" *(American Society of Cybernetics,* Vol. 8, Nos. 1-4, 1976); "Managing Change" *(Journal of the Society of Internal Auditors,* 1977); *Planning Change* (The Hampton Institute, 1978); *Grow or Die: The Unifying Principle of Transformation* (Random House, 1973); *Creative Alternatives and Decision-Making* (Mankato State University, 1974).

LANDAU, ERIKA
Director
The Young Persons' Institute
    for the Promotion of Art and Science
Museum Haaretz Tel-Aviv
P.O.B. 17068, Tel-Aviv, Israel

Born: 1931, Vienna, Austria

Telephone: (03) 427014

Profession: Psychotherapist; art history educator

Field of specialization: Education—creativity, giftedness, games; Psychotherapy—future-oriented and prophylaxia through potential talents development.

Education: M.A., Psychology and History, University of Tel-Aviv, 1965; Ph.D., Psychology and Art History, Ludwig-Maximillian University, 1968.

Professional employment: Tel-Aviv University, Department of Psychotherapy: Supervisor (1972-). Young Persons' Institute for the Promotion of Art and Science: Director (1968-).

Professional activities: Private practice in psychotherapy; intercultural survey "Children Ask Questions About the Future"; Scientific Secretary of the Israel Association for Futures Research; Member, FORUM, Human Dialogue on Important Contemporary Issues and Problems and on the Future of Man, New York.

Publications: Co-author, "Creativity and Self-actualization in the Aging Personality" (*American Journal of Psychotherapy*, January 1978); "Creative Thinking as Existential Therapy" (*Confinia Psychiatrica*, Basel, 21: 1978); *Psychologie der Kreativitat [Psychology of Creativity]* Ernst Reinhardt Verlag, Munchen-Basel, 1969); *Creativity* (Gome, Tel-Aviv, 1973); "The Creative Approach to Psychotherapy" (*American Journal of Psychotherapy*, October 1973); *Facing Death Experience* (B. Zerikower, Tel-Aviv, 1974); "On the Creative Experiences of Beholders of Visual Art" (*Leonardo*, England, 1975).

LANDSBERG, HANS H.
Born: 1913, Germany

Senior Fellow and Co-Director
Center for Energy Policy Research
Resources for the Future, Inc.
1755 Massachusetts Avenue, N.W.
Washington, D.C. 20036, U.S.A.
Telephone: (202) 462-4400

Profession: Economist

Field of specialization: Natural resources and materials policy; technology assessment; energy economics and policy.

Education: Law, Universities of Freiburg, Heidelberg, Berlin (1931-33); B.Sc., Economics, London School of Economics, 1936; M.A., Columbia University, 1941.

Professional employment: Resources for the Future, Inc.: Senior Fellow and Co-Director, Center for Energy Policy Research (1976-); Co-Director, Energy and Materials Division (1973-1976); Director, Resource Appraisal Program (1960-1973). Gass, Bell and Associates, Consulting Economists: Economist (1956-59). Office of the Economic Adviser to the Israel Government, Washington, D.C.: Economist (1950-55). U.S. Department of Commerce, Office of International Trade (1949-50). Italian Technical Delegation, Washington, D.C. (1947-48). Office of Strategic Services, Washington, D. C., Africa, Italy (1942-45). National Bureau of Economic Research, New York (1939-42). National Research Project on Technology and Employment Opportunities, WPA, Philadelphia (1936-39).

Professional activities: Member, Board of Editors, *Daedalus* (1977-); member, Advisory Board, Institute of Energy Analysis, Oak Ridge, Tennessee (1976-); member, Advisory Board, Center for Energy Studies, University of Texas (1977-); co-chairman, International Materials Conference, Nuclear Regulatory Commission (March 1979); member, Editorial Board, *Science* (1975-78); member, Editorial Board, *Resources Policy*.

Publications: Co-author, *The Agricultural Potential of the Middle East* (Elsevier, 1971); editor, *Review of FEA National Energy Outlook 1976* (National Technical Information Service, 1977); "Materials: Some Recent Trends and Issues" (*Science*, Vol. 191, February 20, 1976); co-author, *Energy and the Social Sciences: An Examination of Research Needs* (Resources for the Future, 1974); co-editor, *The No-Growth Society* (W. Norton, New York, 1974).

LASZLO, ERVIN
Born: 1932, Budapest, Hungary

Special Fellow
United Nations Institute for Training and Research
801 United Nations Plaza
New York, New York 10017, U.S.A.
Telephone: (212) 754-8635/6

Profession: Philosopher, futurist, policy analyst

Field of specialization: Long-term global futures; social change; the new international economic order; international and United Nations affairs.

Education: Artist Diploma, Music, Royal Academy, Budapest, 1947; Docteur es-Lettres et Sciences Humaines, Philosophy, Sorbonne, University of Paris, 1970.

Professional employment: United Nations Institute for Training and Research: Special Fellow

(1975-76). State University of New York, Geneseo: Professor of Philosophy (permanent, on leave). Portland State University: Visiting Professor of Systems Science (as of September 1976). Indiana, Northwestern, and Gothenburg: Visiting Professor (1967-74). Princeton and Yale: Visiting Fellow (1966-73).

Professional activities: Project Director, "Progress in the Establishment of the New International Economic Order: Obstacles and Opportunites" (September 1977-December 1980); representative of UNITAR to various United Nations organizations and committees; consultant to the U.N. Conference on Science and Technology; teaching, lecturing and writing on areas of interest and activity.

Publications: Principal author, *Goals for Mankind: Report to the Club of Rome* (Dutton/Signet Books, 1977, 1978); *The Inner Limits of Mankind: Heretical Reflections on Contemporary Values, Culture and Politics* (Pergamon Press, 1978); editor, *Goals in a Global Community* (2 Vols.) (Pergamon Press, 1977, 1978); *Introduction to Systems Philosophy* (Harper Torchbooks, 1973); *A Strategy for the Future* (Braziller, 1974); *The Systems View of the World* (Braziller, 1972); *System Structure and Experience* (Gordon and Breach, 1969); *Individualism, Collectivism and Poltical Power* (Nijhoff, 1963).

LEACH, GERALD ADRIAN

Born: 1933, Colombo, Sri Lanka

Senior Fellow
International Institute for Environment and Development
10 Percy Street
London W1, England

Telephone: (01) 580-7656

Profession: Energy policy and analysis

Field of specialization: Energy analysis and descriptions of alternative energy supply/demand scenarios.

Education: B.A., Natural Sciences, Clare College, University of Cambridge, 1955.

Professional employment: International Institute for Environment and Development: Senior Fellow (1974-). Science Policy Research Unit, University of Sussex: Visiting Fellow (1972-74). *The Observer*: Science Correspondent (1969-72). *New Statesman*: Science Correspondent (1963-69). *Discovery*: Editor (1959-63).

Professional activities: Currently working on alternative energy scenarios for Western Europe and North America and on energy development for rural areas of the Third World; has researched and written extensively on several specific areas of energy (transport, food production, energy analysis) and on resource-development-environment issues; Advisory Editor on science to Penguin Books, Ltd.

Publications: *A Low Energy Strategy for the United Kingdom* (Science Reviews/IIED, January 1979); coauthor, *Energy: Global Prospects 1985-2000* (McGraw-Hill, 1977); *Energy and Food Production* (IPC Business Press, Ltd., 1976); "Net Energy Analysis: Is It Any Use?" (*Energy Policy*, December 1975); *The Biocrats* (Cape; Penguin; McGraw-Hill; Droemer Verlag; Mondadori; Editions Seuil, 1969-70).

LECHT, LEONARD A.

Born: 1920, Providence, Rhode Island, U.S.A.

Director, Special Research Projects
The Conference Board
845 Third Avenue
New York, New York 10022, U.S.A.

Telephone: (212) 759-0900

Profession: Economist

Field of specialization: Concerned with impact of changes in makeup of labor force for social and economic activity in next decades; technologies of occupational procedures and their uses in planning.

Education: B.A., Sociology, University of Minnesota, 1942; Ph.D., Economics, Columbia University, 1953.

Professional employment: The Conference Board: Director, Special Research Projects (1974-). National Planning Association: Director, Center for Priority Analysis (1963-74). Long Island University: Professor, Chairman, Economics Department (1954-63). Carleton College: Assistant Professor (1953-54). University of Texas: Assistant Professor (1949-53).

270

Professional activities: Research on effects of slow or rapid growth in recovery from current recession on employment in different occupations (1976); completing study of changes in occupational characteristics and their implications for manpower, educational planning in next decade; lecturer, New School for Social Research (1976); Adjunct Professor, Temple University (1967-68); consultant and speaker to public and private agencies in fields of manpower, planning, and priorities.

Publications: Co-author, *Planning Ahead for the 1980's: Changes in Occupational Characteristics* (The Conference Board, 1976); *Occupational Choices and Training Needs: Prospects for the 1980's* (Praeger, 1977); *Dollars for National Goals: Looking Ahead to 1980* (John Wiley, 1974); *Evaluating Vocational Education Policies and Plans for the 1970's* (Praeger, 1974); *Manpower Needs for National Goals in the 1970's* (Praeger, 1964); *Goals, Priorities and Dollars—The Next Decade* (Free Press, 1966); *Experience Under Railway Labor Legislation* (Columbia University Press, 1951).

LENK, HANS A. P.　　　　　　　　　　　　　　　**Born:** 1935, Berlin, Germany
Professor
Department of Philosophy
Karlsruhe University
Kaiserstrasse 12
D7500 Karlsruhe, Federal Republic of Germany　　　　**Telephone:** (0721) 608-2149

Profession: Philosopher; sociologist

Field of specialization: Epistemology; philosophy of the social and systems sciences and of technology; value systems and moral philosophy; analytical philosophy and logic; formal methods in sociology.

Education: Habilitation in Sociology, 1969, Technical University of Berlin.

Professional employment: Karlsruhe University: Full Professor of Philosophy (1969-); Dean of Humanities and Social Sciences (1973-75). University of Massachusetts: Visiting Professor (1976). University of Illinois: Visiting Professor (1973). Technical University of Berlin: Universitatsdozent (1967); Assistant Professor (1962).

Professional activities: Philosophy of the Social and systems sciences (1976-); action theories in an inter-disciplinary perspective (1975-76); philosophy of technology (1972-75); foundation of logical constants (1964-68); philosophical problems of explanation, prediction and planning (1969-72); achievement principle and motivation in a philosophical perspective (1972-75); has published 30 books as author and editor and more than 300 articles.

Publications: *Erklaerung—Prognose—Planung [Explanation—Forecasts—Planning]* (Rombach, Freiburg, 1972); *Pragmatische Philosophie [Pragmatic Philosophy* (Hoffman and Campe, Hamburg, 1975); co-author and editor, *Technokratie als Ideologie [Technocracy as Ideology]* (Kohlhammer, Stuttgart, 1973); *Normenlogik [Logic of Norms]* (Dokumentation Saur, Munich, 1974); co-author and editor, *Systemtheorie als Wissenschaftsprogramm [Systems Theory as a Scientific Program]* (Athenaeum, Frankfurt, 1978); co-author and editor, *Handlungstheorien Interdisziplinaer [Theories of Action in Interdisciplinary Perspective* (Fink, Munich, 1977, 4 vols.).

LENZ, RALPH C., JR.　　　　　　　　　　　　**Born:** 1919, Beatrice, Nebraska, U.S.A.
Senior Research Engineer
University of Dayton Research Institute
300 College Park Drive
Dayton, Ohio 45469, U.S.A.　　　　　　　　　　**Telephone:** (513) 229-3036

Profession: Technology analyst

Field of specialization: Technological forecasting; technology assessment.

Education: Aeronautical Engineering, University of Cincinnati, 1943; M.S., Industrial Management, Massachusetts Institute of Technology, 1959.

Professional employment: University of Dayton Research Institute: Senior Research Engineer (1975-). Aeronautical Systems Division, U.S. Air Force: Assistant Deputy for Development Planning (1963-74); Chief, Plans Division (1957-62). Wright Air Development Center, U.S. Air Force: Chief, Research Plans (1954-56); Structures Engineer (1946-53). Glenn L. Martin Company: Senior Quality Engineer (1943-45).

Professional activities: Flight vehicle technology assessment and forecasting, AF Office of Scientific Research;

satellite communications forecast, NASA-Lewis; electronic U.S. Telephone and Telegraph Corporation and DuPont Textile Fibers Department; lectures frequently on trend extrapolation methods of technological forecasting and has published several articles on this topic; co-founding editor of *Technological Forecasting and Social Change* (1969-71).

Publications: Co-author, *Predicting the Diffusion Rate of Industrial Innovations* (University of Dayton Research Institute, March 1978); co-author, *Technology Systems Division Report 62-414, 1962); A Development of Explicit Methods in Technological Forecasting* (Master's Thesis, MIT, 1959).

LEONARD, GEORGE B.

Box 509
Mill Valley, California 94941, U.S.A.

Born: 1923, Macon, Georgia, U.S.A.

Telephone: (415) 383-1480

Profession: Author; cultural analyst

Field of specialization: Cultural evolution in terms of education, sexuality, sports and games, lifestyle, energy utilization, social organization and consciousness.

Education: A.B., English, University of North Carolina.

Professional employment: Self-employed: Author, Lecturer, Workshop Leader (1970-). *Look* Magazine: Senior Editor (1953-70). United States Air Force: Intelligence Analyst (1950-53); Combat Pilot (1943-45).

Professional activities: President-Elect, Association for Humanistic Psychology (1978-79); Vice President, International Movement Arts Center (1976-); has written numerous articles for *Harper's, Atlantic, Saturday Review, New York, Esquire, Reader's Digest* (1971-) and numerous analytical articles and special issues of *Look* Magazine (1953-70); Vice-President, Esalen Institute (1965-69); frequently gives workshops in relaxation, conflict resolution, stress reduction and alternative ways of being, based on insights from the art of aikido; co-owner of a school, Aikido of Tamalpais.

Publications: *The Transformation* (Delacorte, 1972); *The Silent Pulse* (Dutton, 1978); *The Ultimate Athlete* (Viking, 1975); *Education and Ecstasy* (Delacorte,1968); *The Man and Woman Thing* (Delacorte, 1970).

LESH, DONALD R.

Executive Director
U.S. Association for the Club of Rome
1735 De Sales Street, N.W., Eighth Floor
Washington, D. C. 20036, U.S.A.

Born: 1931, Berwyn, Illinois, U.S.A.

Telephone: (202) 638-1029

Profession: Non-profit policy analysis and editing

Field of specialization: Public education on future issues; changes in U.S. values and norms; information for decision-makers.

Education: B.A., English, University of Rochester, 1953; M.A., Russian Studies, Harvard University Graduate School, 1959; Ph.D. Candidate, Slavic Languages and Literatures, Harvard University Graduate School, 1959-60; Graduate Student, Moscow State University, Moscow, USSR, 1960-61.

Professional employment: U.S. Association for The Club of Rome: Executive Director (1977-). Potomac Associates: Vice-President (1970-77). Administrative Aide to U.S. Senator Mike Gravel, Alaska (September-December, 1970). Department of State: Foreign Service Officer (1961-70).

Professional activities: Observer, United Nations Conference on the Human Environment, Stockholm, Sweden (1972); participant and speaker, Wilton Park Conference on Problems of Economic and Social Development, Sussex, England (1973); panel participant, Amerika Haus conference on *The Limits to Growth*, Frankfurt, Germany (1973); participant, Special Meeting of The Club of Rome on the New International Order, Algiers, Algeria (1976); periodic liason with Canadian Association for The Club of Rome in Ottawa and Montreal, Canada (1977-); writer, periodic newsletter, U.S. Association for the Club of Rome.

Publications: Editor, *A Nation Observed: Perspectives on America's World Role* (Potomac Associates, 1974); co-author with Walter Slocombe, Lloyd A. Free, and William Watts, "The Pursuit of National Security: Defense and the Military Balance" (*Policy Perspective 1976/3*, Potomac Associates, 1976); co-author with Gladwin Hill and Lloyd A. Free, "Protecting the Environment: Progress, Prospects, and the Public View" (*Policy Perspective 1976/4*, Potomac Associates, 1976); co-author with Edwin L. Dale, Jr. and Lloyd A. Free, "Priorities in an Uncertain Economy: Inflation, Recession and Government Spending" (*Policy Perspective 1976/5*, Potomac Associates, 1976).

LESOURNE, JACQUES FRANCOIS

Born: 1928, La Rochelle, France

Director, INTERFUTURES
Organization for Economic Cooperation and Development
176, Avenue Charles de Gaulle
92200 Neuilly-sur-Seine, France

Telephone: 747 12-80

Profession: Economist

Field of specialization: Systems analysis; econometrics; prospective.

Education: Ecole Polytechnique, Paris; Ingenieur des Mines.

Professional employment: Organization for Economic Cooperation and Development: Director, IN-TERFUTURES research project on the future development of advanced industrial societies in harmony with that of developing countries (1976-). SEMA-METRA International: President (1958-76). French National Coal Board (1954-57).

Professional activities: Vice Chairman of the International Institute for Applied Systems Analysis, Vienna, Austria; Chairman of the Association Francaise pour le Developpement de l'Analyse de Systemes, France; Professor of Economics at the Conservatoire National des Arts et Metiers, Paris.

Publications: *The Management Revolution* (1970); *Modeles de croissance de l'entreprise [Models of Business Growth]* (1972); *Cost-Benefit Analysis and Economic Theory* (1975); *Les systemes du destin [Systems of Destiny]* (1976); *A Theory of the Individual for Economic Analysis* (1977).

LESSE, STANLEY

Born: 1922, Philadelphia, Pennsylvania, U.S.A.

Editor-in-Chief
American Journal of Psychotherapy
114 East 78th Street
New York, New York 10021, U.S.A.

Telephone: (212) 288-4466

Profession: Neurologist-psychiatrist

Field of specialization: Medicine; values; psychiatry-neurology; futures methodology; education.

Education: B.A., Chemistry, University of Pennsylvania, 1942; M.D., Jefferson Medical College, 1945; Med. Sc. D., College of Physicians and Surgeons, Columbia University, 1955.

Professional employment: Neurological Institute of New York, Columbia Presbyterian Hospital: Attending Neurologist (1953-). Private practice of Neurology and Psychiatry (1952-). *American Journal of Psychotherapy*: Editor-in-Chief (1959-). Association for the Advancement of Psychotherapy: President (1964-).

Professional activities: Scientific Council, World Future Studies Federation; Board of Directors, International Federation for Medical Psychotherapy; Commission on Therapy, American Psychiatric Association; current research on future of health science, future of education, psychotropic drugs, psychotherapy, and neurology; active in international psychotherapy; lecturer at many medical colleges in U.S. and abroad; Visiting Professor of Psychiatry, King George Medical College, Luchnow, India (1975); has published more than 200 articles dealing with futures, psychotherapy, psychotropic drugs, neuropathology, psychosociology, and education.

Publications: "The Preventive Psychiatry of the Future" (THE FUTURIST, Vol. 10, No. 5, October 1976); "Factors Influencing Sexual Behavior in Our Future Society" (*American Journal of Psychotherapy*, Vol. 30, July 1976); "Human Needs: The Determining Factors" (*Futures*, Vol. 8, December 1976); co-author, "Medicine and Our Future Society" in *Mankind 2000* (Allen and Unwin, London, 1969); "Future-Oriented Psychotherapy" (*American Journal of Psychotheraphy*, Vol. 25, 180, 1971).

LINDAMAN, EDWARD B.

Born: 1920, Davenport, Iowa, U.S.A.

President
Whitworth College
Spokane, Washington 99251, U.S.A.

Telephone: (509) 489-3550

Profession: Educational administrator

Field of specialization: Impact of science and technology on human values; citizen participation.

Education: —

Professional employment: Whitworth College: President (1970-). Rockwell International: Director, Program Planning, Apollo Spacecraft Project (1962-69); Manager, Master Planning, Minuteman Guidance and Control Systems (1958-61).

Professional activities: Consultant, Office of Technology Assessment (1977-); founding member, Association of Futures-Invention Facilitators; member, Policy Board of Project Change in Liberal Education, Association of American Colleges (1975-76); member, Commission on Liberal Learning, Association of American Colleges (1975-76); Chairperson, National Goals Steering Committee for years 1979-1984, National Council of YMCA's (1976-80); Chairperson, Board of Directors, Northwest Regional Foundation, Spokane (1974-76); member, Board of Advisers, Northwest Institute of Applied Social Sciences (1976); Chairman, Alternatives for Washington 1985, Governor's Citizen Task Force (1973-75); has lectured extensively on the relationship between religion and science in the context of our responsibility to the future; conducts courses in futuristics at Whitworth College and consults with business organizations in the Pacific Northwest on future planning; conducts workshops on futures invention for churches, YMCA's and educational groups in the western United States.

Publications: *Thinking in the Future Tense* (Broadman Press, Nashville, Tennessee, 1978); *Space: A New Direction for Mankind* (Harper and Row, 1969).

LINDSEY, GEORGE ROY

Born: 1920, Toronto, Ontario, Canada

Chief
Operational Research and Analysis Establishment
101 Colonel By Drive
Ottawa, Ontario, Canada K1A 0K2

Telephone: (613) 992-5025

Profession: Operational Research and Systems Analyst

Field of specialization: Strategic studies; futures studies; implication of technology for international stability.

Education: B.A., Mathematics and Physics, University of Toronto, 1942; M.A., Experimental Physics, Queens University, 1946; Ph.D., Nuclear Physics, University of Cambridge, 1950; National Defence College, 1966; Public Service Bicultural Course, Quebec, 1971.

Professional employment: Operational Research and Analysis Establishment: Chief (1974-). Defence Research Analysis Establishment: Chief (1967-74). Operational Research Group, SACLANT ASW Centre, La Spezia, Italy: Head (1961-64). Defence Systems Analysis Group: Director (1959-61). Royal Canadian Air Force Air Defence Command: Senior Operational Research Officer (1954-59). Defence Research Board of Canada (1950-74).

Professional activities: Currently director of operational research analysis program for Canadian Department of National Defence; designing futures research programme for Institute for Research on Public Policy; operational research on strategic and tactical problems of military process (1943-); Past President, Canadian Operational Research Society (1961).

Publications: Co-author, *The Dynamics of the Nuclear Balance* (Cornell University Press, 1974); co-author, *Le Feu Nucleaire [Nuclear Fire]* (Seuil, Paris, 1973); "The Limitation of Military Space Vehicles" (*Air Force College Journal*, Toronto, 1961); "The Stability of Countries of Various Sizes" (*Proceedings of the Fifth International Conference of Operational Research*, 1970); "How Dangerous Is Nuclear Proliferation?" (*Science Forum*, Vol. 8, No. 1, 1975).

LINNEMANN, HANS
Director
Economic and Social Institute
Free University
P.O. Box 7161
Amsterdam, The Netherlands

Born: 1931, Rotterdam, Netherlands

Telephone: (20) 5484622

Profession: Economist

Field of specialization: Economic development; agriculture and natural resources.

Education: Ph.D., Economics, Netherlands School of Economics, Rotterdam, 1966.

Professional employment: Free University, Amsterdam, Department of Economics: Professor of Development Economics (1966-). Netherlands School of Economics, Rotterdam: Lecturer and Senior Lecturer, Economics (1958-66).

Professional activities: Member of an interdisciplinary research team studying the long-term development of food production and consumption in the world; teaching and research in international development problems; United Nations assignments in economic planning (1959-64).

Publications: Co-author, *MOIRA-Model of International Relations in Agriculture* (North-Holland, Amsterdam, 1979); co-author, "To Grow or Not to Grow: Is That the Question?" (*Anticipation*, May 1974); *An Econometric Study of International Trade Flows* (North-Holland, Amsterdam, 1966); co-author, with Jan Tinbergen, *Shaping the World Economy* (Twentieth Century Fund, New York, 1962).

LINOWITZ, SOL M.
Senior Partner
Coudert Brothers
One Farragut Square South
Washington, D.C. 20006, U.S.A.

Born: 1913, Trenton, New Jersey, U.S.A.

Telephone: (202) 783-3010

Profession: Attorney

Field of specialization: Law, international affairs, Latin America.

Education: A.B., Hamilton College, 1935; J.D., Cornell Law School, 1938.

Professional employment: Coudert Brothers—An International Law Firm: Senior Partner (1969-). Organization of American States: U.S. Ambassador (1966-69). Inter-American Committee of the Alliance for Progress: U.S. Representative (1966-69). Xerox Corporation: Chairman of the Board, previously Chairman of Executive Committee and General Counsel (1955-66). Harris, Beach, Wilcox, Dale and Linowitz (Rochester, New York): Senior Partner (1958-66).

Professional activities: Co-chairman (formerly Chairman), National Urban Coalition; President, Federal City Council; Chairman, National Council of Foreign Policy Association; Chairman, Commission on U.S./Latin American Relations; Memberships: Board of Directors, Time, Inc., World Future Society, Pan American World Airways; co-negotiator, Panama Canal treaties; member, National Commission on Critical Choices for Americans, Council of Foreign Relations.

Publications: Author of articles in professional journals.

LINSTONE, HAROLD A.
University Professor and Director, Futures Research Institute
Portland State University
P.O. Box 751
Portland, Oregon 97207, U.S.A.

Born: 1924, Hamburg, Germany

Telephone: (503) 229-4960

Profession: Planner; systems analyst

Field of specialization: Technological forecasting; futures methodology; corporate planning; technology assessment.

Education: B.S., Geophysics, City College of New York, 1944; M.A., Mathematics, Columbia University, 1947; Ph.D., Mathematics, University of Southern California, 1954.

Professional employment: Portland State University: University Professor and Director, Futures Research Institute (1977-); Professor and Director, Systems Science Ph.D. Program (1970-77). Lockheed Aircraft Corporation: Associate Director of Corporate Planning—Systems Analysis (1963-70). Rand Corporation: Senior Research Scientist (1961-63). Hughes Aircraft Company: Head, Corporate Planning Staff and Operations Analysis Group (1949-61).

Professional activities: Editor, *Technological Forecasting and Social Change*, an international journal (1969-); President, Systems Forecasting, Inc. (1969-); Director, Center for Technological and Interdisciplinary Forecasting, Tel Aviv University (1971-72); consultant (1961-).

Publications: Co-editor with M. Turoff, *The Delphi Method: Techniques and Applications* (Addison-Wesley Publishing Co., 1975); co-editor with D. Sahal, *Technological Substitution* (Elsevier, 1976); co-editor with W.H.C. Simmonds, *Futures Research: New Directions* (Addison-Wesley Publishing Co., 1977); "Planning: Toy or Tool?" *(IEEE Spectrum*, April 1974); "Four American Futures: Reflections on the Role of Planning" *(Technological Forecasting and Social Change*, Vol. 4, No. 1, 1972); "A University for the Post-Industrial Society" *(Technological Forecasting and Social Change*, Vol. 1, No. 3, 1970).

LIPINSKI, ANDREW J.

Born: 1920, Poznan, Poland

Senior Research Fellow
Institute for the Future
2740 Sand Hill Road
Menlo Park, California 94025, U.S.A.

Telephone: (415) 854-6322

Profession: Research fellow

Field of specialization: Elicitation, processing and aggregation of expert judgement; calibration of experts; modeling; communication of results to decision makers.

Education: B.S., 1946, Diploma, 1947, Electrical Engineering, Imperial College of Science and Technology, London, England.

Professional employment: Institute for the Future: Senior Research Fellow (1969-). Stanford Research Institute: Research Analyst (1965-69). Lenkurt Electric Company, Planning Department: Research Analyst (1961-65). Canadian Westinghouse Company, Electronics Division, General Telecommunications Department: Manager (1958-61).

Professional activities: Future of the United Kingdom (1978); working on impact of societal, economic, and regulatory changes on the future of large corporations; work in the fields of future-oriented methodology, satellite communications and telecommunications.

Publications: Co-author with H. M. Lipinski, "Canadian Policy Options in Computer Communications" *(Background Papers: The Canadian Computer/Communications Task Force*, 1974); co-author with D.A. Dunn, "Economic Considerations in Computer-Communication Systems" *(Computer-Communication Networks*, 1973); co-author with H. M. Lipinski and R.H. Randolph, "Computer-Assisted Expert Interrogation: A Report on Current Methods Development" *(Technological Forecasting and Social Change*, Vol. 5, No. 1, 3-18, 1973).

LIPPITT, GORDON L.

Born: 1920, Fergus Falls, Minnesota, U.S.A.

Professor of Behavioral Science
George Washington University
2131 G Street, N.W.
Washington, D.C. 20036, U.S.A.

Telephone: (301) 320-4409

Profession: Educator

Field of specialization: Futures methodology; organization development; leadership development for the future; images of potential analysis for organizations and groups.

Education: B.S., Counselling and Guidance, Springfield College, 1942; B.D., Psychology of Religion,

Yale University, 1945; M.A., Educational Psychology, University of Nebraska, 1947; Ph.D., Social Psychology, American University, 1959.

Professional employment: George Washington University: Professor of Behavioral Science (1960-). National Education Association: Program Director (1950-59). Union College: Assistant Professor of Psychology (1949-50). University of Nebraska: Instructor (1945-49). New Haven YMCA: Executive Director (1942-45).

Professional activities: Study of consulting process, Academy of Management (1973-76); study of multidisciplinary problem solving, "multocular process" (1971-76); study of "criteria for effective resource developments," American Society of Training and Development (1975-76); Past President, American Society of Training and Development (1969); Chairman, Consulting Division, Academy of Management (1975); Executive Committee, Society of Personnel Administration (1964-65).

Publications: *Visualizing Change—Model Building* (University Associates, 1973); *Organizational Renewal* (Prentice-Hall, 1969); editor, *Optimizing Human Resources* (Addison-Wesley Publishing Co., (1971); editor, *Management Development and Training Handbook* (McGraw-Hill, 1975); *Quest for Dialogue* (Development Publications, 1965).

LITTLE, DENNIS LLOYD
Specialist in Futures Research
Congressional Research Service
U.S. Library of Congress
Washington, D.C. 20540, U.S.A.

Born: 1938, Minneapolis, Minnesota, U.S.A.

Telephone: (202) 426-6498

Profession: Policy analyst

Field of specialization: Futures research; strategic planning and public administration.

Education: A.B., 1960, M.A., 1962, Georgetown University; graduate courses in Business, Public Administration and Urban Planning at Wayne State University and the University of Michigan; doctoral program, School of Public Administration, University of Southern California.

Professional employment: Congressional Research Service, Library of Congress: Management Staff and Specialist in Futures Research (1975-). Office of Administration, Social Security Administration: Program Analyst, Long Range Planning Staff (1973-74). Commonwealth of Pennsylvania: Commissioner, Office of Income Maintenance (1972-73). The Institute for the Future: Research Associate (1969-72). Metropolitan Fund (Urban Affairs Foundation): Program Associate (1968-69). Ford Motor Company: Supervisor, Administrative Section, Purchasing, later Coordinator, Program Timing Department, Product Development Office (1962-68).

Professional activities: Design, manage, and execute various interdisciplinary research projects with a futures perspective; established and developed the Futures Research Group at the Congressional Research Service; adjunct faculty, School of Public Administration, University of Southern California and Policy Sciences Program, University of Maryland, Baltimore County (present); consultant on various futures projects such as: International City Manager's Association (Urban 2000), Midwest Research Institute (Kansas City Tomorrow), National Institute of Public Administration (President's Management Intern Program), United States Department of Agriculture (Renewable Natural Resources), and Edison Electric Institute (Future of Economic Growth); member and chairman, Public Service Futures Committee, American Society for Public Administration; member, World Future Society and awarded Society's Distinguished Service Award in 1975.

Publications: "Post-Industrial Society and What It May Mean" a review of Daniel Bell's *The Coming of Post-Industrial Society: A Venture in Social Forecasting* (THE FUTURIST, December 1973); *Renewable Natural Resources: Some Emerging Issues*, a report to the Senate Committee on Agriculture, Nutrition, and Forestry, 96th Congress, 1st session; *Long Range Planning*, a report to the Subcommittee on the Environment and the Atmosphere of the Committee on Science and Technology, U.S. House of Representatives, 94th Congress, 2nd session; *Computer Simulation Methods to Aid National Growth Policy*, a report to the Subcommittee on Fisheries and Wildlife Conservation and the Environment of the Committee on Merchant Marine and Fisheries, U.S. House of Representatives, 94th Congress, 1st session; co-editor with Walter A. Hahn, "Public Administration in the Third Century" (a symposium, *Public Administration Review*, September-October, 1976).

LIVINGSTON, DENNIS
Marlboro College
Marlboro, Vermont 05344 U.S.A.

Born: 1940, New York, New York, U.S.A.

Telephone: (802) 254-2393

Profession: Political scientist; policy analyst/consultant

Field of specialization: World order; international environment/marine affairs; science fiction and utopian literature; alternative lifestyles; intermediate technology; technology assessment; community and Third World economic development; future studies education.

Education: B.A., Political Science, University of California-Santa Barbara, 1961; Ph.D., Political Science, Princeton University, 1967.

Professional employment: Marlboro College: Visiting Professor of Social Science (1978-79). Rensselaer Polytechnic Institute: Assistant Professor of Political Science (1974-78). Self-employed as a consultant on education for alternative futures (1972-74). Center for Marine Affairs, Scripps Institute of Oceanography, San Diego; Post-Doctoral Fellow (1972). Case Western Reserve University: Assistant Professor of Political Science (1968-71). University of California-Davis: Assistant Professor of Political Science (1964-68).

Professional activities: Member of American Political Science Association, International Studies Association, World Future Society, Science Fiction Research Association, Society for Social Studies of Science; conducts courses on "limits to growth and world order," "science, technology and public policy," "food and the global community," "the politics of outer space," "science, technology, and values," "science fiction," and "appropriate technology and the politics of decentralization"; ongoing research projects on policy and long-range implications of appropriate technology, global pollution and world order, decentralization and the steady state society, and use of science fiction in futures research; developed slide show presentation on "Images of the Future" using illustrations from science fiction magazines to analyze alternative futures open to society.

Publications: Co-author, *Technological Choices and Development Strategies in Developing Countries* (National Science Foundation funded research report, October 1978); "The Utility of Science Fiction" in Fowles, *Handbook of Futures Research* (Greenwood Press, 1978); "Science Fiction as an Educational Tool" in Alvin Toffler's *Learning for Tomorrow* (Random, 1974); "International Technology Assessment and the United Nations System" (*Proceedings of the American Society of International Law*, 1970).

LOVERIDGE, DENIS JOHN
Manager, Business Development
Pilkington Brothers Ltd.
Watson Street
St. Helens, Merseyside
United Kingdom

Born: 1930, Batugajah, Malaysia

Telephone: 744-28882 ext. 6132

Profession: Generalist; policy analyst

Field of specialization: Social philosophy; values; corporate/national futures; energy; communication; methodology.

Education: B.Sc., General, London Universities External, 1953.

Professional employment: Pilkington Brothers Ltd.: Manager, Business Development (1971-). British Coal Utilization Research Association: Project Coordinator, Process Development Group (1957-71). Vokes Ltd.: Research Officer (1956-57). Royal Artillary: Surveyor (1953-55). F.W. Berk and Co. Ltd.: Analytical Chemist (1947-53).

Professional activities: Working on social futures for the 1980's-90's (1973-); United Kingdom Associate of the Institute for the Future, Menlo Park, California, for a study of the future of the United Kingdom (1977-); Planning Manager to Pilkington Cemfil Project (1971-77); the future of the television receiver manufacturing industry (1972-73).

Publications: "Values and Futures" in *Futures Research: New Directions*, Simmonds and Linstone, eds. (Addison-Wesley, 1978); co-author with P. Holroyd, "Industry and Higher Education Alternatives" in *Higher Education Alternatives*, Stephens and Roderick, eds. (Pergamon Press, 1978); "Futures Research and Corporate Planning" (lecture to Administrative Staff College, Henley, 1977); "Project Control: A Commentary Based on Industrial and Research Experience" (paper to the Royal Aeronautical Society Symposium, March 1977); "Installing Data Logging" (*Engineering, 1968*).

LOVINS, AMORY B.
British Representative
Friends of the Earth
9 Poland Street
London, W1V 3DG, England

Born: 1947, Washington, D.C., U.S.A.

Telephone: (01) 439-9247; 434-1684

Profession: Consultant physicist

Field of specialization: Energy and resource strategies, particularly those based on efficient use and renewables.

Education: Chemical Physics, Linguistics, Law, Harvard College, 1964-65 and 1966-67; Chemical Physics, Linguistics, Law, Medicine, Magdalen College, Oxford, 1967-69; M.A., Biophysics, Merton College, Oxford.

Professional employment: Academic, governmental, and intergovernment organizations in many countries: Consultant (1974-). Friends of the Earth: British Representative (1971-). University of California at Berkeley: Regents' Lecturer on Energy and Resources (1978). Camp Winona, Bridgton, Maine: Mountain Guide (Summers, 1966-). Academic, governmental, and industrial research organizations in the U.S.A.: Consultant Experimental Physicist (1965-68).

Professional activities: Active in energy policy at a technical and political level in about 15 countries, both privately and via International Project for Soft Energy Paths (IPSEP); co-editor, *Soft Energy Notes*, IPSEP (1978-); work on energy and allied topics; research and writing on nuclear proliferation and its links with domestic energy policy, policy instruments for clearing institutional barriers, and other specialized energy topics; numerous lectures and publications; various consultative groups and advisory boards.

Publications: *Soft Energy Paths: Toward a Durable Peace* (Friends of the Earth, San Francisco; Ballinger, 1977; Harper and Row, 1979); "Soft Energy Technologies" (*Annual Review of Energy*, Vol. 3, 1978); "Cost-Risk-Benefit Assessments in Energy Policy" (*George Washington Law Review*, Vol. 45 1977); co-author and co-photographer, *Eryri, the Mountains of Longing* (Friends of the Earth, San Francisco; McCall; Allen and Unwin, 1971).

LOYE, DAVID
Co-Director
Institute for Futures Forecasting
25700 Shafter Way
Carmel, California 93923, U.S.A.

Born: 1925, Palo Alto, California, U.S.A.

Telephone: (408) 624-8337

Profession: Social psychologist

Field of specialization: Futures forecasting; the psychology of ideology; social dynamics theory.

Education: B.S., Psychology, Dartmouth College, 1948; M.A., Psychology of Personality, Ph.D., Social Psychology, New School for Social Research.

Professional employment: Institute for Futures Forecasting: Co-Director (1978-). University of California at Los Angeles (UCLA) School of Medicine: Research Director, Program on Psychological Adaptation and the Future (1974-79); Research Psychologist, Department of Psychiatry (1974-). Princeton University: Visiting Lecturer (1973-74). Educational Testing Service: Professional Associate (1967-73).

Professional activities: Conducting developmental research for new Ideological Matrix Prediction (IMP), Hemispheric Consensus Prediction (HCP), Person-Situation Prediction (PSP), and Social Dynamics Prediction (SDP) methods of futures forecasting; writing *The Psychology of the Middle* and *The Social Motor;* research on ideology and social dynamics base to forecasting at Princeton University (1972-74), UCLA (1974—); lecturing on effecting social change; television effects on adults; left-right and forebrain functioning in forecasting (1971-78); former Chairman, Los Angeles Chapter, Society for the Psychological Study of Social Issues (1976-77).

Publications: *The Knowable Future: A Psychology of Forecasting and Prophecy* (Wiley-Interscience, 1978); *The Leadership Passion: A Psychology of Ideology* (Jossey-Bass, 1977); *The Healing of a Nation* (Norton, 1971; Delta, 1972); co-author with Milton Rokeach, "Ideology, Belief Systems, Values and Attitudes" in *The International Encyclopedia of Neurology, Psychiatry, Psychoanalysis and Psychology* (Van Nostrand-Reinhold, 1976); co-author with Harry Harman and Carl Helm, *Computer-Assisted Testing* (Educational Testing Service, 1968).

MACKENSEN, RAINER ULRICH
Professor of Sociology
Technische Universitat Berlin
Dovestr. 1-5
1 Berlin 10, BRD 1000
Federal Republic of Germany

Born: 1927, Greifswald, Germany

Telephone: (030) 314-3255

Profession: Sociologist

Field of specialization: Urban and regional planning; demography.

Education: Dr. Phil., Philosophy, University of Tuebingen, 1954; Venia Legendi, Sociology and Demography, University of Muenster, 1967; Professor Ordinarius, Sociology, Technische Universitat, Berlin, 1968.

Professional employment: Technische Universitat Berlin, Institute of Sociology: Managing Director (1978-); Professor of Sociology (1974-).

Professional activities: Project Director, Migration in Federal Germany (finished 1976); Project Director, Population Project Group, Werner Reimers Foundation.

Publications: Co-author and editor, *Dynamik der Bevolkerungsentwicklung [Dynamics of Population Growth]* (Carl Hanser Verlag, Munchen, 1973); *Probleme Regionaler Mobilitat [Problems of Regional Mobility]* (Otto Schwartz Verlag, Gottingen, 1975); co-author, *Gesellschaftliche Bedurfnislagen [The Situation of Social Needs]* (Otto Schwartz Verlag, Gottingen, 1975); co-author and editor, *Alternativen fur die Verstadterung Europas [Alternatives to the Urbanization of Europe]* (Zentrum Berlin fur Zukunftsforschung, 1975).

MACNULTY, CHRISTINE A. RALPH
Many Futures
4, St. Katherine's Road
Henley-on-Thames, Oxfordshire
RG9, 1PJ United Kingdom

Born: 1945, Salford, Lancaster, United Kingdom

Telephone: Henley 2519

Profession: Management consultant

Field of specialization: Scenario development; strategy development and assessment; forecasting; long range planning.

Education: Mathematics, London University; courses at several U.S. universities.

Professional employment: Many Futures: Partner (1972-). Strategic Resources Group: Associate (1972-74). International Research and Technology Corp.: Senior Staff Member (1969-72). Plessey Radar Ltd.: Systems Analyst (1967-69).

Professional activities: Consultant to Taylor Woodrow Construction Ltd. (1977-); lecturer on scenario development and social forecasting at Bradford University Management Centre each December and June since June 1976; Consultant to Programmes Analysis Unit (February 1976-September 1977); lecturer on scenario development as part of the corporate planning process, Administrative Staff College (February 1977); consultant to many U.S. corporations and government agencies (1969-75).

Publications: "Scenario Development for Corporate Planning" (*Futures*, IPC Press, April 1977); co-author and editor, *Industrial Applications of Technological Forecasting* (John Wiley and Sons, 1971); *Politics and the Businessman to 1990* (Many Futures Report, 1975).

MADEIRA, THOMAS ROBERTS
Planning Supervisor
Philadelphia Architects' Workshop
401 North Broad Street
Philadelphia, Pennsylvania 19108, U.S.A.

Born: 1947, Philadelphia, Pennsylvania, U.S.A.

Telephone: (215) 574-9491

Profession: Urban Planner

Field of specialization: Long-range futures; social and educational planning; housing and finance.

Education: A.B., Sociology, Princeton University, 1969; M.A., Urban and Regional Planning, Nottingham University, 1972.

Professional employment: Philadelphia Architects' Workshop: Planning Supervisor (1977-). London Borough of Lambeth: Senior Planning Officer (1974-76). Halpern and Partners, London: Planner (1972-74). Harbeson, Hough, Livingston and Larsen, Philadelphia: Researcher (1969-70).

Professional activities: Directing community planning and development studies for advocacy planning and design center; free lance lecturing on future studies and consultant in futures with relevance to urban policy and development; Member of the Royal Town Planning Institute, participated in over 25 planning and development studies in four countries (since 1969).

Publications: —

MALEK, IVAN

Born: 1909, Zabreh, Czechoslovakia

Director, Senior Scientist
Academician
Czechoslovac Academy of Sciences
Narodni tr. 3, 11000
Praha 1, Czechoslovakia
Na dolinach 18
Praha 4, 14700, Czechoslovakia

Telephone: 4370 92

Profession: Medical doctor; microbiologist

Field of specialization: Single cells (bacteria, yeast, algae, fungi) as a source of protein food or fodder; planning of science; development of creativity as a main factor of human progress; role of health care in development of healthy and efficient human population.

Education: Medical Doctor, Charles University, Praha, 1932; Doctor of Sciences, 1952, Academician, 1952, Czechoslovac Academy of Sciences.

Professional employment: Microbiological Institute, Czechoslovac Academy of Sciences: Director, Senior Scientist (1963-69) (1973-). Czechoslovac Academy of Sciences: Vice-President (1961-69). Biological Institute, CSAV: Director (1952-63) (1950-). Charles University, Medical Faculty, Microbiology: Professor (1945-), Associate Professor (1945-48); University Assistant (1933-45).

Professional activities: Plan of organization of socialist health care (1941-65); planning science (1947-); biology for the future of mankind (1950-); The Biological Productivity and Human Welfare (Int. Biological Program) (1965-75); study of the factors of developing creative abilities in man (1967-); Secretary, Vice-President, International Union of Biological Science (IUBS) (1964, 1967-70); member of the Continuing Committee of the Pugwash Conferences (1960-73); member of the Governing Board of Stockholm International Peace Research Institute (SIPRI) (1965).

Publications: "Creativity and the Social Change" in Nobel Symposium 14, *The Place of Value* (Almquist and Wisell, Stockholm, 1970); *Biology for the Future* (published in Czechoslovakian, Russian and German, Publishing House, Czechoslovac Academy of Sciences, 1961); "World Order and the Responsibility of Scientists" in *Conditions of World Order*, Daedalus Library 10 (1966, 1968).

MALITZA, MIRCEA

Born: 1927, Oradea, Romania

Professor
Division for Systems Studies
University of Bucharest
14 Academiei
Bucharest, Romania

Telephone: 50 27 90

Profession: Mathematician

Field of specialization: Futures methodology; learning theories; games, coalitions, bargaining.

Education: M.S., 1950, Ph.D., Mathematics, University of Bucharest.

Professional employment: University of Bucharest: Professor, Division of Systems Studies (1972-); Assistant Professor (1950). Ministry of Education: Minister (1970-72). Ministry of Foreign Affairs: Deputy Minister (1962-70); Counsellor, U.N. Mission, New York (1956-61).

Professional activities: Course on "Mathematical Models in Social Sciences" (1972); research on learning theories, new mathematical concepts in social sciences, and theory of decisions under uncertainty; lecture on the "Mathematical Approaches to International Relations" (International Seminar, Romania, 1974).

Publications: *The Chronicle of the Year 2000* (Romanian edition, 1969; also published in Hungarian, Slovak, German, Polish, and Spanish); co-author, *Mathematics of Organization* (Abacus Press, England, 1974); "The Theory and Practice of Negotiations" (Bucharest, Ed. Pol., 1972); co-author, "Triads—Coalition and Connection in Games" (Ed. Stiintifica, Bucharest, 1973); *Gray Gold*—Three volumes of essays (Ed. Dacia, 1971, 72, 73).

MALLMANN, CARLOS ALBERTO
Executive President
Fundacion Bariloche
Casilla de Correo 138
San Carlos de Bariloche, Rio Negro 8400, Argentina

Born: 1928, Martinez, Buenos Aires, Argentina

Telephone: 48017; 18321

Profession: Physicist

Field of specialization: Quality of life and development; science policy.

Education: Ph.D., Physics and Mathematics, University of Buenos Aires, 1952.

Professional employment: Fundacion Bariloche: Head, Technological Transfer Program (1975-); Executive President (1966-75; 1978-). Synergic Developments Group: Researcher (1978). Bariloche Atomic Center: Director (1962-66). Atomic Energy Commission: Research Director (1961-62). Argonne National Laboratory, U.S.A.: Researcher (1958-61).

Professional activities: Currently working on a Latin American Model and studies of quality of life and development; 15 years of low-energy nuclear physics research and five years of science policy research.
Publication: *On the Formalization of a Dynamic and Systemic View of Synergic Human-Needs-Satisfaction-Oriented Developments* (December 1977); co-author, *Human Synergy as the Ethical and Esthetical Foundation of Development* (June 1978); *Needs-Satisfaction-Oriented Alternative Societies* (February 1978); *Appropriate—Synergy-Oriented—Technology for Industrialized Nations: A View from the Developing Countries* (March 1978); *Quality of Life and Development Alternatives* (Fundacion Bariloche, 1975).

MANDEL, THOMAS FREDERICK
Policy Analyst
Stanford Research Institute
333 Ravenswood Avenue
Menlo Park, California 94025, U.S.A.

Born: 1946, Chicago, Illinois, U.S.A.

Telephone: (415) 326-6200 x2365

Profession: Futurist

Field of specialization: Futures research, forecasting, long-range planning, and scenario generation methods and applications; policy analysis, especially in energy and transportation areas; future of the automobile; social impact assessment; entertainment and leisure technology.

Education: B.A., Futuristics, University of Hawaii, 1972; work in progress toward M.S., Cybernetic Systems, San Jose University.

Professional employment: Stanford Research Institute: Policy Analyst (1974-). DCM Associates, San Francisco: Consultant (intermittently, 1973-). Self-employed: Planning Consultant (1973-).

Professional activities: Current and recent research projects: analysis of long-range energy demand scenarios for California, especially transportation demands; alternative futures of automobiles in the U.S.; long-range alternative futures of U.S. transportation energy demand; technology forecasts in recreation and transportation areas; future of the U.S. automobile industry; future of leisure, recreation, and entertainment in the U.S.

Publications: Co-author, *Driven: The American Four-Wheeled Love Affair* (Stein and Day, 1977); *Future Technology in the California Desert* (Recreation, Agriculture and Transportation) (SRI International for the Bureau of Land Management, August, 1978); "U.S. Urban Transportation in the Early 21st Century" (*TOTAL Information,* France, Fall, 1978); "Getting Your Ideology Straight: What the Government Thinks Cars Will Look Like in the Next Decade" (*Car and Driver,* 1977); co-author, *Transportation in America's Future: Potentials for the Next Half Century* (SRI International for the U.S. Department of Transporation, 1977).

282

MARIEN, MICHAEL DAVID

Born: 1938, Washington, D.C., U.S.A.

Director
Information for Policy Design
Webster Road
Lafayette, New York 13084, U.S.A.

Telephone: (315) 677-9278

Profession: Social scientist; futures researcher

Field of specialization: Futures documentation; social role of future studies and policy studies; future studies methodology; social forecasting; trend analysis; social systems; cultural evolution; decentralization.

Education: B.S., Cornell University, 1959; M.B.A., Organization Theory, University of California-Berkeley, 1964; Ph.D., Social Science/National Planning, Syracuse University, Maxwell Graduate School of Citizenship and Public Affairs, 1970.

Professional employment: World Future Society: Director of Information Studies and editor of Future Survey (1978-). Information for Policy Design: Director (1974-). World Institute Council: Project Director (1972-74). Educational Policy Research Center, Syracuse University Research Corporation: Research Fellow (1968-72). University of California, Statewide Budget Office: Budget Analyst (1962-64).

Professional activities: Teaching course on "The Literature of Future Studies and Policy Studies," Syracuse University, School of Information Studies (Spring 1979); participant, First and Second General Assemblies, World Future Society and 1977 and 1978 conferences, Canadian Association for Futures Studies; contributor to the World Future Society's *The Future: A Guide to Information Sources*, editor, *Public Policy Book Forecast* (October 1977-October 1978).

Publications: "The New Path of Progress and the Devolution of Services" (*Social Policy*, Vol. 9, No. 2, November/December 1978); "The Two Visions of Post-Industrial Society" (*Futures*, Vol. 9, No. 5, October 1977); "Who's Who in Future Studies" (*Futures*, Vol. 9, No. 6, December 1977); compiler, *Societal Directions and Alternatives: A Critical Guide to the Literature* (Information for Policy Design, May 1976); compiler, "A World Institute Guide to Futures Periodicals" (*Fields Within Fields*, No. 12, Summer 1974); *Alternative Futures for Learning: An Annotated Bibliography of Trends, Forecasts, and Proposals* (Syracuse University, Educational Policy Research Center, 1971).

MARKLEY, O. W. ("MARK")

Born: 1937, Detroit, Kansas, U.S.A.

Associate Professor
Studies of the Future Program, University of Houston at Clear Lake City
2700 Bay Area Boulevard
Houston, Texas 77058, U.S.A.

Telephone: (713) 488-9250

Profession: Professor of futures research

Field of specialization: Methodology of forecasting, impact assessment, and strategic planning; transpersonal creativity and consciousness research.

Education: B.S., Mechanical Engineering, San Diego State University, 1962; M.S., Comprehensive Engineering Design, Stanford University; M.A., 1967, Ph.D., 1968, Social Psychology, Northwestern University.

Professional employment: University of Houston at Clear Lake City; Associate Professor (1978-). Management Awareness, Inc.: President (1978-). Stanford Research Institute, Center for the Study of Social Policy: Senior Policy Analyst (1973-78); Systems Analyst (1969-73). San Jose State University, Cybernetic Systems Program: Adjunct Professor (1974-). Western Behavioral Sciences Institute and Center for Studies of the Person: Postdoctoral Fellow (1968-69). Predoctorate employment in engineering and computer programming.

Professional activities: Currently teaching courses in forecasting, monitoring, assessment, systems analysis, transpersonal knowledge processes and task group dynamics; consultant to institutions such as SRI International, Battelle Laboratories, Department of Energy; study of feasibility of using minimum standards as a way to develop social indicators for the Environmental Protection Agency (1975); study of "social consequences of changing images of man" for the C.F. Kettering Foundation (1974-).

Publications: "Human Consciousness in Transformation" in *Human Systems in Transition,* Jantsch and Waddington (Addison-Wesley, 1976); *Changing Images of Man* (Policy Research Report Number Four, Stanford Research Institute, May 1974); "Alternative Future Histories: Methods, Results, and Educational Policy Implications" in *Long Range Policy Planning in Education* (Organization for Economic Cooperation and Development, 1973); *Contemporary Societal Problems* (Policy Research Report Number Two, Stanford Research Institute, June 1971); *Minimum Standards for Quality of Life* (Environmental Protection Agency, May 1975).

MARSH, JOHN S.
Associate Professor
Department of Geography
Trent University
Peterborough, Ontario, Canada

Born: 1942, England

Telephone: (705) 748-1211

Profession: Geographer

Field of specialization: Parks and recreation; history; planning; management and forecasting.

Education: B.A., Geography, University of Reading, U.K., 1963; M.Sc., Geography, University of Alberta, 1965; Ph.D., Geography, University of Calgary, 1971.

Professional employment: Trent University: Associate professor (1978-); Assistant professor (1971-78).

Professional activities: Research on a "National Park History of Canada"; teaches "Recreation Geography," "Geography of Future Environment"; editor, "Park News"; member, Canadian Association of Geographers and the World Future Society.

Publications: "Trends and Future Problems in North American Outdoor Recreation" (Transactions 41st North American Wildlife and Natural Resources Conference, 1976); co-author, "Recreation in Consumer and Conserver Societies" *(Alternatives,* 1978); "Maintaining the Wilderness Experience in Canada's National Parks" in Nelson's *Canadian Parks Perspective* (Harvest-House, 1970); "Land Use in Canada's National Parks" *(Alternatives,* Vol. 1, No. 3, 1972).

MARSTRAND, PAULINE KENDRICK
Senior Fellow
Science Policy Research Unit
University of Sussex
Falmer, Brighton
England

Born: 1927, London, England

Telephone: 0273. 686758

Profession: Hydrobiologist; science policy analyist

Field of specialization: Environmental evaluation of industrial policy; alternative technical choices.

Education: B.Sc., Zoology, 1951, M.Sc., Applied Hydrobiology, London University.

Professional employment: Science Policy Research Unit: Senior Fellow (1974-), Fellow (1969-74); various secondary schools; science teacher (1956-69).

Professional activities: Social and Technical Alternatives for the Future (1974-); Human Life and Safety in Relation to Technical Change (1969-73); Safety in the Home (1973-74); Vice-Chairman, Committee of Environment Division (1976-), secretary, Working Party, Biology in Water Industry (1969-72), chairman, Committee, Biologists in Water Industry (1972-77), member of Council (1973-77), Institute of Biology; consultant to UNIDO/UNEP, Triple Impact Project (June-July 1974); convenes and teaches undergraduate courses on "Science and Environment" "Industry, Resources and Environment" "Economics of Industry and Environment" and involved with post-graduate teaching and research; associated with

Science in a Social Context (SISCON) project of Bradford and Manchester Universities, producing teaching materials for transdiciplinary courses.

Publications: "Ecological and Social Evaluation of Industrial Development" (*Environmental Conservation*, Winter 1976); co-author, "World Food: Crisis or Plenty?" (*Food Policy*, in press); co-author, "When Enough is not Enough" chapter in *World Futures: The Great Debate*, Freeman and Jahoda, eds., (Martin Robertson, London, 1978); co-author and editor, *Environmental Pollution Controls* (Allen and Unwin, London, 1974).

MARTEL, LEON CHARLES

Executive Vice President
Hudson Institute
Quaker Ridge Road
Croton-on-Hudson, New York 10520, U.S.A.

Born: —

Telephone: (914) 762-0700

Profession: Political scientist; policy analyst

Field of specialization: International politics, intelligence, Soviet studies; future studies.

Education: B.A., Philosophy, Dartmouth College; M.A., Political Science, Columbia University; Certificate of Russian Institute, Columbia University; Ph.D., Political Science, Columbia University.

Professional employment: Hudson Institute: Executive Vice-President (1976-); Deputy to Director (1975-76); Professional Staff (1974-75). Hofstra University: Faculty, Political Science (1965-74).

Professional activities: Administration and research management; research, writing and speaking on Soviet military affairs, intelligence and various future studies; taught courses on international politics, Soviet politics, American politics, American foreign policy and political methodology (1945-74).

Publications: *Lend-Lease Loans and the Coming of the Cold War: A Study in the Implementation of Foreign Policy* (Westview Press, forthcoming in 1979); co-author with Herman Kahn and William Brown, *The Next 200 Years: A Scenario for America and the World* (William Morrow, 1976); "The Growth of Growth" (*Futures*, April 1977).

MARTINO, JOSEPH P.

Research Scientist
Research Institute
University of Dayton
Dayton, Ohio 45469, U.S.A.

Born: 1931, Warren, Ohio, U.S.A.

Telephone: (513) 229-3036

Profession: Operations analyst

Field of specialization: Technological forecasting; techno-economic planning.

Education: A.B., Physics, Miami University, Ohio, 1953; M.S., Electrical Engineering, Purdue University, 1955; Ph.D., Mathematics, Ohio State University, 1961.

Professional employment: University of Dayton Research Institute: Research Scientist (1975-). Air Force Avionics Laboratory: Staff Scientist (1972-73). Air Force Office of Research Analyses: Operations Analyst (1968-71). Air Force Office of Scientific Research: Operations Analyst (1963-67).

Professional activities: Consulting, research, and teaching in technological forecasting, R and D management, and long-range planning; Associate Editor, *Technological Forecasting and Social Change*; Technological Forecasting Editor, THE FUTURIST; Editorial Advisory Board Member, *Transactions on Engineering Management*; Secretary (1973), Vice Chairman (1974), Chairman (1975) of Dayton Chapter, Engineering Management Society; Board of Directors, Military Operations Research Society (1967-71), Vice President (1970-71); has written and lectured extensively on methods of technological forecasting and applications to long-range planning.

Publications: *Technological Forecasting for Decisionmaking* (American Elsevier, 1972); editor, *Proceedings, First, Second and Third Symposia on Long Range Forecasting* (U.S. Government Printing Office); "Science and Society in Equilibrium" (*Science*, August 1969); "A Survey of Behavioral Science Contributions to Laboratory Management" (*Transactions on Engineering Management*, August 1973); "Technological Forecasting for R and D Planning" (*Technological Forecasting*, Vol. 2, 1971).

MARUYAMA, MAGOROH
Professor of Administrative Sciences
Southern Illinois University
Carbondale, Illinois 62901, U.S.A.

Born: 1929, Tokyo, Japan

Telephone: (618) 453-3307

Profession: Anthropologist

Field of specialization: Cultural alternatives; urban and regional planning,; international develpment.

Education: B.A., Mathematics, University of California-Berkeley, 1951; Ph.D., Philosophy, University of Lund, Sweden, 1959.

Professional employment: Southern Illinois University: Professor of Administrative Sciences (1979-). University of Oregon: Visiting Professor of Sciology (1978). University of Missouri: Bernardin Dis- 'tinguished Visiting Professor of Anthropology and Architecture (1976-77). Portland State University: Professor of Systems Science (1973-76). Antioch College: Visiting Professor of Philosophy (1971-72). University of Hawaii: Visiting Research Fellow in Culture and Mental Health Program (1970-71). Brandeis University: Research Associate, Lemberg Center for the Study of Violence (1967-69). San Francisco State University: Associate Professor of Psychology (1965-67. Stanford University: Research Associate, Institute for the Study of Human Problems (1962-64). University of California, Berkeley: Research Psychologist, Institute of Human Development (1960-62).

Professional activities: Fellow, American Anthropological Association; member: American Association for the Advancement of Science, American Psychological Association, World Futures Studies Federation; NASA/Stanford project on extraterrestrial community design (1975); consultant: Canadian Federal Ministry of State for Urban Affairs (1974-75), Corps of Engineers (1972-74), National Bureau of Standards (1971), Office of Economic Opportunities (1965-67).

Publications: Editor, *Cultures of the Future* (Mouton, 1979); "The Second Cybernetics" (*American Scientist*, April 1963); "Human Futuristics and Urban Planning" (*American Institute of Planners Journal*, October 1973); "Hierarchists, Individualists and Mutualists: Three Paradigms Among the Planners" (*Futures*, (April 1974); "Paradigmatology and Its Applications to Cross-Professional Communication" (*Cybernetica*, 1974); "Designing a Space Community" (*Futurist*, October 1976); "Heterogenistics: An Epistemological Restructuring of Biological and Social Sciences" (*Acta Biotheoretica*, 1977); "Heterogenistics and Morphogenetics: Toward a New Concept of the Scientific" (*Theory and Society*, January 1978).

MASINI, ELEONORA BARBIERI
Secretary General
World Future Studies Federation (WFSF)
Casella Postale 6203
Roma Prati
Rome, Italy

Born: 1928, Quirigna, Guatemala

Telephone: (06) 872529

Profession: Lawyer; Secretary General, WFSF

Field of specialization: Futures methodologies; needs and values; education; women's role in society.

Education: Degree in Law, Rome University, 1953; specialization course in Comparative Law, Rome University, 1954; informal studies in philosophy and psychology.

Professional employment: World Future Studies Federation: Secretary General (1975-). Gregoriana University: Director, course in social forecasting (1978-). IRADES: Responsible for social forecasting studies (1968-75).

Professional activities: Directed research on "children's images of the future" for UNESCO (1972-78); research on "women's changing role in Italy" for Centro Italiano Femminile (1972-78); subproject "Visions of Desirable Societies" in project "Goals, Processes and Indicators of Development" of the U.N. University (1978-); seminars in future studies, Universita Gregoriana (1976-77); organization of Fifth (1976) and coordinator of Sixth (1978) World Conference on Future Studies for WFSF.

Publications: *Space for Man* (Edizioni Previsionali, Roma, 1973); *Social and Human Forecasting* (Edizioni Previsionali, Roma, 1973); *Social Indicators and Forecasting—Forecasting Methods* (Edizioni Paolini, 1977).

MASON, ROY E.

President
Tricentennial Development Corporation
P.O. Box 558
Arlington, Virginia 22216, U.S.A.

Born: 1938, Houston, Texas, U.S.A.

Telephone: (202) 232-2011

Profession: Architect/consultant

Field of specialization: Future architecture; alternative energy; land development; film making; futures research.

Education: B. Architecture, Texas Technological College, 1961; Master of Architecture, Yale School of Architecture, 1962.

Professional employment: Roy Mason Associates: President (1978-). Tricentennial Development Corp.: President (1978-). Future Options Room: Director of Planning (1975-).

Professional activities: Editor of *Habitats Tomorrow* newsletter; set designs for *Star Trek* (the movie, 1978); developing first planned solar community on east coast (1977-); designing alternative energy houses; designing urban strategy center for Canadian Ministry of Urban Affairs; developing Option Rooms for corporate and governmental clients; Art Director of the World Future Society and Architectural Editor of *The Futurist;* design and, in some cases, construction of 60 homes in the Washington, D.C. area; design of innovative housing for low income groups in the U.S. and abroad; lectures and writes on the future of architecture; designing and encouraging the development of ecological, self-sufficient communities.

Publications: Editor and co-author, *Toward the Future* (16mm documentary film, 1978); *Future Architecture* (slide show, revised 1978); "Biological Architecture: A Partnership of Nature and Man" (THE FUTURIST, June 1977); "Architecture Beyond 2000" (THE FUTURIST, October 1975); "Underground Architecture" (THE FUTURIST, February, 1976); "Areas Within a City Might Specialize" (THE FUTURIST, October 1969).

MASTON, ROBERT E.

President
Futuremics, Inc.
1629 K Street, N.W.
Washington, D.C. 20006, U.S.A.

Born: 1924, Chicago, Illinois, U.S.A.

Telephone: (202) 667-5620

Profession: Linguistics and psychology

Field of specialization: Program development; learning systems; management.

Education: B.A., 1946, B.D., 1947, University of Dubuque; M.A., Linguistics, 1952, Ph.D., 1962, University of Michigan.

Professional employment: Futuremics, International: Founder and President (1970). Futuremics Research Institute: Founder and Executive Director (1976-). Migrant Division, Office of Economic Opportunity: Special Consultant (1969-). Bay Tech Associates, Inc.: Director of Planning (1968). Peace Corps: Training Officer, Korea Programs (1966-70). Council of the Southern Mountains: Consultant to and Director of Planning (1968). Previous professional positions with Harvard/Radcliffe (Peace Corps Internship Program), University of Hawaii, Laubach Literacy Fund, University of Maryland, English Language Services, Eastern Michigan University, George Peabody College for Teachers (Korea contract), Instituto Technologico del Noreste, Mexico, University of Michigan, Habibia College, Afghanistan, etc.

Professional activities: Conducts seminars, learning labs, management workshops, and a consulting program with Futuremics, Inc.; activities with Futuremics Research Institute involve programs and projects of an educational nature to help individuals, groups, and organizations prepare for the future; consultant to various groups, organizations, universities, and corporations in program design, training in planning techniques, community development, and human relations.

Publications: "Careers in the Future: Education for Preferable Futures" (*Liberal Education*, Vol. 62, No. 2, May 1976); "Instructional Technology and Language Learning: A Report to the Academy for Educational Development" in *The Study of the President's Commission on Education Technology* (Washington, D.C., 1978); co-author, with D.N. Larson and W. A. Smalley, *Manual of Language Learning* (Toronto Institute of Linguistics, 1958); "New Directions in English Teaching" (*National University Newspaper*, University Press, June 1962).

MASUDA, YONEJI
President
Institute for Information Society
Fujimura Bldg. 2-15-29 Shinjuku Shinjukuku
Tokyo, Japan

Born: 1909, Tokyo, Japan

Telephone: (03) 341-8515

Profession: Techno-economist

Field of specialization: Societal impact of computer communication technology.

Education: A.B., China Economy, Toa Dobun Shoin University, 1943.

Professional employment: Institute for Information Society: President (1977-). Japan Computer Usage Development Institute: Executive Director (1965-77). Aichi Industrial University: Chief Professor of Management Science (1962-65). Japan Productivity Center: Chief Researcher (1956-62).

Professional activities: Development of "Target Setting Policy Model Building and Scheduling System" (1972-); study on "Business Forecasting Toward 1985" (1975); consultation on "Local Information Service Project" for Swedish government (1975); member of Information Committee, Council on Industrial Structure, Ministry of Industry and Trade (1974-75); has conducted a study on "The Plan for Information Society" (1972-73); presentations at various international conferences including Stockholm (1974), Tokyo (1978), The International Congress of Cybernetics and Systems, Amsterdam (1978), Brazilian Telecommunication Congress, Brazil (1978).

Publications: "Privacy in the Future Information Society" (*Proceedings of the International Congress of Cybernetics and Systems,* August 1978); "Future Perspectives for Information Utility" (*Proceedings of the International Conference on Computer Communication,* September 1978); *The Information Economics* (Sangyo Noritsu College, 1976); "The Conceptual Framework of Information Economics" (*IEEE Transaction on Communications,* October 1975); "Automated States vs. Computopia: Unavoidable Alternatives for the Information Era" (presentation to the World Future Society Second General Assembly June 1975).

MAYNARD, RICHARD G.
Manager
Policy Support and Special Studies Division
House Information Systems
House of Representatives Office Building, Annex No. 2, Room 3641
Washington, D. C. 20515, U.S.A.

Born: 1940, Windsor, Vermont, U.S.A.

Telephone: (202) 225-0201

Profession: Information technology; systems analysis; operations research.

Education: Field of specialization: Information technology; simulation modeling; visual communications (computer graphics); systems analysis.

Education: B.A., Government, Dartmouth College, 1962; Cert., Economics, Anthropology, University of Sao Paulo, Brazil, 1965; M.A., Economics, University of Pennsylvania, 1969.

Professional employment: House of Representatives, House Information Systems: Manager of Policy Support and Special Studies Division (1977-); Senior Information System Specialist (1973-77). Applied Urbanetics: Senior Research Analyst/Marketing (1971-73). Department of Defense: Operations Research Analyst (1970-71). EDP Technology: Systems Analyst (1969-70).

Field of specialization: Information technology; simulation modeling; visual communications (computer graphics); systems analysis.

Professional activities: Implementing information technology including computer graphics for U.S. Congress (1975-); President, Washington, D.C. Chapter of the World Future Society (1976-); Program Committee, Second General Assembly of the World Future Society (June 1975).

Publications: —

MAYUR, RASHMI

Director
Urban Development Institute
181, Rewa, Haji Ali
Bombay 400 026
India

Born:—

Telephone: 352912

Profession: Urban systems scientist and environmental planner.

Field of specialization: Technology assessment; urban planning.

Education: M.A., Economics and Psychology, Bombay University; Ph.D., Urban Sciences, New York University, 1967.

Professional employment: Urban Development Institute: Director (present). Futurology Panel, Government of India: Member.

Professional activities: Coordinator, World Future Society, Bombay Chapter.

Publications: *The Profile of Urbanization in India;* "The Coming Third World Crisis" (THE FUTURIST, October 1975); co-author, "International Migration of Talented Personnel" (U.N. Secretary General's Report, May 1973); editor, *Whither Bombay?* (Bombay Pradesh Congress Committee, 1975); *Crime, Violence and Tensions in Bombay.*

MCDANIEL, ROBERT

Associate Professor
Department of Geography
Social Science Centre
University of Western Ontario
London, Ontario, Canada

Born: 1926, Winnipeg, Manitoba, Canada

Telephone: (519) 679-6629

Profession: Geographer; futurist

Field of specialization: Regional analysis and development; spatial futuristics.

Education: B.A., Geography, 1953, M.A., 1954, University of Western Ontario; A.B.D., Regional Science, University of Pennsylvania.

Professional employment: University of Western Ontario: Associate Professor (1961-). Canadian Army: Lieutenant (1948-59).

Professional activities: Developing new futures course in geography (1976); study of changing urban system characteristics (1975); study of past, present, and future patterns of global spatial organization and control (1970-); construction of regional geocoded information system (1967-70); Lake Erie Region input-output study (1967); member, Canadian Association for Futures Studies.

Publications: "How Information Structures Influence Spatial Organization" in *Human Geography in a Shrinking World* (Duxbury, 1975); "Geographic Research Opportunities with Real-Time Information Systems" (*Ontario Geography*, University of Western Ontario, No. 2, 1969); co-author, *A Systems Analytic Approach to Economic Geography* (Commission on College Geography, 1968).

MCGRAW, JOHN G.

Professor
Departments of Philosophy and Interdisciplinary Studies
Loyola Campus, Concordia University
7141 Sherbrooke Street West
Montreal, Quebec
H4B IR6 Canada

Born: Minneapolis, Minnesota, U.S.A.

Telephone: (514) 482-0320 Ext. 412

Profession: Philosophy professor

Field of specialization: Axiology; futurontology; phenomenology of affectivity; philosophical anthropology; philosophy of religion; and political philosophy.

Education: B.A., Political Science, University of Notre Dame, South Bend, 1956; Ph.B., Ph.L., Philosophy, Pontifical Institute of Philosophy, Chicago, 1959 and 1960; Ph.D., Philosophy, Angelicum University, Rome, 1963.

Professional employment: Concordia University, Loyola Campus: Philosophy Professor (1965-). Marygrove College, Detroit, Michigan: Professor, Department of Philosophy (1963-65).

Professional activities: Coordinator, Montreal membership, World Future Society (1970-); Member, Canadian Association for Futures Studies; will teach "Future Studies" (1976-77) and has taught "Futurontology" (alternative futures from ontological, metaphysical, and axiological perspectives—1970-74); principal current research on putatively new view of personality and personality development (The Theory of Positive Disintegration).

Publications: "Poverty: No Place in Cybernetic Era" (Association for Systems Management, January and March, 1972); "Technologic Man" (*The Happening*, January 1974); "Secular, Religious Thinkers Delve Into Man's Future" (*The Montreal Star*, November 1969); "Desintegration Positive et les Niveaux de Developpement de L'Amour" [*"Positive Disintegration and the Levels of Development of Love"*] (*Les Editions Saint-Yves*, August 1970); "A Philosophical Approach to Contemporary Physical Education and Athletics" (*Gymnasium*, Spring 1969).
(From the first edition. Corrections not received by press time.)

MCHALE, MAGDA CORDELL

Born: 1921, Nove-Zamky, Czechoslovakia

Acting Director
Center for Integrative Studies
Library Building, Room 571
University of Houston
Houston, Texas 77004, U.S.A.

Telephone: (713) 749-1121

Profession: Artist; trend analyst

Field of specialization: Social and cultural trends; future of women; human requirements.

Education: M.A. equivalence, various institutions.

Professional employment: Center for Integrative Studies, College of Social Sciences, University of Houston: Acting Director (1979-) and Senior Research Associate (1977-). Center for Integrative Studies, School of Advanced Technology, State University of New York: Senior Research Associate (1968-77). World Resources Inventory, Southern Illinois University: Consultant (1962-68). Freelance, London, England: Artist/Design and Communications Consultant (1950-62).

Professional activities: Research on world trends and developments; consultant to the United Nations; member, Board of Directors, *Futuribles*, Paris; member U.S. Association for the Club of Rome; Vice-President, World Future Studies Federation, Rome; planning consultant, Third Biennial Woodlands Conference on Growth Policy, Woodlands; fellow, Royal Society of Arts, England; commissioned by the Population Reference Bureau, Washington, D.C. to produce for the International Year of the Child 1979, a three-part study on children.

Publications: Co-author, *Children in the World* (Chartbook), *The World of Children* (Population Bulletin Series), and *1979 World's Children Data Sheet* (Population Reference Bureau, Washington D.C., 1979); co-author, *Basic Human Needs: A Framework for Action* (Transaction Books, 1977); co-author, *Futures Directory* (Westview Press, 1977); co-author, *Human Requirements, Supply Levels and Outer Bounds* (Aspen Institute for Humanistic Studies Program in International Affairs, Princeton, N.J., 1975); co-author, *Women in World Terms: Facts and Trends* (Center for Integrative Studies, Houston, Texas, 1975).

MCLEAN, JOHN MICHAEL

Born: 1948, London, England

Research Fellow
Institute for Research on Public Policy
3535 Chemin Queen Mary
Montreal, Quebec
H3V 1H8 Canada

Telephone: (514) 342-9121

Profession: Systems Analyst

Field of specialization: Technical change in the electronics industry and its social and economic impact; the methodology of mathematical modelling.

Education: B.Sc., Logic, 1970, M.Phil., History and Social Studies of Science, 1978, University of Sussex.

Professional employment: Science Policy Research Unit, University of Sussex: Research Fellow (1975-78). UNESCO: Consultant, Methods and Analysis Dept. (1974). Department of Health and Social Security, United Kingdom: Principal Administrative Officer (1973). International Computers Ltd.: Sales Engineer (1970-72).

Professional activities: Work for Institute for Research on Public Policy on the impact of microelectronics on the structure of the Canadian economy; Series editor, "Library of New Technologies," Macmillan Press, London; Editorial Board Member, "Applied Mathematical Modelling," IPC Press, London; Consultant for "Science and Technology in the New Socio-Economic Contest" activity, OECD, Paris.

Publications: Co-author with P. Shepherd, *Demystifying Models* (Macmillan Press, to be published in 1979); "Getting the Problem Right—A Role for Structural Modelling" in *Futures Research: New Directions*, Linstone and Simmonds, eds., (Addison-Wesley, 1978); co-author, *The Impact of Microelectronics on the United Kingdom Economy* (Occasional Paper No. 7, Science Policy Research Unit, 1978); co-author with M. Hopkins, "The World Food Crisis: Projections, Models and Paradigms" (*Annals of the New York Academy of Sciences*, September 1975); The Computerisation of Social Research" in *Demystifying Social Statistics* (Pluto Press, 1978).

MCLUHAN, HERBERT MARSHALL

Professor
St. Michaels College
University of Toronto
Toronto, Ontario, Canada

Born: 1911, Edmonton, Alberta, Canada

Telephone: -—-

Profession: Author and professor

Field of specialization: Communications

Education: B.A., 1932, M.A., 1934, University of Manitoba; B.A. 1936, M.A., 1939, Ph.D., 1942, Cambridge University.

Professional employment: St. Michaels College, University of Toronto: Professor (1952-); Faculty (1946-52). Assumption University: Associate Professor (1944-46). University of St. Louis: Instructor (1937-44). University of Wisconsin: Member of the Faculty (1936-37).

Professional activities: Chairman, Ford Foundation Seminar on Culture and Communication (1953-55); co-editor (1954-59), editor (1964-), *Explorations Magazine;* appointment by President of University of Toronto to create new Centre for Culture and Technology to study psychic and social consequences of technologies and media (1963); appointment to Schweitzer Chair in the Humanities, Fordham University, New York (1967-68); Eugene McDermott Professorship, University of Dallas, Irving, Texas (1975).

Publications: Co-author with Kathryn Hutchon and Eric McLuhan, *City as Classroom* (Book Society of Canada, 1977); co-author with Barrington Nevitt, *Take Today: The Executive as Dropout* (Harcourt, Brace, Jovanovich, 1972); *War and Peace in the Global Village* (McGraw-Hill, 1968); *The Medium is the Message* (Bantam Books, 1967); *Understanding Media (McGraw-Hill, 1964); The Gutenberg Galaxy: The Making of Typographic Man* (University of Toronto Press, 1962).

MEADOWS, DENNIS LYNN

Professor of Engineering
Dartmouth College
Murdough 337
Hanover, New Hampshire 03755, U.S.A.

Born: 1942

Telephone: (603) 646-3551

Profession: Professor, Institute Director

Field of specialization: Methodology of social system simulation, documentation and implementation of computer model-based social policy, soft energy systems.

Education: B.A., Chemistry, Carleton College, 1964; Ph.D., Management, Massachusetts Institute of Technology, 1969.

Professional employment: Dartmouth, Thayer School of Engineering: Associate Professor and Professor of Engineering (1972-). Massachusetts Institute of Technology: Assistant Professor of Management (1969-72).

Professional activities: Director, Research Program on Technology and Public Policy; Member of the Council on Foreign Relations; energy policy consultant to several legislative, executive and corporate organizations; Director, Club of Rome project on "The Limits to Growth."

Publications: Co-author, *The Limits to Growth* (Universe Books, A Potomac Associates book, 1972); editor, *Toward Global Equilibrium* (Wright-Allen Press, 1973); co-author, Dynamics of Growth in a Finite World (Wright-Allen Press, 1974); co-author, "The Transition to Coal" (*Technology Review*, October-November, 1975); *Dynamics of Commodity Production Cycles* (Wright-Allen Press, 1970); editor, *Alternatives to Growth-I* (Ballinger Books, 1977).

MEADOWS, DONELLA H.
Associate Professor
Department of Environmental Studies
Dartmouth College
Hanover, New Hampshire 03755, U.S.A.

Born: 1941, Elgin, Illinois, U.S.A.

Telephone: (603) 646-3551

Profession: System Dynamicist

Field of specialization: Biophysics—enzymology, spectroscopy; systems analysis—demography, environmental studies, agriculture and land use, computer simulation, system dynamics.

Education: B.A., Chemistry, Carleton College, 1963; Ph.D., Biophysics, Harvard University, 1968.

Professional employment: Dartmouth College: Associate Professor of Environmental Studies (1972-). Advanced Study Institute: Lecturer, System Dynamics (1972-). East-West Population Institute: Senior Fellow (1973-74). Massachusetts Institute of Technology: Research Associate, Nutrition and Food Science (1970-72). Travel—Research Program in India and Ceylon (1969-70). Harvard University; Post-doctoral Research Fellow (1969). Merck, Sharp and Dohme: Research Chemist (1967-68). Argonne National Laboratory: ACM Fellow (1962-63).

Professional activities: Currently working on a survey of policy-oriented models and modeling methods on a study of population and development in Village India, and on case studies of the U.S. agricultural system (1976-); teaching systems theory, simulation, and environmental policy at undergraduate and graduate levels; National Board of Directors, Zero Population Growth (1972-73); Task Force on Human Resources, Executive Office of Environmental Affairs, State of Massachusetts (1972); Board of Directors, Center for Growth Alternatives (1973-75).

Publications: Co-author, *The Limits to Growth* (Universe Books, 1972); co-author, *Dynamics of Growth in a Finite World* (Wright-Allen Press, 1974); editor, *Toward Global Equilibrium* (Wright-Allen Press, 1973); *Food and Population Policies for the United States* (University Press of New England, 1976); *Equity, the Free Market and the Sustainable State* (in press, 1976).

MEIER, RICHARD L.
Professor
College of Environmental Design
University of California-Berkeley
Berkeley, California 94720, U.S.A.

Born: 1920, Kendallville, Indiana, U.S.A.

Telephone: —

Profession: Planner

Field of specialization: Resource-conserving urban design; general systems models; simulations of complex organizations.

Education: Science, Northern Illinois State Teachers College; B.S., Chemistry, University of Illinois-Urbana, 1940; M.S., 1942, Ph.D., 1944, Chemistry, University of California-Los Angeles.

Professional employment: University of California-Berkeley: Professor of Environmental Design

(1967-). University of Michigan: Research Social Scientist (1957-67). University of Chicago: Assistant Professor, Social Science (1950-56). Manchester University, U.K.: Fulbright (1949-50). Federation of American Scientists: Executive Secretary (1947-49). Standard Oil of California: Research Chemist (1943-47).

Professional activities: Teaching courses on "Environmental Policy Planning," "Climatological Effects Upon Environmental Controls," "Architectural Research Methods and Documentation," "Futures of Urbanism and the City"; research on "Social Uses for Ultra-Modern Science and Technology"; simulations of "Community and Social Organization" (1969-73); strong futures interest in finding the best paths to ease into a steady state for human settlements, especially in the poorer parts of the world.

Publications: *Planning for an Urban World—Design of Resource-Conserving Cities* (MIT Press, 1974); *Science and Economic Development—New Patterns for Living* (MIT Press, 1956, 1966); *Developmental Planning* (McGraw-Hill, 1965); *A Communications Theory of Urban Growth* (MIT Press, 1962); "Communications Stress" (*Annual Review of Ecology and Systematics*, 1972); "A Stable Urban Ecosystem" (*Science*, 1976).

MENASANCH, ROSA MENASANCH
Secretary-General de Honor
Club de Amigos de la Futurologia
(Club of Friends of the Future)
Gran Via 608, 80D
Barcelona 7, Spain

Born: 1916, Tarragona, Spain

Telephone: 318 21 53

Profession: Professor; organizer of associations.

Field of specialization: Organization of projects for associations; especially interested in politics of the future and education of the future.

Education: Professor, Superior School, French Institute.

Professional employment: Asociacion para la Mujer Efectiva [Association for the Effective Woman]: Vice President and Founder (1971). Asociacion de Amigos de la India [Friends of India Association]: Secretary General and Founder (1967-72). Asociacion de Amigos del UNICEF [Friends of UNICEF Association]: Vice President and Founder (1961-67). Club de Amigos de la UNESCO [Friends of UNESCO Club]: Secretary General and Founder (1961-64). Asociacion de Amigos de las Naciones Unidas [Association of Friends of the United Nations]: Secretary General and Founder (1960-65).

Professional activities: Secretary General de Honor and Founder of the Club de Amigos de la Futurologia (1973-78); member, World Future Studies Federation; participant in the Rome conference (1973); attended the Congress of the World Federation of Associations for the United Nations, New York (1963). "In Mexico, where I lived from 1941-49 as a political refugee of the Spanish Civil War, I belonged to various associations for children, youth, and the advancement of women, as well as cultural and philosophical organizations."

Publications: *Solo Ante el Mundo [Alone Before the World]* (Costa-Amic, Mexico, 1965); *Cuento de Navidad [A Tale of Christmas]* (Una Revista de Mexico, 1947); *Hacia el Futuro [Towards the Future]* (Una Revista de Mexico, 1948); *Recuerdos [Memories]* (Una Revista de Mexico, 1948); *Aurora [Dawn]* (Una Revista de Mexico, 1949).

MENDELL, JAY STANLEY
Professor
Business Administration
Florida Atlantic University
Boca Raton, Florida 33065, U.S.A.

Born: 1936, New York, New York, U.S.A.

Telephone: (305) 395-5100

Profession: Professor

Field of specialization: Business futurism; visionary and creative management; strategy; corporate identity; planning for an uncertain future, emerging issues scanning and corporate response.

Education: B.A., Rensselaer Polytechnic Institute, 1956; M.A., Vanderbilt University, 1958; Ph.D., Physics, Rensselaer Polytechnic Institute, 1964.

Professional employment: Florida Atlantic University, Business Administration: Professor (1976-); Associate Professor (1975-76). Florida International University: Associate Professor, Technology (1973-75). Pratt and Whitney Aircraft: Senior Analyst (1963-73).

Professional activities: Editorial Chairman, *Business Tomorrow* (1978-); contributing editor, *Planning Review* (1974-); innovation editor, THE FUTURIST (1969-); Editorial Board Member, *Technological Forecasting and Social Change* (1970-77); President, Jay S. Mendell & Associates, consulting futurists; professional workshop leader and convention speaker.

Publications: Co-author, *The Have-to-Innovate Book* (in preparation); "The Practice of Intuition" (*Handbook of Futures Research*, 1978); "The Actuary as Futurist" (*Society of Actuaries Record*, 1976); co-author, *Early Warning Signals—A Course on Information on the Future* (World Future Society, 1975); co-author, "What Futurists Can Learn from Creative Problem Solvers" in *The Next 25 Years: Crisis and Opportunity* (World Future Society, 1975).

MENDLOVITZ, SAUL H.

Born: 1925, Scranton, Pennsylvania, U.S.A.

Vice-Chairman of the Board
Institute for World Order, Inc.
1140 Avenue of the Americas
New York, New York 10036, U.S.A.

Telephone: (212) 575-0055

Profession: Professor of World Order Studies

Field of specialization: Value systems; futures modeling.

Education: B.A., Syracuse University, 1947; J.D., Law, 1953, M.A., Sociology, 1961, University of Chicago.

Professional employment: Columbia University: Ira D. Wallach Chair of World Order Studies (1978-79). Institute for World Order: President (1974-77). Rutgers Law School: Professor of International Law (1961-). New York University, Center for International Studies: Senior Fellow (1967-68).

Professional activities: Director, World Order Models Project—an effort by a team of global scholars to define preferred worlds for the 1990s, and an international system guided by the values of peace, social and economic justice and ecological balance (1969-); Consultant, Social Science Advisory Board, U.S. Arms Control and Disarmament Agency (1970-74); Member, Executive Council, American Society of International Law (1966-72); Vice Chairman, Subcommittee on Disarmament of the Committee on Arms Control and Disarmament, American Bar Association.

Publications: General editor of series, *Preferred Worlds for the 1990's* (6 volumes, The Free Press, New York, 1975-79); editor, *On the Creation of a Just World Order* (The Free Press, 1975); co-author, *Regional Politics and World Order* (W.H. Freeman, 1973); co-author, *Strategy of World Order* (4 volumes, World Law Fund, 1972).

MENDRAS, HENRI

Born: 1927, Paris, France

Director, Centre National de la Recherches Scientifique (CNRS)
Head, Groupe de Recherches Sociologiques
Bt G Universite de Paris X
Rue de Rouen
Nanterre-Cedex 92001, France

Telephone: 725 92 34

Profession: Sociologist

Field of specialization: Rural sociology

Education: Doctor of Letters, University of Paris, Sorbonne; Diploma, Institute of Political Sciences; Graduate degree in Philosophy, Sorbonne.

Professional employment: Institut d'Etudes Politiques: Professor (1956-). Centre National de la Recherches Scientifique: Director (1972-); Senior Specialist (1962); Specialist (1957); Research Assistant (1954).

Professional activities: Head, Sociological Research Group, CNRS; Co-Director of the CEUCORS research project on the future of rural communities in industrial societies; Head, sociological project on "Continuous Observation of Change," CNRS; Member of the Board, *Futuribles*; Director, sociology series, A. Colin Collection.

Publications: *La fin des paysans [The Vanishing Peasant] (MIT Press); Elements de sociologie [Elements of Sociology]* (A. Colin, Paris, 1977); *Les collectivites rurales francaises, I and II [French Rural Communities]* (A Colin, Paris, 1971-73); co-author, *Terre, paysan et politique [Land, Peasant, and Politics]*, studies presented by a research group under the direction of H. Mendras, *et al.; Les societes paysannes [Peasant Societies]* (A. Colin, Paris, 1976).

MESAROVIC, MIHAJLO D.
Director
Systems Research Center
Case Western Reserve University
10900 Euclid Avenue
Cleveland, Ohio 44106, U.S.A.

Born: 1928, Zrenjanin, Yugoslavia

Telephone: (216) 368-4576

Profession: Systems engineer; mathematician

Field of specialization: Multilevel hierarchical systems theory applied to biological urban and global systems; technology and policy assessment; computer modeling applied to policy analysis and decision-making; long range (50 years) alternative policy assessment.

Education: Dipl. Ing., Electrical Engineering, 1951, Ph.D., Technical Science, 1955, Serbian Academy of Sciences; Post-doctoral Fellow, Sloan School of Management, Massachusetts Institute of Technology, 1958-59.

Professional employment: Case Western Reserve University: Director, Systems Research Center (1966-); Professor of Engineering and Mathematics (1959-); Chairman, Systems Engineering Department (1967-72). Nikola Tesla Institute, Belgrade: Director, Control Systems Department (1955-57). Technical University of Belgrade: Docent (1955-58).

Professional activities: Director, Phosphorus Pollution Control in Lake Erie Basin and Water Quality Management Project (1972-); Director, Long Range U.S. Food Policy Assessment Project (1974-); Co-Director, with Eduard Pestel, Multilevel Regionalized Global Modeling Project (1971-); teaching seminars in complex systems and systems theory; founder and editor, *Mathematical Systems Theory Journal*; Member, Club of Rome, Institute for Electrical and Electronics Engineers, and Association for Computing Machinery.

Publications: Co-author, *Mankind at the Turning Point* (E. P. Dutton and Co., 1974); co-author, *General Systems Theory: Mathematical Foundations* (Academic Press, 1975); co-author, *Theory of Multilevel Hierarchical Systems* (Academic Press, 1970); editor, *Multilevel Regionalized World Model* (International Institute of Applied Systems Analysis, Laxenburg, Austria, 1974); *Control of Multivariable Systems* (MIT Press and John Wiley, 1960).

(From the first edition. Corrections not received by press time.)

MESTHENE, EMMANUEL G.
Distinguished Professor of Philosophy
Rutgers, The State University
93 New Street
Newark, New Jersey 07102, U.S.A.

Born: 1920, New York, New York, U.S.A.

Telephone: (201) 648-5533

Profession: Philosopher

Field of specialization: Technology and social change; technology and values; technology and religion.

Education: B.S., Philosophy, 1948, M.A., 1949, Ph.D., 1964, Columbia University.

Professional employment: Rutgers—The State University of New Jersey: Distinguished Professor Philosophy (1977-); Dean, Livingston College, Professor of Philosophy (1974-). Harvard University: Director, Harvard Program on Technology and Society (1964-74). The Rand Corporation: Research Staff Member, Economics Department (1953-64). Organization for Economic Cooperation and Development, Paris: Staff

Director, ad hoc Advisory Group on Science Policy, and Secretary, First International Ministerial Meeting on National Policies for Science and Technology (1962-64).

Professional activities: Currently research and teaching; formerly chief academic and administrative officer of one of four undergraduate colleges at Rutgers; as director of the Harvard University Program on Technology and Society organized and administered long-term, university-wide program of research on the interaction of technological change and social, economic, and political change; taught courses on technology and society and on science and public policy; for OECD prepared and wrote report on major policy issues relating to science and technology, both nationally and internationally, and on the general orientation objectives of IECD activities in science; White House Staff Assistant to the President for Science and Technology (1960).

Publications: *Technological Change: Its Impact on Man and Society* (Harvard University Press, 1970); *How Language Makes Us Know* (The Hague: Martinus Nijhoff, 1964); editor, *Technology and Social Change* (Bobbs-Merrill, Indianapolis, 1967); editor, *Ministers Talk About Science* (OECD, Paris, 1965); "On the Ideal-Real Gap" in *The Corporate Society*, Robin Marris, ed. (Macmillan, London, 1974).

MICHAEL, DONALD NELSON

Born: 1923, Chicago, Illinois, U.S.A.

Program Director
Center for Research on Utilization of Scientific Knowledge
426 Thompson Street
Ann Arbor, Michigan 48106, U.S.A.

Telephone: (313) 764-2554

Profession: Educator

Field of specialization: Technology and social change; social psychology of long-range planning; social construction of reality and social change.

Education: S.B., Physics, Harvard, 1946; M.A., Sociology, University of Chicago, 1948; Ph.D., Social Psychology, Harvard, 1952; D.Sc. (Honorary), Marlboro College, 1964.

Professional employment: University of Michigan: Professor of Psychology, Department of Psychology; Professor of Planning and Public Policy, School of Natural Resources; Program Director, Center for Research on Utilization of Scientific Knowledge, Institute for Social Research (1966-). Institute for Policy Studies: Resident Fellow(1963-66).Peace Research Institute: Director (1961-63). The Brookings Institution: Senior Staff Member and Project Coordinator (1959-61).

Professional activities: Fellow: American Association for the Advancement of Science; Society for the Psychological Study of Social Issues. Contributing editor, *Communication* (1974-). Member: Membership Committee, U.S. Association for the Club of Rome (1976-); The Club of Rome (1970); Editorial Advisory Board, *World Futures Journal* (1976-); Oak Ridge National Laboratory/National Science Foundation Environmental Program Advisory Group (1971-74); task force on "The Information Process and Its Impacts on Policy-Making Centers During the Next Twenty Years," The Conference Board, Inc. (1970-71); Working Group on Social Impact of Computers and Working Group on Values and Rights, Commission on the Year 2000, American Academy of Arts and Sciences (1968-). Consultant, Institute for the Future (1968-).

Publications: *On Learning to Plan—and Planning to Learn: Social Psychological Aspects of Changing Toward Future-Responsive Societal Learning* (Jossey-Bass, San Francisco, 1973); *The Unprepared Society: Planning for a Precarious Future* (Basic Books, Inc., New York, 1968; Harper and Row Colophon paperback No. CN 200, New York, 1970); *The Next Generation: The Prospects Ahead for the Youth of Today and Tomorrow* (Random House, New York, 1965; Vintage paperback No. 273, 1965); "Cybernation: The Silent Conquest" (*Computers and Automation*, Vol. 11, No. 3, March 1962); *Proposed Studies on the Implications of Peaceful Space Activities for Human Affairs* (The Brookings Institution, Washington, D.C., December 1961).

MICHAELIS, MICHAEL

Born: 1919, Berlin, Germany

Senior Consultant
Arthur D. Little, Inc.
1735 Eye Street, N.W.
Washington, D.C. 20006, U.S.A.

Telephone: (202) 223-4400

Profession: Agent-for-Change (social and technical)

Field of specialization: Innovation policy formulation; technology assessment; catalyzing innovative and beneficial change in both public and private sectors of society.

Education: B.Sc., Engineering, University of London, 1941.

Professional employment: Arthur D. Little, Inc.: Senior Consultant (1972-); Manager, Washington Operations (1963-72); Senior Associate (1951-61). White House Panel on Civilian Technology: Executive Director and Special Assistant to President's Science Advisor (1961-63). United Kingdom Atomic Energy Authority: Director, Physics Division (1949-51). General Electric Company of England: Group Leader, Research Labs (1935-49).

Professional activities: Member, Board of Directors, World Future Society (1969-); Director, Interdisciplinary Communications Associates, Inc. (1968-); Executive Director, Research Management Advisory Panel, U.S. House of Representatives, Committee on Science and Technology (1963-); extensive lecturing and writing on process of change and innovation; member, advisory and standing Committees of National Planning Association, Committee for Economic Development, Chamber of Commerce of the U.S., National Academy of Science; consultant to Organization for Economic Cooperation and Development, Paris (1962-65); member, Technical Advisory Board to U.S. Department of Commerce (CTAB) (1978-).

Publications: Co-author *Barriers to Innovation: Opportunities for Public Policy Changes* (National Science Foundation, 1973); *Federal Funding of Civilian Research and Development* (U.S. Department of Commerce, 1975); "Technology for Business" (White House Conference on Industrial World Ahead, 1972); "The Management of Change" (THE FUTURIST, February 1971); Chairman, *Criteria for Federal Support of Research and Development* (U.S. Chamber of Commerce, 1965).

MIHANOVICH, CLEMENT SIMON   **Born:** 1913, St. Louis, Missouri, U.S.A.
Professor of Sociology
Saint Louis University
221 North Grand Boulevard
St. Louis, Missouri 63103, U.S.A.   **Telephone:** (314) JE5-3300

Profession: Sociologist

Field of specialization: Value systems; futures methodology.

Education: B.S. in Ed., 1935, M.A., Sociology, 1936, Ph.D., 1939, Saint Louis University.

Professional employment: Saint Louis University: Professor of Sociology (1947-); Chairman of Department (1940-64); Associate Professor (1943-47); Assistant Professor (1940-43); Graduate Fellow (1936-37).

Professional activities: Police-community relations consultant (1955-); futures studies consultant (1967-); teaches courses in futures studies including "Basic Principles," "Methods," "Norms and Values," "Constructing Alternative Futures."

Publications: *Social Problems* (Bruce Company, 1950); *Principles of Juvenile Development* (Bruce Company, 1950); *Social Theorists* (Bruce Company, 1955); *Marriage and Family* (Bruce Company, 1956); co-author and editor, *European Economic Community* (1960).

MILES, IAN DOUGLAS   **Born:** 1948, Gloucester, United Kingdom
Research Fellow
Science Policy Research Unit
Mantell Building
University of Sussex
Brighton
Sussex, United Kingdom   **Telephone:** (0273) 68 67 58

Profession: Social researcher

Field of specialization: Ideology in/of futures research; social indicators; social and political theory for scenario analysis; political economy of state; character structure in comtemporary social formations.

Education: B.Sc., Psychology, University of Manchester, 1969.

Professional employment: University of Sussex, Science Policy Research Unit: Research Fellow (1972).

Professional activities: Working for UNITAR Project (technology, income distribution and North-South relations) on various aspects of scenario analysis (economic crisis, international relations, political change); teaching includes course on "Social and Technological Forecasting"; working on alternative compendium of social statistics on the state of Britain.

Publications: Editor, with John Irwine and Jeff Evans, *Demystifying Social Statistics* (Pluto Press, London, 1979); co-author, *World Futures: The Great Debate,* edited by C. Freeman and M. Jahoda (Martin Robertson, London, 1978); co-author, *Uses and Abuses of Forecasting,* edited by T. Whiston (Macmillan, London, 1979); *The Poverty of Prediction* (Saxon House/Lexington Books, 1975); Chapters 10, 11, etc., in *The Art of Anticipation,* edited by S. Encel, P. Marstrand, W. Page (Martin Robertson, 1975); editor with C. Freeman, M. Jahoda, *Progress and Problems in Social Forecasting* (Social Science Research Council, 1976).

MILLER, LEWIS   **Born:** 1922, Saint John, New Brunswick, Canada
General Manager
Research and Planning Division
Ontario Educational Communications Authority
2180 Yonge Street
Toronto, Ontario, Canada, M4S 2C1   **Telephone:** (416) 484-2724

Profession: Philosopher

Field of specialization: Alternative futures and the role of the media; educational broadcasting.

Education: B.A., Honours, Philosophy, Dalhousie University, Halifax, Canada, 1950; M.A., Honours, Philosophy, 1952, Ph.D., 1962, University of Edinburgh, Scotland.

Professional employment: Ontario Education Communications Authority: General Manager, Research and Planning Division (1973-); Director of Programming \(1970-73).\ University of Toronto: Associate Professor of Philosophy (1965-70); Director of Extension, Scarborough College (1964-66); Assistant Professor of Philosophy (1964-65). Canadian Broadcasting Corporation: Program Organizer (1957-64). University of New Brunswick: Associate Professor of Philosophy and Head of Department (1954-57).

Professional activities: Manager of Research and Planning Division responsible to the Ontario Educational Communications Authority for formative and summative project research, for basic background policy research, statistical research (audience research) and for long-term basic planning; delivered paper, "Open Education in Ontario: The OECA as Catalyst," to international conference of the Society of Motion Picture and Television Engineers, Toronto, 1974; paper, "Television and Its Effects on Children" to the First Congress on Education, Toronto, 1978; paper, "Value Judgements in Planning" to National Planners' Conference, Toronto, 1977.

Publications: Editor, *Alternative Futures and the Role of the Media* (Ontario Educational Communications Authority, 1975); co-author, "Canada," one part of three-part study in *Adult Education and Television* (National Institute of Adult Education, England and Wales, under auspices of UNESCO, 1966); editor, *Educational Television,* an abstract of proceedings of International Educational Television Conference in Newfoundland (Queen's Printer, Ottawa, 1966); "Catch 2020" (paper prepared for the workshop, The Transition to a Conserver Society, for the Ontario Educational Communications Authority, 1974).

MISCHE, GERALD F.   **Born:** 1926, St. Cloud, Minnesota, U.S.A.
President
Global Education Associates
552 Park Avenue
East Orange, New Jersey 07017, U.S.A.   **Telephone:** (201) 675-1409

Profession: World order analyst

Field of specialization: World order futures; development of multi-issue grass-roots movement for world order in North America, Europe and "Third World" countries.

Education: Economics, St. Cloud State; B.A., Social Science and Philosophy, Maryknoll College, 1952; M.I.A., International Affairs, Columbia University, 1969.

Professional employment: Global Education Associates: President (1973-). Institute for World Order: Staff Associate (1972-73). Association for International Development: Co-founder and Director (1957-67). Mexican Social Action Project: Director (1955-56).

Professional activities: Conducting world order workshops and consulting on world order strategies throughout the United States; taped seven half hour programs on world order for CBS-TV Summer Semester (1978); developing "issue monographs" on world order (1978-79); conducting and designing conferences on world order in East Africa, Europe, Japan, the Philippines and Latin America (1978-79); conducted world order conferences in India (1975-77) and in Europe (1975-77); lectures on "international development" and "world order" throughout the United States.

Publications: Co-author, *Toward a Human World Order* (Paulist Press, 1977); co-author, *Hunger and World Order* (Whole Earth Papers, 1977); "Toward a Human World Order" (*New Frontiers in Education,* 1977); co-author, *Housing and World Order* (Whole Earth Papers, 1977); a series of World Order Working Papers (Global Education Associates, 1974-).

MISCHE, PATRICIA MARY SCHMITT
Director, Educational Development
Global Education Associates
552 Park Avenue
East Orange, New Jersey 07017, U.S.A.

Born: 1939, Shakopee, Minnesota, U.S.A.

Telephone: (201) 675-1409

Profession: Educator; writer; editor

Field of specialization: World order; value systems; human development.

Education: B.A., English, Education, Sociology, College of Saint Benedict, 1961; British Education, University of London, 1961; African Studies, Education, University of East Africa, Makerere, Uganda, 1961; M.A., Comparative and International Education, Columbia University Teacher's College, 1969.

Professional employment: Global Education Associates: Co-founder and Director, Educational Development (1973-). Georgetown University: Adjunct Faculty (summer) (1974-). Seton Hall University: Adjunct Faculty (summer) (1974-). Essex County Community College: Adjunct Faculty (1971-72). Clark School: Teacher (1971-72). Riverside Church School, New York: Teacher (1970-71). Association for International Development: Co-director, Buffalo office (1964-66). Mukuma Girls Secondary School, Kenya: Teacher (1962-63).

Professional activities: Editor, *The Whole Earth Papers* (1977-); researching women and alternative futures and human development and world order; consulting for schools, colleges on curriculum development in peace, justice and world order studies; speaking on peace, justice and world order and world futures issues; teaching courses on world order and peace education in Elementary and Early Childhood at Georgetown and Seton Hall Universities; founded and directed Institute on Peace, Justice and Human Values conducted annually at Seton Hall University; director of an International Mobile Institute featuring international, intergenerational participation and a mutual educational dynamic; conducted workshops in the U.S., Europe, India and Africa on world order and alternative futures.

Publications: Co-author, *Toward a Human World Order* (Paulist Press, 1977); "Women, Power and Alternative Futures" *The Whole Earth Papers* (Global Education Associates, May 1978); "Parenting in a Hungry World" in *The Earth is the Lord's,* Mary Evelyn Jegen, editor (Paulist Press, 1977); "A Cloud Over Family Life" (*Sign,* May 1977); "World Hunger: Putting the Question to Ourselves: (*Sign,* June 1975).

MITCHELL, ARNOLD
Director, Values and Lifestyles Program
SRI International
333 Ravenswood Avenue
Menlo Park, California 94025, U.S.A.

Born: 1918, New York, New York, U.S.A.

Telephone: (415) 326-6200

Profession: Social economist

Field of specialization: Changing values and lifestyles; futures methodologies; societal trends; corporate uses of values information.

Education: A.B., English, Amherst College, 1940.

Professional employment: SRI International: Director, Values and Lifestyles Program (1978-); Senior Social Economist (1967-78); Program Manager, Long-Range Planning Service (1958-67); Coordinator, Research Communication (1955-58).

Professional activities: Research: diagnosis and forecasting of trends in the values and lifestyles of Americans, and application of this information in a variety of corporate activities (1978-); long-range planning; corporate strategies; studies of quality of life; changing consumption patterns.

Publications: *Consumer Values: A Typology* (SRI Values and Lifestyles Program, 1978); co-author, *The Art of Exploratory Planning* (SRI Business Intelligence Program, 1976); co-author, *Handbook of Forecasting Techniques* (SRI for Department of the Army, 1975); co-author with Duane S. Elgin, "Voluntary Simplicity" (THE FUTURIST, Vol. 11, No. 4, August 1977); *American Values* (SRI Long-Range Planning Service, 1968).

MITCHELL, FERD H., JR.   **Born:** 1938, Mobile, Alabama, U.S.A.
Academic Administrator
Department of Family Practice
University of California at Davis
2221 Stockton Blvd.
Sacramento, California 95817, U.S.A.   **Telephone:** (916) 453-2820

Profession: Health systems administrator; planning and policy analyst; educator

Field of specialization: Strategic planning and forecasting methodologies; multi-organizational systems predictive models; organizational decision-making processes; health systems planning, development and operations.

Education: B.S., Physics, University of Florida, 1959; M.S., Physics, University of California, Los Angeles, 1962; Ph.D., University of Alabama, 1965.

Professional employment: University of California at Davis: Academic Administrator (1976-). Health Application Systems: Vice-President (1973-76). General Research Corporation: Director, Southeast Operations (1969-73). IBM Coproration: Manager (1966-69). Florida State University: Assistant Professor (1965-66).

Professional activities: Currently working on a broad-scope health planning research project in conjunction with an international study group (1975-); teaching courses in health systems and policy analysis (1976-); administration of innovative medical education and health service delivery programs (1973-); performance of health planning and evaluation studies as a consultant to the U.S. Department of Health, Education and Welfare (1972-76); manager of interdisciplinary consultant groups (1967-76).

Publications: "Anticipation Versus Results: An Approach to Improved Program Forecasting" (*American Journal of Health Planning*, April 1978); co-author, "The Health Care Team" chapter in *Family Medicine: Principles and Practice*, R. Taylor, editor (Springer-Verlag, 1978); co-author, "Primary Care: Whose Responsibility and Who Should Deliver It? (*Health Planning and Primary Care*, American Association of Comprehensive Planners, 1977); "The Use of Multi-Organizational Systems Models in Health Planning" (Annual Meeting of the American Public Health Association, 1978).

MOBLEY, LOUIS R.   **Born:** 1915, Atlanta, Georgia, U.S.A.
President
Mobley and Associates, Inc.
5000 Sheppard Lane
Ellicott City, Maryland 21043, U.S.A.   **Telephone:** (301) 531-5593

Profession: Consultant

Field of specialization: Value systems; policy consulting; organization and management systems.

300

Education: B.S., Mechanical Engineering, Georgia Institute of Technology, 1938.

Professional employment: Mobley, Luciani Associates: President (1975-78). Mobley and Associates, Inc.: President (1970-78). IBM Corporation: Director of the IBM Executive School and a variety of operating and educational assignments (1938-70).

Professional activities: Management consulting and contract work on values, policy making, and quality of work life (1970-78); American Excellence Board (1977-78); Earth Society Board (1975-78); Engineers Council for Professional Development (1950-53); American Society for Training and Development (1950-65); New York Management Development Study Group (1953-58); member, Church Executive Development Board (1965-72).

Publications: Co-author, *Personal Values and Corporate Ethics* (Herder and Co., Vienna, Austria, 1971); co-author, *The Values Option Process* (Society for General Systems Research, 1978).

MOLES, ABRAHAM A.

Born: 1920, Paris, France

Director
Institute of Social Psychology
University of Strasbourg
12 Rue Goethe
Strasbourg, France 67000

Telephone: (88) 35 43 00

Profession: Social psychologist

Field of specialization: Methodology of future studies; quality of life; communication ecology; micropsychology and theory of actions.

Education: M.A., Mathematics and Physics, 1940, M.A. Philosophy and Psychology, 1946, Paris; Ingenieur IEG, Grenoble, 1941; Doctorat d'Etat Sciences Physiques, 1952, Doctorat d'Etat et Lettres, Paris, 1955.

Professional employment: Director of the Institute of Social Psychology, Universite Louis Pasteur, Strasbourg (1966-); Senior Professor (1970-); Maitre de Conference (1966-70); Dozent Hochschule fur Gestaltung, Ulm, Germany (1961-68); Charge de recherche CNRS (1945-57); Attache au Service de recherche de L'ORTF (1948-65); Directeur Scientifique du Laboratoire Scherchen (1950-60); Ingenieur (1946-55).

Professional activities: Currently working on "mediators" such as messages, objects, acts, and environment which in mass society insert themselves between the individual and the social system; develops systematically the applications of the results of his Information Theory (structuralism) which he first applied to the aesthetic perception; conducts graduate courses on these themes at his institute as well as in various seminars in Paris and abroad; methodology of Delphi Methods in connection with Regnier's Colored Abacus (scalogram); Professor at San Diego State University (1976-77); consultant various industries (marketing and publicity) (1955-); seminar on futurology ("The Future in Society") (1963-65).

Publications: *Theorie des Actes [Theory of Actions]* Vol. 1 (Casterman, 1977); *Micropsychology*, Vol. 1, (Denoel, 1975); *Information Theory and Aesthetic Perception* (Illinois Press, 1966); *Sociodynamique de la Culture [Sociodynamics of Culture]* (Ed. Mouton, 1962); *Theorie des Objets [Theory of Objects]* (Ed. Universitaires, 1972); *Psychologie de l'Espace [Pyschology of Space]* (Ed. Casterman, 1972).

MOLITOR, GRAHAM THOMAS TATE

Born: 1934, Seattle, Washington, U.S.A.

President
Public Policy Forecasting, Inc.
9208 Wooden Bridge Road
Potomac, Maryland 20854, U.S.A.

Telephone: (301) 762-5174

Profession: Lawyer; educator; business executive

Field of specialization: Public policy forecasting; socio-political forecasting; world food and nutrition; consumer policy and environmental affairs; population; structure of government; structure of private enterprise; value systems.

Education: B.A., Political Science/History, University of Washington, 1955; L.L.B., Law, American University, 1963.

Professional employment: Public Policy Forecasting, Inc.: President (1977-). General Mills, Inc.: Director, Government Relations (1970-77). White House: Director of Research, White House Conference on the Industrial World Ahead (1971-72). Nabisco: Washington Counsel and Assistant Director of Government Relations (1964-69). American University: Instructor/Adjunct Professor (1968-75). U.S. Congress: Legislative Assistant (1960-63).

Professional activities: Currently working on studies for the Library of Congress on rural-urban trends, population, political democratization, and social welfare trends; consultant to several major U.S. corporations and universities; Chairman, Second General Assembly of the World Future Society, June 1975.

Publications: "How to Anticipate Public Policy Changes" (*Advanced Management Journal*, Summer 1977); "Choosing Our Environment: Can We Anticipate the Future?" (Panel on Environmental Science and Technology, Senate Committee on Public Works, February 1976); "A Look at Government: Forecasting Public Policy Developments" (*Technology Assessment*, 1973); "The Implications of Zero Population Growth" (*Alternative Futures and Environmental Quality*, May 1973); "A Hierarchy of Needs and Values" in *The Quality of Life Concept: A Potential New Tool for Decision Makers* (Environmental Protection Agency, March 1973); "The Coming World Struggle for Food" (THE FUTURIST, Vol. 8, No. 4, August 1974).

MONETA, CARLOS J.

Born: 1938, Buenos Aires, Argentina

Special Fellow
United Nations Institute for Training and Research (UNITAR)
801 United Nations Plaza
New York, New York 10017, U.S.A.

Telephone: (212) 754-8633

Profession: Political scientist (international relations)

Field of specialization: International politics analysis: the potential impact of world order studies on the international arena.

Education: Licenciado, International Relations, University of Salvador, Buenos Aires, Argentina, 1965; M.A., International Relations, University of Pennsylvania, 1967; Ph.D. candidate, Political Science, New York University, 1978.

Professional employment: UNITAR: Special Fellow, Research Department (1977-). Center of Economic and Social Studies of the Third World, Mexico: Researcher, Area NIEO (1976-77). University of California at Los Angeles; Visiting Professor (1976). University of Salvador, Buenos Aires, Argentina: Professor of International Relations (1970-75). National Commission of the Measure of Silver, Argentina: President (1973-74).

Professional activities: Currently working at UNITAR on studies of "the future of Latin American regional cooperation and the role of U.N." and "impact of world order studies on policy-making"; member, World Future Studies Federation; research, lecturing and writing on the new international economic order, the present and future of the Third World, the future of the Antartic and southern Atlantic region, relations between South America and Black Africa, the Middle Powers, and foreign policy of Brazil and Argentina.

Publications: "El uso de los modelos de simulacion global como instrumentos politicos en el orden mundial: algunas consideraciones preliminares" ["The Use of Global Simulation Models and How They Instrument Politics in the World Order: Some Preliminary Considerations"] (*Mundo Nuevo: Revista de Estudios Latino-americanos*, Univ. Simon Bolivar, Caracas, Venezuela, No. 2, 1978); co-author, *La Atlantartida: un espacio geopolitico [La Atlantartida: A Geopolitical Space]* (Edit. Pleamar, Buenos Aires, Argentina, 1978); "Antartida Argentina: los problemas de 1975-1990" ["Antartida Argentina: The Problems of 1975-1990"] (*Estrategia*, Buenos Aires, No. 31-32, November-December, 1974; January-February, 1975); co-author, *The Impact of the Cold War* (Kennikat Press, Edit. Siracusa, Barclay, Port Washington, New York, 1977); co-author, *De la dependencia a la liberacion: la politica exterior de America Latina [From Dependence to Liberation: The Political Exterior of Latin America]* (Edit. Astrea, Buenos Aires, 1973).

MORRIS, GEOFFREY KEITH

Born: 1932, London, England

Director of Research
Matrix Corporate Affairs Consultants
4 Cromwell Place
London S.W. 7, England

Telephone: —

302

Profession: Researcher

Field of specialization: Futures, environmental, sensitivity analysis.

Education: B.A., History, Downing College, Cambridge, 1956.

Professional employment: Matrix: Director of Research (1973-). IBM, United Kingdom Ltd.: External Affairs (1970-73); Research Planning Manager (1966-70); Advertising and PublicationsManager.

Professional activities: Lecturing.

Publications: - -

M'PHERSON, PHILIP KEITH   **Born:** 1927, London, United Kingdom
Professor of Systems Science
The City University
Northampton Square
London, EC1V OHB, United Kingdom   **Telephone:** (01) 253 4399

Profession: Systems engineer

Field of specialization: Decision models for policy research and systems design; value systems; dynamics and management of technological change; technological assessment.

Education: Marine Engineering, 1944-48, Ordnance Engineering, 1949-51, Royal Naval Engineering College; M.S., Instrumentation Laboratory, Massachusetts Institute of Technology, 1955; M.A., Special Award, Oxford University, 1965.

Professional employment: City University, London: Professor of Systems Science (1967-). International Institute of Applied Systems Analysis (1976-77). Oxford University: Fellow, St. Johns College (1965-67). United Kingdom Atomic Energy Authority: Leader, Dynamics Group (1959-65). Royal Navy: Lt. Commander (1955-59); Lieutenant (1948-55).

Professional activities: Decision model for science policy and research portfolio selection (1973-); value calculus for multi-attribute evaluation (1975-); integrated model of technological change (1976-); dynamics of technological change and improvement (1977-); Fellow of Institute of Marine Engineers (1978-), Institute of Measurement and Control (1978-), Institution of Mechanical Engineers (1967-), and Operations Research Society, U.K. (1974-); Companion of Nautical Institute (1978-); courses in systems engineering design and systems management (1967-); has written some 35 research reports for the Royal Navy, U.K. Atomic Energy Authority and the Science Research Council.

Publications: "Modeling Technological Change" (*Proceedings IFAC/IFORS Workshop on Systems Analysis Applications to Complex Programs,* Poland, June 1977); "A Value Calculus for Dealing with Subjective Criteria in Decision Making" (International Congress of Cybernetics and Systems, Bucharest, August 1975); "A Perspective on Systems Science and Systems Philosophy" (*Futures,* 1974); "Systems Theoretic Concepts of Systems Engineering" in *Advances in Cybernetics and Systems Research* (Transcripta Books, 1973).

MUSHKAT, MARI'ON   **Born:** 1919, Poland
The Israeli Institute for the Study of International Affairs
Tel Aviv POB 17027, Israel 61170   **Telephone:** (03) 414256 or (03) 420743

Profession: International lawyer; peace and future researcher

Field of specialization: Underdevelopment; disarmament; and other peace and future research issues.

Education: Ph.D., Political Science, University of Nancy, France, 1947; L.L.D., Law, University of Warsaw, 1949.

Professional employment: Tel-Aviv University: Professor of International Law and International Organization (1957-). The Institute for the Study of International Affairs: Academic Director (1963-). University of Warsaw: Professor of International Law (1951-56).

Professional activities: Currently cooperating in research programs of the Institute for the Study of International Affairs on the metamorphosis of the present international community following the diffusion of economic and military power (1977-), and on the European Community from an economic towards a political union (1978-).

Publications: *The Dynamics of the International Community* (Academic Publishers, 1976); *Humanitarian Law and the Law of War—New Developments* (The German Yearbook of International Law, Kiel, 1978); *The Future of Disarmament and the Military Establishment* (Co-Existence, Glasgow, 1978); *From the Law of Nations Through Peace Research and Planning to Futurology* (Co-Existence, Glasgow, 1971); *Underdevelopment—A Threat to International Security* (Die Dritte Welt, Koln, 1974).

MYRDAL, ALVA REIMER
Vaesterlaanggatan 31
S 11129, Stockholm, Sweden

Born: 1902, Uppsala, Sweden

Telephone: (08) 21 36 41

Profession: Diplomat; educator; sociologist; writer

Field of specialization: Disarmament; peace research.

Education: B.A., Stockholm University, 1924; Rockefeller Fellow, United States, 1929-30; University of Geneva, 1930-31; M.A., Uppsala University, 1934.

Professional employment: University of Texas at Austin: Co-holder of the Tom Slick Professorship in International Peace (Spring term, 1978). Wellesley College: Visiting Distinguished Slater Professor (1976). Massachusetts Insitute of Technology: Visiting Professor (May 1974, March 1975, May 1975). Center for the Study of Democratic Institutions: Visiting Fellow (1973-74). Cabinet Minister, Church Affairs (1969-73). Cabinet Minister, Disarmament (1966-73). Ambassador-at-Large (1961-66). Member of Parliament, Senate (1962-70). Ambassador to Nepal (1960-61). Minister to Burma (1955-58). Ambassador to India, Minister to Ceylon (1955-61). Training College for Preschool Teachers, Stockholm: Director (1936-40). Workers Education Association, Stockholm: Teacher (1924-32).

Professional activities: Chairman of Government Delegation for Expanding International Laws Against Brutality in War (1972-73); Chairman of Government Commission on Studies of the Future (1971-72); Chairman of the U.N. Committee on Disarmament and Development (1972); Chairman, Swedish Labor Party and Confederation of Trade Unions, Work Group on Reforms for Increased Equality (1968-73); Chairman, Government Commission on Separation of Church and State (1968-72).

Publications: *The Game of Disarmament* (second edition, Pantheon Books, 1978, also published in Swedish and Japanese); co-author, *Towards Equality: The Alva Myrdal Report* (Prisma, Stockholm, 1971, also published in German and Portuguese); co-author, *To Choose a Future* (Royal Ministry for Foreign Affairs, Stockholm, 1974); "The Right to Conduct Nuclear Explosions" (SIPRI paper, 1975); co-author with V. Klein, "Women's Two Roles" (revised edition, 1968); "Disarmament—Reality or Illusion?" (1965); "Nation and Family" (second edition, 1965); co-author with Dean Rusk and A. Altmeyer, "America's Role in International Social Welfare" (1954).

MYRDAL, GUNNAR
Professor of International Economics
Stockholm University
Institute for International Economic Studies
Fack, S-104 05 Stockholm 50, Sweden

Born: 1898, Gustafs Parish, Sweden

Telephone: —

Profession: Lawyer; economist

Field of specialization: International economics; world poverty.

Education: Law Degree, Stockholm University, 1923; Juris Doctor Degree in Economics, Stockholm University, 1927; studied in Germany and Britain, 1925-29; Rockefeller Fellow, United States, 1929-30.

Professional employment: Stockholm University: Professor of International Economics (1961-); Director, Institute for International Economic Studies (1961-). New York City University: Distinguished Visiting Professor (1974-75). Center for the Study of Democratic Institutions: Visiting Research Fellow (1973-74). Twentieth Century Fund: Directed a comprehensive study of economic trends and policies in South Asian countries (1957). Minister of Commerce, Sweden (1945-47). United

Nations Economic Commission for Europe (1947-57). Swedish Senate: Member (elected in 1934 and again in 1942).

Professional activities: Member, British Academy, American Academy of Arts and Sciences, The Royal Swedish Academy of Sciences, Fellow of the Econometric Society, Honorary Member of the American Economic Association; founded the Institute for International Economic Studies at Stockholm University (1961) and is still a member of its Directorate; Member of the Board of the Stockholm International Peace Research Institute.

Publications: *Against the Stream: Critical Essays on Economics* (Pantheon Books, New York, 1973); *The Challenge of World Poverty: A World Anti-Poverty Program in Outline* (Pantheon Books, New York, 1970); *Objectivity in Social Research* (Pantheon Books, New York, 1969); *Challenge to Affluence* (Pantheon Books, New York, 1963); *Beyond the Welfare State: Economic Planning and Its International Implications* (Yale University Press, 1960); *Value in Social Theory* (Harper and Bros., New York, 1958); *An International Economy: Problems and Prospects* (Harper and Bros., New York, 1956).

NANUS, BURT
Director
Center for Futures Research
University of Southern California
Los Angeles, California 90007, U.S.A.

Born: 1936, New York, New York, U.S.A.

Telephone: (213) 741-5229

Profession: Management scientist; policy analyst

Field of specialization: Futures methodology; corporate and government planning processes; impact of computers on society.

Education: M.E., Mechanical Engineering, Stevens Institute of Technology, 1957; M.S., Industrial Management, Massachusetts Institute of Technology, 1959; D.B.A., Quantitative Analysis, University of Southern California, 1967.

Professional employment: University of Southern California: Associate Professor of Management (present); Director, Center for Futures Research (1971-); Senior Research Associate, Public Systems Research Institute (1969-71). Planning Technology, Inc.: President (1967-69). Systems Development Corporation: Senior Tech. Advisor to Management (1962-67). Univac Division, Sperry Rand Corporation: Manager, Advanced Educational Techniques (1959-62).

Professional activities: Principal researcher on studies of multinational computers and new communities; Chairman, The Institute of Management Sciences, College on Planning (1975-76); consultant to many corporations and government agencies on planning processes; teaches courses and executive workshops in futures research; organized U.S.C. Center for Futures Research (1971-); conducted a study of Impact of Year 2000 on Mental Retardation for President's Commission on Mental Retardation (1974); many studies in fields of computers, work and leisure, and corporate planning.

Publications: "Management Training in Futures Concepts" (*Futures*, June 1977); "Futures Research in an Academic Setting" (WORLD FUTURE SOCIETY BULLETIN, March-April 1977); co-author, *The Social Implications of Use of Computers Across National Boundaries* AFIPS Press, 1973); "The Future-Oriented Corporation" (*Business Horizons*, February 1975); co-author, *Management Games* (Reinhold Publishing Company, 1961).

NELSON, RUBEN FREDERICK WERTHENBACH
President
Square One Management Ltd.
No. 302, 100 Gloucester Street
Ottawa, Ontario, Canada K2P 0A4

Born: 1939, Calgary, Alberta, Canada

Telephone: (613) 236-9712

Profession: Consulting futurist; social researcher; policy analyst; management consultant; theologian

Field of specialization: The foundations of public policy; cultural crises and transformations; designing conferences.

Education: Hon. B.A., Philosophy, Queen's University, Kingston, Ontario, 1961; Special Student, Indian Religions, United Theological College, India, 1963; Testamur, Systematic Theology, Queen's Theological College, Ontario, 1974.

Professional employment: Square One Management Ltd.: President (1971-). Privy Council Office, Ottawa: Social Policy Consultant (1970-71). University of Calgary: Director, University Centre (1968-70). Queens University: Senior Instructor (1966-68).

Professional activities: Continuing research into cultural crises and shifting paradigms of thought and action; designing conferences; conducting seminars on fundamental social change and organizational renewal; conference speaker; President, Canadian Association for Futures Studies.

Publications: "Stumbling Towards Responsible Enterprise" (*CA Magazine*, November 1978); *The Illusions of Urban Man* (Macmillan Company of Canada, 1976); 'Acting on Our Own Best Advice" (*Social Sciences in Canada*, 1976); "Running to Catch Up" (*Canadian Public Administration*, 1973); "Society: Today and Tomorrow," in *You Have a Right To Be Here* (United Church of Canada, 1973); "Reading as if it Matters" (*Futures Canada*, 1978).

NERFIN, MARC PAUL
International Foundation for Development Alternatives
2 place du Marche
1260 Nyon, Switzerland

Born: 1930, Geneva, Switzerland

Telephone: (22) 61 82 82

Profession: Adviser; writer; organizer

Field of specialization: New approaches to development and international relations; interface between research and decision-making.

Education: Maturite, B.A., Humanities, College de Geneve, 1949; Licence, M.A., History, Universite de Geneve, 1955.

Professional employment: Free lance consultant, including several U.N. agencies (present). Dag Hammarskjold Project on Development and International Cooperation: Director (1975). U.N. Conference on the Human Environment: Executive Assistant to the Secretary-General (1970-72). Study of the Capacity of the U.N. Development System: Adviser to the Commissioner (1968-69). U.N. Department of Economic Affairs: Adviser (1966-68). U.N. Economic Commission for Africa, Addis Ababa: Adviser (1963-65). Professor and journalist in Tunisia (1958-62).

Professional activities: President, International Foundation for Development Alternatives; member, Editorial Committee, *Development Dialogue*, journal of the Dag Hammarskjold Foundation; member Scientific Committee, Development Studies Institute, Geneva; Member of the Jury, Prix Futuribles, Paris; Senior Fellow, International Development Research Centre, Ottawa (1973); missions and visits to about 60 countries in all continents.

Publications: Editor, *Another Development: Approaches and Strategies* (The Dag Hammarskjold Foundation, Uppsala, Sweden, 1977; Spanish edition, Siglo XXI, Mexico); editor, "What Now—Another Development" (*Development Dialogue*, 1975); *Entretiens avec Ahmed Ben Salah sur la dynamique socialiste dans la Tunisie des annees 1960 [Conversations with Ahmed Ben Salah on the Socialist Dynamic in Tunisia During the 1960s]* (Maspero, Paris, 1974); co-author, *The Study of the Capacity of the United Nations Development System* (United Nations, New York, 1969).

NICHOLSON, SIMON
The Open University
Oxford Research Unit
Boars Hill
Oxford, United Kingdom

Born: 1934, London, United Kingdom

Telephone: 0865-730731

Profession: Artist

Field of specialization: The interactive arts and community participation in futures.

Education: First year A.R.C.A., Sculpture Department, Royal College of Art, London, 1953; B.A. and M.A., Department of Prehistoric Archeology and Anthropology, Trinity College, Cambridge, 1957.

306

Professional employment: The Open University, Faculty of Technology: Lecturer; member, Oxford Research Unit (1971-). University of California-Los Angeles: Visiting Professor, School of Architecture and Urban Planning (1974). Ontario Institute for Studies in Education: Visiting Professor (1973). Harvard University, Carpenter Center for the Visual Arts: Visiting Associate Professor (1971). University of California-Santa Barbara: Lecturer, College of Creative Studies (1969). University of California-Berkeley: Lecturer, College of Environmental Design (1965-67). Moore College of Art: Visiting Professor in Sculpture (1964-65).

Professional activities: Futures Exhibitions, The Athens International Symposium, *The Child in the World of Tomorrow*, July 1978; *Play in Human Settlements* [Le jeu dans-les establissements humaines], 7th World Conference, Ottawa, August 1978.

Publications: *Whatever Will Be...* (The Open University Press, 1977); *The Empty Box* (The Open University Press, 1976); co-author, *Community Participation in City Decision Making* (The Open University Press, 1974); co-author, *Art Is Not Yesterday* (The Open University Press, 1976); *"No Vanished Futures": The Future of Communication: Cultural Identity in an Interdependent World* (World Future Studies Federation, Rome, 1979).

NIGHTINGALE, DONALD VICTOR   **Born:** 1944, Niagara-on-the-Lake, Ontario, Canada
Associate Professor
School of Business
Queen's University
Kingston, Ontario, Canada K7L 3N6   **Telephone:** (613) 547-5867

Profession: Psychologist

Field of specialization: Work organizations, democracy in the workplace

Education: B.A., Psychology, University of Western Ontario, 1967; Ph.D., Psychology, University of Michigan, 1971.

Professional employment: Queen's University: Associate Professor (1973-). University of Ottawa: Assistant Professor (1971-73).

Professional activities: Teaching courses on futures research; conducting research on industrial democracy; Member of Executive, Canadian Association of Futures Studies; Vice President, Administrative Sciences Association of Canada.

Publications: - -

NILSSON, SAM   **Born:** 1931
Director
International Federation of Institutes for Advanced Study (IFIAS)
Ulriksdals Slott
171 71 Solna, Sweden   **Telephone:** (08) 85 01 15

Profession: Physicist

Field of specialization: Advanced research in the natural and social sciences; research and human needs; science and society; commercial development of innovations in advanced technologies.

Education: M.A., Mechanical Engineering; Ph.D., Physics and Mathematical Physics; D. Science, Physics.

Professional employment: IFIAS: Director (1972-); Feasibility Study of IFIAS (1971-72).

Professional activities: Member, Advisory Board, Gulbenkian Institute for Science and Society, Lisbon, Portugal (1977-); foreign member, National USSR Organizing Committee for U.N. Conference on Science and Technology for Development, 1979 (1977-); U.N. Educational, Scientific and Cultural Organization, program on "research and human needs": senior consultant (1976-78), member of committee of advisors (1977). Member of the Board: Inventor Invest Company, Ostersund, Sweden (1974-); Innovation Development Institute, Stockholm, Sweden (1974-).

Publications: Co-author, with Dr. E. Block, *The Future Threat or Opportunity* (in Swedish, 1970); co-editor, with Professor Arne Tiselius, *The Place of Value in a World of Facts* (Nobel Symposium 14, 1971); co-editor with Professor T. Segerstedt, *Man, Environment and Resources* (Nobel Symposium 29, 1975).

NOSAL, CZESLAW S.

Technical University of Wroclaw
Wybrzeze Wyspianskiego 27
50-370 Wroclaw, Poland

Born: 1942, Wojtkowa, Poland

Telephone: 203757

Profession: Psychologist

Field of specialization: Human problem solving methodology; futures methodology; human information processing (work, education, creative thinking, communication networks); behavioral sciences methodology; systems approach; science policy.

Education: Educational College, 1961; M.A., 1966, Ph.D., 1971, Psychology, University of Poznan.

Professional employment: Technical University of Wroclaw: Research Worker (1972-). University of Poznan: Research Worker (1966-71).

Professional activities: Research projects concerning influence of ability on problem solving (1971-1974); theory of human information processing (1975-1976); psychological aspects of communication in science (1977-); educational planning in technology and medicine (1972-76); human needs and technology planning (1972-74); heuristics methods in futures methodolgy (1972-74).

Publications: *Work Psychology: Organization of Human Mental and Behaviorial Activity* (Technical University of Wroclaw Press, 1977); *Psychology of Human Mind: Abilities, Cognitive Styles, Information Processing* (Tech. Univ. Of Wroclaw Press, 1978); "Dynamics of Problem Solving and Cognitive Abilities" (*Polish Psychology Bulletin,* 1974); "Diagnosis of Creative Personality: Stimulation of Creativity" (*Prace Naukoznawcze i Prognostyczne,* No. 13, 1975).

NYHEIM, JAN HENRIK

Norsk rikskringkasting [Norwegian Broadcasting Corporation]
Bjornstjerne Bjornsons Plass
Majorstua—Oslo 3, Norway

Born: 1933, Baerum, Norway

Telephone: (02)46 98 60

Profession: Long range planner (corporate planner)

Field of specialization: Communications technology, development, uses, implications and consequences; communications policy on a national and international level; the relationship between the application of communication technology and society.

Education: Magister Artium (Ph.D.), Political Science, University of Oslo, 1962.

Professional employment: Norwegian Broadcasting Corporation: Long range planner (1970-). NAVF (Norwegian Research Council for the Sciences and Humanities): Director, Social Studies Section (1968-69). University of Arhus, Denmark: Assistant Professor, Political Science.

Professional activities: Currently working on TELSAM, a study initiated by the Norwegian PTT authorities on the relationship between application of new telecommunication services on society in general and planning processes in particular (1977-); presently President of the SEFREM (Norewegian Society for Future Studies).

Publications: Editor, *Teletjenester, samfunnsutvikling og samfunnsplanlegging [Teleservices, Development and Planning for Society]* (Televerket, Norwegian PTT, June 1978); *Kommunikasjon og fremtid [Communications Technology and the Future]* (SEFREM, Ingeniorforlaget, 1975); "Nordsat: The Nordic Satellite Broadcasting System" (*Satellite Communications,* April 1978); "Long-range Planning in Broadcasting: A Help or a Headache?" (*EBU Review,* June 1977); *Cable: Channels, Sources and Choices* (International Broadcast Institute, 1976).

ODUM, HOWARD THOMAS

Graduate Research Professor
Systems Ecology and Energy Analysis
Department of Environmental Engineering Sciences
University of Florida
Gainesville, Florida 32611, U.S.A.

Born: 1924, Durham, North Carolina, U.S.A.

Telephone: (904) 392-0847

Profession: Systems ecologist; professor

Field of specialization: Systems ecology; energy analysis; biological oceanography

Education: A.B., Zoology, University of North Carolina, 1947; Ph.D., Zoology, Yale University, 1951.

Professional employment: University of Florida: Graduate Research Professor, Environmental Engineering Sciences (1970-); Director, Center for Wetlands (1972-). University of North Carolina: Professor of Ecology (1966-70). Puerto Rico Nuclear Center: Chief Scientist (1963-66). University of Texas: Director, Institute of Marine Science (1956-63). Duke University and Duke Marine Center: Assistant Professor (1954-56). University of Florida: Assistant Professor (1950-54). U.S. AAF Tropical Weather School, Canal Zone: Meteorologist (1944-45).

Professional activities: Principal investigator, projects utilizing wetlands as waste interface with society, energy analysis of system of humanity and nature, and models affecting public policy; completing a book on ecological and general systems; teaching courses on systems ecology, energy analysis, and ecological engineering.

Publications: *Environment, Power and Society* (John Wiley, 1971); co-author, *Energy Basis of Man and Nature* (McGraw-Hill, 1976); co-editor, *A Tropical Rain Forest* (Division of Technical Information, Atomic Energy Commission, 1970); "Energy Analysis, Energy Quality, and Environment" (AAAS Selected Symposium No. 9 Energy Analysis, 1978); co-author, *Coastal Ecological Systems of the United States* (Report to Federal Water Pollution Control Administration, Vol. 1-3, published by the Conservation Foundation, 1974).

OGDEN, FRANK **Born:** 1920, Toronto, Ontario, Canada
Xanada-Canada
P.O. Box 3608
MPO Vancouver, British Columbia, Canada V6B 3Y6 **Telephone:** (604) 688-7103

Profession: Consultant

Field of specialization: Communications; visionary development.

Education: University of Manitoba.

Professional employment: Self-employed as private consultant (1948-).

Professional activities: Consultant to 25 companies in Canada, U.S., Caribbean and South Pacific; "Aquatic Village" housing project; Third Millennium Project.

Publications: Co-author, *The Use of LSD in Psychotherapy and Alcoholism* (Bobbs-Merrill,1967).

OKITA, SABURO **Born:** 1914, Dairen, China
Chairman
The Japan Economic Research Center
Nikkei Building, 9-5, Otemachi 1-chome
Tokyo 100, Japan **Telephone:** (03) 270-7376

Profession: Economist

Field of specialization: International economic relations; food, energy and natural resources.

Education: B.E., Engineering Faculty, Tokyo University, 1937; Doctor of Economics, Ministry of Education, 1962; Doctor of Laws, Honorary, University of Michigan, 1977.

Professional employment: Japan Economic Research Center: Chairman (1973-). Overseas Economic Cooperation Fund: President (1973-77). Japan Economic Research Center: President (1964-73). Economic Planning Agency, Planning Bureau and Developing Bureau: Director General (1956-63).

Professional activities: Member, United Nations Committee for Development Planning (1966-); member, Japan Society for Future Studies (1968-); member, Pearson Commission for International Development (1968-69); member, Expert Group of OECD on Science Policy in the 1970s (1969); lecturer, FAO McDougall Memorial Lecture (1973); lecturer, Azad Memorial Lecture (1977).

OLIVERA, JULIO H. G.
Professor
Faculty of Economic Science
University of Buenos Aires
Cordoba 2122
Buenos Aires, Argentina

Born: 1929, Santiago del Estero, Argentina

Telephone: 46-2023

Profession: Economist

Field of specialization: Economic theory; monetary economics; economic systems.

Education: Doctor in Law and Social Sciences, University of Buenos Aires, 1954.

Professional employment: University of Buenos Aires: Full Professor of Economic Theory, Faculty of Economic Science (1960-); Director, Institute for Economic Research (1962-); Professor of Economics (1956-60).

Professional activities: Member of the Council, Econometric Society (1976); Member of the Honorary Editorial Advisory Board, *World Development* (1971-); Member of the Academie Internationale des Sciences Politiques (1964-); Member of The Club of Rome (1968-); Rector (President), University of Buenos Aires (1962-65); President of the Latin American Union of Universities (1963-64); Member of the Executive Committee, International Economic Association (1965-71); Secretary of State for Science and Technology (1973-74).

Publications: "Supply of Statistics and Choice of Economic Policies in Developing Countries" (*International Social Science Journal*, 1976); "Structural Economics and Linear Systems" (*Economic Notes,* 1977); "Cyclical Growth Under Collectivism" (*Kyklos*, 1960); "Structural Inflation and Latin American Structuralism" (*Oxford Economic Papers*, 1964); "Die Universitat als Produktionseinheit" ["The University as a Production Unit"] (*Weltwirtschaftliches Archiv*, 1967); "On Passive Money" (*Journal of Political Economy*, 1970); "On Bernoullian Production Sets" (*Quarterly Journal of Economics*, 1973).

O'NEILL, GERARD KITCHEN
Professor
Physics Department
Princeton University
Jadwin Hall, Box 708
Princeton, New Jersey 08540, U.S.A.

Born: 1927, New York, New York, U.S.A.

Telephone: (609) 452-4347

Profession: Physics professor

Field of specialization: High energy physics research; research on applications of space technology to astronomy and space colonization.

Education: B.A., High Honors, Physics, Swarthmore College; Ph.D., Physics, Cornell University, 1954.

Professional employment: Princeton University: Professor (1965-); Associate Professor (1959-65); Physics Instructor (1954).

Professional activities: Experimental research, high energy physics—elementary particle physics (1963-); research on applications of space technology to astronomy and space colonization (1968-); particle accelerator design (1954-69); storage ring design and development (1956-65); Fellow of the American Physical Society; member, American Institute of Aeronautics and Astronautics.

Publications: *The High Frontier* (Bantam Books, 1978); "The Low (Profile) Road to Space Manufacturing" (*Astronautics and Aeronautics*, March 1978); "The Storage Ring Synchotron: Device for High-Energy Physics Research" (*Physics Review*, 102,5,1418, 1956); "Storage Rings for Electrons and Protons" (*Proceedings*, International Conference on High-Energy Accelerators and Instrumentation, 1959); co-author, "Wide Angle Electron Scattering on the Princeton-Stanford Storage Rings" (Oxford International Conference on Elementary Particles, September 1965); "The Colonization of Space" (*Physics Today*, September 1974); "Space Colonies and Energy Supply to the Earth" (*Science*, Vol. 190, December 1975).

310

O'TOOLE, JAMES JOSEPH

Center for Futures Research
University of Southern California
Graduate School of Business Administration
Los Angeles, California 90007, U.S.A.

Born: 1945, San Francisco, California, U.S.A.

Telephone: (213) 741-5229

Profession: Social anthropologist, policy analyst

Field of specialization: Sociology of work; relationship of business and society.

Education: B.A., Humanities, University of Southern California, 1966; D. Phil., Social Anthropology, Oxford University, 1970.

Professional employment: University of Southern California: Associate Professor (1977-); University of Southern California, Center for Futures Research: Director, Third Twenty Year Forecast (1976); Assistant Professor of Management (1973-77). Aspen Institute: Director, Project on Education, Work and the Quality of Life (1973). Department of Health, Education and Welfare: Chairman, Secretary's Committee on Work in America (1971-73); Special Assistant to the Secretary (1970-71). President's Commission on Campus Unrest: Coordinator, General Field Investigations (1970).

Professional activities: Member, Board of Directors, American Association for Higher Education (1977-79); Director, "Twenty Year Forecast of the Future of Business-Government Relations"; Program Chairman, 1977 National Conference of the American Association for Higher Education; Director, "Twenty Year Forecast—Energy and Social Change" (1974-75); wrote and lectured extensively on manpower planning, job redesign and the future of education and work (1972-75).

Publications: *Work, Learning and the American Future* (Jossey-Bass, 1977); "Tenure: A Concientious Objection" (*Change*, June-July 1978); "The Immobilized State" (*Harvard Business Review*, March-April 1979); co-author, *Work In America* (MIT Press, 1973); co-author, *Energy and Social Change* (MIT Press, 1974); *Watts and Woodstock: Identity and Culture in the U.S. and South Africa* (Holt, Rhinehart and Winston, 1973).

OVERHOLT, WILLIAM HENRY

Researcher
Hudson Institute
Quaker Ridge Road
Croton-on-Hudson, New York 10520, U.S.A.

Born: 1945, Lexington, Virginia, U.S.A.

Telephone: (914) 762-0700

Profession: Political scientist; policy analyst

Field of specialization: National security planning; economic development planning; country risk studies.

Education: B.A., Social Studies, Harvard, 1968; M. Phil., 1970, Ph.D., 1972, Political Science, Yale University.

Professional employment: Hudson Institute: Researcher (1971-). Columbia University, Research Institute on International Change: Research Associate (1975-78). Yale University, Political Science Department: Teaching Assistant, Teaching Associate (1969-70). Institute for Defense Analyses: Researcher (1968).

Professional activities: Editor, "Global Political Assessment," a semi-annual report (1976-78).

Publications: Editor and co-author, *Asia's Nuclear Future* (Westview Press, 1977); editor and co-author, *The Future of Brazil* (Westview Press, 1978); *South Korea in U.S. Foreign Policy* (1979); *The Rise of the Pacific Basin* (Pacific Community, 1974).

OZBEKHAN, HASAN

Professor
University of Pennsylvania
400 Vance Hall
3733 Spruce Street
Philadelphia, Pennsylvania 19174, U.S.A.

Born: 1921, Istanbul, Turkey

Telephone: (215) 243-5739

Profession: Planner; consultant

Field of specialization: Planning; social systems; methodology.

Education: License, Political Science/Law, University of Paris; B.Sc., Economics, University of London, 1943.

Professional employment: University of Pennsylvania: Professor (1971-). H. Ozbekhan and Associates: President (1969-). Systems Development Corporation: Director of Planning (1963-69). General Electric Company: Special Consultant (1955-63).

Professional activities: Teaching Planning Theory, Corporate Planning, Multinational Corporations, Systems Theory; current research on planning methodology; Research Director and Member of the Executive Committee of The Club of Rome (1968-70); Research Head, International Functions of Paris (1970-73); consultant to French and Turkish governments and various multinational firms.

Publications: "Toward a General Theory of Planning" (*Perspectives of Planning*, OECD, 1970); "Planning and Human Action—Hierarchically Organized Systems in Theory" (1972); "Organized Systems in Theory and Practice" (1972); "Predicament of Mankind—TIMS Management Lines" (1975); "Thoughts on the Emerging Methodology of Planning Systems and Management" (1974).

OZMON, HOWARD

Born: Portsmouth, Virginia, U.S.A.

Professor of Education
School of Education
Virginia Commonwealth University
Richmond, Virginia 23284, U.S.A.

Telephone: (804) 770-8296

Profession: Professor of Education

Field of specialization: Utopias; future of education.

Education: A.B., Philosophy, University of Virginia, 1954; M.A. and Ed.D., Philosophy of Education, Columbia University, 1962.

Professional employment: Virginia Commonwealth University: Professor of Education (1970-). Chicago State University: Chairman and Professor of Education (1968-70). University of Virginia: Associate Professor of Education (1964-67).

Professional activities: Regional Coordinator, World Future Society (1970-); speaker, consultant, and writer on the future of education (1970-); Fellow, Philosophy of Education Society (1961-).

Publications: *Dialogue in the Philosophy of Education* (Charles E. Merrill, 1972); co-author, *Philosophical Foundations of Education* (Charles E. Merrill, 1976); *Utopias and Education* (Burgess, 1969); *Twelve Great Philosophers* (Oddo, 1968); *Contemporary Critics of Education* (Interstate, 1970).

PADDOCK, WILLIAM CARSON

Born: 1921, Minneapolis, Minnesota, U.S.A.

Box 593259
Miami, Florida 33159, U.S.A.

Telephone: (202) 338-8690

Profession: Agronomist

Field of specialization: Tropical agricultural development; basic food crop production; problems related to the world food/population equation.

Education: B.S., Botany, Iowa State University, 1944; Ph.D., Plant Pathology, Cornell University, 1950.

Professional employment: Consultant: 1964-. National Academy of Sciences: Head, Latin American Affairs (1962-64). Escuela Agricola Panamericana, Tegucigalpa, Honduras: Director (1958-62). International Cooperation Administration, Guatemala: Agronomist (1955-58).

Professional activities: Director, Iowa State University Guatemala Tropical Research Station, Antigua, Guatemala; Professor of Plant Pathology, Iowa State University; Assistant Professor of Plant Pathology, Pennsylvania State University; writes and consults on problems related to basic food production in the tropics.

Publications: Co-author, *Hungry Nations, 1* (Little, Brown, 1964); co-author, *Famine-1975, America's Decision Who Will Survive* (Little, Brown, 1967); co-author, *We Don't Know How: An Independent*

Audit of What They Call Success in Foreign Assistance (Iowa State University Press, 1973); co-author, *Time of Famine* (Little, Brown, 1976).
(From the first edition. Corrections not received by press time.)

PAGE, R. WILLIAM
Research Fellow
Science Policy Research Unit
University of Sussex
Falmer, Brighton
Sussex, England BNZ 9RF

Born: 1946, London, United Kingdom

Telephone: (0273) 68 6758

Profession: University research fellow

Field of specialization: Medium and long-term outlook for supply, trade and consumption of metals.

Education: B.A., Social Psychology, University of Sussex, 1969.

Professional employment: University of Sussex, Science Policy Research Unit: Research Fellow (1971-). Post Office Telecommunications: Market Researcher in M.R. and Forecasting Division (1970-71). Political and Economic Planning Ltd.: Researcher (1970).

Professional activities: Working on the SPRU "Social and Technological Alternatives for the Future" program; initially worked on population forecasting methodology, including a "hindsight" study, and on cost-benefit analysis technology; working on non-renewable (non-fuel) minerals since 1972, including hindsight, role of mining in UDC's, demand forecasting methodology; currently running two undergraduate courses, "Project Evaluation and Social Cost-Benefit Analysis" and "Materials and the Future."

Publications: "The United Kingdom Balance of Payments and the Substitution and Recycling of Metals" (*SPRU*, for the National Economic Development Office, 1976); "Some Non-Fuel Minerals: Alternatives for the Next 75 Years" in *World Futures—The Great Debate*, Jahoda and Freeman, eds., (Martin Robertson, 1978); "Long-term Forecasts for Metals: The Track Record, 1910-1960" (SPRU Occasional Paper No. 6, 1978); "Mining and Development: Are they Compatible in South America?" (*Resources Policy*, December 1976); co-author, *Thinking About the Future: A Critique of "The Limits to Growth"*, H.S.D. Cole et al., eds., (Sussex University Press and Universe Books as *Models of Doom*, 1974); co-author, with C. de Houghton and G. Streatfeild, *...And Now The Future* (Political and Economic Planning, 1971); editor, with S. Encel and P. K. Marstrand, *The Art of Anticipation* (Martin Robertson, 1975); co-author, with C. Barker, "OPEC as a Model for Other Mineral Exporters" (*Institute of Development Studies Bulletin*, October 1974).

PAGE, TALBOT
Visiting Associate
Environmental Quality Laboratory
California Institute of Technology
Pasadena, California 91125, U.S.A.

Born: 1940, Philadelphia, Pennsylvania, U.S.A.

Telephone: (213) 795-6811

Profession: Economist

Field of specialization: Environmental economics; long term, latent hazards; intemporal equity.

Education: B.A., Mathematics, Harvard, 1962; Ph.D., Economics, Cornell, 1972.

Professional employment: California Institute of Technology: Visiting Associate in Economics (1977-). Resources for the Future: Senior Research Associate (1975-77), Research Associate (1971-77).

Professional activities: Teaching a course entitled "Environmental Economics" (1978); working on research projects "pesticide contaminants in breast milk" and "ozone depletion and the fair distribution of risk"; research proposal reviewer for the National Science Foundation (1975-); consultant to the Office of Technology Assessment (1977-) and the Energy, Resources, Conservation and Development Commission, State of California (1978-); member, Subcommittee on Concepts (BEIR), Assembly of Life Sciences (1975-) and Study on Principles of Decision Making for Regulating Chemicals in the Environment (1975), National Academy of Sciences; member, Advisory Committee on Materials, Office of Technology Assessment (1975-77).

Publications: *Conservation and Economic Efficiency* (Johns Hopkins Press, 1977); co-author with Robert Harris and Nancy Reiches, "Carcinogenic Hazards of Organic Chemicals in Drinking Water", in

Origins of Human Cancer (Cold Spring Harbor Laboratory, 1977); *Economics of Involuntary Transfers: A Unified Approach to Pollution and Congestion Externalities* (Springer-Verlag, 1973); co-author, "On the Foundations of Intertemporal Choice" (*American Journal of Agricultural Economics*, 1978); "A Generic View of Toxic Chemicals and Similar Risks" (*Ecology Law Quarterly*, 1978).

PAIGE, GLENN DURLAND

Born: 1929, U.S.A.

Professor
Department of Political Science
University of Hawaii
2424 Maile Way
Honolulu, Hawaii 96822, U.S.A.

Telephone: (808) 948-8357

Profession: Political scientist

Field of specialization: Political leadership and nonviolent political alternatives.

Education: A.B., Politics, Princeton University, 1955; M.A., Regional Studies—East Asia, Harvard University, 1957; Ph.D., Political Science, Northwestern University, 1959.

Professional employment: University of Hawaii: Professor of Political Science (1967-). Princeton University: Associate Professor (1965-67); Assistant Professor (1961-65). University of Minnesota: Assistant Professor of Public Administration (1959-61). Graduate School of Public Administration, Seoul National University: Research Adviser (1959-61).

Professional activities: Developing courses on nonviolent political alternatives from the perspective of a nonviolent political science (1977-); courses on the scientific study of political leadership as a source of creative potential for transition to more desirable futures (1968); Program chairman, Hawaii State Governor's Conference on the Year 2000 (August 1970); participant in the second International Future Research Conference, Kyoto (1970) and the third World Future Research Conference, Bucharest (1972); together with Glenda Hatsuko Paige made the inaugural presentation of the Futures Party at the "International Conference on Malaysia in the Year 2001," Kuala Lumpur (August 1975).

Publications: "On Values and Science: The Korean Decision Reconsidered" (*American Political Science Review*, December 1977); *The Scientific Study of Political Leadership* (Free Press, 1977); editor, *Political Leadership* (Free Press, 1972); editor, *Hawaii 2000: Continuing Experiment in Anticipatory Democracy*, (University Press of Hawaii 1973); *Political Leadership in the Future Informational Society* in Japanese (Gakken Publishing Co., 1975).

PARRY, RENEE-MARIE CROOSE (nee HAUSENSTEIN)

Born: 1922, Munich, Germany

81 Onslow Square
London SW7 3LT, England

Telephone: (01) 584 8661

Profession: Free lance writer, lecturer, and reporter

Field of specialization: Value systems, particularly evolutionary ethics with a view to human survival and development; the Christian Marxist dialogue and hence Christian socialism; the socio-political system and ethic of the Chinese People's Republic.

Education: History of Art, German Literature, and Languages, University of Munich, 1938-40. Emigrated to Brazil (1942) and then to U.S. (1946) due to racial persecution.

Professional employment: Office for Refugees, Migration and Voluntary Assistance, Foreign Operations Administration, Washington, D.C.: Special Assistant to the Director (1953-55). Various positions in business and industry in the U.S. (1950-52). Catholic War Relief Services, New York: Resettlement of displaced persons (1949-50). Language tutor in Rio de Janeiro, Brazil, and Washington, D.C. (1942-49).

Professional activities: Founder and Honorary Secretary, People for a Non-nuclear World (1977-); Founder and Acting Secretary, Parliamentary Liaison Group for Alternative Energy Strategies (1977-); free-lance lecturer, writer, and reporter on a variety of subjects pertaining to futures research (1974-); current research on values for the Fourth World on "alternative movements" and on the thought of Teilhard de Chardin and related thinkers; Founder and former Honorary Secretary of The Teilhard Centre for the Future of Man, London (1964-74); editor, color insert of *The Teilhard Review* (summer 1968-74); member of The World Future Studies Federation, The Society for Anglo-Chinese Understanding, U.K., and Amnesty International; member, Steering Committee, World Future Society, London Group; cooperates with *Resurgence,* Journal of the Fourth World, London.

Publications: "Human Needs and the New Society" in *Human Needs, New Societies, Supportive Technologies,* Vol. I (Irades, Rome, 1974, and *The Teilhard Review,* Vol. IX, No. 3, 1974); "Values of the Fourth World" (*Christian Action Journal,* London, May 1976); "The Promethean Situation—Are We Going Towards a Biological Slum?" (*The Teilhard Review,* Vol. X, No. 11, Summer 1975); "The Limits to Medicine" (*Futures,* Vol. VII, No. 4, August 1975); many articles, conference reports and reviews in *The Teilhard Review* (1966-75) and some in *Futures* (1974-75).

PARSONS, JACK   **Born:** 1920, Kirkby-in-Ashfield, England
Senior Lecturer and Deputy Director
David Owen Centre for Population Studies
University College
Cardiff, Wales   **Telephone:** Cardiff 44211

Profession: Social demographer

Field of specialization: Population control and socio-economic stabilization.

Education: B.A. (Honours), Philosophy and Politics, University College, Keele, 1955.

Professional employment: David Owen Centre for Population Studies: Senior Lecturer in Population Studies and Deputy Director (1975-). Brunel University: Lecturer in Social Institutions, School of Social Sciences (1960-75). National Coal Board: Sociological Research Officer (1956-60). Various Civil Engineering Firms: Site Engineer (1946-51). Royal Air Force: Air Pilot (1941-46). Various Engineering Firms: Artisan (1934-41).

Professional activities: Principal activity at present is coordinating and improving a new interdisciplinary post-graduate diploma course in population studies, mainly for Third World people engaged in population control programs. Main research areas are: competitive breeding, socio-economic stabilization, and the ecology of liberty,with emphasis on migration control. Founder-member and council member of the Conservation Society (1967-75); population consultant and member, Liberal Party Environment Panel (1971-75); founder and convenor, Brunel Environment Group (1972-75); member, Friends of the Earth and Conservation Tools and Technology; delivered a paper at the World Population Conference, Bucharest; numerous public lectures and radio and TV talks on population/environmental topics; interested in intermediate technology and learning to run a small farm appropriately.

Publications: Co-author, *Human Fertility Control: Theory and Practice* (Butterworths, London, 1979); co-author, *Crisis in Britain's Sociological Perspective* (Reading University Press, 1977); "Reflections on Demophobia" (*Intercom,* Washington, D.C., September 1978); "What Malthus Really Said" (*People,* 4, No. 4, 1977); "Malthus: The Man Behind the Myth" (*People,* 4, No. 3, 1977).

PECCEI, AURELIO   **Born:** 1908, Turin, Italy
The Club of Rome
163, Via Giorgione
Rome 00147, Italy   **Telephone:** (06) 540 68 72

Profession: Industrial manager (retired)

Field of specialization: The human condition in our time.

Education: Doctor, Economics, University of Turin, 1930.

Professional employment: Italconsult, Rome: Chairman of the Board (1971-); President (1957-74). Fiat, Turin: Member, Management Committee (1930-73). Fiat, Buenos Aires: Chairman of the Board (1953-73). Olivetti, Ivrea: President (1963-67).

Professional activities: Inspirer and co-founder of The Club of Rome; devotes time to the study of the macroproblems of the technological age and of the fundamental changes required in human society in order to find adequate answers to these problems; promoter of the International Institute for Applied Systems Analysis (Vienna) and of the International Institute for the Management of Technology

(Milan); member of the Board of Trustees of the International Institute for Environment and Development (London), and the World Wildlife Fund (Morges), the International Ocean Institute (Malta), the International Federation of Institutes for Advanced Study (Stockholm), and the Population Institute (Washington).

Publications: *The Chasm Ahead* (Macmillan Press, 1969): *The Human Quality* (Pergamon Press, 1977). Translation of these books in many languages; numerous articles and essays in journals and magazines.

PESSOLANO, F. JOHN

Born: 1926, New Kensington, Pennsylvania, U.S.A.

Counselor in Public Relations
F. John Pessolano
333 East 46th Street
New York, New York 10017, U.S.A.

Telephone: (212) 490-1826

Profession: Counselor in public relations and public affairs; teacher

Field of specialization: Futures methodologies and applications; management information systems; the communications function.

Education: B.S., Biology, 1948, M.A. English, 1950, University of Pittsburgh.

Professional employment: F. John Pessolano: Counselor in Public Relations and Public Affairs (1959-). Pace University: Adjunct Assistant Professor (1978-). New York University, Business and Management Programs: Designer and Instructor, Career Development Programs in Public Relations (1975-). University of Pittsburgh: Lecturer (1953-54). University of Kansas: Instructor (1951-53).

Professional activities: Director, Delphi Study "The Future of Public Relations" (1978-79); directing futures research for Public Relations Society of America (1978-); contributing editor, *Business Tomorrow* (1978-); member, National Accreditation Board and Planning Committee for 31st National Conference "Preparing for the 80s" Public Relations Society of America (1978); consultant to the National Science Foundation on technology assessment "Life Extending Technologies" (1977); co-designed, "Early Warning Signals" Seminars, American Management Associations (1976).

Publications: "Reading the Social and Business Environment" (*Public Relations Review,* 1978); "The Practitioner as Futurist" (*Public Relations Journal,* 1978); editor, *Options for the Future* by Thomas E. Jones (W.H. Freeman, to be published in 1979); co-author, "Mismanaging Change with Safe Decisions and Used-Up Ideas" (*The President,* Summer 1977); co-author, "Management and the Scrutable Future" (*Managers' Forum,* February 1977).

PETERSON, RUSSELL WILBUR

Born: 1916, Portage, Wisconsin, U.S.A.

President
National Audubon Society
950 Third Avenue
New York, New York, 10022, U.S.A.

Telephone: (212) 832-3200

Profession: Chemist; association executive

Field of specialization: Technology assessment; environmental protection.

Education: Ph.D., Chemistry, University of Wisconsin, 1942.

Professional employment: National Audubon Society: President (1979-). U.S. Congress, Office of Technology Assessment: Director (1978-79). New Directions: President (1976-78). President's Council on Environmental Quality: Chairman (1973-76). Rockefeller Commission on Critical Choices for Americans: Chairman, Executive Committee (1973). State of Delaware: Governor (1969-73). Du Pont Company, Development Department, Research and Development Division: Director (1942-68).

Professional activities: Board of Directors: American Association for the Advancement of Science (1978-), World Wildlife Fund (current), Population Crisis Committee (current), U.S. Association for the Club of Rome (current); Regional Vice-Chairman, National Municipal League (current); Chairman, Textile Research Institute (1961-63); Director, Tri-County Conservancy of the Brandywine (1968-76); Vice-Chairman, Save Our Seas (1972-73); President, Three-S-Citizens Campaign, correction system in

316

Delaware (1960's); Chairman, National Advisory Committee on Criminal Justice Standards and Goals (1971-73); Vice-Chairman, U.S. Delegation to U.N. World Population Conference, Bucharest (1974); Vice-Chairman, U.S. Delegation to U.N. World Conference on Human Settlements (1976).

Publications: "Surviving the Technological Imperative" (*Chemical Engineering Progress,* June 1978); "Family Planning in Poor Nations" (*New York Times,* August 2, 1976); "The Role and Responsibility of the U.S. in Coping with the World Problematique" (*Congressional Record,* June 8, 1977); "Threats to World Security—A Chemist's View" (*Chemical and Engineering News,* June 20, 1977); "Wildlife and the Man in the Street" (*Vital Speeches of the Day,* November 15, 1976).

PHELPS, JOHN BEDFORD   **Born:** 1929, Sioux City, Iowa, U.S.A.
Consultant
Hudson Institute
Croton-on-Hudson, New York 10520, U.S.A.   **Telephone:** (914) 762-0700

Profession: Physicist; futurologist

Field of specialization: General futurology; technology (especially physical science developments); models, methodology and theory; economics; social theory.

Education: B.A., Physics and Mathematics, Morningside College, 1948; M.A., Physics, Colorado College, 1951; M.S., Physics, 1953, Ph.D., Theoretical Biophysics, 1959, Yale University.

Professional employment: Hudson Institute: Consultant (1977-). Advanced Research Projects Agency: Consulting Scientist, Editor and Futurologist (1968-); Physicist and Assistant to Director (1964-68). Morningside College: Lecturer in Future Studies (1976). Editor-in-Chief: *New American Encyclopedia* (1971-73). Institute for Defense Analyses: Senior Staff Manager (1961-64). Ohio State University: Research Associate (1958-61).

Professional activities: Consulting for Hudson Institute on models and theory, technology, economics, and social trends (1977-); lecturing and writing; consultant, lecturer and panelist on nuclear weapons and arms control (1955-70); member, American Association for the Advancement of Science, Arms Control Association, World Future Society.

Publications: Articles in various journals (including *Scientific American* and *New Scientist*) and numerous papers and reports.

PHILLIPS, BERNARD S.   **Born:** 1931, New York, New York, U.S.A.
Professor
Department of Sociology
Boston University
100 Cummington Street
Boston, Massachusetts 02215, U.S.A.   **Telephone:** (617) 353-2592

Profession: Sociologist

Field of specialization: Sociology of the future.

Education: B.A., Sociology, Columbia University, 1952; M.A., Sociology, Washington State University, 1954; Ph.D., Sociology, Cornell University, 1956.

Professional employment: Boston University: Professor of Sociology (1961-). University of Illinois: Assistant Professor of Sociology (1958-61). University of North Carolina: Assistant Professor (1956-58).

Professional activities: Presently teaching courses entitled "Sociology of the Future" (twice a year) and "Theories of Social Change" (one a year); co-founder of the section of the American Sociological Society on "Sociological Practice" (1976-77).

Publications: *Worlds of the Future: Exercises in the Sociological Imagination* (C.E. Merrill, 1972); *Sociology: Consciousness, Imagination, Practice* (McGraw-Hill), forthcoming; *Social Research: Strategy and Tactics,* Third Edition, (MacMillan, 1976); editor, *Sociological Practices* (semi-annual journal) (Human Sciences Press, 1977-78).

PICKARD, JEROME PERCIVAL

Senior Analyst
Appalachian Regional Commission
1666 Connecticut Avenue, N.W.
Washington, D.C. 20235, U.S.A.

Born: 1916, Chicago, Illinois, U.S.A.

Telephone: (202) 673-7849

Profession: Economic geographer, regional development

Field of specialization: Regional, urban and economic development; population and its future projections—regional and metropolitan; urbanization, settlement patterns and land use.

Education: A.A., Chemistry, University of Chicago, 1935; B.A., 1947, M.S., 1949, Geography, University of Wisconsin; Ph.D., Geography, Syracuse University, 1954; Fulbright Scholar, University of Oslo, 1950-51.

Professional employment: Appalachian Regional Commission (1970-). U.S. Department of Housing and Urban Development: Director, Program Analysis and Evaluation Staff DUS (1967-70). Urban Land Institute: Research Director (1960-67). Hammer and Company Associates: Research Director (1959-60). Washington Board of Trade: Research Director, Economic Development Committee (1954-59).

Professional activities: Development of population projections for Appalachian Region; projection methodologies for Appalachian land use and settlement patterns: conducted a course on regional development at George Washington University (1975); Ad Hoc Interagency Committee on Futures Research (1971); Federal Committee on Standard Metropolitan Statistical Areas (1976-); Research Advisory Committee, Task Force on Economic Growth and Opportunity, U.S. Chamber of Commerce (1965-67); Committee on Land Use Statistics, Resources for the Future (1962-65).

Publications: *Dimensions of Metropolitanism*, two volumes, Research Monographs, 14, 14A (Urban Land Institute, 1967-68); "U.S. Metropolitan Growth and Expansion 1970-2000, with Population Projections" in *Population, Distribution and Policy*, Vol. V, Commission Research Reports (The Commission on Population Growth and the American Future, 1973); "Subnational Population Distribution Trends, Their Projections and Implications" (U.S. House Subcommittee on Census and Population Hearings, January 1976); *Appalachia—A Reference Book* (Appalachian Regional Committee, December 1978, second edition).

PIOTET, FRANCOISE ODETTE

Agence nationale pour l'amelioration des conditions de travail (ANACT)
16-18 rue Barbes
Montrouge, France 92120

Born: 1943, Casablanca, Morocco

Telephone: 657-1300

Profession: Sociologist

Field of specialization: Professional relations in the public and nationalized sectors; organization of work.

Education: Doctorate in Sociology, University of Paris, Sorbonne, 1971; Law Graduate, Faculty of Law, Paris, 1968; Graduate, Institute of Political Studies, Paris, 1968.

Professional employment: ANACT: charge de mission (1977-); Conservatoire National des Arts et Metiers, Laboratoire de Sociologie du Travail: Teaching Assistant (1973-); Indian Ocean: Assistant (1969-72).

Professional activities: Instructor, Institute of Political Studies; current research on the new forms of work organization in France; thesis on change in a rural commune of southeast France (1971); "The Future of Work" (Commissariat General du Plan, 1975); contractual scenario on the future of professional relations (SESAME DATAR, 1976).

Publications: Co-author, *La Prospective du Travail [The Future of Work]* (La Documentation Francaise, 1976); "Negociation collectives et conditions de travail" ["Collective Bargaining and Work Conditions"] (*Liasons sociales*, June 1978); "L'attitude de femmes a l'egard du travail" ["Attitudes of Women Concerning Work"] (*Projet*, September 1977).

PLATT, JOHN

Department of Anthropology
University of California at Santa Barbara
Santa Barbara, California, 93106, U.S.A.

Born: 1918, Jacksonville, Florida, U.S.A.

Telephone: (805) 961-2017

Profession: Social philosopher

Field of specialization: Science and society; rates of social change.

Education: B.S., 1936, M.S., 1937, Physics, Northwestern University; Ph.D., Physics, University of Michigan 1941.

Professional employment: University of California at Santa Barbara: Lecturer (1977-). University of Michigan, Mental Health Research Institute: Research Scientist (1965-77). University of Chicago: Professor of Physics and Bio-Physics (1945-6E). Northwestern University: Instructor of Physics (1943-45). University of Minnesota: Research Fellow in Physics (1941-43).

Professional activities: Consultant, lecturer and author on the interaction between science and society; taught courses on "Global Problems and the Future;" conducted research in theoretical chemistry and the biophysics of perception.

Publications: *The Step to Man* (John Wiley and Sons, 1966); *Perception and Change* (University of Michigan Press, 1970); *The Excitement of Science* (Houghton Mifflin, 1962); editor, *New Views of the Nature of Man* (University of Chicago Press, 1965).

POHL, FREDERIK
386 West Front Street
Red Bank, New Jersey, 07701, U.S.A.

Born: 1919, New York, New York, U.S.A.

Telephone: unlisted

Profession: Writer

Field of specialization: Science fiction; normative forecasting.

Education: Self-educated.

Professional employment: Bantam Books: Science Fiction Editor (1973-78). Ace Books: Executive Editor (1971-72). Galaxy Magazine: Editor-in-Chief (1960-69).

Professional activities: President, Science Fiction Writers of America (1974-76); Member of Council, The Authors Guild (1976-); U.S. Chairman, First World Science Fiction Writers Conference (1976); various books in preparation.

Publications: Co-author, with C. M. Kornbluth, *The Space Merchants* (Ballantine Books, 1953); *The Best of Frederik Pohl* (Nelson Doubleday, 1975); *The Early Pohl* (Doubleday and Co., 1976); *Man Plus* (Random House, 1976); *Gateway* (St. Martin's Press, 1977); *The Way The Future Was* (Del Ray, 1978); *Jem* (St. Martin's Press, in press, 1979).

POLAK, FRED L.
Parkbud 26
Wassenaar, The Netherlands

Born: 1908, Amsterdam, The Netherlands

Telephone: 1751/78207

Profession: Social scientist

Field of specialization: Image of the future through history; future evolution of society.

Education: Ph.D., University of Amsterdam, 1947. Doctoral thesis on the evolution of science and society in the world of tomorrow.

Professional employment: Polak has held various positions in government and education, including serving as Managing Director of the Netherlands Central Planning Bureau, personal advisor to the Dutch Minister of Education, plenipotentiary of the Dutch government to promote full employment, and Professor of Sociology at the University of Rotterdam.

Professional activities: Currently active as a director of a Dutch Institute for the Exploration of the Future, and with the International Society for Technology Assessment. Has served as local coordinator for the World Future Society, and as President of Mankind 2000 International. Associated with the Center for Advanced Study in the Behavioral Sciences at Stanford University (1954-55). Lecturer, Syracuse University (Fall 1975-76). Continuously devoted to studying and writing on the future of man and society.

Publications: *Slow Motion Man* (Elsevier, 1977); *The Most Audacious Challenge: Is the New Astrophysical Sky in Harmony with God?* (Styhoff, 1979); *The New World of Automation* (3rd edition, 1979); *Die Toekomst Is Verleden Tijd [The Image of the Future]* (Dutch original translated into English and published in 1973 by Elsevier, Amsterdam); *Prognostics* (Elsevier, 1971); "Toward the Goal of Goals" in *Mankind 2000* (Mankind 2000 International, 1969).

POOL, ITHIEL DE SOLA   **Born:** 1917, New York, New York, U.S.A.
Professor of Political Science
Massachusetts Institute of Technology (E53-401)
Cambridge, Massachusetts 02139, U.S.A.   **Telephone:** (617) 253-3124

Profession: Professor of Political Science

Field of specialization: Communications.

Education: B.A., Political Science, 1938, M.A., 1939, Ph.D., 1952, University of Chicago.

Professional employment: Massachusetts Institute of Technology: Arthur and Ruth Sloan Professor of Political Science (1953-). Keio University, Tokyo: Visiting professor (1976). Churchill College, Cambridge University: Fellow (1977). Stanford University, Hoover Institute: Associate Director, RADIR project (1949-53). Hobart College: Assistant Professor (1942-48.).

Professional activities: Currently conducting research on the social impact of communications systems; Fellow, American Academy of Arts and Sciences; Member, American Political Science Association, Council on Foreign Relations, American Association for Public Opinion Research, American Sociological Association; Surgeon General's Scientific Advisory Committee on Television and Social Behavior (1970-71); Trustee, International Broadcast Institute; Woodrow Wilson Award for the best political science book of 1963.

Publications: Co-author, *American Business and Public Policy* (1963); co-author, *Candidates, Issues and Strategies;* co-author and editor, *Handbook on Communications;* co-author, *The People Look at Educational Television;* co-author and editor, *Talking Back;* co-author and editor, *The Social Impact of Television* (MIT Press, 1976).

POQUET, GUY RENE   **Born:** 1945, Morteau, France
Research Officer
Association Internationale Futuribles
55 rue de Varenne
75007 Paris, France   **Telephone:** (1) 222 63 10

Profession: Social scientist

Field of specialization: Value systems and social dynamics; environment and quality of life; resources management; futures methodology.

Education: Bachelor of Laws, 1968, Master of Laws, Economic and Political Science, 1970, University of Law, Paris.

Professional employment: International Association Futuribles: Research Officer (1975-). French Ministry of Industry and Research: Member of Cabinet (1972-75). French Ministry of Defense: News Editor and Press Attache (1971-72.) French Ministry of Industry and Research: News Editor (1970-71).

Professional activities: Research project in progress, "French Conserver Society: Scenarios" (completion for 1979); seminar on "Methodology of Future Studies" (1978); Editor of *Futur-Informations* Newsletter; contributor to various periodicals including *Futuribles, 2000,* and *International Social Science Journal;* work group leader for "The Future of Lifestyles" and "Dynamics of Human Needs"; Chief editor of *Developpement industriel et scientifique [Industrial and Scientific Development Journal]* (1970-71).

Publications: "The Limits of Global Modelling" (*International Social Science Journal* (UNESCO), (1978); *Economies of Raw Materials* (DEMP/Futuribles Report, 1977); *Le probleme alimentaire mondial [The World Food Problem]* (UNITAR/Futuribles Report, 1977); *L'environnement dans les modeles mondiaux [The Environment of World Models]* (2000, 1977); co-author, *Vivre en Europe: notes sur l'evolution des modes de vie en Europe de l'Ouest [To Live in Europe: Notes on Change in Life-Styles in Western Europe]* (Futuribles Report, 1977).

PRESSMAN, NORMAN E. P.

Born: 1939, Montreal, Quebec, Canada

Associate Professor
School of Regional and Urban Planning
University of Waterloo
Waterloo, Ontario, Canada N2L 3G1

Telephone: (519) 885-1211 ext. 2149

Profession: Planner; urban designer

Field of specialization: History of city development; new communities planning; urban design and redevelopment; urban growth strategies; international comparative development design and policy.

Education: B. Architecture, McGill University, 1962; M. Architecture, Urban Design, Cornell University, 1969; Cert. U.S.P., Urban/Social Planning, Manchester University, U.K., 1970.

Professional employment: University of Waterloo: Associate Professor, Urban and Regional Planning (1971-). Syracuse University: Assistant Professor, Planning (1969-71). Borough of North York, Toronto: Senior Planner (1966-67). Worked in France, England, Israel in architecture, urban design, urban/regional planning and policy development (1962-66).

Professional activities: Research project, Urban Innovation in Louvain-la-Neuve (a new community in Belgium), sponsored by CMHC, Ottawa; editor-in-chief, *Contact* (1973-); research on "Social Planning Prerequisites for New and Expanded Communities" (Ministry of State for Urban Affairs, Ottawa); teaches courses in history of urban planning, planning and development of new communities regional planning and international development (1972-).

Publications: Editor, "New Communities in Canada: Exploring Planned Environments" (*Contact*, August 1976); editor, "International Settlement Strategies: Social Perspectives on Planned Development" (*Contact*, December 1978); "Canadian New Town Policy" in *International Urban Growth Policies: New Town Contributions*, G. Golany, ed., (John Wiley, 1978); *Planning New Communities in Canada* (Ministry of State for Urban Affairs, Ottawa, August 1975); *Social Planning Prerequisites for New and Expanded Communities* (University of Waterloo, July 1975).

PRITCHARD, COLIN LEONARD

Born: 1943, Bradford, Yorkshire, United Kingdom

Director Society, Religion and Technology Project
Church of Scotland Home Board
121 George Street
Edinburgh, EH2 4YN Scotland

Telephone: (031) 225-5722

Profession: Chemical Engineer

Field of specialization: Storage and industrial use of energy from diffuse sources; technology assessment — the impact of technological innovations on society, human life, communities and religious thought.

Education: B.A., Natural Sciences, 1963, M.A., Chemical Engineering, 1967, University of Cambridge; Ph.D., Chemical Engineering, Indian Institute of Technology, Delhi, 1969.

Professional employment: University of Edinburgh: Lecturer in Chemical Engineering (1978-), Church of Scotland Home Board: Director, Society, Religion and Technology Project (1975-), Courtlands Ltd.: Plant Manager (1973-75); Section leader (1970-73); Chemical engineer (1975-76).

Professional activities: Executive Group, Center for Human Ecology, Edinburgh University (1978-); teaching open courses at Edinburgh University; Delphi Study project, "Scotland Towards a Just and Sustainable Society"; steering a cooperative, practical program on "Conservation Technology—Design for the Future."

Publications: "Science, Faith and the Vision of a New Society" (SPCK *Theology*, March 1977); *Engineering Implications of Novel Energy Concepts* (Institution of Electrical Engineers, London, 1979); editor and co-author, "Renewable Energy Sources in Highland Communities" (SRT Project, Jan. 1978); "The Concept of Employment in a Sustainable Industrial Society" in *Appropriate Technology for the UK* (University of Newcastle-on-Tyne, March 1976); *Half the Loaf—A Study of the World Food Crisis* (The St. Andrew Press, Edinburgh, 1975).

PROSKE, RUEDIGER K. A.
Norddeutscher Rundfunk
Projekt Studio
92 Rodenbekerstrasse
2 Hamburg 65, Federal Republic of Germany

Born: 1916, Berlin, Germany

Telephone: (040) 604 9798

Profession: Science journalist

Field of specialization: Future energy sources, weapons technology, studies on different forms of post-industrial societies, future prospects of bio-sciences.

Education: Political Science, Economics, University of Toronto, 1941-44; Private studies in mathematics, University of Saskatoon, 1944-46.

Professional employment: Nordwestdeutscher Rundfunk [Northwest German Radio]: Deputy Editor-in-Chief (1952-56). Norddeutsches Fernsehen [North German Television]: Editor-in-Chief (1957-63). Since then working as author, director, producer.

Professional activities: TV documentary series (60 programs) "Searching for the World of Tomorrow"; writing a book on "Evolution—Yesterday, Today Tomorrow"; have finished editing 15 volume book series, Current Science.

Publications: *Auf der Suche Nach der Welt von Morgen [Searching for the World of Tomorrow]* (Olde Hansen Verlag, 1968); *Am Ende Unserer Zukunft? [At the End of Our Future?]* (Olde Hansen Verlag, 1972); *Unsere Welt: Gestern, Heute, Morgen [Our World: Yesterday, Today, Tomorrow]* (Bertelsmann Verlag, 1968); *Station Mond [Moon Station]* (Franz Schneider Verlag, 1969); regular newspaper column in *Handelsblat* on the future aspects of current affairs (1969-71).

PURDY, JUDSON DOUGLAS
Associate Professor
Department of History and Comparative Education
Faculty of Education, University of Western Ontario
London, N6G 2H6, Ontario, Canada

Born: 1932, Saint John, New Brunswick, Canada

Telephone: (519) 679-3767

Profession: Historian; educator

Field of specialization: Educational futures; futures methodology; utopian futures.

Education: B.A., History, 1953, M.A., 1954, University of New Brunswick; Ph.D., History, University of Toronto, 1962.

Professional employment: University of Western Ontario: Associate Professor (1968-). Pickering College (Prep. School): History Master (1956-68).

Professional activities: Teaching courses in Canadian educational history with futures components; Editorial Board, *Bulletin of Canadian Futures Association*; offering a course entitled "Alternative Futures in Education" (beginning September 1976).

Publications: To date all publications have been strictly of the traditional historical type.

PYKE, DONALD L.
Coordinator of Academic Planning
University of Southern California
Los Angeles, California 90007, U.S.A.

Born: 1921, Lafayette, Indiana, U.S.A.

Telephone: (213) 746-7801

Profession: Systems analyst; planner

Field of specialization: Futures methodology; socio-technological forecasting.

Education: B.S., Public Service Engineering, 1946, M.S., Engineering Mechanics, 1953, Purdue University.

Professional employment: University of Southern California: Coordinator of Academic Planning (1970-). TRW Inc.: Manager, Technical Liaison and Forecasting (1969-70); Assistant to Vice-President, R and D (1963-69); Manager, Administration-Intellectronics Lab (1955-62). System Development Corporation: Technical Assistant to Senior Vice-President and other staff positions (1962-63). Dartmouth and Purdue Universities: Faculty and administrative positions (1948-55).

Professional activities: Co-founder and past President of the World Future Society's Los Angeles Chapter (1967-); advisor, Twenty-Year Forecast, Center for Futures Research, USC (1973-); environmental planning for USC neighborhood (1973-); Coordinator, USC Advisory Committee for Academic Planning (1970-); Committee on Technology Forecasting, National Research Council (1969); Social and Technology Forecasting Consultant to Southern California Edison (1973-75); organized and conducted TRW's Probes I and II (1965-71).

Publications: *Probe II* (TRW Publication, 14 volumes, December 1970); *The Public Research Library of the Future* (University of Southern California Internal Document, 1975); *Comprehensive Technological Forecasting* (USC Center for Futures Research, September 1973); "Mapping—A System Concept for Displaying Alternatives" (*Technological Forecasting and Social Change*, Vol. 2, 1971; also a chapter in *A Guide to Practical Future" (Harvard Business Review*, May-June 1969).

QUISTWATER, JACK RAIMOND
Director of Liberal and General Studies
Sheridan College of Applied Arts and Technology
Trafalgar Road
Oakville, Ontario L6H 2L1, Canada

Born: 1934, Antwerp, Belgium

Telephone: (416) 845-9430

Profession: Director, Liberal and General Studies

Field of specialization: Technology assessment, science-society interaction, individual responses to future change.

Education: B.A. (Honours), Chemistry, University of Vancouver, 1954; M.Sc., Physical Chemistry, University of British Columbia, 1958; Ph.D., Physical Chemistry, University of London, England, 1966.

Professional employment: Sheridan College: Director of Liberal and General Studies (1975-); Chairman, School of Applied and Liberal Studies (1971-75); Student Progress Advisor (1970-71); Teaching Master (1968). Arthur D. Little, Ltd., Edinburgh, Scotland: Senior Research Scientist (1966-68). Ministry of Technology, London: Senior Scientist Officer (1964-66).

Professional activities: Mainly interested in the development of scientific and technological awareness in students, as part of their general education component.

Publications: —

RAIFFA, HOWARD
Professor
John Fitzgerald Kennedy School of Government
Harvard University
Cambridge, Massachusetts 02138, U.S.A.

Born: 1924, New York, New York, U.S.A.

Telephone: (617) 495-4724

Profession: Decision analyst

Field of specialization: Decision analysis; policy analysis; operations research.

Education: Ph.D., Mathematics, University of Michigan, 1951.

Professional employment: Harvard University: Professor (1957-). International Institute for Applied Systems Analysis: Director (1972-75).

Professional activities: —

Publications: Co-author, *Games and Decision* (Wiley, 1957); *Decision Analysis* (Addison Wesley, 1968); co-author, *Decision Analysis with Multiple Objectives* (Wiley, 1976); co-author, *Applied Statistical Decision Theory* (MIT Press, 1961); co-author, *Introduction to Statistical Decision Theory* (McGraw Hill, 1964).

(From the first edition. Corrections not received by press time.)

RAKSASATAYA, AMARA

Professor
National Institute of Development Administration
Bangkok 24, Thailand

Born: 1933, Nan, Thailand

Telephone: 3777401

Profession: Public administrator

Field of specialization: Value systems; development administration; political development; social planning.

Education: B.A., Honors, Political Science, Chulalongkorn University, 1954; M.A., 1957, Ph.D., 1960, Government, Indiana University.

Professional employment: National Institute of Development Administration: Professor (1967-); Dean, School of Public Administration (1969-74); Director of Training (1968); Director of Research (1967). United Nations Asian and Pacific Development Administration Centre (UNAPDAC), Kuala Lumpur: Expert (1974-78).

Professional activities: Consultant, UNAPDAC (1978-79); research projects on rural development and civil service studies; teaching in the fields of policy development, rural development and personnel administration; policy development and analysis (1974-76).

Publications: *Policy Analysis and Development in Thailand* (in Thai, UNACDA Report to Government of Thailand, 1975); editor, *Rural Development Training in Thailand* (UNACDA, Kuala Lumpur, 1977); editor, *Rural Development: Training to Meet New Challenges* (5 volumes, UNAPDAC, Kuala Lumpur, 1978); *Utilization of Resources and Conservation of Environment* (in Thai, Krungthep Press, Bangkok, 1977); *Futures of Thailand: Toward Social Justice for the Masses* (in Thai, Army Education Department, Bangkok, 1976).

RENFRO, WILLIAM L.

Analyst
The Futures Research Group
Congressional Research Service
Library of Congress
Washington, D.C. 20540, U.S.A.

Born: 1945, West Palm Beach, Florida, U.S.A.

Telephone: (202) 426-6498

Profession: Analyst in futures research

Field of specialization: Futures research in the legislative environment.

Education: B.S., Physics, Rensselaer Polytechnic Institute, 1967; Graduate School of Physics, Yale University; J.D., School of Law, University of Connecticut, 1972; M.S., Nuclear Engineering, Rensselaer Graduate Center, 1972.

Professional employment: Library of Congress, Congressional Research Service: Analyst in Futures Research (1976-). The Futures Group: Senior Analyst (1973-76). Private practice of law (1972-73). Combustion Engineering: Staff Physicist (1968-69).

Professional activities: Congressional foresight (1977-78); impact forecasts (1977-); Futures Information Retrieval System (FIRST) (1976-); Energy Related Goals and Opportunities (1973); Future of Life Insurance Industry (1973); Prepaid Legal Services (1974); Court Caseloads and Work Loads (1975).

Publications: "The Future and Congressional Reform" (*American Bar Journal*, April 1978); "How Congress is Exploring the Future" (THE FUTURIST, April 1978); *Forecasting and Futures Research in Congress: Background and Prospects* (Congressional Research Service, September 1977); *Foresight: Congress Looks to the Future* (Congressional Research Service, February 1977); co-author, "Futures in the Political Process" in *Handbook for Futures Research*, J. Fowles, ed. (Greenwood Press, 1977).

RESCHER, NICHOLAS

University Professor of Philosophy
University of Pittsburgh
5818 Aylesboro Avenue
Pittsburgh, Pennsylvania 15217, U.S.A.

Born: 1928, Hagen, Germany

Telephone: (412) 521-6768

324

Profession: Philosopher

Field of specialization: Theory of knowledge; philosophy of science.

Education: B.S., Mathematics, Queens College, 1949; Ph.D., Philosophy, Princeton University, 1951.

Professional employment: University of Pittsburgh: Professor of Philosophy (1961-). Lehigh University: Associate Professor of Philosophy (1957-61). Rand Corporation: Research Mathematician (1954-56).

Professional activities: Currently teaching philosophy and philosophy of science; conducting research on scientific progress; Editor, *American Philosophical Quarterly*; Secretary-General, International Union of History and Philosophy of Science, an organ of UNESCO (1969-75).

Publications: *Cognitive Systemization* (Blackwells, Oxford, 1978); *Scientific Progress* (Blackwells, 1978); *Scientific Explanation* (Free Press, 1970); *Welfare* (The University of Pittsburgh Press, 1972); *Introduction to Value Theory* (Prentice Hall, 1969); editor, *Values and the Future* (Free Press, 1969).

RITTERBUSH, PHILIP C.
THOR, Inc.
Suite 402 2030 M Street, N.W.
Washington, D.C. 20036, U.S.A.

Born: 1936, Orange, New Jersey, U.S.A.

Telephone: (202) 466-3860

Profession: Educator

Field of specialization: Studying ways to develop regional resource and enviornmental information systems to convey development options to the general public and involve them in decision-making.

Education: B.A., Interdisciplinary Cultural Studies, Yale University, 1958; D. Phil., History and Philosophy of Science, University of Oxford, 1961.

Professional employment: *Social Innovation*: Editor and Director of the Archives (1971-). Smithsonian Institution: Staff Assistant to Secretary and Director of Academic Programs (1964-70). U.S. Senator Thomas J. McIntyre: Legislative Assistant (1962-63).

Professional activities: Communications consultant to the Science Museum of Virginia, the Electric Power Research Institute and the Neurosciences Research Program; design and sponsorship of institutional innovations in the popularization of knowledge and experiential education; research on theories of social change; editor, *Prometheus*, quarterly review of literature on institutional change (since 1971).

Publications: "Public Involvement," in *Strategies for Europe: A Review of Science and Technology Policies*, ed., M. Goldsmith, (Pergamon Press, 1978); editor, *Technology as Institutionally Related to Human Values* (Acropolis Books, 1974); *The Art of Organic Forms* (Smithsonian Institution, 1968); *Overtures to Biology* (Yale University Press, 1964).

ROBERTSON, JAMES HUGH
7 St. Ann's Villas
London W11 4RU, United Kingdom

Born: 1928, Huddersfield, England

Telephone: (01) 603 6572

Profession: Generalist

Field of specialization: Holistic approaches to social change and the transition to post-industrial society.

Education: First Class Honours, Greats (Literae Humaniores), Balliol College, Oxford, 1950.

Professional employment: Independent writer and speaker (1973-). Inter-Bank Research Organization: Director (1968-73). Scientific Control Systems Ltd.: Senior Consultant (1965-68). British Central Government: Administrative Civil Servant (1953-65).

Activities: Independent lecturing, speaking and seminars; writing on the future of industrialized societies; policy research and analysis, systems analysis, studies of government, business and financial organization and institutions (1953-73); co-founder, Turning Point network; council member, British Futures network; member, Scientific and Medical network.

Publications: *The Sane Alternative* (self-published, 1978); *Power, Money and Sex* (Marion Boyars, London, 1976); *Profit or People?* (Calder and Boyars, London, 1974); co-author, *The Future of London as an International Financial Centre* (HMSO for the Cabinet Office, London, 1973); *Reform of the British Central Government* (Charles Knight/Chalto and Windus, London, 1971).

ROEMER, KENNETH MORRISON

Born: 1945, East Rockaway, New York, U.S.A.

Associate Professor
Department of English
University of Texas at Arlington
Arlington, Texas 76019, U.S.A.

Telephone: (817) 273-2692

Profession: Editor; English professor

Field of specialization: American utopian literature.

Education: B.A., English, Harvard College, 1967; M.A., American Civilization, 1968, Ph.D., 1971, University of Pennsylvania.

Professional employment: University of Texas at Arlington: Associate Professor of English (1974-); Assistant Dean, Graduate School (1975-77); Assistant Professor (1971-74). University of Pennsylvania: Teaching Assistant (1969-70).

Professional activities: Designed special course "Build Your Own Utopia"; editor, "News Center" for Fall and Spring issues of *Alternative Futures* (1978); book review editor, *American Literary Realism* (1978-).

Publications: *The Obsolete Necessity: America in Utopian Writings* (Kent State University Press, 1976); editor, *The Human Drift*, by K.C. Gillete (1976); *America as Utopia: Collected Essays* (Burt Franklin, 1979).

ROGGE, PETER G.

Born: 1931, Bremerhaven, Germany

PROGNOS AG, European Center for Applied Economic Research
Viaduktstrasse 65/Steinengraben 42
Basel CH-4011, Switzerland

Telephone: (061) 22 40 70

Profession: Economist

Field of specialization: Economic forecasting; strategical planning for government and business; business cycle analyses and forecasting.

Education: Doctor of Political Affairs (Economics and Business), Universities of California, Gottingen, Freiburg i. Br., Basel, 1957.

Professional employment: Swiss Bank Corporation Consultants Group: Chairman (1977-). PROGNOS AG: Vice Chairman (1977-); Managing Director (1962-77); Project Manager (1960-62). LIST Society: Senior Economist (1957-59).

Professional activities: Member of Board of Directors of several major consulting organizations in Switzerland and Germany in the fields of economic forecasting, management consulting, industrial and technological planning; permanent activity as lecturer on economic policy as well as economic growth and business cycle problems at numerous institutions in various countries; direct consulting work for large industrial and servicing organizations in the fields of medium and long term planning; member of the board, The Swiss Society for Future Studies and The Society for Future Studies of the Federal Republic of Germany.

Publications: *Tendenzwende-Wirtschaft nach Wachstrum und Wunder [Trend Changes: Commerce after Growth and Boom]* (Verlag Bonn Aktuell, Stuttgart, 1975); *Wirtschaftlichkeit an den Grenzen des Wachstums [Economy at the Limits of Growth]* (RKW Landesgruppe Baden-Wurttemberg, 1972); *Der Weg in die Zukunft: Zukunftsorientierte Unternehmensfuhrung [The Road to the Future: Future-oriented Management]* (Rudolf Poensgen Foundation, Dusseldorf, 1970); *Unternehmerisches Planen—Die Suche nach dem Trend [Business Planning: Searching for the Trend]* (Verlag Ex Libris, Zurich); *Langfristige Entwidklungsperspektiven der Bundesrepublik [Long-range Development Perspectives for the Federal Republic of Germany]* (Gesellschaft fur Konsum-, Markt- und Absatz-forschung, 1970).

ROSE, CHARLIE

Born: 1939, Fayetteville, North Carolina, U.S.A.

Member of Congress
U.S. House of Representatives
218 Cannon House Office Building
Washington, D.C. 20515, U.S.A.

Telephone: (202) 225-2731

Profession: Lawyer; Member of U.S. House of Representatives

Field of specialization: The political process (application of new technology into the Congress with a goal of improving communication within the institution and with the public).

Education: A.B., Davidson College, 1961; L.L.B., University of North Carolina, 1964.

Professional employment: United States House of Representatives: Member (1973-). Private legal practice, Fayetteville, North Carolina (1970-72) (1964-67); Twelfth Judicial Circuit, State of North Carolina: Chief District Court prosecutor (1967-70).

Professional activities: Chairman, Policy Group of Information and Computers, Committee on House Administration; chairman, Subcommittee on Evaluation, Permanent Select Committee on Intelligence; chairman, Subcommittee on Dairy and Poultry, Committee on Agriculture; member, Democratic Steering and Policy Committee; chairman, Telecommunications Advisory Committee to the Governor of North Carolina; first member of Congress to acquire a computer terminal, establish a mobile District office, and communicate with constituents via satellite; founder and board member of three ad hoc policy groups within the House, the Congressional Clearinghouse on the Future, the Congressional Clearinghouse on Women's Rights and the Congressional Rural Caucus.

Publications: —

ROSEN, STEPHEN
Future Facts
150 West End Avenue
New York, New York 10023, U.S.A.

Born: 1934, New York, New York, U.S.A.

Telephone: (212) 580-0717

Profession: Physicist; consultant; author

Field of specialization: Market planning; communications; high-technology; products and services.

Education: B.S., Physics and Mathematics, Queens College, City University of New York, 1955; M.A., Physics, Bryn Mawr College, 1958; Ph.D., Physics, Adelphi University, 1966.

Professional employment: Marketing and Planning Group, Inc.: Vice President (1970-). Hudson Institute: Senior Professional Staff (1969-1970). State University of New York: Professor (1962-67). Institut D'Astrophysique: Research Scientist (1968).

Professional activities: Public lectures (Program Corporation of America, Hartsdale, N.Y.); television production of science documentaries; management consulting activities for AT&T, IBM, GT&E, Xerox Corp. and other Fortune 100 companies; member, New York Academy of Sciences and The Institute of Management Sciences.

Publications: *Weathering: How Our Atmosphere Conditions Your Body, Your Mind, Your Moods, —and Your Health* (Evans and Co., forthcoming); *Future Facts: The Way Things are Going to Work in the Future in Technology, Medicine, Science and Life* (Simon & Schuster, 1976); also articles and essays in *The Wall Street Journal, The New York Times,* Field newspaper syndicate and other magazines.

ROSENFELD, ALBERT
25 Davenport Avenue
New Rochelle, New York 10805, U.S.A.

Born: 1920, Philadelphia, Pennsylvania, U.S.A.

Telephone: (914) 235-2033

Profession: Writer-editor; biophilosopher

Field of specialization: Biomedical research and its impact on society; science and human values; public understanding of science.

Education: B.A., History and Social Science, 1950, D. Lett., Hon., 1970, New Mexico State University.

Professional employment: *Geo Magazine:* Consulting Editor (1978-). *Saturday Review:* Science Editor (1972-). The National Foundation—March of Dimes: Consultant on Future Programs (1973-). The University of Texas, Medical Branch; Visiting Professor and Adjunct Assistant Professor (1972-). Drexel University: Adjunct Professor of Biophilosophy (1971-74). *Family Health Magazine:* Managing Editor (1970-71). *Life Magazine:* Science Editor (1957-69).

Professional activities: Board of Trustees, Totts Gap Institute for Human Ecology; Professional Advisory

Board, The Foundation of Thanatology; Scientific Advisory Board, The Center for Preventive Psychiatry (1970-); Bioethics Advisor, *Modern Medicine* (1975-77); Executive Board, Council for the Advancement of Science Writing (1968-); Board of Advisors, National Center for Bioethics, Drew University (1974-); President, Council for the Advancement of Science Writing (1968-72); Senior Research Associate in Contemporary Ethics, Manhattanville College (1973-74); Consulting Editor, *Physicians World* (1972-74); has won a half dozen writing awards, including the Lasker Award with a special citation for "Leadership in Medical Journalism"; member, World Future Society and numerous other associations.

Publications: Co-author and editor, *Mind and Supermind: A Saturday Review Report* (Holt, Rinehart & Winston, 1977); co-author and editor, "God and Science: New Allies in the Search for Values"—special section (*Saturday Review*, December 10, 1978); *Prolongevity* (Alfred A. Knopf, 1976); *The Second Genesis: The Coming Control of Life* (Prentice-Hall, 1969); *The Quintessence of Irving Langmuir* (Pergamon Press, 1966); "The Control of Life"—a four-part series of articles (*Life Magazine*, 1965); "Mind and Supermind," "Inside the Brain," "The Psychotherapy Jungle,"—a series of three special sections (*Saturday Review*, 1975-76).

ROTHGAENGER, KLAUS

Boessnerstrasse 3
D-8400 Regensburg, Federal Republic of Germany

Born: 1936, Hamburg, Germany

Telephone: (0941) 21824

Profession: Architect; designer-grad.

Field of specialization: (Non-professional) Architecture assessment; balance of energy (consumption + dissipation equals demand) in architecture; communication problems in working process; natural protection and ecological problems in urbanism district; activities for "green" politics at Bavaria (1978); since 1976 owner of a little farm near Regensburg.

Education: Architecture and Design, Werkkunstschule Krefeld, Germany (1963-).

Professional employment: Architect at offices of free architects in Hamburg and Regensburg, Germany (1963-).

Professional activities: Architectural planning and construction (1963-). Gesselschaft fur Zukunftsfragen (GZ) Germany (1972-); World Future Studies Federation, Paris (1973-); Ornithologische Arbeitsgemeinschaft Ostbayern, Germany [Ornithological Studies Taskforce of Eastern Bavaria] (1974); Bund Naturschutz—Bayern—Germany [Bavarian Environmental Protection League], Germany (1976); Gessellschaft fur Sonnenenergie [Association for Solar Energy], Germany (1976).

Publications: "Institutes for Social Research Must Prepare Assistance for Behavior Suitable to All Events" (Proceedings of III World Future Studies Conference, 1972); "Brauchen wir die Energie, die wir verbrauchen?" [Do We Need the Energy that We Use?"] in "Zukunft Energie" (Gesselschaft fur Zukunftsfragen, 1975), and others.

ROY, ROBIN

Lecturer
Faculty of Technology
The Open University
Walton Hall
Milton Keynes, MK7 6AA, United Kingdom

Born: 1946, London, United Kingdom

Telephone: 0908 74066

Profession: Lecturer in Technology and Design

Field of specialization: Social implications of technology; design research and methods; food resources for the United Kingdom; alternative technology.

Education: B.Sc., Mechanical Engineering, 1967, M.Sc., Design Technology, 1968, Ph.D., Design Technology, 1970, Manchester University.

Professional employment: The Open University: Lecturer, Faculty of Technology (1971-). State University of New York at Buffalo: Visiting Lecturer, "Bases for Futures" course (1970).

Professional activities: Member, Open University Alternative Technology Group (1976-); course team chairman, "Control of Technology" course (1975-78); course team author, "Man-Made Futures" course (1972-75); consultant, Food Policy Unit, Earth Resources Research Ltd. (1975-); Membership Secretary,

Design Research Society (1973-77); course team author, "Man-Made World" Foundation course (1971-73); author of several articles on a method of technology assessment using simulated transport and information systems.

Publications: Editor, *The Politics of Technology* (Longmans/Open University Press, 1977); co-author, *Government and Technology*, T361 Units 3-4 (Open University Press, 1978); co-author, *Arms Control* T361 Unit 13 (Open University Press, 1978); co-editor, *Man-Made Futures: Readings in Society, Technology and Design* (Hutchinson/Open University Press, 1974); co-editor, *The Future of Food* (Open University Press, 1975).

RUGGLES, RUDY L., JR.
President
Hudson Institute, Inc.
Quaker Ridge Road
Croton-on-Hudson, New York 10520, U.S.A.

Born: 1938, Evanston, Illinois, U.S.A.

Telephone: (914) 762-0700

Profession: Policy analyst

Field of specialization: —

Education: B.S., Physics, Harvard College, 1960; M.B.A., Harvard Business School, 1966.

Professional employment: Hudson Institute, Inc.: President (1975-); Executive Vice President (1974-75); Vice President, Res. Management (1974); Senior Member, Prof. Staff (1971-74). Hudson Research Services, Inc.: President (1975-). IBM Corporate Headquarters: Exploratory Planning Consultant (1966-71). IBM Systems and Comp. Dev. Labs.: Senior Associate Physicist (1960-64).

Professional activities: American Physical Society; Scientific Research Society of America (RESA); Ends of the Earth; International Institute for Strategic Studies; North American Society for Corporate Planning, Director of the New York Chapter; Director of Affiliate Artists, Inc.; American Association for the Advancement of Science; also holds two patents as a result of work involving x-ray and infrared studies of silicon and integrated device design and development.

Publications: "Six Business Lessons from the Pentagon" (*Harvard Business Review*, also included in *Business Strategy*, H. Igor Ansoff, ed., Penguin Press, 1969); "Developing Systems for Strategic Planning" (*Long Range Planning Journal*, June 1971), numerous other articles in journals such as *IEEE Electron Device Journal*.

RUZIC, NEIL PIERCE
President
Island for Science, Inc.
P.O. 527
Beverly Shores, Indiana 46301, U.S.A.

Born: 1930, Chicago, Illinois, U.S.A.

Telephone: (219) 874-5139

Profession: Scientist; executive.

Field of specialization: Space-technology; technology utilization consultant to NASA; mariculture, wind energy augmentation, solar desalination, rare animal breeding, marine pharmaceuticals, and insect biocontrol for Island for Science, Inc. (Bahamas).

Education: B.S., Journalism, Science, and Psychology (three degrees), Northwestern University, 1950.

Professional employment: Island for Science, Inc.: President (1978-). Neil Ruzic and Co.: President (1972-78). Industrial Research, Inc.: President (1958-72). IIT Research Institute: Director of Publications (1952-58).

Professional activities: Developed systems for interdisciplinary research and production on Little Stirrup Cay, Bahamas, including seaweed shrimp open-ocean mariculture, delta wing augmented windmill systems, solar desalination using hybrid solar humidifier and vacuum, raising rare zoo animals, insect bio-control using pheromones, and mass screening of sea organisms for marine pharmaceuticals; National Aeronautics and Space Administration, technology transfer consultant (1972-78); founder and publisher of *Industrial Research, Oceanology International, Electro-Technology* and other magazines; holds first U.S. patent for a device to be used exclusively on the moon, a lunar cryostat.

Publications: *Where the Winds Sleep* (Doubleday, 1970); *The Case for Going to the Moon* (Putman, 1965); *Spinoff 1976* (NASA, 1976); *A Blueprint for an Island for Science* (Neil Ruzic and Co., 1977); *There's Adventure in Meteorology, There's Adventure in Civil Engineering* (Popular Mechanics Press, 1959).

RYAN, ROBERT DALE

Chairman
Department of Technology
St. Cloud State University
St. Cloud, Minnesota 56301, U.S.A.

Born: 1931, Newman Grove, Nebraska, U.S.A.

Telephone: (612) 255-2107

Profession: Mathematician; administrator

Field of specialization: Technology assessment; futures methodology; approriate technology; general futures education.

Education: B.A., Physical Science, Wayne State College, 1955; M.S., Industrial Education, 1957, Ed. D., Industrial Education and Psychology, 1964, University of North Colorado.

Professional employment: St. Cloud State University: Chairman, Department of Technology (1962-). Community College, Alpena, Michigan: Dean of Students, Coordinator of Technical Technology (1959-62). University of Minnesota: Professor of Mathematics and Engineering Graphics (1957-59). High School, Scottsbluff, Nebraska: Instructor, Mathematics (1955-57).

Professional activities: Vice-President, Minnesota Futures Society, Central Region (1976); President, North Central Region, National Association of Industrial Technology (1976); currently working on academic program development at St. Cloud University (1976-); St. Cloud Area Energy Commission, (1977-); had lectured extensively on technology and the future, leisure, changing labor force and population.

Publications: "Toward a Future Studies Program" (*Man, Society and Technology*, 1978); co-author, "Future Alternatives for Industrial Arts" (ACIATE, 1976); co-author, *Advancing Technology: Its Impact on Society* (William C. Brown Co., 1971); "Drafting Aid Transparencies," (Instruct-A-Kits, St. Cloud, Minnesota, 1966); "Educated Leisure" (*Industrial Arts Journal*, 1966); "Technology and Religion" (*Minnesota Pastors Newsletter*, 1972).

SABATO, JORGE ALBERTO

Member, Board of Directors
Fundacion Bariloche
Newbery 2875
Buenos Aires, Argentina

Born: 1924, Argentina

Telephone: 771-4524

Profession: Metallurgist

Field of specialization: Technology policy and technology assessment.

Education: Professor, Physics, Instituto del Profesorado, 1947.

Professional employment: Fundacion Bariloche: Member, Board of Directors (1966-). Universite de Montreal: Visiting Professor (1977-79). Atomic Energy Commission of Argentina: Chief, Technology (1960-70).

Professional activities: Currently writing a book on nuclear energy and underdevelopment; consultant to U.N., Andean Pact, and the InterAmerican Bank.

Publications: *Transferencia de Technologia [Transference of Technology]* (Centro Estudios del Tercer Mundo, Mexico, 1978); *Energia Nuclear y Desarrollo Industrial[Nuclear Energy and Industrial Development]* (Organizacion de Estados Americanos, Washington, 1978); "El pensamiento latinoamericano en la problematica ciencia y technologia-desarrollo-dependencia" ["Latin American Thought Concerning the Problems of Science, Technology, Development and Dependency"] (*Paidos*, Buenos Aires, 1975); "The Use of Science to Manufacture Technology" (*Impact*, Paris, 1974); has published more than 50 papers in different international journals.

SAHAL, DEVENDRA
Senior Research Fellow
International Institute of Management
Griegstrasse 5-7
West Berlin 33, Federal Republic of Germany

Born: 1949, Jaipur, Raj, India

Telephone: (030) 826-3071

Profession: Professor

Field of specialization: National science and technology policy; R and D management; developmental studies; general systems theory.

Education: B.S., Mechanical Engineering, Banaras Hindu University, 1970; M. Phil., Nuclear Physics, 1973, Licentiate of Technology, 1973, Doctor of Technology, Industrial Engineering, 1974, Helsinki University.

Professional employment: International Institute of Management, Berlin: Senior Research Fellow (1977-). Portland State University, Systems Science Phd Program: Assistant Professor and Research Associate (1974-77). Yleistekniikka, Valmet Nokia and Tampella Corporations, Technical Research Center of Finland: Engineer and Research Scientist (1970-74).

Professional activities: Currently working on three studies, "Stochastic Models of Evolutionary Processes in the Design of Engineering Systems," "Generalized Theory of System Similitude," and "Elements of a Stochastic Systems Theory"; conducts graduate courses on "Cybernetics" and "General Systems" at Portland State University.

Publications: "A Theory of Measurement of Technology" (*International Journal of Systems Science,* 1977); "Toward a Theory of Systems" (*General Systems Yearbook,* 1977); "Principles of Regulation and Control" (*Kybernetes,* 1978); "Cross-Impact Analysis and Prediction of Technological Development" (*IEEE Transactions on Engineering Management,* 1975); "Elements of an Emerging Theory of Complexity" (*Cybernetica,* 1976).

SAINT-GEOURS, JEAN
President
SEMA (Metra International)
16, rue Barbes
Montrouge, France

Born: 1925, Bordeaux, France

Telephone: 657 13 00

Profession: Economist

Field of specialization: Social accounts; monetary and fiscal policy.

Education: Diplome, Etudes Superieures Droit et Economie, Paris; Diplome, Institut d'Etudes Politiques, Paris. Ecole Nationale Administration.

Professional employment: SEMA (Metra International): Chairman and President (1976-). Credit Lyonnais: Executive General Manager (1968-75). Forecast and Planning Department, Ministry of Finance: Head (1965-68).

Professional activities: Chairman and President of SEMA (data processing, management development of human resources, marketing, economic studies, planning and development); Professor of Economic Policy, Institut d'Etudes Politiques, Paris; Vice-President, Association Internationale Futuribles; member of The Club of Rome.

Publications: *Pour une economie du vouloir [For an Economy of Willpower]* (Calmann-Levy, 1976); *La politique economique [Economic Policy]* (Sirey, 1969-73); *Vive la societe de consomation [Long live the Consumer Society]* (Hachette, 1971); co-author, *Pour nationaliser l'etat [To Nationalize the State]* (Le Seuil, 1969); "Les lancianantes theses de M. Rueff [Mr. Rueff's Painful Arguments] (*Analyse et Prevision,* 1969).

SAINT-PAUL, RAYMOND HENRI
Professor
Conservatoire National des Arts et Metiers
292 Rue Saint-Martin
75003 Paris, France

Born: 1927, Toulouse, France

Telephone: 27124-14 poste 522

Profession: Economist

Field of specialization: R and D management; technological forecasting; technology assessment; futures methodology.

Education: Doctorat es-sciences economiques, 1957; Doctorat en droit, Law, 1953; Public Policy, Institut etudes politiques, 1951.

Professional employment: Conservatoire National des Arts et Metiers: Professor (1971-); Associate Professor (1967). Commissariat General au Plan: Economist (1955).

Professional activities: Teaching in various universities; directing research in R and D management; consultant to private firms, public institutions and international organizations.

Publications: Co-author, *Innovation et evaluation technologique [Technological Innovation and Evaluation]* (Entreprises Modernes d'Editions, Paris, 1975).

SALK, JONAS

Founding Director
The Salk Institute
Post Office Box 1809
San Diego, California 92112, U.S.A.

Born: 1914, New York, New York, U.S.A.

Telephone: -

Profession: Physician; scientist; educator.

Field of specialization: Alternative human values for improving the quality of life for the individual and for the species.

Education: B.S., College of the City of New York, 1934; M.D., New York University College of Medicine, 1939.

Professional employment: The Salk Institute: Fellow and Director (1963-); University of California, San Diego: Adjunct Professor of Health Sciences (1970-); Director of Virus Research Laboratory, School of Medicine (1947-63). University of Michigan, Department of Epidemiology, School of Public Health: Fellow, Research Associate, Assistant Professor of Epidemiology (1942-47).

Professional activities: Currently engaged in writing about the prospects and alternatives for the future of man. Founding Director of the Salk Institute, which brings together scientists and scholars from different fields of biological research who share a concern for the implications of their work for man and society. Personally involved in research programs aimed at understanding and manipulating the immune system, as this may have a bearing on the control of autoimmune and neoplastic diseases, such as multiple sclerosis and cancer. While at the University of Pittsburgh conducted studies on poliomyelitis which pointed the way toward the development of a vaccine for paralytic polio. Member, Expert Advisory Panel on Virus Diseases, World Health Organization (1951-).

Publications: *Man Unfolding* (Harper and Row, 1972); *The Survival of the Wisest* (Harper and Row, 1973).

SALOMON, JEAN-JACQUES

Head
Science Policy Division
Organization for Economic Cooperation and Development
2, rue Andre Pascal
Paris 16e, France

Born: 1929, Metz, France

Telephone: 524 9340

Profession: Philosopher and historian of science

Field of specialization: Science and technological policy.

Education: Licence es-Lettres, Philosophy, Faculte des Lettres, Sorbonne, 1953; Doctorat es-Lettres et Sciences Humaines, 1970, Certificat d'Etudes Superieures d'Ethnologie, 1954, Sorbonne.

Professional employment: Organization for Economic Cooperation and Development: Head, Science Policy Division. Conservatoire National des Arts et Metiers: Professor of Technology and Society.

Professional activities: Currently working on science and technology in relation to economic growth; problems of technological innovation in the framework of the current social and economic changes.

Publications: *Science and Politics* (Macmillan Press, England and MIT Press, 1970): *International Scientific Organizations* (OECD, 1966); editor, *Problems of Science Policy* (OECD, 1968); director, *The Research System* (Vol. I, 1972, Vol. II, 1973; Vol. III and General conclusions, 1974, OECD).

SCARDIGLI, VICTOR

Centre de Recherche sur le Bien-Etre (CEREBE)
140 Rue du Chevaleret
Paris 75013, France

Born: 1938, Skikda, Algeria

Telephone: (1) 584 14 20

Profession: Sociologist

Field of specialization: Ways of life and social change; inequalities and social policies.

Education: B.A., Psychology, 1959, B.S., Biology, 1960, Ph.D., Sociology, 1974, Sorbonne.

Professional employment: Centre de Recherche sur le Bien-Etre: Maitre de Recherche (1978-). Centre de Recherches sur la Consommation: Director, Division Analyse Sociale et Prospective (1967-78). Societe d'Economie et de Mathematique Appliquees: Researcher (1964-67). Cie des Machines Bull.: Researcher (1961-62).

Professional activities: Comparisons of ways of life (behaviors and attitudes) in Europe; consumption patterns and their evolution in the Third World.

Publications: *Ways of Life and Social Change in Western Europe* (Commission of the European Communities, 1976); *Ascension Sociale et Pauvrete [Social Mobility and Poverty]* (Centre National de la Recherche Scientifique, 1978); "Comment vous vivrez dans diz ans" ["How You Will Live in Ten Years"] (*L'Expansion*, October 1975).

SCHAFF, ADAM

President
Board of Directors
European Coordination Centre for Research
   and Documentation in Social Sciences
Grunangergasse 2
Vienna 1010, Austria

Born: 1913, Lwow, USSR

Telephone: 52 43 33

Profession: Philosopher

Field of specialization: Social philosophy and philosophy of language.

Education: M.A., Juridical Sciences, University of Lwow, 1931; Dr. Philosophical Sciences, Institute of Philosophy, Academy of Sciences of the USSR.

Professional employment: European Coordination Centre for Research and Documentation in Social Sciences: President, Board of Directors. Polish Academy of Sciences: Member (1951-). University of Vienna: Professor of Philosophy (1974).

Professional activities: Research on problems of alienation.

Publications: *Structuralism and Marxism* (Pergamon Press, 1978); *Alienation as a Social Phenomenon* (Pergamon Press, in print); *The Marxist Theory of Truth* (Warsaw, 1956); *Introduction to Semantics* (Pergamon Press, 1963); *Marxism and the Human Individual* (McGraw Hill, 1973); *History and Truth* (Pergamon Press, 1976).

SCHALLER, LYLE EDWIN

Parish Consultant
Yokefellow Institute
530 N. Brainard Street
Naperville, Illinois 60540, U.S.A.

Born: 1923, Lime Ridge, Wisconsin, U.S.A.

Telephone (312) 355-0817

Profession: Clergyman

Field of specialization: Social indicators; urban planning; religion and life; institutional change.

Education: B.S., 1948, M.S., 1949, History, M.S., Political Science, 1952, M.S., Regional and City Planning, 1956, University of Wisconsin; B.D., Theology, Garrett Theological Seminary, 1957.

Professional employment: Yokefellow Institute: Parish Consultant (1971-). Evangelical Theological Seminary: Professor (1968-71). Regional Church Planning Office: Church Planner (1960-68). Methodist Church: Pastor (1955-58). City of Madison, Wisconsin: City Planner (1951-54).

Professional activities: Parish consultant, lecturer, author (1971-78); recipient of the Louis Brownlow Award from the American Society for Public Administration (1965); H. Paul Douglass lecturer for the Religious Association (1974); editor, Creative Leadership Series, Abingdon (1978-80).

Publications: *Community Organization* (Abingdon, 1966); *The Impact of the Future* (Abingdon, 1969); *The Change Agent* (Abingdon, 1972); *The Decision-Makers* (Abingdon, 1974); *Understanding Tomorrow* (Abingdon, 1976).

SCHMACKE, ERNST STEPHAN
Born: 1924, Hamburg, Germany

Director
DEMAG AG
Wolfgang-Reuter-Platz
D-4100 Duisburg 1, Federal Republic of Germany **Telephone:** 203/605-1

Profession: Journalist

Field of specialization: —

Education: Dr. Phil., Hamburg University, 1950.

Professional employment: DEMAG AG: Director (1966-).

Professional activities: Publications (1966-76); Founding member of the German Society for Future Problems *[*Gesellschaft fur Zukunftsfragen*]* (1967-).

Publications: Editor, *Zukunft im Zeitraffer [The Future in Time Accelerator]* (Droste, 1967); editor, *1980 ist morgen [1980 Is Tomorrow]* (Droste, 1969); *Fahrplan in die Zukunft [Travel Plan into the Future]* (Droste, 1970); *German Provinces on the Way to the Year 2000*, book series (Droste, 1969-74).

SCHULZE, LOTHAR GUNTHER
Born: 1921, Adorf Sachsen, Germany

Secretary
Kommunikationszentrum fur Zukunfts—und Friedensforschung in Hannover GmbH
[Communications Center for Future and Peace Research in Hannover, Inc.]
Glockseestrasse 33 i. Hs. Gaswerk
3000 Hannover 1, Federal Republic of Germany **Telephone:** (0511) 32 44 88

Profession: Physicist

Field of specialization: General problems of futurology and peace research.

Education: Diploma, Physics, 1950, Doctor, Horticulture, 1954, Technische Universitat, Hannover.

Professional employment: Communications Center for Future and Peace Research in Hannover, Inc.: Secretary (1976-). Association for the Advancement of Futures and Peace Research; Promoter and President (1964-). Institute of Radiation Biology, Hannover: Scientist (1958-64). Fa. Harting, Espelkamp: Development Engineer (1957-58). Institute for Technology in Horticulture, Hannover: Scientist (1951-57).

Professional activities: Vice-President of the Association for Future Studies, Berlin (1976); working on problems of futurology and public perception (1968-).

Publications: "Zwolf Thesen zur Zukunfts—und Friedensforschung" ["Twelve Theses Concerning Future and Peace Research"] (*Zukunfts—und Friedensforschung—Information*, 1968); "Zukunftssicherung als Vermittlungsproblem" ["Future Security as a Problem of Mediation"] (Zukunfts—und Friedensforschung—Information, 1977); *Die Zukunft geht uns alle an [The Futures Concerns Us All]* (published by the author, 1976).

SCHUMACHER, DIETER
Chamber of Commerce and Industry
Hans Boecklerstrasse 4
Heidelberg
D6900 West Germany

Born: 1936, Krefeld, Germany

Telephone: (6221) 25753

Profession: Innovation consultant

Field of specialization: Innovation research, technology transfer, small industry, developing countries, science policy design.

Education: Ph.D., Physics, University of Stuttgart, 1965.

Professional employment: IHK Rhein Neckar [Chamber of Commerce and Industry]: Director, Innovation service (1976-). Systemplan, Heidelberg: Director (1972-76). Bundeskanzlerant, Bonn: Consultant (1970-72). Dornier System, Friedrichhafen: Assistant General Manager (1968-70). Centre d'Etudes Nucleaires, Grenoble: Coll. Etr. (1966-68). Max Planck Institut fur Metallforschung, Stuttgart: Research Assistant (1962-66).

Professional activities: Research on technology transfer in urban problems (1976), technological change and international relations (1976), public administration of science and technology (1976), the future of physics, European science and technology policy (1974-75), and domestic technology transfer (1973-75).

Publications: *Perspektiven einer Internationalen Forschungs und Technologiepolitik [Prospects for an International Research and Technology Policy]* (Verlag Schwartz, Gottingen, 1975); editor, *Technology Assessment and Quality of Life* (Elsevier, Amsterdam, 1973).

SCHWARTZ, BERTRAND
Universite Paris IX Dauphine
Place Marechal de Lattre de Tassigny
F-75116 Paris, Cedex, France

Born: 1919, Paris, France

Telephone: 553 50 20

Profession: Professor of Education Sciences

Field of specialization: Future of education; relations between the different levels of education; innovation.

Education: Engineering degree, Ecole Polytechnique, Paris; Doctorat d'Etat, University of Paris.

Professional employment: University Presidents' Conference: Consultant on Continuing education (present). Council of Europe: Director of the project, "Continuing Education" (1972-77). Ministry of Education: Consultant on continuing education (1968-75). National Institute for the training of Adults: Director (1963-69). University Center for Economic and Social Cooperation: Director (1960-71).

Professional activities: Consultant on Continuing Education, University Presidents Conference; current research, "A Study of Educational Policies for Adult Education in the Universities."

Publications: Numerous articles on the future of education; *A New School* (Flammarion, 1977); *L'Education Demain [Education Tomorrow]* (Aubier Montaigne, Paris, 1972); *Retour a l'Ecole [Return to School]* (Organization for Economic Cooperation and Development, Washington, 1973).

SCHWARTZ, PETER
Senior Policy Analyst
SRI International
Center for the Study of Social Policy
333 Ravenswood Avenue
Menlo Park, California 94025, U.S.A.

Born: 1946, Germany

Telephone: (415) 326-6200 ext. 3986

Profession: Policy analyst

Field of specialization: Futures methodology; scenarios; appropriate technology; value change; science policy.

Education: B.S., Aeronautical Engineering, Rensselaer Polytechnic Institute, 1968.

Professional employment: SRI International: Senior Policy Analyst (1973-). Pacific House: Research Analyst (1972-73). University of California, Davis: Assistant Dean of Students (1969-72).

Professional activities: Research on long term directions of societal change and the implications for current decision making (for various clients on several projects); co-leader, "Alternative Futures for Environmental Policy Planning: 1975-2000" (1975); leader, "Assessment of Future National and International Problem Areas" project, National Science Foundation (1977); co-leader, Department of Transportation's study "Transportation in America's Future: Potentials for the Next Half Century" (1977).

Publications: Co-author, "In Search of Tomorrow's Crisis" (THE FUTURIST, October, 1977); co-author, "Toward a Doctrine for Futures Research" (*Futures*); "When Less is More and More is Less" (*San Francisco Examiner*); co-author, "The Problem of Critical Problem Selection" in *Futures Research*, Linstone and Simmonds, editors (1977); co-author, "The Future of Futures Research" in *Handbook of Futures Research*.

SCHWARZ, STEPHAN
Head Librarian
Royal Institute of Technology Library
Valhallavagen 81
Stockholm, Sweden S-10044

Born: 1932, Vienna, Austria

Telephone: (08) 7877080

Profession: Librarian

Field of specialization: Epistomological and ethical problems in planning and futures studies; practical problems of library administration; library information and science.

Education: Ph.D., Mathematics, 1959, Ph.D., Physics, 1967, University of Stockholm.

Professional employment: Royal Institute of Technology Library: Head Librarian (1973-). Research Institute for National Defense: Senior Research Officer (1969-73). Organization for Economic Cooperation and Development, Paris: Deputy Head of Information Centre (1966-69).

Professional activities: Research and administration; university courses; experimental nuclear physics; planning theory and futures studies.

Publications: In physics, library and information science and long-range planning. Editor of "Stockholm Papers in Library and Information Science" and "Stockholm Papers in History and Philsophy of Technology." Editor or co-editor of collective volumes including "The Interactive Library" (1975), "Knowledge and Concepts in Future Studies" (1976), "Trends in Planning" (1977), "Library Services in Transition" (1978) and "Knowledge and Development: Reshaping Library and Information Services for the World of Tomorrow" (1978).

SEABORG, GLENN THEODORE
Professor
Lawrence Berkeley Laboratory
University of California
Berkeley, California 94720, U.S.A.

Born: 1912, Ishpeming, Michigan, U.S.A.

Telephone: (415) 843-2740, Extension 5661

Profession: Chemist; educator

Field of specialization: Energy problem; the environment; resources; recycling.

Education: A.B., Chemistry, University of California-Los Angeles, 1934; Ph.D., Chemistry, University of California-Berkeley, 1937.

Professional employment: University of California (1939-); University Professor (1972-). U.S. Atomic Energy Commission: Chairman (1961-71). University of California-Berkeley: Chancellor (1958-61)/Lawrence Berkeley Laboratory: Associate Director (1954-61, 1972-); Director, Nuclear Chemistry Division (1946-58, 1972-75). University of Chicago, Metallurgical Laboratory: Head, Plutonium Chemistry Work (1942-46).

Professional activities: Research at Lawrence Berkeley Laboratory on transuranium elements; President, American Chemical Society (1976); member, Board of Directors of The World Future Society (1969-) and the California Council for Environmental and Economic Balance (1974-); Chairman of the Board, American Association for the Advancement of Science (1973), President (1972); President, Fourth United Nations International Conference on the Peaceful Uses of Atomic Energy (1971); member of the National Committee on America's Goals and Resources (1962-64) and the President's Science Advisory Committee (1959-61).

Publications: Co-author, *Man and Atom* (E. P. Dutton and Company, 1971); co-author, *Education and the Atom* (McGraw Hill, 1964); *Nuclear Milestones* (W. H. Freeman and Company, 1972); co-author, *Elements of the Universe* (E. P. Dutton and Company, 1958).

SECOMSKI, KAZIMIERZ
Born: 1910, Kamiensk, Poland

Council of Ministers Office
Al. Ujazdowskie 1
Warsaw 00-583
Poland

Telephone: 21-66-72

Profession: Economist

Field of specialization: Economic and social policy; national economic planning.

Education: B.A., Higher School of Commerce, 1937; Ph.D., Main School of Commerce, 1939.

Professional employment: Council of Ministers, Deputy Prime Minister (1976-); Planning Commission at the Council of Ministers, First Deputy Chairman (1971-76); Main School of Planning and Statistics, Warsaw: Professor, Chair holder (1946-).

Professional activities: Polish Academy of Sciences: Member (1961-); Deputy Scientific Secretary (1969-70); Member Presidium (1972-); Chairman, Committee on Economic Sciences (1966-); Chairman, Committee "Poland 2000" (1969-); Polish Economic Society, Chairman Main Council (1966).

Publications: *The Theory of Socio-Economic Policy* (1976); *Spatial Planning and Policy—Theoretical Foundations* (1974); *Prognostics* (1971); *Foundations of Long Range Planning* (1966); *Capital Investments Planning* (1954).

SELAN, VALERIO
Born: 1927, Cuneo, Italy

Director
Cnos-Tecnoservizi
Viale Astronomia 30
Rome, Italy 00114

Telephone: 5903469

Profession: Economist

Field of specialization: Technology assessment

Education: —

Professional employment: Cnos-Technoservizi: Director (1976-). Futuribili: Vice-Manager (1960-71).

Professional activities: University of Rome, research in public finance; transfer of technologies; technological assessment; future research; regional planning; public finance.

Publications: —

SETH, SATISH CHANDRA
Born: 1932, Abbotabad, India

Member-Secretary
Department of Science and Technology
Technology Bhavan, New Mehrauli Road
New Delhi-110029, India

Telephone: 662626

Profession: Futurologist and Science Administrator with the Government of India.

Field of specialization: Developing an infra-structure for futurology in India and its various States, Universities and Institutes of Advanced Learning; futures research; methodological questions; rural development; social change.

Education: B.Sc., First Division, NREC College, Khurja (UP) India, 1951; M.A., First Class First, University of Agra, India, 1953; Ph.D., Political Science, University of Agra, India, 1959; Ph.D., Public Administration, University of Manchester, U.K., 1962.

Professional employment: Department of Science and Technology: Member-Secretary, NCST Panel on Futurology (1978-). Administrative Reforms Commission on India: Special Assistant and Advisor to Study Teams (1970-78). Ministry of Education: Under Secretary to the Government of India and Section Chief (1966-70). Indian Institute of Public Administration, New Delhi: Senior Research Officer (1964-66). University of Manchester: Visiting Research Fellow (1962-64).

Professional activities: Present activity involves promotion of quantitative research in Futurology, supervision and guidance of eleven technical sub-groups in the field of 1) energy, 2) food, 3) rural development, 4) urbanology, 5) housing, 6) transportation, 7) communication, 8) management, 9) education, 10) health, and 11) water, and running the Futurology panel; conducting Futurology workshops; thematic and awareness, setting up of Futurology Centres and Futurology Committees in different parts of India; guidance to the Indian Council of Management and Future; professional research in the field of public administration, administrative reforms, social change, management of educational problems at the primary, secondary and university level, promotion of Indian Society of Training and Development (promoting professional management in India); Editor-in-Chief, *Indian Administrative and Management Review*, and *Indian Review of Management and Review*.

Publications: Central Administrative Organisation in India and in some other Commonwealth Countries (Asia Publishing House Strand, London); co-author, *Understanding British Government System* (Allied Publishers, Delhi, 1964); *Public Administration: Yesterday and Today* (Agra University Press, 1965); editor, *Base Paper on NCST Panel on Futurology*; wrote and edited several official documents in the field of futures research in the series "An Outlook for India's Future: 2000 A.D." (Department of Science and Technology, Government of India).

SETHI, BRIJ BHUSHAN
Head
Department of Psychiatry
King George's Medical College
Lucknow, U.P., India

Born: 1932, Rawalpindi, Pakistan

Telephone: 82415

Profession: Psychiatrist

Field of specialization: Changing family patterns and psychiatric illness.

Education: MBBS, King George's Medical College, Lucknow, 1956; M.Sc., Psychiatry, 1960, D.Sc., Psychiatry, 1963, University of Pennsylvania; Certification by the American Board of Psychiatry and Neurology, 1960; M.R.C., Psychiatry, England, 1972; F.A.P.A., 1973; F.R.C. Psychiatry, England, 1976.

Professional employment: King George's Medical College, University of Lucknow: Professor and Head, Department of Psychiatry (1971-); Professor of Psychiatry (1967-71); Lecturer in Psychiatry (1963-64). University of Pennsylvania Medical School: Instructor and Associate in Psychiatry (1960-61). Malvern Institute for Psychiatric and Alcohol Studies: Staff Psychiatrist (1960-63).

Professional activities: Editor-in-chief, *Indian Journal of Psychiatry* (1977-); participant: IV International Congress of Psychosomatic Medicine, Kyoto, Japan (1977), VI World Congress of Psychiatry of the World Psychiatric Association, Hawaii (1977), Rome Special World Conference of Future Research on Human Needs—New Societies—Supportive Technologies (1973); Visiting Professor at Mount Sinai Medical School (1974), Albany Medical College (1976), University of British Columbia (1971), National Institute of Mental Health (1971).

Publications: "Psychiatry in the Year 2000" (paper presented at VI Conference of the World Psychiatric Association, Hawaii, 1977); "Child Psychiatry in India" (chapter in a book published by PJK Publications, September 1975); "Psychiatry in India: Theory and Practice" (*American Journal of Psychotherapy*, 1974); "Future of Psychiatry" (*Tribuna Spain*, February 1974); "Impact of Technology on Man: Social, Cultural and Behavioral Effects and the Need for New Technologies" (paper presented at the Rome Special World Conference on Future Research, 1973).

SHANE, HAROLD GRAY　　　　　　　　　**Born:** 1914, Milwaukee, Wisconsin, U.S.A.
University Professor of Education
School of Education
Indiana University
Bloomington, Indiana 47401, U.S.A.　　　　　**Telephone:** (812) 337-2230/1067

Profession: Professor of Education

Field of specialization: Significance of the future for U.S. and international education.

Education: B.E., University of Wisconsin-Milwaukee, 1935; M.A., 1939, Ph.D., 1943, Ohio State University.

Professional employment: Indiana University: University Professor of Education (1965-); Dean, School of Education (1959-65). Northwestern University: Professor of Elementary Education and School Administration (1949-59). Winnetka, Illinois, Public Schools: Superintendent (1946-49). Ohio State Department of Education: State Supervisor of Elementary Education (1942-43).

Professional activities: Coordinating National Education Association Study of Goals for 2001 A.D. (1975-77); teaching futures course at Indiana University (1975-); Board of Directors, National Society for the Study of Education (1976-79), Chairman (1967-68, 1973-74); Review Council, Association for Supervision and Curriculum Development (1976-81), President-elect, President, and Past President (1972-75); Editorial Consultant, *Phi Delta Kappan* (1975-).

Publications: Numerous publications, some most directly related to the future are: "America's Next 25 Years: Some Implications for Education" (*Phi Delta Kappan*, Vol. 58, September 1976); *Curriculum Change: Toward the 21st Century* (NEA, Washington, D.C., 1977); "Looking to the Future: Reassessment of Education Issues of the 70's" (*Phi Delta Kappan*, Vol. 54, January 1973); *The Educational Significance of the Future* (Phi Delta Kappan, Bloomington, Indiana 1973); "Education for Tomorrow's World" (THE FUTURIST, Vol. 7, June 1973).

SHARIF, NAWAZ M.　　　　　　　　　　　**Born:** 1942, Khulna, Bangladesh
Professor of Industrial and Systems Engineering
Asian Institute of Technology
P.O. Box 2754
Bangkok, Thailand　　　　　　　　　　　　**Telephone:** 516-8311

Profession: Teacher; consultant

Field of specialization: Technology management; systems modeling; computer simulation.

Education: B.Sc., Mechanical Engineering, Bangladesh Engineering University, 1964; M.E.A., Engineering Administration, George Washington University, 1967; Ph.D., Industrial Engineering, Texas A & M University, 1969.

Professional employment: Asian Institute of Technology: Professor (1979-); Associate Professor (1975-78); Assistant Professor (1972-75). Bangladesh Engineering University: Assistant Professor (1970-72). Investment Advisory Centre of Pakistan: Consultant (1969-70).

Professional activities: Teaching graduate level courses; supervising master and doctoral degree research; Chairman, Computer Applications Division; Director, Regional Computer Center; Consultant to OECD, UNIDO, INSEAD.

Publications: Basic models chapter in *Technological Substitution* (American Elsevier, 1976); co-author, "Stochastic Network Technique for Technological Forecasting" (*Technological Forecasting and Social Change*, 1977); co-author, "Determinants for Forecasting Technological Substitution" (*Technological Forecasting and Social Change*, 1978); editor, *Systems Models for Decision Making* (AIT-Pergamon, 1978); co-author, "A Generalized Model for Forecasting Technological Substitution" (*Technological Forecasting and Social Change*, 1976).

SHELDON, ELEANOR BERNERT　　　　　**Born:** 1920, Hartford, Connecticut, U.S.A.
President
Social Science Research Council
605 Third Avenue
New York, New York 10016, U.S.A.　　　　　**Telephone:** (212) 557-9521

Profession: Sociologist

Field of specialization: Demography; social indicators; evaluation research.

Education: A.A., Colby Junior College, 1940; A.B., Sociology, University of North Carolina, 1942; Ph.D., Sociology, University of Chicago, 1949.

Professional employment: Social Science Research Council: President (1972-). Russell Sage Foundation: Sociologist and Executive Associate (1961-72). University of California-Los Angeles, School of Nursing: Associate Research Sociologist and Lecturer (1957-61). UCLA, Department of Sociology: Research Associate and Lecturer in Sociology (1955-61).

Professional activities: Member, Advisory Committee on Research Applications Policy, National Science Foundation (1975); member, Assembly of Behavioral and Social Sciences, National Research Council (1973-78); Board of Directors, The Rand Corporation (1972-); Board of Directors, U.N. Research Institute for Social Development (1973-); Second Vice-President, Population Association of America (1970-71).

Publications: Editor, *Indicators of Social Change: Concepts and Measurements* (Russell Sage Foundation, 1968); editor, *Family Economic Behavior* (J. B. Lippincott Co., 1973); co-author, "Notes on Social Indicators: Promises and Potential" (*Policy Science*, 1970); co-author, "Social Reporting for the 1970s: A Review and Programmatic Statement" (*Policy Science*, 1972); co-author, "Social Indicators" (*Science*, 1975).

SHONIKER, ROBERT GEORGE
President
R.G. Shoniker and Associates, Inc.
Suite 101, 20 Pine Crescent
Toronto, Ontario, Canada

Born: 1946, Oshawa, Ontario, Canada

Telephone: (416)699-1492

Profession: Management consultant

Field of specialization: Marketing and financial strategies for future consumer markets.

Education: B. Comm. (Hon.), Marketing, 1969, M.B.A., Finance, 1970, Queen's University at Kingston.

Professional employment: R.G. Shoniker and Associates, Inc.: President (1975-). Curshon, Inc.: President (1976-). Burns Bros. and Denton Ltd.: Senior Analyst (1970-75).

Professional activities: Member, Financial Analyst Federation, Toronto Society of Financial Analysts, Distilled Spirits Council of the United States, Inc., Canadian Association for Future Studies, Toronto Futures Society; consulting for several major consumer companies resulting in research projects such as: "Soft Drinks Beyond the Pepsi Generation," "Spirits, Beer, Wine Or?" "Business Strategy for a Maturing Consumer Market," "Tomorrow's Beer Consumer," "The Hospitality Industry 1990"; consultant to Royal Commission on Corporate Concentration (1975-76).

Publications: *A Maturing Consumer Market: A Life Cycle Approach* (Dominion Securities Limited, 1977); *A Report on Rothman's Pall Mall of Canada Limited* (Royal Commission on Corporate Concentration, 1978); *The Home Centre Life Cycle* (Draper Dobie Limited, 1976).

SHOSTAK, ARTHUR B.
Professor
Department of Psychology and Sociology
Drexel University
Philadelphia, Pennsylvania 19104, U.S.A.

Born: 1937, Brooklyn, New York, U.S.A.

Telephone: (215) 895-2466

Profession: Sociologist

Field of specialization: Social impact assessment; new towns planning; blue collar lifestyles; men's issues; space colony lifestyles; social indicators and "quality of life" research.

340

Education: B.S., Industrial and Labor Relations, Cornell University, 1958; Ph.D., Sociology, Princeton University, 1961.

Professional employment: Drexel University: Professor (1967-). University of Pennsylvania: Assistant Professor (1961-67).

Professional activities: National Science Foundation Faculty Research Fellowship (Summers 1976-78); Consultant to Mathtect and Housing and Urban Development (Fall 1977-Summer 1978); appointed to the Governor's Commission on Higher Education (1977-); Executive Council, Environmental Section, American Sociological Association; President, Pennsylvania Sociological Society (1976-77).

Publications: *Blue Collar Life* (Random House, 1968); *Modern Social Reforms* (Macmillan, 1974); editor, *Our Sociological Eye* (Alfred, 1977); editor, *Putting Sociology to Work* (David McKay, 1974); editor, *Sociology in Action* (Dorsey, 1966).

SICINSKI, ANDRZEJ
Born: 1924, Warsaw, Poland
Head
Division for Lifestyles Studies
Institute of Philosophy and Sociology
Polish Academy of Sciences
Nowy Swiat 72
Warsaw 00-330, Poland
Telephone: 26-76-42

Profession: Social scientist

Field of specialization: Futures methodology; changes in culture and life-style.

Education: M.A., 1952, Ph.D., 1961, Sociology, The University of Warsaw; Civil Engineer, Warsaw Polytechnical Institute, 1953; Docent, Sociology, Polish Academy of Sciences, 1971.

Professional employment: Institute of Philosophy and Sociology, Polish Academy of Sciences: Head of the Division for Lifestyles Studies (current); Head of the Group for Social Prognoses (past). Committee "Poland 2000," Polish Academy of Sciences: Member of the Presiding Board; Chairman of the Commission of Theory and Methodology (1975-).

Professional activities: Project on lifestyles in Poland and Scandinavia (1975-); project on methodology of social prognoses (1974-); university course and seminar of social prognostication (1971-); Member of the Executive Committee, World Future Studies Federation.

Publications: Co-editor and co-author, *Images of the World in the Year 2000* (Mouton, The Hague, Paris, 1976); editor and co-author, *Styl Zycia: Koncepcje i Propozycje [Style of Life: Conceptions and Proposals]* (1976); "The Concepts of 'Need' and 'Value' in the Light of the System Approach" (*Social Science Information*, 17, 1, 1978); *Prognoses and Science*, in Polish (1970); editor, *Studies in Social Prognostics*, in Polish (1972).

SILVERNAIL, DAVID LEE
Born: 1946, Osceola, Wisconsin, U.S.A.
Assistant Professor of Curriculum and Instruction
University of Southern Maine
Bailey Hall 510
Gorham, Maine 04038, U.S.A.
Telephone: (207) 780-5303

Profession: Educator

Field of specialization: Values assessment, especially futuristic values; global perspectives education.

Education: A.B., Philosophy, 1969, M.S., Secondary Education, 1975, Ed.D., Curriculum and Instruction, 1977, Indiana University.

Professional employment: University of Southern Maine: Assistant Professor of Curriculum and Instruction (1977-). Indiana University, Phi Delta Kappa Commission on Lifelong Learning Curriculum Models: Research Assistant (1974-77). Southeastern School Corporation: Social Studies Teacher (1969-74).

Professional activities: Research project on assessment of teachers' futuristic values; graduate courses in research and curriculum.

Publications: "The Assessment of Teachers' Future World Perspective Values" (*Journal of Environmental Education*, 1978); "Global Perspectives Education: In Need of a Futuristic Values Position" (*Futurics*, 1978; "Adapting Education to a Changing World" (THE FUTURIST, Vol. 11, No. 6, December 1977); co-author, "Foreign Language Study for a World in Transition" in *The Language Connection: From the Classroom to the World* (National Textbook Co., New York, 1977); co-author, "An Approach to Globan Studies: Balancing Problems and Promises" in *Global Studies: Problems and Promises for Elementary Teachers* (Association for Supervision and Curriculum Development, Washington, D.C., 1976).

SILVIO, CECCATO

Universita degli Studi di Milano
Via Festa del Perdono, 3
Milano, Italia

Born: 1914, Montecchio M. (Vicenza), Italy

Telephone: (02) 8846

Profession: Cyberneticist; linguist

Field of specialization: Analysis and mechanization of thought and language processes; studies and research on attitudes and values.

Education: Degree in Law, 1937; Ph.D. in Theoretical Philosophy, 1960; Studies in Musical Composition.

Professional employment: Center of Cybernetics and Linguistic Activities: Director (1958-). Institute of Technology of Education: Director (1973). University of Modern Languages: Professor of Linguistics (1971).

Professional activities: Director of a project on a universal language based on a serial order of the things to be named (1965); director of a project for examining the emotional aspects in educational communication (1974); studies and research on linguistic and aesthetic communications, mainly in music and design (1973); director of a project on mechanical translation (American Air Forces, Euratom, and CNR, 1958-64); Professor of Theoretical Philosophy (1948-62); director of the Quarterly Review, *Methodos* (1949-62).

Publications: *Un Tecnico fra i filosofi [A Technician Among Philosophers]*, two volumes (Marsilio, Padova, 1962-64); *Cibernetica per tutti [Cybernetics for Everyone]*, two volumes (Feltrinelli, Milano, 1964-66); *La terza cibernetica [The Third Cybernetics]* (Feltrinelli, Milano, 1974); *La mente vista da un cibernetico [The Mind Viewed by a Cyberneticist]* (ERI, Roma-Torino, 1972); *Il maestro inverosimile [The Improbable Teacher]*, two volumes (Bompiani, Milano, 1972).

SIMMONDS, WALTER H. C.

Industrial Programs Office
National Research Council of Canada
Montreal Road
Ottawa, Ontario
K1A 0R6 Canada

Born: 1917, London, United Kingdom

Telephone: (613) 993-1506

Profession: Policy analyst; generalist and synthesist

Field of specialization: The value, private and social, of R and D; the new framework for conditions of continuing change; industry futures through the behavior pattern, ecological, systems approaches; futures methodologies; national goals; manpower planning.

Education: B.A., 1939, B.Sc., 1940, M.A., 1943, Chemistry, Oxford University; B.A. (Hon.), Sociology, Sir George Williams University, 1970; Associate Member, 1945, Member, 1955, Chemical Engineering, Chartered Engineer, 1966, Institution of Chemical Engineers.

Professional employment: National Research Council: Industrial Programs Office (1970-). Canadian Industries Ltd.: Corporate Planning (1956-70). Dominion Tar and Chemical Ltd.: Assistant to Director of Research (1952-56). University of Durham: Associate Professor of Chemical Engineering (1946-52). Lever Brothers and Unilever Ltd.: Research Chemist, Development Engineer (1940-46).

Professional activities: Member, The McHales Bio-resources Development Conference (1978); keynote address to the Ausimm-Aime Joint Conference on International Resource Development, Canberra (1978); National Science Foundation, Project Knowledge 2000 (1976); founding member, Canadian Association for

The Club of Rome; World Future Studies Federation Council; Advisory Board, *Technological Forecasting and Social Change;* World Future Society; Futures Network, U.K.; Canadian Association for Futures Studies; Society for General Systems Analysis; New York Academy of Sciences; adviser and consultant to governments, industry, nonprofit associations, and universities; Vice-Chairman, Innovation Canada (1970-75); member, The Innovation Group (1970-71).

Publications: Co-editor, with H.A. Linstone, *Futures Research: New Directions* (Addison-Wesley, Reading, Massachusetts, 1977); "Minimum Disturbance Social Change" *(Futures Canada,* Vol. 2, No. 3, 6-9, 1978); "Impact of New External Values on Industrial R and D" *(Resources Management,* Vol. 21, No. 3, 29-33, 1978); "Environmental and Social Responsibilities in Future International Resource Management" *(Proceedings of the Joint International Conference on Resource Management,* Ausimm-Aime, Canberra, Australia, May 1978); "The Analysis of Industrial Behavior and Its Use in Forecasting" *(Technological Forecasting and Social Change,* Vol. 3, 1972).

SIMMONS, WILLIAM W.

President
Applied Futures, Inc.
22 Greenwich Plaza
Greenwich, Connecticut 06830, U.S.A.

Born: 1912, Lansdowne, Pennsylvania, U.S.A.

Telephone: (203) 661-9710

Profession: Business planner; consultant

Field of specialization: Business planning systems, from very basic five-year planning systems to the incorporation and use of more innovative techniques such as environmental scanning, Delphis, technology forecasting.

Education: Electrical Engineering Degree, Swarthmore College, 1934.

Professional employment: Applied Futures, Inc.: President (1972-). International Business Machines: Director of Exploratory Planning, Corporate Planning, Product Planning (1952-71).

Professional activities: Honorary Chairman of International Affiliation of Planning Societies; consulting with clients, including Peat, Marwick, Mitchell and Company, Computer Sciences, Provident National Bank in Philadelphia; Advisory Board, Prospects for Mankind; President NASCP (1968); Chairman of the International Affiliation of Planning Societies (1970-72).

Publications: "A Strategic Planning Program for the Next Decade" *(American Management Journal,* January 1976); "What the Future Holds for Today's Managers" *(Manager's Forum,* Vol. 2, No. 1, January 1975); "Main Forms of Futures Research" *(European Business,* Summer 1972); "Practical Planning" *(Long Range Planning,* Vol. 5, No. 2, June 1972); *So You Want To Have a Long-Range Plan* (Planning Executives Institute, Winter, 1978).

SINE, THOMAS WILLIAM

World Concern
19303 Fremont Ave. N.
Seattle, Washington 98133, U.S.A.

Born: 1936, Pocatello, Idaho

Telephone: (206) 546-7209

Profession: Futurist; development planner

Field of specialization: Futures invention; Third World development planning; educational planning; design of alternative human delivery systems.

Education: B.A., Communications, Cascade College, 1958; M.A., Counseling, California State University, 1968; Ph.D., History and Futures, University of Washington, 1978.

Professional employment: World Concern: Research and Planning (1976-). University of Washington: Instructor in Futurism (1976-). Weyerhauser Corporation: Consultant in Futures (1974-76). Washington 2000: Director (1973-74).

Professional activities: Teaching futures courses, University of Washington (1976-); applying futures methodology to Third World development (1976-); studying the history and the future of images and ideas (1976-); conducting futures workshops at World Concern to promote economic justice, simplification of lifestyle, and new responses to increasing human needs in developing nations.

Publications: "Megamachine and the Future of the Schoolhouse" (*Phi Delta Kappan*, March 1974); editor, *Prospectus-Washington 2000* (State of Washington, 1973).

SIRKIN, ABRAHAM MEYER
Consultant on International Affairs
6525 Wiscasset Road
Bethesda, Maryland 20016, U.S.A.

Born: 1914, Barre, Vermont, U.S.A.

Telephone: (301) 229-7498

Profession: Policy planner and analyst

Field of specialization: International communications and telecommunications policy; economic development; value systems and human rights.

Education: B.A., Social Sciences, Columbia College, 1935; M.S., Journalism, Graduate School of Journalism, Columbia University, 1936.

Professional employment: U.S. Department of State: Consultant (1974); member, Policy Planning Staff (1972-74). American Embassy, Athens: Counselor for Public Affairs (1967-72). U.S. Consulate, Madras, India: Director, U.S. Information Service (1963-66). U.S. Information Agency: Long Range Planning Officer (1957-61).

Professional activities: Study on communications policy planning, Department of State (May-July 1978); political and economic human rights project, International Commission of Jurists (1978-); consultant, Human Rights Seminar, Aspen Institute (May-August 1977); consultant and editor, Resource Sensing for Development, National Academy of Sciences (September 1975-January 1977); consultant, Interdependence Project, Aspen Institute (February-August 1975).

Publications: Editor, *Resource Sensing from Space: Prospects for Developing Countries* (National Academy of Sciences, 1977); *Living With Interdependence: The Decades Ahead in America* (Aspen Institute for Humanistic Studies, 1975); *Elements of a U.S. Human Rights Strategy* (Aspen Institute for Humanistic Studies, 1978); "Satellite Communications: Hopes and Fears" (International Educational and Cultural *Exchange*, Winter 1978).

SJOERDSMA, ANDRE C.
Managing Director
Future Shape of Technology Foundation
Prinsessegracht 23
The Hague, The Netherlands

Born: 1926, Amersfoort, The Netherlands

Telephone: (070) 646800

Profession: Electronics Engineer

Field of specialization: Future technological developments and their social consequences.

Education: IR, Electronics, Delft Technological University, 1958.

Professional employment: Future Shape of Technology Foundation: Managing Director (1968-). Royal Netherlands Air Force: Major (1960-68). Royal Military Academy and Royal Netherlands Air Force: Subs. Officer Ranks (1948-68).

Professional activities: Currently conducting studies in transportation, energy, environment, food, communication, health, spatial planning, and materials; consulting and lecturing; has worked on quality assurance in NATO projects.

Publications: Editor, *Energy Conservation: Ways and Means* (Future Shape of Technology Foundation, 1974); "Non-Conventional Energy Resources" (*Essobron*, July 1974); *Technology in a Post-Industrial Society* (TNO Project, November 1975); *R & D and Change in Social Goals* (OECD Report, January 1972); "Eldo-Rockets for a Space Program" (*De Militaire Spectator*, November 1967).

SKINNER, B. F.
Professor of Psychology Emeritus
Harvard University
Kirkland Street
William James Hall
Cambridge, Massachusetts 02138, U.S.A.

Born: 1904, Susquehanna, Pennsylvania, U.S.A.

Telephone: (617) 495-3888

Profession: Psychologist

Field of specialization: Analysis of behavior; design of cultures; education.

Education: A.B., English, Hamilton College, 1926; M.A., 1930, Ph.D., 1931, Psychology, Harvard University.

Professional employment: Harvard University: Professor of Psychology Emeritus (1974-); Professor of Psychology (1948-74). Indiana University: Chairman and Professor of Psychology (1945-48). University of Minnesota: Instructor—Associate Professor (1936-45).

Professional activities: Currently writing and lecturing; teaching and research (1936-74).

Publications: *Behavior of Organisms* (Appleton-Century-Crofts, 1938); *Walden Two* (Macmillan, 1948); *Science and Human Behavior* (Macmillan, 1953); *Beyond Freedom and Dignity* (Knopf, 1971); *About Behaviorism* (Knopf, 1974); *Particulars of My Life* (Knopf, 1976); *The Shaping of a Behaviorist* (Knopf, 1979).

SKOE, ANDERS S.
Economist/Planner
British Columbia Telephone Company
Marketing, Floor 11
3777 Kingsway
Burnaby, British Columbia, V5H 3Z7 Canada

Born: 1943, Stavanger, Norway

Telephone: (604) 432-3981

Profession: Economist

Field of specialization: Technology assessment; corporate planning; value systems; futures methodology.

Education: B.A., Economics, University of Manchester, England 1967; Candidate for Masters Degree, Communications, Simon Fraser University, British Columbia.

Professional employment: British Columbia Telephone Company: Economist/Planner (1976-). Trans-Canada Telephone System: Economist/Planner (1975-76). British Columbia Telephone Company: Economist (1969-75). Government of Saskatchewan: Policy Analyst (1967-69).

Professional activities: Member at large for British Columbia, Canadian Association for Future Studies (1978-); President, Vancouver Chapter, World Future Society (1973-75).

Publications: - -

SKOLIMOWSKI. HENRY K.
Department of Humanities
College of Engineering
The University of Michigan
Ann Arbor, Michigan 48104, U.S.A.

Born: 1930, Warsaw, Poland

Telephone: (313) 764-1420

Profession: Professor of Philosophy

Field of specialization: Technology and man, alternative futures; futures methodology; eco-philosophy; philosophy of architecture.

Education: B.Sc., 1954, M.Sc., 1956, Civil Engineering, Warsaw Institute of Technology; M.A., Philosophy and Logic, Warsaw University, 1959; D. Phil., Philosophy, New College, Oxford University, 1964.

Professional employment: University of Michigan: Professor (1970). University of Southern California: Associate Professor (1965-70); Assistant Professor (1964-65). Linacre College, Oxford University: Research Fellow (1968-69). Columbia University: Senior Research Fellow (Summer, 1969). Clare Hall, Cambridge University: Research Fellow (1970-71). St. Anthony's College, Oxford University: Research Associate (Spring, Summer, 1973).

Professional activities: Co-ordinator, Science, Technology and Future Societies, Faculty Seminar, University of Michigan (1972-); teaching courses on "Technology and Man" and "Alternative Futures," University of Michigan (1971-); member, Task Force on Appropriate Technology of the United States Senate (1977-); member, Editorial Board, *Research in Philosophy and Technology* and *The Teilhard Review;* associate editor, *The Ecologist;* delivered papers and addresses on philosophy of technology, technology assessment, appropriate technology, and alternative futures, and had numerous articles published in these and related fields; trustee, Cosanti Foundation.

Publications: "The Structure of Thinking in Technology" in *Philosophy and Technology,* Mitcham and Mackey, eds. (Free Press, 1972); "The Twilight of Physical Descriptions and the Ascent of Normative Models" in *Models, Norms and Applications,* E. Laszlo, ed. (George Braziller, 1973); "Knowledge and Values *(The Ecologist,* January, 1975); *Ecological Humanism* (monograph) (Gryphon Press, 1976); "Epistemological Aspects of Technology Assessment" in *Futures Research: New Directions,* Linstone and Simmonds, eds. (Addison-Wesley, 1977).

SMIL, VACLAV

Born: 1943, Plzen, Czechoslovakia

Associate Professor
University of Manitoba
Department of Geography
Winnipeg, Manitoba
R3T 2N2 Canada

Telephone: (204) 474-9351

Profession: Professor

Field of specialization: Energy analysis; system energetics; China's energy; food energy.

Education: M.S., Geography, Carolinum University, Prague, 1965; Ph.D., Geography, Penn State University, 1972.

Professional employment: University of Manitoba: Associate Professor (1972-). Board of the Chief Architect, Most, Czechoslovakia: Consultant (1966-69). Military Geographical Institute, Prague: Editor (1965-66).

Professional activities: "China's Energy Technology," a study for the United States Congress (1978); China's Food" and "China from Space" books in progress (1978-79); teaching courses on energy, energy analysis and China.

Publications: *China's Energy* (Praeger Publishers, 1976); *Energy and the Environment: A Long-Range Forecasting Study* (University of Manitoba, 1974); editor, *Energy in the Developing World* (Oxford University Press, 1979); and numerous other articles dealing with energy, China, environment and development in a wide variety of journals.

SNYDER, DAVID PEARCE

Born: 1938, Indianapolis, Indiana, U.S.A.

Senior Planning Officer
U.S. Internal Revenue Service
1111 Constitution Avenue, N.W.
Washington, D.C. 20224, U.S.A.

Telephone: (202) 566-4740

Profession: Planning Officer, consulting futurist

Field of specialization: Personal, institutional and community social value systems and decision processes; information/communication technology; futures teaching; public policy analysis; future of the family.

Education: B.A., Government, Antioch College, 1961; Graduate work, Public Administration, George Washington University, 1962-63; Graduate work, Public Affairs, American University, 1962-64; Graduate Certificate, Systems Analysis, University of California-Irvine, 1968-69.

346

Professional employment: Consulting futurist (1977-). U.S. Internal Revenue Service: Senior Planning Officer (1973-); Chief, Information Systems (1971-73); Chief, Records and Paperwork Management (1969-73); Management Analysis Officer (1966-68). Rand Corporation: Consultant (1968-69). U.S. Office of Economic Opportunity: Community Development Consultant (1964-65).

Professional activities: Assistant Director for Socio-Political Programs and Director of two one-week courses in Socio-Political Forecasting each year, Industrial Management Center, Inc. (1975-); Vice-President, Washington, D.C. Chapter of the World Future Society (1971-); Associate Editor, *The Bureaucrat* (1972-); member and co-chairman, Review Committee, Futurics Survey Course, Second General Assembly of the World Future Society (June 1975); instructor in futures programs for the U.S. Federal Executive Institute and the U.S. Civil Service Commission (1971-).

Publications: Co-author and editor, *The Family in Post-Industrial America: Fundamental Issues for Policy Analysis* (Westview Press, 1979); "The Corporate Family: A Look at a Proposed Social Invention" (THE FUTURIST, December 1976);Informing the Decision-Makers" (World Future Society *BULLETIN;* co-author and editor, *The Future of the Bureaucracy* (Sage Publications, Beverly Hills, 1974); co-author, *Studies in the Quality of Life* (D.C. Heath, Inc., 1972); co-author, "Computers, Personal Privacy and the Treatment of Information as an Economic Commodity," chapter in *Operations Research in Law Enforcement, Justice and Societal Security*, Kamrass, Ed. (Lexington Books, D.C. Heath, Inc., 1976); "Controlling Computer Abuse: The Need for a Rational Perspective" (*Creative Computing Magazine*, December 1975).

SOCIAS, JUAN
Advisor
Estudios Prospectivos
Apartado Chaco 61.486
Caracas 106
Venezuela

Born: 1943, Santiago, Cuba

Telephone: (02) 74.88.54, 74.69.53

Profession: Planner

Field of specialization: Futures methodology; long range planning; communications.

Education: Bachelor, Social Communications, Andres Bello University; Master, Ed. Planning, Simon Rodriquez University; Ph.D., Southeastern University, 1978.

Professional employment: Simon Rodriquez University: Program Director (1973-78). Center of Studies on the Future of Venezuela: Advisor (1969-78). Simon Bolivar University: Advisor, Latin American Study (1975). Andres Bello University: Coordinator, Social Sciences School (1971-74).

Professional activities: Research projects on the future of Venezuela (1976-78); consulting on future problems (1969-78); Professor of social planning (1971-76); research on communications and the future (1969); research on A Paradigm for Venezuela (1970-71).

Publications: Editor, *Sociedad en Crisis? [Is Society in Crisis?]* (OESE, Caracas, 1973; co-author, *Futuro de la Com. Social en Venezuela [The Future of Social Communication in Venezuela]* (CEFV-UCAB, Caracas, 1970); "El Futuro como Ciencia y A. Latina" ["The Future as a Science and Latin America"] (*Revista Interciencia*, Caracas, Vol. 2:1, February 1977); "Herman Kahn canta un Requiem al Petroleo" ["A Requiem to Oil by Herman Kahn"] (*Revista Resumen* No. 182, April 1977).

SOLEM, ERIK
Defence Scientist
Directorate of Strategic Analysis
Operational Research and Analysis Establishment (ORAE)
Department of National Defence
Ottawa, Ontario, Canada K1A OK2

Born: 1938,Norway

Telephone: (613) 992-7236

Profession: Political scientist; strategic analyst

Field of specialization: Defence and strategic questions concerning energy and resources, long-term forecasting and planning, nuclear matters, and influence of scientific and technological advances; futures methodology; technological forecasting and assessment.

Education: B.A., Political Science and Economics, University of Manitoba, Canada, 1964; M.A., Advanced European Political Studies, Faculty of Social Sciences, Leicester University, United Kingdom, 1966; D. Phil. (Oxon), Politics, Oxford University, 1974.

Professional employment: National Defence, Directorate of Strategic Analysis, ORAE, Ottawa, Canada: Defence Scientist (1974-). U.N. Institute for Training and Research (UNITAR), New York: Staff Member and Research Associate (1972-74). Kansas State University: Post-Doctoral Fellow, Department of Political Science, and Research Associate, Departments of Political Science and Physics (1970-72).

Professional activities: Designs and teaches university courses, and lectures on futures and forecasting; cross-national research projects, international conferences, and meetings on nuclear materials control and regulation, peace research, political and economic integration, and community building; working on a book of *Theories of Fascism*; work for UNITAR: Commission on the Future; enhancing efficiency of U.N. structures and methods; social and political forecasting; energy resources allocation, control and utilization; regional integration and community building, and economic, political and social development; working visits to International Atomic Energy Agency (1971) and European Atomic Energy Community (1971) on question of safeguarding strategic nuclear materials.

Publications: *The Nordic Council and Scandinavian Integration* (Praeger Publishers, New York, 1977); "Energy Sources and Global Strategic Planning" in *Impact of Science on Society* (Vol. 26, No. 112, January-April, 1976, U.N. Educational, Scientific and Cultural Organization, Paris); "Some Future Uses of Analytic Forecasting" in *Environmental Assessment of Socio-Economic Systems*, Burkhardt and Ittelson, editors, (North Atlantic Treaty Organization Conference Series II: System Sciences, Plenum Press, New York and London, 1978); "Alternative Approaches to Technology Assessment" in *Technology Assessment and the Oceans*, Wilmot and Slingerland, editors, (IPC Science and Technology Press, United Kingdom, 1977); "Future Applications of Political Science" (*Futures*, Vol. 8, No. 4, August 1976).

SOMIT, ALBERT
Executive Vice President and Professor of Political Science
State University of New York at Buffalo
503 Capen Hall
Buffalo, New York 14260, U.S.A.

Born: 1919, Chicago, Illinois, U.S.A.

Telephone: (716) 636-2901

Profession: Political scientist; university administrator

Field of specialization: Futures; biopolitics.

Education: A.B., 1941, Political Science and History, Ph.D., 1947, Political Science, University of Chicago.

Professional employment: Netherlands Institute for Advanced Studies: Fellow (1978-79). State University of New York at Buffalo: Executive Vice President (1970); Professor of Political Science (1966-); Chairman, Political Science Department (1966-69). New York University: Director of Doctoral Programs, Graduate School of Public Administration (1962-66).

Professional activities: Chairman, Biology and Politics Research Committee, International Political Science Association (1976); Member, Directing Group, Programme on Institutional Management in Higher Education, OECD (1973-); Chairman, Specialists' Panel on "Biology and Politics" (1970), Meeting of International Political Science Association, Montreal (1973) and Munich (1970); technical consultant, International Seminar on Student Life (International Union of School and University Health and Medicine) under auspices of World Health Organization and UNESCO (1971-).

Publications: Co-author, "Methodological Problems Associated with a Biologically-Oriented Social Science" (*Journal of Social and Biological Structures*, No. 1, 1978); co-author, *The Literature of Biopolitics, 1963-1977* (Center for Biopolitical Research, DeKalb, IL., 1978); editor, *Biology and Politics: Recent Explorations* (Mouton Press, Paris, 1976); editor, *Political Science and the Study of the Future* (Dryden Press, Hinsdale, Illinois, 1973); "Reports of Two Key SSRC Committees: Back to the Drafting Board?" (*Political Science*, Vol. 8, No. 1, Winter 1975); review article, "Biopolitics" (*British Journal of Political Science*, Vol. 2, Part 2, April 1972); "One of the Reviewed Reviews" (*Political Science*, Vol. 7, No. 4, Fall 1974).

SORENSEN, ARNE
President
Society for Futures Research
Ribe Landevej 3
Dk-6100
Haderslev, Denmark

Born: 1906, Louns, Denmark

Telephone: (04) 52 09 60

Profession: Anthropologist

Field of specialization: Value systems; futures methodology.

Education: —

Professional employment: College for the Future: President (1973-76). Society for Futures Research, Denmark: President (1968-).

Professional activities: Secretary-General, World Future Studies Federation (1970-72); Member of the Danish Parliament (1943-47) and of the Danish Government (1945); Member of the Danish Resistance Council (1943-45); studied and lived or traveled in many countries (1930-76).

Publications: Has written twelve books in Danish on cultural and social analyses.
(From the first edition. Corrections not received by press time.)

SPENGLER, JOSEPH JOHN
Professor of Economics Emeritus
Department of Economics
Duke University
Durham, North Carolina 27706, U.S.A.

Born: 1902, Piqua, Ohio, U.S.A.

Telephone: (919) 684-3936

Profession: Professor of Economics Emeritus

Field of specialization: Demography; problems of aging

Education: A.B., Economics, 1926, M.A., 1929, Ph.D., 1930, Ohio State University.

Professional employment: Duke University: Associate Professor, Professor (1934-); James B. Duke Professor (1972); retired in 1972. University of Arizona: Assistant and Associate Professor (1930-32, 1933-34). Ohio State University: Instructor (1928-30).

Professional activities: Research in demography and aging and in the history of economic ideas.

Publications: Author, co-author or editor of some ten books and about 250 articles dealing with problems in demography, age structure, natural resource use and with economic thought and its history; *Facing Zero Population* (Duke University Press, Durham, N.C., 1978); *France Faces Depopulation* (Duke University Press, Durham, N.C., 2nd edition, 1978); *Population and America's Future* (W. H. Freeman, San Francisco, 1975); *Population Change, Modernization and Welfare* (Prentice-Hall, Englewood Cliffs, N.J., 1974); *Indian Economic Thought* (Duke University Press, Durham, N.C., 1971); editor, *Zero Population Growth: Implications* (Carolina Population Center, Chapel Hill, N.C., 1975).

SPENGLER, MARIE
Social Policy Analyst
SRI International
333 Ravenswood Avenue
Menlo Park, California 94025, U.S.A.

Born: 1944, Oakland, California, U.S.A.

Telephone: (415) 326-6200

Profession: Social policy analyst

Field of specialization: Values and lifestyles; futures research; relationship between social change and the business world.

Education: B.S., Business Administration, University of California at Berkeley, 1966; M.B.A., Harvard University, 1976.

Professional employment: SRI International: Social Policy Analyst (1976-). GMV Counseil: Senior Consultant (1972-74). IBM: Systems Engineer (1966-71).

Professional activities: Sensitizing corporations to changes in values and lifestyles through seminars and research projects; involved in societal futures work and scenario writing.

Publications: —

SPILHAUS, ATHELSTAN

National Oceanic and Atmospheric Administration
Department of Commerce
6010 Executive Blvd.
Rockville, Maryland 20852, U.S.A.

Born: 1911, Cape Town, Union of South Africa

Telephone: (301) 443-8923

Profession: Scientist

Field of specialization: Oceans; meteorology.

Education: B.Sc., University of Cape Town, 1931; M.S., Massachusetts Institute of Technology, 1933; D.Sc., University of Cape Town, 1948.

Professional employment: National Oceanic and Atmospheric Administration: Consultant (1974-). Woodrow Wilson International Center for Scholars: Fellow (1971-74). American Association for the Advancement of Science: Chairman (1971); President (1970); President-Elect (1969). Aqua International, Inc.: President (1969-70). The Franklin Institute: President (1967-69). University of Minnesota: Dean, Institute of Technology (1949-66). New York University: Director of Research (1946-48); Professor of Meteorology (1937-48). Woods Hole Oceanographic Institution: Investigator in Physical Oceanography (1938-60).

Professional activities: Member, Council on Trends and Perspectives, Chamber of Commerce of the United States; member, Advisory Panel, Committee on Science and Astronautics, House of Representatives; member, National Science Board (1966-72); member, Board of Trustees, The International Oceanographic Foundation; inventor of the Bathythermograph and the Spilhaus Space Clock.

Publications: *Waste Management—The Next Industrial Revolution* (1966); *Experimental Cities* (1966); *The Ocean Laboratory* (1966); *Turn to the Sea* (1959); *Satellite of the Sun* (1958); *Meteorological Instruments* (1953); *Weathercraft* (1951); *Workbook on Meteorology* (1942); "Our New Age"—a Sunday illustrated feature on science.

STEFFES, DALE WILLIAM

President
Planning and Forecasting Consultants
908 Town and Country Blvd.
Houston, Texas 77024, U.S.A.

Born: 1933, Olpe, Kansas, U.S.A.

Telephone: (713) 467-4732

Profession: Forecaster; strategic planner

Field of specialization: Formal forecasting systems—interrelationships between six prime INFLUENCES: social, political, technological, ecological, economic, and natural resources; formal planning systems within specific infrastructures under the six prime INFLUENCES.

Education: B.S., Mechanical Engineering, 1958, B.S., Business Administration, 1959, Kansas State University; B.Th., Theology, St. Thomas University, 1972.

Professional employment: Planning and Forecasting Consultants: President (1973-). Panhandle Eastern Pipe Line Co.: Senior Planner (1968-73); Senior Project and Design Engineer (1959-68).

Professional activities: Conducting multiclient studies for major corporations such as: World and U.S. Energy Studies, Coal Industry and Coal Transportation Studies; lectured to professional societies on coal transportation, technology forecasting, scenario planning, and energy; founder (1969), director (currently), Houston Chapter of the World Future Society; president, Houston National Association of Business Economist (1973); director, North American Society of Corporate Planning (1974); member, Executive Committee, Future Studies Committee, Houston Chamber of Commerce; member of several professional associations.

Publications: "Western (U.S.) Coal Market Study" (private, May 1978); "The United States Energy Strategic Playbook" (private, January 1977); "Rail Transportation of Western Coal and Other Com-

350

modities" (private, April 1975); "World Petroleum Supply and Demand" (private, February 1974); "A Coal Slurry Pipeline from the Western States" (private, March 1974).

STEVENSON, HUGH ALEXANDER

Born: 1935, Peterborough, Ontario, Canada

Assistant Dean, Faulty of Education and Associate Professor
Althouse College
Faculty of Education
University of Western Ontario
London, Ontario, Canada N6G 1G7

Telephone: (519) 679-6025

Profession: Educator, historian, author

Field of specialization: Educational futures; policy development; futures information analysis.

Education: B.A., Psychology and Philosophy, 1958, M.A., History, 1960, Dip. Ed., Education, 1967, University of Western Ontario.

Professional employment: University of Western Ontario: Assistant Dean, Faculty of Education and Associate Professor, History and Comparative Education Department (1969-); Program Coordinator (1974-75). Lakeport Secondary School: Acting Head, History Department (1968-69). Prince of Wales College (now University of Prince Edward Island): Instructor, History Department (1963-65).

Professional activities: President and Interim Executive, Canadian Association for Futures Studies (1976-77); teaches courses on "Policy Making in Canadian Education," "Political Organization of Education," "Research Design," "Contemporary Issues in Education," "History of Canadian Education," "Alternative Futures in Education," and "Utopian Thought and Education"; Director, Canadian Education and the Future Project (1970-72); varied consultantships on educational publishing, information research and policy development.

Publications: Co-editor with J.D. Wilson, and co-author, *Precepts, Policy and Process: Perspectives on Contemporary Canadian Education* (Alexander, Blake Associates, 1977); editor, *Alternatives Canada* (Alexander, Blake Associates, 1976); "Policy-Making in Contemporary Canadian Education: The Failure of Traditional Professional and Political Mechanisms" (*Canadian Society for the Study of Education Bulletin,* Vol. 2, No. 5, March 1975); "Ten Years to Know Where" in *The Failure of Educational Reform,* D. Myers, ed. (McClelland and Stewart Ltd., 1973); co-author, with W.B. Hamilton, and editor, *Canadian Education and the Future: A Select Annotated Bibliography 1967-71* (University of Western Ontario, 1972); author and co-editor, with F.H. Armstrong and J.D. Wilson, *Aspects of Nineteenth Century Ontario: Essays Presented to James J. Talman* (University of Toronto Press, 1974).

STOEBER, GERHARD J.

Born: 1933, Essen, NRW, Germany

Director, SYSTEMPLAN e.V.
Institute for Environmental Research and Development Planning
Tiergartenstrasse 15
D-6900 Heidelberg 1, Federal Republic of Germany

Telephone: (6221) 49021-22

Profession: Economist; sociologist; policy consultant

Field of specialization: Urban and regional development planning; technology assessment; technology transfer; industrial development policy; organization of planning in government and public administration; developing countries; human mobility research.

Education: M.A., Economics, University of Munich, 1959; Sociology, University of Frankfurt, 1961; Ph.D., Political Economy, University of Basle, Switzerland, 1963.

Professional employment: SYSTEMPLAN e.V., Institute for Environmental Research and Development Planning: Director (1972-). Planning Department, Federal Chancellor's Office: Senior Adviser (1967-71). Studiengruppe fuer Systemforschung [Study Group for Systems Research]: Senior Scientist (1968-71). University of Karlsruhe, Institute for Urban and Regional Planning: Head, Regional Planning Research Group (1964-67). University of Frankfurt, Institute for Social Research: Research Scientist (1960-64).

Professional activities: Member of the Executive Committee and Scientific Director, SYSTEMPLAN (1972-); director of project, "Man and Industry in Future Europe" of Plan Europe 2000, European Cultural

Foundation (1974-76); member, Integration Committee for Plan Europe 2000 (1974-76); member of the Executive Board, German Committee for European Cultural Cooperation (1972-77); consultant for regional development planning in developing countries (1972-); Fellow, Center for Human Mobility (1975-77); consultant for OECD and U.N. on technology assessment and urban development issues (1970-75); lecturer at University of Karlsruhe and University of Stuttgart on urban and regional planning, systems analysis (1965-70); President of Salzburg Assembly on Impacts of New Technology (1970-74); Preparatory Committee for HABITAT—The U.N. Conference on Human Settlements (1974-75).

Publications: *Das Standortgefuge der Grossstadtmitte [The Structure of the Central Metropolis]* (Europaische Verlagsanstalt, Frankfurt, 1964); "Technischer Fortschritt als Determinante und Instrument der Stadtentwicklung" *["Technological Progress as the Cause and Effect of Urban Development"]* (*Stadtbauwelt* 21, 1969); "Forschung und Innovation" *["Research and Innovation"]* (*Forschungspolitik*, Heft 9, 1969); editor, *Technology Assessment and Quality of Life* (Elsevier, Amsterdam, 1973); co-author, *Regional Planning in Developing Countries* (Federal Ministry for Economic Cooperation, 1974).

STOKES, BRUCE EDWARD

Born: 1948, Butler, Pennsylvania, U.S.A.

Researcher and Director of Outreach
Worldwatch Institute
1776 Massachusetts Avenue, N.W.
Washington, D.C. 20036, U.S.A.

Telephone: (202) 452-1999

Profession: Researcher

Field of specialization: Population; community participation in development.

Education: B.S.F.S., International Affairs, Georgetown University, 1970; M.A., International Affairs, Johns Hopkins University, 1974.

Professional employment: Worldwatch Institute: Researcher and Director of Outreach (1974-).

Professional activities: —

Publications: *Worker Participation* (Worldwatch Papers, December 1978); *Local Responses to Global Problems* (Worldwatch Papers, February 1978); *Filling the Family Planning Gap* (Worldwatch Papers, May 1977); co-author, *22 Dimensions of the Population Problem* (Worldwatch Papers, March 1978).

STOVER, JOHN G.

Born: 1947, Pittsburgh, Pennsylvania, U.S.A.

Manager, Analytic Services
The Futures Group
124 Hebron Avenue
Glastonbury, Connecticut 06033, U.S.A.

Telephone: (203) 633-3501

Profession: Futures research; policy analyst

Field of specialization: Development planning; futures methodology.

Education: B.S., Chemistry, Case Western Reserve University, 1969; M.A., Futures Research, Campus Free College, 1975.

Professional employment: The Futures Group: Manager, Analytic Services (1973-). Peace Corps (1969-72).

Professional activities: Study and communication of the impacts of rapid population growth on development, Agency for International Development (1977-80); application of venture analysis to analysis of public and private return, Department of Energy (1977-78); development of forecasting service-FUTURSCAN, The Futures Group (continuing); methodology development-trend impact analysis, probabilistic system dynamics, decision modeling; lectured and written extensively on futures methodology.

Publications: "The Use of Probabilistic System Dynamics in the Analysis of National Development Policy: A Study of Economic Growth and Income Distribution in Uruguay" (Summer Computer Simulation Conference, July 1975); "Including Future Events in System Dynamics Models" (*Management Science*, forthcoming); co-author, "Cross Impact Analysis" in *Handbook of Futures Research*, J. Fowles, ed. (Greenwood Press, 1978); "The Use of Decision Modelling for Substitution Analysis"(*Technological Forecasting and Social Change*, forthcoming); co-author, "Using Perceptions and Data about the Future to Improve the Simulation of Complex Systems" (*Technological Forecasting and Social Change*, 1976.)

STREATFEILD, GUY FREDERICK   **Born:** 1945, Chiddingstone, Kent, England
Assistant Director
Center for Integrative Studies
College of Social Studies
University of Houston
Houston, Texas 77004, U.S.A.   **Telephone:** (713) 749-1121

Profession: Research associate

Field of specialization: —

Education: B.Sc., Social Science, Southampton University, 1967.

Professional employment: Center for Integrative Studies, State University of New York: Assistant to the Director (1974-76). Mankind 2000 Association: Executive Secretary (1973). *Futures*, IPC Science and Technology Press: Editor (1968-73).

Professional activities: Recent research contributions to reports on "International Survey of Futures Studies," "Women in World Terms: Facts and Trends," "Basic Human Needs, A Framework for Action" (1977-78), and "Children Worldwide: Facts and Trends" (1978).

STRZELECKI, JAN WLADYSLAW   **Born:** 1919, Warsaw, Poland
Research Sociologist
Instytut Socjologji
Polska Akademia Nauk
Nowy Swiat 72
Warsaw, Poland   **Telephone:** 39-88-31

Profession: Sociologist

Field of specialization: Value systems—organization and change; alternative post-industrial societies.

Education: M.A., Sociology, Warsaw University, 1949; Ford Foundation Grant, Sociology, University of California at Berkeley, 1958-59; Ph.D., Sociology, Warsaw University, 1964.

Professional employment: Polish Academy of Sciences: Styles of Life Research Team, Institute of Sociology (1975-); Member, Committee of the Year 2000 (1967-77); Industrial Sociology Research Team, Institute of Sociology (1963-68).

Professional activities: Research on past and current concepts of social progress; preparing collection of essays on future images in socialist thought; member of the Editorial Board and writer of *Nowa Kultura* (1955-61) and of *Literatura* (1971-74).

Publications: *American Anxieties* (Polish Publishing House, 1962); *Continuities I and II* (Polish Publishing House, 1969, 1974); editor, *Jean Jaures, Selected Works* (Ksiazka i Wiedza, 1970); "Ossowski's Projective Sociology" (*Odra* No. 1, 1975); "Lyrical Imagination in Socialist Thought" (Unpublished, 1978).

STULMAN, JULIUS   **Born:** 1906, New York, New York, U.S.A.
President
World Institute Council
171 West Street
Brooklyn, New York 11222, U.S.A.   **Telephone:** (212) 383-5000

Profession: Author

Field of specialization: Futures methodology systems.

Education: New York University, 1923-25.

Professional employment: Self employed: always involved in lumber manufacture distibution, insurance interests, terminal operations, transportation, management counselling (largely for government agencies). Father of the containerization concept.

Professional activities: Currently President of the World Institute Council.

Publications: *Evolving Mankind's Future* (Lippincott, 1967); *Main Currents in Modern Thought* (publisher for 25 years); *Fields Within Fields* (publisher); *Man, Mankind, The Universe* (1968); *Economic Fluctuation* (1968); *The Methodology of Pattern* (1972); *The Third Industrial Revolution* (1973); *The Key to Mankind's Emergence* (The World Institute, 1974).

SUCHODOLSKI, BOGDAN
Polish Academy of Science
Nowy Swiat 72
Warsaw, Poland

Born: 1903, Sosnowiec, Poland

Telephone: 39-20-27

Profession: Educationist; philosopher

Field of specialization: Education; philosophical anthropology; civilization of the future.

Education: Ph.D., Warsaw University, 1925; postgraduate studies in universities in Cracow, Berlin, and Paris.

Professional employment: Polish Academy of Science: Member of Praesidium (current); Interdisciplinary Committee, Poland 2000, Member of Praesidium (current). Warsaw University: Professor (1946-68).

Professional activities: Research on the philosophy of man; studies on education for the future; modern values.

Publications: *Wychowanie dla przyszlosci [Education for the Future]* (Warszawa, Panstwowe Wydawn, Naukowe, 1947, 1959, 1968; translations in Hungarian, Italian, Spanish); *U podstaw materialistycznej teorii wychowania [Foundations of the Materialist Theory of Education]* (1957; translations in German, Spanish, Italian, Portuguese); *Narodziny nowozytnej filozofii czlowieka [The Birth of the Modern Philosophy of Man]* (1963, 1968; translations in Serbian and French); *Swiat czlowieka a wychowanie [The Human World and Education]* (1967; translation in Spanish); *Labirynty wspolczesnosci [Labyrinths of the Modern Time]* (1972, 1974); *Oswiata i czlowiek przyszlosci [Education and the Man of the Future]* (Warszawa, Ksiazka i Wiedza, 1974); *Kim jest czlowiek? [Who is a Man?]* (1974, 1976).

SURREY, ARTHUR JOHN
Senior Fellow
Science Policy Research Unit
University of Sussex
Falmer, Brighton
Sussex, England

Born: 1933, London, England

Telephone: 0273 686758

Profession: Economist; policy analyst

Field of specialization: Energy economics and policy, national and international.

Education: Honours, B.Sc., Economics, London School of Economics, 1956.

Professional employment: Science Policy Research Unit, University of Sussex: Senior Fellow (1969-). House of Commons Select Committee on Science and Technology: Specialist Advisor (1974-). Department of Economic Affairs: Government Economic Adviser (1966-69). National Institute of Economic and Social Research: Research Fellow (1964-66). Central Electricity Generating Board: Economist in Development Policy Branch (1961-64). British Railways: Management Trainee (1956-59); Economist (1959-61).

Professional activities: Specialist advisor to the Energy Resources Inquiry of the House of Commons Select committee on Science and Technology (1974-); leading Energy Research Programme at Science Policy Research Unit (1969-); consultant to various organizations.

Publications: In collaboration with P.L. Cook, *Energy Policy: Strategies for Uncertainty* (Martin Robertson, Ltd., 1977); *The World Market for Electric Power Equipment: Rationalization and Technical Change* (Science Policy Research Unit, 1972); "The Future Growth of Nuclear Power" (*Energy Policy*, two parts, September and December 1973); "Japan's Uncertain Energy Prospects: The Problems of Import Dependence" (*Energy Policy*, September 1974); co-author, "Energy R and D: A United Kingdom Perspective" (*Energy Policy*, September 1974).

354

SWAGER, WILLIAM LEON
Assistant Manager, Department of Metallurgy
Battelle-Columbus
505 King Avenue
Columbus, Ohio 43201, U.S.A.

Born: 1921, Ft. Wayne, Indiana, U.S.A.

Telephone: (614) 424-7567

Profession: Materials policy analyst

Field of specialization: Technological forecasting and assessment; qualitative relevance trees and other structuring methods; methodologies for policy analysis.

Education: B.S., Chemical Engineering, Purdue University, 1942.

Professional employment: Battelle Memorial Institute-Columbus: Assistant Manager, Department of Metallurgy (1974-); Research Marketing Analyst (1970-74); Manager, Technical Economics (1960-70); Manager, Management Research Division (1957-60); Manager, Operations Research Division (1953-57); Engineering Economic Division (1948-53). Allied Chemicals, General Chemical Division: Engineering and Administrative assignments (1943-48).

Professional activities: Currently conducting research on models for resource analysis based on the entire materials cycle, including energy and environmental wastes (1975-); Advisory Board, *Technological Forecasting and Social Change;* chairman, Group 5, Program Committee, Management, American Institute of Chemical Engineers (1970-75); chairman, Central Ohio Chapter, Society for the Advancement of Management.

Publications: "A Return to the Home Grown" in *Planning for Corporate Growth,* S. Singhui and S. Jain, eds. (Planning Executive Institute, 1974); "Technological Forecasting and Goal Setting" (IEEE 1973 Intercon Technical Papers, March 1973); "Strategic Planning I: The Roles of Technological Forecasting," "Strategic Planning II: Policy Options," "Strategic Planning III: Objectives and Program Options" *(Technological Forecasting and Social Change,* (1972).

SZALAI, ALEXANDER
Scientific Counselor
Group for Science Planning and Organization
Hungarian Academy of Sciences
Munnich Ferenc-utca 18
Budapest V, H-1051, Hungary

Born: 1912, Budapest, Hungary

Telephone: 318-385, 123-022

Profession: Sociologist

Field of specialization: Sociology and application of mathematical methods in the social sciences; futures research; impact of scientific and technological development on society; communications research; methodology of cross-national comparative social research.

Education: Dr. Phil., Philosophy and Psychopathology, University of Zurich, 1934; Doctorate in Philosophical Sciences and Academy Membership, Hungarian Academy of Sciences, 1948.

Professional employment: Hungarian Academy of Sciences, Research Group on Science Organization: Scientific Counselor (1972-). Karl Marx University of Economic Sciences: Professor of Sociology (1972-). United Nations Institute for Training and Research: Deputy Directory of Research (1966-72). Philosophical Faculty, Roland Eotvos University: Professor of Sociology and Director of the Sociological Institute (1946-56).

Professional Activities: Honorary Special Fellow of the United Nations Institute for Training and Research (1972-); member, Standing Committee on Comparative Research, International Social Science Council (1966-); member of the Council, International Sociological Association (1964-); consultant to the Hungarian National Technological Development Board (1963); Director of the Multi-National Comparative Time-Budget Research Project, Vienna Centre of the International Social Science Council (1964-72).

Publications: *Media Abundance and the Future of Mass Communications* (International Media Congress, Neustift, September 1978); "Prognostic Analysis of Complex Social Effects of New Technologies" *(Problems of the Science of Science, Polish Quarterly,* 5th Special Issue, 1977); *Changes in the Valuation of Human Life and of*

Human Life Stages (6th International Conference, ICUS, San Francisco, November 1977); "Forecasting in the United Nations" in *The United Nations and the Future* (U.N. Institute for Training and Research, New York, 1977).

TAIT, JANICE JOHNSON

Born: 1929, Brantford, Ontario, Canada

Senior Policy Analyst
Surface Administration
Transport Canada
Tower C, Place de Ville
Ottawa, Ontario K1A ON5 Canada

Telephone: (613) 996-4180

Profession: Futures Research

Field of specialization: Conceptual and morphological analysis; futures methodology and public education; developing networks.

Education: B.A., Honors, Philosophy and History, University of Toronto, 1951; Certificat, French, Universite de Geneve, 1962; Diploma, Philosophy and Psychology, University of London, 1971.

Professional employment: Transport Canada, Surface Administration: Senior Policy Analyst (1978-). Government of Canada, Privy Council Office: Study Team on Quebec/Ottawa Relations (1977-78). Transportation Department Agency: Chief, Futures Research (1976-77). Department of Environment: Policy Analyst (1975-76); Senior Advisor, Advanced Concepts Center (1973-75). Teacher for eight years— History, English, French, Future Studies.

Professional activities: Member, Board of Association for Canadian Future Studies; recently completed a study on the automobile system in Canada, *The Car Affair*; active in futures group in Ottawa; Chairperson, Montreal Association for Future Studies.

Publications: *Some Ways of Thinking about the Future* (Department of Environment, June 1974); *Future Studies—A New Growth Industry* (Survey, Department of the Environment, June 1974); *Non-Renewable Resources—What Alternatives?* (Department of Environment, August 1974); "Cities Fit to Live In" (*Optimum*, January 1976); co-author, *Fourth Quarter Century Trends* (Department of Environment Document, 1976).

TANNER, W. LYNN

Born: 1938, Provo, Utah, U.S.A.

The University of Calgary
Calgary, Canada T2N 1N4

Telephone: (403) 284-5685

Profession: Public administration

Field of specialization: Organizational psychology and technology assessment (values and cultural shifts and the potential impact of technological change and their development on society); management team building and organizational development; cultural myths and verbal blindness (early warning systems); changing sex roles and their impact on modern society.

Education: B.A., Political Science and Economic Finance, 1964, M.P.A., Public Administration and Finance, 1966, Brigham Young University; Ph.D., Public Administration and Organization Development, Syracuse University, Maxwell School, 1975.

Professional employment: Faculty of Management, The University of Calgary: Associate Professor (1977-). Florida International University: Coordinator, Public Administration Program (1972-77). Syracuse University: NDEA Fellow, Maxwell School (1969-72). Pan American World Airways: Senior Financial Analyst (1968-69); Manager, Customer Operations, Nairobi, Kenya (1967-68).

Professional activities: Currently working on learning theory and the role of national myths in formal organizations; developing theory constructs for management planning in complex technological societies; developed graduate courses on technology and values in modern society at Florida International University (1973-76); conducted early warning systems seminars for The World Future Society and others; has lectured and written on the future of management, values, and technological change, changing male/female sex roles and their impact on organizational structures; developed courses and seminars on life career assessment and planning in modern society; organization development editor, *Planning Review*; editorial board of newsletter, *Business Tomorrow*.

Publications: Co-author, "Early Warning Signals: Management and the Scrutable Future" *(Managers' Forum,* **AMA,** February 1977); co-author, *Mismanaging Change with Safe Decisions and Used-Up Ideas* (American Management Association, Summer 1977); co-author, "Organization Development at the Grass Roots: First Line Management Team Building in a Public Housing Project" in *Organization Development in Public Administration* (Marcel Dekker, New York, 1978); co-author, "The Positive Consciousness Process: A Tool for Planners" *(Planning Review,* September 1978); co-author, *Adapting and Testing Business Management Programs for Educational Administration* (American Educational Research Association Clearinghouse, 1972); co-author, *Evaluation for Center of Planning and Development of the American Management Association* (U.S. Office of Education, 1971); co-author, "Process Is More Important than Product or Throw Out the Plan and Keep the Planner" *(Planning Review,* July 1975).

TARTER, DONALD EDWARD
Associate Professor
Department of Sociology
University of Alabama at Huntsville
Huntsville, Alabama 35807, U.S.A.

Born: 1938, Murfreesboro, Tennessee, U.S.A.

Telephone: (205) 895-6190

Profession: Sociologist

Field of specialization: Technology assessment (space technology as a major focus); behavior technology.

Education: B.S., Sociology, Middle Tennessee State University, 1960; Ph.D., Sociology, University of Tennessee, 1966.

Professional employment: University of Alabama in Huntsville: Assistant Professor and Associate Professor (1966-); Chairman, Department of Sociology (1968-74). Middle Tennessee University: Instructor (1964-66).

Professional activities: Teaching courses in futuristics and space and society; serving on Aerospace and Society National Technical Committee, American Institute of Aeronautics and Astronautics; serving as an organizer for conferences on and about futuristic issues; coordinator for two Congressional Seminars on the future of space technology sponsored by the Committee for the Future.

Publications: "Heeding Skinner's Call: Toward the Development of a Social Technology" *(The American Sociologist,* November 1973); "Toward Prediction of Attitude-Action Discrepancy" *(Social Forces,* July 1969); "Attitude: The Mental Myth" *(The American Sociologist,* August 1970); "Pragmatic Sociology: Sociology and the Behavior Modification Movement" *(Louisiana State University Journal of Sociology,* March 1971); "Group Incentive Techniques in Undergraduate Teaching" *(Change* Magazine, Special Report on Teaching Undergraduate Sociology, July 1977).

TAYLOR, GORDON RATTRAY
c/o Coutts and Company
10 Mount Street
London W1, England

Born: 1911, Eastbourne, United Kingdom

Telephone: Author

Profession: Author

Field of specialization: Understanding social change.

Education: Radley College; Trinity College, Cambridge.

Professional employment: Full-time author (1966-). *Horizon:* Editor (1964-66). British Broadcasting Corporation: Writer and Creator of science TV programs (1958-66); Chief Science Advisor (1963-66).

Professional activities: Editorial consultant, *Discovery* (1963-65), *Science Journal* (1965-68); devised British pavilion display for Turin Fair (1961); adivsor, Triumphs of British Genius exhibition; lecture tours in U.S.; Founder and Past-President, International Science Writers Association; contributor to numerous journals and periodicals including *Encounter, The Observer* and *Futures.*

Publications: The Biological Time Bomb (New American Library, 1968); *The Doomsday Book* (New American Library, 1970); *Rethink: A Paraprimitive Solution* (Secker and Warburg, London, 1972; E.P. Dutton, 1973); *How to Avoid the Future* (Secker and Warburg, London, 1975); *A Salute to British Genius* (Secker and Warburg, London, 1977).

TAYLOR, HAROLD

Born: 1914, Toronto, Ontario, Canada

Director
Center for International Service
The College of Staten Island
130 Stuyvesant Place
Staten Island, New York, 10301, U.S.A.

Telephone: (212) 390-7856

Profession: Educator; writer

Field of specialization: International education; transfer of technology

Education: B.A., 1935, M.A., 1936, Philosophy, University of Toronto; Ph.D., Philosophy, University of London, England, 1938.

Professional employment: Visiting lecturer in colleges and universities in the U.S. and abroad (1959-79). Sarah Lawrence College: President (1945-59). University of Wisconsin: Member, Department of Philosophy (1939-45).

Professional activities: The College of Staten Island, City University of New York, Distinguished Professor of Social Sciences (1975-79); development of a technology curriculum for foreign students; research study on education of teachers; director of a pilot project for a world college (1963); member of various boards, including the Institute for World Order, New York Studio School, College for Human Services and the League for Industrial Democracy.

Publications: *Students Without Teachers* (McGraw-Hill, 1969); *The World as Teacher* (Doubleday, 1969); *How to Change Colleges* (Holt Rinehart Winston, 1971); *On Education and Freedom* (University of Southern Illinois Press, 1967); *Art and the Intellect* (Doubleday, 1966); editor, *The Idea of a World University* (University of Southern Illinois Press, 1967).

TAYLOR, THEODORE B.

Born: 1925, Mexico City, Mexico

Mechanical and Aerospace Engineering Department
Princeton University
Princeton, New Jersey 08540, U.S.A.

Telephone: (609) 452-5146

Profession: Physicist

Field of specialization: Nuclear power risks and safeguards; space technology; solar energy systems; technology assessment; futures methodology.

Education: B.S., Physics, California Institute of Technology, 1945; Physics, University of California-Berkeley, 1946-49; Ph.D., Theoretical Physics, Cornell University, 1954.

Professional employment: Princeton University: Visiting Lecturer (1976-). International Research and Technology Corporation: Chairman of the Board (1967-76). Defense Atomic Support Agency: Deputy Director—Scientific (1964-66). General Atomic: Senior Research Advisor (1956-64). Los Alamos Scientific Laboratory: Staff Member (1949-56). Radiation Laboratory, University of California: Research Assistant (1946-49).

Professional activities: Assessment of worldwide use of solar energy, as consultant to the Rockefeller Foundation (1977-78); assessment of solar energy use in the United States, Ford Foundation/Princeton University (1977-78); undergraduate courses at Princeton University on nuclear energy, comparisons of alternative energy sources, and solar energy (1976-78); voluntary speaker for U.S. Information Service in India, Indonesia, Singapore, Malaysia, and Thailand, lecturing on future energy alternatives, solar energy, and technology assessment (1977-78); member of the Ford Foundation/Resources for the Future Study Group on Energy: The Next Twenty Years (1978); survey of uses of biomass in the less developed countries, as a consultant to the U.S. Office of Technology Assessment (1978); Technical Director, "Project Orion for Propulsion of Large Space Vehicles by Nuclear Explosions" (1957-64); design of fission weapons (1949-56); one of recipients of the Atomic Energy Commission's Ernest O. Lawrence Memorial Award for work on design of nuclear weapons and Triga Research Reactor (1965).

Publications: *An Assessment of Solar Energy Technology for Worldwide Use* (Report for the Rockefeller Foundation, February 1979); "The Ultimate Source: The Case for Solar Energy" (*Skeptic Magazine*, March/April 1977); co-author, *Nuclear Proliferation* (McGraw-Hill, 1977); co-author with M. Willrich, *Nuclear Theft: Risks and Safeguards* (Ballanger, 1974); co-author with C. Humpstone, *The Restoration of the Earth* (Harper and Row, 1973); "Strategies for the Future" (*Saturday Review/World*, December 1974); "Nuclear Safeguards" (*Annual Review of Nuclear Science*, 1975); "Propulsion of Space Vehicles" (*Perspectives in Modern Physics*, Interscience, 1966).

TEBICKE, HAILE LUL
Born: 1933

Commissioner
Ethiopian Science and Technology Commission (ESTC)
P.O. Box 2490
Addis Ababa, Ethiopia

Telephone: 11 62 41

Profession: Electrical engineer

Field of specialization: Technology assessment; generation of environmentally sound, socio-economically appropriate technology in Ethiopia.

Education: B.Sc., Power Engineering, Manchester University, 1955; M.Sc.D.I.C., Electrical Power Systems, Imperial College of Science and Technology, 1969.

Professional employment: ESTC: Commissioner (1975-). Addis Ababa University: Assistant Professor (1969-75). Ethiopian Electric Light and Power Authority, Power Plant Division: Head (1958-67). Brown, Boveri and Co., Switzerland: Apprentice Engineer (1955-57).

Professional activities: Chairman, National Science and Technology Council (1975-); Commissioner, Ethiopian Science and Technology Commission (1975-); President, Ethiopian Association-of Engineers and Architects (1970-71); member, World Future Society (1968-).

Publications: —

TEIGE, PETER J.
Born: 1947, Cambridge, Massachusetts, U.S.A.

Research Analyst
SRI International
Center for the Study of Social Policy
333 Ravenswood Avenue
Menlo Park, California 95112, U.S.A.

Telephone: (415) 326-6200

Profession: Futures research analyst

Field of specialization: Futures research; values and lifestyles; general systems; appropriate technology; consciousness research.

Education: B.A., Distributed Studies, University of Colorado, 1971; M.S. (candidate), Cybernetic Systems, San Jose State University.

Professional employment: Center for the Study of Social Policy: Research Analyst (1975-).

Professional activities: California Energy Futures Study (1978); Future Canadian Social Issues (1978); Emerging National Issues (1977-78); Transportation in America's Future—The Next 50 Years (1976); Future National and International Problem Areas (1977); Potential Use and Changes in the Automobile System in America (1977).

Publications: Co-author, "The Problem of Critical Problem Selection" in *Futures Research: New Directions,* Linstone and Simmonds, eds. (Addison-Wesley, 1977); co-author, "In Search of Tommorrow's Crises" (THE FUTURIST, October 1977).

TEXTOR, ROBERT BAYARD
Born: 1923, Cloquet, Minnesota, U.S.A.

Professor
School of Education and
Department of Anthropology
Stanford University
Stanford, California 94305, U.S.A.

Telephone: (415) 497-3008

Profession: Anthropologist; educator

Field of specialization: Cultural and ethnographic futures research; Southeast Asian national and regional futures; Third World futures; futures education; theories of sociocultural change; theories of development.

Education: A.B., Asian Studies, University of Michigan, 1945; Ph.D., Cultural Anthropology, Cornell University, 1960.

Professional employment: Stanford University: Professor, Education and Anthropology (1964-); Associate Professor (1964-68). Harvard University: Resident Fellow in Statistics (1962-64). Peace Corps, Washington, D.C.: Consultant on Training and Programs (1961-62). Yale University: Resident Fellow and Associate in Southeast Asian Studies (1959-61).

Professional activities: Ethnographic futures research concerning national and regional futures for Thailand, Malaysia, Singapore, Indonesia, Philippines (1977-); teaching courses in Cultural Approaches to Alternative Futures, Ethnographic Futures Research, and Education and Sociocultural Change; President, Council on Anthropology and Education (1974-75); research on development, cultural change, education, and religion — Thailand, Malaysia, Indonesia (1952-); Civilian Education Official, Allied Occupation of Japan (1946-48); currently collaborating with President Francis L.K. Hsu of the American Anthropological Association in the production of an anthology on new paradigms (including futures-oriented ones) in sociocultural anthropology with publication expected in 1980.

Publications: "Cultural Futures for Thailand: An Ethnographic Inquiry" (*Futures*, October 1978); *A Guide to Ethnographic Futures Research* (forthcoming in 1979); "Ethnographic Futuristics and the Anticipation of Culture Conflict in Asia" (Japanese Association for Asian Studies, Proceedings of Tokyo Conference, February 1978); "Ethnographic Futuristics and the Future of Southeast Asian Studies" (Proceedings of the Conference on Southeast Asian Studies, Kota Kinabalu, Malaysia, November 1977) (to be published by the University Malaya Press); co-author, *A Cross-Polity Survey* (MIT Press, 1963).

THAPAR, ROMESH

Born: 1922

Editor and Publisher
Seminar, The Monthly Symposium
Post Box 338
New Delhi, India

Telephone: 46534

Profession: Writer and commentator; policy analyst

Field of specialization: Political and economic development; value systems; alternative societies.

Education: B.A. (Hons.), Punjab University, 1942.

Professional employment: *Seminar*, The Monthly Symposium: Editor and Publisher. Active in journalism for some 25 years.

Professional activities: Vice-President, World Future Studies Federation (1976-); member of the Nehru Memorial Museum and Library (1966-76); member Executive Board of the Indian National Commission for Cooperation with UNESCO (1967); member of the Indian delegation to the UNESCO General Conference in 1966 and 1972; former Chairman of the National Book Development Board and Director of the National Book Trust; has had a close association with the theater, with filmmaking and broadcasting; helped with the reorganization of the infrastructure of tourism in the country as Chairman of the nationally owned India Tourism Development Corporation (1967-70); Director of the India International Centre, New Delhi, for six years; Chairman of the Committee on National Awards for Films and the Committee for Excellence in Printing and Designing; sponsor of UNESCO's "Design for Living" project; member of The Club of Rome and active in the debate on the problems of the future since 1965.

Publications: Editor and publisher, *Seminar*, The Monthly Symposium; *India in Transition* (Current Book House, Bombay); *The Indian Dimension* (Vikas, New Delhi, 1977); *The Waste and the Want* (Orient Loncemans, Delhi, 1978).

THEOBALD, ROBERT

Born: 1929, Madras, India

Participation Publishers
Box 2240
Wickenburg, Arizona 85358, U.S.A.

Telephone: (602) 684-7861

Profession: Generalist

Field of specialization: Creating ways in which people can invent myths, images, paradigms which will make life worth living in the future as we move from the industrial era to the communications era.

360

Education: M.A., Economics, Cambridge, England, 1952; Public Policy, Harvard University, 1957-58.

Professional employment: Self-employed: President, own company (1959-). O.E.E.C.: Administrator (1953-57).

Professional activities: Creative linkage system to bring together those who believe we are passing through a transformation period; currently consulting, speaking, and writing; specific concerns have been with resource distribution, citizen participation, new styles of information movement, and education.

Publications: *Beyond Despair* (New Republic, 1976); *An Alternative Future for America's Third Century* (Swallow, 1976); editor, *Futures Conditional* (Bobbs-Merrill, 1970); co-editor, *The Failure of Success* (Bobbs-Merrill, 1972); editor, *The Guaranteed Income* (Doubleday, 1966).

THIEMANN, HUGO ERNST
Nestle S.A.
Avenue Vevey
1800 Vevey, Switzerland

Born: 1917, St. Gallen, Switzerland

Telephone: (021) 51 01 12

Profession: Member of management committee, counsellor

Field of specialization: Futures studies and long-range planning.

Education: Diploma in Electrical Engineering, 1939, Dr. es. sc. tech., 1947, Ecole Polytechnique Federale, Zurich; Dr. es. sc. honoris causa, University of Geneva, 1965.

Professional employment: Member of the Swiss Science Council (1978-). Nestle Alimentana S.A.: Counselor to Top Management (1974-). Battelle Institute, Geneva: Director General (1954-74); Head, Applied Physics and Engineering Division (1953-54). Dr. E. Gretener S.A.: Head, Television Group—EIDOPHOR (1951-53). Institute of Applied Physics, EPF-Zurich: Assistant to Director, then Section Leader (1940-51).

Professional activities: Currently acting as counsellor to the top management of Nestle Alimentana in questions of long-range planning and in charge of prospective studies (1974-); member of the Executive Committee of The Club of Rome (1968-); Fellow of The Institute of Electrical and Electronics Engineers (1972-); has specialized in various fields of applied physics, optics and television.

Publications: "Neue Ziele fur die Industriegesellschaft," ["New Goals for Industrial Society"] an address on the occasion of awarding the Sandoz Prize, (Schweiz. Handelskammer in Oesterreich—Offizieller Monatsbericht, Wein, 1978); "The Mission of the Food Industry," lecture presented at the 7th European Food Symposium, Holland, 1977, (*Lebensm.-Wiss.u.-Technol.* 11, 1978); "Science: A Consequence of Science Policy or an Expression of Civilization?" (ASP, Amsterdam, 1972); "Nouvelles Contraintes pour les Technologies d'Avenir" ["New Constraints for Future Technologies"] (Polyrama, No. 11, December 1972); "New Frontiers for Research and Development" (Proc. Roy. Instn., Great Britain, 44, No. 204, 1971).

THOMPSON, FRED G.
Privy Council Office
Langevin Block
Ottawa, Ontario, Canada K1A 0A3

Born: 1914, Toronto, Ontario, Canada

Telephone: (613) 593-4846

Profession: Engineer

Field of specialization: Futures methodology; technological forecasting; long-range planning; industrial engineering.

Education: B.A. Sc., Engineering, University of Toronto, 1937.

Professional employment: Privy Council Office: Futures and Special Projects (1978-). Canada Post Office: Assistant to the Director, Systems Research and Development (1974-). Economic Council of Canada: Project Research (1963-74). Stevenson and Kellogg, Ltd.: Management Consulting (1960-63, 1951-57).

Professional activities: Past President of Canadian Association for Futures Studies (1977-78); advisor on futures and strategic planning for Post Office operations (1974-76); project on quality of working life (1974-76); currently coordinator, Ottawa Futures Society; has conducted several seminars on futures (1974-76);

survey of futures activities in Canadian business and government (1972); survey of long-range planning and manpower planning procedures in Canadian business (1971).

Publications: Co-author, *Meeting Managerial Manpower Needs* (Economic Council of Canada, Ottawa, 1971); co-author, *Long Term Forecasting in Private and Public Organizations in Canada* (Economic Council of Canada, 1972); *Saskatchewan Seminar on Futures Forecasting* (Canadian Plains Research Center, Regina, Saskatchewan, 1974).

THOMPSON, GORDON BRUCE

Born: 1925, Toronto, Ontario, Canada

Communication Engineer
Bell Northern Research
P.O. Box 3511, Station C
Ottawa, Ontario
K1Y 4H7 Canada

Telephone: (613) 596-6282

Profession: Engineer

Field of specialization: Interaction between information technology and socio-economic systems.

Education: BASc., Engineering Physics, University of Toronto, 1947.

Professional employment: Bell Northern Research: Communication Studies (1963-). Northern Electric: Supervisor, Audio and Video Product and System Design (1955-63); Development Engineer (1947-54).

Professional activities: Director, Gordon V. Thompson Ltd., music publishers; Governor, International Council on Computer Communication; member, Association of Professional Engineers of Ontario; member, Canadian Association for Futures Studies and the World Future Society; Editorial Board, *Data Networks* (published by North Holland); Committee on Social Implications of Technology, IEEE Communications Society.

Publications: "The Information Society, Where Consumerism and Cottage Industry Meet" (*Canadian Journal of Information Science*, Spring 1976); "An Analysis of Some Factors Affecting the Evolution of an Information Society" (Third International Conference on Computer Communications, Toronto, August 1976 and International Council on Computer Communications, Washington, D.C.); "Electronic Funds Transfer Systems and Responsive Mass Media" (Proceedings of the 1976 National Telecommunications Conference, 1976, Vol. II, published by IEEE, New York); "Towards a Clever Data Network" (*Computer Networks*, September 1976, North Holland Publishing Company); "The World Turned Upside Down" (*Telecommunications Policy*, March 1977, IPC Science and Technology Press Ltd.).

THOMPSON, WILLIAM IRWIN

Born: 1938, Chicago, Illinois, U.S.A.

Chairman
Board of Directors
The Lindisfarne Association
47 W. 20th Street
New York, New York 10011, U.S.A.

Telephone: (516) 283-8210

Profession: Educator

Field of specialization: Cultural history.

Education: B.A., Philosophy, Pomona College, 1962; M.A., 1964, Ph.D., 1966, Cornell University.

Professional employment: The Lindisfarne Association: Chairman, Board of Directors (1973-). Syracuse University: Visiting Professor of Religion (1973). York University: Professor of Humanities (1972-73); Associate Professor (1968-72). Massachusetts Institute of Technology: Associate Professor of Humanities (1968); Instructor (1965-66).

Professional activities: Founding Director, Lindisfarne Association (1973); member, Foundation for Integration Education, New York; Fellow, Society for Arts, Religion, and Contemporary Culture; Colleague, The Cathedral Church of St. John the Divine, New York City.

Publications: *Darkness and Scattered Light: Four Talks on the Future* (Doubleday 1978); *Evil and World Order* (Harper and Row, 1976); *Passages About Earth: An Exploration of the New Planetary Culture* (Harper and Row, 1974); *At the Edge of History* (Harper and Row, 1971); *The Imagination of an Insurrec-*

362

tion: *Dublin, Easter, 1916* (Oxford University Press, 1967); "Lindisfarne: A Planetary Community" (THE FUTURIST, February 1975).

THOMSON, IRENE TAVISS
Associate Professor of Sociology
Farleigh Dickinson University
Madison, New Jersey 07922, U.S.A.

Born: 1941, New York, New York, U.S.A.

Telephone: (201) 377-4700 ext. 378

Profession: Sociologist

Field of specialization: Technology and society, individual and society, value change.

Education: B.A., Sociology, Brooklyn College, 1962; Ph.D., Sociology, Harvard University, 1967.

Professional employment: Farleigh Dickinson University: Associate Professor (1977-); Assistant Professor (1975-77); American Academy of Arts and Sciences: Executive Associate (1974-75). Harvard University: Lecturer, Sociology (1972-74); Research Associate, Program on Technology and Society (1966-72).

Professional activities: Teaching course on technology and society at Fairleigh Dickinson University (Spring 1976); Organizer, American Sociological Association Session on Social Consequences of Science and Technology (Summer 1976); consulting with Harvard University's Program on Information Technologies and Public Policy (1974-76).

Publications: *Our Tool-Making Society* (Prentice-Hall, 1972); editor, *The Computer Impact* (Prentice-Hall, 1970); co-editor, with Everett Mendelsohn and Judith Swazey, *Human Aspects of Biomedical Innovation* (Harvard University Press, 1971); "Futurology and the Problem of Values" (*International Social Science Journal*, December 1969); "Changes in the Form of Alienation" (*American Sociological Review*, February 1969).

THRING, MEREDITH WOOLDRIDGE
Head
Department of Mechanical Engineering
Queen Mary College
London University
Mile End Road
London E1 4NS, England

Born: 1915, Melbourne, Australia

Telephone: (01) 980-4811

Profession: Professor and engineering prophet

Field of specialization: Engineering ethical innovation.

Education: B.A., Physics, 1937, Sc.D., Engineering, 1964, Cambridge University.

Professional employment: Queen Mary College: Head of Mechanical Engineering Department (1964-). Sheffield University: Head of Department of Fuel Technology and Chemical Engineering (1953-64). British Iron and Steel Research Association: Head of Physics Department and Assistant Director (1946-53). British Coal Utilization Research Association: Combustion Research (1937-46).

Professional activities: Sceptology (1964-); research on telchiric mining (1970-), low energy farming, low energy ship propulsion and low energy drying; President, Institute of Fuel (1962-63); work on continuous steel making (1960-70); currently writing a book on the future of civilization, to be called "The Engineer Conscience."

Publications: *Man, Machines and Tomorrow* (Routledge and Kegan Paul Ltd., 1973); *Machines: Masters or Slaves of Man?* (Peter Peregrinus, Ltd., 1973); co-author, *How to Invent* (Macmillan, 1976); co-editor, *Energy and Humanity* (Peter Peregrinus Ltd., 1974); *The Science of Flames and Furnaces*, second edition (Chapman Hall, 1962).

TINBERGEN, JAN
University of Rotterdam
Burgemeester Oudlaan 50
Rotterdam 3016
The Netherlands

Born: 1903, The Hague, The Netherlands

Telephone: (010) 145511

Profession: Emeritus Professor

Field of specialization: Income redistribution.

Education: Dr. of Physics, Mathematics and Natural Science, University of Leiden.

Professional employment: University of Leiden: Professor (1973-75). University of Rotterdam: Professor (1933-73). Netherlands Central Planning Bureau: Director (1945-55).

Professional activities: At present conducting private scientific research; Coordinator, Project RIO (Reviewing the International Order), Report to The Club of Rome (1974-76).

Publications: *Business Cycles in the U.S.A.* (League of Nations, 1939, Agathon Press, New York 1968); *Economic Policy: Principles and Design* (North Holland, 1956, American Elsevier, 1967); *Lessons from the Past* (Elsevier, 1963); *Shaping the World Economy* (Twentieth Century Fund, 1962); *Income Distribution* (North Holland, American Elsevier, 1975).

TOFFLER, ALVIN

Bantam Books, 666 Fifth Avenue
New York, New York 10019, U.S.A.

Born: 1928, New York, New York, U.S.A.

Telephone: (212) 765-6500

Profession: Author

Field of specialization: Social change.

Education: B.A., English, New York University, 1949; several honorary degrees.

Professional employment: *Fortune* Magazine: Associate Editor (1959-61).

Professional activities: Principal organizer of the Committee on Anticipatory Democracy (1975-); plenary session speaker at the Second General Assembly of the World Future Society (June 1975); consultant to Rockefeller Brothers Fund, Institute for the Future, A.T. & T., System Development Corporation, Education Facilities Laboratories, Inc., and other companies, foundations, and organizations; frequent contributor to various periodicals; Visiting Professor, Cornell University (1969); Visiting Scholar, Russell Sage Foundation (1969-70); Board of Trustees, Antioch University; Board of Advisors, Center for Governmental Responsibility; International Committee, Futuribles; International Committee, Nevis Institute; Contributing Editor, *Futurics;* Contributing Editor, *Art News.* In a 1965 article entitled, "The Future as a Way of Life" (*Horizon,* Summer 1965), Toffler coined the term "future shock," which he defined as "the shattering stress and disorientation that we induce in individuals by subjecting them to too much change in too short a time."

Publications: *The Eco-Spasm Report* (Bantam Books, Inc., 1975); editor, *Learning for Tomorrow* (Random House, 1973); editor, *The Futurists* (Random House, 1972); *Future Shock* (Bantam Books, 1971); editor, *The Schoolhouse in the City* (Praeger, 1968); *The Culture Consumers* (St. Martin's Press, 1965; Literary Guild Selection, 1965; Penguin Books, 1965, Random House, 1972).

TONCHEV, LIUBEN ALEXIEV

Academy for Social Sciences and Management
21 Pionerski Pat St.
Sofia, Bulgaria

Born: 1925, Svoghe, Bulgaria

Telephone: 5 68 11 ext. 279

Profession: Political scientist

Field of specialization: Futures methodology and management

Education: Economist, Foreign Trade Department, Institute of Economics, Karl Marx University, 1952.

Professional employment: Academy for Social Sciences and Management: Associate Professor, Theory of Management and Operation Research (1974-); Head, Section for Social Forecasting (1970-74).

Professional activities: Improvement of management cycle and forecasting; chairman, Science and Methodology Council, "Georgi Kirkov" Society; currently lecturing on theory of management for graduate and postgraduate courses at the Academy and carrying out research work on the problems of the nature, laws, principles and technology of social economic forecasting.

Publications: *Operation Research* (Sofia, 1969); *Cybernetics: Theoretical Basis of Automation* (Sofia, 1972); *Forecasting of the Social Processes* (Sofia, 1971); *Problems of Forecasting in Bulgaria* (Sofia, 1974);

Foundations of the Socialist Way of Life (Sofia, 1977); *Problems of the Theory of Management* (Sofia, 1972); *Social Forecasting* (Sofia, 1977); *Foundations of the Operation Research* (Sofia, 1978); *Futurism, Futurology, Deideologisation and Some Previsions About Management in the Communist Society* (Sofia, 1976).

TUGWELL, FRANKLIN

Born: 1942, San Juan, Puerto Rico

Associate Professor
Department of Government
Pomona College and Claremont Graduate School
Carnegie Hall
Claremont, California 91711, U.S.A.

Telephone: (714) 626-8511

Profession: Political scientist; policy analyst

Field of specialization: Political futures; international oil; private sector/state relations; Latin America.

Education: B.A., Government, Columbia College, 1963; M.A., Government, 1964, Ph.D., Political Science, 1969, Columbia University.

Professional employment: Pomona College: Associate Professor (1968-).

Professional activities: Currently teaching, consulting (mainly on energy policy matters), and writing; teaches a course on the study of the future (1969-).

Publications: Editor, *Search for Alternatives: Public Policy and the Study of the Future* (Winthrop, 1973); *The Politics of Oil in Venezuela* (Stanford University Press, 1975).

TUROFF, MURRAY

Born: 1936, San Francisco, California, U.S.A.

Professor
New Jersey Institute of Technology
323 High Street
Newark, New Jersey 07102, U.S.A.

Telephone: (201) 645-5352

Profession: Computer and information science

Field of specialization: Delphi; computerized conferencing; futures methodology; information systems.

Education: B.A., Math-Physics, University of California-Berkeley, 1958; Ph.D., Physics, Brandeis, 1965.

Professional employment: New Jersey Institute of Technology: Professor (1972-). Office of Emergency Preparedness: Senior Operations Research Analyst (1968-73). Institute for Defense Analyses: Research Scientist (1964-68). International Business Machines: Systems Engineer (1960-64).

Professional activities: Computerized Conferencing and Communications Center, New Jersey Institute of Technology: Director; consultant to various public and private organizations on computerized conferencing, Delphi design, corporate planning, cross impact, management of information systems, design of interactive systems, technological forecasting and assessment; originated the "Policy Delphi Technique," which is an extension of the Delphi method for use in policy and decision analyses.

Publications: Co-author, *The Network Nation* (Addison Wesley, 1978); "The EIES Experience" (Bulletin of ASIS, June 1978); co-author, *The Delphi Method: Techniques and Applications* (Addison Wesley, 1975); "Technological Forecasting and Assessment: Science and/or Mythology?" (*Journal of Technological Forecasting and Social Change*, Vol. 5, 1973); "The Future of Computerized Conferencing" (THE FUTURIST, August 1975).

UMPLEBY, STUART A.

Born: 1944, Tulsa, Oklahoma, U.S.A.

Assistant Professor
School of Government and Business Administration
George Washington University
Washington, D.C. 20052, U.S.A.

Telephone: (202) 676-7530

Profession: System scientist

Field of specialization: General systems theory; cybernetics; computer conferencing; development strategies; citizen participation.

Education: B.S., Mechanical Engineering, 1967, A.B., 1967, A.M., 1969, Political Science, Ph.D., Communications, 1975, University of Illinois at Urbana.

Professional employment: George Washington University: Assistant Professor of Management Science (1975-). University of Illinois: Res. Assistant in Communications (1970-75); Instructor of Political Science (1968-70). Institute for the Future: Research Associate (summer, 1970). Westinghouse Electric: Engineer (summer, 1966).

Professional activities: Moderator of a National Science Foundation supported computer conference among general systems theorists (1977-79); consultant to the Institute of Cultural Affairs (1976-); Steering Committee, Washington, D.C. Chapter of the World Future Society (1977-); coordinator of the annual meeting of the Society for General Systems Research (1977); Director, Alternative Futures Project, University of Illinois (1970-75).

Publications: "Is Greater Citizen Participation in Planning Possible and Desirable?" (*Technological Forecasting and Social Change,* 1972); "Second Order Cybernetics and the Design of Large Scale Social Experiments" (Conference Proceedings, Society for General Systems Research, 1975); "Information Theory and Consumer Action" (*Business and Society Review,* 1972); "Citizen Sampling Simulations: A Method for Involving the Public in Social Planning" (*Policy Sciences,* 1970); "Clandestine Techniques as Social Technology" (*Society,* 1973).

VACCA, ROBERTO
3, Via Oddone di Cluny
Rome, Italy

Born: 1927, Rome, Italy

Telephone: (06) 571264

Profession: Systems analyst

Field of specialization: Design of large technological systems; analysis of interaction between large (urban) systems in congested areas.

Education: Electrical Engineering, 1951, Libera docenza in Automation of Computation, 1960, Rome University.

Professional employment: Compagnia Generale Automazione: General Manager (1962-75). National Research Council of Italy: Research scientist, computers (1955-62). Various Italian industries: systems designer—power (1951-55).

Professional activities: Currently working as a consultant on systems aspects of human settlements, territorial planning, industrial development for various Italian regions and industries; also working on construction of a mathematical model of interactions among large systems in congested areas and consequent systems downgrading; has lectured and written on future of high technology societies; taught a course on electronic computers, Rome University (1960-66).

Publications: *The Coming Dark Age* (Doubleday and Company, 1973); *Manuale per un'improbabile salvezza [Handbook for an Improbable Salvation]* (Mondadori, Milan, Italy, 1974); "The Future of Urban Planning" (Appendix to Italian National Report to U.N. Habitat Conference on Human Settlements, Vancouver, Canada, 1976); "A Systems Approach to the Problem of Avoidance, Prevention and Resistance to Terrorism" (Symposium at Glassboro State College, New Jersey, on Terrorism in the Contemporary World, 1976).

VALASKAKIS, KIMON
Director, GAMMA
University of Montreal and McGill University
3535 Queen Mary, Suite 210
Montreal, Quebec, Canada

Born: 1941, Greece

Telephone: (514) 343-7020

Professions: Director of GAMMA and professor of economics.

Field of specialization: Conservation; information economy; international development (integrated approach); methodology.

Education: B.A., Economics/Philosophy, American University, Cairo; Law, Bachelier en Droit, Paris; Ph.D., Economics, Cornell University.

Professional employment: University of Montreal/McGill University: Director, GAMMA (1976-). University of Montreal: Associate Professor of Economics (1972-); Associate Director, Centre de Recherches en Dev. Econ. (1970-72).

Professional activities: Project Director, "Conserver Society Project," GAMMA Project for Federal Government of Canada; Associate Director, "Future Alternatives Quebec 1995," GAMMA Project for Quebec Government; in the process of publishing a book on the conserver society.

Publications: *La Societe de Conservation [The Conserver Society]* (Editions Quinze, Montreal, 1978; Harper and Row, New York, 1979); "Eclectics" *(Futures,* December 1975); "The Chronospace" *(Futures,* June 1976); "Prospective, Retrospective, Perspective" *(Actualite Economique,* June 1975); "Elements of an Interdisciplinary Future Studies Methodology" *(CIBA Foundation Symposium,* Elsevier-North Holland, 1975).

VALLEE, JACQUES F.
President
INFOMEDIA Corporation
430 Sherman Avenue
Palo Alto, California 94306, U.S.A.

Born: 1939, Pontoise, France

Telephone: (415) 321-2682

Profession: Computer scientist

Field of specialization: Teleconferencing; information systems; networking; UFO's; parapsychology.

Education: B.S., Mathematics, University of Paris, 1959; M.S., Astrophysics, University of Lille, 1961; Ph.D., Computer Science, Northwestern University, 1967.

Professional employment: INFOMEDIA Corporation: President (1976-). Institute for the Future: Senior Research Fellow (1972-76). Stanford Research Institute: Research Engineer (1971-72). Stanford University: Manager, Information Systems (1969-71).

Professional activities: Member, Association for Computing Machinery (1965-); member, Editorial Board, *Telecommunications Policy* (1976-); U.S. Delegate to ISO (International Vocabulary of Information Processing, 1969-71); Chairman, ISO working group on software terminology (1971); received the Jules Verne Prize for the best science-fiction novel in French for 1961.

Publications: Co-author, *Electronic Meetings* (Addison-Wesley, 1978); *Messengers of Deception* (And/Or Press, 1979); "The Forum Project" *(Computer Networks* Vol. 1, No. 1, 1976); "Network Conferencing" *(Datamation,* May 1974); *The Invisible College* (E. P. Dutton and Co., 1976).

VAN DAM, ANDRE
Director of Planning for Latin America
CPC International, Inc.
Cerrito 866
Buenos Aires, Argentina

Born: 1918, Rotterdam, The Netherlands

Telephone: 46-3555

Profession: Corporate planner; economist

Field of specialization: Long-range planning for the developing countries of Latin America, Africa, and Asia.

Education: Faculty of Economics, University of Geneva, Switzerland; also B.A. in French and similar degrees in English and Spanish.

Professional employment: CPC International, Inc.: Corporate Planner (1960-). With other agro-industrial transnational corporations in Western Europe and Latin America (1945-60).

Professional activities: Economic and socio-political forecasting and futures research into the development process of the Third World, and into the role of private enterprise therein; lectures on that topic in

North and South America and Europe; cooperates with numerous private and public international organizations.

Publications: Has published in 150 specialized journals, in eight languages and in 40 countries on the emerging North-South interdependency and its far-reaching ripple effect.

VAN HULTEN, MICHEL

Euro Action Sahel Acord
Prins Hendrikkade 48
Amsterdam, Netherlands

Born: 1930, Batavia, Indonesia

Telephone: (020) 24 43 66

Profession: Representative in Mali

Field of specialization: Urban planning; constraints; public policy.

Education: M.A., Social Geography, 1958, Ph.D., Philosophy, 1962, University of Amsterdam.

Professional employment: Euro Action Sahel Acord: Representative in Mali (1978-). Ministry of Transport and Public Works: Secretary of State (1973-77). Parliament-Second Chamber: Member (1972-73). Parliament First Chamber: Member (1971-72). Fondation Europenne de la Culture: Director of Urbanization Project, Plan Europe 2000 (1969-73). Rijksdienst Ysselmeerpolders (Zuyderzee Development Corporation): Head, Social-Economic Study Department (1965-69). University of Amsterdam: Research Assistant, Social Geographic Institution (1962-67). Provincial Council for Agriculture: Secretary (1961-62).

Professional activities: Organization of development activities and advisement on the future for a developing nation.

Publications: *De collectivisatie van de landbouw in de Volksrepubliek Polen, 1944-1960 [The Collectivization of Agriculture in the Polish People's Republic, 1944-1960]* (Ph.D. Thesis, University of Amsterdam, 1962); editor, *Urban Core and Inner City* (E. J. Brill, Leiden, 1967); editor, *Citizen and City in the Year 2000* (Kluwer, Deventer, 1971); *"Gratis" Openbaar Vervoer ["Free" Public Transport]* (Kluwer, Deventer, 1972).

VAN STEENBERGEN, BART

Department of Sociology
University of Utrecht
Heidelberglaan 2
Utrecht, The Netherlands

Born: 1940, The Hague, The Netherlands

Telephone: (30) 531973

Profession: Sociologist; futurist

Field of specialization: Design of future societies; global models, futures methodology; utopian thought.

Education: Ph.D., Sociology, University of Utrecht, 1967; Sociology, Temple University, Philadelphia, 1967-68.

Professional employment: Princeton University: Visiting Fellow (1979). University of Utrecht, Department of Sociology: Instructor (1971-). Werkgroep 2000: Secretary of Studies (1968-71).

Professional activities: Research projects on: "Scenarios" for the Netherlands Physical Planning Agency (1977-); "visions of desirable societies" for the World Future Studies Federation and the United Nations University (1978-); "changing consumption patterns" for the Netherlands Scientific Council for Government Policy (1977-78); "alternative society designs" (1978-79); and "the second wave of global models" (1977-78).

Publications: Co-author, *De Tweede Golf Wereldmodellen [The Second Wave of Global Models]* (in Dutch, Contact, Amsterdam, Spring 1979); editor and co-author, "De Toekomst van de Arbeid, Verslag van een Scenario Workshop" ["The Future of Work, Report of a Scenario Workshop"] in *Reports of Research Unit Planning and Policymaking* (1978); co-author, *Naar de Toekomst Leven [Living Towards the Future]* (in Dutch, Bosch and Keuning, Baarn, The Netherlands, 1978); "Voluntary Simplicity as a New Lifestyle" (*Alternatives*, Spring 1979).

VANSTON, JOHN H. JR.

Born: 1928, Sherman, Texas, U.S.A.

President
Technology Futures, Inc.
10 Red Bud Cove
Austin, Texas 78746, U.S.A.

Telephone: (512) 471-4049

Profession: Research engineer; educator

Field of specialization: Technology forecasting; technology assessment.

Education: B.S., General Engineering, U.S. Military Academy, 1950; M.S., 1960, N.E., 1963, Nuclear Engineering, Columbia University; Ph.D., Mechanical Engineering, University of Texas at Arlington, 1974.

Professional employment: Technology Futures, Inc.: President (1978-). University of Texas at Austin, Center for Energy Studies: Director, Division of Technology Forecasting and Assessment (1973-). University of Texas at Austin, Mechanical Engineering Department: Assistant Professor (1972-77). United States Army Special Weapons Test Program: Test Director (1967-70).

Professional activities: Manager, Department of Energy study on institutional/legal considerations in the development of geopressured geothermal energy sources (June 1978-June 1979); Manager, Exxon Corporation sponsored study of effects of energy facility delays (September 1977-September 1978); conduct industrial and university courses in Technology Forecasting and Assessment (1972-); consulted with organizations including National Bureau of Standards, Pan Handle-Eastern Pipeline, Technical Association of Pulp and Paper Industry, and the Austrailian National Government (1972-); developed technique for computer forecasting of large scale, high technology development (Partitive Analytical Forecasting) (1972-76); assisted in Office of Technology Assessment analysis of first two ERDA budgets (1974-75); conducted study of coal/methanol slurries for Texas Utilities, Co. (1976-77).

Publications: "PAF-A New Probabilistic, Computer-Based Technique for Technology Forecasting" (*Technological Forecasting and Social Change*, Volume 10, 1977); co-author, "Alternate Scenario Planning" (*Technological Forecasting and Social Change*, Volume 10, 1977); "Texas Nuclear Power Policies: A Study of Alternatives" (special issue on Energy Policy, *Management Science*, 1978); co-author and co-editor, *A Feasibility Study for Enhancing the Development of Fusion Energy* (Electric Power Research Institute, 1978)

VESTER, FREDERIC

Born: 1925, Saarbrucken, Germany

Director
Studiengruppe für Biologie und Umwelt gemeinnutzige GmbH
[Study Group for Biology and the Environment, Inc.]
Nussbaumstrasse 14
D-8000 Munich 2, Federal Republic of Germany

Telephone: (089) 53 50 10

Profession: Biochemist; publicist; policy analyst; writer; environmentalist

Field of specialization: Environmental problems, impacts on society, systems research.

Education: Chemistry, Universitat Mainz; Licencie es sciences, Sorbonne, Paris; Ph.D., Universitat Hamburg; Lecturer, Universitat Konstanz.

Professional employment: Study Group for Biology and Environment, Ltd.: Founder and Director (1970-). Max Planck Institute for Protein Research: Member (1965-70). Universitat des Saarlandes: Assistant (1957-65). Yale Medical School, New Haven: Post-doctoral fellow (1955-57). University of Heidelberg, Cancer Research Institute: Assistant (1953-55).

Professional activities: Member of the Federal Research Institute for Rural Studies and Land Use, and other councils; current research project: the cybernetical approach to the ecology of rural areas; studies in the field of environmental problems; consulting in environmental problems; scientific and school films; cancer research.

Publications: *Bausteine der Zuknuft [Building Blocks of the Future]* (S. Fischer Verlag, 1968); *Das Uberlebensprogramm [The Survival Program]* (Kinder-Verlag, 1972); *Das kybernetische Zeitalter [The Age of Cybernetics]* (S. Fischer-Verlag, 1974); *Denken-Lernen [Thinking-Learning-Forgetting]* (DVA, 1975); *Ballungsgebiete in der Krise [Urban Systems in Crisis]* (bilingual) (DVA 1976); *Unsere Welt—ein vernetztes System [Our World—A Network System]* (Klett-Cotta, 1978).

VICKERS, CHARLES GEOFFREY   Born: 1894, Nottingham, England
Little Mead
Manor Road
Reading, RG8 9ED, England   **Telephone:** Goring 2933

Profession: Writer

Field of specialization: Systems theory applied to human social systems, especially value systems.

Education: B.A., 1919, M.A., 1953, Humanities, Oxford University.

Professional employment: Writer; retired administrator and lawyer.

Professional activities: Currently writing and consulting in fields of policy-making, planning, and professional education; member, British National Coal Board (1945-55); Deputy Director, Ministry of Economic Warfare I/C Economic Intelligence (1941-45); private legal practice (1920-40).

Publications: *The Art of Judgment* (Chapman and Hall, London, Basic Books, New York, 1965); *Towards a Sociology of Management* (Chapman and Hall/Basic Books, 1967); *Value Systems and Social Process* (Tavistock Publications, London/Basic Books, 1968); *Freedom in a Rocking Boat* (Allen Lane and Basic Books, 1970, Penguin Books, 1973); *Making Institutions Work* (Associated Business Programmes, London, 1973, and Halstead Press, New York, 1974).

VLACHOS, EVAN   Born: 1935, Athens, Greece
Professor of Sociology and Civil Engineering
Department of Sociology
Colorado State University
Fort Collins, Colorado 80523, U.S.A.   **Telephone:** (303) 491-6089

Profession: Sociologist

Field of specialization: Technology assessment; social forecasting; natural resources analysis; utopian thought.

Education: LL.B., Law, University of Athens, 1959; M.A., 1962, Ph.D., 1964, Sociology, Certificate, Russian Studies, 1964, Indiana University.

Professional employment: Colorado State University: Professor of Sociology and Civil Engineering (1967-); Assistant Professor (1966-67). Pierce College: Assistant Professor (1964-66).

Professional activities: Consultant to National Science Foundation (1978-79), Corps of Engineers (1978-79), Department of Transportation (1977), and U.N. Educational, Scientific, and Cultural Organization; teaching and lecturing on technology assessment and futurism.

Publications: Co-author, *Technology Assessment for Water Supplies* (Water Resources Publication, 1978); "Metaphors, Scenarios and the Planning of the Future" in *Population and Development* (1974); "The Use of Scenarios for Social Impact Assessment" in *Methodology of Social Impact Assessment*, Fiusterbush and Wolf (1977); "Icons of the Future and Scenarios of the Apocalypse"; in *American Sociological Association Seminar on Sociology of the Future* (1972); "The Future in the Past" in *Cultures of the Future*, M. Maruyama (1978).

VON LAUE, THEODORE H.   Born: 1916, Frankfurt/Main, Germany
Professor of History
Clark University
950 Main Street
Worcester, Massachusetts 01610, U.S.A.   **Telephone:** (617) 793-7213

Profession: Historian

Field of specialization: Russian history; interaction of cultures in area of modern Ghana; comparative historical studies; future projection of historial trends, global perspectives.

Education: A.B., 1939, Ph.D., 1944, History, Princeton University; Certificate, Russian Institute, Columbia University, 1948.

Professional employment: Clark University: Professor of History (1970-). Washington University, St.

Louis, Missouri: Professor of History (1964-70). University of California-Riverside: Professor of History (1955-64).

Professional activities: Current research projects on "interaction of European and African cultures in area of modern Ghana," and a "historical assessment of present and future in global context." My interest in the future is a continuation of my work as a historian. All uses of history point to the future, as all men live for the future, i.e., forward, away from the past, knowingly or unknowingly. Conversely, all future projections are based on past experience; they imply (or sometimes openly state) an interpretation of the past. The present is characterized by a universal break with national and cultural pasts; we live in the age of beginning globalization, for which no separate pasts have prepared us and for which no common past yet exists. I am trying to explore that condition as a key to the future."

Publications: *The Global City* (Lippincott, 1969).

VRANKEN, JAN
Faculty of Political and Social Sciences
University of Antwerp (UFSIA)
Rodestraat 14
2000 Antwerpen, Belgium

Born: 1944, Vucht, Maasmechelen, Belgium

Telephone: (031) 32 39 23

Profession: Social scientist

Field of specialization: Poverty; structure of modern society; social policy and planning; structuralist methods in the social sciences.

Education: Cand., Political Social Sciences, 1964, Lic., Social Sciences, 1966, Cand., Economics, 1967, Catholic University Leuven; Ph.D., Political and Social Sciences, 1977, University of Antwerp (UIA), Department of Political and Social Sciences.

Professional employment: University of Antwerp (UFSIA): Research Director (1978-); First Assistant (1972); Teaching Assistant (1968).

Professional activities: International comparative study on persisting poverty (1978-80); "Social Problems, Social Policy and Social Planning: An Introduction" (1979-80); "Social Welfare Organization in Belgium" (paper for the Belgian-Dutch Congress on Sociology); Director of National Welfare Organization for Migrant Workers (1977-); course on "The Structure of Modern Society" (1974-); scientific consultant for diverse welfare organizations; member of the editorial staff of *De Nieuwe Maand;* study of the future (the structure of society, social security, and methodological problems, 1968-72).

Publications: *Poverty in the Welfare State: An Analysis of its Historical and Structural Dimensions* (doctoral dissertation, in Dutch, Antwerp, UIA, 1977); co-author, *On "Differential Participation" and Living Conditions of the Poor in Belgium* (in Dutch, Brussels, VWEC, 1979); co-author, *Introduction a la Planification Sociale [Introduction to Social Planning]* (SESO—UFSIA, 1971); co-editor, *Armoede in Belgie [Poverty in Belgium]* (De Nederlandsche Boekhandel, 1975); "The Future as a Part of the Social Environment" in *Science, Man and his Environment* (Beograd, Science and Society Association, 1971).

WAGAR, W. WARREN
Professor of History
Department of History
State University of New York at Binghamton
Binghamton, New York 13901, U.S.A.

Born: 1932, Baltimore, Maryland, U.S.A.

Telephone: (607) 798-3098

Profession: Historian

Field of specialization: Normative futures; history of futurist thought.

Education: A.B., History, Franklin and Marshall College, 1953; M.A., History, Indiana University, 1954; Ph.D., History, Yale University, 1959.

Professional employment: State University of New York at Binghamton: Professor of History (1971-). University of New Mexico: Associate Professor, Professor (1966-71). Wellesley College: Instructor, Assistant Professor, Associate Professor (1958-66).

Professional activities: Member, Advisory Board, *Alternative Futures: The Journal of Utopian Studies* (1977-); member, American Historical Association and The World Future Society; member, Board of Directors, Council for the Study of Mankind (1967-); consultant to various publishers, research institutes; book reviewer for several magazines and journals; occasional guest lecturer; researcher in progress on visions of the end of the world.

Publications: *World Views: A Study in Comparative History* (Holt, Rinehart and Winston, 1977); *Building the City of Man: Outlines of a World Civilization in 20th-Century Thought* (Houghton Mifflin, 1963); *Good Tidings: The Belief in Progress from Darwin to Marcuse* (Indiana University Press, 1972); H.G. *Wells and the World State* (Yale University Press, 1961); editor, *Science, Faith, and Man: European Thought Since 1914* (Harper and Row, 1968).

WAGENFUHR, HORST

Born: 1903, Langewiesen, Germany

Wickert Institute Tubingen fur wirtschaftliche Zukunftsforschung
[The Wickert Institute of Tubingen for Futures Research in Economics]
Wilhelmstrasse 102
D 7400 Tubingen, Federal Republic of Germany

Telephone: (07071) 2 23 18

Profession: Economic analyst and forecaster

Field of specialization: Futures research, especially in the fields of economics and sociology.

Education: Attended Universities of Berlin, Erlangen, Innsbruck, Jena, Kiel, Leipzig, Wien.

Professional employment: The Wickert Institute Tubingen fur wirtschaftliche Zukunftsforschung.

Professional activities: Numerous research projects with The Wickert Institute (see publications); co-publisher and co-editor, *Zeitschrift fur Markt- Meinungs- und Zukunftsforschung [Periodical for Market, Opinion, and Futures Research].*

Publications: *Westdeutschlands wirtschaft zwischen wunsch und wirklichkeit [West Germany's Economy Between Wish and Reality]* (Wickert Institute, Report 1975); *Gesellschaft und wirtschaft im zukunftigen Deutschland [Society and Economy in the Future Germany]* (Wickert Institute, Report 85); *Gegenwartige Situation un Zukunftsfragen [Current Conditions and Future Questions]* (Wickert Institute, Report Pharma 85); *Report zur Energiekrise—Fakten, Vorschlage und futurologische Aspekte [Report on the Energy Crisis: Facts, Proposals, and Future Aspects]* (Wickert Institute); *Dynamik von morgen [Dynamics of Tomorrow]* (Wickert Institute, Report Technik 1999); *Wirtschaftliche Zukunftsforschung—Eine Einfuhrung in Theorie und Praxis [Futures Research in Economics—An Introduction to Theory and Practice]* (Wickert Institute); *Vom Wesen der Zeit—aphorismen [The Nature of our Times—Aphorisms]* (Wickert Institute); *Zukunft in Wort und Zahl—Deutschlands Wirtschaft 1970-2000 [The Future in Words and Numbers—Germany's Economy Between 1970 and 2000]* (Wickert Institute).

WAGSCHAL, PETER H.

Born: 1944, New York, New York, U.S.A.

Director, Future Studies Program
School of Education
University of Massachusetts
Amherst, Massachusetts 01003, U.S.A.

Telephone: (413) 545-0981

Profession: Educator

Field of specialization: "Radical" futures and their impact on educational systems.

Education: B.A., Social Relations, Harvard University, 1966; M.A., Education, Stanford University, 1967; Ed.D., Education, University of Massachusetts, 1969.

Professional employment: University of Massachusetts: Associate Professor and Director, Future Studies Program (1975-); Assistant Professor (1969-75); Lecturer (1968-69).

Professional activities: Study of two possible energy-futures for Franklin County, Massachusetts, sponsored by the National Endowment for the Humanities (1978-79); conducts courses on future studies and conferences/workshops/teacher-education programs on future studies and education (1975-); contributing editor, *Education Tomorrow* (1978-); Director, Learning Tomorrows Conference (April 1978); Board of

372

Advisors, Toward Tomorrow Fair (Summer 1977, 1978); Board of Advisors, Forum on Appropriate Technology, National Science Foundation (October 1978).

Publications: Editor, *Learning Tomorrows: Perspectives on the Future of Education* (Praeger Publishing Company, Spring 1979); editor and co-author, *R. Buckminster Fuller on Education* (University of Massachusetts Press, Fall 1979); "The Future of American Education" (*Learning Tomorrows*, Praeger, Spring 1979); "Illiterates with Doctorates" (THE FUTURIST, August 1978).

WAKEFIELD, RICHARD P.

Born: 1921, Sheffield, Massachusetts, U.S.A.

Center for Studies of Metropolitan Problems
National Institute of Mental Health
Room 15-99, 5600 Fishers Lane
Rockville, Maryland 20857, U.S.A.

Telephone: (301) 443-3373

Profession: Plans and Process Analyst

Field of specialization: Processes and general systems (elements, variables, relationships, alternatives, values); human systems (social, organizational, communications, programs); preventive health and mental health; synergy and symbiosis; anticipatory processes; organization development and evolution.

Education: A.B., Romance Languages, Harvard College, 1947; MCP, City Planning, Harvard Graduate School of Design, 1950; Psychology and Social Sciences, Russell Sage, 1959-61; Human Development Education, University of Maryland, 1965-66.

Professional employment: National Institute of Mental Health: Urban Planner (1965-). General Electric Company: Managerial semanticist and project analyst (1956-65). U.S. Post Office: Chief, Planning Section, Bureau of Facilities (1953-56). Arlington County, Virginia: Principal Planner and Assistant Planner (1950-53); City of Cambridge, Massachusetts: Research Analyst, Planning Board (1949-50). Office of Strategic Services, U.S. Army: Radio operator (1943-45).

Professional activities: Federal Interagency Committee on Education, Subcommittee on Environmental Education (1975-); interagency discussion group on environmental design research (1978-); member, Society for General Systems Research (1956-); member, American Institute of Planners (1950-); Chairman, Ad Hoc Interagency Committee for Futures Research (1970-); Chairman, Human Values Group, Washington, D.C. (1968-); consultant/respondent, National Commission for Protection of Human Subjects of Biomedical and Behavioral Research (1975-); member, Organizing Committee, 1976 International Society for Technology Assessment Congress, Ann Arbor, Michigan, October 1976 (1975-); representative of NIMH/DHEW, Working Group for U.N. Conference on Human Settlements (1976).

Publications: "Business Planning as a Process" (*Marketing Times*, General Electric, January 1961); "Images of Man and the Future of Human Disciplines" (*Proceedings: International Futures Research Conference*, Kyoto, Japan, 1970); co-author, "A Futures-Creative and Values-Sensitive Policy Science Paradigm" (Rome Special World Conference on Futures Research, September 1973); "Research Needs Concerning Emergent Forces in Human Values" (Third World Futures Research Conference, Bucharest, September 1972).

WAKEFIELD, ROWAN ALBERT

Born: 1919, Great Barrington, Massachusetts, U.S.A.

President
Wakefield Washington Associates, Inc.
1129 20th Street, N.W., Suite 504
Washington, D.C. 20036, U.S.A.

Telephone: (202) 833-9880

Profession: Management consultant

Field of specialization: Planning energy and economic growth—research, development, technology transfer, and education; planning future of higher education; forecasting trends relating to family and public policy; changing relationship between the corporation and the government.

Education: B.A., Political Science, Williams College, 1942.

Professional employment: Wakefield Washington Associates, Inc.: President (1975-). Center for Policy Process: Director (1974-75); Center for Government-Education Relations: Director (1973-75). Aspen

Institute for Humanistic Studies: Executive Vice-President (1970-73). State University of New York, Washington Office: Director (1965-70).

Professional activities: Co-editor, the *American Family*, bimonthly newsletter on family and public policy, current actions and future trends; Washington representative of several universities and corporations, analyze and forecast nature of relationship between these institutions and the federal government; helping to plan the Adelphi University Center for Energy Studies (1975-); participated in the design and implementation of alternative policy processes project for the White House Domestic Council staff while Director of Center for Policy Process (1974-75); helped conceptualize and administer "A Program of Education for a Changing Society," a program exploring education future, sponsored jointly by the Aspen Institute, Educational Testing Service, and Institute for Educational Development (1972-73); helped to plan and carry out seminars for the Aspen Institute on the future of the broadcasting industry and humanistic implications of the space program (1970-73); member, Board of Directors, World Future Society.

Publications: Co-author with Catherine Allen and Gail Washchuck, *Family Research: An Analysis and Guide to Federal Funding* (forthcoming in 1979); "Focus on Washington" (regular column, *Grants Magazine*).

WARD, BARBARA (LADY D.B.E. JACKSON)

Born: 1914, England

President
The International Institute for Environment and Development
10 Percy Street
London W1P ODR, England

Telephone: —

Profession: Author and economist

Field of specialization: World problems of environment and development.

Education: Convent of Jesus and Mary, Felixstowe; Lycee Moliere and the Sorbonne, Paris; die Klause, Jugenheim, Germany; Somerville College, Oxford, Exhibitioner; Honorary Degree in Philosophy, Politics and Economics, 1935.

Professional employment: International Institute for Environment and Development: President (1973-). Columbia University: Albert Schweitzer Professor of International Economic Development (1968-73). Carnegie Fellow (1959-67). Harvard University: Visiting Scholar (1957-68). *The Economist:* Assistant Editor (1939). Cambridge University: Lecturer, University Extension Courses (1936-39).

Professional activities: Member, Pontifical Commission for Justice and Peace (1967-); President, Conservation Society (1973-); Member, Royal Institute of International Affairs (1943-44, 1973-); Governor, Sadler's Wells and the Old Vic (1944-53); Governor of BBC (1946-50); Editor, *The Widening Gap* (1971).

Publications: *The Home of Man* (1976); co-author, with Rene Dubos, *Only one Earth* (1972); *Spaceship Earth* (1966); *The Rich Nations and the Poor Nations* (1962) and many others.

WARD, JONATHAN

Born: 1941, Illinois, U.S.A.

Executive Producer
Special Events
CBS News
524 W. 57th Street
New York, New York 10019, U.S.A.

Telephone: (212) 975-2905

Profession: Writer; reporter; producer

Field of specialization: Continuing study of the philosophical, logical and scientific principles of prediction; collecting oral accounts of futurists and forecasting.

Education: Mathematics/Philosophy of Science, Grinnell College; Journalism, University of Illinois; Computer Science, New School for Social Research.

Professional employment: CBS News: Executive Producer, Special Events (1974-); reporter, "The Future File," and Director, Program Services (1971-74). Field Television, Chicago: Writer, Director (1968-71).

Professional activities: Researching past predictions from classical times to present; book in press on the history of the future; writes and produces broadcasts on the future and trends for CBS; lecturing on social futures and trends in communications; speaker on the future for Sunpapers Journalism Series, University of Michigan Future World series, University of Pennsylvania Herbert Spenser series.

Publications: "The Future File" (*Innovation Magazine*, 1973-74); "Kahnversation—The Savoring of America" (*Intellectual Digest*); "Peter Goldmark's New Rural Society" (*Intellectual Digest*); co-author, *Dreams Must Explain Themselves* (Algol Press, 1975).
(From the first edition. Corrections not received by press time.)

WASKOW, ARTHUR I.

Public Resource Center
1747 Connecticut Avenue, N.W.
Washington, D.C. 20009, U.S.A.

Born: 1933, Baltimore, Maryland, U.S.A.

Telephone: (202) 483-7902

Profession: Historian

Field of specialization: Relation of religious and political change, especially in the U.S.; future of U.S. foreign policy; future of American Jewish community; future of Middle East.

Education: B.A., History, Johns Hopkins, 1954; M.A., 1956, Ph.D., 1963, U.S. History, University of Wisconsin.

Professional employment: Public Resource Center: Resident Colleague (1977-). Institute for Policy Studies: Resident Fellow (1963-1977). Peace Research Institute: Senior Research Staff (1961-63). U.S. House of Representatives: Legislative Assistant (1959-61).

Professional activities: Project on American Jewish institutions (1977-); project on energy transition at the community level (1977-); project on "The Religious Search Toward Social Justice" (1975-); Editorial Board, *Peace and Change* (1973-); lecturer at campuses, synagogues on religious change; future of Judaism and peace in the Middle East (1973-); Executive Committee, Consortium on Peace Research, Education and Development (1972-75); Secretary-Treasurer, Conference on Peace Research in History (1966-69).

Publications: *Godwrestling* (Schocken Books, 1978); "The Future of Jewish Peoplehood" (Public Resource Center, 1977); *The Bush is Burning* (Macmillan, 1971); "Messianism and the New Halacha" (*Response*, Spring 1974); "Notes from 1999" (*Working Papers*, Spring 1973); *From Race to Sit-In, 1919 and the 1960's* (Doubleday, 1966); *The Limits of Defense* (Doubleday, 1962).

WATERLOW, CHARLOTTE MARY

Browne and Nichols School
Gerry's Landing
Cambridge, Massachusetts 02138, U.S.A.

Born: 1915, Lewes, England

Telephone: (617) 547-6100

Profession: School teacher; writer on world affairs

Field of specialization: World problems, especially those concerning the gulf between the rich and the poor countries; philosophy of history (especially with regard to the question, where are we going?); comparative religion.

Education: B.A., History Tripos, First Class, 1936, M.A., 1953, Cambridge University; Dip. Ed., London University, 1954; Awarded M.B.E. (Member of British Empire) by George VI, 1950.

Professional employment: Browne and Nichols School: History Teacher (present position). Notre Dame University, British Columbia, Canada: Assistant Professor of History (1967-69). Guildford Girls' Grammar School, England: Head of History Department (1954-67). Foreign Office, London: Administrative Grade Officer (1945-53). Ministry of War Transport, London: Administrative Grade Officer (1941-45).

Professional activities: Member, Board of Directors and Executive Committee of the United Nations Association of Greater Boston (1973-); member, World Federalists Association of New England (1975-); Core Member of Goals for Global Society project, sponsored by The Club of Rome; currently writing a book to be called *New Vision: The Coming Convergence of Western Humanism, Marxism and Religion to Save the World from Doom*.

Publications: *Superpowers and Victims: The Outlook for World Community* (Prentice-Hall, 1974); *Europe 1945 to 1970* (Methuen, London, 1973); *India* in "The World in Transformation Series" (Ginn, London, 1969); *Tribe, State and Community: Contemporary Systems of Government and Justice* (Methuen, London, 1967); "Values and Models for a Global Community" in *The Next 25 Years: Crisis and Opportunity* (World Future Society, 1975).

WATT, KENNETH E. FERGUSON

Born: 1929, Toronto, Ontario, Canada

Professor
Department of Zoology
University of California
Davis, California 95616, U.S.A.

Telephone: (916) 752-1558

Profession: Systems ecologist

Field of specialization: Systems simulations of countries and groups of countries

Education: B.A. (Hon.), Biology, University of Toronto, 1951; Ph.D., Zoology (Ecology), University of Chicago, 1954; LL.D., Honorary, Simon Fraser University, 1970.

Professional employment: University of California at Davis, Department of Zoology: Professor (1965-); Associate Professor (1963-65). Canadian Department of Forestry: Head, Statistics (1960-63). Canadian Department of Agriculture: Senior Biometrician (1957-60). Ontario Department of Lands, Research Division: Biometrician (1954-57).

Professional activities: Conducting statistical analyses and building simulation model for world system (1978); Head, Interdisciplinary Systems Group (1968-75); research and consulting for government and corporations (1974-).

Publications: "The Structure of Post-Industrial Economies" (*Journal of Social Biological Structure,* 1978); co-author, "A Simulation of the Use of Energy and Land at the National Level" (*Simulation,* 1975); *The Titanic Effect* (Sinauer, 1974); co-author, *The Unsteady State* (University of Hawaii Press, 1977).

WEAVER, JOHN JACOB

Born: 1911, Dayton, Ohio, U.S.A.

Archdeacon for the Future
Episcopal Diocese of California
1055 Taylor Street
San Francisco, California 94108, U.S.A.

Telephone: (415) 776-6611

Profession: Episcopal priest

Field of specialization: Education; genetics engineering; violence; guaranteed income; institutional change; technology; human values; new issues of capitalism; energy; drugs; ekistics; economics; noetics; alternatives for the aged; extra-terrestrial; work and leisure; theology and the Third World; food and hunger; political decision-making; female worthwhileness.

Education: B.A., Otterbein College, 1934; STB, Episcopal Theological School, Cambridge, Massachusetts, 1939; D.D., Church Divinity School of the Pacific, Berkeley, California, 1969.

Professional employment: Archdiocese of California: Archdeacon for the Future (1966-); Chief Executive of the Planning Council; Archdeacon for Personnel (1973-1975). Diocese of Michigan: Dean of Cathedral Church of St. Paul (1947-64). Diocese of Ohio: Rector of Trinity Church (1939-47). Leave of absence during war years: Protestant Chaplain in the U.S. Army (1942-46). Chaplain to Archbishop of Canterbury (1945).

Professional activities: Member: Joint Doctoral Program, Cybernetic Systems, San Jose State College; Policy Advisory Committee on the College of Agricultural and Environmental Sciences, University of California-Davis; World Future Society; American Ontoanalytic Association; National Council on Drug Abuse of the Chicago Psychiatric Foundation and Ontoanalytic Institute. Chairman, Board of Trustees, "The California Center on Environment"; Founder of Common College and Nairobi College; Presiding Bishop's personal representative to the U.N. Conference on Human Environment, Stockholm (1972); U.S.A. Club of Rome.

Publications: Collator, *Annual Conference of Episcopal Cathedral Deans* (MPB Booklet, April 1967); collator, *Know Ye the Truth* (MPB Booklet, January 1973); collator, *Limits of Obsession*, Harlan Cleveland (MPB Booklet, December 1971); *Institutions Will Change and the Military Will Change* (MPB Booklet, June 1976).

WEAVER, ROY A.
Assistant Professor
School of Education, WPH 702h
University of Southern California
University Park
Los Angeles, California 90007, U.S.A.

Born: 1947, Huntington, Indiana, U.S.A.

Telephone: (213) 741-2044

Profession: Educator, curriculum specialist

Field of specialization: Educational alternatives; relationships among cross-age and cross-cultural images of the future.

Education: B.S., Education, 1969, M.A., Curriculum and Instruction, 1971, Ball State University; Ed.D., Curriculum and Instruction, Indiana University, 1975.

Professional employment: University of Southern California: Assistant Professor (1975-). Indiana University: Administrative Assistant (1974-75); Teaching Assistant (1973-74).

Professional activities: Completing several studies including "Work That Doesn't Exist...But Will" a survey of potential changes in work, and "Cross-Age and Cross-Cultural Views of the Future" a comparative analysis of five cultures and three age groups' views of future alternatives; teaching a course each fall titled "Futures Studies in Curriculum and Instruction"; presented numerous speeches and papers.

Publications: Editor, Futures Theme Issue of the *Educational Research Quarterly* (Winter, 1977); "Whither Goest Futur-(es)-(ism)-(ology)-( ) in Education" (Educational Research Quarterly, Winter 1977); co-author, "Educational Futures" in *Handbook of Futures Research*, J. Fowles, ed. (Greenwood Press, 1978); co-author, "An Outline of a Rationale for Comprehensive Long-Range Educational Planning for California" (paper for the State Commission on Educational Planning and Innovations, December 1977); co-author, "Beyond Darth Vader, R2D2 and 3CPO: Future Studies in the Social Science Curriculum" (*California Social Science Review*, Summer 1978).

WEBBER, JAMES B.
1303 Massachusetts Avenue
Lexington, Massachusetts 02173, U.S.A.

Born: 1931, Philadelphia, Pennsylvania, U.S.A.

Telephone: (617) 862-5315

Profession: Management consultant

Field of specialization: The utilization of futures studies in organizations; the policy process in corporations, hospitals, colleges and governments; implementation of future-oriented planning—approaches, tools, and skills.

Education: B.S., Mechanical Engineering, University of Pennsylvania, 1953; M.B.A., Business Administration, Harvard Graduate School of Business, 1961.

Professional employment: Self-employed: Management Consultant (1975-). Cambridge Research Institute: Director (1970-75). Materials Analysis Company: Executive Vice President (1969-70). Raychem Corporation: Director of Industrial Relations (1967-69); Director of Manufacturing (1963-67).

Professional activities: Conducts course for the Industrial Management Center on "Socio-Political Inputs to Technological Forecasting" (1973-76); Course Director for the Bureau of Health Planning and Resources Development on "Strategy Formulation and Implementation" (1975-76); Visiting Research Associate, Center for Policy Alternatives, Massachusetts Institute of Technology (1976); Founder and first President, Boston/Cambridge Chapter, World Future Society (1971-72); has lectured on "The Plight of Institutions, A Comparative Study" (March 1976); "Environmental Scanning" (February 1976); "The Nature of the Future"; "The Future of American Business" (December 1974).

Publications: Co-author, "Effective Planning Committees for Hospitals" (*Harvard Business Review*, May/June 1974); "Planning from the Outside In" (*Management Review*, American Management Association, March 1974); co-author, *What You Should Know about the Value Added Tax* (Dow Jones/Irwin, 1973); co-author, *New England Deaconess Hospital* (Cambridge Research Institute, 1972); "Intelligent vs. Reasonable Decision Making" (*Media Industry Newsletter*, Spring 1975).

WEINER, EDITH M.

Born: 1948, Brooklyn, New York, U.S.A.

Executive Vice President
Weiner, Edrich, Brown, Inc.
303 Lexington Avenue
New York, New York 10016, U.S.A.

Telephone: (212) 889-7007

Profession: Management consultant

Field of specialization: Interested in all aspects of science and technology; politics and government; social sciences; business and economics.

Education: B.A., Psychology, City College of New York, 1969.

Professional employment: Weiner, Edrich, Brown, Inc.: Exeuctive Vice President (1977-). Institute of Life Insurance: Program Director, Trend Analysis Program (1970-77).

Professional activities: Writes and lectures for both the business and academic communities on various aspects of futures research, from specific topics to corporate use of long-range planning; member, Board of Directors, Union Mutual Life Insurance Co. (1978-); member, U.S. Association for the Club of Rome (1978-); designs and participates in strategic scanning systems for client organizations.

Publications: "Some Thoughts on Women...and Insurance Marketing" (*Insurance Marketing*, September 1978); "The Future and the Audiovisual Profession" (*Photomethods*, January 1978); *The Changing World of the Employee*, Trend Analysis Report No. 7 (Institute of Life Insurance, September 1973); *The Life Cycle—New Trends in Life Stages and Living Patterns*, Trend Analysis Report No. 8 (Institute of Life Insurance, 1974); *Innovative Technologies*, Part I (Health), Part II (Information), Trend Analysis Reports No. 10 and 11 (Institute of Life Insurance, Winter and Spring 1975); *A Culture in Transformation— Toward a New Social Ethic*, Trend Analysis Report No. 12, (Institute of Life Insurance, Fall 1975).

WEINGARTNER, CHARLES

Born: 1922, New York, New York, U.S.A.

Professor of Education
College of Education
University of South Florida
Tampa, Florida 33620, U.S.A.

Telephone: (813) 974-2100

Profession: Professor

Field of specialization: Educational futures, especially uses of electronic information-instruction systems.

Education: B.S., 1950, M.A., 1951, Communication, Syracuse University; Ed.D., Communication, Teachers College, Columbia University, 1958.

Professional employment: University of South Florida: Professor of Education (1970-). Queens College, City University of New York: Professor of Education (1965-70). New York University, Linguistics Demonstration Center: Associate Director (1964-65). State University of New York: Professor of English and Education (1962-64). University of Chicago, Committee on Institutional Cooperation-Big Tent: Staff Associate (1961-62).

Professional activities: Teaching educational futures (1978); assessing current thinking among futurists relative to educational futures (1979); extensive speaking on education and the future; conducting courses on mass media and communication technology and social effects.

Publications: Co-author, *The School Book* (Dell, 1973); co-author, *Teaching as a Subversive Activity* (Dell, 1973); "Schools and the Future" in *The Future of Education* T. Hipple, editor (Goodyear, 1973); "Communication, Education, and Change" in *The Radical Papers* H. Sobel, editor (Harper and Row, 1972); "No More Pencils, No More Books, No More Teachers' Dirty Looks" (*Proceedings of the Educational Futures Conference, 1978*, University of Houston, in press).

WEIZSACKER, CARL FRIEDRICH FREIHERR V.

Born: 1912, Kiel, Germany

Director
Max-Planck Institute on the Preconditions of Human
   Life in the Modern World
Riemerschmidstrasse 7
D 813 Starnberg, Federal Republic of Germany

Telephone: 08151/1491

Profession: Physicist; philosopher

Field of specialization: Physics; philosophy.

Education: Studied physics at the Universities of Berlin, Gottingen, and Leipzig, 1929-33; Ph.D., Leipzig, 1933. Presented thesis, University of Leipzig, 1936.

Professional employment: Max-Planck Institute on the Preconditions of Human Life in the Modern World: Director (1970-). University of Hamburg: Professor of Philosophy (1957-69). Max-Planck Institute for Physics, Gottingen: Department Head (1946-57). University of Gottingen: Honorary Professorship (1946-57). University of Strasbourg: Associate Professor (1942-44). Kaiser Wilhelm Institut, Berlin: Lecturer (1936-42).

Professional activities: Advisory activities in politics and related fields; projects with the Max-Planck Institute.

Publications: *The History of Nature* (Routledge and Kegan Paul, London, 1951); *The World View of Physics* (Routledge and Kegan Paul, London, 1951); *The Relevance of Science* (Harper and Row, 1964); *Die Einheit der Natur [The Unity of Nature]* (Hanser, Munich, 1972); *The Politics of Peril* (Seabury Press, New York, 1978); *Der Garten des Menschen [The Garden of Mankind]* (Hanser, Munich, 1978).

WELLESLEY-WESLEY, JAMES FRANK   **Born:** 1926, London, England
Executive Director
Mankind 2000
1 rue aux Laines
1000 Brussels, Belgium   **Telephone:** —

Profession: —

Field of specialization: Human development.

Education: Eton College.

Professional employment: —

Professional activities: Mankind 2000: Executive Director (1970-); Executive Secretary (1965-70).

Publications: —
(From the first edition. Corrections not received by press time.)

WESCOTT, ROGER WILLIAMS   **Born:** 1925, Philadelphia, Pennsylvania, U.S.A.
Professor and Chairman
Anthropology Department
Drew University
Madison, New Jersey 07940, U.S.A.   **Telephone:** (201) 377-3000

Profession: Anthropologist

Field of specialization: Extraterrestrial community planning.

Education: B.A., English, 1945, M.A., Indology, 1947, Ph.D., Linguistics, 1948, Princeton University; B. Litt., Anthropology, Oxford University, 1952.

Professional employment: Drew University: Professor and Chairman, Anthropology Department (1966-). Southern Connecticut State College: Chairman, Social Science Department (1962-66). Michigan State University: Director, African Language Program (1957-62). Boston University: Assistant Professor, Human Relations (1953-57).

Professional activities: President, Linguistics Association of Canada and U.S. (1976-); Director, Teilhard Association for Future of Man (1974-); organized Drew University Conference on the Future (1972); President, School of Living, Brookville, Ohio (1961-65); Director, Union of Exploratory Educators, New York (1963-64); has taught futuristics course and published futuristics articles since 1969.

Publications: *The Divine Animal* (Funk and Wagnalls, 1969); co-author and editor, *Language Origins* (Linstok Press, 1974); *A Bini Grammar* (U.S. Office of Education, 1963); *Visions: Selected Poems* (Oryx Press, 1975); *A Comparative Grammar of Albanian* (U. Microfilms, 1955).

WICKERT, GUNTER

Born: 1928, Erfurt, Germany

Wickert Institute Tubingen fur wirtschaftliche Zukunftsforschung
[The Wickert Institute of Tubingen for Futures Research in Economics]
Wilhelmstrasse 102
D 7400 Tubingen, Federal Republic of Germany

Telephone: (07071) 2 23 18

Profession: Market and opinion research

Field of specialization: Futures research in the fields of sociology and economics.

Education: Attended the Universities of Basel, Gottingen, Heidelberg, Jena, Leipzig, Tubingen.

Professional employment: The Wickert Institute Tubingen fur wirtschaftliche Zukunftsforschung.

Professional activities: Numerous research projects with the Wickert Institute (see publications); publisher and editor, *Zeitschrift fur Markt-, Meinungs- und Zukunftsforschung [Periodical for Market, Opinion, and Futures Research]*.

Publications: Editor, *Westdeutschlands wirtschaft zwischen wunsch und wirklichkeit [West Germany's Economy Between Wish and Reality]* (Wickert Institute, Report 1975); editor, *Gesellschaft und wirtschaft im zukunftigen Deutschland [Society and Economy in the Future Germany]* (Wickert Institute, Report 85); editor, *Gegenwartige Situation und Zukunftsfragen [Current Conditions and Future Questions]* (Wickert Institute, Report Pharma 85); editor, *Report zur Energiekrise—Fakten, Vorschlage und futurologische Aspekte [Report on the Energy Crisis—Facts, Proposals, and Future Aspects]* (Wickert Institute); *Dynamik von morgen [Dynamics of Tomorrow]* (Wickert Institute, Report Technik 1999).

WIDMAIER, HANS PETER

Born: 1934, Lorrach, Baden, Germany

Professor of Economics
University of Regensburg
Lehrstuhl fur Volkswirtschaftslehre
[Chair for Political Economy]
Universitatsstrasse
84 Regensburg, Federal Republic of Germany

Telephone: (0941) 9432709

Profession: Economist

Field of specialization: Anthropology; social policy; economics.

Education: Ph.D., University of Basle.

Professional employment: University of Regensburg: Full Professor of Economics (1968-). Basle Center for Economic Research: Director (1964-68). Organization for Economic Cooperation and Development, Paris: Consultant (1961-64).

Professional activities: Chairman of the Social Policy Committee of the Verein fur Sozialpolitik [Society for Socio-Politics] (1975); Member, Institute International de Finances Publiques (1973-); co-editor, *Social Indicators Research*—an international and interdisciplinary journal for quality of life measurement; Member, Academy for Regional Research and Planning, Committee on Regional Educational Planning within the Frame of Development Planning (1973-); main teaching activities—economic policy, social policy, labour economics and economics of education, infrastructure planning, planning in socialist countries, and educational planning; main research activities—problems of political economy of political processes, problems of the future distribution between private and public goods, labour market research, and educational planning and labour market problems.

Publications: *Sozialpolitick im Wohlfahrtsstaat—Zur Theorie politischer Guter [A Theory of Social Policy in the Welfare State]* (Beitrag zum Weltkongress 1978 der Soziologen in Uppsala, Sweden, Vol. 14-19, August 1978); "Basic Needs in the Social and Educational Sector and State Policy: An Alternative to the Human-Capital Approach," seminar on long-term prospects for the development of education (International Institute for Educational Planning (IIEP), Paris, Vol 23-26, October 1978; IIEP/S48/32A); co-author, "Public versus Private Expenditures, General Prospective View, Plan Europe 2000" in *The Future is Tomorrow* (M. Niihoff, The Hague, 1972).

WIKSTROM, SOLVEIG RAGNBORG

Born: 1931,Atland,Finland

Professor
Department of Business Administration
University of Lund
Fack
S-22005 Lund, Sweden

Telephone: (046) 124100

Profession: Professor of consumer affairs

Field of specialization: Consumer policy analysis; systems analysis; long-range planning; future studies; technology assessment applied to the relationship of business, governmental agencies, and consumers.

Education: Master of Science, Business Administration/Consumer Behavior, The Business School of Abo Akademi, Finland, 1957; Ph.D., Business Administration/Consumer Affairs/Consumer Behavior, The Business School of Abo Akademi and the Business School of Gothenburg, Sweden, 1961.

Professional employment: University of Lund, Department of Business Administration: Professor of Marketing and Consumer Affairs (1978-). Stockholm University, Department of Management Science: Associate Professor, Research Project Manager and Thesis Advisor (1969-78). Swedish Government's Department of Commerce: Part-time consultant and advisor (1973-76). Gutenberghs Reklam Advertising Agency: Marketing Manager and Special Consultant to the Board of Directors (1967-68). Swedish Government's Department of Finance and Department of Commerce: Full-time consultant and advisor (1964-67). Tornbloms Annonsbyra Advertising Agency: Marketing Manager of Consumer Products (1960-64).

Professional activities: Currently working on an opionions survey of Swedish public, business and regulator attitudes towards consumer-related issues; member, Swedish Futures Association (1972); initiator and manager of a research program, "Methods for Improving the Quality of Life Content in Consumption" (1973-); conducts graduate courses on long-range planning, future studies and consumer economics; manager of an interdisciplinary seminar on consumer affairs and consumer research, 1975); has written and lectured extensively on the future of business environment, retailing and the consumers situation.

Publications: Editor and co-author, *In the Consumer's Interest—Business, Enterprises, Consumers and Agencies from a Consumer's Perspective* (Business and Social Research Institute (SNS), Stockholm, April 1979); co-author, "Models for Consumer Intervention in Planning Retail Services" in *The Swedish Retail System in the 1980's* (Marketing Techniques Center, Spring 1979); co-author, "Harmonizing the Views of Business and Consumers on Social Responsibility in Marketing" in *Future Directions of Marketing* (Marketing Science Institute, 1978); "The Convenience Goods Distribution Now and in the Future: A Model and an Overall Analysis from the Consumer's Point of View" (Government Commission Report, Appendix A, 1975); *The Food Marketing Process: A Future Study* (Bonniers, 1973).

WILLIAMS, CHARLES W.

Born: 1931, New Orleans, Louisiana, U.S.A.

President
Charles W. Williams, Inc. (Policy Research and Assistance)
801 North Pitt Street, Suite 117
Alexandria, Virginia 22314, U.S.A.

Telephone: (703) 548-2501

Profession: Policy Research

Field of specialization: Policy planning and forecasting for government and business

Education: B.S., Business Administration, University of Alabama, 1953; NIPA Fellow, Public Administration and Political Science, Stanford University, 1964; Economics of National Security, Industrial College of the Armed Forces.

Professional employment: Charles W. Williams, Inc.: President (1973-). Stanford Research Institute: Deputy Director, Center for the Study of Social Policy (1971-73). President's Advisory Council on Management Improvement: Research Director (1971). The White House: Staff Director, National Goals Research Staff (1969-71). National Science Foundation: Staff Associate, Office of Planning and Policy Studies (1965-69).

Professional activities: —

Publications: "Inventing a Future Civilization" (THE FUTURIST, August 1972); "Whither Private Enterprise: What is Happening to Our Quality of Life?" (Speech before the Financial Management Institute, Northeastern Conference, Montreal, Canada, June 7, 1975).

WILSON, ALBERT GEORGE
Director
Research Program Studies
P.O. Box 113
Topanga, California 90290, U.S.A.

Born: 1918, Houston, Texas, U.S.A.

Telephone: (213) 455-1764

Profession: Mathematician; morphologist

Field of specialization: Methodologies of futures research, especially morphological construction; epistemology of systems theory and futures research; worldviews and their value systems.

Education: B.S., Electrical Engineering, Rice Institute, 1941; M.S., Mathematics, 1942, Ph.D., Mathematics and Physics, 1947, California Institute of Technology.

Professional employment: Research Program Studies: Director (1978-); Associate Director (1969-1977). McDonnell-Douglas Corporation: Director, Environmental Sciences Laboratories, The Douglas Advanced Research Laboratories (1966-69). The Rand Corporation: Senior Research Staff, Environmental Sciences (1957-65). Mt. Wilson and Palomar Observatories: Staff Member (1947-53).

Professional activities: Associate, Institute for Advanced Systems Studies, California Polytechnic, working on designs of training models for environmental education; Visiting Professor, University of Southern California, conducting graduate course on "Patterns of the Future" (1970-); Editorial Board, *Technological Forecasting and Social Change* (1974-); consultant, Institute for the Future, on designs for the institutionalization of change (1969-70); conducted graduate courses at University of California-Los Angeles on "Technological Forecasting" (1970, 1972), "Fundamentals of Futures Research" (1971), "Introduction to General Systems Theory" (1973); consulted on futures-related problems with industrial, educational and governmental bodies; has lectured and written widely on technical and popular futures topics.

Publications: Co-editor, *Hierarchical Structures* (American Elsevier, New York, 1969); co-editor, *New Methods of Thought and Procedure* (Springer-Verlag, New York, 1967); "Systems Epistemology" in *The World System*, Laszlo, Ed. (Braziller, New York, 1973); co-author, "Futures Orientation" in *Human Futuristics*, Maruyama and Dator, Eds. (University of Hawaii, 1971); co-author, *Relativity and the Question of Discretization in Astronomy* (Springer-Verlag, Berlin, 1970).

WILSON, DONALD N.
President
Institute for Canadian Futures
2323 Confederation Parkway, No. 206
Mississauga, Ontario
L5B 1R6 Canada

Born: 1943, Toronto, Ontario, Canada

Telephone: (416) 276-2660

Profession: Economist; policy analyst

Field of specialization: Long range public policy design; impact analysis of technological innovation and development computer simulation of socio-economic systems.

Professional employment: Institute for Canadian Futures: President, Senior Research Fellow (current).

Education: —

Professional activities: Currently designing a "Canada's Future Options Project" and "A Survey of Businesses in Canada"; implementing a "Municipal Energy Budget", an energy simulator for the design of energy efficient urban systems; conducts long range corporate planning seminars and has developed a long range corporate model known as "Corporate Structural Modelling"; presently publishing the *Canadian Futures Journal.*

Publications: Co-author, *A Suggested Municipal Energy Model: Alternative Energy Policies for Local Governments* (Institute for Canadian Futures Press, 1978); editor, *Get It Together: Tri Level Planning* (Institute for Canadian Futures Press, 1977); *A Suggested Model for a National Goals and Priorities Study* (Institute for Canadian Futures Press, 1977); *A Framework for Municipal Economic Planning* (Institute for Canadian Futures Press, 1977); *A Proposed Model for the Institute for Canadian Futures* (Institute for Canadian Futures Press, 1977).

WILSON, DONNA

Born: 1931, Omaha, Nebraska, U.S.A.

Associate
Institute for Advanced Systems Studies
California State Polytechnic University
3801 West Temple Avenue
Pomona, California 91768, U.S.A.

Telephone: (714) 598-4536

Profession: Psychologist; educator

Field of specialization: Psychological types; group dynamics; futures education.

Education: B.A., Astronomy, University of California-Los Angeles, 1961; Graduate Studies, Psychology and Philosophy, UCLA and Loyola University.

Professional employment: Institute for Advanced Systems Studies, California State Polytechnic University: Associate (1976-). Eomega Grove: Counselor (1969-76). Douglas Advanced Research Laboratories: Research Associate (1966-69). The Rand Corporation: Research Staff, Aero-Astronautics Department (1957-65).

Professional activities: Educational consultant, design of curricula, counseling, human relations workshops, group creativity seminars (current); has conducted graduate courses at University of California-Los Angeles, "Machine, Myth, Metaphor" (1973), "Technology and Social Forecasting" (1970-1972); Visiting Fellow, Institute for Man and Science, conducted workshops on "Ecology and Economics" and "Alternative Futures for America (1967-69).

Publications: Co-editor, *Hierarchical Structures* (American Elsevier, New York, 1969); co-author, *Toward the Institutionalization of Change* (Institute for the Future, 1970); "Forms of Hierarchy" (*General Systems Yearbook*, Vol. XV, 1970); co-author, "The Four Faces of the Future" (*Technological Forecasting and Social Change*, 1975); "Competing Images of the Future" (in press).

(From the first edition. Corrections not received by press time.)

WILSON, IAN. H.

Born: 1925, Pinner, England

Consultant
Public Policy Research
General Electric Company
3135 Easton Turnpike
Fairfield, Connecticut 06431, U.S.A.

Telephone: (203) 373-2920

Profession: Corporate planner; policy analyst

Field of specialization: Socio-political trends and their impact on business and education; changing value systems.

Education: M.A., Philosophy/History, Oxford University, 1947.

Professional employment: General Electric Company: Consultant, Public Policy Research (1976-); Staff Associate, Business Environment Research (1974-75); Consultant, Business Environment Studies (1967-73); Consultant, Management Development (1963-67); various public relations positions (1954-63).

Professional activities: Developing "futures modules" for management education courses for General Electric Management Development Institute (1977-78); currently working on analyses of present and future public policy issues impacting business, and on socio-political forecasting (1976-); major studies for General Electric on aspects of future business environment (changing value systems, future minority environment, women's rights, inflation, future consumer markets) (1967-72); frequent lectures and writing on socio-political forecasting and corporate planning; Chairman, Citizens Advisory Committee on Long Range School Goals, Westport, Connecticut (1967-69).

Publications: "The Future of the World of Work" (*Advanced Management Journal*, Autumn 1978); *Corporate Environments of the Future: Planning for Major Change* (The Presidents Association, 1976); co-author, *The Business Environment of the 70s* (McGraw-Hill, 1970); "Socio-political Forecasting: New Dimension in Corporate Planning" (*Michigan Business Review*, July 1974); "The New Reformation" (THE FUTURIST, June 1971).

WINIECKI, JAN STANISLAW

Associate Professor
Polish Institute of International Affairs
P.O. Box 1000
la Warecka Street
00-950 Warsaw, Poland

Born: 1938, Sopot, Poland

Telephone: 26-30-21

Profession: Economist; policy analyst

Field of specialization: Long term trends in the world economy; international economics including multi-national business; technology transfer; forecasting methodology; global modelling; forecasting of international economic and political relations.

Education: Foreign Trade Department, Main School of Planning and Statistics, 1955-57; M.A., Law and Administration Department, 1964, LL.D. International Organizations, 1971, Post-doctoral Degree, Political Science Department, 1978, Warsaw University.

Professional employment: Polish Institute of International Affairs: Associate Professor, Head, Inter-disciplinary Forecasting Group (1973-). Center for Scientific, Technological and Economic Information, Warsaw: Head, Department of Economic Policy (1972-73). Central Council of Trade Unions, Economic Analysis Department: Economic Analyst (1965-71).

Professional activities: "The Future of Multinational Corporation in International System" research project (1977-80); continuing research on: 1) medium-term prospects of the Western economies-growth inflation, and employment, 2) long-term structural change in world production and trade; "Prognostics and Politics-Prognosological Studies in International Relations" book in progress (1978-79); Executive Secretary, Commission on International Problems, Committee "Poland 2000" of the Polish Academy of Sciences (1977-); written extensively on international economic relations, especially on the position of the United States and Japan, on international transfer of technology, and on methodological and theoretical problems of forecasting in international relations-political and economic.

Publications: *Economic Instruments of Foreign Policy in International Politics* (in Polish, PIIA, Warsaw, 1975); "The U.S. in International Economic Relations: Trends and Perspectives" (*International Affairs*, No. 11, 1974); "External Economic Relations of Japan after the Energy Crisis" (*International Affairs*, No. 1, 1976); co-author, "Multilateral Transfer of Skills and Knowledge" in *Problems of Scientific and Technological Progress* (PSP, 1977); "On Limitations and Possibilities of Forecasting in International Relations" (Conference Papers, Volume I, 1976).

WITT-HANSEN, JOHANNES

Professor
Institute of Philosophy
University of Copenhagen
Kobmagergade 50
1150 Copenhagen K, Denmark

Born: 1908, Levring, Denmark

Telephone: (01) 134570

Profession: Professor of philosophy

Field of specialization: Value systems; futures methodology; ecology.

Education: B.A., Physics/Chemistry, 1930, M.A., 1949, Ph.D., 1959, Philosophy, University of Copenhagen.

Professional employment: University of Copenhagen: Professor, Institute of Philosophy (1959-); Assistant Professor (1957-59). Folks' High School: Teacher (1934-57).

Professional activities: Member, Board of *Danish Yearbook of Philosophy* (1966); member, Board of Poznan Studies in the Philosophy of the Sciences and the Humanities (1975); investigation of the impact of mathematical and physical science on Marxian social science (1957-); investigation of the relationship between futures research in Western Europe and the Communist countries (1967-); member, Academy for Futures Research, Copenhagen (1967-); author of Introduction and editor of the first Danish edition of *Karl Marx: Capital I-III* (1970-72).

Publications: *Historical Materialism: The Method, The Theories*, Book I (Munksgaard, 1960); *On Generalization and Problems of Generalization in Mathematical and Historical Sciences*, in Danish (Festskrift, University of Copenhagen, 1963); *Historical Materialism: Marx's Social Science, Its Philosophy and*

Method, in Danish (Berlingske Forlag, Copenhagen, 1973); author and editor, "Marxian Methodology and the Research of Futures" (*Danish Yearbook of Philosophy,* 1973); "The Futurologist, in Time and the Philosophies" (UNESCO, 1977).

WOODWARD, DOUGLAS
Born: 1933, England

Long Range Planning Directorate
Policy Research and Strategic Planning Branch
Health and Welfare Canada
Government of Canada
Brooke Claxton Building Room 1344
Ottawa, Ontario, Canada K1K 4A8

Telephone: (613) 992-4962

Profession: Strategic Long-range planner

Field of specialization: Socio-economic effects of science and technology progress. Human side-effects of the inability of large businesses, industries and governments to cope with contemporary and emerging social values in an increasingly complex and unmanageable world.

Education: B.Comm., Sir George Williams University, 1967; Certificate in Policy Analysis/-Econometrics, University of Toronto, 1974; Corporate Planning, Centre d'Etudes Industrielles, Geneva, 1975.

Professional employment: Health and Welfare Canada: Senior Planning Officer (1977-). Treasury Board Secretariat, Government of Canada: Chief, Futures Research and Forecasting (1974-77); Head, Planning Section (1971-74). Public Service Commission, Government of Canada: Staff Consultant (1970-71).

Professional activities: Co-Vice-President, Futures Research Committee, International Sociological Association. Activities directed towards an understanding of the appropriate methods and strategies to synthesize the futures research strategy and planning relating human futures to coping with scientific and technological progress.

Publications: Editor, *Canadian Agriculture in the Seventies* (Queens Printer for Canada, 1970); *Quality of Working Life: Concept and Implications for Personnel Policy* (Treasury Board, 1975); *Disability Insurance Plan: Analysis of Variables Contributing to Claims* (Treasury Board, 1974); co-author, *Towards the Future—A Socio-Political Exploration* (unpublished, 1976); *A Futures Report to Aid Long-Term and Strategic Planning in the Personnel Policy Branch* (Treasury Board, 1975).

WREN-LEWIS, JOHN
Born: 1924, Rochester, England

Ragged Mountain Center
2613 P Street, N.W.
Washington, D.C. 20007, U.S.A.

Telephone: (202) 338-7450

Profession: Freelance writer and lecturer

Field of specialization: Future directions in science and technology; changing public attitudes to science and technology; the future of religion in society; the future of human consciousness.

Education: B.Sc., Applied Mathematics, Imperial College, London University, 1945.

Professional employment: Self-employed: Freelance writer and lecturer (current position). Imperial Chemical Industries, Ltd., England: Editor and Social Studies Specialist, *Year 2000 Study* (1963-71); Acting Administrator of Central Laboratory (1960-62); Chairman of Committee on Scientific and Technical Computer Applications (1955-60); R & D Administrator (1946-55).

Professional activities: Current studies: healthy versus neurotic elements in current movements for greater awareness of nature; relationship between belief in immortality and social consciousness; current anti-scientific attitudes; and dreams as a tool for forecasting future social trends. Governor of Manchester College, Oxford (1968-72); External Examiner in Social Science and Technology, Loughborough University (1970-72); lecturer in New Movements in Theological Thought, University of Edinburgh (1964); first Chairman of the Association for Humanistic Psychology, Great Britain (1971).

Publications: *What Shall We Tell the Children?* (Constable, London, 1971); "Faith in the Technological Future," in *The Futurists,* Alvin Toffler, Ed. (Random House, 1972); "Teaching Scientists to

Future-Think," in *Learning for Tomorrow*, Alvin Toffler, Ed. (Random House, 1973); "Love's Coming-of-Age," in *Psychoanalysis Observed*, Charles Rycroft, Ed. (Penguin Books, 1966); *God in a Technological Age*, booklet (Forward Movement Publications, 1965).

YANKELOVICH, DANIEL

Born: 1924, Boston, Massachusetts, U.S.A.

President
Yankelovich, Skelly and White, Inc.
575 Madison Avenue
New York, New York 10022, U.S.A.

Telephone: (212) 752-7500

Profession: Social scientist

Field of specialization: How attitudes, values and beliefs influence social change.

Education: B.A., Social Relations, 1946, Rantoul Fellow in Clinical Psychology, 1948-50, Harvard University; Philosophy, Sorbonne, 1950-52.

Professional employment: Yankelovich, Skelly and White: President (1958-). New York University: Professor (1969-). Nowland and Company: Research Director (1952-58).

Professional activities: Currently working on a grant from Ford Foundation, "Response to Shortages in Three Industrial Countries" and continuing studies of political indicators in the U.S., life-styles and value changes in the U.S., and changing public demands on the corporation.

Publications: Co-author, *Ego and Instinct* (Random House, 1970); *The New Morality* (McGraw-Hill, 1974); *Changing Values on Campus* (Simon and Schuster, 1972); co-author, *Work, Productivity and Job Satisfaction* (Psychological Corporation, 1975).

(From the first edition. Corrections not received by press time.)

YOUNG, DAVID LESLIE

Born: 1945, London, United Kingdom

Manager, Market Research
Telecom Australia
16th Floor, 518 Little Bourke St.
Melbourne, Victoria
3000, Australia

Telephone: (03) 602-2604

Profession: Organizational psychologist

Field of specialization: Social forecasting; sociotechnical systems analysis; futures methodology; organizational development; social research methodology.

Education: B. Comm (Honours), Economics and Social Psychology, University of New South Wales, 1967; M.A. (Honours), Social Psychology, Macquarie University, 1971.

Professional employment: Telecom Australia: Manager, Market Research (1977-); Social Scientist, Telecom 2000 Project (1974-77). Mitchell College: Lecturer, Organizational Psychology (1972-74). CDC (Australia): Lecturer, Software/Student Counsellor (1970-72). Macquarie University: Tutor, Psychology (1968-79).

Professional activities: Research on effects of television (1973-); lecturer in social technical systems, Royal Melbourne Institute of Technology (1978); lecturer in organizational development (1976-); Bathurst-Orange Growth Centre Study (commissioned by Australian Government Cities Commission) (1973); lecturer, "Coping with Change," Sydney University (1972; Chairman, Regular Officer Development Committee, Search Conference, Department of Defense (1977).

Publications: "The Ecology of Telecommunications" in *Technology vs. Society* (Queensland University Press, in press); "Social Futures" chapter 1 of *Telecom 2000* (Australian Government Printer, 1976); co-author, "Computer Communications" and "Introduction of New Services" chapters in *Telecom 2000* (Australian Government Printer, 1976); *The Future of Entertainment* (UNESCO, 1977); co-author, "The Curriculum Disciplines Evaluation Analogue" (*Journal of Advanced Education*, 1973).

386

ZEMAN, ZAVIS PETER
Project Leader
Institute for Research on Public Policy
3535 Queen Mary Road, No. 514
Montreal, Quebec
H3V 1H8 Canada

Born: 1937, Prague, Czechoslovakia

Telephone: (514) 342-9121

Profession: Policy analyst

Field of specialization: Technology pre-assessment; futures methodology; long-range planning; systems theory.

Education: Diploma, Economic Engineering, 1960, C.Sc., Civil Engineering, Czech Technical University; Diploma, Systems Dynamics, MIT, 1971; Postgraduate courses, Philosophy of Science, McGill University.

Professional employment: Institute for Research on Public Policy: Project Leader (1977-). University of Montreal: Visiting Professor (1972-76); Project Manager (1969-72). Concordia University: Research Consultant (1969). Northumberland Consultants: Research Engineer (1967-69).

Professional activities: Responsible for "OMENA" project (impacts of technological and economic changes on Canadian society), a series of early warning probes into world processing, new world monetary system, seabed mining, home computer, transborder data flows and other topics; participation in the electronic information exchange system; teaching graduate courses in systems theory; research in systems; lectures and presentations; member of a dozen learned and professional societies.

Publications: Co-author, *Place in the Sun: Canada as a Resource Supplier for Japanese Economy* (Institute for Research on Public Policy, 1978); numerous other publications not relevant to present futures work.

ZIEGLER, WARREN LEIGH
Director
The Futures-Invention Project
1250 South Williams Street
Denver, Colorado 80210, U.S.A.

Born: 1927, New York, New York, U.S.A.

Telephone: (303) 733-1854

Profession: Policy analyst; educator

Field of specialization: Long-term participatory planning; civic literacy and citizen participation; policy analysis and formulation in education and lifelong learning; futures-invention in all domains (e.g., health, education, criminal justice, ecology/environment, the future of cities and communities, religion, etc.).

Education: B.A., Liberal Arts, 1948, M.A., Social Science, 1951, University of Chicago.

Professional employment: The Futures-Invention Project, Syracuse Research Corporation: Director (1975-). The Futures-Invention Associates: President (1977-). Syracuse University: Associate Professor of Education (adjunct); School of Education (1969-). Educational Policy Research Center, Syracuse Research Corporation: Co-director (1969-74). Agency for International Development, State Department: Associate Director of Personnel for Manpower Development (1966-68).

Professional activities: Currently conducting futures-invention projects and workshops around the country with a wide variety of education, government, religious, community organizations; conducting graduate seminars in futures-invention and policy at various universities; emphasizing research and writing on the future of lifelong learning and post-secondary education, on civic literacy and participatory planning; educational policy analysis, Syracuse Research Corporation (1969-74); manpower and personnel, Agency for International Development (1965-68); international development, U.S. Peace Corps, Nigeria (1963-65).

Publications: *The Art of Futures-Invention* (The Futures-Invention Associates, June 1977); *A Mindbook for Futures-Inventors* (The Futures-Invention Associates, June 1978); co-author with Grace M. Healey, *Adult Learning and the Future of Post-Secondary Education* (ERIC Clearinghouse on Career Education, April 1977); *On Civic Literacy* (Educational Policy Research Center, Syracuse, New York, July 1974); "Planning as Action: Techniques of Inventive Planning Workshops" in *Participatory Planning in Education* (OECD, Paris, 1974).

ZUCKERMAN, PETER

Secretary-Treasurer
World Future Society
4916 St. Elmo Avenue
Washington, D.C. 20014, U.S.A.

Born: 1929, Budapest, Hungary

Telephone: (301) 656-8274

Profession: Association executive

Field of specialization: Management; planning; systems analysis.

Education: B.S., 1957, M.B.A., 1959, Business Administration, University of California-Los Angeles.

Professional employment: World Future Society: Secretary-Treasurer (1966-). EDP Technology, Inc.: Management Consultant (1968-72). System Development Corporation: Management Consultant (1966-68). Northrop Corporation: Systems Analyst (1965-66). North American Aviation: Systems Analyst (1962-65).

Professional activities: Secretary-Treasurer, World Future Society (1966-); Project Manager: "An Introduction to the Study of the Future" (1976-77); "Information Sources for the Study of the Future" (1976-77); "Model Cities Program Information System" (1969-72).

Publications: *Systems Life Cycle Standards* (Brandon/Systems Press, 1970).

RESEARCH PROJECTS

RESEARCH PROJECTS

The projects listed here represent only a small sampling of the hundreds of studies now being conducted by government, business, and educational institutions in many countries. This selection is offered solely to suggest the scope and variety of current futures research. The projects are listed alphabetically by organization rather than by subject.

Where available, the following information is provided for each project listed:

Name of performing organization
Mailing address
Name of sponsor
Title of project
Name and title of principal investigator(s)
Expected period of effort
Project budget
Summary of project approach and objectives

Performing organization: Academy for Contemporary Problems, 1501 Neil Avenue, Columbus, Ohio 43201, U.S.A.

Sponsor: German Marshall Fund of the United States

Title of Project: The Trinational Cities Exchange

Principal Investigator (s): Gail G. Schwartz, Director

Period of Effort: May 1978 through 1979   **Budget:** No answer

Summary of Project: This project compares urban problems and strategies for dealing with them, in the United States, West Germany and Great Britain, with the purpose of selecting strategies in one or more countries suitable for "exporting" to one or more of the other countries.

Performing organization: Arab Educational, Cultural and Scientific Organization, Science Unit, Tahrir Street 109, Giza, Egypt

Sponsor: Arab League Educational, Cultural and Scientific Organization (ALECSO)

Title of Project: Content and Prerequisites for Successful Undertaking of a Study of Science and Technology in Arab Region by the Year 2000

Principal Investigator (s): Ali Nassar and Hussam Mandour

Period of Effort: November 1978 to November 1979   **Budget:** $30,000

Summary of Project: A growing number of Arab organizations and institutes are interested in long-term predictions and forecasting. In recent discussion on the future of science and technology in Arab regions there was an agreement on the necessity of formulating clear ideas on the concepts of science and technology future potentials, the necessary information system, preconditions of successful application of the available techniques for investigating the distant future, and how such investigations could be undertaken in the form of a comprehensive analysis taking into account development scenarios of the Arab region.
The project contains studies and seminars designed for participants of different levels, which contribute to the above mentioned objectives.

Performing organization: Arab League Educational, Cultural and Scientific Organization (ALECSO), 109 Tahrir Street, Dokki, Giza, Egypt.

Sponsor: Arab League Educational, Cultural and Scientific Organization (ALECSO)

Title of Project: Environmental Considerations in Development Planning

Principal Investigator (s): Samir I. Ghabbour, Consultant, Environmental Programmes, ALECSO

Period of Effort: January 1977 to December 1981   **Budget:** $80,000

Summary of Project: The entire Arab World, no matter what differences may exist between its countries in physical, social and economic conditions, is preoccupied for many years now with development, because Arabs feel that their position in the modern world is out of proportion to their resources and does not satisfy their legitimate ambitions. Development is mainly the rationalization of the use of resources, maximization of their yield, and sustainability, for the welfare of the Arab citizen wherever he is. Thus our preoccupation with development should be accompanied by our concern not to destroy or spoil our environment. The dilemma is to reconcile two aims: the developmental experience in the Arab World has shown that there could be no hope of conserving the environment if millions of our citizens live the way they do now; at the same time, there is no hope in a uni-lateral development which cares only about capital and profit and does not ensure its continuity by conserving the environment.

Performing organization: Arab League Educational, Cultural and Scientific Organization (ALECSO), 109 Tahrir Street, Dokki, Giza, Egypt

Sponsor: ASPEN Institute and UNEP

Title of Project: Technologies for the Satisfaction of Basic Human Needs in the Arab Region

Principal Investigator (s): O.A. El-Kholy

Period of Effort: February 1978 to February 1980   **Budget:** $120,000

Summary of Project: Although a number of Arab countries are endowed with large reserves of mineral resources, and others with large tracts of cultivable land, the majority of their populations still rank within the less affluent sections of the world population and their basic human needs are not adequately met. The constraint is no longer colonialism, lack of capital, lack of know-how, etc., as it used to be a few decades ago, but rather lack of the suitable technologies for the introduction of modern production methods which should maximize yields without harming the basic life-support systems of production. The project aims at paving the way for the formulation of plans to create this technology.

Performing organization: Arab League Educational, Cultural and Scientific Organization (ALECSO), 109 Tahrir Street, Dokki, Giza, Egypt

Sponsor: ALECSO, Arab League Economic Council, and Arab League HQ

Title of Project: Science and Technology in the Arab Region in the year 2000

Principal Investigator(s): O.A. El-Kholy

Period of Effort: October 1974 to October 1980   **Budget:** $100,000

Summary of Project: Arab nations stand at an important crossroads in history, related to the special position of the Arab World on one hand, and, on the other, to the general conditions of development in the world at large, which tend to widen the gap between rich, industrial and poor, developing nations. These conditions emanate from two main factors: (a) the increasing dependence on science and technology to meet the requirements of pressing development needs, and (b) the tendency of states to coalesce into regional collectives in order to be able to compensate for their individual lack of expertise by scientific, economic and political cooperation.

Performing organization: Austrian Institute for Economic Research, Arsenal Objekt 20, Postfach 91, Vienna, Austria, A-1103

Sponsor: The Institute

Title of Project: Medium Term Forecasts for the Austrian Economy

Principal Investigator(s): Jiri Skolka

Period of Effort: Permanent task, starting 1978   **Budget:** No answer

Summary of Project: The Institute regularly prepares medium-term forecasts of the future development of the Austrian economy. The macroeconomic forecasts concentrate on the estimation of the likely rate of the GDP growth and on the development of final demand components (private, consumption, gross fixed capital formation, exports). The specific topics are, *inter alia,* the forecasting of energy demand, manpower supply, agricultural output, public expenditure, structure of manufacturing industry, etc. The results are published in the Institute's journal *Monatsberichte.*

Performing organization: Gerald O. Barney & Associates, Inc., c/o Council on Environmental Quality, 722 Jackson Place, N.W., Washington, D.C. 20006, U.S.A.

Sponsor: Council on Environmental Quality

Title of Project: Global 2000 Study

Principal Investigator(s): Gerald O. Barney, Study Director

Period of Effort: October 1977 through October 1978   **Budget:** No answer

Summary of Project: In his May Environmental Message, President Carter directed the Council on Environmental Quality and the Department of State, working in cooperation with the Environmental Protection Agency, the National Science Foundation, the National Oceanic and Atmosphere Administration, and other appropriate agencies to make a one-year study of the probable changes in the world's population, natural resources and environment through the end of the century. The study is to serve as the foundation of the Government's longer-term planning. To answer the President's directive, the study will draw upon existing models and projection tools, giving first priority to capabilities within the Government. While most projection and modeling capabilities now available are restricted to relatively narrow disciplines or subjects, the study will draw these single-purpose projections together as consistently as possible into an integrated whole. The results of this process will be compared with those of large-scale systems-models such as that developed by Professor Mihajlo Mesarovic at Case Western Reserve University. A number of these large systems-models will be analyzed as possible approaches to the kind of integrated analyses required for longer-range planning. The study will identify scarcities and problems which may become serious by 2000 and the years following the turn of the century, to the extent that these can be identified in this brief analysis. The study will also suggest ways in which the effectiveness and efficiency of longer-range planning can be increased and will identify research priorities in science, technology and other areas.

Performing organization: Battelle Columbus Laboratories, 2030 M Street, N.W., Washington, D.C. 20036, U.S.A.

Sponsor: National Science Foundation

Title of Project: An Agenda for Technology Assessment in the Materials Field

Principal Investigator (s): A.N. Christakis, Research Leader, Futures and Policy Research

Period of Effort: July 1977 to May 1978   **Budget:** $70,000

Summary of Project: This project is based on a study for the derivation of topics for technology assessment through the application of a systematic methodology. The methodology is based on the use of science forums to engage experts in forecasting and assessing technology candidates in the context of a hypothetical scenario. The area of technology of the topics in this study is materials, but the procedure should be equally applicable to other fields. The relative urgency for assessment of the "TA Candidates" was determined through statistical analysis of ratings assigned to the candidates at a science forum, by experts representing two points of view: science and technology on the one hand, and social science on the other.

Performing organization: Battelle Columbus Laboratories with the University of Michigan, 2030 M Street, N.W., Washington, D.C. 20036, U.S.A.

Sponsor: Environmental Protection Agency

Title of Project: Coal Technology Assessment

Principal Investigator (s): Richard S. Davidson, A.N. Christakis, K. Kawamura

Period of Effort: November 1977 to July 1980   **Budget:** $1,500,000

Summary of Project: The expected future demand for coal would require developing not only new technology for coal mining, transportation, conversion, and utilization, but also new infrastructure to manage them. However, providing sound guidance for policy decisions regarding the balance between the forecasted energy demand and the protection of the quality of the environment has been the source of much debate in the United States. The U.S. Environmental Protection Agency intends to provide such guidance through a 2-1/2 year study recently started in November 1977, at Battelle's Columbus Laboratories and the University of Michigan.

The study utilizes the futures-creative** methodological approach that the Battelle-Michigan team has adopted. Three principal aspects of the TA approach adopted are: (a) a technical analysis based on scientific knowledge and data, (b) a policy analysis focusing on the major political issues and alternative futures, and (c) a social learning process and the involvement of the interested parties. **See M. Boroush, K. Chen, and A.N. Christakis, *Technology Assessment: Creative Futures*, to be published during 1978.

Performing organization: Battelle Columbus Laboratories, 2030 M. Street, N.W., Washington, D.C. 20036, U.S.A.

Sponsor: National Science Foundation

Title of Project: Forecasting Science and Industry

Principal Investigator (s): A.N. Christakis, Research Leader, Futures and Policy Research

Period of Effort: January 1977 to May 1977   **Budget:** $70,000

Summary of Project: This project was undertaken to forecast the future of science and industry and the relationship between the two, for the decade 1980 to 1990. The project had both a methodological purpose and a substantive objective. Methodologically its purpose was to devise an approach to make such forecasts, and to render them credible and plausible through a dialogue among experts. For the substantive objective, the following five industries were

394

selected jointly with NSF for the forecasts: chemicals, electronics, health care delivery, metals and transportation equipment; and two sciences were chosen to be forecast: chemistry and materials science.

Performing organization: Brookings Institution, 1775 Massachusetts Ave., N.W., Washington, D.C. 20036, U.S.A.

Sponsor: Brookings Institution

Title of Project: The Baby Boom Generation: An Economic "History"

Principal Investigator (s): Louise B. Russell

Period of Effort: July 1978 to July 1980 **Budget:** No answer

Summary of Project: Do changes in the age structure of the population have important effects on the economy, and, if so, what are the nature and magnitude of those effects? Louise B. Russell will examine these questions by focusing on the baby boom generation—the group of people born during the years 1946-65—and following this cohort through its life cycle from childhood to old age. Since the first members of this cohort reached the age of 30 in 1976 and the last are only about 10 years old, the study will be only in part a true history. It will apply what is known about the relationships between age structure and economic phenomena to suggest what the economic future of this generation, and because of this generation, the future of the economy, may be.

Performing organization: Center for Futures Research, University of Southern California, Los Angeles, California 90007, U.S.A.

Sponsor: Fifteen major corporations

Title of Project: The Future Environments of International Trade

Principal Investigator (s): Selwyn Enzer, Principal Investigator

Period of Effort: August 1977 to September 1978 **Budget:** $80,000

Summary of Project: This project is designed to provide a multidisciplinary analysis of alternative means of restructuring international trade to permit world markets to operate effectively over the long-term while enabling the poor nations to repay their debts and achieve self-sufficiency. Issues include the nature and magnitude of busines opportunities and problems resulting from a new world economic order, and long-term implications for inflation, capital markets, raw material availability and foreign investments.

Performing organization: Center for Futures Research, University of Southern California, Los Angeles, California 90007, U.S.A.

Sponsor: Ten corporations

Title of Project: Interax

Principal Investigator (s): Selwyn Enzer, Principal Investigator

Period of Effort: January 1978 to January 1979 **Budget:** $80,000

Summary of Project: This is a major methodology development project aimed at developing a large general purpose interactive cross-impact model capable of being linked to existing strategic planning models. It will include a large data base, computer program, operating manual and all software for conducting interactive analyses.

Performing organization: Centre International de Recherche sur l'Environnement et le Developpement (International Center for Research on Development and the Environment), 54, boulevard Raspail, 75270 Paris Cedex 06, France

Sponsor: CNUCED

Title of Project: Energy Demand in the Third World and Investment Requirements

Principal Investigator (s): J.C. Hourcade

Period of Effort: November 1977 tu January 1979   **Budget:** No answer

Summary of Project: This project begins with three contrasting scenarios for development and seeks to define the energy styles corresponding to each, and to evaluate the investment flows required for these energy futures.

Performing organization: Centre International de Recherche sur l'Environnement et le Developpement (International Center for Research on Development and the Environment), 54, boulevard Raspail, 75270 Paris Cedex 06, France

Sponsor: International Foundation for a Different Development

Title of Project: "Tomorrow Today": Social Experimentation, Changes in Life-Style and Development

Principal Investigator (s): I. Sachs, M. Schiray

Period of Effort: January 1978 continuing   **Budget:** No answer

Summary of Project: Creation of an information network to identify social experiments having a basically innovative character. Detailed study of a certain number of particularly important cases. Organization in several industrialized countries of public debates with many different types of voluntary groups. Study of the role and methods of communications and exchange that might lead to social experimentation.

Performing organization: Centre for Policy Research, 27, Paschimi Marg, Vasant Vihar, New Delhi 110057, Delhi, India

Sponsor: Centre for Policy Research

Title of Project: Dynamics of Rural Futures

Principal Investigator (s): P.N. Rastogi, Professor

Period of Effort: May 1, 1978 to December 31, 1978   **Budget:** $30,000

Summary of Project: This study aims at developing a computer simulation model of rural systems at village and block level to examine its course over a period of the next three to five decades. The system is sought to be viewed as a comprehensive whole in terms of the demographic factors, production, productivity, income, poverty, employment, migration, health, literacy, housing and rural social tensions. These factors would cover the rural population strata—large, medium, small and marginal farmers, landless labour and artisans individually and collectively. The course of the system as a whole would be traced under a variety of scenarios corresponding to the nature and dimensions of the measures of planned change. The impact of the people's participation in development, diverse administrative measures, political and socio-economic factors would be sought to be assessed through policy simulation experiments on the model. The study is designed for providing the preview of the possible rural future over the next 30 to 50 years.

Performing organization: Centre for Policy Research, 27, Paschimi Marg, Vasant Vihar, New Delhi, 110057, Delhi, India

Sponsor: Centre for Policy Research

Title of Project: Employment Policy

Principal Investigator (s): V. Subramaniam, Visiting Professor, Centre for Policy Research

Period of Effort: April 1, 1977 to June 30, 1979   **Budget:** $25,000

Summary of Project: The study proposes to examine the creation of about six million new jobs every year during the next 25 years based on the assumption that the labour force during this period will increase by about 150 million persons. These issues will be examined with special reference to the work done in Maharashtra under the Employment Guarantee Scheme and the ILO's experiments in India.

Performing organization: Centre for Policy Research, 27, Paschimi Marg, Vasant Vihar, New Delhi 110057, Delhi, India

Sponsor: Centre for Policy Research

Title of Project: Investment Policy for Agricultural Development

Principal Investigator (s): P.N. Rastogi, Professor, Indian Institute of Technology, Kanpur

Period of Effort: May 15, 1977 to September 14, 1977   **Budget:** $25,000

Summary of Project: This study covers the investment problems of Indian agricultural sector over the next 10-15 years or so. The thrust of the study is to look into the specific forms of investments especially in irrigation, fertilizers, pesticides, seeds, power and also the prospect of employment in the agriculture sector.

Performing organization: Centre for Policy Research, 27, Paschimi Marg, Vasant Vihar, New Delhi 110057, Delhi, India

Sponsor: Family Planning Foundation, New Delhi

Title of Project: Population Policy - 2000 A.D. - A Study of the Relationship Between Population and Economic Development

Principal Investigator (s): V.A. Pai Panandiker, Director, Centre for Policy Research and P.D. Malgavkar, Visiting Professor, Centre for Policy Research

Period of Effort: December 1, 1977 to May 31, 1979   **Budget:** $95,000

Summary of Project: The objective of the study is to examine: (1) Whether it is feasible to bring about a more effective relationship between economic development and population growth? Specially what would be the relationship of the various economic indicators of investments, income generation, employment, policy on industrial development, food production, regional development, etc. on the population policy. (2) What is the relationship between population growth and the ability of a country to provide the minima to the people? In particular, how the population below the poverty line can be ensured the minimum levels of consumption within the next 25 years and implications thereof to the population policy? (3) To examine the problems of the rate of population growth and income levels. In particular whether a relationship can be established between higher income and the reduction in the rate of population growth. (4) To study the factors designed to improve the quality of life not only in terms of the minimum needs but other items as well for the population over the next 25 years. (5) To study the issues pertaining to internal security arising out of the population growth, especially the areas of the country where the rate of growth may not be commensurate with the population increase which in turn may lead to the problems of internal security, law and order, etc.

Performing organization: Centre for Policy Research, 27, Paschimi Marg, Vasant Vihar, New Delhi 110057, Delhi, India

Sponsor: Centre for Policy Research

Title of Project: Towards an Industrial Policy-2000 A.D.

Principal Investigator (s): P.D. Malgavkar, Visiting Professor, Centre for Policy Research; V.A. Pai Panandiker, Director, Centre for Policy Research

Period of Effort: January 1, 1975 to September 30, 1978   **Budget:** $50,000

Summary of Project: The study looks into the basic objectives and prerequisites for a successful industrial policy up to the year 2000 A.D. This study places at the very core of industrial policy the four key socio-economic objectives of meeting: (a) the minimum needs of the masses, (b) the strategic requirements of the nation, (c) the export objectives and the research and development goals to be abreast of the developed nations by the 21st century.

The study suggests the need for effective population control and food production to provide the basis for economic development. It also brings to the limelight the crucial problem of unemployment facing the country and the scale of effort which will be required to meet the challenge from now on to the end of the century.

Performing organization: Centre for Policy Research, 27, Paschimi Marg, Vasant Vihar, New Delhi 110057, Delhi, India

Sponsor: Centre for Policy Research

Title of Project: Towards New Horizons in Agricultural Production: 2000 A.D.

Principal Investigator (s): C.H. Shah, Professor, Bombay University; S.D. Sawant, Bombay University

Period of Effort: July 1, 1976 to June 30, 1978   **Budget:** $25,000

Summary of Project: This study probes into the question on the supply side with the help of a series of seven scenarios, each one with different assumption. These scenarios which are based on projections as well as on linear programming exercises seek to answer: (1) What would be the future level of production if the past repeats into the future? (2) Can the country meet the minimum food needs by utilizing fully the irrigation potential? (3) What will be the impact of high yielding varieties or the new technology now in the pipeline on the food production? (4) Will the supply of fertilizers restrict the total food production despite the promise of the new technology? The seven scenarios used in this study may briefly be described as follows:

In the first scenario past trends for each component for each State have been projected for the future. It is an aggregate of production for each crop for each State that gives production level for the country as a whole.

Scenario 2 departs from the first one only in regard to the extent of area under irrigation.

Scenario 3 assumed that level of yields attained by the first generation of high yielding varieties may represent the average for entire area for the year 2000 A.D.

Scenario 4 provides the gains of the efficient allocation of scarce resources.

Scenario 5 uses the same constraints as scenario 4. The available labour supply projected for the year 2000 A.D. has been introduced as an additional constraint.

Scenario 6 is an extension of scenario 5. Instead of maximising the difference between the output and inputs, the total output is maximised, subject to the constraints of available levels of scarce resources and the need to meet the minimum food requirements.

Scenario 7 takes off the constraint regarding the supply of fertilizers. It postulates that fertilizers would be available in adequate quantity to maximise the production with given land and irrigation facilities.

Performing organization: Centre for World Food Studies, c/o Free University, P.O. Box 7161, Amsterdam, The Netherlands

Sponsor: Dutch Government, University of Wageningen, Free University in Amsterdam

Title of Project: Integrated Modelling Effort of Linking Country Models in an International Multi-Country Multi-Commodity Framework

Principal Investigator (s): Wonter Tims, Doeke Faber, C.T. de Wit

Period of Effort: 1976 to 1981-82   **Budget:** No answer

Summary of Project: With emphasis on agriculture, the research team is compiling country models for different countries. Agricultural knowledge will be inputted concerning soils and climate, production levels attainable at certain physical investment levels. The international framework to which country models will be linkable consists of a general equilibrium model for international trade relations.

Performing organization: Club d'Amics de la Futurologia (Club of Friends of Futurology,) Gran Via, 608 - 80 D, Barcelona, Spain

Sponsor: Same

Title of Project: The Structures of Power and the Universal Problematic

Principal Investigator (s): Rosa Menasanch, Secretary General of Honor and the Departments of Politics and Prospectives of the Club

Period of Effort: January 1978 to May 1978   **Budget:** No answer

Summary of Project: The purpose of this project is to study and systematize in the first place, what are the principle structures of power. After isolating the principle problems on the the universal level that effect humanity, we intend to see in what degree these structures of power, in their livelihood, influence and to what extent a change of the same things is necessary in order to approach a more realistic solution at the same time. Lastly we propose a series of alternatives that can help bring about this change.

Performing organization: The Club of Rome, Via Giorgoine, 163, Rome, 00147 Italy

Sponsor: The Club of Rome

Title of Project: Learning

Principal Investigator (s): Mircea Malitza, James Botkin, Mahdi Elmandjra

Period of Effort: January 1977 to January 1979   **Budget:** No answer

Summary of Project: Research and reflections on adaptive and anticipatory learning capability of individuals and society and how it can be developed in harmony with rapidly and radically changing realities.

Performing organization: The Club of Rome Learning Project, Harvard Education School, Nichols House, Cambridge, Massachusetts 02138, U.S.A.

Sponsor: The Club of Rome

Title of Project: Learning to Bridge the Human Gap

Principal Investigator (s): Mircea Malitza, James W. Botkin and Mahdi Elmandjra

Period of Effort: February 1977 to February 1979   **Budget:** No answer

Summary of Project: This study will attempt to create a new focus to clarify, study, and improve our capacity to cope with urgent world-wide problems. The authors start from the premise that human learning has not kept pace with the challenge of global issues and in fact the stagnation of learning sytems is one cause of the overwhelming complexity of the world problematique. In defining *learning* as the basic process, the authors make a break from earlier definitions, popularly associated with schooling, and predicated in the literature on the self-maintenance of learning systems. The great changes in the environment require a focus that highlights learning as a restructuring and value transforming process in an individual's interaction with society. Not only individuals learn, but societies learn as well. An effective process of learning has as key features: participation and anticipation, resulting in autonomy and reciprocity.
The Report will be aimed at increasing the awareness of the link between learning and global issues but at the same time will attempt to throw new light on the actions necessary to improve the formal and non-formal educational systems as part of the learning mechanisms of society.
The Report, to be published in a book of 200 pages for a wide audience, will have a parallel *Yearbook* of scientific articles contributing to the study of learning as explored by scholars in various disciplines.

Performing organization: The Club of Rome, Via Giorgione, 163, Roma, 00147 Italy

Sponsor: The Club of Rome

Title of Project: World Capital Requirements and Capital Formation

Principal Investigator (s): Orio Giarini

Period of Effort: January 1978 to June 1979   **Budget:** No answer

Summary of Project: Reflections on material resources (both natural endowment and capital accumulation) available to meet the growing needs and wants of a quickly expanding world population.

Performing organization: Contracultura Center, C.C. Central 1332, 1000 Buenos Aires, Argentina

Sponsor: Rolanroc Club

Title of Project: Pro-World 99

Principal Investigator (s): Anonymous

Period of Effort: May 1979 to 1999   **Budget:** No answer

Summary of Project: The purpose of this project is to coordinate several groups of researchers and voluntary teams with "flowing" members, covering three main areas: 1) analysis of a) current trends in Argentine Society and its unavoidable failures, b) possible trends in the same society and a feasible two decade model. 2) development of a "future consciousness" regarding the construction of a pilot town. 3) projection of the results to other Latin American countries.

Performing organization: Cornell University, Program on Science, Technology and Society, 614 Clark Hall, Ithaca, New York 14853, U.S.A.

Sponsor: National Science Foundation

Title of Project: An Exploratory Analysis and Assessment of Electronic Message Transfer

Principal Investigator (s): Raymond Bowers and Arnim H. Meyburg

Period of Effort: September 1, 1978 to February 1, 1980   **Budget:** $85,960

Summary of Project: The objective of the proposed research is to identify and provide some answers to some central questions regarding the use of electronic communications as a substitute for present mail freight transportation needs. A central but not exclusive component of the research will be the potential which electronic mail handling schemes have for conserving energy and other resources. Also considered will be alternative providers for mail service. Furthermore, the researchers will compile an inventory of potential social impacts, and place them in a cost/benefit framework.

Performing organization: Council on Foreign Relations, 58 East 68th Street, New York, New York 10021, U.S.A.

Sponsor: Council on Foreign Relations

Title of Project: The 1980's and Beyond

Principal Investigator (s): Richard H. Ullman (Director), Miriam C. Camps, William Diebold, Jr., David C. Gompert, Catherine B. Gwin, Roger Hansen, Edward L. Morse

Period of Effort: 1973 continuing   **Budget:** $1,300,000

Summary of Project: The 1980s Project resulted from the wide recognition that many of the assumptions, institutions, and policies that have governed international relations during the past 30 years are outmoded. The Project seeks to identify those future conditions and the kinds of adaptations they might require. In scope, it is the most ambitious research program ever undertaken by the 55-year-old Council on Foreign Relations.

Most of the Project's studies are prescriptive rather than merely descriptive or predictive. "They focus not simply on likely results of present trends extrapolated into the future but rather on what a desirable future would be so that trends can be 'steered' to those ends."

The Project has given special attention to such problems as: (a) controlling nuclear weapons and other weapons of mass destruction (b) coordinating economic policies with regard to such common world problems as inflation and unemployment; (c) reforming the international monetary system to make its cost and benefits more equitable; (d) reforming the international trading system, with special regard to raw materials, agricultural products, and East-West trade; (e) containing the spread and limiting the violence of armed conflict, and controlling world traffic in arms; (f) coping with international problems posed by national claims to ocean and seabed resources, atmospheric and water pollution, population growth, and scarcities of foodstuffs, fuels, and other raw materials; (g) reducing international terrorism and governmentally sponsored subversion; (h) monitoring governmental violations of human rights and inducing compliance with common standards; and (i) addressing the claims of less developed states for a larger proportion of the world's wealth and for greater participation in decisions affecting their welfare.

There will be no single final report on the Project's "findings." An effort will be made, however, to combine the many specialized studies into a small number of synthesizing, or integrating, books prepared by staff members and others. They will focus on North-South relations, human rights, the reform of international institutions and the creation of new ones to meet predictable problems of the midterm future and problems of peacekeeping and peacemaking.

Performing organization: Dartmouth College, Research Program on Technology and Public Policy, Box 8000, Hanover, New Hampshire 03755, U.S.A.

Sponsor: Department of Energy

Title of Project: Long-term Energy Economy Interactions

Principal Investigator (s): Dennis and Donella Meadows

Period of Effort: October 1, 1978 to December 30, 1981   **Budget:** No answer

Summary of Project: A system dynamics simulation model is being developed to project the consequences of increased energy costs, shortages, and capital requirements on GNP growth, composition, and distribution through 2025 in the United States.

Performing organization: Decision Sciences Corporation, Suite 528, Fox Pavilion, Jenkintown, Pennsylvania 19046, U.S.A.

Sponsor: Internal and several local governments

Title of Project: Fiscal Impact Analysis System (FIAS)

Principal Investigator (s): Donald F. Blumberg

Period of Effort: January 1973 continuing   **Budget:** $2.5 million

Summary of Project: Comprehensive study to develop a sophisticated computerized model of local government including: the community structure, the governmental structure, the environment, the private sector in order to forecast future scenarios as a function of change in any one component. The system, called the Fiscal Impact Analysis System/Environmental Impact Assessment System (FIAS/ENIAS) is now being used as a planning tool by several local governments.

Performing organization: Decision Sciences Corporation, Suite 528, Fox Pavilion, Jenkintown, Pennsylvania 19046, U.S.A.

Sponsor: Internal and 12 industrial firms

Title of Project: Health Care/Pharmaceutical Markets

Principal Investigator (s): Donald F. Blumberg and D. Cohn

Period of Effort: January 1977 to December 1979 **Budget:** $1.5 million

Summary of Project: To fully forecast the future of the U.S. (domestic) and international health care and medical market structure and trends for the period from 1978-1990 on a year by year basis. Includes extensive field surveys, 10 separate major mail questionnaires, directed to all major segments of the industry, and the development of a comprehensive computer model.

Consequences and Policy Implications of Increased Unionization of Personnel Involved with the Court System in the United States George Cole December 1976 to December 1978No answer The unionization of court employees could create problems that may affect not only labor relations in the judicial arena, but also the normative context within which justice is administered. The purpose of this work, now in progress, is to study the consequences and implications of increased unionization of personnel involved with state and local court systems in the United States. The structure and scope of collective bargaining arrangements will be described, along with their impact on the institutions and persons involved; and likely future conditions both internal and external to the court systems, that might lead to a growth in unionization of court and legal services personnel will be forecast. The scope and form of possible union growth also will be evaluated and the consequences of the evolution in light of the forecast will be described. Important issues and problems likely to arise under the forecasted conditions will be spotlighted, and policy guidelines for their resolution will be developed.

Performing organization: Delegation a l'amenagement du territoire et a l'action regionale (DATAR) Systeme d'etudes du scheme d'amenagement de la France (SESAME), 48 Bd de Latour Maubourg, 75 007, Paris, France

Sponsor: DATAR

Title of Project: Life Styles and Area Planning

Principal Investigator (s): No answer

Period of Effort: May 1978 to May 1979 **Budget:** No answer

Summary of Project: Deep transformation of the French society for 20 years have caused the rise of new claims about environmental quality. Life styles have changed and at the same time the environmental needs have changed. The Area Planning is now facing two problems: How is it possible to take into account these life styles? Which policies to choose in order to fit future life styles? SESAME will study how value systems appear and spread and at which socio-cultural resistances these value systems come up against. This research is a part of the research worked out by DATAR on that subject.

Performing organization: Delegation a l'amenagement du territoire et a l'action regionale (DATAR) Systeme d'etudes du scheme d'amenagement de la France (SESAME), 48 Bd de Latour Maubourg, 75 007, Paris, France

Sponsor: DATAR

Title of Project: Prospective Research on Agriculture

Principal Investigator (s): No answer

Period of Effort: May 1978 to May 1979 **Budget:** No answer

Summary of Project: Research and development on the foreseeable results of current technological research in the agricultural field in France and in the other industrialized countries. The purpose is to appreciate the impact on national economy of the place of France in the international agricultural market and especially on the agricultural activities and to examine consequent possibilities and new constraints for the different French regions.

Performing organization: Delegation a l'amenagement du territoire et a l'action regionale (DATAR) Systeme d'etudes du scheme d'amenagement de la France (SESAME), 48 Bd de Latour Maubourg, 75 007, Paris, France

Sponsor: DATAR

Title of Project: Scenarios on Employment

Principal Investigator (s): No answer

Period of Effort: April 1977 to June 1978 **Budget:** No answer

Summary of Project: Elaboration of three scenarios around the year 2000 according to different socio-political assumptions, according to international environment (insertion in international division of labour) which relates to volume, sectorial and spatial repartition and qualification of the active population. The scenarios approach more qualitative problems relative to behaviour facing work, to job dividing and to social relations.

Performing organization: Delegation a l'amenagement du territoire et a l'action regionale (DATAR) Systeme d'etudes du scheme d'amenagement de la France (SESAME), 48 Bd de Latour Maubourg, 75 007, Paris, France

Sponsor: DATAR

Title of Project: Scenarios on Transportation

Principal Investigator (s): No answer

Period of Effort: May 1978 to May 1979 **Budget:** No answer

Summary of Project: SESAME will propose scenarios on transportation based on research and development already done for the scenarios on employment (international assumptions and constraints, evaluation of industrial activities and services related to transportation). Contrasted assumptions will be introduced according to degree of voluntarism for area planning and state interventionism for transportation. At the same time these scenarios will allow the evaluation of constraints and consequences of "economic rationality" on organisation of transportation systems. They will allow the appreciation of effects of different policies of area planning on transporters and on the state transportation policy.

Performing organization: Forecasting International, Ltd., 1001 North Highland Street, Arlington, Virginia 22201, U.S.A.

Sponsor: United States Coast Guard

Title of Project: Forecast of Surveillance-related Program Standards

Principal Investigator (s): Charles McFadden

Period of Effort: September 1978 to April 1979 **Budget:** No answer

Summary of Project: This study will develop a U.S. Coast Guard Surveillance Research and Development Program, based upon an analysis of current surveillance requirements. These will be considered in conjunction with relevant trends and potential events in order to project requirements to the year 2005. An examination of emerging technologies and the existing and planned R&D efforts of other federal agencies will permit the identification of gaps which must be addressed in the USCG program.

Performing organization: Forecasting International, Ltd., 1001 North Highland Street, Arlington, Virginia 22201, U.S.A.

Sponsor: National Science Foundation

Title of Project: The Potential Influence of Social, Economic, Regulatory and Technological Factors on Scientific & Technical Communications Through 2000 A.D.

Principal Investigator (s): Norman Nisenoff

Period of Effort: September 1978 to March 1981 **Budget:** No answer

Summary of Project: The purpose of the project is to improve our understanding of the interaction of technological and non-technological factors influencing future changes in the scientific and technical information (STI) transfer process. This research will examine the influence of social, economic, regulatory and technological events upon established trends in the processing and distribution of STI, and predict the consequences of such trends and possible future events. The trends studied will relate to both capabilities and needs within predicted environments for the years 1980, 1990 and 2000, corresponding to the occurrence or non-occurrence of selected subsets of events.
Descriptions of alternative futures will be developed by the application of trend analysis and cross-impact analysis using existing data bases as a nucleus. This is to be augmented by individual as well as collective judgment during a workshop session involving expert consultants.

Performing organization: Forecasting International, Ltd., 1001 North Highland Street, Arlington, Virginia 22201, U.S.A.

Sponsor: United States Coast Guard

Title of Project: A Study of the Influence of Emerging Technologies and Other Factors on the People and Management of the Coast Guard

Principal Investigator (s): Marvin J. Cetron

Period of Effort: September 1978 to December 1979 **Budget:** No answer

Summary of Project: The tasks to be performed in this study include the identification of trends and events pertinent to Coast Guard personnel and management procedures; development of a structured description of areas of USCG concern in this context; an analysis of the impact of selected trends and events upon those areas of concern, and a synthesis and elaboration of these findings in a form appropriate for utilization in USCG planning and policy making.

Performing organization: Foundation Reshaping the International Order (RIO), Weena 700, P.O. Box 299, 3000 AG Rotterdam, The Netherlands

Sponsor: Government of Norway

Title of Project: The 'Like-Minded' Countries and The New International Order

Principal Investigator (s): Antony J. Dolman

Period of Effort: January 1978 continuing **Budget:** $40,000

Summary of Project: The project sets out to identify innovative and politically feasible ways whereby the group of so-called 'like-minded' countries could more creatively respond to assisting the Third World in its technological transformation. Such a transformation, aimed at reducing the technological dependence of the developing countries through the strengthening of their own autonomous technological capacities, is considered an essential of attempts to shape a more equitable international order. For the purposes of the project, 'like-minded' group is defined to include Finland, Denmark, Netherlands, Norway and Sweden.

Performing organization: Fundacion America Latina 2001, Apartado Aereo 854, Bogota, Colombia, Calle 10 No. 3-61, Bogota, Colombia

Sponsor: Fundacion America Latina 2001

Title of Project: Prospective, theoretical foundations and methodological significance

Principal Investigator (s): Horacio H. Godoy

Period of Effort: August 1978 to August 1979 **Budget:** $12,000

Summary of Project: 1. Theoretical foundations of prospective studies:
1.1 Special characteristics: a. World dimension (the world as a unit of analysis and as an optional unity); b. Long-term (25 to 30 years); c. Multisectorial analysis; d. Transdisciplinary approach; e. Practice oriented.
1.2 Prospective: a. Neither fatalism nor eutopic thinking; b. Prospective and future reality; c. The possible, the probable and the desirable futures.
1.3 Prospective thinking: a. Epistemology of practical knowledge; b. Projection and prospective; c. Mathematical models and normative models; d. Theoretical objections.
1.4 The critical realism and the future: a. Exploratory and normative prospective; b. Projection and prospective; c. Mathematical models and normative models; d. Theoretical objections.
1.5 Theoretical relation between diagnosis, transition and building of models.
1.6 The philosophical basis of prospective thinking: Towards a theory of prospective knowledge.

Performing organization: The Futures Group, 76 Eastern Blvd., Glastonbury, Connecticut 06033, U.S.A.

Sponsor: Department of Transportation

Title of Project: Alternatives for Major Changes in Urban Transportation

Principal Investigator (s) : W. Donald Goodrich, Manager, Transportation Studies

Period of Effort: October 1976 to July 1978   **Budget:** No answer

Summary of Project: The goal of this study, now nearing completion, is to address new transport technologies, transportation service improvements, and novel nontransport measures as alternatives to current planning in an effort to define actions that can substantially modify urban transportation systems in the overall direction of enhanced societal benefits. The impact and feasibility of these actions will be determined within a 30-year frame. The analysis will be conducted in terms of likely technological, socioeconomic, and environmental consequences, including specification of key issues, interest groups, and impacts. The results will be formulated as a selected set of brief scenarios whose policy implications can be discerned.

Performing organization: The Futures Group, 76 Eastern Blvd., Glastonbury, Connecticut 06033, U.S.A.

Sponsor: U.S. Department of Transportation and National Highway Traffic Safety Administration (NHTSA)

Title of Project: An Analysis of Corporate Strategies of Automotive Manufacturers

Principal Investigator (s) : Harold S. Becker, Executive Vice President, Principal Investigator; Ralph King, Assistant Principal Investigator

Period of Effort: October 1977 to March 1979   **Budget:** No answer

Summary of Project: The objective of this study is to develop means for assessing the corporate decisionmaking process for domestic and foreign automotive manufacturers. The study will identify and assess possible product planning, marketing, manufacturing, engineering and financial strategies that domestic and foreign auto manufacturers might adopt in response to the market place, federally-mandated automotive fuel economy standards and other government policies such as a gasoline tax or an automotive excise tax.

Performing organization: The Futures Group, 76 Eastern Blvd., Glastonbury, Connecticut 06033, U.S.A.

Sponsor: National Science Foundation

Title of Project: Consequences and Policy Implications of Increased Unionization of Personnel Involved with the Court System in the United States

Principal Investigator (s) : George Cole

Period of Effort: December 1976 to December 1978   **Budget:** No answer

Summary of Project: The unionization of court employees could create problems that may affect not only labor relations in the judicial arena, but also the normative context within which justice is administered. The purpose of this work, now in progress, is to study the consequences and implications of increased unionization of personnel involved with state and local court systems in the United States. The structure and scope of collective bargaining arrangements will be described, along with their impact on the institutions and persons involved; and likely future conditions both internal and external to the court systems, that might lead to a growth in unionization of court and legal services personnel will be forecast. The scope and form of possible union growth also will be evaluated and the consequences of the evolution in light of the forecast will be described. Important issues and problems likely to arise under the forecasted conditions will be spotlighted, and policy guidelines for their resolution will be developed.

Performing organization: The George Washington University, The Program of Policy Studies in Science and Technology, Library Room 714, Washington, D.C. 20052, U.S.A.

Sponsor: National Science Foundation

Title of Project: An Exploratory Technology Assessment of Computer Assisted Makeup and Imaging Systems (CAMIS) for Printing On Demand

Principal Investigator (s): Vary T. Coates, Henry B. Freedman, Robert W. Anthony

Period of Effort: July 1978 to October 1979   **Budget:** No answer

Summary of Project: The CAMIS project will explore and assess emerging technologies in the printing, publishing, and information fields which will provide printed information at the time it is requested, thus printing on demand. The project will provide a comprehensive framework within which each stakeholder and issue can be understood in their policy perspective; give particular attention to potential impacts on the printing industry and the associated labor force, as a major segment of the national economy and as a craft and trade integral to the national culture; identify latent stakeholder groups as well as those already organized and represented; anticipate the possible issues lying just around the corner from the more immediate controversies already engaged; enhance public awareness and informed discussion of the inter-relatedness of the many apsects of information's role and influence on society; assemble the many opinions and expectations surrounding the continued development of CAMIS into a coherent and documented report; and to provide a series of workshop forums for stakeholders and those knowledgeable on various aspects of CAMIS development to exchange views and explore options.

Performing organization: Group for Future Research, Dimitrov ter 8, 1093 Budapest, Hungary, H-1093

Sponsor: Karl Marx University of Economic Sciences and Hungarian Academy of Sciences

Title of Project: Complex Research of Remote Future

Principal Investigator (s): Geza Kovacs, Professor (Head of the group), Erzsebet Novaky, Senior Lecturer; Attila Korompai and Eva Hideg, Researchers, Gabor Nemethi, Assistant

Period of Effort: Continuous   **Budget:** No answer

Summary of Project: This project includes the following: — theoretical-methodological aspects of future research, especially that of comprehensive, complex future research, — interaction and alternatives of processes of natural, technical, economic and social development, — the consistency of different parts of shapes of the future and those of prognoses and plans, — the role of space and time factors in the future development.

Performing organization: Hudson Institute, Quaker Ridge Road, Croton-on-Hudson, New York 10520, U.S.A.

Sponsor: Arizona Tomorrow, Inc.

Title of Project: Arizona Tomorrow, A Precursor of Postindustrial America

Principal Investigator (s): Paul Bracken

Period of Effort: May 1977 to January 1979   **Budget:** No answer

Summary of Project: Arizona is currently the fastest growing state in the nation. This study examines where this growth may lead in the 21st century. The possibility that Arizona in particular and much of the Southwest in general may be a precursor of life in Postindustrial America receives special emphasis. The basis for this conjecture is the successful fusion of life-style factors with modern technology that occurs there. In general, life-style factors are dominant. It is this particular trend that is expected to increase in the future.

The study projects alternative Arizona futures including politics, life-style, water issues, urbanization, Indian affairs, energy and economics. The general viewpoint is that the resolution and development of these trends in Arizona has broader significance for advanced capitalist societies around the world. Note: The study will appear in book form in early 1979 as *Arizona Tomorrow* by Paul Bracken (Boulder: Westview Press, 1979).

Performing organization: Hudson Institute, Quaker Ridge Road, Croton-on-Hudson, New York 10520, U.S.A.

Sponsor: Hudson Institute

Title of Project: The Future of Australia

Principal Investigator (s): Rudy Ruggles, Herman Kahn, Thomas Pepper

Period of Effort: No answer   **Budget:** No answer

Summary of Project: Funded by a group of corporations, the Institute is undertaking a comprehensive study of Australia's future business environment, including political trends, economic development, international economic relationships, business regulations, labor movements and other issues. In particular, Australia's special problems, it's potential role in the Pacific Basin region and alternative government policies are being examined. The study hopes to provide business and government officials with a context useful to them in their normal planning and evaluations, in the form of background data and projections. It will also serve as a useful and interesting account of Australia for use by the general public.

Performing organization: Hudson Institute, Quaker Ridge Road, Croton-on-Hudson, New York 10520, U.S.A.

Sponsor: Health, Education and Welfare, New York State and Westchester County governments, and United Way of Westchester

Title of Project: The Future Need for Social Services in Westchester County, New York

Principal Investigator (s): Jane Newitt

Period of Effort: April 1978 to February 1979   **Budget:** No answer

Summary of Project: Trend-line analysis and speculation on the five, ten, and twenty-five year future of Westchester County in its metropolitan and regional setting. The objective is to assist long-range planning by local governmental and voluntary-sector social service agencies.

Performing organization: Hudson Institute, Quaker Ridge Road, Croton-on-Hudson, New York 10520, U.S.A.

Sponsor: National Institutes of Health

Title of Project: Generational Crowding

Principal Investigator (s): Irving Leveson

Period of Effort: To July 1979   **Budget:** No answer

Summary of Project: This current project for the National Institutes of Health entails examining the impact of fluctuations in the number of persons in an age group (e.g., the baby boom) on the incomes, labor force participation, birth rates and other economic, social and demographic variables.

Performing organization: IAURIF — Institut d'Amenagement et d'Urbanisme de la region Ile de France (Paris), (Institute for Planning and Urban Affairs in the Ile de France Region), 21-23, rue Miollis, 75732 Paris Cedex 15, France.

Sponsor: Region d'Ile de France (Ile de France Region)

Title of Project: Ten Million Inhabitants Projected for the Paris Region. Town and regional planning in zero demographic growth

Principal Investigator (s): Jacques Foucher, Study Director

Period of Effort: January 1978 through December 1978   **Budget:** No answer

Summary of Project: The study deals with "Region d'Ile de France," surrounding the Parisian metropolis where almost ten million people live. Its purpose is to forecast the consequences of regional zero demographic growth upon the regional urban system (job needs, housing development, needs for public services and infrastructures), upon the living environment and upon the main public development schemes now being implemented (such as new towns). Three scenarios will be examined. All of them will start from the hypothesis of zero demographic growth.

Performing organization: Institute for the Future, 2740 Sand Hill Road, Menlo Park, California 94025, U.S.A.

Sponsor: National Defense University with the United States Department of Agriculture, Defense Advanced Research Projects Agency and National Oceanic and Atmospheric Administration

Title of Project: Climate Change to the Year 2000

Principal Investigator (s): Hubert Lipinski, Roy Amara

Period of Effort: March 1977 to September 1978   **Budget:** No answer

Summary of Project: In the second phase of a study on "Climate Change to the Year 2000," the Institute is examining the likely impact on changing climatic conditions on selected crops in specific countries. Through the use of a structured questionnaire, information on crop yields was elicited from a carefully selected group of agricultural experts. The 15 particular country-crop combinations examined were: Argentina, corn and wheat; Australia, wheat; Brazil, soybeans; Canada, wheat; India, rice and wheat; People's Republic of China, rice and winter wheat; U.S., corn, soybeans, spring and winter wheat; and USSR, spring and winter wheat. For each of the 15 country-crop combinations, two types of estimates were obtained: the first dealt with the influence of technology on crop yields to the year 2000 and the second with the effects of temperature and precipitation changes on crop yields. To determine crop yields under each of the climate scenarios generated in the first phase of the study, the research team developed a methodology for linking the crop yield matrices with the climate parameters to obtain a frequency distribution of yield for each scenario.

Performing organization: Institute for the Future, 2740 Sand Hill Road, Menlo Park, California 94025, U.S.A.

Sponsor: Multi-client study

Title of Project: The Future of the United Kingdom

Principal Investigator (s): Andrew J. Lipinski, Senior Research Fellow

Period of Effort: January 1978 to Spring 1979   **Budget:** No answer

Summary of Project: Intended for senior executives in industrial corporations, financial institutions, and government agencies, this study addresses the future prospects for the United Kingdom in the last two decades of this century. The main emphasis in the study is on the 1985-90 time frame. Unique features of the study include: It utilizes the most qualified persons from a wide range of disciplines in the United Kingdom and abroad to evaluate the probability of many different futures for the United Kingdom, futures possibly ranging from the very favorable to the very dismal; it combines the use of scenarios with the more rigorous approach of decision analysis; in a 1979 concluding workshop the sponsors will be shown how to use the study results in making strategic decisions involving choices among two or more sets of uncertainties — for example, locating a future society in the United Kingdom or France.

Performing organization: Institute for the Future, 2740 Sand Hill Road, Menlo Park, California 94025, U.S.A.

Sponsor: National Science Foundation

Title of Project: Interactive Group Modeling: A New Methodology for Computer-Based Scientific Communication

Principal Investigator (s): Roy Amara, Hubert Lipinski

Period of Effort: July 1977 to July 1981   **Budget:** $400,000 (4 years)

Summary of Project: The intent of this project, which is an outgrowth of previous Institute research in computer conferencing, is to improve the ways in which computer-based models are constructed and used to facilitate input to the modeling effort from individuals and groups who may be geographically separated. Leading from an analysis of the basic components of modeling, Institute researchers are attempting to provide protocols and procedures that can assist in the documentation and validation of models, help control their costs, and improve interaction among the people who build and use them. The project includes software design, development of evaluation procedures using groups engaged in modeling, and extended field testing.

Performing organization: Institute for the Future, 2740 Sand Hill Road, Menlo Park, California 94025, U.S.A.

Sponsor: Exxon Education Fund

Title of Project: Teleconferencing in Postsecondary Education

Principal Investigator (s): Robert Johansen, Maureen McNulty

Period of Effort: October 1977 to July 1978 **Budget:** No answer

Summary of Project: The focus of this study is on current and potential uses of teleconferencing in postsecondary education. Based on a survey of over 50 institutions using teleconferencing media (audio, video, and computer-based group communication), the report provides organizations considering implementing or expanding the use of electronic media in education with guidelines for successful applications. The guidelines encourage planners to consider ways to improve teleconferencing skills, implement systematic evaluations, determine cost-effectiveness, take advantage of media mixes, and expand interorganizational communication. The research team explored the limitations and advantages of these media, discussing a range of instructional, administrative, student service, and interorganizational applications. In the light of information about current societal trends and projections of likely developments over the next 10 years, the researchers offer future visions of the impact of electronic media on postsecondary institutions.

Performing organization: Institute for Future Research, Giesebrechtstrasse 15, D 1000 Berlin 12, Federal Republic of Germany

Sponsor: Federal Environment Agency, Berlin

Title of Project: Action-Groups in the Area of Environmental Protection

Principal Investigator (s): Walter Andritzky, Ulla Wahl-Terlinden

Period of Effort: January 1977 through October 1977 **Budget:** $50,000

Summary of Project: Three hundred and thirty questionnaires were sent as a representative survey-research among 2,600 action-groups, asking questions of organisation, internal democracy, number of members, the success, cooperation with other groups, etc.

Basic data about the structure of "Citizen Initiatives" in the BRD was gathered.

In the second part of the project, the authors developed a multidimensional approach of citizen's participation in governmental planning processes.

Performing organization: Institute for Future Research (IFZ) GmbH, Giesebrechstrasse 15, D 1000 Berlin 12, Federal Republic of Germany

Sponsor: Heinrich-Hertz-Institut fuer Nachrichtentechnik

Title of Project: Investigation into the Possibilities of Implementing Two-way Cable TV in Order to Close Relationships Between Local Government and Citizenry

Principal Investigator (s): Helgomar Pichlmayer

Period of Effort: January 1977 through May 1977 **Budget:** $70,000

Summary of Project: Subject of Investigation: The subject of investigation was an analysis of the possibilities present in implementing a two-way cable television system directed at improving the capacity of local government to recognize and satisfy demands of its citizens. It was necessary to determine which areas, within these fields of inter-activity, could be included in the range of services offered by a future cable television system. Furthermore statistical and systems-analytical dimensions were derived from simple studies by different government services, which enable conclusions regarding the technical layout to be made.

Procedural Methods: In agreement with grantee, five government agencies in daily contact with the public were chosen. They were chosen according to frequency and future development of this contact, the homogeneity/heterogeneity of the people using the agency, the potential of the information carriers, the manner in which the contact is carried out, etc. Within these areas individual processes were studied more exactly and their procedures recorded. They were queried quantitively and qualitatively through interviews with their respective specialists. They were checked and supplemented by evaluating secondary statistics.

Performing organization: Institute for Future Research, Giesebrechtstrasse 15, D 1000 Berlin 12, Federal Republic of Germany

Sponsor: Deutsche Unilever GmbH, Hamburg

Title of Project: Pre-Retirement Program for Industrial Manager

Principal Investigator (s): Hans Buchholz, Ralf Schroter, Dieter Kolb, Jochen Kruger

Period of Effort: May 1977 through December 1979 **Budget:** $80,000

Summary of Project: In the first two phases of the project an empirical survey about the possible problem of a crisis after retirement has been carried out, to bring approval of hypothesis that (a) the crisis after retirement is a problem of general importance, (b) managers tend to inhibit the problem, (c) managers and pensioners can contribute to solution strategies, (d) a preparation program is needed, and (e) the start of consciousness raising must be dated in the early process of management development.

Performing organization: Institute for Future Research (IFZ) GmbH, Giesebrechtstrasse 15, D 1000 Berlin 12, Federal Republic of Germany

Sponsor: Heinrich-Hertz-Institut fuer Nachrichtentechnik

Title of Project: Social and Economic Aspects Regarding the Implementation of CATV Field Projects in West Germany

Principal Investigator (s): K. Dette, J. Kratzsch, H. Pichlamayer

Period of Effort: April 1978 to July 1978 **Budget:** $15,000

Summary of Project: Four small Feasibility Studies have been made concerning (a) cost-benefit-analysis of cable-TV-projects as a means to evaluate the "project-success"; (b) a design of an economic methodology to measure regional incentives and spatial effects cable-TV can develop (c) data protection aspects of a two-way cable-TV project, and (d) a display of framework to guess future environment, the municipality and the citizen surrounded by cable-TV. The scenario-method was chosen.

Performing organization: Institute for Future Research, Giesebrechstrasse 15, D l000 Berlin 12, Federal Republic of Germany

Sponsor: Ministry of Family, Youth and Health Affairs

Title of Project: The Social Framework of Leisure-activities and the Public Planning of Leisure Conditions

Principal Investigator (s): Walter Andritzky

Period of Effort: January 1971 through May 1976 **Budget:** $25,000

Summary of Project: The aim of the project was to discover whether it is more effective to create special facilities in which to spend leisure time or to improve the other conditions of social life in the population. The areas of housing in the metropolitan areas and the countryside, the influences of family-socialization and secondary socialization and the interdependency of working conditions with the different forms of leisure-behavior were analyzed.

Performing organization: Institute for Future Research, Giesebrechtstrasse 15, D-l000 Berlin 12, Federal Republic of Germany

Sponsor: Volkswagen Foundation

Title of Project: Workshop in the Residential Quarter — Training of Social Skills with Foreign Workers

Principal Investigator (s): Ralph Schroeter, Walter Andritzky

Period of Effort: June 1976 through May 1978 **Budget:** $400,000

Summary of Project: The claim of the project is not to integrate the foreign workers into the German population. That seems to be impossible, because they do not want to spend their whole life in Germany. They only want to work for five to seven years in Germany and then return home. The social and cultural differences between their home-countries and Germany are particularly significant so they live in a social ghetto, especially the Turkish people. It is necessary to develop a meeting-center in this ghetto to mediate basic knowledge of language and social skills. We have created two meeting-places which we call "LEARNSTATT" in the quarter where 37% of the population are foreigners. There the people meet and participate in sessions together with a German facilitator to solve some problems. (Problems related to the Labour Office, the police, the landlord, the neighbors, etc.) Through this service they may overcome their social isolation and find a new way of communication with the other foreign German people in the quarter and with the complicated bureaucracy. This approach aims to help foreigners solve their everyday problems, make new friends and keep their original identity.

Performing organization: Institute for Futures Studies, Vester Farimagsgade 3, DK-1606 Copenhagen V, Denmark

Sponsor: Danish Agricultural and Veterinary Research Council

Title of Project: Delphi Study of Danish Agricultural Research

Principal Investigator (s): Niels de Bang, Erik Juul Jorgensen

Period of Effort: October 1977 to February 1979 **Budget:** No answer

Summary of Project: The purpose of the study is to encircle the most important research breakthroughs which might take part over the period 1985-2000. The Delphi study is carried out in a panel of 100 research associates representing agriculture, horticulture, and silviculture.

Performing organization: Institute for Futures Studies, Vester Farimagsgade 3, DK-1606 Copenhagen V, Denmark

Sponsor: Council of Technology

Title of Project: Future Conditions for the Iron and Metalworking Industry in 10-15 Years and Connected Development Trends

Principal Investigator (s): Erik Juul Jorgensen and Thorkil Kristensen

Period of Effort: May 1977 to June 1978 **Budget:** No answer

Summary of Project: The evaluation of the future development is based on analyses of the iron and metalworking industry itself and of the economic and political factors which affect input and output. As to input labour, raw materials, energy, investments and sub-supplies are subject to analysis. As to output, sales of finished goods and sub-supplies on the home market and on existing and new export markets are studied. Technological aspects are subject to analysis by a group of institutes at the Technical University of Denmark, the Technological Institute and the Danish Welding Institute.

Performing organization: Institute for Futures Studies, Vester Farimagsgade 3, DK-1606 Copenhagen V, Denmark

Sponsor: Danish Defence's Research and the Danish Ministry of Education

Title of Project: International Economic Interdependence and Influence

Principal Investigator (s): Allan G. Ottsen, Project Manager; Johan Peter Paludan, Kristian Richard Petersen

Period of Effort: June 1978 through December 1979 **Budget:** No answer

Summary of Project: The primary purpose is to analyse the international economic interdependence and influence on a country basis by means of a thorough trend correlation based on statistical and political analysis, hereby enabling a country-by-country assessment of sensitivity and vulnerability. Initial studies will focus on crucial single goods and world trade.

Performing organization: Institute for Futures Studies, Vester Farimagsgade 3, DK-1606 Copenhagen V, Denmark

Sponsor: Institute for Futures Studies

Title of Project: Perspectives for Economic and Political Development

Principal Investigator (s): Thorkil Kristensen, Erik Juul Jorgensen, Bent Ryd Svensson, Rolf Jensen

410

Period of Effort: Mid-1975 continuing **Budget:** No answer

Summary of Project: Reports are published in March and September each year. The purpose is to provide quantified analyses and studies of the international developments in order to minimize the degree of uncertainty existing as to the future. The material is placed at the disposal of our member enterprises in such a way that they either directly or after adjustments may use it in their budgeting and strategical planning. The reports contain forecasts for the short, medium, and long-term economic and political developments in the countries and regions which are most important for the Danish economy.

Performing organization: Institute for Research on Public Policy, 3535, chemin Queen Mary, Suite 514, Montreal, Quebec H3V 1H8, Canada

Sponsor: Canadian Federal Government

Title of Project: Social Impacts on Canada's Alternative Energy Sources 1975-2025

Principal Investigator (s): Rick Clayton, Project Leader, Futures Studies Program

Period of Effort: June 1977 to March 1979 **Budget:** No answer

Summary of Project: The objective of this research is to identify the long-run energy-supply options available to Canada, and the public policy issues and life-style impacts such possible energy changes would mean. A number of alternative quantitative "scenarios" are being drawn up, each one revealing a different "mix" of energy supplies, and charting how such supplies would be put to practical use by final consumers. Each scenario spells out likely relative prices, relative "mix" of supplies and the issues and impacts each raises. A summing-up also indicates what common policy action is likely to be required by Canadian governments taking into consideration all possibilities revealed in the scenarios.

Performing organization: Institute for Research on Public Policy, 3535, chemin Queen Mary, Suite 514, Montreal, Quebec H3V 1H8, Canada

Sponsor: Canadian Federal Government

Title of Project: Social Trends in Canada

Principal Investigator (s): Marc Laplante, Project Leader, Futures Studies Program

Period of Effort: September 1977 to December 1979 **Budget:** No answer

Summary of Project: The study on social trends, historical as well as future, is aimed at providing means to evaluate social changes in Canadian society. The final document, scheduled for late 1979, will be destined, in particular, for decision-makers at all levels of public and private intervention. In its first stage, the project undertakes a secondary analysis of data already available in Canada. The comparative method is often credited with placing Canada's position in research to other countries and exposing the differences and similarities between regions of a country.

Such a study also provides an excellent occasion to evaluate the ability of actual social statistics to further the analysis and decisions of men of action. The study is proceeding in collaboration with public and private organizations who specialize in gathering data. Eventually, research and special investigation will be undertaken in Canada in order to acquire missing data and to improve the effectiveness of certain indicators. Commencing October 1978, the preliminary results of this research will be circulated in a quasi-monthly publication of IRPP entitled: SOCIOSCOPE.

Performing organization: Institute for Research on Public Policy, 3535, chemin Queen Mary, Suite 514, Montreal, Quebec, H3V 1H8, Canada

Sponsor: Canadian Federal Government

Title of Project: Technological and Economic Impacts on Canada

Principal Investigator (s): Zavis P. Zeman, Project Leader, Futures Studies Program

Period of Effort: May 1977 to December 1979 **Budget:** No answer

Summary of Project: The project studies foreseeable critical impacts of technological and economic changes on Canadian society. It is based on the conviction that international transfers of technology have been and will continue to create deep-seated changes in the international economic order.

The project is carried out in a series of mostly qualitative short-term studies pre-assessing the emerging technological and economic developments five to ten years into the impacts of the future.

Growth scenarios for the Canadian economy in the 1980s, the changing international monetary environment, electronic work processing, home terminals, transborder data flows, the information marketplace, impacts of seabed mining on Canadian nickel industry, the future of Japanese trading companies, the future development of Japan and the consequences for Canada of the shift of the locus of the United States towards the sunbelt states are issues that have been studied so far.

Performing organization: The Institute for World Order, 1140 Avenue of the Americas, New York, New York 10036, U.S.A.

Sponsor: The Institute for World Order

Title of Project: Transnational Academic Program (TAP)

Principal Investigator (s): Burns Weston, Director, TAP

Period of Effort: 1963 through 1980   **Budget:** No answer

Summary of Project: The Transnational Academic Program has sought to promote world order education at all levels and in all parts of the world thereby providing students with the opportunity to study ways in which the world might be responsibly restructured so as to alleviate large scale global problems in the areas of peace, social justice, economic well-being, and ecological balance. TAP has trained thousands of secondary, college, and university teachers through workshops and consultations. It has helped to initiate world order and related courses in more than 500 colleges and universities, and has established world order studies centers/programs at seven major American universities. *World Food/Hunger Studies* and *Peace and World Order Studies: A Curriculum Guide* are among the more than 50 instructional tools TAP has prepared.

Performing organization: The Institute for World Order, 1140 Sixth Avenue, New York, New York 10036, U.S.A.

Sponsor: The Institute for World Order

Title of Project: World Order Models Project (WOMP)

Principal Investigator (s): Rajni Kothari and Saul Mendlovitz

Period of Effort: 1967 to 1980   **Budget:** No answer

Summary of Project: WOMP brings together distinguished scholars and public figures from eight major regions of the world. Their task is to develop ways of restructuring the political, economic, and social system so as to cope with the problems of war, social injustice, poverty, and ecological decay. With reference to his particular area, each scholar undertakes to: (1) diagnose these major global problems and their relationship to the existing social system; (2) design or prescribe preferred alternative systems capable of coping with them; and (3) propose general transition steps leading from the current international system to the preferred worlds.

The work of WOMP is being published in a series of books under the umbrella title *Preferred Worlds for the 1990s*. In addition, WOMP produces instructional materials, a global policy quarterly journal, *Alternatives*, an annual *State of the Globe Report*, and a series of position papers on the major issues facing humanity over the next 15 years.

Performing organization: International Federation of Institutes for Advanced Study and Aspen Institute for Humanistic Studies, 1919 14th St., No. 811, Boulder, Colorado 80302, U.S.A.

Sponsor: —

Title of Project: Consequences of a Hypothetical World Climate Scenario Based on an Assumed Global Warming Due to Increased Carbon Dioxide

Principal Investigator (s): Not yet determined

Period of Effort: Three years, starting date not yet determined   **Budget:** No answer

Summary of Project: The purposes of the planned study are to: 1) assess the social, political, economic and technical issues posed by a postulated warm climate scenario that is assumed to be the consequences of the carbon dioxide increase; 2) consider what alternatives there are for social and political action to ameliorate any adversity suggested by the climate scenario; and 3) make suggestions of an optimum organization to conduct the study.

Performing organization: The Israeli Institute for the Study of International Affairs (IISIA)

Sponsor: The Economics Department of the Jewish Agency

Title of Project: The Role of International Law in Building the New International Economic Order

Principal Investigator (s): M. Mushkat

Period of Effort: To December 1979   **Budget:** No answer

Summary of Project: The purpose of this study is to investigate the changing role of international organizations and international law in reconstructing the present world order and making it an instrument linking development to social justice and international security.

This is the first part of a more general project entitled "The Functions of the Law of Property as an instrument of building a future-oriented international community." Some excerpts of the study were published in review in the book *The Dynamics of the International Community* (Dekel Academic Press, Tel Aviv, 1977).

Performing organization: Kent State University, Institute for 21st Century Business, Kent, Ohio 44242, U.S.A.

Sponsor: Kent State University Foundation

Title of Project: Proposed Plans for Reorganizing States of the United States and the Effects on Business

Principal Investigator (s): Donald F. Mulvihill

Period of Effort: May 1976 to January 1979   **Budget:** No answer

Summary of Project: An analysis of six plans to make fewer, larger, and possibly more economically sound, political subdivisions at the state level in the United States and projects as to how such changes would affect business operations.

Performing organization: Kent State University, Institute for 21st Century Business, Kent, Ohio 44242, U.S.A.

Sponsor: Kent State University Foundation

Title of Project: Recognition of Futures Research by Large Corporations and by Colleges of Business Administration

Principal Investigator (s): Donald F. Mulvihill

Period of Effort: May 1978 to May 1979   **Budget:** No answer

Summary of Project: This is an ongoing study of how and why large firms are recognizing the need for long-range economic forecasting, technological forecasting, technological assessment, and new product development. The *Fortune* 500 corporations were questioned on a two-step sequential questionnaire basis. One hundred and forty responded to the first inquiry; 94 returning completed questionnaires, of which 49 have responded to the second questionnaire. Some indicated a preference for a personal interview and these will be made as time permits. Schools of business were also queried as to courses offered in the fields indicated above. Twenty-one accredited schools offer at least one course in this area and one school offered five courses. Fourteen others indicated futures studies were integrated into other courses.

Performing organization: Max-Planck-Institut zur Erforschung der Lebensbedingungen der wissenschaftlich-technischen Welt (Max Planck Institute for Research on Living Conditions in the Scientific-Technical World) Riemerschmid-Str. 7, D-813 Starnberg, Federal Republic of Germany

Sponsor: Max-Planck-Gesellschaft

Title of Project: See summary of project

Principal Investigator (s): Horst Afheldt

Period of Effort: No answer **Budget:** No answer

Summary of Project: Problem: Will forward defense of Western Europe in the nineties be feasible by the means employed today: heavy units, highly mobile, dependent on difficult logistics and air support? Or do such means imply the risk of intolerable devastation?

The project is to study latest technological developments (automatisation, miniaturisation of weapons) which seem to favour defense and to develop a new strategic concept: territorial defense by small units equipped with highly sophisticated technology ("techno-commandos").

Performing organization: MIT System Dynamics Group, E40-253, Massachusetts Institute of Technology, Cambridge, Massachusetts 02139, U.S.A.

Sponsor: Various corporations, foundations and individuals

Title of Project: National Model Project

Principal Investigator (s): Jay W. Forrester, Nathaniel Mass, Peter Senge, Alan Graham, Gilbert Low

Period of Effort: 1972 continuing **Budget:** No answer

Summary of Project: The MIT System Dynamics Group is working on the development of the National Model, a computer simulation of the structure and dynamics of the national economy. The model will provide insight into the complex interrelationship of forces that determine socio-economic behavior, and will make possible the testing of corporate and governmental policy alternatives. The methodology used is that of System Dynamics, designed for better understanding of the behavior of complex systems.

Performing organization: The MITRE/Metrek Corporation, 1820 Dolley Madison Boulevard, McLean, Virginia 22101, U.S.A.

Sponsor: Department of Energy

Title of Project: Solar Energy: A Comparative Analysis to the Year 2020

Principal Investigator (s): Gerald E. Bennington, Associate Department Head, Advanced Energy and Resource Systems Analysis Department

Period of Effort: October 1975 through November 1978 **Budget:** Approximately $1.9 million

Summary of Project: The Metrek Division of The MITRE Corporation was funded by the Division of Solar Energy of the United States Energy Research and Development Administration to perform a comparative analysis and potential market impact assessment of solar energy technologies and to use this analysis in examining alternative recommendations for the planning of the research, development, and demonstration program for solar energy technologies. Metrek developed an energy data base, two primary scenarios reflecting trends in demand and energy prices, and a computer simulation model. The energy data base contains engineering cost data on designs derived from reviews of the latest available information and studies from the federal solar program. The two scenarios are: (1) A scenario which incorporates the proposals in the National Energy Plan as proposed in April 1977 and (2) a scenario reflecting recent trends [since 1973] in energy prices, policy and technology. Projections of solar energy utilization and market impact are made by computer simulations of regional market decisions to purchase solar or conventional technologies in each market sector on a year-by-year basis to the year 2020. The Metrek study was carried out in 1977 and is based on information available as of April 1977. Since that time, Presidential and Congressional initiatives and additional technical information have produced changes in policy that are not incorporated in the work presented in this document. Results of analyses to examine the impact of these changes and program thrusts will be presented in subsequent reports.

Performing organization: The National Center for Research in Vocational Education, 1960 Kenny Road, Columbus, Ohio 43210, U.S.A.

Sponsor: National Institute of Education

Title of Project: Contents and Methods of Career Preparation: Transferable Skills

Principal Investigator (s): Frank C. Pratzner, Project Director; William L. Ashley, Acting Project Director

Period of Effort: June 1978 to November 1979   **Budget:** No answer

Summary of Project: The Transferable Skills project is building upon earlier exploratory studies of occupational change and transferable skills. The project is attempting to determine how application of transferable skills and occupational adaptability in educational and training programs can help improve the development of human resources to meet the future needs of the labor market, as well as empower the individual to cope successfully with future occupational changes. Issues of particular interest include patterns of job mobility, the transferability of skills, the transfer of learning to application, teaching for transfer, and the nature of occupational adaptability. Project activities, past and current, have resulted in a number of publications and products, and are available through the National Center's Information Series.

Performing organization: National Institute for Research Advancement, 37F. Mitsui Bldg. 2-1-1, Nish-Shinjuku, Shinjuku-ku, Tokyo, Japan 160

Sponsor: National Institute for Research Advancement

Title of Project: Choice of a Long-Term Energy Strategy

Principal Investigator (s): Masao Sakiska, President of NIRA

Period of Effort: January 1975 to January 1977   **Budget:** 120 million yen

Summary of Project: The National Institute for Research Advancement (NIRA) had been engaged in a comprehensive energy project since January 1975. Our aim had been to study long-term energy issues by taking into consideration the importance of energy problems in the coming years. The objectives of this project are to investigate supply-demand situations of energy in Japan in the years 1985 and 2000, and to identify appropriate alternatives for long-term energy policy by analyzing relevant problems. The project was done in cooperation with seven research institutes.

Performing organization: National Institute for Research Advancement, 37F. Mitsui Bldg. 2-1-1, Nishi-Shinjuku, Shinjuku-ku, Tokyo, Japan 160

Sponsor: National Institute for Research Advancement

Title of Project: Japan Toward the 21st Century

Principal Investigator (s): Junnosuke Kishida, Vice-President of NIRA and Chief Editorial Writer of Asahi Newspaper

Period of Effort: September 1975 to March 1978   **Budget:** 300 million yen

Summary of Project: The National Institute for Research Advancement (NIRA) recognizes Japan will face, in the years ahead, various problems of considerable magnitude—political, economic and social. NIRA, therefore, aimed to identify these long-term problems and classify them so that the basic data and reference material may be presented to the people in such a manner that they may suggest appropriate new courses for future development. With this task in mind, NIRA had been engaged in a comprehensive large-scale research project with the cooperation of many experts and research institutes in Japan and abroad.

Performing organization: National Research Council of Canada, Montreal Road, Ottawa, Ontario, Canada K1A OR6

Sponsor: National Research Council

Title of Project: The Private and Social Returns to R&D and Their Value to Society

Principal Investigator (s): W.H.C. Simmonds

Period of Effort: 1978 continuing   **Budget:** No answer

Summary of Project: The production of benefits through research and development for the customer, which the performer of the research and development cannot capture through the market system, is not yet officially accepted within government. Three methods for evaluating such benefits exist—the economist's consumer surplus, direct calculation when sufficient facts are available, and econometric estimates. The most benefit today is probably the net generation of new, permanent jobs to replace those being lost. Such evaluations require the development of a new broader analytical framework for dealing with the impact of technology and science during a period of continuing change. Steps to implement this are being initiated.

Performing organization: Planning and Forecasting Consultants, 908 Town and Country Boulevard, Suite 120, Houston, Texas 77024, U.S.A.

Sponsor: Various Utilities and Coal Companies

Title of Project: Rail Transportation of Western Coal and Other Commodities 1975 to 1995

Principal Investigator (s): Dale W. Steffes

Period of Effort: January 1975 to June 1975   **Budget:** Multi-client funding, $5,000 each

Summary of Project: In 1974, the energy philosophy, at that time, was to utilize the western coal reserves of the United States to resolve the energy crisis. This raised the concern of how to transport this coal. P&FC had previously conducted a multi-client study of coal slurry pipelines and then realized that utilities and slurry proponents did not understand the railroads. Therefore, a study was conducted to clarify pricing philosophy of railroad rates, capacity of the railroads, and the amount of coal the railroads would likely transport in the time frame studied.

Performing organization: Planning and Forecasting Consultants, 908 Town and Country Blvd., Suite 120, Houston, Texas 77024, U.S.A.

Sponsor: Utilities and Energy Companies

Title of Project: The United States Energy Strategic Playbook

Principal Investigator (s): Dale W. Steffes

Period of Effort: November 1976 to February 1977   **Budget:** Multi-client funding, $5,000 each

Summary of Project: The purpose of the study was to understand the domestic energy situation so that logical actions could be taken by those funding companies. In this report the individual growth rates for markets, forms and sources were determined. Individual state energy requirements were projected, and specific states were identified where energy growth would be negative. Also, an energy cost sheet was developed for the years 1975 and 1985, in which it was determined that the energy required to fuel our economy would increase from 11.2% of GNP to 13.8% of GNP in 1985. However, this increase in cost would make the United States more self sufficient and our energy reserves would be enhanced.

Performing organization: Planning and Forecasting Consultants, 908 Town and Country Blvd., Houston, Texas 77024, U.S.A.

Sponsor: Various National and International Energy Companies

Title of Project: United States Refinery Requirements to 1990

Principal Investigator (s): Paul S. Strain

Period of Effort: September 1978 to January 1979   **Budget:** Multi-client funding, $6,000 each.

Summary of Project: The purpose of this study is to investigate the probable evolution of the United States refinery industry in a time frame reaching out to 1990. The industry exists in an interlocking set of matrices of economics, technological, political, sociological factors which determine the direction and scope of its development. Increasingly it is becoming involved in world economics and political forces. This study will simplify this complex by selecting the more important options and challenges and discard those of lesser significance. In this way the problem can be reduced to considering a number of variables and options which can be comprehended. In this manner the questions of growth and expansion, crude supplies and prices, market for products, and refinery costs and prospective government regulations will be dealt with and appropriate scenarios developed.

Performing organization: Planning and Forecasting Consultants, 908 Town & Country Blvd., Suite 120, Houston, Texas 77024, U.S.A.

Sponsor: Various National and International Energy Companies and Domestic Utilities

Title of Project: World Energy Supply and Demand to 1990

Principal Investigator (s): Dale W. Steffes

Period of Effort: September 1978 to January 1979   **Budget:** Multi-client funding, $6,000 each

Summary of Project: The purpose of this study is to investigate the likely outcome between the supply of energy and the demand for energy worldwide to 1990. With world economics uncertain, and new sources of energy becoming available, and better energy technology being developed, P&FC will determine what sources will be produced and at what price. Most energy pronouncements by government or industrial managements are to influence behavior one way or another. This study is not intended to predict good or bad, rather it is to predict what is likely to happen and then individual sponsors can take offensive or defensive measures.

Performing organization: Polish Academy of Sciences, Division for Lifestyles Studies, Institute of Philosophy and Sociology, Nowy Swiat 72, Warsaw, 00-330, Poland

Sponsor: Polish Academy of Sciences

Title of Project: Changes of Lifestyles

Principal Investigator (s): Andrzej Sicinski

Period of Effort: 1976 to 1980   **Budget:** No answer

Summary of Project: The project is part of a cross-national comparative study initiated by the Division for Lifestyles Studies, Institute of Philosophy and Sociology.

Performing organization: Portland State University, P.O.B. 751, Portland, Oregon 97207, U.S.A.

Sponsor: National Science Foundation

Title of Project: The Use of Structural Modeling for Technology Assessment

Principal Investigator (s): Harold A. Linstone, Director, Futures Research Institute

Period of Effort: October 1976 through June 1978   **Budget:** $140,000

Summary of Project: A survey and evaluation of structural modeling tools to develop a rough overview and insight into the behavior of complex systems—with particular emphasis on applications to technology assessment. The tools are geometric and semi-quantitative in nature; examples are Interpretive Structural Modeling (ISM), KSIM, SPIN, QSIM, IMPACT and ELECTRE. The basic building blocks are trees and hierarchies, directed graphs and networks. A misfit variable concept (SOPA) and cross-impact analysis techniques have also been studied. Guidelines for users are developed to help them in a first-cut study of complex systems encountered in technology assessment and related impact problems.

Performing organization: Presidial Committee on the Impact of Science and Technology on Society, Hungarian Academy of Sciences, Budapest/Chairman: Professor Alexander Szalai, Attila-ut 125, H-1012 Budapest, Hungary

Sponsor: Hungarian Academy of Sciences

Title of Project: Forecasting the Probable Development of Scientific Research in the Main Fields of Actual or Potential Research Activity in Hungary

Principal Investigator (s): Alexander Szalai, Member of the Hungarian Academy of Sciences, Adviser to the HAS Research Group on Science Organization, Professor of Sociology/Karl Marx University of Economic Sciences, Budapest/President of the Hungarian Sociological Association

Period of Effort: November 1978 to December 1980   **Budget:** No answer

Summary of Project: This project is a follow-up to a much smaller pilot project of similar nature undertaken in 1975 with a time-horizon of 1990. The present project's time-horizon is the year 2000 and its results should contribute to the governmental work on long-range/up to the year 2000/national socio-economic planning centralized in the National Planning Office.

The project does *not* encompass the whole R&D, only "R." Thus, it does *not* extend to technological developmental work. However, research in the humanities and in the social sciences/e.g., sociology, economics, law, etc./is part of "scientific research" as understood in Hungary.

The project is concentrated on those fields of research which are for theoretical or practical reasons of considerable actual or potential relevance and importance to Hungarian scientific and socio-economic development. It is therefore selective in its coverage of fields of research and takes into account the limits of the scientific and socio-economic resources and also the needs of this relatively small and not very affluent country. A great variety of forecasting methods and techniques will be used—from conceptual and mathematical modelling, cross-impact matrices, Delphi, scenarios, etc., to brainstorming.

Performing organization: Science Policy Research Unit, Mantell Building, University of Sussex, Falmer, Brighton, Sussex, BN1 9RF, United Kingdom

Sponsor: United Kingdom Social Science Research Council

Title of Project: Forecasting in the Food and Agriculture Sector

Principal Investigator (s): P. K. Marstrand

Period of Effort: 1977 to 1979 **Budget:** No answer

Summary of Project: This project has been concentrating on microbial protein, with particular reference to the ecological and social effects of introducing a new technology. The purpose of the work is to develop methods of assessing what happens when a new process or technology is introduced into society, and to test ideas developed during the work done earlier for the United Nations Environment Programme on the textile industry in Thailand. Microorganisms such as yeasts, fungi and algae will grow on almost any organic substrate and, when harvested and dried, provide a powder rich in protein. Recent increases in prices of traditional sources of protein for animal feeds and requirements to treat organic waste-waters have made processing of wastewater into microbial protein more attractive than hitherto, and three United Kingdom firms: British Petroleum, Imperial Chemical Industries and Shell, have just introduced or are about to introduce food materials produced in this way. A literature survey is in progress. Research scientists have been interviewed and patents for processes taken out since 1920 to the present have been listed. Interviews are being arranged with people in the producing companies and with firms using the products for feed formulation.

Performing organization: Science Policy Research Unit, Mantell Building, University of Sussex, Falmer, Brighton, Sussex BN1 9RF, United Kingdom

Sponsor: United Kingdom Social Science Research Council

Title of Project: Forecasting the Long-Term Supply of and Demand for Metals

Principal Investigator (s): R. W. Page

Period of Effort: 1977 to 1979 **Budget:** No answer

Summary of Project: This project is an examination of the factors that may influence the long-term supply of, and demand for, metals, encompassing factors largely internal to the sector (e.g., reserves and extraction technology, conservation and substitution), as well as the more external ones (e.g., the political influences on investment and trade, or economic growth rates). The overall conclusions compare the broad alternatives of mining more or using less, in the context of wider perspectives on future world development. In addition prospects for the world tin industry are being examined. The first stage of the work looked ahead about 20 years at the problems and opportunities that may arise in the world supply of, and demand for, tin; and then at what decisionmakers could do now in the light of that analysis. A draft report has now been prepared.
A hindsight review of materials forecasting is now complete. It concerns forecasts of the long-term supply of and demand for metals. About 150 past forecasts were located, going back as far as the turn of the century. The objective was to see what lessons, if any, could be learned for application to current materials forecasting exercises. The main conclusions were that a surprising number of the individual forecasts in these publications have proved correct (over 70%), that more sophisticated methods do not lead to more accurate forecasts, and that some specific developments have been continually wrongly forecast.

Performing organization: Science Policy Research Unit, Mantell Building, University of Sussex, Falmer, Brighton, Sussex, BN1 9RF, United Kingdom

Sponsor: Programmes Analysis Unit (UK)

Title of Project: The Future of Industrial Societies

Principal Investigator (s): J. I. Gershuny

Period of Effort: 1977 to 1979 **Budget:** No answer

Summary of Project: The first part of this study was mainly concerned with the collection of aggregate data on historical patterns of change in industrial employment, occupational status, consumption patterns of industrial productivity for the United Kingdom, and to a lesser extent, for other Organization for Economic Cooperative Development (OECD) countries. The major output of the work so far is a book *After Industrial*

Society? published by Macmillan in May 1978. It presents findings which challenge, in some important respects, the conventional view of the future of developed economies. It suggests, not the emergence of a post-industrial service economy, but the precise contrary. Where we would expect, according to the current dogma, to find a considerable rise in the consumption of services by households, we find instead a remarkable fall in service consumption as a proportion of the total. Instead of buying services, households seem increasingly to be buying (in effect investing in) durable goods which allow final consumers to produce services for themselves. A large proportion of the increase in service employment over the last decade can be explained, not by service consumption, but by the increasing need of manufacturing industry for managers and for salesmen, as part of the drive for efficient production of consumer durables. This is in effect a self-service economy, with paid employment concentrating in technical and managerial occupations in manufacturing industry, while services are produced outside the formal economy, through direct labour, using capital machinery installed in the household. There is every reason to expect this trend to continue, since it is driven by two economic processes whose direction cannot be expected to vary: on the one hand, technical innovation leading to cheaper and improved capital equipment; on the other, rising labour costs. In its conclusion the book briefly outlines a novel view of the future—a developed dual economy. The argument centers on: (a) increasingly capital intensive and automated production of what are in effect capital goods for installation in the household; (b) an increasing proportion of final production being carried out in the home.

Performing organization: Science Policy Research Unit, Mantell Building, University of Sussex, Falmer, Brighton, Sussex, BN1 9RF, United Kingdom

Sponsor: United Kingdom Social Science Research Council

Title of Project: Images of the Future: Their Influence and Organisation

Principal Investigator (s): H.S.D. Cole

Period of Effort: 1978 to 1979   **Budget:** No answer

Summary of Project: This project is intended to link work on the transmission of images of the future through society with work on the organisation and methods of forecasting. It is intended as a contribution to the understanding of the organisation of policy research into these issues and is based on the hypothesis that images of the future provide a significant influence for good or bad on the direction of policy research. Policymakers and policy researchers in different countries and at different times often have very different images of their country's and the world's future. Such images are transmitted through society and help to condition personal and policy choices. If short-term goals in specific policy areas are set within visions of long-term social change, then images of the future provide a structure for decision-making. They may suggest possibilities, determine expectations and set boundaries on what people believe to be possible, and thus be tied to the ultimate consequences of policies on physical and social environment. This working hypothesis will be investigated and its significance considered for the organisation of policy oriented research.

Performing organization: Science Policy Research Unit, Mantell Building, University of Sussex, Falmer, Brighton, Sussex BN1 9RF, United Kingdom

Sponsor: United Kingdom Social Science Research Council

Title of Project: Industrial Work Styles: Stress or Strife?

Principal Investigator (s): T. G. Whiston

Period of Effort: 1977 through 1979   **Budget:** No answer

Summary of Project: This study attempts to examine relationships between industrial workstyles in "mechanised" industry and educative potential and background of employees. Consideration will be given to future mechanisation and automation trends and the implications for skill patterns, against a backcloth of ongoing educative developments. The project is intended to consider fairly broad social, educative and technological issues.

Performing organization: Science Policy Research Unit, Mantell Building, University of Sussex, Falmer, Brighton, Sussex BN1 9RF, United Kingdom

Sponsor: National Coal Board; British Petroleum Ltd; United Kingdom Atomic Energy Authority; Central Electricity Generating Board; British Gas Corporation; Department of Energy; Electricity Council

Title of Project: Long-term Supply and Demand for Energy

Principal Investigator (s): A. J. Surrey, J. H. Chesshire

Period of Effort: 1977 through 1979   **Budget:** No answer

Summary of Project: This project is an analysis of possible long-term demand and supply developments and their policy implications for the depletion of North Sea oil and gas, Research and Development and energy conservation. The first part of this work, comprising an analysis of energy consumption in the year 2000 for each of the principal sectors of final demand and their aggregation into a national energy balance, has been completed. Other studies include an analysis of the national stock of industrial boilers, started at the end of 1977, and a comparative study of electricity consumption in the major Organization for Economic Cooperative Development (OECD) countries, which will examine the effects of different levels of appliance ownership, growth in output and disposable incomes, and relative electricity prices. The aim of the boiler study is to cast more light on a large segment of the industrial crude heat market, including technical change, efficiency and the choice of fuel. The aim of the electricity study is to examine the scope for further electricity growth, which is relevant for decisions affecting nuclear power and the coal industry.

Performing organization: Science Policy Research Unit, Mantell Building, University of Sussex, Falmer, Brighton, Sussex BN1 9RF, United Kingdom

Sponsor: United Kingdom Social Science Research Council

Title of Project: Obsolescence, Product Life and Consumerism

Principal Investigator (s): T. G. Whiston

Period of Effort: 1977 to 1979   **Budget:** No answer

Summary of Project: This study is concerned with the socio-economic, technological and resource-energy factors which are pertinent to "optimal product life" and total systems costing. It seeks to relate legislative frameworks and market pressures with consideration of conservation and optimal use of materials, energy and manpower. Besides attempting to define more clearly the criteria of "optimality," the study has the broader aim of examining the relationships between current futures/forecasting literature with actual ongoing policy and societal trends.

The project is concentrating on the automobile industry in the United Kingdom and the United States and interviews have been conducted with government, legislative, and producer and consumer organisations in both countries.

Performing organization: Science Policy Research Unit, Mantell Building, University of Sussex, Falmer, Brighton, Sussex BN1 9RF, United Kingdom

Sponsor: United Kingdom Social Science Research Council

Title of Project: Quality of Life, Indicators and Models of Social Change

Principal Investigator (s): I. D. Miles

Period of Effort: 1971 to 1979   **Budget:** No answer

Summary of Project: In earlier work it was recognized that different social philosophies entail both different conceptions of the nature of social systems, and different evaluations of means and ends in intervening in them. This recognition has been used by Miles as the basis for developing a forecasting methodology which involves contrasting three such social philosophies, here called 'world views.' A conservative, a reformist and a radical 'world view' have been illustrated by reference to political principles and the types of sociological and economic analysis typically drawn upon or developed by the proponents of each. These three 'world views' are employed as self-consistent sets of assumptions and prescriptions which could add substance to the profiles which take into account both conclusions concerning physical possibilities for the world emerging from the work of colleagues, and the implications of each 'world view' for the processes in which changes in international economic growth and inequality might come about. Work has also been continuing on more specific issues concerning social indicators. Miles has been collaborating with two other social scientists in editing a book entitled *Demystifying Social Statistics.* This is a collection of original and critical papers on the history, model of production, and ideological components of social statistics and quantitative social research. Current plans for the development of social forecasting work include studies of the reciprocal interactions between technological and economic changes and changes in socio-cultural life, politics and state policy. Social indicator research will be both a tool in this work, a source of data concerning processes of social change, and an object of study.

Performing organization: Science Policy Research Unit, Mantell Building, University of Sussex, Falmer, Brighton, Sussex, BN1 9RF, United Kingdom

Sponsor: United Kingdom Social Science Research Council

Title of Project: Social and Technological Alternatives for the Future

Principal Investigator (s): M. Jahoda, T. G. Whiston, P. K. Marstrand, H.S.D. Cole, R. W. Page, I. D. Miles

Period of Effort: 1971 to 1979   **Budget:** No answer

Summary of Project: During 1977-78 much of the work centered around studies of the uses and abuses of forecasting. Previous work has demonstrated that forecasting is as necessary in the modern world as it is difficult to do, assess and use. Accordingly, the group was engaged in a collection of case histories of a variety of forecasting exercises and their analysis. Different though these selected cases are in scope and topic, each one aims to deal with as many as possible of the following basic issues: the nature of the forecast (including dates, time span and subject matter); the qualifications of the forecasters and their position within the field with which they deal; the initiator(s) of the forecasts; the financial support for the forecast; the original purpose of the forecast and reasons for continuing or stopping the exercise; the rationale, if any, for the choice of forecasting techniques; evidence, if any, on the impact of the forecast on policy-makers; the relation between forecasters' and policy-makers' biases in the forecast and its use, if any; criteria for 'goodness' of forecast. These case studies, their analysis and any general points which emerge will be published in a book, entitled provisionally "Uses and Abuses of Forecasting."

Performing organization: Science Policy Research Unit, University of Sussex, Mantell Building, Falmer, Brighton, Sussex BN1 9RF, United Kingdom

Sponsor: United Nations Institute for Training and Research

Title of Project: Towards a Model of Technology for Basic Needs

Principal Investigator (s): H.S.D. Cole and J. A. Clark

Period of Effort: 1977 to 1979   **Budget:** No answer

Summary of Project: A conclusion of previous studies was that technological change is not well accounted for within global models as they are currently constructed. This study is geared towards the investigation of the technological questions in relation to future alternative paths of development, with the conflict of goals and current limitations of data and theory in mind. It is intended both as a contribution to the world models debate and as part of a continued evaluation of the usefulness of macro-models and the understanding of technological choice.

Methodologically the study is an attempt to confront the "macro-micro" problem. It links together previous work carried out on scenario analysis, mathematical modelling and the evaluation of technologies.

In the first phase, the work brings together theoretical and empirical findings. The empirical basis is provided by existing studies on the transfer, innovation and diffusion of know-how and their socio-economic implications in developing countries.

The theoretical work develops the structure of the Bariloche model introducing, in addition, economic relations between trade patterns, distribution of income, and substitution between capital and labour coefficients in a general equilibrium model based on the empirical findings discussed above. Particular attention is paid to the possible patterns of demand compatible with the other variables. The study will take into consideration patterns of growth that may involve comparison between growth paths directed towards the satisfaction of basic needs and others to a maximisation of GNP (Gross National Product) indices. The formal structure developed on the basis of currently available studies is intended to provide a contribution to further empirical studies of technology. The study will examine the relative merits of various approaches to the inclusion of micro-data into macro-models.

Performing organization: The Secretariat for Futures Studies, Fredsgatan 2, 111 52 Stockholm, Sweden

Sponsor: The Secretariat for Futures Studies

Title of Project: Care in Society—A Future Study on Care and Need for Care

Principal Investigator (s): M. Lagergren, Director, Birgitta Johansson-Hedberg, Lena Lundh, Marianne Parmsund, Christer Sanne

Period of Effort: November 1977 to November 1980   **Budget:** 800,000 Swedish Crowns yearly

Summary of Project: The purpose of the project is to study the long-term consequences of current policies and the long-term choices in the field of care—health care, social care, care for the elderly, for the children, etc. The future care problems are seen in the full context of society: Which are the qualities of society that create the need for care? What are the possibilities of prevention? Which role does the social network play in determining the need for public action? How should the public health care be organized to meet the need of care in the future?

Performing organization: The Secretariat for Futures Studies, P.O. Box 7502, 103 92 Stockholm, Sweden

Sponsor: Secretariat for Futures Studies

Title of Project: Forecasting and Political Futures Planning

Principal Investigator (s): Lars Ingelstam, Patrik Engellau, Simon Andersson

Period of Effort: 1977 to 1979   **Budget:** Approximately $150,000

Summary of Project: The purpose of the project is to study the conditions for political futures planning in the Swedish society. The center of interest is therefore located in the administrative, organizational and technical environment around the central organs of the government.

Forecasting is a basic tool for political futures planning. A number of minor studies will be carried out regarding the nature of forecasts presented to the political decision-makers. A special object of such studies will be what methodological or other influences unduly limit the scope of choice for the decision-makers. The project will also study what possibilities now exist for national planning and to what extent these may be considered sufficient in other contexts.

Performing organization: The Secretariat for Futures Studies, P. O. Box 7502, S-103 92 Stockholm, Sweden

Sponsor: The Secretariat for Futures Studies

Title of Project: Sweden in a New International Economic Order

Principal Investigator (s): Soren Ekstrom

Period of Effort: 1978 to 1981   **Budget:** No answer

Summary of Project: The project is initiated with a view to provide information on Sweden's role in a new international economic order. As a starting point, the proposals advanced by the developing countries for change of the world order have been analysed. The major changes in the world economy during the last 10-15 years, and in the Swedish economy itself, are then to be analysed. On the basis of that different possible scenarios for the development of the world economy during the next 15-20 years will be formulated and implications for the Swedish economy discussed.

Performing organization: The Secretariat for Futures Studies, P. O. Box 7502, 103 92 Stockholm, Sweden

Sponsor: Secretariat for Futures Studies

Title of Project: The Vulnerable Society

Principal Investigator (s): Ola Svenson, Ann-Kristin Wentzel

Period of Effort: 1977 to 1979   **Budget:** 230,000 Swedish Crowns

Summary of Project: In this project, the society is investigated mainly from one aspect—the vulnerability. The work includes a brief review of the vulnerability of different parts of the society. The issues are social and psychological as well as technical and ecological. The report to be published in Swedish.

Performing organization: Stichting Toekomstbeeld der Techniek (The Future Shape of Technology Foundation), Prinsessegracht 23, The Hague, The Netherlands

Sponsor: No answer

Title of Project: Physician and Data Handling

Principal Investigator (s): R.G.F. De Groot

Period of Effort: No answer   **Budget:** No answer

Summary of Project: The delivery of health care and medical care can be improved by more and better use of data handling. Future developments are being explored in adaptation of hardware and software to the individual physician.

Performing organization: Stichting Toekomstbeeld der Techniek (The Future Shape of Technology Foundation), Prinsessegracht 23, The Hague, The Netherlands

Sponsor: No answer

Title of Project: Urban Housing

Principal Investigator (s): J. Overeem

Period of Effort: End 1978   **Budget:** No answer

Summary of Project: History and future of urban housing and living is being explored and indications are given for long term planning in urban projects.

Performing organization: Swiss Association for Future Research, Weinbergstrasse 17, CH-8623, Wetzikon, Switzerland

Sponsor: Swiss Association for Future Research

Title of Project: Combination of Future Research Methods

Principal Investigator (s): P. Dubach, B. Fritsch, G. Kocher

Period of Effort: Autumn 1978 to 1980   **Budget:** 10,000 Swiss francs

Summary of Project: Combination of methods for future research to obtain better results. Methods and combinations for prospective, perspective and prognosis.

Performing organization: United Nations Institute for Training and Research (UNITAR), 801 United Nations Plaza, New York, New York 10017

Sponsor: UNITAR and the Center for the Economic and Social Study of the Third World (Mexico) (CESSTW)

Title of Project: Progress in the Establishment of the New International Economic Order (NIEO): Obstacles and Opportunities

Principal Investigator (s): Ervin Laszlo, UNITAR Special Fellow, Project Director and Jorge Lozoya, CESSTW, Project Co-Director

Period of Effort: September 1977 to September 1980   **Budget:** No answer

Summary of Project: The project investigates the principal types of obstacles blocking progress in the establishment of the NIEO, as well as the alternative policy measures which could facilitate progress. The project uses a network of over 60 individual and institutional research teams in all parts of the world, and is coordinated by a central project staff in New York (UNITAR) and Mexico (CESSTW). Its publications will be published by UNITAR and Pergamon Press, and are expected to include four or more volumes of studies. They are aimed at informing the debates leading toward the adoption of a new Programme of Action on the NIEO at the Special Session of the United Nations General Assembly in 1980.

Performing organization: University of Dayton Research Institute, 300 College Park Avenue, Dayton, Ohio 45469, U.S.A.

Sponsor: National Science Foundation

Title of Project: Electronic Information Exchange in Futures Research

Principal Investigator (s): Joseph P. Martino

Period of Effort: October 1977 through March 1979   **Budget:** No answer

Summary of Project: This research utilizes the computer conferencing facility at New Jersey Institute of Technology to conduct an 18-month conference among futures researchers in the United States and Europe. The purpose of the conference is to test certain hypotheses regarding the relationship between means of communication and the productivity of scientific workers.

Performing organization: University of Dayton Research Institute, 300 College Park Avenue, Dayton, Ohio 45469, U.S.A.

Sponsor: National Science Foundation

Title of Project: Indices of Technological Change

Principal Investigator (s): Joseph P. Martino

Period of Effort: September 1978 through August 1981   **Budget:** No answer

Summary of Project: To develop leading indicators of technological change within various industries. Indicators being examined include patents, R&D expenditures, and publication of technical papers. During the first phase of the study, ten industries will be examined. Later phases of the study will examine the generalizability of the results to other industries.

Performing organization: University of Southern California, Center for Futures Research, University Park, Los Angeles, California 90007, U.S.A.

Sponsor: 18 major U.S. corporations

Title of Project: Emerging Social and Worker Entitlements

Principal Investigator (s): James O'Toole, Director, Twenty Year Forecast Project

Period of Effort: October 1978 to October 1979   **Budget:** $100,000

Summary of Project: The study focuses on the long-term trend by which personal needs and privileges are transformed into social rights, particularly in the workplace. The research explores the new rights that might emerge in the next twenty years, how the costs will be shared between the private and public sectors, and what the consequences are likely to be for business and society.

Performing organization: University of Southern California, Center for Futures Research, University Park, Los Angeles, California 90007, U.S.A.

Sponsor: 15 major U.S. corporations

Title of Project: The Future Environments of International Trade

Principal Investigator (s): Selwyn Enzer, Associate Director, CFR

Period of Effort: October 1977 to February 1978   **Budget:** $85,000

Summary of Project: The study explores alternative means of structuring international trade to permit world markets to function smoothly over the long term while enabling the poor nations to repay their debts. The research should improve understanding of the nature and magnitude of business opportunities and problems arising from a new world economic order, and the long term impacts upon domestic inflation, capital markets, balance of trade, foreign investment, and raw material availability and cost.

Performing organization: University of Southern California, Center for Futures Research, University Park, Los Angeles, California 90007, U.S.A.

Sponsor: 10 major corporations

Title of Project: The Future of Network Information Services

Principal Investigator (s): Herbert Dordick, Burt Nanus

Period of Effort: August 1976 to December 1978   **Budget:** $120,000

Summary of Project: This project is designed to explore the long-run significance of network information services (NIS) or those services that permit information users to interact directly with one or more computers, associated information files and problem-solving algorithms from remote terminals. The study explores ways that NIS may evolve, how it might relate to other industries, governments and institutions and how NIS might impact upon the economic and social fabric of the nation.

Performing organization: University of Southern California, Center for Futures Research, University Park, Los Angeles, California 90007, U.S.A.

Sponsor: National Science Foundation

Title of Project: Technology Assessment of the Personal Computer and Society

Principal Investigator (s): Jack M. Nilles, Director, Office of Interdisciplinary Programs; Paul Gray, Senior Research Associate, CFR

Period of Effort: August 1978 to August 1979   **Budget:** No answer

Summary of Project: The study examines the long-term impacts of inexpensive general purpose computer systems in home and office. Estimates will be made of the impacts of such a technology on a wide range of business and social variables including public policy, computer costs, the office of the future, personal recordskeeping, recreation, etc.

Performing organization: Wickert Institute fur Markt-, Meinungs-und wirtschaftliche Zukunftsforchung (Wickert Institute for Market, Opinion, and Business Futures Research), Wilhelmstrasse 102, 7400 Tubingen, West-Germany

Sponsor: Thirty business firms and associations

Title of Project: Quo Vadis: A Study of Dynamic Future Models for the Germany Federal Republic

Principal Investigator (s): H. Wagenfuhr and Gunter Wickert

Period of Effort: May 1978 through December 1978   **Budget:** 80,000 Deutsche Marks

Summary of Project: From a variety of starting assumptions, mathematical and psychological factors will be used to construct models of possible future developments in the German Federal Republic. Follow-up reports may modify these models in actual practice. Although grounded upon statistical information, the models will also incorporate results obtained from representative opinion polls and multiple choice questionnaires.

Performing organization: Charles W. Williams, Inc., 801 North Pitt Street, Suite 117-118, Alexandria, Virginia 22314, U.S.A.

Sponsor: Various United States government agencies

Title of Project: Long Range Perspectives

Principal Investigator (s): Charles W. Williams

Period of Effort: January 1977 continuing   **Budget:** No answer

Summary of Project: Worldwide regional trend analyses and forecasts of long-range developments in major global issues which will have a significant impact upon the future world environment. Studies assess policy implications of future world developments in terms of operational functions and tasks.

Performing organization: Charles W. Williams, Inc., 801 North Pitt Street, Suite 117-118, Alexandria, Virginia 22314, U.S.A.

Sponsor: United States Coast Guard

Title of Project: Long Range Planning Framework

Principal Investigator (s): Charles W. Williams

Period of Effort: September 1976 to April 1977 **Budget:** Approximately $55,000

Summary of Project: A set of formal objectives and supporting functions for the United States Coast Guard based on a scenario of the most desirable future for the service.

Performing organization: World Institute Council, 171 West Street, Brooklyn, New York 11222, U.S.A.

Sponsor: World Institute Council

Title of Project: Research of Methodology of Pattern on Urban Development Especially New York City

Principal Investigator (s): No answer

Period of Effort: No answer **Budget:** No answer

Summary of Project: The establishment of a world institute, an association of the earth's most gifted people, utilizing an intercultural, interdisciplinary systems approach in dealing with mankind's social problems in the context of rapid and continual change. The ultimate goal is the formation of a new frame of reference that will call forth holistic behavior benefitting the human being and civilization rather than individuals or individual communities.

Performing organization: Worldwatch Institute, 1776 Massachusetts Ave., N.W., Washington, D.C. 20036, U.S.A.

Sponsor: Worldwatch Institute

Title of Project: Technology and Society

Principal Investigator (s): Colin Norman

Period of Effort: September 1977 through September 1979 **Budget:** No answer

Summary of Project: Colin Norman is considering some of the connections between technology and society—the criteria that have been used for choosing technologies, and those that should be considered (energy use, employment impacts, ecological sustainability, and social equity). The final results are expected to be published in 1979 just before the United Nations Conference on Science and Technology for Development.

Performing organization: Wroctaw Technical University, Forecasting Research Center, Wybrzeze Wyspianskiego 27, 50-370 Wroctaw, Poland

Sponsor: Ministry for Higher Education, Science and Technology

Title of Project: Scientific and Creative Function of Scientific Libraries in the System of Sciences

Principal Investigator (s): Karol Grombiowski

Period of Effort: July 1977 through December 1979 **Budget:** No answer

Summary of Project: Various functions and developmental trends in scientific libraries created and operating under Polish conditions in the 19th and 20th centuries. Based on these data, future trends for the 21st century are indicated.

Performing organization: USSR Academy of Sciences, Section on Social Forecasting, Institute of Social Research, Novo-Cheremushki, 46 Moscow, 117418 USSR

Sponsor: USSR Academy of Sciences

Title of Project: Methodological Approaches to the Building of Society Way of Life Forecasting Initial Model

Principal Investigator (s): USSR Government

Period of Effort: 1976 to 1980 **Budget:** No answer

Summary of Project: The purpose of this study is to examine several approaches to the building of society's way of life initial model as a system of social indicators for the subsequent transformation of this system into forecasting exploratory and normative models of society's way of life. Those examined are:

comparative analysis of existing systems, content-analysis of relevant information sources, expert panels, Delphi techniques, simulation, questionnaires, cross-impact analysis.

Performing organization: State University of Utrecht, Institute of Sociology, Research Unit Planning and Policymaking, Heidelberglaan 2, Utrecht, The Netherlands

Sponsor: Dutch Physical Planning Agency (RPD)

Title of Project: Scenario Methods Research Project

Principal Investigator (s): P. Thoenes, H. A. Becker, H. de Vries

Period of Effort: January 1978 to mid-1980   **Budget:** No answer

Summary of Project: The research unit is working on scenarios for the spatial development in the Netherlands. This project, a joint-venture of both the Dutch Physical Planning Agency and the State University, should comprise the following: (a) a thorough analysis of the present society and an indication of the developments that will be or become important for the society in the next ten years; (b) the development of methods that can be used for designing scenarios; (c) the design of a number of alternative futures, in which the spatial consequences of societal developments are incorporated. So far, two reports have been published.

BOOKS AND REPORTS

BOOKS AND REPORTS

The titles listed here have been chosen to indicate the range and variety of non-fiction books and reports about the future, and include many of the works that have been most influential in shaping the field. To make this list as useful as possible to non-specialists, almost all the titles listed are English-language publications. In many instances, brief annotations have been provided.

Where available, the following information is included for each book and report listed:

Author, editor, translator or compiler
Title
Place of publication
Publisher
Date of first publication

Abler, Ronald F., Donald G. Janelle, Allen K. Philbrick, and John W. Sommer. *Human Geography in a Shrinking World*. N. Scituate, Massachusetts: Duxbury, 1975.

Abt, Clark C. *Serious Games*. New York: Viking Press, 1970.

> This book describes games that are used as learning devices both in schools and in policy-making situations. The author is president of Abt Associates, a consulting firm in Cambridge, Massachusetts. Abt says that games permit players to test situations and "solutions" that are either irreversible or too risky or expensive to test in the real world. They offer an opportunity for virtually risk-free, active exploration of serious intellectual and social problems. The book is generally readable although moderately technical in places.

Ackoff, Russell L. *Redesigning the Future: A Systems Approach to Societal Problems*. New York: John Wiley, 1974.

Adams, John, John Hayes, and Barrie Hopson. *Transition: Understanding and Managing Personal Change*. Montclair, New Jersey: Allanheld, Osmun & Co., 1977.

Alter, Steven. *The Mathematics of Time-Dependent Cross-Impact Modeling*. Los Angeles: Center for Futures Research, 1976.

Alter, Steven. *Systems and Modeling Issues Related to Time Dependent Cross-Impact Models*. Los Angeles: Center for Futures Research, 1977.

Amalrik, Andrei. *Will the Soviet Union Survive Until 1984?* New York: Harper and Row, 1970.

Amelio, Ralph J. *Hal in the Classroom: Science Fiction Films*. Dayton, Ohio: Pflaum Publishing, 1974.

American Association of University Women. *Exploring American Futures*. Publication 592. Washington, D.C.: American Association of University Women, 1975.

American Society of Landscape Architects Foundation. *Information, Perception, and Regional Policy*. Prepared for the National Science Foundation. NSF/RA-760064. Washington, D.C.: U.S. Government Printing Office, 1975.

Amis, Kingsley. *New Maps of Hell: A Survey of Science Fiction*. New York: Harcourt, Brace, 1960.

Anderson, Stanford, ed. *Planning for Diversity and Choice: Possible Futures and Their Relations to the Man-Controlled Environment*. Cambridge, Massachusetts: MIT Press, 1968.

Andriole, Stephen J. *Progress Report on the Development of an Integrated Crisis Warning System*. McLean, Virginia: Decisions and Designs, Inc., 1976.

Annan, Chairman Lord. *Report of the Committee on the Future of Broadcasting*. London: HMSO, 1977.

Argenti, John. *Systematic Corporate Planning*. New York: Halsted Press, 1974.

Armbruster, Frank E. *Our Children's Crippled Future: How American Education Has Failed*. New York: Quadrangle, 1977.

Armstrong, J. Scott. *Long Range Forecasting: From Crystal Ball to Computer*. New York: Wiley-Interscience, 1978.

> A complete guide and reference source covering forecasting methods in the social and management sciences. Research was drawn from economics, sociology, psychology, and a wide range of other fields.

Armytage, W. H. G. *Yesterday's Tomorrows: A Historical Survey of Future Societies*. Toronto: University of Toronto Press, 1968.

Arnstein, Sherry P. and A. Christakis. *Perspectives on Technology Assessment*. Jerusalem: Science and Technology Publishers, 1975.

Ascher, William. *Forecasting: An Appraisal for Policy-Makers and Planners*. Baltimore, Maryland: The Johns Hopkins University Press, 1978.

    In this innovative study, William Ascher examines the records of expert forecasting of national trends in population, economics, energy, transportation, and technology over a 50-year period. He has identified factors associated with greater accuracy as well as with systematic biases and he finds that the methodological sophistication of computer models is relatively unimportant compared to the core assumptions concerning the broad context of a trend. Ascher shows that for each trend the distinctive approach curve relating the reduction in forecast errors to the approach of the target date can enable policy-makers to evaluate the accuracy of forecasts of specific length. And in some cases policy-makers can predict the likely accuracy and biases of forecasts according to their sources and methodology.

Ash, Brian. *Who's Who in Science Fiction*. New York: Taplinger, 1976.

Avery, Norman E. *Time Out for Tomorrow*. Belt, Montana: Janher Publishing Co., 1977.

Aviation Futures to the Year 2000. Washington, D.C.: Federal Aviation Administration, 1977.

Ayres, Robert U. *Technological Forecasting and Long-Range Planning*. New York: McGraw-Hill, 1969.

    This book outlines the methods used in technological forecasting in a systematic way. It also describes various failures of technological forecasting and the epistemology of forecasting. Although now somewhat dated, the book is a highly useful and authoritative introduction to its subject.

Baade, Fritz. *The Race to the Year 2000*. Garden City, New York: Doubleday, 1962.

Bacheller, Martin. *The Hammond Almanac*. New York: Signet, 1978.

    Billed as book of a million facts, records, and forecasts, this 1979 edition of the Hammond Almanac contains a special section on the future written by the staff of the World Future Society.

Bagdikian, Ben H. *The Information Machines: Their Impact on Man and the Media*. New York: Harper and Row, 1971.

    This book provides a view of the future of communications, prepared by a distinguished journalist who spent two years at the Rand Corporation in Santa Monica, California, where he directed a study of the impact of future technology of the gathering and dissemination of news. Bagdikian followed up his Rand study with detailed studies of seven newspapers. His Rand research included a Delphi poll on the future of communications.

Baier, Kurt, and Nicholas Rescher, eds. *Values and the Future*. New York: Free Press, 1969.

    This is a collection of 17 essays by such futurists as Theodore Gordon, Olaf Helmer, Bertrand de Jouvenel, Kenneth Boulding, and others. The book is introduced by Alvin Toffler, who describes the "value impact forecaster" as "a profession of the future." Also included is "a questionnaire study of American values by 2,000 A.D." by Nicholas Rescher. The volume concludes with two bibliographies dealing with technological progress, future-oriented studies, and the theory of value.

Barnett, H. G. *Innovation: The Basis of Cultural Change*. New York: McGraw-Hill, 1953.

Barney, Gerald O. *The Unfinished Agenda: The Citizen's Policy Guide to Environmental Issues*. New York: Crowell, 1977.

Barney, Gerald O., ed. *The Global 2000 Report to the President of the U.S.: Entering the 21st Century*. 2 vols. Elmsford, New York: Pergamon Press, Inc., 1979.

Basile, Paul S., ed. *Energy Supply-Demand Integrations to the Year 2000: Global and National Studies,* Third Technical Report of the Workshop on Alternative Energy Strategies. Cambridge, Massachusetts: The MIT Press, 1977.

Basiuk, Victor. *Technology, World Politics and American Policy.* New York: Columbia University Press, 1977.

Victor Basiuk, a consultant in science, technology, and national security policy examines the effect that future technological developments will have on international politics and social patterns. Basiuk details how future technological developments will further the stalemate between the United States and the Soviet Union and increase global interdependence and then examines the social characteristics of the various industrial powers that will hinder or help them cope with future technological change.

Bauer, Raymond. *The Corporate Social Audit.* New York: Russell Sage Foundation, 1973.

Bauer, Raymond, Richard Rosenbloom, and Laure Sharp. *Second Order Consequences.* Cambridge, Massachusetts: M.I.T. Press, 1969.

Bauer, Raymond, ed. *Social Indicators.* Cambridge, Massachusetts: M.I.T. Press, 1966.

Raymond Bauer, a psychologist professor at the Harvard Business School, and Bertram Gross, an academician in the field of public administration, contribute major essays to this volume, which introduces the general topic of social indicators. This book was financed by a grant from the National Aeronautics and Space Administration to the American Academy of Arts and Sciences in Boston. NASA is only one of a number of U.S. agencies that have been interested in social indicators, that is, statistics, on the many aspects of our society that are not covered by the traditional census statistics and economic indicators.

Bean Louis H. *The Art of Forecasting.* New York: Random House, 1969.

Beckerman, Wilfred. *Two Cheers for the Affluent Society.* New York: St. Martin's Press, 1974.

Wilfred Beckerman, Head of the Department of Political Economy at University College in London, argues that the anti-growth camp is selfish, misinformed about pollution, and often flatly wrong in its facts. Chief among the errors of the anti-growth camp is the failure to credit mankind with any innovativeness. A solution, he says, lies not in stunting the output of goods and services, but in allocating them optimally.

Beckwith, Burnham P. *Government by Experts: The Next Stage in Political Evolution.* New York: Exposition Press, 1972.

Beckwith, Burnham P. *The Next 500 Years: Scientific Predictions of Major Social Trends.* New York: Exposition Press, 1967.

This book contains more than 1,000 specific forecasts about what may happen in human society during the next five centuries. The book analyzes major social trends and covers such topics as population, education, and knowledge, religion, the relationship of work and leisure, etc. In general, the forecast is optimistic and the forecasts appear highly integrated; that is, they tend to jibe fairly well with each other. The book is tightly written and stimulating but somewhat lacking in evidence to support its assertions.

Beer, Stafford. *Platform for Change.* London: John Wiley, 1975.

Belch, Jean. *Contemporary Games.* Detroit, Michigan: Gale Research Company, 1973.

Bell, Daniel. *The Coming of Post-Industrial Society: A Venture in Social Forecasting.* New York: Basic Books, 1973.

This book contains most of the concepts that sociologist Bell has developed in recent years. Scholarly and well-documented, it offers a thoughtful analysis of the great social trends that are shaping our future society. Bell argues that people can make meaningful forecasts about the future of modern society if they take the trouble to understand fully the present conditions of that society and the trends visibly at work in it.

Bell, Daniel. *The Cultural Contradictions of Capitalism.* New York: Basic Books, 1976.

Bell argues that capitalism may destroy itself if the polarities between its affective and rational elements are not reconciled. He says that capitalism as an economic system requires ever greater applications of rationality to solve problems of organization and deficiency and to find the right balance between cost and benefit. On the other hand, capitalist *culture* places an ever-greater emphasis on such values as self-fulfillment and personal gratifications. As these two tendencies grow stronger, the rift between them widens. This book continues the analysis of Bell's earlier work, *The Coming of Post-Industrial Society.* Bell describes the split character of the new capitalism of abundance: it demands a Protestant ethic in production, but encourages a fun ethic in consumption. Bell argues that modern society can best be analyzed by thinking of it as "an uneasy amalgam of three distinct realms: the social structure (principally the techno-economic order), the polity, and the culture." The three realms are ruled by contrary principles: efficiency, equality, and self-realization or self-gratification.

Bell, Daniel, ed. *Toward the Year 2000: Work in Progress.* Boston: Houghton Mifflin, 1968.

This is the first report of the Commission on the Year 2000, formed in 1965 by the American Academy of Arts and Sciences and chaired by sociologist Daniel Bell. The volume summarizes the dialogue that occurred at the working sessions of the Commission in October 1965 and in February 1966. The book also includes a number of papers ranging from Leonard J. Duhl's ideas on planning to David Riesman's "Thinking on Meritocracy." This book is a highly compact compendium of stimulating ideas.

Bell, Gwen, ed. *Strategies for Human Settlements: Habitat & Environment.* Honolulu, Hawaii: The University Press, 1976.

Bell, Wendell, and James A. Mau, eds. *The Sociology of the Future.* New York: Russell Sage Foundation, 1971.

Thirteen social scientists discuss the 1970s and the study of the future. The book offers a theory of social change based on the concept of the image of the future together with research strategies for studying the future. The book contains an annotated bibliography on social science studies of the future.

Bennis, Warren G., and Phillip E. Slater. *The Temporary Society.* New York: Harper and Row, 1968.

Beres, Louis R., and Harry R. Targ, ed. *Planning Alternative World Futures: Values, Methods and Models.* New York: Praeger Publishers, Inc., 1975.

This collection of essays addresses the concept and design of alternative futures for such world problems as international and national security systems, populations, diminishing natural resources, environmental deterioration, and the widening gap between rich and poor.

Berry, Adrian. *The Next Ten Thousand Years: A Vision of Man's Future in the Universe.* New York: E. P. Dutton, 1974.

The author, a fellow of Britain's Royal Astronomical Society, explores such possibilities as a colonization of Venus, factories on the moon, intelligent life on other planets and the extensive use of space ships. The book offers an optimistic and imaginative view of the possibilities of outer space. The emphasis is heavily on technology as the means for achieving "ever more magnificent achievements."

Best, Fred, ed. *The Future of Work.* Englewood Cliffs, New Jersey: Prentice-Hall, 1973.

Bete, Channing L. *Education 2000+ : Some Ideas Subject to Change Without Notice About the Future of Education.* Greenfield, Massachusetts: Channing L. Bete Co., 1969.

Bhagwati, Jagdish N., ed. *Economics and World Order: From the 1970s to the 1990s.* London: Macmillan, 1972.

Bloomfield, Lincoln P., and Charles W. Yost, eds. *The Future of the U.N.* Boulder, Colorado: Westview Press, 1977.

Bookchin, Murray. *Our Synthetic Environment.* Rev. ed. New York: Harper and Row, 1974.

Boot, J. C. G. *Common Globe or Global Commons: Population Regulation.* New York: Marcel Dekker, 1974.

Boucher, Wayne, ed. *The Study of the Future: An Agenda for Research.* Washington, D.C.: U.S. National Science Foundation, 1977.

Boulding, Kenneth E. *The Meaning of the Twentieth Century: The Great Transition.* New York: Harper and Row, 1964.

> The author, a University of Colorado economist, argues that mankind is in a transition from civilized to "post-civilized" society and that he needs to avoid four "traps": (1) the war trap ("a major nuclear war would unquestionably set back the transition to a post-civilized world by many generations . . . "); (2) the population trap (Attempts to help people through medical services, says Boulding, could lead to disastrous overpopulation.); (3) the technological trap ("Technology at the present time, even the highest technology, is largely dependent for its sources of energy and materials on accumulations in the earth which date from its geological past. In a few centuries, or at most a few thousand years, these are likely to be exhausted."); and (4) the entropy trap (Borrowing a term from thermodynamics, Boulding suggests that the human potential may gradually diminish. To avoid these traps, Boulding believes that man should use all his intellectual resources to create an image of the future, or set of long-range goals, which would stress the infinite possibilities open to him.).

Bowman, Jim, Fred Kierstead, Chris Dede, & John Pulliam. *The Far Side of the Future: Social Problems and Educational Reconstruction.* Washington, D.C.: The World Future Society, 1978.

> A forceful, innovative proposal for the reconstruction of society through education. The authors outline a comprehensive model for transcending traditional education and emphasize the evolutionary changes that will help facilitate living and learning alternatives.

Brameld, Theodore. *The Teacher as World Citizen: A Scenario of the 21st Century.* Palm Springs, California: ETC Publications, 1976.

> Written as if by a citizen of the "World Community of Nations" which is functioning successfully in this imaginary year 2000. Brameld says that he is attempting to build on the work of Edward Bellamy, author of *Looking Backward.*

Bright, James R. *A Brief Introduction to Technology Forecasting Concepts and Exercises.* Austin, Texas: The Pemaquid Press, 1972.

> James Bright is Professor of Technology Management at the University of Texas's Graduate School of Business Administration and president of the Industrial Management Center in Hilton Head, South Carolina. Since 1967 he has organized a series of seminars on technology forecasting and assessment. An integral part of Bright's seminars is the workshop in which students execute exercises based on case histories. Some of the most useful exercises are reproduced in this volume. Each group of exercises is preceded by a brief explanation of how forecasting techniques should be applied to the exercise, and in the process Bright offers some very clear explanations of the forecasting techniques now in use.

Bright, James R. *Practical Technology Forecasting: Concepts and Exercises.* Austin, Texas: Sweet Publishing Co., 1978.

> This workbook on technology forecasting begins with a brief introduction to the history, possibilities, and limitations of forecasting, and traces a clear and informative path through the field's most modern and exciting techniques.

Bright, James R., ed. *Technological Forecasting for Industry and Government.* Englewood Cliffs, New Jersey: Prentice-Hall, 1968.

> This volume resulted from Bright's May 1967 seminar at the Lake Placid Club in New York and provides a number of authoritative papers by professional forecasters.

Bronwell, Arthur B., ed. *Science and Technology in the World of the Future.* New York: John Wiley, 1970.

> This volume brings together a number of authoritative and generally readable papers. Especially useful are the state-of-the-art summaries and the accompanying speculation for the various technological fields, such as transportation, biomedical engineering, science, cities, the oceans, etc.

Brown, Harrison. *The Challenge of Man's Future.* New York: Viking Press, 1954.

> This book by a California Institute of Technology geochemist has proved a durable classic which had its 15th printing in 1967. The book discusses the major problems facing modern man such as rising population, the need to increase the food supply, dwindling supplies of fossil fuels and the limited supplies of mineral resources. Brown sees three possible futures: (1) the reemergence of an agrarian world following a nuclear holocaust, which Brown regards as the most likely possibility, (2) a completely controlled, collectivized industrial society, and (3) a fully industrialized world in which everyone leads a good life.

Brown, Harrison. *The Human Future Revisited: The World Predicament and Possible Solutions.* New York: Norton, 1978.

> In recent decades a most significant development in human history has been taking place: it is the fissioning of the world into two megacultures— the rich and the poor. What are the consequences for the future of these two distinct cultures cohabiting the earth? In this book the situation is examined in terms of the growth of population and affluence, changing technologies, energy, food resources, weaponry, and the changing global environment.

Brown, Harrison, James Bonner, and John Wier. *The Next Hundred Years.* New York: Viking Press, 1957.

> This volume results from a series of discussions between the authors, who are all professors at the California Institute of Technology, and the chief executives of thirty major corporations. The book focuses on trends in (1) availability of material resources and skilled manpower, (2) population growth and food production, and (3) the availability of creative people to solve technical dilemmas.

Brown, Harrison, and Edward Hutchings, Jr. *Are Our Descendents Doomed? Technological Change and Population Growth.* New York: Viking Press, 1972.

Brown, Harrison, *et al. The Next Ninety Years.* Pasadena, California: California Institute of Technology, 1967.

> This volume results from a conference held in March 1967 in which the authors reviewed the forecasts that they had made 10 years earlier. Two basic surprises emerged: the fantastically rapid growth of population, which greatly exceeded the rates imagined earlier, and the revolution in the world energy picture brought about by the rapidly decreasing cost of nuclear power. The authors found two major disappointments: first, agriculture production had increased less rapidly than had been anticipated; second, while the technologically developed West was getting richer more rapidly than was thought possible, the poorer nations of the world were not sharing significantly in the bounty.

Brown, Lester R. *In the Human Interest: A Strategy to Stabilize World Population.* New York: W. W. Norton, 1974.

Brown, Lester R. *Seeds of Change: The Green Revolution in the 1970s.* New York: Praeger, 1970.

> This volume, which describes the "green revolution," made its appearance in 1969 when a number of Asian countries had made a great deal of progress with the "miracle seeds" of

wheat and rice. Taking an optimistic view of the food problem at that time, Brown focused on what he called "second-generation problems"—the problems of providing adequate water and fertilizer, warding off dangerous plant diseases, learning to manage land under new conditions of continuous cropping, etc. The problem which seemed to worry Brown the most at the time this book was written was how to employ surplus rural people and give them sufficient buying power so that they can buy the additional foods which the owners of land produce.

Brown, Lester R. *The Twenty Ninth Day: Accommodating Human Needs and Numbers to the Earth's Resources.* New York: W.W. Norton & Co., 1978.

> This book provides a bridge between ecologists and economists and an analysis of the four principal biological systems on which humanity depends— fisheries, forests, grasslands and croplands. The head of Worldwatch Institute demonstrates very explicitly that demands at current levels of population and per capita consumption often exceed the long-term carrying capacity.

Brown, Lester R. *World Without Borders.* New York: Random House, 1972.

> This book offers an overview of the current world situation regarding population, food production, pollution, etc. The author argues for an expanded world communication system, with English as the international lingua franca, and new supranational institutions such as a world environmental agency and international research institutes. The book is reasonably optimistic in its outlook, partly because Brown spells out a number of possible solutions to international dilemmas.

Brown, Lester R., with Erik P. Eckholm. *By Bread Alone.* New York: Praeger, 1974.

Brown, Seyom. *New Forces in World Politics.* Washington, D.C.: Brookings Institution, 1974.

Brubaker, Sterling. *In Command of Tomorrow: Resource and Environmental Strategies for Americans.* Baltimore, Maryland: Johns Hopkins University Press, 1975.

Brzezinski, Zbigniew. *Between Two Ages: America's Role in the Technetronic Era.* New York: Viking Press, 1970.

> The author, a professor of government at Columbia University, argues that a community of developed nations, including the Soviet Union and the United States, could work out solutions to world problems. He believes that such a community could successfully aid the underdeveloped nations and counter "the global tendencies toward chaos."

Bundy, Robert, ed. *Images of the Future: The 21st Century and Beyond.* Buffalo, New York: Prometheus, 1976.

Burhoe, Ralph Wendell, ed. *Science and Human Values in the 21st Century.* Philadelphia: Westminster Press, 1971.

Butler, William F., and Robert A. Kavish. *How Business Economists Forecast.* Rev. ed. Englewood Cliffs, New Jersey: Prentice-Hall, 1974.

Calder, Nigel, ed. *Unless Peace Comes: A Scientific Forecast of New Weapons.* New York: Viking Press, 1969.

Calder, Nigel, ed. *The World in 1984.* Two vols. Baltimore, Maryland: Penguin Books, 1965.

> These volumes include 100 short articles originally published in the British journal *New Scientist* during 1964. The authors generally do their forecasting in their own narrow areas, with little attempt to look beyond the confines of their disciplines, but the overall impact of this work is to provide a sense of a very rapid change now occurring in the many different aspects of human life.

Callaway, Col. Jack, G. *Korea: Future Problems, Future Policies.* National Security Affairs Monograph, 77-3, Washington, D.C.: National War College, 1977.

436

Calvert, Geoffrey N. *Pensions and Survival: The Coming Crisis of Money and Retirement.* Toronto, Ontario, Canada: Maclean-Hunter Limited, 1977.

Camilleri, Joseph A. *Civilization in Crisis.* New York: Cambridge University Press, 1977.

Campbell, Angus, Philip E. Converse, and Willard L. Rodgers. *The Quality of American Life: Perceptions, Evaluations, and Satisfactions.* New York: Russell Sage Foundation. 1976.

   This book, based on research conducted by the Institute for Social Research at the University of Michigan, covers such topics as the residential environment, the experience of work, marriage and family life, and personal resources and competence. The authors devote separate chapters to the situation of women and black people.

Campbell, Carlos C. *New Towns: Another Way to Live.* Reston, Virginia: Reston, 1976.

   Carlos Campbell, an urban planner and resident of Reston, Virginia, here describes the new communities that have developed in the United States over the past two decades. Highly opinionated, the book offers a view of what life is really like in the new towns.

Carter, Paul A. *The Creation of Tomorrow.* Columbia University Press, 1977.

Case, Charles W., and Paul A. Olson, eds. *The Future: Create or Inherit.* Lincoln, Nebraska: University of Nebraska Printing Service, 1974.

Center for Futures Research, University of Southern California. *The Twenty Year Forecast Project—The Future Environments of International Trade.* Los Angeles: Center for Futures Research, 1977.

Center for Futures Research, University of Southern California. *The Twenty Year Forecast Project—The Future of Government Corporate Relations.* Los Angeles: Center for Futures Research, 1976.

Cetron, Marvin J. *Technological Forecasting: A Practical Approach.* New York: Gordon and Breach, 1969.

   The author, president of Forecasting International of Arlington, Virginia, has set out to write a primer which would answer essential questions that a research manager would have about how technological forecasters go about their work, the basic methods they employ, and what one might expect them to deliver. The examples derived primarily from the defense arena, since the author was employed by the U.S. Navy.

Cetron, Marvin J., and Harold F. Davidson. *Industrial Technology Transfer.* Leyden, The Netherlands: Noordhoff International Publishing, 1977.

Cetron, Marvin J., and Christine A. Ralph. *Industrial Applications of Technological Forecasting: Its Utilization in R and D Management.* New York: John Wiley, 1971.

Chaplin, George, and Glenn D. Paige, eds. *Hawaii 2000: Continuing Experiment in Anticipatory Democracy.* Honolulu, Hawaii: University Press of Hawaii, 1973.

Chartham, Robert. *Your Sexual Future.* New York: Pinnacle Books, 1972.

Chase, Stuart. *The Most Probable World.* New York: Harper and Row, 1968.

   Social critic and economist Chase, a professional writer for about half a century, outlines the basic characteristics of tomorrow's world. He concentrates attention on ten areas: (1) technological advances; (2) population growth; (3) diminution of individual living space; (4) going urbanization; (5) peaceful use of atomic energy; (6) the increasing mix of private and public enterprise; (7) the impact of automation on man; (8) the arms race; (9) mixed trends in nationalistic orientations; and (10) the development of a global community. In an optimistic epilogue Chase describes a world characterized by environmental beauty, a world language, reduced population growth, new towns, material abundance, and world order.

Chen, Kan. *Growth Policy: Population, Environment, and Beyond.* Ann Arbor, Michigan: University of Michigan Press, 1974.

Chinoy, Ely, ed. *The Urban Future.* New York: Lieber-Atherton, 1973.

Chodak, Szymon. *Societal Development: Five Approaches with Conclusions from Comparative Analysis.* New York: Oxford University Press, 1973.

Chou, Marylin, David P. Harmon, Jr., Herman Kahn, and Sylvan H. Wittwer. *World Food Prospects and Agricultural Potential.* New York: Praeger Publishers, 1977.

Christian, James L. *Extra-Terrestrial Intelligence: The First Encounter.* Buffalo, New York: Prometheus, 1976.

Churchman, C. West, ed. *World Modeling: A Dialogue.* New York: American Elsevier, 1976.

Ciba Foundation Symposium. *The Future as an Academic Discipline.* Amsterdam: Elsevier, 1975.

This volume summarizes a symposium in London on the study of the future in an educational setting. The participants include such distinguished figures as Harold Shane, Professor of Education, Indiana University; British biologist and Nobel prize winner C. H. Waddington, and many others.

A Citizen's Guide to the Future. Greenville, South Carolina: Skip Everett, 1977.

Clareson, Thomas D. ed. *Many Futures, Many Worlds.* Kent, Ohio: Kent State University Press, 1977.

Clark, John, and Sam Cole, with Ray Curnow, and Mike Hopkins. *Global Simulation Models: A Comparative Study.* Chichester, England: John Wiley, 1976.

Clarke, Arthur C. *Profiles of the Future.* Rev. ed. New York: Harper and Row, 1973.

This is a new edition of one of the classics of futurist literature. The book was originally published in 1963 and some of the things that Clarke spoke of have already come true. The first two chapters explore the question of why prophets in the past often failed to foresee the future. Clark attributes this to (1) a failure of nerve and (2) a failure of imagination. In the one case, the would-be prophet has all the facts but cannot see that they point to an inescapable conclusion. In the other case, the prophet does not have the facts, and can't imagine them. Later chapters explore such topics as transport, ground-effect machines, ocean mining, space, etc. This exceptionally well-written and scientifically balanced book presents the author's imaginative forecasts for the next 150 years. Clarke maintains that it is impossible to predict the actual future in any detail but one can delineate general direction that development might take and indicate what are possibilities.

Clarke, Robin, ed. *Notes for the Future.* New York: Universe Books, 1975.

Cleveland, Harlan. *The Future Executive.* New York: Harper and Row, 1972.

Cleveland, Harlan. *The Third Try at World Order: U.S. Policy for an Interdependent World.* New York: The Aspen Institute for Humanistic Studies, 1977.

Coates, Vary T. *Technology and Public Policy: The Process of Technology Assessment in the Federal Government.* Two vols. Washington, D.C.: George Washington University, 1972.

Cohn, Alvin W. *The Future of Policing.* Beverly Hills, California: Sage Publications, 1978.

Cole, Dandrige M. *Beyond Tomorrow: The Next 50 Years in Space.* Amherst, Wisconsin: Amherst Press, 1965.

Cole, H. S. D., C. Freeman, M. Jahoda, and K. L. R. Pavitt, eds. *Models of Doom: A Critique of the Limits to Growth.* New York: Universe Books, 1973.

> The Club of Rome's widely publicized work on *The Limits to Growth* suggested that computer simulations of global conditions indicate that the world ecosystem is approaching collapse. In this book, 13 Sussex University scientists argue that the Club's world model did not accurately reflect reality and their policy recommendations are a counsel of despair, impossible to implement.

Cole, Sam. *Global Models and the International Economic Order.* Oxford, England: Pergamon, 1977.

Commission on Population Growth and the American Future. *Population and the American Future.* Report of the Commission. Washington, D.C.: U.S. Government Printing Office, 1972.

Commoner, Barry. *The Closing Circle: Nature, Man, and Technology.* New York: Knopf, 1971.

The Conference Board. *Information Technology: Some Critical Implications for Decision-Makers.* Report 537. New York: The Conference Board, 1972.

The Conference Board. *Perspectives for the 70s and 80s: Tomorrow's Problems Confronting Today's Management.* New York: The Conference Board, 1970.

Conger, D. Stuart. *Social Inventions.* Prince Albert, Canada: Saskatchewan Newstart, 1970.

> This report, prepared by a Canadian government official, surveys social inventions now employed in human society and also speculates on inventions that may occur in the future.

Cook, Earl. *Man, Energy, Society.* San Francisco, California: W. H. Freeman & Co., 1976.

Cornish, Edward. *1999: The World of Tomorrow.* Washington, D.C.: The World Future Society, 1978.

> This anthology of articles from THE FUTURIST is divided into four sections: "The Future as History," "The Future as Progress," "The Future as Challenge," and "The Future as Invention." The subjects covered include economic visions, architecture, medicine, space colonies, energy, education, sex, work, appropriate technology, the automated office, and social inventions.

Cornish, Edward. *The Study of the Future: An Introduction to the Art and Science of Understanding and Shaping Tomorrow's World.* Washington, D.C.: The World Future Society, 1977.

> A general introduction to futurism and future studies. Chapters discuss the history of the futurist movement, ways to introduce future-oriented thinking into organizations, the philosophical assumptions underlying studies of the future, methods of forecasting, current thinking about what may happen as a result of the current revolutionary changes in human society, etc. The volume also includes detailed descriptions of the life and thinking of certain prominent futurists and an annotated guide to further reading.

Council of Europe. *Long-term Planning and Forecasting in Europe 1968-70.* Strasbourg, France: Council of Europe, Directorate of Political Affairs, 1970.

Cournand, Andre, and Maurice Levy, eds. *Shaping the Future: Gaston Berger and the Concept of Prospective.* New York: Gordon and Breach Science Publishers, 1973.

Crosson, Pierre R., and Kenneth D. Frederick. *The World Food Situation: Resources and Environmental Issues in the Developing Countries and the United States.* Washington, D.C.: Resources for the Future, 1977.

Dag Hammarskjold Foundation. *Another Development, Strategies.* Uppsala, Sweden: Dag Hammarskjold Foundation, 1977.

Dalkey, Norman C., Ralph Lewis, Daniel Rourke, and David Snyder. *Studies in the Quality of Life: Delphi and Decision Making.* Lexington, Massachusetts: Lexington Books, 1972.

Daly, Herman E., ed. *Toward a Steady-State Economy*. San Francisco: W. H. Freeman, 1973.

> This book seeks to present a single coherent point of view—that of a steady-state economy, which is based on both physical and ethical first principles. Daly, a Louisiana State University economist, says that "we absolutely must revise our economic thinking, so that it will be more in conformity with the finite energy and resource limits of the earth, and with the finite limits of man's stomach." This volume, which constitutes a vigorous attack on "growthmania," includes such articles as "The Economics of the Coming Spaceship Earth" by Kenneth E. Boulding, "Buddhist Economics," by E. F. Schumacher, and Daly's own paper "The Steady-State Economy: Toward a Political Economy of Biophysical Equilibrium and Moral Growth."

Dantzig, George L., and Thomas L. Saaty. *Compact City: A Plan for a Livable Urban Environment*. San Francisco: W. H. Freeman, 1973.

Dark, Harris Edward. *Auto Engines of Tomorrow: Power Alternatives for Cars to Come*. Bloomington, Indiana: Indiana University Press, 1975.

Darwin, Charles G. *The Next Million Years*. Garden City, New York: Doubleday, 1953.

Davis, Douglas. *Art and the Future: A History/Prophecy of the Collaboration Between Science, Technology and Art*. New York: Praeger, 1973.

Decoufle, Andre-Clement. *La Prospective*. Paris: Presses Universitaires de France, 1972.

de Jouvenel, Bertrand. *The Art of Conjecture*. New York: Basic Books, 1967; first published by Editions du Rocher, 1964.

> Originally published in France in 1964, this book has become one of the classics of futurist literature. De Jouvenel, widely known as an economist and philosopher, regards looking into the future as an art rather than a science. After laying the philosophical groundwork for the new emerging field, he urges the creation of a "forecasting forum" to develop the art for government, industry, and people at large.

de Jouvenel, Bertrand. *La Civilisation de Puissance*. Paris, France: Fayard, 1976.

> This latest book by French futurist Bertrand de Jouvenel (economist, political scientist and editor of the journal *Futuribles)* is not yet available in English.
> Focusing on the impact of new technologies on man's beliefs and values, de Jouvenel discusses the concept of "progress" and man's changing view of his own place in the biosphere, and reviews the significance of today's world-wide economic instability for our attempts to plan for the future.

deNeufville, Judith Innes. *Social Indicators and Public Policy: Interactive Processes of Design and Application*. Amsterdam: Elsevier, 1975.

Deutsch, Karl W., ed. et. al. *Problems of World Modeling: Political and Social Implications*. Cambridge, Massachusetts: Ballinger Publishing Co., 1977.

Dickson, Paul. *The Electronic Battlefield*. Bloomington, Indiana: Indiana University Press, 1976.

Dickson, Paul. *The Future File: A Guide for People with One Foot in the 21st Century*. New York: Rawson Associates Publishers, Inc., 1977.

> This book is divided into two sections. The first part gives an overview of today's futurism and the futurists, featuring the kinds of driving ideas, personalities, envisioned world, concepts of the future, and specific forecasts that make the whole business tick. Added is a collection of specific predictions made by various authorities. The second part is an almanac and directory of the future, which features a "yellow pages" section listing futures groups, futuristic games, charts about the future, and models for writing future scenarios.

Dickson, Paul. *The Future of the Workplace*. New York: Weybright and Talley, 1975.

Dickson, Paul. *Think Tanks*. New York: Atheneum, 1971.

> This volume describes, in a rather breezy style, the activities of the Rand Corporation, System Development Corporation, Hudson Institute, Institute for the Future, Urban Institute, etc. One chapter, entitled "Prospecting the Future," focuses special attention on futuristics.

Didsbury, Howard F. *The Study of the Future—A Manual for Teachers*. Washington, D.C.: The World Future Society, 1979.

> A brief complementary volume to the *Student Handbook for the Study of the Future*, this manual contains course outlines, research suggestions, teaching aids, bibliographic additions, and more.

Didsbury, Howard F. *The Study of the Future—Study Guide for Students*. Washington, D.C.: The World Future Society, 1979.

> A supplement to the World Future Society's *The Study of the Future*, this volume is designed to assist the student in developing a sound basic understanding of the field of futuristics. Contains essay and discussion suggestions, examinations of futurist forecasting methods, additional essays, and much more.

Dolotta, T. A., M. I. Bernstein, R. S. Dickson, Jr., N. A. France, B. A. Rosenblatt, D. M. Smith, and T. B. Steel, Jr. *Data Processing in 1980-1985*. New York: John Wiley, 1976.

> The authors see mounting pressures being put on the data-processing industry for new services in the next five to ten years. Workers using computer technology will increase rapidly, making simplified end-use procedures imperative. "Hardware," or engineering costs, have already been eclipsed by "software," or programming costs, and the "software" will come in for major attention by the experts, in an effort to raise it from a craft to a science. The authors foresee steady growth in the world economy and an increasing demand for data processing equipment and services for the world's expanding needs.

Doxiadis, Constantinos. *Ekistics: An Introduction to the Science of Human Settlements*. New York: Oxford, 1968.

Dror, Yehezkel. *Crazy States: A Counterconventional Strategic Problem*. Lexington, Massachusetts: Heath, 1971.

Dror, Yehezkel. *Design for Policy Sciences*. New York: American Elsevier, 1971.

Dror, Yehezkel. *Public Policy-Making Reexamined*. San Francisco: Chandler Publishing Company, 1968.

Dror, Yehezkel. *Ventures in Policy Sciences: Concepts and Applications*. New York: American Elsevier, 1971.

Drucker, Peter F. *The Age of Discontinuity*. New York: Harper and Row, 1969.

> Economist Drucker describes four areas of significant discontinuity: (1) new technologies—not embroiderments on old ones, but entirely new ones—which will bring about new industries and render some existing ones obsolete; (2) the world economy, which is becoming a single market, one "global shopping center"; (3) highly organized power concentrations to which all our social tasks have been entrusted, but concerning which there is increasing disillusionment; and (4) the centrality of knowledge, which Drucker views as the most important of the four discontinuities. "Knowledge during the last decades," Drucker says, "has become the central capital, the cost center, the crucial resource of the economy. This changes labor forces and work, teaching and learning, the meaning of knowledge and its politics." Drucker anticipates an upcoming period of change in the world economy with four new industries becoming major forces: those based on information, oceans, materials, and the megalopolis. Drucker forecasts that the knowledge industry will account for one-half of the total national product in the late 1970s.

Drucker, Peter F., ed. *Preparing Tomorrow's Business Leaders Today*. New York: Harper and Row, 1969.

Duke, Richard D. *Gaming: The Future's Language.* New York: Sage Publications, 1974.

Dumont, Rene. *L'Utopie ou la Mort! [Utopia or Else!]* New York: Universe Books, 1975; originally published in French by Editions du Seuil, 1973.

Dunstan, Maryjane, and Patricia Garlan. *Worlds in the Making: Probes for Students of the Future.* Englewood Cliffs, New Jersey: Prentice-Hall, 1970.

Eckholm, Erik P. *Losing Ground.* New York: W. W. Norton, 1976.

> Eckholm, a researcher with the Worldwatch Institute, gives an eyewitness report on the catastrophic damage now being done to the earth's agricultural lands by the tilling of mountainsides, the overgrazing of range lands, and the wanton destruction of tropical rain forests. Eckholm says the world is inexorably proceeding toward Malthusian disaster unless monumental land-use reforms are instituted.

Edison Electric Institute. *Economic Growth in the Future.* New York: McGraw-Hill, 1976.

> Contrasting scenarios are examined to show the main arguments for and against policies of unrestricted growth, no growth and limited growth. The volume should be of great interest to any futurist, both as a reference tool and as a starting point for discussion.

Edmunds, Stahrl W. *Alternative U.S. Futures: A Policy Analysis of Individual Choices in a Political Economy.* Santa Monica, California: Goodyear Publishing, 1978.

Eldredge, H. Wentworth. *Taming Megalopolis.* Two vols. Garden City, New York: Doubleday, Anchor, 1967.

Elgin, Duane S., David C. MacMichael, and Peter Schwartz. *Alternative Futures for Environmental Policy Planning: 1975-2000.* Prepared by Stanford Research Institute for Environmental Protection Agency. EPA-540/9-75-027. Washington, D.C.: U.S. Government Printing Office, 1975.

Ellul, Jacques. *The Technological Society.* New York: Knopf, 1964.

Enzer, Selwyn, *Beyond Bounded Solutions.* Los Angeles, California: Center for Futures Research, 1977.

Enzer, Selwyn. *Neither Feast Nor Famine.* Lexington, Massachusetts: Lexington, 1978.

Enzer, Selwyn. *The Role of Futures Research in Corporate Planning.* Los Angeles: University of Southern California, Center for Futures Research Publication, 1975.

Enzer, Selwyn and Steven Alter. *INTERAX — An Interactive Environmental Simulator for Corporate Planning.* Los Angeles: Center for Futures Research. 1977.

Enzer, Selwyn, Dennis Little, and Frederick D. Lazar. *Some Prospects for Social Change by 1985 and Their Impact on Time-Money Budgets.* Report S-25. Middletown, Connecticut: Institute for the Future, 1972.

Esfandiary, F.M. *Esfandiary Trilogy: Up-Wingers; Telespheres; Optimism One.* New York: Fawcett Books, 1977.

> This three-volume set presents the thinking of one of the most optimistic futurists, who offers a vision of the future when almost everything is possible and human beings can realize hitherto undreamt-of-capacities.

Ettinger, Robert. *The Prospect of Immortality.* New York: Doubleday, 1964.

Etzioni, Amitai. *Genetic Fix.* New York: Macmillan, 1973.

Eurich, Alvin C., ed. *Campus 1980: The Shape of the Future in American Higher Education.* New York: Delacorte Press, 1968.

Eurich, Alvin C., ed. *High School 1980: The Shape of the Future in American Secondary Education.* New York: Pittman, 1970.

Evans, Wayne O., and Nathan S. Kline, eds. *Psychotropic Drugs in the Year 2000.* Springfield, Illinois: Charles C. Thomas, 1971.

Ewald, William R., ed. *Environment and Change: The Next Fifty Years.* Bloomington, Indiana: Indiana University Press, 1968.

> This volume presents some of the papers submitted to the American Institute of Planners' 1967 conference in Washington, D.C. Included are papers by Bertrand de Jouvenel, "On Attending to the Future," and Joseph Sittler, "The Role of the Spirit in Creating the Future Environment." (This is a companion volume to Ewald's *Environment and Policy: The Next Fifty Years.)*

Ewald, William R., ed. *Environment and Policy: The Next Fifty Years.* Bloomington, Indiana: Indiana University Press, 1968.

> Like its companion volume, *Environment and Change,* this book presents papers commissioned for the American Institute of Planners' 50th Anniversary Conference in 1967. Included are papers by William H. Stewart on "Health: The Next 50 Years," Kevin Lynch on "The Possible City," and Charles Abrams on "Housing in the Year 2000."

Ewald, William R., ed. *Environment for Man: The Next Fifty Years.* Bloomington, Indiana: Indiana University Press, 1967.

Fabun, Don. *The Dynamics of Change.* Englewood Cliffs, New Jersey: Prentice-Hall, 1967.

Falk, Richard A. *A Study of Future Worlds.* New York: Free Press, 1975.

> A professor of international law, Richard Falk details the structures and functions of new world organizations required to eliminate poverty, injustice, war, and environmental imbalance. Since today's major problems defy national solutions, the author proposes a reformed and integrated world policy. He suggests setting minimal goals compatible with present political realities adhering to a strict time frame, to the 1990s, and he develops a strategy for moving from the present to the future.

Falk, Richard A. *This Endangered Planet: Prospects and Proposals for Human Survival.* New York: Random House, 1972.

> A Princeton University professor discusses the growing need for world order and some of the inter-relationships involved in the global ecological crisis. He offers alternative images of the future—a period of desperation leading to annihilation in the 21st century and an optimistic scenario of world transformation which would usher in an era of world harmony in the 21st century.

Farmer, Richard N. *The Real World of 1984: A Look at the Foreseeable Future.* New York: David McKay, 1973.

Farrell, Edmund J. *Deciding the Future: A Forecast of Responsibilities of Secondary Teachers of English 1970-2000 A.D.* Report 12. Urbana, Illinois: National Council of Teachers of English, 1971.

Feinberg, Gerald. *The Prometheus Project: Mankind's Search for Long-Range Goals.* New York: Doubleday, Anchor, 1969.

> The author, a Columbia University physicist, argues that the emerging unity of mankind makes it desirable to create long-term goals for the whole world, thereby giving man a clear sense of purpose. The book classifies and analyzes goals, distinguishing between individual

goals and collective goals as well as intermediate and final goals. He proposes a "Prometheus Project" as "a cooperative effort by humanity to choose its long-term goals."

Feingold, Norman, and Alice Fins. *Your Future in More Exotic Occupations.* New York: Richards Rosen Press, 1978.

Felix, Fremont. *World Markets of Tomorrow.* New York: Harper and Row, 1972.

Ferkiss, Victor. *The Future of Technological Civilization.* New York: George Braziller, 1974.

The author calls for a new world view, "ecological immanentism," in order to bring about the peaceful revolution needed for human development on a finite planet. He argues that "the essence of humanity's current crisis is that we have allowed our collective destiny to be determined by the political philosophy usually called liberalism, which holds that the prime purpose of society is to encourage individual self-aggrandizement." In addition to liberalism, Ferkiss attacks other conventional ideologies such as Marxism, socialism, and anarchism. None of these ideologies, Ferkiss believes, can possibly cope with the crisis now gripping the world. But mankind can survive, he argues, through an "immanent revolution" that will involve a radical restructuring of society.

Ferkiss, Victor C. *Futurology: Promises, Performances, Prospects.* Beverly Hills, California: Sage Publications, 1977.

One of The Washington Papers written for the Center for Strategic and International Studies, Georgetown University, this book presents a survey of the art and science of predicting the future.

Ferkiss, Victor. *Technological Man: The Myth and the Reality.* New York: George Braziller, 1969.

Victor Ferkiss, a professor of government at Georgetown University, argues that world prospects for the long-run future are hopeful, if civilization safely survives the dangers of the near term. What is needed, he suggests, is "technological man"—a wise world citizen who can understand technology and the earth's environment as a complex system. At present, the world is dominated by what Ferkiss calls "bourgeois" man. Bourgeois man does not understand the modern world or see it in its totality and therefore uses technology piecemeal for selfish and limited purposes rather than for the general good of mankind. Ferkiss argues for a new philosophy based on three tenets: (1) "A new naturalism" (Man is viewed as an integral part of nature and must live in harmony with it.); (2) "A new holism" (Everything in the universe is interconnected.); and (3) "A new immanentism" (The whole is created from within.).

Finland 1990: Economic Prospects. Helsinki, Finland: Economic Planning Centre, 1977.

Flechtheim, Ossip K. *History and Futurology.* Meisenheim am Glan, Germany: Verlag Anton Hain, 1966.

This is a collection of essays by a professor of political science who has taught in the United States and Germany. Ossip Flechtheim published a prophetic article entitled "Teaching the Future" in a relatively obscure U.S. publication in 1943. In this article he called for the development of courses dealing with the future. Later he published other articles on what he called "futurology." This volume of essays, written primarily between 1941 and 1952, is about equally divided between history and futurology. During the late 1960s, the author founded the German journal *Futurum,* a scholarly journal devoted to studies of the future.

Ford, Barbara. *Future Food: Alternate Protein for the Year 2000.* New York: William Morrow & Co., 1978.

Ford, George A. and Gordon L. Lippitt. *Planning Your Future: A Workbook for Personal Goal Setting.* LaJolla, California: University Associates, Inc., 1976.

Two persons who developed new careers on several occasions have written a step-by-step workbook on formulating life goals and how to attain them. They take the participant through sequential tasks and exercises that help in self-understanding and the planning of day-to-day and broad-life goals.

Forecasting International. *A Report of the State-of-the-Art in Technological Forecasting and Which Forecasts are Available for Use in the Technology Incentives Program*. Arlington, Virginia: Forecasting International, 1972.

Forrester, Jay W. *Industrial Dynamics*. Cambridge, Massachusetts: MIT Press, 1961.

Forrester, Jay W. *Urban Dynamics*. Cambridge, Massachusetts: MIT Press, 1969.

Forrester, Jay W. *World Dynamics*. Cambridge, Massachusetts: Wright-Allen Press, 1971.

> Jay Forrester, Professor of Management at the Massachusetts Institute of Technology, has developed a technique known as "System Dynamics" to simulate the functioning of factories, cities, and the world as a whole. The computer simulation of the world, described in this book, suggests that man may now be living in a golden age that will soon disappear. The simulation of world trends indicates that catastrophe looms if man does not drastically slow down the growth of population and industrialization. Forrester's colleague, Dennis Meadows, used system dynamics in the now famous "Limits to Growth" study that became widely discussed in the early 1970s.

Fowles, Jib, ed. *Handbook of Futures Research*. Westport, Conn: Greenwood Press, 1978.

> Forty-six of the world's most prominent futurists including Arthur C. Clarke, Herman Kahn, and Barry Commoner have contributed to this comprehensive collection of contemporary futures scholarship.

Francoeur, Robert T. *Eve's New Rib: Twenty Faces of Sex, Marriage, and Family*. New York: Harcourt Brace Jovanovich, 1972.

> This book by a biology professor suggests possible future patterns of marriage and parenthood, including group marriage, trial marriage, unisex marriage, contract marriages, etc.

Francoeur, Robert T. *Utopian Motherhood: New Trends in Human Reproduction*. New York: Doubleday, 1970.

Francoeur, Robert T. and Anna K. *The Future of Sexual Relations*. Englewood Cliffs, New Jersey: Prentice-Hall, 1974.

Friends of the Earth. *Progress: As If Survival Mattered*. San Francisco, California: Friends of the Earth, 1978.

Freeman, Christopher and Marie Jahoda. *World Futures: The Great Debate*. New York: University Books, 1978.

Fuller, R. Buckminster. *Operating Manual for Spaceship Earth*. Carbondale, Illinois: Southern Illinois University Press, 1969.

Fuller, R. Buckminster. *Utopia or Oblivion: The Prospects for Humanity*. New York: Bantam, 1969.

Fuller, R. Buckminster, and Robert Marks. *The Dymaxion World of Buckminster Fuller*. Carbondale, Illinois: Southern Illinois University Press, 1960; New York: Doubleday, Anchor, 1973.

Furnas, Clifford C. *America's Tomorrow*. New York: Funk and Wagnalls, 1932.

Furnas, Clifford C. *The Next Hundred Years: The Unfinished Business of Science*. New York: Reynal and Hitchcock, 1936.

Gabel, Medard. *Energy, Earth and Everyone: A Global Energy Strategy for Spaceship Earth*. San Francisco: Straight Arrow Books, 1975.

> An associate of comprehensive designer Buckminster Fuller, Medard Gabel describes today's wasteful shortlived energy systems and presents a global energy development strategy that insures a continuing supply of relatively clean energy by 1985 through the substitution of alcohol, methane, hydrogen, electricity, and solar heat for the combustion of coal, petroleum, natural gas, and nuclear energy. The book offers a sampling of the Fullerian ap-

proach to world problems. In this book, Fuller and the author make a special attempt at reaching the young people, whom they regard as the most hopeful segment of society.

Gabor, Dennis. *Innovations: Scientific, Technological, and Social.* New York: Oxford University Press, 1970.

> This book offers a short description of 137 inventions and innovations that may occur in the future. Gabor freely offers his judgments on the desirability of the innovations he describes. For example, he is pleased that the prospects for automated language translaters are dim, because "if such devices were successful, it would discourage young people from being linguists." More desirable, in Gabor's opinion, are such items as holographic identification cards and the surveillance of streets by television cameras. Other innovations on Gabor's list include electric transmission of newspapers, semi-automation of repairs, photon rockets, and non-fattening foods.

Gabor, Dennis. *Inventing the Future.* New York: Knopf, 1964.

> Dennis Gabor, a Nobel prize-winning physicist, has popularized the phrase "inventing the future." He argues that it is not possible to predict what will happen in the future, but it is possible to create the future through imagination and effort. In this book, Gabor argues that civilization faces three dangers: nuclear war, overpopulation, and "the age of leisure." Gabor suggests that men may be able to cope with the first two dangers more easily than with the third, because of its novelty. In recent decades, man has moved rapidly toward the abolition of work but has done little to prepare himself for leisure. Gabor argues for more creative imagination both in short-range social engineering and in long-term visions of the future.

Gabor, Dennis. *The Mature Society.* New York: Praeger, 1972.

Garlan, Patricia, and Maryjane Dunstan, with Dyan Pike. *Star Sight: Visions of the Future.* Englewood Cliffs, New Jersey: Prentice-Hall, Inc., 1977.

Geiger, Theodore. *The Fortunes of the West: The Future of the Atlantic Nations.* Bloomington, Indiana: Indiana University Press, 1973.

George Washington University Program of Policy Studies in Science and Technology. *Social Impacts of Civil Aviation and Implications for R&D Policy.* Washington, D.C.: George Washington University, 1971.

George Washington University Program of Policy Studies in Science and Technology. *Some Implications of the Technology Assessment Function for the Effective Public Decision-Making Process.* Washington, D.C.: George Washington University, 1971.

Gerba, John, ed. *Alternative Futures and Environmental Quality.* Washington, D.C.: Environmental Protection Agency, 1973.

Gerba, John, ed. *The Quality of Life Concept: A New Tool for Decision Makers.* Washington, D.C.: Environmental Protection Agency, 1973.

Giglio, Ernest D., and John J. Schrems, eds. *Future Politics.* Berkeley, California: McCutchan, 1971.

Glasser, Ralph. *The Net and The Quest: Patterns of Community and How They Can Survive Progress.* New York: Pica Press, 1978.

> A social psychologist and economist, Glasser writes on the growing concern about the destructive impact of development policies on the values of societies in the Third World as well as advanced countries. Places do exist that live a pre-industrial life and the author here reports on an intimate study he made of one such place, a group of poor hill villages in Southern Italy.

446

Glenn, Jerome and George Robinson. *Space Trek: The Endless Migration.* Harrisburg, Pennsylvania: Stackpole Books, 1978.

> This book hopes to provide insight into all the questions and problems attendant upon men's peaceful use of space in this solar system and beyond. Among the questions brought into focus are: Can humanity migrate to space in a civilized manner without real star wars? What are the justifiable economic, political, and philosophical reasons for undertaking such a vast project?

Glines, Don E. *Educational Futures I: Imagining AND Inventing; Educational Futures II: Options AND Alternatives; Educational Futures III: Change AND Reality.* Millville, Minnesota: Anvil Press, 1978.

Goble, Frank. *Beyond Failure: How To Cure a Neurotic Society.* Ottawa, Illinois: Caroline House, 1977.

Goldsmith, Edward. *The Stable Society.* Wadebridge, U.K.: Wadebridge Press, 1978.

Goldsmith, Edward, *et al. A Blueprint for Survival.* Boston: Houghton Mifflin, 1972.

Goldsmith, Maurice, ed. *The Predicament of Mankind.* Guildford, Surrey: IPC Science and Technology Press, Ltd., 1974.

Gompert, David C., Michael Mandelbaum, Richard L. Garwin, and John H. Barton. *Nuclear Weapons and World Politics: Alternatives for the Future.* New York: McGraw-Hill Book Co., 1977.

Goran, Morris. *The Future of Science.* Rochelle Park, New Jersey: Hayden Book Company, 1971.

Gordon, Theodore J. *A Discussion of Some Methods of Technology Assessment.* Report 138-01-17. Glastonbury, Connecticut: The Futures Group, 1974.

Gordon, Theodore J. *The Future.* New York: St. Martin's Press, 1965.

> Theodore Gordon, now President of the Futures Group, a private forecasting and consulting firm in Glastonbury, Connecticut, wrote this book in the early 1960s. Then a space scientist, Gordon provided a general discussion of various aspects of the future. In addition to discussing such possible technological achievements as man-made life in the laboratory, the discovery of extraterrestrial life forms, and the attainment of immortality, Gordon focused on such problems as individual freedom and the future of religion and morality.

Gorney, Roderic. *The Human Agenda.* New York: Simon and Schuster, 1972.

Graduate Research Center of the Southwest. *Goals for Dallas.* Dallas, Texas: Graduate Research Center of the Southwest, 1966.

Gray, Elizabeth and David D., and William F. Martin. *Growth and Its Implications for the Future.* Branford, Connecticut: The Dinosaur Press, 1975.

Green, Thomas, ed. *Educational Planning in Perspective: Forecasting and Policy Making.* Guildford, Surrey: IPC Science and Technology Press Ltd., 1971.

Gribbin, John. *Forecasts, Famines and Freezes: Climate and Man's Future.* New York: Walker, 1976.

> Scientist John Gribbin began piecing together the global weather picture from isolated reports in the early 1970s. After gathering much first-hand information and conferring with outstanding climatologists in many parts of the world, he has synthesized a concise report. The likelihood of food shortfalls caused by weather is very great, he says, and man must arrange contingency plans or suffer dire consequences.

Gross, Bertram, ed. *A Great Society.* New York: Basic Books, 1968.

Grunig, James E. ed. *Decline of the Global Village: How Specialization is Changing the Mass Media.* New York: General Hall Publishers, 1976.

Hagerty, Herbert G. *Forward Deployment in the 1970's and 1980's.* National Security Affairs Monograph, 77-2. Washington, D.C.: The National War College, 1977.

Hahn, Walter A., and Kenneth F. Gordon, eds. *Assessing the Future and Policy Planning.* New York: Gordon and Breach, 1973.

> This volume consists of papers presented at a conference organized by the Washington, D.C., chapter of the Institute of Management Sciences, the World Future Society, and the National Bureau of Standards in Gaithersburg, Maryland, in March 1970. The contents include papers by Joseph P. Martino on "Methods of Technological Forecasting," Jack W. Carlson on "Impact of Future Forecasts on Federal Policy," and Charles W. Williams, Jr., on "The Role of National Goals Research."

Hake, Barry J. *Does Education Have a Future?* The Hague: M. Nijhoff, 1975.

Halacy, Daniel S. *Genetic Revolution: Shaping Life for Tomorrow.* New York: Harper and Row, 1974.

Hall, Peter G., ed. *Europe 2000.* London: Duckworth, 1976.

Hardin, Garrett. *The Limits to Altruism.* Bloomington, Indiana: Indiana University Press, 1977.

Harkins, Arthur M., ed. *1971 American Anthropological Association Experimental Symposium on Cultural Futurology: Pre-Conference Volume.* Minneapolis, Minnesota: Office for Applied Social Science and the Future, University of Minnesota, 1971.

Harkins, Arthur, and Magoroh Maruyama. *1972 American Anthropological Experimental Symposium on Cultural Futuristics: Pre-Conference Volume.* Minneapolis, Minnesota: Office for Applied Social Science and the Future, University of Minnesota, 1972.

Harman, Willis W. *Alternative Futures and Educational Policy.* Menlo Park, California: Stanford Research Institute, 1970.

Harman, Willis W. *An Incomplete Guide to the Future.* San Francisco: San Francisco Book Company, 1976.

> Author Harman, director of Stanford Research Institute's Social Policy Research Center, here offers a synthesis of his thinking to date. Harman foresees a radical restructuring of human society in the years ahead.

Hayashi, Yujiro, ed. *Perspectives on Post-Industrial Society.* Tokyo: University of Tokyo Press, 1970.

Hayes, Denis. *Rays of Hope: The Transition to a Post-Petroleum World.* New York: W.W. Norton & Company, 1977.

Heathers, Glen, Jane Roberts and JoAnn Weinberger. *Educators Guide for the Future.* Philadelphia, Pennsylvania: Research for Better Schools, Inc., 1977.

Heer, John E. Jr., and Joseph D. Hagerty. *Environmental Assessments and Statements.* New York: Van Nostrand Reinhold, 1977.

Heilbroner, Robert L. *Business Civilization in Decline.* New York: W.W. Norton & Co., 1976.

Heilbroner, Robert L. *The Future as History.* New York: Grove Press, 1961.

> Economist Heilbroner criticizes America's historic optimism and belief in the goodness in the future. He argues that the U.S. future will be shaped by such trends as the development of military technology to the point where war has become too dangerous to solve problems, the urgent demands of the developing nations for a share of economic goods, and rapid growth which makes it difficult to respond properly to change.

Heilbroner, Robert L. *An Inquiry into the Human Prospect.* New York: W. W. Norton, 1974.

> Economist Heilbroner suggests that mankind may not be able to take the measures necessary to surmount the present world crisis without repressive rule by governments capable of rallying obedience far more effectively than is possible in a democratic setting. Heilbroner discusses in some detail four "threats to mankind"—overpopulation, war, pollution, and knowledge. Knowledge, in the form of science and technology, is not ominous in and of itself, but has been and will continue to be used injudiciously. This is one of the most bleakly pessimistic books that has appeared in recent years.

Hellman, Hal. *Biology in the World of the Future.* New York: M. Evans and Company, 1971.

> This is one of a series of volumes describing various aspects of the future. The books are well illustrated and suitable for high school-age people as well as adults.

Hellman, Hal. *The City in the World of the Future.* New York: M. Evans and Company, 1970.

Hellman, Hal. *Communications in the World of the Future.* New York: M. Evans and Company, 1975.

Hellman, Hal. *Energy in the World of the Future.* New York: M. Evans and Company, 1973.

Hellman, Hal. *Feeding the World of the Future.* New York: M. Evans and Company, 1972.

Hellman, Hal. *Transportation in the World of the Future.* New York: M. Evans and Company, 1974.

Helmer, Olaf. *The Future State of the Union and Its Relevance to the Planning Process.* Los Angeles: University of Southern California, Center for Futures Research Publication, 1974.

Helmer, Olaf. *On the Future State of the Union.* Report R-27. Menlo Park, California: Institute for the Future, 1972.

Helmer, Olaf. *Orienting Education Toward the Future.* Los Angeles: Center for Futures Research, 1977.

Helmer, Olaf. *Social Technology.* New York: Basic Books, 1966.

> Olaf Helmer, once Chief Mathematician at the Rand Corporation, was one of the principal founders of the Institute for the Future and the co-inventor of the now-famous Delphi technique of polling experts on their opinions about the future. He now is a professor at the University of Southern California's Center for Futures Research. This volume brings together several of his early papers on forecasting, including the now classic Delphi study that he and Theodore Gordon published in 1964.

Henderson, Hazel. *Creating Alternative Futures: The End of Economics.* New York: Berkley Publishing Co., 1978.

Henley, Stephen P., and James R. Yates. *Futurism in Education: Methodologies.* Berkeley, California: McCutchan, 1974.

Henshel, Richard L. *On the Future of Social Prediction.* Indianapolis, Indiana: Bobbs-Merrill, 1976.

Heppenheimer, T.A. *Colonies in Space.* Harrisburg, Pennsylvania: Stackpole, 1977.

Herman, Stewart, James S. Cannon with Alfred J. Malefatto. *Energy Futures: Industry and the New Technologies.* New York: INFORM, Inc., 1976.

Hetman, Francois. *Le Langage de la Prevision [The Language of Forecasting].* Paris: SEDEIS, 1970.

> This is a combined French and English dictionary of forecasting with a vocabulary in German. The author, a member of the Paris group headed by Bertrand de Jouvenel, offers extensive quotes and excerpts from authors who have used the various terms he seeks to define.

Hillegas, Mark R. *The Future as Nightmare: H. G. Wells and the Anti-Utopians*. New York: Oxford University Press, 1967.

Hirsch, Fred. *Social Limits to Growth*. Cambridge, Massachusetts: Harvard University Press, 1976.

Hirsch, Werner Z., *et al. Inventing Education for the Future*. San Francisco: Chandler, 1967.

Hitch, Charles J., ed. *Resources for An Uncertain Future*. Baltimore, Maryland: The Johns Hopkins University Press, 1978.

Horn, Robert E. *The Guide to Simulations/Games for Education and Training*. Cranford, New Jersey: Didactic Systems, 1977.

Hostrop, Richard W. *Foundations of Futurology in Education*. Palm Springs, California: ETC Publications, 1973.

Hottovy, Tibor C. *Forecasting and Long Term Planning in Sweden, A Review*. Stockholm: The National Swedish Institute for Building Research, 1975.

Hough, Granville W. *Technology Diffusion: Federal Programs and Procedures*. Mt. Airy, Maryland: Lomond Systems, Inc., 1975.

House, Peter. *The Urban Environmental System: Modeling for Research, Policy-Making and Education*. Beverly Hills, California: Sage Publications, 1973.

Hubbard, Barbara. *The Hunger of Eve*. Harrisburg, Pennsylvania: Stackpole, 1976.

Barbara Hubbard, widely known in futurist circles, tells the story of her life and development as an evolutionary thinker. This autobiography is enlivened by many intimate descriptions of well-known figures ranging from Jonas Salk and Abraham Maslow to Elizabeth Taylor and Dwight Eisenhower.

Hubbard, Earl. *The Creative Intention*. New York: Interbook, 1974.

Hubbard, Earl. *Our Need for New Worlds*. New York: Interbook, 1976.

Philosopher-prophet Earl Hubbard argues that mankind needs to move into the universe, thereby creating a new universal species rather than one that is merely terrestrial. This short book offers a distillation of Hubbard's thinking.

Hubbard, Earl. *The Search Is On: A View of Man's Future from the New Perspective of Space*. Los Angeles: Pace Publications, 1969.

Hudson Institute. *1973 Synoptic Context on the Corporate Environment: 1975-1985*. Five vols. Croton-on-Hudson, New York: Hudson Institute, 1975.

The Human Resources Research Council of Alberta. *Social Futures Alberta 1970-2005*. Edmonton, Canada: The Human Resources Research Council of Alberta, 1970.

Hunter, John O. *Values and the Future: Models of Community College*. Sherman Oaks, California: Banner Books International, 1977.

Ingelstam, Lars. *Some Future Perspectives on Health and Care Development: A Swede's View*. Stockholm, Sweden: Secretariat for Futures Studies, 1977.

Ingelstam, Lars E., ed. *To Choose a Future*. Stockholm: Ministry of Foreign Affairs/Secretariat for Future Studies, 1974.

IRADES (Instituto Ricerche Applicate Documentazioni e Studi). *Human Needs, New Societies, Supportive Technologies*. Project 30. Rome: IRADES, Institute of Research and Education in Future Studies, 1974.

IRADES (Instituto Ricerche Applicate Documentazioni e Studi). *Social and Human Forecasting: Documentation 1975*. Rome: Edizioni Previsionali, 1975.

> This is a directory of people and organizations active in the futures field. IRADES, an Italian organization, began publishing such directories in 1971 but by 1976 it was uncertain whether the project would continue. The directory covers most of the major nations of the world.

Jantsch, Erich. *Design for Evolution: Self-Organization and Planning in the Life of Human Systems*. New York: George Braziller, 1975.

Jantsch, Erich. *Technological Forecasting in Perspective*. Paris: Organization for Economic Cooperation and Development, 1967.

Jantsch, Erich. *Technological Planning and Social Futures*. New York: John Wiley, 1972.

Jantsch, Erich, and Conrad H. Waddington, eds. *Evolution and Consciousness: Human Systems in Transition*. Reading, Massachusetts: Addison-Wesley, 1976.

Johansen, Robert, Jacques Vallee, and Kathleen Spangler. *Electronic Meetings: Technical Alternatives and Social Choices*. Reading, Massachusetts: Addison-Wesley, 1978.

Johnson, Warren. *Muddling Toward Frugality*. San Francisco, California: Sierra Club Books, 1978.

Joint Economic Committee. *U.S. Long Term Economic Growth Prospects: Entering a New Era*. Washington, D.C.: Joint Economic Committee, 1978.

Jones, Christopher J. *Design Methods: Seeds of Human Futures*. London: John Wiley, 1970.

Jones, Harry, and Brian Twiss. *Forecasting Technology for Planning Decisions*. England: Macmillan Press, 1978.

Jones, Martin V. *A Technology Assessment Methodology: Some Basic Propositions*. Washington, D.C.: The Mitre Corporation, 1971.

Judge, Anthony J., ed. *Yearbook of World Problems and Human Potential*. Brussels: Mankind 2000/Union of International Associations, 1976.

Jungk, Robert. *Everyman Project: A World Report on Resources for a Humane Society*. New York: Liverright, 1977.

Jungk, Robert, and Johan Galtung, eds. *Mankind 2000*. London: Allen and Unwin, 1969.

> This volume contains 35 papers which emerged from the first international research conference held in Oslo in 1967.

Kahn, Herman. *The Emerging Japanese Superstate*. Englewood Cliffs, New Jersey: Prentice-Hall, 1970.

Kahn, Herman, ed. *The Future of the Corporation*. New York: Mason and Lipscomb, 1974.

Kahn, Herman, et. al. *The Next 200 Years: A Scenario for America and the World*. New York: William Morrow Co., 1976.

> The authors predict that the world's population increase will slow down and that prosperity will remain a viable possiblity for all nations. Their studies suggest that economic growth will continue well into the next century, eventually reaching a worldwide plateau characterized by affluence and a universally high standard of living.

Kahn, Herman. *World Economic Development: 1979 and Beyond*. Boulder, Colorado: Westview Press, 1979.

> A general survey of the world economy in the context of its long-term development. Kahn presents a generally optimistic view, arguing that people will become increasingly wealthy in the years ahead.

However, the advanced capitalist nations will experience "malaise" during the final decades of the 20th century with a number of other nations making faster progress.

Kahn, Herman, and B. Bruce-Briggs. *Things to Come: Thinking about the Seventies and Eighties.* New York: Macmillan, 1972.

> This volume appeared in 1972, five years after the earlier Hudson Institute volume, *The Year 2000,* and is shorter and somewhat less ponderous than its predecessor. The book presents a later stage in the evolving view of Kahn and his colleagues. The basic long-term multifold trend of western culture is described again with certain modifications based on suggestions developed in the wake of the earlier volume. Over all, the volume seems somewhat more optimistic in tone than *The Year 2000,* but not so optimistic as the later volume, *The Next 200 Years,* which appeared in 1976.

Kahn, Herman, William Brown, and Leon Martel. *The Next 200 Years.* New York: William Morrow and Company, 1976.

> Kahn and his Hudson Institute colleagues here present a highly optimistic view of America's future. They express confidence that Americans will become increasingly wealthy and that the problems associated with shrinking supplies of fossil fuels and increasing pollution can be overcome.

Kash, Don E., et. al. *Our Energy Future.* Tulsa, Oklahoma: University of Oklahoma, 1976.

Kasper, Raphael, ed. *Technology Assessment: Understanding the Social Consequences of Technological Applications.* New York: Praeger, 1972.

Kastens, Merritt L. *Long-Range Planning for Your Business: An Operating Manual.* New York: AMACON, 1976.

Kateb, George, ed. *Utopia.* Chicago: Aldine, 1971.

Kates, Robert W. *Risk Assessment of Environmental Hazard.* Somerset, New Jersey: John Wiley and Sons, 1978.

Kauffman, Draper L. *Futurism and Future Studies: Developments in Classroom Instruction.* Washington, D.C.: National Education Foundation, 1976.

Kauffman, Draper L. *Teaching the Future: A Guide to Future-Oriented Education.* Palm Springs, California: ETC Publications, 1976.

> A practical handbook for classroom teachers interested in future-oriented education, with an emphasis on teaching methods and resources which have proven effective and flexible. The book contains many exercises on ways of thinking about the future, applicable on a wide range of grade levels and classroom settings. It also has a scenario for role-playing and a guide to literature, films, and simulation games.

Kemeny, John G. *Man and the Computer.* New York: Charles Scribners, 1972.

Kettle, John. *Footnotes on the Future.* Toronto, Canada: Methuen Publishers, 1970.

Koberg, Don & Jim Bagnall. *The Universal Traveler: A Soft-Systems Guide to Creativity, Problem-Solving and the Process of Reaching Goals.* Los Altos, California: William Kaufmann, 1976.

Koberg, Don & Jim Bagnall. *Values Tech.* Los Altos, California: William Kaufmann Inc., 1976.

Kosolapov, V. *Mankind and the Year 2000.* Moscow: Progress Publishers, 1976.

Kostelanetz, Richard, ed. *Beyond Left and Right: Radical Thought for our Times.* New York: William Morrow, 1968.

Kostelanetz, Richard, ed. *Human Alternatives: Visions for Us Now*. New York: William Morrow, 1971.

Kostelanetz, Richard, ed. *Social Speculations: Visions for Our Time*. New York: William Morrow, 1971.

This is an anthology of future-oriented writings ranging from Buckminster Fuller on "Our Spaceship Earth" to Burnham Beckwith talking about "Life in A.D. 2500." The emphasis here is on readable and imaginative writings.

Kothari, Rajni. *Footsteps into the Future: Diagnosis of the Present World and a Design for an Alternative*. New York: Free Press, 1974.

LaConte, Ronald T., and Ellen LaConte. *Teaching Tomorrow Today: A Guide to Futuristics*. New York: Bantam, 1975.

Lakey, George. *Strategy for a Living Revolution*. San Francisco: W. H. Freeman, 1973.

A prominent Quaker activist outlines a nonviolent path to social transformation, focusing specifically on how the United States can be remade without resorting to self-defeating cataclysm, and how the strategy for nonviolent revolution in the U.S. relates to struggles in other countries—particularly to those in the Third World. The book includes previously unpublished case material on little-known nonviolent struggles and fresh interpretations of some famous ones.

Land, George T. Lock. *Grow or Die: The Unifying Principle of Transformation*. New York: Random House, 1973.

Landsberg, Hans H., Leonard L. Fischman, and Joseph L. Fisher. *Resources in America's Future*. Baltimore, Maryland: Johns Hopkins Press, 1963.

Lanford, H. W. *Technological Forecasting Methodologies: A Synthesis*. New York: American Management Association, 1972.

Lapp, Ralph. *The Logarithmic Century*. Englewood Cliffs, New Jersey: Prentice-Hall, 1973.

Laszlo, Ervin. *Goals for Mankind: A Report to the Club of Rome*. New York: E.P. Dutton, 1977.

Ervin Laszlo, a Professor of Philosophy, and his fellow contributors here offer "an atlas of national and regional goals" with separate chapters on goals in many different areas of the world. The book also describes "new horizons" for mankind through global goals for security, food, energy and resources, and development.

Laszlo, Ervin. *A Strategy for the Future: The Systems Approach to World Order*. New York: George Braziller, 1974.

Laszlo, Ervin. *The Systems View of the World*. New York: George Braziller, 1972.

Laszlo, Ervin, and Judah Bierman, eds. *Goals in a Global Community (Volume II—The International Values and Goals Studies)*. Elmsford, New York: Pergamon Press, Inc., 1978.

Second volume of papers from which Laszlo created *Goals for Mankind*. Presents some 30 international values and goals studies representing beliefs and desires in all parts of the global community.

Lauda, Donald P., and Robert D. Ryan. *Advancing Technology: Its Impact on Society*. Dubuque, Iowa: William C. Brown, 1971.

Lawless, Edward W. *Technology and Social Shock*. New Brunswick, New Jersey: Rutgers University Press, 1977.

Lecht, Leonard A. *Changes in National Priorities During the 1960s: Their Implications for 1980*. Washington, D.C.: National Planning Association, 1972.

Lecht, Leonard A. *Dollars for National Goals: Looking Ahead to 1980*. New York: John Wiley, 1974.

Lecht, Leonard A. *Goals, Priorities and Dollars: The Next Decade.* New York: Free Press, 1966.

Lecht, Leonard A. *Manpower Needs for National Goals in the 1970s.* New York: Praeger, 1969.

Leonard, George B. *The Transformation: A Guide to the Inevitable Changes in Humankind.* New York: Dell, Delacorte Press, 1972.

Leontief, Wassily. *Future of the World Economy: A United Nations Study.* New York: Oxford University Press, 1977.

Levine, Arthur L. *The Future of the U.S. Space Program.* New York: Praeger, 1975.

Lindaman, Edward B. *Space: A New Direction for Mankind.* New York: Harper and Row, 1969.

Lindaman, Edward B. *Thinking in the Future Tense.* Nashville, Tennessee: Broadman Press, 1978.

Leff, Herbert L. *Experience, Environment, and Human Potentials.* New York: Oxford University Press, 1978.

Linstone, Harold A., and Devendra Sahal, eds. *Technological Substitution: Forecasting Techniques and Applications.* New York: American Elsevier, 1976.

> The editors state that technological forecasting is accomplished basically by keeping a watchful eye on processes of utilizing natural resources. Efficient processes supersede inefficient processes; scarce materials are replaced by abundant materials as soon as technology develops efficient means of processing the new material. The book presents a series of mathematical models of representative areas of technological forecasting, such as "System Dynamics Modeling for Forecasting Multilevel Technological Substitution," "The International Diffusion of New Technology," and "Substitution of Mechanical Corn Pickers by Field Shelling Technology." It ends with a discussion of the future that emphasizes the inherent substitutability of one resource material for another, contingent on available energy. The authors state that if man can develop an infinite energy source such as solar or fusion power, a stable steady-state technology could be worked out that would serve him for centuries.

Linstone, Harold A., and W.H. Clive Simmonds, eds. *Futures Research: New Directions.* Reading, Massachusetts: Addison-Wesley Publishing Co., 1977.

Linstone, Harold A., and Murray Turoff, eds. *The Delphi Method: Techniques and Applications.* Reading, Massachusetts: Addison-Wesley, 1975.

> This volume constitutes a handbook on the Delphi Method, a polling technique designed to overcome some of the problems associated with earlier ways of compiling a consensus view of possible future developments. In their introduction, Linstone and Turoff discuss the characteristics and evolution of the Delphi technique. Later chapters contain essays on the philosophy of Delphi, and evaluation of the approach and the use of cross-impact analysis. In one section, contributors discuss Delphi applications to such subjects as drug-abuse policy, the culprit environment, plastics and competing materials, and the future of the steel and ferroalloy industries.

Lippitt, Gordon L. *Visualizing Change: Model Building and the Change Process.* Fairfax, Virginia: Learning Resources Center, National Training Laboratory, 1973.

> Gordon Lippitt, a professor at George Washington University, discusses ways in which a manager, consultant, or change agent can more effectively "picture" the change he is planning, so that those involved can understand the goals to be attained and forces that might resist the changes.

Liston, Robert A. *Promise or Peril?: The Role of Technology in Society.* New York: Thomas Nelson, Inc., 1976.

Little, Dennis. *Urban Simulation and Policy Analysis.* Middletown, Connecticut: Institute for the Future, 1971.

Lovins, Amory B. *Soft Energy Paths: Toward a Durable Peace.* Cambridge, Massachusetts: Ballinger, 1977.

Lovins, Amory B. and John H. Price. *Non-Nuclear Futures: The Case for an Ethical Energy Strategy.* Cambridge, Massachusetts: Ballinger Publishing Co., 1975.

Loye, David. *The Knowable Future: A Psychology of Forecasting and Prophecy.* New York: Wiley-Interscience, 1978.

Lundberg, Ferdinand. *The Coming World Transformation.* Garden City, New York: Doubleday, 1963.

Lundborg, Louis B. *Future Without Shock.* New York: W. W. Norton, 1974.

McCall, Robert, and Isaac Asimov. *Our World in Space.* Greenwich, Connecticut: New York Graphic Society, 1974.

> This large format volume presents 72 color pages and 40 black and white illustrations by space artist Robert McCall, who offers an exhilarating vision of man's future in space. The text is provided by Isaac Asimov, who offers speculations on the colonization of the moon and Mars, voyages to the outer reaches of the solar system, and the exploration of distant star systems.

McHale, John. *A Continuation of the Typological Survey of Futures Research.* Binghamton, New York: State University of New York, Center for Integrative Studies, 1972.

McHale, John. *The Ecological Context.* New York: George Braziller, 1970.

> This volume epitomizes McHale's world-encompassing view of human problems. Like his long-time collaborator, R. Buckminster Fuller, McHale approaches ecological and economic questions with a thoroughly planetary perspective, drawing data from the widest number of sources. This volume revises and expands his 1967 report for the World Resources Inventory.

McHale, John. *The Future of the Future.* New York: George Braziller, 1969.

> John McHale, artist, sociologist, and futurist, argues that mankind is headed toward a planetary society, and it is important that we begin to think and plan and act in terms of the shared planetary culture of the future. He argues that we must learn to anticipate and plan for the future because we will have the future that we learn to imagine and create.

McHale, John. *World Facts and Trends.* New York: Collier Books, 1972.

> This volume brings together McHale's thought provoking chart of world trends, such as the increase in the speed of travel, rising water consumption, advances in life expectancy, etc.

McHale, John and Magda Cordell McHale. *Basic Human Needs: A Framework for Action.* New Brunswick, New Jersey: Transaction Books, 1978.

McHale, John, and Magda Cordell McHale. *Futures Directory.* Boulder, Colorado: Westview Press, 1977.

McLaughlin, Curtis P., and Alan Sheldon. *The Future and Medical Care: A Health Manager's Guide to Forecasting.* Philadelphia: Ballinger Publishing Company, 1974.

Madden, Carl H. *Clash of Culture: Management in an Age of Changing Values.* Washington, D.C.: National Planning Association, 1972.

Maddox, John. *The Doomsday Syndrome.* New York: McGraw-Hill, 1972.

Marien, Michael. *Alternative Futures for Learning: An Annotated Bibliography of Trends, Forecasts, and Proposals.* Syracuse, New York: Educational Policy Research Center, 1971.

Marien, Michael. *Societal Directions and Alternatives: A Critical Guide to the Literature.* LaFayette, New York: Information for Policy Design, 1976.

Marien, Michael, and Warren Ziegler. *The Potential of Educational Futures.* Worthington, Ohio: Charles A. Jones, 1972.

Marland, Sidney P., Jr. *Career Education: A Proposal for Reform.* New York: McGraw-Hill, 1974.

Martin, James. *Future Developments in Telecommunications.* (Second Edition) Englewood Cliffs, New Jersey: Prentice-Hall, 1977.

Martin, James. *The Wired Society.* Englewood Cliffs, New Jersey: Prentice-Hall, 1978.

Martin, Marie. *Films on the Future.* Washington, D.C.: World Future Society, 1977.

Martino, Joseph P. *Technological Forecasting for Decisionmaking.* New York: American Elsevier, 1972.

Martino, Joseph P., ed. *An Introduction to Technological Forecasting.* New York: Gordon and Breach, 1972.

> This is a collection of articles on technological forecasting by a variety of experts. Examples: "Industrial Implications of Technical Forecasting" by William L. Swager, "Prospects of Technological Progress" by Olaf Helmer, and "Thinking About Future Social Development" by Joseph M. Goldsen.

Maruyama, Magoroh, and James A. Dator. *Human Futuristics.* Honolulu, Hawaii: University of Hawaii Press, 1971.

Maruyama, Magoroh, and Arthur Harkins, eds. *Cultures Beyond the Earth: The Role of Anthropology in Outer Space.* New York: Vintage Books, 1975.

Maruyama, Magoroh, and Arthur Harkins, eds. *Cultures of the Future.* Chicago: Aldine, 1976.

Masuda, Yoneji. *The Plan for Information Society.* Tokyo: Japan Computer Usage Development Institute, 1973.

Maxmen, Jerrold S. *The Post-Physician Era: Medicine in the Twenty-First Century.* New York: John Wiley, 1976.

> In 50 years, doctors will be obsolete, replaced by computers and a new breed of health care professional called "the medic," predicts Maxmen, who is himself a physician. He goes on to describe in detail his vision of the Post-Physician Era—the organizational issues that could arise, the interface of medicine and communication technology, the future of the health care professions, the biomedical revolution with its ethical implications, and the necessary changes in medical education. In the final chapter, he suggests that humanity must redefine its identity and learn to live harmoniously with the machine if we are to survive in a technological society.

Mead, Margaret. *Culture and Commitment: A Study of the Generation Gap.* New York: Doubleday, Natural History Press, 1970.

> In this essay Mead presents her theory of prefigurative, cofigurative and postfigurative cultures. In the (postfigurative) cultures of the past, the central figures were the elders who had learned the most and were able to do the most with what they had learned. In the postfigurative society now emerging, the focus is on children who represent the world that is to come.

Mead, Margaret. *World Enough: Rethinking the Future.* Boston: Little, Brown, 1975.

Mead, Shepherd. *How to Get to the Future Before It Gets to You.* New York: Basic Books, 1974.

Meadows, Dennis, ed. *Alternatives to Growth — I.* Cambridge, Massachusetts: Ballinger Books, 1977.

Meadows, Dennis L., ed. *Toward Global Equilibrium.* Cambridge, Massachusetts: Wright-Allen, 1973.

Meadows, Dennis L., *et al. Dynamics of Growth in a Finite World.* Cambridge, Massachusetts: Wright-Allen, 1973.

> This fairly technical volume is the third book to be written on the problem of growth by the system dynamics group at M.I.T. under the leadership of Jay W. Forrester. *Dynamics of Growth* reinforces the premises of its predecessors, *Limits to Growth* and *Toward Global Equilibrium: Collected Papers:* Uncontrolled growth will lead inexorably to world destruction. The models simulate man's total interaction with his environment and show possible global outcomes.

Meadows, Donella H., Dennis L. Meadows, Jorgen Randers, and William W. Behrens, III. *The Limits to Growth.* New York: Universe Books, 1972.

> This is the report prepared by Dennis Meadows and his colleagues on The Club of Rome study of world trends. The researchers used the computerized system-dynamics technique developed by Professor Jay Forrester. The report argues that if present patterns of rapid population and capital growth are allowed to continue, the world faces "a disastrous collapse."

Medawar, Peter B. *The Future of Man.* New York: Basic Books, 1961.

Mendlovitz, Saul H., ed. *On the Creation of a Just World Order: Preferred Worlds for the 1990s.* New York: Free Press, 1975.

> In this volume, scholars from Japan, India, and the United States, Africa, Western Europe, Latin America and China developed the theme "Preferred Worlds for the 1990s." Mendlovitz, who is the director of the World Order Models Project says in his introduction: "I believe that global community has emerged and global government is not far behind. Hopefully, this set of global essays will contribute to the creation of the social processes necessary for a just and peaceful world order."

Mesarovic, Mihajlo, and Eduard Pestel. *Mankind at the Turning Point: The Second Report to The Club of Rome.* New York: E. P. Dutton/Reader's Digest Press, 1974.

> Whereas *The Limits to Growth,* The Club of Rome's first report, urged an immediate slowdown of economic growth, this second report concludes that a new differentiated kind of growth is required, balancing world population, food, energy, and world wealth distribution. The nature of many global crises, the authors state, lies in some form of uncontrolled and undifferentiated growth, one of the most critical aspects of which is the growth in world population. Based on the results of the World Modeling Project, Mesarovic and Pestel observed that the long-term interests of all the nations and peoples of the world would be best served by encouraging rational decision-making procedures based on worldwide and long-term perspectives.

Messolonghites, Louisa, ed. *Alternative Pursuits for America's Third Century.* Washington, D.C.: U.S. Government Printing Office, 1974.

Mesthene, Emmanuel G. *Technological Change: Its Impact on Man and Society.* Cambridge, Massachusetts: Harvard University Press, 1970.

Mesthene, Emmanuel G., ed. *Technology and Social Change.* Indianapolis, Indiana: Bobbs-Merrill, 1967.

Michael, Donald N. *The Next Generation: The Prospects Ahead for the Youth of Today and Tomorrow.* New York: Random House, Vintage Books, 1963.

Michael, Donald N. *On Learning to Plan — And Planning to Learn.* San Francisco, California: Jossey-Bass, Inc., 1973.

Michael, Donald N. *The Unprepared Society: Planning for a Precarious Future.* New York: Basic Books, 1968.

Social psychologist Michael of the University of Michigan says the world is woefully unequipped to do the kind of radical long-range planning that is needed to cope with the stupendous changes ahead. Michael sees a profound societal crisis arising from "our growing intention to undertake long-range planning and our unpreparedness to do it well." Preparing students for tomorrow requires that the teacher teach *styles* of life as much or more than the "facts" of life, Michael believes.

Michael, Donald N., ed. *The Future Society.* Chicago: Aldine, 1970.

Miles, Rufus E., Jr. *Awakening from the American Dream—The Social and Political Limits to Growth.* New York: Universe Books, 1976.

Formerly a top career official of the U.S. Department of Health, Education, and Welfare and later president of the Population Reference Bureau, Rufus Miles currently is senior fellow and lecturer at the Woodrow Wilson School of Public and International Affairs at Princeton University. In this book he analyzes 22 determinants that have brought American society to its present state. He believes that American society is highly vulnerable to further social deterioration, sabotage, and breakdown. This highly pessimistic work may be contrasted with Herman Kahn's highly optimistic volume, *The Next 200 Years.*

Miller, David C., and Ronald L. Hunt. *The Advent Futures Studies and Research Curriculum Guide.* San Francisco: DCM Associates, 1973.

Miller, David C., and Ronald L. Hunt. *The Advent Futures Studies and Research Learning Resources Guide.* San Francisco: DCM Associates, 1973.

Miller, James G. *Living Systems.* New York: McGraw Hill Book Co., 1978.

Miller, Samuel, and Pamela Roby. *The Future of Inequality.* New York: Basic Books, 1970.

The Mitre Corporation. *Technology Assessment: Will It Help Resolve the Energy-Environment Conflict?* U.S.-Japan Joint Symposium. McLean Virginia: The Mitre Corporation, 1974.

Moffitt, Donald, ed. *The Wall Street Journal Views America Tomorrow.* New York: AMACON, 1977.

Montana, Patrick J. and Margaret V. Higginson. *Career Life Planning for Americans: Agenda for Organization and Individuals.* New York: AMACON, 1978.

Mood, Alexander M. *The Future of Higher Education: Some Speculations and Suggestions.* New York: McGraw-Hill, 1973.

Moore, Patrick. *The Next Fifty Years in Space.* New York: Taplinger, 1978.

Morphet, Edgar L., and David L. Jesser, eds. *Designing Education for the Future.* Seven vols. New York: Citation Press, 1967, 1968, 1969.

Mueller, Peter. *The Future Role of Nuclear Power: A Time for Choosing.* Toronto, Canada: Canadian Institute of International Affairs, 1977.

Muller, Herbert J. *Uses of the Future.* Bloomington, Indiana: Indiana University Press, 1974.

Murray, Bruce C. *Navigating the Future.* New York: Harper and Row, 1975.

Bruce Murray, Director of the Jet Propulsion Laboratory at the California Institute of Technology, challenges both the doomsday prophets and the fantasists by presenting his own "rationally optimistic" view of mankind's options for survival. Murray believes that man's best hope lies in a "World Confederation" of diverse peoples existing in largely autonomous states. The World Confederation would not be a Utopia, but simply "the least unsatisfactory means of governing a world racked by widespread social dissatisfaction and

458

by ecological problems of unprecedented magnitude.'' He examines other scenarios, explaining why they are less probable or satisfactory.

Nanus, Burt. *The Future-Oriented Corporation.* Los Angeles: University of Southern California, Center for Futures Research Publication, 1974.

Nanus, Burt. *Management Training in Futures Concepts.* Los Angeles: Center for Futures Research, 1977.

Nanus, Burt. *Problems in Long-Range Economic Forecasting.* Los Angeles: Center for Futures Research, 1977.

National Academy of Engineering, Committee on Public Engineering Policy. *A Study of Technology Assessment.* Report for the Committee on Science and Astronautics, U.S. House of Representatives. Washington, D.C.: U.S. Government Printing Office, 1969.

National Academy of Sciences. *Technology: Processes of Assessment and Choice.* Report for the Committee on Science and Astronautics, U.S. House of Representatives. Washington, D.C.: U.S. Government Printing Office, 1969.

National Commission on Supplies and Shortages, Advisory Committee on National Growth Policy Processes. *Forging America's Future: Strategies for National Growth and Development.* Washington, D.C.: U.S. Government Printing Office, 1976.

National Goals Research Staff. *Toward Balanced Growth: Quantity with Quality.* Washington, D.C.: U.S. Government Printing Office, 1970.

Negley, Glenn. *Utopian Literature: A Bibliography.* Lawrence, Kansas: Regents Press of Kansas, 1978.

North, Michael, ed. *Time Running Out? Best of Resurgence.* New York: Universe, 1977.

North, Robert C. *The World That Could Be.* New York: Norton, 1978.

Novick, David. *World of Scarcities.* New York: Halsted Press, 1976.

Office of Technology Assessment, U.S. Congress. *Annual Report to the Congress.* Washington, D.C.: U.S. Government Printing Office, 1975.

Office of Technology Assessment, U.S. Congress. *An Assessment of Community Planning for Mass Transit.* Washington, D.C.: U.S. Government Printing Office, 1976.

Office of Technology Assessment, U.S. Congress. *Automated Guideway Transit: An Assessment of PRT and Other New Systems.* Washington, D.C.: U.S. Government Printing Office, 1975.

Office of Technology Assessment, U.S. Congress. *Coastal Effects of Offshore Energy Development: Oil and Gas Systems.* Washington, D.C.: U.S. Government Printing Office, 1976.

Office of Technology Assessment, U.S. Congress. *Drug Bioequivalence.* Washington, D.C.: U.S. Government Printing Office, 1974.

Office of Technology Assessment, U.S. Congress. *Energy, the Economy, and Mass Transit.* Washington, D.C.: U.S. Government Printing Office, 1975.

Office of Technology Assessment, U.S. Congress. *The Financial Viability of Conrail.* Washington, D.C.: U.S. Government Printing Office, 1975.

Office of Technology Assessment, U.S. Congress. *Oil Transportation by Tankers: An Analysis of Marine Pollution and Safety Measures.* Washington, D.C.: U.S. Government Printing Office, 1975.

Office of Technology Assessment, U.S. Congress. *Requirements for Fulfilling a National Materials Policy.* Washington, D.C.: U.S. Government Printing Office, 1975.

Office of Technology Assessment, U.S. Congress. *A Review of National Railroad Issues.* Washington, D.C.: U.S. Government Printing Office, 1975.

Ofshe, Richard. *The Sociology of the Possible.* New York: Prentice-Hall, 1970.

Ogburn, William F. *On Culture and Social Change: Selected Papers.* Chicago: Phoenix Books, 1964.

Ogburn, William F., with J. L. Adams and S. Colum Gilfillan. *The Social Effects of Aviation.* Boston: Houghton Mifflin, 1946.

O'Neill, Gerard K. *The High Frontier: Human Colonies in Space.* New York: William Morrow & Co., 1977.

Ophuls, William. *Ecology and the Politics of Scarcity.* San Francisco, California: W.H. Freeman, 1977.

Orhauer, H., H. Wiberg, A. Sicinski, and J. Galtung, eds. *Images of the World in the Year Two Thousand: A Comparative Ten-Nation Study.* Atlantic Highlands, New Jersey: Humanities Press, 1976.

Ostheimer, Nancy C., and John M. Ostheimer, eds. *Life or Death: Who Controls?* New York: Springer, 1976.

> An anthology designed as an introduction to life-and-death issues which have been given a new urgency by recent technological breakthroughs and increasing concern about over-population. Divergent viewpoints on abortion, eugenic manipulation, euthanasia, and compulsory sterilization are offered by Elizabeth Kubler-Ross, Garrett Hardin, Paul and Anne Ehrlich, Charles Frankel, Marya Mannes, and many others. The epilogue surveys current public attitudes towards these issues.

O'Toole, James. *Different Assumptions, New Tools: A Futurist's Perspective on Employment and Economic Growth.* Los Angeles: Center for Futures Research, 1976.

O'Toole, James. *Energy and Social Change: Summary of First Twenty Year Forecast Project.* Los Angeles: University of Southern California, Center for Futures Research Publication, 1975.

O'Toole, James. *The Twenty Year Forecast Project.* Los Angeles: University of Southern California, Center for Futures Research Publication, 1974.

Owen, Henry, and Charles L. Schultze. *Setting National Priorities: The Next Ten Years.* Washington, D.C.: The Brookings Institution, 1976.

Ozmon, Howard. *Utopias and Education.* Minneapolis, Minnesota: Burgess, 1969.

Peccei, Aurelio. *The Chasm Ahead.* New York: Macmillan, 1969.

Peccei, Aurelio *The Human Quality.* Elmsford, New York: Pergamon Press, 1977.

> The President of the Club of Rome here tells the story of his life, thinking, and creation of the Club of Rome.

Perelman, Lewis J. *Global Mind: Beyond the Limits to Growth.* New York: Mason/Charter Publishers, Inc., 1976.

Perloff, Harvey, ed. *The Future of the U.S. Government: Toward the Year 2000.* New York: George Braziller, 1971.

> This is a report of the United States task force of the Commission on the Year 2000 of the American Academy of Arts and Sciences. The book includes 19 essays plus panel discussions. The book's editor is Harvey F. Perloff, Dean of the School of Architecture and Urban

460

Planning at the University of California at Los Angeles. Perloff says that the activities of the task force centered on two themes: (1) the most significant problems and critical issues that the government of the United States will have to face and (2) the institutional changes and processes needed to enable the government to cope effectively with these changes.

Peters, Ted. *Futures—Human and Divine.* Atlanta, Georgia: John Knox Press, 1978.

Phillips, Bernard S. *Worlds of the Future: Exercises in the Sociological Imagination.* Columbus, Ohio: Charles E. Merrill, 1972.

Pickard, Jerome P. *U.S. Metropolitan Growth and Expansion 1970-2000.* The Commission on Population Growth and the American Future Research Reports. Washington, D.C.: U.S. Government Printing Office, 1973.

Pirages, Dennis Clark, ed. *Sustainable Society: Implications for Limited Growth.* New York: Praeger, 1977.

Pirages, Dennis C., and Paul R. Ehrlich. *Ark II. Social Response to Environmental Perspectives.* New York: Viking Press, 1974.

Platt, John. *Perception and Change: Projections for Survival.* Ann Arbor, Michigan: The University of Michigan Press, 1970.

Platt, John. *The Step to Man.* New York: John Wiley, 1966.

These essays, by a humanistic scientist long associated with the University of Michigan, take a searching look at the nature of man and his organizations and how they are changing. Platt suggests that the danger of the human race extinguishing itself cannot long continue. "No one lives very long walking on loose rocks at the edge of a precipice. Either, very soon, in ten or 20 years, or in 30 or 40, we fall over the nuclear precipice, or else, very soon, before that time runs out, we argue some sense into our collective heads and move back from danger." If humanity survives the next generation or so, Platt suggests it will move into a "steady-state" of history, when new ways of creative leisure and interaction will provide "the most interesting and satisfying ways of life."

Pohl, Frederik. *The Way the Future Was: A Memoir.* New York: Ballantine Books, 1978.

Polak, Fred L. *The Image of the Future: Enlightening the Past, Orienting the Present, Forecasting the Future.* Two vols. New York: Oceana Publications, 1961.

Dutch scholar Fred Polak examines here the various "images of the future" which man has constructed in the past. His retrospect encompasses Hellenic, Persian, Jewish, and Christian myths, as well as the imagistic historical periods of the middle ages, the Renaissance, the Enlightenment and the Age of Progress. He believes that modern man's "imaging" faculty is now seriously impaired. He attributes this primarily to the rise of de-Utopianism, that is, the trend towards believing that the future offers neither a heaven in the sky nor a utopia on earth. Polak believes that "the task before us is to reawaken the almost dormant awareness of the future and to find the best nourishment for a starving social imagination."

Polak, Fred L. *Prognostics: A Science in the Making Surveys and Creates the Future.* Amsterdam: Elsevier, 1971.

Dutch scholar Polak here offers a philosophical discussion of the future as a field of study. He argues that only by freeing ourselves of the dogmatism of the past can we comprehend the full spectrum of the future and realize its full potential.

Prehoda, Robert W. *Designing the Future: The Role of Technological Forecasting.* Philadelphia: Chilton Books, 1967.

Technological forecaster Robert Prehoda presents a rationale for man's potential ability to foresee accurately the future capabilities and results of applied science. The book defines technological forecasting as "the description or prediction of a foreseeable invention, specific scientific refinement, or likely scientific discovery that promises to serve some useful function." Prehoda describes several approaches to technological forecasting; his primary technique is through what he calls "the Hahn-Strassmann point." The name comes from the Hahn-Strassmann experiments in 1938, which showed the possibility of uranium fission. His method is to look for analogous situations, i.e., laboratory achievements which show the possibility of some major advance on a practical scale, then forecast the practical results which could be based on this laboratory achievement. About two-thirds of the book is devoted to examining various fields of science which, in Prehoda's opinion, have passed Hahn-Strassmann points, and which will therefore lead to major advances in the practical sphere.

Prehoda, Robert W. *Extended Youth: The Promise of Gerontology*. New York: Putnam, 1968.

President's Commission on National Goals. *Goals for Americans*. New York: Prentice-Hall, 1960.

President's Research Committee on Social Trends. *Recent Trends in the United States*. New York: McGraw-Hill, 1933.

Ridker, Ronald G. *Population, Resources and the Environment*. The Commission on Population Growth and the American Future Research Reports. Washington, D.C.: U.S. Government Printing Office, 1972.

Ritterbush, Philip C., and Martin Green, eds. *Technology as Institutionally Related to Human Values*. Washington, D.C.: Acropolis Books, 1974.

Rivers, Patrick. *The Survivalists*. New York: Universe, 1976.

Robertson, James. *The Sane Alternative*. London, England: James Robertson, 1978.

Robinson, Timothy C.L., ed. *The Future of Science: 1975 Nobel Conference*. New York: Wiley-Interscience, 1977.

Roemer, Kenneth M. *The Obsolete Necessity: America in Utopian Writings 1888-1900*. Kent, Ohio: Kent State University Press, 1976.

The author analyzes the writings of a "utopian era" in the United States (1888-1900) when some 160 utopian, partially utopian, or anti-utopian works were published. Roemer reasons that the utopian writings can help understanding of early attempts to define the "American Dream" as well as present-day hopes and fears about the future.

The Rome World Special Conference on Futures Research, 1973. *Human Futures*. London: IPC Business Press, 1974.

Rosen, Stephen. *Future Facts*. New York: Simon and Schuster, 1976.

Billed as "a forecast of the world as we will know it before the end of the century," this book describes over 300 specific products, concrete ideas, and detailed processes that may be part of life in the 21st century, if not before. Among the "Future Facts" are Artificial Life, Nuclear-Powered Artificial Heart, "Electric Aspirin," Solar Power from Satellites, Quick-Ripening Produce, Deep-Sea Food Storage, Protein from Wastes, Flying Trains, Car Radar and Sonar, Chemical Transfer of Learning, Nonlethal Weapons, Ultrasonic Sewing, a Mobile Bridge, Portable Telephones, Life-Cycle Insurance, Remote Cassette Vendors, a "People Washer" Egg, Electric Toilet, and Disappearing Plastic. Each Future Fact is explained in terms of a problem, its solution, and the person or agency responsible for creating the innovation.

Rosenfeld, Albert. *Prolongevity*. New York: Alfred A. Knopf, 1976.

Science writer Rosenfeld describes current attempts to extend the span of human life by controlling the aging process. He suggests that human life can and will be longer in the future.

462

Rosenfeld, Albert. *The Second Genesis: The Coming Control of Life.* Englewood Cliffs, New Jersey: Prentice-Hall, 1969.

> Albert Rosenfeld, formerly science editor of *Life* magazine, here focuses public attention on man's rapidly growing ability to control the nature of life. He also describes the critical ethical problems raised by the new scientific capabilities.

Rostow, W.W. *Getting From Here to There: America's Future in the World Economy.* New York: McGraw-Hill, 1978.

Rowe, William D. *An Anatomy of Risk.* New York: John Wiley and Sons, 1977.

Rubin, Louis, ed. *The Future of Education: Perspectives on Tomorrow's Schooling.* Boston, Massachusetts: Allyn & Bacon, 1975.

Rushmer, Robert F. *Humanizing Health Care: Alternative Futures for Medicine.* Cambridge, Massachusetts: MIT Press, 1975.

> This book is concerned with displaying the full range of options and alternatives for health care. It clarifies the issues and suggests strategies by which society can make optimal choices for safeguarding the future health of the people. The options are examined on the basis of cost/benefit and value-added criteria in order to establish priorities for implementation.

Sagan, Carl. *The Cosmic Connection: An Extraterrestrial Perspective.* Garden City, New York: Doubleday, Anchor Press, 1973.

Sagan, Carl, and I. S. Shklovskii. *Intelligent Life in the Universe.* San Francisco: Holden-Day, 1966.

Salk, Jonas. *Survival of the Wisest.* New York: Harper and Row, 1973.

Sauvy, Alfred. *Zero Growth?* New York: Praeger, 1976.

Schaller, Lyle E. *Impact of the Future: Trends Affecting the Church of Tomorrow.* Nashville, Tennessee: Abingdon Press, 1969.

Schaller, Lyle E. *Understanding Tomorrow.* Nashville, Tennessee: Abingdon Press, 1976.

Schmalz, Anton B., ed. *Energy: Today's Choices, Tomorrow's Opportunities.* Washington, D.C.: The World Future Society, 1974.

> This volume contains 47 articles by outstanding authorities and includes a foreword by Gerald Ford and an epilogue by John W. Gardner, chairman of Common Cause. Published in conjunction with the World Future Society's Energy Forum, April 1974, the book examines the energy question from eight perspectives: some new dimensions, resources, technology, economics, humanities, policy, implementation, and transitions.

Schneider, Stephen H. with Lynne Mesirow. *The Genesis Strategy: Climate and Global Survival.* New York: Plenum Press, 1976.

Schon, Donald A. *Beyond the Stable State.* New York: Random House, 1971.

Schon, Donald A. *Technology and Change: The New Heraclitus.* New York: Dell, Delta, 1967.

Schumacher, E. F. *Small Is Beautiful: Economics as if People Mattered.* New York: Harper and Row, 1973.

> This is a collection of essays by a German-born British economist who has attracted a wide following in recent years. This book sums up his thinking about economics and society. He urges the decentralization of industry and an emphasis on providing jobs for people rather than increasing productivity. Schumacher is an advocate of what he has termed "intermedi-

ate technology"—technology that is neither primitive nor highly advanced—as a means for
revitalizing the villages of the underdeveloped world.

Schwarz, Stephan, ed. *Knowledge and Concepts in Future Studies.* Boulder, Colorado: Westview Press, 1976.

Schwitzgebel, Robert and Ralph, eds. *Psychotechnology: Electronic Control of Mind and Behavior.*
Winston, New Jersey: Holt, Rinehart and Winston, 1973.

Seaborg, Glenn T., and W. R. Corliss. *Man and Atom.* New York: E. P. Dutton, 1971.

Seifert, Harvey. *Reality and Ecstasy: A Religion for the 21st Century.* Philadelphia: Westminster Press
1974.

Shane, Harold G. *Curriculum Change Toward the 21st Century.* Washington, D.C.: National Education
Association, 1977.

In his latest book, Shane examines the responses of an international panel of educators and other
leaders to questions regarding the content and direction of education in the years to come. The report
concludes by proposing 28 cardinal premises to guide curriculum development for the future.

Shane, Harold G. *The Educational Significance of the Future.* Bloomington, Indiana: Phi Delta Kappa
Educational Foundation, 1973.

The author, a professor of education at Indiana University, prepared this report for the U.S.
Commissioner of Education on the basis of interviews with more than 80 futurists. The book
offers a compact digest of what futurists are thinking about the future and specifically about
education.

Sheldon, Eleanor, and Wilbert Moore. *Indicators of Social Change.* New York: Russell Sage
Foundation, 1968.

Simmons, W.W. *Exploratory Planning: Briefs of Practices.* Oxford, Ohio: Planning Executive Institue, 1977.

Simonds, John Ormsbee. *Earthscape: A Manual of Environmental Planning.* New York: McGraw Hill Book
Company, 1978.

Smil, Vaclav. *Energy and the Environment: A Long-Range Forecasting Study.* Winnipeg, Canada:
University of Manitoba, 1974.

Somit, Albert, ed. *Political Science and the Study of the Future.* Hinsdale, Illinois: Dryden Press, 1974.

Spekke, Andrew A., ed. *The Next 25 Years: Crisis and Opportunity.* Washington, D.C.: The World
Future Society, 1975.

This volume is a selection of 47 papers submitted to the World Future Society's Second
General Assembly, June 1975. The meeting was the largest gathering of futurists ever held
(approximately 2,800 attendees). The papers were selected for their general interest and
relevance to the theme of the meeting—a look at the prospects for mankind during the final
quarter of the 20th century.

Spengler, Joseph J. *Population and America's Future.* San Francisco: W. H. Freeman, 1975.

Stanford Research Institute, Center for the Study of Social Policy. *Changing Images of Man.* Prepared
for the Charles F. Kettering Foundation. Menlo Park, California: Stanford Research Institute, 1974.

Stavrianos, L. S. *The Promise of the Coming Dark Age.* San Francisco: W. H. Freeman, 1976.

Stephens, James C. *Managing Complexity: Work, Technology, Resources, and Human Relations.* Lomond, 1977.

464

Stevenson, Hugh A. *Alternatives Canada.* London: Alexander, Blake Associates, 1976.

Stevenson, Hugh A., and William B. Hamilton, eds. *Canadian Education and the Future: A Select Annotated Bibliography, 1967-71.* London, Ontario, Canada: University of Western Ontario, 1972.

Stevenson, Hugh A. and J. Donald Wilson, compilers and eds. *Precepts, Policy and Process: Perspectives on Contemporary Canadian Education.* London, Ontario: Alexander, Blake Associates, 1977.

Stine, G. Harry. *The Third Industrial Revolution.* New York: Putnam, 1975.

> An aeronautical engineer argues that many of the environmental crises facing earth can be solved by the development of space industry. Raw materials can be obtained from the moon and asteroid belt. Future space transportation systems will allow the shipment of refined metals or finished products to the earth's surface at a reasonable cost.

Streatfeild, Guy F. . . . *And Now the Future: A PEP Survey of Futures.* London: PEP, 1971.

Stulman, Julius. *Evolving Mankind's Future: The World Institute: A Problem-Solving Methodology.* Philadelphia: Lippincott, 1968.

Stulman, Julius, and Ervin Laszlo, eds. *Emergent Man: His Chances, Problems and Potentials.* New York: Gordon and Breach, 1973.

Sullivan, Edward A. *The Future: Human Ecology and Education.* Palm Springs, California: ETC Publications, 1975.

Sullivan, William G. and Wayne Claycombe. *Fundamentals of Forecasting.* Reston, Virginia: Reston Publishing Co., 1977.

Swan, Christopher and Roaman, Chet. *YV 88: An Eco-Fiction of Tomorrow.* San Francisco, California: Sierra Club Books, 1977.

Syed Kechik Foundation. *Malaysia 2001: A Preliminary Inquiry.* Kuala Lumpur: Banyan Productions, 1978.

Tavel, Charles H. *The Third Industrial Age: Strategy for Business Survival.* Homewood, Illinois: Dow Jones-Irwin, 1975.

> The author, educated in Switzerland and present Chairman of the European Common Market Committee on Industrial Innovation, has traveled widely in the world's industrial community and gained many insights into new trends and directions. He divides the modern history of business into three industrial ages: the Age of the Entrepreneur, the Age of the Manager, and, since the early 1970s, the Age of the Strategist. The corporation in the Age of the Strategist will be characterized more by the personality of its chief executive than was the case in the second age. The chief executive will need a broad sweep of mind and outstanding creative ability in order to compete in an increasingly competitive business world. The author offers a wealth of insights and suggestions for the successful executive in the Age of the Strategist.

Taylor, Gordon Rattray. *The Biological Time Bomb.* New York: New American Library, 1968.

Taylor, Gordon Rattray. *The Doomsday Book: Can the World Survive?* New York: New American Library, 1970.

Taylor, Gordon Rattray. *How to Avoid the Future.* London: Secker and Warburg, 1975.

Taylor, Gordon Rattray. *Rethink: A Paraprimitive Solution.* New York: E. P. Dutton, 1973.

Taylor, John G. *The Shape of Minds to Come.* New York: Weybright and Talley, 1971.

Taylor, Theodore B., and Charles C. Humpstone. *The Restoration of the Earth*. New York: Harper and Row, 1973.

> Nuclear physicist Taylor and his lawyer colleague, Charles Humpstone, here propose a comprehensive program to eliminate pollution. They describe the procedures and institutions needed to achieve that goal. Based on the "containment principle," the program requires that all pollutants be recycled or captured and stored.

Teich, Albert, ed. *Technology and Man's Future*. New York: St. Martin's Press, 1972.

Teilhard de Chardin, Pierre. *The Future of Man*. London: Collins, 1964.

Theobald, Robert. *An Alternative Future for America*. Chicago: Swallow Press, 1968.

> This is a collection of essays and speeches presenting Theobald's concepts of how America can create a better future for itself. The collection reflects his view that the United States needs to effect a basic change in its economic, social, and educational thinking or undergo some kind of collapse. One change that Theobald views as essential is the establishment of the right of every American to an income sufficient for him to live in dignity. He would not lose this right even if he did no work whatsoever. This basic economic security would enable each individual to do what he personally feels to be important. Theobald is convinced most people will want to work at tasks even if there is no economic necessity for them to do so.

Theobald, Robert. *An Alternative Future for America's Third Century*. Chicago, Illinois: Swallow, 1976.

Theobald, Robert. *Beyond Despair*. Washington, D.C.: New Republic, 1976.

> This volume summarizes Robert Theobald's thinking on the social and economic problems that the United States currently faces and how they might be overcome. He urges new thinking for the new "communications era."

Theobald, Robert, ed. *Futures Conditional*. New York: Bobbs-Merrill, 1972.

> This is an anthology of poems, cartoons, and essays dealing with the future, education, revising the U.S. Constitution, and pollution. The selections presented here are chosen to suggest four basic postures taken toward the future: (1) positive extrapolists—those who assume that the future will be fundamentally like the present only "better"; (2) negative extrapolists—those who believe that the future will be essentially "more of the same" only "worse"; (3) the romantics who feel that things will resolve themselves happily somehow if everyone just does his own thing; and (4) the systemic thinkers (such as Theobald) who believe that the future is ours to shape but that many hard choices and hard work are required.

Theobald, Robert, and J. M. Scott. *TEG's 1994: An Anticipation of the Near Future*. New York: Swallow Press, 1972.

> British socio-economist Theobald and his anthropologist wife here present a "participation book" in which a number of collaborators have worked to create a vision of the future as seen through the eyes of a woman named TEG. Teg is a girl of twenty who in 1994 receives a one-year fellowship from the Orwell Foundation, established in 1984 to celebrate man's survival to that much-dreaded year. During her year of worldwide travel, study and investigation, Teg "reviews" the history of previous years, much as Edward Bellamy did in his famed *Looking Backward*.

Thomson, Sir George. *The Foreseeable Future, Rev. ed.*. Cambridge, England: Cambridge University Press, 1960.

> Nobel prize-winning British physicist Sir George Thomson published this book in 1955. The author focused on sources of energy, transportation, communication, meteorology, natural resources, food production, and intellectual development. Two decades after his book appeared, a reviewer in THE FUTURIST reported that Thomson's twenty-year-old forecasts had generally turned out to be remarkably accurate: Thomson had correctly foreseen the energy crisis in the 1970s and the triumph of the computer.

Thompson, William Irwin. *Darkness and Scattered Light: Speculations on the Future.* New York: Doubleday, 1977.

Thring, M. W. *Man, Machines and Tomorrow.* London: Routledge and Kegan Paul, 1973.

Tinbergen, Jan, coordinator. *Reshaping the International Order. A Report to the Club of Rome.* New York: E.P. Dutton & Co., Inc.,1976.

Toffler, Alvin. *Eco-Spasm Report.* New York: Bantam Books, 1975.

In this short work, Toffler argues that the world faces more than an economic upheaval but something far deeper. "What is happening, no more, no less," he says, "is the breakdown of industrial civilization on the planet and the first fragmentary appearance of a wholly new and dramatically different social order: a super-industrial civilization that will be technological but no longer industrial."

Toffler, Alvin. *Future Shock.* New York: Random House, 1970.

A best-seller that has sold some six million copies and been translated into 20 languages, *Future Shock* argues that increasing numbers of people are suffering from the impact of too rapid social change. Toffler argues that the problem may become increasingly severe in the years to come. A final chapter, "The Strategy of Social Futurism," proposes a number of ways in which society can learn to cope with future shock. The author outlines his ideas about how to make democracy more anticipatory in its character.

Toffler, Alvin, ed. *The Futurists.* New York: Random House, 1972.

In this anthology of writings by a number of well-known futurists, readers will find an introduction to many strains of current futurist thinking. Selections range from Arthur Clarke writing on "hazards of prophecy" to Kenneth Boulding describing "the economics of the coming spaceship earth."

Toffler, Alvin, ed. *Learning for Tomorrow: The Role of the Future in Education.* New York: Random House, 1974.

This anthology is essentially a call for "education in the future tense." The central thesis is that all education springs from images of the future, and all education creates images of the future. The volume includes a "Status Report, Sample Syllabi, and Directory of Future Studies" by Billy Rojas and H. Wentworth Eldredge.

Tompkins, Robert. *Futurescapes: Explorations in Fact and Fiction.* Agincourt, Ontario, Canada: Menthuen Publications, 1977.

Toynbee, Arnold. *Surviving the Future.* New York: Oxford University Press, 1971.

Tugwell, Franklin, ed. *Search for Alternatives: Public Policy and the Study of the Future.* Cambridge, Massachusetts: Winthrop Publishers, 1973.

This anthology of futurist writing includes many frequently quoted articles, such as "On the Epistemology of the Inexact Sciences" by Olaf Helmer and Nicholas Rescher, "What We Must Do" by John Platt, and "The Counter-Intuitive Behavior of Social Systems" by Jay W. Forrester.

Turn, Rein. *Computers in the 1980s.* New York: Columbia University Press, 1974.

Tuve, George L. *Energy, Environment, Populations, & Food: Our Four Interdependent Crises.* New York: Wiley-Interscience, 1976.

Underwood, Robert, ed. *The Future of Scotland.* London: The Nevis Institute, 1977.

United Nations Commission for Europe. *Coal: 1985 and Beyond: A Perspective Study.* Oxford: Pergamon Press, 1978.

Urban, G. R., ed., in collaboration with Michael Glenny. *Can We Survive Our Future?* New York: St. Martin's Press, 1971.

Urban Land Institute. *Management and Control of Growth.* Three vols. Washington, D.C.: The Urban Land Institute, 1975.

U.S. Congress, House, Committee on Science and Astronautics. *Technical Information for Congress: Report to the Subcommittee on Science, Research, and Development, Rev. ed..* Washington, D.C.: U.S. Government Printing Office, 1971.

U.S. Congress, House, Merchant Marine and Fisheries Committee, Subcommittee on Fisheries and Wildlife Conservation and the Environment. *Computer Simulation Methods to Aid National Growth Policy.* Washington, D.C.: U.S. Government Printing Office, 1975.

U.S. Congress, Senate, Committee on Rules and Administration, Subcommittee on Computer Services. *Hearing on S. 2302.* 92nd Cong. Washington, D.C.: U.S. Government Printing Office, 1972.

U.S. Department of Agriculture. *Alternative Futures for U.S. Agriculture.* Washington, D.C.: U.S. Government Printing Office, 1975.

U.S. Department of Health, Education and Welfare. *Toward a Social Report.* Washington, D.C.: U.S. Government Printing Office, 1969.

U.S. Department of Transportation. *National Transportation Trends and Choices to the Year 2000.* Washington, D.C.: U.S. Government Printing Office, 1977.

U.S. Interagency Task Group on Technological Forecasting in the U.S. Federal Government. *The Role of the Federal Government in Technological Forecasting.* Report to the President's Committee on Manpower and to the National Commission on Technology, Automation and Economic Progress. Washington, D.C.: U.S. Government Printing Office, 1966.

U.S. National Resources Committee, Subcommittee on Technology. *Technological Trends and National Policy.* Washington, D.C.: U.S. Government Printing Office, 1937.

Vacca, Roberto. *The Coming Dark Age.* New York: Doubleday, 1973.

> The collapse of modern technology and modern life is forecast in this book by Italian computer scientist Roberto Vacca. He says that all the major systems on which modern life depends—transport, electricity, garbage removal, etc.—are hopelessly overloaded and about to crack. He says the breakdown will come sometime between 1985 and 1994 and will begin in the United States and Japan. A crisis in one system will aggravate the collapse of another and then another until the catastrophe becomes worldwide. The result of the collapse, Vacca suggests, will be a new dark age. Monastic communities for survival will be located in high places, because heights are easiest to defend. In the monasteries a few people may be able to preserve the remnants of civilization until a new renaissance dawns.

Valaskakis, K. et. al. *The GAMMA Report on the Conserver Society. The Selective Conserver Society.* Volume 1. Montreal: GAMMA, 1977.

Vanston, John, Jr., Dudley L. Poston, and W. Parker Frisbee. *Technology Assessment of Portable Energy RDT&P: University Team Report.* Report for the National Aeronautics and Space Administration. NASA CR-137655. Austin, Texas: The University of Texas at Austin, Center for Energy Studies, 1975.

Waddington, C.H. *The Man-Made Future.* New York: St. Martin's Press, 1978.

Wagar, W. Warren. *Building the City of Man: Outlines of a World Civilization.* New York: Grossman Publishers, 1971.

The author, a professor of history at the State University of New York at Binghamton, focuses on major trends in recent human history and then projects his own "blueprint for a global society" into the future. Wagar says that "the enemy of modern civilization is something quite commonplace and utterly impersonal. I shall not be clever. The enemy is change. The enemy is the geometrically accelerating pace of change in the growth of all the powers of mankind."

Wagar, W. Warren. *The City of Man: Prophecies of a World Civilization in Twentieth-Century Thought*. Boston: Houghton Mifflin, 1963.

Ward, Barbara. *The Home of Man*. New York: W. W. Norton & Co., Inc., 1976.

Ward, Barbara, and Rene Dubos. *Only One Earth*. New York: W. W. Norton, 1972.

Ward, Hiley H. *Religion 2101 A.D.: Who or What Will Be God?* Garden City, New York: Doubleday, 1975.

Waterlow, Charlotte. *Superpowers and Victims: The Outlook for World Community*. Englewood Cliffs New Jersey: Prentice-Hall, 1974.

Watt, Kenneth E. F. *The Titanic Effect: Planning for the Unthinkable*. New York: E. P. Dutton, 1974.

Kenneth Watt, a professor of zoology at the University of California at Davis, argues that the world is in the grips of a critical disease, characterized by excessive, undirected, and destructive growth. The world's planners are failing to take adequate steps to deal with the disease because of a basic human tendency to ignore potential enormous disasters as "unthinkable," since they have never happened before. Consequently, appropriate counter-measures are not taken. Watt urges adopting the point of view of ecology and systems analysis to make more accurate future projections, plan accordingly, and use vital resources effectively.

Watt, Kenneth, E. *The Unsteady State: Environmental Problems, Growth, and Culture*. Honolulu, Hawaii: University Press of Hawaii, 1977.

Weaver, W. Timothy. *Delphi: A Critical Review*. EPRC Research Report RR-7. Syracuse, New York: Syracuse University Research Corporation, Educational Policy Research Center, 1972.

Western, John S. and Paul R. Wilson. *Planning in Turbulent Environments*. University of Queensland Press, 1977.

Wheelwright, Steven C., and Spyros Makridakis. *Forecasting Methods for Management*. Second Edition. New York: Wiley-Interscience, 1977.

White House Conference on the Industrial World Ahead. *A Look at Business in 1990*. Washington, D.C.: U.S. Government Printing Office, 1972.

Whiting, Allen S., and Robert F. Dernberger. *China's Future: Foreign Policy and Economic Development in the Post-Mao Era*. New York: McGraw-Hill, 1977.

Whittaker, James B. *Strategic Planning in a Rapidly Changing Environment*. Lexington, Massachusetts: D.C. Heath and Co., 1978.

Wilcox, Howard A. *Hothouse Earth*. New York: Praeger, 1975.

The author, Director of the U.S. Navy's Ocean Farm Project, says that as man utilizes increasing amounts of energy from fossil fuels, nuclear reactors, and geothermal sources, he will release enough heat into the atmosphere to melt the polar ice caps and inundate the world's seaports and vast areas of valuable land. He urges that man turn to solar energy for his needs, since there is an unlimited supply and its use would not contribute *additional* heat, since the sun heats the earth regardless of human use of solar power. The author sees open-ocean "farms" producing vast quantities of plant material for food, fuel, and industrial raw material as the most efficient way to utilize solar energy.

Wilson, Carroll, ed. *Energy: Global Prospects 1985-2000.* New York: McGraw-Hill, 1977.

Wilson, Ian H. *Corporate Environments of the Future: Planning for Major Change.* New York: The Presidents Association, 1976.

Wilson, Kenneth D., ed. *Prospects for Growth: Changing Expectations for the Future.* New York: Praeger Publishers, Inc., 1977.

Winner, Langdon. *Autonomous Technology: Technics-out-of-Control as a Theme in Political Thought.* Cambridge, Massachusetts: The MIT Press, 1977.

Wolstenholme, Gordon, ed. *Man and His Future.* Ciba Foundation Volume. Boston: Little, Brown, 1963.

Woodward, Herbert. *Capitalism Can Survive in a No-Growth Economy.* Stamford, Connecticut: Bookdale Press, 1977.

World Food and Nutrition Study: The Potential Contributions of Research. Washington, D.C.: National Academy of Sciences, 1977.

World Future Society. *The Future: A Guide to Information Sources.* Washington, D.C.: The World Future Society, 1979.

World Future Society. *Resources Directory for America's Third Century: Part I—An Introduction to the Study of the Future* and *Part II—Information Sources for the Study of the Future.* Prepared under a grant from the National Science Foundation and the Library of Congress, Congressional Research Service. Washington, D.C.: World Future Society, 1977.

The Year 2000 and the Prospect for American Women. Washington, D.C.:Congressional Research Service, Library of Congress, 1977.

Young, David P. *A New World in the Morning: The Biopsychological Revolution.* Philadelphia: Westminster Press, 1972.

Young, Michael. *The Rise of the Meritocracy.* Baltimore, Maryland: Penguin Books, 1961.

> In this satirical essay, a British sociologist suggests that seniority might eventually be abandoned as a means of determining status. Young points out that throughout history, age has been the most enduring social class. Every aristocracy, plutocracy, or bureaucracy has also been a gerontocracy. But in a rapidly changing society the young are more at home than the old and can learn things for the first time easier than the old can unlearn and learn again for the second or third time. In the future, Young suggests, older people will increasingly find themselves taking orders from younger people; bank presidents will become tellers and professors may become teaching assistants.

Zaltman, Gerald, and Robert Duncan. *Strategies for Planned Change.* New York: John Wiley & Sons, 1977.

Zuckerman, David W., and Robert E. Horn. *The Guide to Simulations and Games for Education and Training.* Lexington, Massachusetts: Information Resources, 1973.

Zurcher, Louis A. *The Mutable Self: A Self-Concept for Social Change.* Beverly Hills, California: Sage Publications, 1977.

PERIODICALS

PERIODICALS

The periodicals listed here include newsletters, magazines, and journals whose primary focus is on the future, either in all its aspects or in one particular aspect. While most of the publications listed here appear in English, foreign language periodicals were also evaluated, and a few of the more prominent and accessible ones have been included.

Where available, the following information is provided for each periodical listed:

Title
Editor
Publisher's name and address
Frequency
Subscription price
Intended audience
Description (including year of first issue and average number of pages per issue)

ALTERNATIVE FUTURES: The Journal of Utopian Studies

Editor: Merritt Abrash, Co-Editor and Alexandra Aldridge, Co-Editor

Publisher: Human Dimensions Center, Rensselaer Polytechnic Institute, Troy, New York 12181, U.S.A.

Quarterly. $8.50 per year—individual, $14—institution (plus $1.50 foreign).

Intended audience: Scholars and non-scholars interested in utopia/future studies

ALTERNATIVE FUTURES is a forum for utopian and futures oriented scholarship and commentary in utopian literature and thought, communitarianism and social experiment, utopian/dystopian science fiction, and non-technical futures inquiry. Includes book reviews, bibliographical information, news center noting professional activities in the utopia/futures field. 128 pages. Published since 1978.

ALTERNATIVES: A Journal of World Policy

Editor: Rajni Kothari and Richard A. Falk

Publisher: Institute for World Order, 777 United Nations Plaza, New York, New York 10017, U.S.A.

Quarterly. $15 per year—individual, $30—libraries and institutions.

Intended audience: Policy-makers, scholars and concerned individuals worldwide

The main purpose of the Journal is to promote wide-ranging discussion and debate on the future of the world from the perspective of a set of values. Principal among these values are autonomy and dignity of the individual and of peoples, equality and justice as principles of social organization, participation in political and economic decision-making structures and in the productive process, elimination of oppression and coercion in human and international affairs, and harmony between man, nature and technology.

The perspective of the Journal will not be confined to foreign or domestic policies of individual nations, but will deal with problems and policies which have worldwide relevance.

The Journal is futuristic in orientation and is actively concerned with shaping and designing the future along preferred lines on the basis of the values outlined above. 125 pages. Published since 1975.

ALTERNATIVES: Perspectives on Society and Environment

Editor: Robert C. Paehlke

Publisher: Alternatives, Inc., c/o Trent University, Peterborough, Ontario, Canada

Quarterly. $7.50 individuals; $12.00 institutions.

Intended audience: Environmentalists, administrators, professionals, academics, teachers, students

Focus is on resource use, population, pollution, conservation and wilderness. The publication emphasizes both natural and social science approaches and a philosophical perspective. Its statement of purpose reads: "The environmental crisis, if it is to be resolved by other means than biological disaster, requires more than mere technical improvements. We must confront the implications it has for our economic structures, our political process and institutions, our living habits, and the moral basis of our philosophy and culture. We must pose and offer imaginative and serious ALTERNATIVES." 52 pages. Published since 1971.

ANALYSEN UND PROGNOSEN (Analyses and Prognoses)

Editor: Ossip K. Flechtheim, Robert Jungk, Hans Buchholz, Bernd P. Spahn, Dieter Kolb

Publisher: Gesellschaft fur Zukunftsfragen (Association for Future Questions), 1 Berlin 12, Giesebrechtstrasse 15, Germany

Bimonthly. $24 per year.

Intended audience: Futures researchers and planners in science, politics, economics, industry, administration and government

ANALYSEN UND PROGNOSEN is a scientific organ containing information about the institutional future research throughout the world. Ten pages or so are devoted to concentrated data from various sources about future development. Two to three articles about research work and scientific results are published in each edition. A literature service is documented. 32 pages. Published since 1968.

ANTICIPATION

Editor: Paul Abrecht

Publisher: Department on Church and Society, World Council of Churches, 150 route de Ferney, 1211 Geneva 20, Switzerland

3 issues per year. Free, contributions welcome.

Intended audience: Approximately 2,000 collaborators around the world interested in study programme on science and technology

ANTICIPATION features collections of papers on Christian social thought in future perspective. They are circulated for the information of participants in the ecumenical enquiry on "The Future of Man and Society in a World of Science-Based Technology." 40 to 45 pages. Published since 1970.

AREAS OF CONCERN

Editor: Harry Hyde, Jr.

Publisher: Harry Hyde, Jr., P.O. Box 47, Bryn Mawr, Pennsylvania 19010, U.S.A.

Monthly. $8 per year.

Intended audience: Concerned citizens—United States and international

"An independent, nationally/internationally circulated newsletter for people who are actively and seriously concerned about problems, challenges, and opportunities of the late 20th century and beyond." Subject matter includes current problems and possible approaches toward their resolution, plus alternative options for the future—in citizen participation, consumer affairs, education, employment, energy, environment, health and social services, human relations, human rights, law enforcement and public safety, national and international security, transportation, urban/community affairs, etc. 6 pages. Published since 1971.

BUDUSHCHEE NAUKI (FUTURE OF SCIENCE) International Yearbook

Editor: E.B. Etingof

Publisher: Znanie, Moscow Tsentre, proezd Serova, D.4, proezd Serova, Moscow

Once a year. 95 Kopecks.

Intended audience: Scientific workers, students, engineers, physicians, agronomists, teachers

This publication contains articles by well-known scholars on all continents of the earth concerning the views of the various sciences, their unsolved problems, new hypotheses, practical scientific means of helping people, in the cause of peace and progress. 288 pages. Published since 1966.

BULLETIN DE LA SOCIETE D'ETUDE DE LA PREVISION ET DE LA PLANIFICATION
(Bulletin of the Society for the Study of Forecasting and Planning)

Editor: P. Goetschin, P. Ruttimann, A. Jenny

Publisher: Society for the Study of Forecasting and Planning, Batiment des Facultes des Sciences humaines, 1015 Lausanne-Dorigny, Switzerland

Quarterly. 30 Swiss francs.

Intended audience: Scholars interested in the future. Universities, industries, commercial

This mimeographed French language bulletin publishes scholarly articles dealing with forecasting and planning, often in a Swiss context. 30 pages. Published since 1974.

BULLETIN OF THE ATOMIC SCIENTISTS

Editor: Ruth Adams

Publisher: James P. Cahill, 1020-24 East 58th Street, Chicago, Illinois 60637, U.S.A.

Monthly. $18—1 year, $32—2 years, $42—3 years.

Intended audience: Scientists and non-scientists concerned about the effects of science and technology on public affairs

Founded in 1945 by Albert Einstein, Leo Szilard, Robert Oppenheimer, and others, the BULLETIN OF THE ATOMIC SCIENTISTS sprang from the desire to tell the world about the new form of energy from the atom. The magazine today explores a wide variety of questions affecting the survival and well-being of mankind. The writers range from knowns to young unknowns offering ideas. The "doomsday clock" which appears monthly on the corner of the BULLETIN is an internationally known symbolic warning of the lateness of the hour as mankind confronts the urgent problems of our times. 64 pages. Published since 1945.

BUSINESS TOMORROW

Editor: Frank Feather

Publisher: The World Future Society, 4916 St. Elmo Avenue (Bethesda), Washington, D.C. 20014, U.S.A.

Bimonthly. $9 for Society members; $12 to non-members and libraries.

Intended audience: Executives, managers, planners, anyone with an interest in the future of business and work

Newsletter covering commerce, manufacturing, marketing, management, and especially the uses of futuristics in business. Also has information on conferences, work and careers, and new trends in the business world. Includes book reviews and short news items as well as signed original short articles. 12 pages. Published since 1978.

CANADIAN FUTURES

Editor: Don Wilson

Publisher: I.C.F. Press Ltd., 2323 Confederation Pkwy, No. 206, Mississauga, Ontario, L5B 1R6, Canada

Bimonthly. $100 per year, including membership.

Intended audience: Politicians, educators, policy designers, community leaders

CANADIAN FUTURES is intended to focus on one general theme in each specific issue. A recent issue focused on "Canada in a Post-Industrial Transition Period." Papers are invited from scholars, journalists and politicians concerned with "Canada's long term future." Published since 1978.

CENTER FOR FUTURES RESEARCH NEWSLETTER

Editor: Burt Nanus

Publisher: Center for Futures Research, University of Southern California, Los Angeles, California 90007, U.S.A.

Bimonthly. Free.

Intended audience: Futures researchers, planners

Bimonthly update of activities of the University of Southern California Center for Futures Research. An annual report is also published with more detailed discussions of projects and listing of more than 50 Center for Futures Research working papers. 2 pages. Published since 1972.

COEVOLUTION QUARTERLY

Editor: Stewart Brand

Publisher: Point Foundation, Box 428, Sausalito, California 94965, U.S.A.

Quarterly. $12 per year.

Intended audience: General

The COEVOLUTION QUARTERLY carries on where the WHOLE EARTH CATALOG left off. The CQ contains articles and reviews of books and tools in the traditional CATALOG categories: whole systems, land use, shelter, soft technology, craft, community, nomadics, communications, and learning. But the CQ runs in a somewhat deeper vein, offering more of what Editor Stewart Brand calls "conceptual news."

In recent issues subjects touched upon included physicist Gerard O'Neill's space colonies, the Gaia Hypothesis (a startling new biological hypothesis about the earth's atmosphere), and an extended conversation between California Governor Jerry Brown and cybernetician Gregory Bateson. There have been articles about personal computers, advanced woodburning, sinsemilla marijuana, and Marlon Brando planning a Whole Earth TV special. 144 pages. Published since 1974.

CONSEQUENCES

Editor: Marvin L. Peebles

Publisher: MLP Enterprises, P.O. Box 31-516, San Francisco, California 94131, U.S.A.

Monthly. Introductory: $1.75/6 months; Regular: $3/6 months, $4.50/yr.

Intended audience: Anyone interested in the consequences of political and social actions

CONSEQUENCES is a political newsletter and a record of and commentary on current events and how they may shape the future. It is designed to provoke and stimulate discussion about the consequences of political and social acts. 2 pages. Published since 1978.

CONSERVATION FOUNDATION LETTER

Editor: Rice Odell

Publisher: The Conservation Foundation, 1717 Massachusetts Avenue, N.W., Washington, D.C. 20036, U.S.A.

Monthly. U.S. rate: $10—1 year, $18—2 years, $25—3 years; foreign rate: $12—1 year, $22—2 years, $31—3 years.

Intended audience: People interested in environmental issues

A monthly report on environmental issues designed for professionals and laymen with a continuing interest in a variety of environmental concerns. Recent subjects included were chemical risks, pollution-control laws, endangered species protection, urban conservation movement, energy, environmental problems in past civilizations and changes in rural land. 8 pages. Published since 1966.

CUADERNOS DE PLANEAMIENTO (PLANNING NOTES)

Editor: Raul Puigbo

Publisher: Planeamiento Editores S.A., Fragata Presidente Sarmiento 2142, Buenos Aires, Argentina

Quarterly. $24 for six issues.

Intended audience: Planning officers (public and private), general audience interested in planning and prospective (futurology)

CUADERNOS DE PLANEAMIENTO publishes articles, reports and book reviews on state and urban zone planning; enterprise planning; public works, energy, ecology, industrial and sectorial planning; human resources and social planning; general futurology; micro and macromodels; basic theory and methodology of planning and futurology; planner and futurologist as a professional. 150 pages. Published since 1976.

CYCLES

Editor: Gertrude F. Shirk

Publisher: The Foundation for the Study of Cycles, Inc., 124 S. Highland Avenue, Pittsburgh, Pennsylvania 15206, U.S.A.

Nine issues a year. $25 per year. Students, instructors and libraries $18.

Intended audience: Scholars, professionals, others interested in cycles

CYCLES reports on results of research into the rhythms, patterns and interrelationships in any time series done by the Foundation, or by other organizations and persons. CYCLES also carries articles on technique, and reports on how extrapolations "come out." 24 pages. Published since 1950.

DATAR Newsletter

Editor: Andre Chadeau

Publisher: DATAR (Delegation a l'Amenagement du Territoire et a l'Action Regionales), 1, avenue Charles-Floquet, Paris 7' France

Quarterly. Cost not given.

Intended audience: English-language readers, particularly businessmen interested in France

An English-language publication designed to inform non-French businessmen about economic, governmental, and other developments in today's France. The main purpose of the publication appears to be to attract foreign capital and business to France. 12 pages.

DEVELOPMENT DIALOGUE

Editor: Sven Hamrell, Olle Nordberg

Publisher: Dag Hammarskjold Foundation, Ovre Slottsgatan 2, S-752 20 Uppsala, Sweden

Biannual. Sent free, particularly to institutions in the Third World, upon application to the Foundation.

Intended audience: Administrators and politicians in both Third World and industrialized countries, officials in international organizations, researchers and other interested persons

DEVELOPMENT DIALOGUE is intended to provide a free forum for critical discussion of development priorities and problems, international development cooperation in general and Nordic development cooperation in particular. 130 pages. Published since 1972.

DEVELOPMENT FORUM BUSINESS EDITION

Editor: William Neddow

Publisher: United Nations Centre for Economic and Social Information, Palais des Nations, CH-21 1211 Geneva 10, Switzerland

Bimonthly. $200 per year, $170 per year for developing countries.

Intended audience: Business community

This publication carries editorial material including country profiles on development and stories of interest to businessmen involved in export. Also all the procurement notices and other advance information relating to loans granted to developing countries by the World Bank, the Inter-American Development Bank and the Asian Development Bank, representing more than 10 billion dollars per year of opportunities.

DISTANCES

Editor: Andre-Clement Decoufle

Publisher: Laboratoire de Prospective Appliquee, Dante no. 6, Paris, France 75005

Monthly. No cost given.

Intended audience: Limited

DISTANCES contains brief notes and chronicles on questions dealing with the history, the epistemology and the sociology of forecasting practices. Eight pages. Published since 1978.

THE ECOLOGIST QUARTERLY

Editor: Edward Goldsmith

Publisher: Ecosystems, 73 Molesworth Street, Wadebridge, Cornwall PL27 7DS, United Kingdom

Four times yearly. Joint subscription with THE NEW ECOLOGIST $16 per year.

Intended audience: "Educated people seeking to understand the world they live in and the global problems their leaders are incapable of interpreting correctly and hence of solving."

EDUCATION TOMORROW

Editor: Al Peakes

Publisher: The World Future Society, 4916 St. Elmo Avenue (Bethesda), Washington, D.C. 20014, U.S.A.

Bimonthly. $9 for Society members; $12 to non-members and libraries.

Intended audience: Teachers, educators, and anyone with an interest in the future of education

Newsletter carrying information and articles about pre-school, primary, secondary, college, university, graduate and continuing education; education to prepare people for the future. Brief articles are solicited from members and interested parties. 8 pages. Published since 1976.

EKISTICS

Editor: P. Psomopoulos

Publisher: Athens Center of Ekistics, P.O. Box 471, Athens, Greece

Ten issues yearly. $36 per year.

Intended audience: Scientists

The EKISTICS journal contains, apart from original articles, a selection of up-to-date information pertaining to the development of human settlements from a variety of fields (social sciences, economics, cybernetics, physical planning, biology, etc.). Each issue is usually devoted to one particular subject. One or more issues cover the activities and scientific studies of the Athens Center of Ekistics and of the World Society for Ekistics, carried out during the year. 48-72 pages. Published since 1956.

ENERGY POLICY: The International Journal for Economics and Planning of Energy

Editor: Lyndon Driscoll

Publisher: IPC Science and Technology Press Limited, Westbury House, Bury Street, Guildford, Surrey, GU2 5AW England

Quarterly. $96.20 four issues.

Intended audience: Government, industry, research and development and policy research

ENERGY POLICY covers the resources and capabilities of particular countries and regions and the increasing independence of their needs. It covers coal, oil, gas, nuclear, hydro and alternative energy sources. It draws together studies by technologists with those of economists, geographers, environmentalists and political scientists. The key foci of ENERGY POLICY are: economics, pricing, investment, forecasting, environment, comparative technologies, national and international politics, geography and transport. 88 pages. Published since 1973.

FASST NEWS

Editor: Student editors, contact Alan Ladwig, President

Publisher: Forum for the Advancement of Students in Science and Technology, Inc., 2030 M Street, N.W. No. 402, Washington, D.C. 20036, U.S.A.

Quarterly. $5 per year.

Intended audience: Individuals and organizations interested in science education and increased opportunities for student participation in science issues.

FASST NEWS serves its readers as a forum for the presentation and discussion of contemporary science issues, including the presentation of conflicting and minority viewpoints. Articles originate from students, press releases and periodicals, and from staff initiatives.

FOOTNOTES TO THE FUTURE

Editor: Darlene M. Hess

Publisher: Futuremics, Inc., 1629 K Street, N.W., Washington, D.C. 20008, U.S.A.

Monthly. $20 per year.

Intended audience: Futurists, business researchers and planners, educators

FOOTNOTES TO THE FUTURE calls attention to significant trends, presents summaries of future-oriented articles in current periodicals, brief notes on meetings, workshops and courses being conducted on future-related topics, short descriptions of new books in the futures field. 4 pages. Published since 1971.

FUTUR INFORMATIONS (Future Information)

Editor: Hugues de Jouvenel

Publisher: Futuribles, 55 rue de Varenne 75007, Paris, France

Monthly. Free to members of the Association Internationale Futuribles as well as (upon request) to selected persons who are engaged in futures studies.

Intended audience: Futurists, corporate planners, public administrators—researchers in general

FUTUR INFORMATIONS is a newsletter which is prepared in cooperation between the International Association FUTURIBLES, the journals FUTURIBLES and 2000 and the Fondation C. N. Ledoux pour les Reflexions sur le Futur (Ledoux Foundation for Thinking about the Future). The bulletin has as its goal the maintenance of contacts established by FUTURIBLES INTERNATIONAL with numerous futures studies groups in France and abroad as well as with the persons who are members of the international network of exchange we have been establishing since 1960. The newsletter is aimed at circulating information on activities related to the future (research programs, training programs, forthcoming conferences, major innovations and future-bearing facts and ideas). 4 pages. Published since 1973.

FUTURE-ABSTRACTS

Editor: Laura Bukkila and Kent Myers

Publisher: Futuremics, Inc., 1629 K Street, N.W., Washington, D.C. 20006, U.S.A.

Monthly. $295 per year, $110 for non-profit organizations and individuals.

Intended audience: Planners, researchers, educators, executives, policy makers, futurists

FUTURE-ABSTRACTS is devoted exclusively to the future. It provides subscribers with futures information and a concise system for accessing it. Included are publications, programs, organizations, data and people. Each abstract, approximately 400 words long, is printed on a 5" x 8" card. Subscriber also receives a file box and a set of tabs which constitute the classification and filing system. The majority of the abstracts are of books and other publications. Most are new titles, but classic works in the futures field are also included. 48 abstracts per issue. Published since 1975.

FUTURE and STARLOG

Editor: Howard Zimmerman

Publisher: Kerry O'Quinn and Norman Jacobs, 475 Park Avenue South, New York, New York 10016, U.S.A.

Eight times yearly. $10.98.

Intended audience: General

FUTURE is a four-color magazine concerned with optimistic future scenarios, space science, and science-fiction (films, TV, books). STARLOG is a four-color magazine concerned with film and television (especially science fiction and fantasy) and some space science. 80 pages. FUTURE published since 1978. STARLOG published since 1976.

FUTURE SURVEY

Editor: Michael Marien

Publisher: World Future Society, 4916 St. Elmo Avenue (Bethesda), Washington, D.C. 20014, U.S.A.

Monthly. $24 per year for WFS members; $36 per year for non-members and libraries.

Intended audience: Futurists, educators, business executives, researchers

Abstract journal covering books and articles just published or about to be published on subjects of special interest to futurists. Each issue covers some 150 abstracts. More than 100 English language periodicals are scanned each month for suitable articles for abstracting, and the book lists of more than 100 publishers are also consulted. Each monthly issue is indexed by subject and author, and cumulative annual indices are included in the subscription price. Abstracts are numbered for quick reference and grouped thematically within general categories to encourage browsing and suggest possible interrelationships.

FUTURES

Editor: Ralph Jones

Publisher: IPC Science and Technology Press Ltd., Westbury House, Bury Street, Guildford, GU2 5AW, England

Bimonthly. $65—individuals.

Intended audience: Academic researchers, policy makers, long-range planners in government, industry, and research

FUTURES covers the methods and practice of long-term forecasting and decision-making on social, economic, and technological questions. It also carries review articles, a science fiction survey, and short reports of work in progress. 88 pages. Published since 1968.

FUTURES CANADA

Editor: Richard L. Henshel

Publisher: Canadian Association for Futures Studies, 302 - 100 Gloucester St., Ottawa, Ontario, Canada K2P OA4

Quarterly. $12 per year.

Intended audience: Futurists and those with like interests

FUTURES CANADA includes news of the Canadian Association for Futures Studies, activities and events of interest to futurists, and several think-pieces. 15 pages. Published since 1976.

FUTURES INFORMATION INTERCHANGE

Editor: William B. Parent

Publisher: University of Massachusetts Future Studies Program, Futures Information Interchange, 162 Hills South, University of Massachusetts, Amherst, Massachusetts 01003, U.S.A.

Semiannual. $2 per year.

Intended audience: Teachers, college professors, government officials, students, general public

The FUTURES INFORMATION INTERCHANGE newsletter is a collection of practical teaching methods and learning activities for introducing future studies into the classroom. Although the newsletter is directed toward primary and secondary teachers, it is intended to be of value to educators at the preschool and university levels as well. The newsletter staff welcomes any specific materials related to future-oriented work in the classroom. 35 pages. Published since 1972.

FUTURES RESEARCH INSTITUTE NEWSLETTER

Editor: Harold A. Linstone

Publisher: Futures Research Institute, P.O.B. 751, Portland State University, Portland, Oregon 97207, U.S.A.

Irregular frequency. No cost given.

Intended audience: Interested individuals and organizations

The newsletter contains news items, recent publications and Institute activities. 2 pages.

FUTURESCOPE

Editor: Raymond Peyton Ewing

Publisher: Kenilworth Institute, 316 Richmond Road, Kenilworth, Illinois 60043, U.S.A.

Twice a year at present, quarterly later. Cost not given.

Intended audience: Business, professional, civic and private persons interested in public policy issues

Highlights future studies, issues, groups which might have impact on the development of public policy. The purpose is to "encourage greater participation of citizens in public policy debate." 4 pages. Published since 1976.

FUTURIBLERNE (Futuribles)

Editor: Board of Danish Future Society

Publisher: Danish Future Society, Sobo Lokker 22, 5683 Haarby, Denmark

Quarterly. 125 Danish kroner

Intended audience: Members of the Danish Future Society

FUTURIBLERNE aims at publishing articles on theoretical and practical aspects of futures research written by leading futurists in Denmark and elsewhere. Recent issues have been on special topics such as: the crisis of legitimacy, hearings on the conditions for east-west transport in Denmark, hearings on the use of gas from the North Sea and on social innovations. 30 pages. Published since 1968.

FUTURIBLES—Analyse—Prevision—Prospective (Futuribles—Analysis—Forecasting—Futures)

Editor: Hugues de Jouvenel

Publisher: Association Internationale Futuribles, 55 rue de Varenne, 75007 Paris, France

Bimonthly. $42.

Intended audience: Executives in business and administration as well as researchers, especially in the future field

The objective of this publication is to provide information, opinions and a platform for reflection on the major problems and choices which might have an impact on the future. The accent is placed on applied futures studies rather than on theoretical studies, although one does not exclude the other. The review addresses itself to problems related to development and growth, quality of life, life-styles, etc. The publication favors pluridisciplinary approaches and insists on diversity in terms of writers' origins (ideology, country, speciality) and topics. One objective is to fill the gap between academic people and practitioners, public and private sectors, French and foreign experiences.

The publication consists of three main parts: articles on major problems and developments which are deemed important for the future, "forum previsionnel"—designed to inform readers about the principal events of interest for the future and to serve as a platform for exchange of opinions about the future, and bibliography. 128 pages. Published since 1975. Created to take the place of the reviews "Analyse et Prevision" (created in 1966) and "Prospectives" (created in 1970).

FUTURICS: A QUARTERLY JOURNAL OF FUTURES RESEARCH

Editor: Scott W. Erickson

Publisher: The Minnesota Futurists, 900 Minnesota Building, St. Paul, Minnesota 55101, U.S.A.

Quarterly. No cost given.

Intended audience: Futurists in the United States and elsewhere

FUTURICS is a quarterly refereed journal which seeks to facilitate communication between researchers, writers and others who are interested in the exploration of alternative futures. Besides articles, the journal prints reactions to articles and ideas, short notes on matters of interest, book reviews and reviews of developments in the field. FUTURICS invites manuscripts from new as well as experienced authors. Since the summer issue of 1978, FUTURICS is being published for the Minnesota Futurists by Pergamon Press. 60 pages. Published since 1976.

FUTURIFIC

Editor: Balint Szent-Miklosy

Publisher: Balint Szent-Miklosy, 150 Haven Avenue, New York, New York 10032, U.S.A.

Monthly. $9 per year. $16 for two years. $21 for three years.

Intended audience: Futurists and the general public

Eight pages. Published since January 1977.

THE FUTURIST

Editor: Edward S. Cornish

Publisher: The World Future Society, 4916 St. Elmo Avenue (Bethesda), Washington, D.C. 20014, U.S.A.

Bimonthly. $18 per year for individuals; $21 for libraries.

Intended audience: People interested in the future

This journal, which has the largest circulation of all future-oriented journals (50,000), reports forecasts made by scientists and others concerning the coming years; explores the possible consequences of these developments on the individual, institutions, and society; and discusses what actions people may take to improve the future. 64 pages, plus cover. Published since 1967.

FUTUROLOGY AND PHILOSOPHY OF TECHNICS

Editor: Manes Fromer

Publisher: Research Center of Futurology and Philosophy of Technics, 46/4 Aronovitz Street, Holon, Israel

Twice yearly. $3 per year.

Intended audience: Scientists, universities, philosophers, futurologists

Recent articles in this publication were on the subject of the three great technological revolutions and the fourth—the spiritual; the biotechnical revolution and the future of sex; and the end of the capitalist-communist era. 36 pages. Published since 1968.

FUTURONTO QUARTERLY

Editor: Frank Feather

Publisher: FUTURONTO, INC., 1207 Linbrook Road, Oakville, Ontario, Canada L6J 2L5

Quarterly. $36 per year (bulk rates on request).

Intended audience: Futurists, planners, business managers, academics, general systems practitioners

FUTURONTO QUARTERLY is a journal covering business planning and management topics which are relevant to the future and are supportable by an open general systems approach to the evolving environment. Its objectives are to provide meaningful and applicable material for practicing managers and business educators. Also publishes results of research projects, programs and activities contracted by FUTURONTO, INC., a futuristic business planning and consulting firm. 36 pages. Published since 1975.

THE GREEN REVOLUTION

Editor: Rari Hok Wats

Publisher: The School of Living, RD 7, Box 388A, York, Pennsylvania 17402, U.S.A.

Monthly, except July and January. $8 per year with School of Living annual membership of $12.

Intended audience: Everyone concerned in humanizing humanity

This periodical consists generally of two-page articles on various problems; contains letters to the editor, book reviews, etc. 36 to 40 pages. Published since 1943.

THE HASTINGS CENTER REPORT

Editor: Margaret O'Brien Steinfels

Publisher: Institute of Society, Ethics and the Life Sciences, 360 Broadway, Hastings-on-Hudson, New York 10706, U.S.A.

Bimonthly. $19 individuals and libraries, $15 full-time students, $30 institutions.

Intended audience: All persons interested in ethical, legal and social implications of advances in the life sciences

The REPORT is devoted entirely to discussions of bioethics. It contains brief, timely articles on new developments, longer essays, reviews, scholarly articles, a regular guide to the most recent literature, specific case studies and a calendar of events across the country. Some of the topics treated include behavior control (psychotropic drugs, psychosurgery, etc.), genetic counseling, genetic engineering, the right to die, abortion, experimentation, research, and population policy. 48 pages. Published since 1970.

IL FUTURO DELL'UOMO (The Future of Man)

Editor: Alessandro Dall'Olio

Publisher: Associazione Teilhard de Chardin: Centro de Ricerca, per il Futuro dell'Uomo (Teilhard de Chardin Association, Research Center for the Future of Man), c/o Instituto Stensen, Firenze, Italy 50129

Quarterly. 4000 Italian lire.

Intended audience: General

This publication, reflecting the interests of the Italian admirers of Father Pierre Teilhard de Chardin, contains both serious articles and book reviews dealing with the broad issues of the human future. 50 pages.

IMPACT OF SCIENCE ON SOCIETY

Editor: Jacques Richardson

Publisher: United Nations Educational, Scientific and Cultural Organization, 7 place de Fontenoy, 75700 Paris, France

Quarterly. $9.50 per year.

Intended audience: People interested in the interface between science-technology and society

This quarterly journal, published in five different language editions (Arabic, English, French, Portuguese and Spanish), offers (1) a dialogue between scientists/engineers and laymen, (2) a continuous transfer of information between the technically advanced and the industrially developing nations, and (3) a constructive guide to understanding an increasingly science-based environment. 100 pages. Published since 1950.

IMPORTANT FOR THE FUTURE

Editor: Joseph Barnea

Publisher: United Nations Institute for Training and Research, 801 United Nations Plaza, New York, New York 10017, U.S.A.

Averages five times a year. $12 yearly.

Intended audience: Policy-makers in international organizations, governments, institutions and companies

Comments and opinion include short articles on developments in the field of natural resources as well as related areas significant for the future. 15 pages. Published since 1975.

INSIGHT

Editor: Courtney A. Stadd

Publisher: National Space Institute, 1911 N. Fort Myer Drive, Suite 408, Arlington, Virginia 22209, U.S.A.

Monthly. National Space Institute members: $15 yearly to adults, $9 to students (18 or younger).

Intended audience: General public

An 8½ x 11 inch, illustrated publication which (1) provides a forum for informed debate on the space program, (2) summarizes the facts and status of particular space issues, (3) includes commentaries from prominent people in the space community, (4) lists space briefs on the more significant space happenings and on NSI news, (5) letters from NSI members, (6) other features. 12 pages. Published since 1975.

INTERFUTURE REPORTS

Editor: Carol-June Cassidy

Publisher: InterFuture, 420 Lexington Avenue, New York, New York 10017, U.S.A.

Annually. $15 including membership in InterFuture Associates.

Intended audience: Students, academics and professionals in intercultural future studies

Reports from undergraduate InterFuture Scholars on their researches on aspects of internationalism, habitat, and individual-and-society in Europe, Africa, and the Caribbean. 25 pages. Published since 1974.

INTERNATIONAL DEVELOPMENT REVIEW

Editor: Andrew E. Rice

Publisher: Society for International Development, International Headquarters, Palazzo Civilta del Lavoro, EUR 00144 Rome, Italy

Quarterly. $12 per year for libraries. Individuals receive only as a part of membership in Society for International Development.

Intended audience: Professionals on Third World and global development problems

Contains articles, book reviews and lists, media commentary, professional news notes. Articles appear in English, French or Spanish with summaries in the other two languages. 80 pages. Published since 1959.

INTERNATIONAL JOURNAL OF GENERAL SYSTEMS

Editor: George J. Klir

Publisher: Gordon and Breach Science Publishers Ltd., 42 William IV street, London WC 2 England or One Park Avenue, New York, New York 10016, U.S.A.

Quarterly. $86.50 yearly.

Intended audience: Academicians and professionals in various disciplines

The journal is currently a source of information concerning advancements in the emerging field of systems problem solving. It covers general problem areas such as systems analysis and design, modeling and simulation, systems complexity and simplification, as well as problems associated with various classes of systems such as adaptive, self-organizing, self-producing or learning systems. Applications of systems thinking and methodology in various areas such as management, engineering, biological and social sciences are particularly emphasized. Also covered are the various aspects of systems education. 64 pages. Published since 1974.

JOURNAL OF SOCIAL POLICY

Editor: R.A. Pinker

Publisher: Cambridge University Press, 32 East 57th Street, New York, New York 10022, U.S.A.

Quarterly. $49 yearly for institutions, $30 for individuals.

Intended audience: Scholars and professionals

A source of information for scholars and professionals in the field of public policy on the development and implementation of public programs in income maintenance, social security, health education, housing and urban planning, social services, income redistribution and social change. Provides a critical analysis of controversies and issues in public policy viewed in cross-national terms. 130 pages. Published since 1972.

JOURNAL OF THE AMERICAN PLANNING ASSOCIATION

Editor: Kenneth Pearlman

Publisher: American Planning Association, 1776 Massachusetts Avenue, N.W., Washington, D.C. 20036, U.S.A.

Quarterly. $18 yearly U.S.A., $22 foreign.

Intended audience: Professional planners, professors of planning and others interested in the development of planning theory

The JOURNAL OF THE AMERICAN PLANNING ASSOCIATION discusses the newest trends and ideas in comprehensive planning and the environmental and social issues affecting urban areas, as well as many other areas of concern to persons interested in the field of urban problem solving. 112 pages. Published since 1925. Formerly the JOURNAL OF THE AMERICAN INSTITUTE OF PLANNERS.

LEEDS FUTURE STUDIES CENTRE NEWSLETTER

Editor: Roland Chaplain

Publisher: Future Studies Centre, 15 Kelso Road, Leeds LS2 9PR, United Kingdom

Bimonthly. $10 per year.

Intended audience: Broad-based

The newsletter usually consists of two pages of introduction about current work at the Centre plus topical issues. The last three or four pages are in the form of a diary of events—local, national, international. A lot of information is packed into the rest of the newsletter—particularly contacts, newsletters, and publications for our reference library. Focus is primarily on intermediate/soft technology in relation to the growing worldwide dialogue between environment and consumer groups, futurists and long-range planners, and workers, trade unions and management in industry about alternative ranges of more desirable products and services both socially and environmentally. Direct involvement of the public in future studies will be particularly stressed. 13 pages. Published since 1974. Bimonthly since September, 1977.

L'HOMME ET L'HUMANITE (Man and Humanity)

Editor: Joseph Foray

Publisher: Federation pour le respect de l'homme et de l'humanite (Federation for the Respect of Man and Humanity), 40 boulevard de Bonne Nouvelle, 75010 Paris, France

Quarterly. 120 French francs.

Intended audience: French readers interested in the relations between Occidental and Non-Occidental worlds

L'HOMME ET L'HUMANITE is the successor to the bulletin of the Centre de Reflexion sur le Monde Non-Occidental (Center for the Non-Occidental World) and presents editorials, viewpoints on various continents, United Nations chronicle, reports on specific international events, positions and propositions, a bibliography and readers mail. 36 pages. Published since 1974.

LONG RANGE PLANNING JOURNAL

Editor: Bernard Taylor

Publisher: Pergamon Press Limited, Headington Hill Hall, Oxford, England 64881

Bimonthly. $90 per year.

Intended audience: Senior managers in industry, administrators in government and academics, and research workers in universities and research groups on an international basis

LONG RANGE PLANNING aims to focus the attention of senior managers, administrators, and academics on the concepts and techniques involved in the development of strategy and the generation of long-range plans. 112 pages. Published since 1968.

MANAGERIAL PLANNING

Editor: Henry C. Doofe

Publisher: Planning Executives Institute, 5500 College Corner Pike (P.O. Box 70), Oxford, Ohio 45056, U.S.A.

Bimonthly. $15 per year.

Intended audience: Corporate and financial planners; budgeters

The objective of MANAGERIAL PLANNING is to promote and disseminate knowledge and information concerning the broad field of managerial planning, budgeting and related disciplines. 40 pages. Published since 1954.

THE NEW ECOLOGIST

Editor: Nicholas Hildyard and Ruth Lumley-Smith

Publisher: Goldsmith, Ecosystems, 73 Molesworth Street, Wadebridge, Cornwall, United Kingdom PL27 7DS

Bimonthly. $9 per year. Joint subscription with THE ECOLOGIST QUARTERLY $16.

Intended audience: Aims at a wider audience than the parent paper with special reference to students and all those engaged worldwide with ecopolitical movements which seek to prompt a saner, less rapacious and more stable ecological future. 36 pages. Previously published as THE ECOLOGIST from 1970 to 1977.

NEW YORK PLANNING REVIEW

Editor: Samuel R. Mozes

Publisher: American Planning Association, 86-10 34th Avenue, Jackson Heights, New York 11372, U.S.A.

Three times yearly. $10 per year to non-members.

Intended audience: Professional planners and related professions

Literary and theoretical publication on urban and regional planning for members of the American Planning Association and other interested subscribers. Features an extensive book review section, with contributors from many states and foreign countries. Strong emphasis on international planning. 100 pages. Published since 1958.

"NEWS CENTER" (Section of ALTERNATIVE FUTURES: THE JOURNAL OF UTOPIAN STUDIES)

Editor: Kenneth M. Roemer (Spring/Fall); Dennis Livingston (Summer/Winter)

Publisher: Rensselaer Polytechnic Institute and the University of Michigan, Human Dimensions Center, Rensselaer Polytechnic Institute, Troy, New York, 12181, U.S.A.

Quarterly. $8.50 for ALTERNATIVE FUTURES.

Intended audience: Scholars and students interested in utopian studies and futures studies.

"NEWS CENTER" began as a separate publication in 1975 (UTOPUS DISCOVERED). In 1978 the newsletter became a feature of ALTERNATIVE FUTURES. In the Spring and Fall, Kenneth Roemer surveys scholarship and conventions relating to utopian studies; in the Summer and Winter, Dennis Livingston surveys publications relating to humanistic futures studies. 10 pages. UTOPUS DISCOVERED published since 1975. "NEWS CENTER" published since 1978.

ORIENTERING OM FREMTIDSFORSKNING

Editor: Torben Bo Jansen

Publisher: Instituttet for Fremtidsforskning (Institute for Futures Studies), Vester Farimagsgade 3, DK-1606 Copenhagen V, Denmark
Six issues annually. $25.50 per year (175 Danish kroner).

Intended audience: Published in Danish as it is solely intended for Scandinavia

ORIENTERING OM FREMTIDSFORSKNING contains abstracts from periodicals/journals concerning futures research, short articles, information on forecasting concerning Danish, Swedish and Norwegian conditions. 80-90 pages. Published since 1974.

PASS-AGE: A FUTURES JOURNAL

Editor: Robert Kahn, Timothy Wessels

Publisher: Earth Metabolic Design, Inc., 431 S. 45th St., Philadelphia, Pennsylvania 19104, U.S.A.

Annual. Price varies per issue.

Intended audience: Educators, futurists

PASS-AGE explores the future, while considering challenges to human society in the present. PASS-AGE is committed to a humane investigation of future possibilities; it hopes that its explorations will challenge others to enter into the futures dialogue. Includes essays, speeches, interviews, poetry, drawings and photography. 100 pages. Published since 1975.

PATTERNS

Editor: Carl Townsend

Publisher: Center for the Study of the Future, 4110 N.E. Alameda, Portland, Oregon 97212, U.S.A.

Bimonthly. $10 per year, U.S.; $13 per year, foreign.

Intended audience: Church leaders

Future-oriented newsletter for Christians studying the future and how the Body of Christ should relate to it. 8 pages. Published since 1973.

PLANNING

Editor: Sylvia Lewis

Publisher: American Planning Association (formerly American Society of Planning Officials), 1313 E. 60th Street, Chicago, Illinois 60637, U.S.A.

12 times per year. Varies from $20 to $40.

Intended audience: City planners, government officials, students, citizen planners

PLANNING includes news, feature articles and book reviews related to city planning, urban affairs and the environment. Although the articles are sometimes of technical nature, they can usually be read by a general audience. 48 pages.

PLANNING REVIEW

Editor: Robert J. Allio

Publisher: Bell PubliCom, 1406 Third National Building, Dayton, Ohio 45402, U.S.A.

Bimonthly. $30 per year.

Intended audience: Managerial decision-makers

PLANNING REVIEW seeks to publish significant and useful articles dealing with the broad field of long-range planning. Manuscripts which discuss new developments in planning theory and practice are included. Also, applications of management science and behavioral science to planning and planning implementation, evaluation of major economic, social, political, and technological trends and forces, developments in merger and acquisition theory and practice. The submittal of original research or analysis and case studies is encouraged. 32 pages. Published since 1972.

POLICY SCIENCES

Editor: Thomas J. Anton

Publisher: Elsevier Scientific Publishing Company, P.O. Box 330, Amsterdam, The Netherlands
Bimonthly. $81.75, institutions; $26.65, personal.

Intended audience: International, systems analysis, policy analysts, policy scientists

POLICY SCIENCES is an international journal devoted to the development and creation of policy scientific approaches to decision-making, management, and social science research (applications, theories, methods). Forecasting counts heavily in these considerations. 130 pages. Published since 1970.

POLICY STUDIES JOURNAL

Editor: Stuart S. Nagel

Publisher: Policy Studies Organization, 361 Lincoln Hall, University of Illinois, Urbana, Illinois 61801, U.S.A.

Quarterly. $10 per year to individuals, $20 per year to libraries and institutions.

Intended audience: Political and social scientists. Also policy-makers and policy-appliers

THE POLICY STUDIES JOURNAL is designed to provide coverage of various public policy topics from political and social science perspective. It is a quarterly primarily consisting of a symposium in each issue on an important policy topic such as environmental protection, poverty, electoral reform, criminal justice, foreign affairs, urban problems, policy analysis, economic regulation, civil liberties, research utilization, education, policy administration, legislative reform, transportation, housing, teaching policy studies, minorities, health, population, policy theory, and food policy. Each issue also contains non-symposium articles, literature reviews, and news concerning policy studies. 150 pages. Published since 1972.

POLSKA 2000 (Poland 2000)

Editor: Antoni Rajkiewicz

Publisher: Ossolineum--–Publishing House of the Polish Academy of Sciences, Palac Kultury i Nauki, Room 2022, Warsaw, Poland 00-901

Irregular—3 or 4 issues per year. Each issue has a different cost.

Intended audience: Scientists and scientific centers, ministries and other institutions, especially government institutions interested in planning and prognostication

This Bulletin contains mainly the results of works of The Research and Prognostics Committee and its commissions, concerning the socioeconomic, health education and cultural development, raw material resources and theory and methodology of prognostication. Published in Polish language, special issues in English and Russian languages. 100 to 400 pages. Published since 1970.

PRACE NAUKOZNAWCZE I PROGNOSTYCZNE (Papers on Science of Science and Forecasting)

Editor: Boleslaw Iwaszkiewicz

Publisher: Politechnika Wroclawska, Wybrzeze Wyspianskiego 27, Wroclaw, Poland 53-370
Quarterly. $2 (40 Polish zloty).

Intended audience: Scientists

This periodical is concerned with science-of-science problems, theory and methodology of science, sociology and psychology of science, management and control of research, technological forecasting, methodology of forecasting, systems and methods of technological forecasting.

Each issue encompasses 5 or 6 papers in Polish, Russian, and English, communications and report notes from the conferences on forecasting sponsored by Polish and foreign research centres, provides book reviews and presents a current analytical bibliography of more interesting papers and books on scientific technological forecasting. 120 pages. Published since 1972.

PRACTICING PLANNER

Editor: Allan A. Hodges, AICP

Publisher: American Planning Association, 1776 Massachusetts Avenue, N.W., Washington, D.C. 20036, U.S.A.

Bimonthly. $15 per year in U.S., $20 overseas.

Intended audience: Professional urban planners, planning commissioners, other municipal and citizen officials interested in land use and planning

PRACTICING PLANNER is a news and feature magazine highlighting what is now happening in the planning field. The material is often presented in case study form. Also, there is coverage of new planning tools and techniques from a how-to-do-it point of view. News in the field is covered and there is a regular legal column which discusses selected cases dealing with issues of growth management. 48 pages. Publication began in 1976. To be merged in July, 1979 with PLANNING (formerly published by the American Society of Planning Officials) as a new monthly magazine published by the new American Planning Association.

PROGNOS EURO-REPORT (Future Trends in Western Europe)

Editor: Aloys Schwietert with permanent research group

Publisher: Prognos AG, Basel, Viaduktstrasse 65, 4000 Basel, Switzerland
Annual. 2,000 Swiss francs.

Intended audience: Company planners, market researchers, planners in government authorities

PROGNOS EURO-REPORT contains the annually updated and revised economic forecasts of PROGNOS for 14 Western European countries and for the United States. It provides a systematic quantitative basis for planning by both private business and associations and government authorities. The report offers forecasts for the next five and ten years on prices, exchange rates, production, employment and productivity (broken down by sectors), private income and expenditure, public expenditure and taxes, investment, exports, imports, population and household data. 480 pages. Published since 1971.

PROGNOSZTIKA (PROGNOSTICS)

Editor: Grolmusz Vince

Publisher: MTA Tudomanyszervezesi Csoport (Institute for Science Organization of the Hungarian Academy of Sciences), Munnich Ferenc utca 18. 1051 Budapest, Hungary

Quarterly. No cost given.

Intended audience: Research managers, research workers, science managers, heads of scientific and educational institutions, planning organizations

PROGNOSZTIKA presents the newest methods and results of forecasting and gives reviews on the Hungarian and international special literature. Gives an opportunity for Hungarian—and sometimes for foreign—representatives of forecasting research to publish papers on their own subject in any field of forecasting. 60 pages. Published since 1969.

RESOURCES

Editor: Joan Tron

Publisher: Resources for the Future, 1755 Massachusetts Avenue, N.W., Washington, D.C. 20036, U.S.A.

Three times a year. Sent at no cost upon request.

Intended audience: General

A bulletin published three times a year, featuring selected brief articles dealing with Resources for the

Future's areas of interest (environment, natural resources, etc.). The views reflected are those of individual staff members and not official points of view adopted by Resources for the Future. 12 pages. Published since 1964.

RESOURCES POLICY

Editor: Lyndon Driscoll

Publisher: IPC Science and Technology Press Ltd., Westbury House, Bury Street, Guildford, Surrey GU2 5AW, United Kingdom

Quarterly. $104 (40 pounds)

Intended audience: Mining engineers, economic geologists, economists, recycling technologists

The journal publishes original manuscripts on the issues affecting future supply of and demand for non-renewable (non-energy) resources. Topics covered include the extent of natural resources and future exploitation; the effects of trading agreements on availability of resources; the role of developing nations; the economics and effects of recycling. Contents also include a current literature survey ("resources reading"); book reviews; and a calendar of related conferences and seminars. 80 pages. Published since 1974.

REVUE 2000

Editor: Gritti Haumont

Publisher: Documentation Francaise (French Government's Printing Office), 55 rue de Varenne, Paris, France

Quarterly. $9.95 yearly (46 French francs).

Intended audience: General

A well-illustrated journal designed for a broad audience. Issues focus on various aspects of the future—transportation, cities, water, waste, etc. 64 pages. Published since 1967.

THE SAGA JOURNAL

Editor: Michael J. Raymond

Publisher: Michael J. Raymond, 4833 Greentree Road, Lebanon, Ohio 45036, U.S.A.

Quarterly. No longer subscription based—sent free to contributors of games, simulations, articles, and reviews for sharing with members.

Intended audience: Educators and game designers

THE SAGA JOURNAL is the chief publication of the Simulation and Gaming Association. "Our basic aim is to provide teachers with low cost educational games for use in their classrooms. Our magazine features teacher designed games and simulations, reviews, evaluation guides, and general interest articles related to educational gaming." 24 pages. Published since 1972.

SCENARIO: A Futures Journal for Educators

Editor: John R. Eggers

Publisher: University of Northern Iowa, UNI Educational Services Center, 120 East State Street, Mason City, Iowa 50401, U.S.A.

Quarterly. $8 per year

Intended audience: Kindergarten-12 classroom teachers, school administrators, higher education

SCENARIO is intended to help educators help youth develop futuristic competencies via futuristic-educational programs and practices. The journal maintains an active advisory board of 10 members who are all involved in varying educational-futures related projects at the K-12 level. Regular features include a "Moon School Report" (school or program involved in implementing futures activities for students), "Future-Scope" (societal trends having educational implications), "Futures Yellow Pages" (human and non-human futures-educational resources), futuristic classroom activities, and essays by futurists-educators. 36 pages. Published since Spring of 1977.

SCIENCE-FICTION STUDIES

Editor: Marc Angenot, Robert M. Philmus, Darko Suvin

Publisher: Darko Suvin, English Department, McGill University, Montreal, Quebec, Canada H3A 2T6

Three times yearly. $8 to United States (surface); $12 to United States (air mail) (50% higher for libraries and other institutions).

Intended audience: People with a serious interest in science fiction

SCIENCE-FICTION STUDIES is a journal devoted to publishing studies, from a variety of perspectives (literary, scientific, sociological, philosophical, etc.), of important science fiction texts and significant science fiction writers. Subscription requests, accompanied by the appropriate remittance, may be sent to: Robert M. Philmus, Department of English, Loyola Campus, Concordia University, Montreal, Quebec, Canada H4B 1R6. 100 pages. Published since 1973.

SEFREM KONTAKT (Newsletter of the Norwegian Society for Future Studies)

Editor: Daniel Liseth

Publisher: Norwegian Society for Future Studies (SEFREM), Box 8231 Hammersborg, Teatergaten 1, Oslo 1, Norway.

Monthly. $20 per year (100 Norwegian kroner).

Intended audience: Members of the Society, press, radio, television

Information on the activities of the Society, abstracts on future studies in Norway and the Scandinavian countries but also Europe and U.S.A. Averages 10 pages. Read also in Sweden and Denmark. Published since 1973.

SIMULATION

Editor: Natalie Fowler, Managing Editor

Publisher: The Society for Computer Simulation (Simulation Councils, Inc.), P.O. Box 2228, La Jolla, California 92038, U.S.A.

Monthly. $38 per year. $25 to members.

Intended audience: Anyone involved in simulation and allied computer arts in all fields

SIMULATION is a medium for exchange of information among simulators, and those concerned with simulation, around the world. It contains articles, surveys, tutorials, technical comments, and other smaller descriptions of theory and application of analog, hybrid, and digital techniques and equipment; application of all kinds of devices to the simulation of dynamic systems; theory, design, and application of simulation systems; and analog, digital, and hybrid computing software and simulation languages. 48 pages. Published since 1963.

SIMULATION IN THE SERVICE OF SOCIETY

Editor: John McLeod, Technical Editor; Suzette McLeod, Managing Editor

Publisher: Society for Computer Simulation, P.O. Box 2228, La Jolla, California 92037, U.S.A.

Monthly. Contact the Society for Computer Simulation for membership requirements and subscription rates.

Intended audience: General

Subjects of this newsletter are selected to cover the latest, most pertinent information available for scientists and laymen who are concerned with societal problems which can be most intelligently attacked if leaders have the improved insight obtainable through computer modeling and simulation. Contains articles, abstracts, book reviews, bibliographies. Appears monthly as a regular feature of SIMULATION, technical journal of the Society for Computer Simulation. Non-technical. 4 pages. Published since 1971.

SOCIAL ALTERNATIVES

Editor: Ralph V. Summy, Margaret Smith, Bruce Dickson

Publisher: Social Alternatives, Department of External Studies, University of Queensland, St. Lucia, Queensland, Australia 4067

Quarterly. $8 per year for individual (Australian); $12 for institution (Australian).

Intended audience: Progressive-minded intellectuals and activists

SOCIAL ALTERNATIVES seeks to break outside the conventional means by which social problems are defined, social policies formulated, strategies designed, and solutions put into effect. The major emphasis of the journal is on the development of alternative proposals to effect social change towards greater freedom, equality, and democracy. While emphasizing such alternatives there is no intention of denying the importance of clarifying the theoretical framework by which social and political issues are discerned and examined. 80 pages. Published since 1978.

SOCIAL INDICATORS NEWSLETTER

Editor: Nancy McManus

Publisher: Social Science Research Council Center for Coordination of Research on Social Indicators, 1755 Massachusetts Avenue, N.W., Washington, D.C. 20036, U.S.A.

Irregular. No charge.

Intended audience: Academics, government officials and others engaged in research on and application of social indicators

The newsletter is about research on social indicators. Its publication is one of the functions for which the Center for Social Indicators was established by the Social Science Research Council in September 1972 under a grant from the Division of Social Sciences of the National Science Foundation. Covers research on social indicators—books, articles, and unpublished writings—and research-related activities such as conferences and sessions at professional meetings. Reports are included on ongoing work and research plans of individuals, organizations, and institutions active in the field, and on problems in indicators research and plans for their resolution. 8 pages. Published since 1973.

SOCIAL INDICATORS RESEARCH

Editor: Alex C. Michalos

Publisher: D. Reidel Publishing Company, P.O. Box 17, Dordrecht, Holland

Quarterly, $20 individual. $60 institution.

Intended audience: Social scientists, policy-makers

SOCIAL INDICATORS RESEARCH describes itself as "An International and Interdisciplinary Journal for Quality-of-Life Measurement." It intends to serve as a "central clearing house" for research dealing with descriptive, evaluative and prescriptive problems related to the measurement of the quality of life. Since the United Nations took an active interest in the 1950s in measuring "levels of living," there has been an increasing amount of research in this field. These days, the field of investigation that the United Nations designated by "levels of living" is more likely to be called the area of social indicators, social reporting, social systems accounting, social bookkeeping or quality-of-life measurement. It is this multi-named and enormously complex area, or set of areas, to which this journal is devoted. 125 pages. Published since 1974.

SOCIAL POLICY

Editor: Frank Riessman

Publisher: Alan Gartner, 33 West 42nd Street, Room 1212, New York, New York 10036, U.S.A.

Five times yearly. $10 per year for individual, $15 for institution.

Intended audience: Those interested in social policy and social change

Deals with social policy, especially in the areas of human services, social change, economics, education, government, health, sexism, race. Regular movie and book reviews. 64 pages. Published since 1970.

SYSTEM DYNAMICS NEWSLETTER

Editor: —

Publisher: System Dynamics Group, Massachusetts Institute of Technology, Building E40-253, Cambridge, Massachusetts 02139, U.S.A.

Annual. $2.75 (plus $0.36 per copy for U.S. postage; overseas orders must include $1.25 surface mailing charge or $5.50 airmail charge per copy ordered).

Intended audience: Persons interested in system dynamics, teachers, and practitioners

The SYSTEM DYNAMICS NEWSLETTER provides information about a wide range of investigations, teaching activities, and applications within the emerging system dynamics profession, as well as facilitating and stimulating communication among system dynamics practitioners. It also furnishes an updated bibliography of books, articles, and theses which deal with topics in system dynamics. 90 pages. Published since 1963.

SZF-BULLETIN (Bulletin of the Swiss Association for Future Research)

Editor: Gerhard Kocher

Publisher: Schweizerische Vereinigung fuer Zukunftsforschung, Weinbergstrasse 17, Wetzikon, Switzerland, CH—8623

Bimonthly. For members only (60 Swiss francs).

Intended audience: All interested in future and futures research

(1) Informs on all futures research in Switzerland and selected futures research abroad. (2) Summarizes all forecasts on Switzerland. (3) Each BULLETIN contains a Swiss bibliography on futures research and planning. (4) Contains a list of articles on those subjects which have been published in Swiss newspapers and journals. (5) Contains a title list of foreign reviews on futures research. (6) Most articles are in German, some are in French or in English. (7) Special subjects. 20 pages. Published since 1972.

TECHNOLOGICAL FORECASTING AND SOCIAL CHANGE

Editor: Harold A. Linstone

Publisher: Elsevier North Holland, Inc., 52 Vanderbilt Avenue, New York, New York 10017, U.S.A.

Quarterly. Two volumes in four issues for $92 (institutions).

Intended audience: Scientists, scholars and others interested in technological forecasting and social change.

An international journal devoted to the methodology of exploratory and normative forecasting to encourage applications to dynamic, integrative planning. Published since 1969.

TECHNOLOGY FORECASTS AND TECHNOLOGY SURVEYS

Editor: Irwin Stambler

Publisher: Willard Wilks, Suite 208, 205 S. Beverly Drive, Beverly Hills, California 90212, U.S.A.

Monthly. $79 per year in United States, $81 in Canada.

Intended audience: Technology and management forecasters, organization planners, scientific and technical managers

Presents news of developments in forecasting methodology, news of forecasting organizations, results of various technological forecast studies, information about major developments in technology that might prove significant to future application trends. 15 pages. Published since 1969.

TECHNOLOGY TOMORROW

Editor: Gary Sycalik

Publisher: The World Future Society, 4916 St. Elmo Avenue (Bethesda), Washington, D.C. 20014, U.S.A.

Bimonthly. $9 for Society members; $12 for non-members.

Intended audience: Persons interested in the future of technology

Newsletter containing signed articles dealing with specific aspects of technology's future. Also includes news items, listings of references, occasional book reviews, summaries of events, and miscellaneous notes of interest. As an amalgamation of several previous newsletters, *Technology Tomorrow* reports on a broad range of disciplines, including communications, food, habitats, health, and resources. 8 to 12 pages. Published since 1976.

THINKING ABOUT THE FUTURE

Editor: Geoffrey N. Calvert

Publisher: Alexander & Alexander Inc., 1211 Avenue of the Americas, New York, New York 10036, U.S.A.

Semi-annually. Free on request.

Intended audience: Business executives, congressmen, universities, libraries

Each issue of THINKING ABOUT THE FUTURE contains one comprehensive carefully researched article about a topic of major importance for the future. 12 pages. Published since 1975.

THRESHOLDS AND TURNINGPOINTS

Editor: David C. Miller

Publisher: David C. Miller, 908 Fox Plaza, San Francisco, California 94102

Monthly. $10 for students; $20 for individuals; $40 for organizations (prepaid only).

Intended audience: Corporate planners, managers, related professions

T&T tracks societal trends. Each issue contains about 100 items, which are concise (10-15 words), with sources given for followup. 4 pages. Published since 1979.

TREND

Editor: Pavel Alexander

Publisher: Center for Information in Science, Technology and Economics, Konviktska 5, Prague 1, Czechoslovakia 113 57

Bimonthly. No cost given.

Intended audience: Professional forecasters and planners in state and economic management, industry, schools

This publication contains a) original articles on methodology of social, economic, science and technology forecasting by Czechoslovak forecasters, articles summarizing results of forecasts; b) information about methodological literature all over the world (articles, books, studies) in form of referents and annotations; c) occasional reports about home events (meetings, etc.) in forecasting. 48 pages. Published since 1969.

TREND DISCONTINUITIES

Editor: Dale W. Steffes

Publisher: Planning and Forecasting Consultants, 908 Town and Country Blvd., Suite 120, Houston, Texas 77024, U.S.A.

Irregular. No charge.

Intended audience: Strategic leaders, selected by Planning and Forecasting Consultants

Planning and Forecasting Consultants issues a trend discontinuity report when it observes an irregularity. The intention is to receive back some information on the concept. This is in a sense a testing of the concept, to determine if it is valid. One page. Published since 1974.

THE TREND REPORT

Editor: -—

Publisher: Center for Policy Process, 1755 Massachusetts Avenue, N.W., Washington, D.C. 20036, U.S.A.

Three times a year. $10,000 annually.

Intended audience: Corporations, government agencies, social institutions

THE TREND REPORT is a forecast and evaluation of social and economic developments in the United States, based on a daily content analysis of the major newspapers in the United States. 200 pages. Published since January 1974.

TURNING POINT NEWSLETTER

Editor: James Robertson

Publisher: TURNING POINT, 7 St. Ann's Villas, London W11 4RU, England

Semiannual, at present (February and September). No formal subscription.

498

Intended audience: Concerned people interested in social change and the post-industrial transition

Newsletter contains information about people, events, activities, publications, ideas, etc.

This newsletter is published by an international network of people whose individual concerns range very widely—environment, sex equality, Third World, disarmament, community politics, appropriate technology and alternatives in economics, health, education, agriculture, religion, etc.,—but who share a common feeling that mankind is at a turning point, with old values, old lifestyles and an old system of society breaking down, and new ones needing help to break through. 16 pages. Published since 1975.

URBAN FUTURES IDEA EXCHANGE

Editor: Laurence A. Alexander

Publisher: Alexander Research and Communications, Inc., 270 Madison Ave., Suite 1505, New York 10016

Bimonthly. $72.00 per year.

Intended audience: Persons interested in the future of urban areas.

URBAN FUTURES IDEA EXCHANGE examines the future, basically up to 20 years ahead, to report on technical, social, economic and other forces which will have an impact on urban areas. It evaluates these for their specific potential urban impacts and for when those impacts will be felt. It suggests strategies and tactics for effectively dealing with those forces and the trends they engender. 6 to 8 pages. Published since 1977.

WHAT'S NEXT?

Editor: Marilyn Gadzuk

Publisher: Congressional Clearinghouse on the Future, 3564 House Annex No. 2, Washington, D.C. 20515, U.S.A.

Monthly. $10 per year (individual); $15 per year (foreign); $50 per year institutional; no charge to members of Congress and staff.

Intended audience: U.S. Congress and staff; other interested persons and groups.

Information about futures research organizations, publications, activities, conferences, citizen participation projects, appropriate technology, etc., and about Capitol Hill activities related to the future. 12 pages. Published since April 1976.

WORKING PAPERS FOR A NEW SOCIETY

Editor: John Case, Managing Editor and Nancy Lyons

Publisher: Lawrence Baker, 4 Nutting Road, Cambridge, Massachusetts 02138, U.S.A.

Bimonthly. $15 per year.

Intended audience: Activists interested in political and public policy reform

WORKING PAPERS attempts to provide a platform for political action for the American left, and in doing so to stimulate meaningful reform. Its articles focus on strategies, reports, ideas, proposals, and interpretations of and for public policy and social change. 80 to 96 pages. Published since 1973.

WORLD FUTURES

Editor: Ervin Laszlo; Jib Fowles, Associate Editor

Publisher: Gordon and Breach, Box 125, University of Houston at Clear Lake City, Houston, Texas 77058, U.S.A.

Semiannually. $38 per year.

Intended audience: Futurists and those interested in the future of international relations and foreign affairs

WORLD FUTURES is dedicated to the clarification of humanity's options and improvement of its prospects through research and debate regarding issues of concern to all peoples. Open to diverse points of view and to various modes of inquiry, it recognizes the need to foster constructive and realistic assessments of the future, and to take all facets of human existence into account, the physical, technological and environmental, as well as the intellectual, ethical and spiritual. To appear initially twice yearly, WORLD FUTURES publishes articles, notes and comments, and book reviews in the field of international futures research and areas of related interest. 80 pages. To begin publishing in 1979.

WORLD FUTURE SOCIETY BULLETIN

Editor: Lane Jennings

Publisher: The World Future Society, 4916 St. Elmo Avenue, Washington, D.C. 20014, U.S.A.

Bimonthly. $12 per year.

Intended audience: Professional futurists, planners and educators

Written for people who have a special interest in the "how to" of future studies. The BULLETIN features technical and scholarly articles on futures-related topics, reviews of recent futurist books, news of interest from the world-wide futurist community, and information about the activities of World Future Society chapters in the United States, Canada and 18 other countries. 48 pages. Published since 1968.

WORLD FUTURE STUDIES FEDERATION NEWSLETTER

Editor: Secretariat of World Future Studies Federation

Publisher: World Future Studies Federation, Casella Postale 6203, Roma—Prati, Italy

Bimonthly. Newsletter sent with membership in World Future Studies Federation.

Intended audience: All persons interested in the future

Informs on members' activities, whether individuals or organizations. Informs on conferences, courses and publications in the field. Offers itself as a forum of exchange of information. 35 pages. Published since 1975.

WORLD ISSUES

Editor: Donald McDonald

Publisher: The Center for the Study of Democratic Institutions, 2056 Eucalyptus Hill Road, Santa Barbara, California 93103, U.S.A.

Bimonthly, with *The Center Magazine* on alternate months. $15 per year.

Intended audience: Informed laymen, academicians, public officials

Reports and papers on a wide variety of subjects including economics, energy, foreign policy. Also book reviews. 32 pages. Published since 1970 (until 1976 as THE CENTER REPORT).

YEARBOOK OF WORLD PROBLEMS AND HUMAN POTENTIAL

Editor: Anthony J. N. Judge

Publisher: Mankind 2000 and Union of International Associations, 1 rue aux Laines, 1000 Brussels, Belgium

Irregular. $65 institutional price.

Intended audience: General reference and those specifically interested in the detailed interrelationships between problems, organizations, and other social resources

The publication is composed of 13 sections each of which is made up of entries with cross-references between them. The sections include: world problems, international organizations, human values, intellectual disciplines, multilateral treaties, occupations, multinational corporations, interdisciplinary concepts, human development concepts, economic sectors, traded commodities, etc. There are a total of 12,884 descriptive entries and 58,195 cross-references. The information is held on computer files to facilitate improvement of the representation of the interlinked networks for which the YEARBOOK functions as a framework. 1100 pages. Publication began in 1976.

EDUCATIONAL COURSES
AND PROGRAMS

EDUCATIONAL COURSES AND PROGRAMS

Courses dealing with the future are now being offered by many elementary schools, high schools and colleges. In addition, some institutions offer programs which integrate several courses into sequence and, in some cases, lead to a degree.

The list is arranged alphabetically by country and is broken down within the United States by state. Within each geographic area, the entries are listed alphabetically by the name of the institution where they are offered. Since few educational institutions publicize their offerings widely, and since new courses and programs are being developed all the time, readers are urged to contact the schools and colleges in their own area for the latest information on courses on the future.

Where available, the following information is provided for each course and program:

Course

Name and address of institution
Course title
Course instructor
Educational level
Date of this offering
Date of first offering
Course description (activities, source materials, and special features)

Program

Name and address of institution
Program title
Program director(s)
Date of first offering
Predominant educational level
Degrees offered
Course titles
Program description

ARGENTINA

FUNDACION ARGENTINA ANO 2000
Leandro Alem 36 10th Piso
Capital Federal
(1003) Argentina

Course title: Introduction to Futuristics

Instructor: Alejandro Piscitelli; Charles Francois

Educational level: Adult

Date of this offering: Fall/Spring, 1978   **Date of first offering:** 1976

Course description: This course is intended to provide a general introduction to futures research. Some of its headings include: future as an object of knowledge; nature of forecasts; historical and scientific prediction; process and action; quantitative forecasts; ecology of ideas; the state of the art in epistemological foundations of forecasting. **Activities:** Short written pieces; lecture-discussion. **Source materials:** Selected articles from THE FUTURIST; Julien, *La Methode des scenarios [The Method of Forecasting]*; Godet, *Crise de la prevision, essor de la prospective [Crisis of the Future]*; Boulding, *The Meaning of the Twentieth Century*. **Special features:** —

AUSTRALIA

MONASH UNIVERSITY
Higher Education Advisory & Research Unit
Wellington Road
Clayton, Victoria
Australia, 3168

Course title: —

Instructor: Terry Hore and Leo West

Educational level: Master's

Date of this offering: July, 1979   **Date of first offering:** March, 1978

Course description: Topics include: introduction to conceptions of the future; basic methodologies; project in educational planning. **Activities:** Lecture-discussion; student presentations; project teams. **Source materials:** Hore, Linke and West, *The Future of Higher Education in Australia*. **Special features:** Projects may be presented via any medium (written, audio, videotape or film.)

BRAZIL

UNIVERSIDADE FEDERAL DO ESPIRITO SANTO
Centro Pedagogico
UFES
Vitoria, Espirito Santo
Brazil 29000

Course title: Alternatives in Education

Instructor: Richard Eugene Andre, Coordinator, Learning Laboratory

Educational level: Master's

Date of this offering: 1978   **Date of first offering:** 1978

Course description: This 10-week course consists of a continuous exploration of alternatives in education and is essentially conducted on a creative problem solving workshop model. Major elements include: learning games and simulations,

504

experiential learning, societal change models and strategies, and alternative institutional models. **Activities:**
Throughout the course students develop projects individually and in small task forces. The projects are intended to gen-
erate alternative futures materials and processes in learning and educational institutional contests. **Source materials:**
Books: Brunner, *A New Theory of Learning*; Freire, *Pedagogy of the Oppressed*; simulations by Andre: *The
Edifice Process; Juxtaposition—The World of Micro-Macro; The Lost Search;* student produced simulation:
The Parting of Apartheid. **Special features:** Several of the materials used or produced in this course are avail-
able in English, although most are presented currently in Portuguese.

CANADA

DAWSON COLLEGE
Center for Continuing Education
350 Selby Street
Montreal, Quebec, Canada H32 1Y9

Date of first offering: 1977

Program title: Future Studies Group

Director: Harry Wagschal, Coordinator of Future Studies

Educational level: College and adult

Degrees offered: —

Course titles: Sociology of Education — The Future of Education; Planetary Consciousness; Alternative Futures; The
Future of the City.

Program description: The Future Studies Group was set up to assist students and the community in clarifying the
significant changes created by technological progress on their own personal and community lives. In addition to regular
courses, the group organizes conferences, study groups, provides consulting services for teachers and educators.

DAWSON COLLEGE
350 Selby Street
Montreal, Quebec
Canada H32 1Y9

Course title: Literature and the Future

Instructor: Steve Bennett

Educational level: College juniors and seniors

Date of this offering: 1978

Date of first offering: 1974

Course description: This course is concerned with the "near" future, in general, especially as seen through the eyes of
novelists. **Activities:** Debates; lectures; role-playing, class discussions. **Source materials:** Huxley, *Brave New
World*; Orwell, *1984*; Callenbach, *Ecotopia*. Toffler, *Future Shock*, Schumacher, *Small is Beautiful*; Pirsig, *Zen
and the Art of Motorcycle Maintenance*; Clarke, *Profiles of the Future*, and others. **Special features:** —

HALTON BOARD OF EDUCATION
2050 Guelph Line
Burlington, Ontario, Canada L7R 3Z2

Date of first offering: 1974

Program title: Futures I: Explorations for Students of the Future

Director: G. Munro, Co-ordinator of Social Studies

Educational level: High school

Degrees offered: —

Course titles: Futures I.

Program description: This course is offered in ten high schools in Halton County. Major topics include
visions of the future, exploring environment, coping with change, and creating the future. Students use a

wide variety of resources including print, film, and multimedia materials to undertake research, use simulations, write scenarios, and make classroom presentations. Students have also put on a Futures Fair.

LORD ELGIN HIGH SCHOOL
5151 New Street
Burlington, Ontario
Canada M8Z 3M9

Date of first offering: September, 1979

Program title: Academy: A Futures Learning Lab for Gifted Learners

Director: Ted Runions

Educational level: High school

Degrees offered: —

Course titles: Basic Methodologies; Anticipating Personal, Societal, and Educational Needs.

Program description: Basics workshop; learning circles; mentor network; research; action-learning. Community experts contribute to the program.

UNIVERSITY OF OTTAWA
Department of Recreology
Tabaret Hall
Laurier Avenue
Ottawa, Ontario
Canada

Course title: Leisure and Canadian Society

Instructor: C. Westland, Professor

Educational level: College juniors and seniors

Date of this offering: Fall, 1978   **Date of first offering:** 1968-69

Course description: Canadian Society: The future of work, free time, population, values, the family, the city. **Activities:** Lecture-discussion. **Source materials:** *Reshaping the International Order; Kahn, The Next 200 Years; The Selective Conserver Society; Perspectives Canada; Values of Mankind.* **Special features:** —

UNIVERSITY OF SASKATCHEWAN
College of Home Economics
Saskatoon, Saskatchewan
Canada S7N OWO

Course title: Current Trends and Methods in Home Economics Education

Instructor: Wanda Young, Associate Professor

Educational level: College juniors and seniors; teacher training: junior to one year beyond baccalaureate

Date of this offering: Fall, 1978   **Date of first offering:** 1966

Course description: Basic Methodologies of Teaching, including scenario, Delphi, presentation on the future; a study of societal trends that affect teaching and home economics; philosophy; preparation of learning package. The main purpose is to review and practice methodology and teaching strategies. **Activities:** Lecture-discussion; action research; scenario writing; oral reports; field trips; media; role playing; drama; resource persons. **Source materials:** Toffler, *Learning About the Future;* THE FUTURIST; World Future Society BULLETIN; *Education Tomorrow; Canadian Futures Association Newsletter;* home economics and family oriented literature. **Special features:** Guest speakers; field trips; student projects.

SIMON FRASER UNIVERSITY
Burnaby, British Columbia
Canada V5A 1S6

Course title: The Study of the Future

Instructor: W. Basil McDermott

Educational level: College juniors and seniors

Date of this offering: 1979-1980   **Date of first offering:** Fall, 1968

Course description: This is a course about the problems one encounters when seeking a set of "better questions" about life. The course consists of lectures and seminars. Students do required reading in order to carry on intelligent discussions. Topics include: Reflections on a decade of future watching; the cathedral of knowledge problem; beyond doomsday, before Utopia; on the foresaking of hope in order to forsake despair also; the case of the vanishing sanctuary; on the law of the conservation of misery and suffering; what does it really mean to "care" about the future?; the survivors and the time capsule: a fable for the future; what are people for? the hidden knowledge problem; Socrates and the soothsayer: on knowing that you do not know; and on the consciousness and control we have not yet acquired. **Activities:** Lecture/seminar; two required essays; required reading before each seminar. **Source materials:** Required texts: Boulding, *The Meaning of the Twentieth Century*; Heilbroner, *An Inquiry into the Human Prospect*; Roszak, *Unfinished Animal: The Aquarian Frontier and the Evolution of Consciousness*; selected reading from books and articles prior to each seminar. **Special features:** —

TRENT UNIVERSITY
Peterborough, Ontario, Canada

Course title: Geography of Future Environments

Instructor: John S. Marsh

Educational level: College juniors and seniors

Date of this offering: 1978-79   **Date of first offering:** 1975

Course description: Trends; Delphi; critical path; lateral thinking; science fiction; computer modelling; scenarios. **Activities:** Five lectures; seminars, displays; 50 percent of course is structured, remainder is free choice. **Source materials:** DeBono, *Lateral Thinking* is main book; Abler et al., *Human Geography in a Shrinking World;* films. **Special features:** Field trips to innovative places and people in Toronto; guest speakers included hazard specialists from army, fire and police organizations commenting on human reactions to disaster and official plans for such events.

UNIVERSITY OF WATERLOO, ONTARIO   **Date of first offering:** 1976
Waterloo, Ontario, Canada N2L 3G1

Program title: Faculty of Environmental Studies

Director: Peter H. Nash, Instructor

Educational level: Undergraduate; master's

Degrees offered: B.E.S. (Geography; City and Regional Planning; and Man/Environment Studies).

Course titles: Introductory courses to the Study of the Future and Alternative Future Environments for departments of Environmental Studies, Geography, Man-Environment Studies, and School of Urban and Regional Planning.

Program description: The introductory course is a non-technical survey of current approaches about refining views of the future: impacts of regional science, ekistics, bioethics, synergetics and prognostics; comprehensive design of optimum environments. Alternative Future Environments seek to analyze ideal environments of the past, including utopian communities, and scrutinize current concepts of future environments. Second semester examines issues in futuristics and their methodological problems, emphasizing resource utilization. Suggested readings: Tugwell, ed., *Search for Alternatives: Public Policy and the Study of the Future;* Cross, ed., *Man-Made Futures: Readings in Society, Technology and Design;* and Garlan and Dunstan, ed., *Star Sight: Visions of the Future.*

UNIVERSITY OF WESTERN ONTARIO
1147 Western Road
London, Ontario, Canada N6G 1Z7

Course title: Alternative Futures in Education

Instructor: Hugh A. Stevenson, Associate Professor of Education

Educational level: Returning professionals

Date of this offering: 1978-79   **Date of first offering:** 1976

Course description: A study of the future as a dimension in educational thought and pedagogical practice. Topics include: future studies; curriculum design; anticipatory planning; educational and societal alternatives; possible teaching techniques. **Activities:** Lecture; discussion; oral, written and visual reports; guest speakers. **Source materials:** Numerous, including Stevenson, ed.: *Alternatives Canada.* **Special features** Extensive individual work in close cooperation with the instructor. Stevenson also teaches future-oriented courses in policy-making in education, contemporary issues in education, utopian thought and education, and independent study.

UNIVERSITY OF WESTERN ONTARIO
London, Ontario, Canada

Course title: Evolving Concepts of Analyzing and Forecasting Spatial Development

Instructor: Robert McDaniel, Associate Professor of Geography

Educational level: Master's and doctorate

Date of this offering: Spring, 1979   **Date of first offering:** 1972

Course description: Regional input-output analysis; interregional linear programming; technological forecasting; network analysis; mosaic synthesis; gravity models. **Activities:** Seminar; discussion; films; audiotapes; computer modeling; student reports. **Source materials:** Books: Abler et al., *Human Geography in a Shrinking World;* Isard, *Introduction to Regional Science;* Beres and Targ, *Reordering the Planet;* Hencley and Yates, *Futurism in Education;* Beer, *Platform for Change* ; films: *Future Shock, Intermediate Technology, The New Alchemists;* magazines: THE FUTURIST, *Futures, Technological Forecasting and Social Change, Antipode, Alternatives.* **Special features:** Lectures by people in computers, electronics, and planning. Field trips to experimental living sites. McDaniel teaches a similiar two-semester course at the senior undergraduate level and a graduate-level course in the design of future spatial systems.

UNIVERSITY OF WINDSOR
Windsor, Ontario
Canada N9B 3P4

Course title: Macro-environmental Psychology (MACENV)

Instructor: William L. Libby, Jr., Professor of Psychology

Educational level: College juniors and seniors

Date of this offering: 1979   **Date of first offering:** 1972

Course description: Basic forecasting and planning methods; alternative futures on level of society (Huxley, *Brave New World* and *Island;* Meadows, *Limits to Growth,* etc.), the city, the local scene, the family and individuals; futures problems and values questions (social traps, "lifeboat ethics"); anticipatory democracy. The university also offers a graduate course, The Social Psychology of Long Range Planning (SPLRP), which deals with the social psychological aspects of long range planning methods, alternative futures, and methods for dealing with values/planning issues. **Activities:** Depending upon enrollment, a variety of activities, including lecture-discussion, workshop, presentation of reports and projects. **Source materials:** Readings chosen from such authors as Huxley, Meadows, Platt, Goldsmith, Henderson, Schumacher, Kahn; films. **Special features:** Guest participants from other disciplines and from the working world who share their experience with students.

COLOMBIA

FUNDACION AMERICA LATINA 2001 [LATIN AMERICAN FOUNDATION 2001]
Calle 10, No. 3-61   **Date of first offering:** August, 1978
Bogota, Colombia

Program title: Prospective, Theoretical Foundations and Methodological Significance

Director: Horacio H. Godoy

Educational level: Post-doctoral

Degrees offered: —

Course titles: Course topics include: theoretical foundations of future research — the prospective approach, the epistemology of praxis, and prospective methodology.

Program description: This is a program of three sessions oriented to the adoption of a formal course on future research at the National University of Colombia. Activities include lecture-discussion. Source materials include a current bibliography with books from the Club of Rome, the Hudson Institute, the National Science Foundation, the World Future Society, and Futuribles. The activities of the Foundation are based on the implementation of projects for research course programming and the organization of seminars.

UNITED KINGDOM

UNIVERSITY OF BRADFORD   Date of first offering: 1975
School of Science and Society
Bradford
West Yorkshire BD7 1DP, England

Program title: Undergraduate Honours Course in Science and Society

Director: Tom Stonier, Chairman, Undergraduate School; Verner Wheelock, Chairman, Postgraduate School

Educational level: College undergraduate; postgraduate

Degrees offered: First class, second class (upper or lower division) and third class honours.

Course titles: The first year consists of a number of compulsory courses including: Natural History of Humanity, Biology of Human Behavior, Energy Studies, Food Technology, Medical Technology, Social Change, etc. The second year contains three parts: compulsory courses: Inter-relationships of Science, Technology and Society and Computers, Statistics and Quantitative Methods; optional courses: Agricultural Science, Engineering Design and Workshop Practice, Aspects of Practical Communications, and Food and Nutrition; and a project. The third year students work outside the school in areas ranging from UK industry to rural development in the Third World. The final year consists of two compulsory courses: Global Society and the Outlook for Human Existence and Ethics and Practice of Decision-Making; optional courses; main emphasis is project work.

Program description: The School of Studies in Science and Society has brought together relevant aspects of science, social sciences, and technology into a new student-oriented interdisciplinary program. The primary aim is to allow students to acquire the terminology and to grasp basic concepts to enable them to communicate effectively with engineers, managers, government officials, educators, etc. Students are trained to move freely across the interface between the sciences, social sciences and humanities. When their interests have matured sufficiently, they can specialize. The program is unique in its strong emphasis on interdisciplinary subjects, its global and future orientation.

CRANFIELD INSTITUTE OF TECHNOLOGY   Date of first offering: 1971
Centre for Transport Studies
Cranfield, Bedford MK43 OAL
England

Program title: MSc in Transport Studies

Director: J.M. Clark

Educational level: Master's

Degrees offered: MSc in Transport Studies

Course titles: Transport System Design and Comparison; Transport Management; Transport Planning Methods.

Program description: This is a one year program culminating in a Master's degree in transport studies. The program provides training in the skills for work in planning, assessment and operations of both passenger and freight transport. The program comprises one term's intensive teaching over a wide range of transport topics, one term of more specialist courses and an extensive introduction to group project work, and two terms in which a personal research project is undertaken and presented as a dissertation. The Centre also has a PhD program and short courses of about a week's duration.

THE OPEN UNIVERSITY
Design Discipline
Faculty of Technology
Walton Hall
Milton Keynes, United Kingdom

Course title: Man-made Futures: Design and Technology

Instructor: Nigel Cross, Team Chairman; David Elliot; Robin Roy.

Educational level: Undergraduate; general

Date of this offering: 1978   **Date of first offering:** 1975

Course description: Technology and Society; Policy and Participation; Design and Technology; Designing the Future; The Future of Shelter, Food, Work; Design and Planning Methods. **Activities:** The course is presented via correspondence materials and BBC TV and radio programmes. Course has three interlinked streams: 1. Theory of technology-society relationships and the future-creating roles of design and planning; 2. "Files" of future-oriented materials in shelter, food and work; 3. Major project-work component based on problem-identification and design methods. **Source materials:** Nine specially published correspondence-study books: Unit 1—*Designing the Future;* Units 2-3—*Technology and Society;* Units 4-5—*Future of Shelter;* Unit 6—*Policy and Participation;* Units 7-8—*Future of Food;* Unit 9—*Design and Technology;* Units 10-11—*Future of Work;* Unit 12—*Project Guide;* Units 13-16—*Design Methods Manual;* simulation-game; *Problem Identification Game;* eleven TV, eight radio programmes; *Man-Made Futures;* edited by Cross, Elliott, Ray. **Special features:** Major part (1/3) of course is student-direct individual project work. Students are all adult (over 21), part-time students. This course is used in some adult-extension courses in USA universities.

UNITED STATES OF AMERICA

ALABAMA

THE UNIVERSITY OF ALABAMA
College of Education
P.O. Box Q
University, Alabama 35486

Course title: Futures Forecasting; Applied Forecasting

Instructor: Bruce Peseau, Professor of Administration and Higher Education and Associate Dean for Administration

Educational level: Doctorate

Date of this offering: 1978   **Date of first offering:** 1974

Course description: These two courses are part of a 27 semester hour sequence of planning courses. Primary topics are the nature of technology and its impact; the technology transfer space as a forecasting hierarchy; technology assessment as the basic analytical process; and selection and use of the appropriate forecasting methods for technology assessment. **Activities:** Lecture-discussion; analytic exercises; brainstorming; films; individual projects applied to real-world problems. **Source materials:** Extensive bibliography—materials are in one location in the library. Required reading: Hencley and Yates, *Futurism in Education;* New York *Times, Technology and Social Change;* Cornisn,

The Study of the Future; films. **Special features:** Specialists visit class; student projects; minimum of five mini-reports on new or developing technologies; cumulative collection of student projects. This seems to improve quality of student projects.

UNIVERSITY OF ALABAMA IN HUNTSVILLE
Huntsville, Alabama 35807

Course title: The Sociology of the Future

Instructor: Donald E. Tarter, Associate Professor, Sociology Department

Educational level: College juniors and seniors

Date of this offering: Fall and Spring quarters, 1978-79 **Date of first offering:** 1972

Course description: Images of the future; technology and social evolution; basic methodologies of futures research; technology forecasting and assessment; issues of growth vs. no growth; the social impact of space technology; speculations on the future of the basic institutions including family, education, economics, politics, religion and cosmology; a look at the deep future. **Activities:** Lecture; discussion; student scenario writing on the next 25 years; guest speakers; integration of class activities with local chapter activities of the World Future Society. **Source materials:** Books: Toffler: *Future Shock;* Clarke: *Profiles of the Future;* Ofshe: *The Sociology of the Possible;* magazine: THE FUTURIST. **Special features** NASA/Marshall Space Flight Center personnel generally speak to class; occasional field trips to NASA, local communes, etc.

ARIZONA

UNIVERSITY OF ARIZONA
Department of Political Science
Tuscon, Arizona 85721

Course title: World Order/Futurism

Instructor: Clifton E. Wilson

Educational level: College juniors and seniors

Date of this offering: Spring semesters, beginning 1980 **Date of first offering:** Spring, 1980

Course description: This course, originally taught as "World Order," now is designed to include futurism. About one half of the course will be future-oriented, and will be taught in Spring, 1980. **Activities:** The course will begin with two or three weeks of lectures and then will include simulations—games, panels, reports, etc. **Source materials:** Books, games, films. **Special features:** —

PHOENIX COLLEGE
3802 North 42nd Place
Phoenix, Arizona 85018

Course title: Dimensions of the Future

Instructor: Ken Conry

Educational level: College freshmen and sophomores

Date of this offering: 1979 **Date of first offering:** 1975

Course description: Topics include: forecasting techniques; future of human relationships; population explosion: myth or reality; solar energy; knowledge explosion—communication revolution; Arizona's future and water; alternative realities—plant emotions, ESP and parapsychology; L-5 society; space colonies; Arcosanti and urban alternatives; terraforming Venus; E.F. Schumacher and economic alternatives. **Activities:** Lecture-discussion; guest speakers; class group work, especially on future wheels and cross-impact matrix. **Source materials:** Cornish, *The Study of the Future;* film *Future Shock;* the game, *Futuribles,* at end of semester. **Special features:** Field trips to Arcosanti

Festival, the water treatment plant at Yuma, Arizona, Understanding Incorporated, etc.; speakers from Arizona Solar Energy Commission, Water Commission, C.A.P.; talks by authors of relevant books.

PIMA COMMUNITY COLLEGE
Downtown Campus
P.O. Box 5027
Tucson, Arizona 85703

Course title: Futurism: A Psychological Perspective

Instructor: Laurence J. Victor

Educational level: College freshmen and sophomores

Date of this offering: Fall, 1978   **Date of first offering:** Fall, 1976

Course description: Emphasis in lectures on educational futures; course uses open format to facilitate self-directed learning; focus on development of alternative perspectives.   **Activities:** Lectures; films; discussions; special projects. **Source materials:** Marien, *Societal Directions and Alternatives;* selected bibliography; THE FUTURIST; *Co-Evolution Quarterly;* articles by instructor (Societal Metamorphosis).   **Special features:**—

SCOTTSDALE COMMUNITY COLLEGE
9000 E. Chaparral Road
Scottsdale, Arizona 85253

Course title: Dimensions of the Future; The Future of Arizona

Instructor: Barry Wukasch; Ken Conry

Educational level: College freshmen and sophomores; adult-general

Date of this offering: 1979   **Date of first offering:** Dimensions-1973 The Future of Arizona-1978

Course description: Course topics include: genetics; forecasting methods; space exploration; extraterrestrial life; solar energy; nuclear energy; financial planning; weapons; cities; other topics as time permits.   **Activities:** Mainly lecture; occasional group projects in class.   **Source materials:** Selected articles assigned by the instructor; Berry, *The Next Ten Thousand Years.*   **Special features:** —

ARKANSAS

UNIVERSITY OF ARKANSAS
GE 245 College of Education
Fayetteville, Arkansas 72701

Course title: Educational Futurism

Instructor: James J. Van Patten, Coordinator of Educational Foundations

Educational level: Doctorate

Date of this offering: 1978   **Date of first offering:** 1974

Course description: This course offers the following topics: definition models, paradigms of futurism; qualitative change; shaping the future; values in the future; technology and humanism; interdependence and human renewal. **Activities:** Lecture-discussion; scenario writing; student oral reports.   **Source materials:** Books, films, simulations from the World Future Society.   **Special features:** Specialists visit class, field trips, student projects presented via many media.

512

CALIFORNIA

CALIFORNIA POLYTECHNIC STATE UNIVERSITY
San Luis Obispo, California 93407

Course title: Future Studies

Instructor: R. L. Rosenberg, Associate Professor, History/Humanities; M. P. Orth, Associate Professor, English

Educational level: College juniors and seniors

Date of this offering: Spring, 1979   **Date of first offering:** Spring, 1976

Course description: Introductory—Futurism and futurists; basic methodologies. **Activities:** Lecture-discussion; scenario writing; students present oral reports. **Source materials:** Texts: Callenbach, *Ecotopia*; Cornish, *The Study of the Future*; Sargent, *Cloned Lives*; Schwartz, ed., *Earth in Transit.* **Special features:** Team-taught by a historian, an art instructor, and an instructor of English literature.

CALIFORNIA STATE UNIVERSITY, DOMINGUEZ HILLS   Date of first offering: 1979
Room G-225, S&BS Building
Dominguez Hills, California 90747

Program title: Future Policy Studies

Director: Linda Groff

Educational level: Undergraduate

Degrees offered: Minor in Future Policy Studies

Course titles: Introduction to Future Studies is a required course for all students in the program. Five additional courses must be selected: two from a core curriculum including: Anthropology of the Future, Economics and the Future, The Future in History, Global Planning and the Future, Sociology and the Future, and Values and the Future; and three from the aforementioned and/or another list including: Technology Policy and the Future, Urbanization and Social Ecology, Utopian and New Communities, Psychology of Consciousness, Environmental Biology, Chemistry for the Citizen, Social Responsibility of Business, etc.

Program description: This is a new interdisciplinary minor program in Future Policy Studies. The purpose is to introduce, and suggest possible solutions for, some of the range of current and projected future problems confronting the world. Future Studies provides a holistic framework for dealing with accelerated change on both the personal and public policy levels. Activities include lecture-discussion, guest speakers, and panels of faculty from all parts of the University.

CALIFORNIA STATE UNIVERSITY, LONG BEACH
1250 Bellflower Boulevard
Long Beach, California 92660

Course title: Science Fiction and Speculative Fantasy (Special Topics)

Instructor: David N. Samuelson, Professor, Department of English

Educational level: College juniors and seniors

Date of this offering: Fall, 1978   **Date of first offering:** Fall, 1968

Course description: Science fiction as science education, social criticism, forecasting, mythic spinoff, escapist nonsense, philosophical expression, and artistic achievement. **Activities:** Lecture-discussion, with student journals and critical papers (Wells and 19th century, comparison of types, evaluation of contemporary examples). **Source materials:** Lawler, ed., *Approaches to Science Fiction*; Scholes et al., *Science Fiction: History—Science—Vision*; Rose, ed., *Science Fiction: A Collection of Essays;* Wells, *The Time Machine*; Lindsay, *Voyage to Arcturus;* Clement, *Mission of Gravity*; Capek. *War with the Newts*; Lem, *Solaris*; Delany, *The Einstein Intersection*; Benford, *In The Ocean of Night.* **Special features:** Samuelson is offering two new courses in the spring of 1979: Space: The Final Frontier (Topics in American Studies); and Wells/Huxley: Critical Studies in Major Authors.

CALIFORNIA STATE UNIVERSITY, LOS ANGELES

Date of first offering: —

5151 State University Drive
Los Angeles, California 90032

Program title: Futures Studies

Director: J. Leonard Steinberg, Professor, School of Education

Educational level: Master's

Degrees offered: M.A. in Urban Studies with special concentration in futures studies

Course titles: Futures studies; forecasting and its implications for educational policy making; seminar in futures studies; future of education in a changing society.

Program description: Program is in planning stages and should be ready for fall of 1979-80.

CALIFORNIA STATE UNIVERSITY, NORTHRIDGE

Department of Sociology
Northridge, California 91330

Course title: Update on Space

Instructor: B. J. Bluth, Associate Professor of Sociology

Educational level: High school; college undergraduate; master's; adult; professionals

Date of this offering: Summer, 1979　　　　　　　　　　　　**Date of first offering:** Summer, 1978

Course description: The overall focus will be the sociological dimension of the move into space — the impact on the quality of life on Earth, the implications of change, the political, cultural, and psychological problems and potentials in new roles, new products, new occupations, new solutions to old problems and new challenges. Main topics include: Science Fiction That Is and Is Not Science Fact; A History of Space Platforms; Design Strategy for Space Habitats; Materials Processing in Space; Solar Power Satellites; Man in Space; Getting to Space — Propulsion; Laser Communications; Shuttle Management Systems; War in Space; Doomsday Projects; Isolation and Confinement; Politics: Government and Space; Life Extension and the Space Age; Mixed Crews in Space and Their Problems (sexually); Social Issues in Space Settlements; Computers and Man in Space, and others. **Activities:** Up-to-date, in-depth briefings by 22 people in NASA, industry, the military, government, and the university on the work they are currently doing related to the settlement and development of space; students taking the course for credit may write projects in areas of their interest, for the Department of Energy SPS Assessment, etc. Students can have lunch in an informal setting and a small group with a few of the speakers. **Source materials:** O'Neill, *The High Frontier;* Heppenheimer, *Space Colonies;* Vajk, *Doomsday Has Been Cancelled;* New Dimensions, *Worlds Beyond;* Stein, *The Third Industrial Revolution;* numerous reprint handouts; films from NASA and industry. Special materials for teachers. **Special features:** Field trips to Jet Propulsion Lab, TRW, and Earth/Space Expo. The course is made possible by grants from Rockwell International, TRW, and Lockheed.

UNIVERSITY OF CALIFORNIA, BERKELEY

Berkeley, California 94720

Course title: Urbanism and the Futures of Cities

Instructor: Richard L. Meier

Educational level: College juniors and seniors

Date of this offering: 1979　　　　　　　　　　　　　　**Date of first offering:** 1977

Course description: Futures material presented throughout the course includes: urban ecosystems analysis; communications theory; organizations theory; field studies. **Activities:** Lecture-discussion; problems; papers. **Source materials:** *Urban Futures Observed—In the Asian Third World;* Abu-Lughad, et al., *Third World Urbanization.* **Special features:** Urban Ecology Laboratory accompanies the course.

514

UNIVERSITY OF CALIFORNIA, LOS ANGELES
Los Angeles, California 90024

Course title: Patterns of Problem Solving

Instructor: Moshe F. Rubinstein

Educational level: College undergraduate

Date of this offering: 1979   **Date of first offering:** 1969

Course description: Discussion of tools and concepts most productive in problem solving and least likely to be eroded with the passage of time. A balance is sought between modeling techniques and attributes of human problem solvers. Topics include language and communication, computers, probability and the will to doubt, probabilistic models, decision-making models, optimization models; dynamic systems models and values. A quarter-long course, offered year round. **Activities:** Lecture-discussion; group work. Students complete a term project using the tools of the course. Peer teaching is an integral part of the course. **Source materials:** Book: Moshe Rubinstein, *Patterns of Problem Solving*; videotape: 19 half-hour lectures on patterns of problem solving by Rubinstein. **Special features:** —

CLAYTON VALLEY HIGH SCHOOL
1101 Alberta Way
Concord, California 94521

Course title: The Future

Instructor: Bill Kepner

Educational level: High school

Date of this offering: —   **Date of first offering:** Fall, 1977

Course description: The future of population, environment, the city, transportation, the family, genetic manipulation and bioethics, lifestyles, work, leisure, media, communication. **Activities:** Discussion based on articles, clippings, audiovisual experiences. Scenario and cross-impact building. **Source materials:** Articles from magazines; study kits: *Redesigning Man, Media & Meaning, Human Values in an Age of Technology, Conflict in American Values*, etc.; films: *Stranger Than Science Fiction, Boomsville, Ultimate Machine*, some NASA films.

EL CAMINO HIGH SCHOOL
14640 Mercado Avenue
La Mirada, California 90638

Date of first offering: 1975

Program title: REAL (Relevant Education through Alternative Learning)

Director: Jerry McCamly, Janis Rosene

Educational level: High school

Degrees offered: —

Course titles: Areas of study: Learning how to learn; relating to self and others; relating through content; valuing; decision-making; producing; consuming; creating; leisure time; futuring. Each learning area incorporates some traditional content areas such as English, social studies, math, etc.

Program description: Students with the help of the teacher develop a learning contract based on competencies: suggested tasks that students can perform to verify their competence. The program uses no textbooks. Students go to the best source: library, college, a person working in a field of student interest, the community, another person who can help with a skill, etc. Program was developed in relation to ideas of Toffler and other futurists.

J.F. KENNEDY HIGH SCHOOL
11254 Gothic Avenue
Granada Hills, California 91344

Course title: Future Studies

Instructor: Shelly Pearson

Educational level: High school juniors and seniors

Date of this offering: 1978   **Date of first offering:** 1975

Course description: This social studies elective changes with the class and current state of the world.   **Activities:** Lecture-discussion; scenario writing; oral reports; group presentations; public opinion polls; audio-visual materials; simulation games; Rockwell International tape and slides on shuttle, etc.   **Source materials:** Toffler, *Future Shock* (book and film); *The City 2001.* Course also uses THE FUTURIST; *Omni; Science Digest; Human Nature; Psychology Today; Los Angeles Times,* and many other publications.   **Special features:** —

POMONA COLLEGE AND CLAREMONT GRADUATE SCHOOL
Claremont, California 91711

Course title: Public Policy and the Study of the Future

Instructor: Franklin Tugwell

Educational level: College freshmen and sophomores

Date of this offering: 1978   **Date of first offering:** 1969

Course description: Forecasting: epistemology and method; substantive topics.   **Activities:** Lecture; discussion; oral reports.   **Source materials:** Tugwell: *Search for Alternatives;* others.   **Special features** —

UNIVERSITY OF REDLANDS
1200 E. Colton Avenue
Redlands, California 92373

Course title: Education in the Future

Instructor: Carol A. Franklin, Assistant Professor of Education; Coordinator of Secondary Education

Educational level: College freshmen and sophomores

Date of this offering: 1978   **Date of first offering:** 1979

Course description: This course is part of a topic freshman seminar program. Courses are: Time: Reflecting on the Future; Curriculum Issues for the Future; Tools, Skills and Techniques in the Future; Who, What is a Futurist? Other courses having futures aspects are interwoven into the curriculum.   **Activities:** Discussion, time-line, values strategies, simulations, science fiction, scenario writing, student developed projects (non-written), brainstorming, alternatives tree, interaction matrix, field trips.   **Source materials:** Toffler, *Learning for Tomorrow*; Romey, *Consciousness and Creativity*; games, *New Town* and *Futuribles*; Kauffman, *Teaching the Future*; THE FUTURIST.   **Special features:** Biofeedback lab; guest lecturer — published science fiction writer; current futurist movies; student presentations; computer simulation projection games.

SAN DIEGO STATE UNIVERSITY
San Diego, California 92182

Course title: Technology and Human Values

Instructor: Willis H. Thompson, Assistant Professor

Educational level: College freshmen and sophomores

Date of this offering: Fall, 1978   **Date of first offering:** 1970

Course description: Student values; introduction to the future; systems analysis; Delphi method; extrapolation; exponential growth; simulation; population; information revolution; problems in media; biological revolution; extended life; energy projections; housing; transportation; clothing; institutional change; case studies on the automobile and the supersonic transport; utopian communities; utopian aspects of Red China; underdeveloped countries; future priorities and normative forecasting.   **Activities:** Lecture; discussion; videotapes; films; field trips.   **Source materials:** Instructor's original text; Portola Institute: *Energy Primer;* Ehrlich: *End of Affluence;* Clark: *Energy for Survival;* selected articles.   **Special features** Individual building projects such as hydroponics, a solar collector, housing models, and others.

UNIVERSITY OF SAN FRANCISCO

University Center Main Lounge
San Francisco, California 94107

Date of first offering: April, 1978

Program title: The Age of Specialization

Director: Ronald Brill, Director of Public Affairs

Educational level: Adult - general

Degrees offered: —

Course titles: —

Program description: The program is a series of public symposia offered twice a year. The format used is a series of speakers, followed by a panel discussion with questions from the audience. The first symposia was titled "Survival of the Generalist in the Age of Specialization"; the second, "The Dilemma of Democracy in the Age of Specialization." Future programs will deal with the "Future of Work"; "Future of Education"; "Design of Our Cities."

SAN JOSE STATE UNIVERSITY

School of Education
Seventh and San Carlos Streets
San Jose, California 95121

Course title: Futures Studies; Advanced Futures Studies

Instructor: Ronald L. Hunt, Professor of Education and Cybernetic Systems

Educational level: Master's

Date of this offering: 1978-79

Date of first offering: 1975

Course description: In the School of Education, Instruction Technology, the sequence of courses is Instructional Technology, Professional Aspects; Instructional Design seminar, etc., including courses in Cybernetic Systems; and Futures Studies courses in Education. The University is now in the process of establishing a minor in future studies that would lead to a B.A., administered in the School of Business, but would be a meta-disciplinary course involving several departments. **Activities:** Lecture-discussion; scenario writing; work with forecasting methods; student reports in multi-media format; emphasis on value structures in future societies; readings from technological forecasting books and articles and science fiction. **Source materials:** Kauffman, *Teaching the Future;* extensive bibliography and professor's collection of books in the field. **Special features:** Visiting specialists from the Institute for the Future in Menlo Park, DCM Associates in San Francisco, etc.

UNIVERSITY OF SOUTHERN CALIFORNIA (USC)

Education, WPH 702h
Los Angeles, California 90007

Course title: Futures Studies in Curriculum and Instruction

Instructor: Roy A. Weaver; Bernard Kirsh

Educational level: Master's; doctorate

Date of this offering: 1978

Date of first offering: 1976

Course description: Course topics include: social events and educational implications; long-range forecasting techniques; model-building; curriculum design for schools for the future. **Activities:** Lecture-discussion; scenario writing; students present oral reports; films, video-cassettes. **Source materials:** Callenbach, *Ecotopia*; Shane, *Curriculum Change Toward the 21st Century*; Hencley, *Futurism: Methodologies*; Cornish, *The Study of the Future.* **Special features:** Trips to Jet Propulsion Lab; Center for Futures Research. Visits by experts in different fields.

SPONTANEOUS COMBUSTION

P.O. Box 4411
San Rafael, California 94903

Date of first offering: 1975

Program title: The Active Classroom

Director: Thomas Farley, Artistic Director/Instructor; Sandra Farley, Managing Director/Instructor; Sally Stockton, Instructor

Educational level: K-12; master's; adult-general, professional; mixed age groups

Degrees offered: —

Course titles: Improvisation and Games; Developing Inter- and Intra-Personal Relationships; Children's Creative Response to Conflict; Developing Dramatic Imagination; Values Clarification; Games Leadership Training; Children's Drama Workshops.

Program description: This is an extension program of the Dominican College of San Rafael. It is offered year round at different times at locations throughout Northern California. The program is not equipment or technology dependent. Individual and group skills for cooperation and mutual support are developed. These inter-personal skills are essential to the survival of human civilization and to the improvement of the quality of life on the planet. Source materials include: *Friendly Classroom for a Small Planet; Non-Violence and Children; Dramatic Imagination; Dealing with Feelings; About Anger,* etc. Some workshops conclude with a presentation or community event.

STANFORD UNIVERSITY
Box 5816
Stanford, California 94305

Course title: Ethics of Development in a Global Environment (EDGE)

Instructor: Kenneth Cooper, Program Coordinator

Educational level: College juniors and seniors, master's and doctorate

Date of this offering: 1978-79   **Date of first offering:** 1973-74

Course description: A year-long interdisciplinary seminar on the processes and rationale for development focusing on the long-term consequences of present-day actions and the global interdependencies of people, resources and lifestyles. The first term is devoted to a discussion of current world trends and a definition of problems related to human survival. The second term concentrates on the role of development and strategies for change using regional and international case studies. The final term explores the relationship of the individual to social change in his own society. **Activities:** Lectures and discussion led by a thirty-member multi-disciplinary faculty group; small student research groups; joint class projects. **Source materials:** Required reading: Brown, *The Twenty Ninth Day;* Lappe, *World Hunger;* Fishlow et al., *Rich and Poor Nations in the World Economy;* recommended: Daly, *Steady State Economics;* extensive reading list. **Special features:** Course is cross-listed in engineering, anthropology, political science, education, and social thought.

COLORADO

INTERNATIONAL GRADUATE SCHOOL OF EDUCATION   **Date of first offering:** Spring, 1974
University Park Place
Parker, Colorado 80134

Program title: Center for Futuristic Studies

Director: Edward C. Pino, President, IGSE

Educational level: Graduate

Degrees offered: Non-degree

Course titles: Alternative Futures in Education.

Program description: The primary activities of the Center include: conducting futures-oriented educational research; translating the messages of the futurists into educational goals for tomorrow's schools; implementing futures-oriented educational programs in the IGSE network of demonstration schools; developing futures-oriented elementary and secondary education programs; conducting national, regional and specialized futuristic workshops for educators; assessing the growth of the quality and numbers of futuristic endeavors in U.S. schools; and publishing futuristic curriculum programs, instructional strategies, and an annual resources index for educators. The graduate-level course is offered in various locations throughout the U.S., Canada, and Europe; academic credit is usually available through nearby institutions. The course focuses on providing participants with the opportunity to learn what the futurists are saying, emphasizing the educational implications, and on having participants develop curricular programs and instructional strategies.

NORTHGLENN SENIOR HIGH SCHOOL
601 W. 100th Place
Denver, Colorado 80221

Course title: Future Studies

Instructor: Larry J. Smith

Educational level: High school

Date of this offering: 1979   **Date of first offering:** 1975

Course description: This course, an integral part of the Social Studies curriculum, is an intensive introduction to the field of future studies, designed and written with instructional/behavioral objectives. **Activities:** The course is a semester in length. Approximately one-half of the course is spent learning tools forecasters utilize (cross-impact matrix, trend extrapolation, simulations, etc.). Remainder of course is specific mini-units (Future of the Family, Future of Work, Bio-medical Technology, etc.). **Source materials:** THE FUTURIST; comprehensive collection of books related to futures. **Special features:** Class visits to planned industrial parks; guest speakers — city planners; visits to solar heated installations in the area.

UNIVERSITY OF SOUTHERN COLORADO
2200 Bonforte Boulevard
Pueblo, Colorado 81001

Course title: English

Instructor: Margaret Senatore

Educational level: College juniors and seniors; adult

Date of this offering: 1978   **Date of first offering:** Spring, 1972

Course description: This course concentrates on population growth; future cities; space colonies; reorganization geopolitically of the U.S.; and life under water. **Activities:** Lecture-discussion; NASA, NOAA films; essay response to two questions: what if...; if *this* continues then...; guest speakers. **Source materials:** Clarke, *Childhood's End*; Pohl, *The Space Merchants*; Herbert, *The Santaroga Barrier*; Elwood, *Six Science Fiction Plays*; U. LeGuin; *The Left Hand of Darkness*. **Special features:** —

CONNECTICUT

UNIVERSITY OF BRIDGEPORT
Management Engineering Program
College of Engineering
220 University Avenue
Bridgeport, Connecticut 06602

Course title: Technological Forecasting and Long Range Planning

Instructor: Phylipp Dilloway

Educational level: Master's

Date of this offering: 1978   **Date of first offering:** 1970

Course description: Fundamentals of forecasting: intuitive, trend extrapolation, normative, monitoring, modeling, scenarios, and cross-impact analysis. The course is typically taken by graduate engineers. Recently a number of political science majors and a municipal employee enriched the class by dealing with political and social systems forecasting. **Activities:** Exercises in connection with course topics; each student prepares a technological forecast at end of semester. **Source materials:** Bright, *Technology Forecasting: Concepts and Exercises* (workbook); Ayers, *Technological Forecasting and Long Range Planning*; Sullivan and Claycombe, *Fundamentals of Forecasting*. Copies of long range plans and audio tape speeches. **Special features:** The university is ideally located for access to corporate planners. One or two are invited as guest speakers and/or critics of the final presentations. Local chapter of WFS is a source of guests and audience for final presentations.

UNIVERSITY OF CONNECTICUT
Box U-33
Storrs, Connecticut 06268

Course title: Futuristics and Secondary Education

Instructor: Ronald T. LaConte

Educational level: Doctorate

Date of this offering: Spring, 1979   Date of first offering: Summer, 1974

Course description: This course examines the trends, developments, projections and forecasts and their potential impact on secondary education. **Activities:** Workshop approach. Some lecture-discussion at outset followed by individualized study as students address problems and issues peculiar to their personal educational concerns (subjects, teaching levels, types of position, etc.). **Source materials:** LaConte, *Teaching Tomorrow Today*; Dickson, *The Future File*; introductory texts; classroom library of over 300 books and well over 1,000 articles available. **Special features:** Varies according to budget, student interests, etc.

MANCHESTER HIGH SCHOOL
134 East Middle Turnpike
Manchester, Connecticut 06040

Course title: Studies in Futuristics

Instructor: Sherrill M. Jamo, Philip Stearns and Maralyn P. Fabian

Educational level: High school juniors and seniors

Date of this offering: Fall, 1978   Date of first offering: Fall, 1976

Course description: Ways of foretelling the future; possibilities and probabilities; my place in one future; how to affect future events today; options and priorities; voluntary simplicity; getting free; a utopian future community; the computer and me. **Activities:** "What if" thinking; intensive letter writing; scenarios; survival gaining; student Delphi survey; guest speakers on world hunger, computers, nuclear energy and others; involvement in school/community project to cause change. **Source materials:** Books: Commoner, *The Closing Circle*; Ehrlich and Ehrlich, *The End of Affluence*; Toffler, *Future Shock*; *Living Poor with Style*; Dickson, *The Future File*; films: *Future Shock*; *Incident at Brown's Ferry*; *The Gene Engineers*; *Pollution: A Matter of Choice, But Is This Progress*; magazines: *Organic Gardening*; THE FUTURIST; *Omni*; *Science News*. **Special features:** Participation in collecting food and money for Food Bank for Manchester hungry; eliminating non-necessary machinery from daily life; fostering independence; sharing with each other.

WESTERN CONNECTICUT STATE COLLEGE
181 White Street
Danbury, Connecticut 06810

Course title: Introduction to Educational Futuristics

Instructor: Thomas M. Butterworth, Associate Professor

Educational level: Master's, professional

Date of this offering: Summer session   Date of first offering: 1977

Course description: This course examines alternative futures for our society and its educational subsystem. Participants imagine possible futures, forecast probable futures, and explore methods for choosing preferable futures in society and education. **Activities:** Delphic exploration of educational futures; scenario writing; simulation gaming on world futures; values clarification exercises; analysis of decisionmaking processes. **Source materials:** *Forecasting the Future*, 5 filmstrips and cassettes; Shane, *The Educational Significance of the Future*; Toffler, *Learning for Tomorrow*; Cornish, *The Study of the Future*. **Special features:** Reports by students of self-initiated projects introducing futurist perspective into educational process. This course is open only to those who have had at least five years experience in educational administration or teaching.

WOOSTER SCHOOL
Ridgebury Road
Danbury, Connecticut 06810

Course title: Alternative Global Futures

Instructor: William A. Nesbitt

Educational level: High school

Date of this offering: Winter, 1979-80

Date of first offering: 1974

Course description: Presentation of the Global Problematique: population, food, energy, resource depletion, arms race, rich-poor gap; scenario writing on pessimistic futures; question of growth—the limits and critiques; scenario writing on optimistic futures. **Activities:** Discussion; interpretation of data; scenario writing; future mapping; simulation games; computer simulations. **Source materials:** Books: Nesbitt and Karls, *Intercom No. 78: Teaching Interdependence;* Brown, *The Twenty Ninth Day;* Gray, Gray and Martin, *Growth and Its Implications for the Future;* Mische and Mische, *Toward a Human World;* Toffler, *Future Shock;* Sivard, "World Military and Social Expenditures, 1978"; Nesbitt, "Data on the Human Crisis"; games: *Limits; The Global Futures Game;* films. **Special features:** The main feature is the use of simulation games to imagine positive alternative futures. An increasingly heavy emphasis is placed on the "small is beautiful" scenario, which encourages individual lifestyle changes.

DISTRICT OF COLUMBIA

AMERICAN UNIVERSITY
School of Business
Washington, D.C. 20016

Date of first offering: 1973

Program title: Master of Business Administration

Director: —

Educational level: Master's and returning professionals

Degrees offered: Master of Business Administration (M.B.A.) with a concentration in management.

Course titles: Ordinary M.B.A. core requirements plus these courses: The Future of Business; Long-range Planning; Complex Organizations; Independent Study in Futuristics.

Program description: These four courses, taught by Professor of Management William E. Halal, are not a formal program leading to a degree in futuristics but are offered to students wishing to pursue this field as part of the ordinary requirements for the M.B.A. degree. Activities include lecture, discussion, scenario writing, forecasting models, planning models, and student projects. Source materials vary with each course.

ANTIOCH UNIVERSITY
Institute for Alternative Futures
1624 Crescent Place, N.W.
Washington, D.C. 20009

Course title: Alternative Futures and the Policy Process

Instructor: Clem Bezold

Educational level: Law School

Date of this offering: 1979

Date of first offering: —

Course description: The purpose of this course is to acquaint law students with possible changes in the legal system and ways to think more effectively about the future. The introduction to the course stresses legal thinking, policy thinking and futures thinking. Students follow up with work in alternative futures, forecasting, policy making in legislatures, policy making in the courts, and the legal "system" and its parts. **Activities:** Readings; oral and written assignments; class discussions and lectures. **Source materials:** Texts: *Proceedings of the Conference on the Future of the Legal System,* Antioch School of Law and the Institute for Alternative Futures, October 1977; Horowitz, *The Courts and So-*

cial Policy; Schwartz, ed., *Law and the American Future; Law in the Future: What Are the Choices?,* supplement to *California State Bar Journal,* July 1976; Bezold, ed., *Anticipatory Democracy;* multiple copies of other readings on reserve in the library. **Special features:** The course is part of a program to integrate futures thinking into the curriculum.

GEORGE WASHINGTON UNIVERSITY
Washington, D.C. 20052

THE AMERICAN UNIVERSITY
Washington, D.C. 20016

Course title: Technology Assessment

Instructor: Vary T. Coates, Associate Director, Program of Policy Studies in Science and Technology, and Joseph F. Coates, Assistant to the Director, U.S. Congress Office of Technology Assessment—George Washington University; David Malone, Division Chairman, Policy and Management Science Division, Center for Technology and Administration—American University.

Educational level: Master's

Date of this offering: 1978-79   **Date of first offering:** 1974

Course description: Instruction in methodology, organization, management, and performance of policy-oriented research on the societal impacts of technological development. The first semester consists of lectures and discussion periods dealing with the concept, rationale, history, and utility of technology assessment, and with technology assessment activities of the national and state governments, the private sector, international organizations, and foreign governments. The second semester is a practicum in which individuals or groups undertake exploratory research projects. **Activities:** Lecture; seminar; student projects; guest speakers. **Source materials:** Francois Hetman, *Society and the Assessment of Technology;* large selection of documents and reprints, many by the course instructors. **Special features:** Course is strongly career-oriented, intended for people aiming for or already involved in policy-oriented and decision-making positions in government, industry and professional policy analysis. Course is offered jointly by George Washington University and The American University. Physical location alternates yearly.

GEORGE WASHINGTON UNIVERSITY
School of Education and Human Development
Washington, D.C. 20052

Course title: Futurism and Education

Instructor: E.P. Kulawiec, Associate Professor of Education

Educational level: Master's and doctorate

Date of this offering: 1978   **Date of first offering:** Spring, 1975

Course description: This graduate education course concentrates on four topics: the future as academic discipline; methodologies (concentrating on scenario writing); contemporary American and world realities; futurism and selected disciplines (science, social sciences, education). **Activities:** Lecture-discussion; wide use of audio-visuals (films, filmstrips, tapes, slides); scenario writing; student reports. **Source materials:** Toffler, *The Futurists;* Ciba Foundation, *The Future as an Academic Discipline;* Kahn, *The Next 200 Years.* **Special features:** A very popular exercise used in 1978 is the cross-reading of prepared scenarios with students supplying variations of endings as drawn by the originator, a kind of see and contrast gaming.

GEORGE WASHINGTON UNIVERSITY
School of Government and Business Administration
Washington, D.C. 20052

                                              Date of first offering: 1975

Program title: General Management Systems and Organizational Cybernetics

Director: Richard F. Ericson, Stuart Umpleby, Elizabeth Adams

Educational level: Master's and doctorate

Degrees offered: M.B.A. in Business Administration; M.P.A. in Public Administration; M.S.A. in Administration; D.B.A. in Business Administration; D.P.A. in Public Administration, all with special concentration in General Management Systems and Organizational Cybernetics.

Course titles: Introduction to General Systems and Cybernetics; Fundamentals of General Management Systems and Organizational Cybernetics; (GEMSOC); Case Studies and Field Research in GEMSOC; Modeling and Simulation; Research Seminar in GEMSOC Theory; Philosophic and Policy Issues in Institutional Articulation.

Program description: The program includes lectures and discussions, group projects, mathematical modeling and computer simulation, research reports and group consulting. Principal books include: Mesarovic and Pestel, *Mankind at the Turning Point;* Ashby, *An Introduction to Cybernetics;* Beer, *Platform for Change;* Forrester, *Principles of Systems;* Ackoff, *Redesigning the Future.* The program has access to a nationwide computer conferencing system linking systems theorists. The evolution of a Washington area agency or firm is a special feature of the program.

FLORIDA

BARRY COLLEGE
11300 N.E. Second Avenue
Miami, Florida 33161

Course title: Future Aspects of Business

Instructor: Mark Weyman

Educational level: College juniors and seniors

Date of this offering: Fall, 1978   **Date of first offering:** 1977

Course description: An overview of current trends and future forecasts in the business and economic world, including topics such as: the future of agribusiness, health care, transportation, energy, construction, and business and economic trends. **Activities:** Lecture; discussion; scenario writing; research reports. **Source materials:** Asimov, *Earth Our Crowded Spaceship;* Schumacher, *Small Is Beautiful;* Cornish, *The Study of the Future.* **Special features:** Field trips to the NOAA installations and to Planet Ocean, an ocean museum.

BELEN JESUIT PREP
824 S.W. 7th Avenue
Miami, Florida 33130

Date of first offering: 1975

Program title: Global Issues Curriculum

Director: Joseph I. Lamas

Educational level: High school

Degrees offered: —

Course titles: —

Program description: Emphasizes the study of alternative world futures: given the present situation of major global issues (overpopulation, hunger and poverty, nuclear proliferation, environmental deterioration, etc.) how are things likely to develop in the future? For the better? For the worse? The Global Issues Curriculum is a four-semester program. Lecture-discussion; simulations; students required to prepare a major research paper. Basic study materials include articles from THE FUTURIST; *1999: The World of Tomorrow;* hand-outs from different sources; films and other audio-visual presentations; several simulations.

CENTRAL FLORIDA COMMUNITY COLLEGE
P.O. Box 1388
Ocala, Florida 32670

Course title: The Future

Instructor: Ernest Jernigan, Professor, Social Sciences Department

Educational level: College sophomores; general; educators for credit and non-credit

Date of this offering: 1978   **Date of first offering:** 1974

Course description: This course represents an examination of alternate futures which may face our society and includes a study of current goals and trends—roles of government, economics, population growth, religion, values, science, conservation, and man's instinct for survival in shaping the future. **Activities:** Lecture-discussion, scenario writing, oral reports on THE FUTURIST, *Science, 1984,* etc., plus a future autobiography. **Source materials:** Cornish, *The Study of the Future;* Schumacher, *Small Is Beautiful;* THE FUTURIST; *The South;* speakers for forums, conferences, institutes. **Special features:** Class visit by policy analyst, speakers; Future Institutes for credit or non-credit. Future Studies Scholarship awarded to three recipients—criteria includes writing an original research paper on the future.

UNIVERSITY OF FLORIDA
Philosophy Department, ASB
Gainesville, Florida 32611

Course title: Environmental Problems and Systems Philosophy

Instructor: Thomas Simon, Philosophy; Howard Odum, Environmental Engineering; John Alexander, Urban Planning

Educational level: College undergraduates; adult - general

Date of this offering: Spring, 1979   **Date of first offering:** 1979

Course description: Course topics include: disciplinary vs. interdisciplinary approaches to solving problems; the systems synthesis; philosophical foundations of systems theory; world modeling; systems approach in disciplines; energy and power; analogue modeling; systems design. This course is an experiment to introduce systems concepts into the general curriculum. **Activities:** Lecture-discussion. **Source materials:** Beishow and Peters, eds., *Systems Behavior*; Odum, *Environment, Power, and Society.* **Special features:** Student design and modeling projects including work on analogue computer.

UNIVERSITY OF FLORIDA
Gainesville, Florida 32611

Course title: Systems Philosophy

Instructor: Thomas W. Simon

Educational level: College juniors and seniors and master's

Date of this offering: Winter, 1978   **Date of first offering:** Winter, 1975

Course description: Systems analysis, especially cybernetics; applications of systems thinking, especially in ecology and futuristics. **Activities:** Lecture-discussion; projects in designing systems. **Source materials:** Ashby, *Introduction to Cybernetics*; Ackoff and Emery, *On Purposeful Systems*; Ackoff, *Design for Future*; Beer, *Platform for Change.* **Special features:** Simon also offers a course on Contemporary Moral Problems including sections on urban planning, values and future, and utopias.

FLORIDA ATLANTIC UNIVERSITY   Date of first offering: 1976
Boca Raton, Florida 33432

Program title: Program in Business Innovation and Strategy

Director: Jay S. Mendell, Visiting Professor

Educational level: College juniors and seniors; master's; professional

Degrees offered: —

Course titles: Various courses are incorporated in the Executive M.B.A. program, the regular M.B.A. program, and Continuing Education in Business.

Program description: Courses can be taken for partial fulfillment of M.B.A. requirements. Workshops can be tailored to the special needs and requirements of individual companies. Resources include the extensive resources of the program director, the Florida futurist community, and those of the university's executive M.B.A. program. The university has no freshman or sophomore years.

FLORIDA STATE UNIVERSITY
Art Education/Craft Design
EDU 123
Tallahassee, Florida 32306

Course title: ATE Graduate seminar

Instructor: Virginia M. Brouch, Department Chairman and Judith A. Kula, Professor — team teaching

Educational level: Doctorate

Date of this offering: Annually   Date of first offering: Summer, 1978

Course description: This course features strategies for eliciting futures responses from learners at all age levels.
Activities: Readings/discussions of available literature; tapes of major speakers (St. Cloud/Clear Lake City Conference); scenario writing; students present oral reports.   Source materials: Esfandiary books; film *Why Man Creates;* some films from World Future Society.   Special features: Instructors hope to develop futures thinking as components of every course at the undergraduate and graduate levels of their program as part of a five-year projection plan for the department.

UNIVERSITY OF SOUTH FLORIDA
College of Education
Tampa, Florida 33620

Course title: Schools and The Future

Instructor: Charles Weingartner

Educational level: Doctorate

Date of this offering: 1978   Date of first offering: 1978

Course description: Concentrates on alternative futures for public schools; alternative methods of developing future scenarios; essential categories for cross impact analyses relating to education; exciting educational future scenarios; scenario development.   Activities: Seminar workshop combining lecture-discussion, scenario writing, student oral reports culminating at the end of quarter in sample scenarios relating to alternative futures—5-10 years ahead.
Source materials: Cornish, *The Study of the Future;* Hipple, *The Future of Education — 1975-2000;* Rubin, *The Future of Education: Perspectives on Tomorrow's School;* current periodicals and future scenarios from the State Education Department.   Special features: Special materials relating to electronic information handling technology, including recent developments in hardware and potential educational applications.

UNIVERSITY OF WEST FLORIDA
9 Mile Road
Pensacola, Florida 32504

Course title: Language of Change; Futuretalk

Instructor: Ron Evans

Educational level: College juniors and seniors, master's, professional

Date of this offering: Once per year on demand   Date of first offering: Fall, 1975

Course description: These seminars in English education concern social future, psychological future, effects of these on language behavior (acquisition, memory coding, conceptualizing, etc.) and the implications of these predictions on education and teacher behavior.   Activities: Reading, discussion-lecture — role playing, scenario writing, project implementation.   Source materials: Farrell, *Deciding the Future; Psychetypes; Language of Change;* Fabun, *Children of Future; EST: Electronic Steersman Theory;* Ernst, *Games Students Play;* Brown, *The Live Classroom;* Samples, *The Metaphoric Mind.*   Special features: Visiting specialists. Futures material is presented throughout the course or as a shorter unit within the course, depending on the level of the course.

GEORGIA

ATLANTA UNIVERSITY
Graduate School of Business Administration
Atlanta, Georgia 30314

Course title: Public Policy and Private Enterprise

Instructor: Ronald W. Hull

Educational level: Master's

Date of this offering: 1978   **Date of first offering:** —

Course description: This course has become future-oriented within the past few years. Discusses questions of public policy in the future of business civilization. Course topics include: optimistic and pessimistic futurists, business alternatives, and a theory of technological development.   **Activities:** Students read and analyze futuristic writers' works; write a scenario of their own situation in 1995; debate the outcome of business civilization.   **Source materials:** Books: Kahn, *The Next 200 Years;* Heilbroner, *Business Civilization in Decline.* The students also use THE FUTURIST, articles and chapters from many sources.   **Special features:** Two speakers from business, one speaking on the optimistic side, one on the pessimistic side.

EMORY UNIVERSITY
Atlanta, Georgia 30322

Course title: Religion, Change and the Future

Instructor: Earl D. C. Brewer, Professor of Sociology and Religion

Educational level: Master's and doctorate

Date of this offering: Spring, 1979   **Date of first offering:** Spring, 1970

Course description: Continuities, changes and future prospects of humanity; ways of visioning the future; religion and future shock; the future of the church, communities, technology, environment, institutions, and people. This is one of the few futuristic courses offered in a seminary. The course is offered every other year.   **Activities:** Lecture-discussion; scenario writing; small group discussions.   **Source materials:** Hiley Ward, *Religion 2101 A.D.;* Toffler, *Future Shock;* Moltmann, *Religion, Revolution, and the Future;* 100 titles on reading list.   **Special features:** Visits by experts in selected fields.

UNIVERSITY OF GEORGIA
           Date of first offering: 1975

Aderhold Hall
Department of Educational Psychology
Athens, Georgia 30602

Program title: Future Problem Solving Program

Director: E. Paul Torrance; J. Pansy Torrance

Educational level: K-12 elementary, intermediate and high school

Degrees offered: —

Course titles: —

Program description: The 1978-79 program involves over 15,000 children in 42 states in a year-long program and is climaxed by an annual bowl and a national scenario writing contest. Activities include creative problem solving, independent study, and scenario writing. Source materials include *Handbook for Training Future Problem Solving Teams* and *Scoring Guide: Future Problem Solving Program;* Practice problems (4 each year with study guides, lists of resources, etc.); scenario writing instructions; videotapes: *Future Problem Solving and Career Education; Children Solve Future Problems.* Local sponsors make use of community resources as appropriate to the exploration and study of a problem.

HAWAII

EAST-WEST CENTER

Date of first offering: 1970-71

1777 East-West Road
Honolulu, Hawaii 96848

Program title: Transnational, Cooperative Problem-oriented Research, Development, and Learning Projects

Director: Jack Lyle, East-West Communication Institute; Verner Bickley, East-West Culture Learning Institute; Lee-Jay Cho, East-West Population Institute; William Matthews, East-West Resource Systems Institute

Educational level: Professional, post-doctoral, pre-doctoral research training

Degrees offered: None

Course titles: Communication Institute: Social Effects of Communication; Communication Process and Context; Communication Policy and Planning; Transnational Knowledge Utilization in Communication. Culture Learning Institute: Methods for Analyzing Cultural Misunderstanding; Culture and the Interactive Process; The Impact of Transnational Interactions: The Problem of Cultural Autonomy; Cultural Problems in Treaty Negotiation; Transcultural/Transnational Education. Population Institute: Development and Application of Techniques in Census, Surveys & Vital Registration; Analysis of Population Growth; Causes and Consequences of Demographic Behavior; Migrants and the City; Policy and Program Analysis. Environment & Policy Institute: Environmental Assessment in Development Planning and Assistance; Extended Maritime Jurisdictions: Environment & Resource Management Policies; Environmental Dimensions of Energy Policy; Methodologies and Information Bases. Resource Systems Institute: Food Systems; Energy Systems; Raw Materials. Centerwide Seminars: Pacific Prospects in Global Perspective (Series).

Program description: The institutes encourage participation in the design, conduct and evaluation of generating, applying, and sharing knowledge about the U.S., Asia and the Pacific aspects of global problems. A list of research and development products is available.

UNIVERSITY OF HAWAII

Date of first offering: 1969

Department of Political Science
2424 Maile Way
Honolulu, Hawaii 96822

Program title: Alternative Futures Program

Director: James A. Dator

Educational level: College undergraduate, master's, doctorate, adult, and returning professionals

Degrees offered: A.B. in Interdisciplinary Studies with a concentration in futuristics; M.A. in political science with a concentration in political futuristics

Course titles: Introduction to Futures Study; Applied Futuristics; Advanced Futuristics; Independent Studies; electives.

Program description: These courses, offered through the political science department, serve as the core courses for the interdisciplinary futuristics degree and as electives for all students. The introductory course consists mainly of lecture, discussion, and audiovisual materials with a futures design final project. The applied course consists entirely of student projects, usually audiovisual or activities to encourage citizen participation in designing their own future. The advanced course focuses on methodology.

MARYKNOLL HIGH SCHOOL

1402 Punahou Street
Honolulu, Hawaii 96822

Course title: Futuristics

Instructor: Andrew W. Corcoran, Vice Principal

Educational level: High school

Date of this offering: 1978-79

Date of first offering: 1970

Course description: Course topics include: introduction to the future (methods of studying); technology and values;

population growth and control; food growth and distribution; urbanization and shelter; transportation/communication; leisure/work; growth vs. no growth; ecology; energy; resource availability; government and institutions; war and peace. **Activities:** Lecture-discussion with related readings; simulation activities, especially in food, population, war and peace; scenario writing; research papers. **Source materials:** Leinwand, ed., *The Future;* Boyer, *Alternative Futures;* Toffler, *Learning for Tomorrow;* LaConte, *Teaching Tomorrow Today;* Schumacher, *Small Is Beautiful;* Orwell, *1984;* Huxley, *Brave New World.* **Special features:** Future studies are also conducted in Theology (especially Resource Depletion, Food Distribution, Nature of Life, etc.), and in Economics.

IDAHO

HIGHLAND HIGH SCHOOL
1800 Bench Road
Pocatello, Idaho 83201

Course title: Future and Science in Society

Instructor: Michael McCarty

Educational level: High school

Date of this offering: Fall, 1979   Date of first offering: 1973

Course description: This mini course in sociology for high school juniors and seniors is offered every other year. Instructor used SRSS Episode Science and Society and studied the future urban development of Pocatello area in the year 2000 A.D. **Activities:** Discussion conducted in small groups; gaming; role-playing. Class used city and county maps to get the urban development future picture. Students sketched Utopias they would like to live in. **Source materials:** THE FUTURIST; SRSS Episode; Toffler, *Future Shock;* filmstrips. **Special features:** —

ILLINOIS

AMERICAN SCHOOL OF MANAGEMENT   Date of first offering: 1979
850 Exchange
Suite L-102
Park Forest South, Illinois 60466

Program title: Future Oriented External Doctorate

Director: William Engbretson

Educational level: Doctorate

Degrees offered: Ph.D. in Administration and Management, D. Adm. (Doctor of Administration)

Course titles: Thematic and topical seminars with a futurist orientation.

Program description: Activities include monthly tutorials and topical seminars by futurists as indicated by student need and interest. ASM's program is an external doctoral degree with a futurist orientation in the generic fields of Administration and Management.

ARLINGTON HIGH SCHOOL
502 W. Euclid Avenue
Arlington Heights, Illinois 60004

Course title: Future Studies

Instructor: Howard Feddema

Educational level: High school juniors and seniors

Date of this offering: Spring, 1979, Fall 1979-80   Date of first offering: Fall, 1977

528

Course description: This course covers basic methodologies—futures wheels, cross-impact matrices, relevance trees, scenarios; limits to growth computer simulation; genetic engineering; space futures; future of family; future of work/employment; future foods/diet; future of architecture. **Activities:** Lecture-discussion; scenario writing; simulations. **Source materials:** Films: *Future Shock; Wild Science; Space: The Final Frontier;* tape/filmstrips: *Redesigning Man; Is Anybody Out There: The Search for Extra-Terrestrial Life; Forecasting the Future; Doomsday 21st Century;* simulations:*Limits;* computer simulation: *Futuribles; Cope;* slides: *Space Colonization; Underground Architecture.* **Special features:** Field trips to Fermi Lab, National Accelerator Lab; films: *Close Encounters of the Third Kind; Coma; Boys From Brazil.* Visit urban planner from Arlington Heights; speakers on future foods, nuclear waste, fibre optics, alternative lifestyles.

BRADLEY UNIVERSITY
Peoria, Illinois 61606

Course title: Geography of the U.S. in the Year 2000

Instructor: C. L. Ulch, Associate Professor of Geography

Educational level: College juniors and seniors

Date of this offering: Spring, 1979 — **Date of first offering:** Spring, 1976

Course description: World models of the future—utopia or doomsday?; Population crisis—truth or hoax?; food for the future; urban lifestyle in the year 2000. **Activities:** Lecture; discussion; student panels; quantitative research. **Source materials:** Meadows *et al.: The Limits to Growth;* Mesarovic and Pestel: *Mankind at the Turning Point;* L. Brown: *By Bread Alone;* F. M. Lappe: *Diet for a Small Planet;* J. Bernard: *Women, Wives, Mothers.* **Special features** Class visits by individuals pursuing alternative life-styles; student preparation of alternative foods.

DEPAUL UNIVERSITY—SCHOOL FOR NEW LEARNING
23 E. Jackson Boulevard
Chicago, Illinois 60604

Course title: Alternative Futures

Instructor: Charles E. Wiberg, Professor of History, North Park College

Educational level: College undergraduate; adult—general

Date of this offering: Fall, Winter, 1978; Academic year 1979-80 — **Date of first offering:** 1978

Course description: The "Limits to Growth" debate—both sides of the argument. Specific attention to problems of population, food supply, non-renewable energy resources, environmental pollution, and the economic, social, and political implications of these problems. Critical examination of alternative scenarios for the future. **Activities:** Lecture-discussion; individual inquiry into specific problems on scenarios (presented in written form). **Source materials:** Heilbroner, *An Inquiry into the Human Prospect;* Meadows, et al. *The Limits to Growth;* Kahn, et al, *The Next 200 Years;* Schumacher, *Small is Beautiful.* **Special features:** —

EASTERN ILLINOIS UNIVERSITY — **Date of first offering:** 1975
School of Technology AAE 101
Charleston, Illinois 61920

Program title: M.S. in Technology

Director: Donald P. Lauda, Dean

Educational level: Master's

Degrees offered: M.S. in Technology

Course titles: This program includes Readings in Technology; Technical Developments in Technology; Contemporary Problems in Technology.

Program description: At the conclusion of this required sequence of courses, each student is knowledgeable in his/her technical area from the past, current status and has it projected into the future. This includes technical content as well as socio/cultural content. Activities include: lecture-discussion; field trips to R & D centers and industries; student projects in which students present the future of their technical area (production or communications or energy/power); books:

Toffler, *Future Shock; Understanding Technology; Technology, Change and Society; Innovations;* films: *Future Shock; Catastrophe or Commitment.*

GOVERNORS STATE UNIVERSITY
Park Forest South, Illinois 60466

Course title: Technological Forecasting

Instructor: Donald R. Herzog

Educational level: Master's

Date of this offering: Winter, 1978   **Date of first offering:** Fall, 1973

Course description: Methods of technological forecasting; applicability in industrial and governmental planning. **Activities:** Lecture; discussion; student research paper presentation. **Source materials:** Bright, ed., *Technological Forecasting for Industry and Government: Methods and Applications;* selected articles from *Futures* and *Technological Forecasting and Social Change.* **Special features:** Emphasis on an energy technology.

HAMPSHIRE JUNIOR - SENIOR HIGH SCHOOL
100 South State Street
Hampshire, Illinois 60140

Course title: Futures

Instructor: John A. Krewer, Project Director; Team members: Jim Feld, Biological Sciences; Pat Tylka, English Department, science fiction, cross-cultural contact; William Stepien, Future City; Fred Rackow, Guidance Department, Future Aptitudes.

Educational level: Intermediate (6-9) and high school (9-12)

Date of this offering: 1978-79   **Date of first offering:** 1973-74

Course description: Thematic approach with units varying each semester. Topics include: biological engineering; genetic screening; science fiction as prophecy; multinational corporations and global responsibility; the Media-2000; human experimentation. **Activities:** Each theme utilizes range of "think tank" techniques including: futures wheels; scenario writing; interaction matrix; decision trees; Delphi process. **Source materials:** Books: Toffler, *Future Shock, Eco-Spasm Report, The Futurists;* DeBono, *New Think;* Ross, *Death and Dying;* Theobald, *Futures Conditional;* THE FUTURIST; games and simulations: *The IQ Game; Drug; Futuribles;* and others; filmstrips/slides: *Redesigning Man; The Control of Life;* and others. **Special features:** Students may take from 5 to 11 quarter hours credit by selecting from 6 mini-courses. All students take basic futures course. Program director and team members have been involved in over 50 teacher in-service and workshop programs on futurizing instruction grades K-12.

NORTH PARK COLLEGE
5125 N. Spaulding Avenue
Chicago, Illinois 60625

Course title: Our Children's World: Calamity or Hope?

Instructor: Charles E. Wiberg, Professor of History

Educational level: Adult - senior citizens

Date of this offering: August 27-31, 1979   **Date of first offering:** 1975

Course description: The course examines and critiques both "limits to growth" and "continuing growth" perspectives. The course covers the problem of exponential growth; the problems of limiting growth; a specific inquiry into the problem of population, food supply, resource depletion, energy, and environmental pollution. Particular attention to economic and social implications. **Activities:** Lecture-discussion. **Source materials:** Heilbroner, *An Inquiry into the Human Prospect;* Meadows, *The Limits to Growth;* Brown, *The Twenty-Ninth Day,* Kahn, *The Next 200 Years.* **Special features:** —

ST. JOSEPH HIGH SCHOOL
4831 S. Hermitage
Chicago, Illinois 60609

Course title: Futuristics

Instructor: Sandra Marie Wisniewski.

Educational level: High school; College freshmen and sophomores

Date of this offering: 1978   **Date of first offering:** 1974

Course description: Introduction to futuristics, technology, improving human life, global problems, space and beyond; science fiction. **Activities:** Presentation of material through films, filmstrips, slides, tapes, lectures, reading and discussion of magazine and newspaper articles and books on each topic as well as science fiction stories. Assimilation of ideas through discussion, oral reports, plays, writing of science fiction short stories, group projects such as building or drawing a home or city of the future, correlation of science fiction stories. Evaluation through teacher and student-made tests.   **Source materials:** Hill, *Reflections of the Future: An Elective Course in Science Fiction and Fact*; Farrell, et al., *Science Fact/Fiction;* Madsen, *Tomorrow: Science Fiction and the Future;* films: 21st Century series from Union Carbide Corp; Shell films; Science fiction; required reading of 8 science fiction books from classroom collection of 300 or from library for book reports and tests.   **Special features:** Field trip to see science fiction film *Encounters of the Third Kind;* class feature film; speakers on abortion, energy.

INDIANA

BALL STATE UNIVERSITY
Muncie, Indiana 47306

Course title: Colloquium on the Future

Instructor: David T. Nelson, Associate Professor of Finance, and Chairperson, Colloquium in Business, Technology and Applied Fields

Educational level: College undergraduate

Date of this offering: 1979   **Date of first offering:** 1970

Course description: Dimensions of future study, thinking for the future, personal and interpersonal relationships, mind and body of future man, education, business, communities of the future, energy alternatives, communications, global perspectives, doing more with less, towards a future for man; additional topics selected by students are also covered. **Activities:** Two-hour presentation weekly session for all 200 students uses lectures, panel presentations, films, slide presentations, guest speakers, live music, student mini-dramas, multi-media, videotapes, and taped music. Weekly one-hour discussion groups of about 50 students are devoted to values clarification and/or forecasting. Weekly study groups of about 20 students concentrate on specific issues. **Source materials:** Nelson, *Approaching the Future*; Toffler, *Future Shock;* Schumacher, *Small Is Beautiful;* Toffler, ed., *Learning for Tomorrow;* films; THE FUTURIST; other futurist books.   **Special features:** Each student is free to choose the medium that best expresses his point of view: fiction, non-fiction, film, slide presentation, artwork, etc.

BURRIS LABORATORY SCHOOL
Ball State University
Muncie, Indiana 47306

Course title: Future Dimensions—A Course in Human Futuristics

Instructor: Carl Keener, Richard Kishel, Wanda Vice (team members)

Educational level: High school

Date of this offering: 1979   **Date of first offering:** 1975

Course description: How to think future; who is a futurist?; theories and process of change; alternative futures; coping with the future; the "good life"; technology and the human environment; behavior and personal relations; biological man and biotechnology; the science of forecasting.   **Activities:** Methodology: inquiry-concept approach; individualized research, synthesis laboratories; creative projects, media productions, experimentation, symposia, simulation-gaming, scenario writing, play production.   **Source materials:** Cornish, *The Study of the Future*, Toffler, *Future Shock;*

Toffler, *The Futurists*, Toffler, *The Eco-Spasm Report*; Rosen, *Future Facts*; Schumacher, *Small Is Beautiful*; Spekke, *The Next 25 Years: Crisis and Opportunity*; Miller, *A Canticle for Leibowitz*; Falk, *This Endangered Planet;* Simulations; films; THE FUTURIST.   **Special features:** Course is taught by an interdisciplinary team and is currently being expanded into a program that includes elementary and middle-school levels. In high school the course is non-graded and open to all ability levels. Students use Delphi technique to research the question, "What are the areas of greatest urgency for study and research for the year 2010?" Field trips; resource persons visit classes. Documentation of project findings via media productions.

INDIANA UNIVERSITY
Bloomington, Indiana 47401

Course title: Educational Futures and the Curriculum

Instructor: Harold G. Shane, Professor of Education

Educational level: Doctorate

Date of this offering: Spring, 1978   **Date of first offering:** Spring, 1976

Course description: Introduction to educational futures and futures research; backgrounds and trends in futures studies; the impact of the future on education; the future as discipline; alternative educational responses to major problems of our age; values for the future; emergent curriculum change.   **Activities:** Lecture; discussion; individual student discussion leadership and reports.   **Source materials:** Shane, *The Educational Significance of the Future;* 1200 titles on reading list.   **Special features:** —

INDIANA UNIVERSITY, PURDUE UNIVERSITY AT INDIANAPOLIS
925 W. Michigan Street
Indianapolis, Indiana 46202

Course title: The Future

Instructor: Richard K. Curtis, Professor of Speech/Communication

Educational level: College juniors and seniors; doctorate

Date of this offering: 1978   **Date of first offering:** 1974

Course description: Why study the future?; the nature of the predictive process; methodological considerations in the study of the future; forecasting the future; education; ecology; cybernetics; energy; communication; urban planning, governance of men; war and peace.   **Activities:** Guest lecturers and panelists from the academic, business, and governmental community. Course begins with full day (6 hours) of orientation, and concludes with another full day, with presentation of term papers by students. Course requires 100 pages of reading, with reports (150 pages for graduate students), 3 mini-papers, and a term paper. In addition, course requires 6 hour-long modules over local educational TV station, prepared by Curtis.   **Source materials:** Comprehensive bibliography of articles and books from which reading may be selected. Color sound films, primarily from university film service.   **Special features:** Course is team-taught and interdisciplinary. Students attend classes on two Saturdays and receive 3 hours credit for the course. This appeals to teachers and others unable to attend class during a regular day — a cross between the Weekend College program and the Extended Degree program. This course is perhaps the most innovative course currently being offered on the campus of 22,000 students.

INDIANA UNIVERSITY, PURDUE UNIVERSITY AT INDIANAPOLIS
School of Education
902 North Meridian
Indianapolis, Indiana 46204

Course title: The Implications of the Future for Educational Planning

Instructor: Philip J. Hobbs and Jean Nicholsen

Educational level: Master's

Date of this offering: —   **Date of first offering:** Summer, 1978

Course description: Considers the influence on educational planning of energy, ecology, population, economics, mobility, communication and technology, and considers alternative designs for the future as related to curriculum change

532

and strategies to cope with such change.   **Activities:** Group projects; lecture-discussion; oral sharing and written reports of review/reaction to books and articles; film festival; forecasting; simulated game; panel and resource speakers. **Source materials:** Text: Shane, *Curriculum Change Toward the 21st Century;* supplementary books: Meadows, *Limits to Growth;* Leonard, *Education and Ecstasy;* Toffler, *Learning for Tomorrow;* Rugg and Shumaker, *The Child-Centered School;* Heilbroner, *An Inquiry into the Human Prospect;* extensive bibliography. **Special features:** Resource speakers; panel of experts on science fiction; group projects involving various media/methods.

ROSE-HULMAN INSTITUTE OF TECHNOLOGY
Date of first offering: 1971-72

5500 East Wabash Avenue
Terre Haute, Indiana 47803

Program title: Center for Technology Assessment and Policy Studies

Director: A. T. Roper, Professor of Mechanical Engineering and Director of the Center

Educational level: College juniors and seniors

Degrees offered: —

Course titles: Technology Assessment; Multi-institutional Technology Assessment; Summer Intern Program in Technology Assessment.

Program description: The quarter-long technology assessment course for Science and Engineering students uses the case study approach and features a five-week micro-assessment. The multi-institutional course focuses on eight-week assessments by joint student teams from Rose-Hulman, Indiana University, Indiana State University, and DePauw University. Other future-oriented courses at Rose-Hulman include problems and future alternatives of the global system, future of the post-industrial state, and political and economic development of the Third World. Projects with state and local policymakers. Summer intern program includes one week micro and five-week mini-assessment (40+ hours per week).

IOWA

HEARTLAND EDUCATION AGENCY
Date of first offering: 1976-77

1921 S.W. 3rd Street
Ankeny, Iowa 50021

Program title: Future Problem Solving Program (Iowa)

Director: Jonathan D. Edwards, Coordinator, Gifted and Talented; Lois Fingerman, President, Iowa Talented and Gifted (ITAG)

Educational level: K-12 Elementary, intermediate and high school

Degrees offered: —

Course titles: —

Program description: Program explained in *Handbook for Training Future Problem Solving Teams* by E. Paul Torrance, J. Pansy Torrance, S. J. Williams, and Ruey-yun Horng. A team of Future Problem Solvers is sponsored by a school and then enters Iowa's first statewide Future Problem Solving Bowl, held in Des Moines. Sponsors learn creative problem solving processes, recognize their creatively gifted students, feel the excitement of students turned on to solving problems they may face as adults. Ten junior (grades 4, 5, 6), ten intermediate (grades 7, 8, 9) and ten senior teams of four students will participate in the Bowl in March. Certificates will be awarded for excellent performance; trophies will be awarded winning teams in each division. Winners of the State Bowl will participate in the National Bowl, April 18-21, in Lincoln, Nebraska. For more information see entry under University of Georgia.

UNIVERSITY OF IOWA
W 303 East Hall
University of Iowa
Iowa City, Iowa 52242

Course title: Futurism in Education

Instructor: Robert M. Fitch, Professor

Educational level: Master's; doctorate; professional; general (adult)

Date of this offering: Spring, 1978   **Date of first offering:** Fall, 1977

Course description: Futurism as a concept; change; methodologies; values and the future; an incomplete guide to the future; research methodology; futurizing the curriculum; projecting alternative educational futures; alternative educational scenarios. **Activities:** Lectures; films; video tapes; computer assisted instruction (computer simulation); individually guided instruction; student reports; scenario writing. **Source materials:** Toffler, *Learning for Tomorrow*; McHale, *The Future of the Future*; Harman, *An Incomplete Guide to the Future*; Baier and Rescher, *Values and the Future*; Bell, *The Coming of Post-Industrial Society*. **Special features:** Computer simulation; computer assisted instruction; distance-learning formats; expertise as appropriate and available as given topics.

UNIVERSITY OF NORTHERN IOWA
Cedar Falls, Iowa 50613

Course title: The Present Predicament of Mankind

Instructor: Josef W. Fox, Professor of Philosophy and the Humanities

Educational level: College juniors and seniors

Date of this offering: Every semester   **Date of first offering:** Fall, 1973

Course description: Population growth; resource depletion; environmental deterioration; nuclear proliferation; institutional reconstruction; values. **Activities:** Lecture-discussion **Source materials:** Ehrlich and Holdren, *Ecoscience: Population, Resources, Environment*; Meadows, *The Limits to Growth*; Kahn, *The Next 200 Years*. **Special features:** —

KANSAS

FORT HAYS STATE UNIVERSITY
Hays, Kansas 67601

Course title: Can Man Survive?

Instructor: G.K. Hulett, Professor of Biology; E.D. Fleharty, Professor of Zoology

Educational level: College juniors and seniors; adults

Date of this offering: 1978   **Date of first offering:** 1971

Course description: The nature of the ecosystem; the evolution of man: societal evolvement; cultural factors affecting man's environmental impact; future alternatives: ecological ethics and the steady-state. **Activities:** Lecture; discussion. **Source materials:** Fleharty and Hulett, *Can Man Survive?* **Special features:** Course has been taught on state-wide TELENET and has been developed for correspondence activities through the University of Kansas. The University also offers two other courses: "A Steady-State Society" offered to college juniors and seniors and those pursuing a master's degree, available since 1976, and a new course offered the first time in the spring of 1979, "Bioethics," offered to college juniors and seniors, those pursuing a doctorate, and adults. This course, taught by E. D. Fleharty, G. K. Hulett and S. G. Tramel, uses films, and the course text is being written by the instructors.

UNIVERSITY OF KANSAS
Lawrence, Kansas 66045

Course title: Communications in the Future

Instructor: William A. Conboy, Professor of Speech Communication and Human Relations

Educational level: College juniors and seniors and master's

Date of this offering: Spring, 1979   **Date of first offering:** 1969

Course description: Personal, social, organizational, and technological models of the future; utopias and dystopias; the future of communication behavior; the future of education; the visions and versions of future-analysts including Fuller, McLuhan, Reich, Skinner, Kahn, Bell, Toffler, and McHale. **Activities:** Lecture; discussion; guest lectures by subject-matter experts; films; future games, including design, construction, and testing of original games by members of the class.   **Source materials:** Books: Toffler: *The Futurists;* Toffler: *Learning for Tomorrow;* Schwartz: *Human Communication and the New Media;* University of Kansas Continuing Education: *2076;* films: *Future Shock; Stranger Than Science Fiction; Ideas in Science Fiction;* multimedia: *Newsweek: 2000 A.D.*   **Special features** Lecture-presentations by science fiction writer, technology assessment expert, future-oriented economist, and future-oriented education specialist; multimedia presentation on Marshall McLuhan by subject-matter expert; original scenarios, sometimes science fiction stories, by students; film and slide-sound presentations by students.

UNIVERSITY OF KANSAS
Lawrence, Kansas 66045

Course title: Intensive English Institute on the Teaching of Science Fiction

Instructor: James Gunn, Professor; Stephen Goldman, Associate Professor

Educational level: College juniors and seniors, master's, doctorate, post-doctoral

Date of this offering: 1979   **Date of first offering:** June, 1975

Course description: This 19-day course provides a background in the history and literary aspects of science fiction upon which teachers can build a course or a foundation for further study. A complete survey of science fiction shows how it functions as literature and how it can be taught. Includes discussion of literary strategies to deal with the future.   **Activities:** Eight to 10 hours a day immersion in science fiction studies. After enrollment 25-30 books are mailed to applicant to be read before arrival at the Institute. Lecture-discussion; speakers.   **Source materials:** Extensive reading before the course; films; Gunn, *Alternate Worlds: The Illustrated History of Science Fiction*; Gunn, (3 volumes) *The Road to Science Fiction*; selected novels.   **Special features:** Intensive, three-week experience; visiting writers and editors; reading list studied before Institute starts; paper prepared after Institute concludes.

LOUISIANA

NORTHWESTERN STATE UNIVERSITY OF LOUISIANA
Natchitoches, Louisiana 71457

Course title: The Management of Change

Instructor: Roger W. Best, Professor and Acting Dean, College of Business

Educational level: College juniors and seniors and master's

Date of this offering: June, 1979   **Date of first offering:** June, 1968

Course description: Planned change; institutional change; technological change; social and behavioral change; managerial roles and change; the individual as change agent; organizational design for change; strategies; technological forecasting.   **Activities:** Discussion; student oral reports; student workbooks and individual forecasts; reading; incidents for future managers.   **Source materials:** Books: Bennis, Benne and Chin, *The Planning of Change;* Basil and Cook, *The Management of Change;* Farmer, *Management in the Future;* Newman, ed., *Managers for the Year 2000;* books by Toffler; magazines: THE FUTURIST; many others.   **Special features:** Each student is expected to prepare a scenario-forecast for the next 15 years in a selected subject area.

MAINE

UNIVERSITY OF MAINE
Shibles Hall
Orono, Maine 04473

Course title: The Future in Education

Instructor: Stanley L. Freeman, Jr., Professor of Education

Educational level: College juniors and seniors; adult

Date of this offering: 1978   **Date of first offering:** 1976

Course description: Course is designed to heighten the awareness of the future as an element of the present, to influence the shape of the future, and to develop ways to bring the future into one's teaching plans. Adults take the same course except for the teaching methods. Course topics include: The future affects our present behavior; limits to growth-necessity for action now; need for alternative futures—methods of creating; methods of "futurizing" teaching. **Activities:** Lecure-discussion of limits to growth, trends in cities; students construct and analyze time line of future events; students complete scenario of arcology construction and simulate political action.   **Source materials:** Kauffman, *Teaching the Future*; Soleri, *City of Man*; THE FUTURIST; film: *1985*.   **Special features:** Students produce teaching plans to infuse the future into teaching/group leadership setting. Plans shared as models with Maine Studies Curriculum Project of State Education Department. The underlying objective is to emphasize citizen involvement in dreaming, choosing, and planning futures.

MARYLAND

CATONSVILLE COMMUNITY COLLEGE
Catonsville, Maryland 21228

Course title: The Future

Instructor: Fred Hickok

Educational level: College freshmen and sophomores

Date of this offering: Spring, 1978   **Date of first offering:**   Spring, 1976

Course description: Possible futures; probable futures; preferable futures; forecasting techniques; various individual subjects.   **Activities:**   Lecture; films; audio and video cassettes; readings; team development of projections in specific fields.   **Source materials:**   Books: Brown, *World Without Borders*; Cornish, *The Study of the Future*; Cornish, ed., *1999: The World of Tomorrow*; Clarke, *Profiles of the Future*; Toffler, ed., *The Futurists*; Toffler, *Future Shock*; Tugwell, ed., *The Search for Alternatives*; films: *Future Shock*; *21st Century* series.
Special features: —

GOUCHER COLLEGE   **Date of first offering:**   1970
Towson, Maryland 21204

Program title: Global Futures

Director: Brownlee Sands Corrin

Educational level: College, adult, and returning professionals

Degrees offered: A.B. in Human Communications

Course titles: Human Communications; Problems of Communications.

Program description: Program includes courses, field research, and communications projects. Source materials include general and technical periodicals, fiction and non-fiction books, and various multimedia materials including slides, films, and audio- and videotapes. Students participate in professional conferences and workshops, hold internships, undertake field research including surveys on citizen attitudes and behavior, and have produced four-minute public service radio and television spots on future problem options.

UNIVERSITY OF MARYLAND
College Park, Maryland 20742

Course title: Futuristics and Feeding Our People

Instructor: Jarvis L. Cain

Educational level: College seniors and graduate students

Date of this offering: Spring, 1979   **Date of first offering:** Spring, 1975

Course description: The world of the futurist; productivity; change and ways of looking at change; physical, human and societal resources; energy; the human feeding problem; current trends in human feeding; the meal concept; synthetic foods; nutrient delivery system; alternative futures. **Activities:** Term paper on selected changes in the food industry by 2000 A.D.; oral presentations by students. **Source materials:** Books: Gardner, *No Easy Victories;* Drucker, *The Age of Discontinuity;* McHale, *Future of the Future;* McHale, *World Facts and Trends;* Toffler, *Future Shock;* Townsend, *Up the Organization;* Tugwell, *Search for Alternatives;* de Jouvenel, *The Art of Conjecture;* selected articles and monographs. **Special features:** —

UNIVERSITY OF MARYLAND
College of Education
College Park, Maryland 20742

Course title: Exploring Our Future

Instructor: Richard L. Hopkins, Associate Professor, Division of Human and Community Resources

Educational level: College juniors and seniors and graduate level

Date of this offering: Spring, 1979   **Date of first offering:** Summer, 1975

Course description: An exploration of predictions about, and methodologies for making predictions about, the human community. Topics include: some views of the future of society; the future of child rearing and education; information exchange systems; social relationships; health and leisure; the exchange of goods and services; housing and clothing in the future; food in the future; science and technology; changing the human being itself; dealing with the future. **Activities:** Readings, oral analyses by students; discussion; student research papers and projects. **Source materials:** Beckwith, *The Next 500 Years;* Toffler, *The Futurists;* about 30 selected articles; about 10 films. **Special features:** —

PRINCE GEORGE'S COUNTY PUBLIC SCHOOLS   Date of first offering: 1970
3940 Elm Street
Upper Marlboro, Maryland 20870

Program title: Industrial Arts Program

Director: W. Harley Smith, Supervisor of Industrial Arts

Educational level: Junior high school

Degrees offered: —

Course titles: Communications Technology; Construction and Living Environments Technology; Manufacturing Technology; Energy and Transportation Technology.

Program description: In each of the above program elements, an emphasis is placed on present and future technology and on a wide variety of present and emerging careers. Students have extensive instruction and hands-on experiences with relevant tools, materials and processes. The program is in the developmental stage and has not been implemented county-wide.

MASSACHUSETTS

CAPE COD COMMUNITY COLLEGE
West Barnstable, Massachusetts 02630

Course title: Future Without Shock

Instructor: Judith M. Barnet, Instructor in Continuing Education

Educational level: Adult — general

Date of this offering: Spring, 1979   **Date of first offering:** —

Course description: Techniques for envisioning the future; imagineering values required for adaptability; cultural, personal facts and theories, hard and soft. **Activities:** Lecture-discussion, group activities (scenarios), films, visiting experts. **Source materials:** Simulation: *Global Futures;* THE FUTURIST. **Special features:** —

FITCHBURG STATE COLLEGE
Fitchburg, Massachusetts 01420

Course title: Future Studies

Instructor: A. Orin Leonard

Educational level: College juniors and seniors

Date of this offering: Spring, 1979   **Date of first offering:** Spring, 1974

Course description: Emphasis is on alternative futures. Students select their own topics: sports, transportation, religion, family, city, ecology, energy, etc. **Activities:** Text; readings; some scenarios; student panel oral presentation; some class discussion; limited lecturing. **Source materials:** Cornish, *The Study of the Future*; Garlan and Dunstan, *Star Sight.* **Special features:** —

UNIVERSITY OF LOWELL
Department of Sociology, North Campus
Lowell, Massachusetts 01854

Date of first offering: 1966

Program title: Futuristics

Director: William S. Harrison

Educational level: College juniors and seniors; adult

Degrees offered: —

Course titles: An Introduction to the Study of Alternative Futures; Alternative Futures; Material Trends; Social and Economic Trends; Political Trends; Towards the Mature Society (Applied Utopianism); Towards Spaceship Earth (World Order).

Program description: This program includes seven courses that may be used towards an A.B. degree in Sociology or as liberal arts electives toward an A.B. or B.S. in other fields. The courses are also offered in evening school as Community Service Programs. Activities include lectures, scenarios, simulations, class seminar discussions and interaction with the University community. Texts used include Cornish, *The Study of the Future;* Dickson, *The Future File;* World Future Society, eds., *1999: The World of Tomorrow;* Koberg and Bagnall, *Values Tech;* Hollister, *You and Science Fiction;* Greenberg, et al., *Social Problems Through Science Fiction;* Gowan, et al., *Moving Toward A New Society.*

MASSACHUSETTS INSTITUTE OF TECHNOLOGY
50 Memorial Drive
Cambridge, Massachusetts 02139

Date of first offering: 1960

Program title: System Dynamics

Director: Jay W. Forrester

Educational level: College juniors and seniors, master's and doctorate

Degrees offered: B.S., M.S., and Ph.D. in management with a concentration in system dynamics

Course titles: Principles of Dynamic Systems I and II; Industrial Dynamics; Application and Implementation of Industrial Dynamics; Dynamics of Health Service Systems; Research Seminar in Dynamics of Management Systems I and II (Economic Dynamics, System Dynamics Policy Analysis).

Program description: Principal activities include computer simulation, individual development of dynamic models, and participation in research programs. Principal books used include: Forrester: *Industrial Dynamics;* Forrester: *Principles of Systems;* Forrester: *Urban Dynamics;* Goodman: *Study Notes in System Dynamics;* Mass: *Economic Cycles: An Analysis of Underlying Causes;* and Meadows and Meadows, eds.: *Toward Global Equilibrium.*

UNIVERSITY OF MASSACHUSETTS
164 Hills House South
Amherst, Massachusetts 01003

Date of first offering: 1969

Program title: Future Studies

Director: Peter Wagschal, Faculty Director

Educational level: College undergraduate, master's, doctorate, and adult

Degrees offered: M.Ed., C.A.G.S. (Certificate of Advanced Graduate Study), and Ed.D. in Education with a concentration in future studies, and Massachusetts elementary and secondary teacher certification

Course titles: Graduate Seminar in Future Studies; Introduction to Future Studies; Future Studies Methods; Foundations of Education for a Changing World; Educational Policy Studies; Student Teaching Internship in Future Studies; Intern Methods and Support; Education, Racism, and Social Change; The Future on Film; Simulation Games for Classroom Use; Alternative Futures of Education; Learning for Tomorrow: A Futures Curriculum; Toward Tomorrow.

Program description: Members of the graduate program are involved in three general areas of study: the development of future-oriented education, the future of education, and long-range social forecasting, as well as teaching and contributing to the program's administration. The undergraduate teacher education program equips prospective teachers with the concepts, skills, resources, and teaching methods needed to create future-oriented curriculum and learning experiences. The in-service teacher education program affords educators the opportunity to earn a master's degree while remaining in their current positions. Program members also offer consulting services to a variety of educational organizations and publish a newsletter.

NORTH SHORE COMMUNITY COLLEGE
3 Essex Street
Beverly, Massachusetts 01915

Course title: Introduction to the Study of the Future

Instructor: Larry E. Myers, Chairman, Interdisciplinary Studies Department; R. E. Baker, Chairman, Division of Humanities and Social Sciences

Educational level: College freshmen and sophomores

Date of this offering: February, 1979   **Date of first offering:** February, 1979

Course description: World crises; technological innovations (Club of Rome, Kahn, etc.); social innovations (changing values, etc.); forecasting for "Fun and Prophet" (techniques, etc.); futuristics and futurists. **Activities:** A combination of lecture-discussion with problem-analysis, using scenarios, Delphi method, etc. **Source materials:** Assigned books: Callenback, *Ecotopia*; Kahn, *The Next 200 Years*; Thomas, *Lives of a Cell*; Clarke, *Childhood's End*; film: *Future Shock*; slide-tape: *Forecasting the Future*. **Special features:** In this first-time offering, possibilities include: selected handouts for analysis and discussion; field trip(s) (New Alchemy Institute, Cape Cod, Maine); seminars led by guest speakers.

MICHIGAN

ANDREWS UNIVERSITY
Berrien Springs, Michigan 49104

Course title: Education Planning and Evaluation; Long-Range Planning

Instructor: Rudolf E. Klimes, Professor of Educatonal Administration

Educational level: Master's and doctorate

Date of this offering: 1978-79, 1979-80   **Date of first offering:** 1975

Course description: These two courses deal with basic planning methodology and futurism. **Activities:** Lecture; discussion; scenario writing; oral and written reports; simulations. **Source materials:** *Futurism in Education; Educational Planning.* **Special features** Group work; creative futurism reports.

CENTRAL MICHIGAN UNIVERSITY
307 Ronan Hall
Mt. Pleasant, Michigan 48859

Course title: Educational Futurism, Professional Studies

Instructor: Roger N. Grabinski, Associate Professor; Co-director of Center for Community Education

Educational level: Master's and specialist

Date of this offering: 1978   **Date of first offering:** 1976

Course description: Educational futurism, professional studies. **Activities:** Lecture-discussion, scenario writing, oral reports, audio visual presentations, independent study. **Source materials:** Cornish, *The Study of the Future; The Future of Education: Perspectives on Tomorrow's Schooling;* Toffler, *The Futurists;* film: *Future Shock;* most of the materials listed by the World Future Society. **Special features:** A variety of outside speakers.

EASTERN MICHIGAN UNIVERSITY
Department of Political Science
Ypsilanti, Michigan 48197

Course title: Politics of the 21st Century

Instructor: Benjamin T. Hourani

Educational level: College juniors and seniors; adult

Date of this offering: Fall, 1980   **Date of first offering:** Fall, 1980

Course description: This course deals with the political long terms effects of present problems of man, society and the state. The major focus is on worldwide transformation and probable political futures. The political implications and possible alternatives to current and emerging trends will be explored. Course topics include: global view of world politics today; futurist research and public policy; socio-political transformation; role of science-technology; role of value systems; global politics; shaping the future of planet Earth. **Activities:** Lecture-discussion; guest speakers; analytic research on trends and implications to current politics. **Source materials:** Bariloche Foundation, *Catastrophe or New Society;* Meadows and Meadows et al., *Limits to Growth;* other works. **Special features:** Researchers from government and universities will be invited guest speakers.

GROSSE POINTE SOUTH HIGH SCHOOL
11 Grosse Pointe Boulevard
Grosse Pointe Farms, Michigan 48236

Course title: America and the Future

Instructor: Robert Bradley

Educational level: High school juniors and seniors

Date of this offering: Spring, 1979   **Date of first offering:** 1975-76

Course description: This American history course is taught chronologically to 1877, then thematically to the 21st century. Themes include: foreign policy, economic history, American art and architecture, politics in America. The final unit is America and the Future. Futures material is introduced into each of the other major themes. **Activities:** Scenario writing; wheels of consequence; extrapolation models; discussion on topics by different authorities: Harry Schwartz— the future of foreign policy; Toffler—anticipatory democracy; Ralph Nader—multi-national corporations, etc.; written reports; planning a utopia. **Source materials:** *Walden II;* Taylor, *The Biological Time Bomb;* Toffler, *Future Shock;* pairs of books for comparison/contrasts: *Brave New World /The Time Machine; 1984/Player Piano; Frankenstein/The Terminal Man.* Slide/cassette tape program on American Architecture, 1870-2000, which includes slides of Soleri's Arcosanti; simulations; selected magazine articles. **Special features:** Videotape of lecture/seminar by Robert Theobald in social studies classes. Strong emphasis on writing skills, particularly in expository essay and the book review.

HOLT SENIOR HIGH SCHOOL
1784 Aurelius Road
Holt, Michigan 48842

Course title: Futuristics

Instructor: Charles L. Green

Educational level: High school

Date of this offering: 1979   **Date of first offering:** 1977

Course description: Course topics include: food for the future; population problem; transportation; medicine; awareness of future shock; science and the future; social problems. **Activities:** Lecture-discussion; forecasting (genius forecasting, trend extrapolation); reading and analysis of magazine articles.   **Source materials:**   Toffler, *Future Shock;* articles from THE FUTURIST; film: *Future Shock;* several Science Screen Reports from Ciba-Geigy films; simulation: *Cope.* **Special features:** —

JOHN D. PIERCE JUNIOR HIGH SCHOOL
5145 Hatchery
Drayton Plains, Michigan 48020

Course title: You and the Future

Instructor: Sherry L. Schiller, Barbara K. Martin, Rochelle Rubin

Educational level: Intermediate 6-9

Date of this offering: Fall, 1978   **Date of first offering:** Fall, 1977

Course description: Topics include: rights and responsibilities, energy and the environment, technology, food, population and health, order and conflict, urbanization, jobs and leisure, mass media and consumerism, the individual of the future.   **Activities:**   A year-long, 4-hour day alternative program for any eighth grader who desires a future-focused alternative to the standard "academic" offerings with credit for language arts, social studies, math, and science. Emphasis is on applying basic skills in real-life problem-solving. The course includes frequent field trips, flexible grouping and scheduling, team-teaching, moral dilemmas, force-field analysis, "real-world challenges," personal and societal goal-setting and self-evaluation, and futures wheels. Students are trying to organize a global organization for young futurists. **Source materials:**   Books: Toffler, *Future Shock*; Orwell, *Animal Farm; Future Shock*, film and simulation; *The Future* (Scholastic); films; filmstrips.   **Special features:**   Students produce their own books and multimedia presentations, including a 25-minute, 3-screen slide-movie-tape; write computer programs; produce a newsletter; conduct community improvement projects; raise ALL operational and instructional material funds for program; involve parents and community in program.

LAMPHERE HIGH SCHOOL
610 West 13 Mile Road
Madison Heights, Michigan 48071

Course title: 21st Century

Instructor: David E. Smith

Educational level: High school

Date of this offering: Spring, 1978   **Date of first offering:** 1969

Course description: Prediction theory, energy, communications, population, transportation, urban development, work and leisure time, education, ecology, privacy, immortality, bioengineering, morality and values, family, future shock, thought and behavior control.   **Activities:**   Lecture-discussion; film presentation, discussion; brainstorming — problem solving; individualized research projects; book reports; scenario writing.   **Source materials:**   A multitude of films, lectures, filmstrips, magazine and newspaper articles.   **Special features:**   Each student is required to analyze and report on one or more books on the future; research and report on a topic dealing with the 21st century; and create an original work dealing with the future, such as a short story, a model city.

OAK PARK HIGH SCHOOL
13701 Oak Park Boulevard
Oak Park, Michigan 48237

Course title: Futuristics

Instructor: Jerry Gutman, Chairman, Social Studies Department; Larry Sabbath, Chairman, Science Department

Educational level: High school

Date of this offering: Fall, 1978   **Date of first offering:** Fall, 1978

Course description: This course introduces students to futuristics and leads to a research paper or project. Topics include: introduction to futuristic problems, values, areas of concern; Who are the futurists? What are futuristic methods? Independent study — research paper or project.   **Activities:**   Seminar; lecture-discussion; simulations; scenario writing; position papers; reports; contacts with futuristic groups; field trips; audio-visual materials.   **Source**

materials: *Futures Conditional; Star Sight;* THE FUTURIST; *Omni; Energy-X* simulation game; *Global Futures* game. **Special features:** Field trips; speakers; independent study reports; future fairs.

OAKLAND UNIVERSITY
School of Education
Rochester, Michigan 48063

Course title: Politics in Education: Designing Educational Futures

Instructor: F. James Clatworthy

Educational level: College juniors and seniors, master's

Date of this offering: Summer, 1979

Date of first offering: 1976

Course description: Main topics include: graphic ontology; question formulation; question critiquing; prioritizing; scenario writing; lateral thinking; creative scenario writing; polarized designs; problem-possibility analysis; policy abstract writing. **Activities:** Workshop-seminar. During workshop phase there are some short lectures, guest speakers on cassette tape and small group leadership skill development. During the seminar phase each participant has an opportunity to teach their problem from an "anticipatory design science" point of view. **Source materials:** Depends on the level. Undergraduates would have more introductory materials in articles and handouts. Graduates would have a series of handouts (excerpts from books and articles) plus the following books: Fuller, *Utopia or Oblivion;* Harman, *An Incomplete Guide to the Future;* Boyer, *Alternative Futures: Designing Social Change;* Toffler, *Learning for Tomorrow;* DeBono, *New Think;* Bowles and Gintis, *Schooling in Capitalist America;* Silberman, *Crisis in the Classroom.* **Special features:** Guest speakers via cassettes; ethnographic research into local school policy formulation by students; flexibility in student presentations to encourage creative communications.

OGEMAW HEIGHTS HIGH SCHOOL
960 S. M-33
West Branch, Michigan 48661

Course title: The Future

Instructor: Richard Overholt, Social Studies Teacher

Educational level: High School

Date of this offering: 1977-78

Date of first offering: 1972

Course description: Introduction (including *Future Shock*), techniques of investigating the future, biology and medicine, technology, global problems, space. **Activities:** Lecture-discussion; simulations; small group presentations. **Source materials:** Toffler, *Future Shock;* Clarke, *Profiles of the Future;* Goddykoontz, ed., *The Future: Can We Shape It?;* Hellfach, *The Future of the Environment; The Future of the Family; The Future of Government; The Future of Work; Futures Handbook;* Kaufman, *Teaching the Future;* King-Hele, *The End of the Twentieth Century;* Stirewalt, *Teaching Futures;* magazine articles; films; filmstrips. **Special features:** Opinion survey given students to find out their reactions to thinking about and discussing the future.

PORT HURON HIGH SCHOOL
2215 Court Street
Port Huron, Michigan 48060

Course title: Futuristics

Instructor: Dick Dougherty, Social Studies Chairman

Educational level: High school juniors and seniors

Date of this offering: 1978

Date of first offering: Fall, 1973

Course description: A one-semester interdisciplinary course. In the first six-seven weeks, students are introduced to global aspects of technology, biogenetics, urban and rural land use patterns, demographics, value aspects including value clarification activities, future cities, and other future-oriented topics. In the last eight-nine weeks, students conduct intensive studies of local future-oriented problems or concerns and report their findings to the community. **Activities:** Simulations; role playing; value clarification activities; scenario writing; Delphi technique; problem-solving. **Source materials:** Books: *Future Shock; The Future: Can We Shape It?;* science fiction; films: *Future*

542

Shock; many others; magazine: THE FUTURIST; many simulations; guest speakers; community interviews. **Special features** Extensive action learning and community involvement. Students spend considerable time outside of school in groups of three-five interviewing community resource people. Each semester study is distributed to members of the community in both written and oral form including publication in the local newspaper and presentations to governmental and service organizations. A class session was filmed by the U.S. Information Agency.

MARYGROVE COLLEGE
8425 W. McNichols Road
Detroit, Michigan 48161

Course title: The Year 2000: Promise or Peril

Instructor: Amata Miller, Adjunct Associate Professor of Economics

Educational level: College juniors and seniors

Date of this offering: Every other year for one semester   **Date of first offering:** 1972

Course description: Topics in this course include: Who are the futurists?; basic methodologies; general overview of the issues; comparison/contrast of views of post industrialists and neo-Malthusians on food, energy and other resources, pollution, socio-economic-political institutions; in-depth study on particular issue by each student. **Activities:** Lecture-discussion; essay writing; oral reports on readings; individual research paper and oral report. **Source materials:** Heilbroner, *Inquiry Into the Human Prospect;* Meadows, *Limits to Growth;* Kahn, *The Next 200 Years;* Mesarovic, *Mankind at the Turning Point;* various issues of THE FUTURIST; filmstrip series: *Lifestyle 2000.* **Special features:** The course is an interdisciplinary one and various faculty members are involved in giving lectures; e.g., a philosopher, a sociologist, a political scientist, a geneticist, a physicist.

MICHIGAN STATE UNIVERSITY   **Date of first offering:** Fall, 1976
Office of Medical Education
Research and Development
A206-A E. Fee Hall
E. Lansing, Michigan 48824

Program title: Social Context of Medicine

Director: Robert C. Brictson

Educational level: Graduate; Program is for medical students pursuing the M.D. degree

Degrees offered: —

Course titles: Topics include: person as an individual; person and family; person and community; health care system in the community; health care system as a community; quality of life and health; future of medicine and health.

Program description: The social context of medicine (SCM) is a program within the Upper Peninsula Medical Education Program (UPMEP). UPMEP is a four-year primary care education track of Michigan State University's College of Human Medicine, conducted jointly with the Upper Peninsula Health Education Corporation. Part of the purpose of UPMEP is to demonstrate that changes in medical education can increase the percentage of medical school graduates practicing primary care in rural under-served areas. SCM attempts to include behavioral science as a distinct element of a comprehensive care clerkship composed of family practice, internal medicine, ob/gyn, pediatrics, psychiatry, surgery, and social context. Two-day seminars expand the program with a variety of topics. Program evaluation consists of examinations, case write-ups, and feedback includes self, peer and preceptor review.

UNIVERSITY OF MICHIGAN
109 E. Madison
Ann Arbor, Michigan 48104

Course title: Computers in College Teaching and Scholarly Work

Instructor: Karl L. Zinn

Educational level: Doctorate

Date of this offering: 1978   **Date of first offering:** 1978

Course description: This course deals with the impact of computers and their use in courses such as technology forecasts; impacts on learning, teaching, administration, institutions, communities; special topics, e.g., computers and women, new organization of knowledge, new media for communication. **Activities:** Demonstration-discussion; individualized group projects. **Source materials:** Nelson, *Computer Lib/Dream Machines;* Nelson, *The Home Computer Revolution;* Seidel, *Computers and Communications; Implications for Education.* **Special features:** Projects using personal computers. An undergraduate version of this course has been offered, giving more attention to personal computer projects and additional attention to social implications. Undergraduate course offers more credit hours.

TEACHING-LEARNING COMMUNITIES

Date of first offering: 1971

Ann Arbor Public Schools
Bach School
600 West Jefferson
Ann Arbor, Michigan 48103

Program title: Teaching-Learning Communities

Director: Carol H. Tice; Jacquenette Locker, and Mary K. Critchell, Field Representatives

Educational level: K-12; College freshmen and sophomores; adult; senior citizens

Degrees offered: —

Course titles: —

Program description: Teacher-Learning Communities is an innovative project of the Ann Arbor Public Schools. It brings the youngest and oldest generations together through integrated arts experiences within the traditional educational structure, and enables both generations to invent the future together. It is multi-cultural and provides for a maximum diversity of values. Source materials include 16mm film produced by University of Michigan, *What We Have;* slide-tape presentation, *Lifelong Learning;* instructional packet of guidelines and resources for setting up the program; *Aide Handbook,* a guide for paraprofessional aides; *Activities Book for* children and grandpersons; evaluation reports.

WEST BLOOMFIELD HIGH SCHOOL

4925 Orchard Lake Road
Orchard Lake, Michigan 48033

Course title: Futuristics

Instructor: James L. Spinelle

Educational level: High school

Date of this offering: 1979

Date of first offering: 1977

Course description: Future technological achievements in a field chosen by the student, such as energy—solar, tidal, geothermal, solar cells, etc.; transportation; communications, etc. **Activities:** The course features a slide-tape program with a minimum of 50 slides and 20 minutes of taped text. Some students have final projects consisting of 30 typewritten pages (40-50 minutes of oral tape) with lead-in music, etc., and over 200 slides, including title slides and special effect slides. **Source materials:** Students write letters of inquiry to institutions and companies working in their project area. **Special features:** Each student chooses what he wants to do: class visits, field trips, etc.

WESTERN MICHIGAN UNIVERSITY

Date of first offering: Winter, 1978

Kalamazoo, Michigan 49008

Program title: Humanistic Future Studies

Director: Rudolf Siebert, Professor of Religion and Society

Educational level: College juniors and seniors

Degrees offered: Minor which can be counted towards an A.B. in any curriculum in the College of Liberal Arts and Sciences or a B.S. in the Colleges of Business or Applied Sciences

Course titles: Introduction to Future Studies; Independent Future Studies; Senior Seminar in Future Studies, which includes Forecasting, Planning, Philosophy of the Future, and Future-Oriented Issues.

Program description: The methodologies of this program are applied as aids to planners and policy-makers in education, the environment , government at all levels, business, industry, the churches, the military, etc. Thus the program is ideally suited for students majoring in many fields. It is also an excellent preparation for graduate work in many areas.

WESTERN MICHIGAN UNIVERSITY
Kalamazoo, Michigan 49008

Course title: Towards 2000: Utopian Visions and Futurism

Instructor: Howard J. Dooley, Assistant Professor in Humanities

Educational level: College juniors and seniors

Date of this offering: 1978-79

Date of first offering: Winter, 1973

Course description: Course is organized dialectically into three basic units: Best of all Possible Worlds—utopian visions from Gilgamesh to the present; Worst of all Possible Worlds—anti-utopian warnings, mostly of 20th century; Futuristics—origins, methods, aspirations, problems, and futuribles. Futuristics section takes first an earth-centered perspective, then a space-centered perspective. Considerable emphasis is given to the limits to growth debate. The course closes with an analysis of the pros and cons of space colonization. **Activities:** Lecture-discussion; students write book reviews; do article abstracts from THE FUTURIST, *Futures, Futuribles, Technological Forecasting and Social Change, Alternative Futures* and other journals. **Source materials:** Book list varies. Titles used in 1978-79: Tod and Wheeler, *Utopia;* Plato, *The Republic;* More, *Utopia;* Bellamy, *Looking Backwards;* Huxley, *Brave New World;* Orwell, *1984;* Miller, *A Canticle for Liebowitz;* Cornish, *The Study of the Future;* Paul and Ann Erhlich, *The End of Affluence;* Kahn, *The Next 200 Years;* Rosen, *Future Facts;* O'Neill, *The High Frontier* and/or Heppenheimer, *Human Colonies in Space;* films: *Limits to Growth; Future Shock; Things to Come* (1936). **Special features:** —

MINNESOTA

COON RAPIDS SENIOR HIGH SCHOOL
Coon Rapids, Minnesota 55433

Course title: Futuristics

Instructor: Kenneth R. Peterson

Educational level: High school seniors

Date of this offering: 1978-79

Date of first offering: 1973

Course description: The acceleration of the rate of change; future shock; futuristics and future thought; spaceship earth; the machine: enemy or ally?; future of the family; future of government. **Activities:** Readings; discussions; simulation games; guest speakers; individual projects; scenario writing. **Source materials:** Judith C. Hellfach series: *Future of the Environment, The Future of Work, The Future of the Family, The Future of the Government;* Fabun, *Dynamics of Change;* Dunstan and Garlan, *Worlds in the Making;* THE FUTURIST; film: *Future Shock.* **Special features:** Use of "Limits to Growth" computer program; major attempt to help students develop a positive image of the future situation.

JOHN F. KENNEDY SENIOR HIGH SCHOOL
9701 Nicollet Avenue South
Bloomington, Minnesota 55420

Course title: Future Studies

Instructor: John Bloom, Roger House, Lois Fennig

Educational level: High school

Date of this offering: 1978-79

Date of first offering: 1973

Course description: Contemporary issues. **Activities:** Lecture-discussion; group activities; computer games; audiovisual presentations and follow-up; community investigation; field trips; student oral projects. **Source materials:** Toffler, *Future Shock;* Dunstan and Garlan, *Worlds in the Making;* Meadows, *Limits to Growth;* Best, *The Future of Work; The Future of the Family;* film: *Future Shock;* computer simulation: *Limits;* slidesound: *An Inquiry into the Future of Mankind;* filmstrips: *Redesigning Man; The American Family: The Challenge of Transition; Population Debate;* slides on Arcosanti. **Special features:** Optional field trips to an experimental solar- and wind-powered home and a planned community; speaker on futuristics.

MARINER HIGH SCHOOL
3551 McKnight Road
White Bear Lake, Minnesota 55110

Course title: Futuristics

Instructor: Robert Gabrick

Educational level: High school

Date of this offering: 1978-1979   **Date of first offering:** 1972-1973

Course description: This course involves the study of alternatives for the future. Emphasis is on content: energy, politics, ecology, shelter, space, transportation, technology, population, economics, leisure time, foods, and life styles. **Activities:** Lecture-discussion; use of "Futures Tools": scenario writing, computer use, matrixes, relevance trees, futures wheels, and trend extrapolation. **Source materials:** Toffler, *Future Shock*; a variety of sci-fi books both fiction and non-fiction; THE FUTURIST; article excerpts from many sources such as *Mother Earth News, Mother Jones, Time*, etc.; films and filmstrips: *Future Shock, Dimensions of Change, Is Anybody Out There?* **Special features:** Guest visits/lectures; field trips to view a media presentation of a power company concerning the future.

MESABI COMMUNITY COLLEGE
Virginia, Minnesota 55792

Course title: Study of the Future

Instructor: Courtney Peterson

Educational level: College freshmen and sophomores; adult

Date of this offering: Winter, 1979   **Date of first offering:** Spring, 1978

Course description: Course titles include: rationale for a study of the future; theoretical framework — general system theory and cybernetics; futures methodology; technology — physical technology and social-cultural technology; futurists and their ideas. **Activities:** Lecture-discussion; small group discussion. **Source materials:** Cornish, *The Study of the Future*; World Future Society, ed., *1999: The World of Tomorrow*; hybrid-delphi game. **Special features:** --

METROPOLITAN STATE UNIVERSITY
Metro Square
7th and Robert
St. Paul, Minnesota 55423

Course title: Futures Studies: An Overview

Instructor: Berenice D. Bleedorn

Educational level: College juniors and seniors

Date of this offering: 1978   **Date of first offering:** Fall, 1975

Course description: This course is an overview. Specific topics featured each quarter depend upon the topics discussed by guest lecturers, and change each quarter. Constants are readings and methodologies. **Activities:** Readings (required and supplementary); discussions; field trips; final papers or projects, strategies and games for futuristic thinking; student journals; films; lectures. Series of public lectures with invited authorities and open to general public. **Source materials:** Toffler, *The Futurists;* Schumacher, *Small Is Beautiful;* films. **Special features:** Cassette tape recordings of student final papers are made available for subsequent classes; tapes of leading lecturers at conferences (Margaret Mead, George Land, Erwin Laszlo, John McHale, etc.); field trips to fresh water biological research center, Oroboros, underground housing, etc.; public lecture series each quarter, with ex-students continuing to participate.

UNIVERSITY OF MINNESOTA
School of Nursing
3313 Powell Hall
500 Essex Street, S.E.
Minneapolis, Minnesota 55455

Course title: The Future Is Now

Instructor: Mary G. Weisensee

Educational level: College juniors and seniors

Date of this offering: Summer, 1979

Date of first offering: Fall, 1975

Course description: This course deals with the implications of various factors on nursing for the next quarter century. Special emphasis is on those aspects of the entire environment which will influence health care needs.   **Activities:** Lecture-discussion, scenario writing, students present oral reports.   **Source materials:** Required reading: Toffler, *Future Shock; The Future is Now,* five articles published by MLN, the Minnesota League for Nursing in 1974; Chaska, *The Nursing Profession;* selected articles from magazines and journals; selected bibliography of other books.   **Special features:** Projects, lecturers, field trips vary with each quarter.

UNIVERSITY OF MINNESOTA

Date of first offering: 1972

College of Education
203-F Burton Hall
Minneapolis, Minnesota 55455

Program title: Concentration in Alternative Social and Educational Futures

Director: Arthur M. Harkins, Associate Professor of Education and Sociology

Educational level: Master's and doctorate

Degrees offered: M.A. and Ph. D. in Education with a concentration in alternative social and educational futures

Course titles: The Master's courses include: Core seminars; foundations courses include general courses for 18 credits: Anthropology of American Education; Introduction to Systems Theory in Social Science and Education; Introduction to Economics of Education; Comparative Philosophies of Education; Seminar—topics in Anthropology and Education and Advanced Sociology of Education; the Doctorate courses include Social Forecasting and Education Futures; Social Design and Education Futures; Seminar on Social and Education Futures; reading list for History and Philosophy of Education; and a supporting program or minor.

Program description: The program is primarily for students interested in alternative models, designs, and paradigms for social and educational futures, and in concept clarification and extension, research, and teaching in an interdisciplinary area. Students are expected to develop supportive specialties in other foundational disciplines within the Social and Philosophic Foundations of Education Program.

MOORHEAD STATE UNIVERSITY

Moorhead, Minnesota 56560

Course title: Sociology of the Future

Instructor: Nancy Parlin, Professor of Sociology

Educational level: College juniors and seniors; master's; adult

Date of this offering: Winter quarter, 1979

Date of first offering: 1974

Course description: This course begins with the sociological imagination, basic concepts for analysis of the future, continues with methodologies and theories, and the interplay of structural and social psychological variables, and ends with alternative models of the future.   **Activities:** Lecture-discussion; exercises using various methodologies. Students write and present a paper describing a possible future change in one social institution and the impacts on other social institutions.   **Source materials:** Texts include Cornish, *The Study of the Future*; Mesarovic and Pestel, *Mankind at the Turning Point*; Phillips, *Worlds of the Future.*   **Special features:** —

MOTLEY HIGH SCHOOL

Box 98
Motley, Minnesota 56466

Course title: 2001 and Science Fiction in Literature

Instructor: Patrick Held, Social Studies Chairperson; Pamela Sachs, English Department Chairperson

Educational level: High school

Date of this offering: 1978

Date of first offering: 1975

Course description: This course serves as an introductory course to the study of the future and futures literature. Topics include: future methodologies; man vs. machine; utopias and dystopias; sci-fi as future study. **Activities:** Scenario writing; oral reports on sci-fi novels; group simulation on future decision making. **Source materials:** Scholastic literature unit; *Newsweek* filmstrip, *2001 A.D.*; Futura City simulation; *Designing Tomorrow Today* slide tape. **Special features:** This course will serve as an introduction to further future study.

ST. CLOUD STATE UNIVERSITY

St. Cloud, Minnesota 56301

Date of first offering: 1978-79

Program title: Futures Studies

Director: Kathleen Redd, Interdisciplinary Studies; Robert Ryan, Chairperson, Department of Technology

Educational level: Undergraduate

Degrees offered: Minor in future studies

Course titles: Technology and the Future; Technology Assessment (Delphi); Appropriate Technologies.

Program description: Class size is limited to 12 and course is mainly lecture, class discussion. The program includes a general study and evaluation of technologies, impacts and futures; concentrates on Delphi Assessment techniques and allows for an assessment study in student's area of interest; examines the evolution of low - medium - high technologies and the impacts; evaluation of appropriate technologies for the 21st century and beyond. Requirements in classes include survey, research, and individual projects - scenario writing, extensive reading and evaluation. One course is taught each quarter — fall, winter and spring.

ST. CLOUD STATE UNIVERSITY

Department of Interdisciplinary Studies
Stewart Hall
St. Cloud, Minnesota 56301

Course title: Images of the Future

Instructor: Kathleen M. Redd, Assistant Professor, Department of Interdisciplinary Studies

Educational level: College juniors and seniors and master's (on an arranged basis)

Date of this offering: Spring quarter, 1979

Date of first offering: 1976

Course description: The course is generally run as a seminar. Course topics include: future focused images; survey of images prevalent in selected cultures; repositories of images of the future; relationship of images of the future to policy making. **Activities:** Research/creative projects; lecture-discussion; heavy use of media; student reports. **Source materials:** Most recent primary text: Bundy, *Images of the Future*; selections from Polak, *The Image of the Future*; have used Kuhn, *Structure of the Scientific Revolution* and Maruyama and Harkins, *Cultures Beyond the Earth*; numerous reprints. **Special features:** Some student projects are multimedia; guest speakers used when available.

ST. OLAF COLLEGE

St. Olaf Avenue
Northfield, Minnesota 55057

Course title: Exopsychology: The Human Factor in Long-Duration Spaceflight and Space Settlement

Instructor: Howard I. Thorsheim

Educational level: College undergraduate

Date of this offering: January, 1979

Date of first offering: January, 1977

Course description: This course is taught during the January interim month. Course topics include: basic methodologies; general systems theory. This course provides an interface of psychology with alternative futures in space. **Activities:** Lecture-discussion; field trips; student papers on selected topics. **Source materials:** Thorsheim et al., *Metaperspectives in Post-Secondary Education* (Paper presented at First Meeting, Education Section, World Future Society, October, 1978); National Academy of Sciences, Space Science Board, *Human Factors in Long-Duration Spaceflight*; Johnson and Holbrow, *Space Settlements: A Design Study* (NASA SP-413); Maruyama and Harkins, eds., *Cultures Beyond the Earth*; Sagan, *The Cosmic Connection*; films: selected NASA films. **Special features:** Conversations with guest speakers via telephone speakerphone connection.

ST. PAUL ACADEMY AND SUMMIT SCHOOL
St. Paul, Minnesota 55105

Date of first offering: 1974-75

Program title: Futures Week in Life and Social Science

Director: 7th and 8th grade teachers

Educational level: Junior high school

Degrees offered: —

Course titles: —

Program description: An annual one-week schoolwide program of films, role playing, computer games, futures wheels, assigned and optional reading, discussion groups, and values clarification activities.

COLLEGE OF ST. THOMAS
Cleveland and Summit
St. Paul, Minnesota 55105

Course title: Current Directions and Dimensions in the Discipline of Creativity

Instructor: Berenice D. Bleedorn

Educational level: Master's

Date of this offering: Fall, 1978

Date of first offering: Fall, 1978

Course description: Problem solving; the creative process; right/left hemisphere dominance; techniques for futuristic thinking; Guilford Model of the structure of the intellect; techniques for process learning; futures leadership for gifted and talented.   **Activities:** Lectures; seminars; group process; discussion; leadership experiences; field trips; problem solving applications and reports; creative thinking exercises (relationships, implications, systems, transformations). **Source materials:** Parnes, Osborn, *Creative Problem Solving Actionbook and Guidebook;* bibliography of literature on creativity; La Conte, *Teaching Tomorrow Today;* Ornstein, *The Psychology of Consciousness;* films; group learning activities—creative thinking/learning techniques and futures studies strategies—future wheel; cross impact matrix.   **Special features:** Field trip to Minnesota Science Museum to view film, *Genesis,* and exhibits; student projects—leadership practice outside of class in student's professional and/ or social community.

MISSISSIPPI

UNIVERSITY OF MISSISSIPPI
University, Mississippi 38677

Course title: Administrative Perspectives of Future of Education

Instructor: Walter M. Mathews, Associate Professor

Educational level: Master's; doctorate

Date of this offering: 1978

Date of first offering: 1976

Course description: A multidisciplinary approach to the study of futures and change as related to education. **Activities:** Lecture-discussion; media development; individual student projects; simulations; imaging; films. **Source materials:** — **Special features:** Course is structured after class meets to tailor it to the people involved. Students have developed individual projects on videotape, slide/tape, audiotape, etc.; faculty members from other disciplines are included as appropriate.

MISSOURI

GLASGOW HIGH SCHOOL
Glasgow, Missouri 65254

Course title: Biology II — Unit on "Science and Technology and the Future"

Instructor: Carla Burres

Educational level: High school

Date of this offering: 1978-79   **Date of first offering:** 1978

Course description: This futures unit is taught within the biology course.   **Activities:** Lecture-discussion; student reports; use of decision trees.   **Source materials:** THE FUTURIST; LaConte, *Teaching Tomorrow Today*; newspaper articles.   **Special features:** —

INSTITUTE FOR EDUCATION IN PEACE AND JUSTICE   Date of first offering: 1973
2747 Rutger
St. Louis, Missouri 63104

Program title: —

Director: Course instructors: Kathleen McGinnis, William Archibald, James B. McGinnis, Greg Stevens

Educational level: Master's and adult

Degrees offered: —

Course titles: Anti-Racist, Anti-Sexist Society; Hunger and Alternative Economic Future; Competition, Cooperation and Alternative Educational Futures.

Program description: Under the broad title of peace education, the Institute's programs center around the themes of alternatives to violence, institutional violence and alternatives, global awareness, alternative world futures, and mutual education. Aimed primarily toward elementary and secondary teachers and administrators, but including religious communities, church study groups, PTAs, and other adult groups, the Institute offers workshops and summer institutes on its basic themes throughout the country. Staff members also teach regularly at Seattle University, Kenrick Seminary (St. Louis, and Webster College, St. Louis). The Institute operates a curriculum center and provides consulting services for many school systems, including the Archdiocesan School Office in St. Louis. Graduate students and a limited number of senior high school students receive school credit for serving as interns. Source materials include: J. McGinnis, *Bread and Justice: Toward a New International Economic Order.*

UNIVERSITY OF MISSOURI   Date of first offering: January-December 1979
Boone County Extension Center
1408-1, I-70 Drive S.W.
Columbia, Missouri 65201

Program title: Increasing Citizen Participation Through the Delphi Technique

Director: Paul A. Lutz, Community Development Specialist, Mid-Missouri Extension Area

Educational level: Adult - general

Degrees offered: —

Course titles: —

Program description: The objective of the program is to identify the preferable Columbia of the future. The program is designed to identify the future problems, issues, or concerns, and 430 people in positions of decisionmaking in the area are being invited to participate in a Delphi inquiry, which will result in information for use as the basis for workshops with members of neighborhood organizations and any other groups who are interested in participating. Depending on the results of the Delphi inquiry, a variety of activities will be used: scenarios, workshops, lectures, discussions, reports, meetings with various boards and commissions of the city, etc. Flexibility is the key, and people in the program are playing it by ear. Books used include: Cornish, *The Study of the Future;* Linstone and Turoff, *The Delphi Method.* A technical advisory committee — 41 faculty members from the five educational institutions in Columbia — will 1) assist in formulating questions and interpreting results; 2) write scenarios; 3) lead workshops and take advantage of any other opportunities to help make people more aware of the future.

UNIVERSITY OF MISSOURI, KANSAS CITY   Date of first offering: 1969
School of Administration
5100 Rockhill Road
Kansas City, Missouri 64113

Program title: Policy and Planning

Director: Reverdy T. Gliddon, Schutte Professor of Management and Public Administration; Professors Karl Johnson, Van E. Rothrock, Robert W. Lewis and Nicholas C. Peroff.

Educational level: Master's; professional

Degrees offered: M.B.A., M.P.A.

Course titles: Economic Policy and Managerial Control; Policy and Administration; Long Range Planning and Forecasting; Science and Public Policy; Research Seminar in Policy Analysis; Urban and Regional Planning for Urban Administrators.

Program description: This program is a graduate concentration in Policy and Planning. The course Long Range Planning and Forecasting deals exclusively with futuristic studies; the other courses all deal at one point or another with them as units inside the course. Students in the planning and forecasting course have access to advice and records of professional specialists through the use of faculty-professional teams. Heavy emphasis is on feasibility of the research strategy. This advanced graduate course requires students to demonstrate strategic support by some forecaster(s)-planner(s) for their project.

ST. LOUIS COMMUNITY COLLEGE AT FOREST PARK
5600 Oakland Boulevard
St. Louis, Missouri 63105

Course title: Future Worlds (Politics and Society of the Future)

Instructor: Jo Clayton, Professor of Political Science

Educational level: College freshmen and sophomores

Date of this offering: Spring, 1979   **Date of first offering:** 1973

Course description: Topics include: technology and the future; environmental strain and the politics of scarcity; power of the multi-nationals; East/West value approaches. **Activities:** Lecture-discussion; films; games; student debate of alternatives. **Source materials:** Required books: Teich, *Technology and Man's Future;* Ophuls, *Ecology and the Politics of Scarcity; Global Reach;* Ratni, *Footsteps Into the Future;* library reserve: Meadows, *The Limits to Growth;* Worldwatch Institute pamphlets; games: *Bafa Bafa;* films: *Future Shock; Still Waters; The Instant Alternative.* **Special features:** —

ST. LOUIS UNIVERSITY   Date of first offering: 1968
221 N. Grand Boulevard
St. Louis, Missouri 63103

Program title: Futures Studies

Director: Clement S. Mihanovich, Professor of Sociology

Educational level: College undergraduate

Degrees offered: A.B. in Sociology with a concentration in futures studies

Course titles: Basic Principles and Procedures; Methods; Values and the Future; Constructing Alternative Futures.

Program description: These four courses together provide the opportunity for studying the future of practically all subject areas and an introduction to all futures research methods. Some general problem areas include: domestic and international politics; human rights; information; education; cybernetics; communications; industry; sociological and ecological revolutions; world development; bioengineering; space; and the individual in mass society. Films, simulations, and oral and written reports are used extensively for teaching methods.

WASHINGTON UNIVERSITY
Graduate Institute of Education
Box 1183
St. Louis, Missouri 63130

Course title: Social Philosophy and Education: Alternative Social and Educational Futures

Instructor: Arthur G. Wirth, Professor

Educational level: College juniors and seniors; doctorate

Date of this offering: 1977-78   **Date of first offering:** Evolving since 1975

Course description: A statement by Daniel Bell sets the theme: The culture is split between the needs for rationality and efficiency versus the needs for wholeness or self-realization. **Activities:** Students look at the schools as work places and see how they are affected by issues in the work world. **Source materials:** Curle, *Education for Liberation*; Harman, *An Incomplete Guide to the Future*; Schumacher, *Small Is Beautiful*; Brown, *The Live Classroom*. Students visit experimental schools in relation to readings. **Special features:** Students make alternative educational and social projections for the 21st Century, using Laszlo, *The Systems View of the World* as a frame of reference.

NEBRASKA

ARBOR HEIGHTS JUNIOR HIGH, WESTSIDE SCHOOLS   Date of first offering: 1975-76
8601 Arbor
Omaha, Nebraska 68124

Program title: Future Studies

Director: Geneve Selsor

Educational level: Intermediate (7, 8, 9)

Degrees offered: —

Course titles: —

Program description: This program, which began as an eighth grade project for selected students and developed under ESEA Title III, is now an integrated part of English, social studies, and science for grades seven, eight, and nine. It is no longer funded under the ESEA Title grant. Activities include field trips, scenario writing, designing, using and evaluating questionnaires, survey and computer gaming, and using the community as a co-educator. Films, books, kits, simulations are used in the curriculum that has been designed for grade level and class work. Activities include either visits to community leaders, urban renewal experts, transportation, ecology and energy experts, and bio-feedback analysts, or the class is visited by these people at various times. Some students this year are participating in the Problem Solving Bowl in Lincoln, Nebraska sponsored by E. Paul Torrance, of the University of Georgia.

UNIVERSITY OF NEBRASKA, OMAHA
Omaha, Nebraska 68182

Course title: Futurism and Education: Learning for Tomorrow/The Role of the Future in Education

Instructor: William G. Callahan, Associate Professor of Special Education

Educational level: Master's

Date of this offering: 1979   **Date of first offering:** 1976

Course description: This course is an overview of futuristics, value systems affecting the future, personal values affecting our own futures orientation, resources available for use in field of futures studies. **Activities:** Phone calls with futurists; discussions held via conference calls with Robert Theobald, Jay Forrester, Ervin Laszlo. Students read material in area and formulated questions to ask the futurists. **Source materials:** Schumacher, *Small Is Beautiful*; Kahn, *The Next 200 Years*; Theobald, *Beyond Despair*, Meadows, *The Limits to Growth*; Toffler, *Future Shock, The Futurists, Learning for Tomorrow*; Shane, *The Educational Significance of the Future*. **Special features:** —

NEVADA

UNIVERSITY OF NEVADA, LAS VEGAS
4505 Maryland Parkway
Las Vegas, Nevada 89145

Course title: Ecofiction

Instructor: Felicia Florine Campbell, English Department

Educational level: College juniors and seniors

Date of this offering: Spring, 1979   **Date of first offering:** 1973

Course description: Environmental problems as they are projected, discussed and sometimes solved in science fiction. **Activities:** Lecture; discussion; student projects including scenario writing, oral reports, films, short stories and plays. **Source materials:** Change every semester. Typical books include: Miller, *A Canticle for Leibowitz;* Fuller, *We Almost Lost Detroit* (non-fiction); Vonnegut, *Cat's Cradle;* Wilson, *The Mind Parasites;* articles from THE FUTURIST. **Special features:** —

NEW HAMPSHIRE

REGIONAL CENTER FOR EDUCATIONAL TRAINING   Date of first offering: 1977
45 Lyme Road
Hanover, N.H. 03777

Program title: Environmental Education for Tomorrow's Needs

Director: Allie Quinn; Karen Burnett, Assistant

Educational level: Teacher training

Degrees offered: —

Course titles: The Institute on the Future of Education: issues explored were regional growth, population and demographic change, impact and promise of technology and resources for the future. Skills for Tomorrow: will offer workshops on regional environmental issues, the communications revolution, "systems" thinking and its integration into curriculum, computers — their concepts and use in education, creative problem solving, and games, simulations and experiential learning in the community.

Program description: This project is financed in large part by the Environmental Education Program of the U.S. Office of Education, sponsored the Regional Center for Educational Training with The Public Affairs Center of Dartmouth College and the Montshire Museum of Science as cooperating agencies. This project assumes that education will be faced with great pressures for change during the near as well as the more distant future; therefore, it is up to educators and other community leaders to take steps now in anticipation of future educational constraints and opportunities. A variety of informal and formal means are utilized to stimulate and encourage dialogue such as: seminars and symposiums; speakers from Dartmouth, government, business and other professions; future wheels; cross impact matrixes; small group discussions; videotapes; field trips; and three primary texts: Kauffman, *Teaching The Future;* Shane, *Curriculum Changes Toward the 21st Century;* and *Readings in Education: Tomorrow's Education.*

NEW JERSEY

BROOKDALE COMMUNITY COLLEGE
Lincroft, New Jersey 07738

Course title: Futures Studies

Instructor: Robert B. Mellert, Assistant Professor, Human Affairs Institute, Department of Interdisciplinary Studies

Educational level: College freshmen and sophomores

Date of this offering: 1978   **Date of first offering:** 1976

Course description: Thinking about the future; basic methodologies; global projections; constructing a future world from a model; analysis of Club of Rome models. **Activities:** Lecture; discussion; case study analysis; Delphi survey; future wheels; cross impact analysis; individual study projects and reports to class. **Source materials:** Books: *Future Shock; Limits to Growth; Mankind at the Turning Point; Population Bomb;* film: *Future Shock;* magazines: *Hastings Report; Development Forum;* THE FUTURIST. **Special features** —

DREW UNIVERSITY
Madison, New Jersey 07940

Course title: Man's Future

Instructor: Roger Wescott, Professor of Anthropology and Linguistics

Educational level: College undergraduate

Date of this offering: Spring, 1979   **Date of first offering:** 1970

Course description: The hazards of prediction; the increasing convergence of science fact and science fiction; man's growing control over his own evolution; the acceleration of social change and cultural innovation; emerging opportunities and dangers for our species. **Activities:** Lecture; discussion; brainstorming; Delphi technique. **Source materials:** Dunstan and Garlan: *Worlds in the Making;* Boulding: *The Meaning of the Twentieth Century;* Clarke: *Profiles of the Future.* **Special features** —

HIGHLAND PARK HIGH SCHOOL
North 5th Avenue
Highland Park, New Jersey

Course title: Toward The Year 2000

Instructor: Joseph Stringer, Jr.

Educational level: High school

Date of this offering: Spring, 1979   **Date of first offering:** 1972

Course description: Units on methodology, technology, family relations, food and energy production, war, utopian designs of dystopian designs, etc. Each of the topics is thought of in a future tense, extrapolating present trends and suggesting alternative possibilities for development. **Activities:** Lecture-discussion; brainstorming on various questions; extrapolation from statistical and/or other data; scenario writing on utopias (or future of education, or family relations, etc.); design of a utopia or dystopia; design of a future newspaper; short stories. **Source materials:** Toffler, *Future Shock;* Huxley, *Brave New World;* Vonnegut, *Player Piano;* Wells, *The Time Machine;* Zamyatin, *We;* magazine articles of current interest; other books with futurist theme. **Special features:** Student designed newspapers; collages; outside speakers.

JERSEY CITY STATE COLLEGE
Jersey City, New Jersey 07305

Course title: Future Society

Instructor: William Dusenberry, Assistant Professor of Sociology

Educational level: College undergraduate

Date of this offering: 1978   **Date of first offering:** Fall, 1977

Course description: The course encourages students to study topics of their own interest. Subjects include population and resource projections. **Activities:** Scenario writing; lectures; student presentations; games; filmstrips. **Source materials:** Books: Orwell, *1984;* Huxley, *Brave New World;* Ehrlich, *Population Bomb; Notes for the Future;* Harper & Row Media Program on the Future; films. **Special features:** Field trips to computer network centers, fast food operations, communications centers. Students create games which are intended to anticipate future decision-making in regard to highway construction, industry, public housing, etc. Students do research papers based on the profession in which they intend to develop a specialization.

KEAN COLLEGE OF NEW JERSEY
Morris Avenue
Union, New Jersey 07083

Date of first offering: 1971

Program title: Program for the Study of the Future

Director: Howard F. Didsbury, Jr., Executive Director

Educational level: College juniors and seniors, master's and adult

Degrees offered: —

Course titles: Dreams and Nightmares: Utopias and History; Planning for Tomorrow Today: Alternative Futures; Interdisciplinary Seminar on Futurism; The Modern Impact of Science and Technology on Culture.

Program description: Course on utopias and dystopias examines conceptions ranging from Plato's to Huxley's with special attention given to economic structures and the emergence of a dystopian tradition in post-industrial civilization. Alternative futures constitutes an introduction to current futures-oriented research. The interdisciplinary seminar focuses on individual student projects, with results presented through suitable media. The course on science and technology may be regarded as an introduction to the program but is not a prerequisite. The program maintains an extensive library of audiotapes and frequently sponsors conferences and symposia on topics which may have a significant impact on society.

MONMOUTH COLLEGE
West Long Branch, New Jersey 07764

Course title: UniEd PALS (Partners All Learning, Social Development Curriculum)

Instructor: Gwen Neser, Associate Professor, Department of Education

Educational level: Pre-service, in-service and graduate education for elementary school teachers

Date of this offering: On-going **Date of first offering:** 1977

Course description: This teacher training program integrates basic skills, performing arts, and human relations around the theme, *We all Live Together* with PALS, a multi-dimensional approach that the child is the symbol of the future. Self-confidence, self-discipline and cooperation are focal objectives. **Activities:** Movement, dance and non-verbal communication techniques; peer teaching, problem solving, choice-making and the joy of learning are integral to PALS. **Source materials:** Records; audio tapes; video tapes; filmstrips; teaching manuals. PALS network through pen/picture, audio/video communication — children throughout the world exchange their PALS experience. **Special features:** This course involves teachers, children and parents and stresses interpersonal/interethnic awareness.

RUTGERS UNIVERSITY
Graduate School of Education
5th & Penn Streets
Camden, New Jersey 08102

Date of first offering: 1971

Program title: Educational Theory

Director: Thomas J. Venables, Coordinator, Graduate Studies in Education

Educational level: Master's

Degrees offered: M. Ed. in Education with special concentration in Educational Theory

Course titles: Philosophy of Education; Urban Education; Creativity and Spontaneity; Simulation and Gaming; Sociology and Anthropology and Education.

Program description: This program uses lecture-discussion, simulation, and small group investigation. The program features critical analysis of current issues in education from a theoretical perspective. It is a highly individualized foundational program with a distinctive urban character.

STEVENS INSTITUTE OF TECHNOLOGY
Hoboken, New Jersey 07030

Course title: Problem Solving I and II

Instructor: Laurence Russ

Educational level: College juniors and seniors

Date of this offering: 1978-79

Date of first offering: 1973

Course description: Future resource allocation; designing for the future. **Activities:** Lecture-discussion; projects.
Source materials: — **Special features:** —

WEST MORRIS MENDHAM HIGH SCHOOL
Mendham, New Jersey 07945

Course title: Literature of the Future

Instructor: James Farrell

Educational level: High school

Date of this offering: 1978-79   **Date of first offering:** Fall, 1973

Course description: Technology and the individual; cities and pollution; population and resources; sociological changes; space travel; solving future conflicts; war and peace. **Activities:** Readings of short stories, drama, poetry, novels, and nonfiction; discussion; research in areas of interest; audiovisual material; media-oriented brainstorming; scenarios; role playing. **Source materials:** Book: *Science Fiction Reader;* teaching kit: Scholastic: *Tomorrow: Science Fiction and the Future;* media kits: *The Year 2000: Can We Survive the Future?; From Wells to Bradbury: The History of Science Fiction.* **Special features** Student projects presented in many media; guest speakers include city planners, computer experts, and a university futurist.

NEW YORK

COLUMBIA UNIVERSITY TEACHERS COLLEGE
New York, New York 10027

Course title: Schooling for the Future

Instructor: Mary Alice White, Professor

Educational level: Master's; doctorate

Date of this offering: Spring, 1979   **Date of first offering:** 1976

Course description: This course concentrates on education for a new set of conditions in all resources: food, energy, nutrition, transportation, social organizations, demands on human behavior. **Activities:** Lecture-discussion; games; written reports of future educational models; exercises in changing behavior; readings. **Source materials:** A wide variety of books, films, simulations; main emphasis on using current magazines and newspapers. **Special features:** Guest lectures where relevant; films.

CONCORDIA COLLEGE
171 White Plains Road
Bronxville, New York, 10708

Course title: Futurology

Instructor: Kenneth J. Doka

Educational level: College juniors and seniors

Date of this offering: January, 1979   **Date of first offering:** January, 1975

Course description: Course topics include: orientations to the future; basic trends, methodologies, forecasting in selected areas. **Activities:** Lecture-discussion; methods exercises; student projects. **Source materials:** Toffler, *Future Shock;* THE FUTURIST, films; speakers. **Special features:** Visit to Sloan Kettering; presentations by policy analyst, planners, etc.

EDWARD B. SHALLOW INTERMEDIATE SCHOOL 227   Date of first offering: December, 1977
6500 - 16 Avenue
Brooklyn, New York 11204

Program title: Future Studies

Director: Donald Del Seni, Principal; Anna Knoll, Learning Center Director

Educational level: Intermediate (6-9)

Degrees offered: —

Course titles: —

Program description: Emphasis is on science fiction, urban planning, global priorities, genetic engineering, environmental awareness, and 21st Century decision making. Activities include learning contracts, futurized curriculum objectives, scenario writing, plays, oral dramatizations, research reports, laboratory objectives and experiments. The materials include Scholastic Multimedia Kits-—Science Fiction, The Future; Human Issues in Science Program; Sunburst Communications - Future Studies Units. Resources include the Learning Center for Independent Study.

GREENPORT PUBLIC SCHOOLS
Front Street
Greenport, New York 11944

Date of first offering: Spring, 1975

Program title: Futurism: A Model Unit

Director: David P. Moore

Educational level: Junior high and high school

Degrees offered: —

Course titles: 7th, 9th, and 12th grade social studies.

Program description: Two-week units in futurism, developed under an ESEA Title III mini-grant, are included in the 7th, 9th, and 12th grade social studies courses. Basic study materials include *Environment: Earth in Crisis* (7th grade), *Science Fiction and the Future* (9th grade) and *The Future: Can We Shape It?* (12th grade), all published by Scholastic Books, and *2000 A.D.,* a multimedia kit published by Newsweek. Activities are used at the individual teacher's discretion and may include student log books included in the Scholastic Books units, surveys of student attitudes toward probable, possible, and preferable futures, forecasting methods, values, problem-solving, and many others.

JERICHO HIGH SCHOOL
Jericho, New York 11753

Course title: Futures Studies

Instructor: Robert Hoffman

Educational level: High school

Date of this offering: 1978-79

Date of first offering: 1971-72

Course description: Biomedical revolution; alternative futures; nature of change; education; food; energy; communications; transportation; family; marriage; sex methodologies; values; work; and leisure. **Activities:** Lecture; discussion; small groups; simulation; audiovisual presentation; projects; model building. **Source materials:** Books: *Worlds in the Making; Teaching Tomorrow Today*; simulations: *I.Q. Game; Futuribles; Cope; Conflict; Utopia Game*; audiovisual: *Redesigning Man; Life Style 2000; Dimension of Change; Future of Family; An Inquiry into the Future of Mankind; Change Here for Tomorrow.* **Special features:** Speakers on Dome East (housing), biofeedback, EST, mind control, marriage and family, education, space, and a corporate trends analysis program; field trip to the Hudson Institute. Hoffman will begin a new class in the fall of 1979 in creative problem-solving, especially concerning the future of Jericho High School.

JUNIPER VALLEY SCHOOL
P.S. 128, Queens
69-26 65th Drive
Howard Beach, Queens, New York 11414

Date of first offering: 1978

Program title: Future Studies

Director: John Iorio, Assistant Principal

Educational level: Elementary (fifth and sixth grades)

Degrees offered: —

Course titles: Topics such as concepts of time, the concept of the future, understanding forecasts, trends, exponential growth, brainstorming and historical "What If's" will be periodically infused into the social studies curriculum.

Program description: The program seeks to develop futuristic thought processes necessary to the child's understanding of forecasting and coping with possible alternative futures. This will be accomplished by creating a school based program of Future Studies which will be piloted in the fifth and sixth grades via infusion into the social studies curricula. Methods and activities include an adapted form of Bundy's attitudinal questionnaire, "What Beliefs About the Future Do You Hold?," as both a pre- and post-unit questionnaire to measure the degree of attitudinal change toward the future. Formal studies begin with reading the first book of Christopher's science fiction trilogy, *The White Mountains*, with follow-up activities. Source materials include *Learning for Tomorrow, Teaching the Future, Groking the Future, Values Clarification,* and *Foundations of Futurology in Education.*

LONG BEACH HIGH SCHOOL
Lagoon Drive West
Long Beach, New York 11561

Course title: Future Shock

Instructor: Jean Boyce, Ann Martin, Robert Nardella, Lorraine Vitale

Educational level: High school

Date of this offering: 1978   **Date of first offering:** 1974

Course description: Decision making; man and machine; redesigning humanity; changing lifestyles. This is an English course taken by 125 tenth graders each semester. A one-semester course. **Activities:** Lecture-discussion takes 20 percent of course time, reports and projects, 10 percent, and individual contracts, 70 percent. **Source materials:** Extensive book list; films; non-print programs from Scholastic Books; simulation: Classroom of the Future. **Special features:** Speaker from local newspaper. Each student produces a project on the future. Great focus is on critical thinking. Course requires weekly writing, work on vocabulary. Comprehension questions for almost everything the class does are available.

MAINE-ENDWELL SENIOR HIGH SCHOOL
Farm-to-Market Road
Endwell, New York 13760

Course title: Futurism in Literature

Instructor: Margaret Burt, English teacher

Educational level: High school seniors

Date of this offering: 1979   **Date of first offering:** 1973

Course description: Students read required books, do in-depth research into the past and the present of some focused aspect of society today, one of strong interest to the individual student, and write an imaginative extrapolation into the 21st century of some aspect of this research — a short story, a newspaper article, diary entries, etc. **Activities:** Lecture-discussion (very light on lecture); research work both in books being studied and in areas of individual interest; strong emphasis on skill-building work of critical analysis, definition, classifying and outlining, essay writing. **Source materials:** Books: Toffler, *Future Shock*; Bradbury, *Fahrenheit 451*; Huxley, *Brave New World*; Orwell, *1984*; Clarke, *Childhood's End*; Bellamy, *Looking Backward*; films: *The Mystery of Life; Alone in the Midst of the Land*; searching for replacements of films on transportation, the cities, undersea, the computer revolution. **Special features:** —

MYNDERSE ACADEMY
Seneca Falls, New York 13148

Course title: Futurism

Instructor: Walter J. Gable, Social Studies Department

Educational level: High school seniors

Date of this offering: September, 1978   **Date of first offering:** September 1975

Course description: Alternative futures scenarios; biological developments; technological implications; cities of the future. **Activities:** Lecture; discussion; scenario writing; simulation games. **Source materials:** Books: *Worlds in the Making; Future Shock; Biological Time Bomb; Limits to Growth*; simulations: *Future Decisions: The I.Q. Game; Immortality; Limits to Growth*; magazine: THE FUTURIST. **Special features** —

558

NEW SCHOOL FOR SOCIAL RESEARCH
66 West 12th Street
New York, New York 10011

Course title: Options for the Future

Instructor: Thomas E. Jones

Educational level: College juniors and seniors, master's, and adult

Date of this offering: Spring, 1978

Date of first offering: 1973

Course description: Current domestic and global problems; the nature of "futurism"; forecasting methodology; systematic analysis of a variety of important, representative forecasts. **Activities:** Lecture; discussion; term paper. **Source materials:** Main texts: Cornish, *The Study of the Future;* Jones, *Options for the Future: An Analysis of Policy-Oriented Forecasts;* sections of following books required reading: Kahn, *The Next 200 Years;* Bell, *The Coming of Post-Industrial Society;* Meadows, et al., *The Limits to Growth;* Brown, *In the Human Interest;* Toffler, ed., *The Futurists;* Theobald, ed., *Futures Conditional;* selected articles from THE FUTURIST and other journals, and various books on reading list. **Special features:** The New School has a Department of Futuristics.

NIAGARA UNIVERSITY
Department of Education
Niagara University, New York 14109

Course title: Education Futures for the 21st Century

Instructor: Carmelo V. Sapone

Educational level: Master's and returning professionals

Date of this offering: 1979

Date of first offering: 1977

Course description: This course provides opportunities to gain skills in dealing with topics that no longer can be solved with a simple answer. Students are exposed to decision-making models: the Delphi; the cross-impact matrix; cross-event matrix; trend analysis matrix; scenario writing; goal-setting models, concepts of leisure, industrial vs. post-industrial society, principles of change, future planning models (in Vitro fertilization, etc.). **Source materials:** Videotapes; movies; lectures; speakers. **Special features:** —

NORTHPORT JUNIOR HIGH SCHOOL
Northport, New York 11768

Course title: People and Technology: Present Into Future

Instructor: Nicholas Econopouly and four student teachers from State University of New York, Stony Brook.

Educational level: Junior high

Date of this offering: 1978-79

Date of first offering: 1974-75

Course description: The course incorporates sections of the Educational Development Center's People and Technology program. The course begins with a study of the natural environment of New York in the pre-Columbian period and then focuses on man and environment in different times and places, strongly emphasizing the influence of technology. Topics include: pre-Columbian New York Indians; the age of whaling in the 19th century; the impact of modern technological systems; local and broader studies projecting into the future. **Activities:** Lecture; discussion; small group seminars; tutorials; manipulative project activities; community interviews; small group field trips; simulation and role playing; readings and thought papers; audio-visuals. **Source materials:** Sound-filmstrips including *People and Technology;* aerial view maps; current periodicals; publications of the Regional Planning Association; teacher-developed simulation activities; portions of selected books. **Special features** Student teachers make possible a great flexibility in methods and use of materials.

PACE UNIVERSITY
Political Studies Program
New York, New York 10038

Course title: 21st Century; The Future of...

Instructor: Linda G. Quest; Paul Conner

Educational level: Undergraduate

Date of this offering: 1979   **Date of first offering:** 1968

Course description: These courses emphasize the political and social impacts of the future: 21st Century Politics, American Politics Re-examined, Politics through Futurism and Science Fiction; Future of...the City, the Third World, International Organizations (and other topics and issues). Substantial emphasis is placed on the future in politics, public myth, revolution or reform. **Activities:** Lecture-discussion, team and individual projects on freshman-sophomore level; seminar-workshops on junior-senior level. Political Activities Group (which is sponsoring a Futures Forum in Spring 1979 to celebrate 10th anniversary of 21st-Century Politics at Pace) and World Politics Society are co-curricular activities. Interfuture is coordinate program for study abroad, usually by juniors. **Source materials:** Books, articles, games, films, interviews, participant-observer data, speculative fiction. **Special features:** City, state, and federal office buildings, and the U.N. and its missions are adjacent or near the campus, enabling students to do fieldwork, internships, and have guest-lecturer programs.

POLYTECHNIC INSTITUTE OF NEW YORK
Graduate School of Management
333 Jay Street
Brooklyn, New York 11201

Course title: Social Forecasting and Planning

Instructor: Thomas E. Jones; Anthony Wiener, program director.

Educational level: Master's

Date of this offering: Fall, 1977   **Date of first offering:** 1970

Course description: This course analyzes selected forecasts in terms of their underlying assumptions; students evaluate methods used to formulate forecasts as well as the ways in which implicit beliefs and values of forecasters can subtly bias forecasts. Students assess alternative futures, survey representative forecasts to show how corporate planners can improve their plans by carefully analyzing alternative futures. **Activities:** Lecture-discussion; students list and analyze factors that should be taken into account in planning for Polytechnic until 1985. **Source materials:** Manuscript of instructor's (T.E. Jones) forthcoming *Options for the Future*; Ackoff, *A Concept of Corporate Planning*; The Conference Board, *Planning and the Corporate Planning Director*; selected book list. **Special features:** —

SCOTIA-GLENVILLE HIGH SCHOOL
Sacandaga Road
Scotia, New York 12302

Course title: Futuristics

Instructor: John Maryanopolis

Educational level: High school

Date of this offering: 1978-79   **Date of first offering:** 1975-76

Course description: Time — Einstein, tachyons; Bio-ethics — biological revolution; Space Colonization — philosophy; visual illusions; individual projects; futurists predictive tooling. **Activities:** Lecture-discussion; scenario writing; individual projects; science fiction reading; futurist vocabulary/jargon building; experiments. **Source materials:** *Science Fact/Fiction;* Whitney computer films; NASA films; *Planet Management Game;* THE FUTURIST; *Mother Earth News; The Humanist.* Extensive bibliography of reading materials. **Special features:** Guest speakers; student slide-tape presentations. A Futures Studies Group has been formed as an outgrowth of this popular class.

SHOREHAM-WADING RIVER SCHOOLS
Rt. 25A
Shoreham, New York 11786

Course title: Futures

Instructor: Herb Meserve

Educational level: Secondary

Date of this offering: 1978-79   **Date of first offering:** 1975

Course description: The course is a year long and includes topics such as: thinking in the future tense; population; food; limits to growth; urban/suburban problem; scenarios for Long Island; systems analysis and technology assessment. **Activities:** Seminars; computer based simulations; paradigm development. **Source materials:** Basic readings include Brown, *The Challenge of Man's Future;* Dunstan and Garlan, *Worlds in the Making;* classroom library; reprints of a variety of articles. **Special features:** —

STATE UNIVERSITY COLLEGE AT BUFFALO NEW YORK

Date of first offering: 1975

Chase Hall
1300 Elmwood Avenue
Buffalo, New York 14222

Program title: Interdisciplinary Center for Creative Studies

Director: Sidney J. Parnes and Ruth B. Noller

Educational level: College undergraduate, master's, post-doctorate, adult, and returning professionals

Degrees offered: M.S. in Creative Studies

Course titles: Four sequential semester-long undergraduate courses in creative studies; independent study; full program of graduate courses.

Program description: An interdisciplinary effort to translate research into the nature and nurture of creative behavior into educational programs. The four core courses are workshops which deal with challenges in students' present and future lives. Many materials used in the classes, including *Guide to Creative Action; Creative Actionbook; Scratching the Surface of Creative Problem-Solving: A Bird's Eye-View of CPS,* and *Toward Super-sanity: Channeled Freedom,* were developed by the program's staff. Advanced students work with these classes, local schools and community organizations, the *Journal of Creative Behavior,* and as research assistants. The program is affiliated with the Creative Education Foundation which has been conducting creativity workshops since 1955.

STATE UNIVERSITY COLLEGE AT POTSDAM, NEW YORK

School of Professional Studies
Pierrpont Avenue
Potsdam, New York 13676

Course title: Learning in the Future; Planning a Futures Curriculum

Instructor: Normal C. Licht, Associate Professor

Educational level: College juniors and seniors; master's

Date of this offering: Fall, 1978   Date of first offering: 1975

Course description: This course helps students anticipate change, develop the ability to relate ideas and information between disciplines, explore ideas, images, models of the future, recognize the continuing impact of technology upon society, examine forecasts in specific problem areas, develop alternative scenarios of the future,and facilitate group interaction. **Activities:** Write 11 short scenarios dealing with specific topics; write final essay discussing specific questions; deliver oral presentation on an article from THE FUTURIST. **Source materials:** Texts: Toffler, *Learning for Tomorrow;* Shane, *The Educational Significance of the Future;* Laconte, *Teaching Tomorrow Today;* Kaufmann, *Teaching the Future.* **Special features:** Tape of brainwashing by William Mayer from Korean prisoners of war; trip to Montreal International Airport; designing city of the future — modeled from "City Building Educational Futures."

SUFFOLK COUNTY, NEW YORK

Date of first offering: 1975

Board of Cooperative Services
Shoreham, New York 11786

Program title: Program for Gifted and Talented

Director: James Releigh; Joseph Connelly; Herb Meserve, Instructor

Educational level: Elementary and secondary

Degrees offered: —

Course titles: —

Program description: This is a summer Institute open to all gifted and talented students in Suffolk County. It is an intensive program in which students meet four hours daily. The primary method of instruction is the seminar with extensive use of computer-based simulations and paradigm development. Basic readings include Brown, *The Challenge of Man's Future*, Dunstan and Garlan, *Worlds in the Making* and a variety of reprints of articles.

SYRACUSE UNIVERSITY
School of Information Studies
113 Euclid Avenue
Syracuse, New York 13210

Course title: The Literature of Future Studies and Policy Studies

Instructor: Michael Marien

Educational level: Graduate

Date of this offering: Spring, 1979   **Date of first offering:** Spring, 1979

Course description: This course seeks to introduce students in librarianship and public policy to the immense variety of sources and the equally immense breadth of content: essentially, an alternative system to classifying knowledge that enables us to better understand the central problems of man, society, and the natural environment. Particular emphasis will be placed on interest groups and ideologies as a fruitful guide to understanding who looks at what problems of the present and future, and how. **Activities:** Lecture, discussion, student papers on similarities and differences of futures literature, broadly defined. **Source materials:** Marien, *Societal Directions and Alternatives: A Critical Guide to the Literature*; World Future Society, *The Future: A Guide to Information Sources*; Fowles, *Handbook of Futures Research*; Linstone and Simmonds, eds., *Futures Research: New Directions*; Freeman, ed., *Policy Studies Review Annual, Vol. 2*; variety of books of various ideologies and topics. **Special features:** —

UNITED STATES MILITARY ACADEMY
West Point, New York 10996

Course title: Political Philosophy

Instructor: Francis P. Butler, Major, U.S. Army, Assistant Professor, Department of Social Science

Educational level: College undergraduate

Date of this offering: 1978-79   **Date of first offering:** —

Course description: Students will be exposed to 27 centuries of thinking, from the sixth century B.C. to the present. Students will also look forward to the thinking and writing that will be coming in the next century. Writing and debating will be emphasized. Students will exchange ideas in the Socratic tradition of the dialectic. **Activities:** Some lectures; discussion and debate; extensive reading; student reports on space age philosophy. **Source materials:** Required reading: Aristotle, *Politics;* Bentham and Mill, *The Utilitarians;* Dostoevsky, "The Grand Inquisitor on the Nature of Man," Locke, *An Essay Concerning Human Understanding*; Nozick, *Anarchy, State and Utopia*; Rawls, *Theory of Justice*; Schumacher, *Small Is Beautiful.* Extensive reading list. **Special features:** Each student assumes the role of a philosopher and proposes and defends his point of view on selected topics. One student "may be" five or six philosophers during the course, depending on topics discussed and philosophers read. Space Age Philosophy paper due at end of course to develop student's own ideas regarding the political implications of future years, emphasizing the effects of Euthenics and Eugenics.

NORTH CAROLINA

ISOTHERMAL COMMUNITY COLLEGE
Box 804
Spindale, North Carolina 28160

Course title: Visions of the Future

Instructor: Barbara Callahan

Educational level: College freshmen and sophomores

Date of this offering: 1978   **Date of first offering:** 1978

562

Course description: The relevance of the study of the future and major methods of forecasting the future; unwanted visions of the future; the Promethean vision; the protean vision; the Sisyphean vision; taming planet Earth. **Activities:** Students contracting for grade A or B are required to do independent research and a class presentation: group/panel discussions on leading futurists and their ideas, creation of futuristic slide/sound presentations, "Tomorrow Teams," which project desirable futures in certain areas.   **Source materials:**   Text: Garlan and Dunstan, *Star Sight: Visions of the Future;* extensive bibliography; simulations: Global Futures.   **Special features:**   Guest speakers; student projects presented via music, original slide programs, art, models, etc.

NORTH CAROLINA STATE UNIVERSITY
Division of University Studies
Raleigh, North Carolina 27650

Course title: Alternative Futures

Instructor: Robert L. Hoffman, Assistant Professor of University Studies

Educational level: College

Date of this offering: Fall, 1978   **Date of first offering:** Fall, 1974

Course description: Topics in this course include: introduction to futures studies; the concept of world view; probable and invented futures; futures studies concepts and forecasting; overview of the contemporary scene; nuclear war and nth country; population and food; environment; energy, resources, and the growth question; the concept of crisis; climate; selected futurist issues; solutions.   **Activities:** Lecture-discussion; students do a critique on one full-length futurist book; students deal with a futurist topic in a short paper.   **Source materials:** Cornish, *The Study of the Future;* Brown, *The Twenty Ninth Day;* reading list.   **Special features:** Occasional guest speakers.

NORTH CAROLINA STATE UNIVERSITY
Division of University Studies
Raleigh, North Carolina 27650

Course title: Technology Assessment

Instructor: Robert L. Hoffman, Assistant Professor of University Studies; Wayland C. Griffith, Professor of Mechanical Engineering and Head, Engineering Design Center

Educational level: Undergraduate

Date of this offering: Spring, 1979   **Date of first offering:** 1973

Course description: Preliminary definition and description of technology assessment. Hindsight: looking at some major technological changes and their impacts. Environmental impact statements; history and politics of technology assessment; appropriate technology.   **Activities:** Lecture-discussion; student teams conducting technology assessments.   **Source materials:**   Hetman, *Society and the Assessment of Technology.* **Special features:** Occasional guest speakers. Students have conducted assessments on microprocessors, returnable bottles, recombinant DNA, and remote sensing from space.

ST. ANDREWS COLLEGE
Laurinburg, North Carolina 28352

Course title: A Look at the Future: Is Pessimism Necessary?

Instructor: W.M. Alexander, Professor of Philosophy

Educational level: College freshmen and sophomores

Date of this offering: Spring, 1978   **Date of first offering:** Spring, 1978

Course description: An examination of the grounds for optimism and pessimism about the future, specifically, criticism of several pessimistic views, including methodological assumptions operating in these views.   **Activities:** Seminar discussion; written essays and critiques; oral reports; small task force research.   **Source materials:** Skinner, *Beyond Freedom and Dignity;* Heilbroner, *An Inquiry into the Human Prospect;* Meadows et al., *The Limits to Growth;* Thompson, *Evil and World Order.*   **Special features:** Visiting resource persons and campus speakers. From 1968 to 1973, St. Andrews required for its B.A., a senior-level course in future studies. Periodically, future studies is now a theme in a required general education course for seniors.

OHIO

CASE WESTERN RESERVE UNIVERSITY
Cleveland, Ohio 44106

Course title: Alternative Future for the Social Work Profession

Instructor: Paul Abels, Professor of Social Work

Educational level: Master's, doctorate, returning professionals

Date of this offering: Spring, 1979   **Date of first offering:** 1972

Course description: Core modules in future studies methods; forecasting; attitudes toward the future; technological change; future orientation in planning; professional trends in social work; ethical practice in the future; alternative futures; alternative modules pursued according to student interest in the future city; quality of life; the future of behavior; the justice system; the health system; the future of minorities; life styles; population; the future of institutions. Emphasis on interdisciplinary approach and action-practice. **Activities:** Lecture; discussion; films; forecasting; research; student presentations. **Source materials:** Books: Spekke, ed.: *The Next 25 Years;* Kuhn: *The Structure of Scientific Revolutions;* Abels' workbook of social work-related articles; miscellaneous fiction; magazine: THE FUTURIST; simulation: *The I.Q. Game.* **Special features** Speakers on the future of mental health; the family; The Club of Rome.

CASE WESTERN RESERVE UNIVERSITY
Department of Anatomy
School of Medicine
Cleveland, Ohio 44106

Course title: Biological Problems of Man in Space

Instructor: Marcus Singer, Department Chairman; J. Richard Keefe.

Educational level: Master's and doctorate

Date of this offering: 1978   **Date of first offering:** —

Course description: Concept of Space Biology; historical background; problems of man in space/solutions; specific biomedical limitations to long-term spaceflight with return to earth; extraterrestrial life potential and certainty. **Activities:** Lecture-discussion; student presentations. Visiting NASA scientists, and other space experimentalists participate. **Source materials:** Films from NASA libraries. Texts include 4-volume series *Foundations of Space Biology and Medicine; U.S. Senate Report on Soviet Space Studies: The Search for Extraterrestrial Intelligence.* Students design experiments to approach solutions to anticipated problems of space flight and space settlements. **Special features:** Student projects are evaluated by outside space authorities.

UNIVERSITY OF CINCINNATI
College of Education
Cincinnati, Ohio 45221

Course title: Futures Studies in Education

Instructor: Geoffrey H. Fletcher and Gary D. Wooddell

Educational level: Master's

Date of this offering: 1978   **Date of first offering:** 1978

Course description: The history of futures studies; basic principles of a futures perspective, futures studies and change, futures studies and the purpose of education, and futures studies in the curriculum. **Activities:** Lecture-discussion; readings; projects/papers; guest lectures; media; activities (forecasting, group dynamics, problem solving). **Sources materials:** Harman, *An Incomplete Guide to the Future;* Cornish, *The Study of the Future;* Shane, *Curriculum Change toward the 21st Century;* film: *Future Shock;* assorted other media; excerpts from other books and from current periodicals. **Special features:** Guest lectures, field trips as applicable; media.

CLEVELAND HEIGHTS HIGH SCHOOL
13263 Cedar Road
Cleveland, Ohio 44118

Course title: Speculative Fiction

Instructor: Betty L. Schwartz

Educational level: High school

Date of this offering: 1978   **Date of first offering:** 1972

Course description: Speculation about the future, based upon science fiction novels, short stories and poetry. Each student presents a project which may concentrate on future of transportation, community, family, etc. There are also many simulations based upon space travel, etc. **Activities:** Lecture-discussion; scenario writing; creative presentations based upon a theme from the literature. **Source materials:** — **Special features:** Student projects via many media.

CLEVELAND STATE UNIVERSITY
Cleveland, Ohio 44115

Course title: Educational Futurism

Instructor: Ernest M. Schuttenberg, Associate Professor of Education

Educational level: Master's and adult

Date of this offering: 1978   **Date of first offering:** 1976

Course description: Students explore the future from at least three points of view: social, political, economic, technological and other factors that may affect the U.S. and the world in the next three decades; implications of alternative future conditions in education; and implications of alternative future conditions for individual decision-making and career planning. **Activities:** Lecture-discussion; each student prepares a book critique, and completes two individual learning projects. **Source materials:** Required texts. Cornish, *The Study of the Future*; Toffler, ed., *Learning for Tomorrow*; supplemental readings from book list. **Special features:** Each students joins a Futures Learning Analysis Group where current issues and trends are discussed. Each group reports to the class at the end of the term.

UNIVERSITY OF DAYTON
300 College Park Avenue
Dayton, Ohio 45469

Date of first offering: 1975

Program title: Management Science

Director: Landis Gephart; Joseph P. Martino, Course Instructor

Educational level: Master's

Degrees offered: —

Course titles: Two futures-oriented courses are included in the Management Science program: Technological Forecasting; Technology Assessment.

Program description: Primary source of students is local industry and government organizations. Students all work full-time, and are taking courses in evenings. Result is highly motivated and intelligent students. Activities in courses are about equally balanced between lecture-discussion and student presentation. Students prepare a term project in each course. The media is selected by students. Source materials include: Martino, *Technological Forecasting for Decision-making;* miscellaneous articles from journals such as *Technological Forecasting and Social Change; Futures.*

UNIVERSITY OF DAYTON
300 College Park Drive
Dayton, Ohio 45469

Course title: Technological Forecasting; Technology Assessment

Instructor: Joseph P. Martino

Educational level: Master's

Date of this offering: — **Date of first offering:** Fall, 1975

Course description: Technological Forecasting: methods of technological forecasting; applications to specific fields; special topics. Technology Assessment: history of technology assessment; case studies of the impacts of technology; assessment techniques; special topics. **Activities:** Courses are based on combination of lecture-discussion, oral reports presented by students, term projects of students, practice sessions using computer terminals, etc. **Source materials:** Technological Forecasting: Martino, *Technological Forecasting for Decisionmaking*; materials from journal *Technological Forecasting and Social Change*. Technology Assessment: selected readings from a wide variety of sources, plus student reports on specific technology assessments sponsored by government agencies. **Special features:** Each student is required to present the results of a project. The two courses listed are electives within the Management Science program. Ultimately the students receive an M.S. in Management Science.

DENISON UNIVERSITY
Granville, Ohio 43023

Course title: The Future As History

Instructor: Bruce E. Bigelow, Associate Professor of History and Director, Denison Simulation Center

Educational level: College juniors and seniors

Date of this offering: Spring, 1978 **Date of first offering:** Spring, 1977

Course description: Basic Methodologies, world political organization, behavior control in the future, population issues, genetic manipulation, issues of technology and computers, health care in the future, alternative lifestyles, future of higher education, drive into space, new or changing ethical implications of future development. **Activities:** Lecture-discussion, with heavy emphasis on the latter, writing of reviews of futurist literature, student projects, community polls and sampling, simulation and values clarification exercises. The course concentrates heavily on the ethical implications of technological development; it attempts to avoid making undue biased judgment about which ethical systems are the best and to force the students to analyze their own ethical bases for judgment. **Source materials:** Cornish, *The Study of the Future*; Ostheimer, *Life or Death—Who Controls?*; Levin, *This Perfect Day*; Ruchmer, *Humanizing Health Care*; Tinbergen, *The RIO Report*; Libby/Whitehurst, *Marriage and Its Alternatives*; Teich, *Technology and Man's Future*; Heppenheimer, *Colonies in Space*; O'Neill, *The High Frontier*; Hardin, *Managing the Commons*; simulations: *Values of the Future; College of the Future;* film: *Tilt; Tragedy of the Commons*. **Special features:** Visits to class by local computer experts, scientists, political analysts; student involvement with community attitudes with surveys.

JOHN CARROLL UNIVERSITY
University Heights, Ohio 44118

Course title: Futures: Past and Present

Instructor: Mary K. Howard, Professor of History

Educational level: College freshmen and sophomores

Date of this offering: Spring, 1979 **Date of first offering:** Fall, 1975

Course description: Rapidly accelerating change and how to deal with it; the major futurists and their methodology; the future of work, leisure, education, the city, and the world food problem. **Activities:** Lecture-discussion; activities from Howard and Franks, *Looking Forward*; Howard and Franks, *The Biological Revolution*; and Franks and Howard, *People, Law and the Futures Perspective*; films; individual projects. **Source materials:** Books: Dunstan and Garlan, *Worlds in the Making*; Mesarovic and Pestel, *Mankind at the Turning Point*; Toffler, *The Futurists*; simulations: *Future Decisions; the I.Q. Game;* and *Educational Horizons;* films: *Future Shock*. **Special features:** Student projects involved developing plans for shaping either personal or societal futures. Howard also teaches an upper-level honors course focusing on methodology, technology, biology, and ethics.

KENT STATE UNIVERSITY
Kent, Ohio 44242

Course title: Business in the 21st Century

Instructor: Donald F. Mulvihill, Professor of Marketing and Coordinator, Institute for 21st Century Business

Educational level: College juniors and seniors and master's

Date of this offering: 1978   **Date of first offering:** Spring, 1971

Course description: Futurists and careers; limits to growth; population and food crisis; pollution; changes in technology; ocean bed activities; developments in space and space movements; development of huge urban areas; political and economic change; possible future state governmental organization in the U.S.; choices for the future; stress throughout on the relationship of these concepts to business. **Activities:** Lecture; discussion; outside resource speakers; films; student reports. **Source materials:** Books: Gray and Martin: *Growth and Its Implications for the Future;* Meadows: *Limits to Growth;* Kostalanetz: *Social Speculations;* Borgstrom: *Too Many;* Toffler: *Future Shock;* films: *The Futurists; Food Revolution; Alone in the Midst of the Land; Introduction to Lasers; Man and the "Second Industrial Revolution"; The Computer Revolution; Energy Crisis; The Deep Frontier; Deep Sea Trawler; Man Invades the Sea; Surviving in Space; Man and His Resources; Boonsville;* various articles. **Special features** —

MAPLE HEIGHTS HIGH SCHOOL
Maple Heights, Ohio 44137

Course title: Futuristics

Instructor: Betty Barclay Franks (on leave 1978-79) and Dale Walter

Educational level: High school

Date of this offering: Fall, 1978; Spring, 1979   **Date of first offering:** Fall 1972

Course description: Coping with change; anticipating change: forecasting and science fiction; evaluating the biological revolution; altering the mind; understanding technological change; using leisure constructively; designing environments; living on spaceship earth. **Activities:** Students view films such as *Future Shock;* write science fiction short stories and scenarios; participate in a Delphi study; become involved in one or more simulations; read science fiction; evaluate possible, probable and preferable futures through brainstorming and values clarification activities; propose solutions to a futures problem and present a written or oral report to the class. **Source materials:** Films: *Future Shock; Stranger than Science Fiction; Man-Made Man; Weird World of Robots; Cities of the Future; The Food Revolution; Energy Sources for the Future; The Ultimate Mystery; Cosmic Zoom;* filmstrips: Center for the Humanities: *The New Genetics; Can We Survive the Future?;* and *An Inquiry into the Future of Mankind: Designing Tomorrow Today;* Denoyer-Geppert: *Lifestyle 2000;* Newsweek: *2000 A.D.;* simulations: *Future Decisions: The I.Q. Game; Global Futures Game; Humanus.* **Special features** Many of the class activities are described in *Looking Forward: A Mini-Course in Future Studies* by Mary Kay Howard and Betty Barclay Franks.

MILFORD EXEMPTED VILLAGE SCHOOL DISTRICT   **Date of first offering:** 1974
c/o Milford Futurology Program
Milford Junior High School
5733 Pleasant Hill Road
Milford, Ohio 45150

Program title: Milford Futurology Program

Director: Geoffrey H. Fletcher, Gary D. Wooddell, Thornton E. Dixon

Educational level: Secondary — junior and senior high school; academically gifted

Degrees offered: —

Course titles: Futurology I (grade 9; academically talented by invitation); Future Studies (grade 9; elective); Futurology II (grade 11, academically talented by invitation); Futures unit (grade 5; gifted program).

Program description: The Milford Futurology Program is one of the oldest interdisciplinary futures programs in the country, and one of the few offered specifically at the junior high level. Main topics include: views of the future (high, low, appropriate technology and extrapolators, revolutionaries, and romantics); biosystems (the beginning of life, mind/brain, and end of life); environmental systems (population/food, energy/resources, ecology/environment, habitat); socio-economic-political systems (government, education, etc.). The program is as experience-oriented as possible. Students design and build a city; they incorporate futures techniques such as forecasting methodologies in their experiences; they are involved in applying futures to the community. Juniors visit three colleges and spend a day as college students. Source materials include: Huxley, *Brave New World;* Vonnegut, *Player Piano; Ecotopia; Dynamics of Change;* exerpts from other books; magazines; films; simulations; filmstrips.

WITTENBERG UNIVERSITY
Springfield, Ohio 45501

Date of first offering: 1973

Program title: Future Studies

Director: George C. Ramsay, Associate Professor of Art

Educational level: College undergraduate

Degrees offered: Minor in Future Studies

Course titles: New Dimensions of Human Experience; New Directions in Music; Art and the Future; Ecological Lifestyles; Alternative Energy Resources; Future World Orders; Self-sufficient Living; Religion and Science; Global Space; The Ethics of Limits.

Program description: Program has strong focus on the humanities. Completion of five courses makes up a minor in Future Studies, including the introductory course on "Images." In addition to the courses offered each term, a shared student-faculty colloquium provides an arena for integrating course material, for considering theoretical and practical future-oriented problems, and for generating individual and group independent study projects.

OKLAHOMA

CASADY SCHOOL
Oklahoma City, Oklahoma 73156

Course title: Society in Change

Instructor: Richard B. McCubbin

Educational level: High school

Date of this offering: Spring, 1979

Date of first offering: 1976

Course description: This is a ten-week course in which students are introduced to the language and methods of possibly determining alternative futures. In the beginning, students are presented with various predictions for the future in the areas of politics, ecology, economics, social change; the remainder of the term is spent studying, researching, discussing, planning alternative futures. **Activities:** Delphi and scenario methods; construct futures wheel; reading and reporting from science fiction; lectures and discussions with people in city government, industry and education; term project is to design a school for the intermediate future—15 to 20 years away. **Source materials:** Science fiction (student's choice); selected magazine articles; film: *Future Shock;* filmstrip: *Lifestyle 2000;* simulation: *The Planet Management Game.* **Special features** Students receive extra credit for additional reading in environmental and futuristic areas.

UNIVERSITY OF OKLAHOMA
820 Van Fleet Oval
Norman, Oklahoma 73069

Course title: Futurology in Education

Instructor: John D. Pulliam, Professor of Education

Educational level: Doctorate

Date of this offering: 1978-79

Date of first offering: Summer, 1964

Course description: Education in the 21st century; alternative learning environments; futuristic technology and research methods. **Activities:** Seminar format; scenario writing; development of futuristic games; analysis of basic works in educational futurism. **Source materials:** Theobald, four books; Platt, two books; Brown, *By Bread Alone;* Bowman, et al., *The Far Side of the Future;* Toffler, *Learning for Tomorrow;* many others. **Special features:** Cooperation with members of the university's College of Environmental Design and with futurists at the University of Houston at Clear Lake City.

UNIVERSITY OF OKLAHOMA
Department of Regional and City Planning
650 Parrington Oval
Norman, Oklahoma 73019

Course title: Futures Study: Methods and Theories

Instructor: Joseph Lee Rodgers, Chairman; Roy W. Reynolds, Course Instructor (Adjunct Assistant Professor)

Educational level: Master's

Date of this offering: Spring, 1978-79   **Date of first offering:** Spring, 1978-79

Course description: This course stresses the importance of general system theory, creative problem-solving process, complementarity of analytic and intuitive cognitive processes, multisensory awareness, and the examination of issues. **Activities:** The course consists of four parts: 1) issues study; 2) rational approaches; 3) speculative/visionary approaches; and 4) synthesis. Methods include inquiry-seminar approach (limited lecture); assignments include a personal journal of thoughts and observations, a project/paper, and an in-class debate. **Source materials:** Cornish, *The Study of the Future*; Kuhns, *The Post-Industrial Prophets*; World Future Society reprints, tapes, films, records. **Special features:** Student journal to record thought development throughout semester; problem-oriented paper or project; field trips (high technology communications media demonstration); multi-media presentations.

OREGON

MARYLHURST EDUCATION CENTER
Marylhurst, Oregon 97036

Date of first offering: Spring, 1978

Program title: Humanities Seminar — 1999: A Futures Exploration

Director: Marilyn Guldan

Educational level: College undergraduate; graduate level; adult

Degrees offered: —

Course titles: —

Program description: The interdisciplinary seminar, "1999: A Futures Exploration," appeals to the off-campus learner. This seminar offers the convenience of home study, including personalized correspondence, and culminates with a live-in workshop at the end of the term. Participants read and reflect throughout the quarter, completing two assignments by mail. In the final weekend participants, faculty, and guest speakers are co-learners from Friday evening through Sunday afternoon. Readings and activities focus on topics such as: What will the future be like? Can I shape my future or must I respond to outside forces? What is meant by transformed humanity? What values, beliefs, and morality will characterize 1999?

PORTLAND STATE UNIVERSITY
P.O. Box 751
Portland, Oregon 97207

Course title: Future of Society

Instructor: Charles D. Bolton

Educational level: College juniors and seniors

Date of this offering: Spring, 1979   **Date of first offering:** 1974

Course description: This course gives an overview of possible changes in society in the future. Topics include: history and method in futurism from industrial to technological society; social meanings of modernization; emerging crises of technological society; possible form of post-industrial society: knowledge base, class structure, value questions, inequality and equalities; form and consciousness in post-industrial society. **Activities:** Lecture-discussion; films. **Source materials:** Teich, *Technology and Man's Future*; Bell, *The Coming of Post-Industrial Society*; Berger, Berger and Kellner, *The Homeless Mind*; Huxley, *Island;* many journal articles. **Special features:** —

PORTLAND STATE UNIVERSITY
P.O. Box 751
Portland, Oregon 97207

Course title: Social Change and the Future of the City

Instructor: Charles D. Bolton

Educational level: Doctorate

Date of this offering: Winter, 1979   **Date of first offering:** 1974

Course description: This course covers social change in regard to the post-industrial society. Topics include: theories of social change; methods of forecasting; urbanization and organization sources of social change; technological society and its emerging problems; capitalism and political society; the transition to post-industrial society; the future of the city; and learning to plan and planning to learn.   **Activities:** Lecture-discussion; oral reports; scenario writing. **Source materials:**   Bell, *The Coming of the Post-Industrial Society*; Michael, *On Learning to Plan and Planning to Learn*; Garner, *Social Change*; Lappe and Collins, *Food First*; Karp, Stone and Yoels, *Being Urban*; many journal articles.   **Special features:**   —

PORTLAND STATE UNIVERSITY
P.O. Box 751
Portland, Oregon 97207

Date of first offering: 1970

Program title: Systems Science Doctoral Program

Director: Harold A. Linstone

Educational level: Doctorate

Degrees offered: Ph.D. in Systems Science with concentrations in forecasting and planning

Course titles: Technological Forecasting; Social Forecasting; Futures Seminar; Systems Approach; Workshop; Modeling and Simulation; Communication; Systems Planning and Management; Information Systems; Operations Research; Computer Technology; Technology Assessment; General Systems and Cybernetics; Advanced Seminar.

Program description: Students may construct programs preparing them either for research in the methodology for treatment of complex systems or for applying the systems approach to vital societal problems. The program also houses the Futures Research Institute and the international journal, *Technological Forecasting and Social Change*. Most students also complete an internship of six to twelve months with a governmental or private organization.

PENNSYLVANIA

LAWRENCE COUNTY DETENTION HOME
Court Street
New Castle, Pennsylvania 16101

Course title: Future Studies

Instructor: Dennis Joura

Educational level: Intermediate (6-9); high school; college freshmen and sophomores

Date of this offering: —   **Date of first offering:** —

Course description: Value clarification; what the future may hold — technology, ecology, politics; personal futures; what can be done now to influence the future. Course includes city planning; house architecture; plotting one's own future; nuclear holocaust; scenarios.   **Activities:** Basically lecture-discussion.   **Source materials:** Science fiction; Scholastic Books, *The Future — Can We Shape It?; Tomorrow* (collection of future oriented short stories).   **Special features:** Basic thrust for the course is value clarification, since the students in the course have very negative future focused role images.

LEHIGH UNIVERSITY
Bethlehem, Pennsylvania 18015

Date of first offering: Fall, 1972

Program title: Humanities Perspectives on Technology

Director: Steven L. Goldman, Andrew W. Mellon Professor in the Humanities; Stephen H. Cutcliffe, Administrative Assistant

Educational level: College undergraduate

Degrees offered: Minor in Technology and Human Values

Course titles: Technology and Its Critics; The Literature of Environment; Science Fiction; Media and Values; The Myth of Knowledge; Leisure in a Technological Society; Utopia: Fictional Ideals and Technological Realities; Self Reliance in a Technological Society; Fiction and the Technological Vision; Sculpture and Technology; Media and the Twentieth Century Vision; Resources and the American Life-style; Media, Technology and Politics; The Machine in America to 1900; The Machine in Modern America; Development of Federal Science Policy; The American Engineer; The Science Technology Establishment and Its Critics; Humanistics in a Technological Society; Independent Study; Electronic Vision: The Contemporary Media of Sight; Science, Technology and Religion; Science, Technology and International Relations; Computer Programming for the Humanities; Computer Applications in the Humanities and Social Sciences; The Ancient City; Electronic Music; War and Non-violent Alternatives in a Techtronic Age; Behavior Control and Human Values; Philosophy of Contemporary Civilization; Medical Ethics; Psychological Perspectives in a Technological Society; Futuristics; Hunger—Challenge to Man; Technology and Religious Thought; Science, Technology and Society; Utopias and Alternative Communities; Social Ecology; The Technological Determinism Debate in Anthropology.

Program description: An interdisciplinary, undergraduate program concerned chiefly with the interrelationships among values, the quality of human life, and technological advance. The program is funded for an initial five-year period by a $500,000 grant from the National Endowment for the Humanities. Some of the courses listed have come and gone, chiefly with their teachers, but most have been absorbed by the appropriate departments after initial funding by the program. Only the Futuristics course focuses entirely on the future; the others tend to be historical and analytical with a unit on the future or with future implications considered as the course proceeds. Student-faculty workshops have guided the development of the program.

LOWER MORELAND HIGH SCHOOL
Huntington Valley, Pennsylvania 19006

Course title: Futurology: The Year 2000

Instructor: Lester Bailey and William Pezza

Educational level: High school seniors

Date of this offering: Spring, 1979   **Date of first offering:** 1970

Course description: Macrohistory—overview of man's evolution; America's evolution; methods of future research; possible causes of future shock; limits of adaptability; biomedical technology; computer technology; systems; alternative life-styles; global concerns; values and valuing; strategies for directorship of preferable futures. **Activities:** Lecture; discussion; debates and symposia; role playing; dramatization; guest speakers; current trend analysis; video presentations; book reviews; strategy assignments; field trips; viewing commercial TV shows. **Source materials:** Books: *Walden II; Future Shock; Greening of America; Bioethics; The Futurists; The Population Bomb; Learning for Tomorrow; The Limits to Growth; Beyond Freedom and Dignity;* films: *Games Futurists Play; Man and the Second Industrial Revolution;* videotapes: *World Hunger—Who Will Survive?; An Interview with Buckminster Fuller; Future Shock; What About Tomorrow?; Helstrom Chronicle; Conservation; Science Fiction or Fact?; The Corporation;* audiotapes: *Alvin Toffler; Toward 1984; Man Planets, Future;* magazine: THE FUTURIST; simulation games: *Humanus; Futuribles.* **Special features** Visits to local science museum and to local colleges to hear noted futurists.

MARYWOOD COLLEGE
2300 Adams Ave.
Scranton, Pennsylvania 18509

Course title: The Future: The Next 200 Years

Instructor: Dorothy A. Haney, Associate Professor of Philosophy and Chairman, Philosophy Department

Educational level: College undergraduate, master's and adult

Date of this offering: 1979   **Date of first offering:** 1976

Course description: Consideration of the future in terms of five great humanizing forces: tool making, language, social organization, education, and man's urge to explain his world. **Activities:** Team teaching in philosophy and history; lecture; discussion; audiovisual materials; critical essays by students on what will and should the future be like.   **Source materials:** Books: Esfandiary: *Up Wingers: A Futurist Manifesto;* Knelman: *1984 and All That;* Kothari: *Footsteps into the Future;* Toffler: *The Futurists;* simulation: *Futuribles;* several sound/filmstrips.   **Special features** A concentrated course offered after participants have been student teaching. Marywood also offers future-oriented courses in Critiques of Contemporary Society, The Peace Mongers and Utopias.

MARYWOOD COLLEGE
2300 Adams Ave.
Scranton, Pennsylvania 18509

Course title: Utopias: Paths to Nowhere

Instructor: Dorothy Haney and Margaret Gannon

Educational level: College undergraduate

Date of this offering: Spring 1979

Date of first offering: 1979

Course description: The course examines the nature of human beings, human values and utopian societies. Several different visions of utopia are considered. Students are asked to construct their own utopia, identifying and justifying the values and organization of their perfect society. Futurist courses also taught at the college include The Peace Mongers and The Future.   **Activities:** Lecture-discussion; strategies for student participation.   **Source materials:** Texts: Schumacher, *A Guide for the Perplexed;* More, *Utopia;* Bellamy, *Looking Backward;* Teilhard, *The Future of Man.* Selected reading list of utopias.   **Special features:** —

MONSIGNOR BONNER HIGH SCHOOL
Garrett Road and Lansdowne Avenue
Drexel Hill, Pennsylvania 19026

Course title: Futurism

Instructor: Edward C. Griffith, Social Studies Department

Educational level: High school

Date of this offering: September, 1979

Date of first offering: 1974

Course description: Various scenarios including Ehrlich and Asimov; concepts of "future shock" including transience; technology and technology assessment; population and national land use; energy; limits to growth; food problems; transportation; genetics; medicine; environment; science fiction.   **Activities:** Scenario writing; oral reports; role playing; filmstrips; films; slides.   **Source materials:** Books: Toffler, *Future Shock;* Norman, *Dimensions of the Future;* films: *Future Shock; Year 1999;* filmstrips: *In Our Own Image; Encounters with Tomorrow; Living with Technology; Science and Society; Forecasting the Future; Is Any Body Out There?; Redesigning Man;* slide-sound: *New Genetics Rights and Responsibilities.*   **Special features:** —

NORTH MIDDLE SCHOOL
R.D. No. 2
Dillsburg, Pennsylvania 17019

Course title: Tomorrow's Mysteries

Instructor: Paula Prober

Educational level: Intermediate — Grades 5-8

Date of this offering: 1979

Date of first offering: 1977-78

Course description: This course involves work with gifted children in grades 5 through 8 — at present sixth graders. Course involves initiating activities — background and discussion; independent projects; a futuristics fair or a schoolwide newsletter as the culmination of the project.   **Activities:** Initiating activities: cross-impact games; "what if" games; grab bag 21st century; vocabulography; time capsule. Independent projects by students: critique of at least five scifi stories; read about and study computers and write a "Guide to the Layman"; 21st century art; TV script for "All in the Family 1991"; etymology — 10 new words that have entered the vocabulary in the last five years; make your own music; etc. Group activities — inquiry sessions; future projection sociodrama; Delphi method; problem solving; population game, etc.   **Source materials:** Course lists teacher resource reading list of books, articles, and newspapers, and a student reading list. Student list includes: Ross-Macdonald, *Life in the Future;* Newman, ed., *1994: The World of*

Tomorrow; Still, *Man: The Next 30 Years*; DeRossi, *Computers: Tools for Today.*   **Special features:** Independent projects include setting up flow charts of "A Morning" as part of the computers section. Speakers for this unit include subjects on history, workings, binary system, and the future.

PENDLE HILL
Wallingford, Pennsylvania 19086

Course title: Where Do I Go From Here?

Instructor: Parker Palmer

Educational level: Adult

Date of this offering: Winter, 1979   **Date of first offering:** Winter, 1975-76

Course description: Work autobiography; skills identification and clustering; matching with future occupations and value systems; systematic targeting; the active job search; survival with your future. **Activities:** Seminar.   **Source materials:** Crystal and Bolles: *Where Do I Go From Here With My Life?* **Special features** Interviews and visits to possible future employment sites. A life/work planning course dealing with future awareness and personal life-careers.

PENNSYLVANIA STATE UNIVERSITY   Date of first offering: 1972
Human Development Building S-210
University Park, Pennsylvania 16802

Program title: Community Systems Planning and Development

Director: Gordon D. Brown

Educational level: Master's and doctorate

Degrees offered: M.S. and Ph.D. in Community Systems Planning and Development, with concentration in health planning and administration, administration of justice, and community social services.

Course titles: Forecasting Methods and Social Policy Planning; Behavioral Assumptions and Strategies in the Process of Planned Change; Community Structure and Social Service Systems; General Systems Perspectives; Analysis of Human Service Systems; Institutional and Political Economics of Social Service Systems.

Program description: The program maintains a strong futures and systems perspective in training professionals for various fields.

PENNSYLVANIA STATE UNIVERSITY
Community Systems Planning and Development Program
S-210 Henderson Building
University Park, Pennsylvania 16802

Course title: Forecasting Methods and Special Policy Planning

Instructor: Fred Eisele; Peter Meyer

Educational level: Master's; doctorate

Date of this offering: 1978-79
                                                      Date of first offering: 1974-75
Course description: Course topics include: role of forecasting in relationship to planning: forecasting methods, trend extrapolation; modeling and simulation, qualitative and holistic methods; forecasting exercises: policy impact forecasts, policy implementation forecasts; forecast evaluations: accuracy, utilization potential. This course is part of the Community Systems Planning and Development Program. Students, especially at the doctoral level, can engage in additional futures and forecasting studies. Some dissertations have included major forecasting elements.   **Activities:** Seminar with faculty lectures as necessary; major student exercises, as listed under course description.   **Source materials:** Baier and Rescher, *Values and the Future*; SRI, *Handbook of Forecasting Techniques*; Bardach, *The Implementation Game*; Glenn, *Cohort Analysis*; Harris, *Social Forecasting Methodologies*; Ferkiss, *Futurology: Promise, Performance, Prospect.* **Special features:** —

PENNSYLVANIA STATE UNIVERSITY
University Park, Pennsylvania 16802

Course title: Geography of the Future

Instructor: Ronald Abler

Educational level: College juniors and seniors

Date of this offering: Spring, 1979 **Date of first offering:** 1972

Course description: Transportation; communications; labor force structure; settlement forms; metropolitan evolution. **Activities:** Lecture; discussion; oral reports; individual research. **Source materials:** General literature; Abler *et al.: Human Geography in a Shrinking World: A Geography of the Future.* **Special features** —

PENNSYLVANIA STATE UNIVERSITY
University Park, Pennsylvania 16802

Course title: Introduction to Community Systems

Instructor: Abram P. Snyder, Associate Professor of Community Development

Educational level: College freshmen and sophomores and adult

Date of this offering: 1978 **Date of first offering:** March, 1975

Course description: Course contains a future-oriented module on land use control systems; topics include: objectives of land use systems; environment—constraints of land use systems; resources—components of land use systems; management of land use control systems. **Activities:** Six 60-minute videotapes; lecture; discussion. **Source materials:** Books: Churchman: *Systems Approach;* Meadows *et al.: Limits to Growth; The Use of Land;* current articles concerning the Pennsylvania situation. **Special features** This module comprises 25% of the course.

SHALER AREA HIGH SCHOOL
1800 Mt. Royal Boulevard
Glenshaw, Pennsylvania 15116

Course title: The Future

Instructor: Thomas J. Wyeth, Elizabeth Spence

Educational level: High school

Date of this offering: 1978 **Date of first offering:** 1972-73

Course description: The course is open to 11th and 12th grade students who want to know and to consider the place of the future in their education and their lives, and who want to identify and promote forces which will create positive opportunities for them and help avoid the threats cited in the forecasts of some pessimistic observers. **Activities:** Small group decision-making activities; role-playing; lecture-discussion; scenario writing; students present oral reports. **Source materials:** Extensive reading list; films; filmstrips and slide programs. Basic texts: Dunstan and Garlan, *Worlds in the Making;* Theobald, *Futures Conditional;* Heilbroner, *The Future as History;* Fabun, *The Dynamics of Change;* Kostelanetz, ed., *Social Speculations.* **Special features:** Through class activities, students will be able to examine and evaluate their own and others' assumptions and perceptions about the future. The course aims to develop futurist skills and attitudes to help students prepare personally and institutionally for "Future Shock."

SLIPPERY ROCK STATE COLLEGE
Slippery Rock, Pennsylvania 16057

Course title: Philosophy and Alternative Futures

Instructor: Robert A. Macoskey, Professor of Philosophy

Educational level: College juniors and seniors, master's, adult—general and professional

Date of this offering: Spring, 1979 **Date of first offering:** Spring, 1972

Course description: This course attempts to do five things: introduce students to major principles of "process philosophy"—the future is open and alternative futures can be invented; identify weaknesses in "reductionist" approach to the world and offer as an alternative— "perspectivism" (Buckminster Fuller); advocate a major, synergistic concept, "interdependence"; demonstrate how "interdependence" pertains to nature and mankind; application of this principle to various aspects of the world.   **Activities:** Lecture-discussion; demonstrations (plays, simulations); role plays, problem solving; aesthetic productions; task forces for special information gathering and report writing; polls/surveys/interviews. **Source materials:**   Principle texts: Laszlo, *Systems View of the World*; Vacca, *The Coming Dark Age*; Stavrianos, *The Promise of the Coming Dark Age*; Schumacher, *Small is Beautiful*; extensive source book list; films/filmstrips (audio-visuals in general); field trips for on-site observation of relevant activities; hardware; software; visiting experts from off campus; faculty from other departments on regular basis; area physicians and surgeons.   **Special feature:**   This course may develop into a master's level program within the next few years. In previous years class has designed education from womb to tomb; designed an intentional community on 140 acres near campus. This year class focuses on alternatives to societal collapse due to over-complexity.

TEMPLE UNIVERSITY
College of Education
Ritter Hall 470
Philadelphia, Pennsylvania 19122

Course title: Perspectives on Tomorrow

Instructor: Elliott Seif, Professor of Education

Educational level: Master's

Date of this offering: Spring, 1979   **Date of first offering:** Spring, 1979

Course description: This course focuses on proposed alternatives for future living as well as dilemmas and choices for future living. Students will attempt to create their own goals for future living based on assumptions explored throughout the course. Course topics include: beliefs and assumptions about the future; present and future problems; trends and scenarios, dealing with dilemmas, personal futures.   **Activities:** Discussion; value clarification; future studies — trend discussions; scenario writing; personal goal setting; simulations.   **Source materials:** Dickson, *The Future File*; World Future Society, *The Future: A Guide to Information Sources; The Survivalists*; Kahn, *The Next 200 Years;* Dunstan and Garlan, *Worlds in the Making, Starsight*, and many others; films; simulations.   **Special features:** Probable field trips to computer center, research centers, special thematic projects.

TEMPLE UNIVERSITY
Date of first offering: Fall, 1979

College of Education
Ritter Hall 470
Philadelphia, Pennsylvania 19122

Program title: Teaching for LIFE (Living in the Future Effectively)

Director: Elliott Seif, Professor of Education

Educational level: Doctorate

Degrees offered: Certificate of Advanced Study - Elementary Education

Course titles: Courses on future living curriculum ideas, English, math, social studies and science education, human development, philosophy of education, thinking and problem solving, and others.

Program description: This program is designed to help educators focus on the needs of children as they face their futures. The program will focus on instructional issues and dilemmas related to the development of a future living education. Students will develop models for future living education ideas. Activities include seminars with many varied activities. Source materials and special features are not decided at present.

WILLIAM PENN CHARTER SCHOOL
3000 West School House Lane
Philadelphia, Pennsylvania 19144

Course title: Global Studies: Alternative World Futures

Instructor: Jacob A. Dresden, Dean of Students and Director of College Placement

Educational level: High school

Date of this offering: Winter, 1978-79   **Date of first offering:** 1972

Course description: Basic units in the course focus on: 1) Evaluation of present world model and its structure, 2) methodologies for creating alternative models, 3) model building — methods, 4) future scenarios through case studies. **Activities:** Basic format — discussion of assigned readings; other methods; debate, values exercises, research into existing alternative models and thinkers; role play.   **Source materials:** Fuller, *Utopia or Oblivion;* Mische, *Toward a Human World Order;* Falk, *This Endangered Planet;* Toffler, *The Futurists;* Toffler, *Learning for Tomorrow.*   **Special features:** Guest speakers; field trip to Fuller's headquarters in Philadelphia; lectures at University of Pennsylvania focused on city in the year 2000 A.D.

RHODE ISLAND

PROVIDENCE COLLEGE
Physics Department
Providence, Rhode Island 02918

Course title: Science and the Future

Instructor: Edwin K. Gora, Professor

Educational level: Undergraduate

Date of this offering: 1979   **Date of first offering:** September, 1978

Course description: This course gives an overview of the history and philosophical roots of futurism, covering early history, coming to the present day, and looking into the future: entropy versus evolution, role of systems approach and cybernetics, 20th century physics and the future, evolution and the future of the universe, biology, psychology, and the future of man—will there be a superman? future of space, science fiction.   **Activities:** Primarily lectures with some discussion; presentation of oral reports by students.   **Source materials:** Dickson, *Future File,* supplemented by handouts based on Toffler, McHale, Meadows, Gabor, Dyson, O'Neill, and others. The Department is working on lecture notes for the course, since they have not found a suitable textbook.   **Special features:** —

SOUTH CAROLINA

AIRPORT HIGH SCHOOL
West Columbia, South Carolina 29169

Course title: The Future

Instructor: Bobbie Hartley

Educational level: High School

Date of this offering: 1978-79   **Date of first offering:** 1975-76

Course description: This nine-week course is designed to make participants aware of the future alternatives they face and allow them to develop those skills needed to deal effectively with their personal futures. Topics include: the nature of change; population dynamics; forecasting and scenarios; alternative life-styles; alternatives to pollution and technology; the future city; the future institutions.   **Activities:** Independent and group work; simulation gaming including role playing; each student develops and presents a prediction of tomorrow through some medium.   **Source materials:** Books: approximately 50 available titles; selected articles from THE FUTURIST; materials from *Newsweek,* The Population Council, and the Population Reference Bureau; films: *Future Shock; The Thinking Machine; Tilt;* and others.   **Special features:** Use of school's videotape system; field trips to institutions and businesses involved in futures studies.

COASTAL CAROLINA COLLEGE
UNIVERSITY OF SOUTH CAROLINA
Conway, South Carolina 29526

Course title: Careers In Education

Instructor: James H. Rex, Chairman, Division of Teacher Education; Stewart Strothers, Team Leader

Educational level: College freshmen and sophomores

Date of this offering: 1978-79   **Date of first offering:** 1975

Course description: Educational Futuristics—curricula, professionalism, student rights, consumerism, methodology, and resources; What Kind of World Do You Want?—a multi-media unit regarding alternative futures. Students react to and discuss popular music, slide-tapes and video-tape scenarios. The course is team-taught/field-based/competency-based.   **Activities:** A team of four instructors utilize a wide range of methodology such as: simulated school board meeting where students present and defend proposals for needed changes in education; lecture-discussion of futuristically oriented popular songs, books, and films.   **Source materials:** Toffler, *Future Shock; Sabertooth Curriculum* films: *Future Shock;* videotapes: *Alternative Schools;* multi-media unit: "What Kind of World Do You Want?" **Special features:** Panel of teachers and administrators discuss realities of the teaching profession at present and how they believe it will change during the next two decades. This is a required introductory experience for all teacher education majors.

FURMAN UNIVERSITY
Greenville, South Carolina 29613

Course title: Sociology of the Future

Instructor: J. Daniel Cover

Educational level: College undergraduate

Date of this offering: Summer, 1979   **Date of first offering:** 1974

Course description: Technology of the future; forecasting methods; principles of social change; limits to growth controversy; biological innovations; future shock.   **Activities:** Lecture; discussion; simulation of global futures; scenario writing; student report on scenario at end of the course.   **Source materials:** Books: Toffler: *Future Shock;* Sorokin: *The Crisis of Our Age;* Meadows: *The Limits to Growth;* Taylor: *The Biological Time Bomb;* films: *Future Shock; Cosmopolis; 1985; Family: Life Styles of the Future; Religion: Making the Scene; Stranger Than Science Fiction; But Is This Progress?; Frank Film; Lapis; Omega; The Communications Explosion; THX 1138;* simulation: *Global Futures Game.*   **Special features** Speakers from Southern Bell Telephone, IBM, Greenville County Planning Commission, a UFO study group, and the Atomic Energy Commission; a NASA telelecture.

UNIVERSITY OF SOUTH CAROLINA
Department of Government and International Studies
Columbia, South Carolina 29208

Course title: The Future of Politics

Instructor: Vukan Kuic

Educational level: College juniors and seniors

Date of this offering: Spring, 1979   **Date of first offering:** 1972

Course description: Topics include: the importance of future studies; the types of future studies; a sample of scenarios; what is technology?; what is work?; what is politics?; work, society, culture and politics.   **Activities:** Lecture-discussion; individual students' project reports.   **Source materials:** Simon, *Work, Society, and Culture;* Sibley, *Nature and Civilization.*   **Special features:** —

SOUTH DAKOTA

DAKOTA WESLEYAN UNIVERSITY
Mitchell, South Dakota 57301

Course title: Choosing Futures

Instructor: Mary Weinkauf, English Department

Educational level: College undergraduate

Date of this offering: January, 1978 Four-week interim   **Date of first offering:** 1978

Course description: Ways of predicting the future; stories of possible futures and essays about change; responsibilities to make decisions now: use of influence; selling the need to direct change.   **Activities:** Lecture-discussion, scenario writing; group project—taping, researching, interviewing; oral reports, questionnaires for self-analysis; game and simulation playing; small group analysis of stories and essays. **Source materials:**   Schumacher, *Small is Beautiful*; Toffler, *The Futurists*; Sheila Schwartz, ed., *Earth in Transit*; THE FUTURIST; *The I-Q Game* filmstrips; *Futuribles* card decision making games; Ray Bradbury tape, *Fantasy and Reality*; I. Asimov tape, *Early Science Fiction*.   **Special features:** Multi-media three-hour presentation on videotape; *Nova* videotapes and *Land of Hype and Glory*; visit by Honeywell engineers and civil defense officer; future music research through listening; taped interviews.

TENNESSEE

SOUTHWESTERN AT MEMPHIS   **Date of first offering:** 1973
2000 North Parkway
Memphis, Tennessee 38112

Program title: Center for the Study of Alternative Futures and Urban Policy Institute

Director: May Maury Harding

Educational level: Adult — government, business, education and civic leadership

Degrees offered: —

Course titles: Workshops to be included: Future Memphis Priorities; Engineering Education in the 1980's (for Christian Brothers College); Inventing the Future: Christian Brothers College in the 1980's (a series of seminars); Memphis in Transition: Building a New Economic Base for the 21st Century (conference).

Program description: The Center conducts seminars, conferences, workshops using trends analysis and futures analysis, interaction, cross-impact, compatibility matrices. Working as individuals, in small groups, and in plenary session, participants present both written and oral reports. Emphasis is on creating own scenarios, monitoring trends and value shifts, drawing from many sources. Occasionally, visiting speakers are invited.

TEXAS

AUSTIN COLLEGE
900 North Grand Avenue
P.O. Box 1601 A.C.
Sherman, Texas 75090

Course title: Sociology of the Future

Instructor: Daniel M. Shores, Associate Professor of Sociology

Educational level: College juniors and seniors, master's

Date of this offering: Spring, 1978   **Date of first offering:** Spring, 1971

Course description: Preview of tomorrow; forecasting; historical methods and current methodology; social change theory; application of theory; futurism in world perspective. **Activities:** Lecture; TV seminar presentations by student groups; simulation games, discussion, Delphi method; films. **Source materials:** Texts: Spekke, ed., *The Next Twenty-Five Years*; Dunstan and Garlan, *Worlds in the Making*; Toffler, *Future Shock*. Supplemental reading: Cornish, *The Study of the Future*; THE FUTURIST, World Future Society BULLETIN, WFS cassette tapes; films; simulation games. **Special features:** Entire course is presented via closed circuit TV (two-way, talkback) among North Texas colleges in addition to classroom students. Guest lectures; TV topic presentations by student teams; field trips; scenario writing.

EAST TEXAS STATE UNIVERSITY
Commerce, Texas 75428

Course title: Shaping the Future

Instructor: Charles Embry, Director, New Center for Learning; Jim Reynolds, course teacher, Director, Academic Advising

Educational level: College undergraduate

Date of this offering: 1979   **Date of first offering:** 1975

Course description: Shaping the Future is the final in a series of courses which compose the alternative general education core curriculum of the New Center for Learning—alternative to distribution requirements. **Activities:** Lecture; lots of discussion; scenario writing and analysis; simulations; lots of *doing*. **Source materials:** Toffler, *Future Shock*; Heilbroner, *An Inquiry into the Human Prospect*; Mesarovic, *Mankind at the Turning Point*; Kahn, *The Next 200 Years*; selections from THE FUTURIST and other magazines and journals; lectures from Stanford Research Institute's *The Changing Images of Man*. **Special features:** Many guest visits by faculty in various fields to explain or argue with various technical or ethical positions. Simulation: class volunteered to isolate themselves for 2½ days to see what it is like to live on scarce resources in crowded conditions.

UNIVERSITY OF HOUSTON AT CLEAR LAKE CITY   **Date of first offering:** 1974
2700 Bay Area Boulevard
Houston, Texas 77058

Program title: Master of Arts or Science in Education: Concentration in Futures Studies

Director: Jim Bowman and Fred Kierstead

Educational level: Master's and adult (community planning workshops)

Degrees offered: M.S. in Education with specialization in Futures Studies

Course titles: Course titles include: Educational/Societal Futures; Reconstructionist Futurism; Technological Forecasting; Futures Change Agents; Seminar in Educational Futures; Changing Images of Man; Study of the Future; Methods of Technological Futures.

Program description: This interdisciplinary program integrates the study of alternatives in education with societal futures. It offers dynamic resources for individuals who want to participate in futures planning through education. Activities include: lecture; dialogue; chronologizing; scenario construction; simulation. Books include: Bowman, et al., *The Far Side of the Future*; Theobald, *TEG's 1994*; Barney, *The Unfinished Agenda* ; Brown, *World Without Borders*. Program includes internships and projects.

UNIVERSITY OF HOUSTON AT CLEAR LAKE CITY   **Date of first offering:** September, 1975
2700 Bay Area Boulevard
Houston, Texas 77058

Program title: Studies of the Future

Director: James C. Coomer

Educational level: Master's

Degrees offered: M.S. in Studies of the Future

Course titles: Introduction to Futures Studies; Communications and Social Change; Technology and Society in the Future; Environmental Management Practices; Environmental Impact Statements; Government Budget Planning and

Analysis; Public Policy Analysis; Public Policy and the Study of the Future; Research Techniques in Government Planning; Theory and Practice of Urban Planning; A Systems Approach; Forecasting Techniques; Reconstructionist Futurism in Education; Data Analysis Techniques; Long-Range Forecasting and Planning; Forecasting By Simulation and Modeling; Science, Technology and Public Policy; Research Techniques in Government Planning; Forecasting Change; Technology and Values; The Utopian Tradition; Health Care Planning; Ecology and Public Policy; Cultural Evolution and Trends; Moral Issues in the Future of Science; Religion and Social Change; Educational Societal Futures; Man's Future in Space; Resources in the Future; International Environmental Problems; Seminar in Futures Studies.

Program description: An interdisciplinary program with 60 degree candidates currently enrolled. Faculty appointed from the university at large.

OUR LADY OF THE LAKE UNIVERSITY
411 S.W. 24th
San Antonio, Texas 78285

Course title: Future Worlds

Instructor: Micheleen Barragy

Educational level: College juniors and seniors

Date of this offering: September, 1978   **Date of first offering:** —

Course description: This course focuses on threats to survival and the general quality of human life by examining value preferences and exploring possible future political and economic activities. The stress is on alternative futures: nature of change, nature of human beings; purpose of life.   **Activities:** Lecture-discussion; oral reports; cross-impact matrix.
Source materials: Cornish, *The Study of the Future*; Falk, *A Study of Future Worlds*; Clarke, *Childhood's End*; filmstrips from Harper & Row; films: *The Man Who Fell to Earth*; *Time and Timbuctu.*   **Special features:** —

RICE UNIVERSITY
Department of Religious Studies
P.O. Box 1892
Houston, Texas 77001

Course title: Futurology and Religion

Instructor: John P. Newport; Nancy Desmond; Doug Szopa

Educational level: College freshmen and sophomores

Date of this offering: 1978   **Date of first offering:** 1977

Course description: This course gives an overview of futurology or futurism, its evolution from pre-scientific and occult futurology to modern futuristics, types of futurists and their visions, areas of speculation, science fiction, and the relation of futurism to the religious perspective.   **Activities:** Lecture-discussion; students present oral reports.
Source materials: Peters, *Futures: Human and Divine;* Harman, *An Incomplete Guide to the Future;* Herberg, *Judaism and Modern Man;* Vaux, ed., *To Create a Different Future.*   **Special features:** Visiting speakers and some field trips.

TARRANT COUNTY JUNIOR COLLEGE
5301 Campus Drive
Fort Worth, Texas 76119

Course title: Futuristics

Instructor: Robert Platt, Director; Gil Desha, Tom Taaffe, Hap Lyda, Bill Holt, Jean Crane, Instructors

Educational level: College freshmen and sophomores; adult

Date of this offering: 1977-78   **Date of first offering:** 1972-74

Course description: This 4-part course presents the opportunity to think about coming changes in the next 50 years, the impact on the environment, values, structures of society, and expected breakthroughs in science.
Activities: Lecture-discussion.   **Source materials:** Handouts, primarily; films; three paperbacks from a list of a dozen or more.   **Special features:** Films are used weekly.

TEXAS A & M UNIVERSITY
College Station, Texas 77843

Course title: Alternative Architecture

Instructor: Peter Jay Zweig

Educational level: Master's and doctorate

Date of this offering: Fall, 1978

Date of first offering: Spring, 1975

Course description: Alternative energy sources; alternative structure; alternative materials; alternative urban and rural designs. **Activities:** Lecture; discussion; visual, oral and written reports; design studio. **Source materials:** *Design With Climate; Whole Earth Catalog; Energy Primer; Energy Directly from the Sun; Frei Otto IL 1-10.* **Special features** Visits to aquaculture facility, greenhouses, methane generators, solar collectors, and local architecture.

UNIVERSITY OF TEXAS AT ARLINGTON
Department of English
UT Arlington
Arlington, Texas 76019

Course title: Build Your Own Utopia

Instructor: Kenneth M. Roemer

Educational level: College juniors and seniors

Date of this offering: Spring, 1978

Date of first offering: Fall, 1976

Course description: This course is designed to help students and instructors clarify and re-examine their ideals and values by asking them to confront hypothetical problems similar to problems confronted by authors of utopian works. Course seeks to introduce students to a variety of utopian works, increase decision-making skills, and improve writing skills. **Activities:** Students in teams work on four problems: various personality theories based on definition of human needs; descriptions of basic marital and family forms as related to a utopian community; campus housing planning (utopian concept on a local level); and illusions of reality, culture and utopia. Students must respond to questions posed at several stages during each of the four stages before receiving feedback. **Source materials:** Johnson, ed., *Utopian Literature;* More, *Utopia;* Bellamy, *Looking Backward;* Skinner, *Walden Two;* Rimmer, *Harrad Experiment;* Le Guin, *The Dispossessed;* Fogarty, ed., *American Utopianism;* film: *Future Shock;* slides; guest lecturers; etc. **Special features:** Guest speakers include writers and planners.

UNIVERSITY OF TEXAS AT AUSTIN
Program in Community College Education
Ed. B. 348
Austin, Texas 78703

Date of first offering: 1960

Program title: Community College Leadership Program

Director: John E. Roueche

Educational level: Doctorate

Degrees offered: Ph.D. in Educational Administration with special concentration in Community College Administration

Course titles: The courses Educational Change and Innovations, and Future Trends in the Community are offered as a shorter unit within the program.

Program description: Students form management teams, invite outstanding authorities to speak to graduate students; some oral student reports. Books used include: *The Far Side of the Future* and *Managers for the Year 2000.* The Community College movement considers adaptability and flexibility to change and future design imperative for fulfilling the comprehensive mission of the institution.

WESTBURY HIGH SCHOOL
5575 Gasmer Road
Houston, Texas 77035

Course title: Advanced Problems in Social Studies: Future Studies

Instructor: Patricia M. Proctor

Educational level: High school

Date of this offering: Spring, 1978-79

Date of first offering: 1976-77

Course description: The course primarily deals with studying forecasts, predictions, assessing techniques and methodology of forecasting in preparing for the future. **Activities:** Brainstorming; students prepare individual and panel oral reports; students keep a scrapbook "Book of the Future" of newspaper and magazine clippings and from it plot trends and get data for several of the course units; lectures on methodologies; Delphi exercise; trend extrapolation; opinion polls by students and their reports on results; read and write science fiction. **Source materials:** Multimedia: *2000A.D.; Beyond City Limits; Redesigning Man; Science and Society; Forecasting the Future; Dimensions of Change; Change Here for Tomorrow;* film: *Future Shock;* simulations: *Cope;* guest speakers. **Special features:** Speakers and fields trips concerning solar heating and air conditioning; speakers for NASA and field trip to the Space Center; speakers and field trip concerning The Woodlands; speakers from major oil companies and from Planning Section of Houston.

UTAH

BRIGHAM YOUNG UNIVERSITY
Department of Spanish and Portuguese
Provo, Utah 84602

Course title: The Media in Foreign Language Education

Instructor: Wendell H. Hall, Associate Professor

Educational level: Doctorate

Date of this offering: Spring, 1979

Date of first offering: Winter, 1978

Course description: The future of education, the future of media and communications. **Activities:** Lecture-discussion; oral reports; projects. (Students will write scenarios next time). **Source materials:** Martin, *The Wired Society;* Kahn, Brown, Martel, *The Next 200 Years;* Kahn and Wiener, *The Year 2000;* film, *Future Shock;* articles from magazines, newspapers; THE FUTURIST. **Special features:** Student projects using media. This is an interdepartmental course, taught to graduate students in German, French, etc., as well as in Spanish.

UTAH STATE UNIVERSITY
College of Education
UMC 28
Logan, Utah 84322

Course title: Future of Education

Instructor: Richard S. Knight and Richard M. Soule

Educational level: College juniors and seniors; master's

Date of this offering: 1979

Date of first offering: 1974

Course description: Alternative futures - images of futurists; science fiction in the classroom; methodologies (Delphi, scenario writing, relevance trees, future wheels, cross-impact, etc.); future of education; futurizing curriculum. **Activities:** Keynote speaker; small group discussions; media; reading and discussing science fiction; model teaching; scenario writing; oral/written plan for implementation; field trip; games/simulations. **Source materials:** Cornish, *The Study of the Future* and Kauffman, *Teaching the Future* are required reading. Extensive bibliography of futurist works on optional basis; films; games. **Special features:** Field trip to the University of Utah medical center, Provo, for hydrogen-fueled automobile, home. (Optional).

582

UNIVERSITY OF UTAH
Department of Sociology
301 Behavioral Science Building
Salt Lake City, Utah 84112

Course title: Sociology of the Future

Instructor: Gerald W. Smith, Thom Kearin

Educational level: College juniors and seniors

Date of this offering: 1979   **Date of first offering:** 1976

Course description: This course is concerned with the future of the American society over the next 30 years, dealing with major alternatives facing the nation and its social systems — an introduction to futures study. **Activities:** Seminar; lecture; student reports (research methodologies) **Source materials:** Kahn, *The Year 2000*; Cornish, *The Study of the Future*; Dickson, *The Future File.* **Special features:** —

VERMONT

HARWOOD UNION HIGH SCHOOL
Route 100
Moretown, Vermont 05660   **Date of first offering:** —

Program title: Approaching the Future

Director: Jonathan S. Weil, Social Studies Department Chairman

Educational level: High school

Degrees offered: —

Course titles: Social Studies courses.

Program description: A series of units that can be integrated into the traditional curriculum or used for alternative education and units in history, economics, political science, psychology, and anthropology. The units are often largely self-taught, using a programmed text, and are open-ended and focus upon the students' perceptions of themselves and their futures at home, on the job, in the community, and in the world. Topics include why not exercises, futures forecasting techniques, where are we headed, who decides, we're all passengers, and what if? doom or bloom. Sub-topics include units on energy, land use, food and nutrition, habitat, and mind control. Methods and activities include reading statistical charts, conducting a Delphi poll, role-playing and simulation, constructing futures wheels, interpretation, translation, and scenario-writing. Source materials include J. Weil and David Victor, *Approaching the Future.*

MARLBORO COLLEGE
Marlboro, Vermont 05344

Course title: Alternative World Futures: Decentralization, World Order, and Limits to Growth

Instructor: Dennis Livingston, Visiting Professor of Social Science

Educational level: College undergraduate

Date of this offering: Spring, 1979

Course description: International political system; limits to growth and other global trends; world order models; decentralist visions and appropriate technology. **Activities:** Whatever structure fits; lecture; discussion; oral reports; student research papers; brainstorming; field visits. **Source materials:** Beres and Targ, *Reordering The Planet*; Schumacher, *Small is Beautiful*; Falk, *A Study of Future Worlds*; LeGuin, *The Dispossessed.* **Special features:** Field trips to local efforts at communal living and small-scale technology.

UNIVERSITY OF VERMONT
College of Education and Social Services Organization
and Human Resource Development Area
228 Waterman Building
Burlington, Vermont 05401

Course title: Seminar in Futurism and Planning

Instructor: Robert Larson, Associate Professor, Administration and Planning

Educational level: Master's, and 30-hour beyond master's (Certificate of Advanced Study—C.A.S.)

Date of this offering: Spring, 1979   **Date of first offering:** 1970

Course description: Examination of knowledge, values, and attitudes relating to the concept of the future; ways of looking at the future; alternative futures; trend analysis; and goal setting in the context of the planning process; forecasting techniques and planning processes applied to educational and social service organizations. **Activities:** Lecture-discussion; small group work; scenario writing; media; guest speakers; student projects applied to real settings. **Source materials:** Brameld, *The Teacher as World Citizen: A Scenario of the 21st Century;* Kahn, et al., *The Next 200 Years;* Michael, *On Learning to Plan and Planning to Learn;* Schumacher, *Small is Beautiful;* film: *Future Shock;* Center for the Humanities, *Toward the Year 2000.* **Special features:** A major focus of the seminar is on the application of futures planning techniques and processes to planning in educational and social service organizations.

VIRGINIA

FORT MYER ELEMENTARY SCHOOL
Arlington, Virginia 22211

Date of first offering: 1971

Program title: Projecting for the Future

Director: Peggy Stephenson

Educational level: Elementary (grades 3 through 6)

Degrees offered: —

Course titles: Course titles vary and have included such topics as Aerospace for the Future, Lifestyle 2000, and Future Communications, *ARTEC* (Arlington Telecommunications System) which was conducted by representatives of the corporation, Math Futurists, especially for gifted math students, and New Views, sponsored by radio personalities and news people.

Program description: The program, held three times a year, consists of mini-courses which are offered once a week for as few as three or as many as seven weeks. Activities include discussions, workshop production, field trips, and the use of audiovisual aids. Outside resource persons frequently direct the courses. Courses have the three goals discussed by Toffler: careers, preparation for the future, and wise use of leisure time. Planning is done by a Future Council composed of teachers, students, parents, and community representatives.

MARY BALDWIN COLLEGE
Staunton, Virginia 24401

Course title: Technology and the Future; History of Science; Science Fiction as History; Folklore as History.

Instructor: Robert H. LaFleur

Educational level: College undergraduate

Date of this offering: 1978   **Date of first offering:** 1975

Course description: Basic literature in the area; reactions to technology; science fiction. **Activities:** Lecture; discussion; field trips; visiting scholars; student reports; simulation; game design. **Source materials:** As wide a variety of monographs, current journalism, literature, art, drama, and music as possible. **Special features:** LaFleur also offers a course on urban society focusing on present and future plans, designs, and problems.

NORFOLK PUBLIC SCHOOLS
School Administration Building
Room 1008
800 E. City Hall Avenue
Norfolk, Virginia 23510

Course title: 7th Grade Decision Making Course

Instructor: Kathleen Schoonmaker, Programs for Gifted/Talented Supervisor; Gloria Hagaus, Social Studies Coordinator; Ann Washington, Programs Gifted/Talented Resource Teacher. 11 Social Studies teachers in 10 junior high schools.

Educational level: 7th grade

Date of this offering: 1978-79

Date of first offering: 1978-79

Course description: This new course takes traditional U.S. history and teaches it from a futuristic point of view. **Activities:** Teaching approach: inquiry learning; creative problem solving process; draw inferences from past; make connections between problems encountered by peoples of the past and contemporary problems. Emphasis is on analysis, synthesis and evaluation. **Source materials:** Books, films, simulations, etc. **Special features:** The following three programs require preparation, hands-on site study and follow-up: Colonial Williamsburg In-Depth Inquiry Approach Program; General Assembly Study and Lynhaven House Study: both include simulations and are based on teaching thinking skills, creative problem solving, using DeBono's thinking skills. Norfolk schools have additional futures courses at other levels.

OLD DOMINION UNIVERSITY
Norfolk, Virginia 23508

Course title: Technology and the Future of Man

Instructor: William B. Jones, Professor of Philosophy

Educational level: College juniors and seniors, master's

Date of this offering: Spring, 1978

Date of first offering: 1974

Course description: Man and technology in historical perspective; technology and change; science, technology and values; technology and contemporary problems; technology and the future. **Activities:** Lecture-discussion; visiting public lectures; oral and audiovisual student reports to class; written reports. **Source materials:** Bronowski, *Science and Human Values*; Burke, ed., *The New Technology and Human Values*; Childe, *Man Makes Himself*; Detweiler et al., eds., *Environmental Decay in Its Historical Context*; Florman, *The Existential Pleasures of Engineering*; Mesthene, *Technological Change*; Mesthene, ed., *Technology and Social Change*; films. **Special features:** Lecture and discussion by visiting specialists and professionals; media use by students and in class presentations.

UNIVERSITY OF RICHMOND
Richmond, Virginia 23173

Course title: Future Policy: Anticipating 2000

Instructor: John W. Outland, Political Science Department

Educational level: College freshmen

Date of this offering: Fall, 1978

Date of first offering: 1973

Course description: The study of the future; the phenomenon of change; coping with change; forecasting methods; global futures, societal futures; personal futures (i.e., dilemma areas and possible responses in each of the last three areas.) **Activities:** Lecture-discussion; oral reports; films; various planning and futurible exercises (*Futuribles*, etc.) **Source materials:** Cornish, *The Study of the Future;* Harman, *An Incomplete Guide to the Future;* Brown, *Human Needs and the Security of Nations* (pamphlet); "A Look into Our Third Century," *Smithsonian* magazine (July 1976). **Special features:** Occasional guest speakers including director of regional planning commission and university instructors in relevant subject areas.

VIRGINIA COMMONWEALTH UNIVERSITY
Richmond, Virginia 23220

Course title: Education and the Future

Instructor: Howard Ozmon

Educational level: Master's

Date of this offering: Spring, 1979

Date of first offering: Summer, 1975

Course description: Forecasting methods; utopias and science fiction; innovations and new technology; future of education; teaching the future. **Activities:** Lecture-discussion; oral and written reports. **Source materials:** Toffler, *Future Shock;* Esfandiary, *Up-Wingers;* Boyer, *Alternative .Futures;* Ozmon, *Utopias and Education.* **Special features:** Course taught every semester.

VIRGINIA COMMONWEALTH UNIVERSITY
812 W. Franklin Street
Richmond, Virginia 23284

Course title: Introduction to the Study of the Future

Instructor: Carol A. Christensen

Educational level: College juniors and seniors; master's

Date of this offering: 1978   **Date of first offering:** 1975

Course description: This course covers the implications of change in the future. Topics include: the philosophies and methodologies of futurism; long-term historical trends; institutional change; marriage and the family; post-industrial society; work and leisure; value changes; the growth/no-growth debate; ethical and distributional questions; appropriate technology; policy questions and directions. **Activities:** Lecture-discussion; journal keeping; students construct scenario sets which are read and evaluated by class members; "show and tell" becomes a central part of the course. **Source materials:** Texts vary from semester to semester. Recent required texts include: Ferkiss, *Futurology*; Kahn, *The Next 200 Years*; Schumacher, *Small is Beautiful*; Sanders, *The Tomorrow File*; articles on a range of subjects and viewpoints; films; video- and audio-tapes. **Special features:** Christensen is also project director for "Futures Report," a series of multi-media presentations and related learning materials designed to encourage discussion about, and planning for, the future in seminars and continuing education sessions for adult lay and professional groups.

WASHINGTON

CENTRAL WASHINGTON STATE COLLEGE
Ellensburg, Washington 98926

Course title: Educational Futurism

Instructor: J. Wesley Crum, Professor of Education

Educational level: Master's

Date of this offering: 1978   **Date of first offering:** 1972

Course description: A study of the literature on alternative futures in American society and their possible impacts upon education. The methods of creative forecasting or futures research. The desirability of deciding between alternative futures in educational organization, administration, curriculum and instruction. Futurism in elementary and secondary schools. **Activities:** Audiovisual presentations; seminars; scenario writing; simple Delphi activities; oral reports. **Source materials:** Books: Hack et al., *Educational Futurism 1985*; Toffler, *Learning for Tomorrow*; Toffler, *The Eco-Spasm Report*; magazines: *Trend*; THE FUTURIST; filmstrips: *Power Struggle; Future Power; On the Public's Shoulders; In the Scientist's Lap; Too Many People; Not Enough Food; Transplants, Machines and People; Tampering with Genes*; films: *Future Shock; The World of Future Shock; Games Futurists Play*; various audiotapes. **Special features:** Each student develops an extensive individual project.

UNIVERSITY OF PUGET SOUND
2122 MacArthur Street West
Tacoma, Washington 98416

Course title: Forecasting and Planning

Instructor: Mitchel F. Bloom, Associate Professor, School of Business and Public Administration

Educational level: College juniors and seniors

Date of this offering: Spring, 1979   **Date of first offering:** 1979

Course description: Main topics include: basic forecasting methodologies including extrapolation, judgment techniques and simulation; world food-population problem; societal futures as envisioned by well-known futurists; accuracy of past forecasts and forecasting techniques; recent forecasts made by instructor and previous students; participation in computerized (EIES) futurist network. **Activities:** Lecture-discussion; oral reports; computer simulations; guest

586

speakers; field exercise in which students perform a forecast for a local business, government agency or non-profit organization. **Source materials:** Ascher, *Forecasting: An Appraisal*; Cornish, *1999: The World of Tomorrow*; Armstrong, *Long Range Forecasting*. **Special features:** Visit to local ecology-oriented commune; visit to major corporate headquarters forecasting/planning group; play *Global Futures* game; experiment with "World 2" model.

WEST VIRGINIA

DAVIS AND ELKINS COLLEGE
Elkins, West Virginia 26241

Course title: The Future

Instructor: Phillips V. Brooks, Dorothy Roberts, Jim Van Gundy, and Thomas Ross

Educational level: College seniors

Date of this offering: Spring, 1979   **Date of first offering:** Spring, 1973

Course description: Probable challenges and opportunities to be confronted in the year 2000; impact of one change in a society on the other elements of society; implications of technology; environmental implications of finite resources; implications of moral and ethical issues and questions; implications for new political and economic structures. **Activities:** Student reports; scenario writing; relevance trees; panel reports; trend exercises; lectures; guest speakers; gaming; films. **Source materials:** Books: LeGuin, *The Dispossessed*; Clarke, *Profiles of the Future*; Hardin and Baden, ed., *Managing the Commons*; Harman, *An Incomplete Guide to the Future*; films: *We; Catastrophe or Commitment; Love-joy's Nuclear War; The War Game; Cosmic Zoom; Power of Ten; But What if the Dream Comes True; A Question of Values*. **Special features:** Four sections offered. Course is in two parts: Trends and Alternatives; Transitions and Scenarios. Guest speakers invited from federal government, private industry, local businessmen, education; and practicing futurists. The course is required of all seniors prior to graduating.

WEST VIRGINIA UNIVERSITY
Suite 609, Allen Hall
Morgantown, West Virginia 26506

Course title: Appropriate Technology

Instructor: Paul W. DeVore, Technology Education Chairman

Educational level: Master's and doctorate

Date of this offering: 1979   **Date of first offering:** Spring, 1977

Course description: A seminar concerned with alternative futures. Strong emphases are social purpose and philosophical position. Concern for global effects of technological choices concerning food, population, energy, resources, environment and quality of human existence. **Activities:** Seminar format with special projects either individual or group. **Source materials:** Selected bibliographies on a range of topics related to alternative futures. **Special features:** Guest lecturers who have had experience in appropriate technology programs in developing countries. Student projects presented and discussed at alternative technology field day.

WEST VIRGINIA UNIVERSITY
Suite 609
Allen Hall
Morgantown, West Virginia 26506
        Date of first offering: 1974

Program title: Public Administration

Director: Herman Mertins, Jr., Chairman

Educational level: Master's

Degrees offered: Master of Public Administration

Course titles: Public Administration and Policy Development; Public Budgeting Personnel; Research.

Program description: Much of the program focuses on future developments and issues in administration with considerable use of futures research methodologies and techniques.

WISCONSIN

GEORGE S. PARKER SENIOR HIGH SCHOOL
3125 Mineral Point Avenue
Janesville, Wisconsin 53545

Course title: Futuristic Literature

Instructor: Katherine M. Conover

Educational level: High school

Date of this offering: 1978-79   **Date of first offering:** Fall, 1973

Course description: This course includes reading and discussing future casting methods; world problems; work/leisure alternatives; communication/transportation alternatives; education alternatives; medical alternatives; alternative lifestyles; future cities; time and space; projecting values. **Activities:** Readings; lecture-discussion; oral reports; drawing and/or building and presenting future city models; values clarification exercises. **Source materials:** Dunstan and Garlan, *Worlds in the Making;* Huxley, *Brave New World;* Orwell, *1984;* Clarke, *2001; Science Fact/Fiction;* THE FUTURIST; Wisconsin Educational TV Network Series: *Futuristics.* **Special features:** Guest speakers from General Motors and Bell Telephone Co.; field trip to Johnson Wax Golden Randelle Theatre in Racine, Wisconsin.

JFK PREP
Box 109
St. Nazianz, Wisconsin 54232

Course title: Three courses: Voluntary Simplicity; Environmental Studies; Energy

Instructor: Melvin Tracy

Educational level: High school

Date of this offering: 1977-78   **Date of first offering:** 1971

Course description: (1) Voluntary Simplicity: types of growth; possible solutions; tenets of voluntary simplicity; design for the future; examples of appropriate technology. (2) Environmental Studies: population; environmental law and environmental impact statements; energy; water quality. (3) Energy: present "crisis"; available sources in use; alternate sources; future scenarios. **Activities:** Lecture-discussion; scenario writing; oral reports. Developed environmental impact statement on proposed school parking lot and defeated project, saving a part of the lawn. **Source materials:** *Limits to Growth; Mankind at the Turning Point;* Ehrlich, *End of Affluence;* Schumacher, *Small is Beautiful;* Commoner, *The Closing Circle; Design for the Real World,* etc.; articles; films; teacher-student developed units. **Special features:** Field trips to Oak Ridge, Tennessee included visits to TVA projects, a coal-powered generator, fusion research facilities and a solar house, in addition to nuclear power plants.

MOUNT MARY COLLEGE
2900 N. Menomonee River Parkway
Milwaukee, Wisconsin 53222

Course title: Multi-Disciplinary Honors Seminar: Future Studies

Instructor: Joan Cook, Associate Professor, English; Angela M. Sauro, Assistant Professor, Biology

Educational level: College juniors and seniors

Date of this offering: 1979   **Date of first offering:** 1974-75

Course description: Course topics include: forecasting techniques, study of environmental problems; using scientific literature, simulation, technology assessment, films, tapes, speakers, science fiction and utopian literature. **Activities:** Some lecture-discussion initially; student input: panel presentations, the technology assessment, group projects to prepare persuasive presentations. **Source materials:** Books: Tuve, *Energy, Environment, Populations,* and *Food;*

Allen, *Science Fiction: The Future*; Huxley, *Brave New World*; Herbert, *Dune*; others on list; film: *Future Shock; Population and America's Future.* **Special features:** Wisconsin Medical College will help with a speaker on recombinant DNA and cloning. They may also serve as one audience for the student presentations at the end of course. This course is an honors program. Because most students are career-oriented and have few options in their programs, more students want to take the course than can fit it into their schedules.

NORTHLAND COLLEGE
Ashland, Wisconsin 54806

Course title: Exploring Alternative Futures

Instructor: Michele Geslin Small, Assistant Professor of English

Educational level: College undergraduate

Date of this offering: Winter, 1979   **Date of first offering:** Fall, 1974

Course description: This is a two-semester course consisting of: Exploring Alternative Futures I; Seminar in Future Studies; Science Fiction and Futurism (the latter two alternate). **Activities:** Lecture-discussion; final project is the writing of a scenario. Students write a journal during the course. **Source materials:** Books: Francoeur, *Eve's New Rib;* Rimmer, *Proposition 31;* Rosenfeld, *The Second Genesis;* Huxley, *Brave New World;* Toffler, ed., *Learning For Tomorrow;* Ehrlich, *The End of Affluence;* Pat, *Alas Babylon;* Farmer, *The Real World of 1984;* Schumacher, *Small Is Beautiful;* films: *How to Make a Woman; Cipher in the Snow; Ark; Joey's World;* selected *NOVA* Programs (PBS); filmstrips and cassettes; games. **Special features:** Visits to class by well-known science fiction writers or futurists.

PHILLIPS HIGH SCHOOL
Phillips, Wisconsin 54555

Course title: Man, Technology and the Future

Instructor: David Peterson

Educational level: High school juniors and seniors

Date of this offering: 1979   **Date of first offering:** 1973-74

Course description: An exploration of man, his machines, and the effect of the use of technology on man's life-style and values. Topics include: science fiction; man and the machine; future studies; ethical dimensions of future problem-solving. **Activities:** Short story writing; logbook; synthesis and analysis of reading materials; simulation; film; lecture; discussion. **Source materials:** *Another Tomorrow; A Science Fiction Reader; Things to Come; Toward the Year 2000; 1984; Brave New World; Cat's Cradle;* many articles and essays. **Special features** —

UNIVERSITY OF WISCONSIN CENTER, BARRON COUNTY

Course title: Futurology

Instructor: Pannier, Crisler, Arnston, Brownlee, Grivna, and Hasman

Educational level: College freshmen and sophomores

Date of this offering: Spring, 1979   **Date of first offering:** 1971

Course description: An interdisciplinary course on possible, probable and desirable future environments, both intermediate and long-range, with special emphases on the next two decades and the effects of rapid technological advances on society. Topics include: the survival of spaceship earth; population and the world problematique; energy; the new biology and human DNA; world food prospects; environmental preservation and economic development; quality of life and human value. **Activities:** Lecture; discussion; student reports. **Source materials:** — **Special features** —

UNIVERSITY OF WISCONSIN, MILWAUKEE
Urban Affairs Department - Bolton Hall
Milwaukee, Wisconsin 53211

Course title: Alternative Urban Futures

Instructor: Wilfred A. Kraegel, Lecturer

Educational level: Master's

Date of this offering: Summer, 1977-1978   **Date of first offering:** 1972

Course description: This course encourages students to explore urban futures—their scope and complexity, their defining and shaping. Course topics include: futures concepts; forecasting methods; urban condition; growth; study of the future; designing a city; urban projects; science fiction views. **Activities:** Lecture-discussion; guest speakers — resource people from the Milwaukee area; students' presentation and discussion of their urban projects. **Source materials:** Cornish, *The Study of the Future;* Schumacher, *Small Is Beautiful;* U.S. Chamber of Commerce, *Economic Growth — New Views and Issues;* Gorham and Glazer, *The Urban Predicament;* Gibson, *Designing the New City.* **Special features:** Several city officials visit class.

UNIVERSITY OF WISCONSIN, OSHKOSH
Algoma Boulevard
Oshkosh, Wisconsin 54901

Course title: Seminar: Futurism in Curriculum and Instruction

Instructor: Leonore W. Dickmann

Educational level: Master's

Date of this offering: 1978   **Date of first offering:** 1976

Course description: Emphasis on thinking about the future, futurology skills, systems, models, preparing educators to meet needs of the future. Topics include: Why teach the future; ways of thinking about the future; who are the futurists; who are the disclaimers; imagining possible, probable and preferable educational futures. **Activities:** Seminar with lecture-discussion; scenario writing; science fiction writing; futures music; writing poetry about the future, etc. **Source materials:** Toffler, *Learning For Tomorrow,* plus extensive bibliography; World Future Society film *Toward The Year 2000;* slides from the Center for Humanities; tapes from the Association for Supervision and Curriculum Development. **Special features:** Student projects are a central part of the course; speakers as available (plus on tape).

UNIVERSITY OF WISCONSIN, OSHKOSH
Oshkosh, Wisconsin 54901

Course title: Telecommunications and the Future

Instructor: Harris N. Liechti, Associate Professor of Speech

Educational level: College juniors and seniors; master's

Date of this offering: Fall, 1978   **Date of first offering:** Spring, 1978

Course description: This course is an exploration into the implications of the electronic communications revolution; the possible and probable near- and long-range futures of telecommunications technology, institutions, and processes; and their impact upon human societies and individuals. **Activities:** Lecture-discussion; students construct personal scenarios; class carries out project of its own choosing. **Source materials:** Hellman, *Communications in the World of the Future;* Clarke, *Profiles of the Future* (rev. ed.) and *Report on Planet Three;* Martin, *Future Developments in Telecommunications* (2nd ed.); film: *Where All Things Belong;* video tapes; magazine articles. **Special features:** Class projects; equipment displays; video tapes; guest speakers; radio programs.

UNIVERSITY OF WISCONSIN, STEVENS POINT
Stevens Point, Wisconsin 54481

Course title: Futures

Instructor: William H. Kirby, School of Education

Educational level: College juniors and seniors

Date of this offering: 1978   **Date of first offering:** 1972

Course description: This course emphasizes futuristic education or material related to a presently living individual's future or to the humanities. Course titles include: general overview of history of the future and current thought; the individual's future; the future of various subjects and areas. **Activities:** Lecture-discussion; scenario writing; students present oral reports; students produce slides, tapes. **Source materials:** Books: Kaufmann, *The Future of the Humanities*; Berry, *The Next 10,000 Years*; Commoner, *The Closing Circle,* and *The Poverty of Power*; Gabor, *Innovations*; Bradbury, *Farenheit 451*; The Club of Rome books and Cole, *Models of Doom*; Koestler, *The Call Girls*; films. **Special features:** Class tries to have faculty from each department or discipline contribute.

UNIVERSITY OF WISCONSIN, STOUT

Date of first offering: 1974

Menomonie, Wisconsin 54751

Program title: Center for Futures Study

Director: Lee Smalley, Co-Director; R.M. Barlow, Co-Director

Educational level: College undergraduate, master's, professionals

Degrees offered: —

Course titles: This program offers facilitation of instruction; program planning; curricular planning; provision of resources to students, professionals and teachers. Program uses workshops, faculty gatherings and extramural talks.

Program description: The Center for Futures Study has as its purpose the provision of resources in futures research, the facilitation of educational and professional planning of programs, curriculum, courses, as well as the instruction of faculty and students in futures research methods. The University also offers two independent courses, "Introduction to Futures Study" and "Advanced Futures Study," both of which focus on orientation to the field, forecasting and policy science. Students work with their major program advisor on a professional projection in their career area.

UNIVERSITY OF WISCONSIN, SUPERIOR

Superior, Wisconsin 54880

Course title: Hells and Heavens in Selected Science Fiction

Instructor: Anne Robb Taylor, Associate Professor of English

Educational level: College freshmen and sophomores

Date of this offering: Winter quarter, 1978-79   **Date of first offering:** Fall, 1974

Course description: Discussions of various science fiction works in four general categories: historical (*Frankenstein,* Verne, Wells, etc.); aliens; heavens or hells; and post-catastrophe. **Activities:** Lecture-discussion; oral and written reports. Emphasis on short stories and novels. **Source materials:** A few changes in texts each time. **Special features:** —

FILMS

FILMS

The primary source for the films listed here was the World Future Society's catalog *Films on the Future* (revised during 1978 for publication in 1979). Because the volume of material made it impractical to screen each film before listing, readers should arrange to preview any film they order to determine its suitability for showing to a particular group. Information on rental costs can be obtained directly from the distributors whose addresses are included at the end of this section.

The films are grouped by subject and are listed alphabetically by title within subject.

Where available, the following information has been provided for each film listed:

    Title/Date of production or release

    Length/Color or black and white

    Producer or sponsor/Series to which film belongs (if any)

    Rental Distributor/Order number

    Description of film contents (from supplier)

AUTOMATION/COMPUTERS

COMPUTER SPEECH (1974)

3 minutes/color

Producer: Bell Systems

Source: Bell Laboratories

Two ways that Bell scientists are studying speech and programming computers to speak like humans.

CYBERNETICA (1974)

20 minutes/technicolor

Producer: British Transport Films for International Union of Railroads

Source: International Film Bureau

Shows ultrasophisticated technology now in use in Europe by railroads. A massive computer network manages such chores as regulating traffic, reading weather conditions, seeing around corners, automatically regulating speed. Freight cars are adroitly shepherded by tiny sensors built into the rail. The sensors can also weigh and identify each car, and speed them up or slow them down to regulate traffic smoothly.

CYBERNETICS (1970)

22 minutes/color

Producer: Budapest Film Studios

Source: McGraw-Hill Films

An introduction to the complexities of cybernetics, that twilight world where man's brain comes into competition with its own creations.

THE INFORMATION MACHINE (1974)

10 minutes/color

Producer: Encyclopaedia Britannica Films

Source: Iowa Films/No. U 20329

Places the computer in historical perspective, showing it to be the culmination of abstractions and measuring tools which man has been developing since primitive times. Shows how we use the computer to define and solve problems.

THE THINKING ? ? ? MACHINES (1969)

15 minutes/color

Producer: Bell Systems

Source: Bell Laboratories

Conveys an understanding of the extent to which machines can take over the functions of the human brain, from simple logic to creative art. Demonstrates its own built-in gifts and limitations.

WEIRD WORLD OF ROBOTS (1969)

26 minutes/color

Producer: CBS: 21st Century Series

Source: McGraw-Hill Films

A film that provides visual evidence of the kinds of performance to be obtained from robots now and in the future. Stimulates creative thinking about the potential achievements of the more extensive partnerships between man and machines in prospect before the year 2000.

BIOLOGY & MEDICAL/BEHAVIORAL SCIENCES

THE BRAIN: CREATING A MENTAL ELITE (1972)

20 minutes/color

Producer: Hobel-Leiterman: Towards the Year 2000 Series

Source: Document Associates

Examines three major areas of brain research. Speculates on the possibility of imprinting knowledge directly on the brain and thus by-passing normal learning procedures.

CENTURY III—THE GIFT OF LIFE (1976)

28 minutes/color

Producer: USIA: Films in America

Source: National Audiovisual Center/No. 008402

Explores controversial questions arising from current medical technology in four key areas: constructive surgery, immunology, cell biology and genetic manipulation. Leading researchers discuss their work and raise the issues of the social and ethical consequences of man's increasing ability to control or drastically alter the human body.

EXPLORING THE HUMAN BRAIN (1977)

18 minutes/color

Producer: Greenhouse Films

Source: BFA Educational Media/No. 11731

The exact function and nature of the brain is one of our continuing mysteries. Today new chemicals and new experimentation with small electrical tools promise to uncover the secrets of intelligence, emotion and control of disease. Such experimentation may help us to reach the limits of our human potential.

EXTENDING LIFE (1976)

15 minutes/color

Producer: Giancarlo Lui, Director

Source: BFA Educational Media/No. 11677

Recent efforts to extend life have raised questions about the nature of man. When do we have the right to extend life? Who decides? What about the problems of increasing population? There are no easy answers.

THE GENE ENGINEERS (1977)

57 minutes/color

Producer: WGBH-TV/The NOVA Series

Source: Time-Life Multimedia

Scientists now have the ability to transfer genes from one creature to another. Man may now be able to perfect plants and animals, to increase food supplies, fight cancer and disease and control human development. But this awesome new power could have terrifying results including deleterious changes in man's own genetic make up. Scientific, moral and legal questions are explored. Award winner.

GENETICS: MAN THE CREATOR (1976)

19 minutes/color

Producer: Hobel-Leiterman

Source: Document Associates

Reports advances and examines the moral implications of genetic engineering. Discusses items such as cloning and the creation of man-animal hybrids. Bronze Medal Winner, Atlanta International Film Festival.

MAN MADE MAN (1967)

25 minutes/color

Producer: CBS: 21st Century Series

Source: McGraw-Hill Films/No. 68908

Film on organ tissue transplants that documents the progress being made in medical technology as it relates to transplantation of artificial organs, tissues and other relatively new precedents in surgical medicine. Investigates surgical problems which have not yet been solved.

MIRACLE OF THE MIND (1975)

19 minutes/color

Producer: CBS: 21st Century Series

Source: McGraw-Hill Films/No. 106564-4

Discusses research into the nature of the brain. Transference of certain substances from one brain to another may be the forerunner of "smart pills," which scientists say may do away with much formal education.

REVOLUTIONS IN SCIENCE (1978)

29 minutes/color

Producer: EMC Film: 20th Century Man Series

Source: University of California EMC/No. 10101

Jacob Bronowski discusses the dilemmas and challenges posed by scientific advancement. Of his work in biology and the processes of creating life he says, "...biological knowledge is not destructive, but it could become dangerous. ...If you want to be protected from evil...do not do anything."

CITIES/URBAN PLANNING

CITIES OF THE FUTURE (1967)

25 minutes/color

Producer: CBS: 21st Century Series

Source: University of California EMC/No. 7422

By the next century, ninety percent of this country's population will live in the cities. This film indicates the probable makeup of a 21st century city, and studies the problems man must face to avoid having the city become a disorganized, unimaginative megalopolis.

DOWN TO EARTH: CITY LIVING (1977)

18 minutes/color

Producer: Joaquin Padro

Source: Pyramid Films/No. 1032

Ecological alternatives for city dwellers.

HABITAT 2000: HUMAN SCALE CITIES (1976)

18 minutes/color

Producer: Hobel-Leiterman: Towards the Year 2000 Series

Source: Document Associates

Moshe Safdie, Paoli Soleri and Christopher Alexander express their views on urban planning and alternatives for the future.

OF PEOPLE, LAND AND PLANNING (1975)

26 minutes/color

Producer: RK Motion Picture Laboratory

Source: University of California EMC/No. 9671

Illustrates a variety of problems associated with land use and planning in Wisconsin. Visually demonstrates some of the consequences of unplanned growth and development. Examines the controversies surrounding such issues as the pressure for recreational areas, the growth of urban sprawl, the loss of farmland and the effects of transportation facilities on planning.

WHERE AIRPORTS BEGIN (1975)

20 minutes/color

Producer: Federal Aviation Administration

Source: Federal Aviation Administration

An airport can be environmentally sound, a good neighbor and an economic stimulus. The key is planning and community interaction. This film shows how two communities successfully planned and developed their airports. A must for any community thinking about upgrading its present airport or building a new one.

THE WRITING ON THE WALL (1978)

50 minutes/color

Producer: British Broadcasting Corporation

Source: Time/Life Multimedia

Is there a relationship between crime and housing design? Here are some illuminating theories about how we are influenced by our architectural surroundings.

COMMUNICATIONS/TRANSPORTATION

COMMUNICATIONS (1970)

23 minutes/color

Producer: American Educational Films

Source: American Educational Films

Explores the exciting possibilities of the new communications media...the laser, the picture phone, credit-data banks and space satellites. Points out some inherent problems and dangers.

COMMUNICATIONS: THE WIRED WORLD (1976)

20 minutes/color

Producer: Hobel-Leiterman: Towards the Year 2000 Series

Source: Document Associates

Looks at some of the methods we will probably use to disseminate information in the future. Law enforcement, medicine, industry, the military and our personal environment will be profoundly affected.

FLYING MACHINES (1978)

28 minutes/color

Producer: NASA

Source: NASA Films

Aviation today and tomorrow. Plans for future research and development in a wide variety of fields. How NASA is looking to solve current aeronautical problems with innovative solutions.

MASS TRANSIT: UP, UP, AND AWAY (1976)

20 minutes/color

Producer: Hobel-Leiterman: Toward the Year 2000 Series

Source: Document Associates

Examines future possibilities in mass transit systems. A computer-controlled car and an underground tube with air sucked out to create a vacuum are among the suggestions explored in this film.

PATHWAYS TO THE WORLD (1978)

28 minutes/color

Producer: Communications Satellite Corporation

Source: Modern Talking Picture Service

A film about communications satellites sponsored by the manager of the 102 nation group which owns the global network for telephone and television service. Arthur C. Clarke, who originated the concept of geostationary communications satellites, opens the film from his home in Sri Lanka.

THE AGE OF SPACE TRANSPORTATION (1976)

20 minutes/color

Producer: NASA

Source: NASA Films

Looks at how space age transportation is making itself felt in health care, education, medical research, communications, earth resources and environment management, manufacturing, astronomy. Takes a particular look at mankind's next giant step in moving around...the space shuttle.

BATE'S CAR (1976)

16 minutes/color

Producer: Arthur Mokin Productions

Source: University of California EMC/No. 9686

Harold Bate, a humorous and creative man in his 70s who lives in rural England, demonstrates and explains the automobile he invented that runs on clean-burning methane gas derived from common barnyard manure. Amusing, informative, and provocative look at one fascinating man's answer to the problems of pollution and fuel shortages.

TO BUILD A POLLUTION-FREE CAR: THE STEAM DREAM MACHINE (1976)

18 minutes/color

Producer: Hobel-Leiterman

Source: Document Associates

Discusses efforts to design a pollution-free car. Harsh controls on city access for cars may be the alternative.

ECOLOGY

HAVE OUR PLANET AND EAT IT TOO (1974)

24 minutes/color

Producer: Churchill Films

Source: Iowa Films/No. U 50342

Studies the conflicts now raging between various theories of land use.

1985 (1970)

56 minutes/color

Producer: Macmillan Films

Source: University of California EMC/No. 7980

Fictionalized news broadcast of ecological crises of 1985, when long-predicted disasters totally devastate environment. Shows poisoned air and water, garbage rotting on city streets, famine, power failures, declaration of martial law. News analysts describe history of environmental neglect as consequences are shown.

A SENSE OF HUMUS (1976)

28 minutes/color

Producer: National Film Board of Canada

Source: Bullfrog Films

We are told that North American farming is the most efficient in the world. This is true if we ignore certain critical aspects of agribusiness, including heavy fuel usage, loss of topsoil and widespread social change which it generates. This film documents another way of farming, organically, without chemcial fertilizers, pesticides or herbicides. Shows how one farmer gets a yield twice the national average on land once classified as unfit for agriculture.

TO DEFEAT THE DOOMSDAY DOCTRINE: THE WORLD ISN'T RUNNING OUT OF EVERYTHING QUITE YET (1976)

20 minutes/color

Producer: Hobel-Leiterman: Target: The Impossible Series

Source: Document Associates

A stimulating film that surveys both pessimistic and optimistic forecasts about the environment and the future of human survival. Shows that the world is more resilient than we thought and that scientists are coming up with new answers.

WHO KILLED LAKE ERIE? (1969)

49 minutes/color

Producer: NBC Films

Source: University of California EMC/No. 7685

Lake Erie represents the first large scale warning that we are in danger of destroying the habitability of the earth. Graphically depicts the pollution of the lake, the results of that pollution, and what is being done about it. Filmed at various cities along the U.S. shores that contribute to the pollution. Makes clear that everyone is to be blamed for the relentless destroying of our natural resources. Award winner.

EDUCATION

GAMES FUTURISTS PLAY (1968)

26 minutes/color

Producer: CBS: 21st Century Series

Source: Iowa Films/No. U50216

Examination of some of the methods being utilized in our search for knowledge of existing and projected problems. "Games" illustrates how these methods assist educators to teach future citizens.

ENERGY

THE ENERGY CONNECTION (1979)

19 minutes/color

Producer: United Ministry in Higher Education

Source: United Ministry in Higher Education

Designed to raise value questions relating to life-styles and resource utilization with particular emphasis on energy. It attempts to relate economic and political patterns to the energy issue.

ENERGY FOR THE FUTURE (1974)

17 minutes/color

Producer: Encyclopaedia Britannica Educational/AGI: Earth Sciences Series

Source: Britannica Films/No. 3348

Surveys possible future energy alternatives including processed coal, shale oils, geothermal heat, nuclear fission and fusion, wind and solar heat. Award winner.

ENERGY IN PERSPECTIVE (1978)

21 minutes/color

Producer: B.P. North America Incorporated

Source: Modern Talking Picture Service/No. 10344

A thought-provoking film about energy. Examines the limits of the world's supply of fossil fuels and considers alternative sources. Emphasizes the need to turn from thoughtless overconsumption to a more intelligent use of energy in the future.

ENERGY: WHAT ABOUT TOMORROW? (1978)

20 minutes/color

Producer: United Nations Films

Source: Barr Films

The days of cheap, seemingly abundant, energy are over and the world is now faced with a search for new energy sources. This film shows worldwide study and use of alternative sources, makes the point that the world cannot pin its hopes on one energy source, for no one source will be sufficient to meet all of our future needs.

ENVIRONMENT/POLLUTION/WEATHER

AIR IS LIFE (1977)

15 minutes/color

Producer: Condor Films

Source: International Film Bureau

Treats the worldwide problem of air pollution. Shows many examples, explores possible solutions. A triple prize winner.

CHOICE STAKES (1975)

10 minutes/color

Producer: Environmental Protection Agency/Pat Oliphant

Source: National AudioVisual Center/No. 009824/GG

An animated film allegory presents man's desire for a richer, fuller material life which inevitably affects the environment. Shows how man must learn to recognize what the choices are and what his decisions will cost him.

A CITY FARMSTEAD (1978)

15 minutes/color

Producer: Steve Greenberg

Source: Phoenix Films/No. 21218

How an old dilapadated Victorian home was transformed in a self-reliant, ecologically sound urban habitat. Among the messages stated; we need to shift to a solar-based economy from our present petroleum based one; we can live in urban areas without having a detrimental impact on ourselves or our environment.

DANGER: RADIOACTIVE WASTE (1977)

50 minutes/color

Producer: NBC

Source: Films Incorporated/No. 3220164

The question of the disposal of the proliferation of radioactive waste is one that has yet to be solved. In the meantime these nuclear wastes multiply and so do the dangers to man and the environment.

POLLUTION OF THE UPPER AND LOWER ATMOSPHERE (1975)

17 minutes/color

Producer: Learning Corporation of America

Source: Learning Corporation of America

Shows how man is creating changes in his own climate. Postulates that if we can more accurately predict the outcome of pollution processes we may be better able to choose environmentally sound options.

SEARCH FOR SURVIVAL (1976)

27 minutes/color

Producer: The Council of California Growers

Source: Association Films, Inc./No. L687

In an overpopulated world endowed with fixed amounts of energy and mineral resources, the U.S. stands out in the development of a renewable resource...food and fiber. Scientists explain how productivity has been increased.

WHITHER WEATHER (1977)

11 minutes/color

Producer: Hubley Studio

Source: Pyramid Films/No. 3403

A film concerned with the affects of climate upon our world and the fact that our earth is one living whole and all the parts are interrelated. A change here effects life there; therefore all nations must respond as one world.

FOOD/POPULATION

DIET FOR A SMALL PLANET (1974)

28 minutes/color ·

Producer: Bullfrog Films

Source: Iowa Films/No. U50379

Discusses the need to reduce meat intake to free more protein for the world's starving peoples. Tells how to get good quality protein from non-meat sources.

EARTH, NO VACANCY: LIMITS TO GROWTH (1976)

19 minutes/color

Producer: Hobel-Leiterman: Towards the Year 2000 Series

Source: Document Associates

Natural resources decline while population increases. Dennis Meadows, author of *Limits to Growth*, discusses the situation. In the future, world governments might have to control child bearing by special permit only.

THE FOOD REVOLUTION (1975)

17 minutes/color

Producer: CBS

Source: McGraw-Hill Films/No. 106566-0

Food synthesis, high-efficiency farming and the use of the sea as a source of food are a few of the techniques being studied as possible answers to the problem of feeding the ever-increasing billions of the world's population. Shows some pilot projects now under way.

HUNGER (1975)

12 minutes/color

Producer: National Film Board of Canada

Source: Learning Corporation of America

A perceptive allegory forecasting the repercussions of over-abundance in a disparate world. Makes brillant use of computer-assisted animation.

HUNGRY PLANET (1976)

29 minutes/color

Producer: Planet Earth, Limited

Source: University of California EMC/No. 9664

Surveys new proposals for solving the interconnected problems that world hunger, overpopulation, inequitable land distribution, and foreign aid programs present for both developed and underdeveloped nations. Contends that the guidelines for developmental foreign aid recently enacted by Congress could—along with cooperation from other countries—lead to agricultural self-sufficiency in the underdeveloped world in less than two decades. Argues for a shift from grain-fed to range-fed beef in the U.S., showing how a shift of only 20 per cent would free enough grain to meet the entire 9 million ton famine-relief need estimated at the last World Food Conference. Wide-ranging, provocative production.

TOMORROW'S CHILDREN (revised) (1978)

17 minutes/color

Producer: Henry Mayer, M.D.

Source: Perennial Education Inc.

A multiple prize winner, this film carries the message that we are destroying our world through overpopulation and environmental pollution. Stresses the need for birth control and education.

TRAGEDY OR TRIUMPH (1975)

28 minutes/black & white

Producer: United Nations; Journal Films

Source: University of Michigan

Deals with the most critical of the world's resources, food. Explains the causes of the problem, considers some answers including the establishment of a world food bank to insure freedom from hunger.

FORECASTS

ETHICS FOR A NEW AGE (1978)

29 minutes/color

Producer: EMC Film: 20th Century Man Series

Source: University of California EMC/No. 10103

Explores violence, the University experience, the role of the individual in society. Bronowski feels our greatest threat is not ecology or the environment but the structure of society.

FUTURISTS (1967)

25 minutes/color

Producer: CBS: 21st Century Series

Source: University of California EMC/No. 7426

Man's future as seen by leaders in science, sociology and government. Current problems are probed and concepts concerning the future of the world and man's capacity for adaptation are discussed.

TECHNOLOGY: CATASTROPHE OR COMMITMENT? (1976)

20 minutes/color

Producer: Hobel-Leiterman: Towards the Year 2000 Series

Source: Document Associates

This film questions the idea that advanced technology offers the ultimate solution to all of society's problems, pointing out that some solutions kill even as they cure. There is a discussion of the dilemma of increasing industrialization and dwindling natural resources.

THINK TANKS: PROPHETS OF THE FUTURE (1976)

20 minutes/color

Producer: Hobel-Leiterman: Towards the Year 2000 Series

Source: Document Associates

In this film the director of the Hudson Institute in New York shares his views on various subjects...future wars, the counter culture, ecology, the changing role of women. He discusses the Institute's main projects of the moment—a year 2000 ideology and The Corporate Environment (1976-1985).

TRENDS (1972)

9 minutes/color

Producer: Learning Corp.

Source: Boston University

An animated film that takes a pointed look at the evolution of man's ideas in several areas. Communication, nutrition, reproduction, weapons. Provocative and thought provoking.

THE UNEXPLAINED (1970)

56 minutes/color

Producer: Encyclopaedia Britannica

Source: University of California EMC/No. 8430

Exploration of the possible and the imaginable featuring many widely recognized scientists and science fiction writers.

HUMAN VALUES

FREE TO BE...YOU AND ME (1974)

42 minutes/color

Producer: ABC

Source: McGraw-Hill Films/No. 106356-0

A self-awareness film that celebrates the human potential, involves children in the endless possibilities of their own uniqueness. A multiple award winner.

THE HANGMAN (1963)

12 minutes/color

Producer: Les Goldman

Source: McGraw-Hill Films/No. 406641

The hangman chooses his next victim from those who remained silent during the execution of his last. Illustrates that failure to choose is a choice itself. Has implications on the social dimensions of human freedom. An award winner.

HUMAN POTENTIAL MOVEMENT: JOURNEY TO THE CENTER OF SELF (1976)

17 minutes/color

Producer: Hobel-Leiterman: Towards the Year 2000 Series

Source: Document Associates

Discusses the human potential movement, its direction and its future possibilities.

INTERNATIONAL RELATIONS/POLITICS

GEOPOLITICS: THE SHAPE OF THINGS TO COME (1976)

20 minutes/color

Producer: Hobel-Leiterman: Towards the Year 2000 Series

Source: Document Associates

Robert Heilbroner and Arnold Toynbee discuss their views of the future world.

TILT (1972)

20 minutes/color

Producer: National Film Bureau of Canada in cooperation with World Bank

Source: University of California EMC/No. 8576

Imaginatively animated satire that questions the attitudes of the affluent nations toward the underdeveloped nations. Humorously shows the foolishness and selfishness of many social and economic ideas thought in the U.S. and

Europe to be rational and humanistic. Makes a plea for sharing and helpfulness among all nations, rich and poor, and for the development of a global consciousness among people. A repeated image of the earth as a ball in a pinball game symbolizes the dangers of current policies and attitudes.

OCEAN/OCEAN SCIENCES

THE LAW OF THE SEA (1974)
28 minutes/color
Producer: United Nations: Journal Films
Source: Iowa Films/No. U50293
Examines traditional and today's claims concerning sea resources. Studies various locales.

MAN IN THE SEA (1972)
26 minutes/color
Producer: Owen Lee (Macmillan)
Source: Macmillan Films
Explores the use of diving as the key to the sea. Shows and describes several kinds of dives. Discusses our potential future in relation to the sea.

OCEANS OF SCIENCE (1974)
26 minutes/color
Producer: National Film Board of Canada
Source: National Film Board of Canada
A look at fisheries science and its effort to ensure that life survives in the seas and inland waters. The film is encouraging evidence that old abuses can be corrected and safeguards established.

WILL THE FISHING HAVE TO STOP? (1976)
31 minutes/color
Producer: WBGH-TV: Nova Series
Source: Time/Life Multimedia
Studies possible solutions to the present threat of disastrous fish shortages. An excellent explanation of what scientists now know about the oceanic food chain.

SOCIOLOGY/LIFE-STYLES/WOMEN

FUTURE SHOCK (1972)
42 minutes/color
Producer: McGraw-Hill
Source: University of California EMC/No. 8613
Imaginative documentation of the rapid social and technological changes now taking place and the illnesses and problems arising from difficulty in adapting to them; based on the book by Alvin Toffler. New scientific possibilities such as organ transplants, computer-created art, rejuvenation surgery, test-tube fertilizations, robots, and a mock genetic supermarket. Questions ethical implications of much of today's research. Also includes scenes of communes, a group-marriage household, student protests, a homosexual wedding ceremony, and other examples of increasingly different social patterns and relationships.

LEISURE (1976)

14 minutes/color

Producer: Bruce Petty/Film Australia

Source: Pyramid Films/No. 1765

A survey of man's encounter with the idea that what he does with his leisure may become the determining factor in society's system of values. A sprightly animated film that introduces some new ideas that call for attention. A double award winner.

NEW AGE COMMUNITIES: THE SEARCH FOR UTOPIA (1978)

40 minutes/color

Producer: Hartley Productions

Source: Hartley Productions

A look at functioning, practical attempts at the Utopian life, both secular and spiritual. We hear what brings people there and holds them together...the economic, philisophical and spiritual beliefs that are the building blocks of new models for a better life.

TOWARD THE FUTURE (1978)

20 minutes/color

Producer: Stowmar Associates for World Future Society

Source: World Future Society

A compelling look at the fascinating field of alternative futures. Shows how everyone can benefit from exposure to the exciting ideas and methods of futuristics. Inspired by the World Future Society book, *The Study of the Future.*

SPACE/SPACE SCIENCES

COSMIC ZOOM (1970)

8 minutes/color

Producer: National Film Board of Canada

Source: McGraw-Hill Films

The movement to or from a point at some speed is an immense one in this film. The aim of this "cosmic zoom" is to give people, especially young people, some idea of the immeasurable grandeur of space and its opposite, the ultimate minuteness of matter. A non-verbal film.

LIFE BEYOND EARTH AND THE MIND OF MAN (1975)

25 minutes/color

Producer: NASA

Source: National AudioVisual Center/No. 009709GA

This important film explores the implications of a fascinating and popular subject: the possibility of extraterrestrial life elsewhere in the universe and within our galaxy. It documents a symposium of preeminent scientists, philosophers, and scholars held on the subject at Boston University on November 20, 1972.

THE PHYSICISTS: PLAYING DICE WITH THE UNIVERSE (1972)

22 minutes/color

Producer: Hobel-Leiterman: Towards the Year 2000 Series

Source: Document Associates

Examines directions in physics research: listening to the universe; trying to communicate with extraterrestrial life; search for the 'quark' and for black holes; speculating about life on other planets; stretching and slowing time; probing the nature of matter. Gold Medal Winner, Atlanta International Film Festival.

POWERS OF TEN (1978)

9 minutes/color

Producer: Charles & Ray Eames

Source: Pyramid Films/No. 2004

A new color production of the 1968 film with a new numbering sequence on the screen. A trip through the universe from the outer galaxies to the nucleus of the atom.

SPACE SHUTTLE (1976)

15 minutes/color

Producer: NASA

Source: NASA Films

Describes the reusable Space Shuttle. Animation shows typical flight mission and planned use of the Shuttle. Concludes with roll-out of first Shuttle Orbiter, the "Enterprise."

UNIVERSE (1976)

28 minutes/color

Producer: NASA

Source: NASA Films

A motion picture that explores almost inconceivable extremes of size and time, from the galaxies to sub-atomic particles. Dramatizes a mysterious and incredibly violent universe.

WHO'S OUT THERE? (1975)

28 minutes/color

Producer: NASA

Source: National AudioVisual Center/No. 009327GG

Orson Wells hosts this voyage from science fiction to science fact. The new view of extraterrestrial life now emerging from the results of probes to the planets is explored. A number of distinguished scientists discuss whether there are other intelligent civilizations in the universe.

TECHNOLOGY/BUSINESS/INDUSTRY

AT HOME 2001 (1967)

25 minutes/color

Producer: CBS: 21st Century Series

Source: University of California EMC/No. 7427

Explores the possibilities for the household of the future in terms of technology and changed patterns of urban living. Present trends are analyzed, the rise in urban population, the multi-family dwelling, the implications of high-speed transportation, and the increase in leisure time. Predicts types of entertainment centers, air conditioners, "domesticated" computers, and housemaid robot in the home.

THE BIG CORPORATION (1976)

57 minutes/color

Producer: British Broadcasting Corporation

Source: Films Incorporated/No. 411-0009

An award winning film that features the history and future development of the big corporation.

CHANGING WORK: AMERICAN WORKERS IN SWEDEN (1976)

40 minutes/color

Producer: Ford Foundation

Source: Films Incorporated

American auto workers react to their experience in a Swedish assembly plant where the traditional assembly line has been replaced by small autonomous work groups.

CONSUMERISM (1976)

20 minutes/color

Producer: Hobel-Leiterman

Source: Document Associates

Consumer groups can and must wield great power in the future. Beginnings are evident today.

COPING WITH TECHNOLOGY: BEYOND BUREAUCRACY TOWARDS A NEW DEMOCRACY (1977)

26 minutes/color

Producer: Hobel-Leiterman

Source: Document Associates

In this film we see that technology is a double-edged sword. It offers new potential achievement but also threatens the individual with loss of control. Several authorities comment on the issue and suggest how we must cope with it.

ERSATZ (1961)

10 minutes/color

Producer: Dusan Vukotic

Source: University of California EMC/No. 8209

Depicts a horrifying make-believe world of plastic inflatable substitutes for everything including man, in which the main character creates and destroys objects and people at will. In the end, however, he is himself destroyed by a stray tack. Winner of numerous international awards.

GAMBLING WITH OUR LIVES (1977)

20 minutes/color

Producer: United Nations Films

Source: Barr Films

Modern technology provides us with an ever-improving standard of living. But while technology has made it possible for us to live better than ever before, it also threatens our existence. We are just beginning to recognize the trade-off we must make between the obvious benefits of progress against the potential hazards to our health.

GROUP DYNAMICS: GROUPTHINK (1973)

22 minutes/color

Producer: Steven Katten

Source: McGraw-Hill Films

An eye-opening look at group decision-making processes. We see some of the problems and see how "groupthink" can generate bad organizational decisions.

THE JOB (1973)

20 minutes/color

Producer: Films Incorporated

Source: Boston University

Today many people are unhappy at their jobs. They want stimulation, challenge, responsibility. Jobs will have to be restructured to meet this need. Bosses should act as group leaders rather than military sergeants. Then the job will become more important and making a living will no longer be separated from living.

MOTIVATION: IT'S NOT JUST THE MONEY (1977)

26 minutes/color

Producer: Hobel-Leiterman

Source: Document Associates

Shows examples of innovative approaches to increase job satisfaction and efficiency. Discusses the far-reaching ideas of Abraham Maslow and Douglas McGregor.

ORGANIZATION DEVELOPMENT AND THE ORGANIZATION OF THE FUTURE (1974)

28 minutes/color

Producer: Development Publications

Source: Development Publications/No. F-6

Features Dr. Gordon Lippitt of George Washington University, a behavioral scientist, who points up nine needs of the organization of the future, explains the characteristics of a future-oriented versus a static organization.

THE OTHER WAY (1975)

26 minutes/color

Producer: British Broadcasting Corporation

Source: Time/Life Multimedia

Explores what economists call an "energy sink"...the consumption of power to build power plants so that increased building can result in a net energy loss. Suggests a radically new approach to industry and agriculture with intriguing examples of the technology which could be adopted as an alternative to today's massive, energy-hungry machines.

RESOURCE RECOVERY IS... (1977)

20 minutes/color

Producer: National Center for Resource Recovery, Inc.

Source: Modern Talking Picture Service/No. 9697

Viewers will learn just what resource recovery is and how it works in its various forms. Examines the outlook for conservation of natural resources through the widespread application of resource recovery.

A TIME OF CHANGES (1977)

15 minutes/color

Producer: Encyclopaedia Britannica

Source: Boston University

Technology has made some working roles obsolete but has created others. This film can spur a young person's imagination to consider jobs that might exist in the future, though not today.

SOURCES

American Educational Films, 132 Lasky Drive, Beverly Hills, California 90212 (213) 278-4996

Association Films, Inc., 866 Third Avenue, New York, New York 10022 (212) 935-4210

Barr Films, P.O. Box 5667, Pasadena, California 91107 (213) 793-6153

Bell Laboratories, Film & TV Division, Room 3C 236, Murray Hill, New Jersey 07974 (201) 582-6504

BFA Educational Media, CBS Educational Publishing, 2211 Michigan Avenue, P.O. Box 1795, Santa Monica, California 90406 (213) 829-2901

Boston University Film Library, 765 Commonwealth Avenue, Boston, Massachusetts 02215. (617) 353-3272

Britannica Films, Encyclopedia Britannica Educational Corporation, 425 North Michigan Avenue, Chicago, Illinois 60611 (312) 321-6800

Bullfrog Films, Inc., Oley, Pennsylvania 19547 (215) 779-8226

University of California, Extension Media Center, Berkeley, California 94720 (415) 642-0460

Development Publications, 5606 Lamar Road, Washington, D.C. 20016 (301) 320-4409

Document Associates, Inc., 211 East 43rd Street, New York, New York 10017 (212) 593-1647

FAA Film Service, 2323 New Hyde Park Road, New Hyde Park, New York 11042 (202) 763-1896

Films Incorporated, 733 Green Bay Road, Wilmette, Illinois 60091 (312) 256-3200

Hartley Productions, Cat Rock Road, Cos Cob, Connecticut 06807 (203) 869-1818

International Film Bureau, Inc., 332 S. Michigan Avenue, Chicago, Illinois 60604 (312) 427-4545

Iowa Films, c/o Audio Visual Center, Media Library C 5 East Hall, The University of Iowa, Iowa City, Iowa 52242 (319) 353-5885

Learning Corporation of America, Customer Service Division, 1350 Avenue of the Americas, New York, New York 10019 (212) 397-9360

McGraw-Hill Films, 1221 Avenue of the Americas, New York, New York 10020 (212) 997-2343

Macmillan Films, Inc., 34 MacQueen Parkway South, Mount Vernon, New York 10550 (914) 664-5051

University of Michigan, Audio Visual Education Center, 416 Fourth Street, Ann Arbor, Michigan 48103 (313) 764-5361

Modern Talking Pictures Service, Inc., 2323 New Hyde Park Road, Hyde Park, New York 11040 (516) 437-6300

NASA Regional Film Libraries, Audiovisual Service Branch, Public Affairs Division, Washington, D.C. 20546 (202) 755-3500

National Audiovisual Center, Washington, D.C. 20409 (301) 763-7420

National Film Board of Canada, 16th Floor, 1251 Avenue of the Americas, New York, New York 10020 (212) 586-2400

Perennial Education Inc., 477 Roger Williams, P.O. Box 855 Ravinia, Highland Park, Illinois 60035 (312) 433-1610

Phoenix Films Inc., 470 Park Avenue, New York, New York 10016 (212) 684-5910

Pyramid Films, Box 1048, Santa Monica, California 90406 (213) 828-7577 Canada: International Tele-Film Enterprises, 47 Densley Avenue, Toronto, Canada M6M 5A8 (416) 241-4483

Time-Life Multimedia, Distribution Center, 100 Eisenhower Drive, P.O. Box 644, Paramus, New Jersey 07652 (201) 843-4545

United Ministry in Higher Education, 2211 East Kenwood Boulevard, Milwaukee, Wisconsin 53211 (414) 962-5461

World Future Society, 4916 St. Elmo Avenue, Washington, D.C. 20014 (301) 656-8274

AUDIOTAPES

AUDIOTAPES

Among the tapes and tape series listed here are many that were produced and recorded for the World Future Society's radio program. Others were prepared as formal lectures or are speeches recorded at conferences.

As in the case of films, the volume of material available made it impractical to attempt to listen to the tapes listed here. Readers should therefore plan to listen to a tape themselves to determine its suitability. The tapes are grouped by subject and listed alphabetically by title within subject. Addresses for all distributors are listed at the conclusion of this section.

Where available, the following information is provided for each tape or tape series listed:

Title/Date
Number of tapes (if a series)/Length (in minutes)
Producer or sponsor/Series title (if applicable)
Distributor/Order number
Description of tape contents (speakers, etc.)

ARTS

THE FUTURE OF THE OBJECT IN ART
THE ARTIST'S OBSESSION

Two one-half hour interviews

Producer: World Future Society

Source: World Future Society/No. T-7802

Ann Truitt, Professor of Art, University of Maryland, commenting on what the world is to do with the outpouring of art objects, says one approach is to move away from the object and to new views of art and the artist. In a personal statement about what drives an artist, Truitt explores creativity and inner tensions.

AUTOMATION/COMPUTERS

THE CHANGING OFFICE

60 minutes

Producer: World Future Society

Source: World Future Society/No. T-7807

Hollis Vail, of the U.S. Department of Interior, and Robert Landau, President of Science Information Association, examine the computer as a new medium of communications to the office and the impact of paper processes, spatial arrangements, and decision processes in light of this new medium.

THE FUTURE OF MANAGEMENT COMMUNICATIONS
THE FUTURE OF THE WIRED CITY

Two one-half hour interviews

Producer: World Future Society

Source: World Future Society/No. T-7406

Murray Turoff, formerly with the Office of Emergency Planning, describes nationwide computer-based systems used during Phase I economic controls. Marvin Cetron, President, Forecasting International, gives a technological assessment of the impacts of telecommunication on cities.

BIOLOGY & MEDICAL/BEHAVIORAL SCIENCES

BRAVE NEW REVOLUTION

27 minutes

Producer: The Center for the Study of Democratic Institutions

Source: The Center for the Study of Democratic Institutions/581

The day is not far off, scientists say, when we will be capable not only of extending our longevity, but also of programming the gender of our offspring. Panelists discuss the social and moral implications of the impending biological revolution.

THE ETHICS OF MEDICINE

41 minutes

Producer: The Center for the Study of Democratic Institutions

Source: The Center for the Study of Democratic Institutions/501

614

A panel of philosophers, lawyers, educators and scientists confront the issues posed to our society by new medical technology. The panel debates the questions of how much a life is worth and when, if ever, it is acceptable for a doctor to "pull the plug."

THE ETHICS OF MIND CONTROL

30 minutes

Producer: The Center for the Study of Democratic Institutions

Source: The Center for the Study of Democratic Institutions/601

Experimentation has shown that electrical brain stimulation and drugs can be helpful in reducing man's more violent tendencies. A noted neuropsychologist expresses concern about the possible misuse of such techniques and argues in favor of a Biological Bill of Rights.

CITIES/URBAN PLANNING

GLOBAL CITY BUILDING: A RETROSPECTIVE VIEW FROM A.D. 2000

72 minutes

Producer: —

Source: Extension Media Center/AT 229

Wilfred Owen, Senior Fellow with the Brookings Institution, takes an imaginary look backward from the year 2000 at the conditions of urban areas across the globe. He sees the apathy of the 70s' having given way to massive rebuilding program, sponsored by both public and private institutions. New concepts of sharing resources and ideas, along with new jobs, will have emerged from this urban reconstruction.

COMMUNICATIONS

MASS MEDIA AND THE FUTURE

29 minutes

Producer: The Center for the Study of Democratic Institutions

Source: The Center for the Study of Democratic Institutions/No. 557

Hugh Downs, who has had a long and varied career in television, discusses his hope that mass media of the future will be used as an agent to link mankind more closely together.

ECOLOGY

THE 29TH DAY
SOME IMPACTS ON THE MARKET ECONOMY

Two one-half hour interviews

Producer: World Future Society

Source: World Future Society/No. T-7801

Lester Brown, President, Worldwatch Institute, discusses some of the trends in our use of resources and warns that we could be at the "29th day" (from a French lesson in mathematics); on the 30th day, human civilization would have exhausted the carrying capacity of the earth's resources. Carl Madden, Professor of Business, American University, comments on how far our life processes, institutional size, secularization and other factors are impacting on the nature of our market system.

EDUCATION

CAREERS TOMORROW
THE UNIVERSITY WITHOUT WALLS

Two one-half hour interviews

Producer: World Future Society

Source: World Future Society/No. T-7704

William Abbott, Associate Editor, *Business Tomorrow*. John Picarelli, Washington International College, explores the shift toward multiple careers and describes an approach to education that not only educates but also prepares for career changes.

EDUCATING PUBLIC POLICY MAKERS IN FUTURISTICS
A SCENARIO FOR THE FUTURE

Two one-half hour interviews

Producer: World Future Society

Source: World Future Society/T-7605

John Ellison, Industrial College of the Armed Forces, discusses the U.S. Military's inclusion of futuristics training as part of its mid-career training for officers. Earl C. Joseph, Sperry Univac, examines the concept of scenarios as tools for thinking about future options.

ENERGY

FUSION ENERGY: POWER OF THE FUTURE

29 minutes

Producer: The Center for the Study of Democratic Institutions

Source: The Center for the Study of Democratic Institutions/No. 572

A cheap, virtually inexhaustible source of power can be attained within 20 years, according to Richard Post of the Lawrence Radiation Laboratory. He describes in non-technical language the potential benefits of fusion, including reduced pollution and safety hazards.

THE FUTURE OF OCEAN THERMAL ENERGY
TAPPING THE WIND

Two one-half hour interviews

Producer: World Future Society

Source: World Future Society/No. T-7601

Robert Cohen, Energy Research & Development Administration, reports on research into the use of ocean temperature differentials for the generation of electricity. Lewis Divone, Chief, Wind Energy Systems, Department of Energy, examines the potential of wind as an energy source.

SMALLER THINGS TO COME

43 minutes

Producer: Center for the Study of Democratic Institutions

Source: Center for the Study of Democratic Institutions/No. 732

Today's energy crisis, says former Interior Secretary Stewart Udall, is just a preview of the long-term fuel shortage which will force major changes in the way we live. In this discussion with Center staff, he presents a capsule history of energy production in the United States, indicts the technological "arrogance" that has led to our present crisis, and offers a blueprint for the complete reorientation of society to enable us to live within our energy means.

ENVIRONMENT/POLLUTION

THE EARTH KILLERS

28 minutes

Producer: Center for the Study of Democratic Institutions

Source: Center for the Study of Democratic Institutions/No. 466

Physicists can blow up the world; bacteriologists can destroy it by disease; pollution can suffocate it; and a population explosion can starve it to death. Lord Ritchie-Calder, science historian, tells John Cogley that the world will continue "mucking things up" unless science comes under public control.

THE EARTH SAVERS

29 minutes

Producer: Center for the Study of Democratic Institutions

Source: Center for the Study of Democratic Institutions/No. 499

Paul Ehrlich, Richard Bellman, Karl Pribram and others analyze in this discussion the failure of the environmental movement and offer various political and industrial strategies to prevent what Ehrlich says will be the "last depression."

GROWTH AND THE COMMUNITY ENVIRONMENT
CAREFUL TECHNOLOGY FOR OUR ENVIRONMENT

Two one-half hour interviews

Producer: World Future Society

Source: World Future Society/No. T-7608

Sydney Howe, Center for Growth Alternatives, examines the community growth phenomena, reactions to it and the need to develop effective ways of controlling it. Joan Nicholson, Bolton Institute, makes a statement about the need to match man's technology with the ecological system with some thoughts about what might be done.

MAN'S IMPACT ON THE ATMOSPHERE

58 minutes

Producer: Center for the Study of Democratic Institutions

Source: Center for the Study of Democratic Institutions/No. 737

A summary of the present status of global air pollution and man's attempts to protect the atmosphere by atmospheric scientist Joseph Knox.

MODELS FOR THE FUTURE

42 minutes

Producer: Center for the Study of Democratic Institutions

Source: Center for the Study of Democratic Institutions/No. 317

Robert Jungk is the founder of Mankind 2000, an institute in Vienna which researches problems of the future. He has high hopes for harmonious environments that will be good to live in because their technological systems will be appropriate to both man and nature.

SURVIVAL OR EXTINCTION: A FINAL CHOICE

27 minutes

Producer: Center for the Study of Democratic Institutions

Source: Center for the Study of Democratic Institutions/No. 500

Actor and conservationist Eddie Albert delivers a moving recitation of human follies in our systematic despoilation of our own environment.

FOOD/POPULATION

POPULATION PATTERNS IN RURAL AMERICA
A POPULATION STRATEGY FOR A FINITE PLANET

Two one-half hour interviews

Producer: World Future Society

Source: World Future Society/No. T-7604

Calvin Beale, Department of Agriculture, Economic Research Service, examines recent demographic trends, suggesting Americans may be reversing their pattern of heading for the big cities. Lester Brown, Overseas Development Council, discusses strategies for food, resource management and environment protection.

THE WORLD FOOD CRISIS AND TRIAGE

77 minutes

Producer: Center for the Study of Democratic Institutions

Source: Center for the Study of Democratic Institutions/No. 734

A debate on the moral aspects of the world food crisis between two adherents of the concept of "triage" (Garrett Hardin and William Paddock) and two who are adamantly opposed to it (Lord Ritchie-Calder and William Murdoch).

HUMAN VALUES

THE HIDDEN REMNANT

43 minutes

Producer: The Center for the Study of Democratic Institutions

Source: The Center for the Study of Democratic Institutions/318

Gerald Sykes speculates on the dehumanization of technologically advanced societies and their potential rescue by the "hidden remnant"—a dedicated group of individuals who refuse to be overwhelmed by the massive problems of their time.

INTERNATIONAL RELATIONS/POLITICS

A REVOLUTIONARY LOOKS AT THE FUTURE

29 minutes

Producer: The Center for the Study of Democratic Institutions

Source: The Center for the Study of Democratic Institutions/574

In this dialogue, author, social historian and revolutionary, Ronald Segal argues that the gap between the rich and the poor in the U.S. has been widening steadily since 1910, that we are in the midst of a social crisis without being aware of it. He also maintains that there is a social crisis of even greater magnitude unfolding on the global scale. He proposes a supranational approach as the best means of solving the impending crisis.

THE WARLESS WORLD

24 minutes

Producer: The Center for the Study of Democratic Institutions

Source: The Center for the Study of Democratic Institutions/10

Walter Millis, military historian, discusses the implications of a world without war for a society that has never existed without it. Millis believes that a warless world will evolve as an outgrowth of the nuclear balance of terror.

OCEAN/OCEAN SCIENCES

THE OCEAN AS A COMMON HERITAGE

44 minutes

Producer: The Center for the Study of Democratic Institutions

Source: The Center for the Study of Democratic Institutions/445

Several international participants conduct a revealing discussion on using ocean resources for the common good. In these discussions, each participant accepts the *idea* of common good, but special interests and biases quickly appear to demonstrate the complexity of the issue.

SOCIOLOGY/LIFE-STYLES/WOMEN

THE EVOLUTION OF SEX AND THE FUTURE OF THE FAMILY

50 minutes

Producer: The Center for the Study of Democratic Institutions

Source: The Center for the Study of Democratic Institutions/No. 748

Today's family is threatened by two fundamental changes: reliable contraceptives and the growth of specialized institutions which do the work of the family outside the home. Anthropologist Paul Bohannan looks at these changes and what impact they may have on the institution of the family and the evolutionary progress of the human species.

FAMILIES OF THE FUTURE

27 minutes

Producer: The Center for the Study of Democratic Institutions

Source: The Center for the Study of Democratic Institutions/603

Sue Dodson, family therapist at the Evergreen Institute, discusses alternatives to the traditional nuclear family, which she feels is finished. She proposes that in order to get over the loss of our family system, we must "evolve another style of life."

THE FUTURE OF THE WORKPLACE
VISIONS OF THE FUTURE

Two one-half hour interviews

Producer: World Future Society

Source: World Future Society/No. T-7806

Paul Dickson, author of "The Future File," reports on developments in the workplace occurring around the world that are relevant to the United States. Sam Love, environmental author and consultant, discusses studies of American values systems as they anticipate the future.

HOW FUTURISTS THINK ABOUT THE FUTURE

60 minutes

Producer: World Future Society

Source: World Future Society/No. T-7701

A discussion between Joseph F. Coates, Office of Technology Assessment, U.S. Congress, and Hollis Vail, U.S. Department of Interior, on how futurists approach the future and some of the methods they use. Intended to orient those unfamiliar with futurist concepts and basic methods.

OPTIMISM VS. PESSIMISM
TALKING ABOUT THE FUTURE

60 minutes

Producer: World Future Society

Source: World Future Society/No. T-7703

Edward S. Cornish, President of the World Future Society, discusses the "attitude struggle" people often have about the future and some of the issues that futurists talk about.

TOWARD A NEUTER GENDER

28 minutes

Producer: The Center for the Study of Democratic Institutions

Source: The Center for the Study of Democratic Institutions/No. 189

Author Elizabeth Mann Borgese argues that historically women have fared better in collective societies rather than individualistic ones. Here she describes a fictional world where women past child bearing age become men. Psychiatrist Ralph Greenson discusses the implications of such a world with her.

SPACE/SPACE SCIENCES

THE SEARCH FOR OUTSIDE LIFE

1 hour 45 minutes

Producer: Extension Media Center

Source: Extension Media Center/AT 393

In this most speculative lecture, Donald Goldsmith, author and scientist, considers the probability of intelligent life in our galaxy. He speculates on the means and implications of communicating with extraterrestrial life.

TECHNOLOGY/BUSINESS/INDUSTRY

THE CRISIS OF IDENTITY IN A WORKLESS WORLD

44 minutes

Producer: The Center for the Study of Democratic Institutions

Source: The Center for the Study of Democratic Institutions/No. 187

Judd Marmor, of the UCLA School of Medicine, contends that discussions of technology all too often ignore the potential psychological dislocation that could occur in a world without work.

THE DANGERS OF TECHNOLOGY

90 minutes

Producer: Pacifica Foundation

Source: Pacifica Tape Library/XZ 0153

Dr. Ernest Schumacher, author of *Small is Beautiful,* discusses his views on appropriate technology and his experiences in Africa where he worked to implement his ideas.

TAPE SERIES
(Assorted Subjects)

ENERGYFEST 1978! (1978)

6 tapes/various lengths

Producer: Audio Village

Source: Audio Village

ENERGYFEST 1978! was a two day fair and celebration of alternative energy technologies, sponsored by the office of Senator Haskell. The following series of audiotapes of lectures given at ENERGYFEST 1978! is available on cassette at a nominal cost by mail.

Dennis Hayes, Senior Researcher of Worldwatch, Coordinator of Earth Day.
Buckminister Fuller, design scientist, philosopher, inventor of geodesic dome, synergetic geometry.
Amory Lovins, author, *Soft Energy Paths,* and *Non-Nuclear Futures,* energy consultant.
Morris Udall, U.S. Representative, former Presidential candidate.
Panel Discussion: Representative Udall, Senator Haskell, Amory Lovins, Frank Kreith, Jerry Plunkett.
World Game: Introduction and documentary of the 1978 Symposium.

THE FIRST CONFERENCE OF THE EDUCATION SECTION OF THE WORLD FUTURE SOCIETY

35 tapes

Producer: Convention Recording Services

Source: Convention Recording Services

A series of 35 tapes recorded from the First Conference of the Education Section of the World Future Society co-sponsored by the World Future Society and the University of Houston at Clear Lake City. The Conference was held October 20-22, 1978 at the University of Houston at Clear Lake City.

3201: The Future of Education: A State of the Union Message. Chris Dede, President, Education Section of the World Future Society, Assistant Professor of Education, University of Houston.
3202: Keynote Address. John McHale, Director, Center for Integrative Studies, University of Houston.
3203: 2001: A Counseling Odyssey. Donald G. Hays, Administrator, Pupil Services, Fullerton Union High School District, Fullerton, California.
   Occupational Adaptability and Transferable Skills: Preparing for Tomorrow's Careers. William L. Ashley, Research Specialist, National Center for Research in Vocational Education, Columbus, Ohio.
   Future-Oriented Counseling. Delores Harms, Professor, University of Wisconsin, Superior, Wisconsin.
3204: The Community College and Future Work. William L. Abbott, Director, American Association of Community Junior Colleges, Washington, D.C.
   Work Values of Youth. James F. Acord, Assistant Professor, Oklahoma State University, Stillwater, Oklahoma.
   Public Learning Network: Agent for Societal Transformation. Francis J. Wuest, Program Director, Kansas City Regional Council for Higher Education, Kansas City, Missouri.
3205: Alternative Futures and the Education of Teachers. Norman Henchey, Associate Dean, Faculty of Education, McGill University, Montreal, Canada.
   Futures Education in a Core Curriculum: A Case Study. Jim Reynolds, Director, New Center for Learning, East Texas State University, Commerce, Texas.
   The Classroom Need Not Be a Battlefield. Phillip A. Sinclair, Professor, Community and Technical College, University of Toledo, Toledo, Ohio.
3206: Education—Communications in the Future: The Government's Role. Robert L. Hilliard, Federal Communications Commission.
   Educational Satellite Project in Appalachia. Nofflet Williams.

3207: The Cell of the Self: A Dynamic Conceptual Educational System of Mind Mechanisms for Continuous Self-Evolution. R. Duncan Wallace, Psychiatrist, Salt Lake City, Utah.

3208: Classroom Teaching and Futurizing. Don Glines, Director, Educational Futures Projects, Sacramento, California.

3209: Teaching to Cope with the Future: Challenges and Possibilities in the Education and Training of Greater Houston Area Public Schools. Billy Reagan, Superintendent, Houston School District, Houston, Texas; Duke Brannen, Professor of Secondary Education, Stephen F. Austin College, Houston, Texas; Dianne Hopper, English Teacher, Cypress-Fairbanks ISD, Houston, Texas; Don Thornton, Assistant Superintendent, Cypress-Fairbanks ISD, Houston, Texas.

3210: Common Characteristics of Utopian and Futuristic Models of Society. Hans Joachim Harloff, Professor, Technische Universitat Berlin, Federal Republic of Germany.

3211: A Dialogue on *The Far Side of the Future*. Jim Bowman, Fred Kierstead, John Pulliam, Chris Dede, Robert Theobald, University of Houston.

3212: Keynote Address. Robert Theobald, Socioeconomist and Author, University of Houston, Houston. Texas.

3213: Models for Future Studies in the Secondary Classroom. Maurice Champagne, Charles Byrne, Howard Feddema, Teachers, High School District 214, Arlington Heights, Illinois.

3214: Educational Futuristics Experientially: A Sampler of Monday Morning Activities. Diane N. Battung, Educational Options Center Coordinator, Unviersity of Southern California, Los Angeles, California.

3215: The School and You in 2002. Jim Isom, Lloyd Longnion and Zelda Rick, Faculty, College of the Mainland, Texas City, Texas.

3216: The Recognition of Futures Research by Large Corporations and by Colleges of Business Administration. Donald F. Mulvihill, Kent State University, Kent, Ohio.
Business Journals and Futurism: Current Status and Suggested Directions. Eugene Laczniak, Marquette University; Robert Lusch, University of Oklahoma, Norman, Oklahoma.
Educational Programs in Administration and Management. Donald Mankin, University of Maryland, University College, College Park, Maryland.

3217: Compact Policy Assessment: Application to Planning for Educational Futures. Barclay M. Hudson, Principal, Hudson and Associates, Santa Monica, California.
Alternative Futures for Adult and Continuing Education in North Carolina: A Delphi Futures Planning Study. Paul F. Fendt, Associate Director of Extension Credit and Certificate Programs, University of North Carolina, Chapel Hill, North Carolina.

3218: Legislative Concerns for the Future of Texas. William P. Hobby, Lieutenant Governor, State of Texas.
The Role of the State Executive in the 21st Century. Stephen C. Oaks, Secretary of State, State of Texas.
The Fiscal Future of Texas. Thomas M. Keel, Legislative Budget Director, State of Texas.

3219: The Three Rs Plus Two Rs: Basics Plus Reasoning and Relating. Clara Orsini-Romano, Principal, Bryan Hills School District, Armonk, New York.

3221: Futuristics: Theory and Application. John Welckle and Penny Damlo, Project Director and Project Instructor, Futuristics, Burnsville Senior High School, Burnsville, Minnesota.

3223: Why Not Add Social Development to Cognition in Public Schooling? John H. Boynton, Graduate Student, School of Social Work, University of Houston, Houston, Texas.
The Problem of Creating Authority in Schools of the Future. William Spady, Senior Research Sociologist, National Institute of Education, Washington, D.C.
A New Public School Compromise for the 21st Century: New Mechanisms for Formulating Educational Policy.
Austin D. Swanson, Professor/Chairman, Department of Educational Administration, State University of New York, Buffalo, New York.

3225: Future of Management: A Delphic Replication, 1970-78. Harvey Nussbaum, Wayne State University, Detroit, Michigan.
Future Business Applications of Delphic Research in Futures Studies. Robert C. Judd, Governors State University, Park Forest South, Illinois.
Planned Innovation. Frank Bacon, Michigan State Unviersity, East Lansing, Michigan.

3226: Women, Education and the Future. Anita Miller, President, National Association of Commissions for Women and Institute for Studies of Equality, Sacramento, California.

3227: No More Pencils, No More Books, No More Teachers' Dirty Looks. Charles Weingartner, Professor of Education, University of South Florida, Tampa, Florida.

3228: A New International Learning Order. James Botkin, Co-author, *The Club of Rome Learning Report*, Cambridge, Massachusetts.

3229: Keynote Address. Ervin Laszlo, Special Fellow, U.N. Institute for Training and Research.

3230: Entrepreneurship and Enterprise Tomorrow: An Inductive Approach to Secondary School Business Education. Timothy S. Mescon and George S. Vozikis, Department of Management, University of Georgia, Athens, Georgia.

Adaptation of Futurist Methods for Classroom Use: Strategy for Future Study in the Secondary School. Eugene Bledsoe, Resident Director, Georgia's Governor's Honors Program, Atlanta, Georgia.

Project REAL: Relevant Education throuth Alternative Learning. Jerry McCamly and Janis Rosene, Team Leader and Teacher, El Camino High School, La Mirado, California.

3231: What is the Future for the Evaluation of Staff Development Programming in Long Term Care Facilities? Nancy E. Hinkley, Director, Nationwide Long Term Care Education Center, Raleigh, North Carolina.

The Future of Quality Day Care Programs. Jacqueline Blackwell, Assistant Professor, Early Childhood Education, Indiana University, Indianapolis, Indiana.

New Strategies for Early Childhood Education. Annie L. Butler, Professor of Education, Indiana University, Indianapolis, Indiana.

3233: Lifelong Learning and the Future of the School: A Critical Analysis. Frank Spikes, Dean, School of Continuing Studies, St. Mary's University, San Antonio, Texas.

Creating a Person-Centered, Growth-Oriented Future in Education. James J. Van Patten, Professor, University of Arkansas, Fayetteville, Arkansas.

Toward a University-Based Flexibility in Lifelong Learning. Arthur W. Eve and Dmitri Gat, Institute for Governmental Services, University of Massachusetts, Amherst, Massachusetts.

3234: Toward the Education of Gifted Children in 2025. Suzanne McFarland, Department of Education, Unviersity of Toledo, Toledo, Ohio.

3235: Federal, State, Local Roles in Educational Management: Appropriate Future Technologies. Nancy L. Knapp, Assistant Professor Educational Administration, Northern Illinois University, DeKalb, Illinois.

3237: Education at the Turn of the Century. Stanley L. Freeman, Professor of Education, University of Maine, Orono, Maine.

The University President as a Midwife to Creative Change. D. J. Guzzetta, President, Unviersity of Akron, Akron, Ohio; and Abdul al-Rubaiy, Acting Director of the Institute for Futures, University of Akron, Akron, Ohio.

3238: Self-Actualizing Education. Harold R. McAlindon, Vice-President, Center for Health Studies, Nashville, Tennessee.

Claiming the Gift of Evolution: Visions of Education that Allow Full Development of Human Potential. Harold L. Hayes, Assistant Professor, Walter State Community College, Greenville, Tennessee.

3239: Roles for Educators in Human Services Futures. Charles W. Case, Dean, College of Education and Community Service, University of Wisconsin, Oshkosh, Wisconsin.

Socrates Revisited? Values Education and the Emergence of a "New Pedagogy" in the Humanities and Social Sciences. Harry G. Wagschal, Coordinator, Futures Studies Group, Dawson College, Montreal, Quebec, Canada.

3240: The Study of the Future in Taiwan, Republic of China. Lai Jin-nan, Professor, Tamkang College, Taipei, Taiwan, Republic of China.

Two Futures for Education-Work Relations: Technocratic versus Socio-Technical Design. Arthur G. Wirth, Professor of Education, Washington Unviersity, St. Louis, Missouri.

Schools for a Space Colony. Alene Faul, Administrative Assistant and Counselor, St. Louis University, St. Louis, Missouri.

THE MACHINE IMAGE

30 minutes

Producer: The Center for the Study of Democratic Institutions

Source: The Center for the Study of Democratic Institutions/Nos. 310-315

An unusual series of six programs about man, work and machines, making effective use of music, dramatized historical incidents and sound effects.

Titles: The Inanimate Slaves
The Machine Universe
Working Man
The New Breed
The War Machine
The City of the Sun

WORLD GAME (1978)

33 tapes/various lengths

Producer: Earth Metabolic Design

Source: Audio Village

A Series of 33 tapes recorded at the World Game Symposium 1978.

Keynote Speech at Toward Tomorrow. Barry Commoner, Biologist, Ecologist.
Introduction to the World Game. Howard Brown, Medard Gabel.
Comprehensive Anticipatory Design Science. Buckminister Fuller.
War Games and the World Game. Francis Kapper, Department of Defense.
Food for Everyone. Medard Gabel.
Soft Energy Paths. Amory Lovins, Alternative energy consultant.
Energy for Survival. Wilson Clark, California state energy advisor.
Science, Technology for Development. Bertrand Chatel, United Nations.
Energy in the Third World. William Knowland. Overseas Development Council.
Synergetics, The Geometry of Thinking. (5 hours) Buckminister Fuller.
The Transition to a Regenerative Resource Economy. Howard Brown.
New Paradigms in Assessing Risk and Economic Futures. Hazel Henderson, Princeton Center for Alternative Futures.
Creating a Visionary Society: Design. John Todd, New Alchemy Institute.
Ron White, U.S. Department of Energy.
Charles Ince, American Institute of Architects Research Corporation.
Energy Equity for Poor. Mary Ann MacKenzie, Community Services Administration.
Underground Designs/Sky Mining. Malcolm Wells, underground architect.
Building Energy Futures. Bruce Anderson.
Demonstrating What We Know. J. Baldwin, *CoEvolution Quarterly*.
Prepositions, Ed Schlossberg, author and Coordinator of first World Game.
World Game Networking. Fred Weibe, United Nations.
Earth Sheltered Construction. Raymond Sterling, Underground Space Center.
Betty Shaw, New England Solar Energy Association.
Appropriate Technology in State Governments. Judy Michalowski, State of California.
J. Baldwin, slide talk on white water rafting, dome-building, design process.
Cooperation in Evolution. Lynn Margulis, author, *Gaia Hypotheses*.
Improving the Human Environment by Design. Fred Dubin, energy analyst.
Architecture and Energy. Richard Stein, author.
Buildings as Organisms. Day Chahroudi. Molecular engineering.
Local Self-reliance as a Development Strategy. Richard Kazis.
Strategy for Urban Self-reliance. Tom Javits, Portola Institute.
Microcomputers as Design Strategy. Albert Doolittle, New Alchemy Institute.
World Game Summary, Group discussion and feedback of participants.

SOURCES

Audio Village, Box 291, Bloomington, Indiana 47401

The Center for the Study of Democratic Institutions, The Fund for the Republic, Inc., P.O. Box 4446, Santa Barbara, California 93103 (805) 969-3281

Convention Recording Services, 1222 Greenbrier, Denton, Texas 76201 (817) 387-9102

Extension Media Center, University of California, Berkeley, California 94720 (415) 642-0460

Pacifica Tape Library, Pacifica Foundation, 5316 Venice Boulevard, Los Angeles, California 90019 (213) 931-1625

World Future Society, 4916 St. Elmo Avenue (Bethesda), Washington, D.C. 20014 (301) 656-8274

GAMES AND SIMULATIONS

GAMES AND SIMULATIONS

The games and simulations listed here were selected mainly by Bruce Bigelow and the Denison Simulation Center, Denison University, Granville, Ohio. This list offers a sampling of items that have proven useful in classroom situations. Teachers and group leaders should try out a game experimentally before introducing it to their students or groups.

The addresses of all distributors are listed at the conclusion of this section.

Where available, the following information has been provided for each item listed:

Name or title/Date of publication
Approximate playing time
Price
Age level of intended users
Distributor
Description of game format and objectives

ADAPT (1975)

5 days suggested

Price: Approximately $12-15, unit price

Age Level: High school through college

Source: Interact

ADAPT is a 4-cycle game. Cycle No. 4 is most related to the area of future studies. This cycle discusses how future societies would adapt to and change their environments. It is suggested that a film on the predictions of the nature of future societies such as *Future Shock* or *1985* be included with the exercise. Authors: Jerry Lipetzky and John Hildebrand.

ALIEN SPACE (1973)

45 minutes to several hours, depending on number of players

Price: $6.00

Age Level: 12 years to adult

Source: Lou Zocchi and Associates

Each player captains his own unique star ship. No two ships are built the same and each has its own special secret weaponry unknown to the other players. Ships move simultaneously over a large table or floor, moving at simulated warp speeds. No ship is powerful enough to go top speed, keep up full shield and fire full strength weapons. So, when a captain compromises some performance feature, in order to spend energy on another, he becomes vulnerable. Optional rules include 3 dimensional combat, repair of damaged ships and fleet size games. Each player is required to announce the compass angle over which his ship is shooting before the simulated shot is laid off from target to victim. Since each ship has a compass circle around it, the string, which simulates the path taken by the announced fire, is stretched over the compass heading announced and must also cross the target ship before a hit can be scored. Practice improves players' abilities to calculate correct angular relationships and geometry can be applied to solve new angular relationships of combat ships. This game has been used in classrooms to increase interest in applied geometry.

BAFA'BAFA' (1973)

1 to 1½ hours

Price: $35.00 complete kit (cassette based)

Age Level: Any group capable of understanding concept of culture

Source: Simile II

The game is designed to increase people's awareness of societal roles and some human traits such as greed, friendliness, helpfulness, etc. Also important for experiencing cultural differences. The game is divided into cultures, Alpha and Beta. Participants learn the rules, customs and values of their culture, then select visitors to "travel" to the other culture. Visitors are generally bewildered and confused by the strangeness of the foreign culture. In the post-game discussion, however, they come to understand the reasons behind the observed behavior.

BALDICER (1975, Third Edition)

2-3 hours

Price: $25 plus shipping

Age Level: High school, college, adult

Source: Educational Manpower, Inc.

The object of the game is "to experience the interdependence of the world economy." Other objectives include: to become more aware of related issues, such as the population explosion, inflation, unequal distribution of resources and technology, and competing styles of economic organization. This simulation makes many assumptions about the nature of the world. After playing the game, it is essential to check the validity of these assumptions. Thus, a sufficient amount of debriefing time must be allotted. Author: Georgeann Wilcoxson.

CASSANDRA (An adaptation of "Humanus") (1972)

1 to 1½ hours with debriefing

Price: Script only: $2 (mimeo); with cassette tape: $5

Age Level: High school through college

Source: Denison Simulation Center

As a result of a world-wide nuclear accident, it is no longer safe for humans to be unprotected from contamination. Therefore, participants are placed in a protected environment that has been provided for them. This cell will be conducive to their continued existence.

Participants in this simulation are controlled by their survival computer, CASSANDRA, which communicates with them through a "voice printout" recorded on tape. CASSANDRA requires that certain decisions be made by the cell if it is to survive. All that remains of the human race resides within the cell. A survival kit is provided; however, it must be located. Participants must respond to "CASSANDRA's" requests. A "new society" is formed on planet Earth.

Experimentation has produced significant positive results from students; this game serves both as a good way to introduce ethical issues associated with futures choices and as a method of creating a sense of unity and comradery among the students in the class. Author: Larry Ledebur.

CLASS STRUGGLE (1978)

1-2 hours

Price: $12 plus shipping and handling

Age Level: All ages (8-80)

Source: In These Times

CLASS STRUGGLE is a board game reflecting the real struggle between the classes in our society. This game has been used extensively in various sociology courses and has been rated very highly. Author: Bertell Ollman.

C.L.U.G. (Community Land Use Game) (1972)

4 hours minimum; may be complete course of study—one semester

Price: $75 complete kit

Age Level: High school through college

Source: Educational Manpower, Inc.

C.L.U.G. is a board game which contains a small number of basic attributes of cities and their surrounding territories on the basis of which players build, operate and maintain their own community. The game is used to explore issues such as environmental pollution, urban politics, transportation, technology and municipal finance. Author: A. J. Feldt.

CONFLICT (1974)

One 4-hour session or 4-8 50-minute sessions

Price: $50.00 for complete kit; $7.50 for directions on how to make your own kit

Age Level: High school and college age students

Source: Simile II

This simulation presents participants with a specific, concrete proposal for maintaining peace in the world. Participating as national leaders in a disarmed world in the year 1999, the players test the five basic mechanisms of Arthur Waskow's disarmament model: 1) The more consensus the more force, 2) Gradual deterrence, 3) Minimal use of force against minimal targets, 4) Major power veto, 5) The veto as law. Sometimes students are able to maintain the peace, but other times the model fails and war breaks out. Whatever the outcome, the experience is an exciting way to involve students in thinking about different ways of structuring the future. Author: Gerald Thorpe.

COPE (1974)

5-20 class hours, with much variation possible

Price: $14.00

Age Level: 8th through 12th grades

Source: Interact

This simulation of change and the future focuses attention on questions such as: What are "good" and "bad" futures? Can we "cause" the kind of future we prefer? Can we adapt quickly enough to accelerating change? First, students read and discuss an article called "Coping With Change." The classroom then becomes a think-tank called Technopolis, in which students live through five future time periods 2000 to 2040 A.D. Students who have experienced the tasks assigned them will know firsthand what "future" shock is all about. A special section assists English teachers in using it in science fiction classes, and it is particularly valuable for teachers who have added urban study units or who wish to expand a traditional unit on work.

DECISION MAKERS (—)

90 minutes

Price: $5.50

Age Level: High school to adult

Source: American Friends Service Committee

The game simulates problems groups face when they try to gain community support for a controversial project. In DECISION MAKERS the interaction between community members seeking change and those whose support is essential for a project to succeed is dramatized. The participants assume roles as residents of a typical suburban community. The group is divided in half. One group becomes Change Agents and the other group Decision Makers. The Change Agents are a local citizens group trying to get a course "Challenges of Peace Building" introduced into the local High School curriculum. The Decision Makers represent the key elements in the community. Parents, teachers, students, school administrators, community leaders' support is needed to introduce the course for 6 weeks, 6 months or one year. A range of topics and emotions are provoked by the interaction. Not only are international issues and community change highlighted but the experience stimulates individuals and heightens a sense of personal awareness and involvement in the process of change.

DIMENSIONS OF CHANGE—HOW TECHNOLOGY SHAPES OUR LIVES (1974)

6 one-hour sessions

Price: $125

Age Level: Grade 7 through adult

Source: Doubleday MultiMedia

The purpose of this series, which includes filmstrips, tapes, and simulation activities, is to present a suggested framework to assist participants in meeting the challenges of the future. Topics dealt with are: Ecology, Shelter, Energy, Food, Mobility and Communications. The entire series could well be used as an introduction for beginning the study of World History, U. S. History, Government, Economics, Political Science, Sociology or Psychology. Author: Don Fabun.

EARTH GAME (1979)

2-4 hours

Price: $9.50

Age Level: 9 years and up

Source: World Future Society

A cooperative game that points to a different attitude toward dealing with the problems of this planet. The players work together as a team, moving about the earth's surface in order to deal with emerging problems. Cards, dice, tokens, a "Spaceship Earth" playing board, and charts with complete rules make up the game's equipment.

EDVENTURE (1974)

3 hours

Price: $60.00 plus $3.00 shipping and handling

Age Level: 16 years through adult

Source: Games Central, c/o Abt Associates Inc.

The basic kit of EDVENTURE is a role-play simulation for 30-45 players. Fifteen different Learner persons present a wide range of education seekers, from the retired businessman who would like to develop a new (possibly lucrative) field of interest to the young divorcee trying to establish herself in a career—all of them engaged in a common pursuit, life-long learning. These Learners interact with 15 educational Institutions, ranging from OmniMedia Network to the Jack-of-all-Trades School to Ivy University. A Learner may decide to work and not to study at all; otherwise, he selects a course and seeks admission at an appropriate Institution. Once admitted, and only if he is able to pay the tuition, the Learner may pass or fail, according to his 'learning type' and the roll of dice. During the simulation, Learners can accumulate surplus income and satisfaction points. Winning at EDVENTURE can be a number of things, depending on how you define the session. One winner could be the richest Learner; another, the most satisfied Learner; yet another, the Institution which filled its maximum enrollment while accommodating the learning style of the greatest number of Learners.

THE END OF THE LINE (1975)

2-3 hours

Price: $75.00 plus postage

Age Level: Junior high through adult

Source: Institute for Higher Education, Research and Services

THE END OF THE LINE is intended to give participants a feel for what it is like to grow old and what it is like to try to help people who are growing old. The game was not designed for play by the elderly themselves but for those who work with the elderly, to sensitize them to the aging process and explore strategies for providing possible services. The reason is obvious: the vivid concreteness of the game is likely to produce a powerful impact on players and may be a traumatic experience for those who face these pains as part of their own everyday reality.

ENERGY AND THE ENVIRONMENT: PRO'S AND CON'S (1976)

Flexible: 1-2 hours with debriefing

Price: $15.95 complete kit for 12 players

Age Level: High school through college

Source: Educational Manpower, Inc.

This simulation deals with vital issues in the areas of energy production and protection of the environment. Role card instructions direct players to take particular stances, sometimes becoming "Devil's Advocates" and other times remaining neutral. The game provides training in the skills of rational debate that sustain a democracy. Developed by Creative Learning Systems, Inc. of Cleveland, Ohio.

EUROPEAN ENVIRONMENT (1974)

2 hours

Price: 50 pence

Age Level: Adult

Source: Conservation Trust

Participants represent the Advisory Council to the Commission for the Environment of the European Community. They are asked to make decisions on energy policy, population policy, water policy, nuclear energy, pollution of the Mediterranean Sea, etc. Frustration is built in because the Council of Ministers of Europe reject some proposals. News bulletins and environmental data are issued every "five years." Author: Michael Bassey.

EXPLOSION (1975)

Takes 5 weeks to play the three phases; however, one phase may be selected

Price: $22

Age Level: Grades 7-12 and college

Source: Educational Manpower, Inc.

A simulation of society's struggle to solve its population problems, 1980-2015. Participants experience the traumas of the population crisis and its social, environmental, and political impact on the Spaceship Earth — a finite system. Players take the role as inhabitants of Scioto, a society whose six regions match six American regions. Phase I: *Social Pressures.* Students become citizens of 1 and 6 Scioto states and complete three research assignments. Phase I ends as the crowded conditions create social unrest. Phase II: *Pacfos.* Scioto creates *Pacfos* (President's Advisory Council for the Future of Scioto), a citizen task-force. Phase III: *Governmental Decision-Making.* Citizens from each state design a bill to solve population-related problems. *De-Briefing:* The simulation ends with a discussion relating Scioto's problems to real world problems. Authors: D. Guida, R. Henke and D. Porter.

FOOD FOR THOUGHT — A Population Simulation Kit (1976)

1 hour

Price: $3 prepaid

Age Level: All ages

Source: Population Institute

FOOD FOR THOUGHT is a role-playing exercise designed to get people thinking about: population growth and distribution, food resources, land use, immigration, family size, overcrowding, environment, etc. The complete kit contains the following: complete instructions for 25 to 100 participants who represent citizens of six major world regions experiencing population and food problems; resource materials including charts, graphs, data sheets and sample scripts. The game provides opportunity for creativity and flexibility. Time projected in this exercise is 1975-2000 A.D.

4000 A.D. (1972)

—

Price: $14.25

Age Level: Middle high school through adult

Source: Educational Manpower, Inc. (EMI)

This is a game of strategy set two thousand years in the future, when men have spread to the planets of other stars hundreds of light-years from earth. An interstellar conflict between worlds is its subject. The concept of star travel by hyper space is the basis of its playing character. Two to four players. Developed by the House of Games, Corp., Ltd.

FUTURA CITY (1973)

Approximately 3-5 classroom sessions

Price: $47.00 with L.P; $49.95 with cassette (Part of the multi-media kit "2000 A.D.")

Age Level: Grade 8 through College

Source: Newsweek Educational Division

Students can be introduced to the process of futures planning, called "anticipatory democracy," through the Newsweek simulation FUTURA CITY, which is a part of a multi-media package "2000 A.D." In preparation for the simulation, students read a short article by Toffler in which he explains the process of anticipatory democracy. Participants then role-play groups in the community whose task it is to plan a future city. This game forces students to weigh present priorities against future plans and is one of the few future-oriented simulations which stresses the concept of the inter-relationship of the *past, present and future.* Students examine their values as they decide what to preserve for the future. A winning team is declared at the conclusion of the simulation, unlike future planning.

FUTURE DECISIONS: THE I.Q. GAME (1975, Second Edition)

2-3 hours

Price: $5.95 or $7.95 with optional cassette tape

Age Level: Middleschool through adult

Source: The Simulation and Gaming Association

This game seeks to reinforce the caveat against ill-considered technological innovation. Players assume the roles of hospital board members or spectators at a meeting of that board. These board members must decide how an "I.Q. Drug" will be administered. Play involves cooperation as board members learn to work together, conflict as observers realize they cannot express their opinions until the debriefing period, and compromise as board members begin to rank the applicants.

The simulation is both a decision-making and values clarification exercise. The tape-recorded debriefing confronts the participants with the long-range consequences of the decisions they have made.

The game includes an introductory essay on the need for future studies, two complete versions of the basic simulation, detailed teacher instruction guides for both versions, all necessary activity forms with student instructions, an optional "radio" script that may be taped, and an annotated bibliography on future studies. May be used in groups from 6 to 600. Author: Betty Barclay Franks.

FUTURE SHOCK (1974)

—

Price: $6.50

Age Level: Adolescent through adult

Source: World Future Society Book Service

This board game takes players through possible events in a person's life, each one constituting a change and requiring some adjustments. The object of the game is to get from start to finish, collecting as much "stability" as possible. Stability is the currency of the game and is collected in the form of "stability cards." These cards change hands as players land on "islands of stability" and "major change" squares; drawing a "future shock" card can eliminate one or all players from the game. Authors: James and Margaret Adams.

FUTURES PLANNING GAME (1976)

Approximately one half hour per exercise

Price: 95¢ each

Age Level: Junior and senior high school

Source: Greenhaven Press

The FUTURES PLANNING GAMES are thirteen separate game brochures, each with brief descriptions of four or five activities. The game titles are: Constructing a Political Philosophy, Planning Tomorrow's Society, Facing the Ecology Crisis, Constructing a Life Philosophy, Planning Tomorrow's Prisons, Determining America's Role in the World, Determining Family and Sexual Roles, Dealing with Death, Protecting Minority Rights, Examining American Values, Dealing with Developing Nations, Determining Economic Values, Preventing Crime and Violence. Students examine the future, values, conflict and change in small groups and attempt to reach a group concensus. These games are highly visual; students with varying reading ability can work together. Teachers can often remove themselves from leadership roles. Authors: David L. Bender, Gary E. McCuen and Dewey Henderman.

FUTURIBLES (1973)

Flexible from 15 minutes to 2 hours

Price: $9.45

Age Level: Senior high through adult

Source: World Future Society Book Service

FUTURIBLES consists of a deck of 288 cards, each citing a projection of some future probability in such areas as communication, energy, food, human experience, learning, natural resources, population, religion, transportation, etc. The cards may be used in many different ways, including games invented by the user group. The leader's guide suggests that players pick seven cards and rank them according to: events most likely to occur, events least likely to occur, events most positive, least positive, etc. FUTURIBLES is an informal and flexible game designed to help people get acquainted with future possibilities, share their feelings about the future and clarify their values regarding the future.

GLOBAL FUTURES GAME (1975, Second Edition)

2-3 hours

Price: $17.75 for complete kit of facilitator manual plus 48 score sheets

Age Level: High school, college & adult

Source: Earthrise, Inc.

The GLOBAL FUTURES GAME is a simulation of present and future world conditions in terms of population, food, technology, education and the relative growth rates of each. Groups of players, representing eight socio-economic world regions barter for resources in 5-year rounds (10 minutes in game time) toward the year 2020. Players make collective policy decisions, avoid "world destruct points," and develop optimal strategies to make all of humanity a success. Players come away from the game having gained insight into the inter-connectedness of global problems and the need for a cooperative effort to solve them. Author: Bill Bruck.

HERSTORY (1972)

5 week period suggested

Price: Approximately $12-15 (unit price)

Age Level: High school through college

Source: Interact

This is a simulation of male and female roles emphasizing the American woman's circumstances, past and present. Male-female pairs study various marital patterns, traditional, androgynous, collective family, living together...Research on 44 hypotheses dealing with society's expected sexual roles... FUTURE FORUM on the sexual roles students want America to have in 2025 A.D....Helps young persons crystallize sexual identity during an era of future shock...This simulation has been used very effectively in conjunction with "Seneca Falls" simulation. Author: Paul DeKock.

HUMANUS (1973)

1½ hours or two 50-minute sessions

Price: $11.50

Age Level: Appropriate for any age group capable of understanding the concept of the future

Source: Simile II

Students participate as "survival cell" group members, the only known survivors of a world-wide catastrophe. They are linked to the outside world, monitored, and controlled by their survival computer, HUMANUS, which communicates to them through a "voice print-out," recorded on tape. HUMANUS requires that certain decisions be made by the cell if it is to survive. Few people can participate in the simulation without being affected by it —generates vigorous discussion and controversy. Can be used with five or more participants. Materials include cassette tape recording plus teacher's manual. Very easy to administer. Authors: Kent Layden and Paul Twelker.

THE HYBRID-DELPHI GAME

1½ to 3 hours

Price: $4.00

Age Level: College age and adults (as young as 16 is feasible)

Source: Jerome Ronald Saroff

Provocative statements about possible future events are used to achieve a priority listing of desirable futures for 20 years off—to simulate decision making and prioritizing. The Delphi technique is combined with face-to-face group negotiation and consensus decision making centered around questions of values and priorities for specified futures.

A 3-round process is involved: 1) individual assignment of desirability ratings to 90 future occurrences, with subsequent display of results to the participants; 2) negotiate (in triads) the 15 most desirable future events; 3) achieve total group consensus on 15 priority futures. Through a system of forced choices, the Hybrid-Delphi Game sensitizes students and/or adults to their own values, alerts them to the consequences of the future, and may help individuals and organizations to establish priorities and "invent" desirable futures. Author: Jerome Ronald Saroff.

INFLATION (1973)

7 major phases of the game —each one requires at least one class period

Price: $23.00

Age Level: Senior high school and college

Source: Paul S. Amidon & Associates, Inc.

INFLATION involves a role-playing activity designed to allow students to participate in some simulated aspects of the complex process of political-economic decision-making. Students are assigned roles representing five major groups in the U.S. economy — the Federal Government, big business, organized labor, special interest groups, and consumers. The Government players are charged with controlling inflation, while other players try to influence the eventual government policy. Developed by Bruce E. Tipple and William E. Miller.

THE INTER-NATION SIMULATION (1966)

—

Price: $73.50 to $82.00 (school price) lower for high school. Class of 30 students needs one Inter-Nation Simulation Kit and one Participant's Manual for each student ($1.68 each, school price)

Age Level: Grade 9 through college

Source: Science Research Associates

Students participate in national politics and international relations. Representing real or fictitious nations, teams act and react to strengthen their country's economy and international prestige.

LIFE CAREERS (1969)

1-6 hours

Price: Approximately $35

Age Level: Grades 7-12 and college

Source: Western Publishing Company, Inc.

LIFE CAREERS involves certain features of the labor market, the education market and the marriage market as they now operate in the United States and as projections indicate they will operate in the future. Participants work with a profile of a fictitious person, allotting his time and activities among school, studying, a job, family responsibilities and leisure. This simulation is appropriate for courses in career planning and any class dealing with social class mobility. Suitable for groups of 2-20. Author: Academic Games Associates.

LIFE-STYLES (1979)

1-3 hours

Price: $2.50

Age Level: Junior high through adult

Source: World Future Society

Against a backdrop of changing world and national conditions, players of the LIFE-STYLES game live imaginary "lives" made up of experiences that could happen to almost anyone, such as starting a second career or having a baby. In response to these experiences, or perhaps just for the sake of change, players may change their marital status as often as they wish, from single to married to living with their lover or to a number of other alternatives. The object of LIFE-STYLES is to live as happily as possible, but its underlying purpose is to help players explore their own ideas of happiness and to examine their reactions to the kinds of personal experiences and world conditions that may occur in the future.

There are no winners or losers in LIFE-STYLES. At the end of the game the players' scores reflect their own feelings about the lives they have led, not an arbitrary point total determined by the cards they have drawn. LIFE-STYLES is a game of exploration, not competition. Developed by staff and members of the World Future Society.

NEW TOWN (1972)

—

Price: $12.00 to $85.00

Age Level: Family Game — Grades 4-6 and junior high: $12.00. Educational Kit — Junior and senior high, civic groups, undergraduate: Maximum of 10 students: $18.00; maximum of 20 students: $32.00. Planners' Set — civic groups, undergraduate and graduate urban planners, local officials (4-20 players): $85.00.

Source: World Future Society Book Service

This educational game originated at Cornell University for those interested in urban planning. The board represents a space that has been allocated for a new town 25 miles from a major city. The object is for players to build a viable new community. NEW TOWN includes board, wooden blocks to represent buildings, paper money, dice, cards and directions. Available in three versions.

NUCLEAR DETERRENCE (1976)

3-5 hours

Price: $2.50 (offered at reproduction costs only)

Age Level: College through adult

Source: Denison Simulation Center

NUCLEAR DETERRENCE is a simulation of defense policy making. It demonstrates the application of deterrence theory with respect to the five nations currently in possession of deliverable nuclear weapons. This is a complete packet as used in the author's International Relations course at Denison University. The author has prepared at least 12 evaluational exercises, two of which deal with "the problems of using fear-producing simulations" and "ethical responses." Author: David Sorenson.

THE PLANET MANAGEMENT GAME (1971)

45 minutes to 1 hour

Price: $30.08 list price — 25% discount $22.56

Age Level: 12 years and up

Source: Houghton Mifflin Company

THE PLANET MANAGEMENT GAME allows players to control an imaginary planet with a population explosion and a pollution problem. Can be played by 2 to 12 players. It links the life sciences with the social and environmental problems of today.

PLAY THE FUTURES GAME (1973) and EXPLORING AMERICAN FUTURES (1972)

1 to several hours

Price: 60 cents for PLAY THE FUTURES GAME and $1.00 per copy for EXPLORING AMERICAN FUTURES

Age Level: —

Source: League of Women Voters of the U.S.

PLAY THE FUTURES GAME is intended to help you organize discussions in your community about the future. It was developed from one brainstorming session involving experts from 12 fields. The text covers only a few of the possibilities the future may hold for us, but it illustrates well the many perspectives from which people are projecting to the year 2000. It is intended to be a teaser—a stimulant to get one interested in the future and to provide ideas for discussion.

EXPLORING AMERICAN FUTURES presents a variety of models of the American society of the future, adapted and tested for use by community groups. It is intended to stimulate and organize our perceptions and expectations of the future. It focuses on critical areas and trends in society both on national and local levels and points up their interrelatedness. It also includes a section designed specifically to help organizations plan. It offers a way to start the task of focusing on the most urgent issues of our nation and our own communities.

636

S.A.F.E. II (SIMULATING ALTERNATIVE FUTURES IN EDUCATION) (1978)

1 to 16 hours, depending on version and desired depth of participants

Price: 3 manuals: $25.00; computer tape: $400.00

Age Level: Adults with university or professional background

Source: Jerry Debenham, University of Utah, Department of Education Administration

S.A.F.E. II is a direct-interaction, time sharing computer simulation of the impact of public educational decisions upon the quality of life in a community. Specifically, it is a game which models the short- and long-range impact on society of decisions which educational leaders might make with respect to possible social, political, educational and technological developments over the next 50 years. Its purpose is to teach 1) decision-making skills, 2) a model of school-society interactions and 3) a range of anticipated future developments in school-society interrelationships. The simulation is designed with change functions so it can be reprogrammed into any new game by simply giving the computer instructions in English. In this way it is completely responsive to the needs of the user and can be applied in decision assistance. A noted side benefit has been the teaching of skills in use of computers and simulations in education. Author: Jerry Debenham.

SEX ROLE OPTIONS: PRO'S AND CON'S (1976)

1-2 hours with debriefing

Price: $15.95 complete kit for 12 players

Age Level: High school through college

Source: Educational Manpower, Inc.

This simulation deals with dramatic issues in the area of equal rights for women. To help participants become more aware of the complexity of the issues and their implications, role card instructions direct players to take particular stances, sometimes becoming "Devil's Advocates". One likely outcome from the play is greater flexibility and understanding between the sexes in "real life" dialogue. Developed by Creative Learning Systems, Inc.

SIMSOC (1978, Third Edition)

6 sessions (50 minutes or more per session — allow 10-15 minutes between sessions)

Price: $5.95

Age Level: High school through college

Source: The Free Press, Division of Macmillan Publishing Co., Inc.

SIMSOC attempts to create a situation in which the student must actively question the nature of the social order and examine the processes of social conflict and social control. Part 6 of the simulation, "Creating a Better Society", qualifies the game to be appropriate for future studies. Members of SIMSOC confront problems of scarcity, social protest, power struggles and the like. SIMSOC is a good simulation in understanding the basic traits in a society. However, students must read and have full knowledge of the rules and an understanding of the game prior to participation. Otherwise, the game can be very puzzling.

SPACE FUTURE (1979)

2-4 hours

Price: $9.50

Age Level: 10 years and up

Source: The World Future Society

Most games depicting humanity's ventures into space involve exploitation of other planets and warfare among the players for domination of space. SPACE FUTURE is based on a cooperative approach. Players individually venture into space on peaceful missions and assist each other in settling and developing other planets. The game equipment consists of a large playing surface, a map of outer space with several planets with resource tokens and several decks of playing cards containing directives and information.

THEY SHOOT MARBLES, DON'T THEY? (1973)

2-5 hours

Price: $40.00

Age Level: Junior high school through adult

Source: Institute for Higher Education, Research and Services

Originally designed to stimulate discussion between police and juvenile delinquents, the game provides an experience base for discussions of social and economic planning as well. This game is useful as a way to explore alternative social and economic futures, presenting a strange social situation, thus providing a gauge of attitudes toward change and perhaps a fresh insight into our own culture.

UTOPIA (1974)

10 to 12 class hours

Price: $10.00

Age Level: 8th-12th grade

Source: Interact

At one time or another, all of us dream of living in a utopia. This simulation gives students the experience not only of "building their castles in the air" but also of "putting foundations under them." UTOPIA opens with a case study analysis to consider what they would do if they were subjects of a professor's experiment in an isolated, self-sufficient environment. After this warm-up, students are "reborn" as adults with occupations in today's society. They have chosen to live in a fertile, yet polluted, valley a wealthy industrialist has donated so that a select group of citizens can start society all over again. Occupations are divided into 4 general categories. Each category is further divided into 8 sub-categories—each sub-category representing the societal interest of a specific occupation. A de-briefing and evaluation session ends the simulation as students discuss whether or not utopian principles can be achieved in today's world.

VALUE OPTION GAMES (1976)

1 to 4 hours

Price: $15.00 per deck, including instructions

Age Level: All ages

Source: Mobley, Luciani & Associates

An involvement experience for 15 or more people that enables them to formulate, clarify or explore new options for values, attitudes or beliefs in any of 13 subject areas. In contrast to learning skills or knowledge from books or lectures, attitudes are learned experientially. Community building and depolarizing experiences are included in the games.

VALUE QUESTIONNAIRES FOR FUTURE STUDIES (1974)

At least 1 hour per topic

Price: $2 per set

Age Level: Junior and senior high through college and adult

Source: EDU-GAME

A series of ten unit-organized questionnaires to stimulate discussion on a variety of topics on the future and its possible effects on human civilization. These values clarification activities can help students confirm or reevaluate personal attitudes. The following units are included: Biology and Genetics, Medicine and Health, Government and International Relations, Money and Banking, Urban Living, Marriage and Family Life, Education, Entertainment and Leisure, New Frontiers, and Predicting the Future.

VALUES AND FUTURE WORLDS (1975)

3-4 hours (may be divided into 2-3 class periods)

Price: $5

Age Level: College

Source: Denison Simulation Center

This simulation is concerned with the potential value structure in our society. Many aspects of the design of this simulation come from a paper by Olaf Helmer called "Simulating the Values of the Future" in Baier and Rescher *Values in the Future*, New York: Free Press, 1969. The simulation requires a planning process in which the participants are asked 1) to make decisions affecting the character of our society; 2) to estimate the societal consequences of these decisions; and 3) to evaluate the desirability of those consequences. Extremely flexible and adaptive to special needs. It may be played either as a relatively short game or as a much longer exercise taking several months to complete. Authors: Bruce E. Bigelow and Larry C. Ledebur.

SOURCES

American Friends Service Committee, Community Peace Action Program, 15 Rutherford Place, New York, New York 10003 (212) 777-4600

Paul S. Amidon & Associates, Inc., 5408 Chicago Avenue, Minneapolis, Minnesota 55417 (612) 690-2401

Conservation Trust, 246 London Road, Earley, Reading RG6 1AJ, England (0734) 663650

Jerry Debenham, Department of Educational Administration, University of Utah, Milton Bennion Hall, Salt Lake City, Utah 84109 (801) 277-1211

Denison Simulation Center, Denison University, Granville, Ohio 43023 (614) 587-0810, Ext. 239

Doubleday MultiMedia, P.O. Box 11607, Santa Anna, California 92705 (714) 557-0403

Earthrise, Inc., P.O. Box 120 Annex Station, Providence, Rhode Island 02901 (401) 274-0011

Educational Manpower, Inc., P.O. Box 4272, Madison, Wisconsin 53711 (608) 274-4180

EDU—GAME, Creative Classroom Activities, P.O. Box 1144, Sun Valley, California 91352

The Free Press Division, Macmillan Publishing Co., Inc., Faculty Service Desk, 866 Third Avenue, New York, New York 10022 (212) 935-2000

Games Central, c/o Abt Associates, Inc., 55 Wheeler Street, Cambridge, Massachusetts 02138 (617) 492-7100, Ext. 377

Greenhaven Press, Inc., 1611 Polk Street, N.E., Minneapolis, Minnesota 55413 (612) 482-1582

Houghton Mifflin Company, One Beacon Street, Boston Massachusetts 02107 (617) 725-5254

Infinity Limited, 1301 Cherokee Avenue, West St. Paul, Minnesota 55118 (612) 330-6042

Institute of Higher Education, Research and Services, University, Alabama 35486 (205) 348-7770

Interact, Box 262, Lakeside, California 92040 (714) 443-0833

In These Times, 1509 N. Milwaukee Avenue, Chicago, Illinois 60622 (312) 489-4444

League of Women Voters of the U.S., 1730 M Street, N.W., Washington, D.C. 20036 (202) 296-1770

Mobley, Luciani and Associates, 16 West 16th Street, New York, New York 10011 (212) 243-1840 or (301) 531-5593

Newsweek Educational Division, Attn: R.N. Burch, Director, 444 Madison Avenue, New York, New York 10022 (212) 350-2620

Population Institute, 110 Maryland Avenue, N.E., Washington, D.C. 20002 (202) 544-3300

Jerome Ronald Saroff, 6246 S.W. 37 Avenue, Portland, Oregon 97221 (503) 246-0947

Science Research Associates/College, 1540 Page Mill Road, Palo Alto, California 94304 (415) 493-4700

Simile II, 218 Twelfth Street, P.O. Box 810, Del Mar, California 92014 (415) 755-0272

The Simulation and Gaming Association, 4833 Greentree Road, Lebanon, Ohio 45036 (513) 423-0036

Western Publishing Company, Inc., School and Library Department, 850 Third Avenue, New York, New York 10022 (212) 753-8500

World Future Society, 4916 St. Elmo Avenue, Washington, D.C. 20014 (301) 656-8274

Lou Zocchi and Associates, Inc., 7604 Newton Drive, Biloxi, Mississippi 39532 (601) 432-2266

OTHER MEDIA

OTHER MEDIA

The 17 items listed in this section include mixed-media packages consisting of audiotapes plus slides, filmstrips, and learning kits. These materials should be previewed to determine their suitability for use by a particular group or age level.

Price information on items (the majority of which are only available for purchase) should be obtained from the distributors whose addresses are provided at the conclusion of this section.

Where available, the following information has been provided for each item listed:

Title/Date
Nature of material (format)
Producer or sponsor
Distributor/order number
Description of program content

AMERICA AND THE FUTURE OF MAN: COURSES BY NEWSPAPER

Learning kit

Producer: University Extension, University of California at San Diego

Source: World Future Society/K 101

This kit of educational materials can be used in or out of the formal classroom. It contains a 59-page booklet of lectures by famous futurists, a 322-page reader containing materials from many sources, a future-oriented game, a study guide and a set of tests. The kit provides a general introduction to the study of the future.

BEYOND CITY LIMITS: TOMORROW'S URBAN SOCIETY

Multimedia kit—1 sound (either record or cassette) and color filmstrip/case study unit/evaluation materials/teacher's guide and storage container

Producer: Newsweek Educational Division

Source: Newsweek Educational Division/No. 711

This multimedia kit helps students understand and evaluate the future of tomorrow's urban societies. The program outlines a range of choices—from restructuring the urban environment to retaining and renewing the city's basic functions.

COMPUTERS AND HUMAN SOCIETY

6 filmstrips/Teacher's Guide

Producer: Harper and Row

Source: Sunburst Communications/No. 079-83

This program provides a framework for assessing the computer's impact and explains in clear, simple terms how they work. Frontiers of computer research are explored and students join in the debate on artificial intelligence. The six parts of the program are: The Ultimate Servant; The Electronic Brain; The Evolution of Intelligence; The Computer Revolution; The Data Explosion and Central Control; Projections for Man and Machine.

DIMENSIONS OF CHANGE

6 filmstrips/Teacher's Guide

Producer: Westport Communications

Source: Sunburst Communications/No. 040-83

This program develops a variety of intriguing proposals, helps students evaluate these proposals and to appreciate the considerable human capacity for creative problem solving. The six topics are: The Man-Made Planet; Shelter; Energy; Food; Mobility; Communications.

DOOMSDAY: 21st CENTURY

2 color filmstrips/cassettes (KCC7650) or records (KCR7650)/Program Guide

Producer: Prentice Hall

Source: Prentice Hall

Predictions of doom are made repeatedly about the not-so-distant future. This film assesses the arguments about population, energy and food and gives students the opportunity to come to their own conclusions about the future doom or survival of the earth.

ECONOMICS AND THE GLOBAL SOCIETY

Multimedia kit—3 sound (record or cassette) and color filmstrips/2 case study units complete with 33 duplicating masters and 12 transparency visuals/simulation materials and storage container.

Producer: Newsweek Educational Division

Source: Newsweek Educational Division/No. 502

This three part series focuses on the underlying concepts of global economic development and interdependence. The first filmstrip, *The Wealth of Nations*, analyzes the basic framework of economic concepts and principles. The second filmstrip *Rich Nations, Poor Nations*, focuses on the emerging and widening gap between the developed and developing nations. *Economic Evolution*, the last in the series, examines the potential for international economic cooperation and the development of a truly global society.

FORECASTING THE FUTURE: CAN WE MAKE TOMORROW WORK?

5 filmstrips/Teacher's Guide

Producer: Harper and Row

Source: Sunburst Communications/No. 077-83

The thesis of this program is that the future can't be predicted, but can be invented. Students learn the importance of deciding what kind of future they want...and of planning for it. Titles of the parts of the program are: Choosing Tomorrow's World; Energy and Human Values; Science, Technology and the Year 2000; The Future of Work; The Family in Transition.

INTRODUCTION TO FUTURISTICS

1-hour tape cassette/book: *1999: The World of Tomorrow*

Producer: The World Future Society

Source: The World Future Society/K-103

The materials included in this package should prove highly useful to people who are just discovering the field of futuristics. The learning kit contains a one-hour tape cassette and a collection of articles from THE FUTURIST covering a wide range of future-related topics. The specific contents are:

Tape recording:
> The Future: Optimism versus Pessimism and Talking About the Future—interviews with Edward S. Cornish, President of the World Future Society. (Note: This tape is the same as T-7703).

Book:
> *1999: The World of Tomorrow*—an anthology of articles from THE FUTURIST. Among the many topics covered in this 160-page book are aviation, architecture, work, sex, forecasting, medicine, space colonies, economic visions, the automated office, education, energy, the oceans, and appropriate technology.

LIVING WITH TECHNOLOGY: CAN WE CONTROL APPLIED SCIENCE?

5 filmstrips/Teacher's Guide

Producer: Harper and Row

Source: Sunburst Communications/No. 074-83

The impact of technology, with special emphasis on the role played in shaping America's character, is demonstrated. Titles in this series are: The Transformation of Society; The American Dream; Implications for the World System; Vulnerability: The System Tested; Visions of the Future.

MARRIAGE AND FAMILY

2 half-hour tapes/series of reprints from THE FUTURIST

Producer: The World Future Society

Source: The World Future Society/K-107

These materials discuss trends and explore possible alternatives in the areas of marriage and family relationships. This kit contains two half-hour interviews and a 20-page collection of articles from THE FUTURIST.

Tape recordings:
> The Future of Family Formation by E. James Liebermann, Psychiatrist.
> Marriage and Divorce Trends by Paul C. Glick, Senior Demographer, Bureau of the Census.

Reprint series:
> "Future of Marriage and Sex"—titles include: Intimate Networks: Will They Replace the Monogamous Family? by James Ramey; Multi-Adult Household: Living Group of the Future by James Ramey; and The Pleasure Bond: Reversing the Anti-Sex Ethic by Robert T. and Anna K. Francoeur.

POPULATION

1-hour tape/series of reprints from THE FUTURIST

Producer: The World Future Society

Source: The World Future Society/K-106

Numerous topics and views on the population crisis are discussed by leading authorities. The learning kit contains a one-hour tape recording, and a 24-page reprint of articles from THE FUTURIST.

Tape recording:
> A Population Strategy for a Finite Planet by Lester Brown, President, Worldwatch Institute.
> Population Patterns in Rural America by Calvin Beale, Department of Agriculture Economic Research Service.

Reprint series:
> "Population and the Future"—titles include: Illegal Immigration: The Hidden Population Bomb by John Huss and Melanie Wirken; Population vs. Standard of Living by Jay W. Forrester; and The Population Problem in 22 Dimensions by Lester R. Brown, Patricia L. McGrath, and Bruce Stokes.

THE POPULATION DEBATE

4 filmstrips/Teacher's Guide

Producer: Westport Communications in association with The Population Institute

Source: Sunburst Communications/No. 041-83

Narrated by Paul Newman and Joanne Woodward, this series documents the world's astonishing population growth and explains the key terms and concepts needed to grasp its significance. Students are encouraged to weigh conflicting views, assess the choices available, and to consider what individuals can do about overpopulation. Titles are: Demography; Ecology and Food; Distribution and Economics; People.

PROJECTIONS FOR THE FUTURE

3 sound slide programs

Producer: Biological Sciences Curriculum Study

Source: Hubbard

Projections for the Future is a series of three sound-slide programs exploring three major alternative models for the future—a growth model, a behavior model and a humanist model. The first shows a continuation of current practices with reliance on more of everything; the second portrays a no-growth or steady state system where behavior modification is the key; and the third model demonstrates a society in harmony with itself and its natural surroundings. An instructional guide is provided with each program.

Titles:
> A Growth Model: 80 35mm slides in a Carousel with sound cassette and record/No. 886.
> A Behavior Model: 80 35mm slides in a Carousel with sound cassette and record/No. 887
> A Growth Model: 132 slides with Carousel, cassette and record/No. 888
> Complete program, including slides, Carousel, cassette and record/No. 885

TOWARD THE YEAR 2000

60-minute audio cassette or video cassette

Producer: Telefutures Incorporated

Source: The World Future Society

In this fascinating television encounter, three famous futurists, Margaret Mead, Herman Kahn and William Irwin Thompson, engage in a wide-ranging, lively and sometimes heated debate on the future of agriculture, the atmosphere, breeder reactors, coal and decentralization, energy, the family, famine, genetic engineering, industrialization, nationalism, nuclear war, the ocean, plutonium, religion, satellites and space colonies.

2000 A.D.

Multimedia kit—1 sound (record or cassette) and full color filmstrip/3 study units/simulation materials and storage container.

Producer: Newsweek Educational Division

Source: Newsweek Educational Division/No. 301

This multimedia kit contains a full overview of ideas about where the future is taking us. Contains 2 case study books, articles by futurists such as Alvin Toffler, a science fiction story, and a simulation game entitled *Futura City*.

WHERE WE LIVE: REGIONAL PLANNING AND THE HOUSING CRISIS

2 color filmstrips/cassettes (KCC6600) or records (KCR6600)/Program Guide

Producer: Prentice Hall

Source: Prentice Hall

At the present rate of growth, American cities are expected to double in size by the year 2000. This filmstrip program examines some of the issues surrounding that potential growth, focusing on environmental and planning concerns.

WORLD RESOURCES AND RESPONSIBILITIES

2 color filmstrips/cassettes (KCC7630) or records (KCR7630) Program Guide

Producer: Prentice Hall

Source: Prentice Hall

In a world afflicted by shortages, distribution of resources becomes a crucial issue. This filmstrip examines the current relationship between the "have" and "have-not" nations and the potential for resource-sharing.

SOURCES

Hubbard, P.O. Box 104, Northbrook, Illinois 60062 (312) 272-7810

Newsweek Educational Division, 444 Madison Avenue, New York, New York 10022 (212) 350-2620

Prentice Hall, 150 White Plains Road, Tarrytown, New York 10591 (914) 631-8300

Sunburst Communications, Room 83, 41 Washington Avenue, Pleasantville, New York 10570 (800) 431-1934

World Future Society, 4916 St. Elmo Avenue (Bethesda), Washington, D.C. 20014 (301) 656-8274

GLOSSARY

GLOSSARY

Following is a list of terms often encountered in futurist literature.

AD-HOCRACY: A system in which work is accomplished on an ad hoc basis, that is, by means of a team assembled to accomplish a specific task. The term contrasts with *bureaucracy*, in which bureaus or departments with relatively constant staffs deal with assigned categories of tasks.

ALTERNATIVE FUTURES: Possible forthcoming developments. The term emphasizes that the future is not fixed: many things *may* occur and people should explore the various possibilities and then seek to realize those that seem most desirable.

ANTI-UTOPIA: A novel or other work that describes, in negative terms, an imaginary society. Aldous Huxley's *Brave New World* and George Orwell's *1984* are anti-utopias. An alternative term is *dystopia*.

BASIC LONG-TERM "MULTIFOLD" TREND: An underlying, many-faceted trend that Western society has experienced over the past few centuries. As described by Herman Kahn and Anthony J. Wiener in their book *The Year 2000,* the trend is toward increasingly sensate cultures, that is, cultures that are empirical, this-worldly, secular, humanistic, pragmatic, utilitarian, contractual, epicurean, or hedonistic.

COMPUTER CONFERENCING: The use of a computer to store, switch, and reference messages between people who employ terminals to communicate with individual users or groups of users. Messages may be retrieved at the convenience of the participants according to subject, date of transmission, or sender/receiver. Unlike ordinary conferences or telephone systems, a computer conference can proceed 24 hours a day, seven days a week, for an indefinite period with the participants at widely separated locations.

CONJECTURE: A surmise or belief concerning a situation, often a possible future development. The French futurist Bertrand de Jouvenel gave prominence to the term in his book *The Art of Conjecture [L'art de la Conjecture],* first published in Monaco in 1964.

COUNTER-INTUITIVE: Contrary to one's natural expectations. The term was popularized by Jay Forrester, Professor of Management at the Massachusetts Institute of Technology in a paper entitled "The Counter-Intuitive Behavior of Social Systems." Forrester pointed out that socioeconomic systems generally do not respond the way people anticipate; as a result, programs undertaken to solve a given problem often fail to solve that problem and even intensify it. For example, a housing project designed to help poor people may actually increase their suffering by concentrating them in a location where they do not have access to jobs; increasing bus fares to raise the revenues of a public transit system which is losing money will often cause a decrease in ridership and a further loss of revenue.

CROSS-IMPACT ANALYSIS: An attempt to identify the various effects that developments have on each other. For example, the development of an improved transportation system may reduce the need for better communications—or vice versa. The structure for accomplishing such an analysis is called a *cross-impact matrix,* in which fields or specific developments are listed along both the horizontal and vertical axes and there are squares or boxes in which the analyst can note the impacts that two variables have on each other.

CYBERNETICS: The field of study that deals with the control processes in systems. The term was coined by Norbert Wiener, who used it to refer to the processes by which information from a system feeds back to control further developments in a system.

DELPHI CONFERENCING: A combination of the Delphi technique and computer conferencing, in which experts are polled (often concerning their beliefs about the future) by means of a computer.

DELPHI TECHNIQUE (or METHOD):   A method of soliciting and aggregating individual opinions or judgments, typically of a group of experts, to arrive at consensus views concerning such things as what may happen in the future. The Delphi technique keeps individual responses anonymous so that social influences (prestige of a certain participant, shyness of certain participants, etc.) are minimized, and poses the questions in a series of rounds. The results of each round are organized and presented to the participants in a carefully structured way.

DISCONTINUITY: A sharp change in nature or direction. For example, a discontinuity occurs when a population stops increasing and begins to decrease.

DOOMSDAY MACHINE (or DEVICE):   A mechanism that would destroy the entire world. The concept emerged among U.S. defense intellectuals thinking about nuclear war and was popularized in the motion picture *Dr. Strangelove.* (q.v.)

DYSTOPIA: An anti-utopia or unfavorable description of an imaginary society.

ECONOMETRIC MODEL: A series of mathematical equations which describe the operations of an economy. The equations can be entered into a computer and a variety of simulations made, using various assumptions (e.g., an income tax increase of $10).

ECOSPHERE: The natural environment in which man lives. The term emphasizes the ecological aspect of the environment, that is, the fact that all the plant and animal life, including man, and the various natural phenomena of air, land, and water are systemically interrelated, so that change in any aspect has an infinite number of impacts on other aspects.

EKISTICS: The science of human settlements. This term was invented by the Greek urban planner Constantinos Doxiadis. The term comes from the Greek *oikos* (house, habitation), the same word from which *economics* and *ecology* are derived.

ENVELOPE CURVE: A curve that summarizes a number of subsidiary curves. For example, an envelope curve may be drawn to represent the increasing speed of travel. For example, envelope curves summarize the subsidiary curves that represent the increase in speed of various transportation technologies—steamships, trains, motor cars, propeller airplanes, jet aircraft, and rockets.

EXPLORATORY FORECASTING: See NORMATIVE FORECASTING.

EXTRAPOLATION: Extending a curve into the future simply by assuming that the variable will continue to change at the same rate and in the same direction. For example, if the population of a city has increased 2% a year and the number of inhabitants is now 1,000,000, one can extrapolate the trend into the future. Such extrapolation would indicate that the population one year from now would be 1,020,000.

FUTURES ANALYSIS: One of a number of terms used to denote the study of the future. The use of the plural "futures" emphasizes the element of choice concerning what the future will be like. See ALTERNATIVE FUTURES.

FUTURE SHOCK: The disorientation that occurs due to rapid social change. The term was coined by Alvin Toffler, author of *Future Shock* (1970), who likened this disorientation to *culture shock,* a term used in anthropology to denote the disorientation that a person from one culture feels when he lives among people who have a different culture.

FUTURES RESEARCH: A term used to denote the study of the future. See FUTURES ANALYSIS, FUTURISTICS, FUTUROLOGY, FUTURICS.

FUTURIBLE: A possible future development. This term was developed by the French futurist Bertrand de Jouvenel from the French words *futur* and *possible.*

FUTURICS: A term used to denote the study of the future.

FUTURISM: The mood or movement that emphasizes the importance of seriously thinking about and planning for the future. (The term also refers to an Italian art movement of the early 20th century.)

FUTURISTICS: The field of study that deals with possible future developments.

FUTUROLOGY: The study of the future. The term appears to have been first used by Ossip Flechtheim, a German-born professor of political science, when he was in the United States during World War II. (Note: Some futurists object to the term on the grounds that it suggests that there is a science of the future. These futurists maintain that ideas about the future are vitally important for decisionmaking, but there can be no science of the future in the sense that there is a science of living things [biology] or the earth [geology], because one cannot study what does not exist.)

GAMING: The use of a game that simulates a real situation. For example, games have been developed to represent the operations of a city government. Different players may play the parts of the mayor, city council, real estate lobby, tenants' association, etc. By playing the game, the players begin to understand more clearly the problems and opportunities of city government.

GENERAL SYSTEMS THEORY: The theory that seeks to explain the behavior of systems, which are aggregates of interacting units. One important aspect of a system is the existence of *feedback,* that is, when one part of a system is acted upon, it reacts, thereby causing numerous other impacts in the system.

GOALS RESEARCH: Research aimed at elucidating the values and purposes of an organization or a community.

GREEN REVOLUTION: The increase in agricultural productivity that occurred in the 1960s, due to the discovery and propagation of new varieties of wheat and rice and to new developments in plant management, fertilizers, pesticides and herbicides, etc. Norman Borlang won the 1970 Nobel peace prize for his work on new grains.

HEURISTIC: Serving to stimulate research or discovery. A number of methods may be used because of their heuristic value, that is, their ability to encourage people to learn a variety of new things. For example, students may be asked to design a model community; in the process, they are led to acquire a wide variety of knowledge about how communities operate, what values are important to the students themselves, etc.

HOLISTIC: Emphasizing the wholeness of a complex system rather than focusing on a portion of the system. The term derives from the Greek word *holos* meaning whole or complete, but because of its similarity to the English word "whole," the word is often erroneously spelled *wholistic.*

INDICATIVE PLANNING: A national planning process which emphasizes agreed-on procedures to achieve given objectives rather than rigid decrees or directives. In France and Sweden, two nations with a history of indicative planning, the government works with private enterprise in setting the national goals and developing the means to reach them.

INTUITIVE FORECASTING: Any method of forecasting that relies on an individual's subjective judgment or personal feelings about what is likely to happen.

LEADING INDICATORS: Statistics that generally precede a change in a situation. For example, an increase in economic activity is typically preceded by a rise in the prices of stocks.

LEAD TIME: The time required for a development to move from conception to completion. In some cases, lead times are very long: building a new power plant, for example, may take 10 years because of the delays occasioned by planning, legal problems, construction, etc.

LINEAR TREND EXTRAPOLATION: Extending a trend in a straight-line fashion. "Linear" forecasting assumes that a trend will continue unchanged into the future; for example, that a city's economy will grow next year by 5% because it has grown 5% a year during the past 10 years.

MEGALOPOLIS: An enormous urban region created by the coalescing of two or more metropolises. Demographers speak of several megalopolises in the United States: the largest extends from Boston to Washington (sometimes called *Boswash*).

652

MODELING: See SIMULATION.

MORPHOLOGICAL ANALYSIS: Any technique which seeks to identify systematically all possible means of achieving a given end. One approach is to create a list of all possible variables so that each can be examined and combinations explored.

NEO-MALTHUSIAN: A modern-day follower of the English economist Thomas Malthus, who believed that population tends to increase faster than food supply and that widespread poverty is inevitable unless population is checked either by reducing the birth rate or by famine, war, and pestilence.

NORMATIVE: Based on what will be needed. A normative forecaster tries to determine what will be required to achieve goals. Normative forecasting is contrasted with *exploratory forecasting,* which seeks to determine what is technologically feasible. "Exploratory and normative methods are not competitive with, or replacements for, one another," writes Joseph Martino in *Technological Forecasting for Decision-making.*   Both are essential and both must be used together. Normally one does not bother to prepare an exploratory forecast of some technology unless there is a normative forecast (at least an implicit one) that the technology will be needed. Likewise, one does not normally prepare normative forecasts without some idea that it will be possible to meet the goals . . . The three most common methods of normative forecasting are relevance trees, morphological models, and mission flow diagrams."

OPERATIONS RESEARCH: The application of mathematical and scientific techniques to resolving complex problems. Operations research developed under military auspices during World War II. The increasing reliance of military and governmental planners on scientific and scholarly expertise led to the establishment by the U.S. Air Force of Project RAND, which later became the RAND Corporation and in turn gave birth to a number of "policy research" institutes.

PARADIGM: A pattern or model representing a situation or condition. As used today, *paradigm* typically refers to a person's basic conception of a certain aspect of reality. He may, for example, view science as the paradigm of knowledge, that is, the way knowledge is or ought to be. The current usage of the term was stimulated by Thomas Kuhn's book *The Structure of Scientific Revolutions.*

PARADIGM SHIFT: A change in an accepted paradigm. This generally refers to a radical change in a large number of people's view of a certain aspect of reality, as when they stop believing that economic growth is good and begin viewing it as potentially harmful.

PERT (PROGRAM EVALUATION AND REVIEW TECHNIQUE):   A group of methods for managing a dispersed and complex program. PERT was originally developed by the Navy's Special Projects Office during the program which led to the building of the Polaris missile. Later PERT was adopted by the Department of Defense and the National Aeronautics and Space Administration as a means of managing complex research and development tasks.

PLANETARY ENGINEERING: The large-scale modification of a planet for human purposes. The term may be applied to large-scale projects on the earth (for example, a sea-level canal through Panama) as well as on other planets.

POST INDUSTRIAL SOCIETY: The most widely used of many titles for a new societal phase that has emerged or is emerging. There are two diametrically opposed usages: (1) indicating a service society or an information society, emerging from a successful industrial era, where the majority of the labor force is in occupations other than agriculture and manufacturing (notably involving knowledge and technology), or (2) indicating a more decentralized society of frugal and ecologically-conscious lifestyles, emerging in the wake of an unsustainable industrialism. The former usage is widely identified with sociologist Daniel Bell, who first used the term in 1959, and fully elaborated on it in *The Coming of Post-Industrial Society* (Basic Books, 1973). The latter usage was originated by Ananda K. Coomaraswamy in Coomaraswamy and Penty, eds., *Essays in Post-Industrialism: A Symposium of Prophecy Concerning the Future of Society* (T.N. Foulis, 1914), and has been employed by many decentralist writers such as Arthur J. Penty, Theodore Roszak, Ivan Illich, Robert Heilbroner, Scott Burns, and William N. Ellis.

PREDICTION: A statement that something will happen in the future. The term *prediction* connotes a greater degree of precision and certainty than does *forecasting*. Today's future-oriented scholars generally avoid making predictions and deal more in terms of *forecasts* or *conjectures*.

PROGNOSTICS: The field that deals with forecasts or study of future possibilities. From *prognosis* meaning "foreknowledge" in Greek. In his book *Prognostics* (Elsevier, 1971), the Dutch scholar Fred L. Polak writes: "In the broad sense prognostics covers *all* the variants and methods of scientific future-thinking."

PROJECTION: A forecast based on current trends.

QUALITY OF LIFE: The extent to which a person enjoys a "good" life. As currently used, the phrase "quality of life" generally emphasizes the non-economic aspects of a person's life, such as the purity of the air, security from crime, effective cultural institutions, and general feelings of satisfaction and well-being.

RELEVANCE TREE: A diagrammatic technique for analyzing systems or processes in which distinct levels of complexity or hierarchy can be identified. A relevance tree for a new drug might start with Biomedical Objectives, under which would be listed Prevention, Diagnosis, Treatment, etc. Under Diagnosis, the tree might branch into Structure, Function, Composition, Behavior, etc. A relevance tree enables an analyst to identify the various aspects of a problem or a proposed solution and thus arrive at a more complete understanding of his subject. This technique is also useful for identifying unintended side-effects of innovations.

SCENARIO: A description of a sequence of events that might possibly occur in the future. A scenario is normally developed by: (1) studying the facts of a situation and (2) selecting a development that might occur, and (3) imagining the range and sequence of developments that might follow. For example, a person charged with protecting a city might first seek to identify the various threats that might occur and what responses the city's agencies might make; he could then imagine what would happen in the event specific challenges to the city's security actually occurred. In this way, the scenario-writer can try to identify potential weaknesses in a city's security system and suggest ways to improve them.

S CURVE: (Also known as *sigmoid curve* from the Greek letter sigma.) A mathematical curve representing a variable which first increases in magnitude at an accelerating rate, decelerates, and eventually grows very little or even declines.

SELF-FULFILLING FORECAST: A forecast that tends to make itself come true. For example, a forecast for rapid growth of a certain city may encourage businesses to locate there, thus causing the forecast to be realized.

SIMULATION: The use of mathematical formulae to replicate or "model" real world processes or behavior. Simple simulation models are used to predict the work flows and staff requirements for bank tellers, supermarket checkout counters, or freeway toll booths. On a far more sophisticated level, econometric forecasters use complex mathematical models of the U.S. economy to evaluate the likely impacts of various policy instruments such as tax increases.

SOCIAL ENGINEERING: The application of social science to the development and improvement of social systems or social behavior.

SOCIAL FORECASTING: The forecasting of developments in society (e.g., changing values, behavior, institutional forms, etc.). The term is often contrasted with technological and economic forecasting.

SOCIAL INDICATOR: A statistical variable relating to the state of society. The crime rate, the level of literacy, and the incidence of alcoholism may be viewed as social indicators. The term social indicators developed as a social equivalent to economic indicators (e.g., unemployment rate).

SPACESHIP EARTH: A paradigm or image of the world, which emphasizes the unity of the world as a single, closed system, thereby emphasizing such factors as the need to keep it free from pollution and

654

to recycle wastes. The image also suggests the unity of mankind on one small planet among millions, dwarfed by the vastness of the universe.

SURMISING FORUM: A forum or center in which people might develop and compare forecasts and ideas about the future. The term was used by French futurist Bertrand de Jouvenel as a translation for *forum previsionnel*.

SYNERGY: The combined action of a number of parts so that the result is greater than the sum total of the separate action of the parts. Originally proposed by Buckminster Fuller as "Synergetics," the characteristics of metallic alloys or structural forms which are stronger than their constituent parts. Today, the concept is expanded to apply to situations in which various forces in combination achieve more than might have been expected.

TECHNOLOGY ASSESSMENT: The evaluation of a technology in terms of its long-range as well as its immediate impacts. The term technology assessment became current through the successful efforts of former Rep. Emilio Q. Daddario to establish an Office of Technology Assessment to assist Congress. Technology assessment advocates have stressed that a technology has many impacts that ordinarily are not adequately considered by the designers and propagators of that technology. A proper assessment would evaluate the long-range, far-reaching, and hidden social as well as economic impacts of a new or proposed technology.

TECHNOLOGICAL (or TECHNOLOGY) FORECASTING: The forecasting of future potential technical developments. A technology forecaster generally makes forecasts concerning how soon various types of technologies will be *possible* and what characteristics they *may* have, rather than what they *will* have, because the actual technology that will be used in the future depends on economic, social, and political considerations which are normally beyond the province of the technology forecaster. For example, a technology forecaster might forecast that it will be possible by the year 2000 to produce electricity from thermonuclear fusion, but whether thermonuclear fusion will actually be used for that purpose may depend on a variety of non-technological considerations.

TIME HORIZON: The farthest distance into the future that one considers in forecasting and planning. A company may be viewed as having a "short time horizon" if it rarely gives serious consideration to events that are forecasted to occur more than two years into the future.

TREND: A change in a variable that takes place over an extended period of time. *Trend* is normally distinguished from *fluctuation,* which is a change that occurs over a brief period of time and often is of no long-term significance. For example, the United States has experienced since the beginning of the 20th century a *trend* toward greater frequency of divorce; in 1946, when soldiers returned from overseas, there was a brief upward *fluctuation* in the divorce rate, which reached a level that did not recur until the 1970s, when the long-term trend reached and surpassed the 1946 level.

TREND EXTRAPOLATION: See EXTRAPOLATION.

WORLD SYSTEM MODEL: A model or simulation that attempts to show the interactions of important global variables, such as population, pollution, economic growth, natural resources, etc. Jay Forrester, Professor of Management at the Massachusetts Institute of Technology, has developed a number of such models, which consist of mathematical equations representing the relationships believed to exist between the variables. A world modeler can try to determine what might happen in the future by feeding various assumptions (e.g., a 20% increase in population) into his model and seeing what happens.

ZERO-SUM GAME: A game in which the cumulative winnings equal the cumulative losses, as in chess. Futurists like to emphasize *non*-zero-sum situations in which everyone (or most parties) win. This is possible when the players do not take from each other but instead cooperate in creating new or larger goods.

GEOGRAPHICAL INDEX

GEOGRAPHICAL INDEX

Individuals and organizations mentioned in the directory are listed by geographic location. The geographic headings which follow are arranged in alphabetical order using the English spelling of each country's name. Within each heading, the names of individuals are listed in regular type and the names of organizations in italics.

658

COLOMBIA

Fundacion America Latina 2001

CZECHOSLOVAKIA

Malek, Ivan

DENMARK

Adler-Karlsson, Gunnar
Kristensen, Thorkil
Sorensen, Arne
Witt-Hansen, Johannes

The Danish Committee on Futures Studies
Instituttet for Fremtidsforskning

EGYPT

El-Kholy, Ussama Amin
Ghabour, Samir Ibrahim
Kassas, Mohamed A.F.

Arab League Educational, Cultural and
Scientific Organization (ALECSO)

ETHIOPIA

Tebicke, Haile Lul

FINLAND

Taloudellinen Suunnittelukeskus

FRANCE

Antoine, Serge
Aujac, Henri
Bize, Rene
Bouladon, Gabriel Antoine
Cassirer, Henry Reinhard
Cazes, Bernard
Cepede, Michel
Crozier, Michel Jean
Decoufle, Andre C.
De Jouvenel, Bertrand
De Jouvenel, Hugues Alain
Delors, Jacques Lucien Jean
Essig, Francois Bernard
Fourastie, Jean Joseph
Friedman, Yona
Gerardin, Lucien A.
Gueron, Georges
Gueron, Jeannine
Hanappe, Paul
Hetman, Francois
King, Alexander
Lesourne, Jacques Francois
Mendars, Henri
Moles, Abraham A.
Piotet, Francoise Odette
Poquet, Guy Rene
Saint-Geours, Jean
Saint-Paul, Raymond Henri
Salomon, Jean-Jacques
Scardigli, Victor

Schwartz, Bertrand

Association Internationale Futuribles
Bureau d'Informations et de Previsions
Economiques
Centre de Recherche sur le Bien-Etre
Centre d'Etude des Consequences Generales
des Grandes Techniques
Centre International de Recherche sur
l'Environnement et le Developpement
Commissariat General du Plan
Delegation a l'Amenagement du Territoire
et a l'Action (D.A.T.A.R.)
Fondation Claude Nicolas Ledoux pour les
Reflexions sur le Futur
Fondation Internationale de l'Innovation
Sociale
Hazan International
INSEAD
Institut de Prospective et Politique de la
Science
Institut Technique de Prevision
Economique et Sociale
International Council of Scientific Unions
(ICSU)
Laboratoire de Prospective Appliquee
Organization for Economic Cooperation
and Development (OECD)
Systeme d'Etudes du Schema General
d'Amenagement de la France (SESAME)
Thomson-CSF, Groupe d'Etudes
Prospectives
United Nations Educational, Scientific and
Cultural Organization (UNESCO)

GERMANY, BERLIN (WEST)

Buchholz, Hans
Flechtheim, Ossip K.
Jungk, Robert
Koelle, Heinz Hermann
Mackensen, Rainer Ulrich
Sahal, Devendra

Gesellschaft fur Zukunftsfragen e.V.
Institut fur Zukunftsforschung
Wissenschaftszentrum Berlin

GERMANY, FEDERAL REPUBLIC OF

Bossell, Harmuth H.
Graul, Emil Heinz
Hubner, Kurt
Kade, Gerhard Paul
Klages, Helmut
Lenk, Hans A.P.
Proske, Ruediger K.A.
Rothgaenger, Klaus
Schmacke, Ernst Stephan
Schulze, Lothar Gunther
Schumacher, Dieter
Stoeber, Gerhard J.
Vester, Frederic
Wagenfuhr, Horst
Weizacker, Carl Friedrich Freiherr von
Wickert, Gunter

Stichting Toekomstbeeld der Techniek
Youth Movement for a New International
    Order (NIO Youth)

NEW ZEALAND

Duncan, James Francis

Commission for the Future

NORWAY

Nyheim, Jan Henrik

Selskapet for Fremtidsstudier (SEFREM)

POLAND

Baworowski, Ludwik Jerzy
Danecki, Jan
Nosal, Czeslaw S.
Secomski, Kazimierz
Sicinski, Andrzej
Strzelecki, Jan Wladyslaw
Suchodolski, Bogdan
Winiecki, Jan Stanislaw

Osrodek Badan Prognostycznych
Polish Academy of Sciences, Institute of
    Philosophy and Sociology, Division for
    Lifestyles Studies
Polish Academy of Sciences, The Research
    and Prognostics Committee, "Poland
    2000"

ROMANIA

Apostol, Pavel A.
Botez, Mihai C.
Malitza, Mircea

SOUTH AFRICA, REPUBLIC OF

Raad vir Geesteswetenskaplike Navorsing
University of Stellenbosch, Unit for
    Futures Research

SPAIN

Menasanch, Rosa Menasanch

Club de Amigos de la Futurologia

SRI LANKA

Clarke, Arthur Charles

SWEDEN

Backstrand, Goran Karl
Block, A. Eskil
Dedijer, Stevan
Hottovy, Tibor C.
Ingelstam, Lars E.
Myrdal, Alva Reimer
Myrdal, Gunnar
Nilsson, Sam
Schwarz, Stephan
Wikstrom, Solveig Rognborg

Centrum for Tvarvetenskapliga Studier av
    Manniskans Villkor
Committee for Future-Oriented Research
Formedlingscentralen for Framtidsstudier
    AB
Forsvarets Forskningsanstalt (FOA)
International Federation of Institutes for
    Advanced Study (IFIAS)
Secretariat for Future Studies

SWITZERLAND

Afheldt, Heik
Altenpohl, Dieter G.
Dubach, Paul
Fontela, Emilio
Fritsch, Bruno
Gabus, Andre M.W.
Garaudy, Roger
Horhager, Axel
Kocher, Gerhard
Lambert-Lamond, Georges M.
Lambo, Thomas Adeoye
Nerfin, Marc Paul
Rogge, Peter G.
Thiemann, Hugo Ernst

Battelle, Geneva Research Centre
International Creative Center (ICC)
Prognos AG, European Center for Applied
    Economic Research
Schweizerische Vereinigung fur
    Zukunftsforschung
St. Galler Zentrum fur Zukunftsforschung

THAILAND

Raksasataya, Amara
Sharif, Nawuz M.

United Nations Asian and Pacific
    Development Institute

UNION OF SOVIET SOCIALIST REPUBLICS

Bestuzhev-Lada, Igor Vassilevich
Dobrov, Gennady Mikhaylovich

Academy of Sciences of the Ukranian SSR,
    Science Policy Studies Department of the
    Institute of Cybernetics
USSR Academy of Sciences, Institute for
    Sociological Research, Section on Social
    Forecasting

UNITED KINGDOM

Berry, Adrian M.
Berry, David John
Calder, Nigel
Chaplain, Roland
Clark, John Albert
Clarke, Ian Frederick
Cole, Hugh Samuel David
Dauman, Jean Victor
Francis, John Michael

Freeman, Christopher
Gershuny, Jonathan Israel
Goldsmith, Edward Rene
Hall, Peter Geoffrey
Jahoda, Marie
Jones, J. Christopher
Jones, Peter Michael Seaton
Kennet (Lord), formerly Wayland Young
King-Hele, Desmond George
Kumar, Jagdish Krishan
Leach, Gerald Adrian
Loveridge, Denis John
Lovins, Amory B.
Mac Nulty, Christine A. Ralph
Marstrand, Pauline Kendrick
Miles, Ian Douglas
Morris, Geoffrey Keith
M'Pherson, Philip Keith
Nicholson, Simon
Page, R. William
Parry, Renee-Marie Croose
Parsons, Jack
Pritchard, Colin Leonard
Robertson, James Hugh
Roy, Robin
Surrey, Arthur John
Taylor, Gordon Rattray
Thring, Meredith Woolridge
Vickers, Charles Geoffrey
Ward, Barbara (Lady D.B.E. Jackson)

*University of Edinburgh, Centre for
  Human Ecology*
The Electrical Research Association Ltd.
*The Findhorn Foundation University of
  Light*
Futures Network
Futures Studies Centre
International Institute for Strategic Studies
The Open University, Design Group
*The Open University, Oxford Research
  Unit*
*David Owen Centre for Population Growth
  Studies*
Policy Studies Institute
*Pugwash Conference on Science and World
  Affairs*
Science Policy Foundation
Social Science Research Council (UK)
Society for Long-Range Planning
*University of Sussex, Science Policy
  Research Unit*

U.S.A.—ALABAMA

Tarter, Donald Edward

U.S.A.—ARIZONA

Theobald, Robert

U.S.A.—CALIFORNIA

Adelson, Marvin

Amara, Roy
Armer, Paul
Beckwith, Burnham Putnam
Bellman, Richard Ernest
Bonner, James
Borgese, Elisabeth Mann
Boucher, Wayne I.
Bradley, Helen Genevieve
Brand, Stewart
Brown, Harrison Scott
Case, Fred E.
Churchman, C. West
Dalkey, Norman C.
Drobnick, Richard Lee
Duhl, Leonard J.
Dunstan, Mary Jane
Elgin, Duane S.
Enzer, Selwyn
Fabun, Don
Gilfillan, S. Colum
Glines, Don E.
Gorney, Roderic
Gray, Paul
Hardin, Garrett
Harman, Willis W.
Helmer, Olaf
Hoos, Ida Russakoff
Jantsch, Erich
Johansen, Robert R.
Kollen, James H.
Leonard, George B.
Lipinski, Andrew J.
Loye, David
Mandel, Thomas Frederick
Meier, Richard L.
Mitchell, Arnold
Mitchell, Fred H., Jr.
Nanus, Burt
O'Toole, James Joseph
Page, Talbot
Platt, John
Pyke, Donald L.
Salk, Jonas
Schwartz, Peter
Seaborg, Glenn Theodore
Spengler, Marie
Teige, Peter J.
Textor, Robert Bayard
Tugwell, Franklin
Vallee, Jacques F.
Watt, Kenneth E. Ferguson
Weaver, John Jacob
Weaver, Roy A.
Wilson, Albert George
Wilson, Donna

Academy of World Studies
*University of California—Los Angeles,
  Department of Psychiatry, Program on
  Psychosocial Adaptation and the Future
  (PSAF)*

*California State Department of Education,
Office of Support Services*
California Tomorrow
*Center for the Study of Democratic
Institutions: The Fund for the Republic,
Inc.*
James L. Creighton
DCM Associates
Educational Futures Projects
*Episcopal Diocese of California, Futures
Planning Council*
Harris International
Infomedia Corporation
Institute for the Future
*Institute for the Study of the Human
Future, Inc.*
Interdisciplinary Systems Group
Public Policy Research Organization
The Rand Corporation
Simulation in the Service of Society
Society for Computer Simulation (SCS)
*University of Southern California, Center
for Futures Research*
*Stanford Research Institute, Business
Intelligence Program*
*Stanford Research Institute, Center for the
Study of Social Policy*

U.S.A.—COLORADO

Bennis, Warren
Boulding, Elise
Boulding, Kenneth Ewart
Vlachos, Evan
Ziegler, Warren Leigh

The Futures-Invention Associates
*International Graduate School of
Education, Center for Futuristic Studies*

U.S.A.—CONNECTICUT

Becker, Harold S.
Bell, Wendell
Bronwell, Arthur B.
Chase, Stuart
Gordon, Theodore Jay
Konetchy, Ronald Dean
Simmons, William W.
Stover, John G.
Wilson, Ian H.

Applied Futures, Inc.
The Futures Group, Inc.
Yankelovich, Skelly and White, Inc.

U.S.A.—DISTRICT OF COLUMBIA

Abbott, William Latham
Arnstein, Sherry Phyllis
Barach, Arnold B.
Best, Fred Joseph
Bezold, Clement
Biderman, Albert D.
Brown, Lester R.

Chacko, George K.
Cheatham, Anne Wilson
Christakis, Alexander N.
Clawson, Marion
Coates, Joseph F.
Coates, Vary T.
Cornish, Edward Seymour
Cornish, Salley Woodhull
Culver, John C.
Daddario, Emilio Quincy
Dixon, John
Eckholm, Erik P.
Edwards, Gregg
Ewald, William Rudolph
Ferkiss, Victor Christopher
Fisher, Joseph Lyman
Fondersmith, John
Gerba, John
Hahn, Walter A., Jr.
Halal, William Emitt
Hitch, Charles Johnston
Hopkins, Frank Snowden
Hubbard, Barbara Marx
Humphries, George E.
Johnston, Denis F.
Kornbluh, Marvin
Lamson, Robert Warren
Landsberg, Hans H.
Lesh, Donald R.
Linowitz, Sol M.
Lippitt, Gordon L.
Little, Dennis Lloyd
Maston, Robert E.
Maynard, Richard G.
Michaelis, Michael
Peterson, Russell Wilbur
Pickard, Jerome Percival
Renfro, William L.
Ritterbush, Philip C.
Rose, Charlie
Snyder, David Pearce
Stokes, Bruce Edward
Umpleby, Stuart A.
Wakefield, Rowan Albert
Waskow, Arthur I.
Wren-Lewis, John
Zuckerman, Peter

*American Council of Life Insurance,
Trend Analysis Program*
*American Enterprise Institute for Public
Policy Research*
The Brookings Institution
Center for Policy Process
*The Center for Strategic and International
Studies/Georgetown University*
Committee for Economic Development
The Committee for the Future
Congressional Clearinghouse on the Future
Congressional Research Service
*Federal Aviation Administration, Office of
Aviation Policy, System Concepts
Branch (AVP-110)*

64

Massachusetts Institute of Technology,
  Research Program on Communications
  Policy
Massachusetts Institute of Technology,
  System Dynamics Group

U.S.A.—MICHIGAN

Aldridge, Alexandra
Chen, Kan
Kaufmann, Felix
Michael, Donald Nelson
Skolimowski, Henryk

U.S.A.—MINNESOTA

Barker, Joel A.
Damlo, Penny Ann
Erickson, Scott William
Harkins, Arthur Martin
Holthusen, T. Lance
Imsland, Donald Orlene
Joseph, Earl C.
Ryan, Robert Dale

Future Systems

U.S.A.—MISSISSIPPI

Mississippi 1990

U.S.A.—MISSOURI

Craver, J. Kenneth
Kauffman, Draper Laurence, Jr.
Mihanovich, Clement Simon

*Institute for Theological Encounter with
  Science and Technology (ITEST)*
Midwest Research Institute

U.S.A.—NEW HAMPSHIRE

Eldredge, H. Wentworth
Meadows, Dennis Lynn
Meadows, Donnella H.

*Research Program on Technology and
  Public Policy*

U.S.A.—NEW JERSEY

Bookchin, Murray
Buchen, Irving H.
Cleveland, Harlan
Darrow, R. Morton
Didsbury, Howard Francis, Jr.
Falk, Richard Anderson
Francoeur, Robert Thomas
Hellman, Hal
Henderson, Hazel
Keller, Suzanne
Mesthene, Emmanuel G.
Mische, Gerald F.
Mische, Patricia Mary Schmitt
O'Neill, Gerard Kitchen
Pohl, Frederik
Taylor, Theodore B.

Thomson, Irene Taviss
Turoff, Murray
Wescott, Roger Williams

*Princeton Center for Alternative Futures,
  Inc.*
*Society for the Investigation of Recurring
  Events*

U.S.A.—NEW YORK

Asimov, Isaac
Bowers, Raymond
Brennan, Donald George
Brown, Arnold
Brown, William M.
Bundy, Robert Franklin
Darling, Charles M. III
Davidowitz, Moshe
Diebold, John
Dubos, Rene
Edrich, Harold
Elton, Martin C.J.
Esfandiary, F.M.
Etzioni, Amitai W.
Eurich, Alvin C.
Feinberg, Gerald
Freeman, Orville Lothrop
Godoy, Horacio Hermes
Gray, Colin S.
Green, Thomas F.
Gross, Bertram
Hamil, Ralph Edward
Harmon, David P., Jr.
Heilbroner, Robert L.
Jones, Thomas Evan
Kahn, Herman
Knoppers, Antonie T.
Kostelanetz, Richard
Land, George Thomas Lock
Laszlo, Ervin
Lecht, Leonard A.
Lesse, Stanley
Marien, Michael David
Martel, Leon Charles
Mendlovitz, Saul H.
Moneta, Carlos J.
Overholt, William Henry
Pessolano, F. John
Phelps, John Bedford
Rosen, Stephen
Rosenfeld, Albert
Ruggles, Rudy L., Jr.
Sheldon, Eleanor Bernert
Somit, Albert
Stulman, Julius
Taylor, Harold
Thompson, William Irwin
Toffler, Alvin
Wagar, W. Warren
Ward, Jonathan
Weiner, Edith M.
Yankelovich, Daniel

The Abend Group
Academy for Educational Development,
    Inc.
Business International Corporation
Center for Policy Research
The College Board, Future Direction for a
    Learning Society
Committee for Economic Development
The Conference Board
Cornell University Program on Science,
    Technology, and Society
The Diebold Group, Inc.
Hudson Institute, Inc.
Information for Policy Design
The Institute on Man and Science
Institute for Society, Ethics and the Life
    Sciences—The Hastings Center
Institute for World Order, Inc.
Interfuture
MPI International, Inc. (Motivation
    Programmers, Inc.)
New York Center for World Game Studies,
    Inc.
Prospective, International Center of
    Research and Communication
Quantum Science Corporation
Risk Studies Foundation
Russell Sage Foundation
Social Impact Assessment Network
United Nations Department of Economic
    and Social Affairs, Population Division
United Nations Institute for Training and
    Research (UNITAR)
Weiner, Edrich, Brown, Inc.
World Institute Council
Yankelovich, Skelly and White, Inc.

U.S.A.—NORTH CAROLINA

Davis, Richard C.
Spengler, Joseph John

U.S.A.—OHIO

Bigelow, Bruce Edward
Franks, Betty Barclay
Martino, Joseph P.
Mesarovic, Mihajlo D.
Swager, William Leon

The Academy for Contemporary Problems
University of Akron Institute for Future
    Studies and Research
Battelle Memorial Institute
University of Dayton Research Institute
Goals for the Greater Akron Area
Institute for 21st Century Business
Management Horizons
National Council for the Social Studies
    (NCSS) Special Interest Group in Future
    Studies
North American Society for Corporate
    Planning
Planning Executives Institute

Predicasts, Inc.
The Simulation and Gaming Association

U.S.A.—OREGON

Linstone, Harold A.

Champoeg II—Oregon 2000 Project
Portland State University, Futures
    Research Institute

U.S.A.—PENNSYLVANIA

Ackoff, Russell L.
Ayres, Robert Underwood
Baier, Kurt E.
Bender, Allan Douglas
Fuller, R. Buckminster
Gappert, Gary M.
Madeira, Thomas Roberts
Ozbekhan, Hasan
Rescher, Nicholas
Shostak, Arthur B.

Movement for a New Society (MNS)
Planning Dynamics, Incorporated
Research for Better Schools, Inc.
School of Living
U.S. Army War College, Strategic Studies
    Institute

U.S.A.—RHODE ISLAND

Carleton, Thomas James

The Institute of Management Sciences
    (TIMS)

U.S.A.—TENNESSEE

Harding, May Maury

U.S.A.—TEXAS

Commer, James Chester
Cook, Earl
Dede, Christopher James
Fowles, Jib
Kozmetsky, George
Markley, O.W. ("Mark")
McHale, Magda Cordell
Roemer, Kenneth Morrison
Steffes, Dale William
Streatfield, Guy Frederick
Vanston, John H., Jr.

Center for Integrative Studies
Goals for Dallas
Houston Chamber of Commerce Future
    Studies Committee and Division
Planning and Forecasting Consultants
Project Forethought Network

U.S.A.—UTAH

Utah Future Study
Utah State Planning Coordinator's Office

U.S.A.—VERMONT

Livingston, Dennis

U.S.A.—VIRGINIA

Bean, Louis H.
Cetron, Marvin Jerome
Gerken, William, Jr.
Mason, Roy E.
Ozmon, Howard
Williams, Charles W.

Decisions and Designs, Incorporated (DDI)
Forecasting International, Ltd.
National Space Institute
Charles W. Williams, Inc.

U.S.A.—WASHINGTON

Lindaman, Edward B.
Sine, Thomas William

Information Futures
Northwest Regional Foundation

U.S.A.—WEST VIRGINIA

Hess, Karl

U.S.A.—WISCONSIN

Kraegel, Wilfred A.

VENEZUELA

Socias, Juan

SUBJECT INDEX

SUBJECT INDEX

This index provides cross-referenced listings for individuals and organizations according to their special area of interest. It is arranged alphabetically by subject heading. Within each heading, the names of individuals are listed in regular type and the names of organizations in italics.

AERO-SPACE

Clarke, Arthur Charles
Gerken, William, Jr.
Graul, Emil Heinz
King-Hele, Desmond George
Koelle, Heinz Hermann
Lenz, Ralph C., Jr.
Ruzic, Neil Price
Sjoerdsma, Andre C.
Tarter, Donald Edward
Taylor, Theodore B.

Dayton, University of, Research Institute
Federal Aviation Administration
Forecasting International, Ltd.
Forum for the Advancement of Students in Science and Technology, Inc.
Future Options Room
Hudson Institute, Inc.
National Space Institute
ORI, Inc.

AFRICA

Ferkiss, Victor
Francois, Charles Oscar
Lambert-Lamond, Georges M.
Lambo, Thomas Adeoye
Moneta, Carlos J.
Van Dam, Andre
Von Laue, Theodore H.

Institut Technique de Prevision Economique et Sociale
Institute for Policy Studies
United Nations Institute for Training and Research (UNITAR)

AGING

Abrams, Mark Alexander
Auerbach, Lewis E.
Darrow, R. Morton
Esfandiary, F.M.
Kraegel, Wilfred A.
Landau, Erika
Spengler, Joseph John

Academy for Educational Development, Inc.
American Council of Life Insurance, Trend Analysis Program
Institute for the Study of the Human Future, Inc.

AGRICULTURE

Bean, Louis H.
Brown, Lester R.
Cepede, Michel
Clark, John Albert
Drobnick, Richard Lee
Freeman, Orville Lothrop
Gordon, Theodore Jay
Harmon, David P., Jr.

Joseph, Earl C.
Landsberg, Hans H.
Linnemann, Hans
Meadows, Donella H.
Paddock, William Carson
Rose, Charlie
Van Dam, Andre
Van Hulten, Michel
Woodward, Douglas

Battelle Memorial Institute
Centre for Policy Research (India)
Fundacion Javier Barros Sierra, A.C.
Futures Group, Inc.
Hudson Institute, Inc.
International Institute for Applied Systems Analysis
National Research Council of Canada
Osterreichisches Institut fur Wirtschaftsforschung
School of Living
Stanford Research Institute, Center for the Study of Social Policy
U.S. Department of Agriculture, Economic Research Service

ANTHROPOLOGY

Harkins, Arthur Martin
King-Hele, Desmond George
Maruyama, Magoroh
Platt, John
Sorensen, Arne
Textor, Robert Bayard
Wescott, Roger Williams
Widmaier, Hans Peter

Werner-Reimers-Stiftung

APPROPRIATE TECHNOLOGY

Bookchin, Murray
Brand, Stewart
Chaplain, Roland
Christakis, Alexander N.
Cordell, Arthur Jason
Curtis, Richard Kenneth
Elgin, Duane S.
Ellis, William N.
Henderson, Hazel
Hess, Karl
Illich, Ivan
Imsland, Donald Orlene
Jones, Peter Michael Seaton
Kapur, Jagdish Chandra
Livingston, Dennis
Lovins, Amory B.
Mallmann, Carlos Alberto
Marstrand, Pauline Kendrick
Mason, Roy E.
Meadows, Dennis Lynn
Mitchell, Arnold
Parsons, Jack
Pritchard, Colin Leonard

Rothgaenger, Klaus
Roy, Robin
Ruzic, Neil Price
Ryan, Robert Dole
Schwartz, Peter
Sjoerdsma, Andre C.
Skolimowski, Henryk
Tebicke, Haile Lul
Teige, Peter J.
Thring, Meredith Woolridge

*Centre International de Recherche sur
l'Environnement et le Developpement*
Findhorn Foundation
Futures Studies Centre (United Kingdom)
Gamma Group
Japan Techno-Economics Society
Northwest Regional Foundation
Open University, Design Group
*Organization for Economic Cooperation
and Development (OECD)*
School of Living
Wakefield Washington Associates, Inc.
Worldwatch Institute

ARCHITECTURE

Dernoi, Louis Antoine
Ewald, William Rudolph
Fondersmith, John
Friedman, Yona
Fuller, R. Buckminster
Hottovy, Tibor C.
Madeira, Thomas Roberts
Mason, Roy E.
Meier, Richard L.
Nicholson, Simon
Pressman, Norman E.P.
Rothgaenger, Klaus

Future Options Room
Institute for Social Engineering, Inc.
International Creative Center
*Systemplan e.V. Institut fur
Umweltforschung und
Entwicklungsplannung*

ARMS CONTROL

Brennan, Donald George
Elmandjra, Mahdi
Feld, Bernard T.
Kennett (Lord)
Lindsey, George Roy
Lovins, Amory B.
Mushkat, Mari'on
Myrdal, Alva Reimer
Phelps, John Bedford
Roy, Robin
Solem, Erik
Taylor, Theodore B.

*Centrum voor Vraagstukken van
Wetenschap en Samenleving*

*Cornell University Program on Science,
Technology, and Society*
*George Washington University Program of
Policy Studies in Science and
Technology*
Institute for Policy Studies
International Institute for Strategic Studies
*Pugwash Conference on Science and World
Affairs*
*Youth Movement for a New International
Order*

ARTS AND ENTERTAINMENT

Berry, David John
Brown, Seyom
Davidowitz, Moshe
Edwards, Gregg
Empain, Louis
Hubbard, Barbara Marx
Jaccai, August T., Jr.
Jones, J. Christopher
Konetchy, Ronald Dean
Kostelanetz, Richard
Landau, Erika
Mandel, Thomas Frederick
Mason, Roy E.
Nicholson, Simon
Rittenbush, Philip C.
Silvio, Ceccato
Young, David Leslie

Balai Seni Toyabungkah
Goals for the Greater Akron Area
International Creative Center
Open University, Oxford Research Unit
Quantum Science Corporation
Square One Management, Ltd.
World Future Society

ASIA

Overholt, William Henry
Smil, Vaclav
Textor, Robert Bayard
Van Dam, Andre

Business International Corporation
*Institut Technique de Prevision
Economique et Sociale*
Japan Economic Research Center
*United Nations Asian and Pacific
Development Institute*
*United Nations Educational, Scientific and
Cultural Organization (UNESCO)*
*United Nations Institute for Training and
Research (UNITAR)*

ASTRONOMY

Berry, Adrian M.
O'Neill, Gerard Kitchen
Wilson, Albert George

ATOMIC ENERGY

Feld, Bernard T.
Fuchs, Georg
Graul, Emil Heinz
Jungk, Robert
Kade, Gerhard Paul
Lindsey, George Roy
Mallmann, Carlos Alberto
Parry, Renee-Marie Croose
Sabato, Jorge Alberto
Seaborg, Glenn Theodore
Solem, Erik
Surrey, Arthur John
Taylor, Theodore B.
Vanston, John H., Jr.

Battelle Memorial Institute
*Centrum voor Vraagstukken van
  Wetenschap en Samenleving*
*Cornell University Program on Science,
  Technology, and Society*
Decisions and Designs, Inc.
Movement for a New Society
Resources for the Future

AUSTRALIA

Drouin, Marie-Josee
Fabun, Don
Young, David Leslie

Hudson Institute, Inc.

AUTOMATION AND ROBOTICS

Asimov, Isaac
Bright, James R.
Diebold, John
Fuller, R. Buckminster
Hoos, Ida Russakoff
Kaya, Yoichi
Michael, Donald Nelson
Polak, Fred L.
Tonchev, Liuben Alexiev

*Bureau d'Informations et de Previsions
  Economiques*
Diebold Group, Inc.
*Stanford Research Institute, Business
  Intelligence Program*

BANKING AND FINANCE

Amara, Roy
Armer, Paul
Becker, Harold S.
Boucher, Wayne I.
Brown, Arnold
Calvert, Geoffrey Neil
Enzer, Selwyn
Feather, Frank
Fritsch, Bruno
Godoy, Horacio Hermes
Kraegel, Wilfred A.
Martel, Leon Charles
Mendel, Jay Stanley

Olivera, Julio H.G.
Robertson, James Hugh
Saint-Geours, Jean
Secomski, Kazimierz
Selan, Valerio
Shoniker, Robert George
Thompson, Gordon Bruce

Battelle Institut e.V.
Business International Corporation
Cambridge Research Institute, Inc.
Future Options Room
Institute for Policy Studies
*National Institute for Research
  Advancement*
Public Policy Research Organization
Quantum Science Corporation
Simulation and Gaming Association
*Stanford Research Institute, Business
  Intelligence Program*

BEHAVIORAL SCIENCES

Bennis, Warren
Calhoun, John Bumpass
Francoeur, Robert Thomas
Lippitt, Gordon L.
Loye, David
Martino, Joseph P.
Nosal, Czeslaw S.
Skinner, B.F.
Tarter, Donald Edward

Battelle Memorial Institute
Harris International
*Institute for Society, Ethics and the Life
  Sciences—Hastings Center*
MPI International, Inc.
*National Science Foundation, Research
  Applications Directorate*
World Man

BIOLOGY

Asimov, Isaac
Bender, Allan Douglas
Bonner, James
Dubos, Rene
Francoeur, Robert Thomas
Ghosh, Samir Kumar
Gorney, Roderic
King-Hele, Desmond George
Malek, Ivan
Meadows, Donella H.
Odum, Howard Thomas
Proske, Ruediger K.A.
Ritterbush, Philip C.
Rosenfeld, Albert
Ruzic, Neil Price
Salk, Jonas
Somit, Albert
Taylor, Gordon Rattray

Battelle Memorial Institute
*Cornell University Program on Science,
  Technology, and Society*

Forrester, Jay Wright
Gappert, Gary M.
Hall, Peter Geoffrey
Imsland, Donald Orlene
Keller, Suzanne
Kozmetsky, George
Mason, Roy E.
Meier, Richard L.
Schumacher, Dieter
Vester, Frederic
Wilson, Donald N.

Academy for Contemporary Problems
Committee for Economic Development
Delegation a l'Amenagement du Territoire
  et a l'Action Regionale
Delft University of Technology
Forecasting International, Ltd.
Futures-Invention Associates
Institute for Canadian Futures
Institute on Man and Science
Institute for Social Engineering, Inc.
Massachusetts Institute of Technology,
  System Dynamics Group
Midwest Research Institute
National Institute for Research
  Advancement
Public Policy Research Organization
Rand Corporation
Resources for the Future
Sociocyberneering, Inc.
Square One Management, Ltd.
Stanford Research Institute, Center for the
  Study of Social Policy
Systeme d'Etudes du Schema General
  d'Amenagement de la France (SESAME)
Systemplan e.V. Institut fur
  Umweltforschung und Entwicklungs-
  plannung
United Nations Educational, Scientific and
  Cultural Organization (UNESCO)
Utah State Planning Coordinator's Office
Werner-Reimers-Stiftung

CLIMATE

Amara, Roy
Bean, Louis H.
Chaplain, Roland
Cleveland, Harlan
Kapur, Jagdrish Chandra
Meier, Richard L.
Rosen, Stephen
Spilhaus, Athelstan

Decisions and Designs, Inc.
International Council of Scientific Unions
International Federation of Institutes for
  Advanced Study

COMMUNICATIONS

Barrett, Francis Dermot
Berry, David John
Bowers, Raymond

Bradley, Helen Genevieve
Brown, Arnold
Cassierer, Henry Reinhard
Chase, Stuart
Cooper, Donald R.
Curtis, Richard Kenneth
Darling, Charles M. III
Dator, James Allen
Day, Lawrence Harvey
Friedman, Yona
Hellman, Hal
Lenz, Ralph C., Jr.
Lipinski, Andrew J.
Loveridge, Denis John
McLuhan, Herbert Marshall
Meier, Richard L.
Michael, Donald Nelson
Miller, Lewis
Moles, Abraham A.
Nicholson, Simon
Nyheim, Jan Henrik
Ogden, Frank
Pessolano, F. John
Pool, Ithiel de Sola
Rosen, Stephen
Silvio, Ceccato
Simmons, William W.
Sirkin, Abraham Meyer
Skoe, Anders S.
Socias, Juan
Szalai, Alexander
Theobald, Robert
Thompson, Gordon Bruce
Turoff, Murray
Wakefield, Rowan Albert
Ward, Jonathan
Wellesley-Wesley, James Frank

Applied Futures, Inc.
Arab League Educational, Cultural and
  Scientific Organization
Association Internationale Futuribles
Center for Integrative Studies
Committee for the Future
Committee for Future Oriented Research
  (Sweden)
Congressional Clearinghouse on the Future
Cornell University Program on Science,
  Technology, and Society
Dayton, University of, Research Institute
Delphi Communications Group
Department of Science and Technology
  (India)
Federal Aviation Administration
Fondation Internationale de l'Innovation
  Sociale
Forecasting International, Ltd.
Forum for the Advancement of Students in
  Science and Technology, Inc.
George Washington University Program of
  Policy Studies in Science and
  Technology

Infomedia Corporation

Dator, James Allen
Dixon, John
Duhl, Leonard J.
Duncan, James Francis
Dunstan, Mary Jane
Emery, Frederick Edmund
Ewald, William Rudolph
Harkins, Arthur Martin
Henderson, Hazel
Hoffman, John David
Holthusen, T. Lance
Jaccai, August T., Jr.
Jungk, Robert
Lamson, Robert Warren
Lindaman, Edward B.
Mische, Gerald F.
Molitor, Graham Thomas Tate
Nightingale, Donald Victor
Paige, Glenn Durland
Ritterbush, Philip C.
Stokes, Bruce Edward
Theobald, Robert
Toffler, Alvin
Umpleby, Stuart A.
Vickers, Charles Geoffrey
Ziegler, Warren Leigh

American Council of Life Insurance,
Trend Analysis Program
Association Internationale Futuribles
Center for Future Management
Center for the Study of Democratic
Institutions
Commission for the Future (New Zealand)
Commission on the Year 2000 (Hawaii)
Congressional Clearinghouse on the Future
Creighton, James L.
D'Amore, L. J., and Associates, Ltd.
Futures Invention Associates
Goals for Dallas
Goals for the Greater Akron Area
Idaho's Tomorrow
Illinois 2000 Foundation
Institute for Alternative Futures
Institute for Applied Systems Analysis and
Prognosis
Japan Techno-Economics Society
Kenilworth Institute
Mississippi 1990
Movement for a New Society
Northwest Regional Foundation
Open University, Design Group
Open University, Oxford Research Unit
Policy Studies Institute (U.K.)
Russell Sage Foundation
Sussex, University of, Science Policy
Research Unit
Youth Movement for a New International
Order

DEMOGRAPHY

Calvert, Geoffrey Neil

Coates, Joseph F.
Johnston, Denis F.
Kraegel, Wilfred A.
Mackensen, Rainer Ulrich
McHale, Magda Cordell
McLean, John Michael
Meadows, Donella H.
Sheldon, Eleanor Bernert
Spengler, Joseph John
Textor, Robert Bayard

Center for Integrative Studies
Institute for Applied Systems Analysis and
Prognosis
Institute for Research on Public Policy
National Planning Association
Policy Studies Institute (U.K.)
Polish Academy of Sciences—"Poland
2000"
Sociaal en Cultureel Planbureau
Social Impact Assessment Network
Social Science Research Council, Center
for Coordination of Research on Social
Indicators
St. Galler Zentrum fur Zukunftsforschung
United Nations Department of Economic
and Social Affairs, Population Division
United Nations Educational, Scientific and
Cultural Organization (UNESCO)
USSR Academy of Sciences, Institute for
Sociological Research
Utah State Planning Coordinator's Office
Worldwatch Institute

DEVELOPING NATIONS

Apostol, Pavel A.
Arvay, Stephen
Backstrand, Goran Karl
Bell, Wendell
Borgese, Elisabeth Mann
Carleton, Thomas James
Choucri, Nazli
Cole, Hugh Samuel David
Darling, Charles M. III
De, Nitish R.
Dedijer, Stevan
Dubach, Paul
Feld, Bernard T.
Freeman, Orville Lothrop
Fritsch, Bruno
Ghabbour, Samir Ibrahim
Ghosh, Samir Kumar
Grinberg, Miguel
Harmon, David P., Jr.
Herrera, Amilcar Oscar
Iyengar, Madhur Srinivas
Kapur, Jagdish Chandra
Knoppers, Antonie T.
Kristensen, Thorkil
Lagos, Gustavo
Lambo, Thomas Adeoye
Leach, Gerald Adrian
Lesourne, Jacques Francois

Linnemann, Hans
Livingston, Dennis
Mallmann, Carlos Alberto
Mayur, Rashmi
Meier, Richard L.
Mische, Gerald F.
Mische, Patricia Mary Schmitt
Muskat, Mari'on
Nerfin, Marc Paul
Olivera, Julio H.G.
Overholt, William Henry
Paddock, William Carson
Parsons, Jack
Raksasataya, Amara
Sabato, Jorge Alberto
Schumacher, Dieter
Sine, Thomas William
Sirkin, Abraham Meyer
Smil, Vaclav
Stoeber, Gerhard J.
Taylor, Theodore B.
Thapar, Romesh
Van Dam, Andre
Van Hulten, Michel
Ward, Barbara
Waterlow, Charlotte Mary

Academy for Educational Development, Inc.
Bureau d'Informations et de Previsions Economiques
Centre International de Recherche sur l'Environment et le Developpement
Fondation Europeenne de la Culture
Foundation Reshaping the International Order
Institut fur Weltwirtschaft
Institut Technique de Prevision Economique et Sociale
Institute for Policy Studies
International Federation of Institutes for Advanced Study
Israeli Institute for the Study of International Affairs
Iyengar, M.S., and Associates, Ltd.
Organization for Economic Cooperation and Development (OECD)
Overseas Development Council
Systemplan e. V., Institut fur Umweltforschung und Entwicklungsplannung
United Nations Asian and Pacific Development Institute
United Nations Educational, Scientific and Cultural Organization (UNESCO)
United Nations Institute for Training and Research (UNITAR)
Wakefield Washington Associates, Inc.
World Future Studies Federation
World Institute Council
Youth Movement for a New International Order

DOCUMENTATION

Clarke, Ian Frederick
Dickson, Paul Andrew
Fondersmith, John
Guy, Cynthia B.
Hamil, Ralph Edward
Jones, Martin V.
Judge, Anthony John
Kocher, Gerhard
Marien, Michael David
McHale, Magda Cordell
Meadows, Dennis Lynn
Schwarz, Stephan
Wellesley-Wesley, James Frank

Applied Futures, Inc.
Arab League Educational, Cultural and Scientific Organization
Association Internationale Futuribles
Battelle Geneva Research Centre
Brookings Institution
California State Department of Education
Congressional Research Service
Contracultura Center
Danish Committee on Futures Studies
Educational Futures Projects
Forsvarets Forskningsanstalt
Futuremics, Inc.
Gesellschaft fur Zukunftsfragen, e.V.
Information for Policy Design
Institute for Research on Public Policy
Institute for 21st Century Business
International Graduate School of Education
International Institute for Strategic Studies
Kommunikationszentrum for Zukunfts-und Friedensforschung in Hannover GmbH
Mankind 2000
National Institute for Research Advancement
National Research Council of Canada
Policy Studies Organization
Predicasts, Inc.
Square One Management, Ltd.
Union of International Associations
United Nations Educational, Scientific and Cultural Organization (UNESCO)
World Future Society
World Problems Project

DRUGS

Ogden, Frank
Weaver, John Jacob

Battelle Memorial Institute
Centre de Recherche sur le Bien-etre
Episcopal Diocese of California
Wickert Institut Tubingen

EARTH SCIENCES

Brown, Harrison Scott
Jones, Martin V.
Vanston, John H., Jr.

680

National Research Council of Canada
Society for the Investigation of Recurring
  Events

ECONOMICS

Acquaviva, Sabino
Adler-Karlsson, Gunner
Aujac, Henri
Ayres, Robert Underwood
Barach, Arnold B.
Baworowski, Ludwik Jerzy
Bean, Louis H.
Beckwith, Burnham Putnam
Borgese, Elisabeth Mann
Boulding, Kenneth Ewart
Brown, Harrison Scott
Bruckmann, Gerhart D.
Calvert, Geoffrey Neil
Cazes, Bernard
Cepede, Michel
Chaplin, George
Chase, Stuart
Clawson, Marion
Cole, Hugh Samuel David
Cornish, Edward Seymour
De Jouvenel, Bertrand
Delors, Jacques Lucien Jean
Drobnick, Richard Lee
Drouin, Marie-Josee
Elmandjra, Mahdi
Essig, Francois Bernard
Fisher, Joseph Lyman
Fontela, Emilio
Fourastie, Jean Joseph
Francois, Charles Oscar
Freeman, Christopher
Freeman, Orville Lothrop
Fritsch, Bruno
Gabus, Andre M.W.
Gappert, Gary M.
Gershuny, Jonathan Israel
Gidai, Erzsebet
Hanappe, Paul
Harmon, David P., Jr.
Heilbroner, Robert L.
Henderson, Hazel
Hetman, Francois
Hitch, Charles Johnston
Horhager, Axel
Jones, Thomas Evan
Kade, Gerhard Paul
Kahn, Herman
Kanamori, Hisao
Kovacs, Geza
Kristensen, Thorkil
Lamontagne, Maurice
Laszlo, Ervin
Lesh, Donald R.
Lesourne, Jacques Francois
Linnemann, Hans
Meadows, Dennis Lynn

Mesthene, Emmanuel G.
Michaelis, Michael
Miles, Ian Douglas
Moneta, Carlos J.
Mushkat, Mari'on
Myrdal, Gunnar
Okita, Saburo
Olivera, Julio H.G.
Overholt, William Henry
Page, Talbot
Phelps, John Bedford
Rogge, Peter G.
Saint-Geours, Jean
Salomon, Jean-Jacques
Schaff, Adam
Secomski, Kazimierz
Skoe, Anders S.
Spengler, Joseph John
Surrey, Arthur John
Thapar, Romesh
Theobald, Robert
Tinbergen, Jan
Wagenfuhr, Horst
Watt, Kenneth E. Ferguson
Wickert, Gunther
Widmaier, Hans Peter
Winiecki, Jan Stanislaw
Witt-Hansen, Johannes

Academy for Contemporary Problems
American Enterprise Institute for Public
  Policy Research
Association Internationale Futuribles
Battelle Geneva Research Centre
Battelle Institute e.V.
Battelle Memorial Institute
Brookings Institution
Bureau d'Informations et de Previsions
  Economiques
Business International Corporation
Central Planning Bureau (Netherlands)
Centre de Recherche sur le Bien-etre
Club of Rome
Commissariat General du Plan
Commission for the Future (New Zealand)
Commission on the Year 2000 (Hawaii)
Committee for Economic Development
Conference Board
Congressional Research Service
Delegation a l'Amenagement du Territoire
  et a l'Action Regionale
Fondation Europeenne de la Culture
Forecasting International, Ltd.
Forsvarets Forskningsanstalt
Foundation Reshaping the International
  Order
Fundacion Argentina Ano 2000
Future Options Room
Future Systems
Futures-Invention Associates
Hazan International
Hudson Institute, Inc.

Kauffman, Draper Laurence, Jr.
Kaufmann, Felix
Kettle, John
Kovacs, Geza
Lindaman, Edward B.
Livingston, Dennis
Maston, Robert E.
Purdy, Judson Douglas
Quistwater, Jack Raimond
Roemer, Kenneth Morrison
Ryan, Robert Dale
Shane, Harold Gray
Snyder, David Pearce
Suchodolski, Bogdan
Toffler, Alvin
Weaver, Roy A.
Wilson, Donna
Wilson, Ian H.
Ziegler, Warren Leigh

Akron, University of, Institute for Future Studies and Research
DCM Associates
Department of Science and Technology (India)
Educational Futures Projects
Future Systems
Institut fur Zukunftsforschung (Berlin)
Institut Technique de Prevision Economique et Sociale
Institute for Alternative Futures
Institute for 21st Century Business
International Graduate School of Education
Kenilworth Institute
National Council for the Social Studies, Special Interest Group in Future Studies
Open University, Design Group
Osrodek Badan Prognostycznych
Planning Dynamics, Inc.
Square One Management, Ltd.
World Future Studies Federation

EDUCATION (Multi-Level)

Apostol, Pavel A.
Barker, Joel A.
Berman, Louise M.
Botkin, James W.
Bundy, Robert Franklin
Cassierer, Henry Reinhard
Cornish, Sally Woodhull
Crealock, Carol Marie
De Jouvenel, Hugues Alain
Delors, Jacques Lucine Jean
Didsbury, Howard Francis, Jr.
Dunstan, Mary Jane
Elboim-Dror, Rachel
Elmandjra, Mahdi
Eurich, Alvin C.
Fuller, R. Buckminster
Glines, Don E.
Green, Thomas F.

Illich, Ivan
Janne, Henri Gustave
Johansen, Robert R.
King, Alexander
Lecht, Leonard A.
Marien, Michael David
Markley, O.W.
Maston, Robert E.
McLuhan, Herbert Marshall
Mensanch, Rosa Mensanch
Michael, Donald Nelson
Mische, Patricia Mary Schmitt
Nosal, Czeslaw S.
Ozmon, Howard
Polak, Fred L.
Schwartz, Bertrand
Seth, Satish Chandra
Shane, Harold Gray
Silvernail, David Lee
Sine, Thomas William
Stevenson, Hugh Alexander
Toffler, Alvin
Wagschal, Peter
Wakefield, Rowan Albert
Weingarten, Charles

Academy for Educational Development, Inc.
Academy of World Studies
Arab League Educational, Cultural and Scientific Organization
Brookings Institution
California, University of, at Los Angeles (UCLA), PSAF Program
California State Department of Education
Center for Policy Research
Club of Rome
College Board
Educational Futures Projects
Episcopal Diocese of California
Fondation Europeenne de la Culture
Forum for the Advancement of Students in Science and Technology, Inc.
Fundacion Javier Barros Sierra, A.C.
Future Options Room
Goals for the Greater Akron Area
INSEAD (European Institute of Business Administration)
Institute for Applied Systems Analysis and Prognosis
Institute on Man and Science
Instituttet for Fremtidsforskning
International Creative Center
International Graduate School of Education
Mankind 2000
New York Center for World Game Studies, Inc.
ORI, Inc.
Overseas Development Council
Polish Academy of Sciences—"Poland 2000"
Research for Better Schools, Inc.

Daly, Herman E.
Durie, Robert Wesley
Feinberg, Gerald
Feld, Bernard T.
Francis, John Michael
Gordon, Theodore Jay
Hamil, Ralph Edward
Hellman, Hal
Hitch, Charles Johnston
Hoos, Ida Russakoff
Illich, Ivan
Jones, Martin V.
Jones, Peter Michael Seaton
Kade, Gerhard Paul
Kapur, Jagdish Chandra
Landsberg, Hans H.
Leach, Gerald Adrian
Loveridge, Denis John
Lovins, Amory B.
Mandel, Thomas Frederick
Mason, Roy E.
Meadows, Dennis Lynn
Odum, Howard Thomas
O'Toole, James Joseph
Parry, Renee-Marie Croose
Pritchard, Colin Leonard
Proske, Ruediger K.A.
Rothgaenger, Klaus
Seaborg, Glenn Theodore
Sjoerdsma, Andre C.
Smil, Vaclav
Solem, Erik
Steffes, Dale William
Surrey, Arthur John
Swager, William Leon
Taylor, Theodore B.
Tebicke, Haile Lul
Teige, Peter J.
Thring, Meredith Woolridge
Tugwell, Franklin
Vanston, John H., Jr.
Wagschal, Peter H.
Waskow, Arthur I.
Watt, Kenneth E. Ferguson
Wickert, Gunther
Wilson, Donald N.

Academy for Contemporary Problems
Battelle Institut e.V.
Battelle Memorial Institute
Center for Strategic and International Studies
Centre International de Recherche sur l'Environnement et le Developpement
Centrum for Tvarvetenskapliga Studier av Manniskans Villkor
Centrum voor Vraagstukken van Wetenschap en Samenleving
Club of Rome
Committee for Economic Development
Dayton, University of, Research Institute
Decisions and Designs, Inc.

Department of Science and Technology (India)
Edinburgh, University of, Centre for Human Ecology
Electrical Research Association, Ltd.
Forecasting International, Ltd.
Formedlingscentralen for Framtidsstudier AB
Fundacion Bariloche
Future Options Room
Futures Group, Inc.
George Washington University Program of Policy Studies in Science and Technology
Gesellschaft fur Zukunftsfragen, e.V.
Hudson Institute, Inc.
Indian Institute of Technology
Institut fur Zukunftsforschung (Berlin)
Institute for Alternative Futures
Institute for Applied Systems Analysis and Prognosis
Institute for Research on Public Policy
Interdisciplinary Systems Group
International Federation of Institutes for Advanced Study
International Institute for Applied Systems Analysis
Israeli Institute for the Study of International Affairs
Iyengar, M.S., and Associates, Ltd.
Japan Economic Research Center
Korea Institute of Science and Technology
Laboratoire de Prospective Appliquee
Midwest Research Institute
National Planning Association
National Research Council of Canada
National Science Foundation, Research Applications Directorate
New York Center for World Game Studies, Inc.
Organization for Economic Cooperation and Development (OECD)
ORI, Inc.
Osterreichische Akademie der Wissenschaften, Institut fur Sozio-okonomische Entwicklungsforschung
Osterreichisches Institut fur Wirtschaftsforschung
Overseas Development Council
Planning and Forecasting Consultants
Planning Dynamics, Inc.
Predicasts, Inc.
Rand Corporation
Research Program on Technology and Public Policy
Resources for the Future
Science Council of Canada
Secretariat for Futures Studies (Canada)
Selskapet for Fremtidsstudier
Sociocyberneering, Inc.
Southern California, University of, Center for Futures Research

Stanford Research Institute, Center for the
  Study of Social Policy
Taloudellinen Suunnittelukeskus
United Nations Institute for Training and
  Research (UNITAR)
United States Congress, Office of
  Technology Assessment
Wakefield Washington Associates, Inc.
Williams, Charles W., Inc.
World Future Society
World Problems Project
Worldwatch Institute
Youth Movement for a New International
  Order

ENGINEERING

Fuller, R. Buckminster
Gerken, William, Jr.
Pritchard, Colin Leonard
Thring, Meredith Woolridge

Battelle Institut e.V.
Battelle Memorial Institute
National Research Council of Canada
National Science Foundation, Research
  Applications Directorate
Rand Corporation
Stichting Toekomstbeeld der Techniek

ENVIRONMENTAL ASSESSMENT

Altenpohl, Dieter G.
Antoine, Serge
Ayres, Robert Underwood
Bookchin, Murray
Bossell, Harmut H.
Brown, Arnold
Calder, Nigel
Calhoun, John Bumpass
Chaplain, Roland
Chen, Kan
Coates, Vary T.
Cook, Earl
Cordell, Arthur Jason
Culver, John C.
Dubos, Rene
Durie, Robert Wesley
Eckholm, Erik P.
Elgin, Duane S.
Ewald, William Rudolph
Feather, Frank
Feinberg, Gerald
Fisher, Joseph Lyman
Gerba, John
Ghabbour, Samir Ibrahim
Gilfillan, S. Colum
Goldsmith, Edward Rene
Graul, Emil Heinz
Hamil, Ralph Edward
Hardin, Garrett
Hayashi, Yujira
Horhager, Axel
Ingelstam, Lars E.

Jupp, George Alexander
Kade, Gerhard Paul
Kane, Julius
Kassas, Mohamed A.F.
Kauffman, Draper Laurence, Jr.
Lamson, Robert Warren
Lesh, Donald R.
Marstrand, Pauline Kendrick
Meadows, Donella H.
Meier, Richard L.
Mesarovic, Mihajlo D.
Molitor, Graham Thomas Tate
Morris, Geoffrey Keith
Odum, Howard Thomas
Page, Talbot
Parsons, Jack
Peterson, Russell Wilbur
Poquet, Guy Rene
Pyke, Donald L.
Raksasataya, Amara
Ritterbush, Philip C.
Rothgaenger, Klaus
Ruzic, Neil Price
Schwartz, Peter
Seaborg, Glenn Theodore
Simmonds, Walter H.C.
Skolimowski, Henryk
Smil, Vaclav
Swager, William Leon
Vester, Frederic
Weaver, John Jacob
Webber, James B.
Wilson, Albert George
Witt-Hansen, Johannes

Arab League Educational, Cultural and
  Scientific Organization
Battelle Memorial Institute
California Tomorrow
Cambridge Research Institute, Ind.
Centre Internationale de Recherche sur
  l'Environnement et le Developpement
Centrum voor Vraagstukken van
  Wetenschap en Samenleving
Commission on the Year 2000 (Hawaii)
Contracultura Center
Cornell University Program on Science,
  Technology, and Society
D'Amore, L. J., and Associates, Ltd.
Edinburgh, University of, Centre for
  Human Ecology
Fondation Europeenne de la Culture
Fundacion Bariloche
Futures-Invention Associates
Hungarian Academy of Science,
  Presidential Committee on the Social
  Impact of Science and Technology
Indian Institute of Technology
Institut fur Zukunftsforschung (Berlin)
Institute for Applied Systems Analysis and
  Prognosis
Institute for the Future
Institute on Man and Science

Institute for the Study of the Human Future, Inc.
Interdisciplinary Systems Group
International Council of Scientific Unions
International Institute for Applied Systems Analysis
Japan Techno-Economics Society
Korea Institute of Science and Technology
National Institute for Research Advancement
National Research Council of Canada
National Science Foundation, Research Applications Directorate
Nucleo Rolanroc
Open University, Oxford Research Unit
ORI, Inc.
Policy Studies Institute (U.K.)
Policy Studies Organization
Resources for the Future
Social Impact Assessment Network
Stanford Research Institute, Center for the Study of Social Policy
Systemplan e.V., Institut fur Umweltforschung und Entwicklungsplannung
Wissenschaftszentrum Berlin
Worldwatch Institute

EUROPE

Auerbach, Philip Hone
Barach, Arnold B.
Bouladon, Gabriel Antoine
Clark, John Albert
Cleveland, Harlan
Cole, Hugh Samuel David
Dauman, Jan Victor
De Jouvenel, Bertrand
De Jouvenel, Hugues Alain
Fontela, Emilio
Gori, Umberto
Hake, Barry John
Hall, Peter Geoffrey
Hetman, Francois
Kennet (Lord)
Lambert-Lamond, Georges M.
Mackensen, Rainer Ulrich
Mihanovich, Clement Simon
Poquet, Guy Rene
Scardigli, Victor
Stoeber, Gerhard J.
Van Hulten, Michel
Von Laue, Theodore H.
Widmaier, Hans Peter

Association Internationale Futuribles
Battelle, Geneva Research Centre
Business International Corporation
Central Planning Bureau (Netherlands)
Club de Amigos de la Futurologia
Fondation Claude Nicolas Ledoux
Fondation Europeene de la Culture
Hazan International

INSEAD (European Institute of Business Administration)
Institut fur Zukunftsforschung (Berlin)
Instituttet for Fremtidsforskning
Policy Studies Institute
Prognos AG, European Center for Applied Economic Research
Science Policy Foundation
Stichting Toekomstbeeld der Techniek
Systemplan e.V. Institut fur Umweltforschung und Entwicklungsplannung
Youth Movement for a New International Order

FAMILY

Best, Fred Joseph
Bestuzhev-Lada, Igor Vassilevich
Cornish, Sally Woodhull
Edwards, Gregg
Ghosh, Samir Kumar
Keller, Suzanne
Mihanovich, Clement Simon
Mische, Patricia Mary Schmitt
Myrdal, Alva Reimer
Sethi, Brij Bhushan
Sheldon, Eleanor Bernert
Snyder, David Pearce
Stokes, Bruce Edward
Wakefield, Rowan Albert

Policy Studies Institute (U.K.)
Polish Academy of Sciences—"Poland 2000"
Prospective, International Center of Research and Communication
United Nations Department of Economic and Social Affairs, Population Division
Wakefield Washington Associates, Inc.
World Future Society

FOOD

Brown, Lester R.
Calvert, Geoffrey Neil
Cepede, Michel
Clark, John Albert
Darrow, R. Morton
Drobnick, Richard Lee
Eckholm, Erik P.
Enzer, Selwyn
Freeman, Orville Lothrop
Harmon, David P., Jr.
Hellman, Hal
Iyengar, Madhur Srinivas
Kristensen, Thorkil
Leach, Gerald Adrian
Linnemann, Hans
Malek, Ivan
Marstrand, Pauline Kendrick
McLean, John Michael
Meadows, Donella H.
Mesarovic, Mihajlo D.

Mische, Gerald F.
Mische, Patricia Mary Schmitt
Molitor, Graham Thomas Tate
Okita, Saburo
Paddock, William Carson
Poquet, Guy Rene
Pritchard, Colin Leonard
Roy, Robin
Shoniker, Robert George
Thiemann, Hugo Ernst
Wikstrom, Solveig Ragnborg

Battelle Memorial Institute
Centre for Policy Research (India)
Club of Rome
Formedlingscentralen for Framtidsstudier
  AB
Fundacion Argentina Ano 2000
Hudson Institute, Inc.
Indian Institute of Technology
Institute for Policy Studies
International Institute for Applied Systems
  Analysis
Iyengar, M.S., and Associates, Ltd.
Massachusetts Institute of Technology,
  System Dynamics Group
Movement for a New Society
National Research Council of Canada
Organization for Economic Cooperation
  and Development (OECD)
Science Council of Canada
United States Congress, Office of
  Technology Assessment
U.S. Department of Agriculture, Economic
  Research Service
World Future Society
World Problems Project
Worldwatch Institute
Youth Movement for a New International
  Order

FORESTRY

Clawson, Marion
De Jouvenel, Bertrand
Eckholm, Erik P.
Fisher, Joseph Lyman

National Research Council of Canada
Stichting Toekomstbeeld der Techniek

FUTURE STUDIES METHODOLOGY

Adelson, Marvin
Aldridge, Alexandra
Amara, Roy
Arnstein, Sherry Phyllis
Asimov, Isaac
Auerbach, Lewis E.
Auerbach, Philip Hone
Backstrand, Goran Karl
Barach, Arnold B.
Barker, Joel A.
Baworowski, Ludwik Jerzy
Becker, Harold S.

Bestuzhev-Lada, Igor Vassilevich
Block, A. Eskil
Bonner, James
Bossell, Harmut H.
Botez, Mihai C.
Boucher, Wayne I.
Boulding, Elise
Bruckmann, Gerhart D.
Buckholz, Hans
Calvert, Geoffrey Neil
Carleton, Thomas James
Case, Fred E.
Cazes, Bernard
Cetron, Marvin Jerome
Chaplain, Roland
Cheatham, Anne Wilson
Chen, Kan
Choucri, Nazli
Christakis, Alexander N.
Coates, Joseph F.
Cole, Hugh Samuel David
Cooper, Donald R.
Cornish, Edward Seymour
Dalkey, Norman C.
Damlo, Penny Ann
Danecki, Jan
Dauman, Jan Victor
Davis, Richard C.
DeCoufle, Andre C.
Dede, Christopher James
De Jouvenel, Bertrand
De Jouvenel, Hugues Alain
Dernoi, Louis Antoine
Dickson, Paul Andrew
Dobrov, Gennady Mikhaylovich
Doyle, Frank
Drouin, Marie-Josee
Dubach, Paul
Duncan, James Francis
Dunstan, Mary Jane
Edwards, Gregg
El-Kholy, Ussama Amin
Elmandjra, Mahdi
Emery, Frederick Edmund
Encel, Solomon
Enzer, Selwyn
Essig, Francois Bernard
Feather, Frank
Flechtheim, Ossip K.
Fontela, Emilio
Fowles, Jib
Francois, Charles Oscar
Franks, Betty Barclay
Fritsch, Bruno
Gabus, Andre M.W.
Garaudy, Roger
Gerardin, Lucien A.
Gerba, John
Ghosh, Samir Kumar
Gidai, Erzsebet
Gilfillan, S. Colum

Williams, Charles W., Inc.
World Future Society
World Future Studies Federation
World Institute Council

GAMES

Bigelow, Bruce Edward
Carleton, Thomas James
Dalkey, Norman C.
Franks, Betty Barclay
Helmer, Olaf
Koelle, Heinz Hermann
Landau, Erika
Malitza, Mircea
Raiffa, Howard

New York Center for World Game Studies,
Inc.
Simulation and Gaming Association
Simulation in the Service of Society
Society for Computer Simulation

GENETICS

Bonner, James
Etzioni, Amitai W.
Francoeur, Robert Thomas

Center for Policy Research
Cornell University Program on Science,
Technology, and Society
Institute for Society, Ethics and the Life
Sciences—Hastings Center
Institute for the Study of the Human
Future, Inc.
United States Congress, Office of
Technology Assessment

GLOBAL MODELING

Ayres, Robert Underwood
Bossell, Harmuth H.
Bruckmann, Gerhart D.
Clark, John Albert
Cole, Hugh Samuel David
Falk, Richard Anderson
Forrester, Jay Wright
Fritsch, Bruno
Fuller, R. Buckminster
Gabus, Andre M.W.
Godoy, Horacio Hermes
Helmer, Olaf
Herrera, Amilcar Oscar
Janne, Henri Gustave
Judge, Anthony John
Kaya, Yoichi
Lagos, Gustavo
Mallmann, Carlos Alberto
Meadows, Dennis Lynn
Mendlovitz, Saul H.
Van Steenbergen, Bart
Watt, Kenneth E. Ferguson
Winiecki, Jan Stanislaw

Center for Integrative Studies

Club of Rome
Fundacion Bariloche
Gesellschaft fur Zukunftsfrage, e.V.
Hungarian Academy of Science,
Presidential Committee on the Social
Impact of Science and Technology
Institute for Applied Systems, Analysis
and Prognosis
Institute of Management Sciences
Institute for World Order, Inc.
Interdisciplinary Systems Group
Laboratoire de Prospective Appliquee
Massachusetts Institute of Technology,
System Dynamics Group
Predicasts, Inc.
Princeton Center for Alternative Futures,
Inc.
Sussex, University of, Science Policy
Research Unit
Worldwatch Institute

GLOBAL SURVIVAL MACROPROBLEM

Botkin, James W.
Bronwell, Arthur B.
Brown, Lester R.
Doyle, Frank
Falk, Richard Anderson
Fontela, Emilio
Gabus, Andre M.W.
Henderson, Hazel
Judge, Anthony John
King, Alexander
Lamontagne, Maurice
Lesh, Donald R.
Meadows, Dennis Lynn
Mendlovitz, Saul H.
Mesarovic, Mihajlo D.
Peccei, Aurelio
Streatfeild, Guy Frederick
Suchodolski, Bogdan
Von Laue, Theodore H.
Ward, Barbara
Waterlow, Charlotte Mary
Weizacker, Carl Friedrich Freiherr von
Wellesley-Wesley, James Frank
Woodward, Douglas

Academy of World Studies
Club de Amigos de la Futurologia
Club of Rome
Foundation Reshaping the International
Order
Fundacion Bariloche
Hudson Institute, Inc.
International Federation of Institutes for
Advanced Study
Mankind 2000
Massachusetts Institute of Technology,
System Dynamics Group
Movement for a New Society
Research Program on Technology and
Public Policy

Interdisciplinary Center for Technological Analysis and Forecasting
Interfuture
International Institute for Applied Systems Analysis
Mankind 2000
Midwest Research Institute
National Research Council of Canada
Northwest Regional Foundation
Open University, Oxford Research Unit
Rand Corporation
Science Council of Canada
Stellenbosch, University of, Unit for Futures Research
World Future Society
World Institute Council

HEALTH AND MEDICINE

Abt, Clark C.
Arnstein, Sherry Phyllis
Baier, Kurt E.
Bender, Allan Douglas
Bize, Rene
Bundy, Robert Franklin
Chacko, George K.
Dalkey, Norman C.
Doyle, Frank
Dubos, Rene
Duhl, Leonard J.
Eckholm, Erik P.
Esfandiary, F.M.
Fuchs, Georg
Gerardin, Lucien A.
Graul, Emil Heinz
Illich, Ivan
Joseph, Earl C.
Kane, Julius
Kaufmann, Felix
Kelty, Miriam Friedman
Kocher, Gerhard
Lambo, Thomas Adeoye
Lesse, Stanley
Malek, Ivan
Mitchell, Ferd H., Jr.
Parry, Renee-Marie Croose
Rosen, Stephen
Rosenfeld, Albert
Salk, Jonas
Thomson, Irene Taviss
Wakefield, Richard P.
Webber, James B.
Woodward, Douglas

Academy for Educational Development, Inc.
American Council of Life Insurance, Trend Analysis Program
Battelle Memorial Institute
Cambridge Research Institute, Inc.
Center for Policy Research
Committee for Future Oriented Research (Sweden)

Cornell University Program on Science, Technology, and Society
Delphi Communications Group
Department of Science and Technology (India)
Futures Group, Inc.
Goals for the Greater Akron Area
Institute for Alternative Futures
Institute for Research on Public Policy
Institute for Society, Ethics, and the Life Sciences—Hastings Center
Institute for Theological Encounter with Science and Technology
International Creative Center
Mankind 2000
National Research Council of Canada
National Science Foundation, Research Applications Directorate
Osterreichische Akademie der Wissenschaften, Institut fur Sozio-okonomische Entwicklungsforschung
Planning Dynamics, Inc.
Rand Corporation
Schweizerische Vereinigung fur Zukunftsforschung
Stanford Research Institute, Business Intelligence Program
Stichting Toekomstbeeld der Techniek
United States Congress, Office of Technology Assessment
World Future Society
World Man
World Problems Project
Worldwatch Institute

HISTORY

Bigelow, Bruce Edward
Clarke, Ian Frederick
Conger D. Stuart
Darrow, R. Morton
Didsbury, Howard Francis
Gilfillan, S. Colum
Heilbroner, Robert L.
Hopkins, Frank Snowden
Illich, Ivan
Jones, Thomas Evan
Kennet (Lord)
Konetchy Ronald Dean
Polak, Fred L.
Purdy, Judson Douglas
Salomon, Jean-Jacques
Spengler, Joseph John
Stevenson, Hugh Alexander
Stulman, Julius
Taylor, Gordon Rattray
Thompson, William Irwin
Tinbergen, Jan
Von Laue, Theodore H.
Wagar, W. Warren
Waterlow, Charlotte Mary

Center for Integrative Studies

694

Janne, Henri Gustave
Jantsch, Erich
Johansen, Robert R.
Jones, Thomas Evan
Joseph, Earl C.
Judge, Anthony John
Jungk, Robert
Kapur, Jagdish Chandra
Kelty, Miriam Friedman
Klages, Helmut
Koelle, Heinz Hermann
Kojarov, Assen Todorov
Konetchy, Ronald Dean
Kozmetsky, George
Land, George Thomas Lock
Laszlo, Ervin
Lenk, Hans A.P.
Leonard, George B.
Lesh, Donald R.
Lesse, Stanley
Loveridge, Denis John
Loye, David
Mallmann, Carlos Alberto
Markley, O.W.
Maruyama, Magoroh
Masini, Eleonora Barbieri
McGraw, John G.
Mendlovitz, Saul H.
Mesthene, Emmanuel G.
Mihanovich, Clement Simon
Mische, Gerald F.
Mische, Patricia Mary Schmitt
Mitchell, Arnold
Mobley, Louis R.
Molitor, Graham Thomas Tate
M'Pherson, Philip Keith
Nilsson, Sam
Parry, Renee-Marie Croose
Peccei, Aurelio
Poquet, Guy Rene
Raksasataya, Amara
Rescher, Nicholas
Ritterbush, Philip C.
Rosenfeld, Albert
Salk, Jonas
Schaff, Adam
Schaller, Lyle Edwin
Schulze, Lothar Gunther
Schwarz, Stephan
Sicinski, Andrzej
Silvernail, David Lee
Silvio, Ceccato
Sine, Thomas William
Sirkin, Abraham Meyer
Skinner, B.F.
Skoe, Anders S.
Snyder, David Pearce
Sorensen, Arne
Spengler, Marie
Strzelecki, Jan Wladyslaw
Stulman, Julius

Suchodolski, Bogdan
Szalai, Alexander
Teige, Peter J.
Thapar, Romesh
Theobald, Robert
Thompson, William Irwin
Thomson, Irene Taviss
Toffler, Alvin
Vickers, Charles Geoffrey
Wagar, W. Warren
Wagschal, Peter H.
Wakefield, Richard P.
Ward, Barbara
Ward, Jonathan
Waterlow, Charlotte Mary
Weaver, John Jacob
Weaver, Roy A.
Weiner, Edith M.
Wellesley-Wesley, James Frank
Wilson, Albert George
Wilson, Ian H.
Witt-Hansen, Johannes
Wren-Lewis, John
Yankelovich, Daniel

Ad Hoc Interagency Committee on Futures Research
Association Internationale Futuribles
Associazione Teilhard de Chardin: Centro di Ricerca sul Futuro dell'Uomo
California, University of, at Los Angeles (UCLA) PSAF Program
Center for Future Management
Center for Integrative Studies
Center for Policy Research
Centre de Recherche sur le Bien-etre
Centrum voor Vraagstukken van Wetenschap en Samenleving
Club of Rome
Commission on the Year 2000 (Hawaii)
Creighton, James L.
Episcopal Diocese of California
Findhorn Foundation
Fondation Europeenne de la Culture
Futures Studies Centre (United Kingdom)
Institute for Applied Systems Analysis and Prognosis
Institute on Man and Science
Institute on Religion in an Age of Science
Institute for Society, Ethics and the Life Sciences—Hastings Center
Institute for the Study of the Human Future, Inc.
Institute for Theological Encounter with Science and Technology
Institute for World Order, Inc.
International Institute for Applied Systems Analysis
Laboratoire de Prospective Appliquee
Mankind 2000
New York Center for World Game Studies, Inc.
Northwest Regional Foundation

INFORMATION TECHNOLOGY

INNOVATION

Gueron, Georges
Hoffman, Ben B.
Kaufmann, Felix
Knoppers, Antonie T.
Lamontagne, Maurice
Land, George Thomas Lock
Lenz, Ralph C., Jr.
Mendell, Jay Stanley
Michaelis, Michael
Nilsson, Sam
Saint-Paul, Raymond Henri
Schaller, Lyle Edwin
Schumacher, Dieter
Schwartz, Bertrand
Simmonds, Walter H.C.
Stoeber, Gerhard J.
Thring, Meredith Woolridge

Abend Group
Harris International
*INSEAD (European Institute of Business
    Administration)*
National Research Council of Canada
*Schweizerische Vereinigung fur
    Zukunftsforschung*
*United States Congress, Office of
    Technology Assessment*

INTERNATIONAL RELATIONS

Adler-Karlsson, Gunnar
Apostol, Pavel A.
Backstrand, Goran Karl
Biderman, Albert D.
Borgese, Elisabeth Mann
Botez, Mihai C.
Botkin, James W.
Boulding, Kenneth Ewart
Brennan, Donald George
Bronwell, Arthur B.
Brown, Lester R.
Brown, Seyom
Chase, Stuart
Choucri, Nazli
Cleveland, Harlan
Cole, Hugh Samuel David
Darling, Charles M. III
Decoufle, Andre C.
De Jouvenel, Bertrand
Drobnick, Richard Lee
Dror, Yehezkel
Drouin, Marie-Josee
Elmandjra, Mahdi
Essig, Francois Bernard
Falk, Richard Anderson
Ferkiss, Victor Christopher
Godoy, Horacio Hermes
Gori, Umberto
Gray, Colin S.
Gross, Bertram
Hanappe, Paul
Harmon, David P., Jr.
Hoffman, Ben B.

Hopkins, Frank Snowden
Ingelstam, Lars E.
Kanamori, Hisao
Kaufmann, Felix
Kaya, Yoichi
Kojarov, Assen Todorov
Kristensen, Thorkil
Lagos, Gustavo
Lambert-Lamond, Georges M.
Lambo, Thomas Adeoye
Laszlo, Ervin
Lesh, Donald R.
Lindsey, George Roy
Linnemann, Hans
Linowitz, Sol M.
Livingston, Dennis
Lovins, Amory B.
Malek, Ivan
Malitza, Mircea
Martel, Leon Charles
Maruyama, Magoroh
Mayur, Rashmi
Mendlovitz, Saul H.
Miles, Ian Douglas
Mische, Gerald F.
Mische, Patricia Mary Schmitt
Moneta, Carlos J.
Mushkat, Mari'on
Myrdal, Alva Reimer
Myrdal, Gunnar
Nanus, Burt
Nerfin, Marc Paul
Okita, Saburo
Overholt, William Henry
Schulze, Lothar Gunther
Schumacher, Dieter
Sirkin, Abraham Meyer
Surrey, Arthur John
Szalai, Alexander
Taylor, Harold
Tinbergen, Jan
Vacca, Roberto
Van Dam, Andre
Ward, Barbara
Wakow, Arthur I.
Winiecki, Jan Stanislaw

*American Enterprise Institute for Public
    Policy Research*
Association Internationale Futuribles
Brookings Institution
*Bureau d'Informations et de Previsions
    Economiques*
Business International Corporation
*Center for Strategic and International
    Studies*
*Center for the Study of Democratic
    Institutions*
*Centre Internationale de Recherche sur
    l'Environnement et le Developpement*
Club de Amigos de la Futurologia
Club of Rome
Commission on the Year 2000 (Hawaii)

Decoufle, Andre C.
Essig, Francois Bernard
Gerba, John
Ghabbour, Samir Ibrahim
Kassas, Mohamed A.F.
Marsh, John S.
Mason, Roy E.
McDaniel, Robert
Meadows, Donella H.
Pickard, Jerome Percival
Rothgaenger, Klaus
Watt, Kenneth E. Ferguson

Centre de Recherche sur l'Environnement et le Developpement
Committee for Future Oriented Research (Sweden)
Institute for Social Engineering, Inc.
International Federation of Institutes for Advanced Study
Laboratoire de Prospective Appliquee
Stanford Research Institute, Center for the Study of Social Policy
Utah Future Study
Utah State Planning Coordinator's Office

LATIN AMERICA

Francois, Charles Oscar
Godoy, Horacio Hermes
Grinberg, Miguel
Herrera, Amilcar Oscar
Lagos, Gustavo
Linowitz, Sol M.
Mallmann, Carlos Alberto
Moneta, Carlos J.
Olivera, Julio H.G.
Sabato, Jorge Alberto
Socias, Juan
Tugwell, Franklin
Van Dam, Andre

Business International Corporation
Fundacion America Latina 2001
Fundacion Argentina Ano 2000
Fundacion Bariloche
Institute for Policy Studies
Nucleo Rolanroc

LAW

Antoine, Serge
Bell, Wendell
Borgese, Elisabeth Mann
Dator, James Allen
Falk, Richard Anderson
Freeman, Orville Lothrop
Godoy, Horacio Hermes
Kojarov, Assen Todorov
Linowitz, Sol M.
Mische, Patricia Mary Schmitt
Mushkat, Mari'on
Myrdal, Gunnar
Renfro, William L.

Academy for Contemporary Problems
American Enterprise Institute for Public Policy Research
Center for Policy Research
Center for the Study of Democratic Institutions
Futures Group, Inc.
Futures-Invention Associates
Institute for Alternative Futures
Midwest Research Institute
National Planning Association
Russell Sage Foundation
Social Science Research Council (U.K.)
Societe d'Etudes et d'Expansion
United Nations Institute for Training and Research (UNITAR)

LIBRARIES

Schwarz, Stephan

International Graduate School of Education

LIFE-STYLES

Best, Fred Joseph
Bestuzhev-Lada, Igor Vassilevich
Bookchin, Murray
Brand, Stewart
Carleton, Thomas James
Chaplain, Roland
De Jouvenel, Hugues Alain
Empain, Louis
Fabun, Don
Francoeur, Robert Thomas
Gorney, Roderic
Leonard, George B.
Livingston, Dennis
Mitchell, Arnold
Poquet, Guy Rene
Roemer, Kenneth Morrison
Shoniker, Robert George
Shostak, Arthur B.
Sicinski, Andrzej
Spengler, Marie
Teige, Peter J.
Toffler, Alvin
Van Steenbergen, Bart
Yankelovich, Daniel

Association Internationale Futuribles
Centre de Recherche sur le Bien-etre
Centre International de Recherche sur l'Environnement et le Developpement
Club of Rome
Commission on the Year 2000 (Hawaii)
Episcopal Diocese of California
Findhorn Foundation
Futures Studies Centre (United Kingdom)
Institute for Research on Public Policy
Mankind 2000
Open University, Oxford Research Unit
Polish Academy of Sciences—Lifestyles Studies

McLean, John Michael
Mesarovic, Mihajlo D.
Raiffa, Howard
Szalai, Alexander
Witt-Hansen, Johannes

Academy of Sciences, Ukranian S.S.R.
Institute of Management Sciences
*International Institute for Applied Systems
   Analysis*

MENTAL HEALTH

Bellman, Richard Ernest
Bize, Rene
Dubos, Rene
Duhl, Leonard J.
Gorney, Roderic
Kelty, Miriam Friedman
Lambo, Thomas Adeoye
Land, George Thomas Lock
Landau, Erika
Lesse, Stanley
Loye, David
Nanus, Burt
Rosenfeld, Albert
Sethi, Brij Bhushan
Wakefield, Richard P.

*California, University of, at Los Angeles
   (UCLA) PSAF Program*
*Institute for Society, Ethics and the Life
   Sciences—Hastings Center*
*Osterreichische Akademie der
   Wissenschaften, Institut fur
   Sozio-Okonomische
   Entwicklungsforschung*
Public Policy Research Organization

MIDDLE EAST

Choucri, Nazli
El-Kholy, Ussama Amin
Ghabbour, Samir Ibrahim
Landsberg, Hans H.
Waskow, Arthur I.

*Academy for Educational Development,
   Inc.*
*Arab League Educational, Cultural and
   Scientific Organization*
*Interdisciplinary Center for Technological
   Analysis and Forecasting*
*International Federation of Institutes for
   Advanced Study*
*Israeli Institute for the Study of
   International Affairs*
*United Nations Institute for Training and
   Research (UNITAR)*

MILITARY AFFAIRS

Biderman, Albert D.
Botez, Mihai C.
Brennan, Donald George
Brown, Seyom

Cleveland, Harlan
Coates, Joseph F.
Dickson, Paul Andrew
Dror, Yehezkel
Gray, Colin S.
Horhager, Axel
Kahn, Herman
King-Hele, Desmond George
Lesh, Donald R.
Lindsey, George Roy
Martel, Leon Charles
Mushkat, Mari'on
Proske, Ruediger K.A.
Ruggles, Rudy L., Jr.
Solem, Erik
Weaver, John Jacob

*American Enterprise Institute for Public
   Policy Research*
Brookings Institution
*Center for the Study of Democratic
   Institutions*
Dayton, University of, Research Institute
Decisions and Designs, Inc.
Forecasting International, Ltd.
Forsvarets Forskningsanstalt
*Interdisciplinary Center for Technological
   Analysis and Forecasting*
International Institute for Strategic Studies
ORI, Inc.
*Pugwash Conference on Science and World
   Affairs*
Rand Corporation
*Sussex, University of, Science Policy
   Research Unit*
*United States Congress, Office of
   Technology Assessment*
*U.S. Army War College, Strategic Studies
   Institute*

MUSEUMS

Holthusen, T. Lance
Joseph, Earl E.
Mason, Roy E.
Taylor, Gordon Rattray

NATIONAL PLANNING

Afheldt, Heik
Auerbach, Lewis E.
Aujac, Henri
Becker, Harold S.
Cazes, Bernard
Chase, Stuart
Culver, John C.
Daddario, Emilio Quincy
Danecki, Jan
Doyle, Frank
Drouin, Marie-Josee
Dubach, Paul
Duncan, James Francis
Durie, Robert Wesley
Elboim-Dror, Rachel

Mushkat, Mari'on
Myrdale, Alva Reimer
Myrdal, Gunnar
Schulze, Lothar Gunther
Solem, Erik
Waskow, Arthur I.

Academy of World Studies
Center for the Study of Democratic
*   Institutions*
Institute for World Order, Inc.
Israeli Institute for the Study of
*   International Affairs*
Kommunikationszentrum fur Zukunfts-und
*   Friedensforschung in Hannover GmbH*
Pugwash Conference on Science and World
*   Affairs*
World Man

PHILOSOPHY

Apostol, Pavel A.
Baier, Kurt E.
Churchman, C. West
Cornish, Edward Seymour
De Jouvenel, Bertrand
Edwards, Gregg
Enzer, Selwyn
Esfandiary, F.M.
Flechtheim, Ossip K.
Green, Thomas F.
Hardin, Garrett
Hubner, Kurt
Illich, Ivan
Jantsch, Erich
Jones, Thomas Evan
Lenk, Hans A.P.
Maruyama, Magoroh
McGraw, John G.
Mesthene, Emmanuel G.
Miller, Lewis
Ozmon, Howard
Rescher, Nicholas
Salomon, Jean-Jacques
Schaff, Adam
Skolimowski, Henryk
Stulman, Julius
Suchodolski, Bogdan
Waterlow, Charlotte Mary
. Weizacker, Carl Friedrich Freiherr Von
Wilson, Albert George
Witt-Hansen, Johannes

Associazione Teilhard de Chardin: Centro
*   di Ricerca sul Futuro dell'Uomo*
Centrum voor Vraagstukken van
*   Wetenschap en Samenleving*
Findhorn Foundation
Institute on Religion in an Age of Science
International Creative Center
Movement for a New Society
Prospective, International Center of
*   Research and Communication*
School of Living

World Future Society
World Man

PHYSICS

Asimov, Isaac
Bowers, Raymond
Brown, William M.
Feld, Bernard T.
Fuchs, Georg
Hellman, Hal
O'Neill, Gerard Kitchen
Phelps, John Bedford
Weizacker, Carl Friedrich Freiherr von

Battelle Memorial Institute
National Research Council of Canada

POLICY ANALYSIS

Abrams, Mark Alexander
Abt, Clark C.
Auerbach, Philip Hone
Ayres, Robert Underwood
Baworowski, Ludwik Jerzy
Becker, Harold S.
Best, Fred Joseph
Bossell, Harmut H.
Botez, Mihai C.
Brown, Arnold
Brown, William M.
Chen, Kan
Coomer, James Chester
Danecki, Jan
Dixon, John
Drobnick, Richard Lee
Dror, Yehezkel
Elboim-Dror, Rachel
Elton, Martin C.J.
Emory, Frederick Edmund
Ewald, William Rudolph
Gerba, John
Gershuny, Jonathan Israel
Glenn, Jerome Clayton
Godoy, Horacio Hermes
Gordon, Theodore Jay
Gori, Umberto
Gray, Colin S.
Hahn, Walter A., Jr.
Hake, Barry John
Hallal, William Emitt
Harman, Willis W.
Harmon, David P., Jr.
Hetman, Francois
Hoffman, John David
Humphries, George E.
Illich, Ivan
Jaumin-Ponsar, Anne Marie
Jones, Peter Michael Seaton
Kollen, James H.
Lamson, Robert Warren
Land, George Thomas Lock
Laszlo, Ervin

Thiemann, Hugo Ernst
Wren-Lewis, John

Academy of Sciences, Ukranian SSR
*Associazione Teilhard de Chardin: Centro
di Ricerca sul Futuro dell'Uomo*
Brookings Institution
*Center for the Study of Democratic
Institutions*
*Centrum voor Vraagstukken van
Wetenschap en Samenleving*
*Cornell University Program on Science,
Technology, and Society*
Fundacion America Latina 2001
Fundacion Javier Barros Sierra A.C.
*George Washington University Program of
Policy Studies in Science and
Technology*
*Hungarian Academy of Sciences, Institute
for Science Organization*
Indian Institute of Technology
*Institut de Prospective et Politique de la
Science*
Institute on Man and Science
Institute on Religion in an Age of Science
*Institute for Society, Ethics and the Life
Sciences—Hastings Center*
*Institute for the Study of the Human
Future, Inc.*
*Institute for Theological Encounter with
Science and Technology*
International Council of Scientific Unions
*International Institute for Applied Systems
Analysis*
Office of Science and Technology Policy
Policy Studies Organization
Public Policy Research Organization
*Pugwash Conference on Science and World
Affairs*
Science Council of Canada
Science Policy Foundaton
*Sussex, University of, Science Policy
Research Unit*
*United Nations Educational, Scientific and
Cultural Organization (UNESCO)*
World Future Studies Federation

SEX

Francoeur, Robert Thomas
Kelty, Miriam Friedman
Leonard, George B.
Lesse, Stanley

SOCIAL FORECASTING

Amara, Roy
Apostol, Pavel A.
Aujac, Henri
Baruchello Terenzi, Barbara
Bean, Louis H.
Best, Fred Joseph
Bestuzhev-Lada, Igor Vassilevich
Block, A. Eskil
Brown, Arnold

Brown, Harrison Scott
Calder, Nigel
Cazes, Bernard
Chase, Stuart
Danecki, Jan
Dauman, Jan Victor
Decoufle, Andre C.
Delors, Jacques Lucien Jean
Dickson, Paul Andrew
Empain, Louis
Encel, Solomon
Erickson, Scott William
Fabun, Don
Ferkiss, Victor Christopher
Fontela, Emilio
Fowles, Jib
Gappert, Gary M.
Gershuny, Jonathan Israel
Gilfillan, S. Colum
Grinberg, Miguel
Hamil, Ralph Edward
Hanappe, Paul
Heilbroner, Robert L.
Hubner, Kurt
Imsland, Donald Orlene
Jones, Thomas Evan
Jungk, Robert
Kahn, Herman
Kanamori, Hisao
Kapur, Jagdish Chandra
Kettle, John
Kostelanetz, Richard
Kraegel, Wilfred A.
Lesourne, Jacques Francois
Little, Dennis Lloyd
Loveridge, Denis John
Loye, David
Mac Nulty, Christine A. Ralph
Marien, Michael David
Martel, Leon Charles
Masini, Eleonora Barbieri
Mendell, Jay Stanley
Michael, Donald Nelson
Miles, Ian Douglas
Molitor, Graham Thomas Tate
Page, R. William
Peccei, Aurelio
Platt, John
Pohl, Frederik
Proske, Ruediger K.A.
Rosen, Stephen
Scardigli, Victor
Schaller, Lyle Edwin
Schmacke, Ernst Stephan
Schwartz, Peter
Shoniker, Robert George
Spengler, Marie
Taylor, Gordon Rattray
Thompson, Gordon Bruce
Toncher, Liuben Alexiev
Vacca, Roberto

Ad Hoc Interagency Committee on Futures
  Research
Association Internationale Futuribles
Battelle Memorial Institute
Brookings Institution
Cambridge Research Institute, Inc.
Center for Future Management
Center for Integrative Studies
Center for Policy Research
Center for the Study of Democratic
  Institutions
Centre de Recherche sur le Bien-etre
Centre d'Etude des Consequences Generales
  des Grandes Techniques Nouvelles
Centre for Policy Research (India)
Club of Rome
Commission for the Future (New Zealand)
Committee for Future Oriented Research
  (Sweden)
Educational Futures Projects
Findhorn Foundation
Fondation Europeenne de la Culture
Fondation Internationale de l'Innovation
  Sociale
Forum for the Advancement of Students in
  Science and Technology, Inc.
Future Systems
Futures Network
Futures Studies Centre (United Kingdom)
Harris International
Hungarian Academy of Sciences,
  Presidential Committee on the Social
  Impact of Science and Technology
Idaho's Tomorrow
Information for Policy Design
INSEAD (European Institute of Business
  Administration)
Institut de Prospective et Politique de la
  Science
Institute for Applied Systems Analysis and
  Prognosis
Institute for Canadian Futures
Institute for the Future
Institute on Religion in an Age of Science
Institute for Research on Public Policy
Interfuture
International Institute for Strategic Studies
Japan Economic Research Center
Korean Society for the Future
Mankind 2000
K. Marx University of Economic Sciences
  (Hungary)
Midwest Research Institute
Movement for a New Society
National Institute for Research
  Advancement
National Research Council of Canada
National Science Foundation, Research
  Applications Directorate
New York Center for World Game Studies,
  Inc.
Organization for Economic Cooperation
  and Development (OECD)

Owen, David, Centre for Population
  Growth Studies
Polish Academy of Sciences—Lifestyles
  Studies
Princeton Center for Alternative Futures,
  Inc.
Public Policy Research Organization
Raad vir Geesteswetenskaplike Navorsing
Rand Corporation
Russell Sage Foundation
Science Policy Foundation
Selskapet for Fremtidsstudier
Simulation and Gaming Association
Simulation in the Service of Society
Sociaal en Cultureel Planbureau
Social Impact Assessment Network
Social Science Research Council (U.K.)
Social Science Research Council, Center
  for Coordination of Research on Social
  Indicators
Societe d'Etudes et d'Expansion
Sociocyberneering, Inc.
Southern California, University of, Center
  for Futures Research
Square One Management, Ltd.
Stanford Research Institute, Center for the
  Study of Social Policy
United Nations Asian and Pacific
  Development Institute
United Nations Educational, Scientific and
  Cultural Organization (UNESCO)
Werner-Reimers-Stiftung
Wissenschaftszentrum Berlin
World Future Society
Yankelovich, Skelly and White, Inc.

SOCIOLOGY

Acquaviva, Sabino
Arvay, Stephen
Bell, Wendell
Best, Fred Joseph
Bestuzhev-Lada, Igor Vassilevich
Biderman, Albert D.
Bookchin, Murray
Eldredge, H. Wentworth
Etzioni, Amitai W.
Fowles, Jib
Friedman, Yona
Ghosh, Samir Kumar
Harkins, Arthur Martin
Henshel, Richard L.
Janne, Henri Gustave
Keller, Suzanne
Klages, Helmut
Kojarov, Assen Todorov
Kumar, Jagdish Krishan
Lenk, Hans A.P.
Mendras, Henri
Mihanovich, Clement Simon
Miles, Ian Douglas
Myrdal, Alva Reimer
O'Toole, James Joseph

Parsons, Jack
Phillips, Bernard S.
Scardigli, Victor
Shostak, Arthur B.
Strzelecki, Jan Wladyslaw
Szalai, Alexander
Tarter, Donald Edward
Wagenfuhr, Horst
Wickert, Gunther

National Council for the Social Studies,
Special Interest Group in Future Studies
Social Science Research Council (U.K.)
USSR Academy of Sciences, Institute for
Sociological Research
Wickert Institut Tubingen

SPACE EXPLORATION

Berry, Adrian M.
Brown, Seyom
Brown, William M.
Buchen, Irving H.
Clarke, Arthur Charles
Erickson, Scott William
Feinberg, Gerald
Forrester, Jay Wright
Gerken, William, Jr.
Glenn, Jerome Clayton
Gordon, Theodore Jay
Hamil, Ralph Edward
Hubbard, Barbara Marx
King-Hele, Desmond George
Koelle, Heinz Hermann
Lindaman, Edward B.
Maruyama, Magoroh
Michael, Donald Nelson
O'Neill, Gerard Kitchen
Proske, Ruediger K.A.
Ruzic, Neil Price
Shostak, Arthur B.
Taylor, Theodore B.
Vallee, Jacques F.
Wescott, Roger Williams

Brookings Institution
Future Options Room
Institute for the Study of the Human
Future, Inc.
National Space Institute

SYSTEMS ENGINEERING

Abt, Clark C.
Amara, Roy
Bossell, Harmut H.
Chacko, George K.
Chen, Kan
Churchman, C. West
Edwards, Gregg
Emery, Frederick Edmund
Feather, Frank
Francois, Charles Oscar
Fuller, R. Buckminster

Goldsmith, Edward Rene
Iyengar, Madhur Srinivas
Kaya, Yoiche
Kozmetsky, George
Laszlo, Ervin
Lenk, Hans A.P.
Mallmann, Carlos Alberto
Maynard, Richard G.
McDaniel, Robert
Meadows, Donella H.
Mesarovic, Mihajlo D.
M'Pherson, Philip Keith
Sahal, Devendra
Stover, John G.
Umpleby, Stuart A.
Vacca, Roberto
Vester, Frederic
Vickers, Charles Geoffrey
Wakefield, Richard P.
Wilson, Albert George
Zeman, Zavis Peter
Zuckerman, Peter

Battelle-Institut e.V.
Massachusetts Institute of Technology,
System Dynamics Group

TECHNOLOGICAL FORECASTING

Abt, Clark C.
Ayres, Robert Underwood
Baworowski, Ludwik Jerzy
Bender, Allan Douglas
Bouladon, Gabriel Antoine
Bright, James R.
Brown, William M.
Cetron, Marvin Jerome
Chacko, George K.
Clarke, Arthur Charles
Craver, J. Kenneth
Davis, Richard C.
Day, Lawrence Harvey
Dede, Christopher James
Diebold, John
Dobrov, Gennady Mikhaylovich
Ferkiss, Victor Christopher
Fowles, Jib
Hetman, Francois
Humphries, George C.
Jantsch, Erich
Joseph, Earl C.
Kaya, Yoichi
King, Alexander
Lenz, Ralph C., Jr.
Linstone, Harold A.
Martino, Joseph P.
Miles, Ian Douglas
Pyke, Donald L.
Rosen, Stephen
Saint-Paul, Raymond Henri
Sharif, Nawaz M.
Simmons, William W.
Solem, Erik

716

Swager, William Leon
Thompson, Fred G.
Turoff, Murray
Vanston, John H., Jr.

Abend Group
Academy of Sciences, Ukranian SSR.
Battelle, Geneva Research Centre
Battelle-Institut e.V.
Battelle Memorial Institute
Bureau d'Informations et de Previsions
  Economiques
Dayton, University of, Research Institute
Diebold Group, Inc.
Forecasting International, Ltd.
Formedlingscentrum for Framtidsstudier
  AB
Hazan International
Hungarian Academy of Sciences, Institute
  for Science Organization
Industrial Management Center, Inc.
Institute for Canadian Futures
Interdisciplinary Center for Technological
  Analysis and Forecasting
Iyengar, M.S., and Associates, Ltd.
K. Marx University of Economic Sciences
  (Hungary)
Massachusetts Institute of Technology,
  System Dynamics Group
ORI, Inc.
Osrodek Badan Prognostycznych
Ostereichisches Institut fur
  Wirtschaftsforschung
Planning and Forecasting Consultants
Portland State University, Futures
  Research Institute
Predicasts, Inc.
Quantum Science Corporation
Stanford Research Institute, Business
  Intelligence Program
Stanford Research Institute, Center for the
  Study of Social Policy
Stichting Toekomstbeeld der Techniek
Sussex, University of, Science Policy
  Research Unit
Taloudellinen Suunnittelukeskus
U.S. Department of Agriculture, Economic
  Research Service
Williams, Charles W., Inc.

TECHNOLOGY ASSESSMENT

Altenpohl, Dieter G.
Armer, Paul
Arnstein, Sherry Phyllis
Arvay, Stephen
Auerbach, Lewis E.
Ayres, Robert Underwood
Becker, Harold S.
Bouladon, Gabriel Antoine
Bowers, Raymond
Bronwell, Arthur B.
Buchen, Irving H.
Buchholz, Hans

Calder, Nigel
Cetron, Marvin Jerome
Chase, Stuart
Chen, Kan
Choucri, Nazli
Christakis, Alexander N.
Clark, John Albert
Coates, Joseph F.
Coates, Vary T.
Carver, J. Kenneth
Daddario, Emilio Quincy
Dauman, Jean Victor
Davis, Richard C.
Day, Lawrence Harvey
Dedijer, Stevan
Dickson, Paul Andrew
Didsbury, Howard Francis, Jr.
Diebold, John
Dobrov, Gennady Mikhaylovich
Doyle, Frank
Dubach, Paul
Durie, Robert Wesley
Edwards, Gregg
El-Kholy, Ussaman Amin
Elton, Martin C.J.
Encel, Solomon
Enzer, Selwyn
Etzioni, Amitai W.
Eurich, Alvin C.
Fabun, Don
Feld, Bernard T.
Francis, John Michael
Francoeur, Robert Thomas
Fritch, Bruno
Gershuny, Jonathan Israel
Gordon, Theodore Jay
Gray, Paul
Gueron, Georges
Gueron, Jeannine
Hahn, Walter A., Jr.
Hardin, Garrett
Hayashi, Yujiro
Hellman, Hal
Helmer, Olaf
Herrera, Amilcar Oscar
Hetman, Francois
Hoos, Ida Russakoff
Hottovy, Tibor C.
Hubner, Kurt
Humphries, George E.
Iyengar, Madhur Srinivas
Jackson, Ray W.
Jones, Martin V.
Jones, Peter Michael Seaton
Kapur, Jagdish Chandra
Kaufmann, Felix
Kelty, Miriam Friedman
King, Alexander
Knoppers, Antonie T.
Kocher, Gerhard
Lamontagne, Maurice

718

Institute for Theological Encounter With
  Science and Technology
Institute for 21st Century Business
Interdisciplinary Center for Technological
  Analysis and Forecasting
International Institute for Strategic Studies
Iyengar, M.S., and Associates, Ltd.
Japan Techno-Economics Society
Korea Institute of Science and Technology
Massachusetts Institute of Technology,
  Research Program on Communications
  Policy
Midwest Research Institute
MPI International, Inc.
National Research Council of Canada
National Science Foundation, Research
  Applications Directorate
Office of Science and Technology Policy
Open University, Design Group
Predicasts, Inc.
Princeton Center for Alternative Futures,
  Inc.
Public Policy Research Organization
Pugwash Conference on Science and World
  Affairs
Regional Research Laboratory Systems
  Planning and Research Management
  Group
Science Council of Canada
Science Policy Foundation
Selskapet for Fremtidsstudier
Social Impact Assessment Network
Stanford Research Institute Business
  Intelligence Program
Southern California, University of, Center
  for Futures Research
Sussex, University of, Science Policy
  Research Unit
Systemplan e.V. Institut fur
  Umweltforschung und
  Entwicklungsplannung
United Nations Educational, Scientific and
  Cultural Organization (UNESCO)
United Nations Institute for Training and
  Research (UNITAR)
United States Congress, Office of
  Technology Assessment
U.S. Army War College, Strategic Studies
  Institute
U.S. Department of Agriculture, Economic
  Research Service
Variflex Corporation
Wickert Institut Tubingen
Williams, Charles W., Inc.
World Future Society
World Future Studies Federation

TECHNOLOGY TRANSFER

Abt, Clark C.
Altenpohl, Dieter G.
Cordell, Arthur Jason
Doyle, Frank
Ellis, William N.

Feld, Bernard T.
Godoy, Horacio Hermes
Hahn, Walter A., Jr.
Humphries, George E.
Kapur, Jagdish Chandra
Knoppers, Antonie T.
Mallmann, Carlos Alberto
Ruzic, Neil Price
Sabato, Jorge Alberto
Schumacher, Dieter
Selan, Valerio
Stoeber, Gerhard J.
Taylor, Harold
Wakefield, Rowan Albert
Winiecki, Jan Stanislaw

Academy for Educational Development,
  Inc.
Forecasting International, Ltd.
INSEAD (European Institute of Business
  Administration)
Japan Economic Research Center
Japan Techno-Economics Society
Korea Institute of Science and Technology
Organization for Economic Cooperation
  and Development (OECD)
Portland State University, Futures
  Research Institute
Systemplan e.V., Institut for
  Umweltforschung und
  Entwicklungsplannung

TELEVISION

Berry, David John
Bradley, Helen Genevieve
Cassierer, Henry Reinhard
Dator, James Allen
Gorney, Roderic
Jaccai, August T., Jr.
Kennet (Lord)
Kettle, John
Miller, Lewis
Nyheim, Jan Henrik
Pool, Ithiel de Sola
Taylor, Gordon Rattray

Massachusetts Institute of Technology,
  Research Program on Communications
  Policy

TRANSPORTATION

Afheldt, Heik
Ayres, Robert Underwood
Becker, Harold S.
Bouladon, Gabriel Antoine
Coates, Vary T.
Francis, John Michael
Gerba, John
Gray, Paul
Hanappe, Paul
Jones, Martin V.
Koelle, Heinz Hermann
Leach, Gerald Adrian

720

Wakefield Washington Associates, Inc.
Weiner, Edrich, Brown, Inc.
World Future Society
Worldwatch Institute

UNITED STATES

Becker, Harold S.
Culver, John C.
Elgin, Duane S.
Gappert, Gary M.
Gray, Colin S.
Gross, Bertram
Hess, Karl
Johnston, Denis F.
Lesh, Donald R.
O'Toole, James Joseph
Pickard, Jerome Percival
Roemer, Kenneth Morrison
Schwartz, Peter
Strzelecki, Jan Wladyslaw
Theobald, Robert
Tinbergen, Jan
Wagschal, Peter
Waskow, Arthur I.
Wilson, Donna
Winiecki, Jan Stanislaw
Yankelovich, Daniel
Academy for Contemporary Problems
Ad Hoc Interagency Committee on Futures
  Research
American Enterprise Institute for Public
  Policy Research
Battelle, Geneva Research Centre
Brookings Institution
Cambridge Research Institute, Inc.
Champoeg II—Oregon 2000 Project
College Board
Congressional Research Service
Goals for Dallas
Goals for the Greater Akron Area
Hudson Institute, Inc.
Illinois 2000 Foundation
Institute for Research on Public Policy
Kenilworth Institute
Massachusetts Institute of Technology,
  System Dynamics Group
Midwest Research Institute
Office of Science and Technology Policy
Predicasts, Inc.
Public Policy Research Organization
Russell Sage Foundation
Social Science Research Council, Center
  for Coordination of Research on Social
  Indicators
United States Congress, Office of
  Technology Assessment
U.S. Department of Agriculture, Economic
  Research Service
Yankelovich, Skelly and White, Inc.

URBAN PLANNING

Afheldt, Heik
Case, Fred E.
Chen, Kan
Clawson, Marion
Cole, Hugh Samuel David
De Jouvenel, Hugues Alain
Dernoi, Louis Antoine
Eiichi, Isomura
Eldredge, H. Wentworth
Ewald, William Rudolph
Fondersmith, John
Francis, John Michael
Fuller, R. Buckminster
Hall, Peter Geoffrey
Hoffman, Ben B.
Hottovy, Tibor C.
Mackensen, Rainer Ulrich
Madeira, Thomas Roberts
Maruyama, Magoroh
Mason, Roy E.
Mayur, Rashmi
Meier, Richard L.
Mesarovic, Mihajlo D.
Pickard, Jerome Percival
Pressman, Norman E.P.
Rothgaenger, Klaus
Schaller, Lyle Edwin
Shostak, Arthur B.
Spilhaus, Athelstan
Stoeber, Gerhard J.
Vacca, Roberto
Van Hulten, Michel

Academy for Contemporary Problems
Committee for Economic Development
Delegation a l'Amenagement du Territoire
  et a l'Action Regionale
Delft University of Technology
Department of Science and Technology
  (India)
Fundacion Javier Barros Sierra A.C.
Institut fur Zukunftsforschung (Berlin)
Institute for Social Engineering, Inc.
National Institute for Research
  Advancement
Prognos AG, European Center for Applied
  Economic Research
Social Science Research Council (U.K.)
Systemplan e.V. Institut fur
  Umweltforschung und
  Entwicklungsplannung
Werner-Reimers-Stiftung

UTOPIAS

Aldridge, Alexandra
Berry, David John
Bestuzhev-Lada, Igor Vassilevich
Clarke, Ian Frederick
Fletchtheim, Ossip K.
Livingston, Dennis
Ozmon, Howard

Purdy, Judson Douglas
Roemer, Kenneth Morrison
Skinner, B.F.
Van Steenbergen, Bart
Vlachos, Evan

WEATHER CONTROL

Brown, Seyom
Chaplain, Roland
Cleveland, Harlan
Jones, Martin V.
Rosen, Stephen

Brookings Institution
International Council of Scientific Unions

WOMEN

Boulding, Elise
Coates, Vary T.
Crealock, Carol Marie
Francoeur, Robert Thomas
Ghosh, Samir Kumar
Hardin, Garrett
Hubbard, Barbara Marx
Jahoda, Marie
Jaumin-Ponsar, Anne Marie
Keller, Suzanne
Masini, Eleonora Barbieri
McHale, Magda Cordell
Menasanch, Rosa Menasanch
Mische, Patricia Mary Schmitt
Myrdal, Alva Reimer
Piotet, Francoise Odette
Rose, Charlie
Streatfeild, Guy Frederick
Weaver, John Jacob
Weiner, Edith M.

Center for Integrative Studies
United Nations Institute for Training and Research (UNITAR)
Werner-Reimers-Stiftung
Worldwatch Institute

WORKPLACE

Abbott, William Latham
Backstrand, Goran Karl
Best, Fred Joseph
Conger, D. Stuart
Crozier, Michel Jean
Danecki, Jan
De, Nitish R.
Dickson, Paul Andrew
Emery, Frederick Edmund
Gappert, Gary M.
Green, Thomas F.
Kumar, Jagdish Krishan
Lagos, Gustavo
Lecht, Leonard A.
Mobley, Louis R.
Nightingale, Donald Victor
O'Toole, James Joseph

Piotet, Francoise Odette
Shostak, Arthur B.
Stoeber, Gerhard J.
Thompson, Fred G.
Wilson, Ian H.
Woodward, Douglas
Yankelovich, Daniel

American Council of Life Insurance, Trend Analysis Program
Committee for Future Oriented Research (Sweden)
Conference Board
Futures Studies Centre (United Kingdom)
Institut de Prospective et Politique de la Science
International Creative Center
Mankind 2000
Secretariat for Future Studies (Sweden)
Southern California, University of, Center for Futures Research
World Future Society

YEAR 2000

Chaplain, George
Culver, John C.
Danecki, Jan
Decoufle, Andre C.
Essig, Francois Bernard
Fabun, Don
Fondersmith, John
Godoy, Horacio Hermes
Hanappe, Paul
Hopkins, Frank Snowden
Kahn, Herman
Kapur, Jagdish Chandra
Nanus, Burt
Paige, Glenn Durland
Seth, Satish Chandra
Sethi, Brij Bhushan
Sicinski, Andrzej
Sine, Thomas William
Stoeber, Gerhard J.
Van Hulten, Michel
Widmaier, Hans Peter
Wren-Lewis, John
Young, David Leslie

Ad Hoc Interagency Committee on Futures Research
Arab League Educational, Cultural and Scientific Organization
Centre for Policy Research (India)
Champoeg II—Oregon 2000 Project
Commission on the Year 2000 (Hawaii)
Delegation a l'Amenagement du Territoire et a l'Action Regionale
Federal Aviation Administration
Formedlingscentrum for Framtidsstudier AB
Iyengar, M.S., and Associates, Ltd.
Japan Economic Research Center
Laboratoire de Prospective Appliquee

K. *Marx University of Economic Sciences*
   (Hungary)
Polish Academy of Sciences—"Poland
   2000"
Raad vir Geesteswetenskaplike Navorsing
Regional Research Laboratory Systems
   Planning and Research Management
   Group
World Future Society

YOUTH

Bestuzhev-Lada, Igor Vassilevich
Michael, Donald Nelson
Mihanovich, Clement Simon

Academy for Contemporary Problems
Fondation Europeenne de la Culture
Forum for the Advancement of Students in
   Science and Technology, Inc.
Nucleo Rolanroc
USSR Academy of Sciences, Institute for
   Sociological Research
Youth Movement for a New International
   Order